If you're looking for more study aids, make sure you check out the Online Learning Center at

www.mhhe.com/mcshane2e

Where you can find

- Additional Chapter Quizzes
- Internet Exercises
- Video Cases
- Additional Readings
- Career Corner
- a Guide to Electronic Research

And introducing our new

- OB Online Interactive Exercises

and much more!

Organizational Behavior

Organizational Behavior

Emerging Realities for the Workplace Revolution

Steven L. McShane
The University of Western Australia

Mary Ann Von Glinow
Florida International University

Boston   Burr Ridge, IL   Dubuque, IA   Madison, WI   New York   San Francisco   St. Louis
Bangkok   Bogotá   Caracas   Kuala Lumpur   Lisbon   London   Madrid   Mexico City
Milan   Montreal   New Delhi   Santiago   Seoul   Singapore   Sydney   Taipei   Toronto

McGraw-Hill Higher Education

A Division of The **McGraw-Hill** *Companies*

ORGANIZATIONAL BEHAVIOR:
EMERGING REALITIES FOR THE WORKPLACE REVOLUTION
Published by McGraw-Hill, a business unit of The McGraw-Hill Companies, Inc., 1221 Avenue of the Americas, New York, NY 10020. Copyright © 2003, 2000 by The McGraw-Hill Companies, Inc. All rights reserved. No part of this publication may be reproduced or distributed in any form or by any means, or stored in a database or retrieval system, without the prior written consent of The McGraw-Hill Companies, Inc., including, but not limited to, in any network or other electronic storage or transmission, or broadcast for distance learning.
Some ancillaries, including electronic and print components, may not be available to customers outside the United States.

This book is printed on acid-free paper.

domestic   3 4 5 6 7 8 9 0 WCK/WCK 0 9 8 7 6 5 4 3 2
international   3 4 5 6 7 8 9 0 WCK/WCK 0 9 8 7 6 5 4 3 2

ISBN   0-07-247008-9

Publisher: *John E. Biernat*
Senior editor: *John Weimeister*
Senior developmental editor: *Christine Scheid*
Senior marketing manager: *Ellen Cleary*
Project manager: *Natalie J. Ruffatto*
Senior production supervisor: *Lori Koetters*
Senior designer: *Jennifer McQueen*
Supplement producer: *Betty Hadala*
Media producer: *Craig Atkins*
Photo research coordinator: *Jeremy Cheshareck*
Photo researcher: *Amy Bethea*
Cover and interior design: *Michael Warrell*
Cover images: *© Photodisc, Inc.*
Typeface: *10/12 New Aster*
Compositor: *GAC Indianapolis*
Printer: *Quebecor World Versailles Inc.*

INTERNATIONAL EDITION ISBN 0-07-115113-3
Copyright © 2003. Exclusive rights by The McGraw-Hill Companies, Inc., for manufacture and export. This book cannot be re-exported from the country to which it is sold by McGraw-Hill. The International Edition is not available in North America.

Library of Congress Control Number: 2002100234

www.mhhe.com

Steven L. McShane

Steven L. McShane is Professor of Management in the Graduate School of Management at the University of Western Australia (UWA). Steve has also taught in the business faculties at Simon Fraser University and Queen's University in Canada. He is a past president of the Administrative Sciences Association of Canada

Steve earned his PhD from Michigan State University, a Master of Industrial Relations from the University of Toronto, and an undergraduate degree from Queen's University in Canada. He receives high teaching ratings from MBA and doctoral students both in Perth, Australia, and in Singapore, where he teaches senior officers in the Singapore Armed Forces.

Steve is also the author of *Canadian Organizational Behavior*, 4th edition (2001), which is McGraw-Hill's best-selling college textbook in Canada. He is co-author with Professor Tony Travaglione of *Organisational Behaviour on the Pacific Rim* (2003), McGraw-Hill's most recent organizational behavior book published in that region. Steve has published several dozen articles and conference papers on the socialization of new employees, gender bias in job evaluation, wrongful dismissal, media bias in business magazines, and other diverse issues.

Along with teaching and writing, Steve enjoys spending his leisure time swimming, bodysurfing, canoeing, skiing, and traveling with his wife and two daughters.

Mary Ann Von Glinow

Mary Ann Von Glinow is the director of the Center for International Business Education and Research (CIBER) and Professor of Management and International Business at Florida International University. She has an MBA and PhD in management science from The Ohio State University and was previously on the business school faculty of the University of Southern California. Dr. Von Glinow was the 1994–95 president of the Academy of Management, the world's largest association of academicians in management. She is also a member of 11 editorial review boards and several international panels. She teaches in executive programs in Latin America, Central America, Asia, the United States, Europe, Africa, and Australia.

In the past six years, Dr. Von Glinow has authored over 70 journal articles and nine books. Her most recent include *Organizational Learning Capability* (Oxford University Press, 1999), in Chinese and Spanish translation, and *Organizational Behavior*, 2nd edition (McGraw-Hill, 2002).

Mary Ann consults to a number of domestic and multinational enterprises, and serves as a mayoral appointee to the Shanghai Institute of Human Resources in China. Mary Ann is actively involved in several animal welfare organizations and received the 1996 Humanitarian Award of the Year from Miami's Adopt-a-Pet

Dedicated with love and devotion to Donna, and
to our wonderful daughters, Bryton and Madison
—SLM

To my family and my virtual, globally distributed
family!
—MAVG

BRIEF CONTENTS

CONTENTS

PART THREE

Team Processes

CHAPTER EIGHT

Foundations of Team Dynamics 224

CHAPTER NINE

Decision Making and Employee Involvement 258

CHAPTER TEN

Creativity and
Team Decision Making   292

CHAPTER ELEVEN

Communicating in
Organizational Settings   320

CHAPTER TWELVE

Organizational Power, Politics, and Persuasion   354

"Emerging realities for the workplace revolution" isn't a marketing slogan; it's a wake-up call for the field of organizational behavior. Knowledge is replacing infrastructure. Self-leadership is superceding command-and-control management. Networks are replacing hierarchies. Virtual teams are replacing committees. Companies are looking for employees with emotional intelligence, not just technical smarts. Globalization has become the mantra of corporate survival. Co-workers aren't down the hall; they're at the other end of an Internet connection located somewhere else on the planet.

Organizational Behavior, Second Edition, is based on these emerging workplace realities. We describe how companies guide workplace behavior through values, how clashing corporate cultures can sink a global merger, and how globalization is driving fundamental organizational changes. We also discuss several emerging concepts that are reshaping the field of organizational behavior, such as knowledge management, emotional intelligence, and appreciative inquiry. This book also presents the new reality that organizational behavior (OB) is not just for managers; it is relevant and useful to anyone who works in and around organizations.

GLOBAL ORIENTATION

Love it or hate it, globalization is part of the emerging reality of organizations. To reflect this emerging reality, *Organizational Behavior,* Second Edition, introduces globalization in the opening chapter and highlights global issues in every chapter. Globalization relates to numerous topics throughout this book, such as personal values across cultures (Chapter 4), the relevance of motivation concepts across cultures (Chapter 5), employee stress in Japan and Spain (Chapter 7), the effect of globalization on virtual teams (Chapter 8), problems with cross-cultural communication (Chapter 11), cross-cultural conflict (Chapter 13), the effect of globalization on organizational change (Chapter 16), and cultural differences in psychological contracts (Chapter 18).

To further emphasize the emerging reality of globalization, every chapter in this edition has one or more Global Connections—highlighted features that link OB concepts to organizational incidents in diverse countries. For example, Global Connections features describe how Japanese firms are taking employees to "smile school" to improve their emotional labor; how Infosys has cre-

GLOBAL CONNECTIONS 13.1

Working Through Culture Clashes in the Renault–Nissan Partnership

Carlos Ghosn experienced more than his share of cross-cultural conflict when French carmaker Renault made him president of its partner, Nissan Motor Company, in Japan. "Certainly many of you have felt the effects of intra-company cultural clashes as your business has become globalized," said the Brazilian-born Renault executive to an audience of automobile executives, consultants, and media. "The results are a waste of talent and a waste of energy."

Ghosn and other French executives were irritated that Nissan's executives seemed to lack a "sense of urgency" to stop seven years of financial losses at Japan's second-largest carmaker. "Even though the evidence is against them, [Nissan executives] sit down and they watch the problem a little bit longer," complains Ghosn.

The Japanese executives were equally disturbed by the French practice of evaluating performance issues across work units. "In a big Japanese company, everyone has their own pigeonhole and their own responsibilities which never impinge on anyone else's, and which means no one questions a colleague's work," explains an anonymous Nissan source.

Conflicts even simmered over traditions involving lunches and meetings. The French executives believe they work better after long lunches, whereas the Japanese executives shovel down their food and get back to work as a show of loyalty. Meanwhile, the Japanese are fond of long meetings because they make their opinions seem valued by the company. This practice irritates the French executives, who prefer quicker decision making.

The good news is that Ghosn seems to be defeating the dysfunctional conflict and saving the Japanese car company through a set of challenging, measurable ob-

Carlos Ghosn experienced plenty of cross-cultural conflict when the Renault executive was transferred to Japan as president of Nissan Motor Company. (© Reuters NewMedia Inc./CORBIS)

jectives called the Nissan Revival Plan. The plan has become a superordinate goal that rallied staff and encouraged them to put aside their cultural differences. "We all knew that in order to develop a plan that would work, we would have to treat natural cultural suspicions and culture clashes as a luxury for rich people," Ghosn explains.

Sources: Y. Kageyama, "Renault Manager Crosses Cultural Divide to Turn Around Nissan," *Associated Press State and Local Wire,* June 25, 2001; O. Morgan, "Nissan's Boy from Brazil Puts Accent on Profits," *The Observer* (UK), May 27, 2001, p. 7; F. Kadri, "Renault-Nissan Two Years On: Being Bi-National Is Not So Simple," *Agence France-Presse,* April 1, 2001; A. R. Gold, M. Hirano, and Y. Yokoyama, "An Outsider Takes On Japan: An Interview with Nissan's Carlos Ghosn," *McKinsey Quarterly,* January 2001, p. 95; "Nissan's Ghosn Calls Cultural Clashes 'A Luxury for the Rich,'" *PR Newswire,* January 18, 2000.

ated a "Silicon Valley culture" in Bangalore, India; how companies in the United Kingdom are improving communication by banning e-mail one day each week; how Ericsson employees in Singapore are building more effective teams; and how Australian travel agency Flight Center has an organizational structure modeled after that of African tribes!

LINKING THEORY WITH REALITY

Every chapter of the second edition of *Organizational Behavior* is filled with real-life examples to make OB concepts more meaningful and to reflect the relevance and excitement of this field. For example, you will read how Capital One Financial has become one of the fastest-growing financial institutions through effective motivation practices; how New Zealand's The Warehouse has become one of the world's top-performing discount department store chains by supporting personal and ethical values; how the Silicon Valley design firm IDEO has become a global icon for innovation by fostering employee creativity; how EDS, the global computer services provider, has become a poster example of organizational turnaround; and how Coca-Cola has decentralized its organizational structure to get back in touch with customers.

These real-life examples appear in many forms. Every chapter of *Organizational Behavior* is filled with photo captions and in-text anecdotes about work life in this new millennium. Each chapter also includes Connections, a special feature that connects OB concepts with real organizational incidents. Case studies and *Business Week* case studies in each chapter also connect OB concepts to the emerging workplace realities. We have tried to ensure that the examples described throughout this book have a balanced, regional representation throughout the United States and around the world. Moreover, these examples cover a wide range of industries—from software to city government, and from small businesses to the Fortune 500.

CONNECTIONS 4.1

Employees Just Want to Have Fun!

It's bonus day at Kryptonite, and CEO Gary Furst is prepared for the occasion. Accompanied by a bagpiper, Furst—dressed up as a Scottish warrior from the movie *Braveheart*, complete with kilt and face paint—hands out the checks. Furst and other executives at the Boston-based bicycle lock maker have also dyed their hair green, held game shows, and hired musicians to entertain the troops. "You really need to find innovative, provocative and fun ways to motivate people," advises Furst. "Work can either be a drag or a lot of fun."

Fun at work? It sounds like an oxymoron. But to attract and keep valuable employees and to help relieve stress, organizations are encouraging employees to participate in—and even create—a little comic relief. Employees at Flanders Electric Motor Service in Evansville, Illinois, have water balloon fights and Nerf ball–throwing contests on Wacky Wednesdays. The co-owner sometimes jumps on a tricycle and pedals around delivering ice cream to Flanders's 190 employees. At Pragmatek, a Minneapolis e-business and consulting firm, employees hold Spam-carving contests. The CoActive Marketing Group in Lincoln Heights, Ohio, has Easter Egg hunts, with money inside the "eggs," and employees sometimes head out to the parking lot to test water balloon rockets.

Southwest Airlines is widely recognized as a pioneer in having fun on the job. During preflight instructions, a flight attendant says: "If there's anything we can do to make this a more pleasant flight, please, please, please hold onto that thought until we get to Houston." When the Southwest Airlines jet is about to land, the captain announces over the intercom, "Flight attendants, prepare your hair for arrival."

These fun and games may seem silly, but some corporate leaders are deadly serious about their value.

Southwest Airlines flight attendants Aimee Behmer (left) and Catrina Brooks ask passengers trivia questions over the airliner's intercom. (© Dean Hoffmeyer © Richmond Times Dispatch)

"It's pretty simple," explains Nathan Rudyk, president of DigIT Interactive Inc. (now part of Quebecor). "If you want to make the most money, you must attract the best people. To get the best people, you must be the most fun."

Sources: H. B. Herring, "Nurturing Your Company's Inner Child: Let There Be Fun!" *New York Times,* September 2, 2001; C. Jones, "Next in Line," *Richmond (VA) Times-Dispatch,* July 29, 2001; M. Shaw, "A Motivating Example," *Network World Fusion,* May 14, 2001; T. Raithel, "Some Companies Work Hard to Help Employees Relax," *Evansville (IL) Courier and Press,* February 11, 2001; D. Emerson, "Employers Urge Playing on the Job," *Business Journal of the Twin Cities (Minneapolis–St. Paul, MN),* September 4, 2000; J. Eckberg, "Playtime—Workers Mix Business, Pleasure," *Cincinnati Enquirer,* July 31, 2000, p. B16; J. Elliott, "All Work and No Play Can Chase Workers Away," *Edmonton (Alberta) Journal,* February 28, 2000.

ORGANIZATIONAL BEHAVIOR KNOWLEDGE FOR EVERYONE

Another distinctive feature of *Organizational Behavior,* Second Edition, is that it is written for *everyone* in organizations, not just managers. The philosophy of this book is that everyone who works in and around organizations needs to understand and make use of organizational behavior knowledge. The new reality is that people throughout the organization—systems analysts, production employees, accounting professionals—are assuming more responsibilities as companies remove layers of bureaucracy and give teams more autonomy over their work. This book helps everyone make sense of organizational behavior and provides the tools needed to work more effectively in the workplace.

CONTEMPORARY THEORY FOUNDATION

Organizational Behavior has a solid foundation of contemporary and classic scholarship. You can see the evidence in the references. Each chapter is based on dozens of articles, books, and other sources. The most recent literature receives thorough coverage, resulting in what we believe is the most up-to-date organizational behavior textbook available. These references also reveal that we reach out to information systems, marketing, and other disciplines for new ideas. At the same time, this textbook is written for students, not the scholars whose work is cited. Consequently, you won't find detailed summaries of specific research studies. Also, the names of researchers or their affiliations are rarely mentioned in the text. The philosophy of this textbook is to present OB scholarship in ways that students will remember long after the final examination.

Consistent with the subtitle of this book, we discuss several emerging workplace realities. For example, this edition dedicates a large part of one chapter to the rapidly growing topic of employee creativity (Chapter 10). It adds a new section on the meaning of money, including how money relates to needs, attitudes, values, and self-identity (Chapter 6). We explore the complex effects of workplace romance on organizational power and politics (Chapter 12) and look at the increasing problem of workplace bullying as a stressor (Chapter 7). Recent attention to entrepreneurship within organizations merits attention in Chapter 5, on employee motivation. The effects of mergers on organizational culture and organizational change are discussed in Chapter 15 and Chapter 16, respectively.

Four emerging topics—knowledge management, information technology, workplace values, and globalization—are woven throughout this edition of *Organizational Behavior.* Knowledge management is introduced in Chapter 1 and is further discussed in the context of individual behavior (Chapter 2), employee involvement (Chapter 9), employee creativity (Chapter 10), organizational communication (Chapter 11), and several other topics. Information technology is another prominent theme throughout this book. For example, we discuss the powerful effects of e-mail, instant messaging, the Web, and other information technology on communication. Virtual teams are discussed in several places, including the limitations of technology on keeping these groups effective. We look at the ups and downs of telecommuting, such as the political risks and distractions of working from home. Workplace values have gained considerable attention recently, so we now emphasize this topic in Chapter 1 and discuss values in the context of many other topics. And, as we mentioned earlier, globalization is an emerging reality that is connected to every chapter in this edition of *Organizational Behavior.*

CHANGES IN THE SECOND EDITION

Organizational Behavior, Second Edition, is the result of reviews over the past two years by more than 80 organizational behavior scholars and teachers. This feedback, along with a continual scan of relevant literature, has resulted in numerous improvements. Instructors will notice that some chapters have been reorganized so that the book is more closely aligned with their preferred sequence of topics. For instance, the topic of creativity and team decision making has its own chapter, reflecting the growing interest in this area. The topics of perceptions, personality, values, ethics, and emotions appear earlier in this edition. Employment relations and career dynamics is now discussed in the final chapter—to launch students from this book to their future. Every chapter has been substantially updated with new conceptual and anecdotal material. All the chapter-opening vignettes and most of the Connections features are new. Over 75 percent of the photographs are new to this edition. Every chapter has numerous content changes and significantly updated references.

Here are some of the more significant improvements within each chapter of this edition:

■ *Chapter 1: Introduction to the Field of Organizational Behavior*—The section on trends in OB now includes workplace values, to reflect the increasing emphasis on personal, cross-cultural, corporate, and ethical values. The open systems section includes discussion of stakeholders. This chapter updates information on intellectual capital and knowledge management.

■ *Chapter 2: Individual Behavior and Learning in Organizations*—This edition introduces coaching as a form of learning and feedback. It adds new information about the ethics of employee monitoring, problems with 360-degree feedback, and the practice of action learning. The section on experiential learning also adds Kolb's model.

■ *Chapter 3: Perception and Personality in Organizations*—This chapter now appears earlier in the textbook to reflect the teaching preferences of many instructors. Social identity theory was introduced in the previous edition and is updated here because of the rapidly growing OB literature on this subject. Splatter vision receives more attention in the section on the perceptual selection process, and the section on self-fulfilling prophecy considers new researching findings. This chapter also provides more detailed information on workforce diversity initiatives.

■ *Chapter 4: Workplace Values, Ethics, and Emotions*—This chapter has also been moved to appear earlier in the book and has been significantly revised. The chapter now begins with a full discussion of workplace values, including the importance of values and alignment of personal, cross-cultural, and organizational values. The section on ethical values is updated. The previous edition was one of the first OB textbooks to discuss workplace emotions in depth; the second edition continues this leadership with new information on emotional intelligence. This chapter also presents cross-cultural information on job satisfaction and provides details of the employee–customer–profit chain theory that connects job satisfaction with customer service.

■ *Chapter 5: Foundations of Employee Motivation*—New to this chapter is information on the trend toward encouraging entrepreneurship within organizations. We also introduce recent information on equity sensitivity and update the discussion of the ethics of inequity and the characteristics of goal setting.

■ *Chapter 6: Applied Motivation Practices*—The most noticeable improvement to this chapter is the new section on the meaning of money, including how money relates to needs, attitudes, values, and self-identity. The topic of organizational rewards receives more coverage, including new material on stock ownership. We also introduce a section on improving the effectiveness of performance-based rewards. The emerging topic of self-leadership is updated.

■ *Chapter 7: Stress Management*—This edition introduces workplace bullying as a stressor. It also adds new information on *karoshi* (death from overwork) in Japan and the loss of siestas in Spain. The discussion of family-friendly and work–life initiatives has been updated. Information on the various ways to manage stress has been updated.

■ *Chapter 8: Foundations of Team Dynamics*—This chapter updates information on virtual teams and introduces the concept of communities of practice. This edition also expands the discussion of building cohesiveness in virtual teams.

■ *Chapter 9: Decision Making and Employee Involvement*—This completely revised chapter recognizes the natural integration of employee participation in the decision-making process. The decision-making material is more solution-oriented. It also updates information on intuition and escalation of commitment, and introduces scenario planning. The employee involvement section adds more information about codetermination and provides a more complete discussion of sociotechnical systems and self-directed work teams. We also add the Vroom–Jago model with a discussion of its employee involvement decision criteria.

■ *Chapter 10: Creativity and Team Decision Making*—This completely revised chapter recognizes the rapidly growing popularity of creativity in the workplace. We give students the latest details on creativity, apparently more than any other OB textbook. The chapter includes discussion of the creative process, personal and work environment conditions supporting creativity, and practices that further leverage the creative potential. Creativity is integrated with team decision making, including updated information on brainstorming and electronic brainstorming.

■ *Chapter 11: Communicating in Organizational Settings*—This chapter features new material on communication competence, instant messaging, and e-zines. The section on electronic mail has been updated, and the literature on the corporate grapevine has been rewritten around Web-based rumor sites and other emerging forms of communication. The section on active listening introduces a new model based on new research from the field of marketing.

■ *Chapter 12: Organizational Power, Politics, and Persuasion*—This edition introduces the emerging topic of workplace romance from the perspective of organizational power. It also revises the discussion of information and power, visibility as a contingency of power, and the political tactic of impression management. The topic of persuasive communication has been moved from the chapter on communicating to this chapter because it provides a better fit with the notion of influence.

■ *Chapter 13: Organizational Conflict and Negotiation*—This chapter provides a fuller overview of the conflict process, with further distinction between task-related and socioemotional conflict. This edition introduces drum circles as a conflict management practice and adds more information on alternative dispute resolution.

■ *Chapter 14: Organizational Leadership*—This edition continues to recognize the trend toward leadership competencies (rather than the historical perspective of leader traits), and the importance of emotional intelligence as a leadership competency. It links the concept of servant leadership to path–goal theory and recognizes the role of self-leadership as a leadership substitute. The topic of gender issues in leadership is updated.

■ *Chapter 15: Organizational Culture*—This chapter now appears earlier (and is introduced in Chapter 1) to reflect widespread interest in having the topic discussed earlier in the book. We have also added new information on cultural language, adaptive cultures, and corporate cults.

■ *Chapter 16: Organizational Change and Development*—This edition updates information on the powerful forces for organizational change and search conferences. The emerging topic of appreciative inquiry has also been revised to reflect recent writing on this important organization development practice.

■ *Chapter 17: Organizational Structure and Design*—This chapter provides new information on the complex balance of centralization and decentralization as well as on the evolution of the client-based divisional structure. This edition also revises the sections on matrix structures and virtual corporations.

■ *Chapter 18: Employment Relationship and Career Dynamics*—This chapter has been moved so that the book finishes with the student's career launch (even for students who are in mid-career). The many changes in this chapter include updated information on psychological contracts, employability, and boundaryless careers. The chapter concludes with a new section on advice for personal career development.

SUPPORTING THE LEARNING PROCESS

The changes described above refer only to the text material. *Organizational Behavior*, Second Edition, also has improved cases, videos, team exercises, and self-assessment exercises.

 Student Learning CD   All new copies of the text are packaged with a special student CD-ROM. This value-added feature includes:

■ Interactive modules that encourage hands-on learning about such topics as motivation, leadership, and organizational communication.
■ Chapter outlines.
■ Interactive chapter quizzes.
■ Videos of real-world companies.
■ Exercises and quizzes that correspond to the CD videos.
■ A special link to McShane/Von Glinow's Online Learning Center and McGraw-Hill's Organizational Behavior Online website.

Chapter Cases and Additional Cases   Every chapter includes one short case that challenges students to diagnose issues and apply ideas from that chapter. Additional cases appear at the end of the book. Several cases are new to this book. Others, such as Arctic Mining Consultants, are classics that have withstood the test of time.

BusinessWeek   *Business Week* **Case Studies**   Found at the end of each chapter, *Business Week* case studies introduce the online full-text article and provide critical thinking questions for class discussion or assignments. These cases encourage students to understand and diagnose real-world issues using organizational behavior knowledge. For example, one case study challenges students to figure out how to motivate employees with stock options when the economy tanks (Chapter 6). Another case study asks students to explain the shifting power dynamics within Yahoo! as the web portal company copes with its new competitive environment (Chapter 12).

TEAM EXERCISE **9.3**

WHERE IN THE WORLD ARE WE?

Purpose This exercise is designed to help you understand the potential advantages of involving others in decisions rather than making decisions alone.

Materials Students require the unmarked map with grid marks (Exhibit 9.8) showing the United States of America. Students are not allowed to look at any other maps or use any other materials. The instructor will provide a list of communities located somewhere on Exhibit 9.8. The instructor will also provide copies of the answer sheet after students both individually and in teams have estimated the locations of communities.

Instructions

■ *Step 1*—Write in Exhibit 9.7 the list of communities identified by your instructor. Then, working alone, estimate the location

in Exhibit 9.8 of these communities, all of which are in the United States. For example, mark a small 1 in Exhibit 9.8 on the spot where you believe the first community is located. Mark a small 2 where you think the second community is located, and so on. Please be sure to number each location clearly and with numbers small enough to fit within one grid space.

■ *Step 2*—The instructor will organize students into approximately equal-sized teams (typically five or six people per team). Working with your team members, reach a consensus on the location of each community listed in Exhibit 9.8. The instructor might provide teams with a separate copy of this map, or each member can identify the team's numbers using a different colored pen on their individual maps. The team's

Team and Self-Assessment Exercises Experiential and self-assessment exercises represent an important part of the active learning process. *Organizational Behavior* facilitates that process by offering one or two team exercises as well as a self-assessment exercise in every chapter. Many of these learning activities, such as Where in the World Are We? (Chapter 9), A Not-So-Trivial Cross-Cultural Communication Game (Chapter 11), and Assessing Your Self-Leadership (Chapter 6), are not available in other organizational behavior textbooks.

Online Learning Center (www.mhhe.com/mcshane2e) *Organizational Behavior* offers a comprehensive and user-friendly Online Learning Center (OLC), which is the perfect solution for Internet-based content. The Student Resources Center of the site follows the textbook chapter by chapter and includes practice questions similar to those found in the test bank, online self-assessments, video cases, links to relevant external websites, and other valuable resources for students.

Margin Notes, Glossary, and Indexes *Organizational Behavior* tries to avoid unnecessary jargon, but the field of organizational behavior (as with every other discipline) has its own language. As an aid in learning this language, key terms are highlighted in bold and brief definitions appear in the margin. These definitions are also presented in an alphabetical glossary at the end of the text. We have also developed comprehensive indexes of content, names, and organizations described in this book.

INSTRUCTOR SUPPORT MATERIALS

Organizational Behavior, Second Edition, includes a variety of supplemental materials to help instructors prepare and present the material in this textbook more effectively. Some restrictions may apply, so please consult your McGraw-Hill representative regarding these resources.

Instructor Online Learning Center (www.mhhe.com/mcshane2e) Along with the Student Resource Center of the OLC (see above), *Organizational Behavior* includes a password-protected website for instructors. The site offers downloadable supplements, sample syllabi, links to OB news, regular updates on concepts and examples discussed in this book, and other resources.

PowerPoint® Presentations (ISBN: 007-247010-0) *Organizational Behavior* offers the most professional-looking and comprehensive set of PowerPoint files in the field of organizational behavior. Each PowerPoint file has more than a dozen slides relating to the chapter, and most files display one or more photographs from the textbook.

Instructor's Resource Manual (ISBN: 007-247012-7)   The *Instructor's Resource Manual i*s written entirely by Steve McShane to ensure that it represents the textbook's content and supports instructor needs. Each chapter includes the learning objectives, a glossary of key terms, a chapter synopsis, a complete lecture outline (in a larger typeface) with thumbnail images of corresponding PowerPoint slides, solutions to the end-of-chapter discussion questions, and comments on photo caption critical thinking questions. It also includes teaching notes for the chapter case, additional cases, team exercises, and self-assessments. Many chapters include supplemental lecture notes and suggested videos. The Instructor's Resource Manual also includes a comprehensive set of transparency masters and notes for the end-of-text cases.

Test Bank (ISBN: 007-247019-4) and Computerized Test Bank (ISBN: 007-247011-9)   The *Test Bank* manual includes more than 2,000 multiple-choice, true-false, and essay questions. Steve McShane wrote all the questions, and the majority of them have been tested in class examinations. Each question identifies the relevant page reference and difficulty level. The entire *Test Bank* manual is also available in a computerized version. Instructors receive special software that lets them design their own examinations from the *Test Bank* questions. It also lets instructors edit test items and add their own questions to the test bank.

ACKNOWLEDGMENTS

Organizational Behavior, Second Edition, symbolizes the power of teamwork. More correctly, it symbolizes the power of a *virtual team*—with Mary Ann Von Glinow in Miami; Steve McShane in Perth, Australia, and Singapore; the editorial crew in Chicago; the copyeditor in Virginia; and the photo researchers in New York.

Superb virtual teams require equally superb team members, and we were fortunate to have this in our favor. Sponsoring editor John Weimeister led the way with unwavering support, while solving the behind-the-scenes challenges that made everyone's life much easier. Christine Scheid, senior developmental editor, was the maestro of talent as she remarkably orchestrated a complex combination of people in this dispersed team. The keen copyediting skills of Alice Jaggard made *Organizational Behavior,* Second Edition, incredibly error-free. Natalie Ruffatto, our project editor, met the challenge of a tight production schedule and persuaded higher authorities to experiment with virtual page-proofing. Jennifer McQueen provided an excellent design and was responsive to our minor suggestions. Amy Bethea, Denise Simmons, and Jeremy Cheshareck triumphed to deliver the many photos that the authors had selected for this edition. Lori Koetters expertly handled the production and printing. Thanks to you all. This has been an exceptional team effort!

As we said earlier, more than 80 instructors around the world reviewed parts or all of *Organizational Behavior,* Second Edition, or its regional editions, over the past two years. Their compliments were energizing, and their suggestions significantly improved the final product. The following people reviewed some or all of the first edition of *Organizational Behavior* after it was published so that we could improve the quality of the second edition:

Elizabeth Abraham
Gustavus Adolphus College

Uzoamaka P. Anakwe
Pace University

Forrest Aven
University of Houston–Downtown

Jean Bartunek
Boston College

Joy Benson
University of Illinois–Springfield

Greg Bier
Stephens College

Weldon M. Blake
Bethune-Cookman College

Antonio Bos
Tusculum College

Richard Brislin
University of Hawaii

Carl R. Broadhurst
Mount Olive College

E. Holly Buttner
University of North Carolina–Greensboro

Michael Camarata
Marywood University

Anthony F. Chelte
Western New England College

Beth Chung
San Diego State University

Cynthia L. Cordes
University of Miami

Jeremy Cripps
Heidelberg College

Roger A. Dean
Washington and Lee University

George E. Dodge
West Texas A&M University

George Dollar
Clearwater Christian College

Sally Dresdow
University of Wisconsin–Green Bay

John A. Drexler, Jr.
Oregon State University

Richard A. Engdahl
University of North Carolina–Wilmington

Ellen Fagenson Eland
George Mason University

Janice M. Feldbauer
Austin Community College

Richard Feltman
San Diego State University

David L. Ford
University of Texas–Dallas

Marilyn L. Fox
Minnesota State University–Mankato

Taggart F. Frost
University of Northern Iowa

Janice S. Gates
Western Illinois University

James P. Gelatt
University of Maryland–University College

Henry Goldman
Touro University International

Eric Goodman
Colorado Technical University

Roger Goodson
College of Notre Dame

Bobby Hall
Wayland Baptist University

Pyung E. Han
Truman State University

Don Harvey
CSUB

Hoyt Hayes
Columbia College

André L. Honorée
Spring Hill College

Eugene Hughes
East Carolina University

Ron Humphrey
Virginia Commonwealth University

Janet S. Jones
Shorter College

Rusty Juban
Dallas Baptist University

Dong I. Jung
San Diego State University

Steven J. Karau
Southern Illinois University

Jennifer Kaufman
Tulane University

Thomas Kolenko
Kennesaw State University

Elliot Kushell
California State University–Fullerton

Katherine Lawrence
University of Michigan

Susan L. Manring
Elon College

Jennifer Martin
York College of Pennsylvania

James C. McElroy
Iowa State University

Janice S. Miller
University of Wisconsin–Milwaukee

Linda Morable
Richland College

Kevin Mossholder
Louisiana State University

Stephanie Naumann
University of the Pacific

Mitchell J. Neubert
Bowling Green State University

James Randall Nutter
Geneva College

Greg Oldham
University of Illinois

Patricia Parker
Maryville University

Ranjna Patel
Bethune-Cookman College

Sheila Petcavage
Cuyahoga Community College

Judy-Lynne Peters
John Jay College of Criminal Justice

Jean Phillips
Rutgers University

Emile Pilafidis
University of La Verne

Kenneth H. Price
University of Texas–Arlington

John Quigley
East Tennessee State University

Elizabeth C. Ravlin
University of South Carolina

Peter Richardson
Southwest Missouri State University

Christine Riordan
University of Georgia

Jill Roberts
Campbellsville University

Lena T. Rodriguez
San Diego State University

Elizabeth J. Rozell
Southwest Missouri State University

John L. Schmidt, Jr.
George Mason University

Michael Shaner
St. Louis University

Jason D. Shaw
University of Kentucky

James Martin Sipos
Regis University

Victoria L. Sitter
Milligan College

Guido H. Slangen
Rensselaer University

Randy Sleeth
Virginia Commonwealth University

Albert C. Smith, Jr.
Radford University

Becky L. Smith
York College of Pennsylvania

Mary Alice Smith
Tarrant County College

John J. Sosik
Penn State University–Great Valley

Marian C. Spataro
University of Arkansas–Little Rock

Christina Stamper
Western Michigan University

Gary Stark
University of Minnesota–Duluth

Susan Stites-Doe
State University of New York–Brockport

Margaret S. Stockdale
Southern Illinois University

Patrick Stubblebine
Miami University

Tom Thompson
University of Maryland–University College

Paul B. Thornton
Springfield Technical Community College

Franki Tomassi
Johnson and Wales University

Bill Turnley
Kansas State University

Mary Uhl-Bien
University of Central Florida

Mathew Valle
Elon College

Donald Vredenburgh
Baruch College

Andrew Ward
Emory University

Ellen Whitener
University of Virginia

Donna Whitney-Bammerlin
Kansas State University

Penny Wright
San Diego State University

   We would also like to thank the following people, who provided detailed comments on either *Organisational Behaviour on the Pacific Rim* (2003) or *Canadian Organizational Behaviour,* 4th edition (2001). Their ideas also found their way into the second edition of *Organizational Behavior.*

Maree Boyle
University of Queensland

Ian Brooks
University of Canterbury

David Brown
La Trobe University

Allan Bull
Macquarie University

Ron Burke
York University

Lorraine Carey
University of Tasmania

Judith Chapman
University of Western Sydney

Liz Creese
RMIT University

John Gilbert
University of Waikato

Howard Harris
University of South Australia

Brad Jackson
Victoria University

Peter Jordan
Griffith University

Alick Kaye
University of South Australia

Beverly Linnell
Southern Alberta Institute of Technology

Peter Lok
University of New South Wales

Gido Mapunda
University of South Australia

Aletta Odendaal
Tech SA

Karl Pajo
Massey University

Wilf Ratzburg
British Columbia Institute of Technology

Rod Salzman
Northern Territory University

Brenda Scott-Ladd
Murdoch University

Michael Sheehan
Griffith University

Richard Sisley
Auckland University of Technology

Conrad Smidt
Rand Afrikaans University

Deb Stewart
Victoria University

Robert Thompson
Queensland University of Technology

Sally Townsend
Swinburne University

Lesley Treleaven
University of Western Sydney

Alvin Turner
Brock University

   Steve would also like to extend special thanks to his students for sharing their learning experience and assisting with the development of the second edition of *Organizational Behavior.* These students include Master of Business Administration students at the University of Western Australia, officers attending his MBA classes at SAFTI Military Institute's Command and Staff College in Singapore, and undergraduate students at Simon Fraser University. They have been warmly receptive to emerging OB concepts, cases and exercises, examination questions, and other pedagogical features of this book. I also extend thanks to my colleagues at the University of Western Australia's Graduate School of Management for their continued support, as well as to my colleagues at Simon Fraser University in Vancouver, Canada. Finally, I am is forever indebted to my wife, Donna McClement, and to our wonderful daughters, Bryton and Madison. Their love and support give special meaning to my life.

Mary Ann would like to thank the many, many students who have used and enjoyed this book. It seems strange when students stop you on the street and say, "I recognize your picture from the book you wrote." However, this experience has happened a number of times now. Thus, it is to the students that I owe many thanks for making this learning journey very exciting! Also, the faculty and staff at Florida International University have been enormously supportive, generously sporting praise for this new contender on the market. Perhaps most of all, I wish to thank Steve McShane for shouldering the bulk of the work, and for being the techno-wizard that he is. Finally, I would like to thank my family—John, Rhoda, Lauren, Lindsay, and Christy—and also some very special folks in my life—Janet, Peter, Bill, Beth, Joanne, Nancy, and Mary, as well as Emma, Zack, Kerry, Molly, Maddie, and Glory. A final word of thanks goes to my CIBER staff—all incredibly talented people. Thank you all for being there for me!

Steven L. McShane
Mary Ann Von Glinow

Introduction

1

Introduction to the Field of Organizational Behavior

AFTER READING THIS CHAPTER, YOU SHOULD BE ABLE TO:

- Define *organizational behavior*.

- Identify three reasons for studying organizational behavior.

- List five emerging trends in organizational behavior.

- Identify the five anchors on which organizational behavior is based.

- Diagram an organization from an open systems view.

- Define *knowledge management* and *intellectual capital*.

- Identify four common ways that organizations acquire knowledge.

The Container Store sells everything you need to organize your life. It is also a model of how to organize people into a highly successful retail business. The company's success begins with a set of humane, do-unto-others values that embrace customers and employees. "It's a quirky, people-oriented, yummy, open culture," says Kip Tindell, who co-founded the Dallas-based company with Garrett Boone over 23 years ago.

Based on the principle that "one great person equals three good people," The Container Store carefully hires people with matching values and a positive work attitude. New recruits then receive over 235 hours of training in the first year, compared with 7 hours average in the retail industry. The Container Store pays its store staff generous salaries—between 50 and 100 percent more than the retail average.

Everyone sees the previous day's sales, their store's sales goal, and the company's expansion plans. They also participate in a daily ritual called "the huddle" to discuss new ways of solving customer needs. "Being well-informed generates that fierce sense of ownership by all employees in our company," Tindell explains. "Customers can feel that energy."

The company also takes empowerment to the extreme. For example, one employee in Chicago reimbursed a customer on the spot for a car seat that got ripped while load-

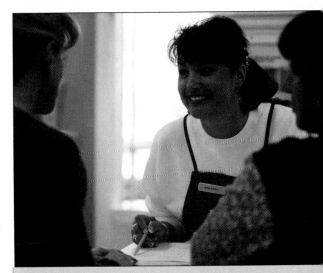

The Container Store has leveraged the power of organizational behavior to become the top-rated company to work for and a powerful competitor in the retail market. (*©Nadia Borowski Scott*)

ing a product into the customer's car. Another employee constructed a custom-made box after it was apparent that the store didn't have a box to suit the shopper's needs. "Everybody we hire, we hire as a leader," says co-founder Boone. "Anybody in our store can take an action that you might think of typically being a manager's action."

The result of these and other organizational practices is that The Container Store is an organizational success story. It recently won the Retail Innovator's Award and an Optimas award for outstanding people-management strategies. It is also the only organization chosen two years in a row by *Fortune* magazine as the best company to work for in America.[1] ■

The Container Store has become a powerful force in the retail industry, but its real power comes from the effective application of organizational behavior theories and concepts. More than ever, organizations are relying on these ideas and practices to remain competitive. For example, The Container Store trains, rewards, and empowers employees. It creates a strong sense of teamwork and emphasizes creativity. The company is driven by a strong set of organizational values that are carefully aligned with the personal values of its employees and the needs of the external environment. The effective leadership of co-founders Kip Tindell and Garrett Boone keep Container Store employees aligned with these values

This book is about people working in organizations. Its main objective is to help you understand behavior in organizations and to work more effectively in organizational settings. Organizational behavior knowledge is not only for managers and leaders. It is relevant and useful for anyone who works in and around organizations. In this chapter, we introduce you to the field of organizational behavior, outline the main reasons you should know more about it, describe the fundamental perspectives behind the study of organizations, and introduce the concept that organizations are knowledge and learning systems.

THE FIELD OF ORGANIZATIONAL BEHAVIOR

organizational behavior
The study of what people think, feel, and do in and around organizations.

Organizational behavior (OB) is the study of what people think, feel, and do in and around organizations. OB scholars systematically study individual, team, and structural characteristics that influence behavior within organizations. By saying that organizational behavior is a field of study, we mean that scholars have been accumulating a distinct knowledge about behavior within organizations—a knowledge base that is the foundation of this book.

By most estimates, OB emerged as a distinct field around the 1940s.[2] However, its origins can be traced much further back in time. The Greek philosopher Plato wrote about the essence of leadership. Aristotle, another respected philosopher, addressed the topic of persuasive communication. The writings of sixteenth-century Italian philosopher Niccolo Machiavelli laid the foundation for contemporary work on organizational power and politics. In 1776, Adam Smith advocated a new form of organizational structure based on the division of labor. One hundred years later, German sociologist Max Weber wrote about rational organizations and initiated discussion of charismatic leadership. Soon after, Frederick Winslow Taylor introduced the systematic use of goal setting and rewards to motivate employees. In the 1920s, Elton Mayo and his colleagues conducted productivity studies at Western Electric's Hawthorne plant. They reported that an informal organization—employees casually interacting with others—operates alongside the formal organization. OB has been around for a long time; it just wasn't organized into a unified discipline until after World War II.

What Are Organizations?

Organizations have existed for as long as people have worked together. Archaeologists have discovered massive temples dating back to 3500 B.C. that were constructed through the organized actions of many people. The fact that these impressive monuments were built suggests not only that complex

The Sydney Olympics is a testament to the power of organizations. The largest peacetime event in the Southern Hemisphere employed 2,400 full-time employees as well as thousands of other people working through suppliers. Several hundred university students were trained to help select more than 50,000 volunteers. The Olympic Village accommodated and fed over 15,000 athletes and representatives from 200 countries. The Sydney Olympics set up the world's largest film processing lab, the world's biggest event website, and one of the world's most sophisticated telecommunications centers. "At the end of the day, this is just a bloody big project," says Sydney Olympics chief of operations Jim Sloman. Of course, complex organizations are not infallible, and the Sydney Olympics was no exception. But in spite of flawed ticketing decisions and other glitches along the way, the Sydney Olympics has become the global standard against which other temporary event organizations are compared.[3] In your opinion, what organizational behavior concepts described in this book would have the greatest influence on the success of the Sydney Olympics and other mammoth projects? (©AFP/CORBIS)

organizations existed, but that the people in them cooperated reasonably well.[4] We have equally impressive examples of contemporary organizations, such as the Sydney Olympics, Hong Kong's new island airport at Chek Lap Kok, and the people who coordinate that complex network of computer connections called the Internet.

"[A] company is one of humanity's most amazing inventions," says Steven Jobs, CEO of Apple Computer and Pixar Animation Studios. "It's totally abstract. Sure, you have to build something with bricks and mortar to put the people in, but basically a company is this abstract construct we've invented, and it's incredibly powerful."[5]

So, what are these powerful constructs that we call **organizations?** They are groups of people who work interdependently toward some purpose.[6] Organizations are not buildings or other physical structures. Rather, they consist of people who interact with each other to achieve a set of goals. Employees

organizations
Groups of people who work interdependently toward some purpose.

have structured patterns of interaction, meaning that they expect each other to complete certain tasks in a coordinated way—in an *organized* way.

Organizations have a purpose, whether it's hosting the world's greatest athletes or selling books on the Internet. Some organizational behavior scholars are skeptical about the relevance of goals in a definition of organizations.[7] They argue that an organization's mission statement may be different from its true goals. Also, they question the assumption that all organizational members believe in the same goals. These points may be true, but imagine an organization without goals: It would consist of a mass of people wandering around aimlessly without any sense of direction. Overall, organizations likely have a collective sense of purpose, even though it is not fully understood or agreed upon.

Why Study Organizational Behavior?

You are probably reading this book as part of a course in organizational behavior. Aside from diploma or degree requirements, why should you or anyone else study OB? After all, who ever heard of a career path leading to a vice president of OB or a chief OB officer?

The main reason for studying organizational behavior is that most of us work in organizations, so we need to understand, predict, and influence the behaviors of others in organizational settings (see Exhibit 1.1). Marketing students learn marketing concepts, and computer science students learn about circuitry and software code. But all of us need organizational behavior knowledge to address the people issues when trying to apply marketing, computer science, and other ideas.

Satisfying the Need to Understand and Predict   All of us have an inherent need to know about the world in which we live. This is particularly true in organizations because of their profound effect on our lives. We feel more

EXHIBIT 1.1

Reasons for studying organizational behavior

comfortable when we can understand why organizational events occur and accurately anticipate future events.[8] The field of organizational behavior uses systematic study to help us understand and predict organizational life. OB's crystal ball isn't perfectly clear because human behavior is influenced by a complex combination of factors. Nevertheless, OB helps us make sense of the workplace and, to some extent, predict what people will do under various conditions.

The OB knowledge presented in this book also gives you the opportunity to question and rebuild your personal theories that have developed through observation and experience. For example, what theories do you hold about effective leadership? Look at "It All Makes Sense," the Self-Assessment Exercise at the end of this chapter. How many of these theoretical statements are true? Even if you answer most of them correctly, the information you will read in this book can further develop and crystallize your personal beliefs so that they more accurately model and predict organizational behavior.

Influencing Organizational Events It's nice to understand and predict organizational events, but most of us want to influence the environment in which we live. Whether you are a marketing specialist or a computer programmer, you need to know how to communicate effectively with others, manage conflict, make better decisions, build commitment to your ideas, help work teams operate more effectively, and so on. OB knowledge will help you influence organizational events. Most organizational behavior scholars take this prescriptive view by concluding their systemic research with specific recommendations for organizational action.[9]

This book takes the view that organizational behavior knowledge is for everyone—not just managers. Indeed, as organizations reduce layers of management and delegate more responsibilities to the rest of the employees, the concepts described in this book will become increasingly important for anyone who works in and around organizations. We all need to understand organizational behavior and to master the practices that influence organizational events. That's why you won't find very much emphasis here on "management." Yes, organizations will continue to have managers ("adult supervision," as young employees cynically call them), but their roles have changed. More important, many employees are now expected to manage themselves. As one forward-thinking organizational behavior scholar wrote many years ago: Everyone is a manager.[10]

EMERGING TRENDS IN ORGANIZATIONAL BEHAVIOR

There has never been a better time to learn about organizational behavior. The pace of change is accelerating, and most of the transformation is occurring in the workplace. Let's take a brief tour through five emerging organizational behavior issues: globalization, the changing workforce, information technology, emerging employment relationships, and workplace values and ethics.

Globalization

In the 1980s, most of Kraft Foods' resources and sales were in the United States, and it competed mainly against Nabisco, General Foods, and other American food processors. The Chicago-based company has since swallowed up these domestic rivals. Today, Kraft is a $35 billion business that battles for global market share against Nestlé, Unilever, Danone, and Fonterra. These competitors are no longer across the street. They are located in Switzerland, UK–Netherlands, France, and New Zealand, respectively.[11]

Kraft employees have experienced the dramatic **globalization** of their organization and the environment in which it operates. Globalization occurs when an organization extends its activities to other parts of the world, actively participates in other markets, and competes against organizations located in other countries.[12] Many firms have had international operations for many years, but these were usually import–export businesses or fairly independent subsidiaries that served local markets. Globalization, on the other hand, connects and coordinates these geographically dispersed segments so that they serve global customers and compete against other global businesses.[13]

Starbucks is another example of a globalized organization. Over the past decade, the Seattle-based coffee merchant has grown from 116 stores in North America to a global brand with 4,600 stores in 21 countries on four continents. The company carefully emphasizes the global tradition of coffee drinking, not its American roots. "It's not an American theme," argues Starbucks chairman Howard Schultz. "It has a universal language because the relevancy of Starbucks, the third place, the quality of the coffee, the social atmosphere, the romance—all of these things are as relevant in Singapore and China as they are in Zurich or Seattle."[14]

Implications for Organizational Behavior   Globalization influences several organizational behavior issues—some good, some not so good. It requires new structures and different forms of communication to assist the organization's global reach. This situation is certainly true at Lend Lease, a real estate and development company. Lend Lease's chairperson is located in Boston, its chief executive and chief financial officer are in London, its headquarters is in Sydney, and members of its senior management committee are "drawn from every corner of the globe."[15] These executives need to adapt innovative ways to communicate and share information.

Globalization often creates new career opportunities and potentially brings in new knowledge to improve the organization's competitive advantage. However, it also leads to more mergers and greater competition, which produces continuous change, layoffs, and other stressful consequences among employees.[16] "Any company, whether international or not, has to look at the way globalization has impacted the way we work," warns an executive at the global health care company GlaxoSmithKline. "And even if you're not global, there's a competitor or customer somewhere who is."[17]

We need to be sensitive to globalization when applying organizational behavior concepts and practices. For the past 40 years, OB scholars have warned that organizational practices in one country may not be applicable elsewhere because of cultural and historical differences.[18] We cannot assume that work teams, employee involvement, stock options, or other organizational behavior practices that work in one country will work as well in other parts of the world.[19] This doesn't mean that we have to reinvent organizational behavior. Rather, globalization emphasizes the need to recognize the contingencies of effective OB practices in different cultures. (The contingency anchor of OB is discussed later in this chapter.)

globalization

When an organization extends its activities to other parts of the world, actively participates in other markets, and competes against organizations located in other countries.

Globalization has important implications for how we learn about organizational behavior. The best-performing companies may be in Finland, Brazil, or India, not just in Illinois or California. That's why you will encounter numerous examples from around the planet in this book. We want you to learn from the best, no matter where their headquarters is located.

The Changing Workforce

Walk into a Wal-Mart store in Washington, D.C., and you might think you have entered a United Nations building. That's because employees come from 45 countries and speak 100 different languages.[20] Like Wal-Mart, most companies in the United States have a multicultural workforce because of the country's increasing demographic diversity. Minorities represent over one-quarter of the American workforce, and the percentage is projected to increase substantially over the next few decades. The Hispanic population is one of the fastest-growing groups in the United States and has replaced African Americans as the second-largest ethnic group.[21] Within the next 50 years, one in four Americans will be Hispanic, 14 percent will be African-American, and 8 percent will be Asian-American. By 2060, non-Hispanic whites will be a minority.

It will be increasingly difficult to discuss ethnic differences as interracial marriages increase. Indeed, scholars are already debating the merits of distinguishing people by their ethnicity.[22] However, as Exhibit 1.2 illustrates, workforce diversity has many other primary and secondary dimensions. The primary dimensions—gender, ethnicity, age, race, sexual orientation, and mental/physical qualities—represent personal characteristics that influence an individual's socialization and self-identity. The secondary dimensions are those features that we learn or have some control over throughout our lives, such as education, marital status, religion, and work experience.

Another form of diversity is the increasing representation of women in the workforce. Women now represent nearly 50 percent of the paid workforce, compared with just 20 percent a few decades ago. Gender-based shifts continue to occur within occupations. For example, women represented only 17 percent of accountants in the United States in the 1960s. Today, over half the accountants are women. Only 9 percent of medical school students in 1970 were women. They now account for 43 percent of medical school enrollments. This is a significant increase, considering that medical economics journals in the 1960s published articles about whether medical training was wasted on women.[24]

Age cohorts represent another primary dimension of workforce diversity. Baby boomers—

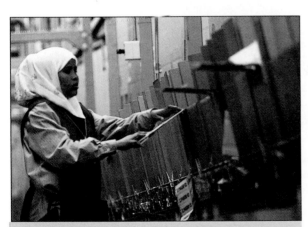

As the workplace becomes more multicultural, corporate leaders need to provide reasonable accommodation for people with diverse backgrounds. That's what Value City Department Stores realized as Asho Ibrahim (shown in photo) and other Muslim employees joined the company. Ibrahim and roughly 200 other Muslim employees in the company's eight distribution centers need to pray five times each day. Value City provides a quiet room so that they can pray during their breaks. Employees also wear clothing mandated by their religious beliefs.[23] What other changes are taking place in organizations to accommodate the increasingly diverse workforce? (©AP/Wide World)

EXHIBIT 1.2

Primary and
secondary dimensions
of workforce diversity

Primary dimension

Secondary dimension

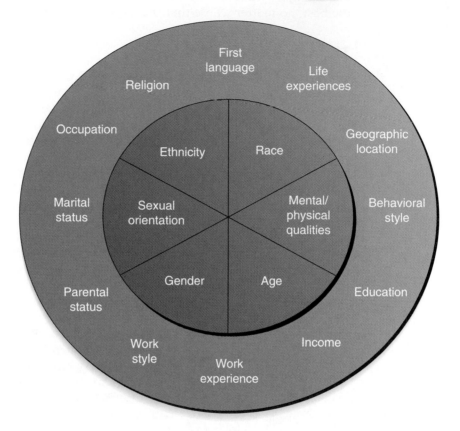

Sources: Adapted from M. Loden, *Implementing Diversity* (Chicago: Irwin, 1996); S. Bradford, "Fourteen Dimensions of Diversity: Understanding and Appreciating Differences in the Workplace," in J. W. Pfeiffer, ed., *1996 Annual: Vol. 2, Consulting* (San Diego: Pfeiffer, 1996), pp. 9–17.

people born between 1946 and 1964—have somewhat different values and expectations in the workplace than Generation-X employees—those born between 1964 and 1977.[25] According to several writers, the typical baby boomer tends to expect and desire more job security (at least, at this stage in his or her career). In contrast, Gen-Xers are typically less loyal to one organization and, in return, expect less job security. Gen-Xers tend to be motivated more by workplace flexibility and the opportunity to use new technology. Baby boomers are more likely to be workaholics, motivated to improve their economic and social status. Some writers are starting to describe how Generation-Y employees (those born in the decade or so after 1978) expect plenty of responsibility and involvement in their employment relationship. While these statements certainly don't apply to everyone in each cohort, they reflect the fact that different generations bring different values and expectations.[26]

Implications for Organizational Behavior Diversity presents both opportunities and challenges in organizations. It can become a competitive advantage by improving decision making and team performance on complex tasks.[27] For many businesses, a diverse workforce is also necessary to provide better customer service in the global marketplace. "We go out of our way to recruit from a melting pot of nationalities," says an executive at Amadeus, a developer of worldwide airline reservation software near Nice, France. "We believe that our product is superior because of the different cultures of the people developing it."[28]

Along with its benefits, workforce diversity presents new challenges. For instance, women have represented a large portion of the workforce for the past two decades, yet they are still underrepresented in senior positions. Most ethnic minorities in the United States also believe that discrimination in the workplace is still common.[29] Various organizational behavior topics, including perceptual distortions (Chapter 3) and organizational politics (Chapter 12) address these issues. Diversity also influences team development (Chapter 8) and the potential for conflict among employees (Chapter 13).

Organizations need to address these potential problems and adapt to emerging workforce needs. For instance, the global consulting firm Cap Gemini Ernst & Young distributes a monthly planning calendar that identifies various religious holidays or ethnic/national celebrations. J. C. Penney executives attend special classes to learn what motivates younger-generation employees. When Siemens AG's nuclear power division in Germany and French nuclear giant Framatome SA merged, executives at the two firms attended cross-cultural sensitivity and team-building classes to minimize cross-cultural conflict.[30]

Emerging Employment Relationships

The workforce isn't the only thing that's changing. After more than 100 years of relative stability, employment relationships are being redefined. Replacing the implied guarantee of lifelong employment in return for loyalty is a "new deal" called **employability.** Employees perform a variety of work activities rather than hold specific jobs, and they are expected to continually learn skills that will keep them employed. Corporate leaders claim that employability is necessary so that organizations can adapt to the rapidly changing business environment. However, as we shall learn throughout this book, employability also has implications for job design, organizational loyalty, career dynamics, and workplace stress.[31]

Another employment shift is the increasing percentage of the workforce in **contingent work**—any job in which the individual does not have an explicit or implicit contract for long-term employment, or one in which the minimum hours of work can vary in a nonsystematic way.[32] By some estimates, more than 15 percent of the U.S. workforce is employed in some sort of contingent work arrangement. Several experts predict that this trend will continue. "We are moving into the age of contractualization where everyone is their own boss," claims a consultant who believes the concept of "employee" is a throwback to industrial revolution servitude.[33]

A new breed of free agents is thriving on the independence and reliance on knowledge that contingent work demands.[34] But contrasting with this optimistic view is the reality that many contingent workers would rather be

employability
An employment relationship in which people are expected to continually develop their skills to remain employed.

contingent work
Any job in which the individual does not have an explicit or implicit contract for long-term employment, or one in which the minimum hours of work can vary in a nonsystematic way.

employed in stable, well-paying jobs. We will learn that contingent work affects organizational loyalty, career dynamics, and other aspects of organizational behavior.

Telecommuting   It's 9 A.M., the beginning of another busy day for Paolo Conconi, the Italian-born owner of Hong Kong electronic-parts maker MPS Electronics. But Conconi doesn't worry about fighting Hong Kong traffic to get to work. His office is at home, far away on the Indonesian island of Bali. Conconi's office is a table by the swimming pool, where he checks e-mail and calls staff and clients in Europe and Asia. "I've organized my work so that I can do it from anywhere," he says. "As long as I have electricity and one or two phone lines, that's all I need."[35]

Paolo Conconi is among the tens of millions of people who have altered their employment relationship through **telecommuting** (also called *teleworking*)—working from home, usually with a computer connection to the office. Technology has untethered some employees so completely from the employer's physical work space that clients and co-workers are oblivious to their true location. For instance, call center operators in Kansas work at home during snowstorms without clients' knowing the difference.[36]

As we move from an industrial to a knowledge-based economy, the number of people who take the information highway to work each day will continue to increase. However, telecommuting poses a number of challenges for organizations and employees.[37] Employers who previously evaluated employees for their "face time"—the amount of time they were physically in the workplace—need to develop outcome-based measures of performance. Evaluating telecommuters is particularly difficult in some Asian cultures where company loyalty is measured by the number of hours at the office.

Employees accustomed to direct supervision need to learn how to manage themselves through self-leadership (see Chapter 6). Many employees complain that telecommuting can be a lonely experience, whereas working at the office is more likely to fulfill a person's social needs. Another problem is that telecommuting creates risks in office politics, a topic we discuss in Chapter 12. As telecommuting increases, employees must also learn how to get things done through **virtual teams**—cross-functional groups that operate across space, time, and organizational boundaries with members who communicate mainly through electronic technologies (see Chapter 8).[38]

Information Technology and OB

By day, Nana Frimpong is the official wood-carver for King Otumfuo Osei Tutu II in the royal Asante court of Ghana, West Africa. But when he isn't carving stools for the king, Frimpong sells his wares over the Internet. Demand from international buyers is so strong that he now employs a staff of 15 carvers. In this country of 19 million people and only 100,000 telephones, Frimpong is somewhat of a celebrity and a role model for the country's potential prosperity. "There are a lot of Nana Frimpongs in the Asante nation," says King Tutu. "Many can be helped through the Internet."[39]

Whether we make fiber-optic routers in California or wooden stools and masks in Ghana, the Internet is changing our lives. It has created opportunities to connect people around the planet and allow small businesses in developing

---

telecommuting
Also called teleworking, it is working from home, usually with a computer connection to the office.

virtual teams
Cross-functional groups that operate across space, time, and organizational boundaries with members who communicate mainly through electronic technologies.

"Can't talk now. I'm in a seminar about improving communication with technology."

(Copyright © 1996. Ted Goff www.tedgoff.com.)

countries to compete in the global marketplace. Information technology is also shaking up traditional organizational behavior concepts within organizations. We have already noted how this technology has given rise to virtual teams and has made it possible for knowledge workers to carry on their business from home or from an Indonesian island. It also increases communication among people with diverse cultural backgrounds and creates new ways to acquire knowledge. In general, information technology challenges traditional business logic regarding how employees interact, how organizations are configured, and how they relate to customers.

network organization

An alliance of several organizations for the purpose of creating a product or serving a client.

Information technology also makes it easier to create a **network organization**—an alliance of several organizations for the purpose of creating a product or serving a client. Cisco Systems, which makes routers and other technology for the Internet, is really a constellation of suppliers, contract manufacturers, assemblers, and other partners connected through an intricate web of information technology. Cisco's network springs into action as soon as a customer places an order (usually through the Internet). Suppliers send the required materials to assemblers, who ship the product directly to the client, usually the same day. Seventy percent of Cisco's product is outsourced this way. In many cases, Cisco employees never touch the product.[40]

Workplace Values and Ethics

At the beginning of this chapter, we read that The Container Store is very careful about hiring the right people. The Dallas-based retailer isn't particularly looking for the job applicant's technical skills. Rather, company founders Kip Tindell and Garrett Boone have emphasized that the best employees bring the same values to the workplace that The Container Store holds up as its corporate values. In other words, the company looks for alignment of values.

values
Stable, long-lasting beliefs about what is important in a variety of situations.

The Container Store and other organizations are paying a lot more attention these days to values in the workplace. **Values** represent stable, long-lasting beliefs about what is important in a variety of situations. They are evaluative standards that help us define what is right or wrong, or good or bad, in the world.[41] Values dictate our priorities, our preferences, and our desires. They influence our motivation and decisions. "Ninety-nine percent of what we say is about values," advises Anita Roddick, founder of the Body Shop.[42]

Cultural, personal, and organizational values have been studied by organizational behavior scholars for several decades.[43] *Cultural values*, which we discuss in Chapter 4 (along with personal and ethical values) represent the dominant prescriptions of a society. They are usually influenced by religious, philosophical, and political ideologies. *Personal values* incorporate cultural values, as well as other values socialized by parents, friends, and personal life events. *Organizational values*, discussed in Chapter 15, on **organizational culture,** are widely and deeply shared by people within the organization.[44]

organizational culture
The basic pattern of shared assumptions, values, and beliefs governing the way employees within an organization think about and act on problems and opportunities.

Importance of Values and Ethics   If values have been studied for so long, why are they just now becoming an emerging issue? One reason is globalization. As organizations expand across cultures, differences in values become more pronounced.[45] Such differences lead to both personal and organizational challenges. At the individual level, employees may find that their personal values conflict with organizational and cross-cultural values.[46] At the organizational level, leaders are looking for ways to integrate (or, at least, coordinate) people with diverse personal and cultural value systems.

Another reason for the recent attention to values is that the old command-and-control system of direct supervision is expensive and incompatible with today's more independently minded workforce. Organizational values represent a subtle, yet potentially effective, alternative. Corporate culture is a deeply embedded form of social control that guides employee decisions and behavior so that they are consistent with the organization's success. For example, The Container Store wants to hire people who value mutual support and customer focus.

ethics
The study of moral principles or values that determine whether actions are right or wrong and outcomes are good or bad.

A third reason why values have become so important is that many societies are putting more pressure on organizations to engage in ethical practices. **Ethics** refers to the study of moral principles or values that determine whether actions are right or wrong and outcomes are good or bad. We rely on our ethical values to determine the right thing to do. Throughout this textbook, you will discover numerous topics that relate to business ethics, such as monitoring employee performance, rewarding people equitably, stereotyping employees, using peer pressure, engaging in organizational politics, and applying organization development practices. Ethics is also discussed in Chapter 4 and is related to corporate culture in Chapter 15.

THE FIVE ANCHORS OF ORGANIZATIONAL BEHAVIOR

Globalization, the changing workforce, emerging employment relationships, information technology, and workplace values are just a few of the issues that we will explore in this textbook. To understand these and other topics, organizational behavior scholars rely on a set of basic beliefs or knowledge structures (see Exhibit 1.3). These conceptual anchors represent the way that OB

The MONY Group's ethics and social responsibility practices strengthen its relationship with both the community and its own employees. The New York–based financial services firm donates $100 to employees who volunteer at least five hours over six months to a nonprofit organization of their choice. MONY employees also volunteer to brighten up school yards (shown in photo) and help students with their reading. "Volunteerism is one element that goes into retaining a good employee," says Lynn Stekis of the MONY Foundation. Carla Cohn, MONY's director of information technology and a volunteer reader to schoolchildren, agrees. "It's another indication of how MONY is not just a company, but also a place that cares about its people and the community," she says.[48] Why do an organization's ethical and social responsibility practices affect its ability to attract and retain employees? *(Courtesy of* Training *magazine)*

researchers think about organizations and how they should be studied. Let's look at each of these five beliefs that anchor the study of organizational behavior.

The Multidisciplinary Anchor

Organizational behavior is anchored around the idea that the field should develop from knowledge in other disciplines, not just from its own isolated research base.[47] In other words, OB should be multidisciplinary. The top part of Exhibit 1.4 identifies the traditional disciplines from which organizational behavior knowledge has developed. For instance, the field of psychology has aided our understanding of most issues relating to individual and interpersonal behavior. Sociologists have contributed to our knowledge of team dynamics, organizational socialization, organizational power, and other aspects of the social system.

The bottom part of Exhibit 1.4 identifies some of the emerging fields from which organizational behavior knowledge is acquired. The communications field helps us understand the dynamics of knowledge management, electronic mail, corporate culture, and employee socialization. Information systems scholars are exploring the effects of information technology on team dynamics, decision making, and knowledge management. Marketing scholars have enhanced our understanding of job satisfaction and customer service, knowledge management, and creativity. Women's studies scholars are studying perceptual biases and power relations between men and women in organizations.

EXHIBIT 1.3

Five conceptual anchors of organizational behavior

EXHIBIT 1.4

Multidisciplinary anchor of organizational behavior

Discipline	Relevant OB topics
Traditional	
Psychology	Motivation, perception, attitudes, personality, job stress, job enrichment, performance appraisals, leadership
Sociology	Team dynamics, roles, socialization, communication patterns, organizational power, organizational structure
Anthropology	Corporate culture, organizational rituals, cross-cultural dynamics, organizational adaptation
Political science	Intergroup conflict, coalition formation, organizational power and politics, decision making, organizational environments
Economics	Decision making, negotiation, organizational power
Industrial engineering	Job design, productivity, work measurement
Emerging	
Communications	Knowledge management, electronic mail, corporate culture, employee socialization
Information systems	Team dynamics, decision making, knowledge management
Marketing	Knowledge management, creativity, decision making
Women's studies	Organizational power, perceptions

The true test of OB's multidisciplinary anchor is how effectively OB scholars continue to transfer knowledge from traditional and emerging disciplines. History suggests that fields of inquiry tend to become more inwardly focused as they mature.[49] It is our hope that OB will avoid this tendency by continuing to recognize ideas from other disciplines.

The Systematic Research Anchor

A second anchor is that organizational behavior researchers believe in the systematic collection of data and information about organizations. In other words, they rely on a set of principles and practices that minimize personal biases and distortions about organizational events. For the most part, they rely on the scientific method by forming research questions, systematically collecting data, and testing hypotheses against those data. OB scholars are also turning to qualitative research methods to make sense of organizations. Qualitative researchers rely on grounded theory and other systematic practices to ensure that they document shared meaning of organizational events. Appendix A at the end of this book provides an overview of research design and methods commonly found in organizational behavior studies.

The Contingency Anchor

contingency approach
The idea that a particular action may have different consequences in different situations.

"It depends" is a phrase that OB scholars often use to answer a question about the best solution to an organizational problem. The statement may frustrate some people, yet it reflects an important way of understanding and predicting organizational events, called the **contingency approach.** This anchor states that a particular action may have different consequences in different situations. In other words, no single solution is best in all circumstances.[50]

Many early OB theorists proposed universal rules to predict and explain organizational life, but there are usually too many exceptions to make these "one best way" theories useful. For example, in Chapter 14 we will learn that leaders should use one style (e.g., participation) in some situations and another style (e.g., direction) in other situations. Thus, when faced with a particular problem or opportunity, we need to understand and diagnose the situation, and select the strategy most appropriate *under those conditions*.[51]

Although contingency-oriented theories are necessary in most areas of organizational behavior, we should be wary about carrying this anchor to an extreme. Some contingency models add more confusion than value over universal ones. Consequently, we need to balance the sensitivity of contingency factors with the simplicity of universal theories.

The Multiple Levels of Analysis Anchor

This textbook divides organizational behavior topics into three levels of analysis: individual, team, and organization (see Exhibit 1.5). The individual level includes the characteristics and behaviors of employees as well as the thought processes that are attributed to them, such as motivation, perceptions, personalities, attitudes, and values. The team level of analysis looks at the way people interact. This level includes team dynamics, decisions, power, organizational politics, conflict, and leadership. At the organizational level, we focus on how people structure their working relationships and on how organizations interact with their environments.

Although an OB topic is typically pegged into one level of analysis, it usually relates to all three levels.[52] For instance, communication is located in this book as a team process, but we also recognize that it includes individual and organizational processes. Therefore, you should try to think about each OB topic at the individual, team, and organizational levels, not at just one of these levels.

The Open Systems Anchor

Hewlett-Packard may have lots of buildings and equipment, but CEO Carly Fiorina says that her job is to nurture something that is alive. "I think that a

---

EXHIBIT 1.5

Three levels of analysis in organizational behavior

company is a living system," says Fiorina. "It is an organism, it is operating in other living systems, and a leader has to think about the company as a living, breathing system."[53] Carly Fiorina is describing the fifth anchor of organizational behavior—the view that organizations are **open systems.**

Organizations are open systems because they take their sustenance from the environment and, in turn, affect that environment through their output. A company's survival and success depend on how well employees sense environmental changes and alter their patterns of behavior to fit those emerging conditions.[54] In contrast, a closed system has all the resources needed to survive without dependence on the external environment. Organizations are never completely closed systems, but monopolies operating in very stable environments can ignore customers and others for a fairly long time without adverse consequences.

As Exhibit 1.6 illustrates, organizations acquire resources from the external environment, including raw materials, employees, financial resources, information, and equipment. Inside the organization are numerous subsystems, such as processes (communication and reward systems), task activities (production, marketing), and social dynamics (informal groups, power dynamics). With the aid of technology (such as equipment, work methods, and information), these subsystems transform inputs into various outputs. Some outputs (e.g., products and services) may be valued by the external environment, whereas other outputs (e.g., work stress, employee layoffs) have adverse effects. The organization receives feedback from the external environment regarding the value of its outputs and the availability of future inputs. This process is cyclical and, ideally, self-sustaining, so that the organization may continue to survive and prosper.

External Environment and Stakeholders   The external environment consists of the natural and social conditions outside the organization. For example, companies depend on physical space, natural resources, and a knowledgeable workforce. Probably the most important component of the external environment is the organization's **stakeholders.** These are the shareholders, customers, suppliers, governments, and any other groups with a vested interest in the organization.[55] Stakeholders influence the firm's access to inputs and

open systems
Organizations that take their sustenance from the environment and, in turn, affect that environment through their output.

stakeholders
Shareholders, customers, suppliers, governments, and any other groups with a vested interest in the organization.

EXHIBIT 1.6

Open systems view of organizations

ability to discharge outputs. Some scholars suggest that each organization's distinctiveness depends on the stakeholders it emphasizes. And unless they pay attention to the needs of stakeholders, organizational leaders may find their business in trouble.

Because organizations operate in a much more complex and turbulent environment than a few decades ago, careful analysis of corporate decisions may be a waste of precious time.[56] Organizations remain responsive by giving employees more freedom to make decisions, allowing them to experiment, and viewing mistakes as learning opportunities. In other words, corporate change occurs more quickly when the people on the frontlines of the changing environment are empowered to make decisions.

Systems as Interdependent Parts   Organizational systems consist of many internal subsystems that need to be continually aligned with each other. As companies grow, they develop more and more complex subsystems that must coordinate with each other in the process of transforming inputs to outputs.[57] These interdependencies can easily become so complex that a minor event in one subsystem may amplify into serious unintended consequences elsewhere in the organization.

British Airways taught its employees about the interdependence of subsystems through a computer simulation. The task involved making "Granny" a happy British Airways passenger while getting her from her home to a particular destination. It isn't as easy as it sounds. When participants use frequent flyer plan incentives to lure Granny onto a particular flight, for example, the computer program quickly points out that this action affects other customers and requires the marketing department to communicate the incentive. Through this exercise, British Airways employees learn how decisions and actions in one subsystem affect not just Granny, but also other people in other parts of the organization.[58]

The open systems anchor is an important way of viewing organizations. However, it has traditionally focused on physical resources that enter the organization and are processed into physical goods (outputs). This outlook was representative of the industrial economy, but not of the new economy, where the most valued input is knowledge. The final section of this chapter introduces the key features of this emerging perspective in organizational behavior.

knowledge management
Any structured activity that improves an organization's capacity to acquire, share, and utilize knowledge in ways that improves its survival and success.

KNOWLEDGE MANAGEMENT

Organizational behavior scholars have built on the open system anchor to create an entire subfield of research dedicated to the dynamics of **knowledge management.** Knowledge management is any structured activity that improves an organization's capacity to acquire, share, and use knowledge in ways that improve its survival and success.[59] The knowledge that resides in an organization is called its **intellectual capital.** Intellectual capital is the sum of an organization's human capital, structural capital, and relationship capital.[60]

intellectual capital
The sum of an organization's human capital, structural capital, and relationship capital.

- *Human capital* is the knowledge that employees possess and generate, including their skills, experience, and creativity.
- *Structural capital* is the knowledge captured and retained in an organization's systems and structures. It is the knowledge that remains after all the human capital has gone home.

- *Relationship capital* is the value derived from an organization's relationships with customers, suppliers, and other external stakeholders who provide added value for the organization. It includes customer loyalty as well as mutual trust between the organization and its suppliers.[61]

Knowledge Management Processes

Intellectual capital represents the *stock* of knowledge held by an organization. This stock of knowledge is so important that some companies try to measure its value.[62] But knowledge management is much more than the organization's stock of knowledge. It is a *process* that develops an organization's capacity to acquire, share, and use knowledge more effectively. This process is often called *organizational learning* because companies must continually learn about their environments in order to survive and succeed through adaptation.[63] The capacity to acquire, share, and use knowledge means that companies have established systems, structures, and organizational values that support the knowledge management process. Let's look more closely at some of the strategies companies use to acquire, share, and use knowledge.

Knowledge Acquisition   Knowledge acquisition includes the organization's ability to extract information and ideas from its environment as well as through insight. One of the fastest and most powerful ways to acquire knowledge is through **grafting**—hiring individuals or buying entire companies.[64] For instance, Nortel Networks quickly moved from telecommunications into fiber-optic gear by acquiring Bay Networks, Qtera Corporation, and other organizations with leading-edge knowledge. Knowledge also enters the organization when employees learn about the external environment. Wal-Mart executives do this by systematically shopping at competitor stores every week. A third knowledge acquisition strategy is experimentation. Companies receive knowledge through insight as a result of research and other creative processes (see Chapter 10).[65]

Knowledge Sharing   Many organizations are reasonably good at acquiring knowledge but waste this resource by not effectively disseminating it. As several executives have lamented: "I wish we knew what we know." Studies report that knowledge sharing is usually the weakest link in knowledge management.[66] Valuable ideas sit idly—rather like unused inventory—or as hidden "silos of knowledge" throughout the organization. One organizational unit might apply useful ideas to improve performance or customer service, whereas a nearby unit has not discovered these better procedures.

Organizations need to improve communication to improve knowledge sharing (see Chapter 11). Global Connections 1.1 describes how Ericsson, the Swedish electronics firm, encourages knowledge sharing mainly through information technology. Some companies encourage knowledge sharing through **communities of practice.** These are informal groups bound together by shared expertise and passion for a particular activity or interest.[67] Great Harvest Bread Company applies this idea by encouraging its 140 highly autonomous franchisees to participate in the company's learning community. This community consists of casual visits, telephone calls, and e-mails to other Great Harvest franchisees. "We had an epiphany a long time ago," says Tom

grafting
The process of acquiring knowledge by hiring individuals or buying entire companies.

communities of practice
Informal groups bound together by shared expertise and passion for a particular activity or interest.

Ericsson Shares the Knowledge

Ericsson values knowledge sharing, but the giant Swedish electronics company is a highly decentralized business spread across many business units and countries. To overcome these distance and functional barriers, Ericsson applies several knowledge-sharing strategies.

A cornerstone of Ericsson's knowledge sharing is providing free Internet access to its employees and their families. The service connects users to Zopps, a virtual community site filled with Ericsson information. The Zopps website invites users to comment on the Ericsson technology and information content, thereby receiving market testing and structured knowledge transfer. "We are really interested in their opinions," says an Ericsson business development executive in Stockholm. "Not so much the technical opinions of our engineers, but their teenage children's ideas of what is good or bad about network technology, content and multimedia."

A second knowledge-sharing venue is Knack, an internal website focused on competence development. To some extent, Knack is an online learning center. However, it is also a place for knowledge transfer through a virtual "coffee shop," where discussion groups and specialist forums are maintained. In this respect, Knack becomes the meeting place of communities of practice. It also provides a knowledge map by listing competence inventories of experts in different fields.

To help the Web-based knowledge connections flow more smoothly, Ericsson brings together project man-

Ericsson, the Swedish electronics giant, relies on several strategies to share knowledge throughout its decentralized business units. (*©Reuters NewMedia Inc./CORBIS*)

agers at the Ericsson Project Management Institute. The explicit objective of these sessions is for project managers to learn new methods and the best practices. Implicitly, the gatherings improve networking, which, in turn, increases knowledge sharing through information technology.

Sources: Based on T. Hellström, "Knowledge and Competence Management at Ericsson: Decentralization and Organizational Fit," *Journal of Knowledge Management* 4 (2000); M. Van Niekerk, "Ericsson Employees Are One Big Internet Family," *The Age (Melbourne),* July 21, 1998, p. 2.

McMakin, chief operating officer of the Dillon, Montana, company. "Owners profit more from each other's experiences than from the 'wisdom' of a central world headquarters."[68]

Knowledge Use Acquiring and sharing knowledge are wasted exercises unless knowledge is effectively put to use. To do this, employees must realize that the knowledge is available and that they have enough freedom to apply it. Effective use of knowledge requires a culture that supports experiential learning (see Chapter 2).

organizational memory
The storage and preservation of intellectual capital.

Organizational Memory

Intellectual capital can be lost as quickly as it is acquired. Corporate leaders need to recognize that they are the keepers of an **organizational memory.** This metaphor refers to the storage and preservation of intellectual capital. It includes information that employees possess as well as knowledge embedded in the organization's systems and structures. It includes documents, objects, and anything else that provides meaningful information about how the organization should operate.

How do organizations retain intellectual capital? One way is by keeping good employees. While many high-tech companies laid off an unprecedented number of people to cut costs during the recent "tech wreck," Apple Computer held on to its talent. "Our main asset is human talent, and we cannot afford to lose it," explains Apple's chief financial officer, Fred Anderson.[69] A second strategy is to systematically transfer knowledge before employees leave. This process occurs when new recruits apprentice with skilled employees, thereby acquiring knowledge that is not documented.

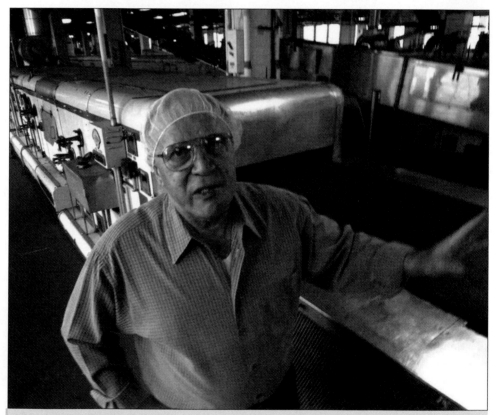

Rod Willcox didn't know how to turn on the lights, let alone operate the equipment, when he first walked into this cracker bakery that Nabisco had shut down a year earlier. Fortunately, Willcox quickly recaptured the lost memory when his company, the Atlantic Baking Group, reopened the East Liberty, Pennsylvania, plant. Willcox simply rehired 40 former Nabisco employees who had worked at the bakery. The former Nabisco workers have been invaluable in redesigning the manufacturing layout and eliminating some kinks in the way things worked under the former owner.[70] Along with keeping (or rehiring) knowledgeable employees, how else can an organization retain organizational memory? (©AP/Wide World)

A third organizational memory strategy is to transfer knowledge into structural capital.[71] This strategy includes bringing out hidden knowledge, organizing it, and putting it in a form that can be available to others. This is what the organizing committee for the Sydney Olympics (SOCOG) did. SOCOG received mostly informal and anecdotal information from the Atlanta Olympics on how to run this type of event. To ensure that future Olympics organizers would have more knowledge, all divisions and functional areas within SOCOG completed extensive templates of how they set up their operations. This effort resulted in 90 manuals that document everything from organizational structure and stakeholders to staffing and budgets.[72]

Before leaving the topic of organizational memory and knowledge management, you should know that successful companies also *unlearn*. Sometimes it is appropriate for organizations to selectively forget certain knowledge.[73] This means that they should cast off the routines and patterns of behavior that are no longer appropriate. Employees need to rethink their perceptions, such as how they should interact with customers and which is the best way to perform a task. As we shall discover in Chapter 16, unlearning is essential for organizational change.

THE JOURNEY BEGINS

This chapter gives you some background about the field of organizational behavior. But it's only the beginning of our journey. Throughout this book, we will challenge you to learn new ways of thinking about how people work in and around organizations. We will also rely on a broad range of firms across the United States and around the planet. You will recognize some companies—such as Ericsson, Boeing, and Southwest Airlines. But we also introduce you to many firms that you probably haven't heard about. Some, such as IDEO and Agilent Technologies, are emerging forces in today's fast-paced world of work. Still others, such as Ipswitch and Animal Logic, are small organizations. Chances are that you will work in a small business, so it makes sense that you should learn about organizational behavior in these operations.

CHAPTER SUMMARY

Organizational behavior is a relatively young field of inquiry that studies what people think, feel, and do in and around organizations. Organizations are groups of people who work interdependently toward some purpose.

OB concepts help us predict and understand organizational events, adopt more accurate theories of reality, and control organizational events more effectively. They let us make sense of the work world, test and challenge our personal theories of human behavior, and understand ways to manage organization activities.

There are several emerging issues and changes in organizational behavior. Globalization requires corporate decision makers to be more sensitive to cultural differences. The workforce is becoming increasingly diverse. Companies and employees must adjust to emerging employment relationships. Information technology has created virtual teams and network organizations. Corporate leaders are paying more attention to values in the workplace.

Organizational behavior scholars rely on a set of basic beliefs to study organizations. These anchors include beliefs that OB knowledge should be multidisciplinary and based on systematic research, that organizational events usually have contingencies, that organizational behavior can be viewed from three levels of analysis (individual, team, and organization), and that organizations are open systems.

The open systems anchor suggests that organizations have interdependent parts that work together to continually monitor and transact with the external environment. They acquire resources from the environment, transform them through technology, and return outputs to the environment. The external environment consists of the natural and social conditions outside the organization. This environment includes stakeholders—any group with a vested interest in the organization. External environments are generally much more turbulent today, so organizations must become adaptable and responsive.

Knowledge management develops an organization's capacity to acquire, share, and use knowledge in ways that improve the organization's survival and success. Intellectual capital is knowledge that resides in an organization, including its human capital, structural capital, and relationship capital. It is a firm's main source of competitive advantage. Organizations acquire knowledge through grafting, individual learning, and experimentation. Knowledge sharing occurs mainly through communication. Knowledge use occurs when employees realize that the knowledge is available and that they have enough freedom to apply it. Organizational memory refers to the storage and preservation of intellectual capital.

KEY TERMS

communities of practice, p. 20

contingency approach, p. 16

contingent work, p. 11

employability, p. 11

ethics, p. 14

globalization, p. 8

grafting, p. 20

intellectual capital, p. 19

knowledge management, p. 19

network organization, p. 13

open systems, p. 18

organizational behavior (OB), p. 4

organizational culture, p. 14

organizational memory, p. 21

organizations, p. 5

stakeholders, p. 18

telecommuting, p. 12

values, p. 14

virtual teams, p. 12

DISCUSSION QUESTIONS

1. A friend suggests that organizational behavior courses are useful only to people who will enter management careers. Discuss the accuracy of your friend's statement.
2. Look through the list of chapters in this textbook; then discuss how information technology could influence each organizational behavior topic.
3. Comment on the accuracy of this statement: Organizational theories should follow the contingency approach.
4. Employees in the water distribution unit of a large city were put into teams and encouraged to find ways to improve efficiency. The teams boldly crossed departmental boundaries and areas of management discretion in search of problems. Employees working in other parts of the city began to complain about these intrusions. Moreover, when some team ideas were implemented, the city managers discovered that a dollar saved in the water distribution unit may have cost the organization two dollars in higher costs elsewhere. Use the open systems anchor to explain what happened here.
5. After attending a seminar on knowledge management, a mining company executive argues that this perspective ignores the fact that that mining companies could not rely on knowledge alone to stay in business. They also need physical capital (such as digging and ore processing equipment) and land (where the minerals are located). In fact, those two factors may be more important than what employees carry around in their heads. Do you agree with the mining executive's statement? Why or why not?
6. Fully describe intellectual capital, and explain how an organization can retain this capital.
7. At a recent seminar on information technology, you heard a consultant say that over 30 percent of U.S. companies use software to manage documents and exchange information, whereas firms in Europe are just beginning to adopt this technology. On the basis of this information, the consultant concluded that knowledge management in Europe is at its beginning stages. In other words, few firms in Europe practice knowledge management. Comment on this consultant's statement.
8. BusNews Corporation is the leading stock market and business news service. Over the past two years, BusNews has experienced increased competition from other news providers. These competitors have brought in Internet and other emerging computer technologies to link customers with information more quickly. There is little knowledge within BusNews about how to use these computer technologies. Based on the knowledge acquisition processes for knowledge management, explain how BusNews might gain the intellectual capital necessary to become more competitive in this respect.

ANCOL CORPORATION

Paul Sims was delighted when Ancol Corporation offered him the job of manager at its Lexington, Kentucky, plant. Sims was happy enough managing a small metal stamping plant with another company, but the invitation to apply to the plant manager job at one of the leading metal fabrication companies was irresistible. Although the Lexington plant was the smallest of Ancol's 15 operations, the plant manager position was a valuable first step in a promising career.

One of Sims's first observations at Ancol's Lexington plant was that relations between employees and management were strained. Taking a page from a recent executive seminar that he attended on building trust in the workplace, Sims ordered the removal of all time clocks from the plant. Instead, the plant would assume that employees had put in their full shift. This symbolic gesture, he believed, would establish a new level of credibility and strengthen relations between management and employees at the site.

Initially, the 250 production employees at the Lexington plant appreciated their new freedom. They felt respected and saw this gesture as a sign of positive change from the new plant manager. Two months later, however, problems started to appear. A few people began showing up late, leaving early, or take extended lunch breaks. Although this represented only about 5 percent of the employees, others found the situation unfair. Moreover, the increased absenteeism levels were beginning to have a noticeable effect on plant productivity. The problem had to be managed.

Sims asked supervisors to observe and record when the employees came or went and to discuss attendance problems with those abusing their privileges. But the supervisors had no previous experience with keeping attendance, and many lacked the necessary interpersonal skills to discuss the matter with subordinates. Employees resented the reprimands, so relations with supervisors deteriorated. The additional responsibility of keeping track of attendance also made it difficult for supervisors to complete their other responsibilities. After just a few months, Ancol found it necessary to add another supervisor position and reduce the number of employees assigned to each supervisor.

But the problems did not end there. Without time clocks, the payroll department could not deduct pay for the amount of time that employees were late. Instead, a letter of reprimand was placed in the employee's personnel file. However, this required yet more time and additional skills from the supervisors. Employees did not want these letters to become a permanent record, so they filed grievances with their labor union. The number of grievances doubled over six months, which required even more time for both union officials and supervisors to handle these disputes.

Nine months after removing the time clocks, Paul Sims met with union officials, who agreed that it would be better to put the time clocks back in. Employee–management relations had deteriorated below the level when Sims had started. Supervisors were overworked. Productivity had dropped due to poorer attendance records and increased administrative workloads.

A couple of months after the time clocks were put back in place, Sims attended an operations meeting at Ancol's headquarters in Cincinnati. During lunch, Sims described the time clock incident to Liam Jackson, Ancol's plant manager in Portland, Oregon. Jackson looked surprised, then chuckled. He explained that the previous manager at his plant had done something like that with similar consequences six or seven years ago. The manager had left some time ago, but Jackson heard about the earlier time clock incident from a supervisor during his retirement party two months ago.

"I guess it's not quite like lightning striking the same place twice," said Sims to Jackson. "But it sure feels like it."

Discussion Questions

1. Use the systems theory model to explain what happened when Ancol removed the time clocks.

2. What changes should occur to minimize the likelihood of these problems in the future?

STAYING PUT IN INDONESIA

BusinessWeek Many of the largest and best-known companies operate on an international scale. Corporations such as General Electric, Coca-Cola, and Exxon Mobil employ people on all continents. They bring to their employers a wide diversity of talents, experience, and cultural norms. A complete understanding of organizational behavior must be able to account for such variation.

This *Business Week* case study describes how organizations remain competitive in international markets. Specifically, it describes the challenges and opportunities facing several businesses with operations in Indonesia, which underwent a great deal of political turmoil following the ouster of President Suharto in 1998. Read through this *Business Week* case study at www.mhhe.com/mcshane2e and prepare for the discussion questions below.

Discussion Questions

1. Apply the open systems model to describe with what elements of the environment the companies described in this article interact. Give an example of how one of these elements might affect organizational behavior in one of the companies mentioned.

2. According to the article's author, why do the companies operate in Indonesia and employ managers from India? What are some management challenges related to this international arrangement?

3. What aspects of knowledge management would be particularly relevant to the organizations described in this article?

Source: Michael Shari, "Staying Put in Indonesia," *Business Week*, September 17, 2001.

HUMAN CHECKERS

Purpose This exercise is designed to help students understand the importance and application of organizational behavior concepts.

Materials Chairs (optional). The instructor has information about the teams' task.

Instructions

■ *Step 1*—Form teams with six students. If possible, each team should have a private location where team members can plan and practice the required task without being observed or heard by other teams.

■ *Step 2*—All teams will receive special instructions in class about the teams' assigned task. All teams have the same task and will have the same amount of time to plan and practice the task. At the end of this planning and practice period, each team will be timed

while completing the task in class. The team that completes the task in the least time wins.

■ *Step 3*—Other than chairs, no special materials are required or allowed for this exercise. Although the task is not described here, students should learn the following rules for planning and implementing the task:

Rule 1—You cannot use any written form of communication or any props other than chairs to assist in the planning or implementation of this task.

Rule 2—You may speak to other students on your team at any time during the planning and implementation of this task.

Rule 3—When performing the task, you must move only in the direction of your assigned destination. In other words, you can only move forward, not backward.

Rule 4—When performing the task, you can move forward to the next space, but only if it is vacant (see Exhibit 1).

Rule 5—When performing the task, you can move forward two spaces, if that space is vacant. In other words, you can move around a student who is one space in front of you to the next space if that space is vacant (see Exhibit 2).

Exhibit 1   **Exhibit 2**

- *Step 4*—When all teams have completed their tasks, the class will discuss the implications of this exercise for organizational behavior.

Discussion Questions

1. Identify organizational behavior concepts that the team applied to complete this task.

2. What personal theories of people and work teams were applied to complete this task.

3. What organizational behavior problems occurred, and what actions were (or should have been) taken to solve them?

TEAM EXERCISE 1.4

DEVELOPING KNOWLEDGE FROM MISTAKES

Purpose The problem that people make from their mistakes isn't so much the mistake itself. Rather, it's that they do not take the time to learn from the mistake. This exercise is designed to help you understand how to gain knowledge from past mistakes in a specific situation.

Instructions

- *Step 1*—The class will be divided into small teams of four to six people. The instructor will identify a situation that students probably have experienced and in which they probably made mistakes. This situation could be the first day at work, the first day of classes, or a social event, such as a first date.

- *Step 2*—After the topic has been identified, each team member writes down an incident in which something went wrong in that situation. For example, if the topic is the first day of classes, someone might note how he or she was late for class as a result of forgetting to set the alarm clock.

- *Step 3*—Each student describes the mistake to other team members. As an incident is described, students should develop a causal map of the incident. They should ask why the problem happened, what the consequences were of this incident, whether it happened again, and so on. The knowledge might not be as obvious as you think. For example, in the incident of being late, the learning might not be that we should ensure the alarm clock is set. It might be a matter of changing routines (going to bed earlier), rethinking our motivation to enroll in a program, and so on.

- *Step 4*—As other incidents are analyzed, the team should begin to document specific knowledge about the incident. Think of this knowledge as a road map for others to follow when they begin their first day of class, first day at work, first date, and the like.

Source: This exercise was developed by Steven L. McShane, based on ideas in P. LaBarre, "Screw Up, and Get Smart," *Fast Company* 19 (November 1998), p. 58.

IT ALL MAKES SENSE?

Purpose This exercise is designed to help you understand how organizational behavior knowledge can help you understand life in organizations.

Instructions Read each of the statements below and circle whether each statement is true or false, in your opinion. The class will consider the answers to each question and discuss the implications for studying organizational behavior. After reviewing these statements, the instructor will provide information about the most appropriate answer. (Note: This exercise may be done as a self-assessment or a team activity.)

1. True False A happy worker is a productive worker.

2. True False Decision makers tend to continue supporting a course of action even though information suggests that the decision is ineffective.

3. True False Organizations are more effective when they prevent conflict among employees.

4. True False It is better to negotiate alone than as a team.

5. True False Companies are most effective when they have a strong corporate culture.

6. True False Employees perform better without stress.

7. True False Effective organizational change always begins by pinpointing the source of the organization's current problems.

8. True False Female leaders involve employees in decisions to a greater degree than do male leaders.

9. True False Thomas Edison is a classic example of the fact that creative people are lone geniuses.

10. True False Top-level executives tend to exhibit Type A behavior patterns (i.e., hard-driving, impatient, competitive, and short-tempered; rapid talkers with a strong sense of time urgency).

11. True False Employees usually feel overreward inequity when they are paid more than co-workers performing the same work.

After studying the preceding material, be sure to check out our website at
www.mhhe.com/mcshane2e
for more in-depth information and interactivities that correspond to this chapter.

Individual Behavior and Processes

2

2

Individual Behavior and Learning in Organizations

AFTER READING THIS CHAPTER, YOU SHOULD BE ABLE TO:

- Describe the four factors that influence individual behavior and performance.

- Identify five types of work-related behavior.

- Define *learning*.

- Describe the A-B-C model of behavior modification.

- Explain how feedback influences individual behavior and performance.

- Identify five elements of effective feedback.

- Describe the three features of social learning theory.

- Discuss the benefits of learning through experience.

Bob Garland was taken aback when executive coach Kathy Lubar suggested he should improve his speaking style. "Why should I have to do that?" wondered the senior manager at accounting firm Deloitte and Touche. "I'm a good speaker already. I've given 300 to 400 speeches over the last 20 years." But after a role-play session with Lubar, Garland realized his speeches were too cerebral and boring. "I thought I was a good speaker," Garland said. "Now, I realize that was not the case at all."

Bob Garland was a skeptic when he started using an executive coach. Now he is a convert, as are a lot of other people. One recent survey estimates that 25 percent of Fortune 500 companies use executive coaches. IBM says it has a competitive advantage by retaining 30 leadership consultants to work with its top 300 executives. At Merrill Lynch, executive coach Don Greene works with stockbrokers and executives, using the same techniques he has applied to Grand Prix drivers, Olympic divers, and Metropolitan Opera divas.

Executive coach Nancy Gerber (left) helps Liz Sanford with her leadership skills after Liz opened her own planning firm in Decatur, Georgia. (© *Jean Shifrin*, The Atlanta Journal-Constitution)

Executive coaches offer accurate feedback, open dialogue, and constructive encouragement to improve the client's performance and personal well-being. They ask provocative questions, offer perspective, and help clients clarify choices. Experts suggest that coaching is an excellent way to improve a person's emotions and interpersonal skills.

Liz Sanford turned to an executive coach when she realized her skills as a boss needed work. "I didn't set clear expectations for people, and I had trouble with the whole facade of being in charge," says the founder of a city and transportation planning firm in Decatur, Georgia. Sanford's leadership skills and confidence improved dramatically after working with personal coach Nancy Gerber. "Coaching is simply a relationship with someone who is paid to tell you the absolute truth," says Gerber.[1] ■

xecutive coaching is a booming business because it potentially addresses some of the drivers of individual behavior and performance that we discuss in this chapter. We begin by introducing a model of individual behavior and performance as well as the main types of work-related behavior. Most elements of the individual behavior model are influenced by individual learning, so the latter part of this chapter discusses the concept of learning and describes four perspectives of learning in organizational settings: reinforcement, feedback, observation, and experience.

MARS MODEL OF INDIVIDUAL BEHAVIOR AND PERFORMANCE

A useful model for understanding the drivers of individual behavior is the MARS model of individual behavior and performance. Exhibit 2.1 illustrates the MARS model, which represents the four factors that directly influence an employee's voluntary behavior and resulting performance—motivation, ability, role perceptions, and situational factors. These four factors are represented by the acronym "MARS" in the model's name.

The MARS model shows that these four factors have a combined effect on individual performance. If any factor weakens, employee performance will decrease. For example, highly qualified salespeople who understand their job duties and have sufficient resources will not perform their jobs as well if they aren't motivated to market the company's products or services. Companies that excel in customer service and employee performance pay attention to all four factors. Global Connections 2.1 describes how paying attention to employee abilities, motivation, role perceptions, and situational factors has helped Singapore Airlines become the world's top-rated airline.

EXHIBIT 2.1   MARS model of individual behavior and performance

The MARS Model Helps Singapore Airlines Soar in Customer Service

Singapore Airlines (SIA) is obsessed with providing exceptional customer service. The island-state's national airline has a limited domestic market, so it competes directly with other airlines for passengers. "Excellent service has been the foundation stone of our success," says a senior SIA executive.

SIA starts its customer service journey by carefully selecting job applicants. Flight attendants are specially screened for their customer-orientation values and other competencies. Prospective managers must pass a series of tests and two interviews. Overall, only 1 in 50 applicants receives a job offer. "Quality people are the company's most important resource, and the most rigorous quality control process we apply is for staff selection," says a former SIA chief executive.

Extensive training is another strategy SIA uses to achieve its high customer service standards. The airline spends 12 percent of payroll on training, compared with 2.3 percent in the average Singaporean firm. Cabin crew complete a five-month course where they learn every possible element of service, from social etiquette to emergency procedures. SIA's most recent training initiative, called Transforming Customer Service, encourages staff to go beyond the routines to serve customers uniquely. "The most important thing that you can do for customers is to make them feel cared for as individuals," explains an SIA executive.

Selection and training guide SIA skills and role perceptions, but the airline also pays attention to employee motivation through companywide financial rewards and a customer-focused culture. As for support through situational factors, SIA, the premier customer for Boeing

Singapore Airlines applies the MARS model of individual behavior to provide exceptional customer service. *(Courtesy of Singapore Airlines)*

777 jets, has one of the world's most modern fleets. The result is an organization that consistently leads the global airline industry in customer service ratings and profitability.

Sources: R. Rosen, P. Digh, M. Singer, and C. Phillips, *Global Literacies* (New York: Simon & Schuster, 2000), pp. 247–48; L. McCauley, "How May I Help You? Unit of One," *Fast Company*, March 2000, p. 93; J. B. Cunningham and P. Gerrard, "Characteristics of Well-Performing Organizations in Singapore," *Singapore Management Review* 22 (January 2000), pp. 35–64; J. Pfeffer, "Seven Practices of Successful Organizations," *California Management Review* 40 (1998), pp. 96–124; B. Davis, "Why Singapore Airlines Is the World's Most Profitable Airline," *Asian Business Review*, December 1996, pp. 34–36.

Employee Motivation

motivation
The forces within a person that affect his or her direction, intensity, and persistence of voluntary behavior.

Motivation represents the forces within a person that affect the direction, intensity, and persistence of his or her voluntary behavior.[2] *Direction* refers to the fact that motivation is goal-oriented, not random. People are motivated to arrive at work on time, finish a project a few hours early, or aim for many other targets. *Intensity* is the amount of effort allocated to the goal. For example, two employees might be motivated to finish their project a few hours early (direction), but only one of them puts forth enough effort (intensity) to achieve this goal. Finally, motivation involves varying levels of *persistence*, that is, continuing the effort for a certain amount of time. Employees may sustain their effort until they reach their goal, or they may give up beforehand. Chapter 5 looks more closely at the conceptual foundations of employee motivation, while Chapter 6 considers some applied motivation practices.

Ability

ability
Both the natural aptitudes and learned capabilities required to success-fully complete a task.

A second influence on individual behavior and performance is the person's ability. **Ability** includes both the natural aptitudes and learned capabilities required to successfully complete a task. *Aptitudes* are the natural talents that help employees learn specific tasks more quickly and perform them better. For example, you cannot learn finger dexterity; rather, some people have a more natural ability than others to manipulate small objects with their fingers. There are many different physical and mental aptitudes, and our ability to acquire skills is affected by these aptitudes. *Learned capabilities* are the skills and knowledge that you have actually acquired—including the physical and mental skills you possess as well as the knowledge you acquire and store for later use.

competencies
The abilities, values, personality traits, and other characteristics of people that lead to superior performance.

Employee Competencies   The external environment is changing so rapidly that many organizations prefer to hire people for their generic competencies rather than for job-specific skills. **Competencies** are the characteristics of people that lead to superior performance.[3] Along with natural and learned abilities, competencies include the person's values and personality traits.

Many firms have identified generic competencies that distinguish outstanding performers across the organization or in broad job groups. Other competencies apply to specific jobs or job groups. Ericsson, the Swedish telecommunications giant, has a competence triangle consisting of three sets of generic and job-specific competencies: technical/professional competence, human competence, and business competence. Technical/professional competence is specific to a particular task or position, such as the person's product knowledge. In its human competence category, Ericsson identifies teamwork, communications, cultural awareness, and other competencies necessary for social interaction. Business competence refers to understanding the business; it includes language skills, customer skills, and general knowledge about the organization.[4]

Person–Job Matching   There are three basic ways to match individuals and their competencies with job requirements.[5] One strategy is to select applicants whose existing competencies best fit the required tasks. This approach includes comparing each applicant's competencies with the requirements of the job or work unit. A second approach is to provide training so that employees develop required skills and knowledge. Canadian Tire, a leading Canadian retailer of automobile and home improvement products, estimates that $50 invested in customer service and related training programs can yield paybacks of $500 a year in increased profits. Academic research also suggests that job-related training improves organizational effectiveness.[6]

The third person job matching strategy is to redesign jobs so employees are given only those tasks that are within their capabilities. MediaOne adopted this strategy after introducing e-mail as a form of customer communication at its call centers. Executives at the U.S. cable television systems company realized that call center staff with strong verbal communication skills aren't necessarily good at written communication. "Many people who can carry on a good conversation on the phone could not put a cogent thought down in writing if they tried," says a MediaOne executive. The company identified employees with strong written communication skills and redesigned their tasks so that they would be responsible for answering e-mail questions.[7]

Role Perceptions

A February cold snap turned a rainy weekend into a citywide skating rink on Monday morning in Madison, Wisconsin. Within hours, emergency crews were scrambling to make the roads safer, while hospital staff worked at full speed to handle the large numbers of emergency room visitors. One hospital spokesperson called it the worst day of ice injuries he had seen. Still, the emergency room staff worked smoothly throughout the day. "The emergency room was a well-oiled machine between nursing staff, medical imaging, and emergency physicians," says Meriter Hospital spokesperson Mae Knowles.[8]

Emergency room staff at Meriter Hospital acted like a "well-oiled machine" not just because they had learned the appropriate skills. They had also developed accurate **role perceptions.** Employees have accurate role perceptions when they understand the specific tasks assigned to them, the relative importance of those tasks, and the preferred behaviors to accomplish those tasks. Role perceptions clarify the preferred direction of effort. For example, retail salespeople need to remember to stock shelves, not just to serve customers. Otherwise, sales are lost if the product isn't on the shelves.[9]

How do organizations improve role perceptions? One strategy is to clearly describe each employee's required responsibilities and to show how those goals relate to organizational goals. Second, employees clarify their role perceptions as they work together over time and receive frequent and meaningful performance feedback.

role perceptions
A person's beliefs about what behaviors are appropriate or necessary in a particular situation, including the specific tasks that make up the job, their relative importance, and the preferred behaviors to accomplish those tasks.

Situational Factors

Job performance depends not just on motivation, ability, and role perceptions. It is also affected by the situation in which the employee works. Situational factors include conditions beyond the employee's immediate control that constrain or facilitate his or her behavior and performance.[10] Some factors—such as time, people, budget, and physical work facilities—are controlled by others in the organization. Corporate leaders need to carefully arrange these conditions so that employees can achieve their performance potential. Lockheed Martin's jet fighter production facility does this by asking employees to identify obstacles created by management that prevent them from performing effectively.[11]

Other situational characteristics—such as consumer preferences and economic conditions—originate from the external environment and, consequently, are beyond the employee's and organization's control. A sales representative may have more difficulty selling the product or service when the economy enters a recession or if the demographics of the sales area indicate fewer people would purchase the item. Rather than create a defeatist attitude, some companies encourage employees to focus on things they can control rather than on the external situational factors.

Motivation, ability, role perceptions, and situational factors affect all conscious workplace behaviors and performance outcomes. In the next section, we introduce the five categories of behavior in organizational settings.

TYPES OF WORK-RELATED BEHAVIOR

People engage in many different types of behavior in organizational settings. Exhibit 2.2 highlights five types of behavior discussed most often in the organizational behavior literature: joining the organization, remaining with the organization, maintaining work attendance, performing required tasks, and exhibiting organizational citizenship.

Joining the Organization

At Dell Computer Corporation, success doesn't sound like a cash register. It sounds more like the clang of a cowbell. Whenever someone with valuable knowledge or experience joins Dell's headquarters, employees ring a bell that symbolically signals the good news. Dell employees celebrate the arrival of key employees because they—and employees of other organizations—need qualified people to perform tasks and acquire knowledge. In fact, attracting and retaining talented employees is one of the top 5 (from a list of 39) nonfinancial factors used by Wall Street's decision makers to pick stocks.[12]

The importance of hiring qualified people is obvious when we consider the consequences of staff shortages. Richcolor, a professional photo lab in Puget Sound, Washington, closed its doors and laid off 50 people because one of the company's two color correctors quit on doctor's orders, and a national search firm couldn't find a replacement. Color correctors look at each frame manually to ensure the colors and shades are just right. "We do not choose to watch Richcolor perform poorly and slowly [lose] its customers and reputation," Richcolor owner Jerry Saunders wrote to customers and employees.[13]

Along with avoiding shortages, effective organizations constantly search for the most qualified people. As consulting firm McKinsey and Company highlighted in its report "The War for Talent," organizations need to acquire knowledge by hiring the best employees. A more recent McKinsey report concludes that successful companies win the talent war by applying many of the

Hospitals across the United States are struggling to find enough nurses to keep beds open. Nursing school enrollment has fallen by 20 percent over the past five years, just as hospitals are expanding capacity to handle the aging population. Hospitals make up for the shortfall by hiring nurses from agencies, but that isn't a long-term solution. "We're all competing for the same shrinking pool of nurses," admits the president of a large nursing agency in Cleveland. Many hospitals provide bonus incentives so that nurses will work overtime. Ironically, the nursing shortage feeds on itself by causing active nurses to leave the profession as a result of burnout. "I think nurses are very frustrated," says Denise Borgman (shown in photo), a charge nurse at Providence Hospital in Southfield, Michigan.[16] What actions would you recommend to a large hospital that faces this shortage of nurses? (© Detroit News/*David Coates*)

ideas in this book—building trust and loyalty, having visionary leaders, offering enriched jobs, financially rewarding performance.[14]

Remaining with the Organization

The war for talent includes keeping the best people, not just hiring them. As we learned in Chapter 1, much of an organization's intellectual capital is the knowledge employees carry around in their heads. Long-service employees, in particular, have valuable information about work processes, corporate values, and customer needs. Very little of this information is documented anywhere. Thus, knowledge management involves keeping valuable employees with the organization. "At 5 p.m., 95% of our assets walk out the door," says an executive at SAS Institute, a leading statistics software firm. "We have to have an environment that makes them want to walk back in the door the next morning."[15]

The problem is that many employees don't return the next morning. The U.S. Bureau of Labor Statistics estimates that the typical American employee holds nine jobs by the age of 32. One large-scale survey reports that nearly half of those currently employed say they are looking around for another job. Over half of the 500 executives recently surveyed worldwide identified retaining talented employees as the top people issue in the company. Even with recent layoffs in some industries, the emerging employability attitude toward work and continuing shortages in some occupations (e.g., information technology, nursing) will keep turnover rates near record levels.[17]

job satisfaction
A person's attitude regarding his or her job and work content.

Why do people quit their jobs? The main cause of turnover is low **job satisfaction**—a person's attitude regarding his or her job and work context (see Chapter 4). Employees become dissatisfied with their employment relationship, which motivates them to search for and join another organization with better conditions. Job dissatisfaction, which "pushes" employees out of their current jobs, has a greater effect on turnover than incentives that "pull" them into new jobs. In other words, the main cause of high turnover isn't that other firms lure away good employees. The main problem is that their current jobs don't motivate good employees to stay.[18]

Maintaining Work Attendance

Along with attracting and retaining employees, organizations need everyone to show up for work at scheduled times. Situational factors—such as a car breakdown, family illness, or a snowstorm—represent a major cause of absenteeism. Recognizing this fact, Xerox minimizes absenteeism by giving all employees free flu shots and health screenings. When the car breaks down or a child is sick, Xerox employees are encouraged to do their work from home. To minimize absenteeism on snowy days, ARO, a call center in Kansas City, also relies on telecommuting.[19]

Motivation is another influence on absenteeism. Employees desiring to temporarily withdraw from stressful or dissatisfying working conditions are more often absent or late for work. Absenteeism is also higher in organizations with generous sick leave because this benefit limits the negative financial impact of taking time away from work.[20]

Performing Required Tasks

task performance
Goal-directed activities that are under the individual's control.

People are hired to perform tasks above a minimum standard. **Task performance** refers to goal-directed activities that are under the individual's control.[21] These include physical behaviors as well as mental processes leading to behaviors. For example, foreign exchange traders make decisions and take actions to exchange currencies. These traders have certain *performance standards;* that is, their behaviors and the outcomes of those behaviors must exceed minimum acceptable levels.

In most jobs, employees are evaluated on several performance dimensions.[22] Foreign exchange traders, for example, must be able to identify profitable trades, work cooperatively with clients and co-workers in a stressful environment, assist in training new staff, and work on special telecommunications equipment without error. Each of these performance dimensions requires specific skills and knowledge. Some are more important than others, but only by considering all performance dimensions can we fully evaluate an employee's contribution to the organization.

Exhibiting Organizational Citizenship

Rick Boomer, head porter at the Empress Hotel in Victoria, Canada, happened to be in the hotel on his day off when a busload of tourists left for the ski resort of Whistler, leaving behind 100 pieces of luggage. Boomer rented a large truck, loaded it himself, took the two-hour ferry ride from Victoria to Vancouver, fought Vancouver's rush-hour traffic, negotiated twisting mountain roads for another two hours, and delivered the luggage to Whistler Mountain ski resort. He took a quick nap, then returned to Victoria for his regular work shift![23]

organizational citizenship
Behaviors that extend beyond the employee's normal job duties.

For the past 60 years, management writers have known that organizations depend on employees who, like Rick Boomer, are willing to "go the extra mile." **Organizational citizenship** refers to behaviors that extend beyond the employee's normal job duties.[24] They include avoiding unnecessary conflicts, helping others without selfish intent, gracefully tolerating occasional impositions, being involved in organizational activities, and performing tasks that extend beyond normal role requirements.[25] Good organizational citizens work cooperatively with co-workers and share resources. They forgive others for mistakes and help co-workers with their problems.

How do employees become good organizational citizens? Rewards and recognition may encourage these behaviors. For example, the New Mexico state government has an "Extra Mile" award for employees who perform beyond the call of duty.[26] However, research has identified two conditions that are essential for organizational citizenship. One of these is the perceived

A traveler from the Middle East had an unusual request when he recently took his family to the Four Seasons hotel in Washington, D.C. "My kids haven't seen Santa Claus since we've arrived," he lamented to the Four Seasons staff. Going beyond the call of duty, assistant front-office manager Liliana Vidal-Quadras (shown in photo) found a costume and an employee to play Santa for a few hours. It's this extra effort that makes the Four Seasons one of the top luxury hotels in the world. Although the pay is adequate, Four Seasons employees engage in organizational citizenship mainly because they are carefully selected for their strong sense of social responsibility and conscientiousness. Vidal-Quadras also says she's treated fairly and has good career opportunities at the hotel chain. In what other ways could Four Seasons employees demonstrate organizational citizenship?[29] *(© Mario Tama)*

fairness of the company's treatment of employees. Organizations encourage organizational citizenship by correcting perceptions of injustice in the workplace. Employees feel a higher sense of obligation to go the extra mile when organizations distribute rewards fairly and have a process in place to correct problems when employees feel unfairly treated. One way to improve organizational citizenship through perceived fairness is to involve employees in decisions that affect them.[27]

The second condition contributing to organizational citizenship is the degree to which employees hold strong ethical values, particularly a sense of social responsibility.[28] **Social responsibility** refers to a person's or an organization's moral obligation toward others who are affected by his or her actions. People with a strong social responsibility norm are more motivated to assist others, whether or not this assistance will ever be repaid, and to avoid behaviors that interfere with others' goals. It is a value learned through lifelong socialization, so organizations might try to hire people with this value.

The five types of workplace behavior and the MARS model of individual performance are related to many topics in this book. One of the more important topics is individual learning because it affects employee ability, role perceptions, and motivation. The rest of this chapter examines the topic of learning in organizational settings.

LEARNING IN ORGANIZATIONS

Most employees appreciate a good paycheck, but an increasing number of them place at least as much value on the opportunity to learn new things at work. "I'm here because I keep learning," says John Waterman, a thirty-something employee. "Whenever I start to get a little bored, a new project comes along with opportunities for learning."[30] **Learning** is a relatively permanent change in behavior (or behavior tendency) that occurs as a result of a person's interaction with the environment.[31] We learn through our senses, such as through study, observation, and experience. Learning becomes evident when the learner behaves differently. For example, we can see that you have learned computer skills if you are operating the keyboard and windows more quickly than before.

Learning influences individual behavior and performance through three elements of the MARS model. First, people acquire skills and knowledge through learning opportunities, which gives them the competencies to perform tasks more effectively. Second, learning clarifies role perceptions. Employees develop a better understanding of their tasks and relative importance of work activities. Third, learning motivates employees. Employees are more motivated to perform certain tasks because they learn that their effort will result in

social responsibility
A person's or organization's moral obligation toward others who are affected by his or her actions.

learning
A relatively permanent change in behavior that occurs as a result of a person's interaction with the environment.

desired performance. Moreover, as in John Waterman's experience, learning generates feelings of accomplishment and other forms of need fulfillment. Learning is also essential for knowledge management—the organization's capacity to acquire, share, and utilize knowledge in ways that improves its survival and success (see Chapter 1).[32]

Learning Explicit and Tacit Knowledge

When employees learn, they acquire both explicit and tacit knowledge. Explicit knowledge is organized and can be communicated from one person to another. The information you receive in a lecture is mainly explicit knowledge because the instructor packages and consciously transfers it to you. Explicit knowledge can be written down and given to others.

However, explicit knowledge is really only the tip of the knowledge iceberg. Most of what we know is **tacit knowledge.**[33] You have probably said to someone: "I can't tell you how to do this, but I can show you." Tacit knowledge is not documented; rather, it is action-oriented and known below the level of consciousness. Some writers suggest that tacit knowledge also includes the organization's culture and a team's implicit norms. People know these values and rules exist, but they are difficult to describe and document.[34]

Tacit knowledge is acquired through observation and direct experience.[35] For example, airline pilots do not learn how to operate a commercial jet through lectures. They master the necessary skills by watching the subtle details as others perform the tasks, and by directly experiencing this complex interaction of behavior with the machine's response. Because most knowledge in organizations is tacit, an important challenge in knowledge management is to make tacit knowledge more explicit so that it may be more easily stored and shared.

Learning tacit and explicit knowledge occurs in many ways. The rest of this chapter introduces four perspectives of learning: reinforcement, feedback, social learning (observation), and direct experience. These activities are not completely separate. For example, feedback can be viewed as a form of reinforcement. Rather, they provide different views of the learning process, and by understanding each of these perspectives, we can more fully appreciate the dynamics of learning.

BEHAVIOR MODIFICATION: LEARNING THROUGH REINFORCEMENT

tacit knowledge
Knowledge embedded in our actions and ways of thinking, and transmitted only through observation and experience.

behavior modification
A theory that explains learning in terms of the antecedents and consequences of behavior.

One of the oldest perspectives on learning, called **behavior modification** (also known as *operant conditioning* and *reinforcement theory*), takes the rather extreme view that learning is completely dependent on the environment. Behavior modification does not question the notion that thinking is part of the learning process, but it views human thoughts as unimportant intermediate stages between behavior and the environment.[36] Our experience with the environment teaches us to alter our behaviors so that we maximize positive consequences and minimize adverse consequences.[37]

Behavior modification emphasizes voluntary behaviors. Researchers call them *operant behaviors* because they "operate" on the environment—they make the environment respond in ways that we want.[38] For example, you put a certain amount of money in a machine and press a certain button so that a particular can of soft drink comes out. You learned from past experience how to cause the environment (the soft drink machine) to deliver that brand of soft drink. Operant behaviors are different from *respondent behaviors*. Respondent behaviors are involuntary responses to the environment, such as automatically withdrawing your hand from a hot stove or automatically contracting your eyes when you turn on a bright light. This book looks at operant behaviors because most learned behaviors in organizational settings are voluntary.

A-B-C's of Behavior Modification

Behavior modification recognizes that behavior is influenced by two environmental contingencies: the antecedents that precede behavior and the consequences that follow behavior. These principles are part of the A-B-C model of behavior modification shown in Exhibit 2.3. The central objective of behavior modification is to change behavior (B) by managing its antecedents (A) and consequences (C).[39]

Antecedents are events preceding the behavior, informing employees that certain behaviors will have particular consequences. An antecedent may be a sound from your computer signaling that an e-mail has arrived or a request from your supervisor to complete a specific task by tomorrow. These antecedents let employees know that a particular action will produce particular consequences. Notice that antecedents do not cause operant behaviors. The computer sound doesn't cause us to open our e-mail. Rather, the sound is a cue telling us that certain consequences are likely to occur if we engage in certain behaviors.

Although antecedents are important, behavior modification focuses mainly on the *consequences* of behavior. Consequences are events following a particular behavior that influence its future occurrence. This concept is based on the **law of effect,** which says that the likelihood that an operant behavior will

law of effect
A principle stating that the likelihood that an operant behavior will be repeated depends on its consequences.

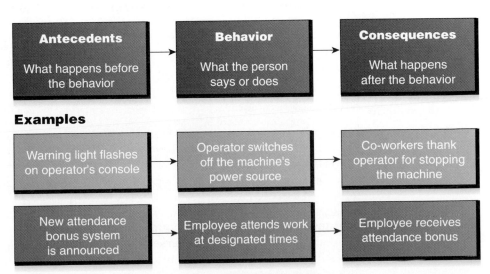

EXHIBIT 2.3

A-B-C's of Behavior Modification

Antecedents What happens before the behavior	**Behavior** What the person says or does	**Consequences** What happens after the behavior

Examples

Warning light flashes on operator's console	Operator switches off the machine's power source	Co-workers thank operator for stopping the machine
New attendance bonus system is announced	Employee attends work at designated times	Employee receives attendance bonus

Sources: Adapted from T. K. Connellan, *How to Improve Human Performance* (New York: Harper & Row, 1978), p. 50; F. Luthans and R. Kreitner, *Organizational Behavior Modification and Beyond* (Glenview, IL: Scott, Foresman, 1985), pp. 85–88.

be repeated depends on its consequences. If a behavior is followed by a pleasant experience, then the person will probably repeat the behavior. If the behavior is followed by an unpleasant experience or by no response at all, then the person is less likely to repeat it. The law of effect explains how people learn to associate behaviors with specific environmental responses. Organizational behavior scholars have identified four types of consequences and five schedules to administer those consequences.

Contingencies of Reinforcement

Behavior modification identifies four types of consequences, collectively known as the *contingencies of reinforcement*, that strengthen, maintain, or weaken behavior. Exhibit 2.4 describes these contingencies: positive reinforcement, negative reinforcement, punishment, and extinction.[40]

■ **Positive reinforcement** occurs when the *introduction* of a consequence *increases or maintains* the frequency or future probability of a behavior. Receiving a bonus after successfully completing an important project usually creates positive reinforcement because it typically increases the probability that you use those behaviors in the future.

■ **Negative reinforcement** occurs when the *removal or avoidance* of a consequence *increases or maintains* the frequency or future probability of a behavior. Supervisors apply negative reinforcement when they stop criticizing employees whose substandard performance has improved. When supervisors withhold criticism, employees are more likely to repeat behaviors that improved their

positive reinforcement
Occurs when the introduction of a consequence increases or maintains the frequency or future probability of a behavior.

negative reinforcement
Occurs when the removal or avoidance of a consequence increases or maintains the frequency or future probability of a behavior.

EXHIBIT 2.4   Contingencies of reinforcement

	Consequence is introduced	No consequence	Consequence is removed
Behavior increases or is maintained	**Positive reinforcement** Example: You receive a bonus after successfully completing an important project.		**Negative reinforcement** Example: Supervisor stops criticizing you when your job performance improves.
Behavior decreases	**Punishment** Example: You are threatened with a demotion or discharge after treating a client badly.	**Extinction** Example: Co-workers no longer praise you when you engage in dangerous pranks.	**Punishment** Example: You give up your "employee of the month" parking spot to this month's winner.

performance.[41] Negative reinforcement is sometimes called avoidance learning because employees engage in the desired behaviors to avoid unpleasant consequences (such as being criticized by your supervisor or being fired from your job).

■ **Punishment** occurs when a consequence *decreases* the frequency or future probability of a behavior. It may involve introducing an unpleasant consequence or removing a pleasant consequence (see Exhibit 2.4). An example of the former would be when an employee is threatened with a demotion or discharge after treating a client badly. The latter form of punishment would occur when a salesperson must give a cherished parking spot to another employee who has higher sales performance for the month.

■ **Extinction** occurs when the target behavior decreases because no consequence follows it. For example, if an employee makes practical jokes that are potentially dangerous or costly, such behavior might be extinguished by discouraging others from praising the employee when he or she engages in these pranks. Behavior that is no longer reinforced tends to disappear; it becomes extinct. In this respect, extinction is a do-nothing strategy.[42]

Comparing Reinforcement Contingencies   In most situations, positive reinforcement should follow desired behaviors and extinction (do nothing) should follow undesirable behaviors, because there are fewer adverse consequences when applying these contingencies compared with punishment and negative reinforcement. However, some form of punishment (dismissal, suspension, demotion, etc.) may be necessary for extreme behaviors, such as deliberately hurting a co-worker or stealing inventory. Indeed, research suggests that, under certain conditions, punishment maintains a sense of equity.[43] Co-workers are often eager to hear about an employee's discipline because it fulfills their need for social justice.

Unfortunately, organizations tend to be inconsistent in their administration of punishment, so justice through discipline is an elusive goal.[44] Moreover, punishment is usually an emotionally charged event that creates negative feelings and undermines the employee's ability to learn from the punishment.[45] In extreme cases, employees develop hostilities toward the organization that may result in aggression and other forms of dysfunctional behavior.

Schedules of Reinforcement

Along with the types of consequences, behavior modification identifies the schedule that should be followed to maximize the reinforcement effect. In fact, some evidence suggests that scheduling the reinforcer affects learning more than the size of the reinforcer does.[46] Behavior modification theorists have identified five schedules of reinforcement. One of these is **continuous reinforcement**—reinforcing every occurrence of the desired behavior. Continuous reinforcement is most effective for learning new behaviors. Employees learn desired behaviors quickly, and when the reinforcer is removed, extinction also occurs very quickly.

The other four schedules of reinforcement are intermittent. They apply the reinforcer after a fixed or variable time (interval) or number of target behaviors (ratio). As illustrated in Exhibit 2.5, a fixed schedule means that the reinforcer occurs after the same number of behaviors or time units, whereas a

punishment
Occurs when a consequence decreases the frequency or future probability of a behavior.

extinction
Occurs when the target behavior decreases because no consequence follows it.

continuous reinforcement
Reinforcing every occurrence of a desired behavior.

EXHIBIT 2.5

Schedules of
reinforcement

	Interval (Time-based)	Ratio (Behavior-based)
Fixed schedule	**Fixed Interval** ▼ ▼ ▼ Week 1 Week 2 Week 3 Example: Weekly paycheck	**Fixed Ratio** ▼ ▼ ▼ 50 Units 100 Units 150 Units Example: Piece-rate pay
Variable schedule	**Variable Interval** ▼ ▼ ▼ 8 17 30 Months Months Months Example: Promotions	**Variable Ratio** ▼ ▼ ▼ 2 8 11 Calls Calls Calls Example: Successful sales calls

**fixed interval
schedule**
Reinforcing behavior
after a fixed time.

**variable interval
schedule**
Reinforcing behavior
after it has occurred
for a varying length of
time around some
average.

**fixed ratio
schedule**
Reinforcing behavior
after a fixed number
of times.

**variable ratio
schedule**
Reinforcing behavior
after it has occurred
a varying number of
times around some
average.

variable schedule means that the reinforcer occurs randomly around an average number of behaviors or time units.

The **fixed interval schedule** occurs when behavior is reinforced after a fixed time. Most people get paid on a fixed interval schedule—their paychecks are received every week or two weeks. As long as the job is performed satisfactorily, a paycheck is received on the appointed day. The **variable interval schedule** involves administering the reinforcer after a varying length of time. Promotions typically follow this schedule—they occur at uneven time intervals. The first promotion might be received after two years of good performance, the next after four years, and the third after 18 months.

The **fixed ratio schedule** reinforces behavior after a fixed number of times. Some piece-rate systems follow a schedule in which employees get paid after they produce a fixed number of units. The **variable ratio schedule** reinforces behavior after a varying number of times. Salespeople experience variable ratio reinforcement—they make a successful sale (the reinforcer) after a varying number of client calls. They might make four unsuccessful calls before receiving an order on the fifth one. This might be followed by 15 unsuccessful sales calls before another sale is made. One successful sale might be made after 10 calls on average, but this does not mean that every 10th call will be successful.

The variable ratio schedule is a low-cost way to reinforce behavior because employees are rewarded infrequently. It is also highly resistant to extinction. Suppose your boss walks into your office at varying times of day. Chances are that you will work consistently better throughout the day than if your boss visits at exactly 11 A.M. every day. If your boss doesn't walk into your office at all on a particular day, you would still expect a visit right up to the end of the day if previous visits were random.

Behavior Modification in Practice

Everyone practices behavior modification in one form or another. We thank people for a job well done, are silent when displeased, and sometimes try to punish those who go against our wishes. Some companies, such as an International Paper plant in Moss Point, Mississippi, provide training programs where supervisors learn about the power of positive reinforcement. David Sulik took one of these courses. Now, the International Paper manager criticizes less and finds many more ways to praise staff for their performance. He can already see the results. "I think they trust me more than in the past," says Sulik.[47]

Behavior modification also occurs in various formal programs to reduce absenteeism, minimize accidents, and improve task performance. When such programs are implemented correctly, the results are generally impressive.[48] For instance, VJS Foods, a British food company, reduced absenteeism by giving employees with perfect attendance each month two chances to win $500, Electric Boat also uses behavior modification principles to minimize sick time among salaried employees at the Groton, Connecticut, shipyard. Top prizes of $2,500 were recently awarded to each of 20 winners drawn from a pool of 955 employees who have not called in sick for at least two years. Auto parts manufacturer Dana Corporation applies behavior modification to reinforce safe work behaviors through a game called safety bingo. Employees can draw a number for their bingo card for every day that the plant has no accident. The employee who fills a bingo card first wins a television set.[49]

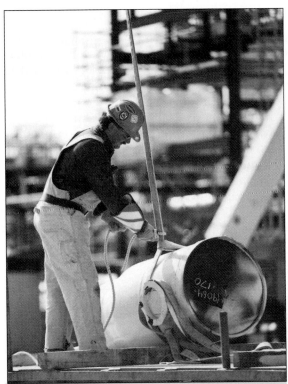

NOVA Chemicals introduced a million-dollar "Recruitment and Retention Program" to reinforce good attendance and continued employment at its construction site in Alberta, Canada. Absenteeism had reached 20 percent on some Fridays before long weekends, threatening the project's completion deadline. NOVA Chemicals' solution was to reward employees who achieved perfect attendance with a chance to win one of ten $1,300 prizes each week. A final draw of four $65,000 grand prizes encouraged employees to stay until the end of their contract. NOVA's behavior modification program cut absenteeism rates by 25 percent and dramatically improved employment levels.[52] Would this type of reinforcement work as effectively for employees in long-term jobs, such as assembly line workers?
(Courtesy of NOVA Chemicals)

Limitations of Behavior Modification In spite of these favorable results, behavior modification is more difficult to apply to conceptual activities than to observable behaviors. For example, it's much easier to reward employees for good work attendance than for good problem solving.[50] A second problem is reward inflation, in which the reinforcer is either quickly forgotten or is eventually considered an entitlement. A bonus that was once an unexpected surprise becomes an expected part of the employment relationship. Withholding the reinforcer may represent extinction, but it feels like punishment.[51]

Behavior modification programs also raise ethical concerns. One issue is that the variable ratio schedule is sometimes viewed as a form of gambling because employees are essentially betting that they will win a lottery or some other reinforcer. A forest products firm that applied this schedule discovered that some employees held strong antigambling beliefs and were upset with the company's behavior modification practices.[53] The other ethical concern is that behavior modification is sometimes viewed as a form of manipulation. It alters human behavior by rearranging incentives and other environmental conditions while ignoring human thoughts and feelings.[54] Behavior modification experts point out that any attempt to change employee behavior is a form of manipulation. No matter how valid this counterargument, behavior modification has an image problem that is difficult to overcome.

LEARNING THROUGH FEEDBACK

feedback

Any information that people receive about the consequences of their behavior.

Feedback is any information that people receive about the consequences of their behavior. Feedback may be an antecedent or a consequence, if we look at it from a behavior modification perspective. However, our discussion of learning through feedback will take a broader view by considering the effects on employee thoughts as well as behaviors.

Feedback influences behavior and task performance through role perceptions, ability, and motivation.[55] It clarifies role perceptions by communicating what behaviors are appropriate or necessary in a particular situation. Feedback improves ability by frequently providing information to correct performance problems.[56] This *corrective feedback* makes people aware of their performance errors and helps them correct those errors quickly. Lastly, feedback is a source of motivation. It fulfills personal needs and makes people more confident that they are able to accomplish certain tasks (see Chapter 5).

Feedback Sources

360-degree feedback

Performance feedback received from a full circle of people around an employee.

Feedback can originate from social or nonsocial sources.[57] Social sources include supervisors, clients, co-workers, and anyone else who provides information about the employee's behavior or results. An increasingly popular strategy is for employees to receive performance feedback from several people. This multisource feedback is called **360-degree feedback** because feedback is received from a full circle of people around the employee, including subordinates, co-workers, project leaders, and customers.[58] Performance reviews are sometimes submitted directly to the employee through an anonymous computer program, or they may be integrated into a single report by the supervisor.

Research suggests that multisource feedback provides more complete and accurate information than that from a supervisor alone.[59] It is particularly useful when the supervisor is unable to observe the employee's behavior or performance throughout the year. Lower-level employees also feel a greater sense of fairness and open communication when they are able to provide upward feedback about their boss's performance.

Multisource feedback also creates challenges.[60] Having several people review so many other people can be expensive and time-consuming. With multiple opinions, the 360-degree process can also produce ambiguous and conflicting feedback, so employees may require guidance to interpret the results. A third concern is that peers may provide inflated rather than accurate feedback to avoid conflicts over the forthcoming year. Connections 2.2 describes a fourth concern, namely, the emotional consequences of giving and receiving critical feedback involving people who work with you.

Personal Challenges of 360-degree Feedback

Multisource feedback systems are spreading like wildfire across the corporate landscape. According to a recent Towers Perrin survey, one-quarter of large U.S. firms rely on 360-degree feedback, up from just 4 percent of these firms five years ago.

But some firms may quickly discover that 360-feedback is not for the faint of heart. "Everybody is a little apprehensive the first time they do this," says Russell Huerta, a senior accounts manager at software maker Autodesk. Even in firms with a supportive culture and in which the feedback is anonymous, employees tend to worry about the repercussions of submitting critical comments.

Receiving feedback is even more difficult than giving it, which creates concerns about interpersonal relations at work. "Initially you do take it personally," admits Huerta. "It's meant to be constructive, but you have to internally battle that." Huerta manages his emotional reaction to the feedback by pretending the advice is about someone else, then learning how to improve his own behavior from that information. "It's almost an out-of-body experience, to take your mind and your emotions out of it," he recommends.

Partners at Baker Botts had plenty of opportunity to practice Huerta's advice. The Houston-based law firm recently started asking nonpartners at the 600-lawyer firm to evaluate the partners. The evaluation form asks associates to rate a partner on office demeanor and approachability, feedback and development, and work assignments and project management. The form also asks for an overall assessment of whether the associate would want to work with that partner in the future.

Richard Johnson, Baker Botts's managing partner, says there was plenty of candid feedback during the first round of upward evaluation. "They were not all positive comments, as you might imagine. Frankly, it smarted a bit, but it's supposed to." He adds that the multisource feedback process is already having a positive effect. "I think we've seen some behavioral change," says Johnson.

Sources: S. Watkins, "Ever Wanted to Review the Boss?" *Investor's Business Daily*, August 10, 2001, p. A1; B. S. Jeffreys, "Lone Star Firms Try Out 360-degree Job Reviews," *The Recorder*, June 22, 2001, p. 3.

Nonsocial Feedback Sources Along with social sources, employees usually receive nonsocial sources of feedback. With a click of the computer mouse, many executives can look at the previous day's sales and compare them with sales of previous dates. The job itself can also be a source of feedback. Many employees see the results of their work effort while they are making a product.

The preferred feedback source depends on the purpose of the information. To learn about their progress toward goal accomplishment, employees usually prefer nonsocial feedback sources, such as computer printouts or feedback directly from the job,[61] because such information is considered more accurate than that from social sources. Corrective feedback from nonsocial sources is also less damaging to self-esteem, because social sources tend to delay negative information, leave some of it out, and distort the bad news in a positive way.[62]

When employees want to improve their self-image, they seek out positive feedback from social sources. It feels better to have co-workers say that you are performing the job well than to discover this information from a computer printout.[63] Positive feedback from co-workers and other social sources motivates mainly because it fulfills social (relatedness) as well as growth needs (see Chapter 5).

Giving Feedback Effectively

Whether feedback is received from a supervisor or from a computer printout, it should be specific, sufficiently frequent, timely, credible, and relevant.

■ *Specific feedback*—Feedback should include specific information, such as "you exceeded your sales quota by 5 percent last month," rather than subjective and general phrases, such as "your sales are going well." Specific information helps employees redirect their efforts and behavior more precisely and gives them a greater sense of accomplishment when the feedback is positive. Also, notice that specific feedback focuses on the task, not the person, thereby reducing the person's defensiveness when receiving negative feedback.

■ *Frequent feedback*—Ideally, employees should be able to monitor their own performance from nonsocial feedback sources. If that isn't possible, then the feedback provider needs to consider the employee's task cycle (how long it takes to complete each task) and task experience. Grocery store cashiers, for instance, have very short task cycles (they finish working with a customer within a few minutes), so they should receive feedback more often than people with long cycles (executives, salespeople). Employees working on new tasks should also receive more frequent feedback because they require more behavior guidance and reinforcement.

■ *Timely feedback*—Feedback should be available as soon as possible so that employees see a clear association between their behavior and its consequences. Computers and other electronic equipment can provide timely feedback, but usually only for routine or standardized information.[64]

■ *Credible feedback*—Employees are more likely to accept feedback (particularly corrective feedback) from trustworthy and credible sources.[65] Multisource feedback has higher credibility because it comes from several people. Employees are also more likely to accept corrective feedback from nonsocial sources (e.g., computer printouts, electronic gauges) because it is not as judgmental.

■ *Relevant feedback*—Feedback must relate to the individual's behavior rather than to conditions beyond the individual's control to ensure that the feedback is not distorted by situational factors.[66] Feedback is also relevant when it is linked to goals. Goals establish the benchmarks (i.e., what ought to be) against which feedback is judged.

Seeking Feedback

So far, we have presented the traditional view that supervisors and others give feedback to employees. However, employees do not just passively receive feedback; they also actively seek it.[67] The most obvious way is through *inquiry*—asking other people about performance and behavior. This feedback-seeking tactic tends to be used when individuals have high self-esteem, expect to receive positive feedback, and work in an organization that values openness.

One of the most common ways to receive feedback is *monitoring*. This approach involves scanning the work environment and the behavior of others for information cues. Executives monitor corporate data to determine whether their strategies have worked. Salespeople monitor the nonverbal cues of customers during a transaction. Monitoring occurs at any time and can be more efficient than relying on others to transmit the information. For instance, production employees can continuously monitor the quality of their work quickly and independently. Although monitoring nonverbal cues of clients and coworkers creates the risk of misinterpreting meaning (see Chapter 11), it has the advantage of avoiding problems with saving face.

Another feedback-seeking strategy is *direct inquiry*. This can be a powerful form of learning in a private setting and when the person providing the feedback communicates the information clearly, yet diplomatically. However, many people have difficulty with direct inquiry when someone has performed a task poorly. Supervisors and co-workers are more likely to provide inaccurate feedback when the information is negative. Moreover, it is more difficult to save face when receiving negative feedback in response to a direct request. A third problem is that inquiry is possible only when someone else is available and has time to answer questions. One solution to these concerns is to retain a coach whose job is to provide candid feedback and guidance to improve performance. The opening vignette in this chapter describes how executive coaches offer honest feedback. They are trained to provide feedback constructively and to build on the employee's strengths rather than criticize his or her weaknesses.

Ethics of Employee Monitoring

From the time you wake up to the time you retire for the day, you leave behind a trail of data for others to gather, merge, analyze, massage, and even sell—often without your knowledge or consent. This type of monitoring applies not just to consumers but also to employees in most organizations. Feedback requires some form of monitoring employee behavior or performance. But technology has raised monitoring to such an advanced science that we need to recognize and respect its ethical implications.[68]

According to a recent survey of 1,600 large and midsize firms, 78 percent of employers monitor their staff by videotaping them on the job or by checking their e-mail, Internet use, or telephone conversations. A few employees at Continental Airlines sued the airline for secretly videotaping them while they worked in an international concierge office. Ameritech Corporation, Bell-South, and other firms have installed global positioning tracking systems in repair vans that can let the company know exactly where drivers are at all times. A Fort Lauderdale construction company places several video surveillance cameras at each building site to monitor the work in case of workers' compensation claims and for other legal protection. Executives at Taco Bell franchises in Southern California can use a password-protected Internet connection to monitor employees and customers. "I could go on vacation and still watch my restaurants," says one vice president at the franchise.[69]

Critics argue that monitoring is an invasion of employee privacy. It symbolizes a lack of trust that undermines the employment relationship. Employers, on the other hand, point out that they need to monitor the workplace to protect company assets, provide a safer work environment, and give employees more accurate feedback about their performance. AT&T Corporation claims that its high-quality customer service is partly due to employee monitoring. "Our quality is quite high, and that's why," says AT&T spokesman Jim McGee. "We keep quite an eye on them."[70] Some research indicates that employees see monitoring as a necessary evil. Although concerned about invasion of privacy, most employees are willing to be monitored when the information is used only for developmental feedback.[71] Still, as technology leads to more sophisticated surveillance, debate about the ethics of employee monitoring will become more intense.

(Copyright © 2001 Ted Goff. www.tedgoff.com)

SOCIAL LEARNING THEORY: LEARNING BY OBSERVING

social learning theory
A theory stating that much learning occurs by observing others and then modeling the behaviors that lead to favorable outcomes and avoiding behaviors that lead to punishing consequences.

Feedback and behavior modification consider learning mainly through direct experience with the environment. However, we also learn by observing the behaviors of other people and the consequences of those behaviors. **Social learning theory** states that much learning occurs by observing others and then modeling the behaviors that lead to favorable outcomes and avoiding behaviors that lead to punishing consequences.[72] There are three related features of social learning theory: behavioral modeling, learning behavior consequences, and self-reinforcement.

Behavioral Modeling

People learn by observing the behaviors of a role model on the critical task, remembering the important elements of the observed behaviors, and then practicing those behaviors.[73] Behavioral modeling works best when the model is respected and the model's actions are followed by favorable consequences. For instance, recently hired college graduates could learn by watching a previously hired college graduate who successfully performs the task.

Behavioral modeling is a valuable form of learning because tacit knowledge and skills are acquired from others mainly in this way. Earlier in this chapter, we explained that tacit knowledge is the subtle information about required behaviors, the correct sequence of those actions, and the environmental consequences (such as a machine response or customer reply) that should occur after each action. The adage that a picture is worth a thousand words applies here. It is difficult to document or explain verbally how a master baker kneads dough better than someone less qualified. Instead, we must observe the subtle actions to develop a more precise mental model of the required behaviors and the expected responses. Behavioral modeling also guides role perceptions, for example, when leaders model the behavior that they expect from others.

Behavioral Modeling and Self-Efficacy Behavioral modeling is valuable because it also enhances the observer's **self-efficacy.** Self-efficacy refers to a person's belief that he or she has the ability, motivation, and resources to complete a task successfully.[74] People with high self-efficacy have a can-do attitude toward a specific task and, more generally, toward other challenges in life.

Behavioral modeling increases self-efficacy because people gain more self-confidence after seeing someone else do a task than if they are simply told what to do. This result is particularly likely when observers identify with the model, such as someone who is the same gender and similar in age, experience, and related features. You might experience self-efficacy when working in a student support group. You form a can-do attitude when another student similar to you describes how he or she was able to perform well in a course that you are now taking. You learn not only what has to be done but also that others like you have been successful at this challenge.

Self-efficacy is also affected by initial experiences when practicing the previously modeled behavior. Observers gain confidence when the environmental cues follow a predictable pattern and there are no surprises when practicing the behavior.[75] For example, computer trainees develop a stronger self-efficacy when they click the mouse and get the same computer response as the model did when performing the same behavior. The expected response gives trainees a greater sense of control over the computer because they can predict what will happen following a particular behavior.

Learning Behavior Consequences

A second element of social learning theory says that we learn the consequences of behavior in ways other than through direct experience. In particular, we learn by logically thinking through the consequences of our actions and by observing the consequences that other people experience following their behavior. First, we logically expect either positive reinforcement or negative reinforcement after completing an assigned task and either punishment or extinction after performing the job poorly.

Second, we learn to anticipate consequences by observing the experiences of other people. Civilizations have relied on this principle for centuries, by punishing civil disobedience in public to deter other potential criminals.[76] Learning behavior consequences occurs in more subtle ways in contemporary organizations. Consider the employee who observes a co-worker receiving a stern warning for working in an unsafe manner. This event would reduce the observer's likelihood of engaging in unsafe behaviors because he or she has learned to anticipate a similar reprimand following those behaviors.[77]

Self-Reinforcement

The final element of social learning theory is *self-reinforcement*. Self-reinforcement occurs whenever an employee has control over a reinforcer but doesn't "take" the reinforcer until having completed a self-set goal.[78] For example, you might be thinking about taking a work break after you finish reading the rest of this chapter—and not before! You could take a break right now, but you don't use this privilege until you have achieved your goal of reading the chapter. The work break is a form of positive reinforcement that is self-induced. You use the work break to reinforce completion of a task.

self-efficacy
A person's belief that he or she has the ability, motivation, and resources to complete a task successfully.

Numerous consequences may be applied in self-reinforcement, ranging from raiding the refrigerator to congratulating yourself for completing the task.[79] Self-reinforcement has become increasingly important because employees are given more control over their working lives and are less dependent on supervisors to dole out positive reinforcement and punishment.

LEARNING THROUGH EXPERIENCE

Mandy Chooi is about to meet with a promising manager who has botched a new assignment. She is also supposed to make a strategy presentation to her boss in three hours, but the telephone won't stop ringing and she is deluged with e-mail. It's a stressful situation. Fortunately, Chooi isn't at her office. Instead, the Motorola human resources executive from Beijing is sitting in a simulation to develop and test her leadership skills. "It was hard. A lot harder than I had expected," says Chooi. "It's surprising how realistic and demanding it is."[80]

Many organizations are discarding the notion that learning is measured by the number of hours employees spend in the classroom. Classrooms transfer explicit knowledge that has been documented, but most tacit knowledge and skills are acquired through experience as well as observation. Much of what we learn in organizations takes place through experience.[81]

Experiential learning has been conceptualized in many ways, but one of the most enduring perspectives is Kolb's experiential learning model, shown in Exhibit 2.6.[82] This model illustrates experiential learning as a cyclical four-stage process. Concrete experience involves sensory and emotional engagement in some activity. It is followed by reflective observation, which involves listening, watching, recording, and elaborating on the experience. The next stage in the learning cycle is abstract conceptualization. This is the stage in which we develop concepts and integrate our observations into logically sound theories.

EXHIBIT 2.6

Kolb's experiential
learning model

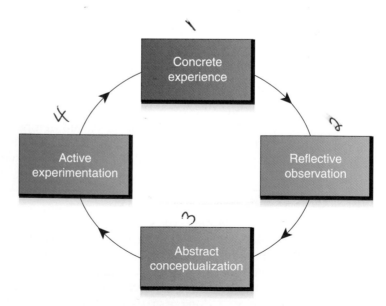

Sources: Based on information in J. E. Sharp, "Applying Kolb Learning Style Theory in the Communication Classroom," *Business Communication Quarterly* 60 (June 1997), pp. 129–34; D. A. Kolb, *Experiential Learning* (Englewood Cliffs, NJ: Prentice Hall, 1984).

The fourth stage, active experimentation, occurs when we test our previous experience, reflection, and conceptualization in a particular context.

Notice from this model that experiential learning includes the polar opposites of concrete and abstract conceptualization. We need to experience concrete reality as well as form abstract concepts from that reality. Experiential learning also involves the polar opposites of active experimentation and passive reflection. People tend to prefer and operate better in some stages than in others as a result of their unique competencies and personality. Still, experiential learning requires all four stages in proper balance.

Experiential Learning in Practice

Learning through experience works best where there is a strong **learning orientation.**[83] Organizations with a strong learning orientation value knowledge management and, in particular, the generation of new knowledge as employees achieve their goals. If an employee initially fails to perform a task, the

learning orientation
The extent that an organization or individual supports knowledge management, particularly opportunities to acquire knowledge through experience and experimentation.

The tranquil Auburn Hills campus of Oakland Community College in Michigan is about to be transformed into a place with arsonists, bound hostages, and terrified bank tellers. It's the site of a mock city designed to provide real-life instruction for police, fire, and emergency medical personnel. Instructors intend to test participants with car crashes, narcotics searches, hostage situations, bank robberies, toxic spills, and fires in the city. The idea behind the $16 million center is that emergency crews need experiential learning to acquire tacit knowledge. "Trying to explain what it's like dealing with a hot fire is like trying to explain what chocolate ice cream tastes like," explains Pontiac fire Battalion Chief Michael Nye. "You have to try it in order to know what it's like."[84] How does this emergency training center apply Kolb's experiential learning model? *(Courtesy of the Combined Regional Emergency Services Training Center)*

experience might still be a valuable learning opportunity. In other words, organizations encourage employees to appreciate the process of individual and team learning, not just the performance results. Organizations achieve a learning orientation culture by rewarding experimentation and recognizing mistakes as a natural part of the learning process. They encourage employees to take reasonable risks to ultimately discover new and better ways of doing things. Without a learning orientation, mistakes are hidden and problems are more likely to escalate or reemerge later. It's not surprising, then, that one of the most frequently mentioned lessons from the best-performing manufacturers is to expect mistakes. "[Mistakes] are a source of learning and will improve operations in the long run," explains an executive at Lockheed Martin. "[They] foster the concept that no question is dumb, no idea [is] too wild, and no task or activity is irrelevant."[85]

action learning
A variety of experiential learning activities in which employees are involved in a "real, complex, and stressful problem," usually in teams, with immediate relevance to the company.

Action Learning   The fastest-growing form of experiential learning in the workplace is called **action learning.** Action learning refers to a variety of experiential learning activities in which employees are involved in a "real, complex, and stressful problem," usually in teams, with immediate relevance to the company.[86] In action learning, the task becomes the source of learning.

Kolb's experiential learning model is usually identified as the main template for action learning.[87] Action learning requires concrete experience with a real organizational problem. The process includes learning meetings, in which participants reflect on their observations regarding the problem or opportunity. The action learning team is responsible for conceptualizing or applying a model to solve the problem or opportunity. Then the team tests the model through experimentation in the real setting. For example, an action learning team at Carpenter Technology was given the challenge to investigate the steel manufacturer's strategy for entry into India. The team investigated the opportunity, wrote up its recommendation, and participated in its implementation.[88]

Action learning is considered one of the most important ways to develop executive competencies.[89] It involves both tacit and explicit learning, forces employees to diagnose new situations, and makes them rethink current work practices. At the same time, the results of action learning potentially add value to the organization in terms of a better work process or service. For example, one of Motorola's action learning teams spent several months learning how to create and manage a software business.[90]

In this chapter, we introduced the behavioral side of organizational behavior, such as the MARS model and types of workplace behaviors. Organizational behavior, however, recognizes that a lot more goes on in organizations beyond behaviors. Over the next two chapters, we look at the fundamental concepts that operate beneath the surface of behavior, including perceptions, personality, values, and emotions.

CHAPTER SUMMARY

Individual behavior is influenced by motivation, ability, role perceptions, and situational factors (MARS). Motivation consists of internal forces that affect the direction, intensity, and persistence of a person's voluntary choice of behavior. Ability includes both the natural aptitudes and learned capabilities to perform a task. Role perceptions are a person's beliefs about what behaviors are appropriate or necessary in a particular situation. Situational factors are environmental conditions that constrain or facilitate employee behavior and performance. These four factors influence various types of behavior, including joining the organization, remaining with the organization, maintaining work attendance, performing required job duties, and exhibiting organizational citizenship.

Learning is a relatively permanent change in behavior (or behavior tendency) that occurs as a result of a person's interaction with the environment. Learning influences ability, role perceptions, and motivation in the MARS model of individual performance. The four main perspectives of learning in organizations are behavior modification (reinforcement), feedback, social learning, and direct experience.

The behavior modification perspective of learning states that behavior change occurs by altering its antecedents and consequences. Antecedents are environmental stimuli that provoke (not necessarily cause) behavior. Consequences are events following behavior that influence its future occurrence. Consequences include positive reinforcement, negative reinforcement, punishment, and extinction. The schedules of reinforcement also influence behavior.

Feedback is any information that people receive about the consequences of their behavior. It affects role perceptions, learning (through corrective feedback), and employee motivation. Employees prefer nonsocial sources of feedback to learn about their goal progress. They prefer positive feedback from social sources to improve their self-image. Effective feedback is specific, frequent, timely, credible, and relevant. Employees seek out feedback, rather than just passively receive it. Although employee monitoring is usually necessary for feedback, it raises ethical concerns.

Social learning theory states that much learning occurs by observing others and then modeling those behaviors that seem to lead to favorable outcomes and avoiding behaviors that lead to punishing consequences. It also recognizes that we often engage in self-reinforcement. Behavioral modeling is effective because it transfers tacit knowledge and enhances the observer's self-efficacy.

Many companies now use experiential learning because employees do not acquire tacit knowledge through formal classroom instruction. Kolb's experiential learning model is a cyclical four-stage process that includes concrete experience, reflective observation, abstract conceptualization, and active experimentation. Action learning refers to a variety of experiential learning activities in which employees solve problems or opportunities, usually in teams, with immediate relevance to the organization.

KEY TERMS

ability, p. 34
action learning, p. 54
behavior modification, p. 40
competencies, p. 34
continuous reinforcement, p. 43
extinction, p. 43
feedback, p. 46
fixed interval schedule, p. 44
fixed ratio schedule, p. 44

job satisfaction,, p. 37
law of effect, p. 41
learning, p. 39
learning orientation, p. 53
motivation, p. 33
negative reinforcement, p. 42
organizational citizenship, p. 38
positive reinforcement, p. 42
punishment, p. 43

role perceptions, p. 35
self-efficacy, p. 51
social learning theory, p. 50
social responsibility, p. 39
tacit knowledge, p. 40
task performance, p.38
360-degree feedback, p. 46
variable interval schedule, p. 44
variable ratio schedule, p. 44

DISCUSSION QUESTIONS

1. An insurance company has high levels of absenteeism among the office staff. The head of office administration argues that employees are misusing the company's sick leave benefits. However, some of the mostly female staff members have explained that family responsibilities interfere with work. Using the MARS model, as well as your knowledge of absenteeism behavior, discuss some of the possible reasons for absenteeism here and how it might be reduced.

2. Organizational citizenship behaviors occur in a variety of settings. Identify specific organizational citizenship behaviors that you have encountered when working with other students on team projects and assignments.

3. You notice that sales representatives in the Pacific Northwest made 20 percent fewer sales to new clients over the past quarter than salespeople located elsewhere in the United States. Use the MARS model to provide possible explanations for

the low performance of the Pacific Northwest sales reps.

4. Customer service reps at Cisco Systems, a major Internet equipment manufacturer, receive 50 points every time they convince a client to click through an online demo rather than place an order over the telephone. If the employees reach a minimum number of sales, they receive at least 1,500 points. These points are later traded in for music CDs (900 points), coffeemakers (2,500 points), and other rewards. What contingency and schedule of reinforcement is Cisco Systems using here?

5. When do employees prefer feedback from nonsocial rather than social sources? Explain why nonsocial sources are preferred under those conditions.

6. Senior officials in a manufacturing firm are increasingly concerned about the liability they face if any of their supervisory staff engage in sexual harassment. The company's attorney says that this risk may be minimized by monitoring supervisory staff with hidden cameras. Discuss the dilemmas that this company might face with employee monitoring in this situation. What is the best solution here?

7. The person responsible for training and development in your organization wants to build a new training center where all employees can receive classroom instruction in new skills and knowledge. Why might this idea be an ineffective approach to learning?

8. A consulting firm has recommended that Big Rock Mining Company should rely on action learning to prepare its technical staff for leadership positions in the organization. The executives complain that action learning takes too long, whereas they could have consultants provide several classroom sessions in less time and at less expense. Discuss the merits of the executives' arguments against action learning.

CASE STUDY 2.1

PUSHING PAPER CAN BE FUN

A large American city government was putting on a number of seminars for managers of various departments throughout the city. At one of these sessions, the topic discussed was motivation—how we can get public servants motivated to do a good job. The plight of a police captain became the central focus of the discussion:

I've got a real problem with my officers. They come on the force as young, inexperienced rookies, and we send them out on the street, either in cars or on a beat. They seem to like the contact they have with the public, the action involved in crime prevention, and the apprehension of criminals. They also like helping people out at fires, accidents, and other emergencies.

The problem occurs when they get back to the station. They hate to do the paperwork, and because they dislike it, the job is frequently put off or done inadequately. This lack of attention hurts us later on when we get to court. We need clear, factual reports. They must be highly detailed and unambiguous. As soon as one part of a report is shown to be inadequate or incorrect, the rest of the report is suspect. Poor reporting probably causes us to lose more cases than any other factor.

I just don't know how to motivate them to do a better job. We're in a budget crunch and I have absolutely no financial rewards at my disposal. In fact, we'll probably have to lay some people off in the near future. It's hard for me to make the job interesting and challenging because it isn't—it's boring, routine paperwork, and there isn't much you can do about it.

Finally, I can't say to them that their promotions will hinge on the excellence of their paperwork. First of all, they know it's not true. If their performance is adequate, most are more likely to get promoted just by staying on the force a certain number of years than for some specific outstanding act. Second, they were trained to do the job they do out in the streets, not to fill out forms. All through their career it is the arrests and interventions that get noticed.

Some people have suggested a number of things, like using conviction records as a performance criterion. However, we know that's not fair—too many other things are involved. Bad paperwork increases the chance that you lose in court, but good paperwork doesn't necessarily mean you'll win. We tried setting up team competitions based upon the excellence of the reports, but the officers caught on to that pretty quickly. No one was getting any type of reward for winning the competition, and they figured, why should they bust a gut when there was no payoff?

I just don't know what to do.

Discussion Questions

1. What performance problems is the captain trying to correct?

2. Use the MARS model of individual behavior and performance to diagnose the possible causes of the unacceptable behavior.

3. Has the captain considered all possible solutions to the problem? If not, what else might be done?

Source: T. R. Mitchell and J. R. Larson, Jr., *People in Organizations*, 3rd ed. (New York: McGraw-Hill, 1987), p. 184. Used with permission.

CASE STUDY 2.2

OFFICE DEPOT'S E-DIVA

BusinessWeek An organization's success follows many individual success stories of the organization's people. For example, Office Depot's winning record in e-commerce has been driven by the actions of its chief of e-commerce, Monica Luechtefeld. Her behavior and knowledge have made Luechtefeld an important strategic asset of Office Depot. She has applied lessons learned from customers and career experiences to develop and implement an unconventional strategy that has moved Office Depot's Internet operations far ahead of those of other online businesses.

This *Business Week* case study describes how Monica Luechtefeld has combined abilities and behaviors to achieve a series of ambitious goals. It identifies significant experiences in Luechtefeld's life and tells how she has learned from them. Read through this *Business Week* case study at www.mhhe.com/mcshane2e and prepare for the discussion questions below.

Discussion Questions

1. Apply the MARS model of individual performance (see Exhibit 2.1) to Luechtefeld's performance at Office Depot. On the basis of the information in the article, how would you rate Luechtefeld's motivation, ability, role perceptions, and situational factors, as defined in the model?

2. The article describes Luechtefeld as an active learner. What kinds of learning has Luechtefeld engaged in? Give an example of each.

3. What lessons has Luechtefeld learned from her experiences? How do these lessons contribute to her performance?

Source: "Office Depot's E-Diva," *Business Week e.biz,* August 6, 2001.

TEAM EXERCISE 2.3

A QUESTION OF FEEDBACK

Purpose This exercise is designed to help you understand the importance of feedback, including problems that occur with imperfect communication in the feedback process.

Materials The instructor will distribute a few pages of exhibits to one person on each team. The other students will require a pencil with eraser and blank paper. Movable chairs and tables in a large area are helpful.

Instructions

- *Step 1*—The class is divided into pairs of students. Ideally, each pair is located in a private area away from other students and where one person can write. One student is given the pages of exhibits from the instructor. The other student in each pair is not allowed to see these exhibits.

- *Step 2*—The student holding the materials will describe each of the exhibits, and the other student's task is to replicate each exhibit accurately. The pair of students can compare the replication with the original at the end of each drawing. They may also switch roles for each exhibit, if they wish. If roles are switched, the instructor must distribute exhibits separately to each student so that they are not seen by the other person. Each exhibit has a different set of limitations, as described below:

  Exhibit 1—The student describing the exhibit cannot look at the other student or his or her diagram. The student drawing the exhibit cannot speak or otherwise communicate with the person describing the exhibit.

  Exhibit 2—The student describing the exhibit may look at the other student's diagram. However, he or she may say only yes or no when the student drawing the diagram asks a specific question. In other words, the person presenting the information can use these words only for feedback and only when asked a question by the writer.

  Exhibit 3 (optional, if time permits)—The student describing the exhibit may look at the other student's diagram and may provide any feedback at any time to the person replicating the exhibit.

- *Step 3*—The class will gather to discuss this exercise. In particular, the class should consider the importance of feedback, the characteristics of effective feedback for individual learning, and the ways in which feedback is a form of reinforcement in behavior modification.

T E A M   E X E R C I S E 2.4

TASK PERFORMANCE

Purpose This exercise is designed to help you understand how specific behaviors are associated with job performance and how people may have different standards or expectations about which behaviors constitute good performance.

Instructions The instructor will identify a job that all students know about, such as a bank teller or course instructor. Students will focus on one performance dimension, such as service skills among cafeteria cashiers, technical skills of computer lab technicians, or lecture skills of professors. Whichever performance dimension or job is chosen for your team, the following steps apply:

- *Step 1*—The instructor identifies a specific job and students are placed into teams (preferably four or five people).
- *Step 2*—Working alone, each student writes down five specific examples of effective or ineffective behavior for the selected job and performance dimension. Each incident should clearly state the critical behavior that made it effective or ineffective (e.g., "instructor sat at desk during entire lecture"; "bank teller chewed gum while talking to client"). The statements should describe behaviors, not attitudes or evaluations.
- *Step 3*—Members of each team jointly number each statement and delete duplicates.

Each behavior statement is read aloud to the team and, without any discussion, each team member privately rates the statement using the seven-point behaviorally anchored rating scale accompanying this exercise. When all statements have been rated, the ratings for each statement are compared. Discard statements about which team members significantly disagree (such as when ratings are two or three points apart).

- *Step 4*—Average the ratings of the remaining statements, and write them at the appropriate location on the accompanying seven-point behaviorally anchored rating scale. An arrow or line should point to the exact place on the scale where the statement's average score is located. (You may want to put the seven-point rating scale and your results on an overhead transparency or flip chart if your results will be shown to the class.)
- *Step 5*—Each team presents its results to the class and describes areas of disagreement. Other class members will discuss their agreement or disagreement with each team's results, including the quality of the statements (e.g., behavior-oriented) and their location on the performance scale.

EXHIBIT 2.7 Behaviorally anchored rating scale

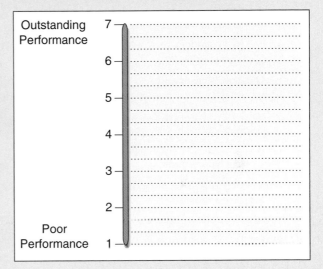

S E L F - A S S E S S M E N T   E X E R C I S E   2.5

ASSESSING YOUR SELF-EFFICACY

Purpose This exercise is designed to help you understand the concept of self-efficacy and to estimate your general self-efficacy.

Overview Self-efficacy refers to a person's belief that he or she has the ability, motivation, and situational contingencies to complete a task successfully. Self-efficacy is usually conceptualized as a situation-specific belief. You may believe that you can perform a certain task in one situation, but are less confident with that task in another situation. However, there is also evidence that people develop a more general self-efficacy that influences their beliefs in specific situations. This exercise helps you estimate your general self-efficacy.

Instructions Read each of the statements below and circle the response that best fits your personal belief. Then use the scoring key in Appendix B of this book to calculate your results. This self-assessment is completed alone so that students rate themselves honestly without concerns of social comparison. However, class discussion will focus on the meaning of self-efficacy, how this scale might be applied in organizations, and the limitations of measuring self-efficacy in work settings.

General self-efficacy scale

To what extent does each statement describe you? Indicate your level of agreement by marking the appropriate response on the right.

	Strongly Agree	Agree	Neutral	Disagree	Strongly Disagree
1. When I make plans, I am certain I can make them work.	☐	☐	☐	☐	☐
2. One of my problems is that I cannot get down to work when I should.	☐	☐	☐	☐	☐
3. If I can't do a job the first time, I keep trying until I can.	☐	☐	☐	☐	☐
4. When I set important goals for myself, I rarely achieve them.	☐	☐	☐	☐	☐
5. I give up on things before completing them.	☐	☐	☐	☐	☐
6. I avoid facing difficulties.	☐	☐	☐	☐	☐
7. If something looks too complicated, I will not even bother to try it.	☐	☐	☐	☐	☐
8. When I have something unpleasant to do, I stick to it until I finish it.	☐	☐	☐	☐	☐
9. When I decide to do something, I go right to work on it.	☐	☐	☐	☐	☐
10. When trying to learn something new, I soon give up if I am not initially successful.	☐	☐	☐	☐	☐
11. When unexpected problems occur, I don't handle them well.	☐	☐	☐	☐	☐
12. I avoid trying to learn new things when they look too difficult for me.	☐	☐	☐	☐	☐
13. Failure just makes me try harder.	☐	☐	☐	☐	☐
14. I feel insecure about my ability to do things.	☐	☐	☐	☐	☐
15. I am a self-reliant person.	☐	☐	☐	☐	☐
16. I give up easily.	☐	☐	☐	☐	☐
17. I do not seem capable of dealing with most problems that come up in life.	☐	☐	☐	☐	☐

Source: Reproduced with permission of authors and publisher from M. Sherer, J. E. Maddux, B. Mercandante, S. Prentice–Dunn, B. Jacobs, and R. W. Rogers, "The Self–Efficacy Scale: Construction and Validation." *Psychological Reports* 51 (1982), pp.663-71. Copyright © *Psychological Reports* (1982).

 After studying the preceding material, be sure to check out our website at
www.mhhe.com/mcshane2e
for more in-depth information and interactivities that correspond to this chapter.

3

Perception and Personality in Organizations

AFTER READING THIS CHAPTER, YOU SHOULD BE ABLE TO:

- Outline the perceptual process.

- Explain how we perceive ourselves and others through social identity.

- Discuss the accuracy of stereotypes.

- Describe the attribution process and two attribution errors.

- Diagram the self-fulfilling prophecy process.

- Discuss the objectives and limitations of diversity initiatives.

- Explain how the Johari Window can help improve our perceptions.

- Identify the Big Five personality dimensions.

- Discuss the psychological dimensions identified by Jung and measured in the Myers-Briggs Type Indicator.

The arrest of nuclear scientist Dr. Wen Ho Lee for allegedly stealing secrets at Los Alamos Nuclear Laboratory raised more than national security concerns. It also opened a long-simmering issue regarding bias against Asian Americans. Government officials deny that Lee, a naturalized U.S. citizen born in Taiwan, was singled out because of his ethnicity, whereas two counterintelligence officers claim Lee's race was a factor.

The U.S. Energy Department says that China recruits ethnic Chinese in the United States for espionage purposes. Others point out that this incident is one more example of the perpetual-foreigner syndrome—that Asian Americans are viewed by others as forever non-American.

Anne Xuan Clark frequently experiences the misperception that she is a foreigner. "I've been told a million times, 'Your English is so good! Where are you from?'" says Clark, a Seattle resident whose ancestors are Vietnamese and Irish. Clark comes from California, but that doesn't satisfy some acquaintances. "No, where are you *really* from?" they ask again.

U.S. Representative David Wu recently experienced perpetual-foreigner bias when he was detained entering the Energy Department building in Washington, D.C. Wu was repeatedly asked if he was an American citizen, even after showing his congressional pass. A recent survey also found that one-third of Americans believe Chinese Americans are more loyal to China than to the United States. "We always knew there was an element of some negative bias . . . but we were startled by the results," says Henry Tang, chairman of a group of prominent Chinese Americans who sponsored the survey.

The arrest of nuclear scientist Dr. Wen Ho Lee for allegedly stealing secrets at Los Alamos raised concerns about the perpetual-foreigner syndrome as a perceptual bias. *(© AFP/ CORBIS)*

"For years, a lot of these things have festered, and it was typical of the Asian way to say nothing," says Kalina Wong, an American-born scientist of Chinese and Hawaiian descent who works at the Livermore nuclear lab. "The whole Chinese spy allegation has set us back further." Wong and eight other Asian-American scientists and engineers at Livermore recently filed a racial discrimination complaint against their employer.[1]

perception
The process of selecting, organizing, and interpreting information in order to make sense of the world around us.

The Greek philosopher Plato wrote long ago that we see reality only as shadows reflecting against the rough wall of a cave.[2] In other words, reality is filtered through an imperfect perceptual process. **Perception** is the process of receiving information about and making sense of the world around us. It involves deciding which information to notice, how to categorize that information, and how to interpret it within the framework of our existing knowledge.

The opening vignette illustrates how perceptions shape opinions, decisions, and actions. Many automatically assume that people who look Chinese must be new to the United States. A few are convinced that Chinese Americans are more Chinese than American in terms of their allegiance. These and other perceptions shape our opinions about people from different backgrounds, as well as our decisions and actions toward them. In this world of increasing cultural diversity and globalization, we need to be particularly aware of the perceptual process and how we can minimize misperceptions of others.

This chapter begins by describing the perceptual process, that is, the dynamics of selecting, organizing, and interpreting external stimuli. Social identity theory is introduced, including how the perceptual process influences our self-perceptions and our perceptions of others. Social identity theory lays the foundation for our coverage of stereotyping, prejudice, and discrimination. The perceptual processes of attribution and self-fulfilling prophecy are described next, followed by an overview of strategies to minimize perceptual problems. Our perceptions of others, as well as most other organizational behavior processes, are influenced by our personality. The final section of this chapter introduces that important concept and its relevance to organizational behavior.

THE PERCEPTUAL PROCESS

As Exhibit 3.1 illustrates, the perceptual process begins when environmental stimuli are received through our senses. Most stimuli are screened out; the

EXHIBIT 3.1

Model of the perceptual process

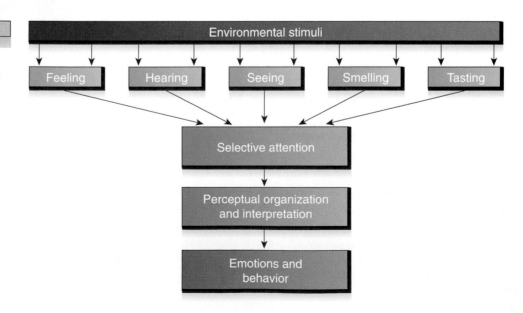

rest are organized and interpreted on the basis of various information-processing activities. The resulting perceptions influence our emotions and behavior toward objects, people, and events.[3]

Selective Attention

Our five senses are constantly bombarded with stimuli. As indicated above, some things get noticed, but most are screened out. A nurse working in post-operative care might ignore the smell of recently disinfected instruments or the sound of co-workers talking nearby. Yet a small, flashing red light on the nurses' station console is noticed immediately because it signals that a patient's vital signs are failing. This process of filtering information received by our senses is called **selective attention.**

One influence on selective attention includes the size, intensity, motion, repetition, and novelty of the target (including people). The red light on the nurses' station console receives attention because it is bright (intensity) and flashing (motion); additionally, it is a rare event (novelty). As for people, we would notice two employees having a heated debate if co-workers normally don't raise their voices (novelty and intensity).

Notice that selective attention is also influenced by the context in which the target is perceived. You might be aware that a client has a German accent if the meeting takes place in Portland, Oregon, but not if the conversation takes place in Germany, particularly if you have been living there for some time. On the contrary, it would be your American accent that others would notice.

Characteristics of the Perceiver　Selective attention depends on more than the object and the context. It is also affected by characteristics of the perceiver. We tend to remember information that is consistent with our values and attitudes and ignore information that is inconsistent with them. For example, interviewers who develop positive feelings toward a job applicant early in the interview tend to subsequently screen out negative information about that candidate.[4] In extreme cases, our emotions screen out large blocks of information that threaten our beliefs and values. This phenomenon, called **perceptual defense,** protects our self-esteem and may be a coping mechanism to minimize stress in the short run.[5]

Selective attention is also affected by our expectations.[6] An African proverb says: "It is on the regular path we take that the wild beast attacks." In other words, through experience, we are conditioned to anticipate routine events. Unique events are excluded from our thoughts—until it is too late. In organizational settings, expectations prevent decision makers from seeing opportunities and competitive threats.

One way to minimize this narrow selective attention is by engaging in **splatter vision**— perceiving everything as a whole rather than focusing on specific elements of the perceptual field. Truck drivers learn to expect the unexpected, such as a child darting out onto the road. Jet fighter pilots constantly check their peripheral vision, not just what's ahead of them. Police detectives try to avoid forming theories too early in criminal investigations with few leads or suspects. "When you get a theory, it can put blinders on to what really happened," explains a detective in one homicide case.[7]

Corporate decision makers should also apply splatter vision to avoid missing unexpected threats and opportunities. They need to avoid relying too

selective attention
The process of filtering information received by our senses.

perceptual defense
A psychological process in which our emotions screen out large blocks of information that threaten our beliefs and values.

splatter vision
The process of perceiving everything as a whole rather than focusing on specific elements of the perceptual field.

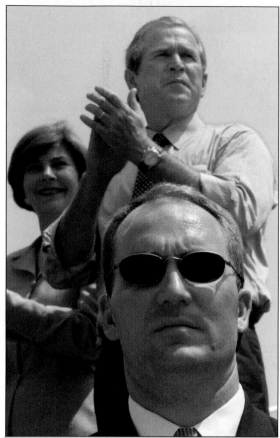

Protecting the president of the United States and other dignitaries is a difficult perceptual job. Secret Service agents must somehow ensure that their selective attention process takes in as much information as possible to identify potential security risks. How do they do this? They practice splatter vision—scanning everything and focusing on nothing. As one agent explains: "Never look through the crowd to find a potential assailant. The sheer number of people will leave you snow-blind." When agents focus on one suspicious character, they develop expectations that focus their attention. That, in turn, causes them to unconsciously screen out most of the other stimuli from the crowd. But with splatter vision, agents don't concentrate on a particular person, so their perceptual process doesn't filter out potentially valuable information.[9] How would splatter vision be useful in organizational settings? *(© AFP/CORBIS)*

much on their familiar expectations. Instead, corporate decision makers should expect the unexpected. They need to develop their "peripheral vision" by keeping an open mind to new information and ideas.

Perceptual Organization and Interpretation

After selecting stimuli, we usually simplify and make sense of them. This process involves organizing the information into general categories and interpreting it. We rely on perceptual grouping principles to organize people and objects into recognizable and manageable patterns or categories. This **perceptual grouping** occurs in a number of ways. It occurs when we make assumptions about people based on their similarity or proximity to others. It also occurs when we think we see trends in otherwise ambiguous information. Another form of perceptual grouping is closure, such as filling in missing information about what happened at a meeting that you missed (e.g., who was there, where it was held).

Perceptual grouping helps us make sense of the workplace, but it can also inhibit creativity and open-mindedness. It puts blinders on our ability to organize and interpret people and events differently. Perceptual grouping is influenced by our broader assumptions and beliefs, known as mental models.

Mental Models Communications guru Marshall McLuhan once wrote that people wear their own set of idiosyncratic goggles. In his colorful way, McLuhan was saying that each of us holds a unique view of what the world looks like and how it operates. These idiosyncratic goggles are known as **mental models**.[8] Mental models are the broad worldviews or "theories in use" that people rely on to guide their perceptions and behaviors. Formed and reinforced through experience, they create the screens through which we select information, the boxes we use to contain that knowledge, and the assumptions we use to interpret events.

Mental models guide our perceptions and alert us to deviations from the past. For example, most of us have a mental model about attending a college lecture or seminar. We have a set of assumptions and expectations about how people arrive, arrange themselves in the room, ask and answer questions,

perceptual grouping
The perceptual organization process of placing people and objects into recognizable and manageable patterns or categories.

mental models
The broad worldviews or "theories-in-use" that people rely on to guide their perceptions and behaviors.

social identity theory
A model that explains self-perception and social perception in terms of the person's unique characteristics (personal identity) and membership in various social groups (social identity).

and so forth. We can create a mental image of what a class would look like in progress. From this mental model, we would immediately notice if something is out of the ordinary, such as whether someone is missing or acting unusual.

Mental models help us make sense of our environment, but they may blind us to seeing that world in different ways.[10] For example, accounting professionals tend to see corporate problems in terms of accounting solutions, whereas marketing professionals see the same problems from a marketing perspective. Mental models also block our recognition of new opportunities. Consider the comment that Harry Warner of Warner Brothers Studios made when soundtracks first appeared for movies in 1927: "Who the hell wants to hear actors talk?" In the 1970s, General Motors continued to build big gas-guzzling cars even though oil prices had significantly altered what consumers were looking for in a vehicle. And as recently as 1996, Microsoft's Bill Gates mocked the commercial viability of the Internet.[11] In each case, mental models blocked the ability to see emerging marketplace realities.

How do we change mental models? It's a tough challenge. After all, we developed models from several years of experience and reinforcement. The first step is to constantly question our existing mental models and assumptions. Working with people from diverse backgrounds is another way to break out of existing mental models. Some companies try to form new mental models by hiring outsiders—people who have not worked in the industry and are therefore free of the dominant perceptions that blind industry veterans. For example, Sony Corporation's video game group successfully launched PlayStation by breaking away from long-established views of the market. They hired people with little or no experience in the video game industry so that the group could see opportunities differently.[12]

SOCIAL IDENTITY THEORY

The perceptual process is more than just placing other people into groups. It is an interactive dynamic between our self-perceptions and our perceptions of others. **Social identity theory** explains this process of self-perception and social perception.[13] According to social identity theory, people develop their self-perceptions through personal identity and social identity. *Personal identity* includes the individual's unique characteristics and experiences, such as physical appearance, personality traits, and special talents. An unusual achievement that distinguishes you from other people becomes a personal characteristic with which you partially identify yourself.

Social identity, on the other hand, refers to our self-perceptions as members in various social groups. For example, one person might have a self-identity as an American, a graduate of the University of Syracuse, and an employee at Cisco Systems. This social categorization process helps us locate ourselves within the social world (see Exhibit 3.2).

People adopt degrees of personal and social identity, depending on the situation.[14] If your organizational behavior class is well represented by gender, race, and specialization (marketing, finance, etc.), then you would tend to identify yourself in terms of personal identity characteristics in that context (e.g., "I'm probably the only one in this class who has trekked through Malaysia's Cameron Highlands!"). On the other hand, if you are a computer science student in a class consisting mostly of business students, then your group

EXHIBIT 3.2

Self-perception and
social perception
through social identity

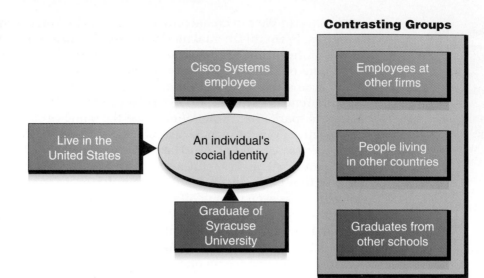

membership—your *social identity*—would dominate your self-perception. In this situation, you would define yourself more by your field of specialization ("I'm from computer science") than by any personal identity characteristics. As your distinguishing social identity becomes known to others, they, too, would likely identify you by that feature.

We tend to perceive ourselves as members of several groups, not just one or two. In this respect, social identity is a complex combination of many memberships determined by personal priorities. But which groups form our social identity? Mainly, we like to have a positive self-image, so we identify with groups that support this positive image. This tendency explains why medical doctors usually define themselves in terms of their profession, whereas people in low-status jobs are less likely to do so. It also explains why some people like to mention their employer and others never mention where they work.[15]

Perceiving Others through Social Identity

Social identity theory explains not only how we develop self-perceptions but also how we perceive others—through the dynamics of social perception. In particular, it describes how and why we categorize others into homogeneous and often less favorable groups. Social identity is a *comparative* process, meaning that we define ourselves in terms of our differences from people who belong to other groups. To simplify this comparison process, we tend to *homogenize* people within social categories. We think that people within our group share certain traits and that people in comparison groups share a different set of traits. Such thinking may be partly true, but we further exaggerate these differences. For example, students from one college often describe students from a rival school (particularly before a sports competition) as though they come from a different planet!

Comparison and homogenization explain why we perceptually group other people and overgeneralize their traits. But we also tend to develop less positive (or sometimes downright negative) images of people outside our social identity groups. Why do we disparage people who are different from us? The answer is

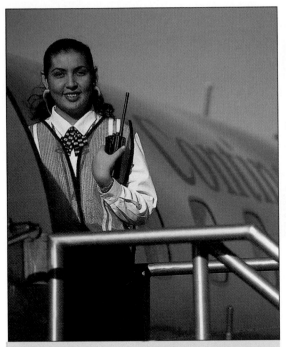

A few years ago, customer service was so bad at Continental Airlines that few employees admitted they worked there. Some employees were so ashamed they actually removed the Continental insignia from their uniforms. "You didn't dare go anywhere with a uniform on," recalls Zack Meza, a Continental reservations agent in Minneapolis. Today, thanks to a dramatic turnaround, Continental Airlines is a leader in customer service, profitability, and employee morale. Employees also have a strong social identity with the Houston-based airline. They proudly show their Continental insignia, and purchases of Continental-labeled items at the company store have increased by 400 percent.[17] In your opinion, what are the benefits of employees' having a strong social identity with their employer? *(Courtesy of Continental Airlines)*

that our self-identity involves contrasting the groups we belong to with other groups. To maintain a positive self-image, we usually construct favorable images of our own social identity group and, as a result, less favorable images of people belonging to other social categories. This tendency is particularly likely when the other groups are in competition and conflict with our social identity groups. The negative image of opponents preserves our self-image while the threat exists.[16]

In summary, the social identity process explains how we perceive ourselves and others. We identify ourselves partly in terms of our memberships in social groups. This comparison process includes creating a homogeneous image of our own social groups and different homogeneous images of people in other groups. We also tend to assign more favorable features to our own groups and less favorable features to other groups. This perceptual process makes our social world easier to understand. However, it also becomes the basis for stereotyping people in organizational settings, which we discuss next.

ERRORS IN THE PERCEPTUAL PROCESS

So far, we have outlined the main elements of social perception in organizations, including selective attention, perceptual organization and interpretation, and social identity processes. You probably noticed already that the perceptual process is less than perfect. People ignore and distort information; then they try to make sense of it in ways that are often different from how other people see the same situation. Over the next several pages, we will more fully explore several explanations of how and why people distort perceptions in organizational settings. Some topics—such as stereotyping and attribution—are natural perceptual processes. We stereotype and make attributions as part of the perceptual process. But these and other perceptual activities are better known for the perceptual errors they create.

Stereotyping in Organizational Settings

stereotyping
The process of assigning traits to people based on their membership in a social category.

Stereotyping is an extension of social identity. It is the process of assigning traits to people on the basis of their membership in a social category.[18] In other words, stereotypes define people by the demographic and organizational groups to which they belong. Exhibit 3.3 illustrates the three steps in the stereotyping process. First, we develop social categories and assign traits that are difficult to observe. For instance, students might form a stereotype that

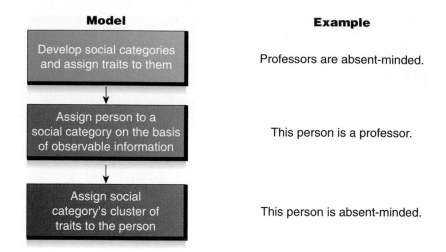

EXHIBIT 3.3

The stereotyping process

Model

Develop social categories and assign traits to them

↓

Assign person to a social category on the basis of observable information

↓

Assign social category's cluster of traits to the person

Example

Professors are absent-minded.

This person is a professor.

This person is absent-minded.

professors are both intelligent and absent-minded. To some extent, these unobservable traits are formed from personal experiences. However, they are influenced just as much by public images, such as movie characters and public figures.

Next, we assign people to one or more social categories on the basis of easily observable information about them, such as their gender, appearance, or physical location. Observable features allow us to assign people to a social group quickly and without much investigation. Lastly, we assign the cluster of traits linked to the social category to people identified as members of that group. For example, we subconsciously assume that professors are absent-minded, at least until we know them better.

How Accurate Are Stereotypes?   Early writers warned that stereotypes were almost completely false or, at best, exaggerated the traits of people in those groups. Scholars now take a more moderate view. They say that stereotypes generally have some inaccuracies, some overestimation or underestimation of real differences, and some degree of accuracy.[19] Still, we should remember that stereotypes are never as accurate as our personal knowledge of an individual.

One problem with stereotyping is that stereotyped traits do not accurately describe every person in that social category. For instance, research has found that people with physical disabilities are stereotyped as being quiet, gentle-hearted, shy, insecure, dependent, and submissive.[20] Although this description may be true of some people, it is certainly not characteristic of everyone who has a physical disability. Another concern with stereotypes is that we often ignore or misinterpret information that is inconsistent with the stereotype.[21] Stereotypes are notoriously easy to confirm because they include abstract personality traits that are supported by ambiguous behaviors.

People also develop inaccurate stereotypes under certain conditions. One condition is the degree to which we interact with people in that group. If we don't communicate with and observe people directly, then we tend to rely on distorted public images of them. Stereotypes are also less accurate when we experience conflict with members of that group. Conflict creates an "us versus them" emotional state that subconsciously distorts the information we assign to the group.

The third problem is that we develop inaccurate stereotypes of groups that enhance our own social identity. Recall from social identity theory that our self-perception is developed by identifying with certain social groups and contrasting them with other groups. This process creates less favorable images of other groups, which involves subconsciously assigning inaccurate traits to people in those different groups.[22]

At this point, you might think we should avoid stereotyping altogether. Unfortunately, it's not that simple. Stereotyping is a natural process to economize mental effort.[23] By remembering information about categories of people rather than about every individual we meet, we use stereotyping to save a lot of investigative work. Moreover, this perceptual process fills in missing information when we lack the opportunity or motivation to know others directly. The good news is that the more we interact with someone, the less we rely on stereotypes to understand that individual. Stereotyping occurs when we lack personal information about the individual or the information is ambiguous. As we get to know someone better, we rely less on our stereotypic perceptions of that individual.[24]

Ethical Problems with Stereotyping Although stereotypes are a natural part of the perceptual process, inaccurate stereotypes raise serious ethical concerns. Perhaps the greatest concern is that stereotyping lays the foundation for **prejudice**—unfounded negative emotions toward people belonging to a particular stereotyped group.[25] For instance, seven African-American employees sued their employer, Georgia Power, for racial discrimination after hangman's nooses were displayed at several power plants. The Alaskan Governor's Commission on Tolerance heard of physical attacks against Native Americans as well as slurs against a city worker because of his sexual orientation. The Hong Kong government doesn't have laws against racial discrimination in the private sector, but it still receives dozens of complaints each year, including reports by Filipino maids of physical abuse and sexual assault from their Hong Kong employers.[26]

Overt prejudice still exists, but it is probably fair to say that most people try to avoid discriminatory behaviors. They support the notion of equality and try to act consistently with this value. People tend to monitor their own emotions and suppress prejudices arising from ingrained stereotypes.[27] Unfortunately, subtle discrimination occurs even when prejudices are minimized, because people rely on stereotypes to establish notions of the "ideal" person in specific roles.[28] A person who doesn't fit the ideal is likely to receive a less favorable evaluation. In the opening vignette in this chapter, U.S. Representative David Wu didn't fit the expected characteristics of an elected representative, so officials at the Energy Department prevented him from entering the building until they were convinced that he wasn't a security threat. Connections 3.1 describes how this stereotyping bias hurts the performance evaluations and employment prospects of older workers.[29]

Before leaving this topic, we should note that stereotyping is also partly responsible for sexual harassment. As we will learn in Chapter 7, sexual harassment refers to unwelcome conduct of a sexual nature that detrimentally affects the work environment or leads to adverse job-related consequences for

prejudice
The unfounded negative emotions toward people belonging to a particular stereotyped group.

An Age-Old Bias in the Workplace

James Brazin's record of 32 positive performance reviews was broken by a C rating in the latest round of evaluations. "My work had always been exceptional and now all of a sudden I'm at the bottom," says the mechanical engineer at Ford Motor Company's Livonia transmission technical center and plant. Brazin, who is 55 years old, thinks age discrimination is a factor. He claims his boss explained his C rating by saying, "You're an old guy just like me."

Ford's revised appraisal system, which forces 10 percent of employees into the bottom rating, has resulted in two class-action lawsuits alleging the system discriminates against older workers like Brazin. The automaker has already settled another age discrimination case in which a supervisor allegedly told an employee that he "was too old to be promoted" at Ford.

Corporate leaders say that there is no age bias, just a few older employees whose skills don't fit current needs. But Bob Shayne will tell you otherwise. The 60-year-old television writer says he is still good at his trade, but networks don't hire older writers. "Maybe I couldn't write 'Friends,'" says Shayne, "but certainly half the shows on television I could write." Fifty writers have filed a class-action lawsuit against television studios and networks, claiming that they have also experienced a systematic and pervasive pattern of age discrimination.

Age bias also seems to plague older employees in the investment industry. For example, Craig Blair (not his real name) worked at several large investment banks, eventually working his way up to the level of senior money market specialist. Then he got pushed out, apparently because he was too old. The 46-year-old was confident about getting a job after interviewing with another investment bank, until a friend told him the news. The friend had overheard a conversation in which the dealer who'd interviewed Blair told someone, "We're not going to hire him. He's too old."

Sources: M. Truby, "Age-Bias Claims Jolt Ford Culture Change," *Detroit News*, April 29, 2001; R. Pogrebin, "At 40, They're Finished, Television Writers Say," *New York Times*, January 30, 2001, p. G9; T. Cole, "Revenge of the Fortysomethings," *Report on Business*, June 2000, p. 34.

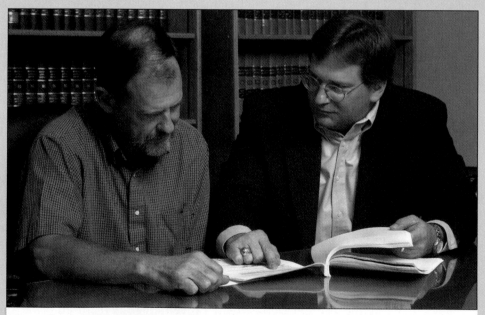

James Brazin (left) believes that age discrimination may be the reason for the C rating on his latest performance review at Ford Motor Company. (© *AP/Wide World*)

its victims. Sexual harassment is mainly caused by the harasser's abuse of power, as we will discuss in Chapter 12. However, it is also more prevalent where the harasser (typically a man) holds sexist motives based on paternalism and gender stereotyping.[30] In other words, harassment is more likely to occur among people who stereotype the victim as subservient and powerless. For example, a study of female firefighters reported that sexual harassment is much more prevalent in fire departments where men hold strong sex stereotypes of women.[31] The implication here is that sexual harassment will continue as long as people maintain sexist perceptions.

Attribution Theory

attribution process

The perceptual process of deciding whether an observed behavior or event is largely caused by internal or external factors.

Our discussion so far has looked mainly at the dynamics of grouping, including social identity and stereotyping. A different perceptual activity, called the **attribution process,** helps us interpret the world around us. The attribution process involves deciding whether an observed behavior or event is caused largely by internal or by external factors.[32] Internal factors originate from within a person, such as the individual's ability or motivation. We make an *internal attribution* by believing that an employee performs the job poorly because he or she lacks the necessary competencies or motivation. External factors originate from the environment, such as lack of resources, other people, or just luck. An *external attribution* would occur if we believe that the employee performs the job poorly because he or she doesn't receive sufficient resources to do the task.

How do people determine whether to make an internal or an external attribution about a co-worker's excellent job performance or a supplier's late shipment? Basically, they rely on the three attribution rules shown in Exhibit 3.4. Internal attributions are made when the observed individual behaved this way in the past (high consistency), he or she behaves like this toward other people or in different situations (low distinctiveness), and other people do not behave this way in similar situations (low consensus). On the other hand, an external attribution is made when there is low consistency, high distinctiveness, and high consensus.

The following example will help clarify the three attribution rules. Suppose that an employee is making poor-quality products one day on a particular machine. We would probably conclude that there is something wrong with the machine (an external attribution) if the employee has made good-quality products on this machine in the past (low consistency), the employee makes good-quality products on other machines (high distinctiveness), and other employees have recently had quality problems on this machine (high consensus). We would make an internal attribution, on the other hand, if the employee usually makes poor-quality products on this machine (high consistency), other employees produce good-quality products on this machine (low consensus), and the employee also makes poor-quality products on other machines (low distinctiveness).[33]

Attributions influence most behaviors and decisions in the workplace.[34] For instance, your co-workers and boss are more likely to get upset with you if they believe your absenteeism or lateness is due to your lack of motivation rather than to traffic, sick children, or other conditions beyond your control. Research has found that employees receive larger bonuses or pay increases

EXHIBIT 3.4   Rules of attribution

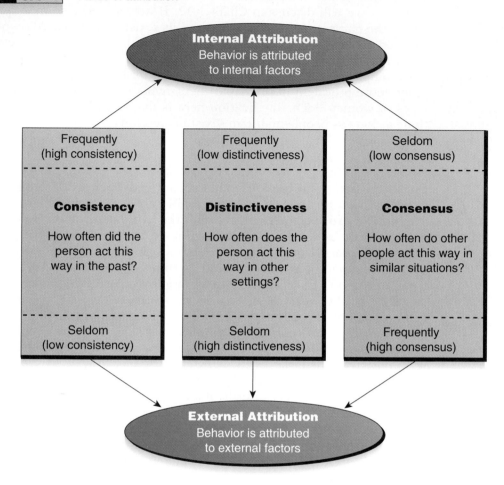

when decision makers attribute good performance to the employee's ability or motivation. Employees also develop a stronger self-efficacy and tend to have higher job satisfaction when they believe positive feedback relates to events within their control rather than to external causes.[35]

fundamental attribution error
The tendency to attribute the behavior of other people more to internal than to external factors.

Attribution Errors   The attribution process is far from perfect. The most fundamental error we make in attribution is called (not surprisingly) **fundamental attribution error**—the tendency to attribute the behavior of other people more to internal than to external factors. If an employee is late for work, observers are more likely to conclude that the person is lazy than to think that external factors may have caused the behavior. Fundamental attribution error occurs where there is limited information about the situational factors affecting other people. The person performing the behavior is naturally more sensitive to situational influences. Fundamental attribution error can lead to disagreement over the degree to which employees should be held responsible for their poor performance or absenteeism.[36] The observer blames the employee's lack of motivation or ability, whereas the employee does not feel

Hong Kong and British Firms Produce Creative External Attributions

To distance themselves from accounting delays and poor profits, some Hong Kong and British executives have a knack for offering unusual external attributions for their performance shortcomings.

Kessel International Holdings Ltd., a Hong Kong manufacturer of battery-operated toys and gadgets, advised shareholders that it couldn't provide its annual figures on time because of "repeated electricity failure in the head office of the company that shut down the company's computer system on various occasions." The electrical failures occurred eight months earlier, but maybe shareholders wouldn't notice this gap.

Interform Ceramics Technologies Ltd. offered a more complex explanation for its late accounting reports. The large Hong Kong ceramics company put its accounting books in storage during a move to a new office. Then, according to a notice to its shareholders, most of its accounting staff left the company. The remaining staff apparently weren't able to retrieve the books, although Interform didn't explain why.

British executives seem to get their financial reports submitted on time, but they are equally adept at distancing themselves from the causes of poor sales or profits. One British IT firm tried to explain how a snowstorm on the East Coast of the United States had somehow undermined its profits for the year. Executives at a brewery blamed their poor results one year ago on mining pit closures in the Northeast and the launch of Britain's National Lottery.

A few years ago, several firms claimed that poor sales were caused by the "Diana effect." DFS, a British furniture chain, explained that customers were too grief-stricken by the death of Princess Diana to think about buying new furniture. DFS executives also suggested that the hot summer weather had led to falling sales.

Sources: J. Ashworth, "Warning: Yet Another Excuse on the Line," *Times of London*, August 8, 2001, p. 20; G. Manuel, "Why Hong Kong Firms Are Late Filing Results," *Asian Wall Street Journal*, August 3, 2001, p. 1.

---

responsible because the behavior seems to be due to factors beyond his or her control.

Another attribution error, known as **self-serving bias,** is the tendency to attribute our favorable outcomes to internal factors and our failures to external factors. Simply put, we take credit for our successes and blame others or the situation for our mistakes. The existence of self-serving bias in corporate life has been well documented. One recent example is a study that monitored a small government organization as it introduced a performance management system. The study found that 90 percent of the employees who received lower-than-expected performance ratings blamed the low ratings on their supervisor, the organization, the appraisal system, or other external causes. Only a handful blamed themselves for the unexpected results.[37] Research has also reported this self-serving bias in corporate annual reports.[38] As we read in Global Connections 3.2, executives in Hong Kong and the United Kingdom have been very creative in identifying external causes for their poor performance.

Aside from these errors, attributions vary from one person to another based on personal values and experiences. For instance, female managers are less likely than male managers to make internal attributions about their job performance.[39] Overall, we need to be careful about personal and systematic biases in the attribution process within organizations.

Self-Fulfilling Prophecy

When Henry Quadracci started Quad/Graphics in the 1970s, he could afford only inexperienced employees, many of whom had low self-esteem. "When

self-serving bias
A perceptual error whereby people tend to attribute their favorable outcomes to internal factors and their failures to external factors.

they come into the employment office, they're not looking at the stars," Quadracci observed. "They're looking at their shoes." But Quadracci saw the potential of these new hires and continually treated them as winners. The strategy worked. Quad/Graphics employees developed confidence and exceptional performance, with the result that the printing firm is one of the largest and most successful in the United States.[40]

Henry Quadracci has been practicing **self-fulfilling prophecy.** Self-fulfilling prophecy occurs when our expectations about another person cause that person to act in a way that is consistent with those expectations.[41] In other words, our perceptions can influence reality. One of the best examples of self-fulfilling prophecy took place in an Israeli Defense Force combat command course. Course instructors were told that one-third of the incoming trainees had high command potential, one-third had normal potential, and the rest had unknown potential. The trainees had been placed randomly into these categories by the researchers, but the instructors were led to believe that the information was accurate. As predicted, high-expectancy soldiers performed significantly better by the end of the course than did others. They also had more favorable attitudes toward the course and the instructor's leadership effectiveness.[42]

The same effect can happen in other organizational situations. If a supervisor believes a new employee won't be able to perform the job, that expectation influences the supervisor's behavior toward the employee and, without the supervisor's realizing it, may cause the recruit to perform the job poorly. Consequently, the supervisor's perception, even if originally incorrect, is confirmed. Exhibit 3.5 illustrates the four steps in the self-fulfilling prophecy process using the example of a supervisor and subordinate.[43]

1. *Expectations formed*—The supervisor forms expectations about the employee's future behavior and performance. These expectations are sometimes inaccurate, because first impressions are usually formed from limited information.
2. *Behavior toward the employee*—The supervisor's expectations influence his or her treatment of the employee.[44] Specifically, a high-expectancy employee (one expected to do well) receives more emotional support through nonverbal cues (e.g., more smiling and eye contact), more frequent

EXHIBIT 3.5

The self-fulfilling prophecy cycle

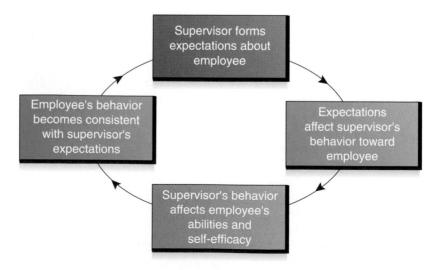

and valuable feedback and reinforcement, more challenging goals, better training, and more opportunities to demonstrate her or his performance.

3. *Effects on the employee*—The supervisor's behaviors have two effects on the employee. First, through better training and more practice opportunities, a high-expectancy employee learns more skills and knowledge than a low-expectancy employee. Second, the employee develops a stronger self-efficacy.[45] Recall from Chapter 2 that high-self-efficacy employees believe they have the ability, motivation, and resources to complete a task successfully.[46] This belief results in higher motivation because employees develop stronger effort-to-performance expectancies and set more challenging goals for themselves.

4. *Employee behavior and performance*—With higher motivation and better skills, high-expectancy employees are more likely to demonstrate desired behaviors and better performance. The supervisor notices this result, which supports his or her original perception.

Self-Fulfilling Prophecies in Practice   Positive self-fulfilling prophecy is a potentially valuable strategy to maximize employee performance and satisfaction. Unfortunately, employees are more likely to be victims of negative self-fulfilling prophecy.[47] How can organizations harness the power of positive self-fulfilling prophecy? Researchers initially recommended that leaders become aware of the Pygmalion effect and learn how to exhibit contagious enthusiasm. Unfortunately, these training programs have had limited success, partly because leaders have difficulty maintaining positive perceptions toward employees who, in their mind, aren't very good.[48]

More recently, experts have recommended a three-pronged approach in which leaders develop positive self-fulfilling prophecies by creating a learning orientation, applying appropriate leadership styles, and building self-efficacy in employees.[49] First, leaders need to develop a learning orientation; that is, they need to appreciate the value of the employee's learning, not just accomplishing tasks (see Chapter 2). Leaders demonstrate a learning orientation by accepting reasonable mistakes as a natural part of the learning process. Second, leaders need to apply appropriate leadership behaviors to all employees. In other words, they practice the contingency approach to leadership that we will learn about in Chapter 14. For employees who are new to the position or task, this approach would usually include leaders' providing frequent, objective feedback and creating a positive relationship by showing support.

The third prong to the positive self-fulfilling prophecy strategy is to teach leaders how to increase employee self-efficacy. As we discussed in Chapter 2, this teaching can occur through behavioral modeling (e.g., having the employee watch someone similar perform the task well) and giving employees the opportunity to practice the task successfully. Self-efficacy can also be increased by convincing doubtful employees using persuasive communication principles (see Chapter 12). Leaders might still harbor negative perceptions of some employees, but this three-pronged approach may partly offset negative self-fulfilling prophecies.

Primacy Effect

The primacy effect relates to the saying that "first impressions are lasting impressions." It is our tendency to quickly form an opinion of people based on

primacy effect
A perceptual error in which we quickly form an opinion of people based on the first information we receive about them.

the first information we receive about them. This rapid perceptual organization fulfills our need to make sense of others and provides a convenient anchor to integrate subsequent information. For example, if we first meet someone who avoids eye contact and speaks softly, we quickly conclude that the person is bashful. It is easier to remember the person as bashful than to recall the specific behaviors exhibited during the first encounter. Unfortunately, once an inaccurate first impression is established, it is difficult to change because people pay less attention to subsequent information and tend to completely ignore information that contradicts the first impression.[50] Thus, the person we think is bashful will have difficulty shaking this first impression.

Under the right circumstances, the primacy effect can be beneficial. Many organizations take extra care to ensure that customers have a positive first experience. They also make sure that employees have a good first impression when they join the firm. For instance, the Royal Bank of Canada invited college students to spend the day rappelling with bank staffers. The idea was to create a first impression that is more consistent with what young people want in an organization. As a Royal Bank recruiter explains: "What that says to prospective employees is, 'We're not necessarily just a bank of blue suits.' "[51]

Recency Effect

recency effect
A perceptual error in which the most recent information dominates our perception of others.

The **recency effect** occurs when the most recent information dominates our perception of others.[52] This effect is stronger than the primacy effect when there is a long delay between the time the first impression is formed and when the person is evaluated. In other words, the most recent information has the greater influence on our perception of someone when the first impression has worn off with the passage of time.

The recency effect is found in performance appraisals, for which supervisors must recall every employee's performance over the previous year. Recent performance information dominates the evaluation because it is the most easily recalled. Some employees are well aware of the recency effect and use it to their advantage by getting their best work on the manager's desk just before the performance appraisal is conducted.

(DILBERT reprinted by permission of United Feature Syndicate, Inc.)

Halo Error

Halo error occurs when our general impression of a person, usually based on one prominent characteristic, colors our perception of other characteristics of that person.[53] If we meet a client who speaks in a friendly manner, we tend to infer a host of other favorable qualities about that person. If a colleague doesn't complete tasks on time, we tend to view his or her other traits unfavorably. In each case, one trait important to the perceiver forms a general impression, and this impression becomes the basis for judgments about other traits. Halo error is most likely to occur when concrete information about the perceived target is missing or we are not sufficiently motivated to search for it.[54] Instead, we use our general impression of the person to fill in the missing information.

Halo error has received considerable attention in research on performance appraisal ratings.[55] Consider the situation in which two employees have the same level of work quality, quantity of work, and customer relations performance, but one tends to be late for work. Tardiness might not be an important factor in work performance, but the supervisor has a negative impression of employees who are late for work. Halo error would cause the supervisor to rate the tardy employee lower on *all* performance dimensions because the tardiness created a negative general impression of that employee. The punctual employee would tend to receive higher ratings on *all* performance dimensions even though his or her performance level is really the same as that of the tardy employee. Consequently, halo error distorts our judgments and can result in poor decision making.

Projection Bias

Projection bias occurs when we believe other people have the same beliefs and behaviors that we have.[56] If you are eager for a promotion, you might think that others in your position are similarly motivated. If you are thinking of quitting your job, you start to believe that other people are also thinking of quitting.

Projection bias is also a defense mechanism to protect our self-esteem. If we break a work rule, projection bias justifies this infraction by claiming that "everyone does it." We feel more comfortable with the thought that our negative traits exist in others, so we believe that others also have these traits.

IMPROVING PERCEPTIONS

We can't bypass the perceptual process, but we should make every attempt to minimize perceptual biases and distortions. This section introduces five strategies to improve our perceptions: introducing diversity initiatives, learning to empathize with others, postponing our impressions of others, comparing our perceptions with those of others, and becoming more aware of our values, beliefs, and prejudices.

Diversity Initiatives

The Charles Schwab Corporation is a leader in promoting women throughout its ranks. Women represent 39 percent of the San Francisco–based brokerage firm's workforce and 36 percent of its corporate officers. More than three-quarters of Schwab's employees ultimately report to a woman. But when asked what formal programs created this notable achievement in a male-dominated industry, Schwab executives respond with incomprehension or irritation. Schwab doesn't have any formal programs; their ability to provide equal opportunity for women is just part of the company's culture. Executives were also surprised when the company won a Catalyst award for the advancement of women. "We didn't think we could win the award because we didn't have any programs," admits Beth Sawi, Schwab's chief administrative officer. "It's a state of mind."[57]

Every organization's ideal would be to have a deeply embedded set of values that embrace workforce diversity, but most firms need some help along the way. That's why more than 75 percent of Fortune 500 companies, as well as many smaller organizations, have introduced various diversity initiatives.[58] The most common initiative is to actively recruit people with diverse backgrounds. Procter & Gamble (P&G) sends out a recruiting team that targets historically black colleges and another team devoted to recruiting Hispanic candidates. To build a long-term relationship with these candidates, P&G brings minority college students into summer camps where they work on assignments that put them in contact with more senior people in the organization. "We're really trying to identify [minority] candidates early so we can develop a relationship long-term and hopefully turn that into long-term employment," explains a P&G recruiting executive.[59]

A second diversity initiative is to provide reasonable accommodation in the workplace. This might involve adjusting work hours for parents so that they can attend to their children, offering job sharing for those who want more work–life balance, or allowing nontraditional breaks for religious reasons. Saima Abbasi has experienced this accommodation as a drive-through teller at Southwest Bank in Clayton, Missouri. Abbasi is a Sunni Muslim, so she is covered from head to toe in traditional dress and is able to take a few short breaks during the day for her zuhur prayers facing Mecca. Executives at Southwest Bank say it hasn't been a problem catering to the diverse needs of their employees.[60]

A third diversity initiative includes various diversity awareness activities, ranging from celebrations of workplace diversity to focused awareness training. Raytheon holds an annual Multicultural Week celebration where employees from different nations proudly show off dresses, artwork, photographs, books, toys, and religious items. Walt Disney World has "hallway celebrations" where employees are encouraged to bring in ethnic dishes and display items for recognized ethnic holidays.[61]

Diversity awareness training takes a more focused approach by sensitizing people about stereotypes and prejudices that may undermine the benefits of diversity. Such training helps dispel myths about people from different backgrounds and sometimes brings out subtle prejudices through role plays and exercises. Diversity awareness training is not intended to correct deep-rooted prejudice or intolerance. In fact, it could make matters worse because highly prejudiced employees are likely to view training sessions as a form of coercion if they are required to attend them.

Diversity awareness training usually tries to change attitudes more than behaviors, which some critics argue results in little real change in the workplace.[62] But supporters suggest that emerging diversity awareness training is

The National Hockey League (NHL) has 600 players from 18 nationalities. Hockey is an aggressive game where players sometimes vent their emotions with racial slurs. "People are always picking on your heritage," says Philadelphia Flyers goalie John Vanbiesbrouck. "We're living in a stereotypical world, where nicknames come before names, and that sometimes leads to other things." To minimize these problems, the NHL requires every player to attend diversity awareness training each year. In these sessions, players learn to appreciate ethnic differences as well as the negative consequences of racial slurs in the NHL . "Obviously, the problem has crept into our game and to pro sports in general," says an NHL player after a diversity awareness session. "There should be a professional respect."[63] Along with this training, what other diversity initiatives could the NHL introduce to minimize ethnic conflict? (© REUTERS/Andy Clark/TimePix)

becoming more experiential and action-oriented. To foster a deeper understanding of differences, United Parcel Service (UPS) and Hoechst Celanese send their senior staff into communities markedly different from their own to educate them about diversity issues. By working with people and groups from backgrounds different from their own, these executives gain a deeper understanding of different perspectives and experiences. "Joining these organizations has been more helpful to me than two weeks of diversity training," concludes a Hoechst Celanese executive.[64]

Empathize with Others

empathy
A person's ability to understand and be sensitive to the feelings, thoughts, and situation of others.

UPS and Hoechst Celanese executives are taking diversity initiatives to the next level by learning how to empathize with people from different backgrounds. **Empathy** refers to a person's ability to understand and be sensitive to the feelings, thoughts, and situations of others.[65] Through empathy, we become more sensitive to external causes of another person's performance and behavior, thereby minimizing attribution errors. Empathy also narrows the psychological distance between prejudiced people and the targets of their prejudice.

Empathy comes naturally to some people. However, the rest of us can develop empathy skills by receiving feedback on how well we seem to empathize.[66] Another way to increase empathy with employees and customers is by "walking in their shoes." Linda Burzynski did this when she became president of Molly Maid. To help her develop a better empathy for employees and customers, Burzynski spent a few weeks working in a frontline job as a maid. "I must admit, I prejudged people, and I ended up being a student," she says of her experience.[67]

Postpone Impression Formation

It is very tempting to put people into categories as soon as possible. After all, the sooner we label them, the sooner we can simplify the world and reduce the tension of uncertainty. Unfortunately, this practice of forming impressions with limited information forces us to rely on inaccurate and overgeneralized stereotypes. A much better perceptual strategy is to postpone impression formation until more information is collected about the individual or situation. By delaying closure, we rely less on stereotyped inferences to understand others.

When working with people from different cultural backgrounds, for instance, we should constantly challenge our stereotypic expectations and actively seek out contrary information. By blocking the effects of stereotypes, first impressions, and other perceptual blinders, we are better able to engage in a developmental learning process that forms a better understanding of others.[68]

Compare Perceptions with Those of Others

Another useful way of reducing perceptual bias is to compare our perceptions with the perceptions other people have about the same target. By sharing perceptions, we learn different points of view and potentially gain a better understanding of the situation. If our colleagues have different backgrounds but similar perceptions of the situation, then there is reason to be more confident in our interpretation. Of course, there is no way to know for sure that our perceptions are correct, but they are less likely to be wrong if people with different backgrounds have the same general interpretation of the situation.

Know Yourself: Applying the Johari Window

Knowing yourself—becoming more aware of your values, beliefs, and prejudices—is a powerful way to improve your perceptions.[69] Suppose that you dislike a particular client who treated you badly a few years ago. If the client meets with you to reestablish the relationship, you might be more open-minded about this business opportunity if you are conscious of these emotions. Moreover, if your colleagues are also aware of your unique values and past experiences, they are more likely to understand your actions and help you improve in the future. If you act harshly toward the troublesome client, for example, your colleagues are likely to understand the reason for your behavior and draw this to your attention.

Johari Window
The model of personal and interpersonal understanding that encourages disclosure and feedback to increase the open area and reduce the blind, hidden, and unknown areas of oneself.

The **Johari Window** is a popular model for understanding how co-workers can increase their mutual understanding.[70] Developed by Joseph Luft and Harry Ingram (hence the name "Johari"), this model divides information about yourself into four areas—open, blind, hidden, and unknown—on the basis of whether your own values, beliefs, and experiences are known to you and to others.

As we see in Exhibit 3.6, the *open area* includes information about you that is known both to you and to others. For example, both you and your co-workers may be aware that you don't like to be near people who smoke cigarettes. The *blind area* refers to information that is known to others but not to yourself. For example, your colleagues might notice that you are embarrassed and awkward when meeting someone confined to a wheelchair, but you are unaware of this fact. Information known to you but unknown to others is found in the *hidden area*. We all have personal secrets about our likes, dislikes, and personal experiences. Finally, the *unknown area* includes your values, beliefs, and experiences that aren't known to you or to others.

The main objective of the Johari Window is to increase the size of the open area so that both you and your colleagues are aware of your perceptual limitations. This is partly accomplished by reducing the hidden area through *disclosure*—informing others of your beliefs, feelings, and experiences that may influence the work relationship. Disclosure must be reciprocal among team members; that is, they should provide information about themselves as you reveal information about yourself. Fortunately, self-disclosure by one person tends to cause others to make a self-disclosure.[71] The open area also increases through *feedback* from others about your behaviors. This information helps you reduce your blind area, because co-workers often see things in you that you do not see. Finally, the combination of disclosure and feedback occasionally produces revelations about information in the unknown area.

EXHIBIT 3.6

Johari Window

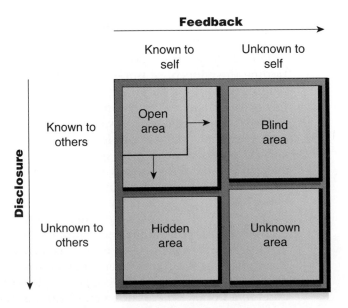

Source: Based on J. Luft, *Group Processes* (Palo Alto, CA: Mayfield, 1984).

Johari Window in Practice   The Johari Window can be found in the diversity awareness activities described earlier. By learning about cultural differences and communicating more with co-workers from different backgrounds, we gain a better understanding of their behavior patterns. The 360-degree feedback process, described in Chapter 2, also applies the Johari Window process, because it represents a structured way to receive feedback from others. A third strategy is to engage in open dialogue with co-workers. As we communicate with others, we naturally tend to disclose more information about ourselves and eventually feel comfortable providing candid feedback to them.

The Johari Window may work well in some cultures, but not in others. It seems to ignore the fact that face-saving is an important cultural value in some Asian countries. The Johari Window also applies strong egalitarian principles—everyone is equal—which conflicts with highly status-oriented cultures. Lastly, in any country, we must remember that everyone needs to have a hidden self. Unfortunately, some organization development practices cross this ethical boundary by trying to invade that private space (see Chapter 15).

No matter which steps are taken to improve the perceptual process, we need to recognize that our perceptions of the world are partly structured by our personality. In fact, an individual's personality traits play a pervasive role in almost every aspect of organizational behavior, from learning processes to one's willingness to adopt a company's cultural values.

PERSONALITY IN ORGANIZATIONS

Jeffrey Mallett is a personality to reckon with in the web-portal business. The president of Yahoo! Inc. is described as a confident, brash, and aggressive competitor who can energize a roomful of staff and be equally blunt and cocky to those who don't see his vision. Since joining Yahoo! soon after its start-up, Mallet's high-octane style earned him the nickname "Sparky." His personality was apparent while he was playing sports in junior high school, where his intensity and confidence easily offset his small stature (he's 5 feet 5 inches tall). "It didn't matter to him that everyone was bigger," recalls a childhood buddy. "Jeff was absolutely fearless."[72]

personality
The relatively stable pattern of behaviors and consistent internal states that explain a person's behavioral tendencies.

It is difficult to describe Jeffrey Mallett—or anyone else—without mentioning the concept of **personality.** Personality refers to the relatively stable pattern of behaviors and consistent internal states that explain a person's behavioral tendencies.[73] Personality has both internal and external elements. External traits are the observable behaviors that we rely on to identify someone's personality. For example, we can see Jeffrey Mallett's confidence in the way he plays ice hockey or speaks to a roomful of employees. The internal states represent the thoughts, values, and genetic characteristics that we infer from the observable behaviors.

An individual's personality is relatively stable. If an individual's personality changes at all, it is only over a very long time or as the result of a traumatic event. Personality explains behavioral tendencies, because a person's behavior is influenced by the situation as well as personality traits. Personality traits are less evident in situations where social norms, reward systems, and other conditions constrain behavior.[74] For example, talkative people remain relatively quiet in a library where "no talking" rules are explicit and strictly enforced.

An individual's personality is both inherited and shaped from the environment.[75] Our personality is partly inherited genetically from our parents.

However, these genetic personality characteristics are altered somewhat by life experiences. Jeffrey Mallett's personality is partly handed down genetically from his parents, but it has also been shaped by a variety of life experiences, such as early friendships and significant events.

Personality and Organizational Behavior

At one time, scholars often explained employee behavior in terms of personality traits and companies regularly administered personality tests to job applicants. This approach changed in the 1960s when researchers reported a very weak relationship between personality and job performance.[76] They cited problems with measuring personality traits and explained that the connection between personality and performance exists only under very narrowly defined conditions. Companies stopped using personality tests because of concerns that these tests might unfairly discriminate against people of color and other identifiable groups.

Over the past decade, personality has regained some of its credibility in organizational settings.[77] Recent studies have reported that certain personality traits predict some work-related behaviors, stress reactions, and emotions fairly well under certain conditions. Scholars have reintroduced the idea that effective leaders have identifiable traits and that personality explains some of a person's positive attitudes and life happiness. Personality traits seem to help people find the jobs that best suit their needs.[78] Although personality is still considered a relatively poor selection test, many companies use personality tests and assessments to hire executives. For instance, Carly Fiorina had to complete a two-hour, 900-question personality test as part of the process to select her as Hewlett-Packard's new chief executive.[79] With these caveats in mind, let's look at the main personality traits and dimensions currently studied in organizational settings.

Big Five Personality Dimensions

Since the days of Plato, scholars have been trying to develop lists of personality traits. About 100 years ago, a few personality experts tried to catalog and condense the many personality traits that had been described over the years. They found thousands of words in *Roget's Thesaurus* and *Webster's Dictionary* that represented personality traits. They aggregated these words into 171 clusters, then further reduced them to five abstract personality dimensions. Using more sophisticated techniques, a recent investigation identified the same five dimensions—known as the **Big Five personality dimensions.**[80] As Exhibit 3.7 shows, these five dimensions are:

- *Conscientiousness*—**Conscientiousness** refers to the extent that people are careful, dependable, and self-disciplined. Some scholars argue that this dimension also includes the will to achieve. People with low conscientiousness tend to be careless, disorganized, and irresponsible.
- *Emotional stability*—People with high emotional stability are poised, secure, and calm. Those with emotional instability tend to be depressed, anxious, indecisive, and subject to mood swings.
- *Openness to experience*—This dimension is the most complex and has the least agreement among scholars. It generally refers to the extent that people are

Big Five personality dimensions
The five abstract dimensions representing most personality traits: conscientiousness, emotional stability, openness to experience, agreeableness, and extroversion.

conscientiousness
A Big Five personality dimension that characterizes people who are careful, dependable, and self-disciplined.

EXHIBIT 3.7

The Big Five
personality
dimensions

Dimension	People who score "high" on this dimension tend to be more:
Conscientiousness	Careful, dependable, self-disciplined
Emotional stability	Poised, secure, calm
Openness to experience	Sensitive, flexible, creative, curious
Agreeableness	Courteous, good-natured, empathic, caring
Extroversion	Outgoing, talkative, sociable, assertive

sensitive, flexible, creative, and curious. Those who score low on this dimension tend to be resistant to change, closed to new ideas, and fixed in their ways.
■ *Agreeableness*—This dimension includes the traits of being courteous, good-natured, empathic, and caring. Some scholars prefer the label "friendly compliance" for this dimension, with its opposite being "hostile noncompliance." People with low agreeableness tend to be uncooperative, short-tempered, and irritable.
■ *Extroversion*—**Extroversion** characterizes people who are outgoing, talkative, sociable, and assertive. The opposite is **introversion,** which refers to those who are quiet, shy, and cautious. This does not mean that introverts lack social skills. Rather, they are more inclined to direct their interests to ideas than to social events. Introverts feel quite comfortable being alone, whereas extroverts do not.

Several studies have found that these personality dimensions affect work-related behavior and job performance.[81] Champions of organizational change (people who effectively gain support for new organizational systems and practices) seem to be placed along the positive end of the five personality dimensions described above.[82] People with high emotional stability tend to work better than others in stressful situations. Those with high agreeableness tend to handle customer relations and conflict-based situations more effectively.

Conscientiousness has taken center stage as the most valuable personality trait for predicting job performance in almost every job group. Conscientious employees set higher personal goals for themselves and have higher performance expectations than do employees with low levels of conscientiousness. High-conscientiousness employees tend to have higher levels of organizational citizenship and are more adaptive to empowerment than to traditional command-and-control organizational structures. Employees with high conscientiousness, as well as agreeableness and emotional stability, also tend to provide better customer service.[83]

extroversion
A Big Five personality dimension that characterizes people who are outgoing, talkative, sociable, and assertive.

introversion
A Big Five personality dimension that characterizes people who are quiet, shy, and cautious.

Jung's Psychological Types and the Myers-Briggs Type Indicator

During the 1920s, Swiss psychiatrist Carl Jung proposed a personality theory that identifies the way people prefer to perceive their environment as well as obtain and process information. Twenty years later, the mother-and-daughter team of Katherine Briggs and Isabel Briggs-Myers developed the **Myers-Briggs Type Indicator (MBTI),** a personality test that measures each of the traits in Jung's model.[84]

Myers-Briggs Type Indicator (MBTI)

A personality test that measures each of the traits in Jung's model.

The MBTI measures how people prefer to focus their attention (extroversion versus introversion), collect information (sensing versus intuition), process and evaluate information (thinking versus feeling), and orient themselves to the outer world (judging versus perceiving). Extroversion and introversion were discussed in the previous section, so let's examine the other dimensions:

■ *Sensing/Intuition*—Some people like collecting information through their five senses. Sensing types use an organized structure to acquire factual and preferably quantitative details. In contrast, intuitive people collect information nonsystematically. They rely more on subjective evidence as well as their intuition and sheer inspiration. Sensers are capable of synthesizing large amounts of seemingly random information to form quick conclusions.

■ *Thinking/Feeling*—Thinking types rely on rational cause–effect logic and scientific research methods (see Appendix A) to make decisions. They weigh the evidence objectively and unemotionally. Feeling types, on the other hand, consider how their choices affect others. They weigh the options against their personal values more than rational logic.

■ *Judging/Perceiving*—Some people prefer order and structure in their relationship with the outer world. These judging types enjoy the control of decision making and want to resolve problems quickly. In contrast, perceiving types are more flexible. They like to adapt spontaneously to events as they unfold and want to keep their options open.

The MBTI questionnaire combines the four pairs of traits into 16 distinct types. For example, corporate executives tend to be ESTJs, meaning that they are extroverted, sensing, thinking, and judging types. Each of the 16 types has its strengths and weaknesses. ENTJs are considered natural leaders, ISFJs have a high sense of duty, and so on. Also, these types indicate a person's preferences, not the way he or she necessarily behaves all the time.

Effectiveness of the MBTI   Is the MBTI useful in organizations? Many business leaders think so. The MBTI is one of the most widely used personality tests in work settings.[85] For example, City Bank and Trust in Oklahoma (now part of BancFirst) used the MBTI to help executives understand each other after the merger of several smaller banks. "[MBTI] really was a breakthrough as far as [our] being able to have empathy for one another," says Bill Johnstone, who was City Bank and Trust president at the time.[86] The MBTI is equally popular for career counseling.

Yet, in spite of its popularity, evidence regarding the effectiveness of the MBTI is mixed.[87] The MBTI does a reasonably good job of measuring Jung's psychological types. There is also some indication that a person's type predicts

At a semiannual retreat in Maine, employees at Thompson Doyle Hennessey & Everest did more than run rapids. Everyone at the Boston real estate company completed the Myers-Briggs Type Indicator and learned how their personalities can help them relate more effectively to each other. For example, the assessments revealed that salespeople don't mind working in a crazed atmosphere, whereas support staff prefer a calmer environment. Both groups now understand each other better.[88] How is the MBTI being used here? Is this an effective use of this instrument?
(Courtesy of Thompson Doyle Hennessey & Everest)

his or her preferences for particular occupations. For example, people who score high on intuition tend to prefer careers in advertising, the arts, and teaching. However, other evidence is less supportive regarding the MBTI's ability to predict job performance.[89] Overall, the MBTI seems to improve self-awareness for career development and mutual understanding, but probably should not be used in selecting job applicants.

Other Personality Traits

The Big Five personality dimensions and the MBTI don't capture every personality trait. We will discuss a few others where they fit specific topics in later chapters, such as need for achievement (Chapter 5), Type A/Type B Behavior Pattern (Chapter 7), and Machiavellianism (Chapter 12). Two other personality traits that you should know are locus of control and self-monitoring.

locus of control
A personality trait referring to the extent to which people believe events are within their control.

Locus of Control   **Locus of control** refers to a generalized belief about the amount of control people have over their own lives. Individuals who feel that they are very much in charge of their own destiny have an *internal locus of control;* those who think that events in their life are due mainly to fate or luck have an *external locus of control.* Of course, externals believe that they control many specific events in their lives—such as opening a door or serving a customer—but they have a general belief that outside forces guide their fate. This belief is particularly apparent in new situations in which the person's control over events is uncertain.

People perform better in most employment situations when they have a moderately strong internal locus of control. They tend to be more successful in their careers and earn more money than their external counterparts. Internals are particularly well suited to leadership positions and other jobs requiring initiative, independent action, complex thinking, and high motivation. Internals are also more satisfied with their jobs, cope better in stressful situations, and are more motivated by performance-based reward systems. This last point was supported in a recent study of Hong Kong bank tellers. Tellers with an internal locus of control had more positive work attitudes following a promotion than did tellers with a more external locus of control.[90]

self-monitoring

A personality trait referring to an individual's level of sensitivity and ability to adapt to situational cues.

Self-Monitoring   **Self-monitoring** refers to an individual's level of sensitivity and ability to adapt to situational cues. High self-monitors can adjust their behavior quite easily and, therefore, show little stability in other underlying personality traits. In contrast, low self-monitors are more likely to reveal their moods and personal characteristics, so it is relatively easy to predict their behavior from one situation to the next.[91]

The self-monitoring personality trait has been identified as a significant factor in many organizational activities. Employees who are high self-monitors tend to be better conversationalists and better organizational leaders; in addition, they perform better in boundary-spanning positions (in which incumbents work with people in different departments or organizations). They are also more likely than low self-monitors to be promoted within the organization and to receive better jobs elsewhere.[92]

Self-monitoring, locus of control, conscientiousness, and the many other personality traits help explain the dynamics of organizational behavior. At the same time, we must be careful about using personality traits to oversimplify a more complex world. Too often, we see problems as personality clashes rather than diagnosing the situation to discover the underlying causes. These personality trait labels can become perceptual blinders that are used to characterize people even after their personal dispositions have changed. As Nobel Prize–winning scholar Herbert Simon warned many years ago, personality is often overused as "a magical slogan to charm away the problems that our intellectual tools don't handle."[93] Personality is only one of the many concepts that we need to understand in organizational behavior.

CHAPTER SUMMARY

Perception involves selecting, organizing, and interpreting information to make sense of the world. Selective attention is influenced by characteristics of the target, the target's setting, and the perceiver. Perceptual grouping principles organize incoming information. This perceptual process is also influenced by our emotions, expectations, and mental models.

According to social identity theory, people perceive themselves by their unique characteristics and memberships in various groups. They also develop homogeneous, and usually positive, images of people in their own groups, and usually less positive homogeneous images of people in other groups. This tendency leads to overgeneralizations and stereotypes.

Stereotyping is the process of assigning traits to people based on their membership in a social category. Stereotyping economizes mental effort and fills in missing information, but it often results in incorrect perceptions about others. These misperceptions may lead to prejudice, more subtle forms of employment discrimination, and sexual harassment.

The attribution process involves deciding whether the behavior or event is due largely to the situation (external attributions) or to personal characteristics (internal attributions). Two attribution errors are fundamental attribution error and self-serving bias.

Self-fulfilling prophecy occurs when our expectations about another person cause that person to act in a way that is consistent with those expectations. Leaders can create positive self-fulfilling prophecies by providing feedback and support, creating a learning orientation, and building the employee's self-efficacy.

We can improve our perceptions in organizational settings through diversity initiatives (including outreach recruitment, reasonable accommodation, and diversity awareness activities) as well as by empathizing with others, postponing our impression of others, comparing our perceptions with those of others, and becoming more aware of our values, beliefs, and prejudices.

Personality refers to the relatively stable pattern of behaviors and consistent internal states that explain a person's behavioral tendencies. It is shaped by both heredity and environmental factors. Personality traits are important for some job design activities, championing organizational change, and matching people to jobs. However, some concerns remain about relying too heavily on personality traits to understand and predict behavior in organizations.

Most personality traits are represented within the Big Five personality dimensions: extroversion, agreeableness, conscientiousness, emotional stability, and openness to experience. Based on Jung's theory of psychological types, the Myers-Briggs Type Indicator measures how people prefer to focus their attention, collect information, process and evaluate information, and orient themselves to the outer world. Locus of control and self-monitoring are two other traits that influence organizational behavior.

KEY TERMS

attribution process, p. 73

Big Five personality dimensions, p. 85

conscientiousness, p. 85

empathy, p. 81

extroversion, p. 86

fundamental attribution error, p. 74

halo error, p. 79

introversion, p. 86

Johari Window, p. 83

locus of control, p. 88

mental models, p. 66

Myers-Briggs Type Indicator (MBTI), p. 87

perception, p. 64

perceptual defense, p. 65

perceptual grouping, p. 66

personality, p. 84

prejudice, p. 71

primacy effect, p. 77

projection bias, p. 79

recency effect, p. 78

selective attention, p. 65

self-fulfilling prophecy, p. 76

self-monitoring, p. 89

self-serving bias, p. 75

social identity theory, p. 67

splatter vision, p. 65

stereotyping, p. 69

DISCUSSION QUESTIONS

1. You are part of a task force to increase worker responsiveness to emergencies on the production floor. Identify four factors that should be considered when installing a device that will get every employee's attention when there is an emergency.

2. Quokka Technologies, Inc., has just acquired a major competitor in the circuit board industry. Although senior executives expected a smooth transition, they soon discovered that employees at each company viewed one another with suspicion and had generally negative perceptions of one another's skills and motives. Use social identity theory to explain why this problem likely exists.

3. During a diversity management session, a manager suggests that stereotypes are a necessary part of working with others. "I have to make assumptions about what's in the other person's head, and stereotypes help me do that," he explains. "It's better to rely on stereotypes than to enter a working relationship with someone from another culture without any idea of what they believe in!" Discuss the merits and problems of the manager's statement.

4. At the end of a professional golf tournament, the previous year's champion explained why he didn't make it into the top five players this time. "I

should have won, because I know the course better than anyone. But I was placed late in the day, so the sun was in a bad position and the winds were stronger. You probably noticed that I had a few bad breaks this time, too. I had a lousy chip shot on the second-round 15th hole because I was distracted by noise from the audience." Use attribution theory to explain the golfer's perceptions of his loss.

5. Self-fulfilling prophecies are common in organizations, but much of the research originated in schools. Discuss how this perceptual process occurs in a college class. How might instructors use self-fulfilling prophecy beneficially?

6. You are the leader of a newly formed project team that will work closely together over the next three months. The seven team members are drawn from as many worldwide offices. They do not know each other and come from different professional specializations. Describe the activities of a one-day retreat that would minimize perceptual errors and potential communication problems among the team members.

7. NanoTech Enterprises wants to hire employees for its new production plant. Employees will have a high degree of autonomy, because the plant uses self-directed work teams. The work also requires employees who are careful because the materials are sensitive to mishandling. Identify one personality trait from the Big Five that may be appropriate for selecting people for these jobs. Describe the trait and fully explain your answer.

8. Look over the four pairs of psychological types in the Myers-Briggs Type Indicator and identify the personality type (i.e., four letters) that would be best for a student in this course. Would this type be appropriate for students in other fields of study (e.g., biology, fine arts) or in graduate-level programs?

CASE STUDY 3.1

NUPATH FOODS, INC.

James Ornath read the latest sales figures with a great deal of satisfaction. The vice president of marketing at Nupath Foods, Inc., was pleased to see that the marketing campaign to improve sagging sales of Prowess cat food was working. Sales volume of the product had increased 20 percent in the past quarter compared with the previous year, and market share was up.

The improved sales of Prowess could be credited to Denise Washington, the brand manager responsible for cat foods at Nupath. Washington had joined Nupath less than two years ago as an assistant brand manager after leaving a similar job at a consumer products firm. She was one of the few women in marketing management at Nupath and had a promising career with the company. Ornath was pleased with Washington's work and tried to let her know this in the annual performance reviews. He now had an excellent opportunity to reward her by offering the recently vacated position of market research coordinator. Although technically only a lateral transfer with a modest salary increase, the marketing research coordinator job would give Washington broader experience in some high-profile work, which would enhance her career with Nupath. Few people were aware that Ornath's own career had been boosted by working as marketing research coordinator at Nupath several years before.

Denise Washington had also seen the latest sales figures on Prowess cat food and was expecting Ornath's call to meet with her that morning. Ornath began the conversation by briefly mentioning the favorable sales figures, and then explained that he wanted Washington to take the marketing research coordinator job. Washington was shocked by the news. She enjoyed brand management and particularly the challenge involved with controlling a product that directly affected the company's profitability. Marketing research coordinator was a technical support position—a "backroom" job—far removed from the company's bottom-line activities. Marketing research was not the route to top management in most organizations, Washington thought. She had been sidelined.

After a long silence, Washington managed a weak "Thank you, Mr. Ornath." She was too bewildered to protest. She wanted to collect her thoughts and reflect on what she had done wrong. Also, she did not know her boss well enough to be openly critical. Ornath recognized Washington's surprise, which he naturally assumed was her positive response to hearing of this wonderful career opportunity. He, too, had been delighted several years earlier about his temporary transfer to marketing research to round out his marketing experience. "This move will be good for both you and Nupath," said Ornath as he escorted Washington from his office.

Washington had several tasks to complete that afternoon but was able to consider the day's events that evening. She was one of the top women in brand management at Nupath and feared that she was being sidelined because the company didn't want women in top management. Her previous employer had made it quite clear that women "couldn't take the heat" in marketing management and tended to place women in technical support positions after a brief term in lower brand management jobs. Obviously, Nupath was following the same game plan. Ornath's comments that the coordinator job would be good for her was just a nice way of saying that Washington couldn't go any further in brand management at Nupath. Washington was now faced with the difficult decision of confronting Ornath and trying to change Nupath's sexist practices or submitting her resignation.

Discussion Questions

1. What symptom(s) exist in this case to suggest that something has gone wrong?

2. Diagnose the underlying problems that have led to these symptoms.

3. What actions should the organization take to correct these problems?

CASE STUDY 3.2

MEET THE NEW HASSO PLATTNER

BusinessWeek Shifting winds are a familiar phenomenon to Hasso Plattner, who spent much of his childhood sailing with his parents. Those early experiences helped equip Plattner for his role at the helm of SAP, the world's third-largest software company, based in Germany. The winds of change blow often and unpredictably in the world of information systems, yet Plattner has so far steered SAP to amazing growth and profitability. As business software has shifted from mainframe computer applications to networks to Internet computing, Plattner's personality characteristics have at times helped him, and at other times hindered his efforts as SAP's co–chief executive.

This *Business Week* case study describes Plattner and the ways he has changed to succeed in a changing business environment. It portrays a confident and forceful manager who has had to learn to share control with others. Read through this *Business Week* case study at www.mhhe.com/mcshane2e and prepare for the discussion questions below.

Discussion Questions

1. According to the author of this article, how have Hasso Plattner's perceptions of his role changed since the 1990s?

2. Consider how the Johari Window applies to Plattner, SAP, and SAP's customers. According to this theory, how can information sharing improve performance within SAP? Based on what you read in this article, are Plattner and SAP applying these principles?

3. What personality characteristics of Plattner does this article describe? How do Plattner's early experiences and culture seem to have shaped aspects of his personality?

Source: S.Baker and S. Hamm, "Less Ego, More Success," *Business Week*, July 23, 2001, pp.56–59.

COMPARING CULTURAL STEREOTYPES

Purpose   This exercise is designed to help you determine the extent that students hold similar cultural stereotypes, and to identify the implications of these stereotypes on attitudes and behavior toward people in other cultures.

Instructions   In the table at right, the names in the left column represent labels that a major consulting project identified with businesspeople in a particular country, based on its national culture and character. These names appear in alphabetical order. In the right column are the names of countries, also in alphabetical order, corresponding to the labels in the left column.

■ *Step 1*—Working alone, students will connect the labels with the countries by relying on their stereotypes of these countries. Each label is associated with only one country, so each label will be connected to only one country, and vice versa. Draw a line to connect the pairs, or put the label number beside the country name.

■ *Step 2*—The instructor will form teams of four or five members. Members of each team will compare their results and try to reach consensus on a set of connecting pairs.

■ *Step 3*—Teams or the instructor will post the results for all to see the extent that students hold common stereotypes about business-

people in other cultures. Class discussion can then consider the reasons the results are so similar or different, as well as the implications of these results for working in a global work environment.

Country stereotypes	
Country label (alphabetical)	**Country name (alphabetical)**
1. Affable humanists	Australia
2. Ancient modernizers	Brazil
3. Commercial catalysts	Canada
4. Conceptual strategists	China
5. Efficient manufacturers	France
6. Ethical statesmen	Germany
7. Informal egalitarians	India
8. Modernizing traditionalists	Netherlands
9. Optimistic entrepreneurs	New Zealand
10. Quality perfectionists	Singapore
11. Rugged individualists	Taiwan
12. Serving merchants	United Kingdom
13. Tolerant traders	United States

Source: Based on R. Rosen, P. Digh, M. Singer, and C. Phillips, *Global Literacies* (New York: Simon & Schuster, 2000).

PERSONALITY ASSESSMENT OF JUNG'S PSYCHOLOGICAL TYPES

Purpose   This self-assessment is designed to help you estimate your psychological type within Jung's model.

Instructions   Circle the word in each pair that most appeals to you or seems most characteristic of you. In some cases, both words may appeal to you or seem characteristic of you; in others, neither word may seem characteristic of you or be appealing. Nonetheless, try to indicate the one word in each pair you prefer. Please work across the page (i.e., begin with the top row across), and answer as quickly as possible. As a rule of thumb, trust your first impressions. After you complete this activity, your instructor will provide instructions on how to score it.

loud—quiet	realistic—intuitive	convincing—touching	systematic—flexible
active—reflective	blueprint—dream	objective—subjective	methodical—curious
gregarious—private	details—pattern	head—heart	organized—spontaneous
outgoing—reserved	sensible—imaginative	just—humane	deliberate—improvising
sociable—detached	practical—creative	principle—passion	exacting—impulsive
external—internal	present—future	fair—tender	definite—tolerant
do—think	factual—symbolic	clarity—harmony	decisive—open-minded
speak—write	specific—general	reason—emotion	plan—adapt
talk—read	formula—hunch	professional—warm	control—freedom
___ ___	___ ___	___ ___	___ ___

Source: B. L. Dilla, G. J. Curphy, R. L. Hughes, R. C. Ginnett, and K. A. Ashley, *Instructor's Manual to Accompany Leadership: Enhancing the Lessons of Experience* (Homewood, IL: Irwin, 1993).

 After studying the preceding material, be sure to check out our website at
www.mhhe.com/mcshane2e
for more in-depth information and interactivities that correspond to this chapter.

CHAPTER 4

Workplace Values, Ethics, and Emotions

Learning Objectives

AFTER READING THIS CHAPTER, YOU SHOULD BE ABLE TO:

■ Identify the different types and levels of values.

■ Define the five main values that vary across cultures.

■ Describe three ethical principles and other factors influencing ethical behavior.

■ Explain how moral intensity, ethical sensitivity, and the situation influence ethical behavior.

■ Discuss the linkages between emotions and behavior.

■ Identify the conditions that require and the problems associated with emotional labor.

■ Outline the dimensions of emotional intelligence.

■ Discuss the effect of job satisfaction on task performance and customer service.

■ Describe five strategies to increase organizational commitment.

Who is the most successful discount retailer in the world? Most people would probably say Wal-Mart or the French giant Carrefour. Yet the best of the breed may be The Warehouse, an Auckland, New Zealand–based company that sells lots of bargain merchandise in 227 distinctive big red, blue, and yellow box stores throughout New Zealand and Australia. The Warehouse was recently praised by *Forbes* magazine as "easily one of the best retail operations in the entire world." *The Wall Street Journal* rated it as the second best performing small-cap company in the Asia-Pacific region.

Founder Stephen Tindall will gladly tell you that the main reason for the company's success is its "people first" values. "We have discovered that our policies of putting team members first . . . makes them feel good about the business they work for," explains Tindall. "This feel-good attitude enables our team members to put the customers first and to provide exceptional service to them."

The Warehouse goes the distance to help employees feel good. Everyone can participate in stock ownership, paid time off for birthdays, and unlimited sick leave. Tindall's own over-the-top optimism also helps. "I always accentuate the positive," says Tindall. "I just don't believe in negative. If something comes along you've just got to climb on top of it."

"People first" values and social responsibility have made The Warehouse in New Zealand one of the world's top-rated discount retailers. *(Courtesy of The Warehouse)*

The Warehouse extends its feel-good values to its responsibility for the community and environment. It has adopted Sweden's "Natural Step" sustainable development process and has commissioned an independent social audit, the results of which will appear in annual reports.

The Warehouse also aims to eliminate landfill waste by 2020. To achieve this daunting "zero waste" objective, 29 stores have odorless worm farms to digest all the organic refuse from the premises. Eight of The Warehouse's stores have already attained the zero waste goal.[1]

T he Warehouse's success isn't due to just low prices and bright red buildings. As founder Stephen Tindall likes to remind everyone, the critical ingredients are hiring and keeping enthusiastic, energized, and loyal staff; applying the "people first" values; and living the ethics of the community. In other words, The Warehouse and other organizations must pay attention to values, ethics, and emotions in the workplace.

This chapter explores the dynamics of these three concepts. The first part of this chapter looks at workplace values. We consider the importance of individual values in organizations, as well as how values differ across cultures. Then, we look at ethical values and behavior, including specific ethical principles, other factors that influence ethical conduct, differences in ethical behavior across cultures, and specific strategies companies use to improve ethical behavior at work. Next, this chapter explores emotions and attitudes in the workplace. We learn how emotions influence behavior and how employees engage in emotional labor and emotional intelligence. We present the basic model of work attitudes and explore key issues regarding two important work attitudes—job satisfaction and organizational commitment.

VALUES AT WORK

The opening vignette describes how employees at The Warehouse apply a core set of organizational values that are consistent with their personal values. Values, which were introduced in Chapter 1, are stable, long-lasting beliefs about what is important in a variety of situations. They are evaluative standards that help us define what is right or wrong, or good or bad, in the world.[2] Values don't just represent what we want; they state what we ought to do—socially desirable ways to achieve those needs. Some people value practicality, whereas others value aesthetics. Some people value frugality; others value generosity. Values dictate our priorities, our preferences, and our actions. "Basic values are at the heart of what influences employees' drives, motivation and behavior," says Kathy Rychel, a partner in the Northbrook, Illinois, consulting firm PeopleWorks.[3]

Values come in many shapes and forms. Aside from the fact that scholars have described more than 100 values over the years, they also distinguished terminal values from instrumental values.[4] *Terminal values* are desired states of existence that we try to achieve. A world of beauty, equality, and wisdom, and a comfortable life are some of the terminal values that people might hold. *Instrumental values*, on the other hand, are desirable modes of behavior that help us reach terminal values. Some instrumental values include being polite, courageous, logical, self-controlled, and ambitious. Organizational behavior scholars tend to focus on instrumental values, possibly because they shape the person's behavior and are most closely associated with organizational objectives.[5]

Values can also be distinguished by different levels at which they operate. Individuals bring *personal values* into the organization, which are formed from past experience and interaction with others. Personal values are also influenced by *cultural values*—the dominant beliefs held by a collective society. As we will learn in this chapter, different societies have different values about how their citizens should and should not act. Yet another level or dimension of values in the workplace is *organizational values*. These are at the heart of organizational culture, which is the basic pattern of shared assumptions, values, and beliefs considered the correct way of thinking about and acting on problems and opportunities facing the organization. Researchers have also investigated *professional values*—the values held within an occupational group.

Lastly, we need to distinguish espoused values from enacted values. *Espoused values* represent the values that we want others to believe we abide by. Individuals, organizations, professions, or even societies might say they value environmentalism, creativity, and politeness, whether or not they really do value these things in practice. Values are socially desirable, so people create a positive public image by claiming to believe in values that others expect them to embrace. *Enacted values*, on the other hand, represent the values in use. They are values we actually rely on to guide our decisions and actions.[6]

The Importance of Values in the Workplace

Values are not new to organizational behavior, but the popularity of this topic has increased noticeably in recent years.[7] One reason is that globalization has raised our awareness of and sensitivity to differences in values across cultures. Organizations rely on individuals to make decisions and take actions that achieve corporate objectives. Global organizations face the challenge of aligning people with diverse values toward a common set of goals, including consistent decisions and actions around the world. But aligning everyone's values may lead to conflict due to differences in personal, organizational, and cultural values.[8]

Second, corporate leaders are looking for better ways to guide employee decisions and behavior. Today's increasingly educated and independent workforce resents the traditional command-and-control supervision, and financial rewards are far from perfect. Values represent a potentially powerful way to keep employees' decisions and actions aligned with corporate goals. Values represent the unseen magnet that pulls employees in the same direction. Values foster a common bond and help ensure that we all pull in the same direction—irrespective of our individual tasks and ranks.[9]

The third reason values have gained prominence is that organizations are under increasing pressure to engage in ethical practices. Ethics refers to the study of moral principles or values that determine whether actions are right or wrong and outcomes are good or bad (see Chapter 1). We rely on our ethical values to determine the right thing to do. Ethical behavior is driven by the moral principles we use to make decisions. These moral principles represent fundamental values.

Aligning Values

A few years ago, Copenhagen Business School professor Peter Pruzan held a seminar on workplace values with executives at a large European-based multinational manufacturing company. Working in teams, the executives developed a list of their five most important personal values. In the afternoon, the teams developed a list of the enacted (not espoused) values of their company. The lists of company values sharply contrasted with the lists of individual values. The personal values list included honesty, love, beauty, peace of mind, and happiness, whereas the company values list included success, efficiency, power, competitiveness, and productivity. After an embarrassing silence, the

CEO briefly spoke, announcing that he would consider resigning. He said that he had actively constructed a monster, a corporate Frankenstein![10]

The CEO of the European firm didn't resign. Instead, the exercise helped him and his executive team become more aware of the importance of aligning personal and organizational values. Without alignment, employees may make decisions that conflict with organizational goals, and they will likely experience higher levels of stress and turnover. Unfortunately, misalignments seem to be common, as the European manufacturing firm realized. One study reported that 76 percent of the managers surveyed believe that a conflict exists between their own ethical beliefs and their company's values. Another study found that managers saw significant differences between their personal values and organizational practices.[11]

Some companies try to avoid or minimize this values misalignment when hiring new staff. Ukrop's Super Markets Inc. is highly respected for its customer service partly because it pays close attention to values alignment when hiring new staff. "[F]irst and foremost, we're looking for people whose values mirror our company's values," says Jacquelin Ukrop, human resource director of the Richmond, Virginia, company. Igus, Inc., takes this values alignment process one step further. Along with a careful selection process, the German manufacturer of polymer bearings and power-supply chains gives job applicants a *schnuppertag*—a sniffing-around day where they can explore, observe, and interview whomever they choose.[12]

Values alignment is also important between the organization and the society in which it conducts its business. Otherwise, the organization may experience conflict with the larger society and have difficulty attracting and retaining talented employees. SC Johnson was aware of this need for alignment for its Australian business. The American household products firm is "a family company with family values." But this is too paternalistic for many Australians, who generally like to separate their work from their personal lives. SC Johnson's solution was to tweak its values somewhat. Rather than hearing that they are part of the SC Johnson family, the company's Australian employees hear about work/life balance and the company's social responsibility. "You can't sell that family company idea in Australia, so we position it as family values with work/life balance," explains an SC Johnson executive.[14] To align company values with cultural values, we need to know about different values in different societies, which we discuss next.

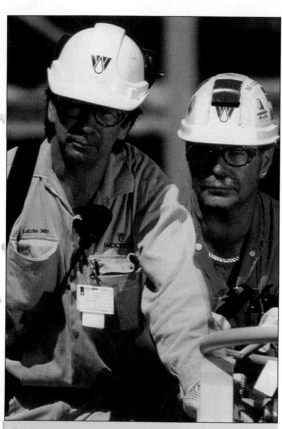

For the past couple of years, Woodside Petroleum has been searching for more than oil and gas deposits. Australia's largest energy company has also been searching its soul for a set of corporate values more closely aligned with the personal values of its employees. Woodside called in consultants to assess the company's "cultural capital" and to identify ways to liberate employees so that their personal values shine through. "In the simplest terms, it is about enabling people to be themselves at work," says a consultant who worked on the transformation.[13] What improvements occur when organizational values are aligned with the personal values of employees? *(Photo courtesy of Woodside Energy)*

Cultural Differences in Values

Not long ago, several Swedish and American employees at Ericsson, the Swedish telecommunications giant, met to resolve a pressing issue. At the end of the discussion, the highest-ranking person in the room—an American—stated his position on the problem. The Americans understood that the senior executive was concluding the debate by making the final decision. The Swedes, on the other hand, left the meeting feeling uneasy that no decision had been made. Scandinavians assume that decisions are made as a group, so they thought the American executive's statements were merely his opinions on the matter.[15]

Anyone who has worked long enough with people in other countries will know that values differ across cultures. As the example above illustrates, people in some cultures value group decisions, whereas others think that the leader should take charge. Meetings in Germany usually start on time, whereas they can typically be half an hour late in Brazil. We need to understand cultural value differences to avoid unnecessary conflicts and subtle tensions between people from different countries. This awareness of differing values is particularly important as companies develop global operations and information technology increases the frequency of cross-cultural communication.

Five Cross-Cultural Values   The dozens of personal values that have been discussed in the literature also apply to cross-cultural values. However, five values have received the most attention and seem to account for a large portion of the differences in the way people think and act across cultures. They include individualism versus collectivism, power distance, uncertainty avoidance, achievement versus nurturing orientation, and long- versus short-term orientation.[16]

- *Individualism versus collectivism*—**Individualism versus collectivism** refers to the degree to which people value individual versus group goals. Collectivists define themselves by their group membership, give group goals priority over their personal goals, put more emphasis on harmonious relationships, and experience more socially based emotions (indebtedness, friendliness). Individualists, on the other hand, view themselves autonomously, give personal goals priority over group goals, put more emphasis on personal achievement, and experience more socially disengaged emotions (pride, anger).[17]

- *Power distance*—**Power distance** is the extent to which people accept unequal distribution of power in a society. Those with high power distance accept and value unequal power, whereas those with low power distance expect relatively equal power sharing. In high power distance cultures, employees are comfortable receiving commands from their superiors, and conflicts are resolved through formal rules and authority. In contrast, participative management is preferred in low power distance cultures, and conflicts are resolved more through personal networks and coalitions.[18]

- *Uncertainty avoidance*—**Uncertainty avoidance** is the degree to which people tolerate ambiguity (low uncertainty avoidance) or feel threatened by ambiguity and uncertainty (high uncertainty avoidance). Employees with high uncertainty avoidance value structured situations where rules of conduct and decision making are clearly documented. They usually prefer direct rather than indirect or ambiguous communications.

individualism versus collectivism
The degree to which people value their individual versus group goals.

power distance
The extent to which people accept unequal distribution of power in a society.

uncertainty avoidance
The degree to which people tolerate ambiguity or feel threatened by ambiguity and uncertainty.

■ *Achievement versus nurturing orientation*—Achievement-oriented cultures value assertiveness, competitiveness, and materialism.[19] They appreciate people who are tough and favor the acquisition of money and material goods. In contrast, people in nurturing-oriented cultures emphasize relationships and the well-being of others. They focus on human interaction and caring rather than competition and personal success.

■ *Long- versus short-term orientation*—People in different cultures also differ in their long- or short-term orientation. Those with a long-term orientation anchor their thoughts more in the future than in the past and present. They value thrift, savings, and persistence, whereas those with a short-term orientation place more emphasis on the past and present, such as respecting tradition and fulfilling social obligations.

Exhibit 4.1 shows how Americans compare with other cultures on these five dimensions. In general, Americans are individualistic with a somewhat low power distance and short-term orientation. They have moderate achievement orientation and have somewhat low uncertainty avoidance (i.e., they can tolerate ambiguity). This information provides the best comparison available of these values across cultures. However, there are at least three limitations that we should keep in mind.[20] First, the information might not be representative because of the restricted group of people surveyed. Specifically, information for the first four scales was collected only from IBM employees in each country; information for the long- versus short-term orientation scale was collected from college students. It is possible that IBM employees and students have values different from those of the general population.

EXHIBIT 4.1   Cultural differences in values

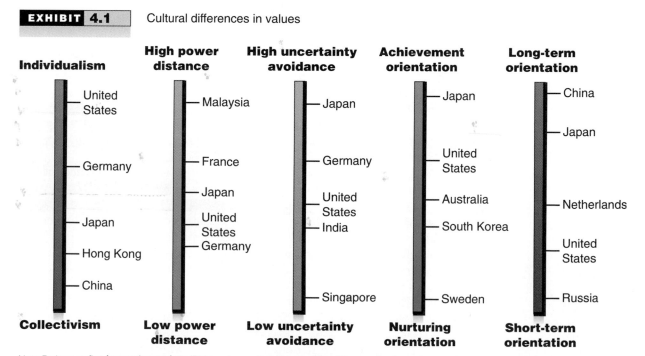

Note: Ratings on first four scales are from IBM employees in these countries. "Germany" refers only to the former West Germany. Data for long– versus short-term orientation are from student samples.
Sources: Based on G. Hofstede, "Cultural Constraints in Management Theories," *Academy of Management Executive* 7 (1993), pp. 81–94; G. Hofstede, "The Cultural Relativity of Organizational Practices and Theories," *Journal of International Business Studies* 14 (Fall 1983), pp. 75–89.

A second concern is that the IBM data are now almost a generation old and some cultures have changed. For instance, there is some evidence that Japan's culture, particularly its younger generation, has become more individualistic in recent years. Additionally, some writers suggest that the global distribution of American culture is creating a more culturally homogeneous world.[21]

A third concern is that these data assume everyone in a society has similar cultural values. This may be true in a few countries, but not in culturally diverse societies. On this point, one study found that there is a wide range of long- versus short-term orientation within the United States, Australia, and Chile. Another study reported significantly different values among Javanese, Batik, and Chinese Indonesians. By attributing certain values to an entire society, we are engaging in a form of stereotyping that limits our ability to understand the more complex reality of that society.[22]

It would be difficult to lure quality engineer Suzanne Suzuki away from her job at Agilent Technologies. That's because the Palo Alto, California–based electronics and communications firm supports Suzuki's volunteer work in training dogs to assist the disabled. Suzuki brings a dog to work each day so that it learns to remain calm and focused in a busy office setting. Agilent also gives Suzuki and other employees up to four hours of paid time off each month to volunteer in their communities. This strong commitment to social responsibility is attractive to employees with the same values. "If employees feel good about us as a company, which is what we hear, they will be happier at work and ultimately do a better job for us," explains the Agilent executive responsible for the company's philanthropic activities.[26] How would supporting employees in volunteer community activities increase their attachment to the organization? (© J. Craig Sweat/Liaison)

ETHICAL VALUES AND BEHAVIOR

Shoppers in several Home Depot outlets throughout the United States recently heard an unusual announcement over the public-address system. "Attention shoppers," began the surprise notice, "on aisle seven you'll find mahogany ripped from the heart of the Amazon." Activists from the Rainforest Action Network had delivered the message electronically by breaking the security code of Home Depot's intercom systems. While Home Depot executives immediately focused on how anyone could gain access to the public-address system, they soon realized the company faced a much larger ethical issue. Home Depot had sold mahogany because it is profitable and in demand. But the intercom incident made these executives aware that they need to consider the ethical consequences of their purchasing and marketing decisions.[23]

Ethics is a natural extension of our discussion of values in the workplace.[24] As we stated earlier in this chapter, ethics refers to the study of moral principles or values that determine whether actions are right or wrong and outcomes are good or bad. Employees and customers value companies and their leaders with ethical values. Indeed, surveys indicate that the employer's integrity is as important to most employees as their income. That's why Home Depot needed to demonstrate its ethical standards by adopting purchasing practices that consider timber reforestation and sustainability.[25]

Social responsibility is associated with business ethics. As we learned in Chapter 2, social responsibility refers to a person's (or an organization's) moral obligation toward others who are affected by his or her actions. People with a strong social responsibility norm are more motivated to assist others, whether or not this assistance will ever be repaid, and to avoid behaviors that interfere with others' goals. The Warehouse, the New Zealand retailer described at the beginning of this chapter, emphasizes social responsibility because it tries to support a sustainable planet and helps the communities in which it does business.

Three Ethical Principles

Philosophers and other scholars have identified several general ethical principles, each with a few variations, that should guide ethical conduct. We can condense most of these principles and variations down to three basic values—utilitarianism, individual rights, and distributive justice.[27] You might prefer one over the others based on your personal values. However, all three principles should be applied to put important ethical issues to the test.

utilitarianism
A moral principle stating that decision makers should seek the greatest good for the greatest number of people when choosing among alternatives.

■ *Utilitarianism*—**Utilitarianism** advises us to seek the greatest good for the greatest number of people. In other words, we should choose the option providing the highest degree of satisfaction to those affected. This is sometimes known as a consequential principle because it focuses on the consequences of our actions, not on how we achieve those consequences. Unfortunately, utilitarianism can occasionally result in unethical choices because it judges morality by the results, not the means of attaining those results. Moreover, it accepts situations in which a few people may be severely oppressed to benefit others.

■ *Individual rights*—This ethical value is the belief that everyone has entitlements that let them act in a certain way. Some of the most widely cited rights are freedom of movement, physical security, freedom of speech, fair trial, and freedom from torture.[28] The individual rights principle is not restricted to legal rights. A person may have a right to privacy, but employers have a right to inspect everyone's e-mail messages. One problem with individual rights is that certain individual rights may conflict with others. The shareholders' right to be informed about corporate activities may ultimately conflict with an executive's right to privacy, for example.

■ *Distributive justice*—This ethical value suggests that inequality is acceptable if (1) everyone has equal access to the more favored positions in society and (2) the inequalities are ultimately in the best interest of the least well-off in society. The first part means that everyone should have equal access to high-paying jobs and other valued positions in life. The second part says that some people can receive greater rewards than others if this benefits those less well-off. For example, employees in risky jobs should be paid more if their risk taking benefits others who are less well-off. The problem with this principle is that society can't seem to agree on what activities provide the greatest benefit to the least well-off.

Moral Intensity, Ethical Sensitivity, and Situational Influences

Ethical values play an important role in ethical behavior, but we also need to consider other factors. The three most important factors are the moral intensity of the issue, the individual's ethical sensitivity, and situational factors.

moral intensity
The degree to which an issue demands the application of ethical principles.

Moral intensity is the degree to which an issue demands the application of ethical principles. The higher the moral intensity, the more that ethical principles should provide guidance to resolve the issue. Stealing from your employer is usually considered high on moral intensity, whereas taking a company pen for personal use is much lower on the scale. Several factors influence the moral intensity of an issue, such as the extent to which the issue clearly produces good or bad consequences, others in the society think it is good or evil, the issue quickly affects people, the decision maker feels close to the issue, and the person is able to influence the issue.[29]

Even if an issue has high moral intensity, some employees might not recognize its ethical importance because they have low ethical sensitivity. **Ethical sensitivity** is a personal characteristic that enables people to recognize the presence and determine the relative importance of an ethical issue.[30] Ethically sensitive people are not necessarily more ethical. Rather, they are more likely to recognize whether an issue requires ethical consideration and can more accurately estimate the moral intensity of the issue. Ethically sensitive people tend to have higher empathy. They also have more information about the specific situation. For example, accountants would be more ethically sensitive regarding accounting procedures than would someone who has not received training in this profession.

The third important factor explaining why good people do bad things is the situation in which the unethical conduct occurs. A few recent surveys have reported that employees regularly experience corporate pressure that leads to selling beyond the customers' needs, lying to the client, or making unrealistic promises. Other surveys have found that most employees believe they experience so much pressure that it compromises their ethical conduct. For instance, nearly two-thirds of the managers in one academic study stated that pressure from top management causes people further down in the hierarchy to compromise their beliefs, whereas 90 percent of top management disagreed with this statement.[31] The point here is not to justify unethical conduct. Rather, we need to recognize the situational factors that influence wrongdoing so that organizations can correct these problems in the future.

ethical sensitivity
A personal characteristic that enables people to recognize the presence and determine the relative importance of an ethical issue.

Cultural Differences in Business Ethics

When Harry Gould, Jr., visited Gould Paper's manufacturing plants in France, he asked his French counterpart to show him the books (financial statements). The French executive casually asked, "Which books do you want to see?" The executive kept three sets of records—one for his family, one for the revenue collector, and the real one. "[The French executive] didn't think anything about that," Gould recalls. "There's a cultural mind-set that has no bearing on the reality we are used to here in the United States."[32]

As Harry Gould discovered, corporate decision makers face a larger set of ethical dilemmas when they enter the global marketplace. The French executive saw little wrong with having three sets of financial records, whereas most Americans would consider this practice of falsifying information highly unethical. This isn't an isolated example. Long ago, the United States made bribery at home or abroad a criminal offense for American companies, whereas it was a legitimate tax deduction in Australia, Germany, Netherlands, and several other countries until a couple of years ago.[33] Various studies have identified differences across cultures regarding attitudes toward software piracy, résumé padding, and a host of other ethical issues.[34]

Do these studies suggest that people in some countries have fewer ethical values? Not necessarily. Research indicates that fundamental ethical principles are fairly similar across cultures, but people interpret the ethical implications of specific situations differently.[35] False financial reporting may be more common in France than in the United States, for example, because French businesspeople might believe it is widely practiced and has little adverse effect on anyone. Americans, on the other hand, are more likely to view false financial reporting as unethical because they believe it has adverse consequences. Thus, financial reporting likely has higher moral intensity in the United States than in some other cultures.

Supporting Ethical Behavior

Almost one-half of all U.S. firms with 50 or more employees have introduced initiatives to support ethical values in the workplace. Ethical codes of conduct are the most common. In fact, 95 percent of the Fortune 500 companies in the United States and 57 percent of the 500 largest companies in the United Kingdom now have codes of ethics. United Technologies, the defense and engineering goliath, has an army of 160 business ethics officers who distribute its code of ethics to employees around the world.[36]

Ethical codes establish the organization's ethical standards, but there is considerable debate about whether they improve ethical conduct.[37] One step beyond ethics codes is to have employees receive ethics training. These seminars typically use case studies to apply and internalize ethical values. Sun Microsystems provides ethics training in the United States and in its Indian operations. "The focus of such training is to educate all employees on Sun's standards of business conduct and code of ethics," explains a Sun executive in India.[38] Some companies further supplement ethics codes and training by requiring employees to sign the ethics code, encouraging them to call a toll-free number when they observe unethical conduct and rewarding them for the ethical performance of their work units.[39]

Values and ethics represent an important part of organizational life. They guide our decisions and actions, and they influence our emotions and attitudes. The latter part of this chapter discusses the dynamics of employee emotions and attitudes.

EMOTIONS IN THE WORKPLACE

emotions
The feelings experienced toward and object, person, or event that create a state of readiness.

Emotions permeate organizational life.[40] A team leader is alarmed that critical supplies have not yet arrived. A new employee is proud to tell friends about being hired by ABC Corporation. A nurse feels sympathy for a patient whose family has not visited the hospital. In each incident, someone has experienced one or more emotions. **Emotions** are feelings experienced toward an object, person, or event that create a state of readiness.[41] Emotional episodes are communications to ourselves. They make us aware of events that may affect important personal goals. In fact, strong emotions demand our attention and interrupt our train of thought. They also create a state of readiness to respond to those events. In other words, they generate the motivation to act toward the object of our attention.[42]

Scholars have organized the different emotions into the six categories shown in Exhibit 4.2.[43] These categories are anger, fear, joy, love, sadness, and

EXHIBIT 4.2	Types of emotions in the workplace

Anger	Fear	Joy	Love	Sadness	Surprise
Disgust Envy Exasperation Irritation Rage Torment	Alarm Anxiety	Cheerfulness Contentment Enthrallment Optimism Pride Relief Zest	Affection Longing Lust	Disappointment Neglect Sadness Shame Suffering Sympathy	(No subcategories of emotion)

Sources: Based on H. M. Weiss and R. Cropanzano, "Affective Events Theory: A Theoretical Discussion of the Structure, Causes, and Consequences of Affective Experiences at Work," *Research in Organizational Behavior* 18 (1996), pp. 1–74; P. Shaver, J. Schwartz, D. Kirson, and C. O'Connor, "Emotion Knowledge: Further Exploration of a Prototype Approach," *Journal of Personality and Social Psychology* 52 (1987), pp. 1061–86.

"Biosensors. The whole company knows instantly when I'm displeased."

(Copyright © 2001 Ted Goff www.tedgoff.com)

surprise. Except for surprise, all these general emotional categories include various specific emotional experiences. For example, researchers have found that alarm and anxiety cluster together to form the general emotional category called fear.

Emotions are experienced through our thoughts, behaviors, and physiological reactions. A person may experience fear in a stressful situation by mentally sensing it, showing it through facial expressions, and developing a faster heartbeat. Facial expressions and other behavior play an interactive role in the emotional experience. For example, you tend to smile when feeling joyful, and this smiling reinforces your feeling of joyfulness. Similarly, your sense of fear is maintained when you notice your heart thumping.

Emotions are directed toward someone or something. We experience joy, fear, and other emotional episodes toward tasks, customers, public speeches we present, a software program we are using, and so on. This contrasts with *moods*, which are less intense emotional states that are not directed toward anything in particular.[44]

Emotions, Attitudes, and Behavior

attitudes
The cluster of beliefs, assessed feelings, and behavioral intentions toward an object.

Emotions are related to **attitudes,** but the two concepts are different. Attitudes represent the cluster of beliefs, assessed feelings, and behavioral intentions toward an object.[45] Emotions are *experiences*, whereas attitudes are *judgments*. We feel emotions, whereas we think about attitudes. We experience most emotions briefly, whereas our attitude toward someone or something is more stable over time.

Imagine hearing that the organization where you work will soon merge with a larger competitor. From this announcement, you might experience surprise, optimism, anger, excitement, or other emotions. These emotions might last a few minutes or perhaps hours, whereas your attitude toward the merger is more complex and stable over time. As illustrated in Exhibit 4.3, attitudes consist of three components:

■ *Beliefs* are your perceptions about the attitude object. For example, you might believe that mergers result in layoffs. Or you might believe that mergers ensure survival in an era of globalization. These beliefs develop from past experience and learning.[46]

■ *Feelings* are the positive or negative evaluations of the attitude object. Some people think mergers are good; others think they are bad. Your like or dislike of mergers represents your assessed feelings toward the attitude object. These evaluations are partly determined by your beliefs regarding the attitude object. If you believe that mergers mainly result in layoffs, then you will likely develop negative feelings toward mergers. Your emotions also shape your feelings. You would likely develop positive feelings toward mergers if you experience the emotions of excitement and optimism when thinking about the merger.[47]

■ *Behavioral intentions* represent your motivation to engage in a particular behavior with respect to the attitude object. You might plan to quit rather than go through the merger. Alternatively, you might intend to e-mail senior executives that this merger was a good decision. These are examples of the behavioral intentions component of attitudes.

Linking Emotions to Behavior Exhibit 4.3 shows how emotions and attitudes affect behavior.[48] First, beliefs influence our feelings toward something

EXHIBIT 4.3

Model of emotions, attitudes, and behavior

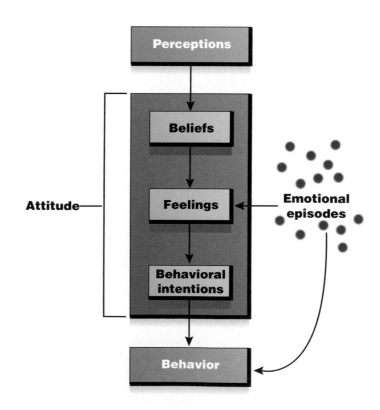

Employees Just Want to Have Fun!

It's bonus day at Kryptonite, and CEO Gary Furst is prepared for the occasion. Accompanied by a bagpiper, Furst—dressed up as a Scottish warrior from the movie *Braveheart*, complete with kilt and face paint—hands out the checks. Furst and other executives at the Boston-based bicycle lock maker have also dyed their hair green, held game shows, and hired musicians to entertain the troops. "You really need to find innovative, provocative and fun ways to motivate people," advises Furst. "Work can either be a drag or a lot of fun."

Fun at work? It sounds like an oxymoron. But to attract and keep valuable employees and to help relieve stress, organizations are encouraging employees to participate in—and even create—a little comic relief. Employees at Flanders Electric Motor Service in Evansville, Illinois, have water balloon fights and Nerf ball–throwing contests on Wacky Wednesdays. The co-owner sometimes jumps on a tricycle and pedals around delivering ice cream to Flanders's 190 employees. At Pragmatek, a Minneapolis e-business and consulting firm, employees hold Spam-carving contests. The CoActive Marketing Group in Lincoln Heights, Ohio, has Easter Egg hunts, with money inside the "eggs," and employees sometimes head out to the parking lot to test water balloon rockets.

Southwest Airlines is widely recognized as a pioneer in having fun on the job. During preflight instructions, a flight attendant says: "If there's anything we can do to make this a more pleasant flight, please, please, please hold onto that thought until we get to Houston." When the Southwest Airlines jet is about to land, the captain announces over the intercom, "Flight attendants, prepare your hair for arrival."

These fun and games may seem silly, but some corporate leaders are deadly serious about their value.

Southwest Airlines flight attendants Aimee Behrner (left) and Catrina Brooks ask passengers trivia questions over the airliner's intercom. *(© Dean Hoffmeyer © Richmond Times Dispatch)*

"It's pretty simple," explains Nathan Rudyk, president of DigIT Interactive Inc. (now part of Quebecor). "If you want to make the most money, you must attract the best people. To get the best people, you must be the most fun."

Sources: H. B. Herring, "Nurturing Your Company's Inner Child: Let There Be Fun!" *New York Times*, September 2, 2001; C. Jones, "Next in Line," *Richmond (VA) Times-Dispatch*, July 29, 2001; M. Shaw, "A Motivating Example," *Network World Fusion*, May 14, 2001; T. Raithel, "Some Companies Work Hard to Help Employees Relax," *Evansville (IL) Courier and Press*, February 11, 2001; D. Emerson, "Employers Urge Playing on the Job," *Business Journal of the Twin Cities (Minneapolis–St. Paul, MN)*, September 4, 2000; J. Eckberg, "Playtime—Workers Mix Business, Pleasure," *Cincinnati Enquirer*, July 31, 2000, p. B16; J. Elliott, "All Work and No Play Can Chase Workers Away," *Edmonton (Alberta) Journal*, February 28, 2000.

or someone. For example, you might think mergers are good (a feeling) because you believe they make companies more globally competitive and thereby improve your career opportunities (a belief).

Emotions also influence our feelings toward the attitude object. If you experience anxiety and irritation about the merger, then you would likely develop negative feelings toward it. Connections 4.1 describes how organizations try to generate positive emotions through various "fun" activities. In each case, the idea is to create emotions that result in favorable judgments about the organization.

Exhibit 4.3 also shows that feelings have a direct influence on behavioral intentions. People with the same feelings may form different behavioral intentions based on their unique past experiences. For instance, some employees who think the merger is bad may intend to quit before the merger proceeds, whereas others might want to complain about the decision. People choose the behavioral intention that they think will work best for them. Although behavioral intentions have the strongest influence on behavior, they are still imperfect predictors, because they relate only to the motivation to act.[49] According to the MARS model (see Chapter 2), behavior also depends on the person's ability, role perceptions, and situational factors.

Lastly, emotions sometimes have a direct effect on behavior. This occurs when people react to their emotions rather than their judgments (attitudes). When upset, an employee might stomp out of a meeting, bang a fist on the desk, or burst into tears. When overjoyed, an employee might embrace a coworker or break into a little dance. These are not carefully thought-out behaviors. They are fairly automatic emotional responses that serve as coping mechanisms in the particular situation.[50]

cognitive dissonance
Occurs when people perceive an inconsistency between their beliefs, feelings, and behavior.

Cognitive Dissonance   Emotions and attitudes usually lead to behavior, but behavior sometimes influences our attitudes through the process of **cognitive dissonance**.[51] Cognitive dissonance occurs when we perceive an inconsistency between our beliefs, feelings, and behavior. This inconsistency creates an uncomfortable tension (dissonance) that we are motivated to reduce by changing one or more of these elements. Behavior is usually the most difficult element to change, particularly when it is known to everyone, was done voluntarily, and can't be undone. Thus, we usually change our beliefs and feelings to reduce the inconsistency.

positive affectivity (PA)
The tendency to experience positive emotional states.

negative affectivity (NA)
The tendency to experience negative emotions.

Emotions and Personality   One last point to remember about the dynamics of workplace emotions is that a person's emotions can result from her or his personality, not just from workplace experiences. **Positive affectivity (PA)** is the tendency to experience positive emotional states. It is very similar to extroversion, described in Chapter 3 as a characteristic of people who are outgoing, talkative, sociable, and assertive. In contrast, some people have a high **negative affectivity (NA),** which is the tendency to experience negative emotions.[52] Employees with high NA tend to be more distressed and unhappy because they focus on the negative aspects of life.

To what extent do these personality traits influence emotions? Some research indicates that a person's level of personal affectivity can predict how he or she will feel about work two years later. Studies of twins raised apart conclude that a person's heredity influences emotions and judgments about work. However, other evidence suggests that the effects of PA and NA are relatively weak.[53] Overall, it seems that PA and NA influence emotions and attitudes in the workplace, but their effects are not as strong as situational factors.

MANAGING EMOTIONS

The Elbow Room Café is packed and noisy on this Saturday morning. A customer at the restaurant in Vancouver, Canada, half shouts across the room for more coffee. A passing waiter scoffs: "You want more coffee, get it yourself!" The customer only laughs. Another diner complains loudly that he and his party are running late and need their food. This time, restaurant manager Patrick Savoie speaks up: "If you're in a hurry, you should have gone to McDonald's." The diner and his companions chuckle.

To the uninitiated, the Elbow Room Café is an emotional basket case, full of irate guests and the rudest staff west of the Canadian Rockies. But it's all a performance—a place where guests can enjoy good food and play out their emotions about dreadful customer service. "It's almost like coming to a theatre," says Savoie, who spends much of his time inventing new ways to insult the clientele.[54]

Whether giving the most insulting service at Elbow Room Café in Vancouver or the friendliest service at The Warehouse in Auckland, employees are usually expected to manage their emotions in the workplace. **Emotional labor** refers to the effort, planning, and control needed to express organizationally desired emotions during interpersonal transactions.[55] When interacting with co-workers, customers, suppliers, and others, employees are expected to abide by *display rules*. These rules are norms requiring employees to display certain emotions and withhold others.

emotional labor
The effort, planning, and control needed to express organizationally desired emotions during interpersonal transactions.

Conditions Requiring Emotional Labor

People experience more emotional labor when their jobs require frequent and long durations of voice or face-to-face contact with clients and others.[56] For instance, caregivers at a nursing home must show courtesy, promote positive emotions, and control the emotions of residents while hiding their own fatigue, anger, and other true emotions. Emotional labor is also more challenging where the job requires employees to display a variety of emotions (e.g., anger as well as joy) and intense emotions (e.g., showing delight rather than forcing a weak smile). Bill collectors face these challenges. They must learn to show warmth to anxious first-time debtors and irritation (but not anger) toward debtors who seem indifferent to their financial obligations.[57]

Jobs vary in the extent to which employees must abide by the display rules. "Smile: we are on stage" is one of the most important rules that employees learn at the Ritz-Carlton in San Francisco and other hotels operated by the venerable hotelier.[58] The extent that someone must follow display rules also depends on the power and personal relationship of the person receiving the service. You would closely follow display rules when meeting the owner of a client's organization, whereas more latitude might be possible when serving a friend.

There are also cross-cultural differences in emotional display norms and values. One survey reported that 83 percent of Japanese believe it is inappropriate to get emotional in a business context, compared with 40 percent of Americans, 34 percent of French, and 29 percent of Italians. In other words, Italians are more likely to accept or tolerate people who display their true emotions at work, whereas such a display would be considered rude or embarrassing in Japan.[59]

Emotional Dissonance

Comedian George Burns once said: "The secret to being a good actor is honesty. If you can fake *that*, you've got it made." Burns's humor highlights the fact that most of us have difficulty hiding our true emotions all the time. Instead, emotions leak out as voice intonations and posture, and in other subtle ways.[60] The problem is particularly true of anger, which is one of the most difficult emotions to control. This conflict between required and true emotions is called **emotional dissonance,** and it is a significant cause of stress and job burnout (see Chapter 7).[61] Emotional dissonance is most common where employees must display emotions that are quite different from their true feelings and where emotional display rules are highly regulated.

emotional dissonance

The conflict between required and true emotions.

Supporting Emotional Labor

Many organizations support emotional labor by teaching employees the subtle behaviors that express appropriate emotions. This training occurs at some airlines where flight attendants and check-in staff complete videotaped exercises and receive feedback on their emotional labor. The feedback helps them learn the subtle art of expressing organizationally desired emotions. Earlier, we mentioned that people in Japan traditionally expect a narrow range of emotional displays. But this norm is changing as companies discover that employee smiles are good for business. Global Connections 4.2 describes how some Japanese companies are sending their employees to "smile school," where they learn the fine art of displaying pleasant emotions.

Along with training, some corporate leaders believe that the best way to support emotional labor is by hiring employees with the right attitude. "Our workers need good customer service skills, and they need to have a good attendance record," explains Steve Hennessy, manager of the Kohl's department store in Whitehall, Pennsylvania. "We hire for attitude and train for skill."[62] Hiring for attitude partly involves matching the individual's values and personality with the job's emotional labor requirements. It also involves hiring people with good emotional intelligence, which we discuss next.

Emotional Intelligence

emotional intelligence (EQ)

The ability to monitor one's own and others' feelings and emotions, to discriminate among them, and to use this information to guide one's thinking and actions.

Each year, the U.S. Air Force hires about 400 recruiters, and each year up to 100 of them are fired for failing to sign up enough people for the service. Selecting and training 100 new recruiters costs $3 million, not to mention the hidden costs of their poor performance. So Rich Handley, head of Air Force recruiting, decided to give 1,200 recruiters a new test that measured how well they manage their emotions and the emotions of others. He discovered that the top recruiters were better at asserting their feelings and thoughts, empathizing with others, feeling happy in life, and being aware of their emotions in a particular situation. The next year, Handley selected new recruiters partly on their results of this emotions test. The result: Only eight recruiters got fired or quit a year later.[63]

To select the best recruiters, the U.S. Air Force considers more than the cognitive intelligence of job applicants; it also looks at their **emotional intelligence (EQ).** EQ is the ability to monitor one's own and others' feelings and emotions, to discriminate among them, and to use this information to guide one's thinking and actions. Emotional intelligence includes the five

Japanese Employees Learn Service with a Smile

Hiroshi Ieyoshi and three dozen other gas station attendants are gathered for some tough after-hours training. They're learning how to smile. "It's easy to say you should smile at the customers," says Ieyoshi, the earnest 33-year-old pump manager after the 90-minute seminar. "But to be honest, it all depends on how I feel at the moment."

Ieyoshi isn't the only one who has trouble smiling at customers. In Japanese culture, hiding your emotions is considered a virtue. The society values group harmony, and any expression of emotion violates that harmony by focusing on the individual's feelings. Now, companies are throwing out the straight-faced tradition and increasing sales with smiling employees.

Leading the smile revolution is Yoshihiko Kadokawa, president of the Smile Amenity Institute and author of *The Power of a Laughing Face*. The former retail executive discovered that even in this dour society, the friendliest clerks consistently have the highest sales. "I have found, through my surveys, that sales personnel could beef up sales by as much as 20% each day by just smiling more at their customers," says Kadokawa.

McDonald's Corporation puts such a premium on smiling faces in Japan that the company screens out those who are too poker-faced. While applicants describe a pleasant experience, interviewers evaluate whether their faces reflect the pleasure they're discussing. McDonald's wants all its employees to provide the friendly service at the price stated on the menu: "Smiles, 0 yen."

In spite of the cultural barriers, some Japanese employees have acquired a natural ability to smile as much as Westerners. In the class of gas station attendants, Kutaro Matsunaga stands out. But he has been practicing for a long time. "[M]y name means 'happy man,' and I always want to make my customers happy," explains Matsunaga, with a smile.

Sources: S. Kakuchi, "Put On a Happy Face," *Asian Business* 36 (March 2000), p. 56; V. Reitman, "Learning to Grin —And Bear It," *Los Angeles Times*, February 22, 1999, p. A1.

Yoshihiko Kadokawa is teaching Japanese employees how to improve customer service through the power of a laughing face. *(Both photos © Ohmori Satoru)*

dimensions illustrated in Exhibit 4.4 and described below. Scholars are beginning to view these dimensions of emotional intelligence in a hierarchy, where self-awareness is the lowest level and social skill is the highest and most complex level of EQ.[64]

■ *Self-awareness*—People with high self-awareness recognize and understand their moods, emotions, and needs. They perceive and anticipate how their actions affect others. Self-aware people are also comfortable talking about and

EXHIBIT 4.4

Dimensions of
emotional intelligence

admitting their limitations, so they know when to ask for help. Notice that this dimension (as well as some other EQ domains described here) is similar to the self-monitoring personality concept that was described in Chapter 3.

■ *Self-regulation*—This is the ability to control or redirect emotional outbursts and other impulse behaviors For example, rather than yelling at a client, you manage to remain calm and later talk out the emotion to a co-worker. Self-regulation includes the ability to suspend judgment—to think through the consequences of the behavior rather than acting on impulse.

■ *Self-motivation*—This includes stifling impulses, directing emotions toward personal goals, and delaying gratification. People with high self-motivation remain optimistic even when they do not achieve their goals.

■ *Empathy*—Empathy was defined in Chapter 3 as the ability to understand and be sensitive to the feelings, thoughts, and situation of others. This dimension doesn't involve adopting other people's emotions; it means being sensitized to them.

■ *Social skill*—This is the ability to manage the emotions of other people. It requires social competence and skills to guide the way other people act. Social skill includes the ability to build networks of relationships and to build rapport—finding common interests with and understanding others. Social skill requires other elements of emotional intelligence, particularly empathy and self-regulation.

EQ has its roots in the social intelligence literature introduced over 80 years ago, but scholars spent most of that time focused on cognitive intelligence (IQ).[65] Now the U.S. Air Force and others are realizing that EQ is just as important as IQ in the performance of most jobs. As we described in Chapter 2, people perform better when their aptitudes—including general intelligence—match the job requirements. But most jobs also involve social interaction, so employees also need emotional intelligence to work effectively in social settings. A recent study of university students reported that those with high EQ try to rebalance their moods to a more positive condition after having a negative experience. Another study found that high EQ people are more successful in many aspects of job interviews. Other studies suggest that women are

Physicians have an above-average IQ (about 120 in the United States), but their average emotional intelligence score (EQ) hovers around 90—well below the population average of 100. "We're taught to look at things analytically, but our biggest difficulties are not analytic," admits Darryl Heustis, M.D., vice president for medical affairs at the Jerry L. Pettis Memorial VA Medical Center in Loma Linda, California. "Without understanding our emotions and others' emotions, we're not going to do as well." Fortunately, Heustis and his medical colleagues are attending special classes at the Veterans Administration where they receive their personal EQ profile and learn to improve their emotional intelligence.[66] Looking at the five emotional intelligence dimensions, explain why it is important for physicians to have a high EQ. *(© Peter Phun/The Press-Enterprise)*

better than men at perceiving emotions, whereas men are better at controlling their emotions.[67]

Improving Emotional Intelligence   Emotional intelligence is related to several personality traits described in Chapter 3, including extroversion, conscientiousness, agreeableness, emotional stability, and openness to experience.[68] Still, EQ can be learned to some extent. Endpoint Research, a Canadian firm specializing in pharmaceutical and biotechnology clinical trials, has put all its 65 employees through the EQ assessment so that they can develop their weak areas. Methodist Hospitals of Dallas has also introduced emotional intelligence training to its management group, with the CEO participating front and center in the program.[69]

Although training programs may help, people don't develop emotional intelligence just by learning about its dimensions. They require personal coaching, plenty of practice, and frequent feedback. Emotional intelligence also increases with age; it is part of the process called maturity.[70] Overall, emotional intelligence offers considerable potential, but we also have a lot to learn about its measurement and effects on people in the workplace.

JOB SATISFACTION AND ORGANIZATIONAL COMMITMENT

Personal values, ethical values, and workplace emotions have a powerful effect on individual behavior in the workplace. They also affect attitudes. As we discussed earlier, attitudes represent the cluster of beliefs, assessed feelings, and behavioral intentions toward an object. Emotions influence attitudes mainly through assessed feelings. In this final section of the chapter, we learn about two important work attitudes: job satisfaction and organizational commitment.

Job Satisfaction

Job satisfaction represents a person's evaluation of his or her job and work context (see Chapter 2).[71] It is an *appraisal* of the perceived job characteristics and emotional experiences at work. Satisfied employees have a favorable evaluation of their job, based on their observations and emotional experiences. Job satisfaction is really a collection of attitudes about specific facets of the job.[72] Employees can be satisfied with some elements of the job while simultaneously dissatisfied with others. For example, you might like your co-workers but are less satisfied with workload or other aspects of the job.

How satisfied are we at work? According to the latest survey from the Gallup Organization (conducted during a faltering economy), 41 percent of Americans are "completely satisfied" and 44 percent are "somewhat satisfied" with their jobs. Indeed, over 85 percent of Americans have been satisfied with their jobs for the past decade or more.[73] Exhibit 4.5 shows that Americans also have the fourth-highest job satisfaction ratings in a recent survey of 39 countries. Only employees in Denmark, India, and Norway say they are happier at work.

Does this mean that we have high job satisfaction? Well, maybe, but probably not as high as these statistics suggest. The problem is that surveys often use a single direct question, such as, "How satisfied are you with your job?" Many dissatisfied employees are reluctant to reveal their feelings in a direct question because this is tantamount to admitting that they made a poor job choice and are not enjoying life. One indication of this inflated rating is that one-third of Americans say they would be happier in another job. Other surveys show that employees rate almost all aspects of the job lower than their overall score.[74] We also need to keep in mind that cultural values make it difficult to compare job satisfaction across countries.[75] People in China, South Korea, and Japan tend to subdue their emotions in public, so they probably avoid extreme survey ratings such as "very satisfied."

Job Satisfaction and Work Behavior   Xerox, Nortel, and Sears, Roebuck and Company are paying a lot more attention to employee satisfaction these days. In each of these firms, executive bonuses are partly determined by the level of job satisfaction indicated in annual employee surveys.[76] The reason for this attention is simple: Job satisfaction affects many of the critical individual behaviors introduced in Chapter 2. Satisfied employees are less likely to quit

EXHIBIT 4.5   Job satisfaction across cultures

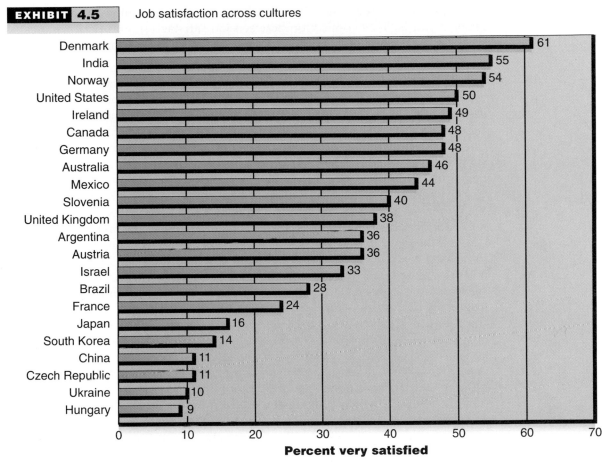

Denmark	61
India	55
Norway	54
United States	50
Ireland	49
Canada	48
Germany	48
Australia	46
Mexico	44
Slovenia	40
United Kingdom	38
Argentina	36
Austria	36
Israel	33
Brazil	28
France	24
Japan	16
South Korea	14
China	11
Czech Republic	11
Ukraine	10
Hungary	9

Percent very satisfied

Source: Based on Ipsos-Reid survey of 9,300 employees in 39 countries in middle of 2000. See "Ipsos-Reid Global Poll Finds Major Differences in Employee Satisfaction around the World," Ipsos-Reid News Release, January 8, 2001.

their jobs, be absent or late for work, steal from their employer, or engage in acts of violence.[77]

Job satisfaction is also an ethical issue. People spend a large portion of their time working in organizations, and many societies now expect companies to provide work environments that are safe and enjoyable. This moral obligation is apparent when an organization has low job satisfaction. The company tries to hide this fact, and when morale problems become public, corporate leaders are usually quick to improve the situation.

But what about job satisfaction and job performance? Is it true that "happy workers are productive workers"? The answer is that researchers have found a weak or negligible association between job satisfaction and task performance.[78] One reason for the weak relationship is that general attitudes (like job satisfaction) don't predict specific behaviors very well. Instead, they affect different people in different ways. One dissatisfied employee may decide to put in less work effort, whereas another dissatisfied employee works productively while looking for employment elsewhere. Another explanation is that job performance leads to job satisfaction (rather than vice versa), but only when performance is linked to valued rewards. High performers receive more rewards and, consequently, are more satisfied than low-performing employees who receive fewer rewards. This connection between job satisfaction and performance is weak because many organizations do not reward good performance.[79]

Job Satisfaction and Customer Satisfaction   Job satisfaction may have a fuzzy effect on job performance, but its influence on customer satisfaction seems to be strong and clear. Marketing experts have developed a model that relates the job satisfaction of employees to customer satisfaction and profitability. As shown in Exhibit 4.6, this employee–customer–profit chain model suggests that increasing employee satisfaction and loyalty results in higher customer perceptions of value, which improves the company's profitability.[80]

The opening vignette in this chapter describes how The Warehouse applies the employee–customer–profit chain model through its "people first" principle. Founder Stephen Tindall believes that companies have happy customers through happy employees. Sears, Roebuck and Company also follows this philosophy. A few years ago, the retail giant calculated that a 5-point improvement on the Sears job satisfaction survey scale would increase customer satisfaction ratings by 1.3 points, which, in turn, would improve revenue growth by 0.5 percent. Gordon Bethune, CEO of Continental Airlines, sums up the equation this way: "We treat our people well, and in turn, they treat our customers well. Happy employees equal customer satisfaction."[81]

There are two main reasons why job satisfaction has a positive effect on customer service. First, job satisfaction affects a person's general mood. Employees who are in a good mood are more likely to display friendliness and positive feelings, which puts customers in a better mood. Second, satisfied employees are less likely to quit their jobs, and longer-service employees have more experience and better skills to serve clients. Lower turnover also gives

EXHIBIT 4.6

The employee–customer–profit chain model

Roger Greene (wearing goggles in photo) isn't taking any chances on poor customer service. The CEO and founder of Ipswitch Inc. has taken all 130 employees—plus one guest each—on a four-day cruise in the Bahamas. The cruise is the Lexington, Virginia, software maker's way of thanking employees for steady financial performance. It's also consistent with Greene's larger objective to keep employees happy so that they will continue to provide exceptional customer service. Ipswitch employees also get five weeks of paid time off, child and elder care, domestic partner benefits, and a concierge service. "If employees are treated well," Greene explains, "they will treat the customers well, and then the profits will come."[82] Along with job satisfaction, what other work attitude described in this chapter might explain why a trip to the Bahamas increases customer satisfaction? *(© John Wilcox, Boston Herald)*

customers the same employees to serve them, so there is more consistent service. There is some evidence that customers build their loyalty to specific employees, not to the organization, so keeping employee turnover low tends to keep customer turnover low.[83]

Improving Job Satisfaction   Given the importance of job satisfaction, how can companies ensure that they have happy workers? The job satisfaction concept is so broad—remember, there are many facets of job satisfaction—that the answer comes from every part of this textbook. Feedback, equity, rewards, leadership, corporate culture, change management, and other topics all implicitly or explicitly refer to job satisfaction as a possible outcome. We must also remember that individual differences, such as personality and personal beliefs, moderate the effects of the work environment on job satisfaction.

Organizational Commitment

Organizational commitment refers to the employee's emotional attachment to, identification with, and involvement in a particular organization.[84] It is the

> **organizational commitment**
> The employee's emotional attachment to, identification with, and involvement in a particular organization.

person's *affective commitment*—his or her loyalty to the organization.[84] Affective commitment can also refer to loyalty toward co-workers, customers, or a profession.[85] In this book, we will concentrate mainly on the employee's overall commitment to the organization.

Along with affective commitment, employees have varying levels of *continuance commitment*.[86] Continuance commitment occurs when employees believe it is in their own personal interest to remain with the organization. In other words, this form of commitment is a calculative bond with the organization rather than an emotional attachment. For example, you may have met people who do not particularly identify with the organization where they work but feel bound to remain there because it would be too costly to quit. Continuance commitment is this motivation to stay because of the high cost of leaving.[87]

Is organizational loyalty declining? Some surveys suggest that organizational commitment has fallen considerably over the past decade, whereas others see no change. Some writers argue that employees are still loyal, but their loyalty is directed more toward their profession, their immediate work unit, or their immediate boss rather than the overall organization.[88]

Consequences of Organizational Commitment   Research suggests that a loyal workforce can be a significant competitive advantage. Employees with high levels of affective commitment are less likely to quit their jobs and be absent from work. Organizational commitment also improves customers' satisfaction because long-tenure employees have better knowledge of work practices and clients like to do business with the same employees. Employees with high affective commitment also have higher work motivation and organizational citizenship.[89]

However, there are potential problems where employees have too much organizational commitment. One potential problem with a highly loyal workforce is that the organization may have very low turnover. This limits the organization's opportunity to hire new employees with new knowledge and fresh ideas. Another concern is that loyalty results in conformity, which holds back creativity. Some critics also argue that organizational commitment is a vestige of the ancient "master–servant" relationship that should be replaced by more professional relationships between employer and employee.[90]

Building Organizational Commitment   Although there are almost as many ways to build organizational loyalty as topics in this textbook, the following activities have been most prominent in the literature:[91]

■ *Fairness and satisfaction*—The most important ingredients for a loyal workforce are positive and equitable work experiences. New employees must believe that the company is fulfilling its obligations.[92] Organizational commitment seems to suffer when people face increased workloads in companies with record profits and senior executives earning lucrative bonuses. Other companies have built commitment by sharing profits and distributing company shares to employees.

■ *Job security*—Layoff threats are one of the greatest blows to employee loyalty, even among those whose jobs are not immediately at risk.[93] Building commitment doesn't require lifetime employment guarantees, but employees should have enough job security to feel some permanence and mutuality in the employment relationship.

◼ *Organizational comprehension*—Affective commitment is a person's identification with the company, so it makes sense that this attitude is strengthened when employees have a solid comprehension of the company. Employees feel disconnected when they don't know what's going on. This uncertainty calls for improved communication processes (see Chapter 11) as well as opportunities to work in various parts of the organization. It also requires more social interaction, particularly where employees are often separated from each other.

◼ *Employee involvement*—Employees feel that they are part of the organization when they make decisions that guide the organization's future. Through participation, employees begin to see how the organization is a reflection of their decisions. Employee involvement also builds loyalty because giving this power is a demonstration of the company's trust in its employees.

◼ *Trusting employees*—**Trust** occurs when we have positive expectations about another party's intentions and actions toward us in risky situations.[94] Trust means putting faith in the other person or group. It is also a reciprocal activity; to receive trust, you must demonstrate trust. Trust is important for organizational commitment because it touches the heart of the employment relationship (see Chapter 18). Employees identify with and feel obliged to work for an organization only when they trust its leaders.

trust
Positive expectations about another party's intentions and actions toward us in risky situations.

Aside from these practices, some firms try to build commitment by tying employees financially to the organization through low-cost loans and stock options. Many knowledge-based firms offer stock options that are vested (withheld) for two or more years. Anglo Irish Bank uses loyalty bonuses to reduce turnover of new staff. People who are hired at the Irish bank receive half of their bonus—which can range up to 50 percent of base salary—after 12 months of employment and the other half 6 months later. "The hope," says an Anglo Irish Bank executive, "is to keep them a little longer."[95]

These "golden handcuffs" do tend to reduce turnover, but they also increase continuance commitment, not affective commitment. Evidence suggests that employees with high levels of continuance commitment have *lower* performance ratings and are *less* likely to engage in organizational citizenship behaviors.[96] Although vested options may be necessary, continuance commitment should not be a substitute for strategies to build and maintain employee loyalty. Employers still need to win employees' hearts (affective commitment) beyond tying them financially to the organization (continuance commitment).

CHAPTER SUMMARY

Values represent stable, long-lasting beliefs about what is important to us. They influence our decisions and interpretation of what is ethical. Some values are terminal, whereas others are instrumental. We also need to distinguish espoused values from enacted values. There are also different levels of values (personal, organizational, professional, and cultural).

Values have become more important in organizations because of globalization, the need to replace command-and-control systems, and the increasing pressure for organizations to engage in ethical practices. Organizations are more effective when they align the company's values with those held by individuals and the society in which they operate.

Five values that differ across cultures are individualism versus collectivism, power distance, uncertainty avoidance, achievement versus nurturing orientation, and long- versus short-term orientation.

Three values that guide ethical conduct are utilitarianism, individual rights, and distributive justice. Three other factors that influence ethical conduct are the extent to which an issue demands ethical principles (moral intensity), the person's sensitivity to the presence and importance of an ethical dilemma, and situational factors that cause people to deviate from their moral values.

People from different cultures tend to act differently when faced with an ethical issue. Although ethical values differ somewhat across cultures, most of this variation is explained by the fact that unique cultural experiences cause people to see different levels of moral intensity.

Emotions are feelings experienced toward an object, person, or event that create a state of readiness. They differ from attitudes, which represent the cluster of beliefs, feelings, and behavioral intentions toward an object. Beliefs are a person's perceptions about an attitude object. Feelings are judgments about our emotional experiences associated with the target. Behavioral intentions represent a motivation to engage in a particular behavior with respect to the target. Emotions usually affect behavior through beliefs, feelings, and behavioral intentions.

Emotional labor refers to the effort, planning, and control needed to express organizationally desired emotions during interpersonal transactions. Emotional labor is more common in jobs with frequent and lengthy customer interaction, where the job requires a variety of emotions displayed, and where employees must abide by the display rules. Emotional labor creates problems because true emotions tend to leak out, and conflict between expected and true emotions (emotional dissonance) causes stress and burnout.

Emotional intelligence is the ability to monitor your own and others' emotions, to discriminate among them, and to use the information to guide your thinking and actions. Emotional intelligence includes self-awareness, self-regulation, self-motivation, empathy, and social skill.

Job satisfaction represents a person's evaluation of his or her job and work context. Job satisfaction affects absenteeism and turnover, and reflects the ethical standards of the organization. Although it has a weak association with task performance, job satisfaction is a strong and clear factor in customer satisfaction.

Affective organizational commitment (loyalty) refers to the employee's emotional attachment to, identification with, and involvement in a particular organization. Affective commitment contrasts with continuance commitment, which is a calculative bond with the organization. Companies build loyalty through fairness and satisfaction, some level of job security, organizational comprehension, employee involvement, and trust. Some companies rely on golden handcuffs, but this approach produces continuance commitment, which tends to reduce job performance.

KEY TERMS

attitudes, p. 107
cognitive dissonance, p. 110
emotional dissonance, p. 112
emotional intelligence (EQ), p. 112
emotional labor, p. 111
emotions, p. 106

ethical sensitivity, p. 105
individualism versus collectivism, p. 101
moral intensity, p. 104
negative affectivity (NA), p. 110
organizational commitment, p. 119

positive affectivity (PA), p. 110
power distance, p. 101
trust, p. 121
uncertainty avoidance, p. 101
utilitarianism, p. 104

DISCUSSION QUESTIONS

1. An American company is beginning to expand operations in Japan and wants you to form working relationships with Japanese suppliers. Considering only the values of individualism and uncertainty avoidance, what should you be aware of or sensitive to in your dealings with these suppliers? You may assume that your contacts hold typical Japanese values along these dimensions.

2. Not long ago, Microsoft set up a program whereby computer science professors would receive $200

for mentioning Microsoft's products at public presentations. The money is used to offset travel costs to attend these sessions. Discuss the ethical implications of this incentive.

3. Compare and contrast moral intensity and ethical sensitivity.

4. After a few months on the job, Susan has experienced several emotional episodes ranging from frustration to joy toward the work she is assigned. Use the model of emotions, attitudes, and

behaviors to explain how these emotions affect Susan's level of job satisfaction with the work itself.

5. The latest employee attitude survey in your organization indicates that employees are unhappy with some aspects of the organization. However, management tends to pay attention to the single-item question asking employees to indicate their overall satisfaction with the job. The results of this item indicate that 86 percent of staff members are very or somewhat satisfied, so management concludes that the other results refer to issues that are probably not important to employees. Explain why management's interpretation of these results may be inaccurate.

6. A recent study reported that college instructors are frequently required to engage in emotional labor. Identify the situations in which emotional labor is required for this job. In your opinion, is emotional labor more troublesome for college instructors or for telephone operators working at a 911 emergency call center?

7. If a co-worker told you that he or she had a high level of emotional intelligence, what would you look for to confirm that statement?

8. Universal Broadcasting Corporation is concerned about losing some of its best technical staff to competitors. Senior executives have decided that the best way to build a loyal workforce is to introduce a deferred profit-sharing plan. Employees would receive half of each year's profit share at the end of the year, but the other half would be paid out over the next two years as trailers. Anyone who leaves, other than as a result of retirement or layoffs, would forfeit some or all of the deferred payments. Explain what effect this plan may have on organizational commitment and employee behaviors.

CASE STUDY 4.1

ROUGH SEAS ON THE LINK650

Professor Suzanne Baxter was preparing for her first class of the semester when Shaun O'Neill knocked lightly on the open door and announced himself: "Hi, Professor, I don't suppose you remember me?" Professor Baxter had large classes, but she did remember that Shaun was a student in her organizational behavior class two years earlier. Shaun had decided to work in the oil industry for a couple of years before returning to school to complete his diploma.

"Welcome back!" Baxter said as she beckoned him into the office. "I heard you were working on an oil rig in the United Kingdom. How was it?"

"Well, Professor," Shaun began, "I had worked two summers in the Texas oil fields and my family's from Ireland, so I hoped to get a job on the LINK650. It's that new WestOil drilling rig that arrived with so much fanfare in the North Sea fields two years ago. The LINK650 was built by LINK, Inc., in Texas. A standard practice in this industry is for the rig manufacturer to manage its day-to-day operations, so employees on the LINK650 are managed completely by LINK managers with no involvement from WestOil.

We all know that drilling rig jobs are dangerous, but they pay well and offer generous time off. A local newspaper there said that nearly a thousand people lined up to complete job applications for the 50 nontechnical positions. I was lucky enough to get one of those jobs.

"Everyone hired on the LINK650 was enthusiastic and proud. We were one of the chosen few and were really pumped up about working on a new rig that had received so much media attention. I was quite impressed with the recruiters—so were several other hires—because they really seemed to be concerned about our welfare out on the platform. I later discovered that the recruiters came from a consulting firm that specializes in hiring people. Come to think of it, we didn't meet a single LINK manager during that process. Maybe things would have been different if some of those LINK supervisors had interviewed us.

"Working on LINK650 was a real shock, even though most of us had some experience working in the oil fields. I'd say that none of the 50 nontechnical people hired was quite prepared for the brutal jobs on the oil rig. We did the dirtiest jobs in the biting cold winds of the North Sea.

Still, during the first few months most of us wanted to show the company that we were dedicated to getting the job done. A couple of the new hires quit within a few weeks, but most of the people hired with me really got along well—you know, just like the ideas you mentioned in class. We formed a special bond that helped us through the bad weather and grueling work.

"The LINK650 supervisors were another matter. They were mean taskmasters who had worked for many years on oil rigs in the Gulf of Mexico or North Sea. They seemed to relish the idea of treating their employees the same way they had been treated before becoming managers. We put up with their abuse for the first few months, but things got worse when the LINK650 was completely shut down twice to correct mechanical problems. These setbacks embarrassed LINK's management and they put more pressure on the supervisors to get us back on schedule.

"The supervisors started to ignore equipment problems and pushed us to get jobs done more quickly without regard to safety procedures. They routinely shouted obscenities at employees in front of others. A couple of my workmates were fired and a couple of others quit their jobs. I almost lost my job one day just because my boss thought I was deliberately working slowly. He didn't realize—or care—that the fittings I was connecting were damaged. Several people started finding ways to avoid the supervisors and get as little work done as possible. Many of my co-workers developed back problems. We jokingly called it the 'rigger's backache' because some employees faked their ailment to leave the rig with paid sick leave.

"On top of the lousy supervisors, we were always kept in the dark about the problems on the rig. Supervisors said that they didn't know anything, which was partly true, but they said we shouldn't be so interested in things that didn't concern us. But the rig's problems, as well as its future contract work, were a major concern to crew members who weren't ready to quit. Their job security depended on the rig's production levels and whether WestOil would sign contracts

to drill new holes. Given the rig's problems, most of us were concerned that we would be laid off at any time.

"Everything came to a head when Bob MacKenzie was killed because someone secured a hoist improperly. Not sure if it was mentioned in the papers here, but it was big news around this time last year. A government inquiry concluded that the person responsible wasn't properly trained and that employees were being pushed to finish jobs without safety precautions. Anyway, while the inquiry was going on, several employees decided to unionize the rig. It wasn't long before most employees on LINK650 had signed union cards. That really shocked LINK's management and the entire oil industry because it was, I think, just the second time that a rig had ever been unionized there.

"Since then, management has been doing everything in its power to get rid of the union. It sent a 'safety officer' to the rig, although we eventually realized that he was a consultant the company hired to undermine union support. Several managers were sent to special seminars on how to manage a unionized workforce, although one of the topics was how to break the union.

"So you see, Professor, I joined LINK as an enthusiastic employee and quit last month with no desire to lift a finger for them. It really bothers me, because I was always told to do your best, no matter how tough the situation. It's been quite an experience."

Discussion Questions

1. Identify the various ways that employees expressed their job dissatisfaction on the LINK650.

2. Shaun O'Neill's commitment to the LINK organization dwindled over his two years of employment. Discuss the factors that affected his organizational commitment.

REVENGE OF THE DOWNSIZED NERDS

BusinessWeek The economic slowdown of 2001 hit the high-tech sector especially hard. Although some people had thought e-commerce would be immune from the punishing downturns of business cycles, many of the layoffs occurred at dot-coms. Newly unemployed high-tech workers in California's Silicon Valley reacted in vastly different ways. Some looked for traditional jobs; others joined the Peace Corps. Some of the most dramatic reactions involved retaliation

This *Business Week* case study discusses the laid-off dot-com workers who sought revenge. It provides several anecdotes of high-tech workers who sabotaged their employers or extorted favorable severance packages. Read through this *Business Week* case study at www.mhhe.com/mcshane2e and prepare for the discussion questions at right.

Discussion Questions

1. From an employer's standpoint, what are the ethical issues in handling an economic downturn by laying off employees? Are the issues different in the case of skilled workers, such as computer experts at a high-tech firm? What values does a company demonstrate when it lays off employees?

2. From the perspective of the employecs described in this article, were these forms of retaliation justifiable? Why or why not? What values are they demonstrating?

3. What were the likely emotions underlying the behavior described in the article? Do you think these emotions represented a high level of emotional intelligence? Why or why not?

Source: Michelle Conlin, "Revenge of the Downsized Nerds," *Business Week,* July 30, 2001.

RANKING JOBS ON THEIR EMOTIONAL LABOR

Purpose This exercise is designed to help you understand the jobs in which people tend to experience higher or lower degrees of emotional labor.

Instructions

- *Step 1*—Individually rank the jobs listed on the next page according to the extent that they require emotional labor. In other words, assign a 1 to the job you believe requires the most effort, planning, and control to express organizationally desired emotions during interpersonal transactions. Assign a 10 to the job you believe requires the least amount of emotional labor. Mark your rankings in column (1).

- *Step 2*—The instructor will form teams of four or five members, and each team will rank the items based on consensus (not simply averaging the individual rankings). These results are placed in column (2).

- *Step 3*—The instructor will provide expert ranking information. This information should be written in column (3). Then students will calculate the differences and record the results in columns (4) and (5). Students then sum the total absolute difference in each of these columns.

- *Step 4*—The class will compare the results and discuss the features of jobs with high emotional labor.

Occupational emotional labor scoring sheet					
Occupation	(1) Individual ranking	(2) Team ranking	(3) Expert ranking	(4) Absolute difference between (1) and (3)	(5) Absolute difference between (2) and (3)
Bartender					
Cashier					
Dental hygienist					
Insurance adjuster					
Lawyer					
Librarian					
Postal clerk					
Registered nurse					
Social worker					
Television announcer					
Total					
				Your score	Team score

S E L F - A S S E S S M E N T   E X E R C I S E   4.4

ETHICS CHECK

Purpose   This exercise is designed to help you assess your ethical response to various business and nonbusiness situations.

Instructions   Read each of the scenarios on the next page and indicate how you would likely respond in each scenario. There is no scoring key for this scale. Instead, the instructor will present the results of other students who have completed this instrument. This exercise is completed alone so that students assess themselves honestly without concerns of social comparison. However, class discussion will focus on business ethics and the issue of ethical sensitivity.

Ethics check scale					
Please indicate the probability that you would take the action indicated at the end of each scenario.	**Yes** ▼	**Probably yes** ▼	**Unsure** ▼	**Probably no** ▼	**No** ▼

1. At work you use many different software packages. Several weeks ago your supervisor ordered a new package for you that several of your colleagues are currently using. The software is now late in arriving. The package would aid you tremendously in completing your current project but is not absolutely necessary. Earlier today your supervisor brought her copy of the software over to you and suggested that you copy it onto your computer for use until your copy arrives. You know that the software is licensed to be installed onto only one computer. Do you copy the software? . . . . ☐ ☐ ☐ ☐ ☐

2. While at lunch with several of your colleagues last week, you overheard a discussion about a client company's financial situation. An accountant working closely with the company noticed significant decreases in sales and receivables. He wasn't sure exactly how bad it was until he heard a rumor at the company about the possibility of filing for bankruptcy. You're now worried because you own a significant block of shares in the company. Do you sell the shares based on this inside information? . . . . ☐ ☐ ☐ ☐ ☐

3. Yesterday you drove to the store with your neighbor and her young son. When you got back out to the car, your neighbor noticed that her son picked up a small item from the store worth about $5 that wasn't paid for. Your neighbor reprimanded the child and then turned to you and said she was ready to go. You asked her if she was going to go back into the store to pay for the item. She said it's not worth the hassle. Do you refuse to drive her home unless she goes back to the store and pays for the item? . . . . ☐ ☐ ☐ ☐ ☐

4. While on a trip out of town on business, you had dinner with your sister. Your company has a policy of reimbursing dinner expenses up to $50 per meal. The total cost for this meal for both you and your sister was $35.70. The cost of your meal alone was $16.30. You know that others in your company routinely submit claims for dinner expenses for nonbusiness parties. Do you claim the entire amount for reimbursement? . . . . ☐ ☐ ☐ ☐ ☐

Source: Adapted from R. R. Radtke, "The Effects of Gender and Setting on Accountants' Ethically Sensitive Decisions," *Journal of Business Ethics* 24 (April 2000), pp. 299–312.

INDIVIDUALISM–COLLECTIVISM SCALE

Purpose This self-assessment is designed to help you identify your level of individualism and collectivism.

Instructions Read each of the statements below and circle the response that you believe best indicates how well each statement describes you. Then use the scoring key in Appendix B to calculate your results for each scale. This exercise is completed alone so that students assess themselves honestly without concerns of social comparison. However, class discussion will focus on the individualism–collectivism values.

Individualism–collectivism scale					
Circle the number that best indicates how well each statement describes you.	**Does not describe me at all** ▼	**Does not describe me very well** ▼	**Describes me somewhat** ▼	**Describes me well** ▼	**Describes me very well** ▼
1. I often do "my own thing."	1	2	3	4	5
2. The well-being of my co-workers is important to me.	1	2	3	4	5
3. One should live one's life independently of others.	1	2	3	4	5
4. If a co-worker gets a prize, I would feel proud.	1	2	3	4	5
5. I like my privacy.	1	2	3	4	5
6. If a relative were in financial difficulty, I would help within my means.	1	2	3	4	5
7. I prefer to be direct and forthright when discussing issues with people.	1	2	3	4	5
8. It is important to maintain harmony within my group.	1	2	3	4	5
9. I am a unique individual.	1	2	3	4	5
10. I like sharing little things with my neighbors.	1	2	3	4	5
11. What happens to me is my own doing.	1	2	3	4	5
12. I feel good when I cooperate with others.	1	2	3	4	5
13. When I succeed, it is usually because of my abilities.	1	2	3	4	5
14. My happiness depends very much on the happiness of those around me.	1	2	3	4	5
15. I enjoy being unique and different from others in many ways.	1	2	3	4	5
16. To me, pleasure is spending time with others.	1	2	3	4	5

Source: T. M. Singelis, H. C. Triandis, D. P. S. Bhawuk, and M. J. Gelfand, "Horizontal and Vertical Dimensions of Individualism and Collectivism: A Theoretical and Measurement Refinement," *Cross-Cultural Research* 29 (August 1995), pp. 240–75. Copyright © 1995 by Sage Publications. Reprinted by permission of Sage Publications, Inc.

After studying the preceding material, be sure to check out our website at
www.mhhe.com/mcshane2e
for more in-depth information and interactivities that correspond to this chapter.

Foundations of Employee Motivation

AFTER READING THIS CHAPTER, YOU SHOULD BE ABLE TO:

■ Define *motivation* and distinguish between content and process theories.

■ Compare the four content theories of motivation.

■ Discuss the practical implications of content motivation theories.

■ Explain how each component of expectancy theory influences work effort.

■ Discuss the implications of expectancy theory.

■ Explain how employees react to inequity.

■ Describe the characteristics of effective goal setting.

Mark Hawkins knows what it's like to be challenged. The senior business analyst joined Capital One a few years ago and has been pushing his potential ever since. "The first few weeks you are playing catch-up, learning about a new industry and organization," says Hawkins, who works at the credit card company's British operations. "But pretty soon you are making decisions about how to take the company forward. There are so many opportunities and you are free to pick up as many projects as you can run with."

Capital One knows how to motivate employees. The Falls Church, Virginia–based firm starts by carefully screening job applicants and selecting those with an inherent entrepreneurial need for achievement. Then, as Mark Hawkins discovered, the company stretches them with challenging goals. "We expect associates to get out of their comfort zones and look for those 'stretch assignments,'" explains a Capital One executive.

Employees are formally evaluated twice each year by supervisors and peers against specific behavioral competencies. They also receive plenty of informal feedback and encouragement. "You have to spend a lot of time working with people and giving them constant feedback," says a Capital One executive. "It makes people feel valued and involved." Employees are also motivated by financial incentives based on individual and organizational performance.

But Capital One's dramatic growth over the past decade creates a challenge for co-founders Richard Fairbank and Nigel Morris. "As we become bigger, we have to make sure we preserve the spirit and the magic of Capital One," Fairbank says. "Now we're at 20,000 [employees], and it still has that entrepreneurial spirit. But it won't be easy."[1] ■

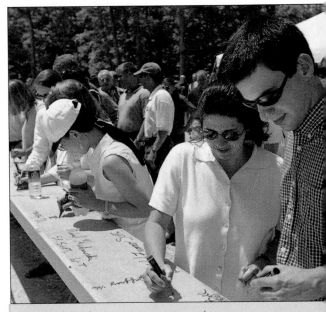

Motivated employees are one reason why Capital One is so successful. In this photo, Dawna DePollo (right) and another Capital One employee are signing their names to the last steel beam on the credit card firm's new building in Richmond, Virginia.
(© Joe Mahoney/Richmond Times Dispatch)

motivation
The forces within a person that affect his or her direction, intensity, and persistence of voluntary behavior.

content theories of motivation
Theories that explain the dynamics of employee needs, such as why people have different needs at different times.

process theories of motivation
Theories that describe the processes through which needs are translated into behavior.

needs
Deficiencies that energize or trigger behaviors to satisfy those needs.

apital One employees are high performers partly because the company has found ways to keep everyone motivated. **Motivation** refers to the forces within a person that affect his or her direction, intensity, and persistence of voluntary behavior.[2] Motivated employees are willing to exert a particular level of effort (intensity), for a certain amount of time (persistence), toward a particular goal (direction). Even when people have clear work objectives, the right skills, and a supportive work environment, they must have sufficient motivation to achieve work objectives.

Most employers (92 percent of them, according to one recent survey) agree that motivating employees has become more challenging.[3] One reason is that many firms have dramatically changed the jobs that people perform, reducing layers of hierarchy, and jettisoned large numbers of employees throughout the process. These actions have significantly damaged the levels of trust and commitment necessary for employees to put out effort beyond the minimum requirements.[4] Some organizations have completely given up on motivation from the heart and, instead, rely on pay-for-performance approaches and layoff threats. These strategies may have some effect (both positive and negative), but they do not capitalize on the employee's motivational potential.

A second problem is that as companies flatten their hierarchies to reduce costs, they can no longer rely on supervisors to practice the old command-and-control methods of motivating employees. This is probably just as well, because direct supervision is incompatible with the values of today's educated workforce. Still, many businesses have not discovered other ways to motivate employees.

Lastly, employee needs are changing. Younger generations of employees are bringing different expectations to the workplace than their baby boomer counterparts.[5] Workforce diversity and globalization have added to this complexity because diverse employees typically have diverse values. Recall from the previous chapter that values represent stable, long-lasting beliefs about what is important in a variety of situations.[6] These values influence what we want, what we need, and what organizations should and should not do to fulfill those needs.

In this chapter, we look at the foundations of employee motivation. Motivation theories fall into two main categories: content theories and process theories. **Content theories of motivation** explain the dynamics of employee needs, such as why people have different needs at different times. By understanding an employee's needs, we can discover the conditions that motivate that person. **Process theories of motivation** do not directly explain how needs emerge. Instead, they describe the processes through which needs are translated into behavior. Process theories of motivation help explain why people behave the way they do. In doing so, they help us understand, predict, and influence employee performance, attendance, work satisfaction, and other outcomes.

CONTENT THEORIES OF MOTIVATION

Most contemporary theories recognize that motivation begins with individual needs. **Needs** are deficiencies that energize or trigger behaviors to satisfy those needs. At some point in your life, you might have a strong need for food and shelter. At other times, your social needs may be unfulfilled. Unfulfilled needs create a tension that makes you want to find ways to reduce or satisfy those needs. The stronger your needs, the more motivated you are to satisfy them. Conversely, a satisfied need does not motivate.[7] In this section, we will look at the four content theories of motivation that dominate organizational thinking today.

Maslow's Needs Hierarchy Theory

One of the earliest and best-known content theories is **needs hierarchy theory.** Developed by psychologist Abraham Maslow, this theory condenses the numerous needs that scholars have identified into a hierarchy of five basic categories.[8] At the bottom are *physiological needs*, which include the need to

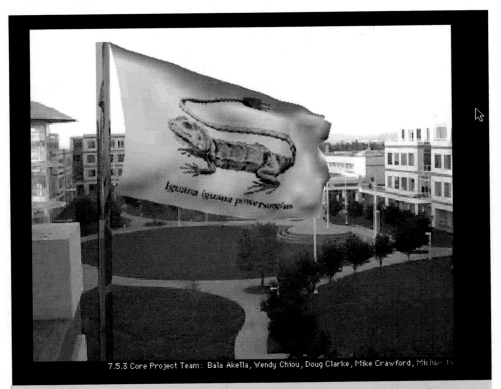

7.5.3 Core Project Team: Bala Akella, Wendy Chiou, Doug Clarke, Mike Crawford, Mich...

Computer programmers like a good paycheck, but they love the recognition found in Easter eggs. Easter eggs are nuggets of graphical graffiti left behind by programmers in most software programs. Click in the right place or type in a special command, and a special message or image will appear. Some Easter eggs are inspired by individual programmers who gain respect by cleverly sneaking them by the quality inspectors. Other Easter eggs are created by the entire development team to fulfill their need for public recognition. For example, this hidden image of Apple Computer's headquarters, complete with a flag that waves in the direction of the user's mouse, scrolls the names of the team that developed the operating system. Software engineers have also introduced Easter eggs in some DVD-formatted movies. What needs are fulfilled when software engineers secretly insert Easter eggs into their programs?[9]

satisfy biological requirements for food, air, water, and shelter. Next come *safety needs*—the need for a secure and stable environment and the absence of pain, threat, or illness. *Belongingness* includes the need for love, affection, and interaction with other people. *Esteem* includes self-esteem through personal achievement as well as social esteem through recognition and respect from others. At the top of the hierarchy is *self-actualization*, which represents the need for self-fulfillment—a sense that the person's potential has been realized.

Maslow recognized that an employee's behavior is motivated simultaneously by several need levels, but behavior is motivated mostly by the lowest unsatisfied need at the time. As the person satisfies a lower-level need, the next higher need in the hierarchy becomes the primary motivator. This concept is known as the **satisfaction-progression process.** Even if a person is unable to satisfy a higher need, he or she will be motivated by it until it is eventually satisfied. Physiological needs are initially the most important, and people are motivated to satisfy them first. As they become gratified, safety needs emerge as the strongest motivator. As safety needs are satisfied, belongingness needs become most important, and so forth. The exception to the satisfaction-progression process is self-actualization; as people experience self-actualization, they desire more rather than less of this need.

Although Maslow's needs hierarchy is one of the best-known organizational behavior theories, the model is much too rigid to explain the dynamic and unstable characteristics of employee needs.[10] Researchers have found that individual needs do not cluster neatly around the five categories described in the model. Moreover, gratification of one need level does not necessarily lead to increased motivation to satisfy the next higher need level. Although Maslow's model may not predict employee needs as well as scholars initially expected, it provides an important introduction to employee needs and has laid the foundation for Alderfer's ERG theory, which has better research support.

Alderfer's ERG Theory

ERG theory was developed by organizational behavior scholar Clayton Alderfer to overcome the problems with Maslow's needs hierarchy theory.[11] ERG theory groups human needs into three broad categories: existence, relatedness, and growth. (Notice that the theory's name is based on the first letter of each need.) As Exhibit 5.1 illustrates, existence needs correspond to Maslow's physiological and safety needs. Relatedness needs refer mainly to Maslow's belongingness needs. Growth needs correspond to Maslow's esteem and self-actualization needs.

Existence needs include a person's physiological and physically related safety needs, such as the need for food, shelter, and safe working conditions. **Relatedness needs** include a person's need to interact with other people, receive public recognition, and feel secure around people (i.e., interpersonal safety). **Growth needs** consist of a person's self-esteem through personal achievement as well as the concept of self-actualization presented in Maslow's model.

ERG theory states that an employee's behavior is motivated simultaneously by more than one need level. Thus, you might try to satisfy your growth needs (such as by completing an assignment exceptionally well) even though your relatedness needs aren't completely satisfied. ERG theory applies the satisfaction-progression process described in Maslow's needs hierarchy model,

satisfaction-progression process
A process whereby people become increasingly motivated to fulfill a higher need as a lower need is gratified.

ERG theory
Alderfer's content motivation theory of three instinctive needs arranged in a hierarchy, in which people progress to the next higher need when a lower one is fulfilled, and regress to a lower need if unable to fulfill a higher one.

existence needs
A person's physiological and physically related safety needs, such as the need for food, shelter, and safe working conditions.

relatedness needs
A person's need to interact with other people, receive public recognition, and feel secure around people.

growth needs
A person's self-esteem through personal achievement as well as the concept of self-actualization.

EXHIBIT 5.1   Content theories of motivation compared

so one need level will dominate a person's motivation more than others. As existence needs are satisfied, for example, related needs become more important.

Unlike Maslow's model, however, ERG theory includes a **frustration-regression process** whereby those who are unable to satisfy a higher need become frustrated and regress to the next lower need level. For example, if existence and relatedness needs have been satisfied, but growth need fulfillment has been blocked, the individual will become frustrated and relatedness needs will again emerge as the dominant source of motivation.

Although not fully tested, ERG theory seems to explain the dynamics of human needs in organizations reasonably well.[12] It provides a less rigid explanation of employee needs than Maslow's hierarchy. Human needs cluster more neatly around the three categories proposed by Alderfer than the five categories in Maslow's hierarchy. The combined processes of satisfaction-progression and frustration-regression also provide a more accurate explanation of why employee needs change over time. Overall, it seems to come closest to explaining why employees have particular needs at various times.

Herzberg's Motivator–Hygiene Theory

Motivator–hygiene theory differs from Maslow's and Alderfer's needs hierarchy models because it does not suggest that people change their needs over time. Developed by OB scholar Frederick Herzberg, this theory proposes that employees are motivated primarily by growth and esteem needs, such as recognition, responsibility, advancement, achievement, and personal growth,

frustration-regression process
A process whereby a person who is unable to satisfy a higher need becomes frustrated and regresses back to the next lower need level.

motivator–hygiene theory
Herzberg's theory stating that employees are primarily motivated by growth and esteem needs, not by lower-level needs.

These factors are called *motivators* because employees experience job satisfaction when the factors are received and are therefore motivated to obtain them. Job satisfaction represents a person's evaluation of his or her job and work context (see Chapter 2).[13] In contrast, factors extrinsic to the work, called *hygienes*, affect the extent to which employees feel job dissatisfaction. Hygienes include job security, working conditions, company policies, coworker relations, and supervisor relations. Improving hygienes will reduce job dissatisfaction, but hygienes will have almost no effect on job satisfaction or employee motivation.[14]

A unique characteristic of motivator–hygiene theory is that it does not view job satisfaction and dissatisfaction as opposites. Improving motivators increases job satisfaction, but it does not decrease job dissatisfaction. Improving hygienes reduces job dissatisfaction, but it does not increase job satisfaction. Job satisfaction is produced by growth fulfillment and other work content outcomes, whereas job dissatisfaction is produced by the work context. Thus, Herzberg's theory differs from Maslow's and Alderfer's hierarchy models by suggesting that growth needs represent the only source of motivation.

Limitations of Motivator–Hygiene Theory   Motivator–hygiene theory offers a unique perspective of employee motivation, but many scholars have concluded that Herzberg's findings are mainly the result of problems with the methodology he used. Other studies have subsequently reported that employees are motivated by more than the job itself. In other words, hygiene factors are widely used to motivate people to join the organization, attend work on time, perform their jobs better, and learn new skills. Financial rewards are also potentially powerful motivators, even though Herzberg saw them mainly as hygienes.[15]

Many high-technology firms have found that younger recruits are motivated as much by a "cool" work environment as by the work they will perform. The work must be interesting, but so should the workplace. That's why, even when the economy turns sour, many organizations continue to provide game rooms, free pizza, and plenty of opportunity to customize the work space.[16] This trend isn't limited to the United States. Entellium, a software firm in Kuala Lumpur, Malaysia, tries to motivate employees with a reception area that looks more like a café. "It's very comfortable and we find the productivity level very high in here," explains Entellium CEO Paul Johnston. "We have basically designed the office to get the best out of our staff."[17]

So why mention Herzberg's theory here? Motivator–hygiene theory casts a spotlight on job content as a dominant source of employee motivation. Before Herzberg's work was published, many researchers were preoccupied with the physical and social context of work. Few writers had addressed the idea that employees may be motivated by the work itself. Motivator–hygiene theory changed this view and has led to considerable study into the motivational potential of jobs.[18] We will look more closely at the motivational aspects of job design in Chapter 6.

McClelland's Theory of Learned Needs

The content motivation models described so far look at the individual's primary or instinctive needs and their relative importance in life. However, people also have secondary needs or drives that are learned and reinforced through childhood learning, parental styles, and social norms. Several learned needs can motivate us at the same time. Psychologist David McClelland devoted his career to studying three secondary needs that he considered particularly important sources of motivation: need for achievement, need for affiliation, and need for power.

need for achievement (nAch)

A learned need in which people want to accomplish reasonably challenging goals through their own efforts, like to be successful in competitive situations, and desire unambiguous feedback regarding their success.

Need for Achievement   The most widely studied learned need is **need for achievement (nAch).** People with a high nAch want to accomplish reasonably challenging goals through their own efforts. They prefer working alone rather than in teams and choose tasks with a moderate degree of risk (i.e., neither too easy nor impossible to complete). High nAch people also desire unambiguous feedback and recognition for their success.[19] Money is a weak motivator, except when it provides feedback and recognition. In contrast, employees with a low nAch have higher motivation when money is used as a financial incentive.

Successful entrepreneurs tend to have a high nAch, possibly because they establish challenging goals for themselves and thrive on competition.[20] Corporate and team leaders should have a somewhat lower nAch because they must delegate work and build support through involvement (characteristics not usually found in high achievers). However, high nAch people may perform well in large companies where they are given considerable independence—as though they are running their own business.[21] Capital One, the financial

Pamela Grof is a successful entrepreneur with a strong need for achievement. Starting at the age of 12, Grof built a series of businesses in Calgary, Canada—ranging from house cleaning to art sales—before launching InterVisual, a Web design firm. InterVisual quickly developed a blue-chip client list and has expanded into other parts of North America. Where did Grof develop her strong need for achievement? "I come from an entrepreneurial family," Grof explains. "I have two brothers and my father who are all in business for themselves. I very much have that business side within me."[22] If need for achievement is learned, how might this need be developed later in life? (*Keith Morison, The Calgary Herald*)

Creating a Company of Entrepreneurs

Matsushita Electric Industrial Company is trying to create a company of entrepreneurs. The Japanese electronics manufacturer, which is best known for its Panasonic and National brand names, is setting up an internal venture capital fund that will provide financial support to employees with creative ideas. "We would be searching for entrepreneurs internally and will venture to create new business areas or develop new business models," says Matsushita president Kunio Nakamura.

Matsushita is not alone in its effort to encourage entrepreneurial spirit within the organization. Seventy percent of the 900 board-level executives recently surveyed in 22 countries say that entrepreneurship is very important to the success of their organization. "Our entrepreneurship has fueled our economic growth over the past years," says Jens Beier, co-CEO and co-founder of the German company IMPRESS.

Companies want more entrepreneurial employees because of their drive to succeed, willingness to take risks, and ability to generate creative ideas. "Entrepreneurship is having an urge towards improvement and having a drive to act within a limited time scale," says

Cor Boonstra, CEO of the Dutch electronics company Philips. The problem, according to the survey, is that few executives think they have an entrepreneurial workforce. On the contrary, one executive in the study suggested that "many organizations and managers beat the entrepreneurial spirit out of employees."

Maintaining an entrepreneurial workforce is also a concern at Accenture, the Chicago-based consulting firm that conducted the survey. "This is a big issue for us," explains Vernon Ellis, Accenture's international chairman in London. "Accenture is founded on entrepreneurial spirit, but now that we have over 75,000 staff, there is a danger that our sheer size and complexity could stifle this."

According to the Accenture report, leaders can create a company of entrepreneurs by clarifying the firm's purpose and shared values, supporting and reinforcing entrepreneurial behavior, and creating small businesses within the larger organization (as Matsushita is doing with its venture capital fund).

Sources: V. Ellis, "Now We All Need to Be Entrepreneurs," *Times of London*, August 22, 2001; Accenture, *Liberating the Entrepreneurial Spirit* (London: Accenture, August 2001); "Matsushita Electric Sets Up 86 Million Dollar Fund for Employees' Ideas," *Agence France-Presse*, January 11, 2001.

---

services company described at the beginning of this chapter, is eager to maintain an entrepreneurial workforce. Global Connections 5.1 reports on how corporate leaders in most countries also want a company of entrepreneurs because of their high need for achievement, willingness to take risks, and ability to provide creative ideas.

One of the most fascinating streams of research has been the effect of nAch on the economic growth and decline of civilizations. One study measured nAch from stories in children's primary-school readers and found that high nAch scores were associated with economic growth in those countries over the next 20 years. Another study that estimated nAch from popular literature in Europe between 1400 and 1830 found that a rise in nAch preceded economic growth by as much as 50 years. A third study reported that nAch (as measured by fourth-grade readers) predicted the number of patents recorded in the United States between 1800 and 1950.[23] Overall, there is convincing evidence that need for achievement is learned, and that this need has a powerful influence on the success of organizations and societies.

Need for Affiliation **Need for affiliation (nAff)** refers to a desire to seek approval from others, conform to their wishes and expectations, and avoid conflict and confrontation. People with a strong nAff want to form positive relationships with others. They try to project a favorable image of themselves and take other steps to be liked by others. Moreover, high nAff employees

need for affiliation (nAff)
A learned need in which people seek approval from others, conform to their wishes and expectations, and avoid conflict and confrontation.

actively support others and try to smooth out conflicts that occur in meetings and other social settings. As Exhibit 5.1 (p. 135) illustrates, need for affiliation is similar to Maslow's belongingness need and Alderfer's relatedness need. The main difference is that need for affiliation is learned rather than instinctive.

High nAff employees tend to be more effective than those with a low nAff in coordinating roles, such as helping diverse departments work on joint projects. They are also more effective in sales positions where the main task is cultivating long-term relations with prospective customers. In general, employees with a high nAff prefer working with others rather than alone, tend to have better attendance records, and tend to be better at mediating conflicts.

Although people with a high nAff are more effective in many jobs requiring social interaction, they tend to be less effective at allocating scarce resources and making other decisions that potentially generate conflict. For example, research has found that executives with a high nAff tend to be indecisive and are perceived as less fair in the distribution of resources. Thus, people in these decision-making positions must have a relatively low need for affiliation so that their choices and actions are not biased by a personal need for approval.[24]

need for power (nPow)

A learned need in which people want to control their environment, including people and material resources, to benefit either themselves (personalized power) or others (socialized power).

Need for Power **Need for power (nPow)** refers to a desire to control one's environment, including people and material resources. People with a high nPow want to exercise control over others and are concerned about maintaining their leadership position. They frequently rely on persuasive communication (see Chapter 12), make more suggestions in meetings, and tend to publicly evaluate situations more frequently. Some people have a high need for *personalized power*. They enjoy their power for its own sake and use it to advance their career and other personal interests. It is a symbol of status and a tool to fulfill personal needs more than a delicate instrument to serve stakeholders. Others mainly have a high need for *socialized power*. They want power as a means to help others, such as by improving society or increasing organizational effectiveness.[25]

Corporate and political leaders have a high nPow that motivates them to influence others—an important part of the leadership process (see Chapter 14).[26] However, McClelland argues that effective leaders should have a high need for socialized rather than personalized power. They should have a high degree of altruism and social responsibility and be concerned about the consequences of their own actions on others. In other words, leaders should exercise their power within the framework of moral standards. The ethical guidance of their need for power develops follower trust and respect for the leader, as well as commitment to the leader's vision.[27]

Learning Needs McClelland argued that achievement, affiliation, and power needs are learned rather than instinctive. Accordingly, he developed training programs that strengthen these needs. In his achievement motivation program, trainees practice writing achievement-oriented stories after reading others and practice achievement-oriented behaviors in business games. They also complete a detailed achievement plan for the next two years and form a reference group with other trainees to maintain their newfound achievement motive style.[28]

These programs seem to work. For example, participants attending a need-for-achievement course in India subsequently started more new businesses,

Killing Motivation with Awards and Recognition

Business is booming in the awards and recognition industry. It seems that everyone is receiving something for her or his job performance. A wastewater treatment plant in Playa del Rey, California, received a shiny new plaque from the American Public Works Association for its "Sludge Out to Full Secondary" project. "We had people thanking their parents," admits the assistant director of the city's bureau of sanitation.

As you might expect, the Awards and Recognition Association (ARA) also dishes out plenty of awards at its annual conference. The top prize is the highly coveted acrylic obelisk for Best New Trophy and Best New Plaque. "It's a big, big, big deal," said the ARA's executive director.

Many organizations continue this award theme in the workplace. There are watches for employees with 25 years of service, plaques for those who avoid an accident, and special dinner ceremonies for those who haven't missed a day of work over the past decade. One publisher even has an "Attaboy" award for the editor who cancels a book that never seems to get written.

But in the midst of this awards hoopla, some corporate leaders have awarded employees with trinkets that don't have much value. Executives at one British firm asked staff to select co-workers for the employee-of-the-month award. Everyone thought that the incentive was so tacky that they chose the worst employees for the award. "The company was surprised at the choices," explains a consultant familiar with the case, "but it didn't dawn on them what was going on."

Companies are handing out plenty of awards and recognition, but how many of these awards actually motivate employees? *(Courtesy of Awards and Recognition Association)*

Barbara Moses also shakes her head at some of the half-baked awards employers have come up with to motivate staff. The workplace consultant recalls particularly a company that awarded a few select employees with alarm clocks embossed with the company's logo. "It completely turned them off," says Moses. "People were saying: 'I work for them, I don't want to wake up to them.'"

Sources: "15 Minutes of Fame—Every 10 Seconds," *Los Angeles Times*, March 20, 2001, p. E1; D. Hawaleshka, "The Power in the Perks," *Maclean's*, May 31, 1999, p. 24; H. Syedain, "The Rewards of Recognition," *Management Today*, May 1995, pp. 72–74.

had greater community involvement, invested more in expanding their businesses, and employed twice as many people as nonparticipants. Research on similar achievement motivation courses for North American small-business owners reported dramatic increases in the profitability of the participants' businesses.

Practical Implications of Content Motivation Theories

Content theories of motivation offer several recommendations. First, corporate leaders need to be sure that rewards fulfill needs. Otherwise, the rewards have little value and, in some cases, employees might try to avoid them. Connections 5.2 describes how companies and industries distribute a wide variety of awards. However, some of these programs backfire because no one looked closely enough to determine whether the recognition was valued by recipients.

Content theories of motivation suggest that different people have different needs at different times. Some employees are ready to fulfill growth needs, whereas others are still struggling to satisfy their minimum existence needs. Needs also change as people enter new stages of their life, so rewards that motivated people at one time may have less motivational value in later years. The second recommendation, then, is to offer employees a choice of rewards. Nortel Networks follows this advice when rewarding length of service. At each five-year service level, employees at the telecommunications company are offered a choice of rewards, including fine art and sculptures, jewelry, timepieces, luggage, and leather portfolios.

Third, content theories of motivation warn against relying too heavily on financial rewards as a source of employee motivation.[29] Although money does motivate employees to some extent, there are potentially more powerful sources of motivation, such as challenging assignments, learning opportunities, and praise from colleagues and corporate leaders.

Content Motivation Theories across Cultures   Are content motivation theories culture-bound? A few scholars think so. They argue that these theories of motivation were developed and tested in North America, so they don't readily apply in cultures with different values.[30] However, some of this criticism has focused on Maslow's needs hierarchy theory, which was rejected by organizational behavior theorists long ago. Thus, it doesn't make sense to complain about the cross-cultural relevance of a theory that doesn't work in the country where it was developed!

Another criticism has been that people in different cultures have different needs. The question is whether these cultural values interfere with the general pattern of developing and fulfilling needs as stated in ERG theory. We don't have much information on this issue, although a few studies have generally found that feelings of achievement and interesting work are the two most important motivating factors in several cultures (e.g., China, Germany, the United States). McClelland's learned needs theory also seems to apply across cultures because much of the work occurred in Europe and India, not just the United States. More recently, scholars have reported that the conceptual structure of need for achievement is consistent across several different cultures, suggesting that its meaning is relevant in other societies.[31] Overall, it is not clear (at least, not as clear as the critics believe) that content motivation theories are culture-bound.

PROCESS THEORIES OF MOTIVATION

expectancy theory
The process motivation theory based on the idea that work effort is directed toward behaviors that people believe will lead to desired outcomes.

At the beginning of this chapter, we distinguished the content theories presented above from process theories of motivation. Content theories explain why people have different needs at different times, whereas process theories describe the processes through which need deficiencies are translated into behavior. Three of the most popular process theories of motivation are expectancy theory, equity theory, and goal setting.

Expectancy Theory of Motivation

Expectancy theory is a process motivation theory based on the idea that work effort is directed toward behaviors that people believe will lead to desired outcomes.[32] Through experience, we develop expectations about whether

EXHIBIT 5.2

Expectancy theory
of motivation

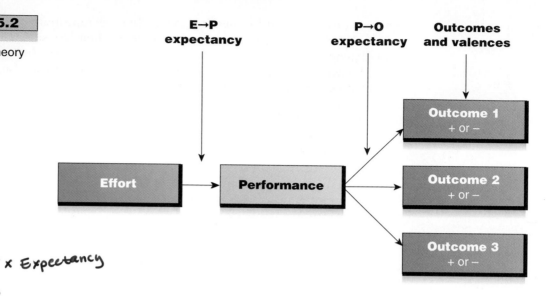

$$\underset{\text{Motivation}}{M} = \underset{\text{Instrumentality}}{I} \times \underset{\text{Valence}}{V} \times Expectancy$$

we can achieve various levels of job performance. We also develop expectations about whether job performance and work behaviors lead to particular outcomes. Finally, we naturally direct our effort toward outcomes that help us fulfill our needs.

Expectancy Theory Model   The expectancy theory model is presented in Exhibit 5.2. The key variable of interest in expectancy theory is *effort*—the individual's actual exertion of energy. An individual's effort level depends on three factors: effort-to-performance (E→P) expectancy, performance-to-outcome (P→O) expectancy, and outcome valences (V). Employee motivation is influenced by all three components of the expectancy theory model. If any component weakens, motivation weakens.

E→P expectancy   The **effort-to-performance (E→P) expectancy** is the individual's perceived probability that his or her effort will result in a particular level of performance. Expectancy is defined as a *probability*, and therefore ranges from 0.0 to 1.0. In some situations, employees may believe unquestionably that they can accomplish the task (a probability of 1.0). In other situations, they expect that even their highest level of effort will not result in the desired performance level (a probability of 0.0). For instance, unless you are an expert skier, you probably aren't motivated to try some of the black diamond ski runs at Vail, Colorado. The reason is a very low E→P expectancy. Even your best effort won't get you down the hill successfully! In most cases, the E→P expectancy falls somewhere between the two extremes.

P→O expectancy   The **performance-to-outcome (P→O) expectancy** is the perceived probability that a specific behavior or performance level will lead to specific outcomes. This probability is developed from previous learning. For example, students learn from experience that skipping class either ruins their chances of receiving a good grade or has no effect at all. In extreme cases, employees may believe that accomplishing a particular task (performance) will *definitely* result in a particular outcome (a probability of 1.0), or they may be-

effort-to-performance (E→P) expectancy
The individual's perceived probability that his or her effort will result in a particular level of performance.

performance-to-outcome (P→O) expectancy
The perceived probability that a specific behavior or performance level will lead to specific outcomes.

lieve that successful performance will have *no effect* on the outcome (a probability of 0.0). More often, the P→O expectancy falls somewhere between the two extremes.

One important issue in P→O expectancies is which outcomes we think about. We certainly don't evaluate the P→O expectancy for every possible outcome. There are too many of them. Instead, we think only about outcomes of interest to us at the time. One day, your motivation to complete a task may be fueled mainly by the likelihood of getting off work early to meet friends. Other times, your motivation to complete the same task may be based more on the P→O expectancy of a promotion or pay increase. The main point is that your motivation depends on the probability that a behavior or job performance level will result in outcomes that you think about.

valence

The anticipated satisfaction or dissatisfaction that an individual feels toward an outcome.

Outcome valences   The third element in expectancy theory is the **valence** of each outcome that you consider. Valence refers to the anticipated satisfaction or dissatisfaction that an individual feels toward an outcome. Valence ranges from negative to positive. (The actual range doesn't matter; it may be from −1 to +1, or from −100 to +100.) An outcome valence is determined by the strength of the person's basic needs that are associated with the outcome. Outcomes have a positive valence when they directly or indirectly satisfy our needs; they have a negative valence when they inhibit need fulfillment. If you have a strong relatedness (social) need, for example, then you would value group activities and other events that help fulfill that need. Outcomes that move you further away from fulfilling your social need—such as working alone from home—will have a strong negative valence.

Notice that some outcomes directly fulfill personal needs, whereas other outcomes indirectly fulfill those needs. You might be motivated to achieve the highest sales in your company this month because "it feels great." This is the direct outcome of growth need fulfillment. At the same time, you might want to be the top salesperson because you will be mentioned in the company magazine, thereby indirectly fulfilling your social needs.

Expectancy Theory in Practice   One of the appealing characteristics of expectancy theory is that it provides clear guidelines for increasing employee motivation by altering the person's E→P expectancies, P→O expectancies, and/or outcome valences.[33] Several practical implications of expectancy theory are listed in Exhibit 5.3 and described below.

Increasing E→P expectancies   E→P expectancies are influenced by the individual's self-efficacy. Recall from Chapter 2 that self-efficacy refers to a person's belief that he or she has the ability, motivation, and resources to complete a task successfully. People with high self-efficacy have a can-do attitude toward a specific task and, in general, toward other challenges in life. Some companies increase this can-do attitude by assuring employees that they have the necessary competencies, clear role perceptions, and favorable situational conditions to reach the desired levels of performance. This involves properly matching employees to jobs on the basis of their abilities, clearly communicating the tasks required for the job, and providing sufficient resources for them to accomplish those tasks.

Counseling and coaching also improve self-efficacy and, consequently, the employee's E→P expectancies regarding specific tasks. Similarly, because E→P

EXHIBIT 5.3   Practical applications of expectancy theory

Expectancy theory component	Objective	Applications
E→P expectancies	To increase the belief that employees are capable of performing the job successful	• Select people with the required skills and knowledge. • Provide required training and clarify job requirements. • Provide sufficient time and resources. • Assign simpler or fewer tasks until employees can master them (shaping). • Provide examples of similar employees who have successfully performed the task. • Provide counseling and coaching to employees who lack self-confidence.
P→O expectancies	To increase the belief that good performance will result in certain (valued) outcomes	• Measure job performance accurately. • Clearly explain the outcomes that will result from successful performance. • Describe how the employee's rewards were based on past performance. • Provide examples of other employees whose good performance has resulted in higher rewards.
Valences of outcomes	To increase the expected value of outcomes resulting from desired performance	• Distribute rewards that employees value. • Individualize rewards. • Minimize the presence of countervalent outcomes.

expectancies are learned, positive feedback typically strengthens employee self-efficacy.[34] Behavior modification and behavioral modeling also tend to increase E→P expectancies in many situations. Finally, some companies involve employees in extreme team-building activities to build their general self-confidence. For example, EMC puts its sales agents through fire-walking sessions. After daring to walk across hot coals, salespeople seem to feel more confident about calling on CEOs rather than meeting with lower-level clients.[35]

Increasing P→O expectancies   The most obvious ways to improve P→O expectancies are to measure employee performance accurately and distribute more valued rewards to those with higher job performance. Many organizations have difficulty putting this straightforward idea into practice. Some executives are reluctant to withhold rewards for poor performance because they don't want to experience conflict with employees. Others don't measure employee performance very well. Chapter 6 looks at reasons rewards aren't connected to job performance.

P→O expectancies are perceptions, so employees should *believe* that higher performance will result in higher rewards. Having a performance-based reward system is important, but this fact must be communicated. When rewards are distributed, employees should understand how their rewards have been based on past performance. In general, companies need to regularly

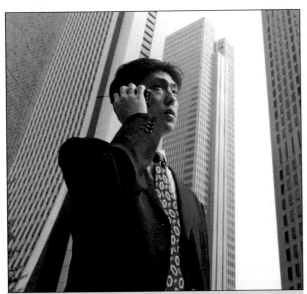

Since World War II, most Japanese employees have enjoyed lifetime employment and seniority-based pay increases. Now, some Japanese firms are questioning whether this traditional employment arrangement sufficiently motivates employees. During Japan's recent economic recession, NEC, Fujitsu, and other companies introduced performance-based incentives for most employees. "The times of endless growth are over, and so are the lifetime employment and seniority wage systems that took growth for granted," says an executive at Toyota Motor Company.[37] On the basis of expectancy theory, do you think that performance-based pay will motivate Japanese employees more or less than the system of lifetime job security and seniority-based pay? (© Daisuke Morita/PhotoDisc)

communicate the existence of a performance-based reward system through examples, anecdotes, and public ceremonies.

Increasing outcome valences Performance outcomes influence work effort only when they are valued by employees.[36] This issue brings us back to what we learned from the content theories of motivation, namely, that companies must pay attention to the needs and reward preferences of individual employees. They should develop more individualized reward systems so that employees who perform well are offered a choice of rewards.

Expectancy theory also emphasizes the need to discover and neutralize countervalent outcomes. These are performance outcomes that have negative valences, thereby reducing the effectiveness of existing reward systems. For example, peer pressure may cause some employees to perform their jobs at the minimum standard even though formal rewards and the job itself would otherwise motivate them to perform at higher levels.

Does Expectancy Theory Fit Reality? Expectancy theory has been a difficult model to test because it must recognize almost every possible performance level and outcome that employees could imagine. Most of the early studies also suffered from measurement and research design problems.[38] Critics have suggested that expectancy theory is culture-bound.[39] Some argue that the theory makes Western-oriented assumptions that employees have strong feelings of personal control. Others claim that expectancy theory applies to individual motivation and, consequently, doesn't work in cultures where people place a higher value on group membership.

In reality, expectancy theory requires neither of the conditions cited as being culture-specific. First, expectancy theory does not assume that people feel complete control over their lives; on the contrary, the E→P expectancy varies directly with the employee's perceived control over the work situation. Second, expectancy theory applies to team and organizational outcomes, not just individual performance. Research indicates that expectancy theory predicts employee motivation in different cultures.[40]

Overall, expectancy theory offers one of the best models available for predicting work effort and motivation. For example, expectancy theory predicts a person's motivation to use a decision support system, leave the organization, and work with less effort in a group setting.[41] All three components of the model have received some research support. There is particularly good evidence that P→O expectancies influence employee motivation.

Equity Theory

Tracy Jones worked through a temporary employment agency in Milwaukee preparing furniture and appliances for shipping. One day, Jones overheard her male co-workers chatting about what good pay they were getting for such easy work. When she asked them what they made, Jones was shocked to learn that the men, who came from the same temp agency, were paid $1.12 an hour more than she was. The agency denied that they paid Jones less, but pay stubs provided by some male co-workers clearly showed otherwise. Jones, the only woman in the group, received lower pay than the men, even though they performed similar work and had no more seniority. This unfair situation motivated Jones to file a pay discrimination complaint with the Equal Employment Opportunity Commission (EEOC).

This recent incident illustrates the dynamics of equity theory in the workplace. Tracy Jones felt an emotional tension created by feelings of inequity, which motivated her to act on those emotions. **Equity theory** explains how people develop perceptions of fairness in the distribution and exchange of resources. As a process theory of motivation, it explains what employees are motivated to do when they feel inequitably treated. For instance, perceived inequities motivated Tracy Jones to correct the inequity by speaking with the temp agency and, when that failed, to file a complaint with the EEOC. Let's look more closely at the four main elements of equity theory: outcome/input ratio, comparison other, equity evaluation, and consequences of inequity.[42]

equity theory
Theory that explains how people develop perceptions of fairness in the distribution and exchange of resources.

Outcome/Input Ratio   The outcome/input ratio is the value of the outcomes you receive divided by the value of inputs you provide in the exchange relationship. Inputs include skills, effort, experience, amount of time worked, performance results, and other employee contributions to the organization. Employees see their inputs as investments into the exchange relationship. For Tracy Jones, these inputs probably included seniority, work effort, and hours of work. Outcomes are the things employees receive from the organization in exchange for the inputs, such as pay, promotions, recognition, or an office with a window. Employees receive many outcomes, so it isn't always easy to determine the overall values. In the case involving Tracy Jones, the main outcome is the paycheck.

Both inputs and outcomes are weighted by their importance to the individual. These weights vary from one person to the next. To some people, seniority is a valuable input that deserves more outcomes from the organization in return. Others consider job effort and performance the most important contributions in the exchange relationship, and give seniority relatively little weight. Similarly, equity theory recognizes that people value outcomes differently because they have different needs. For example, it accepts that some employees want time off with pay, whereas others consider this a relatively insignificant reward for job performance.

Comparison Other   Equity theory states that we compare our situation with that of a comparison other.[43] However, the theory does not identify the comparison other. It may be another person, a group of people, or even yourself in the past. It may be someone in the same job, another job, or another organization. Like Tracy Jones, we tend to compare ourselves with others who are nearby, are in similar positions, and have similar backgrounds.[44] This tendency probably occurs because it is easier to get information about co-workers than from people working elsewhere.

People in senior positions compare themselves more with their counterparts in other organizations. Chief executives have no direct comparison within the firm, so they tend to compare themselves with other CEOs. Some research suggests that employees frequently collect information on several referents to form a generalized comparison other.[45] For the most part, however, the comparison other varies from one person to the next and is not easily identifiable.

Equity Evaluation   We form an equity evaluation after determining our own outcome/input ratio and comparing it with the comparison other's ratio. Let's consider the incident involving Tracy Jones again. Jones felt *underreward inequity* because she discovered that male co-workers received higher outcomes (pay) for inputs that were probably identical to hers. This condition is illustrated in Exhibit 5.4 (a).

In the *equity condition*, Jones would believe that her outcome/input ratio is similar to that of her male co-workers. This situation would occur if the male co-workers received the same pay as Jones for the same amount of effort and/or seniority—the condition depicted in Exhibit 5.4 (b). Feelings of equity would also occur if the male co-workers were paid more than Jones but had higher seniority or performed more difficult tasks.

Lastly, it is possible that some of the male co-workers experienced *overreward inequity,* as illustrated in Exhibit 4.3 (c), when they learned about how much more they were earning than was Tracy Jones. However, as we learn next, over-reward inequity isn't as common as underreward inequity.

The equity theory model recognizes that the individual makes more complex equity evaluations when he or she and the comparison other have different outcomes and inputs. Because the model compares outcome/ input *ratios,* not simply *amounts,* equity can occur even when the amounts of inputs and outcomes are unequal. For instance, we feel equitably treated when we work harder than the comparison other and receive proportionally higher rewards as a result.

Consequences of Inequity   People feel an uncomfortable emotional tension when they perceive inequity. If this tension is strong enough, it motivates employees to take steps to reduce the inequity. There are six possible ways to reduce feelings of inequity:[46]

■   *Changing inputs*—Underrewarded workers tend to reduce their effort and performance if the outcomes don't affect their paycheck. Overpaid workers

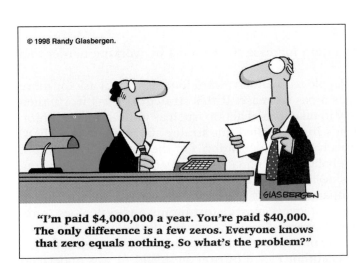

© 1998 Randy Glasbergen.

"I'm paid $4,000,000 a year. You're paid $40,000. The only difference is a few zeros. Everyone knows that zero equals nothing. So what's the problem?"

(© 1998 Randy Glasbergen. Reprinted with special permission from www.glasbergen.com)

EXHIBIT 5.4

Equity theory model

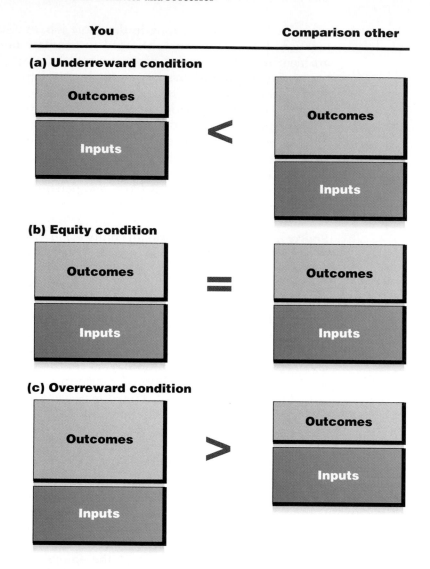

sometimes (but not very often) increase their inputs by working harder and producing more.

■ *Changing outcomes*—People with underreward inequity might ask for more desired outcomes, such as a pay increase. If this strategy doesn't work, then employees are more likely to take formal action, such as joining a labor union to demand changes.[47] Tracy Jones applied this strategy by going to the EEOC in the expectation of receiving compensation for the pay discrimination. Some employees try to rebalance the equation by misusing sick leave, using facilities for personal business, or stealing company property. At the extreme, a few people damage company property to get even with the employer.[48]

■ *Changing perceptions*—Employees may distort inputs and outcomes to restore equity feelings.[49] Overrewarded employees typically follow this strategy because it's easier to increase their perceived inputs (seniority, knowledge, etc.) than to ask for less pay. As author Pierre Burton once said: "I was underpaid for the first half of my life. I don't mind being overpaid for the second half."[50]

■ *Leaving the field*—Some people try to reduce inequity feelings by getting away from the inequitable situation. Thus, equity theory explains some instances of employee turnover and job transfer. This approach also explains why an underrewarded employee might take more time off from work even though he or she is not paid for the absenteeism.

■ *Acting on the comparison other*—Equity is sometimes restored by changing the comparison other's inputs or outcomes. If you feel overrewarded, you might encourage the referent to work at a more leisurely pace. If you feel underrewarded, you might subtly suggest that the overpaid co-worker should be doing a larger share of the workload.

■ *Changing the comparison other*—If we can't seem to alter the outcome/input ratio through other means, we might eventually replace the comparison other with someone having a more compatible outcome/input ratio. As mentioned earlier, we sometimes rely on a generalized comparison other, so feelings of inequity may be reduced fairly easily by adjusting the features of this composite referent.

The Ethics of Inequity   Inequity in the workplace isn't just about employee motivation. It also relates to the organization's ethical conduct through the distributive justice rule described in Chapter 4.[51] Recall that this principle suggests that inequality is acceptable if (1) everyone has equal access to the more favored positions in society and (2) the inequalities are ultimately in the best interest of the least well-off in society. The first part means that everyone should have equal access to higher-paying jobs and other valued positions in life. The second part says that some people can receive greater rewards than others if this situation benefits those less well-off. Employees in risky jobs should be paid more if this inequality benefits others who are less well-off.

Applying the distributive justice rule is challenging because it is difficult to determine how much the least well-off benefit from those who receive higher rewards. Consider the business jet and $200 million bonus that Steve Jobs received for turning around Apple Computer. If Jobs hadn't stepped in as CEO, Apple might be history today. Instead, it grew faster than most other computer makers. Does this make Jobs's bonus fair or unethical?[52]

People are asking similar questions about how much is a fair level of executive pay. A bankruptcy judge recently questioned the fairness of a $2 million bonus plan for executives at troubled bicycle maker Schwinn/GT. The executives had asked the judge to keep details of the bonus confidential, perhaps worried about the ethics of rewarding executives who led the firm into bankruptcy.[53] A few executives are also worried about the ethics of executive pay. "Frankly, I've been amazed, appalled and awed by the levels of compensation of a number of CEOs that have walked away with incredibly munificent packages clearly not based on performance," exclaims John N. Lauer, head of Oglebay Norton Company. Lauer works without a salary at the Cleveland-based industrial minerals and shipping firm. Instead, he receives dividends from $1 million in shares bought with his own money as well as bonuses from specific performance-based targets.[54]

Individual Differences in Equity   So far, we have described equity theory as though everyone has the same feelings of inequity in a particular situation. The reality, however, is that not everyone shares the same interpretation of fairness.

equity sensitivity
Our outcome/input preferences and reaction to various outcome/input ratios.

We vary in our **equity sensitivity**, that is, our outcome/input preferences and reaction to various outcome/input ratios.[55] At one end of the equity sensitivity continuum are the "benevolents"—people who are tolerant of situations where they are underrewarded. They might still prefer equal outcome/input ratios, but they don't mind if others receive more than they do for the same inputs. In the middle are people who fit the standard equity theory model. These "equity sensitives" want their outcome/input ratio to be equal to the outcome/input ratio of the comparison other. As the ratios become different, these people feel an uncomfortable tension. At the other end are the "entitleds." These people feel more comfortable in situations where they receive proportionately more than others. They might accept having the same outcome/input ratio as others, but they would prefer receiving more than others performing the same work.[56]

Why are some people benevolents and others entitleds? Personality is one factor. Research has found that benevolents have more of an internal locus of control whereas entitleds tend to have an external locus of control. Benevolents also have higher levels of conscientiousness and agreeableness. Cultural values seem to be another influence on equity sensitivity. One study reported that Chinese employees had more of a benevolent orientation, whereas British and French employees were more entitlement-oriented. This difference may be due to the strong collectivist and power distance values in China.[57]

Equity Theory in Practice   Equity theory has received considerable support in research and practice. Organizational behavior researchers have applied the equity theory model to explain why baseball players change teams, why employees steal from their employer, why people become hostile at work, and why employees enact numerous other behaviors.[58] One of the clearest lessons from equity theory is that we need to continually treat people fairly in the distribution of organizational rewards. If feelings of inequity are sufficiently strong, employees may put less effort into the job, leave the organization, steal resources or time (e.g., absenteeism), or join a labor union to correct these inequities.

Unfortunately, maintaining feelings of equity is not an easy task. Surveys report that about half of all employees feel underpaid.[59] One reason, as we discussed above, is that people have different levels of equity sensitivity, so they react differently to the same situation. Employees also have unique opinions regarding which inputs should be rewarded (e.g., seniority versus performance) and which outcomes are more valuable than others.[60] Overall, trying to maintain feelings of equity in the workplace will probably always be challenging.

Goal Setting

Mitel Corporation has a secret weapon to keep project deadlines on time. In the cafeteria is an enormous digital clock—7 feet long and 1 foot tall—that measures everything from tenths of a second to days in a year. Beside the clock is a whiteboard that lists interim deadlines for all major projects at the telecommunications development company. Whenever a team misses a deadline, Mitel executives put a red slash through the date for everyone to see. Employees initially complained, but the results have silenced the critics. Mitel's average length of product development time has dropped from 70 to 50 weeks.[61]

Mitel and other organizations have discovered that goal setting is one of the most effective theories of motivation in organizations.[62] **Goals** are the immediate or ultimate objectives that employees are trying to accomplish from their

goals
The immediate or ultimate objectives that employees are trying to accomplish from their work effort.

goal setting
The process of motivating employees and clarifying their role perceptions by establishing performance objectives.

work effort. **Goal setting** is the process of motivating employees and clarifying their role perceptions by establishing performance objectives. Goal setting potentially improves employee performance in two ways: (1) by stretching the intensity and persistence of effort and (2) by giving employees clearer role perceptions so that their effort is channeled toward behaviors that will improve work performance.

Some companies apply goal setting through a formal process known as **management by objectives (MBO).** There are a few variations of MBO programs, but they generally identify organizational objectives, then cascade them down to work units and individual employees. MBO also includes regular discussion of goal progress.[63] Although MBO has been criticized for creating too much paperwork, it can be an effective application of goal setting.

Characteristics of Effective Goals Goal setting is more complex than simply telling someone, "Do your best." Instead, organizational behavior scholars have identified specific conditions to maximize task effort and performance: specific goals, relevant goals, challenging goals, goal commitment, participation in goal formation (sometimes), and goal feedback.[64]

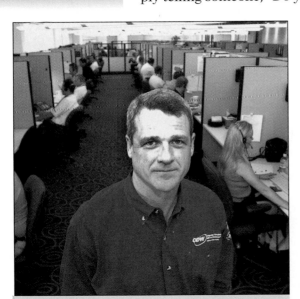

By setting specific challenging goals for its employees, CDW Computer Centers Inc. has become a leading direct marketer of computers and peripherals. "We set BHAGS—which are big, hairy, aggressive goals," says John A. Edwardson (front in photo), president and CEO of the Vernon Hills, Illinois, company. "The current BHAG is $11 million in bonuses shared with the employees of the company when we hit $7 billion in revenue." Edwardson explains that the previous stretch goal was called 5432, which referred to $5 million in bonuses for $3 billion in sales by 2000. CDW employees exceeded that goal, which nearly tripled the company's revenue from three years earlier.[66] To what extent is this goal-setting process compatible with the characteristics of effective goals? *(© Jim Robinson/Tribune)*

Specific goals Employees put more effort into a task when they work toward specific goals rather than "do your best" targets. Specific goals have measurable levels of change over a specific time, such as "reduce scrap rate by 7 percent over the next six months." Specific goals communicate more precise performance expectations, so employees can direct their effort more efficiently and reliably.

Relevant goals Goals must also be relevant to the individual's job and within his or her control. For example, a goal to reduce waste materials would have little value if employees don't have much control over waste in the production process. This goal characteristic is similar to the need for relevant feedback that we discussed in Chapter 2.

Challenging goals Employees tend to have more intense and persistent work effort when they have challenging rather than easy goals. Challenging goals also fulfill a person's need for achievement or growth needs when the goal is achieved.[65] Capital One, the financial services firm described in the opening vignette in this chapter, motivates employees by stretching their potential. This process typically occurs through stretch goals—goals that are challenging enough to stretch the employee's abilities and motivation toward peak performance. "We set stretch goals that many people thought to be impossible, and we made those goals part of our culture," explains John Chambers, chief executive

management by objectives (MBO)
A participative goal-setting process in which organizational objectives are cascaded down to work units and individual employees.

of Cisco Systems. Stretch goals are effective if employees receive the necessary resources and are not overstressed in the process.[67]

Goal commitment   Of course, there are limits to challenging goals. At some point, goals become so difficult that employees are no longer committed to achieving them. At that point, work effort falls dramatically, as we see in Exhibit 5.5. This condition is the same as the E→P expectancy that we learned about in the section on expectancy theory.[68] The lower the E→P expectancy that the goal can be accomplished, the less committed (motivated) the employee is to the goal. The optimal level of goal difficulty is the area in which the goal is challenging but employees are still committed to achieving it.[69] There is also evidence that high-self-efficacy employees are more likely to accept their goals because they believe they can choose successful strategies to reach those goals.[70] Those with low self-efficacy, on the other hand, tend to be in a panic when given a unique goal when the means to achieve that goal aren't obvious.

Participation in goal formation   Another way to build or maintain commitment to goals is to ensure that employees are involved in the goal-setting process.[71] Participation in goal formation tends to increase goal commitment because employees take ownership of the goal, a result that is less likely with goals that are merely assigned by supervisors. In fact, employees in today's workforce increasingly expect to be involved in goal setting and other decisions that affect them. Participation may also improve goal quality, because employees have valuable information and knowledge that may not be known to those who initially formed the goal. Thus, participation ensures that employees buy into the goals and have the competencies and resources necessary to accomplish them.

Goal feedback   Feedback is another necessary condition for effective goal setting. In particular, experts emphasize that effective goal setting requires measurable feedback that matches the specific metrics of the goal. As we discussed in Chapter 2, feedback is a powerful source of learning. In terms of goal setting, feedback lets us know whether we have achieved the goal or are

EXHIBIT 5.5

Effect of goal difficulty on performance

properly directing our effort toward it. Feedback is also an essential ingredient in motivation because our growth needs can't be satisfied unless we receive information on goal accomplishment.

Goal-Setting Applications and Limitations   Goal setting has a few limitations. One problem is that when goals are tied to monetary incentives, many employees tend to select easy rather than difficult goals.[72] In some cases, employees have negotiated goals with their supervisor that have already been completed! Employees with high self-efficacy and need for achievement tend to set challenging goals whether or not they are financially rewarded for their results. Nevertheless, employers should typically separate goal setting from the pay-setting process to minimize the politics of goal setting.[73]

Another limitation is that we can't apply goal setting to every performance dimension of every job. Many dimensions of job performance have difficult-to-measure, complex, and long-term performance outcomes. The result is that goal setting potentially focuses employees on a narrow subset of short-term performance indicators. The saying "What gets measured, gets done" applies here. Thus, goal setting may cause more performance problems in the long term than it solves in the short term. Aside from these concerns, goal setting is one of the tried-and-true theories in organizational behavior. It is widely supported by research and is generally successful in practice.

COMPARING MOTIVATION THEORIES

Exhibit 5.6 summarizes the central ideas behind the four content and three process theories of motivation presented in this chapter. As you can see, each

EXHIBIT 5.6   Comparing employee motivation theories

Motivation theory	Type	Central idea
Maslow's needs hierarchy	Content	People try to satisfy a higher need when a lower need is fulfilled (satisfaction-progression).
Alderfer's ERG theory	Content	Satisfaction-progression (see above); also, people focus on a lower need if unable to satisfy a higher need (frustration-regression).
Herzberg's motivator–hygiene theory	Content	Motivators (job content, recognition) motivate and satisfy, whereas hygiene factors (work relations, work environment) can create or reduce dissatisfaction but do not motivate.
McClelland's learned needs theory	Content	Some needs are learned rather than instinctive, and more than one need can motivate at the same time.
Expectancy theory	Process	Motivation is determined by perceived expectancies, outcome values, and a rational decision-making process.
Equity theory	Process	Perceived equity is formed from outcome/input ratios with a comparison other, and people are motivated to reduce perceived inequities.
Goal setting	Process	Clear, relevant goals increase motivation and performance by stretching the intensity and persistence of effort and by clarifying role perceptions.

of the process theories provides a unique perspective of employee motivation. Each looks at different variables in the workplace and the minds of employees. As for the content theories, Alderfer's ERG theory builds on Maslow's needs hierarchy theory. McClelland's learned needs theory is somewhat more distinctive because it suggests that some needs are acquired (learned) rather than instinctive.

CHAPTER SUMMARY

Work motivation refers to the forces within a person that affect his or her direction, intensity, and persistence of voluntary behavior in the workplace. As a new generation of employees enters the workplace and as globalization creates a more diverse workforce, companies need to rethink their motivational practices.

Content motivation theories explain why people have different needs at different times. Process theories of motivation describe the processes through which needs are translated into behavior.

According to Maslow's needs hierarchy theory, the lowest needs are initially most important, but higher needs become more important as the lower ones are satisfied. Alderfer's ERG theory is a content motivation theory that groups human needs into a hierarchy of three broad categories: existence, relatedness, and growth. It also suggests that those who are unable to satisfy a higher need become frustrated and regress to the next lower need level. Herzberg's motivator–hygiene theory states that people are motivated only by characteristics of the work itself, whereas hygiene factors only reduce dissatisfaction. However, evidence suggests that hygienes can motivate to some extent. McClelland's learned needs theory argues that people have secondary needs or drives that are learned rather than instinctive, including need for achievement, need for affiliation, and need for power.

One of the main implications of content motivation theories is that different people have different needs at different times. These theories also warn us against relying too heavily on financial rewards as a source of employee motivation. Although some scholars argue that content motivation theories are culture-bound, the evidence so far suggests otherwise.

Expectancy theory states that work effort is determined by the perception that effort will result in a particular level of performance (E→P expectancy), the perception that a specific behavior or performance level will lead to specific outcomes (P→O expectancy), and the valences that the person feels for those outcomes.

The E→P expectancy is increased by improving the employee's ability and confidence to perform the job. The P→O expectancy is increased by measuring performance accurately, distributing higher rewards to better performers, and showing employees that rewards are performance-based. Outcome valences are increased by finding out what employees want and using these resources as rewards.

Equity theory explains how people develop perceptions of fairness in the distribution and exchange of resources. The model includes four elements: outcome/input ratio, comparison other, equity evaluation, and consequences of inequity. The theory also explains what people are motivated to do when they feel inequitably treated. Equity theory relates to the ethical principle of distributive justice. Recent debates about the fairness of executive pay reveal that it is difficult to reach consensus on how much pay is fair. People react differently to inequitable situations on the basis of their equity sensitivity. These differences are influenced by personality and cultural values.

Goal setting is the process of motivating employees and clarifying their role perceptions by establishing benchmarks against which growth needs are fulfilled. Goals are more effective when they are specific, relevant, challenging, accepted by the employee, and accompanied by meaningful feedback. Participative goal setting is important in some situations. Goal setting is usually less effective when tied to financial rewards. It also creates the risk of focusing employees on measurable dimensions of their job to the detriment of more complex and long-term performance dimensions.

KEY TERMS

content theories of motivation, p. 132

effort-to-performance (E→P) expectancy, p. 142

equity sensitivity, p. 150

equity theory, p. 146

ERG theory, p. 134

existence needs, p. 134

expectancy theory, p. 141

frustration-regression process, p. 135

goal setting, p. 151

goals, p. 151

growth needs, p. 134

management by objectives (MBO), p. 151

motivation, p. 132

motivator–hygiene theory, p. 135

need for achievement
(nAch), p. 137

need for affiliation (nAff), p. 138

need for power (nPow), p. 139

needs, p. 132

needs hierarchy theory, p. 133

performance-to-outcome (P→O)
expectancy, p. 142

process theories of
motivation, p. 132

relatedness needs, p. 134

satisfaction-progression
process, p. 134

valence, p. 143

DISCUSSION QUESTIONS

1. This chapter begins by stating that motivating employees has never been more challenging. Do you agree with this statement? Are there any other reasons employees might be more (or less) difficult to motivate today than, say, 20 years ago?

2. Think about your personal level of needs for achievement, power, and affiliation. What factors in your past have caused you to experience high, moderate, or low levels of each? Which of these needs would you like to increase or decrease in the future?

3. As a team leader, you notice that one employee isn't putting much effort into the team project because she doesn't believe she has the ability to contribute anything valuable. Using your knowledge of expectancy theory's E→P expectancy, identify four ways that you might increase this person's motivation to contribute to the team.

4. Use all three components of expectancy theory to explain why some employees are motivated to show up for work during a heavy storm whereas others don't make any effort to leave home.

5. Several service representatives are upset that the newly hired representative with no previous experience will be paid $1,000 a year above the usual starting salary on the pay range. The department manager explained that the new hire would not accept the entry-level rate, so the company raised the offer by $1,000. All five reps currently earn salaries near the top of the scale ($10,000 higher than the recruit), although they all started at the minimum starting salary a few years earlier. Use equity theory to explain why the five service representatives feel inequity in this situation.

6. Inequity occurs in the classroom as well as in the workplace. Identify classroom situations in which you had feelings of inequity. How might instructors minimize these inequitable situations?

7. In some countries, employees believe that pay levels should be determined partly by the number of children in the employee's family. They believe that co-workers with more children need more money to support their families, so they should receive higher pay. Discuss this idea in the context of the equity theory model.

8. Cyber Cellular, Inc., wants to introduce a goal-setting program to improve motivation and performance among its 30 research and development (R&D) staff. Specifically, it wants to impose a minimum goal of two new patents per employee in the R&D unit each year, as well as specific goals that would minimize costs in that work unit. Use your knowledge of goal setting to discuss the potential problems and solutions to consider in this proposal.

CASE STUDY 5.1

THE REGENCY GRAND HOTEL

The Regency Grand Hotel, a five-star hotel in Bangkok, was established 15 years ago by a local consortium of investors and had been operated by a Thai general manager since that time. The hotel was one of Bangkok's most prestigious hotels, and its 700 employees enjoyed the prestige of being associated with the hotel. The hotel provided good employee benefits, above-market-rate salaries, and job security. In addition, a good year-end bonus amounting to four months' salary was rewarded to employees regardless of the hotel's overall performance during the year.

Recently, the Regency was sold to a large American hotel chain that was very keen to expand its operations into Thailand. When the acquisition was announced, the general manager decided to take early retirement when the hotel changed ownership. The American hotel chain kept all the Regency employees, although a few were transferred to other positions. John Becker, an American with 10 years of management experience with the hotel chain, was appointed the new general manager of the Regency Palace Hotel. Becker was selected as the new general manager because of his previous successes in integrating newly acquired hotels in the United States. In most of the previous acquisitions, Becker took over operations with poor profitability and low morale.

Becker is a strong believer in empowerment. He expects employees to go beyond guidelines and standards to consider guest needs on a case-by-case basis. That is, employees must be guest-oriented at all times so as to provide excellent customer service. From his U.S. experience, Becker had found that empowerment increases employee motivation, performance, and job satisfaction, all of which contribute to a hotel's profitability and customer service ratings. Soon after becoming general manager of the Regency Palace, Becker introduced the practice of empowerment to replicate the successes that he had achieved back home.

The Regency Grand Hotel had been very profitable since it opened 15 years ago. The employees always worked according to management's instructions. Their responsibility was to ensure that the instructions from their managers were carried out diligently and conscientiously. Innovation and creativity were discouraged under the previous management. Indeed, employees were punished for their mistakes and discouraged from trying out ideas that had not been approved by management. As a result, employees were afraid to be innovative and to take risks.

Becker met with the Regency's managers and department heads to explain that empowerment would be introduced in the hotel. He told them that employees must be empowered with decision-making authority so that they could use their initiative, creativity, and judgment to satisfy guest needs and to handle problems effectively and efficiently. However, he stressed that the more complex issues and decisions were to be referred to superiors, who were to coach and assist rather than provide direct orders. Furthermore, Becker stressed that although mistakes were allowed, making the same mistake more than twice would not be tolerated. He advised his managers and department heads not to discuss with him minor issues or problems and not to consult with him on minor decisions. Nevertheless, he told them that they were to discuss important, major issues and decisions with him. He concluded the meeting by asking for feedback. Several managers and department heads told him that they liked the idea and would support it, while others simply nodded their heads. Becker was pleased with the response and was eager to have his plan implemented.

In the past, the Regency had emphasized administrative control, resulting in many bureaucratic procedures throughout the organization. For example, the front counter employees needed to seek approval from their manager before they could upgrade guests to another category of room. The front counter manager would then have to write and submit a report to the general manager justifying the upgrade. Soon after his meeting with managers, Becker reduced the number of bureaucratic rules at the Regency and allocated more decision-making authority to frontline employees. This action upset those employees who previously had decision-making power over these issues. As a result, several of these employees left the hotel.

Becker also began spending a large portion of his time observing and interacting with the employees at the front desk, in the lobby, in the restaurants, and in various departments. This direct interaction with Becker helped many employees understand what he wanted and expected of them. However, the employees had difficulty trying to distinguish between major and minor issues and decisions. More often than not, supervisors would reverse employee decisions by stating that they were major issues requiring management approval. Employees who displayed initiative and made good decisions in satisfying the needs of the guests rarely received any positive feedback from their supervisors. Eventually, most of these employees lost confidence in making decisions and reverted to relying on their superiors for decision making.

Not long after the implementation of the practice of empowerment, Becker realized that his subordinates were consulting him more frequently than before. A majority of them came to him with minor issues and consulted with him on minor decisions. He had to spend most of his time attending to his subordinates. Soon he began to feel highly frustrated and exhausted, and very often would tell his secretary that "unless the hotel is on fire, don't let anyone disturb me."

Becker thought that the practice of empowerment would benefit the overall performance of the hotel. However, contrary to his expectation, the business and overall performance of the hotel began to deteriorate. There was an increasing number of guest complaints. In the past, the hotel had minimal guest complaints. Now there was a significant number of formal written complaints every month. Many other guests voiced their dissatisfaction verbally to hotel employees. The number of mistakes made by employees was on the increase. Becker was very upset when he realized that two local newspapers and an overseas newspaper had published negative feedback on the hotel in terms of service standards. He was most distressed when an international travel magazine voted the hotel "one of Asia's nightmare hotels."

The stress levels of the employees were continually mounting since the introduction of the practice of empowerment. Absenteeism due to illness was increasing at an alarming rate. In addition, the employee turnover rate reached an all-time high. The good working relationships that were established under the old management had been severely strained. The employees were no longer united and supportive of each other. They were quick to point fingers at or to back-stab one another when mistakes were made and when problems occurred.

Discussion Questions

1. Identify the symptoms indicating that problems exist in this case.
2. Diagnose the problems in this case using organizational behavior concepts. (Your instructor may restrict this case analysis to motivational topics or may ask you to consider other topics in this book in your analysis.)
3. Recommend solutions that overcome or minimize the problems and symptoms in this case.

Note: This case was written by Lisa Ho under the supervision of Steven L. McShane, The University of Western Australia. It is based on true events, but the industry and names have been changed.

CASE STUDY 5.2

HE POURS GAS ON THE FIRE

BusinessWeek Most people think of motivation as the condition of being all fired up—filled with enthusiasm and energy to achieve a goal. In an organization, employees who are all fired up with the company's mission will presumably work very hard, doing their jobs plus a little extra. Mark Walsh, chairman of VerticalNet, decided that his e-commerce firm "needed additional gasoline poured on the fire." So Walsh turned to a man with a gasoline-like effect, Joseph Galli Jr. Galli was already famous for stirring up enthusiasm in the successful launch of Black & Decker's line of professional-quality tools, sold under the DeWalt brand. Walsh hired Galli to perform a similar feat for VerticalNet's online business communities.

This *Business Week* case study describes what Joseph Galli Jr. has begun to do as VerticalNet's chief executive officer. It details his plans for the company, as well as earlier experiences that have shaped his style as a motivator. Read through this *Business Week* case study at www.mhhe.com/mcshane2e and prepare for the discussion questions below.

Discussion Questions

1. What needs or motivators seem to be at work in motivating Galli? In motivating his employees?
2. How has Galli applied expectancy theory in motivating his employees?
3. What role does goal setting play in motivation at VerticalNet? Do Galli's goals for VerticalNet meet the requirements of effective goals?

Source: Amy Barrett, "He Pours Gas on the Fire," *Business Week*, December 11, 2000.

BONUS DECISION MAKING

Purpose This exercise is designed to help you understand the elements of equity theory and how people differ in their equity perceptions.

Instructions Four managers in a large national insurance company are described below. The national sales director of the company has given your consulting team (first individually, then together) the task of allocating $100,000 in bonus money to these four managers. It is entirely up to your team to decide how to divide the money among these people. The only requirements are that all the money must be distributed and that no two branch managers can receive the same amount. The names and information are presented in no particular order. You should assume that economic conditions, client demographics, and other external factors are very similar for these managers.

- *Step 1*—Students will form teams of four or five people. Working alone, read the information about the four managers. Then, in the "Individual decision" column in the "Bonus allocation form," fill in the amount you would allocate to each manager.
- *Step 2*—Still working alone, fill in the "Equity inputs form." First, in the "Input factor" column, list in order of importance the factors you considered when allocating these bonus amounts (e.g., seniority, performance, age). The most important factor should be listed first and the least important last. Next, in the "Input weight" column, estimate the percentage weight that you assigned to each factor. The total of this column must add up to 100 percent.
- *Step 3*—After individually allocating the bonus money and determining the input factors and weights, team members will compare their results and note any differences. Then team members will reach a consensus on the bonus amount that each manager should receive. These amounts will be written in the "Team decision" column.
- *Step 4*—The instructor will call the class together to compare team results and note dif-

ferences in inputs and input weights used by individual students. Discussion of these results in terms of equity theory will follow.

Manager Profiles

Bob B. Bob has been in the insurance business for over 27 years and has spent the past 21 years with this company. A few years ago, Bob's branch typically made the largest contribution to regional profits. More recently, however, it has brought in few new accounts and is now well below average in terms of its contribution to the company. Turnover in the branch has been high, and Bob doesn't have the same enthusiasm for the job as he once did. Bob is 56 years old and is married with five children. Three children are still living at home. Bob has a high school diploma as well as a certificate from a special course in insurance management.

Edward E. In the two years that Edward has been a branch manager, his unit has brought in several major accounts and now stands as one of the top units in the country. Edward is well respected by his employees. At 29, he is the youngest manager in the region and one of the youngest in the country. The regional director initially doubted the wisdom of giving Edward the position of branch manager because of his relatively young age and lack of experience in the insurance industry. Edward received an undergraduate business degree from a regional college and worked for five years as a sales representative before joining this company. Edward is single and has no children.

Lee L. Lee has been with this organization for seven years. The first two years were spent as a sales representative in the office that she now manages. According to the regional director, Lee rates about average as a branch manager. She earned an undergraduate degree in geography from a major university and worked as a sales representative for four years with another insurance company before joining this organization. Lee is 40 years old, is divorced, and has no children. She is a very ambitious person but sometimes has problems working with her staff and other branch managers.

Sandy S. Sandy is 47 years old and has been a branch manager with this company for 17 years. Seven years ago, her branch made the lowest contribution to the region's profits, but the branch's profitability has steadily improved and is now slightly above average. Sandy seems to have a mediocre attitude toward her job but is well liked by her staff and other branch managers. Her experience in the insurance industry has been entirely with this organization. She previously worked in nonsales positions, and it is not clear how she became a branch manager without previous sales experience. Sandy is married and has three school-age children. Several years ago, Sandy earned a diploma in business from a nearby community college by taking evening courses.

Bonus allocation form		
Name	**Individual decision**	**Team decision**
Bob B.	$_____	$_____
Edward E.	$_____	$_____
Lee L.	$_____	$_____
Sandy S.	$_____	$_____
Totals	$100,000	$100,000

Equity inputs form	
Input factor*	**Input weight****
_____	_____%
_____	_____%
_____	_____%
_____	_____%
_____	_____%
Total	100%

*List factors in order of importance, with most important factor listed first.
**The weight of each factor is a percentage ranging from 1 to 100. All factor weights together must add up to 100 percent.

S E L F - A S S E S S M E N T   E X E R C I S E   5.4

MEASURING YOUR GROWTH NEED STRENGTH

Purpose This self-assessment exercise is designed to help you to estimate your level of growth need strength.

Instructions People differ in the kinds of jobs they would most like to hold. The descriptions and choices in the exercise give you a chance to say just what it is about a job that is most important to you. For each entry, two different kinds of jobs are briefly described. Please indicate which of the two jobs you personally would prefer if you had to make a choice between them. For each pairing, pay attention only to the characteristics listed; assume that everything else about the jobs is the same.

After circling each answer, use the scoring key in Appendix B to calculate your results for this scale. This exercise is completed alone so that students assess themselves honestly without concerns of social comparison. However, class discussion will focus on the growth need strength concept and its implications.

Growth need strength scale						
Job A	**Strongly prefer A**	**Slightly prefer A**	**Neutral**	**Slightly prefer B**	**Strongly prefer B**	**Job B**
A job where the pay	1	2	3	4	5	A job where there is considerable opportunity to be creative and innovative

—continued

Growth need strength scale (cont.)						
Job A	Strongly prefer A	Slightly prefer A	Neutral	Slightly prefer B	Strongly prefer B	Job B
A job where you are often required to make important decisions	1	2	3	4	5	A job with many pleasant people to work with
A job in which greater responsibility is given to those who do the best work	1	2	3	4	5	A job in which greater responsibility is given to loyal employees who have the most seniority
A job in a firm that is in financial trouble and might have to close down within the year	1	2	3	4	5	A job in a firm that is are not allowed to have any say whatever in how your work is scheduled or in the procedures to be used in carrying it out
A very routine job	1	2	3	4	5	A job where your co-workers are not very friendly
A job with a supervisor who is often very critical of you and your work in front of other people	1	2	3	4	5	A job that prevents you from using a number of skills that you worked hard to develop
A job with a supervisor who respects you and treats you fairly	1	2	3	4	5	A job that provides constant opportunities for you to learn new and interesting things
A job where there is a real chance you could be laid off	1	2	3	4	5	A job with very little chance to do challenging work
A job in which there is a real chance for you to develop new skills and advance in the organization	1	2	3	4	5	A job that provides lots of vacation time and an excellent benefits package
A job with little freedom and independence to do your work in the way you think best	1	2	3	4	5	A job where working conditions are poor
A job with very satisfying teamwork	1	2	3	4	5	A job that allows you to use your skills and abilities to the fullest extent
A job that offers litttle no challenge	1	2	3	4	5	A job that requires you to be completely isolated from co-workers

Source: Developed by J. R. Hackman and G. R. Oldham as part of the Job Diagnostic Survey instrument. The authors have released any copyright ownership of this scale (see J. R. Hackman and G. Oldham, *Work Redesign* [Reading, MA: Addison-Wesley, 1980], p. 275).

MEASURING YOUR EQUITY SENSITIVITY

Purpose This self-assessment exercise is designed to help you to estimate your level of equity sensitivity.

Instructions Read each statement below and circle the response that you believe best reflects your position regarding that statement. Then use the scoring key in Appendix B to calculate your results. This exercise is completed alone so that students assess themselves honestly without concerns of social comparison. However, class discussion will focus on equity theory and the effect of equity sensitivity on perceptions of fairness in the workplace.

Equity sensitivity scale					
Circle the number indicating the extent that you agree or disagree with each statement.	Strongly agree ▼	Agree ▼	Neutral ▼	Disagree ▼	Strongly disagree ▼
1. I prefer to do as little as possible at work while getting as much as I can from my employer.	1	2	3	4	5
2. I am most satisfied at work when I have to do as little as possible.	1	2	3	4	5
3. When I am at my job, I think of ways to get out of work.	1	2	3	4	5
4. If I could get away with it, I would try to work just a little bit slower than the boss expects.	1	2	3	4	5
5. It is really satisfying to me when I can get something for nothing at work.	1	2	3	4	5
6. It is the smart employee who gets as much as he or she can while giving as little as possible in return.	1	2	3	4	5
7. Employees who are more concerned about what they can get from their employer rather than what they can give to their employer are the wisest.	1	2	3	4	5
8. When I have completed my task for the day, I help out other employees who have yet to complete their tasks.	1	2	3	4	5
9. Even if I receive low wages and poor benefits from my employer, I would still try to do my best at my job.	1	2	3	4	5
10. If I had to work hard all day at my job, I would probably quit.	1	2	3	4	5
11. I feel obligated to do more than I am paid to do at work.	1	2	3	4	5
12. At work, my greatest concern is whether or not I am doing the best job I can.	1	2	3	4	5
13. A job that requires me to be busy during the day is better than a job that allows me a lot of time for loafing.	1	2	3	4	5
14. At work, I feel uneasy when there is little work for me to do.	1	2	3	4	5
15. I would become very dissatisfied with my job if I had little or no work to do.	1	2	3	4	5
16. All other things being equal, it is better to have a job with a lot of duties and responsibilities than one with few duties and responsibilities.	1	2	3	4	5

Source: Reprinted from *Journal of Management*, Vol. 26, K. S. Sauleya and A. G. Bedeian, "Equity Sensitivity: Construction of a Measure and Examination of Its Psychometric Properties," pp. 885–910. Copyright © 2000, with permission from Elsevier Science.

After studying the preceding material, be sure to check out our website at

www.mhhe.com/mcshane2e

for more in-depth information and interactivities that correspond to this chapter.

Applied Motivation Practices

AFTER READING THIS CHAPTER, YOU SHOULD BE ABLE TO:

- Explain how money and other financial rewards affect our needs and emotions.

- Discuss the advantages and disadvantages of the four types of rewards.

- Identify four commonly applied team or organizational-level performance-based rewards.

- Describe five ways to improve reward effectiveness.

- Discuss the advantages and disadvantages of job specialization.

- Diagram the job characteristics model of job design.

- Identify three strategies to enrich jobs.

- Describe the five elements of self-leadership

- Explain how mental imagery improves employee motivation.

Casey Crook recently went home very happy from her job at IKEA. So did 400 other employees at IKEA's home furnishings store in Renton, Washington. Every year, the store holds a special Bonus Day in early December when the store hands over the entire day's sales (except sales tax) to its employees. Office workers, accountants, and other nonsales employees all pitch in, doing anything from helping clerks to loading cars with merchandise.

All full- and part-time IKEA employees who have worked at the Renton store since the beginning of August receive a bonus. The amount is determined half by a management assessment of that person's performance and half by the person's years of service at the store and the number of hours worked. The most recent Bonus Day at the Renton store brought in $1.1 million sales, which gave Crook a bonus of nearly $10,000.

IKEA employees have a lot to smile about from the bonus they receive in the store's annual Bonus Day event. *(Courtesy of IKEA)*

IKEA held a similar one-time worldwide Big Thank You Bonus day to usher in the new millennium. The Scandinavian company pledged the entire day's sales to its 44,000 employees at the 152 stores around the world. IKEA rang up $80 million (800 million Swedish kronor) in sales, nearly doubling its previous one-day record. Every full-time employee received a bonus of $1,800 (about half that amount for part-time staff). Employees in lower-income countries earned up to a maximum of three months' salary.

"Saturday proved to be an overwhelmingly positive day for everyone at IKEA," said an IKEA executive of the worldwide bonus day event. "IKEA employees worked tirelessly throughout the day and well into the night, showing the same enthusiasm that has helped make the company so successful."[1]

IKEA didn't become the world's largest home furnishings retailer by paying big bonuses and salaries. Yet employee reaction to the Scandinavian company's bonuses suggests that *money does matter* to IKEA's employees. The first part of this chapter looks at the complex dynamics of reward systems. We look at the meaning of money and other financial rewards, the different types of rewards and their objectives, and the characteristics of effective reward implementation.

Of course, reward systems are not the only way to motivate employees. Thus, we consider two other applied motivation practices: job design and self-leadership. The second part of this chapter examines the dynamics of job design, specific job design strategies to motivate employees, and the effectiveness of recent job design interventions. The final part of this chapter introduces the emerging concept of self-leadership. This section explains how employees motivate themselves through personal goal setting, constructive thought patterns, designing natural rewards, self-monitoring, and self-reinforcement.

THE MEANING OF MONEY IN THE WORKPLACE

Money and other financial rewards are a fundamental part of the employment relationship. Organizations distribute money and other benefits in exchange for the employee's availability, competencies, and behaviors. Rewards try to align individual goals with corporate objectives and to provide a return for the individual's contribution. This concept of economic exchange can be found across cultures. The word for "pay" in Malay and Slovak means to replace a loss; in Hebrew and Swedish it means making equal.[2]

But money is not just an economic medium of exchange in the employment relationship. It is a symbol with much deeper and more complex meaning.[3] It affects our needs, our emotions, and our self-identity. As one scholar wrote: "Money is probably the most emotionally meaningful object in contemporary life: only food and sex are its close competitors as common carriers of such strong and diverse feelings, significance, and strivings."[4]

Money and Employee Needs

Money potentially satisfies a variety of needs. Money is strongly linked to the fulfillment of existence needs because it allows us to buy food and shelter. This connection might explain why people in low-income countries tend to value money more than people in high-income countries.[5] Some people also see money as a symbol of respect and status, thereby fulfilling some social needs. For others, money symbolizes personal accomplishments and, consequently, relates to growth needs. People with a high need for achievement are not motivated primarily by money (see Chapter 5), but they do value money as a source of feedback and a representation of goal achievement. In other words, money is a way of "keeping score" of their successes.

Money Attitudes and Values

Money tends to create strong emotions and attitudes. Some people are preoccupied with money. Others are nervous with money and its responsibilities. One large-scale study revealed that money generates a variety of emotions, most of which are negative, such as anxiety, depression, anger, and helpless-

Most of the cars in ARCNET's employee parking lot look alike. That's because the New Jersey architectural engineering firm gives every employee—from secretaries to the president—keys to a new BMW after one year of employment. ARCNET CEO Al Galdi (being interviewed in photo) offers this dreamy perk as a way to motivate employees to stay with the company. Each vehicle is leased for about $9,000 per year, including insurance. Galdi frequently asks employees if they would rather have the cash, but most prefer the BMWs. "I see the effect already," says Galdi. "My employees want to work harder and it's a benefit when it comes to recruiting."[6] Would a luxury car satisfy the same needs as a cash reward? *(Courtesy of ARCNET)*

ness. Money is associated with greed, avarice, and, occasionally, generosity. Some OB scholars have studied the money ethic, that is, the extent to which people believe money is a representation of their success, is not evil, and should be budgeted carefully.[7]

Cultural values seem to influence attitudes toward money. In Chapter 4, we described how people in China, Hong Kong, Japan, and other countries with a long-term orientation value thrift, savings, and persistence. Not surprisingly, they also give money a high priority in their lives.[8] In contrast, Scandinavians, Australians, and New Zealanders have a strong egalitarian value that discourages people from talking openly about money or displaying their personal wealth. This value is sometimes know as the "tall poppy" syndrome because the culture knocks down those who try to stand out from the others.[9]

Money and Self-Identity

People tend to identify themselves in terms of their ownership and management of money. Some individuals see themselves as hoarders of or worriers about money, whereas others will tell you they are compulsive shoppers or spendthrifts. Research on marital relationships shows that couples tend to adopt polarized roles (and, consequently, self-identities) regarding their management and expenditure of money.[10] The same polar relationships might exist in the workplace, although we haven't found any research on this topic.

Men are more likely than women to emphasize money in their self-identity. One large-scale survey of people in 43 countries revealed that men attach more importance or value to money than do women in every country except India, Norway, and Transkei.[11] Two recent surveys found that money was a much higher priority for men than for women.[12] Why do men identify more with money? Some writers suggest that men are more likely to believe that money equals power and that power is the path to respect. Other research has found that, compared with women, men are more confident managing their money and are more likely to use money as a tool to influence and impress others.[13]

The bottom line is that money and other financial rewards do much more than pay employees back for their contributions. They fulfill a variety of needs, influence emotions, and shape or represent a person's self-identity. This knowledge is important to remember when distributing rewards in the workplace. Over the next several pages, we look at various types of rewards and how to improve the implementation of performance-based rewards.

TYPES OF REWARDS AND THEIR OBJECTIVES

Organizations reward employees for their membership and seniority, job status, competencies, and performance. Each reward objective has its advantages and disadvantages, as Exhibit 6.1 summarizes.

EXHIBIT 6.1   Reward objectives, advantages, and disadvantages

Reward objective	Advantages	Disadvantages
Membership/seniority	• May attract applicants • Minimizes stress of insecurity • Reduces turnover	• Doesn't directly motivate performance • May discourage poor performers from leaving • Golden handcuffs may undermine performance
Job status	• Tries to maintain internal equity • Minimizes pay discrimination • Motivates employees to compete for promotions	• Encourages political tactics to increase job worth • Creates psychological distance between employees and executives
Competencies	• Improves workforce flexibility • Tends to improve quality • Is consistent with employability	• Measurement of competencies may be subjective • Skill-based pay plans are expensive
Task performance	• Motivates task performance • Attracts performance-oriented applicants • Organizational rewards create an ownership culture • Pay variability may avoid layoffs during downturns	• May weaken motivation of job itself • May distance reward giver from receiver • May discourage creativity • Viewed as quick fix, but doesn't solve real cause of problem

Membership- and Seniority-Based Rewards

The largest portion of most paychecks is determined by membership and seniority. Employees receive fixed hourly wages or salaries, and many benefits are the same for everyone in the firm. Other rewards increase with seniority, such as the amount of paid vacation time. Clark County and other communities in Nevada offer employees longevity pay. For example, an employee earning $50,000 receives an additional $2,500 each year after 10 years of service and $5,700 per year after 20 years of service. Japanese firms typically increase every employee's pay rate for each year on the job or for age, although some companies are moving toward more performance-based pay.[14]

Advantages and Disadvantages   Membership-based rewards may attract job applicants, particularly when the size of the reward increases with seniority. They also provide a level of security that minimizes stress and builds loyalty.[15] Seniority-based rewards reduce turnover because the cost of quitting increases with the employee's length of service. However, membership-based rewards do not directly motivate job performance. Membership-based rewards also discourage poor performers from quitting because they seldom have better job offers. Instead, the good performers are lured to better-paying jobs. Lastly, as we learned in Chapter 4, some of these rewards are golden handcuffs. They discourage people from leaving the organization, but they also undermine job performance through continuance commitment.

Job Status–Based Rewards

Almost every organization rewards employees for the status of their jobs in the organization. Firms often rely on **job evaluation** to evaluate the worth of each job within the organization. Jobs have more value and are placed in higher pay grades if they require more skill and effort, have more responsibility, and have difficult working conditions. Organizations that don't rely on job evaluation still tend to reward job status on the basis of pay survey information about the external labor market. People in some higher-status jobs are also rewarded with large offices, company-paid vehicles, and exclusive dining rooms.

job evaluation
Systematically evaluating the worth of jobs within an organization by measuring their required skill, effort, responsibility, and working conditions. Job evaluation results create a hierarchy of job worth.

Advantages and Disadvantages   Job evaluation and job status-based pay motivate employees to compete for positions higher up in the organizational hierarchy. Membership-based rewards also try to maintain *internal equity;* that is, they try to make pay levels fair across different jobs within the organization. This process also tries to minimize pay discrimination by ensuring that jobs dominated by women receive similar pay as jobs dominated by men in the organization. For instance, the Hong Kong government recently brought in job evaluation experts to determine whether people in female-dominated civil service jobs are paid the same as people in male-dominated jobs with similar values (as measured by job evaluation ratings).[16]

Despite these advantages, job status–based pay and benefits create a psychological distance between employees and management, thereby inhibiting communication across these groups. Status-based pay also reinforces the traditional hierarchy and is inconsistent with flatter organizational structures and increased emphasis on knowledge rather than position. Lastly, job evaluation systems motivate employees to increase their pay rate by exaggerating job duties and hoarding resources. "People knew they could change their pay by rewriting their job description, not by raising their productivity," says an executive at Seattle-based clothing retailer Eddie Bauer.[17] This consequence has led Eddie Bauer and other organizations to shift from job status–based to competency-based rewards.

Competency-Based Rewards

Competencies are the skills, knowledge, and other underlying characteristics that lead to superior performance (see Chapter 2).[18] Competency-based pay rewards employees for their skills, knowledge, and traits that lead to desired behaviors. How do firms reward employees for their competencies rather than status? They flatten the organizational hierarchy, reduce the number of pay grades, and reward employees for their demonstrated competencies, such as customer service, technical knowledge, and creativity.[19] Clothing retailer Eddie Bauer did this by reducing its pay structure to three broad bands: entry, intermediate, and specialist. Employees increase their pay by increasing their skills within each band. This structure motivates employees to acquire skills and knowledge by moving laterally through several jobs, rather than waiting for promotion up a tall career ladder.

skill-based pay
Pay structures in which employees earn higher pay rates with the number of skill modules they have mastered.

Skill-based pay plans represent a variation of competency-based pay. In skill-based pay plans, employees' pay rates increase with the number of skill modules they master.[20] Through special training and job rotation, employees learn how to operate another machine or complete another set of tasks. The employee's pay rate depends on the number of skill modules that he or she has mastered, not on the specific job performed on a particular day.

Marley Cooling Tower Company in Olathe, Kansas, has a skill-based reward system involving more than 30 skill modules in its production operations. Each skill module is worth between 30 and 75 cents per hour, depending on its level of difficulty. Employees at the cooling tower manufacturer who have mastered all 30 skill modules earn more than twice as much as unskilled staff. Marley employees perform only one skill module at a time, but they are paid for the number of skill modules they are capable of performing.[21]

Advantages and Disadvantages   Competency-based rewards improve workforce flexibility because employees possess a variety of skills to move into different jobs as demands require. Product or service quality tends to improve because employees with multiple skills are more likely to understand the work process and know how to improve it.[22] Competency-based rewards are also consistent with employability. This emerging view asserts that employees are not hired to perform a specific job for life; rather, they perform a variety of tasks and therefore must continual learn skills that will keep them employed (see Chapter 1). One potential problem with competency-based pay is that measuring competencies can be subjective, particularly when the competencies are personality traits or values.[23] Skill-based pay systems measure specific skills, so they are usually more objective and accurate. However, they are expensive because employees spend more time learning new tasks.

Performance-Based Rewards

Bank One wants its Ohio workforce to be a powerful sales force. Employees receive $50 for every friend or family member who becomes a Bank One customer. The employee who signs up the most new customers wins a $2,500 shopping spree; a dozen runners-up each receive $1,000. Bank One's reward plan is part of a trend toward more performance-based rewards. Performance-based rewards have existed since Babylonian days in the twentieth century B.C.[24] Today, they come in more varieties than ever before. Exhibit 6.2 lists the most common types of individual, team, and organizational performance-based rewards.

Individual Rewards   One of the oldest performance-based rewards is the *piece rate*, which calculates pay by the number of units the employee produces. *Commissions* pay people on the basis of sales volume rather than units produced. For example, sales associates at department store chain Hudson Belk earn commissions in addition to their salary for the value of merchandise they sell to customers.[25] *Royalties* pay individuals a percentage of revenue from the resource or work ascribed to them. Some mining companies pay their exploration geologists royalties from the mineral deposits they discover. *Merit pay*—increasing the individual's pay on the basis of performance appraisal results—was common during times of high inflation, but most organizations now offer re-earnable *bonuses* for accomplishing specific tasks or achieving certain goals.

Team Rewards   A decade ago, most institutional brokers on Wall Street were paid individual commissions. Today, the top dozen firms have shifted to salary and bonuses determined by team and organizational performance. Similar changes are occurring in retail brokerages as Merrill Lynch and other firms move brokers into teams.[26]

gainsharing plan
A reward system that rewards team members for reducing costs and increasing labor efficiency in their work process.

Companies across the United States are shifting from individual to more team-based reward systems.[27] One of the most popular team-based rewards is the **gainsharing plan.** Gainsharing motivates team members to reduce costs and increase labor efficiency in their work process. Typically, the company shares the cost savings with employees for one or two years.[28] An unusual example of gainsharing was recently introduced at St. Joseph's Hospital in Atlanta, Georgia. Cardiac surgeons can cut about $2,000 out of the $15,000 cost

EXHIBIT 6.2

Types of performance-based rewards

- Organizational rewards
  - Stock ownership
  - Stock options
  - Profit sharing
- Team rewards
  - Gainsharing
  - Bonuses
- Individual rewards
  - Piece rate
  - Commissions
  - Royalties
  - Bonuses

Team and organizational incentives keep Steel Dynamics profitable at a time when many American steel mills are in trouble. "You'll rarely see people standing around doing nothing," says Bob Soden, manager of engineering and services at the Butler, Indiana–based mini-mill. "Everyone is motivated by the pay systems to get in there and lend a hand when something breaks." Steel Dynamics production employees can double their $10 per hour base pay when the mill achieves production level targets. They earn another bonus by reducing input costs during production. Everyone from office assistants to workers running furnaces gets stock options twice a year. The company also hands out profit sharing bonuses across the workforce. Thanks to these financial incentives, the average Steel Dynamics employee (excluding officers) earns nearly $65,000 each year."[29] Why would Steel Dynamics rely on team and organizational rewards rather than individual rewards to motivate employees? *(Courtesy of Steel Dynamics, Inc.)*

of a heart bypass surgery operation by using less expensive sutures and avoiding opening supplies that aren't used. St. Joseph encourages this cost savings by paying surgeons 50 percent of the cost savings. Because of the emphasis on safety, this particular application of gainsharing required a special ruling from the U.S. government. "We're not withholding (services)," explains the surgeon who devised the pay plan. "We're just reducing waste."[30]

Gainsharing plans tend to improve team dynamics and pay satisfaction. They also create a reasonably strong E→P expectancy (see Chapter 5) because much of the cost reduction and labor efficiency is within the team's control. In other words, team members quickly learn that their work efficiencies increase the size of the gainsharing bonus.[31] One concern, however, is that gainsharing plans may increase workloads and reduce customer service in the long run as employees find ways to cut costs in the short term.

Organizational Rewards   IKEA's Big Thank You Bonus, described at the beginning of this chapter, is typical of the emerging trend toward organizational rewards. The most common organizational rewards are employee stock ownership plans, stock options, and profit sharing plans.

> **employee stock ownership plans (ESOPs)**
> A reward system that encourages employees to buy shares of the company.

■ **Employee stock ownership plans (ESOPs)** _—Qualified Pension Plans_ encourage employees to buy shares in the company, usually at a discounted price or with a no-interest loan from the company. Employees are subsequently rewarded through dividends and market appreciation of those shares. There are currently 10,000 ESOP plans representing 10 million employees throughout the United States. Most of these are in privately held companies, but you will also find ESOPs at Procter & Gamble, Home Depot, and other publicly traded firms.[32]

> **stock options**
> A reward system that gives employees the right to purchase company stock at a future date at a predetermined price.

■ **Stock options** are a variation of ESOPs that give employees the right to purchase company stock at a future date at a predetermined price.[33] For example, your employer might offer you the right to purchase 100 shares at $50 two years or more from now. If the stock price two years from now is above $50, you could exercise your options by purchasing the shares from the company at $50 and selling them at a profit. If the price is below $50, you would wait until the stock price rises above that amount or let the options expire. Most North American high-technology firms offer stock options because they instantly connect new employees to the organization's success. As Global Connections 6.1 describes, stock options are also gaining popularity throughout Asia.

> **profit sharing**
> A reward system that pays bonuses to employees based on the previous year's level of corporate profits.

■ **Profit sharing** plans pay bonuses to employees on the basis of the previous year's level of corporate profits. These plans are most often found in firms that use teams and face plenty of competition, such as Southwest Airlines and Steel Dynamics. Tien Wah Press, a Malaysian printing company, also has a profit sharing plan that annually distributes a percentage of pretax profits to its 3,000 employees in Malaysia, Singapore, and Indonesia.[34]

How effective are organizational rewards? The evidence is mixed. The positive news is that ESOPs and stock options tend to align employee behaviors more closely with organizational objectives. In other words, they create an ownership culture in which employees feel aligned with the organization's success. According to one study, productivity rises by 4 percent annually at ESOP firms, compared with only 1.5 percent at non-ESOP firms. Profit sharing tends to create less of this ownership culture effect. However, it has the advantage of automatically adjusting employee compensation with the firm's prosperity, thereby reducing the need for layoffs or negotiated pay reductions during recessions.[35]

The main problem with organizational-level rewards is that employees often perceive a weak connection between individual performance and corporate profits or the value of company shares. Even in small firms, the company's stock price or profitability is influenced by economic conditions, competition, and other factors beyond the employee's immediate control. These organizational-level rewards also fail to motivate employees when

The Stock Option Generation Arrives in Asia

Most of the 3,000 staff at Micron Semiconductor's production plant in Singapore are keeping a close watch on the company's stock price. That's because the U.S.-based high-technology company recently gave every employee around the world options to buy 25 shares per year over the next four years at the fixed price of US$28.56 per share. If the stock price on the market is higher, employees immediately earn the difference. Micron's Singapore staff keep track of the company's stock performance with a scrolling electronic board on the cafeteria wall.

Micron employees are the latest group to become "Soggies"—the stock option generation. PepsiCo, the U.S. soft drink company, first granted stock options to employees worldwide back in 1989, making it a Soggie pioneer in Asia. Lucent Technologies granted 100 stock options to each of its 100,000 employees when it split

away from AT&T in 1996. By 2000, the shares were worth nearly 10 years of wages for most Lucent employees in Thailand. "I still can't believe it," says Khun Taen, who works at Lucent's manufacturing plant near Bangkok.

Singapore Press Holdings and Singapore Airlines, two of the island-state's largest companies, have followed the American trend by distributing stock options to all employees. So did Cable & Wireless HKT, Hong Kong's telephone company, to replace the "thirteenth month" paycheck that all employees traditionally received. HKT's employees complained about losing their guaranteed bonus but are now seeking more stock options. "[HKT employees] will be actively seeking stock options—unlike our passive response before," says a union representative.

Sources: H. Chow, "All Micron Staff Get Stock Options," *Straits Times (Singapore)*, November 14, 2000; Y. Cohen, "Stock Options Trickle Down to Thai Workers," *Christian Science Monitor*, March 27, 2000; Y. Ghahremani, "In the Company of Millionaires," *Asiaweek*, March 17, 2000, pp. 42 ff.

profits are negligible or in bear markets, when stock prices decline. Indeed, morale may suffer in companies with these plans.[36]

Improving Reward Effectiveness

Performance-based rewards have been criticized for a variety of reasons.[37] One concern is that they distract employees from the motivation that comes from serving customers or achieving challenging objectives. Rewards also potentially create relationship problems. One study of performance-based pay reported that conflict increased between supervisors and staff when performance appraisal results were used to determine pay increases. It also created tensions between "star" employees and those with lower performance.[38]

A third criticism of performance-based pay systems is that they discourage creativity and risk taking because employees are less likely to explore new opportunities outside the realm of rewarded behavior or results. Lastly, many corporate leaders use rewards as quick fixes, rather than carefully diagnosing the real causes of the undesirable behavior. For example, one company hands out cash to employees who arrive early at company meetings and fines those who arrive late.[39] The company would be better off identifying the causes of lateness and changing the conditions, rather than using money to force a solution to the problem.

These concerns do not necessarily mean that we should abandon performance-based pay. On the contrary, evidence indicates that the top-performing companies around the world are more likely to have performance-based rewards.[40] Reward systems do motivate most employees, but only under the right conditions. Here are some of the more important strategies to improve reward effectiveness.

Link Rewards to Performance   Employees with better performance should be rewarded more than those with poorer performance.[41] This simple principle is a logical conclusion of both behavior modification (Chapter 2) and expectancy theory (Chapter 5), yet it seems to be unusually difficult to apply. A recent survey reported that one-third of the 770 U.S. and Canadian firms studied paid rewards to people who didn't meet minimum performance standards. This situation occurs partly because it is difficult to measure the many elements of job performance and organizational citizenship. Moreover, research suggests that performance-pay decisions are biased by organizational politics.[42]

How can we improve the pay-for-performance linkage? First, bias in pay systems can be minimized by introducing gainsharing, ESOPs, and other plans that rely on objective performance measures. Second, where subjective measures of performance are necessary, companies should rely on multiple sources of information. In other words, use 360-degree feedback to minimize biases from any single source (see Chapter 2). Third, companies need to apply rewards soon after the performance occurs, and in a large enough dose (such as a bonus rather than a pay increase) that employees can see the reward.[43]

Ensure That Rewards Are Relevant   Companies need to align rewards with performance within the employee's control. The more employees see a direct connection between their daily actions and the reward, the more they are motivated to improve performance.[44] Sears, Roebuck and Company rewards senior executives for corporate performance because they have some control over the Chicago-based retail giant's overall success. Bonuses for department sales managers, on the other hand, are on the basis of profits and customer satisfaction in their departments, but not for Sears's overall corporate performance.[45] Reward systems also need to correct for situational factors. Salespeople in one region may have higher sales because the economy is stronger there than elsewhere, so sales bonuses need to be adjusted for those economic factors.

Use Team Rewards for Interdependent Jobs   Organizations should use team (or organizational) rewards rather than individual rewards when employees work in highly interdependent jobs.[46] One reason is that individual performance is difficult to measure in these situations. For example, you can't determine how well one employee in a chemical processing plant contributes to the quality of the liquid produced. It is a team effort. A second reason is that team rewards tend to make employees more cooperative and less competitive. People see that their bonuses or other incentives depend on how well they work with co-workers, and they act accordingly.

The third reason for having team rewards is that they support employee preferences for team-based work arrangements. This result was found in a study of Xerox customer service representatives. The Xerox employees assigned to teams with purely team bonuses eventually accepted and preferred a team structure, whereas those put in teams without team rewards did not adapt as well to the team structure.[47]

Ensure Rewards Are Valued   It seems obvious that rewards work best when they are valued. Yet recall from Chapter 5 that companies sometimes make false assumptions about what employees want, with unfortunate consequences. The solution, of course, is to ask employees what they value. Campbell Soup did this when it introduced a special team reward program at one of its distribution centers. Executives at the food company thought distribution staff would want money as the top reward. Instead, employees said they wanted leather jackets with the Campbell Soup logo on the back as the winning team's prize.[48]

Watch Out for Unintended Consequences   Performance-based reward systems sometimes have unexpected—and undesirable—effects on employee behaviors.[49] Consider the pizza company that decided to reward its drivers for on-time delivery. The plan got more hot pizzas to customers on time, but it also increased the accident rates of its drivers because the incentive motivated them to drive recklessly.[50] Connections 6.2 describes a few other examples where reward systems had unintended consequences. The solution here is to carefully think through the consequences of rewards and, where possible, test incentives in a pilot project before applying them across the organization.

Beyond Money and Other Financial Rewards

At the beginning of this chapter, we said that money and other financial rewards have a complex effect on the needs, emotions, and self-identity of employees. Money also seems to have become a top priority when forming the employment relationship. "Show me the money"—the often repeated phrase from the film *Jerry Maguire*—captures this emerging reality as companies offer more signing bonuses, stock options, and BMWs.

But money isn't the only thing that motivates people to join an organization and perform effectively. "High performers don't go for the money," warns William Monahan, CEO of Oakdale, Minnesota–based Imation Corporation. "Good people want to be in challenging jobs and see a future where they can get even more responsibilities and challenges." Rafik O. Loutfy, a Xerox research center director, agrees with this assessment. "Our top stars say they want to make an impact—that's the most important thing," he says. "Feeling they are contributing and making a difference is highly motivational for them."[51] In other words, Imation, Xerox, and other companies motivate employees mainly by designing interesting and challenging jobs, which we discuss next.

JOB DESIGN

job design
The process of assigning tasks to a job, including the interdependency of those tasks with other jobs.

Organizational behavior scholars generally agree that the deepest passion for performing a job well comes from the work itself. **Job design** refers to the process of assigning tasks to a job, including the interdependency of those tasks with other jobs. A *job* is a set of tasks performed by one person.[52] Some jobs have very few tasks, each requiring limited skill or effort. Other jobs involve very complex tasks requiring highly trained tradespeople or professionals.

Information technology has transformed many jobs over the past couple of decades. It has increased responsibility and autonomy for many employees by improving direct access to information. Yet these same computer networks

When Rewards Go Wrong

There is an old saying that "what gets rewarded, gets done." But what companies reward isn't always what they had intended for employees to do. Here are a few dramatic examples:

- Toyota rewards its dealerships on the basis of customer satisfaction surveys, not just car sales. What Toyota discovered, however, is that this strategy motivates dealers to increase satisfaction scores, not customer satisfaction. One Toyota dealership received high ratings because it offered free detailing to every customer who returned a "Very Satisfied" survey. The dealership even had a special copy of the survey showing clients which boxes to check off. This tactic increased customer ratings, but not customer satisfaction.

- A building design company implemented an incentive plan that encouraged its engineers to design buildings so that they would be built below budget. One creative employee achieved this goal by simply scaling down the building's walls and ceilings by an inch or two. This approach saved thousands of dollars for the company and earned the engineer a sizable bonus, until the company and client discovered the shrunken results.

- Some investment analysts warn that stock options motivate executives to improve the value of the company's stock, not necessarily the company's long-term success. At IBM, stock-optioned executives have spent almost $39 billion repurchasing IBM stock from the market over the past five years. This amount is significantly more than the $33 billion IBM invested in its entire research and development budget over that same time span. The buyback rewarded IBM executives through improved stock

Customer service incentives may have rewarded the wrong behavior at Toyota dealerships. (© John Thoeming)

prices, but probably didn't help IBM's development of new products and services for future profitability.

- Donnelly Mirrors introduced a gainsharing plan that motivated employees to reduce labor but not material costs. Employees at the automobile parts manufacturer knew they worked faster with sharp grinding wheels, so they replaced the expensive diamond wheels more often. This action reduced labor costs, thereby giving employees the gainsharing bonus. However, the labor savings were easily offset by much higher costs for diamond grinding wheels.

Sources: D. S. Hilzenrath, "Financial 'Performance' Options Getting a Second Look," *Washington Post*, April 1, 2001, p. H1; C. Teasdale, "Not All Firms Find Variable Pay Plans Pay Off," *St. Louis Business Journal*, September 28, 1998; F. F. Reichheld, *The Loyalty Effect* (Boston, MA: Harvard University Press, 1996), p. 236; D. R. Spitzer, "Power Rewards: Rewards That Really Motivate," *Management Review*, May 1996, pp. 45–50.

have reduced personal control in other jobs by monitoring employee actions, keystrokes, and whereabouts. The amount of personal control available to employees depends on how the technology is implemented.[53] Employability is another influence on job design. Employees are no longer hired into specific, narrowly defined jobs. Instead, they hold generic titles (associates, team members) and are expected to perform several clusters of tasks.[54]

Whether the change occurs through information technology or workforce flexibility, job design often produces an interesting conflict between the employee's motivation and ability to complete the work. To explain this issue more fully, we begin by describing early job design efforts aimed at increasing work efficiency through job specialization.

Job Design and Work Efficiency

Cindy Vang sits in a blue vinyl chair at Medtronic's assembly line in Minneapolis, Minnesota. Using a pair of tweezers, she loads 275 feedthroughs—tiny needlelike components for pacemakers and neurostimulators—onto a slotted storage block. She fills a block in about 15 minutes, then places the completed block on a shelf, and loads the next block.[55]

Cindy Vang works in a job with a high degree of **job specialization.** Job specialization occurs when the work required to build a pacemaker—or any other product or service—is subdivided into separate jobs assigned to different people. Each resulting job includes a very narrow subset of tasks, usually completed in a short cycle time. Cycle time is the time required to complete the task before starting over with a new work unit. For Cindy Vang, the cycle time for loading each feedthrough is a few seconds.

The economic benefits of dividing work into specialized jobs have been described and applied for at least two centuries. Over 2,300 years ago, the Chinese philosopher Mencius and the Greek philosopher Plato noted that division

job specialization
The result of division of labor in which each job now includes a subset of the tasks required to complete the product or service.

These sewing machine operators on the main assembly floor of the United International Corporation garment plant in Saipan (a U.S. territory in the Pacific Ocean) have a high degree of job specialization. An employee might complete each work unit (a piece of clothing) in a few minutes.This specialization improves work efficiency, but it can also lead to boredom and repetitive strain injuries. Some garment plants have introduced team-based work and job rotation to offset these problems, but some sewing jobs involve specialized work. How does job specialization improve work efficiency for sewing machine operators? *(© AP/Wide World)*

EXHIBIT 6.3

Horizontal and vertical job specialization

of labor improves work efficiency. In 1436 A.D., the waterways of Venice became an assembly line loading 10 galleons in just six hours. Over 200 years ago, economist Adam Smith described how 10 pin makers working alone could each produce no more than 20 pins per day. But Smith also described a factory where 10 pin makers collectively produced as many as 48,000 pins per day because they performed specialized tasks, such as straightening, cutting, sharpening, grinding, and whitening the pins.[56]

Why does job specialization potentially increase work efficiency? One reason is that employees have fewer tasks to juggle and therefore spend less time changing activities. They also require fewer physical and mental skills to accomplish the assigned work, so less time and fewer resources are needed for training. A third reason is that employees practice their tasks more frequently with shorter work cycles, so jobs are mastered quickly. Lastly, work efficiency increases because employees with specific aptitudes or skills can be matched more precisely to the jobs for which they are best suited.[57]

Adam Smith's example of pin manufacturing mainly describes *horizontal job specialization,* in which the basic physical behaviors required to provide a product or service are divided into different jobs (see Exhibit 6.3). With horizontal job specialization, employees perform fewer tasks. *Vertical job specialization,* on the other hand, refers to separating physical tasks from the administration of those tasks (planning, organizing, scheduling, etc.). In other words, vertical job specialization divorces the "managing" job functions from the "doing" job functions.

Scientific Management   One of the strongest advocates of job specialization was Frederick Winslow Taylor, an industrial engineer who introduced the principles of **scientific management** in the early 1900s.[58] Scientific management involves systematically partitioning work into its smallest elements and standardizing tasks to achieve maximum efficiency. Taylor advocated vertical job specialization so that detailed procedures and work practices are developed by engineers, enforced by supervisors, and executed by employees. He also applied horizontal job specialization, such as narrowing the supervisor's role to such a degree that one person manages operational efficiency, another manages inspection, and another is the disciplinarian. Through scientific management, Taylor also popularized many organizational practices that are commonly found today, such as goal setting, employee training, and incentive systems.

scientific management
Involves systematically partitioning work into its smallest elements and standardizing tasks to achieve maximum efficiency.

There is ample evidence that scientific management has improved efficiency in many work settings. One of Taylor's earliest interventions was at a ball bearing factory where 120 women each worked 55 hours per week. Through job specialization and work efficiency analysis, Taylor increased production by two-thirds using a workforce of only 35 women working fewer than 45 hours per week. Taylor also doubled the employees' previous wages. No doubt, some of the increased productivity can be credited to improved training, goal setting, and work incentives, but job specialization also contributed to the success of scientific management.

Problems with Job Specialization   Job specialization tries to increase work efficiency, but it doesn't necessarily improve job performance because job specialization ignores the effects of job content on employees.[59] Some jobs—such as Cindy Vang's task of loading feedthroughs—are so specialized that they are tedious, trivial, and socially isolating. Job specialization was supposed to let companies buy cheap, unskilled labor. Instead, many have to offer higher wages—some call it *discontentment pay*—to compensate for the job dissatisfaction of narrowly defined work.[60] Job specialization also costs more in terms of higher turnover, absenteeism, sabotage, and mental health problems. Work quality is often lower with highly specialized jobs because employees see only a small part of the process. As one observer of automobile assembly line work reports: "Often [employees] did not know how their jobs related to the total picture. Not knowing, there was no incentive to strive for quality—what did quality even mean as it related to a bracket whose function you did not understand."[61]

Perhaps the most important reason job specialization has not been as successful as expected is that it ignores the motivational potential of jobs. As jobs become specialized, the work tends to become easier to perform, but it is less motivating. As jobs become more complex, work motivation increases, but the ability to master the job decreases. Maximum job performance occurs somewhere between these two extremes, where most people can eventually perform the job tasks efficiently, yet the work is interesting.

Job Design and Work Motivation

Industrial engineers may have overlooked the motivational effects of job characteristics, but these effects are now the central focus of many job design changes.[62] Frederick Herzberg cast a spotlight on the motivational potential of job content with his motivator–hygiene theory, described in Chapter 5.[63] It might seem rather obvious to us today that the job itself is a source of motivation, but it was radical thinking when Herzberg proposed the idea in the 1950s.

Herzberg's writing and subsequent research by organizational behavior scholars has led to the **job characteristics model,** shown in Exhibit 6.4. This model details the motivational properties of jobs as well as specific personal and organizational consequences of these properties.[64] The job characteristics model identifies five core job dimensions that produce three psychological states. Employees who experience these psychological states tend to have higher levels of internal work motivation (motivation from the work itself), job satisfaction (particularly, satisfaction with the work itself), and work effectiveness.

job characteristics model
A job design model that relates the motivational properties of jobs to specific personal and organizational consequences of these properties.

EXHIBIT 6.4   The job characteristics model

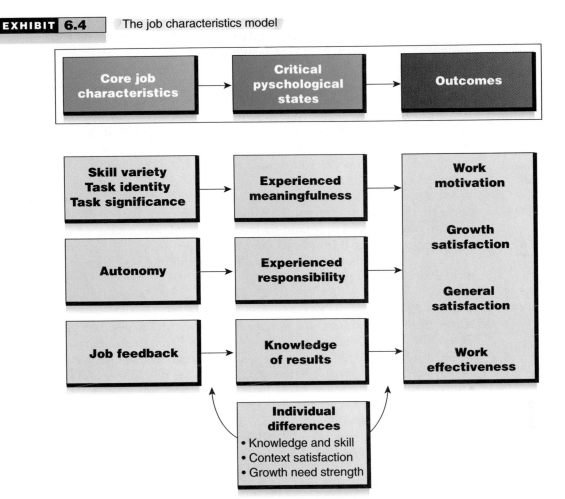

Source: J. R. Hackman and G. Oldham, *Work Redesign* (Reading, MA: Addison-Wesley, 1980), p. 90. Used with permission.

Core Job Characteristics   The job characteristics model identifies five core job characteristics (see Exhibit 6.4). Under the right conditions, employees are more motivated and satisfied when jobs have higher levels of these characteristics.

■ **Skill variety** refers to using different skills and talents to complete a variety of work activities. For example, salesclerks who normally only serve customers might be assigned the additional duties of stocking inventory and changing storefront displays.

■ **Task identity** is the degree to which a job requires completion of a whole or identifiable piece of work, such as doing something from beginning to end, or where it is easy to see how one's work fits into the whole product or service. An employee who assembles an entire computer modem rather than just soldering in the circuitry would develop a stronger sense of ownership or identity with the final product.

■ **Task significance** is the degree to which the job has a substantial impact on the organization and/or larger society. For instance, Medtronic executives

skill variety
The extent to which employees must use different skills and talents to perform tasks within their job.

task identity
The degree to which a job requires completion of a whole or identifiable piece of work.

task significance
The degree to which the job has a substantial impact on the organization and/or larger society.

autonomy
The degree to which a job gives employees the freedom, independence, and discretion to schedule their work and determine the procedures used in completing it.

job feedback
The degree to which employees can tell how well they are doing based on direct sensory information from the job itself.

realize that Cindy Vang (described earlier) and many other employees have low skill variety, so they have special sessions where patients give testimonials to remind staff of their task significance. "We have patients who come in who would be dead if it wasn't for us," says a Medtronic production supervisor. Little wonder that 86 percent of Medtronic employees say their work has special meaning and 94 percent feel pride in what they accomplish.[65]

■ **Autonomy** is the degree to which the job provides employees with freedom, independence, and discretion in scheduling the work and determining the procedures to be used to complete the work. In autonomous jobs, employees make their own decisions rather than relying on detailed instructions from supervisors or procedure manuals.

■ **Job feedback** is the degree to which employees can tell how well they are doing on the basis of direct sensory information from the job itself. Airline pilots can tell how well they land their aircraft, and physicians can see whether their operations have improved the patient's health. Some research suggests that task feedback has an important effect on reducing role ambiguity and improving job satisfaction.[66]

Critical Psychological States   The five core job characteristics affect employee motivation and satisfaction through three critical psychological states.[67] One of these is *experienced meaningfulness*—the belief that one's work is worthwhile or important. Skill variety, task identity, and task significance contribute directly to the job's meaningfulness. If the job has high levels of all three characteristics, employees are likely to feel that their job is highly meaningful. Meaningfulness drops as the job loses one or more of these characteristics.

Work motivation and performance increase when employees feel personally accountable for the outcomes of their efforts. Autonomy directly contributes to this feeling of *experienced responsibility*. Employees must be assigned control of their work environment to feel responsible for their successes and failures. The third critical psychological state is *knowledge of results*. Employees want information about the consequences of their work effort. Knowledge of results can originate from co-workers, supervisors, or clients. However, job design focuses on knowledge of results from the work itself.

Individual Differences   Job redesign doesn't increase work motivation for everyone in every situation. Employees must have the required skills and knowledge to master the more challenging work. Otherwise, job redesign tends to increase stress and reduce job performance. A second condition is that employees must be reasonably satisfied with their work environment (e.g., working conditions, job security, salaries) before job redesign affects work motivation. A third condition is that employees must have strong growth needs. People with strong growth needs have satisfied their relatedness or existence needs, and are looking for challenges from the work itself (see Chapter 5). In contrast, improving the core job characteristics will have little motivational effect on people who are focused primarily on existence or relatedness needs.[68]

Increasing Work Motivation through Job Design

Three main strategies are used to increase the motivational potential of jobs: job rotation, job enlargement, and job enrichment. This section also identifies several ways to implement job enrichment.

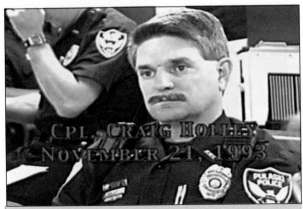

Police officers in Pulaski, Tennessee, are feeling plenty of task significance, thanks to a unique video program that shows them at work. For nine months, a reserve officer videotaped staff in field assignments, office work, meetings, and organized events of fellowship. With inspirational background music, the final program featured each officer in the course of his or her duties. Officers were clearly moved when the tape was presented for the first time at the year-end holiday party. Everyone received a copy with thanks for her or his contribution to the community. Pulaski's recently retired assistant police chief sums up the video's effect: "The video allows officers to see themselves through the eyes of others; realize how important their work appears to others; understand how integral their contribution is to accomplishing the goals of the agency; and recognize how vital they are to the everyday operations of the department."[70] In what other ways might a police department increase officer perceptions of the task significance among police officers and other staff? *(Carl Sutton, © 1999 Almost Life Size Productions)*

job rotation
The practice of moving employees from one job to another.

job enlargement
Increasing the number of tasks employees perform within their job.

Job Rotation **Job rotation** is the practice of moving employees from one job to another. Consider a large one-hour photo finishing retail outlet where one employee interacts with customers, another operates the photo finishing machine, and a third puts the finished product into envelopes and files them for pickup. Job rotation would occur where employees move around those three jobs every few hours or days.

Moving employees around different jobs might reduce job boredom, but most organizations introduce job rotation mainly to develop a flexible workforce. Employees become multiskilled, so they can fill in vacancies and staff shortages. A third reason for introducing job rotation is to reduce the incidence of repetitive strain injuries. Carrier Corporation uses job rotation for this reason. The air conditioning manufacturer identified complementary jobs so that employees move around to different jobs to use different muscles, thereby reducing strain on one muscle.[69]

Job Enlargement Rather than rotating employees through different jobs, **job enlargement** combines tasks into one job. This approach might involve combining two or more complete jobs into one, or just adding one or two more tasks to an existing job. Either way, the job's skill variety has increased because there are more tasks to perform. A recent example of job enlargement is video journalists who perform tasks previously handled by a three- or four-person news crew. As Exhibit 6.5 illustrates, a traditional news team consists of a camera operator, a sound and lighting specialist, and the journalist who writes and presents or narrates the story. Video journalists perform all these tasks. Some are even using notebook computers with video software to edit the final report in the field, then upload the story to the television network using wireless technology.

Job enlargement significantly improves work efficiency and flexibility. However, research suggests that simply giving employees more tasks only minimally improves motivation, performance, and job satisfaction. Instead, these benefits result only when skill variety is combined with more autonomy and job knowledge.[71] In other words, employees are motivated when they have a variety of tasks *and* have the freedom and knowledge to structure their work to achieve the highest satisfaction and performance. These job characteristics are at the heart of job enrichment, which we discuss next.

Job Enrichment **Job enrichment** occurs when employees are given more responsibility for scheduling, coordinating, and planning their own work.

EXHIBIT 6.5

Job enlargement of video journalist

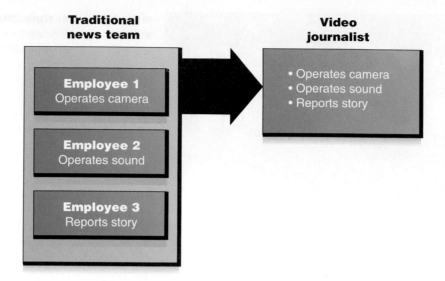

Traditional news team

Employee 1
Operates camera

Employee 2
Operates sound

Employee 3
Reports story

Video journalist

• Operates camera
• Operates sound
• Reports story

job enrichment
Employees are given more responsibility for scheduling, coordinating, and planning their own work.

empowerment
A feeling of control and self-efficacy that emerges when people are given power in a previously powerless situation.

Although some writers suggest that job enrichment is any strategy that increases one or more of the core job characteristics, Herzberg strongly argued that jobs are enriched only through autonomy and the resulting feelings of responsibility.[72] Notice that this definition of job enrichment relates directly to *vertical job loading* because it reverses vertical job specialization, which was described earlier. There are numerous ways to enrich jobs, but we will discuss the three most popular methods: empowering employees, forming natural work units, and establishing client relationships.

Empowering employees Karl Heid keeps a laminated card in his wallet signed by the CEO of Ford Motor Company. It says: "Don't ask, just do it." The miniature agreement gives the material handling supervisor the right to put his good ideas into action and the responsibility to be accountable for the results. DaimlerChrysler is doing the same thing right down to the plant floor. "A trend has been to give more responsibility to the [plant] floor and to cascade that responsibility down to empower our people," says a DaimlerChrysler spokesperson.[73]

Ford, DaimlerChrysler, and many other organizations are trying to empower employees. The definition of **empowerment** is still under discussion, but we will cautiously define empowerment as a feeling of control and self-efficacy that emerges when people are given power in a previously powerless situation.[74] Karl Heid and other empowered employees are given autonomy—freedom, independence, and discretion over their work activities. They are assigned work that has high levels of task significance—importance to the organization and society. Empowered employees also have control over performance feedback, which guides their work. Notice from the definition that empowered employees have feelings of self-efficacy; that is, they believe that they are capable of successfully completing the task (see Chapter 2). When these ingredients are in place, empowerment can have a noticeable effect on employee motivation and performance.[75]

Forming natural work units Another way to enrich jobs is to group tasks into a natural grouping, such as completing a whole task. An example of forming a natural work unit would be assembling an entire computer modem

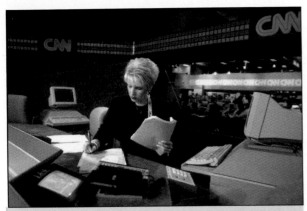

Traditionally, television networks required up to four people to shoot a news clip: a reporter, camera operator, sound operator, and lighting person. Now, CNN and other companies want one video journalist to perform all four jobs. "Look for the quick introduction of small, high-quality DV cameras and laptop editing equipment, enabling us to deploy smaller reporting teams, one or two people at a time, when it makes sense," CNN executives wrote in a recent memo to employees. "[C]orrespondents would do well to learn how to shoot and edit . . . and smart shooters and editors will learn how to write and track." The memo continues by saying that "CNN will always value exceptional ability, [but] the more multi-talented a newsgatherer, the more opportunity the News Group will provide that person."[77] According to the job characteristics model, how would the video journalist job have more motivational potential than each of the more specialized jobs?
(© Ted Thai/TimePix)

rather than just some parts of it. Or it might involve assigning employees to a specific client group, such as managing entire portfolios for specific clients rather than taking random client calls from a customer service pool. Forming natural work units gives jobholders stronger feelings of responsibility for an identifiable body of work. They feel a sense of ownership and, therefore, tend to increase job quality. Forming natural work units increases task identity and task significance because employees perform a complete product or service and can more readily see how their work affects others.

Establishing client relationships As mentioned, some natural work units assign employees to a specific client group. However, establishing client relationships takes this process one step further by putting employees in *direct contact* with their clients rather than using the supervisor as a go-between. The key factor is direct communication with clients. These clients submit work and provide feedback directly to the employee rather than through a supervisor. By being directly responsible for specific clients, employees have more information and can make decisions affecting those clients.[76]

Brooklyn Union, a New York gas company, has enriched the jobs of field distribution crews by establishing client relationships. At one time, these crews would only install pipes from the main lines to the house. A customer service representative would then come into the house to finish the work. Now, the distribution employees do the entire job and work directly with customers. After the distribution employees have installed the pipes, they clean off their shoes and enter the house to unlock the gas, relight the pilot light, and check the results. The customer deals with one person or crew, and the field staff feel a stronger sense of obligation to their client.[78]

Job Design Prospects and Problems

Job rotation, enlargement, and enrichment are now common in the United States. Research suggests that job design interventions have a much higher survival rate than most other work interventions and are generally effective. In particular, employees with high growth needs in enriched jobs have higher job satisfaction and work motivation, along with lower absenteeism and turnover. Productivity is also higher when task identity and job feedback are improved. Product and service quality tend to improve because job enrichment increases the jobholder's felt responsibility and sense of ownership over the product or service. Quality improvements are most apparent when employees complete a natural work unit or establish client relationships.[79]

Obstacles in Job Design In spite of these potential benefits, job design is not easy to implement. Objective measures of job characteristics are expensive, and the *perceived* job characteristics measures typically used by scholars and consultants may be distorted by the employee's attitudes regarding other aspects of the job.[80] Job design interventions also face resistance to change. Some supervisors don't like job redesign interventions because they change their roles and may threaten job security.[81] Labor union leaders have been bitter foes of job specialization and scientific management, yet many are concerned that job enrichment programs are management ploys to get more work out of employees for less money. Unskilled employees may lack the confidence or growth need strength to learn more challenging tasks. Skilled employees are known to resist job redesign because they believe the intervention will undermine their power base and force them to perform lower-status work.[82]

Lastly, an ongoing dilemma with job design is finding the ideal balance between job enrichment and specialization. There are several competing factors to consider. Specialized jobs may improve work efficiency, but performance may fall if this specialization reduces employee motivation. Job enrichment may increase motivation, but performance may fall if employees lack the skills necessary to perform these challenging tasks. Job enrichment may increase recruiting and training costs, whereas job specialization may increase payroll costs if companies provide discontentment pay to entice people into boring jobs.[83] Job enrichment improves product quality, but error rates may increase when tasks become so challenging that employees lack the necessary skills or experience stress.[84] Of course, job specialization also increases stress if employees do not make effective use of their talents in narrowly defined jobs.

MOTIVATING YOURSELF THROUGH SELF-LEADERSHIP

While most companies are busy finding new "carrots" to motivate employees, Key Resources is teaching its employees to motivate themselves. On their first day of work at the Atlanta-based company, new recruits are brought to a quiet room and asked to write down what they want to do and achieve, from personal to professional goals. "The intention is to give them a process, a formula to set and achieve goals," explains Key Resources chief executive Jeff Moore. "People are self-motivated."[85]

Jeff Moore recognizes that employees motivate themselves and direct their own behavior most of the time. According to a recent survey, corporate leaders also identify self-motivation as one of the most important features to look for in new hires.[86] This is probably because direct supervision is becoming too expensive and is incompatible with the values and expectations of today's workforce.

The emerging view is that employees should manage themselves most of the time through **self-leadership**—the process of influencing oneself to establish the self-direction and self-motivation needed to perform a task.[87] This concept includes a tool kit of behavioral activities borrowed from social learning theory (Chapter 2) and goal setting (Chapter 5). It also includes constructive thought processes that have been studied extensively in sports psychology. Overall, self-leadership takes the view that individuals mostly regulate their own actions through these behavioral and cognitive (thought) activities.

Although we are in the early stages of understanding the dynamics of self-leadership, the five main elements of this process have been identified

self-leadership
The process of influencing oneself to establish the self-direction and self-motivation needed to perform a task.

EXHIBIT 6.6 Elements of self-leadership

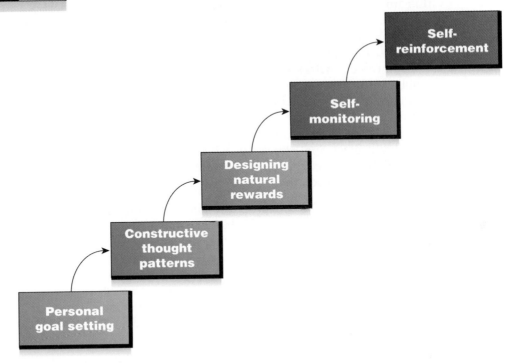

(Exhibit 6.6). These elements, which generally follow each other in a sequence, include personal goal setting, constructive thought patterns, designing natural rewards, self-monitoring, and self-reinforcement.[88]

Personal Goal Setting

The first step in self-leadership is to set goals for your own work effort. This step applies the ideas we learned in Chapter 5 on goal setting, such as identifying goals that are specific, relevant, and challenging. The main difference between personal goal setting and our previous discussion is that goals are set alone, rather than assigned by or jointly decided with a supervisor. According to the self-leadership literature, effective organizations establish norms whereby employees have a natural tendency to set their own goals to motivate themselves.[89]

self-talk
Talking to ourselves about our own thoughts or actions for the purpose of increasing our self-efficacy and navigating through decisions in a future event.

Constructive Thought Patterns

Before beginning a task and while performing it, employees should engage in positive (constructive) thoughts about that work and its accomplishment. In particular, employees are more motivated and better prepared to accomplish a task after they have engaged in positive self-talk and mental imagery.

Positive Self-Talk   Do you ever talk to yourself? Most of us do, according to a recent study of undergraduate students.[90] **Self-talk** refers to any situation in which we talk to ourselves about our own thoughts or actions. Some of this internal communication assists the decision-making process, such as weighing the advantages of a particular choice. Self-leadership is mostly interested in evaluative self-talk, in which you evaluate your capabilities and accomplishments.

The problem with most evaluative self-talk is that it is negative; we criticize much more than encourage or congratulate ourselves. Negative self-talk undermines our self-efficacy, which, in turn, undermines our potential for performing a particular task.[91] In contrast, positive self-talk creates a can-do belief and thereby increases motivation by raising our E→P expectancy. We often hear that professional athletes psych themselves up before an important event. They tell themselves that they can achieve their goal and that they have practiced enough to reach that goal. They motivate themselves through self-talk.

Mental Imagery   You've probably heard the phrase "I'll cross that bridge when I come to it." Self-leadership takes the opposite view. It suggests that we need to practice a task mentally and imagine performing it successfully beforehand. This process is known as **mental imagery.**[92]

As you can see from this definition, mental imagery has two parts. One part involves practicing the task mentally, anticipating obstacles to goal accomplishment, and working out solutions to those obstacles before they occur. By mentally walking through the activities required to accomplish the task, we

mental imagery
Mentally practicing a task and visualizing its successful completion.

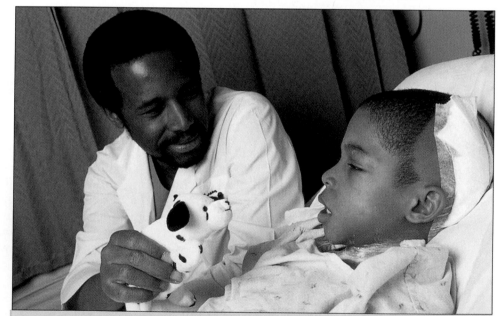

As one of the world's leading neurosurgeons, Dr. Ben Carson uses mental imagery to visualize each medical operation he performs—up to 500 of them each year. "I think through every procedure: how I expect it to go, how long each phase will last, when I can move on to the next one," explains the chief of pediatric neurosurgery at Johns Hopkins Hospital in Baltimore. Carson also imagines the worst thing that could happen, and what he should do if it does. "I always anticipate the worst-case scenario," says Carson.[93] How might Dr. Carson apply other elements of the self-leadership model in his work? *(Courtesy of Carson Scholars Fund)*

begin to see problems that may occur. We can then imagine what responses would be best for each contingency.[94]

While one part of mental imagery helps us anticipate things that could go wrong, the other part involves visualizing successful completion of the task. We imagine the experience of completing the task and the positive results that follow. Everyone daydreams and fantasizes about being in a successful situation. You might imagine yourself being promoted to your boss's job, receiving a prestigious award, or taking time off work. This visualization increases goal commitment and motivates us to complete the task effectively.

Designing Natural Rewards

Self-leadership recognizes that employees actively craft their jobs. To varying degrees, they can alter tasks and work relationships to make the work more motivating.[95] One way to build natural rewards into the job is to alter the way a task is accomplished. People often have enough discretion in their jobs to make slight changes to suit their needs and preferences. For instance, you might try out a new software program to design an idea, rather than sketching the image with pencil. By using the new software, you are adding challenge to a task that may have otherwise been mundane.

Self-Monitoring

Self-monitoring is the process of keeping track of one's progress toward a goal. In the section on job design, we learned that feedback from the job itself communicates whether we are accomplishing the task successfully. Self-monitoring includes the notion of consciously checking that naturally occurring feedback at regular intervals. It also includes designing artificial feedback where natural feedback does not occur. Salespeople might arrange to receive monthly reports on sales levels in their territory. Production staff might have gauges or computer feedback systems installed so that they can see how many errors are made on the production line. Research suggests that people who have control over when they receive performance feedback perform their tasks better than those with feedback assigned by others.[96]

Self-Reinforcement

Self-leadership includes the social learning theory concept of self-reinforcement. Self-reinforcement occurs whenever an employee has control over a reinforcer but doesn't take the reinforcer until completing a self-set goal (see Chapter 2).[97] A common example is taking a break after reaching a predetermined stage of your work. The work break is a self-induced form of positive reinforcement. Self-reinforcement also occurs when you decide to do a more enjoyable task after completing a task that you dislike. For example, after slogging through a difficult report, you might decide to spend time doing a more pleasant task, such as catching up on industry news by scanning websites.

Self-Leadership in Practice

It's too early to say that every component of self-leadership is useful, but evidence suggests that these practices generally improve self-efficacy, motivation, and performance. Studies in sports psychology indicate that self-set goals and constructive thought processes improve individual performance. For example, young ice-skaters who received self-talk training improved their performance one year later. Self-talk and mental imagery have also improved performance of tennis players and female college swimmers. Indeed, studies show that almost all Olympic athletes rely on mental rehearsal and positive self-talk to achieve their performance goals.[98]

One of the few studies in organizational settings reported that new employees who practiced self-set goals and self-reinforcement had higher internal motivation. Another study found that airline employees who received constructive thought training experienced better mental performance, enthusiasm, and job satisfaction than co-workers who did not receive this training.[99]

People with a high degree of conscientiousness and internal locus of control are more likely to apply self-leadership strategies. However, one of the benefits of self-leadership is that it can be learned. Training programs have helped employees improve their self-leadership skills. Organizations can also encourage self-leadership by providing sufficient autonomy and establishing rewards that reinforce self-leadership behaviors. Employees are also more likely to engage in self-monitoring in companies that emphasize continuous measurement of performance.[100] Overall, self-leadership promises to be an important concept and practice for improving employee motivation and performance.

Self-leadership, job design, and rewards are valuable approaches to motivating people in organizational settings. However, they are not the only ways to motivate. Motivation is derived from a person's unique combination of natural and learned needs. Each of these needs can be fulfilled in many ways and from various sources. In some respects, many of the topics covered later in this book—such as team cohesiveness and corporate culture—also affect employee motivation.

CHAPTER SUMMARY

Money and other financial rewards are a fundamental part of the employment relationship. They also potentially fulfill existence, relatedness, and growth needs. People experience various emotions and hold many attitudes toward financial rewards. They also tend to identify themselves in terms of how much money they have acquired and dispersed.

Organizations reward employees for their membership and seniority, job status, competencies, and performance. Membership-based rewards may attract job applicants, and seniority-based rewards reduce turnover. However, they are more likely to discourage turnover among those with the lowest performance. Rewards on the basis of job status try to maintain internal equity and motivate employees to compete for promotions. However, job status-based rewards can lead to organizational politics and create a psychological distance between employees and management.

Competency-based rewards are becoming increasingly popular because they improve workforce flexi-

bility and are consistent with the emerging idea of employability. However, competency-based rewards tend to be measured subjectively and can result in higher costs as employees spend more time learning new skills.

Piece rates, commissions, and other individual performance-based rewards have existed for centuries and are widely used. Many companies are shifting to team-based rewards, such as gainsharing plans, and to organizational rewards, such as employee stock ownership plans (ESOPs), stock options, and profit sharing. ESOPs and stock options create an ownership culture, but employees often perceive a weak connection between individual performance and the organizational reward.

Financial rewards have been criticized for being used as quick fixes. There is also a risk that they distract employees from the motivational potential of the work, create a psychological distance between the person giving and the person receiving the reward, and discourage creativity and risk taking. To improve reward effectiveness, organizational leaders should ensure that rewards are linked to work performance, are aligned with performance within the employee's control, are valued by employees, and do not have unintended consequences. Additionally, leaders should ensure that team rewards are used where jobs are interdependent.

Job design involves assigning tasks to a job and distributing work throughout the organization. Job specialization, which subdivides work into separate jobs for different people, increases work efficiency because employees master the tasks quickly, spend less time changing tasks, require less training, and can be matched more closely with the jobs best suited to their skills. However, job specialization may reduce work motivation, create mental health problems, lower product or service quality, and increase costs through discontentment pay, absenteeism, and turnover.

Contemporary job design strategies reverse job specialization through job rotation, job enlargement, and job enrichment. The job characteristics model is a template for job redesign that specifies core job dimensions, psychological states, and individual differences. Companies often enrich jobs through empowering employees, forming natural work units, and establishing client relationships.

Self-leadership is the process of influencing oneself to establish the self-direction and self-motivation needed to perform a task. This process includes personal goal setting, constructive thought patterns, designing natural rewards, self-monitoring, and self-reinforcement. Constructive thought patterns include self-talk and mental imagery. Self-talk refers to any situation in which a person talks to him- or herself about his or her own thoughts or actions. Mental imagery involves practicing a task mentally and imagining performing it successfully beforehand.

KEY TERMS

autonomy, p. 180

employee stock ownership plans (ESOPs), p. 171

empowerment, p. 183

gainsharing plan, p. 169

job characteristics model, p. 178

job design, p. 174

job enlargement, p. 181

job enrichment, p. 183

job evaluation, p. 167

job feedback, p. 180

job rotation, p. 181

job specialization, p. 176

mental imagery, p. 186

profit sharing, p. 171

scientific management, p. 177

self-leadership, p. 184

self-talk, p. 185

skill variety, p. 179

skill-based pay, p. 168

stock options, p. 171

task identity, p. 180

task significance, p. 180

DISCUSSION QUESTIONS

1. As a consultant, you have been asked to recommend either a gainsharing or a profit sharing plan for employees who work in the four regional distribution and warehousing facilities of a large retail organization. Which reward system would you recommend? Explain your answer.

2. Some city councils pay bonuses to parking contractors when they issue more than a predetermined minimum number of parking fines each month. Discuss the benefits and potential problems associated with this reward system.

3. Yakka Tire Corporation has redesigned its production facilities around a team-based system. However, the company president believes that employees will not be motivated unless they receive incentives on the basis of their individual performance. Give three explanations why Yakka Tire should also introduce team-based rewards in this setting.

4. Under what conditions would job specialization be most appropriate?

5. Most of us have watched pizzas being made while we are waiting to pick one up from a pizza shop. What level of job specialization do you usually notice in these operations? Why does this high or low level of specialization exist? If some pizza shops have different levels of specialization than others, identify the contingencies that might explain the differences.

6. In a large grocery store, cashiers spend most of their time at the cash register, stock handlers focus on moving goods from the storeroom onto the shelves, and cleaners keep the area clean. But Aldi, a German-based company, has opened grocery superstores where cashiers are asked to bring stock from storage areas, stock shelves, and clean the floors at the end of the day. Use the job characteristics model to explain the implications of Aldi's revised job description for cashiers.

7. Tomorrow, you present your first report to senior management to extend funding for your unit's special initiative. All the materials are ready for the

presentation. Following the five steps in self-leadership, describe how you can prepare for that meeting.

8. Several elements of self-leadership are derived from concepts presented earlier in this book.

Identify those concepts and explain how they are applied in self-leadership.

CASE STUDY 6.1

KEEPING SUZANNE CHALMERS

Thomas Chan hung up the telephone and sighed. The vice president of software engineering at Advanced Photonics Inc. (API) had just spoken to Suzanne Chalmers, who called to arrange a meeting with Chan later that day. She didn't say what the meeting was about, but Chan almost instinctively knew that Suzanne was going to quit after working at API for the past four years. Chalmers is a software engineer in Internet Protocol (IP), the software that directs fiber-optic light through API's routers. It is very specialized work, and Suzanne is one of API's top talents in that area.

Thomas Chan had been through this before. A valued employee would arrange a private meeting. The meeting would begin with a few pleasantries; then the employee announces that he or she wants to quit. Some employees say they are leaving because of the long hours and stressful deadlines. They say they need to decompress, get to know the kids again, or whatever. But that's not usually the real reason. Almost every organization in this industry is scrambling to keep up with technological advances and the competition. They would just leave one stressful job for another one.

Also, many of the people who leave API join a start-up company a few months later. These start-up firms can be pressure cookers where everyone works 16 hours each day and has to perform a variety of tasks. For example, engineers in these small firms might have to meet customers or work on venture capital proposals rather than focus on specialized tasks related to their knowledge. API has over 1,000 employees, so it is easier to assign people to work that matches their technical competencies.

No, the problem isn't the stress or long hours, Chan thought. The problem is money—too much

money. Most of the people who leave are millionaires. Suzanne Chalmers is one of them. Thanks to generous stock options that have skyrocketed on the stock markets, many employees at API have more money than they can use. Most are under 40 years old, so they are too young to retire. But their financial independence gives them less reason to remain with API.

The Meeting

The meeting with Suzanne Chalmers took place a few hours after the telephone call. It began like the others, with the initial pleasantries and brief discussion about progress on the latest fiber-optic router project. Then, Suzanne made her well-rehearsed statement: "Thomas, I've really enjoyed working here, but I'm going to leave Advanced Photonics." Suzanne took a breath, then looked at Chan. When he didn't reply after a few seconds, she continued: "I need to take time off. You know, get away to recharge my batteries. The project's nearly done and the team can complete it without me. Well, anyway, I'm thinking of leaving."

Chan spoke in a calm voice. He suggested that Suzanne should take an unpaid leave for two or maybe three months, complete with paid benefits, then return refreshed. Suzanne politely rejected that offer, saying that she needs to get away from work for a while. Thomas then asked Suzanne whether she was unhappy with her work environment—whether she was getting the latest computer technology to do her work and whether there were problems with co-workers. The workplace was fine, Susanne replied. The job was getting a bit routine, but she had a comfortable workplace with excellent co-workers.

Chan then apologized for the cramped work space, due mainly to the rapid increase in the number of people hired over the past year. He suggested that if Suzanne took a couple of months off, API would give her special treatment with a larger work space with a better view of the park behind the campuslike building when she returned. She politely thanked Chan for that offer, but it wasn't what she needed. Besides, it wouldn't be fair to have a large work space when other team members work in smaller quarters.

Chan was running out of tactics, so he tried his last hope: money. He asked whether Suzanne had higher offers. Suzanne replied that she regularly received calls from other companies, and some of them offered more money. Most were start-up firms that offered a lower salary but higher potential gains in stock options. Chan knew from market surveys that Suzanne was already paid well in the industry. He also knew that API couldn't compete on stock option potential. Employees working in start-up firms sometimes saw their shares increase by five or ten times their initial value, whereas shares at API and other large firms increased more slowly. However, Chan promised Suzanne that he would recommend that she receive a significant raise—maybe 25 percent more—and more stock options. Chan added that Chalmers was one of API's most valuable employees and that the company would suffer if she left the firm.

The meeting ended with Chalmers promising to consider Chan's offer of higher pay and share options. Two days later, Chan received her resignation in writing. Five months later, Chan learned that after a few months traveling with her husband, Chalmers joined a start-up software firm in the area.

Discussion Questions

1. Do financial rewards have any value in situations such as this, where employees are relatively wealthy?

2. If you were Thomas Chan, what strategy, if any, would you use to motivate Susan Chalmers to stay at Advanced Photonics Inc.?

3. Of what importance is job design in this case?

CASE STUDY 6.2

SAVAGED BY THE SLOWDOWN

BusinessWeek During the business boom of the 1990s, many companies used stock options to attract and reward employees. A stock option gives its owner the right to buy a specified amount of stock at a specified price during a specified time period. When stock prices were soaring, the value of an employee's stock options might rise along with the market to a million dollars or more. When stock prices peaked and fell, however, the value of the options could fall to zero—and sometimes stock ownership involved hefty tax bills in spite of its worthlessness. Worse yet, many employees who were used to being courted by employers began to experience shrinking bonuses and even layoffs. In this environment, what can an employer offer the remaining employees to keep them motivated, even as they shoulder the responsibilities of their laid-off colleagues?

This *Business Week* case study describes the challenges of motivating employees in a slowing economy. The examples of worried, debt-burdened employees illustrate the need for motivational tools that are appropriate for this situation. Read through this *Business Week* case study at www.mhhe.com/mcshane2e and prepare for the discussion questions below.

Discussion Questions

1. How have changing income levels affected the employees described in this article? Consider the effects on their motivation at work, as well as the effects on them personally.

2. According to the examples in this article, what are some disadvantages of rewards linked to a company's profits or stock price? How might an employer address these disadvantages?

3. What do you think are appropriate ways to motivate the employees described in this

article? Consider both rewards and job-related sources of motivation.

Source: Michelle Conlin, "Savaged by the Slowdown," *Business Week,* September 17, 2001.

T E A M   E X E R C I S E   6.3

IS STUDENT WORK ENRICHED?

Purpose   This exercise is designed to help students learn how to measure the motivational potential of jobs and to evaluate the extent that jobs should be further enriched.

Instructions   Being a student is like being an employee in several ways. You have tasks to perform, and someone (such as your instructor) oversees your work. Although few people want to be students most of their lives (the pay rate is too low!), it may be interesting to determine how enriched your job is as a student.

- *Step 1*—Students are placed into teams (preferably four or five people).
- *Step 2*—Working alone, each student completes both sets of measures in this exercise.

Then, using the guidelines below, they individually calculate the score for the five core job characteristics as well as the overall motivating potential score for the job.

- *Step 3*—Members of each team compare their individual results. The group should identify differences of opinion for each core job characteristic. They should also note which core job characteristics have the lowest scores and recommend how those scores could be increased.
- *Step 4*—The entire class will then discuss the results of the exercise. The instructor may ask some teams to present their comparisons and recommendations for a particular core job characteristic.

Job Diagnostic Survey						
Circle the number on the right that best describes student work.	Very little ▼		Moderately ▼			Very much ▼
1. To what extent does student work permit you to decide on your own how to go about doing the work? ... 1	2	3	4	5	6	7
2. To what extent does student work involve doing a whole or identifiable piece of work, rather than a small portion of the overall work process? 1	2	3	4	5	6	7
3. To what extent does student work require you to do many different things, using a variety of your skills and talents? 1	2	3	4	5	6	7
4. To what extent are the results of your work as a student likely to significantly affect the lives and well-being of other people (e.g., within your school, your family, society)? 1	2	3	4	5	6	7
5. To what extent does working on student activities provide information about your performance? 1	2	3	4	5	6	7
Circle the number on the right that best describes student work.	Very inaccurate ▼		Uncertain ▼			Very Accurate ▼
6. Being a student requires me to use a number of complex and high-level skills. 1	2	3	4	5	6	7

(continued)	Very inaccurate ▼			Uncertain ▼			Very Accurate ▼
7. Student work is arranged so that I do *not* have the chance to do an entire piece of work from beginning to end.	7	6	5	4	3	2	1
8. Doing the work required of students provides many chances for me to figure out how well I am doing.	1	2	3	4	5	6	7
9. The work students must do is quite simple and repetitive.	7	6	5	4	3	2	1
10. How well the work of a student gets done can affect a lot of other people.	1	2	3	4	5	6	7
11. Student work denies me any chance to use my personal initiative or judgment in carrying out the work.	7	6	5	4	3	2	1
12. Student work provides me the chance to completely finish the pieces of work I begin.	1	2	3	4	5	6	7
13. Doing student work by itself provides very few clues about whether or not I am performing well.	7	6	5	4	3	2	1
14. As a student, I have considerable opportunity for independence and freedom in how I do the work.	1	2	3	4	5	6	7
15. The work I perform as a student is *not* very significant or important in the broader scheme of things.	7	6	5	4	3	2	1

Source: Adapted from the Job Diagnostic Survey, developed by J. R. Hackman and G. R. Oldham. The authors have released any copyright ownership of this scale (see J. R. Hackman and G. Oldham, *Work Redesign* [Reading, MA: Addison-Wesley, 1980], p. 275).

Scoring Core Job Characteristics Use the following set of calculations to score the core job characteristics for the job of being a student. Use your answers from the Job Diagnostic Survey that you completed above.

$$\text{Skill variety (SV)} \qquad \frac{\text{Question } 3 + 6 + 9}{3} = \underline{\hspace{2cm}}$$

$$\text{Task identity (TI)} \qquad \frac{\text{Question } 2 + 7 + 12}{3} = \underline{\hspace{2cm}}$$

$$\text{Task significance (TS)} \qquad \frac{\text{Question } 4 + 10 + 15}{3} = \underline{\hspace{2cm}}$$

$$\text{Autonomy} \qquad \frac{\text{Question } 1 + 11 + 14}{3} = \underline{\hspace{2cm}}$$

$$\text{Job feedback} \qquad \frac{\text{Question } 5 + 8 + 13}{3} = \underline{\hspace{2cm}}$$

Calculating Motivating Potential Score (MPS) Use the formula on p.194 and the results above to calculate the motivating potential score. Notice that skill variety, task identity, and task significance are averaged before being multiplied by the scores for autonomy and job feedback.

$$\left(\frac{SV + TI + TS}{3} \right) \times \text{autonomy} \times \text{job feedback}$$

$$\left(\frac{\underline{} + \underline{} + \underline{}}{3} \right) \times \underline{} \times \underline{} = \underline{}$$

SELF-ASSESSMENT EXERCISE 6.4

WHAT IS YOUR ATTITUDE TOWARD MONEY?

Purpose This exercise is designed to help you understand the types of attitudes toward money and to assess your attitude toward money.

Instructions Read each statement below and circle the response that you believe best reflects your position regarding that statement. Then use the scoring key in Appendix B to calculate your results. This exercise is completed alone so that students assess themselves honestly without concerns of social comparison. However, class discussion will focus on the meaning of money, including the dimensions measured here and other aspects of money that may have an influence on behavior in the workplace.

Money Attitude Scale					
Circle the number that best reflects the extent you agree or disagree with each statement.	Strongly Agree ▼	Agree ▼	Neutral ▼	Disagree ▼	Strongly Disagree ▼
1. I sometimes purchase things because I know they will impress other people.	1	2	3	4	5
2. I regularly put money aside for the future.	1	2	3	4	5
3. I tend to get worried about decisions involving money.	1	2	3	4	5
4. I believe that financial wealth is one of the most important signs of a person's success.	1	2	3	4	5
5. I keep a close watch on how much money I have.	1	2	3	4	5
6. I feel nervous when I don't have enough money.	1	2	3	4	5
7. I tend to show more respect to people who are wealthier than I am.	1	2	3	4	5
8. I follow a careful financial budget.	1	2	3	4	5
9. I worry about being financially secure.	1	2	3	4	5
10. I sometimes boast about my financial wealth or how much money I make.	1	2	3	4	5
11. I keep track of my investments and financial wealth.	1	2	3	4	5
12. I usually say I can't afford it, even when I can afford something.	1	2	3	4	5

Sources: Adapted from J. A. Roberts and C. J. Sepulveda, "Demographics and Money Attitudes: A Test of Yamauchi and Templer's (1982) Money Attitude Scale in Mexico," *Personality and Individual Differences* 27 (July 1999), pp. 19–35; K. Yamauchi and D. Templer, "The Development of a Money Attitudes Scale," *Journal of Personality Assessment* 46 (1982), pp. 522–28.

SELF-ASSESSMENT EXERCISE 6.5

ASSESSING YOUR SELF-LEADERSHIP

Purpose This exercise is designed to help you understand self-leadership concepts and to assess your self-leadership tendencies.

Instructions Read each statement below and circle the response that you believe best reflects your position regarding that statement. Then use the scoring key in Appendix B to calculate your results. This exercise is completed alone so that students assess themselves honestly without concerns of social comparison. However, class discussion will focus on the meaning of each self-leadership concept, how this scale might be applied in organizations, and the limitations of measuring self-leadership in work settings.

Self-leadership questionnaire					
Circle the number that best reflects your position regarding each statement.	Describes me very well ▼	Describes me well ▼	Describes me somewhat ▼	Does not describe me well ▼	Does not describe me at all ▼
1. I try to keep track of how I am doing while I work. . . .	5	4	3	2	1
2. I often use reminders to help me remember things I need to do.	5	4	3	2	1
3. I like to work toward specific goals I set for myself. . .	5	4	3	2	1
4. After I perform well on an activity, I feel good about myself.	5	4	3	2	1
5. I seek out activities in my work that I enjoy doing. . . .	5	4	3	2	1
6. I often practice important tasks before I do them. . . .	5	4	3	2	1
7. I usually am aware of how I am performing an activity.	5	4	3	2	1
8. I try to arrange my work area in a way that helps me positively focus my attention on my work.	5	4	3	2	1
9. I establish personal goals for myself.	5	4	3	2	1
10. When I have successfully completed a task, I often reward myself with something I like.	5	4	3	2	1
11. When I have a choice, I try to do my work in ways that I enjoy rather than just trying to get it over with.	5	4	3	2	1
12. I like to go over an important activity before I actually perform it.	5	4	3	2	1
13. I keep track of my progress on projects I am working on.	5	4	3	2	1
14. I try to surround myself with objects and people that bring out my desirable behaviors.	5	4	3	2	1
15. I like to set task goals for my performance.	5	4	3	2	1
16. When I do an assignment especially well, I like to treat myself to something or an activity I enjoy.	5	4	3	2	1
17. I try to build activities into my work that I like doing. . .	5	4	3	2	1
18. I often rehearse my plan for dealing with a challenge before I actually face the challenge.	5	4	3	2	1

Source: C. C. Manz, *Mastering Self-Leadership: Empower Yourself for Personal Excellence* (Englewood Cliffs, NJ: Prentice Hall, 1992). Used with permission of the author. The scale presented here excludes the self-punishment dimension found in the SLQ1 instrument because it is not calculated in the SLQ1 total score. The designing natural rewards dimension presented here is measured by items in the third dimension of the SLQ2 instrument.

After studying the preceding material, be sure to check out our website at
www.mhhe.com/mcshane2e
for more in-depth information and interactivities that correspond to this chapter.

Stress Management

AFTER READING THIS CHAPTER, YOU SHOULD BE ABLE TO:

- Define *stress* and describe the stress experience.

- Outline the stress process from stressors to consequences.

- Identify the different types of stressors in the workplace.

- Explain why the same stressor might produce different stress levels in different people.

- Discuss the physiological, psychological, and behavioral effects of stress.

- Identify five ways to manage workplace stress.

Sammy Fong has coped with floods, earthquakes, and other crises for the California Department of Water Resources. But nothing compares with the intensity of his new job as an energy buyer for the State of California. "It's hard to convey the stress," says Fong, who must buy up enough energy supply to meet California's energy demand. "Your adrenaline's flowing, your senses are alive . . . and the gravity of everything is hanging over you."

Power shortages and sudden spikes in energy prices have put added pressure on Fong and his co-workers in Sacramento to make the right decisions. Wrong choices can cost millions or result in rolling blackouts. Trading room supervisors try to alleviate the stress by scrawling humorous messages on the wall or offering fun prizes, such as riding the boss's Harley-Davidson. They also watch for symptoms of burnout. "With the long hours, people start to get rummy after a while, and that's when it's time to rotate them out," says Fong.

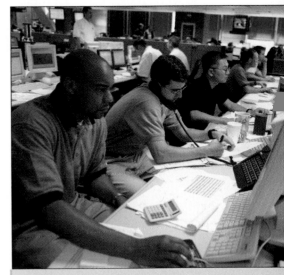

These energy traders at Houston-based Reliant Energy experience intense stress that wears out many of them within 10 years. (© *Smiley N. Pool*/The Houston Chronicle)

On Louisiana Street in Houston, America's center for energy trading, many energy traders wear out within 10 years. They are replaced by energetic newcomers, but it doesn't take long before they also feel stressed from the intense bartering and 24/7 schedule. "The money is so good, it's worth being obsessed and not taking vacations," says Robin Conner, a 30-year-old trader at Reliant Energy. "But it can wear you out. You get home at night and you don't even want to talk anymore. I want to soak in a tub for five hours."

Axia Energy trader Ken Merideth has the same feelings. "I am so burned out at the end of the day, I don't even want to make a decision about what to eat for dinner," he admits.[1]

The stress associated with energy trading has both short- and long-term effects on employees in this industry. But work-related stress is becoming an epidemic in almost every organization. According to a major survey by the Families and Work Institute, 28 percent of employees often or very often feel overworked or overwhelmed by work. Another recent survey suggests that over half of American employees say they work under a great deal of stress. The American Institute of Stress estimates that work-related stress costs American businesses about $300 billion each year in lower productivity and higher absenteeism, turnover, alcoholism, and medical costs.[2]

Chronic work-related stress is not just an American affliction. Japan's Institute of Life and Living reports that 68 percent of Japanese often feel worried and anxious, up from 37 percent a decade earlier. A study sponsored by the Canadian Heart and Stroke Foundation found that almost one-third of employees in that country regularly have difficulty coping with the demands of their jobs. Nearly two-thirds of Australian employees say they are under extreme stress at work. An international study reported that people born after 1955 are up to three times as likely to experience stress-related disorders as were their grandparents. At the Escorts Heart Institute in Delhi, India, routine cardiac screenings indicate that most executives are in the advanced stages of stress. "Corporate India is finally waking up to the fact that a lot of human potential is being drained away because of stress and burnout," says Shekhar Bajaj, CEO of the Indian consumer electronics manufacturer Bajaj Electricals.[3]

In this chapter, we look at the dynamics of work-related stress and how to manage it. The chapter begins by describing the stress experience. Next, the causes and consequences of stress are examined, along with the factors that cause some people to experience stress when others do not. The final section of this chapter looks at ways to manage work-related stress from either an organizational or an individual perspective.

WHAT IS STRESS?

stress

An individual's adaptive response to a situation that is perceived as challenging or threatening to the person's well-being.

Stress is an adaptive response to a situation that is perceived as challenging or threatening to the person's well-being.[4] As we shall see, stress is the person's reaction to a situation, not the situation itself. Moreover, we experience stress when something is perceived to interfere with our well-being, that is, with our need fulfillment. Stress has both psychological and physiological dimensions. Psychologically, people perceive a situation and interpret it as challenging or threatening. This cognitive appraisal leads to a set of physiological responses, such as higher blood pressure, sweaty hands, and faster heartbeat.

We often hear about stress as a negative consequence of modern living. People are stressed from overwork, job insecurity, information overload, and the increasing pace of life. These events produce *distress*—the degree of physiological, psychological, and behavioral deviation from healthy functioning.[5] There is also a positive side of stress, called *eustress*, that refers to the healthy, positive, constructive outcome of stressful events and the stress response. Eustress is the stress experience in moderation, enough to activate and motivate people so that they can achieve goals, change their environments, and succeed in life's challenges. In other words, we need some stress to survive. However, most research focuses on distress, because it is a significant concern in organizational settings.[6] Employees frequently experience enough stress to hurt their job performance and increase their risk of mental and physical health problems. Consequently, our discussion will focus more on distress than on eustress.

General Adaptation Syndrome

The stress experience was first documented 50 years ago by Dr. Hans Selye, a pioneer in stress research.[7] Selye determined that people have a fairly consistent physiological response to stressful situations. This response, called the **general adaptation syndrome,** provides an automatic defense system to help us cope with environmental demands. Exhibit 7.1 illustrates the three stages of the general adaptation syndrome: alarm reaction, resistance, and exhaustion. The line in this exhibit shows the individual's energy and ability to cope with the stressful situation.

general adaptation syndrome

A model of the stress experience, consisting of three stages: alarm reaction, resistance, and exhaustion.

Alarm Reaction   In the alarm reaction stage, the perception of a threatening or challenging situation causes the brain to send a biochemical message to various parts of the body, resulting in increased respiration rate, blood pressure, heartbeat, and muscle tension, as well as other physiological responses. At first, the individual's energy level and coping effectiveness decrease in response to the initial shock. Extreme shock, however, may result in incapacity or death because the body is unable to generate enough energy quickly enough. In most situations, the alarm reaction alerts the person to the environmental condition and prepares the body for the resistance stage.

Resistance   The person's ability to cope with the environmental demand rises above the normal state during the resistance stage because the body has activated various biochemical, psychological, and behavioral mechanisms. For example, we have a higher than normal level of adrenaline during this stage, which gives us more energy to overcome or remove the source of stress. However, our resistance is directed to only one or two environmental demands, so we become more vulnerable to other sources of stress. This

EXHIBIT 7.1

Selye's general adaptation syndrome

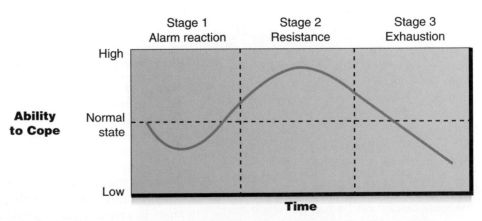

Source: Adapted from J. L. Gibson, J. M. Ivancevich, and J. H. Donnelly, *Organizations: Behavior, Structure, Processes,* 7th ed. (Burr Ridge, IL: Irwin, 1994), p. 265.

Janice Howell experienced all three stages of the general adaptation syndrome from teaching 28 students, 11 of them with learning or behavioral difficulties, at a primary school in Wales. She initially had the assistance of an English-language teacher, but that teacher took long-term leave and was not replaced. Unable to cope with the additional workload, Howell had a nervous breakdown. After recovering several months later, Howell complained to the school about the intolerable stress. Rather than providing support, the school added two more troubled kids to Howell's class. One new student to Wales ran away one morning and was seen playing near dangerous mudflats. Although he was taken home safely, no one told Howell until the end of the day. This incident led to Howell's second breakdown, effectively ending her career. "From being a confident, well-adjusted teacher who enjoyed her job, I became depressed and dysfunctional," says Howell, who was awarded U.S.$180,000 in compensation for her stress. "It got to the stage that I was physically unable to enter the classroom."[10] How does the exhaustion stage of the general adaptation syndrome relate to the consequences of stress discussed later in this chapter? *(Ian Nicholson/PA Photos)*

situation explains why people are more likely to catch a cold or other illness when they have been working under pressure.

Exhaustion   People have a limited resistance capacity, and if the source of stress persists, they will eventually move into the exhaustion stage as this capacity diminishes. In most work situations, the general adaptation syndrome process ends long before total exhaustion. Employees resolve tense situations before the destructive consequences of stress become manifest, or they withdraw from the stressful situation, rebuild their survival capabilities, and return later to the stressful environment with renewed energy. However, people who frequently experience the general adaptation syndrome have increased risk of long-term physiological and psychological damage.[8]

The general adaptation syndrome describes the stress experience, but this is only part of the picture. To effectively manage work-related stress, we must understand its causes and consequences as well as individual differences in the stress experience.

STRESSORS: THE CAUSES OF STRESS

Stressors, the causes of stress, include any environmental conditions that place a physical or emotional demand on the person.[9] There are numerous stressors in organizational settings and other life activities. Exhibit 7.2 lists the four main types of work-related stressors: physical environment, role-related, interpersonal, and organizational stressors.

Physical Environment Stressors

Some stressors, such as excessive noise, poor lighting, and safety hazards, are found in the physical work environment. For example, a study of textile workers in a noisy plant found that their levels of stress measurably decreased when they were supplied with ear protectors. Another study reported that clerical employees experience significantly higher stress levels in noisy open offices than in quiet areas.[11] Physical stressors also include poorly designed office space, lack of privacy, ineffective lighting, and poor air quality.

Causes and consequences of stress

Work-related stressors

Physical environment stressors

Role-related stressors

Interpersonal stressors

Organizational stressors

Individual differences

Stress

Nonwork stressors

Consequences of distress

Physiological
• Heart disease
• Ulcers
• High blood pressure
• Headaches
• Sleep disturbances
• More illness

Psychological
• Job dissatisfaction
• Depression
• Exhaustion
• Moodiness
• Burnout

Behavioral
• Lower job performance
• More accidents
• Faulty decisions
• Higher absenteeism
• Workplace aggression

stressors
The causes of stress, including any environmental conditions that place a physical or emotional demand on the person.

role conflict
Conflict that occurs when people face competing demands.

role ambiguity
Uncertainty about job duties, performance expectations, level of authority, and other job conditions.

Role-Related Stressors

Role-related stressors include conditions where employees have difficulty understanding, reconciling, or performing the various roles in their lives. The four main role-related stressors are role conflict, role ambiguity, workload, and task control.

■ *Role conflict*—**Role conflict** occurs when people face competing demands.[12] *Interrole conflict* exists when employees have two roles that conflict with each other. For example, sales staff in the U.S. banking industry experience interrole conflict trying to balance the needs of their bank and the needs of customers.[13] Role conflict also occurs when an employee receives contradictory messages from different people about how to perform a task (called *intrarole conflict*) or work with organizational values and work obligations that are incompatible with his or her personal values (called *person-role conflict*).[14]

■ *Role ambiguity*—**Role ambiguity** exists when employees are uncertain about their job duties, performance expectations, level of authority, and other job conditions. This ambiguity tends to occur when people enter new situations, such as joining the organization or taking a foreign assignment, because they are uncertain about task and social expectations.[15]

■ *Workload*—Work underload, receiving too little work or having tasks that do not sufficiently use your talents, is a possible stressor. However, work overload

Karoshi: Death by Overwork in Japan

Nobuo Miuro was under a lot of pressure from his employer to get a new restaurant ready for its launch. The interiors fitter from Tokyo worked late, sometimes until 4:30 in the morning. After one such marathon, Miuro caught a few hours of sleep, then returned for another long day. But he didn't get very far. The 47-year-old suddenly took ill and keeled over while picking up his hammer and nails. He died a week later. The coroner's verdict was that Miuro died of *karoshi*—"death by overwork."

Karoshi accounts for nearly 10,000 deaths each year in Japan. Research indicates that long work hours cause unhealthy lifestyle behaviors, such as smoking, poor eating habits, lack of physical exercise, and insufficient sleep. This lifestyle results in weight gain, which, along with stressful working conditions, damages the cardiovascular system and leads to strokes and heart attacks.

Karoshi came to the public spotlight in the 1970s when Japan's economy was booming, but the country's current recession is making matters worse. Companies are laying off employees and loading the extra work onto those who remain. Performance-based expectations are replacing lifetime employment guarantees, putting further pressure on employees to work long hours. Many also blame Japan's "samurai spirit" culture, which idealizes long work hours as the ultimate symbol of company loyalty and personal fortitude. "Being exhausted is considered a virtue," explains a Japanese psychiatrist.

So far, only 17 percent of Japanese firms offer overstressed employees some form of counseling. However, the Japanese government has launched an advertising campaign encouraging people to call a "karoshi hotline" for anonymous help. The families of deceased workaholics, including Nobuo Miuro's relatives, are also taking action by suing the employers for lack of due care.

Sources: "Trend of Caring for Employees Waning among Japan's Companies," *Japan Weekly Monitor*, May 14, 2001; C. Fukushi, "Workplace Stress Taking Toll on Women's Health," *Daily Yomiuri (Japan)*, April 21, 2001; S. Efron, "Jobs Take a Deadly Toll on Japanese," *Los Angeles Times*, April 12, 2000, p. A1; M. Millett, "Death of a Salaryman," *The Age (Melbourne)*, April 11, 2000, p. 15; E. Addley and L. Barton, "Who Said Hard Work Never Hurt Anybody?" *The Guardian (UK)*, March 13, 2001; M. Shields, "Long Working Hours and Health—1994–1997 Data," *Health Reports* 11 (Fall 1999), pp. 3–48.

is a far more common stressor these days. Employees have either too much to do in too little time, or they work too many hours on the job. Long work hours lead to unhealthy lifestyles, which, in turn, cause heart disease and strokes. As Global Connections 7.1 describes, work overload is such a problem in Japan that death from overwork has its own name—*karoshi*.

■ *Task control*—Employees are more stressed when they lack control over how and when they perform their tasks as well as the pace of work activity.[16] Work is potentially more stressful when it is paced by a machine or involves monitoring equipment, or when the work schedule is controlled by someone else. Information technology has this effect on office workers because they are always on call through e-mail, pagers, and cell phones. "I resent the fact that you can't get away today," says Pat Boyce, a medical equipment installer in Ohio who relies on his cell phone. "It's always there. You can be found at any time."[17]

Interpersonal Stressors

Interpersonal stressors include ineffective supervision, office politics, and other conflicts we experience with people. Call center employees are stressed from uncooperative customers and high productivity quotas. "260 calls a day from rude and angry people . . . it's hard to deal with at times," concludes one call center employee.[18] The trend toward teamwork also seems to generate more interpersonal stressors because employees must interact more with co-workers.[19]

Sexual Harassment   Laura Flannery was experiencing a lot of stress at the small Long Island manufacturing plant where she worked. The stress wasn't from her sales job; it was from an older male co-worker who would frequently drop by her office to boast about his sexual prowess and proposition her. Flannery recorded some of his lewd remarks so that the company owner would stop the problem, but no action was taken. "I was miserable whenever I saw him," says Flannery, "but I needed the job."[20]

Laura Flannery has experienced the stress of **sexual harassment**—unwelcome conduct of a sexual nature that detrimentally affects the work environment or leads to adverse job-related consequences for its victims. One form of sexual harassment, called *quid pro quo*, includes situations in which a person's employment or job performance is conditional on unwanted sexual relations (e.g., a male supervisor threatens to fire a female employee if she does not accept his sexual advances). Laura Flannery experienced the second and more common form of sexual harassment, called *hostile work environment*. This form of harassment includes sexual conduct that interferes unreasonably with an individual's work performance or creates an intimidating, hostile, or offensive working environment.[21]

However, sexual harassment is more than a legal issue. It is a serious interpersonal stressor.[22] Victims of sexual harassment experience trauma (especially from rape or related exploitation) or must endure tense co-worker relations in a hostile work environment. Moreover, they are expected to endure more stress while these incidents are investigated. This is particularly true in Japan and other countries where women who complain of harassment are sometimes stigmatized by friends and co-workers. "Companies don't want to hire 'dangerous women,' who make a fuss about sexual harassment," says Moeko Tanaka, the pen name of a Japanese woman who won a case of harassment against a prefecture governor.[23]

Workplace Violence   Another serious interpersonal stressor is the rising wave of physical violence in the workplace.[24] In the United States, 1,000 employees are murdered on the job each year and 2 million others experience lesser forms of violence. For instance, the National Institute of Occupational Safety and Health (NIOSH) estimates that more than 9,000 nurses and other health care workers are injured or verbally or physically attacked on the job *every day*.[25] But workplace violence isn't highest in the United States. According to research published by the International Labor Organization, employees in France, Argentina, Romania, Canada, and England have a higher incidence of workplace assaults and sexual harassment.[26]

Employees who experience violence usually have symptoms of severe distress after the traumatic event.[27] It is not uncommon for these primary victims to take long-term disability. Some never return to work. Workplace violence is also a stressor to those who observe the violence. After a serious workplace incident, counselors assist many employees, not just the direct victims. Even employees who have not directly experienced or observed violence may show signs of stress if they work in high-risk jobs. For example, one study reported that the greatest cause of work-related stress among British bus drivers was their perceived risk of physical assault.[28]

Workplace Bullying   Although less dramatic than violence, workplace bullying is becoming so common that it is considered a more serious interpersonal

sexual harassment

Unwelcome conduct of a sexual nature that detrimentally affects the work environment or leads to adverse job-related consequences for its victims.

workplace bullying
Offensive, intimidating, or humiliating behavior that degrades, ridicules, or insults another person at work.

stressor. **Workplace bullying** refers to offensive, intimidating, or humiliating behavior that degrades, ridicules, or insults another person at work.[29] The incidence of bullying reported in university studies ranges from 5 percent among hospital workers in Finland to 40 percent of federal court employees in Michigan (within the past five years). People with higher authority are more likely to engage in bullying or incivility toward employees in lower positions. Women are more likely than men to be targets of bullying.[30] Research indicates that most victims experience stress and its consequences following incidents of bullying. They also have more absenteeism and, back on the job, have impaired decision making, lower work performance, and more work errors.[31]

Bullying has become enough of a concern that Scandinavian countries have passed laws against it.[32] Some organizations have also taken steps to minimize the incidence of incivility. For example, Quaker Oats explicitly advises in its code of conduct that employees must treat each other with consideration, respect, and dignity. Past behavior is the best predictor of future behavior, so companies should carefully screen applicants in terms of past incidents. Feedback, particularly the 360-degree variety (see Chapter 2), lets employees know when their behavior is out of line. Lastly, organizations should have a grievance, mediation, or other conflict resolution process that employees trust when they become victims of workplace bullying.[33]

Organizational Stressors

Organizational stressors come in many forms. As we shall learn in Chapter 16, most forms of organizational change are stressful. Mergers and acquisitions are increasingly common organizational stressors, as are most other forms of organizational change. Downsizing (reducing the number of employees) is extremely stressful to those who lose their jobs. Layoff survivors also experience stress. For example, the company nurse at one high-tech firm discovered that the percentage of employees suffering from high blood pressure doubled after the company laid off 10 percent of its workforce. A study in Finland reported that long-term sick leave taken by surviving government employees doubled after a major downsizing.[34] As Connections 7.2 describes, the stress experienced by layoff survivors is due mainly to higher workloads, feelings of guilt, increased job insecurity, and the loss of friends at work.

Nonwork Stressors

Work is usually the most stressful part of our lives, but it's not the only part. We also experience numerous stressors outside organizational settings. Employees do not park these stressors at the door when they enter the workplace. The stressors carry over and ultimately affect work behavior. Moreover, the stress model shown earlier in Exhibit 7.2 has a two-way arrow, indicating that stressors from work spill over into nonwork and conflict with each other. The three main work–nonwork stressors are time-based, strain-based, and role behavior conflict.[35]

Time-Based Conflict   Jennifer Kelly knows all about the stress of trying to balance time at work with family. The graphic designer in New Jersey works 52 hours a week, sleeps about 6 hours a night and, in her words, is "frazzled

The Stress of Surviving Layoffs

Janet Driscoll enjoyed her job as marketing manager at Sega Software in Reston, Virginia—until the company laid off most of her staff. Sega was acquired by a large corporation, which slashed Driscoll's budget and left her to do the work of several people. But the toughest part of the downsizing was seeing her staff leave. As employees cleaned out their desks, Driscoll retreated to her office and cried. The experience was so heart-wrenching that Driscoll quit her job and moved to Colorado.

People who are laid off experience considerable stress, but so do the layoff survivors. Some of the stress is simply from the chaos of change. "Most people have their heads down, they're in shell shock during layoffs," says Dick Fincher, a consultant in Phoenix, Arizona, and survivor of 20 layoffs at various large employers. Others, such as Janet Driscoll, experience stress from losing friends and co-workers.

Patricia Baccus, who has 28 years of seniority at Virginia-based Viasystems Technologies Corporation, experienced layoff survivor stress from her feelings of guilt. "You felt a little guilty because you still had a job and there were those that didn't," she says after the circuit board manufacturer slashed half of its workforce. "I think it's going to be a long time before the hurt goes away."

For Mike Hewitt, being a layoff survivor meant coping with the stress of overwork. "When we were really busy and had a tough time keeping up with all the work coming in, I was probably working 40 hours a week," recalls the director of client services for Renaissance Worldwide in Cary, North Carolina. Following the layoffs at the information technology consulting firm, he was given tasks performed by former co-workers. "Now that business is down 15 percent, I'm working 60 hours a week," he says.

Janet Driscoll (shown here saying good-bye to a co-worker) quit her job at Sega Software because the stress of being a layoff survivor was too much. (© Paul Corbit Brown)

Sources: K. S. Rives, "Tired, Overworked and Stressed Out," *Raleigh (NC) News and Observer*, July 15, 2001, p. E1; J. Magruder, "Pink-Slip Blues Touch Entire Office," *Arizona Republic*, July 4, 2001, p. E1; S. Schafer, "Moving Up, Then Moving Out," *Washington Post*, May 8, 2001, p. E1; M. McCance, "Post-Layoff Workplace Stress," *Richmond (VA) Times Dispatch*, February 11, 2001, p. E1.

and tired." With clients all over the world, Kelly has a 24/7 schedule, leaving little time for family. "When I'm with them [the children], I'm so tired sometimes that I can't take them anywhere or do anything fun," admits Kelly.[36]

Jennifer Kelly has to contend with *time-based conflict*—the challenge of balancing the time demanded by work with family and other nonwork activities. This stressor is particularly noticeable in employees who hold strong family values. Time-based conflict largely explains why stress increases with the number of hours of paid employment and the amount of business travel or commuting time. Inflexible work schedules and rotating shift schedules also take a heavy toll because they prevent employees from effectively juggling work and nonwork.[37] Time-based conflict is more acute for women than for men because housework and childcare represent a "second shift" for many women in dual-career families.[38] Until men increase their contribution to homemaking and business learns to accommodate the new social order, many of these "supermoms" will continue to experience "superstress."

Strain-Based Conflict   *Strain-based conflict* occurs when stress from one domain spills over to the other. Relationship problems, financial difficulties, and loss of a loved one usually top the list of these nonwork stressors. New responsibilities, such as marriage, birth of a child, and a mortgage, are also stressful to most of us. Stress at work also spills over to an employee's personal life and often becomes the foundation of stressful relations with family and friends. One study found that fathers who experience stress at work engage in dysfunctional parenting behaviors, which then lead to their children's behavior problems in school.[39]

Role Behavior Conflict   A third work–nonwork stressor, called *role behavior conflict*, occurs when people are expected to enact different work and nonwork roles. People who act logically and impersonally at work have difficulty switching to a more compassionate behavioral style in their personal lives. For example, one study found that police officers were unable to shake off their professional role when they left the job. This role conflict was confirmed by their spouses, who reported that the officers would handle their children in the same manner as they would people in their job.[40]

Stress and Occupations

Several studies have attempted to identify which jobs have more stressors than others.[41] These lists are not in complete agreement, but Exhibit 7.3 identifies a representative sample of jobs and their relative levels of stress. You should view this information with some caution, however. One problem with rating occupations in terms of their stress levels is that a particular occupation may have considerably different tasks and job environments across organizations

EXHIBIT 7.3   Stressors in occupations

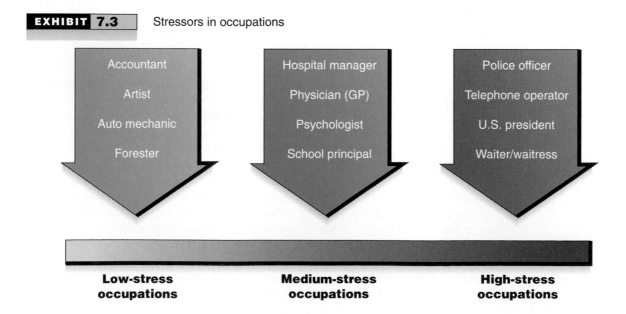

and societies. A police officer's job may be less stressful in a small town, for instance, than in a large city where crime rates are higher and the organizational hierarchy is more formal.

Another important point to remember when looking at Exhibit 7.3 is that a major stressor to one person is insignificant to another. In this respect, we must be careful not to conclude that people in high-stress occupations actually experience higher stress than people in other occupations. Some jobs expose people to more serious stressors, but careful selection and training can result in stress levels no different from those experienced by people in other jobs. The next section discusses individual differences in stress.

INDIVIDUAL DIFFERENCES IN STRESS

As indicated earlier in this chapter (see Exhibit 7.2), individual characteristics moderate the extent to which people experience stress or exhibit a specific stress outcome in a given situation. Two people may be exposed to the same stressor, such as having too many deadlines, yet they experience different stress levels or different stress symptoms.[42]

People exposed to the same stressors might have different stress symptoms for three reasons. One reason is that each of us perceives the same situation differently. People with high self-efficacy, for instance, are less likely to experience stress consequences in that situation because the stressor is less threatening.[43] Self-efficacy refers to a person's belief that he or she has the ability, motivation, and situational contingencies to complete a task successfully (see Chapter 2). Similarly, some people have personalities that make them more optimistic, whereas others are more pessimistic (see Chapter 3). Those with pessimistic dispositions tend to develop more stress symptoms, probably because they interpret the situation in a negative light.[44]

A second reason some people have more stress symptoms than others in the same situation is that people have different thresholds of resistance to a stressor. Younger employees generally experience fewer and less severe stress symptoms than older employees because they have a larger store of energy to cope with high stress levels. This explains why exercise and healthy lifestyles, discussed later in this chapter, are one way to manage stress. People who exercise regularly and have other healthy lifestyle behaviors are also less likely to experience negative stress outcomes.

A third reason people may experience the same level of stress and yet exhibit different stress outcomes is that they use different coping strategies.[45] Some employees tend to ignore the stressor, hoping that it will go away. This is usually an ineffective approach, which would explain why they experience higher stress levels. There is some evidence (although still inconclusive) that women cope with stress better than their male counterparts. Specifically, women are more likely to seek emotional support from others in stressful situations, whereas men try to change the stressor or use less effective coping mechanisms.[46] However, we must remember that these coping strategies are not true for all women or men.

Type A and Type B Behavior Patterns

A 52-year-old systems analyst collapsed on a downtown sidewalk. An ambulance crew discovered he had blood flow problems to his heart, so they strapped him to a gurney and hooked him up to a heart monitor. In spite of his confinement and health condition, the systems analyst tried to make business calls on his mobile telephone while the ambulance was racing him to the nearest hospital.[47]

type A behavior pattern

A behavior pattern associated with people having premature coronary heart disease; type A's tend to be impatient, lose their temper, talk rapidly, and interrupt others.

This systems analyst probably has a **type A behavior pattern.** Type A people are hard-driving, competitive individuals with a strong sense of time urgency. They tend to be impatient, lose their temper, talk rapidly, and interrupt others during conversations (see Exhibit 7.4).[48] In contrast, those with a **type B behavior pattern** are less competitive and less concerned about time limitations. They tend to work steadily, take a relaxed approach to life, and be even-tempered. Type B people may be just as ambitious to achieve challenging tasks, but they generally approach life more casually and systematically than do type A people. The important distinction, however, is that type B people are less likely than type A people to experience distress and its physiological symptoms (such as blood flow problems to the heart) when exposed to a stressor.

Regarding job performance, type A people tend to work faster than type B people, choose more challenging tasks, have higher self-motivation, and be more effective in jobs involving time pressure. On the other hand, type A people are less effective than type B people in jobs requiring patience, cooperation, and thoughtful judgment.[49] Type A people tend to be irritable and aggressive, so they generally have poorer interpersonal skills.

CONSEQUENCES OF DISTRESS

The general adaptation syndrome introduced at the beginning of this chapter describes how chronic stress diminishes the individual's resistance, resulting in adverse consequences for both the employee and the organization. This results in a variety of physiological, psychological, and behavior consequences.

EXHIBIT 7.4   Characteristics of type A and type B behavior patterns

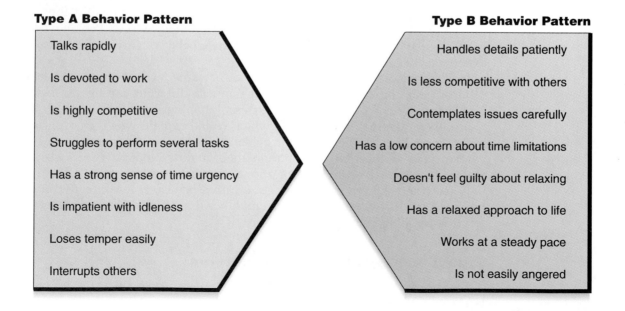

Type A Behavior Pattern

Talks rapidly

Is devoted to work

Is highly competitive

Struggles to perform several tasks

Has a strong sense of time urgency

Is impatient with idleness

Loses temper easily

Interrupts others

Type B Behavior Pattern

Handles details patiently

Is less competitive with others

Contemplates issues carefully

Has a low concern about time limitations

Doesn't feel guilty about relaxing

Has a relaxed approach to life

Works at a steady pace

Is not easily angered

Physiological Consequences

Stress takes its toll on the human body. Studies have found that medical students who are anxious about their exams are more susceptible to colds and other illnesses.[50] Many people experience tension headaches due to stress. Others get muscle pain and related back problems. These physiological ailments are attributed to muscle contractions that occur when people are exposed to stressors.

Cardiovascular disease represents one of the most disturbing effects of stress in modern society.[51] Strokes and heart attacks were rare a century ago but are now the leading causes of death among American adults. Stress also influences hypertension (high blood pressure). Hypertension has decreased in recent years as a result of better lifestyles and medical treatment. Still, nearly one-quarter of all American adults are treated for this condition.[52]

Medical researchers believe that the long-term effect of stress on the heart goes something like this: Whenever people are stressed, their blood pressure goes up and down. That frequent pressure change causes injury to the blood vessel walls, which eventually makes them constrict and function abnormally. Over time, this sequence leads to heart disease. Unfortunately, we often can't tell when we are physiologically stressed. For example, researchers have found that people think they are in a low-stress state when, in fact, their palms are sweating and their blood pressure has risen.[53]

Psychological Consequences

Stress produces various psychological consequences, including job dissatisfaction, moodiness, and depression.[54] Emotional fatigue is another psychological consequence of stress and is related to job burnout.

Job Burnout   **Job burnout** refers to the process of emotional exhaustion, depersonalization, and reduced personal accomplishment resulting from prolonged exposure to stress.[55] The phrase "job burnout" didn't exist 40 years ago; now it's heard in everyday conversations. Job burnout is a complex process that includes the dynamics of stress, coping strategies, and stress consequences. Burnout is caused by excessive demands made on people who serve or frequently interact with others. In other words, burnout is mainly due to interpersonal and role-related stressors.[56] For this reason, it is most common in helping occupations (e.g., nurses, teachers, police officers).

Exhibit 7.5 diagrams the relationship among the three components of job burnout. *Emotional exhaustion,* the first stage, plays a central role in the burnout process.[57] It is characterized by a lack of energy and a feeling that one's emotional resources are depleted. Emotional exhaustion is sometimes called compassion fatigue because the employee no longer feels able to give as much support and caring to clients.

Depersonalization follows emotional exhaustion and is identified by the treatment of others as objects rather than people. Burned-out employees become emotionally detached from clients and cynical about the organization. This detachment reaches the point of callousness, far beyond the level of detachment normally required in helping occupations. For example, a burned-out nurse might coldly label a patient as "the kidney in room 307."

type B behavior pattern
A behavior pattern of people with low risk of coronary heart disease; type B's tend to work steadily, take a relaxed approach to life, and be even-tempered.

job burnout
The process of emotional exhaustion, depersonalization, and reduced personal accomplishment resulting from prolonged exposure to stress.

EXHIBIT 7.5

The job burnout process

Interpersonal and role-related stressors

Emotional exhaustion

Depersonalization

Reduced personal accomplishment

Physiological, psychological, and behavioral consequences

Depersonalization is also apparent when employees strictly follow rules and regulations rather than try to understand the client's needs and search for a mutually acceptable solution.

Reduced personal accomplishment, the final component of job burnout, refers to the decline in one's feelings of competence and success, and becomes evident in feelings of diminished competency. In other words, the person's self-efficacy declines (see Chapter 2). In these situations, employees develop a sense of learned helplessness as they no longer believe that their efforts make a difference.

© 2001 Randy Glasbergen.
www.glasbergen.com

"It's a smoke detector. The boss thinks I might be headed for a burnout."

(Copyright © Randy Glasbergen. Reprinted with special permission from www.glasbergen.com)

Behavioral Consequences

When stress becomes distress, job performance falls and workplace accidents are more common. High stress levels impair our ability to remember information, make effective decisions, and take appropriate action.[58] You have probably experienced this level of distress in an exam or emergency work situation. You forget important information, make mistakes, and otherwise draw a blank under intense pressure.

Overstressed employees also tend to have higher levels of absenteeism. One reason is that stress makes people sick. The other reason is that absenteeism is a coping mechanism. At a basic level, we react to stress through fight or flight. Absenteeism is a form of flight—temporarily withdrawing from the stressful situation so that we have an opportunity to re-energize. Companies may try to minimize absenteeism, but it sometimes helps employees avoid the exhaustion stage of the stress experience (see Exhibit 7.1).[59]

Workplace Aggression   Workplace aggression is more than the serious interpersonal stressor described earlier. It is also an increasingly worrisome consequence of stress.[60] Aggression represents the fight (instead of flight) reaction to stress. In its mildest form, employees engage in verbal conflict. They fly off the handle and are less likely to empathize with co-workers. Occasionally, the combination of an individual's background and workplace stressors escalate this conflict into more dangerous levels of workplace hostility.

Co-worker aggression represents a relatively small proportion of workplace violence, but these behaviors are neither random nor inconsequential. Like most forms of organizational behavior, co-worker aggression is caused by both the person and the situation.[61] Although certain individuals are more likely to be aggressive, we must remember that employee aggression is also a consequence of extreme stress.[62] In particular, employees are more likely to engage in aggressive behavior if they believe they have been treated unfairly, experience other forms of frustration beyond their personal control, and work in physical environments that are stressful (e.g., hot, noisy).

MANAGING WORK-RELATED STRESS

A recent Christmas holiday season was a nail-biter for Sharon Milligan. The 28-year-old retail director for New York fashion house Nicole Miller agonized as daily sales of the company's 14 stores fell below the previous year's numbers. She had to personally tell employees at the store in Scottsdale, Arizona, that the boutique there would be closed. A store scheduled for opening in Florida was delayed, missing a crucial weekend of holiday sales. Three days before Christmas, Milligan sat in the doctor's office with a fever and sore throat. "I just crashed," she says. Milligan flew to Jamaica the day after Christmas and slept through the first three days of her long-awaited vacation.[63]

Sharon Milligan was fortunate. She was able to manage her stress before matters got worse. Unfortunately, many of us deny the existence of our stress until it is too late. This avoidance strategy creates a vicious cycle because the failure to cope with stress becomes another stressor on top of the one that created the stress in the first place. The solution is to discover the tool kit of effective stress management strategies identified in Exhibit 7.6, and to

EXHIBIT 7.6

Stress management
strategies

determine which ones are best for the situation.[64] As we look at each approach, keep in mind that the organization and the employees have joint responsibility for effective stress management. Moreover, managing stress often includes more than one of these strategies.

Remove the Stressor

From this list of stress management strategies, some writers argue that the *only* way companies can effectively manage stress is by removing the stressors that cause unnecessary tension and job burnout. Other stress management strategies may keep employees "stress-fit," but they don't solve the fundamental causes of stress.[65]

One way for organizations to manage stress is to investigate the main causes of stress in their workplace. Good Hope Hospital in the United Kingdom is conducting such an audit by asking staff to complete confidential questionnaires to identify when and how they experience stress.[66] In general, research has found that one of the most powerful ways to remove workplace stressors is to empower employees so that they have more control over their work and work environment (see Chapter 6).[67] Role-related stressors can be minimized by selecting and assigning employees to positions that match their competencies. Noise and safety risks are stressful, so improving these conditions would also go a long way to minimize stress in the workplace. Workplace bullying can be minimized through clear guidelines for behavior and feedback to those who violate those standards.

Employees can also take an active role in removing stressors. If stress is due to ambiguous role expectations, for example, we might seek out more information from others to clarify these expectations. If a particular piece of work is too challenging, we might break it into smaller sets of tasks so that the overall project is less threatening or wearing. We can minimize workplace violence by learning to identify early warning signs of aggression in customers and co-workers and by developing interpersonal skills that dissipate aggression.

Family–Friendly and Work–Life Initiatives   As a consultant with a major firm, David Peterson worked on a long-term assignment in another city and flew home on weekends. But on one of those weekends, he overheard one of his two-year-old twin daughters ask his wife, "Does Daddy live here anymore?" That question changed Peterson forever. His children were growing up fast, and he didn't want to miss out on those special moments. So Peterson decided to form the North Highland Company, an independent management and technology consulting firm with a unique policy. The Atlanta-based company makes work-related travel completely voluntary. In fact, when work started coming in from other cities, North Highland set up separate offices with local consultants so that no one had to travel. "Consulting work is very stressful and travel is an additional strain, especially when you get to the point where you have a family and lots of responsibilities at home," says Peterson.[68]

North Highland and many other organizations have applied specific policies to help employees maintain a work–life balance. Many companies claim to offer a work–life balance, yet Americans are working more hours than ever and some employees complain that much of the rhetoric doesn't match corporate practices. Five of the most common work–life balance initiatives are flexible

On this workday afternoon, when many auto executives aren't even thinking about heading home, Mark-Tami Hotta is engaged in a rousing game of Daddy Elephant–Baby Elephant with his kids. The chief program engineer for the Ford Windstar minivan leaves work early three days each week as part of the company's effort to improve work–life balance. Hotta is starting to change Ford's culture away from one that praises long work hours as a badge of honor. For example, Hotta initiated an event where 250 people on the Windstar team agreed to get their assignments completed and be out of the building by 3 P.M. on Valentine's Day. The exercise was so successful that Ford's entire North America car group did the same on the Friday before Memorial Day.[71] What other activities would encourage busy Ford executives to balance their work with nonwork? (© D. Guralnick/Detroit News)

work time, job sharing, telecommuting, personal leave programs, and child care support.

■ *Flexible work time*—Many firms are flexible with regard to the hours, days, and amount of time employees want to work.

■ *Job sharing*—Job sharing splits a career position between two people so that they experience less time-based stress between work and family. They typically work different parts of the week, with some overlapping work time in the weekly schedule to coordinate activities.[69]

■ *Telecommuting*—Chapter 1 described how an increasing number of employees are telecommuting. This reduces the time and stress of commuting to work and makes it easier to fulfill family obligations, such as temporarily leaving the home office to pick up the kids from school. Research suggests that telecommuters experience a healthier work–life balance.[70] However, telecommuting may increase stress for those who crave social interaction. It also isn't a solution for child care.

■ *Personal leave programs*—Employers with strong work–life values offer extended maternity, paternity, and personal leaves to care for a new family or take advantage of a personal experience. The U.S. Family and Medical Leave Act gives expectant mothers (and anyone considered to have an illness) 12 weeks of unpaid, job-protected leave. However, almost every other developed nation requires employers to provide paid maternity leave.[72] Increasingly, employees require personal leave to care for elderly parents who need assistance.

■ *Child care support*—Nearly one-quarter of American employees have on-site or subsidized child care facilities. Child care support reduces stress because employees are less rushed to drop off their children and less worried during the day about how well they are doing.[73]

Withdraw from the Stressor

Removing the stressor may be the ideal solution, but that option is often not feasible. An alternative strategy is to permanently or temporarily remove employees from the stressor. Permanent withdrawal occurs when employees are transferred to jobs that better fit their competencies and values.

Temporary Withdrawal Strategies   Temporarily withdrawing from stressors is the most frequent way that employees manage stress. Nortel Networks has a relaxation room complete with comfy chairs and comedy videos where employees can temporarily escape from the hassles of work. Washrooms are becoming increasingly popular retreats for American employees, particularly as

Keep the Stress-Busting Siesta in Modern Spain

María José Mateo is defying a force that has ruled Spain for centuries. The 29-year-old bank employee is trying to stay awake during the afternoon. She and many other Spaniards are giving up their siesta—a two- or three-hour mid-afternoon break when employees head home for a hot meal, followed by a restful nap.

Customers in other European countries increasingly expect Spanish employees to answer the telephone throughout the day. Companies are also discouraging these long breaks in an attempt to increase productivity. TotalFina, the French oil company, gives its Spanish managers and salespeople coupons for nearby fast-food outlets—a hint that they should have a power lunch, not a power nap. Commuting is also killing siestas. Employees don't have time to commute twice each day through traffic-clogged Madrid and Barcelona.

Ironically, the siesta is disappearing just when people in other countries are discovering the health benefits of a midday snooze. American studies report that the nervous system needs a long break at night and a shorter one somewhere between 2 P.M. and 5 P.M. A smattering of American firms, such as Burlington Northern Santa Fe Railway, have established napping policies. Kodak, PepsiCo, IBM, and Pizza Hut offer courses teaching employees how to take power naps at work. Deloitte Consulting has gone as far as setting up nap rooms.

Fede Busquet, a former tanning salon owner, may have found a solution to Spain's siesta dilemma. Busquet realized that Spaniards still need their siesta when he noticed rows of parked cars along Barcelona's streets with men sleeping inside around midday. He thought these people might prefer a more comfortable place for a power nap near their office.

Busquet set up two dozen parlors where, for 1,000 pesetas (U.S.$7), customers get a 10-minute massage in an ergonomic chair, then an hour in that same chair to

Masseurs Remco Rafina, left, and Eva Pacheco give two people a special siesta massage in a newly opened massage parlor in Madrid, Feb. 3, 1999. For 1,000 pesetas ($7, 6 euros) customers get a 10-minute massage in an ergonomic chair, then an hour in that same chair to sleep or rest. Those in a hurry can stay half as long for half the price. *(AP Photo/Paul White)*

sleep or rest. Those in a hurry can stay half as long for half the price. Business is booming. It seems that Spaniards still need their midday siesta, but something quicker and closer to the office.

Sources: L. Stevens, "Believers in the Midday Doze Are Stripping Away Stigma of Siestas**,**" *Fort Worth (TX) Star-Telegram*, March 24, 2001; R. Hogan, "A Daytime Nap Could Make You More Productive," *Los Angeles Times,* January 15, 2001; S. M. Handelsblatt, "Stressed Out and Stranded in Barcelona?" *Wall Street Journal Europe*, August 4, 2000, p. 32; R. Boudreaux, "Spaniards Are Missing Their Naps," *Los Angeles Times*, March 28, 2000; D. Woolls, "Spanish Entrepreneur Finds Market Niche in Siesta Deprived," *Deseret News (Salt Lake City, UT)*, March 22, 1999.

open work spaces replace private offices.[74] Siestas provide midday sleep breaks for employees in Spain and other Mediterranean countries. However, as Global Connections 7.3 describes, Spanish employees are under pressure to give up their cherished siesta because of globalization and urbanization, just as other countries discover the benefits of these power naps.

Vacations represent somewhat longer temporary withdrawals from stressful conditions. Richer Sounds has eight holiday homes around the world, and all 300 employees at the U.K. hi-fi retailer are entitled to one week each year in one of these properties at no charge. "I'd far rather someone was using these places than being at home," says Richer Sounds managing director David Robinson. "That way, when they come back, they're relaxed and firing on all cylinders."[75] Nearly one-third of the best 100 companies to work for in America offer sabbaticals to long-service employees.[76] Sabbaticals represent an extended version of vacations, whereby employees take a few months of paid leave after several years of service.

Change Stress Perceptions

Employees often experience different levels of stress in the same situation because they perceive it differently. Consequently, stress can be minimized by changing perceptions of the situation. This strategy does not involve ignoring risks or other stressors. Rather, it involves strengthening our self-efficacy and self-esteem so that job challenges are not perceived as threatening.

Humor can help in this regard. Consider Shirley Cayton, director of nursing at Presbyterian Hospital in Matthews, North Carolina. When work gets tense, colleagues encourage Cayton to put on fuzzy kitty slippers—the ones that are three sizes too large and have jingly bells. "I feel silly, all dressed up in a business suit and wearing the slippers," she admits. But this little silliness breaks the sober business pressure and provides a little levity in the office.[77]

Several elements of self-leadership described in Chapter 6 can alter employee perceptions of job-related stressors. For example, mental imagery can reduce the uncertainty of future work activities. A study of newly hired accountants reported that personal goal setting and self-reinforcement can reduce the stress that people experience when they enter new work settings.[78] Positive self-talk can potentially change stress perceptions by increasing our self-efficacy and by helping us develop a more optimistic outlook, at least in that situation.

Control the Consequences of Stress

Coping with workplace stress also involves controlling its consequences. Research indicates that physical exercise reduces the physiological consequences of stress by helping employees lower their respiration, muscle tension, heartbeat, and stomach acidity.[79] Beyond fitness programs, some companies offer wellness programs that educate and support employees in better nutrition and fitness, regular sleep, and other good health habits.[80] Another way to control the physiological consequences of stress is through relaxation and meditation. Generally, these activities decrease the individual's heart rate, blood pressure, muscle tension, and breathing rate.[81]

employee assistance programs (EAPs)
Counseling services that help employees overcome personal or organizational stressors and adopt more effective coping mechanisms.

Many large employers offer **employee assistance programs (EAPs).** EAPs are counseling services that help employees overcome personal or organizational stressors and adopt more effective coping mechanisms. Most EAPs are broad-brush programs that counsel employees on any work or personal problems. Family problems often represent the largest percentage of EAP referrals, although this varies with industry and location. EAPs can be one of the most effective stress management interventions where the counseling helps employees understand the stressors, acquire stress management skills, and practice those skills.[82]

Receive Social Support

Social support from co-workers, supervisors, family, friends, and others is one of the more effective stress management practices.[83] Social support refers to the person's interpersonal transactions with others and involves providing either emotional or informational support to buffer the stress experience.

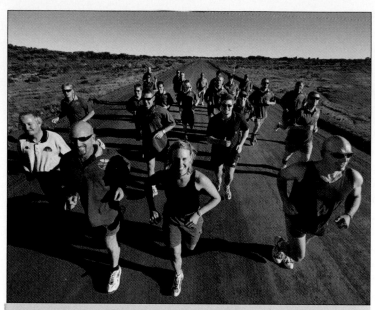

Employees at Homestake's Darlot gold mine are running for their lives. Each week, Fleta Solomon (center) and other exercise physiologists are flown into the mine site in Australia's outback to help the 190 miners and other staff improve their health and fitness. Along with organizing training runs, the physiologists check employee posture on the job, test cholesterol levels, and give lunchtime lectures on nutrition and coping with shift work. Darlot's mine manager hopes this health and fitness campaign will result in healthier employees who, in turn, experience less stress and have fewer accidents.[86] In your opinion, what else could Homestake do to help the Darlot mine employees minimize stress? (© R. Taylor/West Australian)

Social support reduces stress in at least three ways.[84] First, employees improve their perception that they are valued and worthy. This, in turn, increases their self-esteem and perceived ability to cope with the stressor (e.g., "I can handle this crisis because my colleagues have confidence in me"). Second, social support provides information to help employees interpret, comprehend, and possibly remove the stressor. For instance, social support might reduce a new employee's stress because co-workers describe ways to handle difficult customers. Finally, emotional support from others can directly help buffer the stress experience. This last point reflects the idea that misery loves company. People seek out and benefit from the emotional support of others when they face threatening situations.[85]

Everyone can practice social support by maintaining friendships. This important way to cope with stress includes helping others when they need a little support from the stressors of life. Organizations can facilitate social support by providing opportunities for social interaction among employees as well as their families. People in leadership roles should also practice a supportive leadership style when employees work under stressful conditions and need this social support. Mentoring relationships with more senior employees may also help junior employees cope with organizational stressors.

CHAPTER SUMMARY

Stress is an adaptive response to a situation that is perceived as challenging or threatening to the person's well-being. Distress represents high stress levels that have negative consequences, whereas eustress represents the moderately low stress levels needed to activate people. The stress experienc, called the general adaptation syndrome, involves moving through three stages: alarm reaction, resistance, and exhaustion.

The stress model shows that stress is caused by stressors. However, the effect of those stressors depends on individual characteristics. Stress affects a person's physiological and psychological well-being, and is associated with several work-related behaviors.

Stressors include any environmental conditions that place a physical or emotional demand on the person. Stressors are found in the physical work environment, the employee's various life roles, interpersonal relations, and organizational activities and conditions. Conflicts between work and nonwork obligations represent a frequent source of employee stress.

Two people exposed to the same stressor may experience different stress levels because they perceive the situation differently, have different threshold stress levels, or use different coping strategies. Employees with type A behavior patterns tend to experience more stress than those exhibiting type B behaviors.

High levels of stress or prolonged stress can cause physiological symptoms, such as high blood pressure, ulcers, sexual dysfunction, headaches, and coronary heart disease. Psychologically, stress reduces job satisfaction and increases moodiness, depression, and job burnout. Job burnout refers to the process of emotional exhaustion, depersonalization, and reduced

personal accomplishment resulting from prolonged exposure to stress. It is mainly due to interpersonal and role-related stressors and is most common in helping occupations. Behavioral symptoms of stress include lower job performance, poorer decisions, more workplace accidents, higher absenteeism, and more workplace aggression.

Many interventions are available to manage work-related stress. Some directly remove unnecessary stressors or remove employees from the stressful environment. Others help employees alter their interpretation of the environment so that it is not viewed as a serious stressor. Wellness programs encourage employees to build better physical defenses against stress experiences. Social support provides emotional, informational, and material resource support to buffer the stress experience.

KEY TERMS

employee assistance programs (EAPs), p. 215

general adaptation syndrome, p. 199

job burnout, p. 209

role ambiguity, p. 201

role conflict, p. 201

sexual harassment, p. 203

stress, p. 198

stressors, p. 201

type A behavior pattern, p. 208

type B behavior pattern, p. 209

workplace bullying, p. 204

DISCUSSION QUESTIONS

1. Use your favorite browser to find one of the many websites on managing stress. Which of the stress management strategies discussed in this chapter receives the most attention? Why, in your opinion, is that particular strategy highlighted more than others?

2. Sally works as an attorney for a leading Washington, D.C., law firm. She was married a few years ago and is currently pregnant with her first child. Sally expects to return to work full-time a few months after the baby is born. Describe two types of work–nonwork conflict that Sally will likely experience during the first year after her return to work.

3. Police officer and waiter are often cited as high-stress jobs, whereas accountant and forester are low-stress jobs. Why should we be careful about describing these jobs as high- or low-stress occupations?

4. Two recent graduates join the same major newspaper as journalists. Both work long hours and have

tight deadlines to complete their stories. They are under constant pressure to scout out new leads and be the first to report new controversies. One journalist is increasingly fatigued and despondent, and has taken several days of sick leave. The other is getting the work done and seems to enjoy the challenges. Use your knowledge of stress to explain why these two journalists are reacting differently to their jobs.

5. Do people with type A personalities make better managers? Why or why not?

6. A friend says that he is burned out by his job. What questions might you ask this friend to determine whether he is really experiencing job burnout?

7. How might fitness programs help employees working in stressful situations?

8. A senior official of a labor union stated: "All stress management does is help people cope with poor management. [Employers] should really be into stress reduction." Discuss the accuracy of this statement.

JIM BLACK: SALES REPRESENTATIVE

Jim Black impatiently drummed the steering wheel and puffed on a cigarette as his car moved slowly northbound along the parkway. Traffic congestion was normal in the late afternoon, but it seemed much heavier today. In any event, it was another irritation that was going to make him late for his next appointment.

As a sales representative at Noram Corporation, Jim could not afford to keep clients waiting. Sales of compressed oxygen and other gases were slow during this prolonged recession. Other compressed gas suppliers were eager to grab new accounts, and it was becoming more common for clients to switch from one supplier to another. Jim pressed his half-finished cigarette against the ashtray and accelerated the car into another lane.

Buyers of compressed gases knew that the market was in their favor, and many were demanding price discounts and shorter delivery times. Earlier in the week, for example, one of Jim's more demanding customers telephoned for another shipment of liquid oxygen to be delivered the next morning. To meet the deadline, Jim had to complete an expedited delivery form and then personally convince the shipping group to make the delivery in the morning rather than later in the day. Jim disliked making expedited delivery requests, even though this was becoming increasingly common among the reps, because it often delayed shipment of Noram's product to other clients. Discounts were even more troublesome because they reduced his commission and, except for very large orders, were frowned upon by Noram management.

Meanwhile, at Noram headquarters where Jim worked, senior managers were putting more pressure on sales reps to produce. They complained that the reps weren't aggressive enough, and area supervisors were told to monitor each sales rep's monthly numbers more closely. Jim fumbled for another cigarette as the traffic stopped momentarily.

Two months ago, the area sales supervisor had "a little chat" (as he called it) with Jim about the stagnant sales in his district and loss of a client to the competition. It wasn't exactly a threat of being fired—other reps also received these chats—but Jim felt nervous about his work and began having sleepless nights. He began making more calls to potential clients but was able to find this time only by completing administrative paperwork in the evenings. The evening work wasn't helping relations with his family.

To make matters worse, Noram's parent company in Germany announced that it planned to sell the U.S. operations. Jim had heard rumors that a competitor was going to purchase the firm, mainly to expand its operations through Noram's Western U.S. sales force and production facilities. The competitor was well established in the eastern United States where Jim worked, and probably wouldn't need a larger sales force there. Jim's job would be in jeopardy if the acquisition took place. Jim felt another headache coming on as he stared at the endless line of red taillights stretching along the highway ahead.

Even if Jim kept his job, any promotion into management would be a long way off if the competitor acquired Noram. Jim had no particular desire to become a manager, but his wife was eager for him to receive a promotion because it would involve less travel and provide a more stable salary (less dependent on monthly sales). Business travel was a nuisance, particularly for out-of-town appointments, but Jim felt less comfortable with the idea of sitting behind a desk all day.

The loud honk of another car startled Jim as he swerved into the exit lane that he was supposed to take (but almost missed). A few minutes later, he arrived at the client's parking lot. Jim rummaged through his briefcase for some aspirin to relieve the headache. He heaved a deep sigh as he glanced at his watch. Jim was 15 minutes late for the appointment.

Discussion Questions

1. What stress symptoms is Jim experiencing?
2. What stressors can you identify in this case?
3. What should Jim do to minimize his stress?

MELTDOWN: ARE YOU LOSING IT?

BusinessWeek In our society, entrepreneurs play the hero's role in business stories. We may revile some for ruthless actions and praise others for generous deeds, but either way, we admire entrepreneurs for creating something out of nothing but their drive and imagination. Playing the heroic role of entrepreneur comes at a price, however. Starting a business is demanding and often isolating—in a word, stressful.

This *Business Week* case study describes the stress facing entrepreneurs and their responses to it. The article includes several examples of entrepreneurs who have struggled with job-related stress, including their accounts of what helped them. Read through this *Business Week* case study at www.mhhe.com/mcshane2e and prepare for the discussion questions below.

Discussion Questions

1. According to the author's descriptions, what stressors affected Scott Corlett, Carol Frank, and Jon Brandt? What were some of the consequences of their stress?

2. How did these entrepreneurs learn to manage their stress? What other ways might they use?

3. According to the article, some people assume that stress and unhappiness are necessary aspects of an entrepreneur's life. Expressing a contrasting viewpoint, mental health consultant Jeffrey P. Kahn says, "I've worked with many successful entrepreneurs. I can't think of one who has been less successful as a result of becoming happier." How do the principles in this chapter support (or not support) these points of view?

Source: W. Smith, "Meltdown: Are You Losing It?" *Business Week*, April 23, 2001.

STRESSED OUT OR NO PROBLEM?

Purpose This exercise is designed to help students understand how people will have different stress reactions to the same stressors.

Instructions

- *Step 1*—Students individually indicate their response to each incident on the scoring sheet.
- *Step 2*—The instructor places students into groups (typically four or five people) to compare their results. For each incident, group members should discuss why each person feels more or less stress. They should pay particular attention to the reasons some students would feel little stress. Specifically, they should examine the extent that each person (a) perceives the situation differently, (b) has more or less tolerance to stressors due to health or need to cope with other problems, and (c) would use different coping strategies to deal with any stress related to the incident.
- *Step 3*—After group members have diagnosed these results, the instructor will bring the class together to compare results and discuss why people react differently to stressors.

Circle the number on the right that best describes the extent to which you would feel stressed in each situation	Very little ▼		Moderately ▼				Very much ▼
1. Your final exam for Economics 200 is in 48 hours, and a bad flu and other assignments have prevented you from studying for it. You know that the instructor will not accept your illness and other assignments as an excuse to have the examination at another time. . . .	1	2	3	4	5	6	7
2. You started work last month as a salesclerk in a small clothing store (men's or women's) and have been asked to mind the store while the other two clerks take their lunch break elsewhere in the shopping mall. During this usually slow time, four customers walk in, each one of them wanting your immediate attention.	1	2	3	4	5	6	7
3. You and two friends are driving in an older van with snow tires to a ski resort in the Canadian Rockies. You took over driving duty at 8 P.M., two hours ago. Your friends are asleep in the backseat while you approach a steep pass. It has been snowing so heavily that you must drive at a crawl to see where you are going and avoid sliding off the road. You passed the last community 30 miles back and the resort is 40 miles ahead (nearly two hours at your current speed).	1	2	3	4	5	6	7
4. You work as an accountant in a large insurance company and for the past month have received unwanted attention several times each week from your supervisor, a married person of the opposite sex. The supervisor regularly touches your shoulder and comments on your looks. You are sure that this behavior constitutes advances rather than just friendly gestures.	1	2	3	4	5	6	7
5. You and your spouse purchased your first home one year ago, a detached house with mortgage payments that your spouse barely covers with his or her take-home pay. The economy has since entered a deep recession, and the company informed you today that you will be laid off in two months.	1	2	3	4	5	6	7

TIME STRESS SCALE

Purpose This self-assessment is designed to help you to identify your level of time-related stress.

Instructions Read each statement below and circle "Yes" or "No." Then use the scoring key in Appendix B to calculate your results. This exercise is completed alone so that students assess themselves honestly without concerns of social comparison. However, class discussion will focus on the time stress scale.

1. Yes No Do you plan to slow down in the coming year?
2. Yes No Do you consider yourself a workaholic?
3. Yes No When you need more time, do you tend to cut back on your sleep?
4. Yes No At the end of the day, do you often feel that you have not accomplished what you had set out to do?
5. Yes No Do you worry that you don't spend enough time with your family or friends?
6. Yes No Do you feel that you're constantly under stress trying to accomplish more than you can handle?
7. Yes No Do you feel trapped in a daily routine?
8. Yes No Do you feel that you just don't have time for fun anymore?
9. Yes No Do you often feel under stress when you don't have enough time?
10. Yes No Would you like to spend more time alone?

Source: Statistics Canada's 1998 General Social Survey. Cited in P. DeMont, "Too Much Stress, Too Little Time," *Ottawa Citizen*, November 12, 1999.

After studying the preceding material, be sure to check out our website at
www.mhhe.com/mcshane2e
for more in-depth information and interactivities that correspond to this chapter.

Team Processes

3

CHAPTER 8

Foundations of Team Dynamics

AFTER READING THIS CHAPTER, YOU SHOULD BE ABLE TO:

- Define *teams*.

- Distinguish departmental teams from team-based organizations.

- Explain why virtual teams are becoming more common.

- Outline the model of team effectiveness.

- Identify six organizational and team environmental elements that influence team effectiveness.

- Explain the influence of the team's task, size, and composition on team effectiveness.

- Describe the five stages of team development.

- Identify four factors that shape team norms.

- List six factors that influence team cohesiveness.

- Discuss the limitations of teams.

- Explain how companies minimize social loafing.

- Summarize the four types of team building.

The Chrysler Division of DaimlerChrysler has discovered how to get new products to market faster, more efficiently, and more in line with customer needs. Their secret weapon? Teams, lot of teams. Chrysler has created 3 types of executive and professional teams, including a senior-level product strategy team; 6 product innovation teams; and 50 component parts teams.

The product strategy team—led by Chrysler Group president Dieter Zetsche—is responsible for the discovery phase of a new vehicle. This group analyzes customer trends, new design ideas, technological innovation, and the economic environment to determine which new vehicle line to develop and build.

Of the six product innovation teams, five represent vehicle groups (small vehicles, trucks, etc.) and a sixth oversees engines and transmissions. These are similar to the platform teams that Chrysler has used for the past decade in product development. However, platform teams focused on design and engineering, whereas product innovation teams will bring marketing and manufacturing people into the product development process earlier.

DaimlerChrysler relies on teams to design and manufacture new vehicles faster, more efficiently, and more in line with customer needs.
(© Alan Levenson/Getty Images)

"We want to ensure a balance between creativity and marketing," says Chrysler Group president and chief executive Dieter Zetsche. Zetsche also expects these teams to reduce product development time from the current average of 24 to 36 months to just 18 months.

Chrysler has also introduced 50 component parts teams that will reduce costs by ensuring that vehicle groups share components. For example, Chrysler now uses about 27 different batteries. The company hopes one of the component teams will cut that number down to about 5 types of batteries.[1]

teams
Groups of two or more people who interact and influence each other, are mutually accountable for achieving common objectives, and perceive themselves as a social entity within an organization.

Teams are replacing individuals as the basic building blocks of organizations. DaimlerChrysler has organized employees from engineering, marketing, purchasing, and other departments into product innovation teams to design and manufacture new vehicles faster and more efficiently. At SEI Investments near Philadelphia, employees work in an open space with desks on wheels so that they can form on-the-fly teams for specific investment projects. AES Corporation, the Virginia-based global power company, relies on teams to operate entire power stations. Flexible Steel Lacing Company in Downers Grove, Illinois, has reorganized its employees into autonomous teams that have almost total control over manufacturing a complete product group.[2]

Teams are groups of two or more people who interact and influence each other, are mutually accountable for achieving common objectives, and perceive

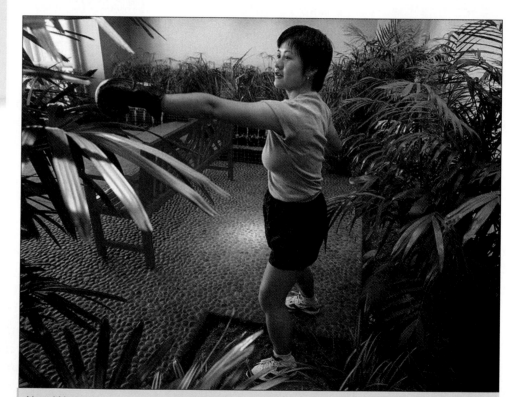

Nortel Networks values teamwork. That's what Phuong Truong discovered when she joined the engineering group at the Internet and telecommunications gear company. Truong (shown here at Nortel's fitness center) is part of a project team of 12 engineers who call themselves the Raptors. No particular reason for the name, except maybe that it sounds ferocious. She recruits new employees for the group and determines who would be an effective team member. Truong also volunteers as a member of the employee satisfaction team that communicates with senior management and employees about job concerns. "We have a big departmental discussion every month to tell us how the team is doing, find out where the team is going, what we are we doing next," explains Truong.[3] Why would Nortel Networks rely on teams rather than individuals to perform these tasks? (© D. Chan / Ottawa Citizen)

themselves as a social entity within an organization.[4] All teams exist to fulfill some purpose, such as assembling a product, providing a service, operating a submarine, or making an important decision. Team members are held together by their interdependence and need for collaboration to achieve common goals. All teams require some form of communication so that members can coordinate and share common objectives. Team members also influence each other, although some members are more influential than others regarding the team's goals and activities.

All teams are **groups** because they consist of people with a unifying relationship. But not all groups are teams; some groups are just people assembled together.[5] For example, employees who meet for lunch are rarely called teams because they have little or no task interdependence (each person could just as easily eat lunch alone) and no purpose beyond their social interaction. Although the terms *group* and *team* are used interchangeably in this book, our main focus is on teams. This is partly because most of the discussion is about task-oriented teams rather than other types of groups, and partly because the term *teams* has largely replaced *groups* in the business language.[6]

As teams become more popular, corporate leaders run the risk of failing to leverage the potential of these groups. For example, research suggests that DaimlerChrysler's cross-functional product innovation teams often fall short of the desired results because corporate leaders ignore the complex conditions that must be in place to make these teams work effectively.[7] This chapter looks at the complex conditions that make teams more or less effective in organizational settings. After introducing the different types of teams in organizational settings, we present a model of team effectiveness. Most of the chapter examines each part of this model, including team and organizational environment, team design, and the team processes of development, norms, roles, and cohesiveness. The chapter concludes by surveying the strategies for building more effective work teams.

groups
People with a unifying relationship.

team-based organization
A type of departmentalization with a flat span of control and relatively little formalization, consisting of self-directed work teams responsible for various work processes.

TYPES OF TEAMS AND OTHER GROUPS IN ORGANIZATIONS

There are many types of teams and other groups in organizations. Permanent work teams are responsible for a specific set of tasks in the organization. For instance, most departments are considered permanent teams because employees interact directly and coordinate work activities with each other, as depicted in Exhibit 8.1(a).[8] Increasingly, employees with different skills work together on work processes. Some hospitals have moved in this direction by forming surgical teams made up of nurses, radiologists, anesthetists, pharmacologists, and others. These people previously worked in departments based on their specialty. Now they work together on a specific work process.

Some companies take this team focus much further by forming a **team-based organization.** Team-based organizations rely extensively on **self-directed work teams (SDWTs)** organized around work processes rather than specialized departments as core work units.[9] These teams complete an entire piece of work requiring several interdependent tasks. They also are fairly autonomous, as indicated by the dashed lines in Exhibit 8.1(b), so there is less need for direct supervision or someone to report continually to the executive team. They are also *cross-functional*. This means that unlike traditional departments where employees have similar competencies (e.g., marketing,

self-directed work teams (SDWTs)
Cross-functional work groups that are organized around work processes, that complete an entire piece of work requiring several interdependent tasks, and that have substantial autonomy over the execution of these tasks.

EXHIBIT 8.1   Departments as work teams

(a) Team-oriented department

(b) Team-based organization

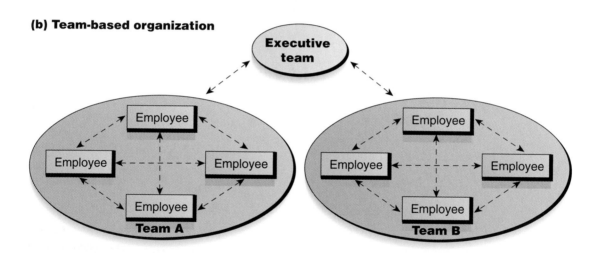

engineering), SDWTs rely on people with diverse and complementary skills, knowledge, and experience. SDWTs are described more fully in the next chapter because they represent the highest level of employee involvement.

Employees often belong to secondary teams that parallel their more permanent positions in the organization. **Quality circles** fall into this category.[10] Quality circles are small teams of employees who meet for a few hours each week to identify quality and productivity problems, propose solutions to management, and monitor the implementation and consequences of these solutions in their work area. Quality circles are usually permanent and typically include co-workers in the same work unit.

Along with permanent teams, organizations rely on temporary teams to make decisions or complete short-term projects. Companies bring together employees from various departments to design a product, solve a client's problem, or search for new opportunities.[11] *Task forces* (also called *ad hoc* teams) are temporary teams that investigate a particular problem and disband when the decision is made. For instance, Royal Dutch/Shell Group formed a cross-functional

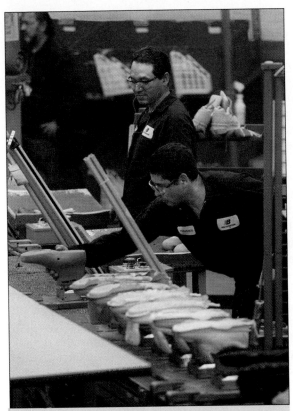

New Balance Athletic Shoe Inc. is competing against low-wage factories in Asia through technology and a team-based organization. Well-trained employees at New Balance's five factories in Massachusetts and Maine operate computerized equipment running up to 20 sewing-machine heads at once. These employees work in teams of five or six people, performing a half-dozen jobs, switching tasks every few minutes, and picking up the slack for one another. New employees receive 22 hours of classroom instruction on teamwork and other techniques and get continual training on the factory floor. This combination of teams and technology allows New Balance to produce a pair of shoes in 24 minutes, compared with nearly three hours in Asian factories.[15] What other advantages would New Balance Athletic Shoe experience with its team-based organization? (© Mark Garfinkel / Boston Herald)

team to improve revenues for its service stations along major highways in Malaysia. This team, which included a service station dealer, a union truck driver, and four or five marketing executives, disbanded after it had reviewed the Malaysian service stations and submitted a business plan.[12]

Skunkworks

Skunkworks are usually (but not always) temporary teams formed spontaneously to develop products or solve complex problems. They are initiated by an innovative employee (a *champion*) who borrows people and resources (called *bootlegging*) to help the organization.[13] Some skunkworks are isolated from the rest of the organization and thus are able to ignore the more bureaucratic rules governing other organizational units. The earliest corporate intranets started as skunkworks, championed by employees with a UNIX computer and free software from universities to create a web server. Skunkworks are responsible for several innovations at 3M Corporation. One example is a special micro-surface mouse pad that has become a commercial success. "Management had no idea the project was being worked on, until it was ready to be launched," explains a 3M executive. "Some lab, some manufacturing, and some marketing people got together as an informal team to do it."[14]

Virtual Teams

When Roger Rodriguez goes to work each day at BakBone Software in San Diego, the client service senior engineer typically picks up customer support problems passed on from colleagues in Lanham, Maryland, and Poole, England. At the end of his workday, Rodriguez passes some of his projects on to BakBone co-workers in Tokyo. Rodriguez must be sure the instructions he sends on to Tokyo are clear because overseas co-workers can't ask him questions in the middle of San Diego's night. Rodriguez also admits that working with distance team members has its challenges. "You don't have the time for open-ended conversation," he says. "You can't informally brainstorm with someone."[16] Roger Rodriguez and his dozen colleagues at BakBone Software are part of the growing trend toward virtual teams. **Virtual teams** are cross-functional groups that operate across space, time, and organizational boundaries with members who communicate mainly through electronic technologies.[17] Some groups become virtual teams when employees telecommute or communicate with team members while

skunkworks
Temporary teams formed spontaneously to develop products or solve complex problems.

visiting clients. BakBone Software created a virtual client support team to benefit from the best possible talent around the world. "Virtual team . . . allow you to draw from a more diverse talent pool because you're hiring in different geographic locations," explains Tim Miller, director of client services at BakBone Software.

Why are virtual teams becoming more common? Emerging information technology has certainly facilitated their development. Recent evidence suggests that effective virtual teams creatively combine e-mail, videoconferencing, intranets, and other traditional electronic communication channels to suit their needs.[18] Virtual teams benefit from the **law of telecosm,** which states that as the web of computer networks expands, distances will shrink and eventually become irrelevant.[19] While distance isn't yet irrelevant, computer connectivity has strengthened bonds among team members in different cities and on different continents. The shift toward knowledge-based rather than production-based work has also made virtual teamwork feasible. Roger Rodriguez's team is able to complete knowledge-based tasks from a distance through information technology, whereas production-based work activities usually require co-location of team members.[20]

Technology and knowledge-based work make virtual teams *possible*, but globalization and the benefits of knowledge sharing and teamwork make them *necessary*. As we described in Chapter 1, globalization has become the new reality in many organizations. As companies open businesses overseas or form tight alliances with companies located elsewhere in the world, there is increasing pressure to form virtual teams that coordinate these operations. For instance, the European Union is providing tens of millions of dollars to fund research into electronic methods of working. The idea is to create virtual teams that leverage their knowledge across the region as well as create more efficient use of transportation systems and office space.[21]

Virtual teams also leverage the benefits of team dynamics. They enable employees in diverse locations to collaborate and make potentially better decisions on complex issues.[22] Virtual teams represent a natural extension of knowledge management because they minimize the "silos of knowledge" problem that tends to develop when employees are geographically scattered. In other words, virtual teams encourage employees to share and use knowledge where geography limits more direct forms of collaboration.

Informal Groups

Along with formal work teams, organizations consist of **informal groups** that exist primarily for the benefit of their members. Informal groups are not specifically formed by organizational decision makers, although their structure may be influenced by the existence of work teams. They shape communication patterns and often create their own set of values that support or oppose the organization's values. Some informal groups, such as the group you meet for lunch, might overlap with the work team. These groups form out of convenience and the need for affiliation. Other groups are bound together for reasons other than social needs. For instance, you might belong to an informal group that shares a car pool and another group that plays together on the company's sports team.

A **coalition** is an informal group that attempts to influence people outside the group by pooling the resources and power of its members. By banding together, coalition members have more power than if each person worked

virtual teams
Cross-functional groups that operate across space, time, and organizational boundaries with members who communicate mainly through electronic technologies.

law of telecosm
States that as the web of computer networks expands, distances will shrink and eventually become irrelevant.

informal groups
Two or more people who interact primarily to meet their personal (rather than organizational) needs.

coalition
An informal group that attempts to influence people outside the goup by pooling the resources and power of its members.

alone to influence others. They also reinforce each other and further mobilize support for their position.[23] The coalition's mere existence can be a source of power by symbolizing the importance or level of support for the issue.

Communities of practice are informal groups bound together by shared expertise and passion for a particular activity or interest.[24] For instance, Schlumberger Ltd. has communities of practice on deepwater drilling, horizontal drilling, deviated wells, and other topics. Employees are connected to the oil-field services firm's web portal where they share knowledge on their daily experiences.[25] In most organizations, communities of practice are informal groups that congregate in person or in cyberspace to share knowledge. People who have a common passion for environmental concerns, for example, might meet twice each month over lunch to share their knowledge. Other communities interact entirely through list servers and websites where participants exchange information on specific technical issues. Many communities of practice extend beyond organizational boundaries, so they represent a source of knowledge acquisition.

> **communities of practice**
> Informal groups bound together by shared expertise and passion for a particular activity or interest.

Why Informal Groups Exist One reason people join informal groups is to fulfill their relatedness needs (see Chapter 5). We meet co-workers for lunch or stop by their work areas for brief chats because this activity satisfies our need for social interaction. Similarly, social identity theory (see Chapter 3) explains that we define ourselves by our group affiliations. If we belong to work teams or informal groups that are viewed favorably by others, then we tend to view ourselves more favorably. We are motivated to become members of groups that are similar to ourselves because this affiliation reinforces our social identity.[26]

Some groups form because they accomplish tasks that cannot be achieved by individuals working alone. Coalitions and other task-oriented informal groups remain intact because members know they cannot achieve the same results alone. When groups are successful, it is easier to attract new members in the future. Informal groups also tend to congregate in stressful situations because we are comforted by the physical presence of other people and are therefore motivated to be near them.[27] This phenomenon explains why soldiers huddle together in battle, even though they are taught to disperse under fire. It also explains why employees tend to congregate when hearing that the company has been sold or that some people may be laid off.

A MODEL OF TEAM EFFECTIVENESS

Why are some teams more effective than others? This question has challenged organizational researchers for some time and, as you might expect, numerous models of team effectiveness have been proposed over the years.[28] **Team effectiveness** refers to how the team affects the organization, individual team members, and the team's existence.[29] First, most teams exist to serve some purpose relating to the organization or other system in which the group operates. Product innovation teams at DaimlerChrysler have been formed to improve the efficiency, speed, and customer delight of new vehicle design. Some informal groups also have task-oriented goals, such as a coalition that wants to persuade senior management to change a corporate policy.

Second, team effectiveness considers the satisfaction and well-being of its members. People join groups to fulfill their personal needs, so it makes sense that effectiveness is measured partly by this need fulfillment. Finally, team

> **team effectiveness**
> The extent to which a team achieves its objectives, achieves the needs and objectives of its members, and sustains itself over time.

**Organizational and
team environment**

- Reward systems
- Communication
  systems
- Physical space
- Organizational
  environment
- Organizational
  structure
- Organizational
  leadership

Team design

- Task characteristics
- Team size
- Team composition

Team processes

- Team development
- Team norms
- Team roles
- Team cohesiveness

Team effectiveness

- Achieve organizational
  goals
- Satisfy member needs
- Maintain team
  survival

effectiveness includes the team's viability—its ability to survive. It must be able to maintain the commitment of its members, particularly during the turbulence of the team's development. Without this commitment, people leave and the team will fall apart. It must also secure sufficient resources and find a benevolent environment in which to operate.

Exhibit 8.2 presents the model of team effectiveness that we will describe over the next several pages. We begin by looking at elements of the team's and organization's environment that influence team design, processes, and outcomes.

ORGANIZATIONAL AND TEAM ENVIRONMENT

Our discussion of team effectiveness logically begins with the contextual factors that influence the team's design, processes, and outcomes. There are many elements in the organizational and team environment that influence team effectiveness. Six of the most important elements are reward systems, communication systems, physical space, organizational environment, organizational structure, and organizational leadership.

■ *Reward systems*—Research indicates that team members tend to work together more effectively when they are at least partly rewarded for team performance. Employees at Jostens, Inc., a manufacturer of school rings and other products, developed a stronger team orientation after the company shifted from individual incentives to a team-based gainsharing plan.[30] This strategy doesn't mean that everyone on the team should receive the same amount of pay based on the team's performance. On the contrary, rewards tend to work better in the United States and other Western societies when individual pay is determined by a combination of individual and team performance.[31]

■ *Communication systems*—A poorly designed communication system can starve a team of valuable information and feedback, or it may swamp it with information overload.[32] Virtual teams in particular require the right combination of communication technologies. For example, virtual team members at BakBone Software stay in touch with others via telephone, e-mail, and a companywide database that tracks specific customer problems.[33] Communication systems are also important when team members are located together. Physical space might be arranged to encourage more face-to-face dialogue. In each of these cases, the team's communication systems are aligned with its task and structure.

◾ *Physical space*—The layout of an office or factory does more than improve communications among team members. It also influences the team's ability to accomplish tasks and shapes employee perceptions about being together as a team. That's why multinational engineering firm Arup moved its Hong Kong headquarters from an aging city high-rise to a suburban site where offices were replaced by low-rise cubicles. The result has been a significant improvement in interaction among team members as well as between teams.[34]

◾ *Organizational environment*—Team success depends on the company's external environment. If the organization cannot secure resources, for instance, the team cannot fulfill its performance targets. Similarly, high demand for the team's output creates feelings of success, which motivates team members to stay with the team. A competitive environment can motivate employees to work together more closely.

◾ *Organizational structure*– Many teams fail because the organizational structure does not support them. Teams work better when there are few layers of management and teams are given autonomy and responsibility for their work. This structure encourages interaction with team members rather than with supervisors. Teams also flourish when employees are organized around work processes rather than specialized skills. This structure increases interaction among team members.[35]

◾ *Organizational leadership*—Teams require ongoing support from senior executives to align rewards, organizational structure, communication systems, and other elements of team context. They also require team leaders or facilitators who provide coaching and support. Team leaders are enablers, meaning that they ensure that teams have the authority to solve their own problems and the resources to accomplish their tasks.[36] Leaders also maintain a value system that supports team performance more than individual success.

TEAM DESIGN FEATURES

Putting together a team is rather like designing a mini-organization. There are several elements to consider, and the wrong combination will undermine team effectiveness. Three of the main structural elements to consider when designing teams are task characteristics, team size, and team composition. As we saw earlier in the team effectiveness model (Exhibit 8.2), these design features affect team effectiveness directly as well as indirectly through team processes. For example, the skills and diversity of team members affect team cohesiveness, but they also have a direct effect on how well the team performs its task. Similarly, the type of work performed by the team (task characteristics) may influence the types of roles that emerge, but it also has a direct effect on the satisfaction and well-being of team members.

Task Characteristics

Teams are generally more effective when tasks are clear and easy to implement, because team members can learn their roles more quickly.[37] In contrast, teams with ill-defined tasks require more time to agree on the best division of labor and the correct way to accomplish the goal. More complex tasks requiring diverse skills and backgrounds further strain the team's ability to develop and form a cohesive unit.

Another important task characteristic is **task interdependence.** High task interdependence exists when team members must share common inputs to their individual tasks, need to interact in the process of executing their work, or receive outcomes (such as rewards) that are determined partly by the performance of others. Teams are well suited to highly interdependent tasks because people coordinate better when working together than separately. Moreover, recent evidence indicates that task interdependence creates an additional sense of responsibility among team members, which motivates them to work together rather than alone.[38] This is why companies organize employees around work processes. Each team is responsible for highly interdependent tasks, so they coordinate the work more efficiently than individuals working in specialized departments.

task interdependence
The degree to which a task requires employees to share common inputs or outcomes, or to interact in the process of executing their work.

Team Size

St. Luke's is a highly successful British advertising agency that relies on self-directed work teams to serve clients. The London-based firm is so team-oriented that it refuses to participate in industry awards that recognize individual achievement. One way that St. Luke's supports team dynamics is through the "35 rule," which states that no team shall have more than 35 members. "When any one group becomes larger than 35 people, it has to split apart, as an amoeba would," explains Andy Law, St. Luke's CEO and co-founder.[39]

Team size is an important concern at St. Luke's. Some writers claim that team size should be limited to 10 or fewer people, making St. Luke's limit of 35 team members far too high. However, the optimal team size depends on several factors, such as the number of people required to complete the work and the amount of coordination needed to work together. The general rule is that teams should be large enough to provide the necessary competencies and perspectives to perform the work, yet small enough to maintain efficient coordination and meaningful involvement of each member.[40]

Larger teams are typically less effective because members consume more time and effort coordinating their roles and resolving differences. Individuals have less opportunity to participate and, consequently, are less likely to feel that they are contributing to the team's success. Larger work units tend to break into informal subgroups around common interests and work activities, leading members to form stronger commitments to their subgroup than to the larger team. Pharmaceutical giant Pfizer Inc. tries to avoid these problems with large teams at its new research facility in Groton, Connecticut, by organizing five to seven scientists into "families" and grouping about 10 families into a "tribe" of 70 people.[41]

Team Composition

Effective teams require individual team members with the motivation and ability to work in a team environment. With respect to motivation, every member must have sufficient drive to perform the task in a team environment. Specifically, team members must be motivated to agree on the goal, work together

Houston's new H-E-B Central Market is a 75,000-square-foot cornucopia of food delights. To support this customer experience, the San Antonio–based grocery retailer carefully hires job applicants (such as Jesus Guevara, shown in photo) who are outgoing and enjoy working in teams. Applicants begin by completing an application form and writing detailed examples of when they used teamwork and communication skills to solve problems on the job. After making the cut, prospective employees are invited back in groups of about eight people and presented with samples of store products. Interviewers observe their willingness to try unusual foods and interact with others. "We want to see who can work together as a team, who's creative and who shows leadership, who's assertive and who's not," says an H-E-B executive. Successful applicants proceed to the third stage where their team, communication, and leadership skills are further assessed through individual interviews.[42] Along with the selection process, how else can companies ensure that employees have the ability and motivation to work in teams?
*(© E. Joseph Deering/*Houston Chronicle*)*

rather than alone, and abide by the team's rules of conduct. Employees with a collectivist orientation—those who value group goals more than their own personal goals (see Chapter 4)—tend to perform better in work teams, whereas those with a strong individualist orientation tend to perform better alone.[43]

Employees must possess the skills and knowledge necessary to accomplish the team's objectives.[44] Each person needs only some of the necessary skills, but the entire group must have the full set of competencies. Moreover, each team member's competencies need to be known to other team members. Team members also need to be able to work effectively with others. They must have sufficient emotional intelligence (see Chapter 4) to manage emotions, as well as conflict management skills to effectively resolve interpersonal differences. Researchers also emphasize the importance of training employees in ways to communicate and coordinate with each other in a team environment.[45]

How do companies ensure that employees have the ability and motivation to work in teams? Team-based reward systems can motivate employees to work with the team rather than focus on individual effort. However, it is often easiest to hire people at the outset who possess team-oriented competencies and values. Anchor Hocking, the glass and plastic kitchenware manufacturer, requires applicants to complete a project in teams while evaluators identify those who work best in a team environment. Candidates also write an essay on what a team environment means to them.[46]

homogeneous teams

Teams that include members with common technical expertise, demographics (age, gender), ethnicity, experiences, or values.

heterogeneous teams

Teams that include members with diverse personal characteristics and backgrounds.

Team Diversity   Another important dimension of team composition is the diversity of team members.[47] **Homogeneous teams** include members with common technical expertise, demographics (age, gender), ethnicity, experiences, or values, whereas **heterogeneous teams** have members with diverse personal characteristics and backgrounds. Should teams be homogeneous or heterogeneous? Both types of teams have advantages and disadvantages, and their relative effectiveness depends on the situation. Heterogeneous teams experience more conflict and take longer to develop. They are susceptible to fault lines—hypothetical dividing lines that may split a team into subgroups along gender, ethnic, professional, or other dimensions. In some situations, these fault lines may eventually split the team apart.[48] In contrast, members of homogeneous teams experience higher satisfaction, less conflict, and better interpersonal relations. Consequently, homogeneous teams tend to be more effective on tasks requiring a high degree of cooperation and coordination, such as the tasks of emergency response teams or string quartets.

Although heterogeneous teams are more difficult to develop, they are generally more effective than homogeneous teams at solving complex problems requiring innovative solutions because people from different backgrounds see a problem or opportunity from different perspectives.[49] Heterogeneous team members also solve complex problems more easily because they usually have a broader knowledge base. A senior executive at Monsanto Corporation sums up this view: "Every time I have put together a diverse group of people, that team has always come up with a more breakthrough solution than any homogeneous group working on the same problem."[50] Finally, a team's diversity may give it more legitimacy or allow its members to obtain a wide network of cooperation and support in the organization.

Team composition, team size, and task characteristics affect team effectiveness directly as well as indirectly through team processes. The four team processes, identified earlier in the team effectiveness model (Exhibit 8.2), are team development, team norms, team roles, and team cohesiveness.

TEAM PROCESSES

Our discussion so far has presented two sets of elements in the team effectiveness model: (1) organizational and team environment and (2) team design. In this section, we introduce the third set of team effectiveness elements, collectively known as team processes. These processes—team development, norms, roles, and cohesiveness—are influenced by both team design and organizational and team environment factors.

Team Development

Team members must resolve several issues and pass through several stages of development before emerging as an effective work unit. They must get to know

EXHIBIT 8.3

Stages of team
development

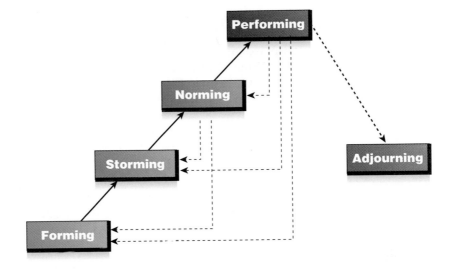

each other, understand their respective roles, discover appropriate and inappropriate behaviors, and learn how to coordinate their work or social activities. This process is ongoing because teams change as new members join and old members leave. The five-stage model of team development, shown in Exhibit 8.3, provides a general outline of how teams evolve by forming, storming, norming, performing, and eventually adjourning.[51] The model shows teams progressing from one stage to the next in an orderly fashion, but the dotted lines illustrate that they might also fall back to an earlier stage of development as new members join or other conditions disrupt the team's maturity.

1. *Forming*—The first stage of team development is a period of testing and orientation in which members learn about each other and evaluate the benefits and costs of continued membership. People tend to be polite during this stage and will defer to the existing authority of a formal or informal leader who must provide an initial set of rules and structures for interaction. Members experience a form of socialization (described in Chapter 18) as they try to find out what is expected of them and how they will fit into the team.

2. *Storming*—The storming stage is marked by interpersonal conflict as members become more proactive and compete for various team roles. Coalitions may form to influence the team's goals and means of goal attainment. Members try to establish norms of appropriate behavior and performance standards. This is a tenuous stage in the team's development, particularly when the leader is autocratic and lacks the necessary conflict management skills.

3. *Norming*—During the norming stage, the team develops its first real sense of cohesion as roles are established and a consensus forms around group objectives. Members have developed relatively similar mental models, so they have common expectations and assumptions about how the team's goals should be accomplished. They have developed a common team-based mental model that allows them to interact more efficiently so that they can move into the next stage, performing.[52]

4. *Performing*—The team becomes more task-oriented in the performing stage. Team members have learned to coordinate and resolve conflicts

more efficiently. Further coordination improvements must occasionally be addressed, but the greater emphasis is on task accomplishment. In high-performance teams, members are highly cooperative, have a high level of trust in each other, are committed to group objectives, and identify with the team. There is a climate of mutual support in which team members feel comfortable about taking risks, making errors, or asking for help.[53]

5. *Adjourning*—Most work teams and informal groups eventually end. Task forces disband when their project is completed. Informal work groups may reach this stage when several members leave the organization or are reassigned elsewhere. Some teams adjourn as a result of layoffs or plant shutdowns. Whatever the cause of team adjournment, members shift their attention away from task orientation to a socioemotional focus as they realize that their relationship is ending.

The team development model is a useful framework for thinking about how teams develop. At the same time, we must keep in mind that it is not a perfect representation of the dynamics of team development.[54] The model does not explicitly show that some teams remain in a particular stage longer than others and that team development is an ongoing process. As membership changes and new conditions emerge, teams cycle back to earlier stages in the developmental process to regain the equilibrium or balance lost by the change (as shown by the dotted lines in Exhibit 8.3).

Team Norms

Have you ever noticed how employees in some departments almost run for the exit door the minute the workday ends, whereas people in the same jobs elsewhere seem to be competing for who can stay at work the longest? These differences are partly due to **norms**—the informal rules and expectations that groups establish to regulate the behavior of their members. Norms apply only to behavior, not to private thoughts or feelings. Moreover, norms exist only for behaviors that are important to the team.[55]

norms
The informal rules and expectations that groups establish to regulate the behavior of their members.

Norms guide the way team members deal with clients, how they share resources, whether they are willing to work long hours, and many other behaviors in organizational life. Some norms ensure that employees support organizational goals, whereas other norms might conflict with organizational objectives. For example, the level of employee absence from work is influenced partly by absence norms in the workplace. In other words, employees are more likely to take off work if they work in teams that support this behavior.[56]

Conformity to Team Norms   Everyone has experienced peer pressure at one time or another. Co-workers grimace if we are late for a meeting or make sarcastic comments if we don't have our part of the project completed on time. In more extreme situations, team members may try to enforce their norms by temporarily ostracizing deviant co-workers or threatening to terminate their membership. This heavy-handed peer pressure isn't as rare as you might think. One survey revealed that 20 percent of employees have been pressured by their colleagues to slack off at work. Half of the time, the peer pressure occurred because colleagues didn't want to look like poor performers against their more productive co-workers.[57]

Elite New Zealand Prison Team's "Culture of Obedience"

Members of a special emergency response team congregated at dawn for a covert mission. The 16 hand-picked and specially trained members based at Paparua Prison, New Zealand, were supposed to reduce prison violence, prevent drugs from entering prisons, and improve prisoner compliance. But the mission on this day was different. The response team was hunting for an escapee—a rooster belonging to a member of the response team that had escaped to a neighboring farm.

This is just one of the bizarre incidents involving the special unit, dubbed the "Goon Squad" by adversaries. The team worked independently of the prison officers and had its own distinctive black uniforms. Unfortunately, a government report also concluded that the team developed a distinctive set of norms, some of which violated corrections department policies.

A government investigation heard claims that the team falsified time sheets, juggled the work roster for personal gain, used department vehicles for personal use, used unnecessary intimidation on inmates, disci-

plined staff inappropriately, and hunted wayward roosters on company time. The special unit also conducted missions in the outside community even though its mandate was restricted to the prison. "Our focus moved to a policeman's role, which we should not have been doing," admits one former member.

None of the members complained during the unit's existence because of "a culture of obedience." For example, when one member refused to go to a party, others in the unit allegedly went to his home, restrained him, hit him over the head with an axe handle, handcuffed him, and dragged him along to the party.

"The most chilling thing about the team was an apparent fear of authority among members, leading to a culture of obedience and silence," says an executive member of the Howard League for Penal Reform. "In effect, they became a law unto themselves."

Sources: Y. Martin, "Goon Squad," *The Press (Christchurch, New Zealand)*, June 9, 2001, p. 2; "'Goon Squad' Prison Staff Disciplined," *New Zealand Press Association*, May 23, 2001; Y. Martin, "Crack Prison Team Members Guilty of Serious Misconduct," *The Press (Christchurch, New Zealand)*, May 24, 2001, p. 1.

Norms are also directly reinforced through praise from high-status members, more access to valued resources, or other rewards available to the team.[58] But team members often conform to prevailing norms without direct reinforcement or punishment because they identify with the group and want to align their behavior with the team's values. This effect is particularly strong in new members because they are uncertain of their status and want to demonstrate their commitment to membership in the team. Global Connections 8.1 provides an extreme example of the consequences of team norms and conformity in organizational settings.

How Team Norms Develop Norms develop as team members learn that certain behaviors help them function more effectively.[59] Some norms develop when team members or outsiders make explicit statements that seem to aid the team's success or survival. For example, the team leader might frequently express the importance of treating customers with respect and courtesy. A second factor triggering the development of a new norm is a critical event in the team's history. A team might develop a strong norm to keep the work area clean after a co-worker slips on metal scraps and seriously injures herself.

Team norms are most strongly influenced by events soon after the team is formed.[60] Future behaviors are influenced by the way members of a newly formed team initially greet each other, where they locate themselves in a meeting, and so on. A fourth influence on team norms is the beliefs and values that members bring to the team. For example, bargaining groups develop norms about appropriate bargaining behavior that are based on each member's previous bargaining experience.[61]

Troubleshooting Dysfunctional Team Norms   Although many team norms are deeply anchored, there are ways to change them or make them less influential on employee behavior. One approach is to introduce performance-oriented norms as soon as the team is created. Another strategy is to select members who will bring desirable norms to the group. If the organization wants to emphasize safety, then it should select team members who already value safety.

Selecting people with positive norms may be effective in new teams, but not when adding new members to existing teams with counterproductive norms. A better strategy for existing teams is to explicitly discuss the counterproductive norm with team members using persuasive communication tactics (see Chapter 12).[62] For example, the surgical team at one hospital had developed a norm of arriving late for operations. Patients and other hospital staff often waited 30 minutes or more for the team to arrive. The hospital CEO eventually spoke to the surgical team about their lateness and, through moral suasion, convinced team members to arrive for operating room procedures no more than 5 minutes late for their appointments.[63]

Team-based reward systems can sometimes weaken counterproductive norms. Unfortunately, the pressure to conform to the counterproductive norm may be stronger than the financial incentive.[64] For instance, employees working in a pajama factory were paid under a piece-rate system. Some individuals in the group were able to process up to 100 units per hour and thereby earn more money, but they all chose to abide by the group norm of 50 units per hour.[65]

Finally, a dysfunctional norm may be so deeply ingrained that the best strategy is to disband the group and replace it with people having more favorable norms. Companies should seize the opportunity to introduce performance-oriented norms when the new team is formed, and to select members who will bring desirable norms to the group.

Team Roles

role
The set of behaviors that people are expected to perform because they hold certain positions in a team and organization.

Every work team and informal group has two sets of roles that help it survive and be more productive. A **role** is the set of behaviors that people are expected to perform because they hold certain positions in a team and organization.[66] One set of roles helps focus the team on its objectives, such as giving and seeking information, elaborating ideas, coordinating activities, and summarizing the discussion or past events (see Exhibit 8.4). The other set of roles tries to maintain good working relations among team members. These relationship-oriented roles include resolving conflicts among team members, keeping communication channels open, reinforcing positive behaviors of other team members, and making team members aware of group process problems when they emerge.

Some team roles are formally assigned to specific people. For example, team leaders are usually expected to initiate discussion, ensure that everyone has an opportunity to present his or her views, and help the team reach agreement on the issues discussed. But team members often take on various roles

EXHIBIT 8.4 Roles for team effectiveness

Role activities	Description	Example
Task-oriented roles		
Initiator	Identifies goals for the meeting, including ways to work on those goals	"The main purpose of this meeting is to solve the problem our client is having with this product."
Information seeker	Asks for clarification of ideas or further information to support an opinion	"Jang, why do you think the client is using the product incorrectly?"
Information giver	Shares information and opinions about the team's task and goals	"Let me tell you what some of my clients did to overcome this problem."
Coordinator	Coordinates subgroups and pulls together ideas	"Susan, will you be meeting with Shaheem's group this week to review common issues with the client?"
Evaluator	Assesses the team's functioning against a standard	"So far, we have resolved three of the client's concerns, but we still have a tough one to wrestle with."
Summarizer	Acts as the team's memory	Person takes notes of meeting and summarizes the discussion when requested.
Orienter	Keeps the team focused on its goals	"We seem to be getting off on a tangent; let's focus on why the product isn't operating properly for our client."
Relationship-oriented roles		
Harmonizer	Mediates intragroup conflicts and reduces tension	"Courtney, you and Brad may want to look at your positions on this; they aren't as different as they seem."
Gatekeeper	Encourages and facilitates participation of all team members	"James, what do you think about this issue?"
Encourager	Praises and supports the ideas of other team members, thereby showing warmth and solidarity to the group	"Tracy, that's a wonderful suggestion. I think we will solve the client's problem sooner than we expected."

Sources: Adapted from information in K. D. Benne and P. Sheats, "Functional Roles of Group Members," *Journal of Social Issues* 4 (1948), pp. 41–49.

informally. Some people like to encourage colleagues to participate more actively. Others prefer to mediate conflicts that may arise among team members. As noted earlier, these preferences are usually worked out during the storming stage of team development. The critical point is that team members need to ensure that these roles are fulfilled so that the team can function effectively.

Team Cohesiveness

team cohesiveness
The degree of attraction people feel toward the team and their motivation to remain members.

Team cohesiveness—the degree of attraction people feel toward the team and their motivation to remain members—is usually an important factor in a team's success.[67] Employees feel cohesiveness when they believe the team will help them achieve their personal goals, fulfill their need for affiliation or status, or provide social support during times of crisis or trouble. Cohesiveness is an emotional experience, not just a calculation of whether to stay with or leave the team. It exists when team members make the team part of their social

EXHIBIT 8.5

Factors contributing to
team cohesiveness

identity (see Chapter 3). Cohesiveness is the glue or *esprit de corps* that holds
the group together and ensures that its members fulfill their obligations.[68]

Causes of Team Cohesiveness   The main factors influencing team cohesiveness are identified in Exhibit 8.5. For the most part, these factors reflect
the individual's identity with the group and beliefs about how team membership will fulfill personal needs.[69] Several of these factors are related to our earlier discussion about why people join informal groups and how teams develop.
Specifically, teams become more cohesive as they reach higher stages of development and are more attractive to potential members.

Member similarity   Homogeneous teams become cohesive more easily than
heterogeneous teams. People in homogeneous teams have similar backgrounds
and values, so they find it easier to agree on team objectives, the means to fulfill those objectives, and the rules applied to maintain group behavior. This
agreement, in turn, leads to greater trust and less dysfunctional conflict within
the group.[70] In contrast, diverse teams are susceptible to the previously described fault lines that psychologically impede cohesiveness, particularly during the early stages of development. The dilemma here is that heterogeneous
teams are usually better than homogeneous teams at completing complex tasks
or solving problems requiring creative solutions.

Team size   Smaller teams tend to be more cohesive than larger teams because it is easier for a few people to agree on goals and coordinate work activities. Nevertheless, the smallest teams are not necessarily the most cohesive,
because not having enough members prevents the team from accomplishing
its objectives. Continued failure may undermine the cohesiveness as members
begin to question the team's ability to satisfy their needs. Thus, team cohesiveness is potentially greatest when teams are as small as possible, yet large
enough to accomplish the required tasks.

Member interaction   Teams tend to be more cohesive when team members
interact with each other fairly regularly. Such interaction occurs when team
members perform highly interdependent tasks and work in the same physical
area.[71] For example, Washington, D.C.–based Chatelain Architects encourages

team interaction with an open office space consisting of low partitions and no special acoustical barriers. Although some might find this arrangement noisy or stressful because of the lack of privacy, it seems to work at this team-oriented architectural firm. "We are always moving around, teaming up and working at other people's desks," says Jill Miernicki, Chatelain Architects' director of business development and environmental initiatives. "It's a very dynamic environment."[72]

The effect of physical proximity on team cohesiveness raises questions about how to maximize cohesiveness in virtual teams.[73] The lack of face-to-face interaction makes it difficult for team members to feel a common bond, even when they work effectively over the Internet. Research suggests that members of virtual teams establish a greater social connection when they have some opportunity to meet face-to-face. The ability to put a face to remote colleagues seems to strengthen the individual's emotional bond to the team. This problem may be worse for telecommuting employees who belong to a team that works in the same physical space. In the long run, these distant workers may feel left out of an otherwise cohesive team.

When Siemens, the German high-technology company, launched a mandatory telecommuting program for its Enterprise Networks group in the United States, productivity dropped and turnover increased. The company's solution was to introduce an annual four-day work-and-play gathering. The annual session provides a much-needed social connection among the 100 people in the work unit; this connection has contributed to lower turnover and higher team cohesiveness. "We feel [the annual meeting is] essential," explains a Siemens executive. "This keeps a touchstone back to other human beings. Cliques can form and people bond, even over the miles."[74]

Somewhat difficult entry   Teams tend to be more cohesive when entry to the team is restricted. The more elite the team, the more prestige it confers on its members and the more its members tend to value their membership in the unit. Existing team members are also more willing to welcome and support new members after they have "passed the test," possibly because they have shared the same entry experience.

One issue is how difficult the initiation should be for entry into the team. Research suggests that severe initiations can potentially lead to humiliation and psychological distance from the group, even for those who successfully endure the initiation.[75] However, as Connections 8.2 describes, the extreme endurance program for Air Force pararescue specialists (PJs) seems to have a strong positive effect on cohesiveness. The explanation here is that this Pipeline training program does not humiliate individuals; rather, it tests the stamina of those who attempt it. Those who endure the two-year program, which has a 90 percent failure rate, feel a special bond with fellow PJs.

Team success   Cohesiveness increases with the team's level of success.[76] Individuals are more likely to attach their social identity to successful teams than to those with a string of failures. Moreover, team members are more likely to believe the group will continue to be successful, thereby fulfilling their personal goals (continued employment, pay bonus, etc.). Team leaders can increase cohesiveness by regularly communicating and celebrating the team's successes. Notice that this can create a spiral effect. Successful teams are more cohesive and, under certain conditions, increased cohesiveness increases the team's success.

Air Force Pararescue Training Creates Cohesiveness

Jason Cunningham's body begged for air. His lungs felt like they would burst, and his brain screamed to swim to the surface for fresh air. But Cunningham ignored these warnings and stayed under until he faded to black. When Cunningham regained consciousness, colleagues were reviving him with an oxygen mask and words of encouragement. "Once you pass out the first time, you get used to it," Cunningham says casually. "It's really not that bad, no big deal."

For most people, drowning ranks pretty high in the "big deal" department. But at the Air Force Pararescue School at Kirtland Air Force Base, New Mexico, it's all part of the learning experience. Air Force pararescue specialists (known as PJs) are extreme emergency medical technicians who locate downed aircrews behind enemy lines, patch them up, and spirit them away to safety.

PJs are also a highly cohesive group of 300 people because they have endured a two-year initiation ritual called the Pipeline, which begins with a two-month-long ordeal of training, including weight-belt swimming, water treading, buddy breathing, and drown-proofing. The underwater school includes such memorable activities as bobbing for precious breaths in the water with your feet bound and your hands tied behind your back. In another segment, trainees are buckled in a mock aircraft that is then dunked and flipped upside down in the water. PJs also get plenty of practice at parachuting, living on meager rations on an island, and handling medical emergencies under difficult conditions.

Air Force pararescue specialists are a highly cohesive group because of their tough initiation into this elite unit. *(Courtesy of Airman)*

It's no wonder that only 10 percent of applicants make it through the Pipeline. Staff Sergeant Doug Isaacks is one of the few who graduated. "All I heard were the statistics, the high washout rates, like only one in a hundred makes it. Nobody gave me much of chance," says Isaacks, who looks as strong as a Clydesdale. "But I did it, and it's one of the greatest moments of my life. It feels great to be part of something special—a brotherhood."

Sources: "Simulated Crash Helps Pararescue People Train," *FDCH Federal Department and Agency Documents*, May 3, 2001; P. McKenna, "Superman School," *Airman*, February 2000, pp. 2–11.

External competition and challenges Team cohesiveness increases when members face external competition or a valued objective that is challenging, such as the threat from an external competitor or friendly competition from other teams. These conditions tend to increase cohesiveness because employees value the team's ability to overcome a threat or competition that they couldn't handle individually. They also value their membership as a form of social support. We need to be careful about the degree of external threat, however. Evidence suggests that teams seem to be less effective when external threats are severe.[77] Although cohesiveness tends to increase, external threats are stressful and cause teams to make less effective decisions under these conditions.

Consequences of Team Cohesiveness Every team must have some minimal level of cohesiveness to maintain its existence.[78] People who belong to high cohesion teams are motivated to maintain their membership and to help the team work effectively. They are generally more sensitive to each other's

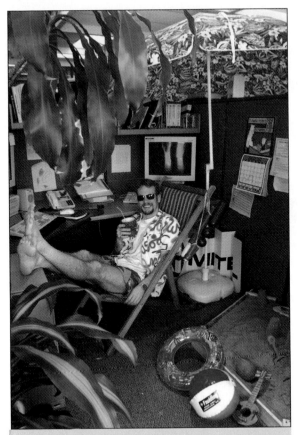

Trevor Pound was looking forward to lying on a Mexican beach for his thirtieth birthday. But the Mitel software engineer's crucial role in a major project put those February vacation plans on hold. Pound barely mentioned his disappointment, but fellow team members at the communications systems firm wanted to make up for his loss. Nearly a dozen co-workers spent a weekend transforming Pound's drab gray cubicle into a colorful oasis. They brought in a 5-foot-wide beach umbrella, a beach chair, a heat lamp, a ukulele, some beach toys, a dozen tropical plants, and over 200 pounds of sand. The culprits even supplied colorful shorts and a Hawaiian-style shirt. The result: Pound celebrated his birthday in an almost tropical setting on that cold winter day. More important, the practical joke expressed the team's support for his loss of personal time.[84] How else do cohesive team members support each other? (© *John Major*/Ottawa Citizen)

needs and develop better interpersonal relationships, thereby reducing dysfunctional conflict. When conflict does arise, members of high cohesion teams seem to resolve the differences swiftly and effectively. Compared with members of low cohesion teams, high cohesion team members spend more time together, share information more frequently, and are more satisfied with each other. They provide each other with better social support in stressful situations.[79]

Cohesiveness and team performance With better cooperation and more conformity to norms, high cohesion teams usually perform better than low cohesion teams.[80] However, the relationship is complex. Exhibit 8.6 illustrates how the effect of cohesiveness on team performance depends on the extent to which team norms are consistent with organizational goals. Cohesive teams will likely have lower task performance when norms conflict with organizational objectives, because cohesiveness motivates employees to perform at a level more consistent with group norms.[81]

THE TROUBLE WITH TEAMS

Scholars and business leaders have long recognized that teams can be a competitive advantage. Yet it is easy to lose sight of the fact that teams aren't always needed.[82] Sometimes, a quick and decisive action by one person is more appropriate. Some tasks are also performed just as easily by one person as by a group. "Teams are overused," admits Philip Condit, CEO of Boeing, Inc. The aircraft manufacturer makes extensive use of teams but knows that they aren't necessary for everything that goes on in organizations. Management guru Peter Drucker agrees. "The now-fashionable team in which everybody works with everybody on everything from the beginning rapidly is becoming a disappointment," he says.[83]

A second problem is that teams take time to develop and maintain. Scholars refer to these hidden costs as **process losses**—resources (including time and energy) expended toward team development and maintenance rather than the task.[85] It is much more efficient for an individual to work out an issue alone than to resolve differences of opinion with other people. The process loss problem becomes apparent when adding new people to the team. The group has to recycle through the team development process to bring

EXHIBIT 8.6

Effect of team
cohesiveness on
task performance

Team norms support company goals	**Moderately high task performance**	**High task performance**
Team norms conflict with company goals	**Moderately low task performance**	**Low task performance**

Low   High
Team cohesiveness

process losses
Resources (including time and energy) expended toward team development and maintenance rather than the task.

everyone up to speed. The software industry even has a name for this problem: Brooks's Law says that adding more people to a late software project only makes it later. Researchers point out that the cost of process losses may be off-set by the benefits of teams. Unfortunately, few companies conduct a cost-benefit analysis of their team activities.[86]

A third problem is that teams require the right environment to flourish. Many companies forget this point by putting people in teams without chang-ing anything else. As we noted earlier, teams require appropriate rewards, communication systems, team leadership, and other conditions. Without these, the shift to a team structure could be a waste of time. At the same time, critics suggest that changing these environmental conditions to improve team-work could result in higher costs than benefits for the overall organization.[87]

Social Loafing

social loafing
A situation in which people exert less effort (and usually perform at a lower level) when working in groups than when working alone.

Perhaps the best-known limitation of teams is the risk of productivity loss due to **social loafing.** Social loafing occurs when people exert less effort (and usu-ally perform at a lower level) when working in groups than when working alone.[88] A few scholars question whether social loafing is very common, but students can certainly report many instances of this problem in their team projects!

Social loafing is most likely to occur in large teams where individual output is difficult to identify, particularly in situations in which team members work alone toward a common output pool (i.e., they have low task interdepen-dence). Under these conditions, employees aren't as worried that their perfor-mance will be noticed. Social loafing is less likely to occur when the task is interesting, because individuals have a higher intrinsic motivation to perform their duties. It is also less common when the group's objective is important, possibly because individuals experience more pressure from other team mem-bers to perform well. Finally, social loafing is less common among members with a strong collectivist value, because they value group membership and be-lieve in working toward group objectives (see Chapter 4).[89]

How to Minimize Social Loafing   By understanding the causes of social loafing, we can identify ways to minimize this problem. Some of the strategies listed below reduce social loafing by making each member's performance more visible. Others increase each member's motivation to perform his or her tasks within the group.[90]

■ *Form smaller teams*—Splitting the team into several smaller groups reduces social loafing because each person's performance becomes more noticeable and important for team performance. A smaller group also potentially increases cohesiveness, so would-be shirkers feel a greater obligation to perform fully for their team.

■ *Specialize tasks*—It is easier to see everyone's contribution when each team member performs a different work activity. For example, rather than pooling their efforts for all incoming customer inquiries, customer service representatives might each be responsible for handling a particular type of client.

■ *Measure individual performance*—Social loafing is minimized when each member's contribution is measured. Of course, individual performance is difficult to measure in some team activities, such as problem-solving projects in which the team's performance depends on one person's discovering the best answer.

■ *Increase job enrichment*—Social loafing is minimized when team members are assigned more motivating jobs, such as jobs requiring more skill variety or having direct contact with clients. However, this strategy minimizes social loafing only if members have a strong growth need strength (see Chapter 6). In general, however, social loafing is less common among employees with high job satisfaction.

■ *Select motivated employees*—Social loafing can be minimized by carefully selecting job applicants who are motivated by the task and have a collectivist value orientation. Those with a collectivist value are motivated to work harder for the team because they value their membership in the group.

TEAM BUILDING

team building
Any formal activity intended to improve the development and functioning of a work team.

Team building is any formal activity intended to improve the development and functioning of a work team. Most team building accelerates the team development process, which, in turn, might reshape team norms or strengthen cohesiveness. Team building is sometimes applied to newly established teams, but it is more common among existing teams that have regressed to earlier stages of team development. Team building is therefore most appropriate when the team experiences high membership turnover or when members have lost sight of their respective roles and team objectives.[91]

Types of Team Building

There are four main types of team building: role definition, goal setting, problem solving, and interpersonal processes.[92] Role definition team building encourages team members to describe perceptions of their own role as well as the role expectations they have of other team members. After discussing these perceptions, team members revise their roles and work toward a common mental model of their respective responsibilities.[93]

Some team-building interventions clarify the team's performance goals, increase the team's motivation to accomplish those goals, and establish a mechanism for systematic feedback on the team's goal performance. This type of intervention is very similar to individual goal setting, described in Chapter 5, except that the goals are applied to teams. Research suggests that goal setting is an important dimension of team building.[94]

A third type of team building examines the team's task-related decision-making process and identifies ways to make it more effective.[95] Each stage of decision making is examined, such as how the team identifies problems and searches for alternatives (see Chapter 9). To improve their problem-solving skills, some teams participate in simulation games that require team decisions in hypothetical situations.[96] As well as helping team members make better decisions, these team-building activities tend to improve interpersonal processes.

The fourth type of team building is interpersonal processes that try to build trust and open communications among team members by resolving hidden agendas and misperceptions. Such activities include **dialogue** sessions, where team members engage in conversations to develop a common mental model of

dialogue

A process of conversation among team members in which they learn about each other's mental models and assumptions, and eventually form a common model for thinking within the team.

Perched on a narrow beam 25 feet above the ground, Wu Xi never stopped thinking about the possibility of falling. The 30-year-old engineer at Ericsson Cyberlab in Singapore was roped together with five colleagues as they scaled their way up a 75-foot pyramid. "I was so scared, but I couldn't give up," says Wu. "My team members held onto me very firmly and they kept encouraging me." Wu Xi and her co-workers climbed over rock walls, inched across planks, scaled cargo nets, and performed other daunting tasks to improve team dynamics at the Swedish telecommunication firm's Asian research unit. "We all made it to the top with lots of difficulties," explains Ericsson Cyberlab director Andreas Fasbender. "But the best part was that you could really achieve more as a team."[97] Which types of team-building processes would this exercise include?
(© Straits Times)

the ideal team process. As they gain awareness of each other's models and assumptions, members eventually begin to form a common model for thinking within the team.[98] Although dialogue is potentially effective, most organizations tend to rely on wilderness team building, paintball wars, and obstacle course challenges to improve interpersonal processes.

Is Team Building Effective?

Team-building activities have become more popular as companies rely increasingly on teams to get the work done. Some organizations are even experimenting with offbeat team-building activities in the hope that these sessions will improve team dynamics. Coca-Cola executives in China participated in a team-building program that included fire-walking. Deloitte Consulting sent some of its California employees on a three-day extreme adventure race. Among other things, the experience included sleeping in trash bags on the dew-soaked ground and huddling together in "puppy piles" to stay warm. Staffordshire County Council in the United Kingdom sent a team of employees to the fire department for the day, where they learned to navigate through a smoke-filled room and battle a controlled towering inferno. "Faced with danger, people have to work together," explains a Staffordshire employee. "They have no other choice."[99]

Are these and more traditional team-building programs effective? Is the money well spent? So far, the answer is an equivocal maybe. Studies suggest that some team-building activities are successful, but just as many fail to improve team effectiveness.[100] One problem is that corporate leaders assume team-building activities are general solutions to general team problems. No one bothers to diagnose the team's specific needs (e.g., problem solving, interpersonal processes) because the team-building intervention is assumed to be a broad-brush solution. In reality, as we just learned, there are different types of team-building activities for different team needs. A mismatch can potentially lead to ineffective team building.[101]

Another problem is that corporate leaders tend to view team building as a one-shot inoculation that every team should receive when it is formed. In truth, team building is an ongoing process, not a three-day jump start. Some experts suggest, for example, that wilderness experiences often fail because they rarely include follow-up consultation to ensure that team learning is transferred back to the workplace.[102]

Finally, we must remember that team building occurs on the job, not just on an obstacle course or in a national park. Organizations should encourage team members to reflect on their work experiences and to experiment with just-in-time learning for team development.

"Let's agree to blame this on Filmore in accounting."

(FARCUS® is reprinted with permission LaughingStock Licensing Inc., Ottawa, Canada. All rights reserved.)

CHAPTER SUMMARY

Teams are groups of two or more people who interact and influence each other, are mutually accountable for achieving common objectives, and perceive themselves as a social entity within an organization. All teams are groups because they consist of people with a unifying relationship. However, not all groups are teams; some groups do not have purposive interaction.

A team-based organization relies on self-directed work teams rather than functional departments as the core work units. Traditional departments may be teams when employees are encouraged to interact directly and to coordinate work activities with each other. However, unlike traditional departments, team-based organizations tend to rely on cross-functional, autonomous teams with less need for supervisors in a communication or coordination role.

Virtual teams operate across space, time, and organizational boundaries with members who communicate mainly through information technologies. They are becoming more common as a result of advances in computer networks, the shift from physical labor to knowledge-based work, corporate globalization, and the need for greater knowledge sharing.

Team effectiveness includes the group's ability to survive, achieve its system-based objectives, and fulfill the needs of its members. The model of team effectiveness considers the team and organizational environment, team design, and team processes. The team or organizational environment influences team effectiveness directly, as well as through team design and team processes. Six elements in the organizational and team environment that influence team effectiveness are reward systems, communication systems, physical space, organizational environment, organizational structure, and organizational leadership.

Three team design elements are task characteristics, team size, and team composition. Teams work best when tasks are clear and easy to implement, and require a high degree of interdependence. Teams should be large enough to perform the work, yet small enough for efficient coordination and meaningful involvement. Effective teams are composed of people with the competencies and motivation to per-

form tasks in a team environment. Heterogeneous teams operate best on complex projects and problems requiring innovative solutions.

The four team processes are team development, norms, roles, and cohesiveness. Teams develop through the stages of forming, storming, norming, performing, and, eventually, adjourning. Some teams remain in a particular stage longer than others, and team development is an ongoing process. Teams develop norms to regulate and guide member behavior. These norms may be influenced by critical events, explicit statements, initial experiences, and members' pregroup experiences. Team members also have roles—a set of behaviors they are expected to perform because they hold certain positions in a team and organization.

Cohesiveness is the degree of attraction people feel toward the team and their motivation to remain members. Cohesiveness increases with member similarity, smaller team size, higher degree of interaction, somewhat difficult entry, team success, and external challenges. Teams need some level of cohesiveness to survive, but high cohesive units have higher task performance only when their norms do not conflict with organizational objectives.

Teams are not always beneficial or necessary. Moreover, they have hidden costs, known as process losses, and require particular environments to flourish. Teams often fail because they are not set up in supportive environments. Social loafing, another potential problem with teams, is the tendency for individuals to perform at a lower level when working in groups than when working alone. Social loafing can be minimized by making each member's performance more visible and increasing each member's motivation to perform his or her tasks within the group.

Team building is any formal activity intended to improve the development and functioning of a work team. Four team-building strategies are role definition, goal setting, problem solving, and interpersonal processes. Some team-building events succeed, but companies often fail to consider the contingencies of team building.

KEY TERMS

coalition, p. 230

communities of practice, p. 231

dialogue, p. 248

groups, p. 227

heterogeneous teams, p. 236

homogeneous teams, p. 236

informal groups, p. 230

law of telecosm, p. 230

norms, p. 238

process losses, p. 246

quality circles, p. 228

role, p. 240

self-directed work teams (SDWTs), p. 227

skunkworks, p. 229

social loafing, p. 246

task interdependence, p. 234

team-based organization, p. 227

team building, p. 247

team cohesiveness, p. 241

team effectiveness, p. 231

teams, p. 226

virtual teams, p. 230

DISCUSSION QUESTIONS

1. Suppose the instructor for this course assigned you to a project team consisting of three other students who are currently taking similar courses in France, Japan, and Brazil. All students speak English and have similar knowledge of the topic. Use your knowledge of virtual teams to discuss the problems that your team might face compared with a team of local students who can meet face-to-face.

2. Informal groups exist in almost every form of social organization. What types of informal groups exist in your classroom? Why are students motivated to belong to these informal groups?

3. You have been put in charge of a cross-functional task force that will develop Internet banking services for retail customers. The team includes representatives from marketing, information services, customer service, and accounting, all of whom will move to the same location at headquarters for three months. Describe the evidence or behaviors that you might observe during each stage of the team's development.

4. You have just been transferred from the Kansas office to the Denver office of your company, a national sales organization of electrical products for developers and contractors. In Kansas, team members regularly called customers after a sale to ask whether the products arrived on time and whether they were satisfied. But in the Denver office, no one seems to make these follow-up calls. A recently hired co-worker explains that other co-workers discouraged her from making those calls.

Later, another co-worker suggests that your follow-up calls are making everyone else look lazy. Give three possible reasons the norms in Denver might be different from those in the Kansas office, even though the customers, products, sales commissions, and other characteristics of the workplace are almost identical.

5. You have been asked to lead a complex software project over the next year that requires the full-time involvement of approximately 100 people with diverse skills and backgrounds. Using your knowledge of team size, how can you develop an effective team under these conditions?

6. You have been assigned to a class project with five other students, none of whom you have met before. To what extent would team cohesiveness improve your team's performance on this project? What actions would you recommend to build team cohesiveness among student team members in this situation?

7. The CEO of Muluwa Railway Corporation wants employees throughout the organization to perform their work in teams. According to the CEO, "teams are our solution to increasing competition and customer demands." Discuss three problems with teams that Muluwa Railway's CEO may not be aware of.

8. The Johari Window, described in Chapter 3, is sometimes used as the foundation for team building. What type of team building would occur through Johari Window activities?

CASE STUDY 8.1

TREETOP FOREST PRODUCTS

Treetop Forest Products Inc. is a sawmill operation in Oregon that is owned by a major forest products company but operates independently of headquarters. It was built 30 years ago and completely updated with new machinery 5 years ago. Treetop receives raw logs from the area for cutting and planing into building-grade lumber, mostly 2-by-4 and 2-by-6 pieces of standard lengths. Higher-grade logs leave Treetop's sawmill department in finished form and are sent directly to the packaging department. The remaining 40 percent of sawmill output consists of cuts from lower-grade logs, requiring further work by the planing department.

Treetop has one general manager, 16 supervisors and support staff, and 180 unionized employees. The unionized employees are paid an hourly rate specified in the collective agreement, whereas management and support staff are paid a monthly salary. The mill is divided into six operating departments: boom, sawmill, planer, packaging, shipping, and maintenance. The sawmill, boom, and packaging departments operate a morning shift starting at 6 A.M. and an afternoon shift starting at 2 P.M. Employees in these departments rotate shifts every two weeks. The planer and shipping departments operate only morning shifts. Maintenance employees work the night shift (starting at 10 P.M.).

Each department, except for packaging, has a supervisor on every work shift. The planer supervisor is responsible for the packaging department on the morning shift, and the sawmill supervisor is responsible for the packaging department on the afternoon shift. However, the packaging operation is housed in a building separate from the other departments, so supervisors seldom visit the packaging department. This is particularly true for the afternoon shift, because the sawmill supervisor is the farthest distance from the packaging building.

Packaging Quality
Ninety percent of Treetop's product is sold on the international market through Westboard Company, a large marketing agency. Westboard represents all forest products mills owned by Treetop's parent company as well as several other clients in the region. The market for building-grade lumber is very price competitive, because there are numerous mills selling a relatively undifferentiated product. However, some differentiation does occur in product packaging and presentation. Buyers will look closely at the packaging when deciding whether to buy from Treetop or another mill.

To encourage its clients to package their products better, Westboard sponsors a monthly package quality award. The marketing agency samples and rates its clients' packages daily, and the sawmill with the highest score at the end of the month is awarded a plaque. Package quality is a combination of how the lumber is piled (e.g., defects turned in), where the bands and dunnage are placed, how neatly the stencil and seal are applied, how accurate the stencil is, and how neatly and tightly the plastic wrap is attached.

Treetop Forest Products won Westboard's packaging quality award several times over the past five years, and received high ratings in the months that it didn't win. However, the mill's ratings have started to decline over the past year or two, and several clients have complained about the appearance of the finished product. A few large customers switched to competitors' lumber, saying that the decision was based on the substandard appearance of Treetop's packaging when it arrived in their lumberyard.

Bottleneck in Packaging
The planing and sawmill departments have increased productivity significantly over the past couple of years. The sawmill operation recently set a new productivity record on a single day. The planer operation has increased productivity to the point that last year it reduced operations to just one (rather than two) shifts per day. These productivity improvements are due to better operator training, fewer machine breakdowns, and better selection of raw logs. (Sawmill cuts from high-quality logs usually do not require planing work.)

Productivity levels in the boom, shipping, and maintenance departments have remained constant. However, the packaging department has recorded decreasing productivity over the past couple of years, with the result that a large backlog of finished product is typically stockpiled outside the packaging building. The morning shift of the packaging department is unable to keep up with the combined production of the sawmill and planer departments, so the unpackaged output is left for the afternoon shift. Unfortunately, the afternoon shift packages even less product than the morning shift, so the backlog continues to build. The backlog adds to Treetop's inventory costs and increases the risk of damaged stock.

Treetop has added Saturday overtime shifts as well as extra hours before and after the regular shifts for the packaging department employees to process this backlog. Last month, the packaging department employed 10 percent of the workforce but accounted for 85 percent of the overtime. This situation is frustrating to Treetop's management, because time-and-motion studies recently confirmed that the packaging department is capable of processing all the daily sawmill and planer production without overtime. Moreover, with employees earning one and a half or two times their regular pay on overtime, Treetop's cost competitiveness suffers.

Employees and supervisors at Treetop are aware that people in the packaging department tend to extend lunch by 10 minutes and coffee breaks by 5 minutes. They also typically leave work a few minutes before the end of their shift. This abuse has worsened recently, particularly on the afternoon shift. Employees who are temporarily assigned to the packaging department also seem to participate in this time loss pattern after a few days. Although they are punctual and productive in other departments, these temporary employees soon adopt the packaging crew's informal schedule when assigned to that department.

Discussion Questions

1. On the basis of your knowledge of team dynamics, explain why the packaging department is less productive than other departments at Treetop.

2. How should Treetop change the nonproductive norms that exist in the packaging group?

3. What structural and other changes would you recommend that could improve this situation in the long term?

CASE STUDY 8.2

DETROIT IS CRUISING FOR QUALITY

BusinessWeek In the 1980s, Detroit automakers were widely criticized for lagging behind the Japanese in most measures of quality. Since then, Ford, General Motors, and DaimlerChrysler have all made strides in quality improvement, often borrowing methods from Japanese manufacturing. Those methods include team-based approaches such as quality circles and cross-functional teams. At the beginning of the twenty-first century, defect rates in U.S. cars are much lower, but the companies still have far to go, and they continue to rely on teams to solve—and prevent—quality problems.

This *Business Week* case study describes efforts by U.S. carmakers to improve quality. It identifies the kinds of problems that are most prevalent and gives examples of team-based solutions. Read through this *Business Week* case study at www.mhhe.com/mcshane2e and prepare for the discussion questions at right.

Discussion Questions

1. What kinds of teams does the author mention in this article? How effective have they been?

2. What are some of the norms that exist at U.S. automakers and in their teams that may have limited their success in improving quality?

3. The article says Chrysler is forming teams for vehicle development. How might participation of employees from the design, engineering, marketing, manufacturing, and purchasing departments prevent "last-minute design changes that lead to errors later on"? What are some advantages and disadvantages of this team approach, compared with letting designers handle this process on their own?

Source: J. Muller, "Detroit Is Cruising for Quality," *Business Week*, September 3, 2001.

TEAM EXERCISE 8.3

TEAM-TRUST EXERCISE

Purpose This exercise is designed to help you understand the role of interpersonal trust in the development and maintenance of effective teams.

Materials The instructor will provide the same 15 objects for each team as well as for the model.

Instructions

■ *Step 1*—The instructor will divide the class into teams of approximately 10 people.

■ *Step 2*—Each team receives 15 objects from the instructor. The same 15 objects are arranged in a specific way on a table at the front of the room (or elsewhere, as designated by the instructor). The table is behind a screened area so that the arrangements cannot be seen by participants from their work areas. The goal of each team is to duplicate the *exact* arrangement (e.g., location, overlap, spacing) of the objects on the table, using its own matching set of objects, within 20 minutes (or other time limit given by the instructor). Participants are allowed one 30-second opportunity at the beginning of the exercise to view the screened table. They may not write, draw, or talk while viewing the screened table. However, each team has *up to two saboteurs*. These are people who have been selected by the instructor (either before the exercise or through notes distributed to all participants). Saboteurs will use any reasonable method to prevent the team from producing an accurate configuration of objects in their work area. They are forbidden to reveal their identities.

■ *Step 3*—At the end of the time limit, the instructor will evaluate each team's configuration and decide which one is the most accurate. The class members will then evaluate their experience in the exercise in terms of team development and other aspects of team dynamics.

Source: This exercise is based on ideas discussed in G. Thompson and P. Pearce, "The Team-Trust Game," *Training and Development*, May 1992, pp. 42–43.

TEAM EXERCISE 8.4

TEAM TOWER POWER

Purpose This exercise is designed to help you understand team roles, team development, and other issues in the development and maintenance of effective teams.

Materials The instructor will provide enough Lego pieces or similar materials for each team to complete the assigned task. All teams should have identical (or very similar) amounts and types of pieces. The instructor will need a measuring tape and stopwatch. Students may use writing materials during the design stage (Step 2 below). The instructor will distribute a Team Objectives Sheet and Tower Specifications Effectiveness Sheet to all teams.

Instructions

■ *Step 1*—The instructor will divide the class into teams. Depending on class size and space available, teams may have between four and seven members, but all teams should be approximately equal in size.

■ *Step 2*—Each team is given 20 minutes to design a tower that uses only the materials provided, is freestanding, and provides an optimal return on investment. Team members may wish to draw their tower on paper or on a flip chart to assist in the tower's design. Teams are free to practice building their tower during this stage. Preferably, teams are assigned to their own rooms so that the design can be created privately. During this stage, each team will complete the Team Objectives Sheet distributed by the instructor. This sheet requires the Tower Specifications Effectiveness Sheet, also distributed by the instructor.

■ *Step 3*—Each team will show the instructor that it has completed its Team Objectives Sheet. Then, with all teams in the same room, the instructor will announce the start of the construction phase. The time elapsed for construction will be closely monitored, and the instructor will occasionally call out time elapsed (particularly if there is no clock in the room).

■ *Step 4*—Each team will advise the instructor as soon as it has completed its tower and will write down the time elapsed that the instructor has determined. The team may be asked to assist the instructor by counting the number of blocks used and the height of the tower. This information is also written on the Team Objectives Sheet. Then the team calculates its profit.

■ *Step 5*—After presenting the results, the class will discuss the team dynamics elements that contribute to team effectiveness. Team members will discuss their strategy, division of labor (team roles), expertise within the team, and other elements of team dynamics.

Source: Several published and online sources describe variations of this exercise, but there is no known origin for this activity.

SELF-ASSESSMENT EXERCISE 8.5

TEAM ROLES PREFERENCES SCALE

Purpose This self-assessment exercise is designed to help you identify your preferred roles in meetings and similar team activities.

Instructions Read each statement below and circle the response that you believe best reflects your position regarding that statement. Then use the scoring key in Appendix B to calculate your results for each team role. This exercise is completed alone so that students assess themselves honestly without concerns of social comparison. However, class discussion will focus on the roles that people assume in team settings. This scale assesses only a few team roles.

Team roles preferences scale					
Circle the number that best reflects your position regarding each statement.	Does not describe me at all ▼	Does not describe me very well ▼	Describes me somewhat ▼	Describes me well ▼	Describes me very well ▼
1. I usually take responsibility for getting the team to agree on what the meeting should accomplish. . . .	1	2	3	4	5
2. I tend to summarize to other team members what the team has accomplished so far.	1	2	3	4	5
3. I'm usually the person who helps other team members overcome their disagreements.	1	2	3	4	5
4. I try to ensure that everyone gets heard on issues. . . .	1	2	3	4	5
5. I'm usually the person who helps the team determine how to organize the discussion.	1	2	3	4	5
6. I praise other team members for their ideas more than do others in the meetings.	1	2	3	4	5
7. People tend to rely on me to keep track of what has been said in meetings.	1	2	3	4	5
8. The team typically counts on me to prevent debates from getting out of hand.	1	2	3	4	5
9. I tend to say things that make the group feel optimistic about its accomplishments.	1	2	3	4	5
10. Team members usually count on me to give everyone a chance to speak.	1	2	3	4	5
11. In most meetings, I am less likely than others to put down the ideas of teammates.	1	2	3	4	5

(continued)

Circle the number that best reflects your position regarding each statement.	Does not describe me at all ▼	Does not describe me very well ▼	Describes me somewhat ▼	Describes me well ▼	Describes me very well ▼
12. I actively help teammates resolve their differences in meetings.	1	2	3	4	5
13. I actively encourage quiet team members to describe their ideas on each issue.	1	2	3	4	5
14. People tend to rely on me to clarify the purpose of the meeting.	1	2	3	4	5
15. I like to be the person who takes notes or minutes of the meeting.	1	2	3	4	5

Team roles preferences scale (cont.)

After studying the preceding material, be sure to check out our website at
www.mhhe.com/mcshane2e
for more in-depth information and interactivities that correspond to this chapter.

9

Decision Making and Employee Involvement

AFTER READING THIS CHAPTER, YOU SHOULD BE ABLE TO:

- Diagram the general model of decision making.

- Explain why people have difficulty identifying problems and opportunities.

- Identify three factors that challenge our ability to choose the best alternative.

- Outline the causes of escalation of commitment to a poor decision.

- Outline the forms and levels of employee involvement.

- Describe sociotechnical systems theory recommendations for more successful self-directed work teams.

- Identify the four contingencies in the Vroom–Jago model that determine the optimal level of employee involvement.

- Discuss the challenges that prevent employee involvement.

Less than two years after its launch, JetBlue has become the buzz of the airline industry. David Neeleman founded the New York–based discount airline using his previous experience launching Morris Air (sold to Southwest Airlines in 1993), then developing WestJet into the most successful discount carrier in Canadian history.

JetBlue's successful start-up is attributed largely to several well-executed decisions. One of the first was to base the business at John F. Kennedy Airport in New York City. New York was one of the few large cities not served by a discount airline, and JFK is less congested than La Guardia. Next, Neeleman and his executive team selected secondary airports near large cities—such as Fort Lauderdale rather than Miami, and Oakland rather than San Francisco—as destinations because they offered lower costs and yet were reasonably convenient for passengers.

Neeleman also decided that JetBlue should use only new aircraft—A320s from Airbus Industrie. His philosophy is that new planes give an airline instant credibility with travelers. Another calculated decision was having luxurious interiors for the all-coach configuration, including wider leather seats, more space between rows, and 24-channel satellite television at every seat. Although JetBlue is a discount carrier, it wants to lure business travelers to its economy service. The plan seems to be working. "We were starved for an airline like this," says one business passenger. "It's hard to compare flying Jet-Blue to [flying] other airlines."

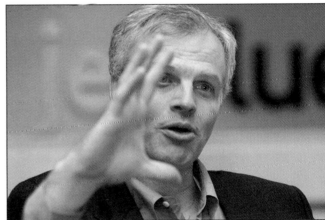

David Neeleman made numerous decisions leading up to the launch of JetBlue, the New York–based discount airline that has taken the industry by storm. (© AP/Wide World)

Not all the decisions about JetBlue were so carefully calculated. For example, JetBlue executives frankly say that some of Neeleman's rejected ideas were a bit wild, such as having separate men's and women's lavatories and serving pizza on planes. "That's why I make sure there are people around me who push back," says Neeleman. One crazy idea that worked was offering naturally blue potato chips free to passengers. The color-coordinated snack was a hit.[1] ∎

decision making
A conscious process of making choices among one or more alternatives with the intention of moving toward some desired state of affairs.

David Neeleman and his executive team made thousands of decisions in launching the hottest airline on the continent. **Decision making** is a conscious process of making choices among one or more alternatives with the intention of moving toward some desired state of affairs.[2] Some of Neeleman's decisions, such as in which city and airport to base the business, followed a careful process of searching for alternatives and weighing the advantages. Other decisions, such as whether to offer blue potato chips or pizza on flights, required the creative exploration of previously untested ideas.

Decisions occur in response to problems or opportunities. A *problem* is a deviation between the current and desired situation.[3] It is the gap between what is and what ought to be. An *opportunity* is a deviation between current expectations and the recognition of a potentially better situation that is neither planned nor expected. In other words, decision makers realize that certain decisions may produce results beyond current goals or expectations. For example, Neeleman saw New York City as an opportunity to launch JetBlue because it was poorly serviced with high-priced airlines.

This chapter begins with an overview of the decision-making process. The model is then examined more critically by identifying the human conditions that impede effective decision making. In today's complex environment, executives can rarely afford to make decisions without some level of employee involvement. The latter part of this chapter explores the forms and levels of employee involvement, including a detailed discussion of self-directed work teams and sociotechnical systems theory. Finally, we discuss the potential benefits and the limitations of employee involvement.

A GENERAL MODEL OF DECISION MAKING

How do people make decisions? The best place to start to answer that question is the general model of decision making shown in Exhibit 9.1.[4] Throughout

EXHIBIT 9.1

General model of decision making

KAARU ISHIKAWA   5 whys   5ˢ

People → Training
Problem
Material

Decision-Making Process

1. Identify problem or opportunity
2. Choose the best decision style
3. Develop alternative solutions
4. Choose the best solution
5. Implement the selected alternative
6. Evaluate decision outcomes

Design → Inputs
People, Method, Equipment
Gathering, material, Environment

this chapter, we'll see that people do not really make decisions this systematically. However, the model provides a useful template for our discussion of the topic and provides some guidance about how to make decisions under certain conditions.[5]

When Albert Einstein was asked how he would save the world in one hour, he replied that he would spend the first 55 minutes defining the problem and the last 5 minutes solving it. Problem identification is the first step in decision making and arguably the most important step. As mentioned above, a problem is a deviation between the current and desired situation. This deviation is a *symptom* of more fundamental causes in the organization. We need to identify the problem correctly to be able to choose the best solution. This process occurs by understanding the underlying causes of the symptoms that catch our attention. The decision process is then directed toward changing the root causes so that the symptoms are reduced or eliminated.[6]

The second step is to determine the most appropriate decision style.[7] One important issue is whether the problem calls for a **programmed** or a **nonprogrammed decision.**[8] A programmed decision follows standard operating procedures. There is no need to explore alternative solutions because the optimal solution has already been identified and documented. For example, when customers call a General Electric answer center, operators key in the problem, and a computer database of 1.5 million issues provides the best solution for the client.[9] In contrast, new, complex, or ill-defined problems require nonprogrammed decisions. In these cases, decision makers must search for alternatives and possibly develop a unique solution. As problems reappear, however, programmed decision routines are formed. In this respect, programmed decisions drive out nonprogrammed decisions because we strive for predictable, routine situations.

The third step in the general decision model is to develop a list of possible solutions.[10] This process usually begins by searching for ready-made solutions, such as practices that have worked well on similar problems. If an acceptable solution cannot be found, then decision makers try to design a custom-made solution or modify an existing one. The fourth step involves choosing the best alternative. In a purely rational process, this step would involve identifying all factors against which the alternatives are judged, assigning weights reflecting the importance of those factors, rating each alternative on those factors, and calculating each alternative's total value from the ratings and factor weights.[11]

In the fifth step, decision makers must rally employees and mobilize sufficient resources to translate their decisions into action. They must consider the motivation, ability, and role perceptions of employees implementing the solution, as well as situational factors to facilitate its implementation (see Chapter 2). The last step in the decision model involves evaluating whether the gap has narrowed between what is and what ought to be. Ideally, this information should come from systematic benchmarks, so that relevant feedback is objective and easily observed.

The general model of decision making seems so logical, yet it is rarely observed in organizations. Decision makers experience a number of personal limitations that make it difficult to identify problems and opportunities, evaluate and choose solutions, and evaluate decision outcomes. Over the next few pages, we look at these challenges and ways to minimize them.

programmed decision

The process whereby decision makers follow standard operating procedures to select the preferred solution without the need to identify or evaluate alternative choices.

nonprogrammed decision

The process applied to unique, complex, or ill-defined situations whereby decision makers follow the full decision-making process, including a careful search for and/or development of unique solutions.

IDENTIFYING PROBLEMS AND OPPORTUNITIES

Problems and opportunities do not announce themselves. They are recognized and ultimately defined by the decision maker. However, people are not perfectly efficient or neutral thinking machines, so problems are often misdiagnosed and opportunities are overlooked. Two factors that interfere with identifying problems and opportunities are the decision maker's imperfect perceptions and diagnostic skills.

Perceptual Biases

People define problems or opportunities on the basis of their perceptions, values, and assumptions. Unfortunately, selective attention mechanisms cause relevant information to be unconsciously screened out. Moreover, employees, clients, and others with vested interests can influence the decision maker's perceptions so that information is more or less likely to be perceived as a problem or an opportunity. Thus, decision making is frequently marked by politics and negotiation.[12]

A broader perceptual challenge is that people see problems or opportunities through their mental models (see Chapter 3).[13] These working models of the world help us make sense of our environment, but they also perpetuate assumptions that blind us to new realities. Connections 9.1 describes how narrow mental models are the source of several famous missed opportunities.

Poor Diagnostic Skills

Perceptual problems block our ability to diagnose problems effectively and to recognize opportunities.[14] People want to make sense of situations, so they quickly define problems on the basis of stereotypes and other unsubstantiated information. They fail to see problems or opportunities as a result of insufficient time or information. Another concern is that organizations are complex systems (see Chapter 1), so decision makers may have trouble identifying where the main causes of problems occur.

Another common diagnostic error is defining problems in terms of their solutions. Someone who says, "The problem is that we need more control over our suppliers" has fallen into this trap. The problem might be that suppliers aren't delivering their product in time, but this statement focuses on a solution. The tendency to focus on solutions is caused by a person's bias for action as well as the need to reduce uncertainty. However, focusing on solution scan short-circuit the problem identification stage of decision making.[15]

The solution-oriented problem also occurs because decision makers receive positive reinforcement from actions that worked in the past. Former Sunbeam CEO Al "Chainsaw" Dunlap saw the appliance

© 1998 Randy Glasbergen.

"My team has created a very innovative solution, but we're still looking for a problem to go with it."

(Copyright © Randy Glasbergen. Reprinted with special permission from www.glasbergen.com.)

Famous Missed Opportunities

Mental models create road maps that guide our decisions. Unfortunately, these maps also potentially block our ability to recognize new problems and opportunities. Here are a few famous examples:

- *L.A. Confidential* director Brian Helgeland approached Hollywood studios about a new film featuring a lowly squire in fourteenth-century England who aspires to be a knight. The squire and his street-smart colleagues (including Geoffrey Chaucer) would do battle on contemporary themes such as youth, freedom, and equality. The entire film would be set to 1970s rock music. The Hollywood studios weren't impressed. "When I pitched it, I couldn't sell it," laments Helgeland. "Some people would laugh and then say, 'What are you really here for?'" Undeterred, Helgeland eventually convinced Columbia Pictures to back the project. The film, *A Knight's Tale*, recouped its $41 million costs in just three weeks and went on to become one of the more successful films of the year.

- Graphical user interfaces, mice, windows, pull-down menus, laser printing, distributed computing, and Ethernet technologies weren't invented by Apple, Microsoft, or IBM. These essential elements of contemporary personal computing originated in the 1970s from researchers at the Xerox Palo Alto Research Center (PARC). Unfortunately, Xerox executives were so focused on their photocopier business that they didn't bother to patent most of these inventions. Xerox has successfully applied some of its laser technology, but the lost value of Xerox PARC's other computing discoveries is much larger than the entire photocopier industry today.

- In 1995, IDEO founder David Kelley was given a personal demonstration of a new mobile computing interface that required the user to learn special shorthand writing. On the basis of his company's experience designing everything from the Apple mouse to stand-up toothpaste tubes, Kelley wasn't impressed. He advised the visitor that this product would have difficulty in the marketplace because people wouldn't take time to learn a new way to use

Brian Helgeland's film *A Knight's Tale* paid for itself in just three weeks even though most Hollywood studio executives rejected the proposal. *(© Photofest)*

a computer. Three years later, in spite of Kelley's predictions, the Palm PDA became one of the world's most popular computing devices.

- When the World Wide Web burst onto the cyberspace scene in the early 1990s, Bill Gates wondered what all the fuss was about. Even as late as 1996, the Microsoft founder lampooned investors for their love-in with companies that made Internet products. However, Gates eventually realized the error in his mental model of computing. Making up for lost time, Microsoft bought Hotmail and other Web-savvy companies, and added Internet support to its Windows operating system.

Sources: C. Sim, "Battling the Odds," *KrisWorld* (Singapore Airlines inflight magazine), September 2001, pp. 8–10; T. Kelley and J. Littman, *The Art of Innovation* (New York: Random House, 2001), pp. 165–66; B. Campbell and M. Conron, "Xerox Ready to Hit Another Home Run," *Ottawa Citizen*, June 28, 1999; O. Port, "Xerox Won't Duplicate Past Errors," *Business Week*, September 29, 1997, p. 98; T. Abate, "Meet Bill Gates, Stand-up Comic," *San Francisco Examiner*, March 13, 1996, p. D1.

manufacturer's problems in terms of the need to slash payroll, just as he had done at Scott Paper and other companies.[16] Other executives introduce a customer service program whenever they face a problem because this solution worked for them in the past. The point here is that decision makers might look at problems from the perspective of their ready-made solutions. Sometimes, they *search* for problems so that they can apply their existing solution.

Identifying Problems and Opportunities More Effectively

Recognizing problems and opportunities will always be a challenge, but the process can be improved through awareness of these perceptual and diagnostic limitations. By recognizing how mental models restrict a person's understanding of the world, decision makers learn to be more open to other perspectives of reality. Perceptual and diagnostic weaknesses can also be minimized by discussing the situation with colleagues. Decision makers discover blind spots in problem identification by hearing how others perceive certain information and diagnose problems.[17] Opportunities also become apparent when outsiders explore information from their different mental models.

Another strategy for problem identification is to create early warning systems. If customer satisfaction ratings drop or costs increase beyond a fixed mark, executive procedures or computer programs can alert decision makers to these concerns. These cues may be determined from past practice or preset goals for major stakeholders (customers, shareholders, employees, etc.). The effectiveness of early warning signs, however, is only as good as the willingness to recognize them. Still, they may help flag problems before a situation deteriorates further.

Computer technology also helps identify opportunities and problems. Some computer programs engage in *data mining*—searching through large databases and organizing this information into meaningful trends. Data mining minimizes perceptual problems that occur with manual searches for trends and patterns in mountains of data.

EVALUATING AND CHOOSING SOLUTIONS

For many years, decision making was studied mainly by economists, who made several assumptions about how people choose among alternatives. They assumed that decision makers have well-articulated and agreed-on organizational goals. They also assumed that decision makers are rational thinking machines who efficiently and simultaneously process facts about all alternatives and the consequences of those alternatives. Finally, these theorists assumed that decision makers always choose the alternative with the highest payoff. These were only hypothetical assumptions, but this rational perspective laid the foundation for popular misconceptions about how people make decisions.

Today, even the economists have cast off these unrealistic assumptions.[18] Instead, they are recognizing that decision making includes a variety of human limitations. Over the past 40 years, organizational behavior researchers have debunked several economic assumptions about decision making, as Exhibit 9.2 highlights.

Problems with Goals

We need clear goals to choose the best solution. Goals identify what ought to be and therefore provide a standard against which each alternative is evaluated. In reality, though, organizational goals are often ambiguous or in conflict with each other. One survey recently found that 25 percent of managers and employees felt decisions are delayed because of difficulty agreeing on what they want the decision to achieve. The problem is compounded when

Traditional economic assumptions versus organizational behavior findings about choosing decision alternatives

organizational members disagree over the relative importance of these goals.[19] It is also doubtful that all decisions are on the basis of organizational objectives; some decisions are made to satisfy the decision maker's personal goals even when they are incompatible with the organization's goals.

Problems with Information Processing

People do not make perfectly rational decisions because they don't process information very well. One problem is that perceptual biases distort the selection and interpretation of information (see Chapter 3). Thus, decision makers are not aware of every piece of information because the selective attention process screens out much of it. Second, decision makers can't possibly think through all the alternatives and their outcomes, so they engage in a limited search for and evaluation of alternatives.[20] For example, there may be dozens of computer brands to choose from, but people typically evaluate only a few of them.

Third, rather than examining all alternatives at the same time, decision makers typically look at alternatives sequentially. As a new alternative comes along, it is immediately compared with an implicit favorite. An *implicit favorite* is an alternative that the decision maker prefers over the others.[21] In some cases, this option is unconsciously chosen long before the formal decision process begins. The implicit favorite becomes a comparison against which all other alternatives are judged. The problem with relying on an implicit favorite is that people unconsciously distort information to make their implicit favorite come out the winner in most comparisons.[22]

Problems with Maximization

satisficing
Selecting a solution
that is satisfactory
or "good enough"
rather than optimal
or "the best."

Decision makers tend to select the alternative that is acceptable or good enough, rather than the best possible solution. In other words, they engage in **satisficing** rather than maximizing. Satisficing occurs because it isn't possible to identify all the possible alternatives, and information about available alternatives is imperfect or ambiguous. Satisficing also occurs because decision makers tend to evaluate alternatives sequentially. They evaluate alternatives one at a time against the implicit favorite and eventually select an option that is good enough to satisfy their needs or preferences. What constitutes a good enough solution depends on the availability of acceptable alternatives. Standards rise when acceptable alternatives are easily found and fall when few are available.[23]

Choosing Solutions More Effectively

Getting around the human limitations of making choices is very difficult, but three strategies worth considering are systematic evaluation, decision support systems, and scenario planning. Systematic evaluation follows a measured and logical process of analyzing the alternatives. In the selection of job applicants, for instance, systematic evaluation would involve (1) identifying the relevant factors against which the applicants are judged; (2) measuring applicants on each factor; (3) weighting the importance of each factor; and (4) computing an overall score for each applicant on the basis of the weights and ratings for each factor.[24]

Dow Chemical relies on systematic evaluation when deciding which information technology projects to pursue. The company has a cross-functional committee that evaluates each proposal using a point system that factors in the quality of the vendors, the logic of the proposal, and Dow's technical and organizational readiness for change.[25] This process tends to minimize the implicit favorite and satisficing problems that occur when relying on general subjective judgments. It also aids information processing because the calculations are made on paper rather than in people's heads.

A second—and often complementary—strategy is to use decision support systems to guide the decision-making process.[26] For example, software developer Cerner Corporation uses a case-based reasoning process at its help desk. Callers' problems or questions are entered in simple English, and the system replies with questions and, eventually, solutions to the problems presented. This decision support system cut in half Cerner's backlog of unresolved client issues and increased customer satisfaction ratings to record high levels.[27] Notice that this decision support software turns a seemingly nonprogrammed decision into a programmed decision. It helps employees systematically identify the problem, which then points to a ready-made solution without the need to evaluate alternatives.

Executives at Ericsson, Royal Dutch/Shell, Noranda, and many other organizations are trying to make better decisions through a third strategy, called **scenario planning**.[28] Scenario planning typically involves thinking about alternative futures and what the organization should do to anticipate and react to those environments. To some extent, scenario planning explores potential problems and opportunities. But it is also a vehicle for choosing the best solutions under possible scenarios long before they occur.

Making Choices with Intuition

A man slipped on a ladder and sliced his arm with broken glass as he fell. Paramedics from the Cleveland fire department arrived within minutes and quickly judged from the pool of blood around the unconscious victim that he had ripped an artery and lost two units of blood. The lead paramedic immediately applied pressure to the man's arm. Medical procedures dictate that the victim should be checked for other injuries before being moved. But the victim would die if he lost much more blood, so the lead paramedic decided to get him immediately into the ambulance. As the vehicle raced to the hospital, a crew member put inflatable pants on the victim to stabilize his blood pressure. Putting the pants on the victim before moving him would have cost precious seconds.[29]

Ten minutes after receiving the call, the paramedics delivered the victim to the hospital. During that time, they made several life-saving decisions without going through the formal decision-making process described at the beginning of this chapter. These paramedics, along with most corporate leaders, will tell you that they don't rely just on systematic evaluation, decision support systems, and scenario planning to make choices. They often rely on their intuition.[30] **Intuition** is the ability to know when a problem or opportunity exists and select the best course of action without conscious reasoning.[31]

There is plenty of debate about the value of intuition. Some scholars warn us that intuition is merely wishful thinking that can have disastrous results. In spite of these warnings, most executives swear by their intuition. Recent studies report that most professionals and executives say they rely on intuition, particularly in combination with more rational decision making.[32] Notice that intuition rarely occurs alone. Decision makers analyze the available information, then turn to their intuition to complete the process.

Should we rely on intuition or view it with caution? The answer is both. It is true that we sometimes justify biased and nonsystematic decision making as intuition. When deciding to invest in a new business, for example, decision makers run the risk of following their emotions rather than the evidence. However, there is also increasing research evidence that intuition is the conduit through which people use their tacit knowledge. Recall from Chapter 2 that tacit knowledge is subtle information acquired through observation and experience that is not clearly understood and therefore cannot be explicitly communicated. This knowledge incorporates logical reasoning that has become habit over time. Thus, intuition allows us to draw on our vast storehouse of unconscious knowledge.[33]

Intuition is particularly valuable when the decision maker has extensive knowledge of the business but lacks detailed knowledge of a new situation.

---

scenario planning
A systematic process of thinking about alternative futures, and what the organization should do to anticipate and react to those environments.

---

intuition
The ability to know when a problem or opportunity exists and select the best course of action without conscious reasoning.

Consider the paramedics described a few paragraphs ago. When arriving at the scene, they didn't have time to collect detailed information about the victim's condition. Instead, they sensed the best solution without consciously thinking through their preference. Through experience, they develop patterns of circumstances that represent templates to be recalled quickly in the future.

Experienced decision makers in other work settings follow this same process. "When you're a start-up, you find that you almost never have all the information you would like to make a decision," says Kirby "Buddy" Pickle, a former Teligent executive who recently started Velocita (formerly PF.Net). "You end up having to work a lot on intuition." Ralph S. Larsen, CEO of Johnson & Johnson, agrees. "Often there is absolutely no way that you could have the time to thoroughly analyze every one of the options or alternatives available to you," says Larsen. "So you have to rely on your business judgment."[34] Certainly, we need to be careful that our gut feelings are not merely perceptual distortions and false assumptions, but we should also recognize the potential value of intuition in making sound choices.

EVALUATING DECISION OUTCOMES

Decision makers aren't always completely honest with themselves when evaluating the effectiveness of their decisions. One concern is that after making a choice, decision makers tend to inflate the quality of the selected alternative and deflate the quality of the discarded alternatives. They ignore or suppress the importance of negative information about the selected alternative and emphasize positive information. This perceptual distortion, known as **postdecisional justification,** results from the need to maintain a positive self-identity.[35] Postdecisional justification gives people an excessively optimistic evaluation of their decisions, but only until they receive very clear and undeniable information to the contrary. Unfortunately, it also inflates the decision maker's initial evaluation of the decision, so reality often comes as a painful shock when objective feedback is finally received.

postdecisional justification
Justifying choices by unconsciously inflating the quality of the selected option and deflating the quality of the discarded options.

Escalation of Commitment

A second problem when evaluating decision outcomes is escalation of commitment. **Escalation of commitment** is the tendency to repeat an apparently bad decision or allocate more resources to a failing course of action.[36] There are plenty of escalation examples around the world. Tokyo's Metropolitan Transport Bureau promised to build a 29-kilometer high-speed subway loop under the city in record time and at enormous profit. Instead, the multibillion-dollar project is way over budget, is more than three years overdue, and won't be profitable until 2040, if ever. Denver's International Airport was supposed to include a state-of-the-art automated baggage handling system. Instead, the project was eventually abandoned, causing the airport to open 16 months late and $2 billion over budget. Global Connections 9.2 describes how the PacifiCat project in British Columbia, Canada, escalated to twice the original cost and produced three ferries that could not be sold. Escalation also occurred years ago when the British government continued funding the Concorde supersonic jet long after its lack of commercial viability was apparent. To this day, some scholars refer to escalation of commitment as the Concorde fallacy.[37]

escalation of commitment
The tendency to repeat an apparently bad decision or allocate more resources to failing course of action.

PacifiCats: An Escalation of Commitment

In the mid-1990s, B.C. Ferries—the government agency that operates the ferry system in British Columbia, Canada—decided to design and build three catamaran-style ferries to carry passengers and vehicles across the 15-mile strait between the city of Vancouver and Vancouver Island. The premier of British Columbia promised that these PacifiCats would travel faster than conventional ferries and cost U.S.$150 million "right down to the toilet paper."

Instead, costs ballooned to nearly U.S.$300 million as the project fell more than two years behind schedule. The first two PacifiCats were plagued by so many mechanical problems that each ferry was under repair half the time. A more devastating discovery was that the PacifiCats had a massive wake that caused ecological and property damage along the shoreline. This made them unsuitable for B.C. waters.

These problems were not unforeseen. During the project's first year, a marine engineer warned that the PacifiCats were not economically feasible and could endanger the public. Soon after, a British shipping journal reported that the ferries would cost much more to build than the original estimates. By the fifth year, the B.C. auditor-general slammed the project, saying that the B.C. Ferries board of directors endorsed the project under government pressure. The board apparently raised concerns about the PacifiCats both before and many times after their decision.

Almost six years after the PacifiCat project was announced, a new premier of British Columbia canceled the program and put the three ferries up for sale at less

The British Columbia government's ill-fated PacifiCat program illustrates the risks and problems associated with decision making. (© R. Allen/Vancouver Province)

than one-quarter of their cost. So far, there are no offers. The former premier, who had supported the PacifiCats until he stepped down for other reasons, was one of the few people who still supported the project.

Sources: C. McInnes and L. Culbert, "Still No Buyers for Three Idled Fastcats," Vancouver Sun, July 5, 2001; K. Fraser, "Ferry-Tale Alarms," Vancouver Province, June 14, 2000; P. Willcocks, "Fast Ferries May Sell for Under $40 Million Each," Vancouver Sun, May 31, 2000; K. Lunman, "B.C. Admits Failure, Puts Fast Ferries up for Sale," Globe and Mail (Toronto), March 14, 2000, p. A1; C. McInnes, "Victoria Sinks Fast Ferries," Vancouver Sun, March 14, 2000; K. Lunman, "B.C. NDP Blasted in Report on Ferries," Globe and Mail (Toronto), October 29, 1999, p. A7.

Causes of Escalating Commitment   Why are people led deeper and deeper into failing projects? Organizational behavior scholars have identified several reasons, including self-justification, gambler's fallacy, perceptual blinders, and closing costs.

Self-justification—Escalation of commitment often occurs because people want to present themselves in a positive light (see Chapter 12).[38] Those who are personally identified with the decision tend to persist because this behavior demonstrates confidence in their own decision-making ability. The B.C. Ferries PacifiCat project probably escalated because it was the former premier's pet project. It was difficult to cancel a symbol of his personal success as a government leader. This persistence is also a decision maker's way of saving face—looking good to avoid the embarrassment of admitting past errors.

Some cultures have a stronger emphasis on saving face than do others, so escalation of commitment is probably more common in those societies.[39]

■ *Gambler's fallacy*—Many projects result in escalation of commitment because decision makers underestimate the risk and overestimate the probability of success. They become victims of the "gambler's fallacy" by having inflated expectations of their ability to control problems that may arise. In other words, decision makers falsely believe that luck is on their side, so they invest more in a losing course of action.

■ *Perceptual blinders*—Escalation of commitment sometimes occurs because decision makers do not see the problems soon enough. Through perceptual defense (see Chapter 3), they unconsciously screen out or explain away negative information. Serious problems initially look like random errors along the way to success. Even when the decision makers see that something is wrong, they believe the information is sufficiently ambiguous that it can be misinterpreted or justified.

■ *Closing costs*—Even when a project's success is in doubt, decision makers will persist because the costs of ending the project are high or unknown. Terminating a major project may involve large financial penalties, a bad public image, or personal political costs. This is probably another explanation why the B.C. Ferries PacifiCat program escalated. Keeping the three ferries in storage would cost U.S.$6 million and leave a reminder of the government's mistake.

Evaluating Decision Outcomes More Effectively

One effective way to minimize escalation of commitment and postdecisional justification is to separate decision choosers from decision evaluators.[40] This strategy tends to avoid the problem of saving face because the person responsible for evaluating the decision would not be concerned about saving face if the project is canceled. In support of this recommendation, a recent study found that banks were more likely to take action against bad loans after the executive responsible had left.[41] In other words, problem loans were effectively managed when someone else took over the portfolio. Similarly, the B.C. Ferries PacifiCat project was canceled only after the premier who started the project stepped down as leader.

A second strategy is to publicly establish a preset level at which the decision is abandoned or reevaluated.[42] This predetermined level is similar to a stop-loss order in the stock market, whereby the stock is sold if it falls below a certain price. The problem with this solution is that conditions are often so complex that it is difficult to identify an appropriate point to abandon a project. A third strategy is to find a source of systematic and clear feedback.[43]

Finally, projects may have less risk of escalation if several people are involved. Other participants continually monitor key decision makers and may notice problems sooner than someone working alone on the project. Employee involvement offers these and many other benefits to the decision making process, as we learn next.

employee involvement
The degree to which employees share information, knowledge, rewards, and power throughout the organization.

EMPLOYEE INVOLVEMENT

Employee involvement (also called *participative management*) refers to the degree to which employees share information, knowledge, rewards, and power throughout the organization.[44] Employees have some level of activity in making decisions that were not previously within their mandate. Employee involvement extends beyond controlling resources for one's own job; it includes the power to influence decisions in the work unit and organization. The higher the level of involvement, the more power people have over the decision process and outcomes. Along with sharing power, employee involvement requires sharing information and knowledge, because employees require more knowledge to make a meaningful contribution to the decision process.

Employee involvement is found in almost every successful American organization. Employees at The Container Store engage in daily "huddles" just before the store opens to hear about yesterday's sales and to discuss new ways of solving customer needs.[45] Teams of nursing staff at Hennepin County Medical Center in Minneapolis work through the logistics and financial implications of their own staffing schedule, a task previously handled only by hospital management. And at First National Bank–Employee Owned, employees take an active role in deciding corporate strategy. The reason, as the company's name implies, is that employees own a majority of shares in the Antioch, Illinois, financial institution.[46]

Why has employee participation become such an important part of corporate decision making? One reason is that employee involvement is an integral component of knowledge management. Corporate leaders are realizing that employee knowledge is a critical resource for competitive advantage, so they are encouraging employees to share this knowledge. E-mail and other forms of information technology have also pushed employee involvement more than we would have imagined a decade ago.

Forms of Employee Involvement

Employee involvement exists in many forms, as we see in Exhibit 9.3.[47] *Formal participation* activities, such as the nursing teams at Hennepin County Medical Center in Minneapolis, are founded on codified policies and institutionalized practices. In other words, the company has established structures and formal expectations that support this form of participation. In contrast, *informal participation* includes casual events, such as approaching a supervisor about an idea or suggestion.

Employee involvement can also be *voluntary* or *statutory*. The Philippines operation of Great Plains Software (now part of Microsoft) applied voluntary employee involvement when it formed a committee to help design the company's new office in Manila.[48] In contrast, joint health and safety committees represent a statutory form of involvement in countries where they are required by law. Statutory involvement is more widespread in Europe, where many countries have codetermination laws.

codetermination
A form of employee involvement required by some governments that typically operates at the work site as works councils and at the corporate level as supervisory boards.

Codetermination varies from one country to the next, but it generally requires employee involvement at both the work site and corporate levels. At the corporate level, employees hold up to half the supervisory board seats in Sweden, Norway, and some other European countries. These boards advise company executives on business issues and make decisions about their salaries. At the work site, codetermination occurs through employee representation committees called *works councils*. The employer must keep the works council informed of financial performance and employment decisions within the organization. It must consult with (not just inform) the council regarding

Form of involvement	Description	Example
Formality		
Formal	Participation is codified policy or institutionalized practice	Self-directed nursing teams make decisions at Hennepin County Medical Center in Minneapolis
Informal	Casual or undocumented activities take place at management's discretion	Employee on the shop floor makes a suggestion to the supervisor
Legal mandate		
Statutory	Government legislates activities	Codetermination is established at Bosch manufacturing plant in Germany
Voluntary	Employees participate without any force of law	Task force on new building design is created at Great Plains Software in the Philippines
Directness		
Direct	Employees are personally involved in decisions	Harley-Davidson employees participate directly in decisions affecting their team's work process
Indirect	Employees participate through representation of peers	Three representatives of pilots and machinists sit on the United Airlines board of directors

matters of employment staffing, work processes, and individual dismissals. In Germany, legislation also requires mutual agreement between the employer and the works council on work hours, use of technology, wages, health and safety, and other "social matters."[49]

In the third form of involvement, employee participation is either *direct* or *representative*. Direct participation occurs when employees personally influence the decision process. For example, Harley-Davidson employees participate directly in decisions affecting their team's work process. Representative participation, on the other hand, occurs when employees are represented by peers. Works councils in the European codetermination system fall into this latter category. United Airlines also has representative participation, where representatives of the pilots association and machinists union have 3 of the 12 seats on the airline's board of directors. This representation occurs because employees own a large portion of outstanding shares of the company.[50]

Levels of Employee Involvement

Levels of employee involvement reflect both the degree of power over the decision and the number of decision steps over which employees can apply that power.[51]

Low Level of Involvement   The *lowest level* of involvement is selective consultation, in which employees are individually asked for specific information or opinions about one or two aspects of the decision. They do not necessarily recommend solutions and might not even know details of the problem for which the information will be used.

Moderate Level of Involvement   A *moderate level* of employee involvement occurs when employees are more fully consulted either individually or in a group. They are told about the problem and offer their diagnosis and recommendations, but the final decision is still beyond their control. Gainsharing, the team-based reward plan described in Chapter 6, involves a moderate level of employee involvement because employees reduce costs through recommendations to senior executives.[52]

The Container Store, American Brass, and Voyant Technologies Inc. encourage a moderate level of employee involvement through a process called **open book management.**[53] Open book management encourages employees to think of financial performance as a game that they can play and win. Employees learn the rules of the game through training to improve their financial literacy. They also receive monthly or quarterly financial data and operating results so that they can keep track of the organization's performance. Employees contribute to the game by recommending ideas that improve those financial results. With their financial training and game-oriented perspective, employees are more likely to make meaningful recommendations that will improve the company's financial performance.[54]

open book management

Involves sharing financial information with employees and encouraging them to recommend ideas that improve those financial results.

High Level of Involvement   The *highest level* of involvement occurs when employees have complete power over the decision process. They discover and define problems, identify solutions, choose the best option, and monitor the results of their decision. These high-involvement conditions are characteristic of the team-based organizations introduced in Chapter 8.[55] Team-based organizational structures rely on self-directed work teams, which we discuss next.

SELF-DIRECTED WORK TEAMS

Surrounded by tall prairie grass, Harley-Davidson's new assembly plant near Kansas City, Missouri, embeds the philosophy of a high-involvement organization. There are no supervisors. Instead, natural work teams of 8 to 15 employees make most day-to-day decisions through consensus. An umbrella group, representing teams and management, makes plantwide decisions. "There is more pressure on employees here because they must learn to do what supervisors did," admits Karl Eberle, vice president and general manager of Harley-Davidson's Kansas City operations. Still, Harley-Davidson is taking employee involvement far beyond the traditional workplace. "There's a lot of work being done to empower the workforce," says Eberle. "But there are very few examples of where they've taken the workforce to run the factory. And that's what we've done."[56]

Harley-Davidson has applied a high level of employee involvement through self-directed work teams (SDWTs), defined in Chapter 8. According to one estimate, 72 percent of Fortune 1,000 companies have at least one SDWT in operation.[57] These formal groups complete an entire piece of work requiring several interdependent tasks and have substantial autonomy over the execution of these tasks. SDWTs vary somewhat from one firm to the next, but they generally have

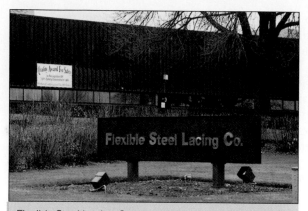

Flexible Steel Lacing Company is becoming a high-involvement workplace through self-directed work teams (SDWTs). The Downers Grove, Illinois, manufacturer of conveyor belt fasteners has moved employees into product teams and out of their previous departments of metal stamping, cold heading, heat treating, machining, and assembly. Each team controls its own production, scheduling, point-of-use inventory, and other decisions in the work process. There are no area managers or supervisors between the teams and the plant manufacturing manager. Each team sets annual performance goals (safety, quality, etc.) and tracks progress toward the goals. The transformation to SDWTs has reduced order fulfillment cycle time by 30 percent and increased plant productivity (sales dollar per employee) by 12 percent over the past three years. Now the company is expanding its high-involvement initiative by introducing SDWTs in purchasing, shipping, facilities, and office areas. This high level of involvement works well at Flexible Steel Lacing Company, but are there organizations where it might be less effective? What types of employees work best in a high-involvement workplace? (Mike Hruby)

the features listed in Exhibit 9.4.[58] First, SDWTs complete an entire piece of work, whether it's a product, a service, or part of a larger product or service. For example, self-directed work teams at Flexible Steel Lacing Company are responsible for making an entire product.

Second, the team—not supervisors—assigns tasks that individual team members perform. In other words, the team plans, organizes, and controls work activities with little or no direct involvement of a higher-status supervisor. Third, SDWTs control most work inputs, flow, and output. "[Teams] have total authority to make all decisions: I mean total, complete authority on every aspect of business," explains Dennis W. Bakke, CEO and co-founder of electrical power company AES Corporation.[59]

Fourth, SDWTs are responsible for correcting work flow problems as they occur. In other words, the teams maintain their own quality and logistical control. Lastly, SDWTs receive team-level feedback and rewards. This point recognizes and reinforces the fact that the team—not individuals—is responsible for the work, although team members may also receive individual feedback and rewards.

You may have noticed from this description that members of SDWTs have enriched and enlarged jobs (see Chapter 6). The team's work is horizontally loaded because it includes all the tasks required to make an entire product or provide the service. It is also vertically loaded because the team is mostly responsible for scheduling, coordinating, and planning these tasks.[60] Self-directed work teams are usually designed around production processes. However, they are also found in administrative and service activities, as Flexible Steel Lacing Company is now doing. Services are well suited to self-directed work teams because members have interdependent tasks, and decisions are frequently made that require the employee's knowledge and experience.[61]

sociotechnical systems (STS) theory
A theory stating that effective work sites have joint optimization of their social and technological systems, and that teams should have sufficient autonomy to control key variances in the work process.

Sociotechnical Systems and SDWTs

How do you create successful self-directed work teams? To answer this question, we need to look at **sociotechnical systems (STS) theory,** which is the main source of current SDWT practices. STS theory was introduced during the 1940s at the Tavistock Institute, where Eric Trist, Fred Emery, and their colleagues had been studying the effects of technology on coal mining in the United Kingdom.[62]

EXHIBIT 9.4

Attributes of
self-directed
work teams

The Tavistock researchers observed that the new coal mining technology (called the "long wall" method) led to lower, not higher, job performance. They analyzed the causes of this problem and established the idea that organizations need joint optimization between the social and technical systems of the work unit. In other words, they need to introduce technology in a way that creates the best structure for semi-autonomous work teams. Moreover, the Tavistock group concluded that teams should be sufficiently independent so that they can control the main variances in the system. This means that the team must control the factors with the greatest impact on quality, quantity, and the cost of the product or service. From this overview of STS theory, we can identify several conditions for successful SDWTs:[63]

■ *Primary work unit*—STS theory suggests that SDWTs work best in a primary work unit, which is any work team that makes a product, provides a service, or otherwise completes an entire work process. By making an entire product or service together, the team is sufficiently independent from other work units that it can make adjustments without affecting or being affected by others too much. At the same time, employees within a primary work unit perform interdependent subtasks, so they have a sense of performing a common task.[64]

■ *Semi-autonomous work groups*—STS theory advocates a team-based structure in which employees in the primary work unit have sufficient autonomy to manage the work process. STS writers call it *collective self-regulation*, which means that the team can decide how to divide work among its members as well as how to coordinate that work. Collective self-regulation is a central feature in self-directed work teams and represents a team-based version of autonomy in job enrichment (see Chapter 6).

■ *Controlling key variances*—STS theory says that productivity improves when the work team has control over key variances. These variances represent the disturbances or interruptions that occur in a work process, such as the mixture of ingredients in soup manufacturing or the courteousness of service at an airline reservations call center. By controlling these factors, work teams control the quantity and quality of output in the work process. In contrast, STS has little advantage when the main causes of good or poor performance are due mainly to technology, supplies, or other factors beyond the team's control.

■ *Joint optimization*—Perhaps the most crucial feature of STS theory is that a balance must be struck between the social and technical systems to maximize the operation's effectiveness.[65] Production demands and social dynamics must be compatible with each other. In particular, the technological system should be implemented in a way that encourages or facilitates team dynamics, job enrichment, and meaningful feedback. This idea of joint optimization was quite radical in the 1940s, a time when many thought there was only one best way to install technology in the workplace and that jobs must be designed around this necessary structure. STS theory, on the other hand, says that companies have considerable latitude in how technology is introduced. In particular, it assumes that technology is flexible enough to support a semi-autonomous, team-based structure.

Sociotechnical Systems Theory in Practice
Hewlett-Packard, Anchor Hocking, the University of Southern California's telecommunications group, L. L. Bean, and many other organizations have successfully applied STS principles to establish a better environment for team-based work.[66] For example, L. L. Bean considered STS principles when redesigning its order fulfillment center. "The technology here is very simple," says Lou Zambello, Bean's senior vice president for operations, about the new process. "The innovative part is adapting it to create a new sociotechnical norm in the new facility. What we did before was like individual swimming in a relay race. Now we do synchronized swimming."[67] In these and other cases, high-involvement team-based structures worked because corporate leaders diagnosed and redesigned the technological structure to ensure that it supported a team-based work environment.

In spite of these successes, some firms have trouble finding the optimal alignment of the social and technical systems. Volvo's Kalmar and Uddevalla plants in Sweden may have demonstrated this point.[68] These plants replaced the traditional assembly line with fixed workstations at which teams of approximately 20 employees assemble and install components in an unfinished automobile chassis. This technological structure creates a strong team orientation, but productivity at the two Volvo plants is among the *lowest* in the automobile industry

Celestica Inc. operates in a competitive environment where technology and employees need careful alignment. To achieve this alignment, the computer and Internet gear manufacturer adopted sociotechnical systems (STS) theory as its template for corporate renewal. Employee study teams mapped work process flows and identified key variances—disturbances or interruptions that occur in a work process. Several changes were introduced that addressed each of the key variances. Permanent self-directed work teams of 15 to 40 people were established to complete each work process. As a result of STS, productivity and quality doubled and job satisfaction increased significantly. As one employee explains: "What I like about the STS process is that the change has been driven by the employees—those responsible for execution—as opposed to management dictating how it's going to be."[69] To what extent has Celestica applied the four STS conditions necessary for successful self-directed work teams? *(Courtesy of Celestica)*

because the technological design is not sufficiently flexible. In other words, in its attempt to accommodate the social system, Volvo's production system may have become technologically too inefficient.

BENEFITS OF EMPLOYEE INVOLVEMENT

For the past half century, organizational behavior scholars have advised that self-directed work teams and other forms of employee involvement offer potential benefits for both employees and their organizations.[70] These benefits include improved decision quality and commitment, as well as employee satisfaction, empowerment, and development.

Decision Quality

Probably the number one reason corporate leaders embrace employee involvement is that it can potentially improve decision-making quality, particularly for complex decisions where employees possess relevant information.[71] Employees are closer to customers and production activities, so they often know where the company can save money, improve product or service quality, and realize unused opportunities.

Employee involvement may improve the quality of decisions in three ways, as Exhibit 9.5 illustrates. First, it may lead to a more accurate definition of the problem. Employees are, in many respects, the sensors of the organization's environment. When the organization's activities misalign with customer expectations, employees are usually the first to know. Employee involvement ensures that everyone in the organization is alerted quickly to these problems.

synergy
A phenomenon in which people generate more and better solutions by working together and sharing ideas than if these people worked alone.

Second, employee involvement potentially can improve the number and quality of solutions generated to organizational problems. In a well-managed meeting, team members create **synergy** by pooling their knowledge to form new alternatives that no one would have designed alone. In other words, several people working together and building on each other's strengths can generate more and potentially better solutions than if these people worked alone. As we noted in the previous chapter, heterogeneous teams—those whose members have diverse backgrounds—tend to develop more innovative solutions to complex problems compared with homogeneous teams.[72]

Third, involving employees in decisions increases the likelihood that the best option will be selected. This tendency occurs because the decision is

EXHIBIT 9.5

How employee involvement improves decision quality

reviewed by people with diverse perspectives and a broader representation of values than if one executive made the choice alone.

Decision Commitment

An old maxim states that the best person to put in charge of a problem is the one most directly affected by its outcome. In other words, employees who are expected to implement organizational decisions should be involved in choosing the course of action. This participation creates psychological ownership of the decision. Rather than viewing themselves as agents of someone else's decision, staff members feel personally responsible for the success of the decision. Consequently, they tend to exhibit less resistance to change and are more motivated to implement the decisions.[73] Employee involvement also increases perceptions of fairness. For example, employees are more likely to believe that a reward system is fair if they had the opportunity to influence the rules for distributing the rewards.[74]

Employee Satisfaction, Empowerment, and Development

Employee involvement tends to improve job satisfaction, organizational commitment, and feelings of empowerment. This improvement, in turn, reduces turnover and increases work motivation.[75] Employee involvement is a form of job enrichment, so its benefits are apparent only when employees receive adequate training, are sufficiently happy with their work context, and have a high growth need strength.

Lastly, we should note that many forms of involvement give employees the opportunity to improve their decision-making skills and prepare for higher levels of responsibility. Team decision making may offer the additional benefits of fostering teamwork and collegiality as co-workers learn more about each other and come to appreciate each other's talents.[76]

CHOOSING THE OPTIMAL LEVEL OF EMPLOYEE INVOLVEMENT

If employee involvement is so wonderful, why isn't everyone in self-directed work teams? The answer is that the optimal level of employee involvement depends on the situation. In other words, as with so many other organizational behavior topics, we need to take a contingency approach to determining the optimal level of employee involvement. Organizational behavior scholars Victor Vroom and Alfred Jago have developed four decision trees to direct us toward the best level of employee involvement under different conditions.[77] Each decision tree considers five levels of employee participation, ranging from purely autocratic to team consensus:

AI   You make the decision alone with no employee involvement.

AII Subordinates provide information that you request, but they don't offer recommendations and they might not be aware of the problem.

CI   You describe the problem to relevant subordinates individually, getting their information and recommendations. You make the final decision, which does not necessarily reflect the advice that subordinates have provided.

CII You describe the problem to subordinates in a meeting, in which they discuss information and recommendations. You make the final decision, which does not necessarily reflect the advice that subordinates have provided.

GII You describe the problem to subordinates in a meeting. They discuss the problem and make a decision that you are willing to accept and implement if it has the entire team's support. You might chair this session, but you do not influence the team's decision.

Exhibit 9.6 presents the most common decision tree, in which the leader faces a problem relevant to employees and has a limited amount of time to make the decision. This model identifies eight factors to consider when deter-

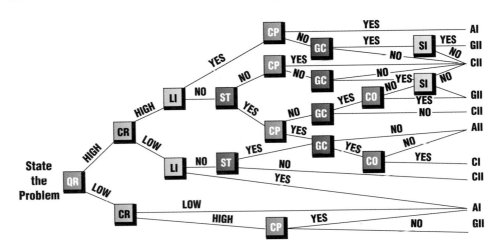

EXHIBIT 9.6

Vroom–Jago time-driven decision tree for employee involvement

QR	**Quality requirement:**	How important is the technical quality of this decision?
CR	**Commitment requirement:**	How important is subordinate commitment to the decision?
LI	**Leader's information:**	Do you have sufficient information to make a high-quality decision?
ST	**Problem structure:**	Is the problem well structured?
CP	**Commitment probability:**	If you make the decision yourself, is it reasonably certain that your subordinate(s) would be committed to the decision?
GC	**Goal congruence:**	Do subordinates share the organizational goals to be attained in solving this problem?
CO	**Subordinate conflict:**	Is conflict among subordinates over preferred solutions likely?
SI	**Subordinate information**	Do subordinates have sufficient information to make a high-quality decision?

Source: V. H. Vroom and A. G. Jago, *The New Leadership: Managing Participation in Organizations* (Englewood Cliffs, NJ: Prentice Hall, 1988), p. 184. © 1987 V. H. Vroom and A. G. Jago. Used with permission of the authors.

mining the optimal level of employee involvement. We begin at the left side of the decision tree and work through the problem attributes to determine the most appropriate level of employee involvement for that problem. A closer look at these questions reveals that they address four key decision issues: decision quality, decision commitment, risk of conflict, and decision structure.

■ Decision quality—Three questions in the Vroom–Jago decision tree consider the effect of employee involvement on decision quality. The first question asks whether the problem has a high or low quality dimension (QR). In other words, is it possible to make a good or bad decision, or are all the options of equal quality? Two other questions ask whether the leader has enough information to make the decision alone (LI) and whether subordinates have enough information to make a high-quality decision (SI). Generally, employee involvement would improve decision quality when the leader does not have enough information and subordinates do have enough to make the decision alone.

■ *Decision commitment*—Two questions address the issue of decision commitment. One question asks whether decision commitment is important (CR); another asks whether employees will be committed to a decision made exclusively by the leader (CP). If employee commitment is important and employees are unlikely to accept the leader's decision, then a higher level of employee involvement is usually necessary.

■ *Risk of conflict*—Two questions refer to the risk of conflict. One question asks whether employee goals are congruent or in conflict with organizational goals (GC). If employees are likely to make a decision contrary to organizational goals, then a lower level of involvement is preferred. Another question asks whether employees will be in conflict with each other when choosing the preferred solution (CO). If conflict is likely, then employees should not make the decision alone.

■ *Decision structure*—One other question in the Vroom–Jago decision tree asks whether the problem is structured (ST). This question refers to the idea presented at the beginning of this chapter that some decisions are programmed whereas others are nonprogrammed. Programmed decisions are less likely to need employee involvement because the solutions are already worked out from past experience.

Overall, the Vroom–Jago decision tree may look like a confusing array of issues, but it breaks down into four important contingencies of employee involvement: decision quality, decision commitment, decision conflict, and decision structure. However, as the next section describes, there are also several challenges to overcome when implementing employee involvement.

OVERCOMING CHALLENGES TO EMPLOYEE INVOLVEMENT

Employee involvement is not a panacea for all organizational problems. In some situations, participation may be useful, but resistance to it could threaten the company's effectiveness in other ways. In other situations, involvement practices are incompatible with the needs and values of the people affected. However, where employee involvement is desirable, corporate leaders need to recognize and overcome at least three potential barriers: cultural differences, management resistance, and employee and labor union resistance.

Cultural Differences

Employee involvement is more compatible with some cultural values than with others.[78] Employee involvement is typically an interpersonal or team-based activity, so it is adopted most readily in cultures with high collectivism. Recall from Chapter 4 that people with a collectivist value appreciate and support their membership in a group. Consequently, they work more comfortably discussing their ideas with co-workers. In contrast, individualistic people may be less comfortable with employee involvement because of their preference to work alone.

Employee involvement also works better in low power distance cultures. Employees with low power distance usually want to be involved in corporate decisions, whereas those in high power distance cultures are more comfortable when supervisors give them directions and answers. Mexico has a very high power distance value system, which explains why firms have difficulty implementing self-directed work teams in that country. One study reported that Mexican employees expect managers to make decisions affecting their work, whereas SDWTs emphasize self-initiative and individual responsibility within teams. Some writers also suggest that SDWTs may be more difficult to apply in China, where traditional cultural values tend to support a rigid social hierarchy.[79]

Aside from these cultural challenges, we should remember that few cultures are so extreme in either collectivism or power distance to prohibit employee involvement. Indeed, there seems to be a cultural shift among younger employees in many countries toward values more compatible with employee involvement. "[Employees] want to function in a more empowerment-driven environment," says Govind Iyer, consultant with search firm Egon Zehnder in India. "[W]hich is not to say they don't want orders; but everybody wants to participate in the decision-making process."[80]

A second consideration is that some forms of employee involvement are less difficult than others to implement across cultures. For instance, open book management seems to work well at Tien Wah Press's printing plants in Malaysia, Singapore, and Indonesia. Supervisors provide financial information to employees every three months, and the reward system seems to motivate employees to suggest ideas for productivity improvement.[81] A third consideration is that people with fairly high power distance and high individualism may adjust over time to a workplace that espouses collectivist and low power distance values. These factors may explain why AES Corporation has successfully introduced a high level of employee involvement at its plants in Argentina, as Global Connections 9.3 describes.

Management Resistance

Poet Robert Frost once wrote, "The brain is a wonderful organ; it starts working the moment you get up in the morning and does not stop until you get into the office."[82] Frost's humor was probably highlighting the fact that many organizations expect employees to park their brains at the door. Indeed, research suggests that supervisors and higher-level managers often resist efforts to involve employees in decision making. They particularly have difficulty making the transition to self-directed work teams.[83]

Their main worry is losing power when employees gain power through participation. Some managers are concerned that their jobs will lose value, whereas

Employee Involvement Powers Up AES Corporation in Argentina

Oscar Prieto was visiting AES Corporation's headquarters in Arlington, Virginia, when a senior executive asked for a volunteer to sit in a meeting. Prieto, a recently hired AES engineer from Argentina, raised his hand. He was soon negotiating with a large European electrical utility over a joint venture in Brazil. Now, two years later, Prieto heads an AES division in Rio de Janeiro that supplies electricity to 8 million homes and businesses. "That's what happens when you raise your hand around here," says Prieto with a smile.

At most companies, Oscar Prieto's personal odyssey would be a fairy tale—far too much new responsibility, far too early in his tenure. At AES, the fast-growing electrical power company, it is standard operating procedure. Lots of companies talk about empowering employees and pushing responsibility out from headquarters. Few companies push as hard or as far as AES. For instance, when AES raised $350 million to finance a joint venture in Northern Ireland, two control room operators led the team that raised the funds. In fact, most of the $3.5 billion that financed 10 new AES power plants was brought in by decentralized teams, not finance specialists.

"The modern manager is supposed to ask his people for advice and then make a decision," says Dennis Bakke, who co-founded AES with Roger Sant in the early 1980s. "But at AES, each decision is made by a person and a team. Their job is to get advice from me and from anybody else they think it's necessary to get advice from. And then they make the decision."

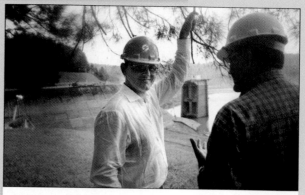

AES Corporation empowers Oscar Prieto (left), his coworkers at this construction project in Brazil, and other AES employees around the globe. (© Christopher Hartlove. Used with permission.)

Oscar Prieto and other managers are quickly learning to continue that power-sharing tradition. When AES took over Argentina's Cabra Corral power plant, Prieto removed the time clocks and bosses, and empowered employees to operate the business. "I trust people—without fear or hesitation," he says. "The best way to let them perform is with absolute freedom: I release you of all constraints, including the constraints imposed by your boss."

Source: Adapted from A. Markels, "Power to the People," *Fast Company* 13 (February–March 1998), pp. 155–65.

---

others believe that they will not have any jobs at all. In a Dutch research and development lab that had restructured to give more power to product development teams, the change made several technical managers feel powerless and frustrated, so they tried to undermine the project leader and the team's success.[84]

Another problem is that supervisors do not know how to become hands-off facilitators of several work teams rather than hands-on supervisors of several employees.[85] This problem was one of the biggest stumbling blocks to self-directed work teams at an automotive parts plant of TRW. Many supervisors kept slipping back into their command-and-control supervisory styles. As one TRW employee explains: "One of the toughest things for some of them was to shift from being a boss to a coach, moving from saying, 'I know what's good for you' to 'How can I help you?'"[86]

Companies need to assure these people that their careers are not threatened. Supervisors also need considerable training to adjust from the command-and-control style to the more ambiguous facilitator style of leadership.

Research suggests that supervisors are less likely to resist employee involvement when they have personally worked in a high-involvement workplace and their own jobs aren't threatened by the change.[87]

Employee and Labor Union Resistance

Employees resist employee involvement for several reasons. Many have been bombarded by previous management fads and do not want to develop false hopes for the latest initiative. Employee involvement also requires new—and usually more ambiguous—role patterns and possibly new skills (e.g., working in teams). Thus, many employees feel uncomfortable as they explore their new roles, and they may be worried that they lack the skills to adapt to the new work requirements.

Labor unions have been strong advocates of joint health and safety committees and supported the early sociotechnical changes in Europe and India. Some union leaders believe that employee involvement is an important right, whereas others have publicly rejected various forms of employee involvement for three reasons.[88] First, they believe that employee involvement programs improve productivity at the price of higher stress levels among employees. This belief is sometimes true. SDWTs and other practices tend to give employees more tasks and responsibilities, a situation that may lead to greater work pressure.

Second, high-involvement practices may require reversing work rules and removing job categories that unions have negotiated over the years. Labor union leaders are concerned therefore that it will be a difficult battle to regain these hard-earned union member rights. Finally, a few union leaders believe that companies use employee involvement programs as a subtle strategy to bypass the union and thereby weaken its power in the workplace.

These union fears are troublesome because employee involvement programs require union support and partnership.[89] Fortunately, there are many examples of successful labor–management initiatives that give employees more control in the workplace. In most cases, labor union resistance was minimized through the slow development of trust between corporate and labor leaders as well as evidence that the company is sincere in its willingness to distribute more power to employees in their work. At the same time, labor union involvement requires labor leaders who perceive the long-term value of employee involvement for their membership and the labor union's survival.

Employee involvement is becoming a pervasive part of organizational life. In fact, it is difficult to think of many organizations in North America where employees are not allowed to express their ideas or be involved in some corporate-level decisions. An organization's competitive advantage is the knowledge and ideas of its employees. Employee involvement provides a conduit for this knowledge. In the next chapter, we will learn how companies further leverage this competitive advantage by supporting creativity.

CHAPTER SUMMARY

Decision making is a conscious process of making choices among one or more alternatives with the intention of moving toward some desired state of affairs. This process involves identifying problems and opportunities, choosing the best decision style, developing alternative solutions, choosing the best solution, implementing the selected alternative, and evaluating decision outcomes.

Perceptual biases and poor diagnostic skills can make it difficult to identify problems and opportunities. We can minimize these challenges by being aware of human limitations, discussing the situation with colleagues, creating early warning systems, and using data mining to systematically identify trends.

Choosing the best solution is often challenging because organizational goals are ambiguous or in conflict, human information processing is incomplete and subjective, and people tend to satisfice rather than maximize. Solutions can be chosen more effectively by systematically identifying and weighting the factors used to evaluate alternatives, using decision support systems to guide the decision process, conducting scenario planning, and using intuition when we possess enough tacit knowledge on the issue.

Postdecisional justification and escalation of commitment make it difficult to evaluate decision outcomes accurately. Escalation is caused mainly by self-justification, the gambler's fallacy, perceptual blinders, and closing costs. These problems are minimized by separating decision choosers from decision evaluators, establishing a preset level at which the decision is abandoned or reevaluated, relying on systematic and clear feedback about the project's success, and involving several people in decision making.

Employee involvement (or participation) refers to the degree that employees share information, knowledge, rewards, and power throughout the organization. It may be formal or informal, direct or indirect, and voluntary or statutory. The level of participation may range from an employee's providing specific information to management without knowing the problem or issue to complete employee involvement in all phases of the decision process.

Gainsharing programs and open book management represent moderate levels of employee involvement. Open book management involves sharing financial information with employees and encouraging them to recommend ideas that improve those financial results.

Self-directed work teams (SDWTs) complete an entire piece of work requiring several interdependent tasks and have substantial autonomy over the execution of these tasks. They assign tasks to team members; control most work inputs, flow, and output; are responsible for correcting problems; and receive team-level feedback and rewards.

Self-directed work teams are more effective when they following the guidance of sociotechnical systems (STS) theory. According to STS theory, teams should be primary work units that involve completion of an entire product or service. They must be sufficiently independent to control the main variances in the system. STS theory calls for a balance between the social and technological systems in the work process, but finding this optimum balance can be difficult.

Employee involvement may lead to higher decision quality, decision commitment, employee satisfaction and empowerment, and employee development in decision-making skills. The Vroom–Jago decision tree guides decision makers through a series of questions to determine the optimal level of involvement. The model mainly considers four contingencies: decision quality, decision commitment, decision conflict, and decision structure.

Although employee involvement is often resisted by management, employees, and labor unions, this conflict can often be resolved through education, training, and trust building. Employees with high individualism and power distance are also less comfortable with some forms of employee involvement.

KEY TERMS

codetermination, p. 271

decision making, p. 260

employee involvement, p. 270

escalation of commitment, p. 268

intuition, p. 267

nonprogrammed decision, p. 261

open book management, p. 273

postdecisional justification, p. 268

programmed decision, p. 261

satisficing, p. 266

scenario planning, p. 267

sociotechnical systems (STS) theory, p. 274

synergy, p. 277

DISCUSSION QUESTIONS

1. A software developer is experiencing an increasing number of customer complaints and a general trend toward lower sales. Describe three reasons executives in this organization might be slow to realize that a problem exists or to identify the main cause(s) of these symptoms.

2. A management consultant is hired by a manufacturing firm to determine the best site for its next

production facility. The consultant has had several meetings with the company's senior executives regarding the factors to consider when making its recommendation. Discuss three decision-making problems that might prevent the consultant from choosing the best site location.

3. A developer received financial backing for a new business financial center along a derelict section of the waterfront, a few miles from the current downtown area of a large European city. The idea was to build several high-rise structures, attract large tenants to those sites, and have the city extend transportation systems out to the new center. The developer believed that others would build in the area over the next decade, thereby attracting the regional or national offices of many financial institutions. Interest from potential tenants was much lower than initially predicted, and the city did not build transportation systems as quickly as expected. Still, the builder proceeded with the original plans. Only after financial support was curtailed did the developer reconsider the project. Using your knowledge of escalation of commitment, discuss three possible reasons the developer was motivated to continue with the project.

4. Ancient Book Company has a problem with new book projects. Even when it is apparent to others that a book is far behind schedule and may not have much public interest, sponsoring editors are reluctant to terminate contracts with authors whom they have signed. The result is that editors invest more time with these projects than with more fruitful projects. Describe two methods that Ancient Book Company can use to minimize this problem of escalation of commitment.

5. When a large insurance company decided to redesign its eating facilities at headquarters, it formed a task force of employees representing different areas of the organization. The group's mandate was to identify features of the cafeteria that would be more enjoyable for employees. Describe the forms and level of employee involvement in this task force.

6. A chicken processing company wants to build a processing plant designed around sociotechnical systems principles. In a traditional chicken processing plant, employees work in separate departments—cleaning and cutting, cooking, packaging, and warehousing. The cooking and packaging processes are controlled by separate workstations in the traditional plant. How would the company change this operation into one that is based on a sociotechnical systems design?

7. Employee involvement applies just as well to the classroom as to the office or factory floor. Explain how student involvement in classroom decisions typically made by the instructor alone might improve decision quality. What potential problems might occur in this process?

8. Sumatra Telecom wants to introduce self-directed work teams (SDWTs) at its operations throughout Indonesia. What potential source of resistance to employee involvement might Sumatra Telecom experience?

CASE STUDY 9.1

EMPLOYEE INVOLVEMENT CASES

Case 1: The Sugar Substitute Research Decision Problem

You are the head of research and development (R&D) for a major beer company. While working on a new beer product, one of the scientists in your unit seems to have tentatively identified a new chemical compound that has a few calories but tastes closer to sugar than current sugar substitutes. The company has no foreseeable need for this product, but it could be patented and licensed to manufacturers in the food industry.

The sugar substitute discovery is in its preliminary stages and would require considerable time and resources before the product would be commercially viable. Further research and development would necessarily take some resources away from other projects in the lab. The sugar substitute project is beyond your technical expertise, but some of the R&D lab researchers are familiar with that field of chemistry. As with most other forms of research, it is difficult to determine the amount of research required to further develop and perfect the sugar substitute. You do not know how much demand is expected for this product. Your department has a decision process for funding projects that are behind schedule. However, there are no rules or precedents for funding projects that would be licensed but not used by the organization.

The company's R&D budget is limited, and other scientists in your work group have recently complained that they require more resources and financial support to get their projects completed. Some of these other R&D projects hold promise for future beer sales. You believe that most researchers in the R&D unit are committed to ensuring that the company's interests are achieved.

Case 2: The Coast Guard Cutter Search Decision Problem

You are the captain of a 200-foot Coast Guard cutter with a crew of 16, including officers. Your mission is general at-sea search and rescue. At 2:00 this morning, while en route to your home port after a routine 28-day patrol, you received word from the nearest Coast Guard station that a small plane had crashed 60 miles offshore. You obtained all the available information concerning the location of the crash, informed your crew of the mission, and set a new course at maximum speed for the scene to commence a search for survivors and wreckage.

You have now been searching for 20 hours. Your search operation has been increasingly impaired by rough seas, and there is evidence of a severe storm building. The atmospherics associated with the deteriorating weather have made communications with the Coast Guard station impossible. A decision must be made shortly about whether to abandon the search and place your vessel on a course that would ride out the storm (thereby protecting the vessel and your crew, but relegating any possible survivors to almost certain death from exposure) or to continue a potentially futile search, with the risks it would entail.

Before losing communications, you received an updated weather advisory concerning the severity and duration of the storm. Although your crew members are extremely conscientious about their responsibility, you believe that they would be divided on the decision of leaving the area or continuing the search.

Discussion Questions (for both cases)

1. To what extent should your subordinates be involved in the decision? (Note: You may assume that both cases have time constraints, so the lowest optimal level of involvement is preferred.) Please choose one of the following:

   A. You make the decision alone with no employee involvement.

   B. Subordinates provide information that you request, but they don't offer recommendations and they might not be aware of the problem.

   C. You describe the problem to relevant subordinates individually, getting their information and recommendations. You make the final decision, which does not necessarily reflect the advice that subordinates have provided.

   D. You describe the problem to subordinates in a meeting, in which they discuss information and recommendations. You make the final decision, which does not necessarily reflect the advice that subordinates have provided.

   E. You describe the problem to subordinates in a meeting. They discuss the problem and make a decision that you are willing to accept and implement if it has the entire team's support. You might chair this session, but you do not influence the team's decision.

2. What factors led you to choose this alternative rather than the others?

3. What problems might occur if less or more involvement (where possible) occurred in this case?

Sources: The Sugar Substitute Research Decision Problem was written by Steven L. McShane, Copyright © 2002. The Coast Guard Cutter Search Decision Problem case is adapted from V. H. Vroom and A. G. Jago, *The New Leadership: Managing Participation in Organizations* (Englewood Cliffs, NJ: Prentice Hall, 1988). © 1987 V. H. Vroom and A. G. Jago. Used with permission of the authors.

THE OILMAN IS A TEACHER

BusinessWeek Most Americans are accustomed to having a voice in many organizational decisions. They may routinely ask questions in classes and offer suggestions in meetings. They write to their representatives in Congress and join committees at school and in their places of worship. In other parts of the world, people expect those in authority to handle most of the decision making. One such place is Russia, so managing a Russian workforce involves very different expectations about decision making.

This *Business Week* case study describes the experiences of Simon G. Kukes, the chief executive of a Russian oil company. Kukes gained much of his business experience in the United States, and on the basis of that experience, he tries to help his managers learn a more egalitarian decision-making style. Read through this *Business Week* case study at www.mhhe.com/mcshane2e and prepare for the discussion questions below.

Discussion Questions

1. What are some pros and cons of trying to increase delegation of the decision-making process at Tyumen Oil Company?

2. How is Simon Kukes trying to develop greater employee involvement in decision making?

3. How well does the Vroom–Jago model apply to selecting an appropriate level of employee involvement at Tyumen Oil?

Source: P. Starobin, "The Oilman Is a Teacher," *Business Week*, June 25, 2001.

WHERE IN THE WORLD ARE WE?

Purpose This exercise is designed to help you understand the potential advantages of involving others in decisions rather than making decisions alone.

Materials Students require the chart with fill-in boxes (Exhibit 9.7) and the unmarked map with grid marks (Exhibit 9.8) showing the United States of America. Students are not allowed to look at any other maps or use any other materials. The instructor will provide a list of communities located somewhere on Exhibit 9.8. The instructor will also provide copies of the answer sheet after students both individually and in teams have estimated the locations of communities.

Instructions

■ *Step 1*—Write in Exhibit 9.7 the list of communities identified by your instructor.

Then, working alone, estimate the location in Exhibit 9.8 of these communities, all of which are in the United States. For example, mark a small 1 in Exhibit 9.8 on the spot where you believe the first community is located. Mark a small 2 where you think the second community is located, and so on. Please be sure to number each location clearly and with numbers small enough to fit within one grid space.

■ *Step 2*—The instructor will organize students into approximately equal-sized teams (typically five or six people per team). Working with your team members, reach a consensus on the location of each community listed in Exhibit 9.7. The instructor might provide teams with a separate copy of this map, or each member can identify the team's numbers using a different colored pen on their individual maps. The team's decision for each location should occur by consensus, not by voting or averaging.

■ *Step 3*—The instructor will provide or display an answer sheet, showing the correct locations of the communities. Using this answer sheet, students will count the minimum number of grid squares between the location they individually marked and the true location of each community. Write the number of grid squares in the second column of Exhibit 9.7, then add the numbers and record the total. Next, count the minimum number of grid squares between the location the team marked and the true location of each community. Write the number of grid squares in the third column of Exhibit 9.7, then add the numbers and record the total.

■ *Step 4*—The instructor will ask for information about the totals, and the class will discuss the implication of the results for employee involvement and decision making.

EXHIBIT 9.7   Selected communities in the United States

Community number	Community name	Individual distance in grid units from the true location	Team distance in grid units from the true location
1			
2			
3			
4			
5			
6			
7			
8			
		Total:	Total:

Copyright © 2002. Steven L. McShane.

EXHIBIT 9.8   The United States of America

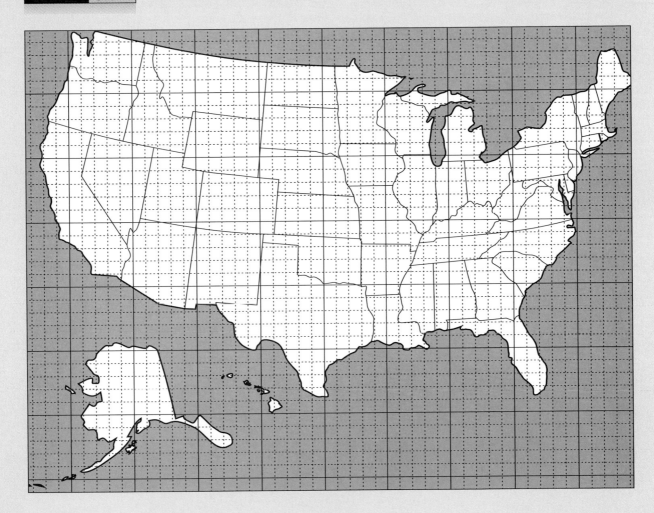

TEAM EXERCISE 9.4

WINTER SURVIVAL EXERCISE

Purpose This exercise is designed to help you understand the potential advantages of involving others in decisions rather than making decisions alone.

Instructions

■ *Step 1*—Read the Situation below. Then, working alone, rank the 12 items shown in the chart below according to their importance to your survival. In the individual ranking column, indicate the most important item with a 1; proceed through to 12 for the least important. Keep in mind why you think each item is or is not important.

■ *Step 2*—The instructor will divide the class into small teams (four to six people). Each team will rank the items and record the numbers in the second column. Team rankings should be based on consensus, not simply by averaging the individual rankings.

■ *Step 3*—When the teams have completed their rankings, the instructor will provide the expert's ranking, which will be entered in the third column.

■ *Step 4*—Each student will compute the absolute difference (i.e., ignore minus signs) between the individual ranking and the expert's ranking, record this information in column four, and enter the total of the absolute values at the bottom of the column.

■ *Step 5*—In column five, record the absolute difference between the team's ranking and the expert's ranking, and enter the total of these absolute values at the bottom of the column. A class discussion will follow regarding the implications of these results for employee involvement and decision making.

Situation You have just crash-landed somewhere in the woods of southern Manitoba or possibly northern Minnesota. It is 11:32 A.M. in mid-January. The small plane in which you were traveling crashed into a small, ice-covered lake. The pilot and copilot were killed. Shortly after the crash, the plane broke through the ice and sank to the bottom of the lake with the pilot's and copilot's bodies inside. Everyone else on the flight escaped to land—dry and without serious injury.

The crash came suddenly, before the pilot had time to radio for help or inform anyone of your position. Since your pilot was trying to avoid a storm, you know the plane was considerably off course. The pilot announced shortly before the crash that you were 45 miles northwest of a small town that is the nearest known habitation.

You are in a wilderness area made up of thick woods broken by many lakes and rivers. The snow depth varies from above the ankles in windswept areas to more than knee-deep where it has drifted. The last weather report indicated that the temperature would reach 5 degrees Fahrenheit in the daytime and minus 15 degrees at night. There are plenty of twigs and dead wood in the area around the lake. You and the other surviving passengers are dressed in winter clothing appropriate for city wear—suits, pantsuits, street shoes, and overcoats. While escaping from the plane, your group salvaged the 12 items listed in the chart below. You may assume that the number of persons in the group is the same as the number in your group, and that you have agreed to stay together.

Source: Adapted from "Winter Survival" in D. Johnson and F. Johnson, *Joining Together,* 3rd ed. (Englewood Cliffs, NJ: Prentice Hall, 1984).

Winter survival tally sheet					
Items	Step 1 Your individual ranking	Step 2 Your team's ranking	Step 3 Survival expert's ranking	Step 4 Difference between steps 1 and 3	Step 5 Difference between steps 2 and 3
Ball of steel wool					
Newspapers					
Compass					
Hand axe					
Cigarette lighter					
45-caliber pistol					
Section air map					
Canvas					
Shirt and pants					
Can of shortening					
Whiskey					
Chocolate bars					
Total					
				Your score	Team score

(The lower the score, the better)

DECISION-MAKING STYLE INVENTORY

Purpose This self-assessment exercise is designed to help you estimate your preferred style of decision making.

Instructions Listed below are statements describing how individuals go about making important decisions. Please indicate whether you agree or disagree with each statement. Answer each item as truthfully as possible so that you get an accurate estimate of your decision-making style. Then use the scoring key in Appendix B to calculate your results. This exercise is completed alone so that students assess themselves honestly without concerns of social comparison. However, class discussion will focus on the decision-making style that people prefer in organizational settings.

Circle the number that best reflects the extent to which you agree or disagree with each statement.	Strongly agree ▼	Agree ▼	Neutral ▼	Disagree ▼	Strongly disagree ▼
1. I make decisions more on facts than on my gut instincts.	5	4	3	2	1
2. I feel more comfortable making decisions in a logical and systematic way.	5	4	3	2	1
3. When making decisions, I rely on my intuition more than anything else.	5	4	3	2	1
4. When I make a decision, it is more important for me to feel the decision is right than to have a rational reason for it.	5	4	3	2	1
5. I won't make a choice that doesn't feel right, even when the facts indicate it is the right choice.	5	4	3	2	1
6. My decision making tends to involve careful analysis of facts and weighting of decision criteria.	5	4	3	2	1
7. When I make a decision, I trust my inner feelings and reactions.	5	4	3	2	1
8. The best decisions I make are based on detailed analysis of factual information.	5	4	3	2	1

Sources: Inspired from ideas in C. W. Allinson and J. Hayes, "The Cognitive Style Index: A Measure of Intuition-Analysis for Organizational Research," *Journal of Management Studies* 33 (1996), pp. 119–35; S. G. Scott and R. A. Bruce, "Decision-Making Style: The Development and Assessment of a New Measure," *Educational and Psychological Measurement* 55 (October 1995), pp. 818–31.

After studying the preceding material, be sure to check out our website at
www.mhhe.com/mcshane2e
for more in-depth information and interactivities that correspond to this chapter.

CHAPTER 10

Creativity and Team Decision Making

AFTER READING THIS CHAPTER, YOU SHOULD BE ABLE TO:

- Define *creativity*.

- Outline the four steps in the creative process.

- Describe the characteristics of creative employees.

- Discuss the workplace conditions that support creativity.

- Identify five problems facing teams when making decisions.

- Compare and contrast the five structures for team decision making.

- Explain why brainstorming may be more effective than scholars originally believed.

IDEO is a global icon for innovation. The Silicon Valley design firm that brought us the Apple mouse, the stand-up toothpaste tube, and 3Com's Palm V handheld has developed several practices to support employee creativity.

Employees work in small, high-autonomous studios that emphasize teamwork and customer focus. "Teams are the heart of the IDEO method," advises Tom Kelley, IDEO's general manager and brother of founder David Kelley. "We believe it's how innovation and much of business take place in the world." IDEO's team members are a diverse group, ranging from engineers to sociologists, who actively search around for ideas in local hardware stores, auto wrecking yards, and toy shops. Each studio also has a "tech box" with hundreds of materials and gizmos to spark ideas.

IDEO team members further improve their creativity through research and prototyping. For example, IDEO staff designed a new bottle top for a wine maker after studying every type of bottle with a closure. They also observed people using toothpaste tubes, which led to their innovation of the pop-on, pop-off cap. IDEO also prototypes its ideas before they are fully developed. Employees take the view that prototype failures are guideposts along the road to innovation.

Brainstorming is probably the

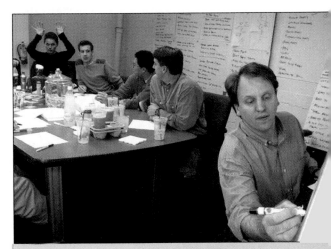

IDEO is a highly innovative product design firm thanks to teamwork, autonomy, brainstorming, and other conditions that support creativity. *(Eric Luse/*San Francisco Chronicle*)*

greatest weapon in IDEO's creative arsenal. Employees typically participate in more than two dozen of these freewheeling sessions each year. A typical brainstormer lasts an hour and produces about 100 ideas. To keep the creative process flowing, employees abide by strict rules of meeting conduct and involve people from many backgrounds. "We've developed a culture of looking broadly for solutions," says Dave Blakely, manager of IDEO's smart products unit. "We're a culture of brainstorming."[1]

I DEO depends on the creativity of its employees to continually push the limits of new product design and materials. But creativity is not restricted to product design companies. In this increasingly knowledge-based economy, creativity is the competitive advantage of every organization.[2] Creativity is part of experimentation in knowledge management (see Chapter 1). It also helps draw in knowledge from the external environment and break down silos of knowledge across work units.

Creativity refers to developing an original product, service, or idea that makes a socially recognized contribution.[3] Although there are unique conditions that support creativity, which we discuss in this chapter, it is really part of the decision-making process described in the previous chapter. We rely on creativity to find problems, identify alternatives, and implement solutions. Creativity is not something saved for special occasions. It is an integral part of decision making.

After describing the creative process, this chapter looks at the characteristics of creative people and the organizational conditions that support creativity. This section is followed by a discussion of specific practices that encourage

creativity
The capacity to develop an original product, service, or idea that makes a socially recognized contribution.

The Boeing Company depends on creative employees to design innovative products, such as the Sonic Cruiser. (This photo shows Boeing Commercial Airplanes president and CEO Alan Mulally with a model of this innovation.) One way the world's largest aerospace company supports innovative ideas is through its Applied Thinking and Creativity Program. Over 2,500 employees have attended these sessions, which include building a stand-alone structure that can balance an egg using only 100 straws and a roll of masking tape. The objective is to help employees understand how each member in their team thinks creatively. "People are creative in different ways," says LeAnn Bornfleth, a co-manager of the Boeing program.[4] In the stages of decision making described in the previous chapter, where would creative thinking apply? (© 2001 The Boeing Company)

creative thought. The latter part of the chapter extends the discussion of creativity to team settings. Specifically, we look at various factors that restrict effective team decision making and creativity; then we examine team structures that help overcome these constraints.

THE CREATIVE PROCESS MODEL

Henry Yuen wanted to record a baseball game on TV while he was out of town, but the scientist had problems setting his VCR properly. While venting his anger, Yuen had an idea. "I thought that taping a program should be as easy as dialing a telephone," he says. So he and co-inventor Daniel Kwoh set out to develop a system that makes VCR recording as simple as making a telephone call. Today, most VCR owners enjoy the fruits of Yuen's creative inspiration through VCR Plus+ (also known as G-code). Users simply punch in the appropriate number from the TV guide listing and the system does the rest.[5]

Henry Yuen's inspiration for VCR Plus+ illustrates the quirky nature of the creative process. Several scholars have attempted over the past century to document the creative process. One of the earliest and most influential models is shown in Exhibit 10.1.[6] This model does not perfectly describe the creative process in every situation. For instance, it ignores team dynamics and the social context in which much creativity occurs (as we learn later in this chapter). Nevertheless, this model has some support and lays a useful foundation for our discussion of creativity.

Preparation

If there is one thing that scholars agree on, it is that preparation is an important condition for creativity. Preparation is the person's or group's effort to acquire knowledge and skills regarding the problem or opportunity.[7] Creativity is not a passive activity. The opening vignette described how IDEO employees generate creative ideas by carefully studying products and observing customers. Creative types also make a point of tearing the problem apart and closely analyzing each component. Preparation involves developing a clear understanding of what you are trying to achieve through a novel solution. It is directed by wishing for something, just as Henry Yuen wished for an easy way to program his VCR.

Incubation

Incubation is the stage of reflective thought. We put the problem aside (sometimes out of frustration), but our mind is still working on it in the background. Some scholars question the importance of incubation for creative insight,

EXHIBIT 10.1

The creative process model

Preparation → Incubation → Insight → Verification

EDS Think Tank Plays through Creative Incubation

Executives at EDS headquarters in Plano, Texas, don't seem to mind if their employees are goofing around in Troy, Michigan. That's because Troy is the site of the computer service firm's new eSpace innovation center, the largest of four such centers EDS is building in the United States and Germany. Blowing bubbles and playing with rubber balls, Lego blocks, and Play-Doh are all part of the incubation process, which should produce more creative ideas for clients.

"The toys give you something to do while you're reflecting and thinking and they trigger new ideas," says team member Renee Guzanek. Guzanek is the group's "lead storyteller," which means she drafts the written work for the projects.

"We're an innovation factory," explains eSpace director Blair Spring. "We're all about collaboration and creativity and inspiration, and the toys are props to stimulate the thought process."

Of course, eSpace offers more than toys and free candy. It also has powerful computers, high-speed Internet access, 24-hour satellite audio and videoconferencing access, and other resources to get prototypes up and running. Employees work with clients to design new products and services more quickly.

"Your brain never stops working around here," said James Wang, a University of Michigan marketing student who works at eSpace as a summer intern.

EDS intern James Wang bounces a ball off his head while incubating new information systems ideas with teammate Jim Sugarman and Gwendolyn Chan. *(Morris Richardson II/The Detroit News)*

Source: C. E. Ramirez, "EDS Brainstorming Team Plots Course for Future," *Detroit News*, August 27, 2001, p. 1; M. Wendland, "EDS Plots to Ignite New Ideas," *Detroit Free Press*, March 1, 2001.

---

whereas others suggest that it plays a powerful role in dissolving previously fixed perspectives about the problem.[8] The important condition here is to maintain a low-level awareness by frequently revisiting the problem. Incubation does not involve forgetting completely about the problem or issue; it simply involves putting the problem on the back burner. The problem is still simmering in your mind, but it is not at the forefront of your attention. Some companies encourage this incubation stage by giving employees the freedom to digress from their work. Connections 10.1 describes how a think tank unit at EDS uses toys and other diversions to support the incubation stage of creativity.

Along with dissolving fixed perspectives of the problem, incubation assists **divergent thinking.** Divergent thinking involves reframing the problem in a unique way and generating different approaches to the issue. This contrasts with *convergent thinking*, which refers to calculating the conventionally accepted "right answer" to a logical problem.[9] Henry Yuen's inspiration for VCR Plus+ and G-coding is an example of divergent thinking because we don't normally think of VCRs in terms of dialing a telephone. Divergent thinking is also responsible for the threaded caps on lightbulbs. Years ago, the experimental bulbs in Thomas Edison's lab kept falling off their fixtures until a technician wondered whether the threaded caps that screwed down tightly on kerosene

divergent thinking

Involves reframing the problem in a unique way and generating different approaches to the issue.

bottles would work on lightbulbs. They did, and the design remains to this day.[10] Divergent thinking breaks us away from existing mental models so that we can apply concepts or processes from completely different areas of life.

Insight

People experience insight at some point during the incubation stage.[11] Insight refers to the experience of suddenly becoming aware of a unique idea. These flashes of inspiration don't keep a particular schedule; they might come to you at any time of day or night. They are also fleeting and can be lost quickly if not documented. For this reason, many creative people keep a journal or notebook nearby at all times so that they can jot down these ideas before they disappear.[12]

Verification

Insights are merely rough ideas. Their usefulness still requires verification through conscious evaluation and experimentation. Henry Yuen's insight that programming a VCR should be like making a telephone call was not a complete solution. Yuen still had to determine whether the idea was feasible as well as to design a workable solution. In other words, verification is the beginning—not the ending—of creativity.

CONDITIONS FOR CREATIVITY

Minnesota Mining & Manufacturing Company (3M) introduces an average of 10 new products every week and generates 30 percent of its annual revenues from products developed within the previous four years.[13] The company achieves these impressive goals by finding creative people and putting them in an environment that encourages creative ideas. In other words, 3M executives have learned that creativity is a function of both the person and the situation. Exhibit 10.2 highlights the main conditions of people and the workplace that affect creativity.

EXHIBIT 10.2

Conditions for creativity

Creative people
- Intellectual abilities
- Relevant knowledge and experience
- Motivation and persistence
- Inventive thinking style

Creative work environment
- Organizational support
- Intrinsically motivating work
- Sufficient time and resources

Increased creativity

Characteristics of Creative People

Everyone is creative, but some people seem to be more creative than others. This fact doesn't mean that organizations should follow the popular notion that creative people are right-brained. The scientific evidence that creativity is a special function of the brain's right hemisphere is quite weak.[14] Anyway, few organizations have the resources to test the brain activity patterns of job applicants. Rather than looking for right-brained people, we should consider the four general characteristics that researchers have identified in creative people: intellectual abilities, relevant knowledge and experience, a strong motivation and persistence, and an inventive thinking style.

Intellectual Abilities   Creative people have the intellectual abilities to synthesize information, analyze ideas, and apply their ideas.[15] First, they are able to synthesize information by connecting seemingly diverse facts into a coherent idea. Like the fictional sleuth Sherlock Holmes, people with synthetic intelligence recognize the significance of small bits of information and are able to connect them in ways that no one else could imagine. Second, creative people use their analytic intelligence—their IQ—to evaluate the potential usefulness of their ideas. Third, creative people have practical ability. They can see how their ideas can be applied in the real world. Equally important, they are able to communicate these abstract ideas so that others understand and support them.

Relevant Knowledge and Experience   Employees are more creative when they possess a good foundation of knowledge and experience on the subject.[16] Some experts suggest that people are most creative after an average of 10 years in a field of inquiry, because discovering new ideas requires knowledge of the fundamentals. For example, the 1960s rock group the Beatles produced most of their songs only after they had played together for several years. They developed extensive experience singing and adapting the music of other people before their creative talents soared.[17]

But lengthy experience isn't always an asset in creativity. Some experts suggest that the more experience we gain, the more we form mental models.[18] Recall from Chapter 3 that these mental models eventually become so ingrained that we cease to question them. This may explain why creative output tends to decline as people move beyond midlife.[19] Although there are exceptions, we tend to become set in our ways and have difficulty breaking out of the mental models learned over the years.

To minimize the problem of mental stagnation, Sony brought in people from outside the music industry to start up its highly successful Sony Music record company. These people had technical knowledge and experience, but not in the music industry, so they didn't have a fixed mental model of what would work. "We didn't want people from the record business," explains a Sony executive. "They would just bring their old ways with them. We wanted people who would have to figure things out all over again, who would question everything, people who 'didn't know any better.' "[20]

Motivation and Persistence   Thomas Edison once remarked that genius is 1 percent inspiration and 99 percent perspiration. He learned this from experience; Edison and his staff discovered hundreds of ways *not* to build a lightbulb before they got it right. Like Edison, creative people are persistent because of their high need for achievement and at least moderate degree of self-confidence.[21] In Chapter 5, we learned that people with a need for achievement want to accomplish reasonably challenging goals. They also have a strong need to assume personal responsibility for their work.[22] This need to achieve, along with at least a moderate level of self-confidence, gives creative people the energy to persist in the face of skeptics and setbacks that litter the path to success.

You can see this persistence in Mike Lazaridis, the founder and co-CEO of Research in Motion (RIM). RIM is leading the way in wireless communication with the BlackBerry, the palm-sized unit that provides instant (always connected) e-mail gratification to mobile people. Lazaridis faced plenty of industry doubters when he first proposed the idea of a handheld wireless communication device a decade ago. Then his company worked through numerous failures before getting closer to Lazaridis's vision. "Mike is one of the most tenacious people I've ever met," says a former Ericsson executive. "[He] keeps grinding towards his goal until he gets there. There were eight or nine failures before BlackBerry. He took lots of at-bats before he hit his home run."[23]

Inventive Thinking Style   Creative people think in novel ways rather than follow set patterns. In other words, they engage in divergent thinking more easily than most other people. Creative people would rather think about creating things than improving on them. They take a broad view of problems, don't like to abide by rules or status, and are less concerned about social approval of their actions.[24] Creative people are risk takers. They are not bothered about working with ambiguous information or issues and are willing to take the chance of making mistakes. The Singapore government's Center for Strategic Process Innovation employs nine such people. These "organizational arsonists" help Singapore government departments reinvent themselves, so they are not bothered by the risks of breaking out of traditional mind-sets.[25]

Animal Logic leads the pack when it comes to trying out new ideas. The Academy Award–winning visual effects company brought us the surreal scenes of old Paris in *Moulin Rouge* (its design team is shown here), the digitally coded dreams in *The Matrix*, and many other creative images. Based in Sydney, Australia, Animal Logic attracts a variety of software programmers, architects, and model makers who don't mind taking risks. Animal Logic executives think the Aussie culture has something to do with their creativity. "All the clichés about Australians are true," says Animal Logic creative director Bruce Carter. "We've got an egalitarian, 'can-do' attitude and a laid-back sense of humor, but we'll only ever measure ourselves against the very best."[27] Aside from national culture, how can companies identify job applicants with an inventive thinking style? *(Courtesy of Animal Logic)*

Creative Work Environment

Hiring creative people will not have the desired results unless they are put in a work environment that supports the creative process.[26] These environmental conditions also improve creativity for other employees. Researchers have identified several workplace conditions that support creativity, including organizational support, intrinsically motivating tasks, and sufficient resources and time.

Organizational Support   The opening vignette in this chapter illustrated how creativity flourishes in organizations with free-flowing communication. These companies also support risk

Canadian Firms Boost Creativity by Minimizing Fear of Failure

Creativity and innovation have made Silent Witness Enterprises a North American leader in video surveillance equipment. "Everyone comes to the office with a mind to be creative," explains Rob Bakshi, CEO of the 125-employee firm in Vancouver, Canada.

"We have a culture that says, 'Nothing is a dumb idea,'" Bakshi explains. "It's always healthy to ask why or why not. And on top of that, when someone does have an idea, we listen. It may be a totally dumb idea, but we look at it."

Sepp's Gourmet Foods also thrives on the creativity of offbeat ideas. "We sometimes talk about having a Department of Wacky Ideas because sometimes the best ideas are the ones that are completely off the wall," says Jim Pratt, CEO of the pâté and meat pie manufacturer. The Vancouver company is working hard to create an organizational environment where employees feel free to try out new product development ideas.

"In our new product development department, the most damaging thing to creativity is if someone has a fear of failure," warns Pratt. "So you have to remove that from your culture. We try to create a culture that says, 'It's okay to fail.'"

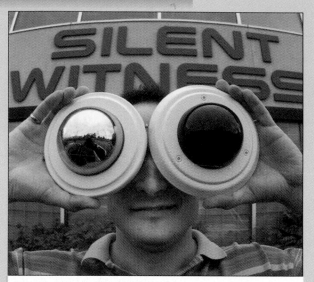

Vancouver-based Silent Witness and Sepp's Gourmet Foods support creativity through a culture that views failure as part of the learning process. (*A. Redekop/ Vancouver Province*)

Source: Adapted from "It's OK to Fail," *Profit Magazine* 18 (November 1999), pp. 25–32.

taking and the inevitable failures that result from those risks. Corporate leaders not only allow employees to make mistakes but also encourage them to try out ideas where failure is more than a remote possibility. "Our beliefs are embedded in our philosophy: failure is not fatal," explains a 3M executive in India. "Innovations are simply chance breakthroughs. And when you take a chance, there is always the possibility of a failure."[28] Global Connections 10.2 describes how two Canadian companies try to minimize the fear of failure through a supportive work environment.

Earlier, we said that creative people are risk takers. Companies can support risk taking by providing a reasonable level of job security. Indeed, research suggests that creative output drops significantly when organizations engage in downsizing, restructuring, and other activities that threaten the individual's employment relationship.[29]

Some companies further encourage risk taking by helping employees break out of their shells. Telus Corporation tries to do this by pushing employees out of their comfort zones with improvisational theater sessions. A theater troupe gets employees at the large Canadian telecommunications provider to act out goofy roles as machines, animals, and other characters. "A necessity for organizations is to empower people to take risks," explains Jay Ono, who leads the corporate improv program. "To foster risk taking, you need a supportive environment where people aren't afraid to express themselves."[30]

Organizational support extends to the roles of project leaders and co-workers.[31] Project leaders must apply enough pressure to complete the project, yet give individuals and teams enough freedom and time, with plenty of support. Team members and other co-workers improve creativity when they trust each other, communicate well, and are committed to the assigned project. In contrast, creativity is undermined when co-workers criticize new ideas, compete against each other, and engage in political tactics to achieve personal goals.

Intrinsically Motivating Work   One of the most important influences on creativity is the job's intrinsic motivation.[32] The job characteristics model (see Chapter 6) helps to explain why job content affects creativity. First, employees tend to be more creative when they believe their work has a substantial impact on the organization and/or the larger society (i.e., task significance). Second, creativity increases with autonomy—the freedom to pursue novel ideas without bureaucratic delays. Creativity is about changing things, and change is possible only when employees have the authority to experiment. Third, creativity is an ongoing learning process, so employees need access to fairly continuous feedback from the job and other sources.

Creative productivity is also higher when people engage in self-set creativity goals, feedback, and other elements of self-leadership (see Chapter 6).[33] This strategy worked for Thomas Edison. By setting goals of one minor invention every 10 days and a major invention every six months, Edison's team produced over 1,000 patents in his lifetime.

In general, jobs encourage creativity when they are challenging and aligned with the employee's competencies.[34] Challenging work pushes employees to draw on their fullest potential. Employees must also have the necessary skills and knowledge, as was noted in the previous section. This alignment of job challenge and employee competencies creates an enjoyable psychological condition called "flow". In a state of flow, our concentration and mental acuity surge and we experience the highest possible sense of involvement in the task.[35]

Sufficient Time and Resources   According to the MARS model, employee performance depends on more than motivation and ability (see Chapter 2). The model indicates that performance also requires sufficient time and resources. The same is true of creativity. People are usually more likely to produce innovative ideas when they have sufficient funds, materials, facilities, information, and time. This requirement doesn't mean that creativity flourishes in the most lavish work settings. Rather, people simply need enough resources to be able to explore alternatives and test their ideas.

Nearly half of advertising and marketing executives say that tight deadlines are the biggest source of creative blocks for their employees. Organizational behavior research supports this concern: Extreme time pressures, unrealistic goals, and ongoing distractions are well-known creativity inhibitors.[36] Although employees need some pressure to produce, companies need to minimize pressure when it strangles creative output.

CREATIVE PRACTICES

Along with hiring creative people and giving them a supportive work environment, organizations apply specific practices that crank up the creative potential.

Entire books have been written on these practices. Some of them work; many lack any empirical validation. The team structures described later in this chapter try to improve creativity and decision making. In this section, we look at three other sets of activities: redefining the problem, associative play, and cross-pollination.

Redefining the Problem

Creativity isn't just a matter of finding a creative solution. It also includes understanding the problem in different ways. One study revealed that successful scientists spend more time than less successful scientists defining and structuring problems before they look for solutions.[37] By redefining the problem, we discover unique solutions from a different perspective.

Consider the following true incident: An automobile executive in Detroit loved his job, but was fed up with his boss. To get away from the tyrant, the executive contacted an executive search firm about finding a job with another firm. That evening, the executive told his wife about calling the headhunter; she, in turn, described her day as a college instructor. By coincidence, her lesson that day was about how to redefine the problem. The executive thought carefully about this idea and, the next day, called the headhunter about a different strategy. Soon after, the executive's surprised boss received and accepted a job offer from the executive search firm. By redefining the problem, the executive got away from the troublesome boss without leaving the job he loved.[38]

Creativity experts have suggested various ways to help people redefine problems. One writer introduced the concept of creative jamming.[39] Based on the metaphor of an improvising jazz group, jamming involves having a group of people giving a problem or idea a thorough workout—passing it around, tearing it apart, putting it back together, turning it over, and so forth. Another suggestion is to schedule some time to look through the notes and files of past projects. After a few months of neglect, these projects might be seen in new ways.[40]

A third strategy, called "tell me, stranger," involves asking people unfamiliar with the issue (preferably with different areas of expertise) to explore the problem. You would state the objectives and give some facts, then let the "stranger" ask questions to further understand the situation. This exchange occurs without your mentioning your current thoughts on the topic. By verbalizing the problem, listening to questions, and hearing what others think, you are more likely to form new perspectives on the issue.[41]

Associative Play

Earlier in this chapter, we learned that divergent thinking involves reframing the problem in a unique way and generating

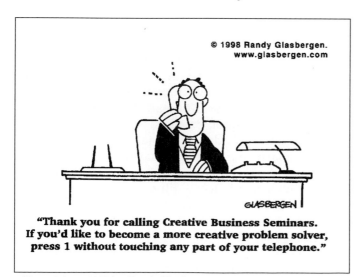

© 1998 Randy Glasbergen.
www.glasbergen.com

"Thank you for calling Creative Business Seminars. If you'd like to become a more creative problem solver, press 1 without touching any part of your telephone."

(Copyright © 1998 by Randy Glasbergen. Reprinted with special permission from www.glasbergen.com.)

different approaches to the issue. Some people are naturally better at divergent thinking, but associative play activities can help others think more divergently.

Monster.com, the online career website, sparks creativity on Monday mornings with a meeting that features Tinker Toys, storytelling, and various games. In the object-oriented chain story, someone brings in several unrelated items— perhaps a fishing pole, a book, a toy—and the group develops a story around them. One person starts by picking an item and telling a story about it. The next person picks another item and adds that item to the first person's story, and so on. The activity gets everyone thinking differently while having fun.[42]

Another form of associative play involves engaging in art or some other creative nonwork activity. Wedgwood, the Irish-based tableware company, brought together its overseas executives in a workshop where they tore up magazines, pasted up pictures, and selected music that represented what they thought the Wedgwood brand should become. This event, along with many discussions, led to a video that depicted the new Wedgwood. "It's pictures, music, it's all the senses, to try to evoke the brand that we're turning into," says Wedgwood's group marketing director.[43]

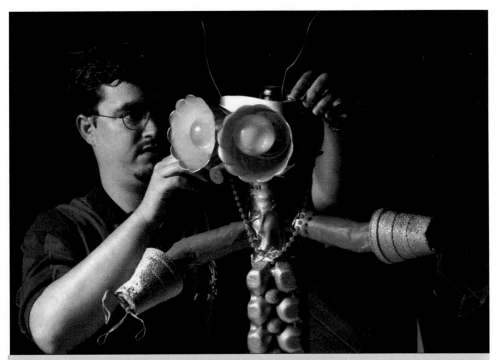

Lion Apparel took its employees to an art school where they transformed wire mesh into alligators and empty paper towel rolls into robots. The Dayton, Ohio–based designer and manufacturer of clothing for firefighters hopes that the creative expression developed in these art sessions will give staff members more divergent thinking back on the job. "This was a way to help them learn to think 'outside the box,'" explains Lion Apparel manager Leise Ling. "To solve the kinds of problems they encounter every hour, they have to be able to think creatively."[44] Explain how attending an art class might improve creativity. Are there situations or conditions in which this strategy wouldn't be very effective? *(Ty Greenlees. Used with permission)*

A third associative play strategy is to use metaphors to compare the situation to something else.[45] A telephone company used this approach to find ways to reduce damage to its pay telephones. Participants were asked to think of a telephone booth as some other object that protects—such as a bank vault or medicine capsule. Then they looked at features of these other objects that might protect telephone booths.

Another structured associative play activity is called *morphological analysis*. Morphology involves listing different dimensions of a system and the elements of each dimension, and then looking at each combination. This type of analysis encourages people to carefully examine combinations that initially seem nonsensical. Tyson Foods, the world's largest poultry producer, recently applied this activity to identify new ways to serve chicken for lunch. The marketing and research team assigned to this task focused on three categories: occasion, packaging, and taste. Next, the team worked through numerous combinations of items in the three categories. This step created unusual ideas, such as cheese chicken pasta (taste) in pizza boxes (packaging) for concessions at baseball games (occasion). Later, the team looked more closely at the feasibility of these combinations and sent them to customer focus groups for further testing.[46]

Cross-Pollination

Another way to spark creativity is to deliberately cross-pollinate ideas and knowledge across the organization.[47] One approach is to ensure that employees work with different people on each project. This diversity of experience improves information sharing and increases the number of perspectives that team members bring to new projects. IDEO, which was described at the beginning of this chapter, uses cross-pollination by encouraging employees to consider how features of one product they've worked on might be relevant to another. For instance, while designing a quieter fan for a computer system, designers might recall how they designed a quieter vacuum cleaner a few months earlier.[48]

Cross-pollination also occurs through formal information sessions where people from different parts of the organization share their knowledge. Mitel, the communications systems designer, holds Demo Days—internal trade shows where Mitel teams exhibit their projects and are encouraged to steal ideas from other groups within the organization.[49] Walt Disney Corporation encourages employees to engage in "displayed thinking" by leaving their work out in the open for others to view and offer comments on. Colleagues are encouraged to leave anonymous notes with suggestions and feedback.

CONSTRAINTS ON TEAM DECISION MAKING AND CREATIVITY

Cross-pollination highlights the fact that creativity rarely occurs alone. Some creative people may be individualistic, but most creative ideas are generated in formal teams and other types of social interaction. Under certain conditions, teams can more effectively identify problems, choose alternatives, and evaluate their decisions. Individual biases are partly or completely offset by the divergent views and experiences of other team members. In spite of these potential advantages, team dynamics can also interfere with creativity and effective decision making. In this section, we look at the main factors that restrict effective creativity and decision making in team settings. In the final section of this chapter, we look at specific team structures that try to overcome these constraints.

Time Constraints

The saying "committees keep minutes and waste hours" reflects the fact that teams take longer than individuals to make decisions.[50] Unlike individuals, teams require extra time to organize, coordinate, and socialize. The larger the group, the more time required to make a decision. Team members need time to learn about each other and build rapport. They need to manage an imperfect communication process so that there is sufficient understanding of each other's ideas. They also need to coordinate roles and rules of order within the decision process.

Another time constraint found in most team structures is that only one person can speak at a time.[51] This problem, known as **production blocking,** causes participants to forget potentially creative ideas by the time it is their turn to speak. Team members who concentrate on remembering their fleeting thoughts end up ignoring what others are saying, even though their statements could trigger more creative ideas.

production blocking
A time constraint in team decision making due to the procedural requirement that only one person may speak at a time.

Thomas Alva Edison wasn't the lone genius that many people assume. Rather, the inventor of over 1,000 patents depended on his team of 14 scientists and technicians who worked closely together in an invention factory. "Edison is in reality a collective noun and means the work of many men," says Francis Jehl, Edison's longtime assistant (seated, fifth from right). Edison and his team of inventors were involved in several projects spanning various fields, all in a single room where they were constantly interacting and helping each other on their projects.[52] In your opinion, was Thomas Edison's innovation team more productive and creative than if each person had worked alone? Why or why not? *(The Smithsonian Institution)*

Evaluation Apprehension

Individuals are reluctant to mention ideas that seem silly because they believe (often correctly) that other team members are silently evaluating them. This **evaluation apprehension** is based on the individual's desire to create a favorable self-presentation and his or her need for social esteem. It is most common in meetings attended by people with different levels of status or expertise, or when members formally evaluate each other's performance throughout the year (as in 360-degree feedback). Evaluation apprehension is a problem when the group wants to generate creative ideas, because these thoughts often sound bizarre or lack logic when presented. Unfortunately, many potentially valuable ideas are never presented to the group because creative thoughts initially seem ridiculous and a waste of time.

Conformity to Peer Pressure

Chapter 8 described how cohesiveness leads individual members to conform to the team's norms. This control keeps the group organized around common goals, but it may also cause team members to suppress their dissenting opinions about discussion issues, particularly when a strong team norm is related to the issue. When someone does state a point of view that violates the majority opinion, other members might punish the violator or try to persuade him or her that the opinion is incorrect. It's not surprising, then, that nearly half of the managers surveyed in one study say they give up in team decisions because of pressure from others to conform to the team's decision.[53] Conformity can also be subtle. To some extent, we depend on the opinions that others hold to validate our own views. If co-workers don't agree with us, then we begin to question our own opinions even without overt peer pressure.[54]

Groupthink

Groupthink is the tendency of highly cohesive groups to value consensus at the price of decision quality.[55] Groupthink goes beyond the problem of conformity. There are strong social pressures on individual members to maintain harmony by avoiding conflict and disagreement. They suppress doubts about decision alternatives preferred by the majority or group leader. Team members want to maintain this harmony because their self-identity is enhanced by membership in a powerful decision-making body that speaks with one voice.[56] Team harmony also helps members cope with the stress of making crucial top-level decisions.

High cohesiveness isn't the only cause of groupthink. It is also more likely to occur when the team is isolated from outsiders, the team leader is opinionated (rather than remaining impartial), the team is under stress due to an external threat, the team has experienced recent failures or other decision-making problems, and the team lacks clear guidance from corporate policies or procedures. Several symptoms of groupthink have been identified and are summarized in Exhibit 10.3. In general, teams overestimate their invulnerability and morality, become closed-minded to outside and dissenting information, and experience several pressures toward consensus.[57]

Most research on groupthink has analyzed policy decisions that turned into fiascoes. The best-known example is NASA's space shuttle *Challenger* explosion

EXHIBIT 10.3   Symptoms of groupthink

Groupthink symptom	Description
Illusion of invulnerability	The team feels comfortable with risky decisions because possible weaknesses are suppressed or glossed over.
Assumption of morality	There is such an unquestioned belief in the inherent morality of the team's objectives that members do not feel the need to debate whether their actions are ethical.
Rationalization	Underlying assumptions, new information, and previous actions that seem inconsistent with the team's decision are discounted or explained away.
Stereotyping of outgroups	The team stereotypes or oversimplifies the external threats on which the decision is based; "enemies" are viewed as purely evil or moronic.
Self-censorship	Team members suppress their doubts to maintain harmony.
Illusion of unanimity	Self-censorship results in harmonious behavior, so individual members believe that they alone have doubts; silence is automatically perceived as evidence of consensus.
Mindguarding	Some members become self-appointed guardians to prevent negative or inconsistent information from reaching the team.
Pressuring of dissenters	Members who happen to raise their concerns about the decision are pressured to fall into line and be more loyal to the team.

Source: Based on I. L. Janis, *Groupthink: Psychological Studies of Policy Decisions and Fiascoes,* 2nd ed. (Boston: Houghton Mifflin, 1982), p. 244.

in 1986.[58] The technical cause of the explosion killing all seven crew members was a faulty O-ring seal that did not withstand the freezing temperatures the night before launch. However, a government commission pointed to a faulty decision-making process as the primary cause of the disaster. Key decision makers at NASA experienced many groupthink symptoms. They were under intense pressure to launch because of previous delays and promises of the space shuttle program's success. Information about O-ring problems was withheld to avoid conflict. Engineers raised concerns about the O-rings before the launch, but they were criticized for doing so.

Group Polarization

group polarization

The tendency of teams to make more extreme decisions than individuals working alone.

Group polarization refers to the tendency of teams to make more extreme decisions than individuals working alone.[59] Exhibit 10.4 shows how the group polarization process operates. Individuals form initial preferences when given several alternatives. Some of these choices are riskier than others, and the average member's opinion leans one way or the other. Through open discussion, team members become comfortable with more extreme positions when they realize that co-workers hold similar opinions. Persuasive arguments favoring the dominant position convince doubtful members and help form a consensus around the extreme option. Finally, individuals feel less personally responsible for the decision consequences because the decision is made by the team.

Social support, persuasion, and shifting responsibility explain why teams make more *extreme* decisions, but why do they usually make *riskier* decisions? The answer is that decision makers often have an illusion of control. They become victims of the gambler's fallacy that they can beat the odds. For example, team members tend to think, "This strategy might be unsuccessful 80 percent

EXHIBIT 10.4

The group polarization
process

of the time, but it will work for us." Thus, team members are more likely to favor the risky option.[60] The result of group polarization is that decision-making
groups sometimes avoid solid opportunities, whereas they bet the company on
risky investments.

TEAM STRUCTURES FOR CREATIVITY AND DECISION MAKING

These problems with team dynamics in decision making may be reduced in a
number of ways. One approach is to ensure that neither the team leader nor
any other participant dominates the process. This limits the adverse effects of
conformity and lets other team members generate more creative and con-
troversial ideas.[61] Another practice is to maintain an optimal team size. The
group should be large enough that members possess the collective knowledge
to resolve the problem, yet small enough that the team doesn't consume too
much time or restrict individual input.[62] Team norms are also important to ensure that individuals engage in critical thinking rather than follow the group's
implicit preferences.

Evaluation apprehension, groupthink, production blocking, and other team
dynamics problems are most common in traditional team meetings where
members meet face-to-face to suggest solutions and debate alternatives. Discussion is usually unstructured, ideas are generated and evaluated simultaneously, and solutions are often suggested long before the problem is sufficiently
understood. Five alternative team structures have been proposed over the
years to improve creativity and decision making in team settings: constructive
controversy, brainstorming, electronic brainstorming, the Delphi technique,
and the nominal group technique.

Constructive Controversy

**constructive
controversy**
Any situation where
people debate their
different opinions
about an issue in a
way that keeps the
conflict focused
on the task rather
than people.

Constructive controversy occurs when team members debate their different
perceptions about an issue in a way that keeps the conflict focused on the task

rather than on people. Through dialogue, participants learn about other points of view, which encourages them to reexamine their basic assumptions about a problem and its possible solution. Controversy is *constructive* because the discussion minimizes negative conflict while discussing differences. This type of dialogue can occur if participants focus on facts rather than people and avoid statements that threaten the esteem and well-being of other team members.[63]

How do we generate constructive controversy? First, decision-making groups should be heterogeneous.[64] As we learned in previous chapters, heterogeneous teams are better than homogeneous teams at perceiving issues and potential solutions from different perspectives.

Second, these heterogeneous team members need to meet often enough to allow meaningful discussion over contentious issues. The team's diversity won't generate constructive controversy if the team leader makes most of the decisions alone. Only through dialogue can team members better understand different perspectives, generate more creative ideas, and improve decision quality.

Third, effective teams generate constructive controversy when individual members take on different discussion roles. Some participants are action-oriented, others insist on reviewing details, one or two might try to minimize dysfunctional conflict, and so on. Where team members have too much agreement, some people should act as *devil's advocates* by challenging the others to explain the logic of their preferences.[65]

Lastly, constructive controversy is more likely to occur when team members think through the consequences of the preferred choice under several scenarios.[66] Before buying another company, for instance, an executive team should consider the wisdom of this decision if the economy stumbles, the government changes, a supply shortage occurs, and so on. Taking different angles also means comparing the preferred alternative against many choices, not just one or two limited options. To identify these varied alternatives, effective teams engage in some form of brainstorming.

Brainstorming

In the 1950s, advertising executive Alex Osborn wanted to find a better way for teams to generate creative ideas.[67] Osborn's solution, called **brainstorming,** requires team members to abide by the four rules displayed in Exhibit 10.5. Osborn believed that these rules encourage divergent thinking while minimizing evaluation apprehension and other team dynamics problems.

brainstorming
A freewheeling, face-to-face meeting where team members generate as many ideas as possible, piggyback on the ideas of others, and avoid evaluating anyone's ideas during the idea-generation stage.

■ *Don't criticize*—The most important rule in brainstorming is that no one should criticize any ideas that are presented. "Once ideas are scrutinized at the moment they are being put forth, people become less forthcoming," warns a creativity facilitator who works with Unilever in India.[68] Without criticism, team members might be more willing to suggest crazy solutions to the problem, which results in a larger number of and potentially better ideas. "[Y]ou can suggest the most stupid things and they can turn out to be incredibly insightful," says Peter Dawe, the British entrepreneur who founded Europe's first commercial Internet service provider, Unipalm-Pipex.[69]

■ *Provide as many ideas as possible*—Brainstorming is based on the idea that quantity breeds quality. In other words, quality increases with the number of ideas presented. This concept relates to the belief that divergent thinking

EXHIBIT 10.5

Rules of
brainstorming

Rules of Brainstorming

1. Don't criticize ideas.

2. Provide as many ideas as possible.

3. Say all ideas that come to mind, no matter how wild.

4. Combine and improve ideas suggested by others.

Source: Based on information in A. F. Osborn, *Applied Imagination,* 3rd ed. (New York: Scribner's, 1963).

occurs after traditional ideas have been exhausted. Therefore, the group should think of as many solutions as possible and go well beyond the traditional solutions to more unusual ideas.

■ *Speak freely*—Brainstorming welcomes wild and wacky ideas, which become the seeds of divergent thinking in the creative process. Crazy suggestions are sometimes crazy only because they break out of the mold set by existing mental models.

■ *Build on the ideas of others*—Team members are encouraged to piggyback or hitchhike, that is, to combine and improve on the ideas already presented. Building on existing ideas encourages the synergy of team processes (see Chapter 9).

Brainstorming is the most popular team structure for encouraging creative ideas. Yet for several years, organizational behavior researchers warned that this practice has several limitations. One concern is that brainstorming rules do not completely remove evaluation apprehension; employees still know that others are silently evaluating the quality of their ideas. Production blocking and related time constraints may prevent all ideas from being presented. Some research reports that individuals working alone produce a larger number of solutions to a problem than if they work together using brainstorming.[70]

Rather than deterring organizations from using brainstorming, these findings should remind us that brainstorming is effective only under the right conditions. As we read in the opening vignette in this chapter, IDEO thrives on brainstorming, mainly because it produces the right environment and structure to make these sessions productive. First, some research has found that brainstorming rules minimize socioemotional conflict among members and improve the team's focus on the required task. Brainstorming participants interact and participate directly, thereby increasing decision acceptance and team cohesiveness.

Evaluation apprehension may be a problem for brainstorming in student research experiments, but it is less of a problem at IDEO, where high-performing teams have a lot of trust and support risky thinking. There is some evidence that effective brainstorming sessions provide valuable nonverbal communication that spreads enthusiasm. Team members share feelings of optimism and excitement that may encourage a more creative climate. Clients are often involved in brainstorming sessions, so these positive emotions may produce higher customer satisfaction than if people are working alone on the product.[71] Overall, brainstorming may prove more valuable to creativity than some of the earlier research indicates.

Electronic Brainstorming

electronic brainstorming
Using special computer software, participants share ideas while minimizing the team dynamics problems inherent in traditional brainstorming sessions.

DaimlerChrysler, Boeing, and many other firms have tried to improve team decision making through **electronic brainstorming.** With the aid of groupware (special computer software for groups), electronic brainstorming lets participants share ideas while minimizing the team dynamics problems inherent in traditional brainstorming sessions.[72] Individuals can enter ideas at any time on their computer terminal. These ideas are posted anonymously and randomly on the screens of all participants. A central convener monitors the entire input to ensure that participants stay focused on the issue.

The greatest benefit of electronic brainstorming is that it significantly reduces production blocking. Participants are able to document their ideas as soon as they pop into their heads, rather than having to wait their turn to communicate.[73] In large groups, this process also supports creative synergy because participants can easily develop new ideas from those generated by other people. Electronic brainstorming also minimizes the problem of evaluation apprehension because ideas are posted anonymously. Research has found that electronic brainstorming generates more ideas than traditional brainstorming and participants seem more satisfied, motivated, and confident in the decision-making exercise than in other team structures.[74]

Despite these advantages, electronic brainstorming is perhaps too structured and technology-bound for most people. Some critics have noted that the additional number of ideas generated through electronic brainstorming is not enough to justify its cost. Another concern is that organizational participants are generally less enthusiastic about electronic brainstorming sessions than are students who participate in research samples.[75] It would seem odd, for example, to advise clients that they conduct an electronic brainstorm rather than talk to each other. The problem is that electronic brainstorming ignores the benefits of social bonding and emotional interaction that occur in face-to-face meetings. Lastly, electronic brainstorming creates political problems because some people may feel threatened by the honesty of some statements and by their inability to control the discussion.

Delphi Technique

Delphi technique
A structured team decision-making process of systematically pooling the collective knowledge of experts on a particular subject to make decisions, predict the future, or identify opposing views.

The **Delphi technique** systematically pools the collective knowledge of experts on a particular subject to make decisions, predict the future, or identify opposing views (called *dissensus*).[76] Delphi groups do not meet face-to-face; in fact, participants are often located in different parts of the world and may not know each other's identity. Moreover, as with electronic brainstorming, participants do not know who "owns" the ideas submitted. Typically, Delphi group members submit possible solutions or comments regarding an issue to the central convener. The compiled results are returned to the panel for a second round of comments. This process may be repeated several more times until consensus or dissensus emerges. Delphi technique helped an electricity supply company understand how to respond to customers who don't pay their bills. It was also used by rehabilitation counselors to reach consensus on rehabilitation credentialing.[77]

Nominal Group Technique

nominal group technique

A structured team decision-making process whereby team members independently write down ideas, describe and clarify them to the group, and then independently rank or vote on them.

Nominal group technique is a variation of traditional brainstorming and Delphi technique that tries to combine individual efficiencies with team dynamics.[78] The method is called *nominal* because participants form a group *in name only* during two stages of decision making. This process, shown in Exhibit 10.6, first involves the individual, then the group, and finally the individual again.

After the problem is described, team members silently and independently write down as many solutions as they can. During the group stage, participants describe their solutions to the other team members, usually in a round-robin format. As with brainstorming, there is no criticism or debate, although members are encouraged to ask for clarification of the ideas presented. In the final stage, participants silently and independently rank or vote on each proposed solution. Ranking is preferred because its forces each person to review carefully all the alternatives presented.[79] Nominal group technique prefers voting or ranking over reaching consensus to avoid dysfunctional conflict that comes with debate.

Nominal group technique tends to produce more and better-quality ideas than do traditional interacting groups.[80] Because of its high degree of structure, nominal group technique usually maintains a high task orientation and relatively low potential for conflict within the team. However, team cohesiveness is generally lower in nominal decisions because the structure minimizes social interaction. Production blocking and evaluation apprehension still occur to some extent.

Throughout this chapter, we have learned various ways to improve creativity in the workplace. We also learned about team dynamics that potentially undermine creativity and decision making, as well as team structures that minimize these problems. However, decisions also require plenty of information sharing, which we discuss in the next chapter on communication in organizations.

EXHIBIT 10.6

Nominal group technique

CHAPTER SUMMARY

Creativity refers to developing an original product, service, or idea that makes a socially recognized contribution. It is an integral part of decision making and an important practice in knowledge management.

The four creativity stages are preparation, incubation, insight, and verification. Preparation is the person or group's effort to acquire knowledge and skills regarding the problem or opportunity. Incubation is the stage of reflective thought, where we put the problem aside but continue to work on it in the back of our mind. Incubation assists divergent thinking, which involves reframing the problem in a unique way and generating different approaches to the issue. Insight is the experience of suddenly becoming aware of a unique idea. These creative thoughts are quickly documented and tested in the verification stage.

Some people are more creative than others. Creative people have the intellectual abilities to synthesize and analyze ideas, as well as to apply their ideas. They possess a good foundation of knowledge and experience on the subject, but not so much that they have formed rigid mental models. Creative people have a high need for achievement and at least a moderate level of self-confidence. Lastly, creative people have an innovative thinking style. They avoid set patterns and are willing to take risks, including the risk of failure.

Organizational support—including support of risk taking, job security, reasonable work pressure, and trustworthy co-workers—increases the level of creativity. One of the most important influences on creativity is the job's intrinsic motivation, including its task significance, autonomy, and job feedback. Challenging work aligned with the person's competencies can generate a state of flow that enhances creative output. A creative work environment also provides sufficient resources and time to accomplish the task.

Corporate leaders can further enhance creativity by encouraging employees to redefine the problem, engage in associative play, and experience cross-pollination. Redefining the problem can occur through jamming sessions where people tear the problem apart, by revisiting old projects, and by having other people look at the problem. Associative play activities include object-oriented chain storytelling, painting, the use of metaphors, and morphological analysis. Cross-pollination occurs when people work with different people on each project and when employees publicly display their projects to others in the organization.

Team decisions are impeded by time constraints, evaluation apprehension, conformity to peer pressure, groupthink, and group polarization. Production blocking—when typically only one person speaks at a time—is a form of time constraint on teams. Evaluation apprehension occurs when employees believe that others are silently evaluating them, so they avoid stating seemingly silly ideas. Conformity keeps team members aligned with team goals, but it also tends to suppress dissenting opinions. Groupthink is the tendency of highly cohesive groups to value consensus at the price of decision quality. Group polarization refers to the tendency of teams to make more extreme decisions than individuals working alone.

Team decision-making problems can be minimized by ensuring that the team leader does not dominate, maintaining an optimal team size, ensuring that team norms support critical thinking, and introducing team structures that support more creative decision making.

Five team structures that potentially improve creativity and team decision making are constructive controversy, brainstorming, electronic brainstorming, the Delphi technique, and the nominal group technique. Brainstorming requires team members to avoid criticizing, provide as many ideas as possible, speak freely, and build on the ideas of others. Electronic brainstorming uses computer software to share ideas while minimizing team dynamics problems. Delphi technique systematically pools the collective knowledge of experts on a particular subject without face-to-face meetings. In nominal group technique, participants write down ideas alone, describe their ideas in a group, then silently rank or vote on the ideas.

KEY TERMS

brainstorming, p. 309

constructive controversy, p. 308

creativity, p. 294

Delphi technique, p. 311

divergent thinking, p. 296

electronic brainstorming, p. 311

evaluation apprehension, p. 306

group polarization, p. 307

groupthink, p. 306

nominal group technique, p. 312

production blocking, p. 305

DISCUSSION QUESTIONS

1. The Chinese word for business is *sheng-yi*, which literally means "to give birth to ideas." Explain how creativity is an inherent part of business decision making.

2. Think of a time when you experienced the creative process. Maybe you woke up with a brilliant (but usually sketchy and incomplete) idea, or you solved a baffling problem while doing something else. Describe this incident to your class, and explain how the experience followed the creative process.

3. Two characteristics of creative people are that they have relevant experience and are persistent in their quest. Does this mean that people with the most experience and the highest need for achievement are the most creative? Explain your answer.

4. One feature of companies that support creativity is that they minimize the employees' fear of failure. Why does this fear affect creativity, and how can organizations minimize the fear? What are the limitations of this creative strategy?

5. Mitel and other companies host internal trade shows, where employees display their knowledge and trade information with other employees. Explain how these internal trade shows improve creativity.

6. Production blocking is often identified as a problem in creativity and team decision making. Describe production blocking, and identify a team structure that minimizes this problem.

7. A senior executive committee wants to make better decisions by practicing constructive controversy. Identify four things that the group must do to increase constructive controversy.

8. Sacramento Resorts, Inc., wants to use brainstorming with its employees to identify new markets for its hotels and services. Advise the Sacramento Resorts executives about the rules to follow for this session, as well as its potential limitations.

CASE STUDY 10.1

EASTERN PROVINCE LIGHT AND POWER

I work as a systems and procedures analyst for the Eastern Province Light and Power Company. The systems and procedures department analyzes corporate policies, procedures, forms, equipment, and methods to simplify and standardize operations. We apply "organized common sense" to develop new practices and to improve old ones.

Requests for analysis of organizational problems are submitted to the systems and procedures department by persons of department head or higher status. Our manager places projects in line for consideration and assigns them to an analyst on the basis of availability; projects are accepted and assigned on the FIFO (first in–first out) method. Projects must undergo analysis, design, and implementation before a change in procedure is realized. What follows is a description of a problem assigned to me. I am in the midst of investigating it right now.

The Problem

For some time, management had been concerned with the inventory carrying charges that accrue when material is stored in company warehouses. Not only is there a cost attached to carrying inventory for future use, but there are additional related costs, such as labor to handle the inventory, warehouse usage in terms of square feet taken up in storage, and clerical time used to account for materials flowing into and out of inventory. One type of material stored is office supplies—pens, writing pads, forms, stationery, envelopes, and dozens of similar items. A desire to reduce the costs of storing these items prompted the head of the department of purchasing and material control to submit a request for a study by systems and procedures.

The request came in the required written form. It described the current procedures, estimated their costs, and invited us to explore ways of changing the procedures to reduce costs. In brief, at the time the study request was submitted, purchases of office supplies were made through 11 vendors. The items were stored in a common warehouse area and disbursed to using departments as requested. As is customary, I convened a meeting of the requesting manager and others who seemed most directly involved in the problem.

The First Meeting

I opened the meeting by summarizing the present procedures for purchasing and storing office supplies and the estimated costs associated with these problems. I explained that we were meeting to explore ways of reducing these costs. I suggested we might try to generate as many ideas as we could without being too critical of them, and then proceed to narrow the list by criticizing and eliminating the ideas with obvious weaknesses.

Just as soon as I finished my opening remarks, the head of purchasing and material control said that we should conduct a pilot study in which we would contract with one of the regular vendors to supply each involved department directly, eliminating company storage of any inventory. The vendor would continue to sell us whatever we usually purchased from it, but would sell and deliver the items to various departments instead of to our central purchasing group. A pilot study with one vendor would indicate how such a system would work with all vendors of office supplies. If it worked well, we could handle all office supplies this way.

She went on to explain that she had already spoken to the vice president to whom she (and, through intermediate levels, the rest of us) reported and that he recognized the potential savings that would result. She also said that she had gone over the idea with the supervisor of stores (who reported to her) and that he agreed. She wanted to know how long it would take me to carry out the pilot study. I looked at a few faces to see if anybody would say anything, but nobody did. I said I didn't know. She said, "Let's meet in a week when you've come up with a proposal." The meeting ended without anything else of any real substance being said.

I felt completely frustrated. She was the highest-ranking person in the meeting. She had said what she wanted and, if her stature wasn't

enough, she had invoked the image of the vice president being in agreement with her. Nobody, including me, had said anything. No idea other than hers was even mentioned, and no comments were made about it.

I decided that I would work as hard as I could to study the problem and her proposed pilot study before the next meeting and come prepared to give the whole thing a critical review.

Between Meetings

I talked to my boss about my feeling that it seemed as though I was expected to rubber-stamp the pilot study idea. I said that I wished he would come to the next meeting. I also said that I wanted to talk to some people close to the problem, some clerks in stores, some vendors, and some buyers in purchasing to see if I could come up with any good ideas or find any problems in the pilot study area. He told me to learn all I could and that he would come to the next meeting.

My experience with other studies had taught me that sometimes the people closest to the work had expertise to contribute, so I found one stores clerk, two buyers, and two vendor sales representatives to talk to. Nobody had spoken to any of them about the pilot study and the general plan it was meant to test. This surprised me a little. Each one of these people had some interesting things to say about the proposed new way of handling office supplies. A buyer, for example, thought it would be chaotic to have 17 different departments ordering the same items. She thought we might also lose out on some quantity discounts, and it would mean 17 times the paperwork. A vendor said he didn't think any vendor would like the idea because it would increase the number of contacts necessary to sell the amount that could be sold now through one contact—the buyer in the purchasing department. A stores clerk said it might be risky to depend on a vendor to maintain inventories at adequate levels. He said, "What if a vendor failed to supply us with, say, enough mark-sensing tools for our meter readers one month, thereby causing them to be unable to complete their task and our company to be unable to get its monthly billings out on time?"

The Second Meeting

Armed with careful notes, I came to the next meeting prepared to discuss these and other criticisms. One of the stores clerks had even agreed to attend so that I could call on him for comments. But when I looked around the conference room, everyone was there except the stores clerk. The head of purchasing and material control said she had talked to the clerk and could convey any of his ideas, so she had told him it wasn't necessary for him to come.

I pointed out that the stores clerk had raised a question about the company's ability to control inventory. He had said that we now have physical control of inventory, but the proposal involved making ourselves dependent on the vendor's maintaining adequate inventory. The head of purchasing and material control said, "Not to worry. It will be in the vendor's own interest to keep us well supplied." No one, including my boss, said anything.

I brought up the subject of selecting a vendor to participate in the pilot study. My boss mentioned that I had told him some vendors might object to the scheme because the additional contacts would increase their costs of sales. The head of purchasing and material control said, "Any vendor would be interested in doing business with a company as big as Eastern Province Light and Power." No further comments were made.

I mentioned that it was the practice of the systems and procedures staff to estimate independently the costs and benefits of any project before undertaking it, and also to have the internal auditing department review the proposal. I said we would need to go ahead with those steps. I asked the head of purchasing and material control to give me the name of somebody in her area I should contact to get the costs of the present system. She said that it really didn't seem necessary to go through all the usual steps in this case since she had already submitted an estimate. Besides, it was only going to be a pilot study. She said, "I think we can all agree on that and just move ahead now with the designation of a vendor." She looked around the table and nobody said anything. She said, "Fine. Let's use Moore Business Forms." Nobody said anything. She then said to me, "OK, let's get back together after you've lined things up."

Discussion Questions

1. Did this group at Eastern Province Light and Power make their decision effectively? Why or why not?

2. Identify any decision-making problems that seem to exist in this case.

3. What team structure would you recommend to make this type of decision in the future?

Source: D. R. Hampton, *Contemporary Management* (New York: McGraw-Hill, 1981). Used with permission.

C A S E   S T U D Y   **10.2**

THE NEW BARRY DILLER

BusinessWeek   In the business world, creative thinking can generate ideas ranging from new products to new ways around a problem to whole new business models. Barry Diller is a television executive known for such thinking. In a career that has taken him from ABC, to Paramount, to a start-up role at Fox, Diller has developed a reputation for creative ideas. More recently, Diller has gone on to lead Home Shopping Network and USA Network.

This *Business Week* case study describes Barry Diller's current business strategy. It focuses on his ideas to build USA Network into a media company that lets television viewers make purchases through their TV sets. Read through this *Business Week* case study at www.mhhe.com/mcshane2e and prepare for the discussion questions below.

Discussion Questions

1. What examples of divergent thinking do the authors describe in this article?

2. The chapter describes several characteristics associated with creative people. Which

of those characteristics does Barry Diller exhibit in this article?

3. How might Diller and USA Network enable employees to work creatively in carrying out Diller's ideas?

Source: Ronald Grover and Tom Lowry, "The New Barry Diller," *Business Week,* September 10, 2001.

TEAM EXERCISE 10.3

THE HOPPING ORANGE

Purpose To help students understand the dynamics of creativity and team problem solving.

Instructions You will be placed in teams of six students. One student serves as the official timer for the team and must have a watch, preferably with a stopwatch timer. The instructor will give each team an orange (or similar object) with a specific task involving use of the orange. The objective is easy to understand and nonthreatening, and will be described by the instructor at the beginning of the exercise. Each team will have a few opportunities to achieve the objective more efficiently.

TEAM EXERCISE 10.4

CREATIVITY BRAINBUSTERS

Purpose To help students understand the dynamics of creativity and team problem solving.

Instructions This exercise may be completed alone or in teams of three or four people. If teams are formed, students who already know the solutions to one or more of these problems should identify themselves and serve as silent observers. When teams are finished (or, more likely, when time is up), the instructor will review the solutions and discuss the implications of this exercise. In particular, be prepared to discuss what helped you solve these puzzles and what may have prevented you from solving them more quickly (or at all).

1. Double Circle Problem Draw two circles, one inside the other, with a single line and with neither circle touching the other (as shown at right). In other words, you must draw both of these

circles without lifting your pen (or other writing instrument).

2. Nine Dot Problem Below are nine dots. Without lifting your pencil, draw no more than four straight lines that pass through all nine dots.

3. Nine Dot Problem Revisited Refer to the exhibit above, and describe how, without lifting your pencil, you could pass a pencil line through all nine dots with three or fewer straight lines.

4. Word Search In the following line of letters, cross out five letters so that the remaining letters, without altering their sequence, spell a familiar English word.

FCIRVEEALTETITVEERS

5. Burning Ropes You have two pieces of rope of unequal lengths and a box of matches. In spite of their different lengths, each piece of rope takes 1 hour to burn; however, parts of each rope burn at unequal rates. For example, the first half of one piece might burn in 10 minutes. How could you use these materials to accurately determine when 45 minutes has elapsed?

TESTING YOUR CREATIVE BENCH STRENGTH

Purpose This self-assessment exercise is designed to help you determine how well you engage in divergent thinking, problem identification, and other creativity practices.

Instructions This self-assessment exercise consists of 12 questions. Write the answer for each question, along with your explanation, on a separate piece of paper. When everyone has finished, the instructor will provide the correct answer for each question, along with an explanation. (Note: This activity may be done as a self-assessment or as a team activity.)

1. There is one word in the English language that is always pronounced incorrectly. What is it?

2. A man gave one son 10 cents, and another son was given 15 cents. What time is it?

3. A boat has a ladder that has six rungs, and each rung is 1 foot apart. The bottom rung is 1 foot from the water. The tide rises at a rate of 12 inches every 15 minutes. High tide peaks in 1 hour. When the tide is at its highest, how many rungs are underwater?

4. There is a house with four walls. Each wall faces south. There is a window in each wall. A bear walks by one of the windows. What color is the bear?

5. Is half of 2 plus 2 equal to 2 or 3?

6. There is a room. The shutters are blowing in. There is broken glass on the floor. There is water on the floor. You find Sloppy dead on the floor. How did Sloppy die?

7. How much dirt would be in a hole 6 feet deep and 6 feet wide that has been dug with a square-edged shovel?

8. Suppose you are in Juneau, Alaska, and drop a bowling ball from a height of three feet into a bucket of water at 45 degrees Fahrenheit. Then, you drop a bowling ball of the same weight, mass, and size from the same height into another bucket at 20 degrees Fahrenheit. Which ball would hit the bottom of the bucket fastest?

9. Explain the significance of the following: The year is 1978, thirty-four minutes past noon on May 6th.

10. What can go up a chimney down but can't go down a chimney up?

11. If a farmer has five haystacks in one field and four haystacks in the other field, how many haystacks would he have if he combined them all in the center field?

12. What is it that goes up and goes down but does not move?

Source: The origin of these brain teasers is unknown. They were distributed by J. Gushue in *St. John's Telegram Online*, April 11, 2000.

ASSESSING YOUR CREATIVE DISPOSITION

Purpose This self-assessment exercise is designed to help you estimate the extent to which you have a creative personality.

Instructions Listed below is an adjective checklist with 30 words that may or may not describe you. Put a mark in the box beside the words that you think accurately describe you. Please do not mark the boxes for words that do not describe you. When finished, you can score the test using the scoring key in Appendix B. This exercise is completed alone so that students assess themselves without concerns of social comparison. However, class discussion will focus on how this scale might be applied in organizations and on the limitations of measuring creativity in work settings.

Adjective checklist

Affected	❏	Honest	❏	Reflective	❏
Capable	❏	Humorous	❏	Resourceful	❏
Cautious	❏	Individualistic	❏	Self-confident	❏
Clever	❏	Informal	❏	Sexy	❏
Commonplace	❏	Insightful	❏	Sincere	❏
Confident	❏	Intelligent	❏	Snobbish	❏
Conservative	❏	Inventive	❏	Submissive	❏
Conventional	❏	Mannerly	❏	Suspicious	❏
Dissatisfied	❏	Narrow interests	❏	Unconventional	❏
Egotistical	❏	Original	❏	Wide interests	❏

Source: Based on information in H. G. Gough, "A Creative Personality Scale for the Adjective Check List," *Journal of Personality and Social Psychology* 37, no. 8 (August 1979), pp. 1398–405.

After studying the preceding material, be sure to check out our website at
www.mhhe.com/mcshane2e
for more in-depth information and interactivities that correspond to this chapter.

11

Communicating in Organizational Settings

AFTER READING THIS CHAPTER, YOU SHOULD BE ABLE TO:

■ Explain the importance of communication and diagram the communication process.

■ Identify four common communication barriers.

■ Describe problems with communicating through electronic mail.

■ Discuss how the law of telecosm will affect organizational communication.

■ Explain how nonverbal communication relates to emotional labor and emotional contagion.

■ Identify two conditions requiring a channel with high media richness.

■ Summarize four communication strategies in organizational hierarchies.

■ Discuss the degree to which men and women communicate differently.

■ Outline the key elements of active listening.

When Pearse Flynn joined Newbridge Networks (now part of Alcatel, the French telecommunications giant) as vice president of European operations, he noticed that employees were communicating in strange acronyms. Even the PowerPoint slides in briefing sessions looked like they were written in a foreign language.

"The only word I understood on the slide was 'Newbridge' down in the corner," jokes the Irish-born Flynn, who has university degrees in applied physics and digital systems. He quickly advised employees to communicate in plain language so that everyone could understand their message. "I said, 'You need to make this so I can explain it to my mother.'"

Flynn further improved communications by changing the physical layout of Newbridge's European headquarters near London. Employees were spread across five buildings, and a security system for each building made it difficult to visit coworkers. Flynn dramatically improved informal communication by reorganizing everyone into one building and moving security to the entrance.

Flynn has a penchant for receiving honest information, so he hands out sticky notes at the end of some meetings and asks employees to write down, after he leaves the room, what was on their minds. "I guarantee you, you do five of those and you'll know what the issues are in the organization," he advises.

Flynn also believes in face-to-face dialogue. When Alcatel acquired Newbridge, Flynn and other executives bused thousands of employees to a nearby stadium to tell them the news in person. "People have to know where they're going, so you have to have a plan and communicate that to people," explains Flynn.

Even as a senior Alcatel executive overseeing 40,000 employees around the

Pearse Flynn tore down communication barriers at French telecommunications giant Alcatel. *(C. Mikula/Ottawa Citizen)*

world, Flynn kept a grueling pace to maintain personal communication. "I make so much of my decisions from the fact that I chat with people, and I pick up what's really going on in people's minds," says Flynn, who is now CEO of Damovo, a global information technology services firm headquartered in Glasgow, Scotland.[1] ■

communication
The process by which information is transmitted and understood between two or more people.

communication competence
A person's ability to identify appropriate communication patterns in a given situation and to achieve goals by applying that knowledge.

Pearse Flynn believes in the power of communication at Alcatel. **Communication** refers to the process by which information is transmitted and *understood* between two or more people. We emphasize the word *understood* because transmitting the sender's intended meaning is the essence of good communication. Pearse Flynn and other leaders of large organizations require innovative strategies to keep communication pathways open. Smaller businesses may have fewer structural bottlenecks, but they, too, can suffer from subtle communication barriers.

In a knowledge-based economy, employees require a high level of communication competence. **Communication competence** refers to a person's ability to identify appropriate communication patterns in a given situation and to achieve goals by applying that knowledge.[2] Competent communicators quickly learn the meaning that listeners take from certain words and symbols, and they know which communication medium is best in a particular situation. Moreover, competent communicators use this knowledge to communicate in ways that achieve personal, team, and organizational objectives. Someone with high communication competence would be better than others at determining whether an e-mail, telephone call, or personal visit would be the best approach to convey a message to an employee. Corporate leaders spend most of their

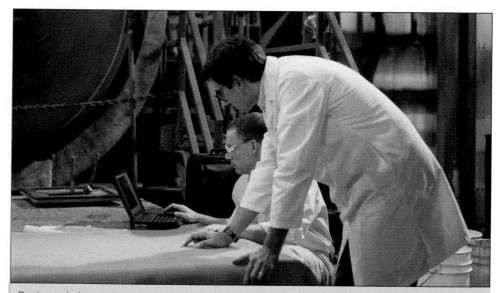

Buckman Laboratories is a pioneer in knowledge management, yet the chemical company sees internal communication as its main strength. "[W]e have designed a system and built a culture that facilitates the communication of whatever is needed across all of the organization's boundaries," explains CEO Robert Buckman. Employees work in 90 countries and spend much of their time with customers. Yet notebook computers connected to Buckman Labs' worldwide information center (called K'netix) allow them to share information quickly. For example, a representative in Indonesia won a $6 million proposal, partly because he requested vital information and received it within eight hours from colleagues in the United States and Europe.[3] What additional ways might Buckman Labs and other companies improve communication across their global operations? *(Courtesy of Buckman Laboratories)*

time and energy communicating with employees and other stakeholders.[4] Consequently, communication competence is particularly important for people in these senior positions.

Communication plays an important role in knowledge management (see Chapter 1).[5] Employees are the organization's brain cells, and communication represents the nervous system that carries information and shared meaning to vital parts of the organizational body. Effective communication brings knowledge into the organization and disseminates it quickly to employees who require that information. Effective communication minimizes the "silos of knowledge" problem that undermines an organization's potential and, in turn, allows employees to make more informed decisions about corporate actions. For instance, British Telecom encourages employees to generate "knowledge moments"—occasions where shared knowledge results in better decisions.[6]

Along with decision making and knowledge management, effective communication coordinates work activities.[7] Through dialogue, co-workers develop common mental models—the broad worldviews that people rely on to guide their perceptions and behaviors—so they can synchronize interdependent work activities through common expectations and assumptions.[8] Lastly, communication is the glue that bonds people together. It fulfills social needs and, as part of the dynamics of social support, eases work-related stress.[9]

This chapter begins by presenting a model of the communication process and discussing several communication barriers. Next, the different types of communication channels, including computer-mediated communication, are described, followed by factors to consider when choosing a communication medium. The chapter then presents some options for communicating in organizational hierarchies and describes the pervasive organizational grapevine. The latter part of the chapter examines cross-cultural and gender differences in communication, as well as strategies to improve interpersonal communication.

A MODEL OF COMMUNICATION

The communication model presented in Exhibit 11.1 provides a useful "conduit" metaphor for thinking about the communication process.[10] According to this model, communication flows through channels between the sender and the receiver. The sender forms a message and encodes it into words, gestures, voice intonations, and other symbols or signs. Next, the encoded message is transmitted to the intended receiver through one or more communication channels (media). The receiver senses the incoming message and decodes it into something meaningful. Ideally, the decoded meaning is what the sender had intended.

In most situations, the sender looks for evidence that the other person received and understood the transmitted message. This feedback may be a formal acknowledgment, such as "Yes, I know what you mean," or indirect evidence from the receiver's subsequent actions. Notice that feedback repeats the communication process. Intended feedback is encoded, transmitted, received, and decoded from the receiver to the sender of the original message.

This model recognizes that communication is not a free-flowing conduit.[11] Rather, the transmission of meaning from one person to another is hampered by *noise*—the psychological, social, and structural barriers that distort and

EXHIBIT 11.1

The communication
process model

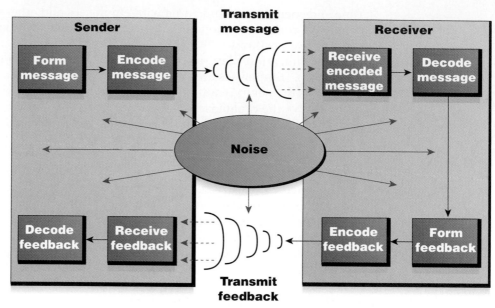

obscure the sender's intended message. If any part of the communication
process is distorted or broken, the sender and receiver will not have a common understanding of the message.

COMMUNICATION BARRIERS (NOISE)

In spite of the best intentions of sender and receiver to communicate, several
barriers inhibit the effective exchange of information. As author George
Bernard Shaw once wrote, "The greatest problem with communication is the
illusion that it has been accomplished." That's why executives at Corning, the
fiber optics manufacturer, follow the "rule of six." Corning CEO John Loose
explains: "When there is a message, to most people, you have to say it six
times. You can't have a meeting one day and check it off. You have to keep going back."[12] This chapter will identify several communication barriers (called
noise in Exhibit 11.1), but four pervasive problems that we discuss in this section are perceptions, filtering, language, and information overload.

Perceptions

As we learned in Chapter 3, the perceptual process determines which messages we select or screen out, as well has how the selected information is organized and interpreted. This process can be a significant source of noise in
the communication process if the sender and receiver have different perceptual frames and mental models. For example, a plant superintendent in a concrete block plant picked up a piece of broken brick while talking with the
supervisor. This action had no particular meaning to the superintendent—just
something to toy with during the conversation. Yet as soon as the superintendent had left, the supervisor ordered a half-hour of overtime for the entire
crew to clean up the plant. The supervisor mistakenly perceived the superintendent's action s a signal that the plant was messy.[13]

Klugey Communication at Microsoft

"Hi Jack, I've worked out a klugey solution to the UI issue," an employee e-mails to a colleague in the next cubicle. "We need to get granular on this. Unfortunately, I'm OOF next week, so you'll have to burn up a few cycles on it. I'm worried that the blue-badges on this project will go totally nonlinear when they realize the RTM date is slipping."*

Welcome to the world of Microspeak—the unofficial language of Microsoft. Employees at the world's largest software company have acquired a lexicon that would baffle researchers at any dictionary publishing company. Microsoft staffers eat their own dog food, dislike weasel users, and avoid getting caught in reality distortion fields. This all makes sense to insiders, but not to people raised in the English language!

Most of this dialogue occurs in cyber media rather than fiber media (paper) or face mail (face-to-face).

That's not to say that Microsoft employees never meet. They do, in small groups around whiteboards in someone's office to share insights, resolve problems, and confirm deadlines. In fact, Microsoft makes sure that employees work at the same location so that they can communicate and solve problems quickly in face-to-face meetings.

*Translation: "Hi Jack, I've worked out a rough solution to the user interface problem. We need to examine the finer details. Unfortunately, I'm away next week, so you need to devote time and energy to this problem. I'm worried that the permanent Microsoft employees on this project will get really angry when they realize that we are getting behind on the released-to-manufacturing date."

Sources: K. Barnes, "The Microsoft Lexicon" (www.cinepad.com/mslex.htm); S. Greenhouse, "Braindump on the Blue Badge: A Guide to Microspeak," *New York Times*, August 13, 1998, p. G1; M. A. Cusumano, "How Microsoft Makes Large Teams Work Like Small Teams," *Sloan Management Review* 39 (Fall 1997), pp. 9–20.

Filtering

Some messages are filtered or stopped altogether on their way up or down the organizational hierarchy. Filtering may involve deleting or delaying negative information, or using less harsh words so that events sound more favorable. Employees and supervisors usually filter communication to create a good impression of themselves to superiors. Filtering is most common where the organization rewards employees who communicate mainly positive information and among employees with strong career mobility aspirations.[14]

Language

Words and gestures carry no inherent meaning, so the sender must ensure the receiver understands these symbols and signs. In reality, lack of mutual understanding is a common reason messages are distorted. Two potential language barriers are jargon and ambiguity.

jargon
The technical language and acronyms as well as recognized words with specialized meaning in specific organizations or groups.

Jargon Jargon includes technical language and acronyms as well as recognized words with specialized meaning in specific organizations or social groups. Connections 11.1 illustrates how "Microspeak"—the strange jargon heard at Microsoft and other high-technology firms—potentially increases communication efficiency when both sender and receiver understand this specialized language. Jargon also shapes and maintains an organization's cultural values as well as symbolizes an employee's self-identity in a group (see Chapter 3).[15]

However, jargon can also be a barrier to effective communication. One example is an incident at Sea Launch, the Long Beach, California–based multinational venture that launches satellites. During a test of a countdown protocol devised by the American staff, the Russian scientists involved with

© 2001 Ted Goff

"That's my commendation for deciphering all the sales talk when we needed to upgrade the computer."

(Copyright © 2001 Ted Goff. www.tedgoff.com)

the project fell into a mysterious funk. When Sea Launch's mission control director Steve Thelin eventually asked why they were acting so moody and distant, the Russians complained that no one told them who Roger was. Everyone had a good laugh when Thelin explained that "roger" is jargon used by the Americans to indicate that they understand what the other person in a transmission is saying.[16]

Ambiguity   We usually think of ambiguous language as a communication problem because the sender and receiver interpret the same word or phrase differently. If a co-worker says, "Would you like to check the figures again?" the employee may be politely *telling* you to double-check the figures. But this message is sufficiently ambiguous that you may think the co-worker is merely *asking* if you want to do this. The result is a failure to communicate.

Ambiguous language is sometimes used deliberately in work settings to avoid conveying undesirable emotions. "Sell" is a word often avoided in the brokerage industry because the overvalued company may be a current or future client. Thus, brokers use more ambiguous language. "'Hold' means 'sell,'" admits one veteran of the brokerage industry. "It's a kind of 'meta' language where you have to look into the meaning behind the word."[17]

Ambiguous language may be a communication barrier, but it is sometimes necessary.[18] Corporate leaders often use metaphors to describe complex organizational values so that they are interpreted broadly enough to apply to diverse situations. Scholars also rely on metaphors because they convey rich meaning about complex ideas. For example, some organizational behavior scholars describe organizations as jazz ensembles or machines to reflect variations of their complex nature.[19]

Information Overload

A year ago, Sean Lapp averaged about 20 e-mails a day. Now, the CEO of the Chicago-based technology company I-Works gets closer to 200 messages daily on his computer. Lapp is also bombarded with dozens of phone calls, voice mails, faxes, paper documents, and other messages every day.[20]

Sean Lapp is not alone. Every day, the average office worker sends and receives more than 150 messages through various media. One survey reports that 49 percent of managers in the United States and several other countries feel they are fairly often or regularly incapable of processing this infoglut. More than 40 percent of them say that receiving so much information weakens their decision-making ability, delays important decisions, and makes it difficult to concentrate on their main tasks. Some medical experts also warn that the bombardment of electronic information is causing memory loss in young people.[21]

Communications guru Marshall McLuhan predicted more than 30 years ago that employees would become overloaded with messages. "One of the effects of living with electric information is that we live in a state of information overload," said McLuhan. "There's always more than you can cope with."[22] **Information overload** occurs when the volume of information received exceeds the person's capacity to process it. Employees have a certain *information-processing capacity*, that is, the amount of information that they are able to process in a fixed unit of time. At the same time, jobs have a varying *information load*, that is, the amount of information to be processed per unit of time.[23]

As Exhibit 11.2 illustrates, information overload occurs when the job's information load exceeds the individual's information-processing capacity. Information overload creates noise in the communication system because information gets overlooked or misinterpreted when people can't process it fast enough. It has also become a common cause of workplace stress.

Information overload is minimized in two ways: by increasing our information-processing capacity and by reducing the job's information load.[24] We can increase information-processing capacity by learning to read faster, scanning documents more efficiently, and removing distractions that slow information-processing speed. Time management also increases information-processing capacity. When information overload is temporary, information-processing capacity can be increased by working longer hours.

We can reduce information load by buffering, summarizing, or omitting the information. Buffering occurs when assistants screen the person's messages and forward only those considered essential reading. Summarizing condenses information into fewer words, such as by providing abstracts and executive summaries rather than the entire document. Omitting is the practice of ignoring less important information. For example, some e-mail software programs have a filtering algorithm that screens out unwanted junk mail (called spam).

information overload

A condition in which the volume of information received exceeds the person's capacity to process it.

EXHIBIT 11.2

Dynamics of information overload

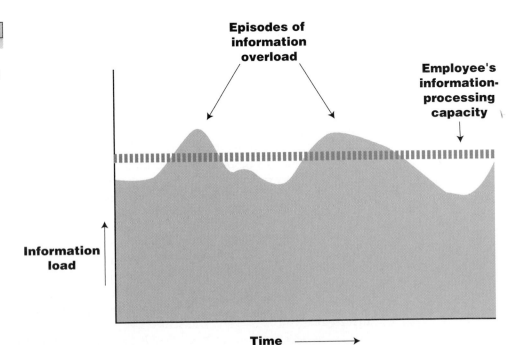

Perceptions, filtering, language, and information overload are not the only sources of noise in the communication process, but they are probably the most common. Noise also occurs when we choose an inappropriate channel through which to send the message. The next section takes a closer look at communication channels.

COMMUNICATION CHANNELS

A critical part of the communication model is the channel through which information is transmitted. There are two main types of channels: verbal and nonverbal. *Verbal communication* includes any oral or written means of transmitting meaning through words. *Nonverbal communication*, which we discuss later, is any part of communication that does not use words.

Verbal Communication

Different forms of verbal communication should be used in different situations. Face-to-face interaction is usually better than written methods for transmitting emotions and persuading the receiver, because nonverbal cues, such as voice intonations and use of silence, accompany oral communications. Moreover, in face-to-face settings, the sender receives immediate feedback from the receiver and can adjust the emotional tone of the message accordingly.

Written communication is more appropriate for recording and presenting technical details, because ideas are easier to follow when written down than when communicated verbally. Traditionally, written communication has been slow to develop and transmit, but electronic mail and other computer-mediated communication channels have significantly improved written communication efficiency.[25]

Electronic Mail

Electronic mail (e-mail) is revolutionizing the way we communicate in organizational settings. According to various estimates, somewhere between 1 trillion and 3 trillion e-mail messages are transmitted each year.[26] It's easy to understand the popularity of e-mail. Messages are quickly formed, edited, and stored. Information can be appended and transmitted to many people with a simple click of a mouse. E-mail is asynchronous (messages are sent and received at different times), so there is no need to coordinate a communication session. This technology also allows fairly random access of information; you can select any message in any order and skip to different parts of a message.

E-mail tends to be the preferred medium for coordinating work (e.g., confirming a co-worker's production schedule) and for sending well-defined information for decision making. The use of e-mail tends to increase the volume of communication and significantly alter the flow of that information throughout the organization.[27] Specifically, it reduces some face-to-face and telephone communication but increases the flow of information to higher levels in the organization. Some social and organizational status differences still exist with e-mail, but they are less apparent than in face-to-face or telephone communication. E-mail also reduces many selective attention biases because it hides age, race, weight, and other features that are observable in face-to-face meetings.

Problems with E-mail Anyone who has used e-mail knows that it has several problems and limitations. Perhaps the most obvious of these is that e-mail contributes to information overload. Many e-mail users are overwhelmed by hundreds of messages each week, many of which are either unnecessary or irrelevant to the receiver. This excess occurs because e-mails can be easily created and copied to thousands of people through group mailbox systems.

A second problem is that e-mail is an ineffective medium for communicating emotions. For example, the emotion of sarcasm is difficult to convey through e-mail because the verbal message requires contrasting nonverbal cues. One scholar quipped that the result "of new information technologies within organizations has not been better communication, only faster misunderstandings." This problem is certainly true at Disney, where e-mail is the source of many conflicts. "Every fight that goes on [at Disney] seems to start with a misunderstanding over an e-mail," says Disney CEO Michael Eisner.[28] E-mail aficionados try to clarify the emotional tone of their messages by combining ASCII characters to form graphic faces called emoticons or "smileys." An entire lexicon of emoticons has developed, including those illustrated in Exhibit 11.3. However, some experts warn that smileys do not always solve the difficult task of communicating emotions through e-mail.[29]

A third problem is that e-mail seems to reduce our politeness and respect for others. This aspect is mostly evident through the increased frequency of **flaming**—the act of sending an emotionally charged message to others. Over half of the people questioned in one survey said they receive abusive flame mail and that men are both the most frequent victims and perpetrators.[30] The main cause of flaming is that people can post e-mail messages before their emotions subside, whereas the sender of a traditional memo or letter would have time for sober second thoughts.

Presumably, flaming and other e-mail problems will become less common as employees receive training on how to use this communication medium. For example, all new staff at the New Jersey Hospital Association (NJHA) attend a session where they learn how to create efficient and flame-proof e-mails.[31] The NJHA training also introduces employees to the largely unwritten and evolving

flaming
The act of sending an emotionally charged message to others.

EXHIBIT 11.3

Icons of emotion (emoticons) in e-mail messages

Icon	Meaning
:-)	Happy
:-}	Smirk
:-(	Unhappy
<:-)	Dumb question
0:-)	Angel (I'm being good)
:-p	Tongue sticking out
:-x	Oops!
{}	Hug
12x—<—@	A dozen roses

Source: Based on R. Peck, "Learning to Speak Computer Lingo," *(New Orleans) Times-Picayune*, June 5, 1997, p. E1; R. Weiland, "The Message Is the Medium," *Incentive*, September 1995, p. 37.

EXHIBIT 11.4

Some basic
e-mail netiquette

- DO fill in the subject line of the e-mail header with an informative description of the message.
- DO keep e-mail messages to fewer than 25 lines—the length of a typical computer screen.
- DO quote the relevant parts (but not necessarily all) of the receiver's previous message when replying to ideas in that message. (The automatic ">" indicates the original message.)
- DO respond to someone's e-mail (where a reply is expected) within one day for most business correspondence.
- DO switch from e-mail to telephone or face-to-face communication when the discussion gets too heated (flaming), the parties experience ongoing misunderstanding, or the issue becomes too complex.
- DON'T forward private messages without the permission of the original sender.
- DON'T send mass e-mails (using group lists) unless authorized to do so and the message definitely calls for this action.
- DON'T send large attachments if the receiver likely has a narrow bandwidth (computer data are transmitted slowly).
- DON'T use e-mail to communicate sensitive issues, such as disciplining someone, or to convey urgent information, such as rescheduling a meeting within the next hour.
- DON'T write messages in ALL CAPITALS because this conveys anger or shouting. (This rule also applies to **boldface** text as e-mail software develops this feature.)
- DON'T use emoticons excessively, and avoid them in formal business e-mails and when there is some chance that the receiver won't know their meaning.

Sources: Based on M. M. Extejt, "Teaching Students to Correspond Effectively Electronically; Tips for Using Electronic Mail Properly," *Business Communication Quarterly* 61 (June 1998), pp. 57+; K. Wasch, "Netiquette: Do's and Don'ts of E-mail Use," *Association Management* 49 (May 1997), pp. 76, 115.

code of conduct for communicating on the Internet, called *netiquette.* Exhibit 11.4 lists a few netiquette rules for e-mail.

Training may reduce some concerns with e-mail, but it cannot correct a fourth problem, namely, that e-mail lacks the warmth of human interaction.[32] As employees increasingly cocoon themselves through information technology, they lose the social support of human contact that potentially keeps their stress in check. Realizing this and other limitations of e-mail, some British companies are banning e-mail one day each week. As Global Connections 11.2 describes, these firms believe that some things are better discussed in person than in cyberspace.

Other Computer-Mediated Communication

IBM executives weren't surprised when a recent survey indicated that IBM employees rated co-workers as one of the two most credible or useful sources of information. What *did* surprise IBM executives was that the other equally credible and important source of information was IBM's intranet.[33] Intranets, extranets, instant messaging, and other forms of computer-mediated communication have fueled the hyperfast world of corporate information sharing.[34] Geographically dispersed work teams can coordinate their work more efficiently through instant messaging software and intranets. Suppliers are networked so tightly through computer-mediated technology that customers see them as one organization (see Chapter 17).

British Firms Encourage Live Conversation with E-mail–Free Fridays

The revolution started on a Friday. A maverick executive at the offices of Camelot, the national lottery operator, issued a startling edict: no more e-mails on the last day of the working week unless totally, absolutely necessary. Staff, it seemed, were forgetting how to talk to each other.

"We needed to make staff more aware of other forms of communication," explains Camelot spokeswoman Jenny Dowden. "If there were elements of the business where you could talk face-to-face instead of sending an e-mail, we wanted to encourage people to do that."

Nestlé Rowntree also decided it was time to discourage e-mail in favor of more personal conversations. By introducing "fewer–e-mail Fridays," the British confectioner hopes its employees will think more carefully about whether they need to copy messages to so many people and whether there are better ways of getting the message across.

"A no–e-mail Friday does two things," explains Andrew Harrison, the marketing director for Nestlé Rowntree. "It removes needless information flow across the organization and it forces people to talk face-to-face and agree on plans mutually. An e-mail ban begins to build a culture of designing and delivering ideas together."

How effective are these edicts to ban or minimize e-mail on Fridays? Camelot restricted its e-mail ban to four Fridays and is "still in the process of reviewing the results." But Jenny Dowden says the 50 e-mails she typically receives dropped to 3 or 4 on Fridays. Nestlé Rowntree executives also say they are noticing changing communication patterns. "People have started to think about how and what they are communicating and are refinding their voices," says one Nestlé manager.

Sources: J. Arlidge, "Office Staff Log Off for E-mail–Free Fridays," *The Observer (London)*, August 12, 2001; N. Muktarsingh, "Companies Rediscover the Power of Speech," *Mail on Sunday (London)*, July 22, 2001, p. 8; O. Burkeman, "Post Modern," *The Guardian (London)*, June 20, 2001.

Instant Messaging   *Instant messaging* appears to be the "next great thing" in technology-based communication. Instant messaging software connects two or more specific people and lets them push messages at each other. If you send an instant message to a co-worker who is connected, your message will instantly pop up on the co-worker's computer monitor (or other communications device). Instant messages are much briefer than e-mail, often relying on acronyms (such as R U THR for "Are you there?"). This efficiency and real-time communication explain why Ernst & Young, State Street Bank, Paine Webber, and other companies have implemented instant messaging. In fact, the number of corporate instant messaging users is expected to skyrocket from the 5.5 million in 2000 to more than 180 million in 2004.[35]

Consider the following example: if you require information for a client, you might log into the instant message service that connects to dozens of other employees in your area. Your message would pop up on their computers instantly, and the information you require could be available within minutes. "No other communications technology operates in situations like that in a time-efficient manner," says Andy Konchan, an executive at the financial planning firm UBS Warburg. "Clients are often taken aback by the speed with which we can now respond to specialized or unusual queries." UBS Warburg has thousands of instant messaging channels representing different knowledge or client interests. The company's 13,000 employees connect to the channels most closely aligned with their area of work.[36]

Instant messaging, e-mail, intranet sites, and other forms of computer-mediated communication each have their own advantages and disadvantages. However, they all have one clear benefit: They seem to reduce time and dissolve

Like most other executives, Adamee Itorcheak carries a laptop computer and cellular telephone almost everywhere he goes. The difference is that Itorcheak lives in Iqaluit, the capital city of Nunavut Territory in northern Canada, and his travels include traditional Inuit hunting trips in the Arctic wilderness. As president of Nunavut's largest Internet service provider and a partner in a high-speed wireless service, Itorcheak is probably the most wired person in the region. He is also wiring together most people in Nunavut, from a fish plant in Pangnirtung to a fishing guide in Clyde River. Through online forums and chat rooms, the people of Nunavut are becoming a more closely knit community. "Here in this huge territory, 20,000 people live in scattered groups," explains Itorcheak. "The Internet is the only way to bring us all together."[37] What are the limitations of Internet-based communication for people who rarely communicate face-to-face? *(Nick Didlick, Vancouver Sun)*

law of telecosm
States that as the web of computer networks expands, distances will shrink and eventually become irrelevant.

distances. This capability relates to the **law of telecosm,** which says that as the web of computer networks expands, distances will shrink and eventually become irrelevant.[38]

You might think that emerging computer-mediated technologies further increase information overload. Although this result is true for some forms of technology, preliminary evidence suggests that Internet-based communication actually *reduces* overload because it offers greater control over the amount of information flow. We decide how much information to receive from the Internet and intranet, whereas there is almost no control over the number of voice mails, faxes, and paper-based memos we receive. This conclusion is supported by a survey of executives in 11 countries. Half of them indicated that the Internet is reducing information overload; only 19 percent claim that it is making matters worse.[39]

Nonverbal Communication

Computer-mediated communication is changing the face of organizations, but it hasn't yet replaced nonverbal communication. Nonverbal communication includes facial expressions, voice intonation, physical distance, and even silence. This communication channel is necessary where physical distance or noise prevents effective verbal exchanges and the need for immediate feedback precludes written communication. But even in close face-to-face meetings, most information is communicated nonverbally.[40] Nonverbal communication is also important in emotional labour—the effort, planning, and control needed to express organizationally desired emotions (see Chapter 4). Employees make extensive use of nonverbal cues to transmit prescribed feelings to customers, co-workers, and others.

Nonverbal communication differs from verbal communication in several ways. First, verbal communication is typically conscious, whereas nonverbal communication is more automatic and unconscious. We normally plan the words we say or write, but rarely plan every blink, smile, or gesture during a conversation. Second, nonverbal communication is less rule-bound than verbal communication. We receive a lot of formal training on how to understand spoken words, but very little on understanding the nonverbal signals that accompany those words. Consequently, nonverbal cues are more ambiguous and more susceptible to misinterpretation.

Nonverbal communication is ambiguous, sometimes with dangerous consequences. Such a situation may have occurred on a Qantas flight as it tried to land on a rainy night at Bangkok International Airport. Less than 10 feet above the rain-soaked runway, the captain told the first officer to abort the landing. As the first officer reached for the thrust lever to pull the Boeing 747 out of its descent, the wheels touched the runway. A few seconds later, the captain decided to land rather than fly around, so he slid his right hand over the top of the first officer's left hand and moved the thrust levers to idle. Unfortunately, the captain didn't say anything as he took this action, which left the first officer unsure about who was in control. During the resulting confusion, no one noticed when the auto-brake system disarmed. The jet slid and shook its way down the runway, eventually stopping on its belly 200 yards past the end of the runway.[42] In your opinion, why didn't the captain use verbal communication when he changed his decision about landing the plane? *(P. Kittiwongsakul/AAP Photo)*

Emotional Contagion What happens when you see a co-worker accidentally bang his or her head against a filing cabinet? Chances are you wince and put your hand on your own head as if *you* had hit the cabinet. This automatic and unconscious tendency to mimic and synchronize our nonverbal behaviors with those of other people is called **emotional contagion.**[41] Emotional contagion is not a disease. It refers to the notion that we tend to "catch" other people's emotions by continually mimicking the facial expressions and nonverbal cues of others. For instance, listeners smile more and exhibit other emotional displays of happiness while hearing someone describe a positive event. Similarly, listeners will wince when the speaker describes an event in which she or he was hurt.

Emotional contagion serves three purposes. First, mimicry provides continual feedback, communicating that we understand and empathize with the sender. To consider the significance of this aspect, imagine if employees remained expressionless after watching a co-worker bang his or her head. The lack of parallel behavior conveys a lack of understanding or caring. Second, mimicking the nonverbal behaviors of other people seems to be a way of receiving emotional meaning from those people. If a co-worker is angry with a client, your tendency to frown and show anger while listening helps you share that emotion more fully. In other words, we receive meaning by expressing the sender's emotions as well as by listening to the sender's words.

Lastly, emotional contagion is a type of social glue that bonds people together. Social solidarity is built out of each member's awareness of a collective sentiment. Through nonverbal expressions of emotional contagion, people see others share the same emotions that they feel. This common or mutual expression of emotions strengthens team cohesiveness by providing evidence of member similarity.

CHOOSING THE BEST COMMUNICATION CHANNELS

Employees perform better if they can quickly determine the best communication channels for the situation and are flexible enough to use different methods, as the occasion requires.[43] But which communication channels are most appropriate? We partly answered this question in our evaluation of the different communication channels. However, two additional contingencies worth noting are media richness and symbolic meaning.

Media Richness

Soon after Ernst & Young encouraged its employees around the globe to form virtual teams, the accounting firm realized that e-mail and voice mail weren't sufficient for these groups. "Try coming to an agreement on the verbiage of a legal contract with a team of lawyers and engineers representing multiple interests using only the telephone and e-mail," quips John Whyte, Ernst & Young's chief information officer. "You can spend weeks sorting through fragmented e-mail conversations or individual phone calls and voice mails." Now employees discuss complex issues through special software that provides a virtual whiteboard on the computer screen and allows real-time chat (instant messaging). It's not quite as good as face-to-face meetings, but it is much better than the previous patchwork of e-mail and telephone calls.[44]

Ernst & Young discovered that some issues require more **media richness** than e-mail and telephone messages can offer. Media richness refers to the medium's *data-carrying capacity*—the volume and variety of information that can be transmitted.[45] Face-to-face meetings have the highest data-carrying capacity because the sender simultaneously uses multiple communication channels (verbal and nonverbal), the receiver can provide immediate feedback, and the information exchange can be customized to suit the situation. Instant messaging would be somewhat lower in the hierarchy, and e-mail is below instant messaging software. Financial reports and other impersonal documents represent the leanest media because they allow only one form of data transmission (written), the sender does not receive timely feedback from the receiver, and the information exchange is standardized for everyone.

Exhibit 11.5 shows that rich media are better than lean media when the communication situation is nonroutine or ambiguous. Nonroutine situations require rich media because the sender and receiver have little common experience and therefore need to transmit a large volume of information with immediate feedback. During emergencies, for instance, you should use face-to-face meetings to coordinate work efforts quickly and minimize the risk of misunderstanding and confusion. Lean media may be used in routine situations because the sender and receiver have common expectations through

EXHIBIT 11.5   A hierarchy of media richness

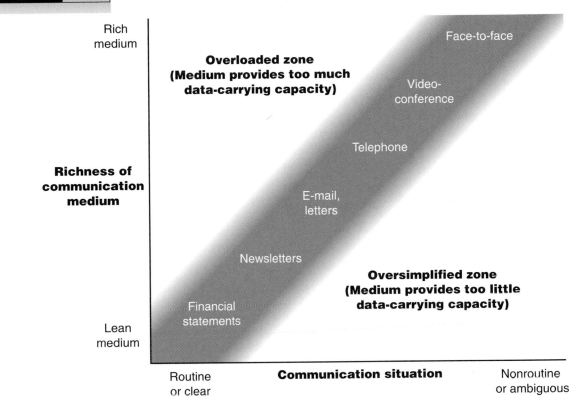

Source: Based on R. Lengel and R. Daft, "The Selection of Communication Media as an Executive Skill," *Academy of Management Executive* 2, no. 3 (August 1988), p. 226; R. L. Daft and R. H. Lengel, "Information Richness: A New Approach to Managerial Behavior and Organization Design," *Research in Organizational Behavior*, 1984, p. 199.

shared mental models.[46] Ambiguous issues, such as Ernst & Young's contract work, also require rich media because the parties must share large amounts of information with immediate feedback to resolve multiple and conflicting interpretations of their observations and experiences. For instance, research indicates that product development presents several ill-defined issues, so team members work better with face-to-face communication than with leaner media.[47]

What happens when we choose the wrong level of media richness for the situation? When the situation is routine or clear, using a rich medium—such as holding a special meeting—would seem like a waste of time. On the other hand, if a unique and ambiguous issue is handled through lean media—such as e-mail—issues take longer to resolve and misunderstandings are more likely to occur. This is the problem that employees at Ernst & Young experienced.

One last point about media richness is that we need to consider previous experience with both the media and the other person in the information exchange. People who have plenty of experience with a particular communication medium can "push" the amount of media richness normally possible through that information channel. Such efficient use of a medium seems to allow more information flow than the channel would allow for people who are new to the medium. Similarly, we can sometimes rely on leaner media when communicating with people who are familiar to us. This familiarity means that the sender and receiver often share common mental models, which reduces the volume of information transmitted.[48]

Symbolic Meaning of the Medium

"The medium is the message."[49] This famous phrase by Marshall McLuhan means that the sender's choice of communication channel transmits meaning beyond the message content. For example, a personal meeting with an employee may indicate that the issue is important, whereas a brief handwritten note may suggest less importance.

The difficulty we face when choosing a communication medium is that its symbolic meaning may vary from one person to the next. Some people view e-mail as a symbol of professionalism, whereas others see it as evidence of the sender's efficiency. Still others might view an e-mail message as a low-status clerical activity because it involves typing.[50] Overall, we must be sensitive to the symbolic meaning of the selected communication medium to ensure that it amplifies rather than contradicts the meaning found in the message content.

COMMUNICATING IN ORGANIZATIONAL HIERARCHIES

In this era when knowledge is competitive advantage, corporate leaders need to maintain an open flow of communication up, down, and across the organization. In this section, we discuss four communication strategies: newsletters and e-zines, work space design, employee surveys, and management by walking around.

Newsletters and E-zines

A decade ago, Hughes Software Systems (HSS) in India had 50 employees and mainly gathered them into a meeting to share company news. Today, HSS employs 1,300 people, so it depends on various electronic and paper media to keep everyone informed. Employees receive hard-copy newsletters about company developments, but they also receive timely information through HSS's intranet. If that's not enough, HSS has an electronic message board called "Junk," where employees share their views on everything from the quality of cafeteria food to ways to get around the electronic blockades HSS has placed on sports websites.[51]

Hughes Software Systems and other large organizations are increasingly applying a multipronged communication strategy to share information with employees. This strategy typically includes both print-based newsletters and web-based electronic newsletters, called e-zines. For example, Hewlett-Packard (HP) posts late-breaking company news every day in its intranet-based publication called *hpNow*. Several times each year, HP employees also receive a print magazine called *Invent*, which features longer, more in-depth articles. HP and other firms have discovered that one communication medium is not enough. Online sources offer instant communication, but many employees still have difficulty reading long articles on a computer screen. Print articles are slower and more costly, but they currently offer more portability than online publications.[52]

Work Space Design

There's nothing like a wall to prevent employees from talking to each other. That's why Phonak, a hearing aid manufacturer in Warrenville, Illinois, has very few walls to block communication. "We're in the communications business," says Phonak CEO Michael R. Jones. "We have no offices and a very open floor plan to foster communication." Other companies have kept the walls up but have rearranged the hallways to support spontaneous, horizontal communication. Seagate Software's offices in Vancouver, Canada, include extrawide hallways so that employees can chat without blocking others. Pearl Assurance, the British financial services group, installed "pit stop" areas along the hallways where people can spontaneously meet and share information.[53]

Do these open-space offices actually improve communication? Anecdotal evidence lends support to the thesis that people communicate more often with fewer walls between them. However, scientific research also suggests that open office design potentially increases employee stress because of the loss of privacy and personal space.[54] Some employees at the offices of TBWA Chiat/Day resorted to making telephone calls in bathroom stalls and under their desks after the Los Angeles advertising firm moved to open offices. The firm has since reverted to a "nesting" model that consists of some private individual space as well as open space for collaboration. According to an analysis of 13,000 employee surveys in 40 major organizations, work space primarily contributes to individual performance by providing a place to concentrate on work without distraction. The second most important influence of work space on performance is how it facilitates informal communication with co-workers. Thus, work space must encourage social interaction, but it also must support a person's need for some privacy.[55]

SEI Investments breaks anyone's stereotype of an investment firm. SEI employees are housed in five colorful buildings in the countryside of Oaks, Pennsylvania. Approximately 150 employees congregate in large, open rooms with windows all around. No walls or cubicle dividers separate work spaces. Each person has a desk on wheels, which is easily moved around to form spontaneous teams. Cables spiral down from the ceilings so that each desk is quickly reconnected to telephone, electricity, and an intranet port in the new location. "It's much, much easier to get things done when everyone is right there working together," says an SEI employee.[56] What are the potential problems of SEI's open office design? *(Tim Hursley/The Arkansas Office)*

Employee Surveys

Many large companies regularly survey employees on a variety of issues. Some surveys measure job satisfaction and loyalty to identify potential morale and employee turnover problems. Companies depend on these job satisfaction surveys for 360-degree feedback for managers, which can influence their performance bonus.

Other organizations use surveys to involve employees in decisions on everything from dress codes to pension plans.[57] For example, Eli Lilly & Company conducted a census of its 14,500 U.S. employees to find out what hours they prefer working. The pharmaceutical company learned that the hours it had mandated for decades were out of date and out of favor. Eli Lilly now offers more flexible hours and optional compressed workweeks.[58]

Management by Walking Around

Cisco Systems is the world's largest manufacturer of routers and other products that run the Internet. Yet John Chambers, Cisco's CEO, doesn't communicate

The uncertain future of Mitsubishi Motors Australia Ltd. (MMAL) has kept CEO Tom Phillips busy as a corporate communicator. When rumors circulated that Mitsubishi headquarters in Japan would shut down the Adelaide-based automaker, Phillips met employees on the assembly line to dispel those myths. When MMAL received a large capital injection, Phillips invited every employee and supplier representative to a meeting (shown in photo) to announce the deal. As the plant thumped to rock music, Phillips led MMAL's 3,200 employees in a human wave, such as the ones seen at sporting events, then told them their future looked stronger than ever. A few months later, when Mitsubishi officially ruled out closing the Adelaide plant, Phillips was quick to communicate the good news to everyone. "I'm going down the (assembly) line tomorrow to shake hands and slap backs," said Phillips when he received the good news.[61] Why should corporate leaders personally meet with employees rather than send a memo under these circumstances? *(Russell Millard/The Advertiser)*

just through e-mail or websites. He believes that executives need to regularly meet face-to-face with employees. In other words, corporate leaders need to practice **management by walking around (MBWA).** Coined several years ago at Hewlett-Packard, MBWA means that executives should get out of their offices and learn from others in the organization through face-to-face dialogue.[59] MBWA minimizes filtering because executives listen directly to employees. It also helps executives acquire a deeper meaning and quicker understanding of internal organizational problems.

MBWA can take many forms. Jonathan Hakim, managing director of Hong Kong start-up incubator tp Labs (a subsidary of techpacific.com), likes to break the ice with employees by breaking out the cue sticks for a game of pool in the company's expansive lounge. Richard Zuschlag, CEO of Acadian Ambulance & Air Med Services Inc. in Louisiana, takes the old-fashioned route by wandering around the company's offices and chatting with employees. "I'm a very curious person," explains Zuschlag. "Just walking around and asking a lot of my dumb questions is how I find out what's going on." John Chambers and other Cisco executives attend monthly "birthday breakfasts" with several dozen employees with birthdays in that month. "The birthday breakfast is the most effective vehicle for getting candid feedback from employees and for discovering potential problems," says Chambers.[60]

COMMUNICATING THROUGH THE GRAPEVINE

Whether or not executives get out of their offices, employees will always rely on the oldest communication channel: the corporate **grapevine.** The grapevine is an unstructured and informal network founded on social relationships rather than organizational charts or job descriptions. According to some estimates, 75 percent of employees typically receive news from the grapevine before they hear about it through formal channels.[62]

Grapevine Characteristics

Early research identified several unique features of the grapevine.[63] It transmits information very rapidly in all directions throughout the organization. The typical pattern is a cluster chain, whereby a few people actively transmit rumors to many others. The grapevine works through informal social networks, so it is more active where employees have similar backgrounds and are able to communicate easily. Many rumors seem to have at least a kernel of truth, possibly because rumors are transmitted through media-rich communication channels (e.g., face-to-face) and employees are motivated to communicate effectively. Nevertheless, the grapevine distorts information by deleting fine details and exaggerating key points of the message.

The problem with some of these earlier findings is that they might not be representative of the grapevine in this era of information technology. E-mail and instant messaging have replaced the traditional watercooler as the main place where people share gossip. Social networks have expanded as employees communicate with each other around the globe, not just around the next cubicle. Vault.com and other public websites have become virtual watercoolers by posting anonymous comments about specific companies for all to view. This technology extends gossip to anyone, not just employees connected to social networks.

management by walking around (MBWA)
A communication practice in which executives get out of their offices and learn from others in the organization through face-to-face dialogue.

grapevine
An unstructured and informal communication network founded on social relationships rather than organizational charts or job descriptions.

For many employees, the corporate grapevine is now connected to the Internet through Vault.com and other websites. The corporate grapevine is "no longer just four staffers huddling around a dusty watercooler," says Vault co-founder Mark Oldman. "Now there are thousands of people around the world comparing notes." Vault.com has message boards for hundreds of companies. Post some hearsay or an opinion about a particular firm and the world will know about it in seconds. "[W]ith the power of the Internet, there is more of a global and real-time flow to rumors and gossip," says Oldman. Vault.com estimates that up to 9 percent of Goldman Sachs employees check in with Vault's Goldman board during any given week.[66] In your opinion, how does the Internet potentially change the pattern of grapevine information and the accuracy of that information? (*Reprinted with permission of Vault.com—The Insider Career Network, www.vault.com*)

Grapevine Advantages and Disadvantages

Should the grapevine be encouraged, tolerated, or quashed? The difficulty in answering this question is that the grapevine has both advantages and disadvantages. One benefit is that the grapevine helps employees make sense of their workplace when the information is not available through formal channels.[64] It is also the main conduit through which organizational stories and other symbols of the organization's culture are communicated (see Chapter 15).

A third advantage of the grapevine is that this social interaction relieves anxiety and fulfills the need for affiliation.[65] This point explains why rumor mills are most active during times of uncertainty. Finally, because the grapevine is most active when employees are anxious, it is a valuable signal for corporate leaders to take appropriate action. Such action may include resolving the problems behind the rumors or communicating more fully through formal networks.

The grapevine is not always beneficial. Morale tumbles when management is slower than the grapevine in communicating information, because the lag suggests a lack of sincerity and concern for employees. Moreover, grapevine information may become sufficiently distorted that it escalates rather than reduces employee anxieties. This result is most likely when the original information is transmitted through several people rather than by one or two people.

Companies have tried to learn the identities of people who post anonymous rumors on websites, but their quest usually fails. City officials in Cascavel, Brazil, have banned employees from engaging in spreading office gossip, but the grapevine will always exist. A better strategy, as mentioned earlier, is to listen to the grapevine as a signal of employee anxiety and then correct the cause of that anxiety. Some companies also listen to the grapevine and step in to correct blatant errors and fabrications. Shaw's Supermarkets Inc. took this approach after a false rumor quickly spread that the West Bridgewater, Massachusetts, grocery store chain was about to be sold. An online newsletter—appropriately called *The Rumor Buster*—was set up to correct this and subsequent errors.[67]

CROSS-CULTURAL AND GENDER COMMUNICATION

In a world of increasing globalization and cultural diversity, organizations face opportunities as well as communication challenges. Employees must become more sensitive and competent in cross-cultural communication. They must also overcome their reluctance to communicate with co-workers from another cultural group. These communication competencies are also gaining importance as companies increasingly work with clients, suppliers, and joint venture partners from other countries.

Language is the most obvious cross-cultural barrier.[68] Words are easily misunderstood in verbal communication, either because the receiver has a limited vocabulary or the sender's accent makes it difficult for the receiver to understand the sound. The issue is further complicated in global organizations where employees from non-English countries often rely on English as the common business language. On top of other communication problems, English words have different meanings across cultures. For example, a French executive might call an event a "catastrophe" as a casual exaggeration, but the term is often taken to mean an earth-shaking event by someone in Germany.[69]

Mastering the same language improves one dimension of cross-cultural communication, but problems may still occur when interpreting voice intonation.[70] A deep voice symbolizes masculinity in North America, but African men often express their emotions using a high-pitched voice. Middle Easterners sometimes speak loudly to show sincerity and interest in the discussion, whereas Japanese people tend to speak softly to communicate politeness or humility. These different cultural norms regarding voice volume may cause one person to misinterpret the other.

Nonverbal Differences

Nonverbal communication is more important in some cultures than in others. For example, people in Japan interpret much of a message's meaning from nonverbal cues. "A lot of Japanese is either unspoken or communicated through body language," explains Henry Wallace, the Scottish-born CEO of Mazda Corporation in Japan.[71] To avoid offending or embarrassing the receiver (particularly outsiders), Japanese people will often say what the other person wants to hear (called *tatemae*) but send more subtle nonverbal cues indicating the sender's true feelings (called *honne*).[72] A Japanese colleague might politely reject your business proposal by saying "I will think about that," while sending nonverbal signals that he or she is not really interested. This difference explains why Japanese employees may prefer direct conversation to e-mail and other media that lack nonverbal cues.

Most nonverbal cues are specific to a particular culture and may have a completely different meaning to people raised in other cultures. For example, most of us shake our head from side to side to say "no," but a variation of head shaking means "I understand" to some people from India. Filipinos raise their eyebrows to give an affirmative answer, yet Arabs interpret this expression (along with clicking one's tongue) as a negative response. Most Americans are taught to maintain eye contact with the speaker to show interest and respect, yet Native Americans, Australian Aborigines, and others learn at an early age to show respect by looking down when an older or more senior person is talking to them.[73]

Even the common handshake communicates different meaning across cultures. Westerners tend to appreciate a firm handshake as a sign of strength and warmth in a friendship or business relationship. In contrast, many Asians and Middle Easterners favor a loose grip and regard a firm clench as aggressive. Germans prefer one good handshake stroke, whereas anything less than five or six strokes may symbolize a lack of trust in Spain. If this isn't confusing enough, people from some cultures view any touching in public—including handshakes—as a sign of rudeness.

Silence and Conversational Overlaps Communication includes the silence between our words and gestures. However, the meaning of silence varies from one culture to another. In Japan, people tend to show respect for the speaker by remaining silent for a few seconds after the person has spoken to contemplate what has just been said.[74] To them, silence is an important part of communication (called *haragei*) because it preserves harmony and is more reliable than talk. Silence is shared by everyone and belongs to no one, so it becomes the ultimate form of interdependence. Moreover, Japanese value empathy, which can only be demonstrated by understanding others without using words.

In contrast, most people in the United States and Canada view silence as a *lack* of communication and often interpret long breaks as a sign of disagreement. For example, after presenting their proposal to a potential Japanese client, a group of American consultants expected to be bombarded with questions. Instead, their proposal was greeted with a long silence. As the silence continued, most of the consultants concluded that the Japanese client disapproved, so they prepared to pack and leave. But the lead consultant gestured them to stop, because the client's face and posture seemed to indicate interest rather than rejection. He was right: When the client finally spoke, it was to give the consulting firm the job.[75]

Conversational overlaps also send different messages in different cultures. Japanese usually stop talking when they are interrupted, whereas talking over the other person's speech is more common in Brazil and some other countries. Talking while someone is speaking to you is considered quite rude in Japan, whereas Brazilians are more likely to interpret this conversational overlap as the person's interest and involvement in the conversation.

Gender Differences in Communication

Soon after Susan Herring joined her first Internet discussion group, she noticed that men were much more likely than women to engage in cantankerous debates with their own combative and condescending e-mail messages. To pique her curiosity, the linguistics professor asked list-group subscribers to tell her what they thought of these e-mail "flame wars." The anonymous, informal poll revealed that men generally accepted this communication style and usually found the barbs entertaining. Most women, on the other hand, were offended or cautious when these debates erupted.[76]

Herring and other scholars have observed that men and women often differ in their communication styles. Whether in a corporate meeting or a virtual chat room, men are more likely than women to view conversations as negotiations of relative status and power.[77] They assert their power by directly giving advice to others (e.g., "You should do the following") and using combative language.

There is also evidence that men interrupt women far more often than vice versa and that they dominate the talk time in conversations with women.

Men tend to engage in "report talk," in which the primary function of the conversation is impersonal and efficient information exchange. This behavior may explain why men tend to quantify information (e.g., "It took us six weeks"). Women also engage in report talk, particularly when conversing with men. But conversations among women tend to have a higher incidence of relationship building through "rapport talk." Thus, women use more intensive adverbs ("I was *so happy* that he completed the report") and hedge their statements ("It seems to be . . ."). Rather than asserting status, women use indirect requests ("Have you considered . . .?"). Similarly, women apologize more often and seek advice from others more quickly than do men. Finally, research supports the belief that women are more sensitive than men to nonverbal cues in face-to-face meetings.[78]

After reading some popular-press books, you would think that men and women come from different planets (Mars and Venus) and require United Nations translators![79] This is not so. Although we have identified several differences, men and women mostly overlap in their verbal communication styles. Some men are very passive conversationalists, and some women are aggressive. Moreover, we know that women (and, to a lesser extent, men) vary their communication styles with the situation.

Both men and women usually understand each other, but there are irritants. For instance, Susan Herring and other women feel uncomfortable with aggressive male communication styles on the Internet. Female scientists have similarly complained that adversarial interaction among male scientists makes it difficult for women to participate in meaningful dialogue.[80]

Another irritant occurs when women seek empathy but receive male dominance in response. Specifically, women sometimes discuss their personal experiences and problems to develop closeness with the receiver. They look for expressions of understanding, such as "That's the way I felt when it happened to me." But when men hear problems, they quickly suggest solutions because this response asserts their control over the situation. As well as frustrating a woman's need for common understanding, the advice actually says, "You and I are different; you have the problem and I have the answer." Meanwhile, men become frustrated because they can't understand why women don't appreciate their advice.

IMPROVING INTERPERSONAL COMMUNICATION

Effective interpersonal communication depends on the sender's ability to get the message across and the receiver's performance as an active listener. In this section, we outline these two essential features of effective interpersonal communication.

Getting Your Message Across

This chapter began with the statement that effective communication occurs when the other person receives and understands the message. To accomplish this difficult task, the sender must learn to empathize with the receiver, repeat the message, choose an appropriate time for the conversation, and be descriptive rather than evaluative.

- ▪ *Empathize*—Recall from Chapter 3 that empathy is a person's ability to understand and be sensitive to the feelings, thoughts, and situation of others. In conversations, empathy involves putting yourself in the receiver's shoes when encoding the message. For instance, be sensitive to words that may be ambiguous or trigger the wrong emotional response.
- ▪ *Repeat the message*—Rephrase the key points a couple of times. The saying "Tell them what you're going to tell them; tell them; then tell them what you've told them" reflects this need for redundancy.
- ▪ *Use timing effectively*—Your message competes with other messages and noise, so find a time when the receiver is less likely to be distracted by these other matters.
- ▪ *Be descriptive*— Focus on the problem, not the person, if you have negative information to convey. People stop listening when the information attacks their self-esteem. Also, suggest things the listener can do to improve, rather than pointing to him or her as the problem.

Active Listening

Darryl Heustis admits that he isn't always good at listening to other people. "I've had the unique ability to start formulating my response before the person is through with the question," says Heustis sheepishly. Fortunately, Heustis, who is the vice president for medical affairs at the Jerry L. Pettis Memorial VA Medical Center in Loma Linda, California, and his colleagues have completed training that helps them listen more actively to what others are saying. "Now, I've learned to practice my listening skills and observation skills. I've improved at watching people carefully, looking for body language and other signals of what they're feeling."[81]

Darryl Heustis and other executives are discovering that listening is at least as important as talking. As one sage wisely wrote: "Nature gave people two ears but only one tongue, which is a gentle hint that they should listen more than they talk."[82] But listening is more than just hearing the other person making sounds; it is a process of actively sensing the sender's signals, evaluating them accurately, and responding appropriately.

These three components of listening—sensing, evaluating, and responding—reflect the listener's side of the communication model described at the beginning of this chapter.[83] Listeners receive the sender's signals, decode them as intended, and provide appropriate and timely feedback to the sender. Active listeners constantly cycle through sensing, evaluating, and responding during the conversation and engage in various activities to improve these processes (see Exhibit 11.6).

Sensing   Sensing is the process of receiving signals from the sender and paying attention to them. These signals include the words spoken, the nature of the sounds (speed of speech, tone of voice, etc.), and nonverbal cues. Active listeners improve sensing by postponing evaluation, avoiding interruptions, and maintaining interest.

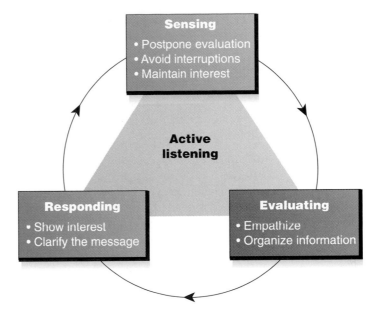

EXHIBIT 11.6

Components of
active listening

Sensing
- Postpone evaluation
- Avoid interruptions
- Maintain interest

Active listening

Responding
- Show interest
- Clarify the message

Evaluating
- Empathize
- Organize information

- *Postpone evaluation*—Many listeners become victims of first impressions (see Chapter 3). They quickly form an opinion of the speaker's message and subsequently screen out important information. Active listeners, on the other hand, try to stay as open-minded as possible by delaying evaluation of the message until the speaker has finished.

- *Avoid interruptions*—Interrupting the speaker's conversation has two adverse effects on the sensing process. First, it disrupts the speaker's idea, so the listener does not receive the entire message. Second, interruptions tend to second-guess what the speaker is trying to say, which contributes to the problem of evaluating the speaker's ideas too early.

- *Maintain interest*—As with any other behavior, active listening requires motivation. Too often, we close our minds soon after a conversation begins because the subject is boring. Instead, active listeners maintain interest by taking the view—probably an accurate one—that there is always something of value in a conversation; it's just a matter of actively looking for it.

Evaluating This component of listening includes understanding the message meaning, evaluating the message, and remembering the message. To improve their evaluation of the conversation, active listeners empathize with the speaker and organize information received during the conversation.

- *Empathize*—Active listeners try to understand and be sensitive to the speaker's feelings, thoughts, and situation. Empathy is a critical skill in active listening because the verbal and nonverbal cues from the conversation are accurately interpreted from the other person's point of view.

- *Organize information*—Listeners process information three times faster than the average rate of speech (450 words per minute versus 125 words per minute), so they are easily distracted. Active listeners use this spare time to organize the information into key points. In fact, it's a good idea to imagine that you must summarize what people have said after they are finished speaking.[84]

Responding   Responding, the third component of listening, refers to the listener's development and display of behaviors that support the communication process. Responsiveness is feedback to the sender, which motivates and directs the speaker's communication. Active listeners respond by showing interest and clarifying the message.

■ *Show interest*—Active listeners show interest by maintaining sufficient eye contact and sending back-channel signals such as "Oh, really!" and "I see" during appropriate breaks in the conversation.

■ *Clarify the message*—Active listeners provide feedback by rephrasing the speaker's ideas at appropriate breaks ("So you're saying that . . . ?"). This response further demonstrates interest in the conversation and helps the speaker determine whether you understand the message.

Communication is a complex process of transmitting and understanding information between two or more people. We communicate to make better decisions, distribute valued knowledge, coordinate work, and fulfill social needs. Communication is also an integral part of most processes to gain power, apply organizational politics, and persuade people to change their beliefs and attitudes. These three processes are the themes of the next chapter.

CHAPTER SUMMARY

Communication supports knowledge management, decision making, work coordination, and the need for affiliation. The communication process involves forming, encoding, and transmitting the intended message to a receiver, who then decodes the message and provides feedback to the sender. Effective communication occurs when the sender's thoughts are transmitted to and understood by the intended receiver.

Several barriers create noise in the communication process. People misinterpret messages because of perceptual biases. Some information is filtered out as it gets passed up the hierarchy. Jargon and ambiguous language are barriers when the sender and receiver have different interpretations of the words and symbols used. People also screen out or misinterpret messages as a result of information overload.

Electronic mail (e-mail) is a powerful way to communicate, and it has changed communication patterns in organizational settings. However, e-mail also contributes to information overload, is an ineffective channel for communicating emotions, tends to reduce politeness and respect in the communication process, and lacks the warmth of human interaction.

Computer-mediated communication gives employees the freedom to communicate effectively from any location. This capability is part of the law of telecosm, which says that distances will shrink and eventually become irrelevant as the web of computer networks expands.

Nonverbal communication includes facial expressions, voice intonation, physical distance, and even silence. Employees make extensive use of nonverbal cues when engaging in emotional labor because these cues help transmit prescribed feelings to customers, co-workers, and others. Emotional contagion refers to the automatic and subconscious tendency to mimic and synchronize our nonverbal behaviors with those of other people.

The most appropriate communication medium depends on its data-carrying capacity (media richness) and its symbolic meaning to the receiver. Nonroutine and ambiguous situations require rich media.

Many organizations rely on a combination of print newsletters and intranet-based e-zines to communicate corporate news. Some companies also try to encourage informal communication through work space design, although open offices run the risk of increasing stress and reducing the ability to concentrate on work. Employee surveys are widely used to measure employee attitudes or involve employees in corporate decisions. Some executives also engage in management by walking around to facilitate communication across the organization.

In any organization, employees rely on the grapevine, particularly during times of uncertainty. The grapevine is an unstructured and informal network founded on social relationships rather than organizational charts or job descriptions. Although early research identified several unique features of the grapevine, some of these features may be changing as the Internet plays an increasing role in grapevine communication.

Globalization and workforce diversity have brought new communication challenges. Words are easily misunderstood in verbal communication, and employees are reluctant to communicate across cultures. Voice intonation, silence, and other nonverbal cues have different meanings and degrees of importance in different cultures. There are also some communication differences between men and women, such as the tendency for men to exert status and engage in report talk in conversations, whereas women use more rapport talk and are more sensitive than are men to nonverbal cues.

To get a message across, the sender must learn to empathize with the receiver, repeat the message, choose an appropriate time for the conversation, and be descriptive rather than evaluative. Listening includes sensing, evaluating, and responding. Active listeners support these processes by postponing evaluation, avoiding interruptions, maintaining interest, empathizing, organizing information, showing interest, and clarifying the message.

KEY TERMS

communication, p. 322

communication competence, p. 322

emotional contagion, p. 334

flaming, p. 329

grapevine, p. 339

information overload, p. 327

jargon, p. 325

law of telecosm, p. 332

management by walking around (MBWA), p. 339

media richness, p. 334

DISCUSSION QUESTIONS

1. A city government intends to introduce electronic mail for office staff at its three buildings located throughout the city. Describe two benefits as well as two potential problems that city government employees will likely experience with this medium.

2. Instant messaging will become an increasingly popular form of information technology over the next few years. What are the advantages and disadvantages of this communication medium compared with e-mail and intranet communication?

3. Marshall McLuhan coined this popular phrase: "The medium is the message." What does the phrase mean, and why should we be aware of it when communicating in organizations?

4. Why is emotional contagion important in organizations, and what effect does the increasing reliance on e-mail have on this phenomenon?

5. An executive recently admitted that she deliberately leaks information through the organizational grapevine before communicating the information through formal channels. The reason, she explains, is to give employees an opportunity to think about the information. "[B]y the time the message is formally announced, everybody has had a chance to think about it and feel like they're on the inside track." Discuss the advantages and limitations of this communication strategy.

6. The Bank of Key Largo (BKL) has just moved into one of the tallest buildings in Miami. Senior management is proud of its decision, because each department is neatly located on its own floor with plenty of closed offices. BKL executives have a breathtaking view from their offices on the top floor. There is even a large BKL branch at street level. Unfortunately, other tenants occupy some floors between those leased by BKL. Discuss the potential effects of this physical structure on communication at BKL.

7. Explain why men and women are sometimes frustrated with each other's communication behaviors.

8. This chapter describes several features of communication in Japan. Discuss three features of communication in Japan that differ from communication where you live.

SEA PINES

The coastal town of Sea Pines, Maine, retained a Boston consulting engineer to study the effect of greatly expanding the town's sewage system and discharging the treated waste into the harbor. At that time, fishermen in the town were experiencing massive lobster kills in the harbor and were concerned that the kills were caused by the effluent from the present Sea Pines sewage treatment plant. They were convinced that any expansion of the plant would further aggravate the problem. The fishermen invited Tom Stone, the engineer, to the monthly meeting of the local fishermen's organization to discuss their concerns. On the night of the meeting, the Legion Hall was filled with men in blue jeans and work jackets, many of whom were drinking beer. An account of this meeting follows, with Fred Mitchell, a local fisherman, speaking first.

Mitchell: Well, as you all know, Mr. Stone has been kind enough to meet with us tonight to explain his recommendations concerning the town's sewage disposal problem. We're all concerned about the lobster kills, like the one last summer, and I for one don't want to see any more sewage dumped into that harbor. [*Murmurs of assent are heard throughout the hall.*] So, Mr. Stone, we'd like to hear from you on what it is you want to do.

Stone: Thank you. I'm glad to get this opportunity to hear your concerns on the lobster situation. Let me say from the outset that we are still studying the problem closely and expect to make our formal recommendation to the town about a month from now. I am not prepared to discuss specific conclusions of our study, but I am prepared to incorporate any relevant comments into our study. As most of you are probably aware, we are attempting to model mathematically, or simulate, conditions in the harbor to help us predict the effects of sewage effluent in the harbor. We . . .

Mitchell: Now wait a minute. I don't know anything about models except the kind I used to make as a kid. [*Laughter.*] I can tell you that we never had lobster kills like we have now until they started dumping that sewage into the

harbor a few years back. I don't need any model to tell me that. It seems to me that common sense tells you that if we've got troubles now in the summer with the lobster, that increasing the amount of sewage by 10 times the present amount is going to cause 10 times the problem.

A Fisherman: Yeah, you don't need to be an engineer to see that.

Stone: Although it's true that we're proposing to extend the sewage system in town, and that the resulting sewage flow will be about 10 times the present flow, the area of the sewage discharge will be moved to a larger area of the harbor, where it will be diluted with much more seawater than in the present area. In addition, if the harbor is selected for the new discharge, we will design a special diffuser to mix the treated sewage effluent quickly with ocean water. As I indicated, we are attempting to use data on currents and water quality that we collected in the harbor and combine that data with some mathematical equations in our computer to help us predict what the quality in the harbor will be.

Mitchell: I don't understand what you need a computer to tell you that for. I've been fishing in this area for over 35 years now, and I don't need any computer to tell me that my lobsters are going to die if that sewage goes into the harbor.

Stone: Let me say before this goes too far that we're not talking about discharging raw sewage into the harbor. The sewage is treated and disinfected before it is discharged.

Mitchell: Isn't the sewage that's being dumped into the harbor right now being treated and disinfected, Mr. Stone?

Stone: Yes, it is, but . . .

Mitchell: The lobsters still die, so it's clear to me that "treated and disinfected" doesn't solve the problem.

Stone: Our model will predict whether the treatment provided will be sufficient to maintain the water quality in the harbor at the state's standard for the harbor.

Mitchell: I don't give a damn about any state standard. I just care about my lobsters and how I'm going to put bread on the table for my kids! You engineers from Boston can come out here spouting all kinds of things about models, data, standards, and your concern for lobsters, but what it really comes down to is that it's just another job. You can collect your fees for your study, go back to your office, and leave us holding the bag.

Stone: Now wait a minute, Mr. Mitchell. My firm is well established in New England, and we didn't get that way by giving our clients that fast shuffle and making a quick exit out of town. We have no intention of leaving you with an unworkable solution to your sewage problems. We also will not solve your sewage problem and leave you with a lobster kill problem. Perhaps I have given you the wrong impression about this modeling. We regard this as one method of analysis that may be helpful in predicting future harbor conditions, but not the only method. We have over 40 years' experience in these harbor studies, and we fully intend to use this experience, *in addition to* whatever the model tells us, to come up with a reasonable solution.

Mitchell: Well, that's all well and good, but I can tell you, and I think I speak for all the lobstermen here, that if you recommend dumping that sewage into the harbor, we'll fight you all the way down the line! [*Shouts of agreement.*] Why can't you pipe the sewage out to the ocean if you're so concerned about dilution? I'm sure that your model will tell you there's enough dilution out there.

Stone: I agree that the ocean would certainly provide sufficient dilution, but the whole purpose of this study is to see if we can avoid a deep ocean outfall.

Mitchell: Why?

Stone: Because the cost of constructing a deep ocean outfall in this area is very expensive—say about $700 per yard. Now, if the length of the outfall is 2,000 yards, don't you think that it makes good sense to spend a few thousand dollars studying the harbor area if we can save you millions?

Mitchell: All that money that you're going to save the town doesn't do much for the lobstermen who'll be put out of business if that sewage goes into the harbor.

Stone: As I said, we wouldn't recommend that if we thought, based on our modeling and our experience in this area, that the quality of water in the harbor would kill any lobster or any other aquatic life.

Mitchell: Well, I'm telling you again, if you try to put that stuff in our harbor, we'll fight you all the way. I think we've made our position clear on this thing, so if there are no further comments, I vote that we adjourn the meeting. [*Seconded.*]

When the meeting ended, the fishermen filed out, talking heatedly among themselves, leaving Mr. Stone standing on the platform.

Discussion Questions

1. What barriers to effective communication exist in this case?

2. How would you overcome or minimize each of these barriers?

Source: This case was written by Terence P. Driscoll. Reprinted from Dalmar Fisher, *Communication in Organizations* (St. Paul, MN: West Publishing, 1981).

C A S E   S T U D Y   11.2

ACROSS THE GEEK DIVIDE

BusinessWeek Miscommunications between engineers and salespeople have been part of business life at least since the Industrial Revolution. In the Internet age, the communication divide between technical and marketing experts has taken on a fresh urgency. High technology permeates the business world. Organizations need technical experts who can help their colleagues and customers use technology well. Often this means that high-tech employees must develop their will to communicate, as well as their ability to do so.

This *Business Week* case study describes organizations committed to developing the communication skills of their technology experts. It gives examples of how computer experts are learning to be communication experts—and how the employees and their companies both benefit. Read through this *Business Week* case study at www.mhhe.com/mcshane2e and prepare for the discussion questions below.

Discussion Questions

1. According to the examples provided by the author, what barriers have prevented effective communication by high-tech workers?

2. In what ways do organizations try to improve communication by their technical experts? Can you think of any additional measures organizations might take?

3. Why are communication skills important for an organization's computer experts? Would it be more reasonable for the organization to let these employees specialize in computer knowledge alone?

Source: T. Forsman, "Across the Geek Divide," *Business Week*, June 26, 2001.

TEAM EXERCISE 11.3

TINKER TOY COMMUNICATION

Purpose This exercise is designed to help you understand the importance of media richness and related issues that affect communication effectiveness.

Materials This activity requires one student on each team to have a cellular telephone that he or she is willing to use for this exercise. (Alternatively, in-house landline telephones or walkie-talkies may be used.) The instructor will provide each team with a set of Tinker Toys, Legos, Mega Blocks, straws, or other materials suitable for building. Each pair of teams must have pieces identical in number, shape, size, and color. This activity also requires either two large rooms or one large room and a few smaller rooms.

Instructions

- *Step 1*—The instructor will divide the class into an even number of teams, each with four or five students. Teams should have the same number of members where possible. Remaining students can serve as observers. Teams are paired (e.g., team 1A and team 1B, team 2A and team 2B, etc.), and each team receives a set of building materials identical to that of the other team in the pair. For example, team 1A would have the same set of materials as team 1B. Teams should check their materials to be sure the

paired team has identical pieces. Each team must have a member with a cellular telephone, and each team should have the telephone number of its paired team.

- *Step 2*—The A teams in each pair are moved to a room near the classroom (or to several small rooms) while the B teams remain in the classroom. Ideally, each team would be assigned to its own small tutorial room, with paired teams located beside each other. If the class has only two rooms, then put one team from each pair in each room.

- *Step 3*—The A teams build a sculpture using *all* the pieces provided. The instructor will set a time limit for this construction (typically about 10 minutes). The B teams, located in another room, must not observe this construction. Ideally, the A team's structure should be able to be moved into the classroom at the end of the exercise.

- *Step 4*—When the A team members have completed their structure, the B team members try to replicate the A team's structure without seeing it. The A team telephones the corresponding B team and verbally describes the structure over the telephone. Only one person from each team may communicate with the other team throughout this exercise. However, the B team communicator conveys the message to other B team members, who are building the replicated structure. The instructor will limit the time allowed for the B team to replicate the structure (about 15 minutes).

- *Step 5*—If the A team structures are sturdy enough, they should be brought into the classroom and placed beside the corresponding B team's replication. The class might want to rate each replication for its similarity to the original structure. The class will then discuss the factors that influence communication in this situation, including the importance of communication media, language, and perceptions.

TEAM EXERCISE 11.4

A NOT-SO-TRIVIAL CROSS-CULTURAL COMMUNICATION GAME

Purpose This exercise is designed to develop and test your knowledge of cross-cultural differences in communication and etiquette.

Materials The instructor will provide one set of question and answer cards to each pair of teams.

Instructions

- *Step 1*—The class is divided into an even number of teams. Ideally, each team would have three students. (Two- or four-student teams are possible if matched with equal-sized teams.) Each team is then paired with another team, and the paired teams (team A and team B) are assigned a private space away from other paired teams.
- *Step 2*—The instructor will hand each pair of teams a stack of cards with the multiple-choice questions facedown. These cards have questions and answers about cross-cultural differences in communication and etiquette. No books or other aids are allowed.
- *Step 3*—The exercise begins with a member of team A picking up one card from the top of the pile and asking the question on that card to the people on team B. The information given to team B includes the question and all alternatives listed on the card. Team B has 30 seconds after the question and alternatives have been read to give an answer. Team B earns one point if the correct answer is given. If team B's answer is incorrect, however, team A earns that point. Correct answers to each question are indicated on the card and, of course, should not be revealed until the question is answered correctly or time is up. Whether or not team B answers correctly, one of its members picks up the next card on the pile and asks the question to members of team A. In other words, cards are read alternately to each team. This procedure is repeated until all the cards have been read or time has elapsed. The team receiving the most points wins.

Important note: The textbook provides very little information pertaining to the questions in this exercise. Rather, you must rely on past learning, logic, and luck to win.

SELF-ASSESSMENT EXERCISE 11.5

ACTIVE LISTENING SKILLS INVENTORY

Purpose This self-assessment exercise is designed to help you estimate your strengths and weaknesses on various dimensions of active listening.

Instructions Think back to face-to-face conversations you have had with a co-worker or client in the office, hallway, factory floor, or other setting. Indicate the extent to which each item below describes your behavior during those conversations. Answer each item as truthfully as possible so that you get an accurate estimate of where your active listening skills need improvement. Then use the scoring key in Appendix B to calculate your results for each scale. This exercise is completed alone so that students assess themselves honestly without concerns of social comparison. However, class discussion will focus on the important elements of active listening.

Active listening skills inventory					
Circle the number to the right that best indicates the extent to which each statement describes your behavior when listening to others.	Not at all	A little	Some-what	Very much	Score
1. I keep an open mind about the speaker's point of view until he or she has finished talking.	0	1	2	3	_____
2. While listening, I mentally sort out the speaker's ideas in a way that makes sense to me.	0	1	2	3	_____
3. I stop the speaker and give my opinion when I disagree with something he or she has said.	0	1	2	3	_____
4. People can often tell when I'm not concentrating on what they are saying.	0	1	2	3	_____
5. I don't evaluate what a person is saying until he or she has finished talking.	0	1	2	3	_____
6. When someone takes a long time to present a simple idea, I let my mind wander to other things.	0	1	2	3	_____
7. I jump into conversations to present my views rather than wait and risk forgetting what I wanted to say.	0	1	2	3	_____
8. I nod my head and make other gestures to show I'm interested in the conversation.	0	1	2	3	_____
9. I can usually keep focused on what people are saying to me even when they don't sound interesting. . . .	0	1	2	3	_____
10. Rather than organizing the speaker's ideas, I usually expect the person to summarize them for me. . . .	0	1	2	3	_____
11. I always say things like "I see" or "uh-huh" so that people know that I'm really listening to them.	0	1	2	3	_____
12. While listening, I concentrate on what is being said and regularly organize the information.	0	1	2	3	_____
13. While the speaker is talking, I quickly determine whether I like or dislike his or her ideas.	0	1	2	3	_____
14. I pay close attention to what people are saying even when they are explaining something I already know.	0	1	2	3	_____
15. I don't give my opinion until I'm sure the other person has finished talking.	0	1	2	3	_____

After studying the preceding material, be sure to check out our website at
www.mhhe.com/mcshane2e
for more in-depth information and interactivities that correspond to this chapter.

12

Organizational Power, Politics, and Persuasion

AFTER READING THIS CHAPTER, YOU SHOULD BE ABLE TO:

- Define *power* and *counterpower.*

- Describe the five bases of power in organizations.

- Explain how information relates to power in organizations.

- Discuss the four contingencies of power.

- Discuss the role of power in sexual harassment.

- Explain how organizational power creates problems in romantic relationships at work.

- Summarize the advantages and disadvantages of organizational politics.

- List six types of political activity found in organizations.

- Describe the conditions that encourage organizational politics.

- Identify ways to control dysfunctional organizational politics.

- Summarize the key features of persuasive communication.

As a corporate road warrior, Jane Buckley knows that she needs to take more than her suitcase and computer on important business trips. The corporate director of strategic solutions for Compass Group, a global food services management provider, also carries one of the most important business tools: her golf clubs. "Our company cares who it does business with and likes to establish long-term relationships with clients," explains Buckley. "Golf is one way of establishing those personal connections."

Networking is an important political activity in the workplace, and many men incidentally or deliberately use golf as a way to build their power base for career advancement. "Men have always used the golf course for networking," says Susan G. Weitzman, a Deerfield, Illinois, business owner who teaches both women and men how to play golf and network successfully on the golf course. "Women need to be there, too."

Carolyn Turknett, executive vice president and co-owner of Turknett Leadership Group in Atlanta, agrees. "Women aren't in on all the informal networks yet," she warns. "A lot goes on on the golf course, but a lot of women still aren't there." Almost 50 percent of women in senior executive positions surveyed in one study say that exclusion from informal networks was a major barrier to the career advancement of women. More startling was that only 15 percent of male CEOs saw this as a problem. In other words, CEOs fail to see that the politics of networking is one of the main reasons women are held back in their careers.

Fortunately, some companies are helping women develop networks inside the organization without learning to play golf. More than one-third of Fortune 500 companies sponsor networks for their female employees. For example, about 3,000 female professionals participate in a women's network at General Electric Corporation.[1] ■

Jane Buckley, an executive with Compass Group, travels with her golf clubs to support the power of networking with colleagues and clients. *(C. Price/ Vancouver Province)*

Golfing isn't usually the first thing that comes to mind when discussing organizational power and politics. Yet playing golf and engaging in other informal networks can make a difference to an individual's career progress and, in some cases, the ability to fulfill job duties. The reality is that no one escapes from organizational power and politics. They exist in every business and, according to some writers, in every decision and action.[2]

We begin this chapter by defining power and presenting a basic model depicting the dynamics of power in organizational settings. We then discuss the five bases of power, as well as information as a power base. Next, we look at the contingencies necessary to translate those sources into meaningful power. Our discussion of power finishes with a look at sexual harassment as an abuse of power, as well as how organizational power complicates office romances. Next, the chapter examines the dynamics of organizational politics, including the various types of political activity, the conditions that encourage organizational politics, and the ways that it can be controlled. The final section of this chapter looks at persuasion as a form of influence. This section introduces a model of persuasion, including characteristics of the communicator, message, medium, and audience.

THE MEANING OF POWER

power

The capacity of a person, team, or organization to influence others.

Power is the capacity of a person, team, or organization to influence others.[3] Power is not the act of changing others' attitudes or behavior; it is only the *potential* to do so. People frequently have power they do not use; they might not even know they have power.

The most basic prerequisite of power is that one party believes he or she is dependent on the other for something of value.[4] This relationship is shown in Exhibit 12.1, where person A has power over person B by controlling something that person B needs to achieve his or her goals. You might have power over others by controlling a desired job assignment, useful information, important resources, or even the privilege of being associated with you! Making matters more complex is the fact that power is ultimately a perception, so people might gain power simply by convincing others that they have something of value. Thus, power exists when others believe that you control resources that they want.[5]

Although power requires dependence, it is really more accurate to say that the parties are *interdependent*. One party may be more dependent than the other, but the relationship exists only when both parties have something of

EXHIBIT 12.1

Dependence in the power relationship

(Used with permission of Rapid Phase Ltd., www.madameve.co.sa)

counterpower

The capacity of a person, team, or organization to keep a more powerful person or group in the exchange relationship.

value to the other. Exhibit 12.1 shows a dotted line to illustrate the weaker party's (person B's) power over the dominant participant (person A). This **counterpower,** as it is known, is strong enough to maintain person A's participation in the exchange relationship. For example, executives have power over subordinates by controlling their job security and promotional opportunities. At the same time, employees have counterpower by controlling the ability to work productively and thereby creating a positive impression of the supervisor to his or her boss. Counterpower usually motivates executives to apply their power judiciously, so that the relationship is not broken.

A Model of Power in Organizations

Power involves more than just dependence. As we see in Exhibit 12.2, the model of power includes both power sources and contingencies. It indicates that power is derived from five sources: legitimate, reward, coercive, expert, and referent. The model also indicates that these sources yield power only under certain conditions. The four contingencies of power include the employee's or department's substitutability, centrality, discretion, and visibility. Finally, as we will discuss later, the type of power applied affects the type of influence the power holder has over the other person or work unit.

SOURCES OF POWER IN ORGANIZATIONS

Over 40 years ago, OB scholars John French and Bertram Raven identified five sources of power within organizations: legitimate, reward, coercive, expert, and referent.[6] Many researchers have studied these five power bases and searched for others. For the most part, French and Raven's list remains intact.[7] The first three power bases are derived from the power holder's position; that is, the person receives these sources of power because of the specific authority or role he or she is assigned in the organization. The latter two sources of power originate from the power holder's own characteristics. In other words, the person brings these sources of power to the organization.[8]

legitimate power

The capacity to influence others through formal authority.

Legitimate Power

Legitimate power is an *agreement* among organizational members that people in certain roles can request certain behaviors of others. This perceived

EXHIBIT 12.2

A model of power
within organizations

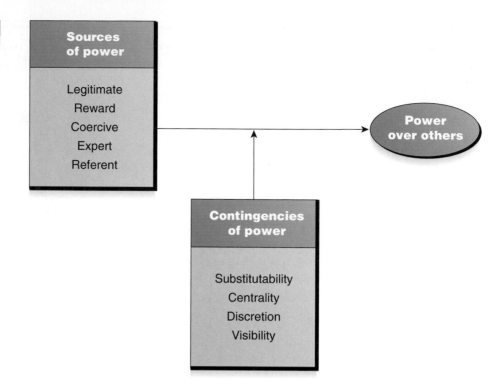

right comes from formal job descriptions as well as informal rules of conduct. Executives have considerable legitimate power, but all employees also have this power based on company rules and government laws.[9] For example, an organization might give employees the right to request customer files if this information is required for their job.

Legitimate power depends on more than job descriptions. It also depends on mutual agreement from those expected to abide by this authority. Your boss's power to make you work overtime depends partly on your agreement to this power. Classic stories of shipboard mutinies, such as *The Caine Mutiny* and *Mutiny on the Bounty*, reveal the limits of legitimate power. Today, employees question their boss's right to make them stay late, perform unsafe tasks, and participate in other activities. Thus, legitimate power is the person's authority to make discretionary decisions as long as followers accept this discretion.[10]

People in high power distance cultures (i.e., those who accept an unequal distribution of power—see Chapter 3) are more likely to comply with legitimate power than are people in low power distance cultures. Legitimate power is also stronger in some organizations than in others. A 3M scientist might continue to work on a project after being told by superiors to stop working on it because the 3M culture supports an entrepreneurial spirit, which includes ignoring your boss's authority from time to time.[11]

In general, employees are becoming less tolerant of legitimate power. Increasingly, they expect to be involved in decisions rather than be told what to do. As one organizational behavior scholar recently concluded: "[C]ommand managers are an endangered species in North America. Their habitat is steadily shrinking."[12] Thus, leadership based on legitimate power, which often guided employee behavior in the past, must be replaced by other forms, particularly expert and referent power, which are described below.

Reward Power

reward power
The capacity to influence others by controlling the allocation of rewards valued by them and removing negative sanctions.

Reward power is derived from the person's ability to control the allocation of rewards valued by others and to remove negative sanctions (i.e., negative reinforcement). Managers have formal authority that gives them power over the distribution of organizational rewards such as pay, promotions, time off, vacation schedules, and work assignments. Employees also have reward power over their bosses through the use of 360-degree feedback systems (see Chapter 2). Employee feedback affects the supervisor's promotions and other rewards, so she or he tends to behave differently toward employees after 360-degree feedback is introduced.

The Caine Mutiny is a classic Pulitzer Prize–winning novel and film about the limits of legitimate power. Captain Queeg (Humphrey Bogart, seated center) is a hard disciplinarian who shapes up the crew of the *Caine*, a battered minesweeper during World War II. However, Queeg's judgment and focus have been impaired by too much combat. After Queeg makes several critical mistakes and becomes obsessed with forcing the crew to search for missing strawberries, some officers fear that their captain is a danger to himself and the crew. Sure enough, a beleaguered Queeg panics during a storm at sea, so two key officers—Lt. Keefer (Fred MacMurray, standing center) and Lt. Maryk (Van Johnson, seated right)—stage a mutiny and assume command. The story illustrates how Queeg's orders and competence tested the limits of his legitimate power over crew members. What "mutinies" have you heard about in more recent organizational settings? What commands triggered employees to refuse to obey their boss? *(Archive Photos/Getty Images)*

Coercive Power

Coercive power is the ability to apply punishment. Managers have coercive power through their authority to reprimand, demote, and fire employees. Labor unions might use coercive power tactics, such as withholding services, to influence management in collective bargaining negotiations. Team members sometimes apply sanctions, ranging from sarcasm to ostracism, to ensure that co-workers conform to team norms. In one survey, more than one-fifth of employees reported that they had been coerced by their co-workers to reduce their work effort.[13]

Some firms rely on the coercive power of team members to control co-worker behavior.[14] Eaton Corporation's forge plant in South Bend, Indiana, may be one of them. "They say there are no bosses here," says an Eaton employee, "but if you screw up, you find one pretty fast."[15]

Expert Power

For the most part, legitimate, reward, and coercive power originate from the position. In contrast, **expert power** originates from within the person. It is an individual's or work unit's capacity to influence others by possessing knowledge or skills that others want.

Employees are gaining expert power as our society moves from an industrial to a knowledge-based economy. The reason is that employee knowledge becomes the means of production, not some machine that the owner controls.[16] Without this control over production,

coercive power
The ability to apply punishment.

expert power
Originates from within the person, and is the individual's or work unit's capacity to influence others by possessing knowledge or skills that they want.

referent power
The capacity to influence others based on the identification and respect they have for the powerholder.

owners are more dependent on employees to achieve their corporate objectives. This situation is quite apparent in nursing, high technology, and a few other industries where the skill shortage is so acute that companies have been forced to limit growth. Except during economic downturns, job applicants can demand generous salaries and preferential working conditions because of their expert power.

Referent Power

People have **referent power** when others identify with them, like them, or otherwise respect them. Like expert power, referent power comes from within the person. It is largely a function of the person's interpersonal skills and usually develops slowly. Referent power is usually associated with charismatic leadership. *Charisma* is often defined as a form of interpersonal attraction whereby followers develop a respect for and trust in the charismatic individual.[17]

Information and Power

Information is power.[18] This phrase is increasingly relevant in a knowledge-based economy. Information power derives from either the legitimate or expert sources of power described above and exists in two forms: (a) control over the flow and interpretation of information given to others and (b) the perceived ability to cope with organizational uncertainties.

Control over Information Flow   SAP, a German business-software company, has developed ways for its employees to receive information directly from corporate headquarters. The company broadcasts the latest news on the car radios of SAP employees, through its intranet site, and in regular e-mails sent directly from SAP's chairman. Most SAP employees appreciate this direct communication, but the company's middle managers have objected to these initiatives. The authority of these middle managers is based partly on their role as a source of information, so their power will diminish as employees receive company news from other sources.[19]

Traditionally, SAP's middle managers have been communication "traffic cops." Their job is to distribute, regulate, and filter out information throughout the organizational hierarchy.[20] This right to control information flow is a form of legitimate power and is most common in highly bureaucratic firms. The wheel formation in Exhibit 12.3 depicts this highly centralized control over information flow. The information gatekeeper in the middle of this configuration—such as the middle managers at SAP—can influence others through the amount, type, and quality of information they receive.

The problem facing these information gatekeepers is that this centralized information control structure is incompatible with knowledge management and team-based organizations. Consequently, SAP and other organizations are encouraging more knowledge sharing by moving toward the all-channel communication structure (see Exhibit 12.3,) in which all employees have relatively equal access to information. This formation allows employees and self-directed work teams to make better decisions. In its purest form, the all-channel network may seem chaotic, so large organizations with bureaucratic cultures tend to slip

EXHIBIT 12.3   Power through the control of information

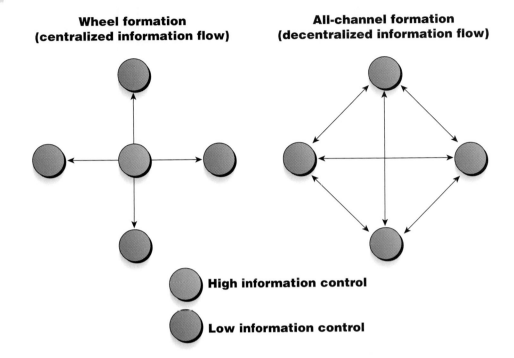

**Wheel formation
(centralized information flow)**

**All-channel formation
(decentralized information flow)**

High information control

Low information control

back into the wheel pattern. The wheel pattern also reemerges because, as we saw at SAP, it confers more power on those who distribute the information.[21]

Coping with Uncertainty   Organizations operate in changing environments, so they require information to reduce the uncertainty of future events. The more the organization can cope with the uncertainty of future events, the more easily it can achieve its goals.[22] Individuals and work units acquire power by helping the organization cope with uncertainty. Coping includes any activity that deals effectively with environmental uncertainties affecting the organization. A groundbreaking study of breweries and container companies identified three general strategies to help organizations cope with uncertainty. These coping strategies are arranged in a hierarchy of importance, with the first being the most powerful:[23]

- *Prevention*—The most effective strategy is to prevent environmental changes from occurring. For example, financial experts acquire power by preventing the organization from experiencing a cash shortage or defaulting on loans.
- *Forecasting*—The next best strategy is to predict environmental changes or variations. In this respect, marketing specialists gain power by predicting changes in consumer preferences.
- *Absorption*—People and work units also gain power by absorbing or neutralizing the impact of environmental shifts as they occur. An example is the ability of maintenance crews to come to the rescue when machines break down and the production process stops.

CONTINGENCIES OF POWER

Let's say that you have expert power by virtue of your ability to forecast and possibly even prevent dramatic changes in the organization's environment. Does this expertise mean that you are influential? Not necessarily. As we saw earlier in Exhibit 12.2, power sources generate power only under certain conditions. The four conditions—called the contingencies of power—are substitutability, centrality, discretion, and visibility.[24] These are not sources of power; rather, they determine the extent to which people can leverage their power bases. You may have lots of expert power, but you won't be able to influence others with this power base if the contingency factors are not in place.

Substitutability

substitutability
The extent to which people dependent on a resource have alternatives.

Substitutability refers to the availability of alternatives. Power is strongest when someone has a monopoly over a valued resource. Conversely, power decreases as the number of alternative sources of the critical resource increases. Substitutability refers not only to other sources that offer the resource, but also to substitutions of the resource itself. For instance, labor unions are weakened when companies introduce technologies that replace the need for their union members. At one time, a strike by telephone employees would have shut down operations, but computerized systems and other technological innovations now ensure that telephone operations continue during labor strikes and reduce the need for telephone operators during normal operations. Technology is a substitute for employees and, consequently, reduces union power.

How do people and work units increase their power through nonsubstitutability? There are several ways, although not all are ethical. We describe some of them here for your information—not necessarily for you to practice.

■ *Controlling tasks*—Professions have legislation preventing outsiders from performing certain tasks within their domain. Attorneys keep paralegals out of certain activities, and doctors keep nurses, midwives, and others away from certain interventions. Certified public accountants require public corporations to use their services in audits.

■ *Controlling knowledge*—Professions control access to the knowledge of their work domain, such as through restricted enrollment in educational programs. Knowledge is also restricted on the job. Several years ago, maintenance workers in a French tobacco processing plant had become very powerful because they controlled the knowledge required to repair the tobacco machines.[25] The maintenance manuals had mysteriously disappeared, and the machines had been redesigned enough so that only the maintenance staff knew how to fix them if they broke down (which they often did). Knowing the power of nonsubstitutability, maintenance staff carefully avoided documenting the repair procedures and didn't talk to production employees about their trade knowledge.

■ *Controlling labor*—Aside from their knowledge resource, people gain power by controlling the availability of their labor. Labor unions attempt to organize as many people as possible within a particular trade or industry so that employers have no other source of labor supply.[26] When unionized workers produce almost all of a particular product or service in a society, then the union has an easier time increasing wages. The union's power during a strike is significantly weakened when the employer can continue production through outside contractors or other nonunion facilities.

While most airline employees have been restless for wage increases after years of modest gains, pilots have the most power to negotiate pay increases. "They have such power because they can ground the airline and in a couple of weeks it will have lost its profits for the entire year," says an airline investment analyst in London. For example, pilots at Germany's Lufthansa Airlines staged two 24-hour strikes that grounded hundreds of flights and cost the airline more than U.S.$23 million. They won pay raises of nearly 30 percent. Pilots are powerful because they have low substitutability (only other pilots can replace them) and high centrality. When pilots go on strike, the effect on the airline is immediate and widespread. Pilot unions further increase their power through centrality by threatening strike action during the peak summer season.[28] What conditions would make pilots less powerful? (© AFP/CORBIS)

■ *Differentiation*—Differentiation occurs when an individual or work unit claims to have a unique resource—such as raw materials or knowledge—that the organization would want. By definition, the uniqueness of this resource means that no one else has it. The tactic here isn't so much the non-substitutability of the resource, but making organizational leaders believe that the resource is unique. Some people claim that consultants use this tactic. They take skills and knowledge that many consulting firms can provide and wrap them into a package (with the latest buzzwords, of course) so that it looks like a service that no one else can offer.

Centrality

Employees and departments have more power as their centrality increases. **Centrality** refers to the degree and nature of interdependence between the power holder and others.[27] Specifically, centrality increases with (a) the number of people affected by your actions and (b) the speed in which other people are affected by your actions. Think about your own centrality for a moment: If you decided not to show up for work or school tomorrow, how many people would be affected, and how much time would pass before they are affected? If you have high centrality, most people in the organization would be adversely affected by your absence, and they would be affected quickly.

Discretion

The freedom to exercise judgment—to make decisions without referring to a specific rule or receiving permission from someone else—is another important contingency of power in organizations. Consider the plight of first-line supervisors. It may seem that they have legitimate power over employees, but this power is often curtailed by specific rules. They must administer programs developed from above and follow specific procedures in their implementation. They administer rewards and punishments, but must abide by precise rules regarding their distribution. Indeed, supervisors are often judged not on their discretionary skills, but

centrality
The degree
and nature of
interdependence
between the
powerholder and
others.

on their ability to follow prescribed rules and regulations. This lack of discretion makes supervisors largely powerless even though they may have access to some of the power bases described earlier in this chapter. "Middle managers are very much 'piggy-in-the-middle,'" complains a middle manager at Britain's National Health System. "They have little power, only what senior managers are allowed to give them."[29]

Visibility

Power does not flow to unknown people in the organization. Someone with valuable knowledge will yield power only when others are aware of it. Someone with higher authority will yield power only when others are aware of his or her position in the organization. Only when a person's or work unit's source of power is visible—when it is known to others—will that source of power be meaningful.[30]

There are many ways to increase your visibility. One strategy is to take people-oriented jobs and work on projects that require frequent interaction with senior executives. "You can take visibility in steps," advises Kerstin Schultz, senior director of global operations at the pharmaceutical firm Searle. "You can start by making yourself visible in a small group, such as a staff meeting. Then when you're comfortable with that, seek out larger arenas."[31]

Another strategy is to work on important tasks. One study revealed that software engineers developing a new color laser printer gained power by working on the most critical components of the project. Corporate leaders paid more attention to engineers working on parts of the project that they believed were most important and faced more crises.[32]

Employees also gain visibility by being, quite literally, visible. Some people strategically move into offices or cubicles where co-workers pass most often (such as closest to the elevator or office lunchroom). Others play the game of face time—spending more time at work and showing that they are working productively. One female engineer on the previously mentioned color laser printer project made a habit of going to the office once each week at 2 A.M., after her boss once saw her working at that hour. "[A]fter the reaction I got from my manager I decided it was important to do that early morning work in the office," explains the engineer. "It is better to be seen here if you are going to work in the middle of the night."[33]

People often use public symbols as subtle (and not-so-subtle) cues to make their power sources known to others.[34] Professionals display their educational diplomas and awards on office walls to remind visitors of their expertise. Some executives still rely on the size of their office and related status symbols to show their legitimate power in the organization. Even the clothing we wear communicates power. Medical professionals wear white coats and have a stethoscope around their neck to symbolize their legitimate and expert power in hospital settings.

mentoring
The process of
learning the ropes of
organizational life
from a senior person
with the company.

Another way to increase visibility is through **mentoring**—the process of learning the ropes of organizational life from a senior person within the company. Mentors give protégés more visible and meaningful work opportunities, and open doors for them to meet more senior people in the organization. Mentors also teach these newcomers political skills and tactics supported by the organization's senior decision makers.[35]

The headquarters of Drake International New Zealand is located in Auckland, but general manager Gary Withers (shown in photo) prefers telecommuting from his home hundreds of miles away in Queenstown. Withers claims that telecommuting keeps him closer to favorite fishing spots and farther away from organizational politics. However, some experts warn that telecommuting doesn't avoid office politics; it creates political liabilities. "Teleworkers left entirely based at home or away from the office tend to miss out on the key informal interaction with colleagues and social aspects of work, and some lose motivation and positioning for promotion," warns Andrew Page, president of the European Community Telework Forum. Val Arnold, senior vice president with Minneapolis-based consulting firm Personnel Decisions International, agrees. "You need to maintain visibility and develop yourself professionally in order to succeed as a telecommuter," Arnold warns.[38] How can telecommuters maintain their visibility to avoid loss of power? *(Southland Times Co. Ltd./Used with permission)*

CONSEQUENCES OF POWER

We use power to influence others, but the type of influence depends on the power source used.[36] Coercive power is generally the least desirable source because it generates resistance by the person or department being influenced. In other words, the targeted person tends to oppose the influence attempt and actively tries to avoid carrying it out. Applying coercive power also reduces trust between the parties and increases employee dissatisfaction. Resistance and distrust also occur when other power bases are used arrogantly or in a manipulative way.

Reward and legitimate power tend to produce compliance, whereby people are motivated to implement the power holder's request for purely instrumental reasons. You will consciously agree to perform an extra task if your boss gives you a bonus for performing that task, but you aren't enthusiastic about it and will certainly do no more than is necessary to receive the reward. Commitment is the strongest form of influence, whereby people identify with the power holder's request and are motivated to implement it even when there are no extrinsic benefits for doing so. Commitment is the most common consequence of expert and referent power. For instance, employees will follow a charismatic leader and do more than is asked because this power base evokes commitment rather than compliance or resistance.

Power also affects the power holder. Chapter 5 described how some people have a strong need for power and are motivated to acquire it for personal or organizational purposes. These individuals are more satisfied and committed to their jobs when they have increased responsibility, authority, and discretion. However, people who acquire too much power often abuse their position to better their personal interests and to gain more power.[37] Powerful employees tend to use their influence more often than is necessary, devalue their less powerful co-workers, and reduce their interpersonal associations with them. They also use their power to acquire more power. If unchecked, powerful employees eventually become even more powerful. In short, there appears to be some truth in Lord Acton's well-known statement that "power tends to corrupt; absolute power corrupts absolutely."[39]

Sexual Harassment: An Abuse of Power

Six weeks after joining a telemarketing firm, Susan (not her real name) started receiving unwanted attention from her boss. The manager asked about her sexual experiences and demanded intimate attention. When the manager tried to kiss her, Susan fled the office, afraid to return to work. When she did return, the manager gave her more difficult work to perform. Six weeks later, he fired Susan for incompetence.[40]

Susan's experience at the telemarketing firm illustrates that sexual harassment not only creates a stressful situation (see Chapter 7), but also constitutes an abuse of power. Sexual harassment includes any unwelcome conduct of a sexual nature that detrimentally affects the work environment or leads to adverse job-related consequences for its victims. According to various estimates, about one-quarter of women in the United States and Canada have been sexually harassed at work. The European Commission reports that up to 65 percent of women in some E.U. countries have been sexually harassed at work. A few European countries have no legislation prohibiting sexual harassment.[41]

Sexual harassment occurs partly because the harasser stereotypes the victim as subservient and powerless (see Chapter 3). Sexual harassment also occurs because the harasser is willing to use his or her power over the victim.[42] This abuse of power is most obvious when the harasser threatens the employee's job security or personal safety through coercive or legitimate power (known as *quid pro quo* harassment). Abuse of power also occurs where sexual harassment takes the form of a hostile work environment, which includes unwelcome conduct, such as telling sexual jokes, leering, and showing pornographic material. A hostile work environment persists because the victim does not have sufficient power to stop the behavior.

Minimizing Sexual Harassment   Organizations accused of sexual harassment pay a tremendous price in public moral embarrassment, loss of talented employees, and financial penalties.[43] Some corporate leaders believe the best solution is to introduce confidential complaint procedures for people who have been sexually harassed. Although such procedures are certainly necessary, they are reactive procedures. Much more important are preventive strategies that reduce the likelihood of sexual harassment incidents.

One way to prevent sexual harassment is to ensure that powerful employees realize how their actions are interpreted by others. Incidents of sexual harassment may seem obvious after the fact, but many harassers really don't realize how their actions are perceived by others at the time, or that they have abused their power in the organization.[44] For example, men often think a comment about an employee's figure is a compliment, whereas female co-workers may feel threatened by these statements because of the harasser's potential use of power if they react defensively. Moreover, executives sometimes forget that they are role models for the entire organization. Their actions signal whether sexual harassment is prohibited or condoned.

Office Romance and Organizational Power

Most contemporary workplaces employ almost as many women as men. They work long hours together, often on collaborative projects requiring frequent interaction. The long days also make it more difficult to meet people outside the workplace. It's little wonder that so many romantic relationships today are started in the workplace. A few recent surveys have estimated that over 40 percent of employees in the United States, Canada, and other countries have dated a co-worker. One poll also found that one-quarter of employees say they have had intimate relations with a co-worker.[45]

The problem with this trend is that office romances don't mix very well with organizational power. One concern is that co-workers tend to think one or both employees in the relationship abuse their power by favoring each other, particularly where one person in the relationship has higher status. Almost 70 percent of employees in one recent survey said they dislike workplace romances between supervisors and subordinates because they can foster favoritism.[46]

A more serious concern is that nearly one-quarter of sexual harassment cases result from workplace romances that went sour.[47] "A lot of sexual harassment complaints result from consensual relationships that went bad," advises a lawyer who specializes in sexual harassment cases. "One of them decides to break it off. The other continues to pursue and it becomes something other than consensual, and the person claims he or she is being sexually harassed."[48]

The risk of sexual harassment is potentially greater in a supervisor–subordinate relationship. If the subordinate ends the relationship, the supervisor might create a hostile work environment through subtle day-to-day decisions. Even when the jilted supervisor acts appropriately, the subordinate may still feel intimidated by the former partner's power over work and career decisions. What should companies do to minimize these power and politics problems with workplace romance? As Connections 12.1 describes, there are several options, some of which are more realistic than others.

Power permeates organizations and has both desirable and adverse effects on employees. But we shouldn't be interested just in who has power. We also need to understand how that power is gained and used to influence others in organizational settings. This understanding relates to the dynamics of organizational politics, which we discuss next.

ORGANIZATIONAL POLITICS

Charlene Pedrolie was ready for trouble when she replaced the old assembly line with a new team-based work structure. As head of manufacturing at Rowe Furniture Company in Virginia, Pedrolie knew there would be glitches and plenty of resistance. Naysayers in the corporate office shook their heads and distanced themselves from Pedrolie's experiment. The computer people wouldn't even respond to her urgent requests for more information. Using her sharpest political skills, Petrolie convinced corporate leaders to fire the firm's computer chief and bring in one of her friends from General Electric, where she had previously worked. Eventually, Petrolie's persistence and political savvy paid off as production employees worked out the kinks in the team-based work processes.[49]

Unplugging the Power and Politics of Workplace Romance

When employees in the Louisiana Community and Technical College System complained of favoritism by college directors who were dating employees, the governing board reacted swiftly by banning these intimate relationships. Any manager and subordinate caught in such a relationship might face termination. However, the ink had barely dried on the policy when some board members discovered that many of the state's college staff dated each other. "We reacted," admits board chairman Kevin McCotter. "We didn't manage this situation. It managed us."

Although some firms actively prohibit amorous relationships, this policy isn't very realistic. There may be too many workplace romances to enforce, as board members at the Louisiana Community and Technical College System discovered. Moreover, these policies don't prevent employees from falling in love with each other; they just keep the relationships quiet.

If prohibiting workplace romances is unrealistic, what steps should organizations take to minimize the risks of sexual harassment and perceived favoritism resulting from workplace romances? Experts suggest that the best policy is to require employees to disclose their intimate relationships with co-workers. In some cases, employees must sign a document indicating that the relationship is consensual. These "love forms" reduce the risk that one party later claims the relationship occurred through an abuse of power.

IMIC Hotels, a hotel management company in Columbia, South Carolina, plans to develop this type of dating policy. "We have a lot of people that tend to hook up, and it scares me with the issue of sexual harassment," admits Angela Ecton, the human resources director responsible for IMIC Hotels' 1,400 employees at 35 locations.

Even with disclosure, office romances can have damaging consequences unless the power dynamics are sorted out. That's why some firms advise employees to remove themselves from a position of power over their partner. For example, when Heather and Mike McClure starting dating at Arthur Andersen Inc., they approached the managing partner for a satisfactory arrangement.

"The partner in charge simply said we couldn't work on accounts together and that I couldn't sit in on any meetings where Heather's name came up for promotion or salary increase," explains Mike McClure, who holds a more senior position at the accounting firm. "For that, I believe, Arthur Andersen is a little ahead of the curve."

Sources: L. G. Klaff, "North Carolina Firms Worried about Sexual Harassment Want Couples to Confess," *Charlotte (NC) Observer*, June 11, 2001; S. Dyer, "Officials Will Reconsider Boss-Employee Dating Ban," *Baton Rouge (LA) Advocate*, October 12, 2000; M. Jameson, "Partners in Work and Play," *Los Angeles Times*, August 16, 1999, p. E1; N. Nejat-Bina, "Employers as Vigilant Chaperones Armed with Dating Waivers: The Intersection of Unwelcomeness and Employer Liability in Hostile Work Environment Sexual Harassment Law," *Berkeley Journal of Employment and Labor Law*, December 22, 1999, pp. 325cf.

organizational politics

The attempts to influence others using discretionary behaviors to promote personal objectives.

As this true story reveals, organizational politics can work either for or against the organization. **Organizational politics** represents attempts to influence others using discretionary behaviors to promote personal objectives.[50] It is the exercise of power to get one's own way, including the acquisition of more power, often at the expense of others. Behaviors are discretionary if they are neither formally prescribed nor prohibited by the organization. For example, the naysayers at Rowe Furniture Company who distanced themselves from Pedrolie probably didn't do anything that was against company policy. They just kept quiet and avoided any image that aligned them with the project.

Organizational Politics: Good or Bad?

Tenneco Packaging has an unusual credo that says, "Management with no fear, egos, or politics."[51] This theme supports the packaging company's quest for a team-based organization with high levels of trust among employees. But should companies try to prevent anyone from engaging in organizational politics? Dysfunctional politics should be discouraged, of course. But we need to

Organizational Politics Saves Apple Computer

Gil Amelio thought that purchasing NeXT Software, Inc., would be his masterstroke to save Apple Computer. Instead, it began a series of political events that would soon have Steven Jobs—who founded both NeXT and Apple—replacing Amelio as Apple's CEO. Steven Jobs started NeXT after he was ousted from Apple in the 1980s. NeXT wasn't very successful, but it had a respectable operating system. Apple was looking for a new operating system, so Jobs convinced Amelio to buy NeXT.

Following the buyout, Amelio invited Jobs to serve as a special adviser, mainly to raise morale among Apple employees and customers. But Jobs quickly became more than a cheerleader. He visited or phoned Amelio several times each week, advising on how to integrate NeXT people and products, cut costs, and redraw the organization chart. He convinced Amelio to put former NeXT people in the top positions. Within a few months, Jobs and his NeXT colleagues held key positions for evaluating and weeding out teams of Apple employees. "NeXT is taking over from inside," said one Apple employee. "It's a Jobs–NeXT regime," said another.

Publicly, Jobs supported Amelio's leadership at Apple. Privately, he ridiculed Amelio's lethargic decision making. Eventually, Jobs demonstrated his nonconfidence in Amelio more publicly by selling the 1.5 million Apple shares he received from the NeXT purchase. This action got the attention of Apple's board of directors. The board removed Amelio and invited Jobs to become Apple's "interim" CEO. Jobs then convinced Apple's current board to resign and picked a new board consisting of friends and allies.

Some writers believed that Amelio's days were numbered and that Jobs was the long-awaited savior for Apple. But in his biography on the experience, Gil Amelio portrayed Jobs as a conniving back-stabber "obsessed with power" who cunningly maneuvered him

Steven Jobs relied on several political tactics to shift from being a special adviser to replacing Gil Amelio as Apple's CEO. *(Reuters/Lou Dematteis/Archive Photos/ Getty Images)*

out of Apple. "I was . . . trapped in a web of plotting as intricate as the War of the Roses," he wrote.

Sources: J. Reingold, "What Gil Amelio Thinks of Steve Jobs and Apple Now," *Business Week*, January 21, 2000; D. Kirkpatrick, "The Second Coming of Apple," *Fortune*, November 9, 1998; D. Takahash, "An Exponential Life and Death," *Electronic Business* 24 (June 1998), pp. 82–88; J. Carlton, "Thinking Different," *Wall Street Journal*, April 14, 1998; J. Mardesich, "Office Gossip Points at Jobs as Mastermind of a Coup," *San Jose (CA) Mercury*, July 10, 1997; B. Schlender, "Something's Rotten in Cupertino," *Fortune*, March 3, 1997, pp. 100–8; J. Pearlstein, "Rumors Fly as Staffers Brace for Apple Cuts," *MacWeek*, February 28, 1997.

recognize that many of our day-to-day actions—the way we dress, how we act toward other people, and so on—are political tactics that help the organization achieve its objectives. In fact, experts suggest that people need to be good politicians, particularly as they reach higher levels in the corporation. "In order to succeed, you really have to understand what the politics of the office are," advises Ingrid Murro Botero, a career consultant in Phoenix, Arizona. "It is a way of life."[52]

Consider the events described in Connections 12.2. It appears that Steven Jobs used organizational politics to regain Apple's top post. Were these tactics good or bad? Many people would argue that Jobs took these steps guided by the belief that Apple's future was in jeopardy with Gil Amelio in charge. In other words, Steven Jobs used political tactics to gain power for the organization's benefit. Apple's sales and profitability soared after Jobs became CEO, so his political activities possibly saved the company. The point here is that some political tactics can help organizations achieve their objectives where traditional influence methods may fail.

Problems with Organizational Politics   Of course, organizational politics is often more of a problem than a benefit. Over one-third of management and nonmanagement employees recently surveyed say that organizational politics is the most common reason for decision-making delays. Another survey estimates that business leaders spent nearly one-fifth of their time dealing with organizational politics.[53] They say this time is consumed addressing several problems created by political behaviors, such as lack of trust, reduced willingness to collaborate, reduced knowledge sharing, and misuse of organizational resources. On top of these problems, employees who experience organizational politics tend to report higher stress, psychological withdrawal, and turnover.[54]

The Ethics of Organizational Politics   How can we tell whether our political actions are good or bad? The answer may be to assess the action against the three ethical standards described in Chapter 4. Generally, a political behavior is ethical only if it satisfies all three moral principles.[55]

1. *Utilitarian rule*—Does the political tactic provide the greatest good for the greatest number of people? If it mainly benefits the individual and possibly harms the welfare of others, then the political behavior is inappropriate.
2. *Individual rights rule*—Does the political tactic violate anyone's legal or moral rights? If the political activity threatens another person's privacy, free speech, due process, or other rights, then it should not be used even if the results might be beneficial to a larger audience.
3. *Distributive justice rule*—Does the political activity treat all parties fairly? If the political behavior benefits those who are better off at the expense of those who are already worse off, then the activity is unethical.

TYPES OF POLITICAL ACTIVITY

So far, we have alluded to the fact that there are various types of political games or tactics found in organizational settings. Organizational behavior scholars have conveniently grouped most of them into the six categories illustrated in Exhibit 12.4.[56]

Attacking or Blaming Others

Probably the most direct and nastiest form of organizational politics is attacking and blaming others. This aspect includes giving rivals a bad image in the eyes of decision makers. Not all blaming is overt. A subtle tactic occurs when people dissociate themselves from undesirable situations or use excuses to form an external attribution of the cause of the problem.[57] You might explain to your boss that a report is late because of lack of support from another

EXHIBIT 12.4

Types of political
behavior in
organizations

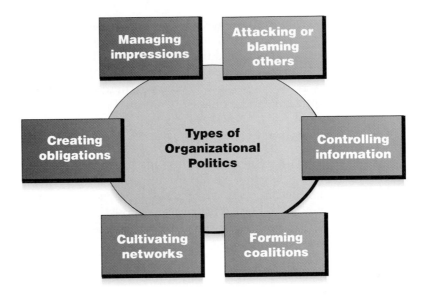

work unit or other conditions beyond your control. In other words, people try to frame their failures in terms of external attributions (see Chapter 3).

Controlling Information

Information is a political tool as well as a source of power.[58] People influence perceptions, limit the opportunities of rival employees, and further increase their power by strategically controlling how information is shared. One poll of British employees reported that almost one-half of them believe that people keep their colleagues in the dark about work issues if doing so helps their own cause.[59] Employees also engage in information politics by organizing meeting agendas to suit their personal interests. For example, they might place a particular issue near the bottom of the agenda so that the committee either doesn't get to it or is too fatigued to make a final judgment. Others arrange meetings in a way that controls who attends.[60]

Forming Coalitions

Cindy Casselman felt that Xerox needed a complete Intranet system for employees to share knowledge, but the communications manager lacked the formal authority to put this WebBoard together. Her solution was to quietly assemble a coalition of people who would benefit from WebBoard. The informal group included an executive who wanted the site to test his unit's work on virtual document delivery systems. Another executive joined the coalition because WebBoard would showcase Xerox's new structure of networked PCs. These and other people gave Casselman enough power to convince her boss to support the project.[61]

Cindy Casselman relied on a coalition to get what she wanted. A coalition attempts to influence people outside the group by pooling the resources and power of its members (see Chapter 8). Creating this informal group is a political tactic because it pools the power of several people toward a common objective that each member is unable to influence alone. By demonstrating their strength in numbers, coalitions also create a sense that an issue has broad appeal and therefore deserves legitimate support.[62] Although coalitions are usually formed with good intentions, one possible problem is that they put pressure on others to change, thereby creating compliance rather than commitment to the change.[63]

Cultivating Networks

The opening vignette in this chapter introduced the notion that golfing—or some other venue for informal networking—can potentially make a difference in your career. This reflects the often-heard statement that it's not what you know but who you know that counts. In other words, employees get ahead not just by developing their competencies. They also need to engage in **networking**—cultivating social relationships with others to accomplish one's goals.

networking
Cultivating social relationships with others to accomplish one's goals.

Networking is an important political practice for three reasons. First, networks consist of people who trust each other, which increases the flow of information among those within the network. The more you network, the more likely you will receive valuable information that increases your expert power in the organization.[64] Second, networking nurtures allies and sponsors, thereby making it easier to get approval for projects and other initiatives. In other words, you tend to receive more support for initiatives from colleagues within the network. Finally, people tend to identify more with partners within their own networks, which increases referent power among people within each network. This network-based referent power may lead to more favorable decisions by others in the network.

Networking is a natural part of the informal organization, yet it can create a formidable barrier to those who are not actively connected to it.[65] As the opening vignette indicated, women have difficulty getting promoted into senior management because they are usually excluded from male networks. That's what Deloitte & Touche executives discovered when they investigated why so many junior female recruits left the accounting and consulting firm before reaching partnership level. Deloitte & Touche now relies on mentoring, formal women's network groups, and measurement of career progress to ensure that female staff members have the same career development opportunities as their male colleagues.[66]

Creating Obligations

The obligation to help someone who has once helped you—called the norm of reciprocity—is deeply embedded in many societies. It is also a political tactic.[67] An employee who has helped someone might later ask that person to put in a good word for or support him or her on a promotion. The indebted co-worker is more likely to agree to this than if there is no debt to repay. Some organizational politicians are able to leverage these debts for a greater return than whatever was given initially.

Managing Impressions

impression management
The practice of actively shaping our public images.

Impression management is the practice of actively shaping our public images.[68] Many impression management activities are done routinely to satisfy the basic norms of social behavior, such as the way we dress and how we behave toward colleagues and customers.[69] Other impression management tactics are done deliberately. Some political tactics described earlier—including blaming others, controlling information, and increasing the visibility of one's power base—are forms of impression management. Maintaining face time—how often others see you in the office—is an important impression management tactic, particularly for telecommuters who otherwise become "out of sight, out of mind" employees.

Some people manage their impressions by padding their résumé. One study of 1.86 million background checks by a U.S. reference-checking firm revealed that about 25 percent of applicants falsify information about work experience and education.[70] In an alarming number of cases, people completely fabricate their credentials and past experience. For example, officials at a medical center in California discovered that its executive director did not have the claimed degrees in psychology and medicine. Instead, he had impersonated medical professionals and had been convicted for armed robbery. Lucent Technologies discovered that a former executive had lied about having a PhD from Stanford University and hid his criminal past involving forgery and embezzlement. Ironically, the executive was most recently in charge of recruiting at Lucent.[71] Global Connections 12.3 describes another extreme example of impression management by a technology entrepreneur in Singapore.

CONDITIONS FOR ORGANIZATIONAL POLITICS

Organizational politics flourishes under the right conditions.[72] One of those conditions is scarce resources. When budgets are slashed, people rely on political tactics to safeguard their resources and maintain the status quo. This condition happened at Exponential Technology, which was working on a superfast chip for the Apple Macintosh. When Apple's future became uncertain, the company hired a second group of engineers to develop a similar chip for the Intel-compatible market. Because of budget restrictions, however, the Mac-compatible engineers did their best to run the new group out of town. "It got really ugly," recalls Exponential CEO Rick Shriner. "It came down to a battle for limited resources." To reduce the political infighting, Shriner moved the Intel group to another city.[73]

Along with resource scarcity, office politics flourishes when resource allocation decisions are ambiguous or complex, or lack formal rules. Decision makers are given more discretion over resource allocation, so potential recipients of those resources use political tactics to influence the factors that should be considered in the decision. Organizational change encourages political behaviors for this reason. Change creates uncertainty and ambiguity as the company moves from an old set of rules and practices to a new set. During these times, employees apply political strategies to protect their valued resources, position, and self-image.

Organizational politics also becomes commonplace when it is tolerated and transparently supported by the organization.[74] Companies sometimes promote people who are the best politicians, not necessarily the best talent to run the company. If left unchecked, organizational politics can paralyze an organization as people focus more on protecting themselves than on fulfilling their roles. Political activity becomes self-reinforcing unless the conditions supporting political behavior are altered.

Taking Impression Management to the Extreme

By any standard, Dennis Lee's résumé is impressive. The 29-year-old co-founder of elipva, a Singapore high-technology start-up firm, says he is a renowned artificial intelligence researcher, the author of several books, and the recipient of numerous awards. One press release from elipva proudly announced that Lee and MIT professor Andersen Dula had won the Innovator 2000 Award from the Massachusetts Institute of Technology and AT&T.

Another press release stated that Lee had won a Stanford University award in connection with Pattie Maes, a renowned MIT researcher in the field of intelligent agents. A third announcement said that Lee had received a rare artificial intelligence award sponsored by the prestigious American Association for Artificial Intelligence (AAAI) and Stanford University. A photo of the AAAI award appeared on Lee's personal website. Lee's résumé also lists books he wrote that were published by well-known publishers. Copies of at least one of these volumes were distributed to the press.

The problem with Dennis Lee's résumé is that it is an elaborate misrepresentation. MIT Media Labs couldn't find any Andersen Dula, and the school didn't hand out an innovation award to Lee. MIT intelligent agents researcher Pattie Maes does exist, but she did not collaborate with Lee on any work. Lee's books looked homemade and carried incorrect publisher names, although no one noticed when copies were distributed. Soon after firing Lee for these falsehoods, elipva also reported that some of Mr. Lee's published writings had been copied from other sources with no credit given.

Lee hasn't explained why he fabricated his past to such an extreme, but his mastery of impression

High-tech entrepreneur Dennis Lee got carried away with impression management. (Straits Times [Singapore])

management certainly worked effectively, for a while. These imaginary achievements helped Lee gain recognition in the media, the venture capital community, and the Singapore Internet community. Lee's reputation grew so highly that he was invited to speak at the Internet World Asia conference and was nominated Internet Visionary of the Year at the Internet World Asia Industry Awards.

Sources: J. Lien, "Some Vital Questions on elipva Still Unanswered," *Business Times (Singapore),* June 5, 2001, p. 12; J. Jaucius, "Internet Guru's Credentials a True Work of Fiction," *Ottawa Citizen,* June 12, 2001; W. F. Tang, "Technopreneur Sacked, Probe Confirms Fraud," *Business Times (Singapore),* May 24, 2001, pp. 1, 2; "BT Search Sparks Probe," *Business Times (Singapore),* May 20, 2001; J. Lien, "Technopreneur Suspended over Alleged Fake Claims," *Business Times (Singapore),* May 19, 2001, pp. 1, 2; "Surprise MIT Award for S'porean," *Straits Times (Singapore),* November 28, 2000, p. 15.

Personal Characteristics

Several personal characteristics affect a person's motivation to engage in organizational politics.[75] Some people have a strong need for personal as opposed to socialized power (see Chapter 5). They seek power for its own sake and use political tactics to acquire more power. People with an internal locus of control are more likely than those with an external locus of control to engage in political behaviors. This does not mean that internals are naturally political; rather, they are more likely to use influence tactics when political conditions are present because, unlike externals, they feel very much in charge of their own destiny.

Machiavellian values

The belief that deceit is a natural and acceptable way to influence others.

Some people have strong **Machiavellian values.** Machiavellianism is named after Niccolò Machiavelli, the sixteenth-century Italian philosopher who wrote *The Prince,* a famous treatise about political behavior. People with high Machiavellian values are comfortable with getting more than they deserve and believe that deceit is a natural and acceptable way to achieve that goal. They seldom trust co-workers and tend to use cruder influence tactics, such as bypassing one's boss or being assertive, to get their own way.[76]

Gender Differences in Organizational Politics   Some experts on gender issues suggest that men and women differ in their use of political tactics. Direct impression management tactics are apparently used more often by men than by women. Specifically, men are more likely to advertise their achievements and take personal credit for successes of others reporting to them. Women are more reluctant to force the spotlight on themselves, preferring instead to share the credit with others.[77]

Men and women also seem to differ in assigning blame.[78] Research suggests that women are more likely to apologize—personally take blame—even for problems not caused by them. Men are more likely to assign blame and less likely to assume it. In fact, some men try to turn their errors into achievements by appearing as the white knight to save the day. This difference is consistent with our discussion of gender communication (Chapter 11), namely, that men tend to communicate and behave in ways that support their status and power.

If they don't rely on blaming or impression management, then which political tactics do women tend to use? Some writers claim that women don't use any political tactics very well in organizations, which has limited their promotional opportunities.[79] More likely, women use indirect impression management as well as forms of networking and coalition building. Of course, we must be careful not to generalize gender differences too much. Some women are very agile corporate politicians, and some men are politically inept in organizations.

CONTROLLING POLITICAL BEHAVIOR

The conditions that fuel organizational politics also give us some clues about how to control dysfunctional political activities.[80] Here are several strategies that should keep dysfunctional politics in check:

- Ensure that there is a sufficient supply of critical resources. This strategy is not easy to apply, but it is possible to ensure that sufficient inventory and cash flow exists in many cases.
- Where resources are necessarily scarce, introduce clear rules and regulations to specify the use of these resources.
- Establish a free flow of information so that the organization is less dependent on a few people at the center of a communications wheel.
- Use effective organizational change management practices—particularly education and involvement—to minimize uncertainty during the change process (see Chapter 16).
- Restructure team and organizational norms (as described in Chapter 8) to reject political tactics that appear to interfere with the organization's goals.

- Select people who have a moderately strong socialized need for power and a relatively low level of Machiavellianism.
- Provide opportunities for open and candid dialogue to resolve conflicts between employees and work units.
- Get employees to monitor the workplace and actively discourage coworkers who engage in political tactics.

INFLUENCING OTHERS THROUGH PERSUASION

persuasive communication
The process of having listeners accept rather than just understand a sender's message.

Organizational politics is not the only way to influence people. Every day, we apply another form of social influence, called **persuasive communication.** The elements of persuasive communication include characteristics of the communicator, message content, communication medium, and the audience being persuaded.[81]

Communicator Characteristics

What makes one person more persuasive than another? One important factor is the communicator's perceived reliability or expertise on the topic. Listeners consider mainly the speaker's credentials and experience, but speech pattern also influences perceived expertise. Specifically, people seem to have expertise when they talk confidently and relatively quickly, use some technical language, and avoid pauses ("umm," "uh") and hedges ("you know," "I guess").[82]

Communicators are more persuasive if they have credibility.[83] For instance, employees are more likely to accept a new policy if it is communicated and supported by a respected peer. Credibility also exists when communicators do not seem to profit from the persuasion attempt as well as when they state a few points against their position. For example, the effective persuader will acknowledge that an opposing position has one or two positive elements. Finally, people who are physically attractive or similar to the listeners tend to be more persuasive because the listeners tend to think such communicators have expertise and trustworthiness.[84]

Message Content

We are persuaded more by the communicator's characteristics when we don't consider the issue extremely important. When the issue is important, however, the message content becomes the critical feature of persuasive communication. The best strategy is to present all sides of the argument. Begin by introducing facts sympathetic to the audience's viewpoint; then shift into the theme of your position. Discussing only one point of view reduces your perceived trustworthiness and gives listeners the feeling of being cornered. When only one side of an argument is presented, the audience reacts by rejecting your information.[85]

Your message should be limited to a few strong arguments, because listeners are more likely to remember these points. The arguments should be repeated, but not to the extent that you are battering listeners over the head with them.[86]

Is it better to be logical or emotional when communicating information? Generally, people should use both tactics. Emotional appeals—such as graphically showing the unfortunate consequences of a bad decision—energize people but may also make them feel manipulated. Combining emotional presentations with logical arguments tends to minimize this problem.[87] Also, emotional appeals should always be accompanied by specific recommendations to overcome the threat. In a safety campaign, for example, employees are persuaded more by graphic pictures of accident victims than by a lecture on recent accident statistics, but only if they are given explicit steps to avoid the danger.[88]

inoculation effect
A persuasive communication strategy of warning listeners that others will try to influence them in the future and that they should be wary about the opponent's arguments.

Finally, persuasive communicators use the **inoculation effect** to ensure that other points of view do not influence listeners. This approach involves warning listeners that others will try to influence them in the future and that they should be wary about the opponent's arguments. This inoculation causes listeners to generate counterarguments to the anticipated persuasion attempts. For instance, a coalition that wants the company to purchase new production equipment might warn senior management about arguments the finance department will use to try to convince them otherwise. This strategy tends to make the finance department's subsequent persuasion attempts less effective.

Communication Medium

In the previous chapter we recommended using two-way verbal communication to persuade or motivate the listener. The personal nature of this medium seems to increase the credibility of the information. Furthermore, it is easier for the sender to determine whether the persuasive message is having the desired effect. Two-way communication also increases the receiver's active participation in the process. As long as this participation does not involve presenting defensive statements, the receiver is more likely to be involved in the conversation and to internalize some of the information presented.

Persuasion may require written documentation, however, when the sender is dealing with technical issues. Whenever written communication is necessary for this purpose, it should be combined with direct discussions for the greatest persuasive effect. The verbal exchange could repeat highlights of the report and provide graphic images for the listener, thereby adding emotional appeal to an otherwise logical message.

Audience Characteristics

Not everyone is equally persuaded by the strategies and conditions that we have described. For example, it is more difficult to persuade people who have high self-esteem.[89] And, as we mentioned above, it is very difficult to persuade those who have been inoculated against your persuasive intent.

CHAPTER SUMMARY

Power is the capacity to influence others. It exists when one party perceives that he or she is dependent on the other for something of value. However, the dependent person must also have counterpower—

some power over the dominant party—to maintain the relationship.

There are five power sources. Legitimate power is an agreement among organizational members that people in certain roles can request certain behaviors of others. Reward power is derived from the ability to control the allocation of rewards valued by others and to remove negative sanctions. Coercive power is the ability to apply punishment. Expert power is the capacity to influence others by possessing knowledge or skills that they want. People have referent power when others identify with them, like them, or otherwise respect them.

Information plays an important role in organizational power. Employees gain power by controlling the flow of information that others need, and by being able to cope with uncertainties related to important organizational goals.

Four contingencies determine whether these power sources translate into real power. Individuals and work units are more powerful when they are nonsubstitutable, that is, when there is a lack of alternatives. Employees, work units, and organizations reduce substitutability by controlling tasks, knowledge, and labor, and by differentiating themselves from competitors. A second contingency is centrality. People have more power when they have high centrality, that is, when a high number of people are affected quickly by their actions.

Discretion, the third contingency of power, refers to the freedom to exercise judgment. Power increases when people have freedom to use their power. The fourth contingency, visibility, refers to the idea that power increases to the extent that a person's or work unit's competencies are known to others. People gain visibility by taking people-oriented jobs, working on important tasks, engaging in face time, using public symbols of their power, and relying on mentors.

Power is applied to influence others, but the type of influence depends on the power source. Coercive power tends to produce resistance; reward and legitimate power result in compliance; expert and referent power produce commitment. People with a high need for power feel more satisfied and committed to their jobs when they have power, but many people tend to abuse their power when given too much of it.

Sexual harassment is a serious abuse of power. It is most obvious when the harasser threatens the employee's job security or personal safety through coercive or legitimate power. Sexual harassment may be minimized by making people aware of their actions.

Organizational power also complicates workplace romances. Co-workers tend to believe that employees in a sexual relationship will abuse their power. If the relationship ends, power imbalances between the two

employees may lead to sexual harassment. Some organizations try to prohibit romantic relationships at work, but experts recommend that employees disclose their relationship and remove themselves from a position of power over their partner.

Organizational politics attempts to influence others through discretionary behaviors that promote personal objectives. People tend to have an unfavorable view of organizational politics, but some political activities benefit the organization. Still, we must always consider the ethical implications of political behaviors, including whether the action provides the greatest good for the greatest number of people, violates anyone's legal or moral rights, and treats all parties fairly.

There are many types of organizational politics. The most common tactics include attacking or blaming others, controlling information, forming coalitions, cultivating networks, creating obligations, and managing impressions.

Organizational politics is more prevalent when scarce resources are allocated using complex and ambiguous decisions, and when the organization tolerates or rewards political behavior. Individuals with a high need for personal power, an internal locus of control, and strong Machiavellian values have a higher propensity to use political tactics. Men tend to engage in explicit impression management (taking credit for successes) and blaming tactics. Women tend to use fewer political strategies.

Dysfunctional organizational politics may be controlled by providing sufficient resources, providing clear rules for resource allocation, establishing a free flow of information, using education and involvement during organizational change, designing norms that discourage dysfunctional politics, selecting people who are less likely to use dysfunctional politics, trying to resolve conflicts before people use political tactics against the other party, and having employees actively discourage co-workers from using dysfunctional politics.

Persuasive communication tries to change behavior by having listeners accept rather than just understand the message. Persuasive communicators have more perceived expertise and credibility. The message content should provide all sides of the argument, limit debate to a few strong points, repeat arguments, combine emotional appeals with logical arguments, and inoculate the listener against opposing arguments. Two-way verbal communication is more persuasive than is written communication.

KEY TERMS

centrality, p. 363

coercive power, p. 359

counterpower, p. 357

expert power, p. 359

impression management, p. 372

inoculation effect, p. 377

legitimate power, p. 357

Machiavellian values, p. 375

mentoring, p. 364

networking, p. 372

organizational politics, p. 368

persuasive communication, p. 376

power, p. 356

referent power, p. 360

reward power, p. 359

substitutability, p. 362

DISCUSSION QUESTIONS

1. What role does counterpower play in the power relationship? Give an example where you have counterpower at school or work.

2. You have just been hired as a brand manager of toothpaste for a large consumer products company. Your job mainly involves encouraging the advertising and production groups to promote and manufacture your product more effectively. These departments aren't under your direct authority, although company procedures indicate that they must complete certain tasks requested by brand managers. Describe the sources of power you can use to ensure that the advertising and production departments will help you make and sell toothpaste more effectively.

3. Suppose you have formal authority to allocate performance bonuses to your employees. What contingencies must exist before this source of power will translate into actual power?

4. Visibility exists in many forms in almost any setting. Without offending any individuals in your class, identify strategies that people use in the classroom to strengthen their power through visibility.

5. The author of a popular-press business book wrote: "Office politics is a demotivator that must be eliminated." He argues that when companies allow politics to determine who gets ahead, employees put their energy into political behavior rather than job performance. Discuss the author's comments about organizational politics.

6. This textbook frequently emphasizes that successful companies engage in knowledge management. What political tactics were described in this chapter that directly interfere with knowledge management objectives?

7. Not long ago, senior executives at a medium-sized company were deciding whether to replace the company's mainframe with a client–server system of microcomputers. During this tense time, the mainframe and microcomputer experts in the information systems department engaged in a heated battle of political infighting by openly badmouthing each other. Meanwhile, people who controlled the mainframe information actively resisted the change to a client–server system, which would effectively allow users to bypass these people. What strategies would you recommend to minimize these incidents of organizational politics?

8. Think back to a time during a lecture when the instructor presented a strong point of view on a particular issue. According to the elements of persuasive communication, what made the instructor's lecture persuasive or not persuasive to you and others in the class?

CASE STUDY 12.1

FOREIGN EXCHANGE CONFRONTATION

I worked in the foreign exchange (FX) back office, where deals done by our 150 dealers were checked, payment instructions were added, and queries were addressed. My job was to resolve problems arising from deals. Much of the time, this meant going upstairs and talking to the dealers. Now, you never told a dealer that he or she was wrong, even when handling those dealers who, throughout the whole of my placement, were never correct. You just briefly stated what the problem was and asked them to kindly look into it.

This particular incident involves Nick, one of the men who always made mistakes. This time he had mixed up the currencies on a deal. The payment was due in half an hour, so it was important to get him to amend the deal. I went up to see him, but Lee, also from the back office, was already talking to him about something else. My problem was urgent, so, rather than return later, I waited for Lee to finish. When Lee left, Nick glanced at me and then, to my surprise, left his desk and went over to another dealer, John, from whom we had heard juicy comments for quite a while. A group of dealers assembled, and I could hear and see from their behavior that they were not discussing business.

I went over and discovered that the reason for their behavior was two pages from *The Sun* newspaper filled with pictures of naked women in various poses. Something inside me just snapped. I told Nick that my job was actually meant as a service to the dealers, to help make them aware of errors before it cost them money. I explained how much work I had to do and how much other dealers appreciated my corrections, so by ignoring me he was not only wasting my time, but his own colleagues' right to the service the back office offers. And with his error statistics, I would imagine he had better things to do than to stare at pictures of naked women.

I turned around, left my sheet of paper on his desk, and departed.

My main emotion both then and now is anger. I felt I had been patient and taken much more abuse and rude behavior than was acceptable. The way Nick ignored me to go and look at photos of nude women in a newspaper was the straw that broke the camel's back. I also felt helpless and vulnerable. They were discussing female anatomy in detail in a room with almost only men, and I knew my views were in the minority.

I was afraid any reaction from me would be ridiculed. Writing about it now, I also feel proud for having had the courage to tell him off.

The foreign exchange dealers, nearly all men, were the most arrogant group of people I have ever come across in my life. If it had not been for my gradually understanding some of the reasons for their behavior, an outburst like the one I have just described would have come much earlier. You need to appreciate the fact that the FX department is, at the moment, one of the best departments with regard to results in this firm and this creates a feeling of invulnerability and extreme self-importance among those working there. Although I did not feel that this situation was a valid excuse for their behavior, I learned to accept it.

The back-office policy was to accept any amount of criticism from the dealers, and then let it all come out afterward when you were safely back at your desk. This policy was no good, as it only helped increase the hostility between dealers and the back office. My telling the dealer off meant that I had broken the main taboo in the office. Over several weeks, I realized that my outburst had earned me much respect. I had done something many of my colleagues had wanted to do for years but dared not do. The risk was smaller for me as I was there only for a short while. So I achieved respect from both the back office and some of the dealers. And perhaps, even more important, I respected myself more for having done what I felt was right.

Discussion Questions

1. Describe the power bases and contingencies of power held by Nick and the back-office person during this incident.

2. How did the back-office person's power change after this incident? Why?

Source: Adapted from Y. Gabriel, "An Introduction to the Social Psychology of Insults in Organizations," *Human Relations* 51 (November 1998), pp. 1329–54.

CASE STUDY 12.2

INSIDE YAHOO!

BusinessWeek   In its early days as a search engine and web portal, Yahoo! was a darling of computer users and investors alike. People lauded the genius of the company's top executives, Timothy Koogle, Jeffrey Mallett, and Jerry Yang. However, that rosy picture began to look gloomy in 2000, following some poor management decisions. With political tactics, managers and board members began to shift the balance of power in the name of saving the company.

This *Business Week* case study describes political behavior that has recently taken place at Yahoo! It details the activities behind the hiring of a new chief executive officer, Terry Semel, and Semel's plans to take charge. Read through this *Business Week* case study at www.mhhe.com/mcshane2e and prepare for the discussion questions at right.

Discussion Questions

1. What sources of power can you identify for Timothy Koogle, Jeffrey Mallett, and Jerry Yang? What sources of power changed during the time described by the author?

2. What *political* objectives would Terry Semel need to have upon taking the CEO's job at Yahoo!? On the basis of the evidence in the article, what types of political activity did Semel engage in?

3. Why do you think organizational politics has played such a significant role during this time in Yahoo!'s existence?

Source: B. Elgin, "Inside Yahoo!" *Business Week*, May 21, 2001.

TEAM EXERCISE 12.3

GENERAL SOFTWARE PRODUCTS: AN IN-BASKET EXERCISE

Purpose This exercise is designed to help you understand the dynamics and feelings of power in an organizational setting.

Materials The instructor will distribute in-basket materials. Teams should have a private area to make their decisions.

Instructions

■ *Step 1*—The instructor will briefly describe what an in-basket exercise is, including the time constraints. Students are then put into groups (typically, four to five people), and each group receives a package with copies of e-mails and memos. (Note: Instead of using teams, your instructor may decide to assign the in-basket exercise to individuals working alone. If so, the following steps still apply, but *Step 2* would refer to individuals.)

■ *Step 2*—Teams have 25 minutes to go through the in-basket, regardless of how many items they actually complete. Please respond to each item in the package.

■ *Step 3*—Immediately after completing the in-basket exercise, each student will individually complete the attitude scale provided by the instructor.

■ *Step 4*—The instructor will debrief students on the exercise.

In-Basket Setting Students take the role of J. Carter, a personal computer (PC) software department manager in General Software Products, one of the companies owned by General Holding Corporation. You are requested to respond to several e-mails, letters, and memos that have been left in your in-basket. General Holding Corporation is a large company that competes in the computer industry.

General Software develops a wide variety of software products. You, J. Carter, have just been promoted from the position of computer games group manager. Your new promotion to department manager represents a natural progression for someone fast-tracking through management levels at General Software Products. Your new position as PC software department manager also carries with it membership in the firm's Software Steering Committee. This committee meets with the firm's chief executive officer, David Brown, to discuss key strategic policy decisions. The previous department manager for PC Software, Sam White, died suddenly of a heart attack three weeks ago, and, as many predicted (including yourself), you were appointed to the position.

Source: D. Eylon and S. Herman, "Exploring Empowerment: One Method for the Classroom," *Journal of Management Education* 21 (February 1999), pp. 80–94. Copyright © 1999 by Sage Publications, Inc. Reprinted by permission of Sage Publications, Inc.

PERCEPTIONS OF POLITICS SCALE (POPS)

Purpose This self-assessment exercise is designed to help you assess the degree to which you view your work environment as politically charged.

Instructions Listed below are statements that might or might not describe the school where you are attending classes. These statements refer to the administration of the school, not the classroom. Please indicate whether you agree or disagree with each statement. Then calculate your score using the scoring key in Appendix B.

Perception of politics scale					
Circle the number that best reflects the extent to which you agree or disagree with each statement about the administration of the school you attend.	Strongly agree ▼	Agree ▼	Neutral ▼	Disagree ▼	Strongly disagree ▼
1. Administrators at this school tend to build themselves up by tearing others down.	5	4	3	2	1
2. Employees at this school are encouraged to speak out frankly even when they are critical of well-established ideas.	5	4	3	2	1
3. There is no place for yes-men here; good ideas are desired even if it means disagreeing with superiors.	5	4	3	2	1
4. Agreeing with powerful administrators is the best alternative in this organization.	5	4	3	2	1
5. There has always been an influential group of administrators at this school that no one ever crosses.	5	4	3	2	1
6. Sometimes it is easier to remain quiet than to fight the system at this school.	5	4	3	2	1
7. It is best not to rock the boat in this organization.	5	4	3	2	1
8. At this school, telling others what they want to hear is sometimes better than telling the truth.	5	4	3	2	1
9. At this school, employees have to follow what they are told rather than making up their own mind.	5	4	3	2	1

Source: Adapted from K. M. Kacmar, "Further Validation of the Perceptions of Politics Scale (POPS): A Multiple Sample Investigation," *Journal of Management* 23 (1997), pp. 627–58.

After studying the preceding material, be sure to check out our website at
www.mhhe.com/mcshane2e
for more in-depth information and interactivities that correspond to this chapter.

13

Organizational Conflict and Negotiation

AFTER READING THIS CHAPTER, YOU SHOULD BE ABLE TO:

- Distinguish task-related from socioemotional conflict.

- Discuss the advantages and disadvantages of conflict in organizations.

- Identify six sources of organizational conflict.

- Outline the five interpersonal styles of conflict management.

- Summarize six structural approaches to managing conflict.

- Outline four situational influences on negotiations.

- Compare and contrast the three types of third-party dispute resolution.

John Crisp wants 12-hour shifts with bigger blocks of time off from work. So would other young employees at Techneglas Inc.'s factory in Columbus, Ohio. The problem is that older Techneglas employees insist on sticking to the current 8-hour shift schedule. They have lived with this schedule for some time, and it lets them work overtime with less fatigue.

That irritates the 24-year-old Crisp and other staff in his age group, who want time off rather than overtime. "The old people don't have a life," snaps Crisp. "Their jobs are their lives." Jackie Beard, another 24-year-old Techneglas employee, agrees. "I've got a life outside of here," says the single mother who is working part-time toward a college degree.

Techneglas is experiencing the rising cacophony of intergenerational conflict. Generation gaps have always existed, but generational conflict is more common today because employees across age groups work together more than ever before. "In the old hierarchical organization, generations were separated," explains Claire Raines, who co-authored a recent book on generational conflict in the workplace. Today, flattened corporate structures and promotions based on merit rather than age are thrusting together employees of different age groups.

Fred Getz, a 50-year-old executive at Robert Half International Inc. in Schaumburg, Illinois, has noticed that younger employees

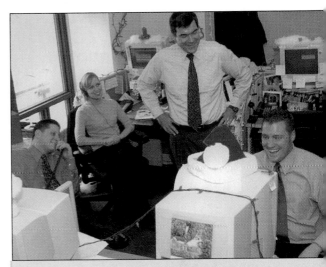

Fred Getz sees plenty of generational differences with his young staff, including (from left in photo) Peter Pacente, Megan Lemerg, and Greg Beardsworth. *(Chicago Tribune photo by Jerry Tomaselli)*

are different, particularly in how they do research. "Someone my age, who takes a more academic approach, is more willing to read and study things," explains Getz. "[Younger employees] don't have time to do a lot of reading."

To minimize conflict resulting from generational differences, Getz recommends adapting to the different needs and work styles of younger employees. "You have to be willing to change with the times and economic circumstances and move ahead," he advises. Larry Sage, a 31-year veteran at Weyerhaeuser in Seattle, follows that advice. "You hang around with these young kids, you learn a lot," says Sage, who listens to younger staff at the forest products company while jogging with them. "That's why I run with them. Otherwise I can't keep up with them."[1]

conflict

The process in which one party perceives that its interests are being opposed or negatively affected by another.

Conflict is a process in which one party perceives that its interests are being opposed or negatively affected by another party.[2] Younger and older employees at Techneglas experience conflict because they perceive that they have opposing interests regarding the shift schedule. Younger employees want a schedule that maximizes their time off; older workers want a schedule that gives them better opportunities for overtime.

This chapter looks at the dynamics of conflict in organizational settings. We begin by describing the conflict process and discussing the consequences and sources of conflict in organizational settings. Five conflict management styles are then described, followed by a discussion of the structural approaches to conflict management. The last two sections of this chapter introduce two procedures for resolving conflict: negotiation and third-party resolution.

THE CONFLICT PROCESS

When we describe an incident involving conflict, we are usually referring to the observable part of conflict—the angry words, shouting matches, and actions that symbolize opposition. But this *manifest conflict* is only a small part of the conflict process. As Exhibit 13.1 illustrates, the conflict process begins with the sources of conflict.[3] Incompatible goals, different values, and other conditions lead one or both parties to perceive that conflict exists. We will look closely at these sources of conflict later in this chapter because understanding and changing the root causes is the key to effective conflict management.

Conflict Perceptions and Emotions

At some point, the sources of conflict lead one or both parties to perceive that conflict exists. They also experience various conflict-laden emotions toward the other party. For example, John Crisp and Jackie Beard were probably frustrated or angry with the older Techneglas employees who opposed their desire for a 12-hour shift schedule.

Task-Related versus Socioemotional Conflict
When asked what Toyota Motor Company does to make great cars, one engineer replied, "Lots of conflict."[4] Toyota employees know that conflict is not always bad. Successful organizations encourage mild forms of conflict without having the situation escalate into an emotional battle between employees or work units. The key is to create *task-related conflict* and to prevent it from escalating into *socioemotional conflict*.[5] Task-related conflict occurs when people disagree about task issues, such as goals, key decision areas, procedures, and the appropriate choice for action. The conflict is separate from them, an object "out there" that must be addressed. This conflict is potentially healthy and valuable because it makes people rethink their perspectives of reality. As long as the conflict remains focused on the issue, new ideas may emerge and the conflict remains controlled.

Unfortunately, conflict often becomes personal. Rather than focusing on the issue, each party perceives the other party as the problem. With socioemotional conflict, differences are viewed as personal attacks rather than attempts to resolve an issue. The discussion becomes emotionally charged, which introduces perceptual biases and distorts information processing.

EXHIBIT 13.1   The conflict process

Manifest Conflict

Conflict perceptions and emotions usually manifest themselves in the decisions and overt behaviors of one party toward the other. These conflict episodes may range from subtle nonverbal behaviors to warlike aggression. Conflict is also manifested by the style each side uses to resolve the conflict, such as whether one side tries to defeat the other or find a mutually beneficial solution. Conflict management styles will be described later in this chapter. At this point, you should know that these styles influence each side's decisions and behaviors. Consequently, they play a critical role in determining whether the conflict will escalate or be resolved quickly.

Conflict Escalation Cycle   The conflict process in Exhibit 13.1 shows arrows looping back from manifest conflict to conflict perceptions and emotions. These loops represent the fact that the conflict process is really a series of episodes that potentially come together into an escalation cycle or spiral.[6] It doesn't take much to start this conflict cycle—just an inappropriate comment, a misunderstanding, or an undiplomatic action. These behaviors communicate to the other party in a way that creates a perception of conflict. Even if the first party did not intend to demonstrate conflict, the second party's response may create that perception.

If the conflict remains task-related, both parties may resolve the conflict through logical analysis. However, the communication process has enough ambiguity that a wrong look or word may trigger an emotional response by the other side and set the stage for socioemotional conflict. These distorted beliefs and emotions reduce each side's motivation to communicate, making it more difficult for them to discover common ground and ultimately resolve the conflict.[7] The parties then rely more on stereotypes and emotions to reinforce their perceptions of the other party. Some structural conditions increase the likelihood of conflict escalation. Employees who are more confrontational and less diplomatic also tend to escalate conflict.[8]

Conflict Outcomes

Angela regards herself as a nice person, but conflict with another employee put her in touch with the darker side of her personality. "I never thought I had this black spot in my soul until this person made my life hell," says the projects officer at a consulting firm. The colleague was a good friend until accusing Angela of "stealing" an important client. Relations deteriorated as the colleague responded by spreading malicious and untrue gossip about Angela. Angela complained, but her superiors didn't act on her complaint for several months. The colleague was eventually fired.[9]

This true incident illustrates how misunderstandings and disagreements escalate into socioemotional conflict, which results in negative outcomes for the organization. "The conflict was bad for business," Angela recalls, "because it affected staff decisions and took the focus off making money." Socioemotional conflict increases frustration, job dissatisfaction, and stress. In the longer term, such conflict leads to increased turnover and absenteeism.[10]

These symptoms are showing up among executives at Walt Disney Corporation. Disney CEO Michael Eisner apparently supports an environment where executives battle each other over scarce resources. Insiders claim that several people have left Disney because constant conflict wears them down.[11] At the intergroup level, conflict with people outside the team may lead to groupthink. The conflict increases cohesiveness within the group, but members value consensus so much that it undermines decision quality.[12]

Given these problems, it's not surprising that people normally associate **conflict management** with reducing or removing conflict. However, task-related conflict should be encouraged under some conditions.[13] Conflict management isn't necessarily about minimizing conflict. It refers to interventions that alter the level and form of conflict in ways that maximize its benefits and minimize its dysfunctional consequences. This sometimes means increasing the level of task-related conflict, which helps people recognize problems, identify a variety of solutions, and better understand the relevant issues. This positive conflict encourages people to consider new perspectives and debate these emerging views.

Constructive controversy is a positive application of conflict.[14] As explained in Chapter 10, constructive controversy helps people learn about other points of view, which encourages them to reexamine their basic assumptions about a problem and its possible solution. You can see this constructive controversy at Tractebel, the Belgian utility and industrial services giant. "If debate doesn't take place, then I make it happen," says Philippe Bodson, the former CEO, who is credited with improving Tractebel's performance. "I push until they react. I want people to speak their mind. That's why I create conflict in meetings. My job is to unveil truth around the table."[15]

Conflict is also beneficial where intergroup conflict improves team dynamics within those units. Teams increase their cohesiveness and task orientation when they face an external threat. Conditions of moderate conflict motivate team members to work more efficiently toward their goals, thereby increasing the team's productivity.

SOURCES OF CONFLICT IN ORGANIZATIONS

If you see manifest conflict in organizations, it is most likely caused by one or more of the six conditions shown in Exhibit 13.2 on p. 390.

conflict management
Interventions that alter the level and form of conflict in ways that maximize its benefits and minimize its dysfunctional consequences.

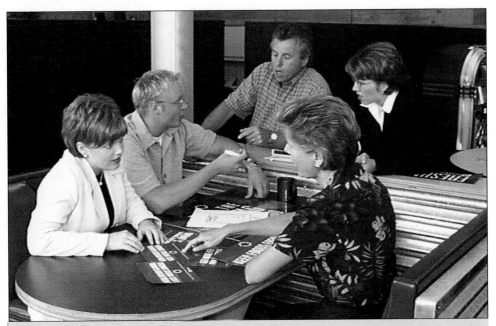

Meyocks & Priebe Advertising encourages constructive controversy. The West Des Moines, Iowa, firm wants its 75 employees to evaluate ideas critically and ensure that dominant participants do not overwhelm these spirited meetings. "We thrive on conflict," says Ted Priebe, president of Meyocks & Priebe. "We actually encourage confrontation as part of our culture. Often there's spirited discussions on what to show the client. It's kind of fun."[16] What conditions must apply to ensure that conflict in these meetings remains task-oriented and doesn't become socio-emotional? *(Courtesy of Meyocks & Priebe Advertising)*

Incompatible Goals

A common source of conflict is goal incompatibility.[17] Goal incompatibility occurs when one employee's or department's personal or work goals seem to interfere with another person's or department's goals. Consider the following situation between "hot-end" and "cold-end" employees at a glass container manufacturer. The hot-end employees form the glass containers and receive a bonus for the number of bottles formed. These bottles work their way to the cold end, where they are packed for shipment. The cold-end employees receive bonuses for minimizing customer complaints and bottle returns, so they weed out jars that don't meet high standards. But the more jars discarded by the cold-end employees, the lower the bonus for the hot-end employees. Conflicts occur when the hot-end employees complain that their cold-end co-workers are too fussy about product quality. Cold-end employees don't like the hot-end employees' questioning their quality control decisions.[18]

Differentiation

Not so long ago, a British automotive company proposed a friendly buyout of an Italian firm. Executives at both companies were excited about the opportunities of sharing distribution channels and manufacturing technologies. But the grand vision of a merged company turned to a nightmare as executives be-

EXHIBIT 13.2

Sources of conflict
in organizations

gan meeting over the details. Their backgrounds and experiences were so different that they were endlessly confused and constantly apologizing to the other side for oversights and misunderstandings. At one meeting—the last, as it turned out—the president of the Italian firm stood up and, smiling sadly, said, "I believe we all know what is the problem here . . . it seems your forward is our reverse; your down, our up; your right, our wrong. Let us finish now, before war is declared."[19]

These automobile executives discovered that conflict is often caused by different values and beliefs due to unique backgrounds, experiences, or training. Mergers often produce conflict because they bring together people with divergent corporate cultures. Employees fight over the "right way" to do things because of their unique experiences in the separate companies. The British and Italian automobile executives probably also experienced conflict due to different national cultures. Cultural diversity makes it difficult to understand or accept the beliefs and values that other people hold toward organizational decisions and events. The partnership of French automaker Renault and Japanese automaker Nissan, described in Global Connections 13.1, provides another rich illustration of conflict due to both national and corporate cultural differences.

Of course, differences also occur within countries. The opening vignette in this chapter described how conflicts occur between older and younger employees. These workplace disputes occur because values, needs, and expectations differ across generations of employees.[20]

Task Interdependence

Conflict tends to increase with the level of task interdependence. Task interdependence exists when team members must share common inputs to their individual tasks, need to interact in the process of executing their work, or receive outcomes (such as rewards) that are determined partly by the performance of others (see Chapter 8).[21] The higher the level of task interdependence, the greater the risk of conflict, because there is a greater chance that

Working Through Culture Clashes in the Renault–Nissan Partnership

Carlos Ghosn experienced more than his share of cross-cultural conflict when French carmaker Renault made him president of its partner, Nissan Motor Company, in Japan. "Certainly many of you have felt the effects of intra-company cultural clashes as your business has become globalized," said the Brazilian-born Renault executive to an audience of automobile executives, consultants, and media. "The results are a waste of talent and a waste of energy."

Ghosn and other French executives were irritated that Nissan's executives seemed to lack a "sense of urgency" to stop seven years of financial losses at Japan's second-largest carmaker. "Even though the evidence is against them, [Nissan executives] sit down and they watch the problem a little bit longer," complains Ghosn.

The Japanese executives were equally disturbed by the French practice of evaluating performance issues across work units. "In a big Japanese company, everyone has their own pigeonhole and their own responsibilities which never impinge on anyone else's, and which means no one questions a colleague's work," explains an anonymous Nissan source.

Conflicts even simmered over traditions involving lunches and meetings. The French executives believe they work better after long lunches, whereas the Japanese executives shovel down their food and get back to work as a show of loyalty. Meanwhile, the Japanese are fond of long meetings because they make their opinions seem valued by the company. This practice irritates the French executives, who prefer quicker decision making.

The good news is that Ghosn seems to be defeating the dysfunctional conflict and saving the Japanese car company through a set of challenging, measurable ob-

Carlos Ghosn experienced plenty of cross-cultural conflict when the Renault executive was transferred to Japan as president of Nissan Motor Company. (© *Reuters NewMedia Inc./CORBIS*)

jectives called the Nissan Revival Plan. The plan has become a superordinate goal that rallied staff and encouraged them to put aside their cultural differences. "We all knew that in order to develop a plan that would work, we would have to treat natural cultural suspicions and culture clashes as a luxury for rich people," Ghosn explains.

Sources: Y. Kageyama, "Renault Manager Crosses Cultural Divide to Turn Around Nissan," *Associated Press State and Local Wire,* June 25, 2001; O. Morgan, "Nissan's Boy from Brazil Puts Accent on Profits," *The Observer (UK),* May 27, 2001, p. 7; F. Kadri, "Renault-Nissan Two Years On: Being Bi-National Is Not So Simple," *Agence France-Presse,* April 1, 2001; A. R. Gold, M. Hirano, and Y. Yokoyama, "An Outsider Takes On Japan: An Interview with Nissan's Carlos Ghosn," *McKinsey Quarterly,* January 2001, p. 95; "Nissan's Ghosn Calls Cultural Clashes 'A Luxury for the Rich,'" *PR Newswire,* January 18, 2000.

each side will disrupt or interfere with the other side's goals.[22] Exhibit 13.3 illustrates the three levels of task interdependence.[23]

▨ *Pooled interdependence*—This is the weakest form of interdependence (other than independence), in which work units operate independently except for reliance on a common resource or authority. Students experience this level of interdependence when they are lined up at the laser printers trying to get their assignments done just before a class deadline. The same thing happens in organizations. Corporate divisions must share scarce resources provided by headquarters, thereby increasing potential conflict.

▨ *Sequential interdependence*—This occurs where the output of one person or unit becomes the direct input for another person or unit. This interdependent

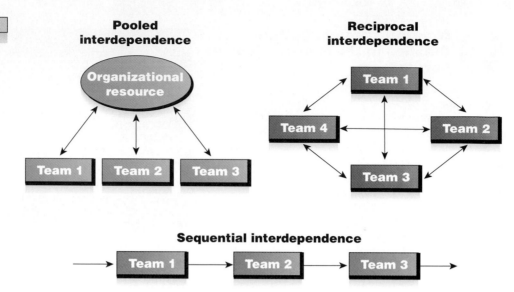

EXHIBIT 13.3

Levels of task
interdependence

Source: Based on J. D. Thompson, *Organizations in Action* (New York: McGraw-Hill, 1967), pp. 54–56.

linkage is found in fish processing plants. Fish are handled by the slitters, then passed to the gutters, who then pass their work to the slimers, who then send their work to the graders.[24]

■ *Reciprocal interdependence*—This is the highest level of interdependence, in which work output is exchanged back and forth among individuals or work units. For example, bus drivers are dependent on the maintenance crews to keep the buses in good repair, and the maintenance crews are dependent on the drivers to operate the vehicles wisely so that their work is minimized.

Scarce Resources

Scarce resources generate conflict because scarcity motivates people to compete with others who also need those resources to achieve their objectives.[25] This situation occurs at Sony's video game group, where the artists who develop "Spawn" and other sci-fi games must compete for resources with the artists who develop sports-related games such as "NFL GameDay." Differentiation partly explains this conflict. "We call them the 'Ghouls and Goblins' and they call us the 'Dumb Jocks,'" laughs the head of the sports group. But the conflict is aggravated by the fact that both groups share a limited budget. "Teams are competing for internal resources for marketing dollars, support for their products," explains a Sony executive. "And they know how much that matters."[26]

Ambiguous Rules

Ambiguous rules—or the complete lack of rules—breed conflict, because uncertainty increases the risk that one party intends to interfere with the other party's goals. Ambiguity also encourages political tactics, and in some cases, employees enter a free-for-all battle to win decisions in their favor. This explains why conflict is more common during mergers and acquisitions. Employees from both companies have conflicting practices and values, and few rules have developed to minimize the maneuvering for power and resources.[27] On the other hand, when clear rules exist, employees know what to expect from each other and have agreed to abide by those rules.

Communication Problems

Conflict often occurs as a result of the lack of opportunity, ability, or motivation to communicate effectively. Let's look at each of these causes. First, when two parties lack the opportunity to communicate, they tend to use stereotypes to explain past behaviors and anticipate future actions. Unfortunately, stereotypes are sufficiently subjective that emotions can negatively distort the meaning of an opponent's actions, thereby escalating perceptions of conflict. Moreover, without direct interaction, the two sides have less psychological empathy for each other.

Second, some people lack the necessary skills to communicate in a diplomatic, nonconfrontational manner. When one party communicates its disagreement in an arrogant way, opponents are more likely to heighten their perception of the conflict. Arrogant behavior also sends a message that one side intends to be competitive rather than cooperative. This attitude may lead the other party to reciprocate with a similar conflict management style.[28] Consequently, as we explained earlier, ineffective communication often leads to an escalation in the conflict cycle.

Ineffective communication can also lead to a third problem: less motivation to communicate in the future. For example, an accountant was verbally abused by an information services manager soon after he was hired. Since then, he has avoided the manager, leaving some problems undetected and unresolved. Another employee reported that the relationship with his manager deteriorated to such an extent that for five months they communicated only by e-mail.[29] These reactions aren't surprising. Socioemotional conflict is uncomfortable, so people are less motivated to interact with others in a conflicting relationship.

Unfortunately, less communication can further escalate the conflict because there is less opportunity to empathize with the opponent's situation and opponents are more likely to rely on distorted stereotypes of the other party. In fact, conflict tends to further distort these stereotypes through the process of social identity (see Chapter 3). We begin to see competitors less favorably so that our self-identity remains strong during these uncertain times.[30]

The lack of motivation to communicate also explains (along with different values and beliefs, described earlier) why conflict is more common in cross-cultural relationships. People tend to feel uncomfortable or awkward interacting with co-workers from different cultures, so they are less motivated to engage in dialogue with them.[31] With limited communication, people rely more on stereotypes to fill in missing information. They also tend to misunderstand each other's verbal and nonverbal signals, further escalating the conflict.

INTERPERSONAL CONFLICT MANAGEMENT STYLES

The six structural conditions described above set the stage for conflict. The conflict process identified earlier in Exhibit 13.1 illustrated that these sources of conflict lead to perceptions and emotions. Some people enter a conflict with

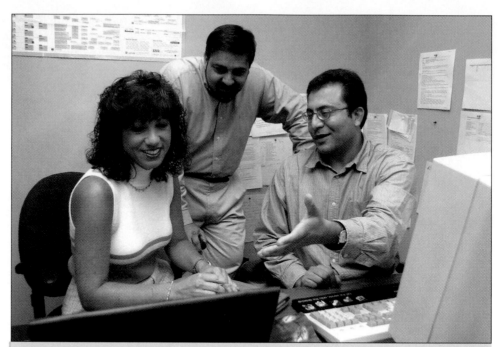

Cross-cultural miscommunication and misunderstanding have resulted in serious conflict at Relativity Technologies. The recently immigrated Russian programmers spoke limited English, so American employees at the Cary, North Carolina, firm, tended to talked down to them. The Russians were also offended when the American co-workers smiled and waved at them in the hallway. Russian employees tend to be serious at work, so these friendly gestures seemed like further evidence that the Americans were mocking them. The Russians eventually threatened to walk off the job. Meanwhile, some of Relativity's newly arrived Indian employees were getting stressed and upset because they worked with an abusive boss and assumed they had no right to protest their ill treatment. "Oh, we had such blowups," admits Relativity CEO Vivek Wadhwa (center), shown here with two Relativity employees.[32] How do misperceptions and miscommunications escalate into full-blown incidents of manifest conflict? *(Los Angeles Times Photo by Jeffrey A. Camarati)*

win–win orientation

The belief that the parties will find a mutually beneficial solution to their disagreement.

win–lose orientation

The belief that the conflicting parties are drawing from a fixed pie, so the more one party receives, the less the other party will receive.

a **win–win orientation.** This is the perception that the parties will find a mutually beneficial solution to their disagreement. They believe that the resources at stake are expandable rather than fixed if the parties work together to find a creative solution. Other people enter a conflict with a **win–lose orientation.** They adopt the belief that the parties are drawing from a fixed pie, so the more one party receives, the less the other party will receive.

Conflict tends to escalate when the parties develop a win–lose orientation because they rely on power and politics to gain advantage. A win–lose orientation may occasionally be appropriate when the conflict really is over a fixed resource, but few organizational conflicts are due to perfectly opposing interests with fixed resources. To varying degrees, the opposing groups can gain by believing that their positions aren't perfectly opposing and that creative solutions are possible. For instance, a supplier and customer may initially think they have opposing interests—the supplier wants to receive more money for the product, whereas the customer wants to pay less money for it. Yet further discussion may reveal that the customer would be willing to pay more if the product could be provided earlier than originally arranged. The vendor may actually value that earlier delivery because it saves inventory costs. By looking at the bigger picture, both parties can often discover common ground.

Adopting a win–win or a win–lose orientation influences our conflict management style, that is, our actions toward the other person. Researchers have categorized five interpersonal styles of approaching the other party in a conflict situation. As we see in Exhibit 13.4, each approach can be placed in a two-dimensional grid reflecting the person's motivation to satisfy his or her own interests (called *assertiveness*) and to satisfy the other party's interests (called *cooperativeness*).[33] Collaboration is the only style that represents a purely win–win orientation. The other four styles represent variations of the win–lose approach. For effective conflict management, we should learn to apply different conflict management styles to different situations.[34]

- *Collaborating*—tries to find a mutually beneficial solution for both parties through problem solving. An important feature of collaboration is information sharing so that both parties can identify common ground and potential solutions that satisfy both (or all) of them.
- *Avoiding*—tries to smooth over or avoid conflict situations altogether. For example, some employees will rearrange their work area or tasks to minimize interaction with certain co-workers.[35]

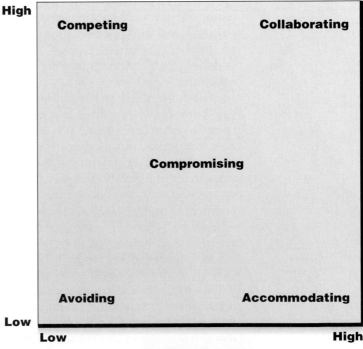

EXHIBIT 13.4

Interpersonal conflict management styles

Source: Adapted from T. L. Ruble and K. Thomas, "Support for a Two-Dimensional Model of Conflict Behavior," *Organizational Behavior and Human Performance* 16 (1976), p. 145.

    ■   *Competing*—tries to win the conflict at the other's expense. This style has the strongest win–lose orientation because it has the highest level of assertiveness and lowest level of cooperativeness.

    ■   *Accommodating*—involves giving in completely to the other side's wishes, or at least cooperating with little or no attention to your own interests.

    ■   *Compromising*—tries to reach a middle ground with the other party. You look for a position in which your losses are offset by equally valued gains.

Choosing the Best Conflict Management Style

Sun Microsystems recently sued memory chip maker Kingston Technology over exclusive rights to a new architecture in memory modules. When the U.S. court threw out Sun's complaint, Kingston co-founder David Sun had another idea; he challenged Sun Microsystems CEO Scott McNealy to a game of golf to settle their differences.[36] A golf game is an unusual way to resolve conflict, but this incident illustrates how people apply different conflict management styles. Ideally, we use different styles under different conditions, but most of us have a preferred conflict management style.

    The collaborative style is usually recognized as the preferred approach to conflict resolution. For example, the collaborative conflict management style results in better joint venture performance.[37] The parties discuss concerns more quickly and openly, seek their partner's opinions, and explain their course of action more fully than when a noncollaborative style is used. However, this style works only under certain conditions. Specifically, it is best when the parties do not have perfectly opposing interests and when they have enough trust and openness to share information. Collaborating is usually desirable because organizational conflicts are rarely win–lose situations. There is usually some opportunity for mutual gain if the parties search for creative solutions.[38]

    You might think that avoiding is an ineffective conflict management strategy, but it may be the best approach when the issue is trivial or as a temporary tactic to cool down heated disputes. However, conflict avoidance should not be a long-term solution because it increases the other party's frustration.

    The competing style of conflict resolution is usually inappropriate because organizational relationships rarely involve complete opposition. However, competing may be necessary when you know you are correct and the dispute requires a quick solution. For example, you might use the competing style when you believe the other party's position is unethical or when it otherwise violates your fundamental values. The competing style may also be necessary when the other party would take advantage of more cooperative strategies.

    The accommodating style may be appropriate when the other party has substantially more power or the issue is not as important to you as to the other party. On the other hand, accommodating behaviors may give the other side unrealistically high expectations, thereby motivating that party to seek more from you in the future. In the long run, accommodating may produce more conflict rather than resolve it.

    The compromising style may be best when there is little hope for mutual gain through problem solving, both parties have equal power, and both are under time pressure to settle their differences. However, compromise is rarely a final solution and may cause the parties to overlook options for mutual gain.

Cultural and Gender Differences in Conflict Management Styles

Cultural differences are more than just a source of conflict. Cultural background also affects the conflict management style we prefer using, because we are more comfortable with conflict management styles that are consistent with our personal and cultural value system.[39]

Research suggests that people from collectivist cultures—where group goals are valued more than individual goals—are motivated to maintain harmonious relations. Consequently, they tend to rely on avoidance or collaboration to resolve disagreements.[40] In contrast, people from individualistic cultures more frequently apply a compromising or competing style. People from collectivist cultures can be just as competitive as are individualists with people outside their group. However, collectivists are generally more likely to avoid confrontation, where possible.

Some writers suggest that men and women also tend to rely on different conflict management styles.[41] Generally speaking, women pay more attention than do men to the relationship between the parties. Consequently, they tend to adopt a collaborative style in business settings and are more willing to compromise to protect the relationship. Men tend to be more competitive and take a short-term orientation to the relationship. Of course, we must be cautious about these observations because gender has a weak influence on conflict management style.

STRUCTURAL APPROACHES TO CONFLICT MANAGEMENT

Conflict management styles refer to how we approach the other party in a conflict situation. But conflict management also involves altering the underlying structural causes of potential conflict. The main structural approaches are identified in Exhibit 13.5. Although this section discusses ways to reduce conflict,

EXHIBIT 13.5

Structural approaches to conflict management

we should keep in mind that conflict management sometimes calls for increasing conflict, mainly by reversing the strategies described over the next few pages.[42]

Emphasizing Superordinate Goals

Carlos Ghosn, described earlier (in Connections 13.1), was able to minimize conflict between French and Japanese executives partly by focusing everyone on the Nissan Revival Plan as a **superordinate goal.** Superordinate goals are common objectives held by conflicting parties that are more important than the departmental or individual goals on which the conflict is based. By increasing commitment to corporatewide goals, employees place less emphasis on and therefore feel less conflict with co-workers regarding competing individual or departmental-level goals.[43] Superordinate goals also potentially reduce the problem of differentiation because they establish a common frame of reference. Heterogeneous team members still perceive different ways to achieve corporate objectives, but superordinate goals ensure they mutually understand and agree on the objectives themselves.

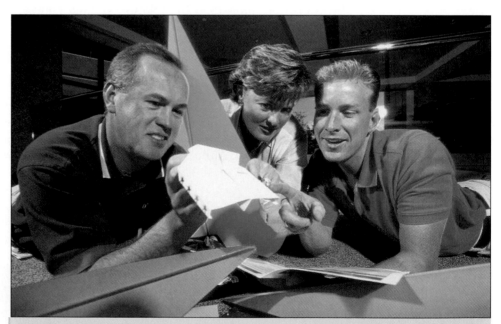

Executives at Tivoli Systems discovered the importance of superordinate goals after participating in an exercise called Paper Airplanes, Inc. Each team at the Austin, Texas, company had 30 minutes to manufacture and sell as many standard-specific planes as possible. The teams initially performed poorly because participants focused on their individual goals. "[T]he biggest problem [was] that you couldn't just focus on your part," explains Tivoli executive Bill Jones (left in photo). Teams eventually won the exercise after their members focused on the organization's success more than their individual tasks. The exercise now represents a reminder that Tivoli employees need to focus on superordinate goals rather than departmental differences. "[W]hen things come up we refer to the exercise to help everyone get on the same page," says Brent Vance (right in photo).[44] In what other ways might the Paper Airplanes exercise reduce dysfunctional conflict? *(Ed Lallo)*

Several research studies indicate that focusing on superordinate goals weakens dysfunctional conflict. One study revealed that marketing managers in Hong Kong, China, Japan, and the United States were more likely to develop a collaborative conflict management style when executives aligned departmental goals with corporate objectives. A U.S. study found that the most effective executive teams consistently apply a superordinate goal strategy. They frame their decisions as collaborations, thereby drawing attention and commitment away from sublevel goals.[45]

Reducing Differentiation

Another way to minimize dysfunctional conflict is to reduce the differences that produce the conflict in the first place.[46] The Manila Diamond Hotel in the Philippines accomplishes this goal by rotating staff across different departments. "In Manila Diamond, there is no turf mentality," explains the hotel's marketing manager. "We all work together. We even share each other's jobs whenever necessary."[47] Similarly, W. L. Gore and Associates reduces differentiation by moving employees around to different teams. The manufacturer of Gore-Tex and other products introduced this team rotation system after it became apparent that employees were becoming too committed to their own team's goals. "You can get a little too focused on your own team and forget the good of the whole company," admits one of Gore's team members.[48]

Improving Communication and Understanding

Communication is critical to effective conflict management. Communication can range from casual gatherings among employees who rarely meet otherwise to formal processes where differences are identified and discussed. Multinational peacekeeping forces work together more effectively when troops eat and socialize together.[49] Given increased opportunity, ability, and motivation to share information, employees develop less extreme perceptions of each other than if they rely on stereotypes and emotions. Direct communication provides a better understanding of the other person's or department's work environment and resource limitations. Ongoing communication is particularly important where the need for functional specialization makes it difficult to reduce differentiation.[50]

Interdepartmental communication includes socializing over a game of Ping-Pong or Foosball. "The more informal communication that happens between various groups in companies, the better they work together as a team," explains Jamey Harvey, CEO of Reston, Virginia–based software maker iKimbo. "Marketing actually understands the intense pressure the development team is under to develop software on time. And the development team understands that the marketing team is spending money that's going to be wasted if the product doesn't come out on time."[51]

Some of the team-building activities described in Chapter 8 help reduce conflict because they help participants understand each other. Siemens AG's nuclear power division in Germany and French nuclear giant Framatome SA took this route when they recently merged. Senior executives at both firms were sent to a retreat an hour outside Paris where they spent a few days in canoe races and blindfolded three-legged races. The consulting firm that operates the

Drumming Out Their Differences

Dozens of businesspeople pour into an auditorium where drums of all types—Latin American congas, African doumbeks, and Brazilian surdos—line the room. The participants anxiously take their seats. Few have played drums before, but they will all play in harmony tonight. They will learn to cooperate and coordinate through the beat of their drums.

Leading the two-hour drumming session is Doug Sole, co-owner of Soul Drums in Toronto, Canada. He starts by pointing randomly to individuals, asking them to play a beat that others will imitate. The rhythm intensifies as others join in, then falls apart into a cacophony. "We're having a communication problem here," Sole interrupts. "If we all start banging our own thing, it's going to be chaos." Sole begins again and repeats the process until the auditorium is filled with the hypnotic beat of strangers working together.

Drum circles represent a metaphor for cooperation, coordination, communication, and teamwork in nontraditional corporate structures. They focus participants on the process of working together, not just on the outcome of achieving a goal. "It forced us to listen to, be dependent on, and have fun with each other," explains Kathleen Ross, an executive at Arbitron, a Maryland-based media research firm whose employees have participated in drum circles.

Onye Onyemaechi, a Nigerian master drummer in California, says that employees often work side by side for years without really getting to know one another. He warns that this lack of unity and understanding hinders the organization's potential, whereas drum circles begin the process of creating harmony among these strangers. "Drum circles bring people together to realize their common base," he advises.

"Drum circles thrive on collaborative creativity, and that is so important in the Internet world," says Christine

Doug Sole and other drum circle facilitators build cooperation and mutual understanding with drumsticks and boomwhackers. *(Gary Diggins, Soul Drums Ltd.; Doug Sole, Mel Bay Productions, Pacific Missouri)*

Stevens, founder of Upbeat Drum Circles in Fort Collins, Colorado. "Drum circles involve creativity and sharing, but they also demonstrate that things need to be coordinated to sound good."

Sources: S. Terry, "Lost in the Rhythm," *Christian Science Monitor,* May 23, 2001, p. 11; R. Segall, "Catch the Beat," *Psychology Today,* July 2000; M. K. Pratt, "A Pound of Cure," *Fast Company,* April 2000; A. Georgiades, "Business Heeds the Beat," *Toronto Star,* August 4, 1999.

retreat also spends time with each group to review the cultural differences between French and German executives.[52]

Another team-building activity that can minimize conflict is the dialogue meeting, in which the disputing parties discuss their differences. Dialogue helps participants understand each other's mental models and fundamental assumptions so that they can create a common thinking process and mental models for the team (see Chapter 8).[53] Several companies, including Toyota, Sony, Microsoft, Dell Computer, and Hewlett-Packard, have introduced yet another conflict-busting activity called drum circles. As Connections 13.2 describes, participants in this unique team-building activity use drums and other percussion instruments to learn the process of working together. It teaches harmony, not only in music, but in how employees communicate and understand each other.

Reducing Task Interdependence

Conflict increases with the level of interdependence, so minimizing dysfunctional conflict might involve reducing the level of interdependence between the parties. If cost-effective, this strategy might occur by dividing the shared resource so that each party has exclusive use of part of it. Sequentially or reciprocally interdependent jobs might be combined so that they form a pooled interdependence. For example, rather than having one employee serve customers and another operate the cash register, each employee could handle both customer activities alone. Buffers also help reduce task interdependence between people. Buffers might involve resources, such as the addition of more inventory between people who perform sequential tasks. We also find human buffers in organizations—people who intervene between highly interdependent people or work units.[54]

Increasing Resources

An obvious way to reduce conflict due to resource scarcity is to increase the amount of resources available. Corporate decision makers might dismiss this solution quickly because of the costs involved. However, they need to compare these costs carefully with the costs of dysfunctional conflict arising out of resource scarcity.

Clarifying Rules and Procedures

Some conflicts arise from ambiguous decision rules regarding the allocation of scarce resources. Consequently, these conflicts can be minimized by establishing rules and procedures. Rules clarify the distribution of resources, such as when students can use the laser printer or for how long they can borrow library books. Consider the following situation that occurred when Armstrong World Industries, Inc., brought in consultants to implement a client–server network. Information systems employees at the flooring and building materials company experienced conflict with the consultants over who was in charge. Another conflict occurred when the consultants wanted to work long hours and take Friday off to fly home. Armstrong minimized these conflicts by spelling out as much as possible in the contract about each party's responsibilities and roles. Issues that were unclear or overlooked in the contract were clarified by joint discussion between two senior executives at the companies.[55]

Rules establish changes to the terms of interdependence, such as an employee's hours of work or a supplier's fulfillment of an order. In most cases, the parties affected by these rules are involved in the process of deciding these terms of interdependence. Because it redefines the terms of interdependence, the strategy of clarifying rules is part of the larger process of negotiation.

RESOLVING CONFLICT THROUGH NEGOTIATION

Think back through yesterday's events. Maybe you had to work out an agreement with other students about what tasks to complete for a team project. Chances are that you shared transportation with someone, so you had to clarify

negotiation
Occurs whenever two or more conflicting parties attempt to resolve their divergent goals by redefining the terms of their interdependence.

the timing of the ride. Then perhaps there was the question of who made dinner. Each of these daily events created potential conflict, and they were resolved through negotiation. **Negotiation** occurs whenever two or more conflicting parties attempt to resolve their divergent goals by redefining the terms of their interdependence.[56] In other words, people negotiate when they think that discussion can produce a more satisfactory arrangement (at least for them) in their exchange of goods or services.

As you can see, negotiation is not an obscure practice reserved for labor and management bosses when hammering out a workplace agreement. Everyone negotiates—every day. Most of the time, you often don't even realize that you are in negotiations.[57] Negotiation is particularly evident in the workplace because employees work interdependently. They negotiate with their supervisors over next month's work assignments, with customers over the sale and delivery schedules of their product, and with co-workers over when to have lunch. And yes, they occasionally negotiate with each other in labor disputes and workplace agreements.

Some writers suggest that negotiations are more successful when the parties adopt a collaborative style, whereas others caution that this conflict management style is sometimes costly.[58] We know that any win–lose style (competing, accommodating, etc.) is unlikely to produce the optimal solution, because the parties have not shared information necessary to discover a mutually satisfactory solution. On the other hand, we must be careful about adopting an openly collaborative style until mutual trust has been established.

The concern with collaboration is that information is power, so information sharing gives the other party more power to leverage a better deal if the opportunity occurs. Skilled negotiators often adopt a *cautiously* collaborative style at the outset by sharing information slowly and determining whether the other side will reciprocate. In this respect, they try to establish trust with the other party.[59] They switch to one of the win–lose styles only when it becomes apparent that a win–win solution is not possible or the other party is unwilling to share information with a cooperative orientation.

Bargaining Zone Model of Negotiations

The negotiation process moves each party along a continuum with an area of potential overlap called the *bargaining zone*.[60] Exhibit 13.6 displays one possible bargaining zone situation. This linear diagram illustrates a purely win–lose situation—one side's gain will be the other's loss. However, the bargaining zone model can also be applied to situations in which both sides potentially gain from the negotiations. As this model illustrates, the parties typically establish three main negotiating points. The *initial offer point* is the team's opening offer to the other party. This point may be its best expectation or a pie-in-the-sky starting point. The *target point* is the team's realistic goal or expectation for a final agreement. The *resistance point* is the point beyond which the team will not make further concessions.

The parties begin negotiations by describing their initial offer point for each item on the agenda. In most cases, the participants know that this is only a starting point that will change as both sides offer concessions. In win–lose situations, neither the target nor the resistance points are revealed to the other

EXHIBIT 13.6   Bargaining zone model of negotiations

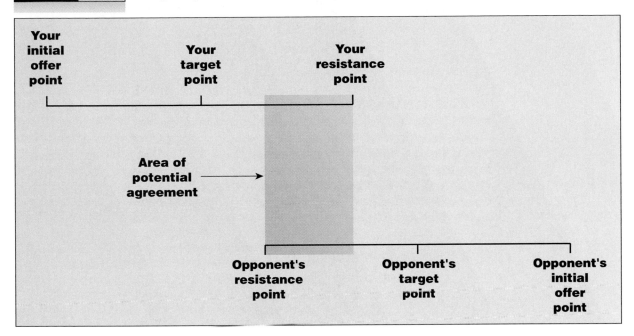

party. However, people try to discover the other side's resistance point because this knowledge helps them determine how much they can gain without breaking off negotiations.

When the parties have a win–win orientation, on the other hand, the objective is to find a creative solution that keeps everyone close to the initial offer points. They hope to find an arrangement by which each side loses relatively little value on some issues and gains significantly more on other issues. For example, a supplier might want to delay delivery dates, whereas delivery times are not important to the business customer. If the parties share this information, they can quickly agree to a delayed delivery schedule, thereby costing the customer very little and gaining the supplier a great deal. On other items (financing, order size, etc.), the supplier might give something with minimal loss even though it is a significant benefit to the business customer.

Situational Influences on Negotiations

The effectiveness of negotiating depends on both the situation and the behaviors of the negotiators. Four of the most important situational factors are location, physical setting, time, and audience.

Location   It is easier to negotiate on your own turf because you are familiar with the negotiating environment and are able to maintain comfortable routines.[61] Also, there is no need to cope with travel-related stress or depend on others for resources during the negotiation. Of course, you can't walk out of negotiations as easily when on your own turf, but this is usually a minor issue. Considering these strategic benefits of home turf, many negotiators agree to neutral territory. Telephones, videoconferences, and other forms of information technology potentially avoid territorial issues, but skilled negotiators usually prefer the media richness of face-to-face meetings.

Physical Setting   The physical distance between the parties and the formality of the setting can influence the parties' orientation toward each other and the disputed issues.[62] So can the seating arrangements. People who sit face-to-face are more likely to develop a win–lose orientation toward the conflict situation. In contrast, some negotiation groups deliberately intersperse participants around the table to convey a win–win orientation. Others arrange the seating so that both parties face a whiteboard, reflecting the notion that both parties face the same problem or issue.

Time Passage and Deadlines   The more time people invest in negotiations, the stronger is their commitment to reaching an agreement. The passage of time increases the motivation to resolve the conflict, but it also fuels the escalation of commitment problems described in Chapter 9. For example, the more time put into negotiations, the stronger the tendency to make unwarranted concessions so that the negotiations do not fail.

Time deadlines may be useful to the extent that they motivate the parties to complete negotiations. However, time deadlines may become a liability when exceeding deadlines is costly.[63] Negotiators make concessions and soften their demands more rapidly as the deadline approaches. Moreover, time pressure inhibits a collaborative conflict management style, because the parties have less time to exchange information or present flexible offers.

Audience Characteristics   Most negotiators have audiences—anyone with a vested interest in the negotiation outcomes, such as executives, other team members, or the general public. Negotiators tend to act differently when their audience observes the negotiation or has detailed information about the process, compared with situations in which the audience sees only the end results.[64] When the audience has direct surveillance over the proceedings, negotiators tend to be more competitive, less willing to make concessions, and more likely to engage in political tactics against the other party.[65] This hardline behavior shows the audience that the negotiator is working for their interests. With their audience watching, negotiators also have more interest in saving face. Sometimes audiences are drawn into the negotiations by acting as a source of indirect appeals. The general public often takes on this role when groups negotiate with governments.[66]

Negotiator Behaviors

Negotiator behaviors play an important role in resolving conflict. Four of the most important behaviors are setting goals, gathering information, communicating effectively, and making concessions.

■ *Planning and setting goals*—Research has consistently reported that people have more favorable negotiation results when they plan and set goals.[67] In particular, negotiators should carefully think through their initial offer, target, and resistance points. They need to check their underlying assumptions, as well as goals and values. Equally important is the need to research what the other party wants from the negotiation.

■ *Gathering information*—"Seek to understand before you seek to be understood." This popular philosophy from management guru Stephen Covey applies to effective negotiations. It means that we should spend more time listening closely to the other party and asking them for details of their position.[68] One way to improve the information-gathering process is to have a team of people participate in negotiations. Asian companies tend to have large negotiation teams for this purpose.[69] With more information about the opponent's interests and needs, negotiators are better able to discover low-cost concessions or proposals that will satisfy the other side.

■ *Communicating effectively*—Effective negotiators communicate in a way that maintains effective relationships between the parties.[70] Specifically, they minimize socioemotional conflict by focusing on issues rather than people. Effective negotiators also avoid irritating statements such as "I think you'll agree that this is a generous offer." Effective negotiators are masters of persuasive communication. In particular, negotiators structure the content of their messages so that their goals are accepted by others, not merely understood (see Chapter 12).[71]

■ *Making concessions*—Concessions are important because they (1) enable the parties to move toward the area of potential agreement, (2) symbolize each party's motivation to bargain in good faith, and (3) tell the other party of the relative importance of the negotiating items.[72] How many concessions should you make? The answer varies with the other party's expectations and the level of trust between you. For instance, many Chinese negotiators are wary of people who change their position during the early stages of negotiations. Similarly, some writers warn that Russian negotiators tend to view concessions as a sign of weakness rather than a sign of trust.[73] Generally, the best strategy is to be moderately tough and give just enough concessions to communicate sincerity and motivation to resolve the conflict.[74] Being too tough can undermine relations between the parties; giving too many concessions implies weakness and encourages the other party to use power and resistance.

THIRD-PARTY CONFLICT RESOLUTION

third-party conflict resolution
Any attempt by a relatively neutral person to help the parties resolve their differences.

Most of this chapter has focused on people directly involved in a conflict, yet many disputes in organizational settings are resolved with the assistance of a third party. **Third-party conflict resolution** is any attempt by a relatively neutral person to help the parties resolve their differences—ranging from formal labor arbitration to informal managerial interventions to resolve disagreements among employees.

There are four main objectives in third-party conflict resolution.[75] One objective is *efficiency*. Those who take the third-party role try to resolve the dispute quickly and with minimum expenditure of organizational resources. Second, conflict resolution should be *effective*, meaning that the process should find the best long-term solution that will correct the underlying causes of the conflict. Third, this process should have outcome fairness. This objective ensures that the parties feel the solution provided by the third-party intervention is fair. Although outcome fairness is similar to effectiveness, they are not the same, because people sometimes think that a solution is fair even though it does not work well in the long term.

Finally, third-party conflict resolution should ensure that the parties feel the dispute resolution process is fair, whether or not the outcome is favorable to them. This objective, known as **procedural fairness,** is particularly important when the third party makes a binding decision to resolve the dispute. In such situations, procedural fairness increases when the third party isn't biased (e.g., doesn't have a vested interest toward one party), is well informed about the facts of the situation, and has listened to all sides of the dispute. It also increases when the decision can be appealed to a higher authority and the third party applies existing policies consistently.[76]

Types of Third-Party Intervention

There are generally three types of third-party dispute resolution activities: arbitration, inquisition, and mediation. These activities can be classified by their level of control over the process and the decision (see Exhibit 13.7).[77]

■ *Arbitration*—Arbitrators have high control over the final decision, but low control over the process.[78] Executives engage in this strategy by following previously agreed upon rules of due process, listening to arguments from the disputing employees, and making a binding decision. Arbitration is applied as the final stage of grievances by unionized employees, but it is also becoming more common in nonunion conflicts. For instance, some workers' compensation boards rely on a process called alternative dispute resolution (ADR), which typically includes mediation followed by arbitration.

■ *Inquisition*—Inquisitors control all discussion about the conflict. Like arbitrators, they have high decision control because they choose the form of conflict resolution. However, they also have high process control because they

---

procedural fairness
Perceptions of fairness regarding the dispute resolution process, whether or not the outcome is favorable to the person.

EXHIBIT 13.7

Types of third-party intervention

choose which information to examine and how to examine it, and generally decide how the conflict resolution process will be handled.

■ *Mediation*—Mediators have high control over the intervention process. In fact, their main purpose is to manage the process and context of interaction between the disputing parties. However, the parties make the final decision about how to resolve their differences. Thus, mediators have little or no control over the conflict resolution decision.

Choosing the Best Third-Party Intervention Strategy

Team leaders, executives, and co-workers regularly intervene in disputes between employees and departments. Sometimes they adopt a mediator role; other times they serve as arbitrators. However, research suggests that people in positions of authority (e.g., managers) usually adopt an inquisitional approach whereby they dominate the intervention process as well as make a binding decision.[79] Managers like the inquisitional approach because it is consistent with the decision-oriented nature of managerial jobs, gives them control over the conflict process and outcome, and tends to resolve disputes efficiently.

However, the inquisitional approach to third-party conflict resolution is usually the least effective in organizational settings.[80] One problem is that leaders who take an inquisitional role tend to collect limited information about the problem using this approach, so their imposed decision may produce an ineffective solution to the conflict. Moreover, employees tend to think that the procedures and outcomes of inquisitions are unfair because they have little control over this approach.

Which third-party intervention is most appropriate in organizations? The answer depends partly on the situation.[81] For example, arbitration is much less popular in Hong Kong than in North America. But generally speaking, for everyday disputes between two employees, the mediation approach is usually best because it gives employees more responsibility for resolving their own disputes. The third-party representative merely establishes an appropriate context for conflict resolution. Although not as efficient as other strategies, mediation potentially offers the highest level of employee satisfaction with the conflict process and outcomes.[82] When employees cannot resolve their differences, arbitration seems to work best because the predetermined rules of evidence and other processes create a higher sense of procedural fairness. Moreover, arbitration is preferred where the organization's goals should take priority over individual goals.

alternative dispute resolution (ADR)

A third-party dispute resolution process that includes mediation, typically followed by arbitration.

Alternative Dispute Resolution   Dallas-based energy services company Halliburton Company and Cleveland-based auto parts and aerospace company TRW, Inc., take third-party resolution one step further through a comprehensive **alternative dispute resolution (ADR)** process. ADR combines third-party dispute resolution in an orderly sequence. ADR typically begins with a meeting between the employee and employer to clarify and negotiate their differences. If this fails, a mediator is brought in to help the parties reach a mutually agreeable solution. If mediation fails, the parties submit their case to an arbitrator whose decision may be either binding or voluntarily accepted by the employer. Some firms (such as TRW) allow employees to take the case to court if they lose the arbitration decision.[83]

When Buddy's Natural Chickens, Inc., opened its plant in Gonzales, Texas, the poultry farming and processing company experienced a rash of workers' compensation claims and other grievances. Before these conflicts could escalate and undermine morale, Buddy's introduced alternative dispute resolution (ADR). This third-party conflict resolution program begins with informal, face-to-face talks between managers and employees. Almost all disputes have been settled at this stage. However, if unresolved, the dispute then moves on to mediation and, finally, to arbitration.[85] Why doesn't the ADR process include inquisition? *(Bob Daemmrich/The Image Works)*

Within this three-step process, ADR takes various forms. Philadelphia Electric (now part of Chicago-based Exelon Corporation) introduced a process whereby employees meet with trained peer coaches who prepare workers for conversations with their supervisors. This tends to increase the success rate of the first stage in the ADR process. Although most ADR systems rely on professional arbitrators, some firms prefer peer arbitrations, which include a panel of co-workers and managers who are not involved in the dispute.[84]

Whether resolving conflict through third-party dispute resolution or direct negotiation, we need to recognize that many solutions come from the sources of conflict that were identified earlier in this chapter. This conclusion may seem obvious, but in the heat of conflict, people often focus on each other rather than the underlying causes. Recognizing these conflict sources is the role of effective leadership, which is discussed in the next chapter.

CHAPTER SUMMARY

Conflict is the process in which one party perceives that its interests are being opposed or negatively affected by another party. The conflict process begins with the sources of conflict. These sources lead one or both sides to perceive a conflict and to experience conflict emotions. This, in turn, produces manifest conflict, such as behaviors toward the other side.

When conflict is task-related, the parties view the conflict experience as something separate from them. Disputes are much more difficult to resolve when they produce socioemotional conflict, where the parties perceive each other as the problem. The conflict process often escalates through a series of episodes and shifts from task-related to socioemotional.

Conflict management maximizes the benefits and minimizes the dysfunctional consequences of conflict. Conflict is beneficial in the form of constructive controversy because it makes people think more fully about issues. Positive conflict also increases team cohesiveness when conflict is with another group. The main problems with conflict are that it may lead to job stress, dissatisfaction, and turnover. Dysfunctional intergroup conflict may undermine decision making.

Conflict tends to increase when people have incompatible goals, different values and beliefs, interdependent tasks, scarce resources, ambiguous rules, and problems communicating with each other. Conflict is more common in a multicultural workforce because of greater differentiation and communication problems among employees.

People with a win–win orientation believe the parties will find a mutually beneficial solution to their disagreement. Those with a win–lose orientation adopt the belief that the parties are drawing from a fixed pie. The latter orientation tends to escalate conflict. Among the five interpersonal conflict management styles, only collaborating represents a purely win–win orientation. The four other styles—avoiding, competing, accommodating, and compromising—adopt some variation of a win–lose orientation. Women and people with high collectivism tend to use a collaborative or avoidance style more than men and people with high individualism.

Structural approaches to conflict management include emphasizing superordinate goals, reducing differentiation, improving communication and understanding, reducing task interdependence, increasing resources, and clarifying rules and procedures. These elements can also be altered to stimulate conflict.

Negotiation occurs whenever two or more conflicting parties attempt to resolve their divergent goals by redefining the terms of their interdependence. Negotiations are influenced by several situational factors, including location, physical setting, time passage and deadlines, and audience. Important negotiator behaviors include planning and setting goals, gathering information, communicating effectively, and making concessions.

Third-party conflict resolution is any attempt by a relatively neutral person to help the parties resolve their differences. The main objectives are to resolve the dispute efficiently and effectively, and to ensure that the parties feel that the process and outcome of dispute resolution are fair. The three main forms of third-party dispute resolution are mediation, arbitration, and inquisition. Managers tend to use an inquisitional approach, although mediation and arbitration are more appropriate, depending on the situation. Alternative dispute resolution applies mediation, but may also involve negotiation and, eventually, arbitration.

KEY TERMS

alternative dispute resolution (ADR), p. 407

conflict management, p. 388

conflict, p. 386

negotiation, p.402

procedural fairness, p. 406

superordinate goal, p. 398

third-party conflict resolution, p. 405

win–lose orientation, p. 394

win–win orientation, p. 394

DISCUSSION QUESTIONS

1. Distinguish task-related from socioemotional conflict, and explain where these two forms fit into the conflict escalation cycle.

2. The president of Creative Toys, Inc., read about cooperation in Japanese companies and has vowed to bring this same philosophy to the company. The goal is to avoid all conflict so that employees will work cooperatively and be happier at Creative Toys. Discuss the merits and limitations of the president's policy.

3. Conflict among managers emerged soon after a Swedish company was bought by a French company. The Swedes perceived the French management as hierarchical and arrogant, whereas the French thought the Swedes were naive and cautious, and lacked an achievement orientation. Describe ways to reduce dysfunctional conflict in this situation.

4. This chapter describes three levels of task interdependence that exist in interpersonal and intergroup relationships. Identify examples of these three levels in your work or school activities. How do these three levels affect potential conflict for you?

5. Jane has just been appointed purchasing manager of Tacoma Technologies Corporation. The previous purchasing manager, who recently retired, was known for his winner-take-all approach to suppliers. He continually fought for more discounts and was skeptical about any special deals

that suppliers would propose. A few suppliers refused to do business with Tacoma Technologies, but senior management was confident that the former purchasing manager's approach minimized the company's costs. Jane wants to try a more collaborative approach to working with suppliers. Will her approach work? How should she adopt a more collaborative approach in future negotiations with suppliers?

6. You are a special assistant to the commander-in-chief of a peacekeeping mission to a war-torn part of the world. The unit consists of a few thousand peacekeeping troops from the United States, France, and four other countries. The troops will work together for approximately one year. What strategies would you recommend to improve mutual understanding and minimize conflict among these troops?

7. Suppose that you head one of five divisions in a multinational organization and are about to begin this year's budget deliberations at headquarters. What are the characteristics of your audience in these negotiations, and what effect might they have on your negotiation behavior?

8. Managers tend to use an inquisitional approach to resolving disputes between employees and departments. Describe the inquisitional approach, and discuss its appropriateness in organizational settings.

CONFLICT IN CLOSE QUARTERS

A team of psychologists at Moscow's Institute for Biomedical Problems (IBMP) wanted to learn more about the dynamics of long-term isolation in space. This knowledge would be applied to the International Space Station, a joint project of several countries that would send people into space for more than six months. It would eventually include a trip to Mars taking up to three years.

IBMP set up a replica of the Mir space station in Moscow. The institute then arranged for three international researchers from Japan, Canada, and Austria to spend 110 days isolated in a chamber the size of a train car. This chamber joined a smaller chamber where four Russian cosmonauts had already completed half of their 240 days of isolation. This was the first time an international crew was involved in the studies. None of the participants spoke English as their first language, yet they communicated throughout their stay in English at varying levels of proficiency.

Judith Lapierre, a French Canadian, was the only female in the experiment. Along with having earned a PhD in public health and social medicine, Lapierre studied space sociology at the International Space University in France and conducted isolation research in the Antarctic. This was her fourth trip to Russia, where she had learned the language. The mission was supposed to have a second female participant from the Japanese space program, but she was not selected by IBMP.

The Japanese and Austrian participants viewed the participation of a woman as a favorable factor, says Lapierre. For example, to make the surroundings more comfortable, they rearranged the furniture, hung posters on the wall, and put a tablecloth on the kitchen table. "We adapted our environment, whereas the Russians just viewed it as something to be endured," she explains. "We decorated for Christmas, because I'm the kind of person who likes to host people."

New Year's Eve Turmoil

Ironically, it was at one of those social events, the New Year's Eve party, that events took a turn for the worse. After drinking vodka (allowed by the Russian space agency), two of the Russian cosmonauts got into a fistfight that left blood splattered on the chamber walls. At one point, a colleague hid the knives in the station's kitchen because of fears that the two Russians were about to stab each other. The two cosmonauts, who generally did not get along, had to be restrained by other men. Soon after that brawl, the Russian commander grabbed Lapierre, dragged her out of view of the television monitoring cameras, and kissed her aggressively—twice. Lapierre fought him off, but the message didn't register. He tried to kiss her again the next morning.

The next day, the international crew complained to IBMP about the behavior of the Russian cosmonauts. The Russian institute apparently took no action against any of the aggressors. Instead, the institute's psychologists replied that the incidents were part of the experiment. They wanted crew members to solve their personal problems with mature discussion, without asking for outside help. "You have to understand that Mir is an autonomous object, far away from anything," Vadim Gushin, the IBMP psychologist in charge of the project, explained after the experiment ended in March. "If the crew can't solve problems among themselves, they can't work together."

Following IBMP's response, the international crew wrote a scathing letter to the Russian institute and the space agencies involved in the experiment. "We had never expected such events to take place in a highly controlled scientific experiment where individuals go through a multistep selection process," they wrote. "If we had known . . . we would not have joined it as subjects." The letter also complained about IBMP's inadequate response to their concerns.

Informed of the New Year's Eve incident, the Japanese space program convened an emergency meeting on January 2 to address the incidents. Soon after, the Japanese team member quit, apparently shocked by IBMP's inaction. He was replaced with a Russian researcher on the international team. Ten days after the fight—a little over a month after the international team began the mission—the doors between the Russian and international crew's chambers were barred at the request of the international research team. Lapierre later emphasized that this action was taken because of concerns about violence, not the incident involving her.

A Stolen Kiss or Sexual Harassment?

By the end of the experiment in March, news of the fistfight between the cosmonauts and the commander's attempts to kiss Lapierre had reached the public. Russian scientists attempted to play down the kissing incident by saying that it involved one fleeting kiss, a clash of cultures, and a female participant who was too emotional.

"In the West, some kinds of kissing are regarded as sexual harassment. In our culture, it's nothing," said Vadim Gushin in one interview. In another interview, he explained: "The problem of sexual harassment is given a lot of attention in North America but less in Europe. In Russia it is even less of an issue, not because we are more or less moral than the rest of the world; we just have different priorities."

Judith Lapierre says the kissing incident was tolerable compared with this reaction from the Russian scientists who conducted the experiment. "They don't get it at all," she complains. "They don't think anything is wrong. I'm more frustrated than ever. The worst thing is that they don't realize it was wrong."

Norbert Kraft, the Austrian scientist on the international team, also disagreed with the Russian interpretation of events. "They're trying to protect themselves," he says. "They're trying to put the fault on others. But this is not a cultural issue. If a woman doesn't want to be kissed, it is not acceptable."

Discussion Questions

1. Identify the different conflict episodes that exist in this case. Who was in conflict with whom?

2. What are the sources or causes of each manifest conflict incident in this case?

3. What conflict management styles did Lapierre, the international team, and Gushin use to resolve these conflicts? What styles would have worked best in these situations?

4. What conflict management interventions were applied here? Did they work? What alternative strategies would work best in this situation and in the future?

Sources: The facts of this case have been pieced together by Steven L. McShane from the following sources: G. Sinclair, Jr., "If You Scream in Space, Does Anyone Hear?" *Winnipeg Free Press,* May 5, 2000, p. A4; S. Martin, "Reining in the Sapce Cowboys," *Globe and Mail (Toronto),* April 19, 2000, p. R1; M. Gray, "A Space Dream Sours," *Maclean's,* April 17, 2000, p. 26; E. Niiler, "In Search of the Perfect Astronaut," *Boston Globe,* April 4, 2000, p. E4; J. Tracy, "110-Day Isolation Ends in Sullen . . . Isolation," *Moscow Times,* March 30, 2000, p. 1; M. Warren, "A Mir Kiss?" *Daily Telegraph (London),* March 30, 2000, p. 22; G. York, "Canadian's Harassment Complaint Scorned," *Globe and Mail (Toronto),* March 25, 2000, p. A2; S. Nolen, "Lust in Space," *Globe and Mail (Toronto),* March 24, 2000, p. A3.

CASE STUDY 13.2

HOW TO BOOST YOUR BARGAINING POWERS

BusinessWeek When conflicts arise because of differences in goals or a shortage of resources, people in organizations often bargain or negotiate their way to a resolution. This behavior is often behind decisions about which projects to fund, how to resolve labor disputes, and whom to promote to key positions. Individuals with skill at negotiating can advance their group's performance, as well as their own careers. For example, skill in negotiating can help a person win a more favorable compensation package.

This *Business Week* case study describes tactics for effective salary negotiations. The author begins with evidence that women on average have been less successful than men in this regard, then summarizes advice aimed at making women more effective negotiators. Read through the *Business Week* case study at www.mhhe.com/mcshane2e and prepare for the discussion questions on page 412.

Discussion Questions

1. What conflicts in organizations create the need for salary negotiations? According to the background in the article, do women typically face additional or different conflicts than men?

2. Of the five conflict management styles shown in Exhibit 13.4, which do you think is (are) represented in this article's advice for negotiation? Which approaches would be most beneficial to the employee? To the employer?

3. On the basis of the chapter's discussion of negotiation, what additional strategies could improve a person's efforts at negotiating a raise?

Source: T. Gutner, "How to Boost Your Bargaining Powers," *Business Week*, October 16, 2000.

TEAM EXERCISE 13.3

UGLI ORANGE ROLE PLAY

Purpose This exercise is designed to help you understand the dynamics of interpersonal and intergroup conflict as well as the effectiveness of negotiation strategies under specific conditions.

Materials The instructor will distribute roles for Dr. Roland, Dr. Jones, and a few observers. Ideally, each negotiation should occur in a private area away from other negotiations.

Instructions

■ *Step 1*—The instructor will divide the class into an even number of teams of three people each. Any students remaining will be given the role of observer. One-half of the teams will take the role of Dr. Roland and the other half will be Dr. Jones. The instructor will distribute roles after the teams have been formed.

■ *Step 2*—Members within each team are given 10 minutes (or other time limit stated by the instructor) to learn their roles and decide on their negotiating strategy.

■ *Step 3*—After reading their roles and discussing strategy, each Dr. Jones team is matched with a Dr. Roland team to conduct negotiations. Observers will receive observation forms from the instructor, and two observers will be assigned to watch the paired teams during prenegotiations and subsequent negotiations.

■ *Step 4*—As soon as Roland and Jones reach agreement or at the end of the time allotted for the negotiation (whichever comes first), the Roland and Jones teams report to the instructor for further instruction.

■ *Step 5*—At the end of the exercise, the class will congregate to discuss the negotiations. Observers and negotiators will then discuss their observations and experiences and the implications for conflict management and negotiation.

Source: This exercise was developed by Robert J. House, Wharton Business School, University of Pennsylvania. A similar incident is also attributed to earlier writings by R. R. Blake and J. S. Mouton.

SELF-ASSESSMENT EXERCISE 13.4

CONFLICT MANAGEMENT STYLE ORIENTATION SCALE

Purpose This self-assessment exercise is designed to help you identify your preferred conflict management style.

Instructions Read each statement in the chart on page 413 and circle the response that you believe best reflects your position regarding that statement. Then use the scoring key in Appendix B to calculate your results for each conflict management style. This exercise is completed alone so that students assess themselves honestly without concerns of social comparison. However, class discussion will focus on the different conflict management styles and the situations in which each is most appropriate.

Conflict management style scale					
Circle the number that best indicates how well each statement describes you.	Rarely ▼				Always ▼
1. If someone disagrees with me, I vigorously defend my side of the issue.	1	2	3	4	5
2. I go along with suggestions from co-workers even if I don't agree with them.	1	2	3	4	5
3. I give and take so that a compromise can be reached.	1	2	3	4	5
4. I keep my opinions to myself rather than openly disagree with people.	1	2	3	4	5
5. In disagreements or negotiations, I try to find the best possible solution for both sides by sharing information.	1	2	3	4	5
6. I try to reach a middle ground in disputes with other people.	1	2	3	4	5
7. I accommodate the wishes of people who have points of view different from my own.	1	2	3	4	5
8. I avoid openly debating issues where there is disagreement.	1	2	3	4	5
9. In negotiations, I hold on to my position rather than give in.	1	2	3	4	5
10. I try to solve conflicts by finding solutions that benefit both me and the other person.	1	2	3	4	5
11. I let co-workers have their way rather than jeopardize our relationship.	1	2	3	4	5
12. I try to win my position in a discussion.	1	2	3	4	5
13. I like to investigate conflicts with co-workers so that we can discover solutions that benefit both of us.	1	2	3	4	5
14. I believe that it is not worth the time and trouble discussing my differences of opinion with other people.	1	2	3	4	5
15. To reach an agreement, I give up some things in exchange for others.	1	2	3	4	5

Sources: Adapted from items in M. A. Rahim, "A Measure of Styles of Handling Interpersonal Conflict," *Academy of Management Journal* 26 (June 1983), pp. 368–76; K. W. Thomas and R. H. Kilmann, *Thomas-Kilmann Conflict Mode Instrument* (Sterling Forst, NY: Xicom, 1977).

After studying the preceding material, be sure to check out our website at
www.mhhe.com/mcshane2e
for more in-depth information and interactivties that correspond to this chapter.

14

Organizational Leadership

Learning Objectives

AFTER READING THIS CHAPTER, YOU SHOULD BE ABLE TO:

- Define *leadership.*

- List seven traits identified with effective leaders.

- Describe the people-oriented and task-oriented leadership styles.

- Outline the path–goal theory of leadership.

- Discuss the importance of Fiedler's contingency model of leadership.

- Contrast transactional with transformational leadership.

- Describe the four elements of transformational leadership.

- Identify three reasons people inflate the importance of leadership.

- Discuss similarities and differences in the leadership styles of women and men.

The world has changed, and so has our concept of effective leadership. That's what consultants Booz Allen & Hamilton and the World Economic Forum's Strategic Leadership Project recently reported. On the basis of interviews with 6,000 executives and employees in several countries, they found that effective leaders subordinate their own egos and, instead, nurture leadership in others throughout an organization.

This new image is a far cry from the command-and-control leaders of yesteryear who took center stage and pretended to have all the answers. "I don't think that dictatorial leaders will survive," warns United Airlines executive Anne Keating. "It's an old-fashioned way of leading people." Wal King, CEO of Leighton Group, agrees: "Leadership style has gone from an autocratic style to encouraging participation to achieve a common outcome."

To achieve a common outcome, leaders must have a sense of direction, the passion to move forward, and the ability to motivate others to lead with them. "A great leader is one who has vision, perseverance, and the capacity to inspire others," says Cynthia Trudell, president of Brunswick Corporation's Sea Ray Group and former CEO of Saturn Corporation. "Above all, I believe the ability to listen is as fundamental as any other skill in the ability to lead," she says.

Personal values also enter most discussions about the emerging definition of leadership. "In my mind, trust, ethics and honesty [constitute] the new 'leadership currency,'" says Gary Irvin, CEO of FORUM Credit Union in Indianapolis. Rich Teerlink, the recently retired CEO of Harley-Davidson, offers a more detailed list of leadership values: "Tell the truth. Be fair. Keep your promises. Respect individuality. If leaders live by those, they can be successful."[1] ▪

"A great leader is one who has vision, perseverance, and the capacity to inspire others," says Cynthia Trudell, president of Brunswick Corporation's Sea Ray Group and former CEO of Saturn Corporation. *(Mike Hungerford)*

What is leadership? The opening vignette illustrates that our concept of leadership is changing, but it remains a complex issue that stirs up plenty of interest and discussion. Reviews of the leadership literature note that scholars do not sufficiently agree on the definition of leadership.[2] Most writers do agree, however, that leaders do not occupy specific positions. Anyone can be a leader throughout the organization. Indeed, the emerging definition is that effective leaders teach and empower their employees to take leadership roles.

leadership
The process of influencing people and providing an environment for them to achieve team or organizational objectives.

We will cautiously define **leadership** as the process of influencing people and providing an environment for them to achieve team or organizational objectives. Effective leaders help groups of people define their goals and find ways to achieve them.[3] They use power and persuasion to ensure that followers have the motivation and role clarity to achieve specified goals. Leaders also arrange the work environment—such as allocating resources and altering communication patterns—so that employees can achieve corporate objectives more easily. No matter how leadership is defined, however, only 8 percent of executives in large firms think their organizations have enough of it.[4] Most are concerned about a lack of leadership talent.

But leadership isn't restricted to the executive suite. Anyone in the organization can be a leader. "We're quite serious when we talk about leadership even to a bench worker on the assembly line," says an executive at General Semiconductor, the New York–based global high-technology company. "Lots of people will say, 'Oh, I'm not a leader,' but when we point out the essence of leadership is influence, they realize everyone has leadership qualities and responsibilities."[5]

Effective self-directed work teams, for example, consist of members who share leadership responsibilities or otherwise allocate this role to a responsible coordinator. Similarly, research indicates that technology champions—employees who overcome technical and organizational obstacles to introduce technological change in their area of the organization—are most successful when they possess the traits and enact the behaviors we associate with effective leadership.[6] Thus, we should not think of leaders only as people at the top of the organization. Anyone can be a leader at an appropriate time and place.

PERSPECTIVES OF LEADERSHIP

Leadership has been contemplated since the days of Greek philosophers, and it is one of the most popular research topics among organizational behavior scholars. This interest in leadership has resulted in an enormous volume of leadership literature, most of which can be split into the five perspectives shown in Exhibit 14.1. Although some of these perspectives are currently more popular than others, each helps us more fully understand this complex issue.

Some scholars have studied the traits or competencies of great leaders, whereas others have looked at their behaviors. More recent studies have looked at leadership from a contingency approach by considering the appropriate leader behaviors in different settings. Currently, the most popular perspective is that leaders transform organizations through their vision, communication, and ability to build commitment. Finally, an emerging perspective suggests that leadership is mainly a perceptual bias. We distort reality and attribute events to leaders because we feel more comfortable believing

EXHIBIT 14.1

Perspectives of
leadership

that a competent individual is at the organization's helm.[7] This chapter explores each of these five perspectives of leadership. In the final section, we also consider whether men and women lead differently in organizational settings.

COMPETENCY (TRAIT) PERSPECTIVE OF LEADERSHIP

Karenann Terrell is a confident leader with an enthusiastic drive to explore new ideas and achieve results. "This is the very best place to do what I do, which is to be very direct, ask hard questions and give hard answers," says the director of e-vehicle product management at DaimlerChrysler. Mark Hogan, president of General Motors' e-commerce unit, where Terrell worked before being lured to DaimlerChrysler, has no doubts about her competencies as a leader. "[General Motors] wanted a culture that was willing and able to move at Internet speed, as opposed to automotive speed," Hogan explains. "Karenann absolutely had that kind of temperament . . . [She leads] with a level of enthusiasm and energy that's breathtaking."[8]

From these accounts, it seems that Karenann Terrell possesses several leadership competencies. Competencies include the knowledge, natural and learned abilities, values, personality traits, and other characteristics of people that lead to superior performance (see Chapter 2).[9] Since the beginning of recorded civilization, people have been interested in personal characteristics that distinguish great leaders. The ancient Egyptians demanded authority, discrimination, and justice from their

Karenann Terrell is well known for her leadership competencies. The director of e-vehicle product management at DaimlerChrysler is self-confident and possesses the motivation to lead. "I live and breathe the ability to make a difference," she says. Terrell also has an unwavering drive that energizes employees to achieve goals and discover new territory in web-based automobile electronics. "[She leads] with a level of enthusiasm and energy that's breathtaking," says Mark Hogan, president of GM's e-commerce unit, where Terrell worked before being lured to DaimlerChrysler. In your opinion, are people like Karenann Terrell born as great leaders, or can companies develop leaders?
(DaimlerChrysler Media Services)

leaders. The Greek philosopher Plato called for prudence, courage, temperance, and justice.[10]

For the first half of the twentieth century, organizational behavior scholars used scientific methods to determine whether certain personality traits and physical characteristics (particularly, the person's height and weight) actually distinguished leaders from lesser souls. A major review in the late 1940s concluded that no consistent list of traits could be distilled from the hundreds of studies conducted up to that time. A subsequent review suggested that a few traits are consistently associated with effective leaders, but most are unrelated to effective leadership.[11] These conclusions caused many scholars to give up their search for personal characteristics that distinguish effective leaders.

Over the past decade, management consultants and organizational behavior scholars have popularized competency-based selection and reward practices. Competencies encompass a broader range of personal characteristics—such as knowledge, abilities, and values—that were not considered by earlier studies on leadership traits. This new generation of leadership experts argues that the earlier studies focused too much on abstract personality traits and the physical appearance of leaders. The recent leadership literature identifies seven competencies that are characteristic of effective leaders.[12] These competencies are listed in Exhibit 14.2 and described briefly below.

■ *Drive*—Leaders have a high need for achievement (see Chapter 5). This drive represents the inner motivation that leaders possess to pursue their goals and encourage others to move forward with theirs. Drive inspires an unbridled inquisitiveness and a need for constant learning. You can see this drive in Karenann Terrell through her energy and enthusiasm at both DaimlerChrysler and General Motors.

EXHIBIT 14.2

Seven competencies of effective leaders

Leadership trait	Description
Drive	The leader's inner motivation to pursue goals
Leadership motivation	The leader's need for socialized power to accomplish team or organizational goals
Integrity	The leader's truthfulness and tendency to translate words into deeds
Self-confidence	The leader's belief in his or her own leadership skills and ability to achieve objectives
Intelligence	The leader's above-average cognitive ability to process enormous amounts of information
Knowledge of the business	The leader's understanding of the company's environment to make more intuitive decisions
Emotional intelligence	The leader's ability to monitor his or her own and others' emotions, discriminate among them, and use the information to guide his or her thoughts and actions

Sources: Most elements of this list were derived from S. A. Kirkpatrick and E. A. Locke, "Leadership: Do Traits Matter?" *Academy of Management Executive* 5 (May 1991), pp. 48–60. Several of these ideas are also discussed in H. B. Gregersen, A. J. Morrison, and J. S. Black, "Developing Leaders for the Global Frontier," *Sloan Management* 40 (Fall 1998), pp. 21–32; R. J. House and R. N. Aditya, "The Social Scientific Study of Leadership: Quo Vadis?" *Journal of Management* 23 (1997), pp. 409–73.

▓ *Leadership motivation*—Leaders have a strong need for power because they want to influence others (see Chapter 5). However, they tend to have a need for "socialized power" because their motivation is constrained by a strong sense of altruism and social responsibility.[13] In other words, effective leaders try to gain power so that they can influence others to accomplish goals that benefit the team or organization.

▓ *Integrity*—This competency refers to the leader's truthfulness and tendency to translate words into deeds. Several large-scale studies have reported that integrity is the most important leadership characteristic. Employees want honest leaders whom they can trust.[14]

▓ *Self-confidence*—Karenann Terrell and other leaders believe in their leadership skills and ability to achieve objectives. They also use impression management tactics (see Chapter 12) to convince followers of their confidence.

▓ *Intelligence*—Leaders have above-average cognitive ability to process enormous amounts of information. Leaders aren't necessarily geniuses; rather, they have superior ability to analyze alternate scenarios and identify potential opportunities.

▓ *Knowledge of the business*—Karenann Terrell and other leaders know the business environment in which they operate. This knowledge assists their intuition, enabling them to recognize opportunities and understand their organization's capacity to capture those opportunities.

▓ *Emotional intelligence*—Effective leaders have a high level of emotional intelligence. They monitor their own and others' emotions, discriminate among them, and use the information to guide their thoughts and actions (see Chapter 4).[15] Emotional intelligence requires a strong self-monitoring personality (see Chapter 3), because leaders must be sensitive to situational cues and readily adapt their own behavior appropriately.[16] It also requires the ability to empathize with others and the social skills necessary to build rapport as well as network with others. The contingency leadership perspective described later in this chapter assumes that effective leaders are high self-monitors, so they can adjust their behavior to match the situation.

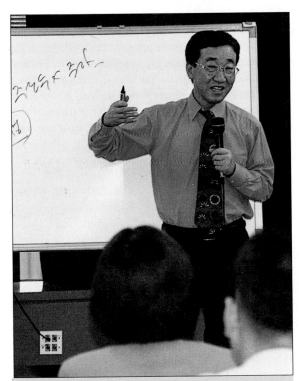

Don't look for Kim Jung-tae in his office. The CEO of Kookmin Bank is busy traveling throughout the company's hundreds of branches and offices, instilling a new way of thinking about banking. "Our bank has to survive doing retail business," explains Kim. "That means customer satisfaction." Kim's marketing savvy and years of experience in the financial services industry make him well suited to lead the largest financial institution in South Korea. Kim also has a strong drive and a high level of integrity, enough to earn the respect of a selection panel that chose him as CEO during a recent merger.[17] What competencies seem to make Kim Jung-tae an effective leader? *(Courtesy of Kookmin Bank)*

Competency (Trait) Perspective Limitations and Practical Implications

One concern with the competency perspective is that it assumes great leaders have the same personal characteristics and all of them are equally important in all situations. This is probably a false assumption; leadership is far too complex to have a universal list of traits that apply to every condition. Some competencies might not be important all the time, although researchers have not yet explored this aspect of traits.

A few scholars have also warned that some personal characteristics might only influence our perception that someone is a leader, not indicate whether the individual really makes a difference to the organization's success.[18] People who exhibit integrity, self-confidence, and other traits are called leaders because they fit our stereotype of an effective leader. Or we might see a successful person, call that person a leader, and then attribute self-confidence and other unobservable traits that we consider essential for great leaders. We will discuss this perceptual distortion more fully toward the end of the chapter. At this point, you should be aware that our knowledge of leadership competencies may be partly due to perceptual distortions.

Aside from these limitations, the competency perspective recognizes that some people possess personal characteristics that offer them a higher potential to be great leaders. The most obvious implication of this is that organizations are relying increasingly on competency-based methods to hire people for future leadership positions.[19] Leadership talents are important throughout the organization, so this recommendation should extend to all levels of hiring, not just senior executives. Companies also need to determine which behaviors represent these competencies so that employees with leadership talents are identified early for promotion.

The competency perspective of leadership does not necessarily imply that great leaders are born, not developed. On the contrary, competencies only indicate leadership potential, not leadership performance. People with these characteristics become effective leaders only after they have developed and mastered the necessary leadership behaviors. People with somewhat lower leadership competencies may become very effective leaders because they have leveraged their potential more fully. Thus, companies must do more than hire people with certain competencies. They must also develop these employees' potential through leadership development programs and practical experience in the field.

BEHAVIORAL PERSPECTIVE OF LEADERSHIP

In the 1940s and 1950s, scholars from Ohio State University launched an intensive research investigation to answer this question: What behaviors make leaders effective? Questionnaires were administered to subordinates, asking them to rate their supervisors on a large number of behaviors. These studies, along with similar research at the University of Michigan and Harvard University, distilled two clusters of leadership behaviors from more than 1,800 leadership behavior items.[20]

One cluster represented people-oriented behaviors, such as showing mutual trust and respect for subordinates, demonstrating a genuine concern for their needs, and having a desire to look out for their welfare. Leaders with a strong people-oriented style listen to employee suggestions, do personal favors for employees, support their interests when required, and treat employees as equals.

The other cluster represented a task-oriented leadership style and included behaviors that define and structure work roles. Task-oriented leaders assign employees to specific tasks, clarify their work duties and procedures, ensure

When Tough Taskmasters Become Abusive Bosses

David Gilmore admits that he can be tough on employees. "I am occasionally a tyrant," confesses the head of Washington, D.C.'s public housing authority. But Gilmore believes that his task-oriented leadership pushes employees just enough to achieve higher performance, and no further. "I try to stretch them as far as they will go without breaking," he says. Gilmore's staff agree with their boss's self-assessment, but that doesn't stop them from teasing the taskmaster. They bought Gilmore a poster from *The Caine Mutiny* and superimposed his face over Humphrey Bogart's as Captain Queeg.

Unfortunately, not everyone has a friendly tyrant for a boss. A recent U.S. Postal Service office report revealed that the postmaster and other managers in Fullerton, California, "used threats, harassment, intimidation and retaliation to control employees' behavior." The postmaster was transferred, and other managers are receiving sensitivity training to develop a more supportive leadership style.

The CEO of Cerner Corporation in North Kansas City, Missouri, recently sent an e-mail missive to 400 managers, warning that employees would be laid off and time clocks installed if staff did not put in more than the usual 40-hour work week. "The pizza man should show up at 7:30 P.M. to feed the starving teams working late," the e-mail stated. "The lot should be half-full on Saturday mornings . . . You have two weeks. Tick, tock." Cerner's shareholders apparently dislike bossy leaders. The medical software firm's stock dropped by 22 percent when the abusive e-mail became public.

These are not isolated cases of abusive bosses. According to one survey, a larger percentage of employees think management abusiveness is higher today than 20 years ago. The most popular explanation is the constant pressure on managers to produce. Most employees recommended better leadership training as well as surveying employees more often for incidents of abuse by their bosses.

Sources: J. Hicks, "Besieged Fullerton Postmaster Reassigned," *Los Angeles Times,* August 28, 2001, p. 2-1; J. Hicks, "Post Office Management Faulted," *Los Angeles Times,* August 18, 2001, p. 2-8; D. Hayes and J. A. Karash, "Harsh E-Mail Roils Cerner," *Kansas City Star,* March 24, 2001, p. A1; D. Armstrong, "Got an Abusive Boss?" *Foxmarketwire.com* (online), February 16, 2000; V. Loeb, "Resident Expert," *Washington Post,* May 7, 1998, p. B1.

that they follow company rules, and push them to reach their performance capacity. They establish stretch goals and challenge employees to push beyond those high standards. The problem with task-oriented leadership is that today's workforce is less receptive to command-and-control leadership. Employees want to participate in decisions rather than receive directives and follow them without question.[21] The other problem is knowing how far to challenge employees. As Connections 14.1 describes, some bosses are friendly tyrants whereas others cross the line to become bullies.

Choosing Task- versus People-Oriented Leadership

Should leaders be task-oriented or people-oriented? This is a difficult question to answer because each style has its advantages and disadvantages. People-oriented leadership is associated with higher job satisfaction among subordinates, as well as lower absenteeism, grievances, and turnover. However, job performance tends to be lower than for employees with task-oriented leaders.[22] Task-oriented leadership, on the other hand, is associated with lower job satisfaction as well as higher absenteeism and turnover among subordinates. But this leadership style also seems to increase productivity and team unity. University students apparently value task-oriented instructors because they want clear objectives and well-prepared lectures that abide by the unit's objectives.[23]

Behavioral leadership scholars reported that these two styles are independent of each other. Some people are high or low on both styles, others are high on one style and low on the other, and most are somewhere in between. The hypothesis that emerged was that the most effective leaders exhibit high levels of both task-oriented and people-oriented behaviors.[24] Out of this hypothesis developed a popular leadership development program, called the **Leadership Grid®** (formerly known as the *Managerial Grid*).[25] Participants assess their current levels of task-oriented and people-oriented leadership; then they work with trainers to achieve maximum levels of concern for both people and production (task).

The problem with the behavioral leadership perspective, as subsequent research has discovered, is it implies that high levels of both styles are best in all situations. In reality, the best leadership style depends on the situation.[26] On a positive note, the behavioral perspective laid the foundation for two of the main leadership styles—people-oriented and task-oriented—found in many contemporary leadership theories. These contemporary theories adopt a contingency perspective, which we describe next.

CONTINGENCY PERSPECTIVE OF LEADERSHIP

The contingency perspective of leadership is based on the idea that the most appropriate leadership style depends on the situation. Most (although not all) contingency leadership theories assume that effective leaders must be both insightful and flexible.[27] They must be able to adapt their behaviors and styles to the immediate situation. This isn't easy to do, however. Leaders typically have a preferred style. It takes considerable effort for leaders to learn when and how to alter their styles to match the situation. As we noted earlier, leaders must have a high emotional intelligence, particularly a self-monitoring personality, so that they can diagnose the circumstances and match their behaviors accordingly.[28]

Path–Goal Theory of Leadership

Several contingency theories have been proposed over the years, but **path–goal leadership theory** has withstood scientific critique better than the others. The theory has its roots in the expectancy theory of motivation (see Chapter 5). Early research by Martin Evans incorporated expectancy theory into the study of how leader behaviors influence employee perceptions of expectancies (paths) between employee effort and performance (goals). On the basis of this perspective, Robert House and other scholars developed and refined path–goal theory as a contingency leadership model.[29]

Path–goal theory states that effective leaders influence employee satisfaction and performance by making their need satisfaction contingent on effective job performance. Leaders strengthen the performance-to-outcome expectancy and valences of those outcomes by ensuring that employees who perform their jobs well have a higher degree of need fulfillment than employees who perform poorly.

Effective leaders strengthen the effort-to-performance expectancy by providing the information, support, and other resources necessary to help employees complete their tasks.[30] Royal Dutch/Shell's leadership development program emphasizes that effective leaders create conditions that enable others to realize their potential in the workplace. The best-performing self-directed

Leadership Grid®
A model of leadership developed by Blake and Mouton that assesses an individual's leadership effectiveness in terms of his or her concern for people and production.

path–goal leadership theory
A contingency theory of leadership based on expectancy theory of motivation that relates several leadership styles to specific employee and situational contingencies.

work teams at Xerox had leaders who gave first priority to arranging organizational support for the team.[31] In other words, path–goal theory advocates **servant leadership.**[32] Servant leaders do not view leadership as a position of power; rather, they are coaches, stewards, and facilitators. Leadership is an obligation to understand employee needs and to facilitate employee work performance. Servant leaders ask, "How can I help you?" rather than expect employees to serve them.

servant leadership
The belief that leaders serve followers by understanding their needs and facilitating their work performance.

Leadership Styles   Exhibit 14.3 illustrates the path–goal theory of leadership. This model specifically highlights four leadership styles and several contingency factors leading to three indicators of leader effectiveness. The four leadership styles are:[33]

■ *Directive*—These are clarifying behaviors that provide a psychological structure for subordinates. The leader clarifies performance goals, the means to reach those goals, and the standards against which performance will be judged. This style also includes judicious use of rewards and disciplinary actions. Directive leadership is the same as task-oriented leadership, described earlier, and echoes our discussion in Chapter 2 on the importance of clear role perceptions in employee performance.
■ *Supportive*—These behaviors provide psychological support for subordinates. The leader is friendly and approachable, makes the work more pleasant, treats employees with equal respect, and shows concern for the status, needs, and well-being of employees. Supportive leadership is the same as people-oriented leadership, described earlier, and reflects the benefits of social support to help employees cope with stressful situations (see Chapter 7).
■ *Participative*—These behaviors encourage and facilitate subordinate involvement in decisions beyond their normal work activities. The leader consults with employees, asks for their suggestions, and takes these ideas into serious consideration before making a decision. Participative leadership relates to the employee involvement concepts and issues described in Chapter 9.

EXHIBIT 14.3

Path–goal
leadership theory

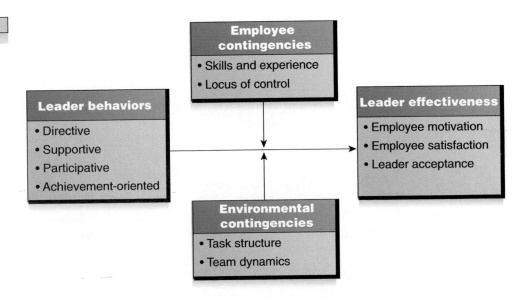

■ *Achievement-oriented*—These behaviors encourage employees to reach their peak performance. The leader sets challenging goals, expects employees to perform at their highest level, continually seeks improvement in employee performance, and shows a high degree of confidence that employees will assume responsibility and accomplish challenging goals. Achievement-oriented leadership applies goal-setting theory (Chapter 5) as well as positive expectations in self-fulfilling prophecy (Chapter 3).

The path–goal model contends that effective leaders are capable of selecting the most appropriate behavioral style (or styles) for a particular situation. Leaders might use more than one style at a time. For example, they might be both supportive and participative in a specific situation.

Contingencies of Path–Goal Theory

As a contingency theory, path–goal theory states that each of these four leadership styles will be effective in some situations but not in others. The path–goal leadership model specifies two sets of situational variables that moderate the relationship between a leader's style and effectiveness: (1) employee characteristics and (2) characteristics of the employee's work environment. Several contingencies have already been studied within the path–goal framework, and the model is open for more variables in the future.[34] However, we will examine only four contingencies here (see Exhibit 14.4).

Skill and Experience   A combination of directive and supportive leadership is best for employees who are (or perceive themselves to be) inexperienced and unskilled. Directive leadership gives subordinates information about how to accomplish the task, whereas supportive leadership helps them cope with the uncertainties of unfamiliar work situations. Directive leadership is detrimental when employees are skilled and experienced because it introduces too much supervisory control.

Locus of Control   Recall from Chapter 3 that people with an internal locus of control believe that they have control over their work environment. Conse-

EXHIBIT 14.4   Selected contingencies of path–goal theory

	Directive	Supportive	Particpative	Achievement-oriented
Employee contingencies				
Skill and experience	Low	Low	High	High
Locus of control	External	External	Internal	Internal
Environmental contingencies				
Task structure	Nonroutine	Routine	Nonroutine	?
Team dynamics	Negative norms	Low cohesion	Positive norms	?

quently, these employees prefer participative and achievement-oriented leadership styles and may become frustrated with a directive style. In contrast, people with an external locus of control believe that their performance is due more to luck and fate, so they tend to be more satisfied with directive and supportive leadership.

Task Structure   Leaders should adopt the directive style when the task is nonroutine, because this style minimizes role ambiguity that tends to occur in these complex work situations (particularly for inexperienced employees).[35] The directive style is ineffective when employees have routine and simple tasks because the manager's guidance serves no purpose and may be viewed as unnecessarily close control. Employees in highly routine and simple jobs may require supportive leadership to help them cope with the tedious nature of the work and lack of control over the pace of work. Participative leadership is preferred for employees performing nonroutine tasks because the lack of rules and procedures gives them more discretion to achieve challenging goals. The participative style is ineffective for employees in routine tasks because they lack discretion over their work.

Team Dynamics   Cohesive teams with performance-oriented norms act as a substitute for most leader interventions. High team cohesiveness substitutes for supportive leadership, whereas performance-oriented team norms substitute for directive and possibly achievement-oriented leadership. Thus, when team cohesiveness is low, leaders should use the supportive style. Leaders should apply a directive style to counteract team norms that oppose the team's formal objectives. For example, the team leader may need to use legitimate power if team members have developed a norm to take it easy rather than get a project completed on time.

Recent Extensions of Path–Goal Theory

The original path–goal theory primarily relates to dyadic relations between a supervisor and an employee.[36] Yet leadership also applies to the work unit and organization. Recognizing this gap, Robert House (who, as mentioned, was a developer of the original path–goal theory) recently extended the model by adding leader styles that apply more to work units and organizations than to individual relations.[37] One of these styles is *networking*, which recognizes that leaders play an important political role. They represent the work unit and engage in political networking activities (see Chapter 12) to legitimize the work unit and maintain positive influences on other areas of the organization. Another style is *value-based leadership*, which includes articulating a vision of the future, displaying passion for this vision, demonstrating self-confidence in the attainment of the vision, communicating the vision, and acting in ways consistent with the vision. This style is the same as the transformational leadership perspective that we describe later in this chapter.

Practical Implications and Limitations of Path–Goal Theory

Path–goal theory reinforces the idea that effective leaders vary their style with the situation. There are times to give directions, times to empathize, times to use stretch goals, and times to involve subordinates in decision making. Path–goal theory also offers a fairly precise set of contingency factors that provide practical advice on when to use various leadership styles.

Path–goal theory has received considerable research support, certainly more than other contingency leadership models.[38] However, one or two contingencies (e.g., task structure) have found limited research support. Other contingencies and leadership styles in the path–goal leadership model haven't received scholarly investigation at all.[39] For example, some cells in Exhibit 14.4 have question marks because we do not yet know how those leadership styles apply to those contingencies. The recently expanded model adds new leadership styles and contingencies, but they have not yet been tested. Until further study comes along, it is unclear whether certain contingencies should be considered when choosing the best leadership style.

Another concern is that as path–goal theory expands, the model may become too complex for practical use. Although the expanded model provides a closer representation of the complexity of leadership, it may become too cumbersome for training people in leadership styles. Few people would be able to remember all the contingencies and appropriate leadership styles for those contingencies. In spite of these limitations, path–goal theory remains a relatively complete and robust contingency leadership theory.

Other Contingency Theories

At the beginning of this chapter, we noted that numerous leadership theories have developed over the years. Most of them are found in the contingency perspective of leadership. Some overlap with the path–goal model in terms of leadership styles, but most use simpler and more abstract contingencies. We will briefly mention two here because of their popularity and historical significance to the field.

situational leadership model
Developed by Hersey and Blanchard, suggests that effective leaders vary their style with the "readiness" of followers.

Situational Leadership Model   One of the most popular contingency theories among trainers is the **situational leadership model,** developed by Paul Hersey and Ken Blanchard.[40] The model suggests that effective leaders vary their style with the readiness of followers. (An earlier version of the model called this concept maturity.) Readiness refers to the employee's or work team's ability and willingness to accomplish a specific task. Ability refers to the extent that the follower has the skills and knowledge to perform the task without the leader's guidance. Willingness refers to the follower's self-motivation and commitment to perform the assigned task. The model compresses these distinct concepts into a single situational condition.

The situational leadership model also identifies four leadership styles— telling, selling, participating, and delegating—that Hersey and Blanchard distinguish in terms of the amount of directive and supportive behavior provided. For example, telling has high task behavior and low supportive behavior. The situational leadership model has four quadrants, with each quadrant showing the leadership style that is most appropriate under certain circumstances.

In spite of its popularity, at least three reviews have concluded that the situational leadership model lacks empirical support.[41] Apparently, only one part of the model works, namely, that leaders should use telling (i.e., a directive style) when employees lack motivation and ability. (That conclusion is also documented in path–goal theory.) The model's elegant simplicity is attractive and entertaining, but other parts don't represent reality very well. The most recent review also concluded that the theory has logical and internal inconsistencies.

Fiedler's Contingency Model   The earliest contingency theory of leadership, called **Fiedler's contingency model,** was developed by Fred Fiedler and his associates.[42] According to this model, leader effectiveness depends on whether the person's natural leadership style is appropriately matched to the situation. The theory examines two leadership styles that essentially correspond to the previously described people-oriented and task-oriented styles. Unfortunately, Fiedler's model relies on a questionnaire that does not measure either leadership style very well.

Fiedler's model suggests that the best leadership style depends on the level of *situational control,* that is, the degree of power and influence that the leader possesses in a particular situation. Situational control is affected by three factors, in the following order of importance: leader–member relations, task structure, and position power.[43] Leader–member relations is the degree to which employees trust and respect the leader and are willing to follow his or her guidance. Task structure refers to the clarity or ambiguity of operating procedures. Position power is the extent to which the leader possesses legitimate, reward, and coercive power over subordinates. These three contingencies form the eight possible combinations of *situation favorableness* from the leader's viewpoint. Good leader–member relations, high task structure, and strong position power create the most favorable situation for the leader because he or she has the most power and influence under those conditions.

Fiedler has gained considerable respect for pioneering the first contingency theory of leadership. His theory, however, has fared less well. As mentioned, the leadership style scale used by Fiedler has been widely criticized. There is also no scientific justification for placing the three situational control factors in a hierarchy. Moreover, it seems that leader–member relations is actually an indicator of leader effectiveness (as in path–goal theory) rather than a situational factor. Finally, the theory considers only two leadership styles, whereas other models present a more complex and realistic array of behavior options. These concerns explain why the theory has limited empirical support.[44]

Changing the Situation to Match the Leader's Natural Style   Fiedler's contingency model may have become a historical footnote, but it does make an important and lasting contribution by suggesting that leadership style is related to the individual's personality and, consequently, is relatively stable over time. Leaders might be able to alter their style temporarily, but they tend to use a preferred style in the long term. More recent scholars have also proposed that leadership styles are "hardwired" more than most other contingency leadership theories assume.[45]

If leadership style is influenced by a person's personality, then organizations should engineer the situation to fit the leader's dominant style, rather than expect leaders to change their style with the situation. A directive leader might be assigned inexperienced employees who need direction rather than seasoned people who work less effectively under a directive style. Alternatively, companies might transfer supervisors to workplaces where the dominant style fits best. For

---

Fiedler's contingency model
Developed by Fred Fiedler, suggests that leader effectiveness depends on whether the person's natural leadership style is appropriately matched to the situation.

instance, directive leaders might be parachuted into work teams with counter-productive norms, whereas leaders who prefer a supportive style should be sent to departments in which employees face work pressures and other stressors.

Leadership Substitutes   So far, we have looked at theories that recommend using different leadership styles in various situations. But one theory, called **leadership substitutes,** identifies contingencies that either limit the leader's ability to influence subordinates or make that particular leadership style unnecessary. When substitute conditions are present, employees are effective without a formal leader who applies a particular style. Although the leadership substitute model requires further refinement, there is general support for the overall notion that some conditions neutralize or substitute for leadership styles.[46]

Several conditions have been identified in the literature that possibly substitute for task-oriented or people-oriented leadership. For example, performance-based reward systems keep employees directed toward organizational goals, so they probably replace or reduce the need for task-oriented leadership. Task-oriented leadership is also less important when employees are skilled and experienced. Notice how these propositions are similar to path–goal leadership theory, namely, in saying that directive leadership is unnecessary—and may be detrimental—when employees are skilled or experienced.[47]

leadership substitutes
A theory that identifies contingencies that either limit the leader's ability to influence subordinates or make that particular leadership style unnecessary.

With no traditional bosses, employees at W. L. Gore & Associates rely on leadership substitutes to get their work done. These substitutes include guidance from co-workers, formal training and socialization, and performance-based rewards. The maker of Gore–Tex and other advanced materials also spends a lot of time hiring people with self-leadership skills.[48] What other leadership substitutes might help teams lead themselves without direct supervision? *(AP/Wide World)*

Leadership substitutes have become more important as organizations remove supervisors and shift toward team-based structures. In fact, an emerging concept is that effective leaders help team members learn to lead themselves through leadership substitutes.[49] Some writers suggest that co-workers are powerful leader substitutes in these organizational structures. Co-workers instruct new employees, thereby providing directive leadership. They also provide social support, which reduces stress among fellow employees (see Chapter 7). Teams with norms that support organizational goals may substitute for achievement-oriented leadership, because employees encourage (or pressure) co-workers to stretch their performance levels.

Self-leadership has also been discussed as a potentially valuable leadership substitute in self-directed work teams.[50] Recall from Chapter 6 that self-leadership is the process of influencing oneself to establish the self-direction and self-motivation needed to perform a task.[51] It includes self-set goals, self-reinforcement, constructive thought processes, and other activities that influence the person's own motivation and behavior. As employees become more proficient in self-leadership, they presumably require less supervision to keep them focused and energized toward organizational objectives.

TRANSFORMATIONAL PERSPECTIVE OF LEADERSHIP

transformational leadership

A leadership perspective that explains how leaders change teams or organizations by creating, communicating, and modeling a vision for the organization or work unit, and inspiring employees to strive for that vision.

As an executive with IBM Global Services, Colleen Arnold saw a unique opportunity to launch an e-business innovation center for the Asia-Pacific region. IBM had contracted 800 information technology (IT) workers to bring together the world's biggest Internet project—the 2000 Sydney Olympics. This valuable pool of talent fit nicely with IBM's need to expand its e-business capability in the region at a time when the industry faced a global IT skills shortage.

Arnold explained her vision to IBM Worldwide, convincing them to leverage this uniquely available talent for an e-business hub. She then convinced her local board of directors to fund the new innovation center, making it the launching pad for an internal corporate culture change that values flexibility, mobility, and customer service. The new e-business center would be free-form and wireless, and would operate around the clock to deliver e-business solutions to customers. Less than two years later, the innovation center became a reality, linking IBM's R&D labs worldwide.[52]

transactional leadership

Leadership that helps organizations achieve their current objectives more efficiently, such as linking job performance to valued rewards and ensuring that employees have the resources needed to get the job done.

Colleen Arnold deomonstrates **transformational leadership.** Through her vision and actions, she created a unique business entity that will eventually spread a new culture and way of working throughout IBM's worldwide operations. Transformational leaders, such as Carly Fiorina (Hewlett-Packard), Herb Kelleher (Southwest Airlines), Carlos Ghosn (Renault–Nissan), and Richard Branson (Virgin), dot the corporate landscape.[53] These people are agents of change. They develop a vision for the organization or work unit, inspire and collectively bond employees to that vision, and give them a can-do attitude that makes the vision achievable.[54]

Transformational versus Transactional Leadership

Transformational leadership is different from **transactional leadership.** Transactional leadership involves managing—helping organizations achieve

Dennis W. Bakke, CEO and co-founder of the global power company AES Corporation, is continually looking for leaders who are both transformational and transactional "We need people who can both lead and manage," says Bakke. "The traditional idea is that a manager takes what is there and makes certain it works well, while a leader takes a visionary look at what is already known to discover something new. But the world changes so much that you can no longer just manage 'what is there.' Leadership that doesn't consider practical execution is ridiculous. It's not either/or. It is much better to think about those two abilities together."[59] How can AES and other organizations ensure that people maintain a balance between transformational and transactional leadership? Or do you think that these roles should occur in different people? *(Courtesy of AES Corporation)*

their current objectives more efficiently, such as by linking job performance to valued rewards and ensuring that employees have the resources needed to get the job done.[55] The contingency and behavioral theories described earlier adopt the transactional perspective because they focus on leader behaviors that improve employee performance and satisfaction.

In contrast, transformational leadership is about leading—changing the organization's strategies and culture so that they have a better fit with the surrounding environment.[56] Transformational leaders are change agents who energize employees and direct them to a new set of corporate values and behaviors. Colleen Arnold is one such leader. The opening story to this section described how she saw a unique opportunity and was able to build commitment from her board and from the Sydney Olympics IT staff to form a new center that would itself further transform IBM worldwide.

Organizations require both transactional and transformational leadership. Transactional leadership improves organizational efficiency, whereas transformational leadership steers companies onto a better course of action. Transformational leadership is particularly important in organizations that require significant alignment with the external environment. Research suggests that organizations that drive societal change—such as environmental organizations—are highly receptive contexts for transformational leadership.[57] Unfortunately, too many leaders get trapped in the daily managerial activities that represent transactional leadership.[58] They lose touch with the transformational aspect of effective leadership. Without transformational leaders, organizations stagnate and eventually become seriously misaligned with their environments.

Transformational versus Charismatic Leadership

One topic that has generated some confusion and controversy is the distinction between transformational and charismatic leadership.[60] A few writers use the terms *charismatic* and *transformational leadership* interchangeably. However, charismatic leadership differs from transformational leadership. As we learned in Chapter 12, *charisma* is a form of interpersonal attraction whereby followers develop a respect for and trust in the charismatic individual. Charismatic leadership, therefore, extends beyond behaviors to personal traits that provide referent power over followers.[61] Transformational leadership, on the other hand, is mainly about behaviors that people use to lead the change process. The remainder of this section will focus on transformational leadership because it offers more specific behavioral implications.

Elements of Transformational Leadership

There are several descriptions of transformational leadership, but most include the four elements illustrated in Exhibit 14.5. These elements are creating a strategic vision, communicating the vision, modeling the vision, and building commitment to the vision.

Creating a Strategic Vision Transformational leaders are the brokers of dreams.[62] They shape a strategic vision of a realistic and attractive future that bonds employees together and focuses their energy toward a superordinate organizational goal.[63] Visions represent the substance of transformational leadership. They reflect a future for the company or work unit that is ultimately accepted and valued by organizational members. Notice that leadership vision is not a mission statement plastered on someone's wall. Rather, it is part of the corporate meaning—the organization's goals and the reason it exists. Strategic visions might originate with the leader, but they are just as likely to emerge from employees, clients, suppliers, or other constituents. They typically begin as abstract ideas that become progressively clearer through critical events and discussions with staff about strategic and operational plans.[64]

There is some evidence that visions are the most important part of transformational leadership.[65] Visions offer the motivational benefits of goal setting, but they are more than mundane goals. Visions are compelling future states that bond employees and motivate them to strive for those objectives. Visions are typically described in a way that distinguishes them from the current situation, yet makes the goal both appealing and achievable.

Communicating the Vision If strategic vision is the substance of transformational leadership, then communicating that vision is the process.

EXHIBIT 14.5

Elements of transformational leadership

Transformational leaders communicate meaning and elevate the importance of the visionary goal to employees. They frame messages around a grand purpose with emotional appeal that captivates employees and other corporate stakeholders. Framing helps transformational leaders establish a common mental model so that the group or organization will act collectively toward the desirable goal.[66] Arthur Blank, the co-founder of home improvement retail giant Home Depot, likes to remind employees that they are "in the business of making people's dreams come true."[67] Blank helps employees see their role toward customers in a different light, one that is much more meaningful and motivating than "selling hammers and nails."

Transformational leaders also bring their visions to life through symbols, metaphors, stories, and other vehicles that transcend plain language.[68] Metaphors borrow images of other experiences, thereby creating richer meaning of the vision that has not yet been experienced. When George Cohen brought McDonald's restaurants to Moscow, he frequently reminded his executive team that they were establishing "hamburger diplomacy." And in the mid-1800s, when ocean transportation was treacherous, Samuel Cunard emphasized that he was creating an "ocean railway." At the time, railroads provided one of the safest forms of transportation, and Cunard's metaphor reinforced the notion to employees and passengers alike that Cunard Steamship Lines would provide equally safe transportation across the Atlantic Ocean.[69]

Modeling the Vision   Transformational leaders not only talk about a vision; they also enact it. They "walk the talk" by stepping outside the executive suite and doing things that symbolize the vision.[70] Moreover, transformational leaders are reliable and persistent in their actions. They stay on course, thereby legitimizing the vision and providing further evidence that they can be trusted. Leaders walk the talk through significant events, but they also alter mundane activities—meeting agendas, office locations, executive schedules—so that they are consistent with the vision and its underlying values. "If you talk about speed in action, yet procrastinate on difficult decisions, you are not believable," warns Percy Barnevik, chairman of the Swiss-Swedish electrical conglomerate ABB. "I and the members of my executive committee must 'walk the talk' and live up to what we say."[71]

Modeling the vision is important because employees and other stakeholders are executive watchers who look for behaviors to symbolize values and expectations. The greater the consistency between the leader's words and actions, the more employees will believe and follow the leader. Walking the talk also builds employee trust because trust is determined partly by the consistency of the person's actions.[72]

Building Commitment to the Vision   Transforming a vision into reality requires employee commitment. Transformational leaders build this commitment in several ways. Their words, symbols, and stories build a contagious enthusiasm that energizes people to adopt the vision as their own. Leaders demonstrate a can-do attitude by enacting their vision and staying on course. Their persistence and consistency reflect an image of honesty, trust, and integrity. Finally, leaders build commitment by involving employees in the process of shaping the organization's vision.

Mauricio Botelho Transforms Embraer into a World Leader

Brazilian aircraft maker Embraer started out as a branch of the Brazilian government responsible for building training aircraft for the nation's air force. Like its counterparts in many other nations, the Brazilian air force wanted the latest technology, so it invested heavily in research and development. However, Embraer became so costly to run that during economic crises in Brazil, the government had to sell it to private-sector investors. The Brazilian government retained only 1 percent ownership plus veto power over executive decisions.

At about that time, Embraer hired Mauricio Novis Botelho to serve as its chief executive officer. Botelho's vision was to remake the struggling operation into a profitable business. Botelho started his efforts at transformation by creating efficiency. The company cut half its workforce and more than one-third of its administrative expenses. At the same time, it slashed its 14-month production lead time to 9 months.

When greater efficiency created the conditions for survival, Botelho could turn more of his attention to the remaining employees. He was concerned that the layoffs had destroyed morale and created persistent anxiety. Seeing that the company had to continue slashing costs, Botelho brought together union and management representatives to negotiate a 10 percent cut in pay and benefits. Botelho expressed pride in his employees' willingness to make this sacrifice: "It shows how committed people are to the future."

That commitment has begun to bear fruit. New aircraft designs have won contracts, and the company has been profitable for several years. Sales have grown,

The transformational leadership of Embraer CEO Mauricio Novis Botelho (center) has turned the once-faltering Brazilian aircraft manufacturer into a global competitor. (© AFP/CORBIS)

and as the company has become one of the world's largest aircraft manufacturers, Embraer has hired employees, surpassing earlier employment levels. Today, Embraer is Brazil's leading exporter, and most observers give the credit to Botelho's leadership.

Sources: "Brazil's Best Companies," *LatinFinance,* March 1, 2001, p. S24; F. Shalom, "Meet Bombardier's Challenger," *Montreal Gazette,* February 3, 2001; L. Rohter, "Brazil's Hot Commodity? Not Coffee or Soccer," *New York Times,* December 31, 2000, sec. 3, p.1; S. Evers, "The Jane's Interview," *Jane's Defence Weekly,* November 6, 1996.

Evaluating the Transformational Leadership Perspective

Transformational leaders do make a difference, according to organizational behavior studies.[73] Subordinates are more satisfied and have higher affective organizational commitment under transformational leaders. They also perform their jobs better, engage in more organizational citizenship behaviors, and make better or more creative decisions. One study also reported that organizational commitment and financial performance seem to increase in branches of a bank where the branch manager completed a transformational leadership training program.[74] Global Connections 14.2 illustrates the effect of transformational leadership on organizational performance. It describes how Mauricio Novis Botelho's leadership transformed Embraer from a bureaucratic (and almost bankrupt) government-owned business to one of the leading aircraft manufacturers in the world.

Transformational leadership is currently the most popular leadership perspective, but it faces a number of challenges. One problem is that some writers engage in circular logic by defining transformational leadership in terms of the leader's success.[75] They suggest that leaders are transformational when they successfully bring about change, rather than whether they engage in certain behaviors we call transformational. Another concern is that the transformational leadership model seems to be universal rather than contingency-oriented. Only very recently have writers begun to explore the idea that transformational leadership is more appropriate in some situations than others.[76] For instance, transformational leadership is probably more appropriate when organizations need to adapt than when environmental conditions are stable. Preliminary evidence suggests that the transformational leadership perspective is relevant across cultures. However, there may be specific elements of transformational leadership, such as the way visions are formed and communicated, that are more appropriate in North America than in other cultures.[77]

ROMANCE PERSPECTIVE OF LEADERSHIP

The competency, behavior, contingency, and transformational leadership perspectives make the basic assumption that leaders make a difference. Certainly, there is evidence that senior executives do influence organizational performance.[78] However, leaders might have less influence than most of us would like to believe. Some leadership experts suggest that three perceptual processes cause people to inflate the importance of leadership in explaining organizational events. These processes, collectively called the romance of leadership, include attribution errors, stereotyping, and the need for situational control.[79]

Attributing Leadership

People have a strong need to attribute the causes of events around them so that they can feel more confident about how to control them in the future. The fundamental attribution error is a common perceptual bias in this attribution process (see Chapter 3). Fundamental attribution error is the tendency to attribute the behavior of other people to their motivation and ability rather than to situational contingencies. In the context of leadership, it causes employees to believe that organizational events are due more to the motivation and ability of their leaders than to environmental conditions. Leaders are given credit or blame for the company's success or failure because employees do not readily see the external forces that also influence those events. Leaders reinforce this belief by taking credit for organizational successes.[80]

Stereotyping Leadership

To some extent, people rely on stereotypes to determine whether their boss is an effective leader. Each of us has preconceived notions about the features and behaviors of an effective leader. These leadership perceptions are based partly on cultural values, so an effective leader in one country might not seem

"A year ago, I was a skinny, green-haired, skate boarding CEO of a dot-com company. But that didn't work out."

(Copyright © Randy Glasbergen. Reprinted with special permission from www.glasbergen.com)

so effective to employees in another country. We rely on stereotypes partly because a leader's success might not be known for months or possibly years. Consequently, employees depend on immediate information to decide whether the leader is effective. If the leader fits the mold, then employees are more confident that the leader is effective.[81]

Need for Situational Control

A third perceptual distortion of leadership suggests that people want to believe leaders make a difference. There are two basic reasons for this belief.[82] First, leadership is a useful way for us to simplify life events. It is easier to explain organizational successes and failures in terms of the leader's ability than by analyzing a complex array of other forces. For example, there are usually many reasons a company fails to change quickly enough in the marketplace, yet we tend to simplify the explanation down to the notion that the company president or some other corporate leader was ineffective.

Second, there is a strong tendency in the United States and similar cultures to believe that life events are generated more from people than from uncontrollable natural forces.[83] This illusion of control is satisfied by believing that events result from the rational actions of leaders. In short, employees feel better believing that leaders make a difference, so they actively look for evidence that this is so.

The romance of leadership perspective questions the importance of leadership, but it also provides valuable advice to improve leadership effectiveness. This approach highlights the fact that leadership is a perception of followers as much as the actual behaviors and characteristics of people calling themselves leaders. Potential leaders must be sensitive to this fact, understand what followers expect, and act accordingly. Individuals who do not make an effort to fit leadership prototypes will have more difficulty bringing about necessary organizational change.[84]

GENDER ISSUES IN LEADERSHIP

Don't ask Betsy Holden whether women lead differently than men lead. The CEO of Kraft Foods argues that there is too much focus on the role of women as business leaders. "Sometimes, there's more emphasis put on the fact that you're a woman than [on] results," she says. "At the end of the day, it's the results that count." So it's not surprising that when Holden was selected as Kraft's next CEO, she was equally delighted to hear that Kraft's board of directors considered several women for the top job and that gender wasn't mentioned during the deliberations. "When I heard that, I said: 'Yes!'" says Holden, pumping her fist. "That's the way it ought to be."[85]

Perhaps it's a sign of improving workplace equality that people don't want to make an issue of gender differences in leadership. However, this topic is worth discussing because OB scholars have reported several important observations on this topic over the years. Moreover, there is still a widespread belief that men and women do lead differently. For example, one recent survey reported that 76 percent of male and female chief executives believe the leadership and management skills of women differ markedly from those of their male counterparts, with women generally seen as consensus builders, better able to "nurture strong interpersonal relationships."[86]

These perceptions are consistent with the views of several writers who suggest that women have an interactive style that includes more people-oriented and participative leadership.[87] They suggest that women are more relationship-oriented, cooperative, nurturing, and emotional in their leadership roles. They further assert that these qualities make women particularly well suited to leadership roles at a time when companies are adopting a stronger emphasis on teams and employee involvement. These arguments are consistent with sex role stereotypes, namely, that men tend to be more task-oriented whereas women are more people-oriented.

Are these stereotypes true? Do women adopt more people-oriented and participative leadership styles? The answer is that male and female leaders are equally people-oriented, but female leaders do tend to be more participative than their male counterparts. Leadership studies in field settings have generally found that male and female leaders do not differ in their levels of task-oriented or people-oriented leadership. The main explanation why men and women do not differ on these styles is that real-world jobs require similar behavior from male and female job incumbents.[89]

Scholars suggest that women are possibly more participative because their upbringing has made them more egalitarian and less status-oriented. There is also some evidence that women have somewhat better interpersonal skills than men, and these skills translate into their relatively greater use of the participative leadership style. A third explanation is that subordinates expect female leaders to be more participative, on the basis of their own sex stereotypes. If a female manager tries to be more autocratic, subordinates are more likely to complain (or use some other power base) because they expect the female executive or team leader to be participative.[90]

Kirsten Feldman has glowing words for everyone on her team who launched Martha Stewart's new company on the New York Stock Exchange. "We had a large team, all of whom are specialists in different aspects of an [initial stock] offering," says the managing director at Morgan Stanley Dean Witter in Manhattan. But Feldman is quick to play down her own lead role on that team: "It's never one person and I wouldn't want to leave that impression." Feldman is known for her participative and people-oriented leadership style. Some people would say that Feldman and other female executives differ from male leaders in the traditionally macho investment industry. Others suggest that men and women adapt similar leadership styles in various situations.[88] In your opinion, do women generally prefer leadership styles that are the same as or different from those of men? *(G. Domenico/The* Ottawa Citizen*)*

Evaluating Female Leaders

For several years, OB scholars warned that female leaders are evaluated slightly less favorably than equivalent male leaders, and this difference is almost completely due to sex stereotype bias. Specifically, women are evaluated negatively when they adopt a stereotypically male leadership style (i.e., autocratic) and occupy traditionally male-dominated positions. These negative evaluations suggest that women "pay the price" for entering traditionally male leadership jobs and for adopting a male-stereotypic leadership style.[91] It also lends further support to our earlier point on why women adopt a more participative style.

However, as the opening vignette in this chapter emphasized, the perceptions of effective leaders are shifting. Followers increasingly expect leaders to support and empower them. These leadership styles are more consistent with how many women prefer to lead and how followers stereotype female leaders. Consequently, several recent surveys reported that women are rated higher than men on most leadership dimensions, including the emerging leadership qualities of coaching, teamwork, and empowering employees.[92]

Whether women or men are better leaders depends, of course, on the individual and on specific circumstances. We should also be careful about perpetuating the apparently false assumption that women leaders are less task-oriented or more people-oriented. At the same time, both male and female leaders must be sensitive to the fact that followers have expectations about how leaders should act, and negative evaluations may go to leaders who deviate from those expectations.

CHAPTER SUMMARY

Leadership is a complex concept that is defined as the process of influencing people and providing an environment for them to achieve team or organizational objectives. Leaders use power and persuasion to motivate followers, and arrange the work environment so that they do the job more effectively. Leaders exist throughout the organization, not just in the executive suite.

The competency perspective tries to identify the characteristics of effective leaders. Recent writing suggests that leaders have drive, leadership motivation, integrity, self-confidence, above-average intelligence, knowledge of the business, and high emotional intelligence.

The behavioral perspective of leadership identified two clusters of leader behavior, people-oriented and task-oriented. People-oriented behaviors include showing mutual trust and respect for subordinates, demonstrating a genuine concern for their needs, and having a desire to look out for their welfare. Task-oriented behaviors include assigning employees to specific tasks, clarifying their work duties and procedures, ensuring that they follow company rules, and pushing

them to reach their performance capacity. This perspective hypothesizes that the most effective leaders exhibit high levels of both types of behaviors, but this notion falsely assumes that one leadership style is best in all circumstances.

The contingency perspective of leadership takes the view that effective leaders diagnose the situation and adapt their style to fit that situation. The path–goal model is the prominent contingency theory that identifies four leadership styles—directive, supportive, participative, and achievement-oriented—and several contingencies relating to the characteristics of the employee and the situation. A recent extension of path–goal theory adds more leader styles and moves the model from a dyadic to a team and organizational level.

Two other contingency leadership theories are the situational leadership model and Fiedler's contingency theory. Research support is quite weak for both theories. However, a lasting element of Fiedler's theory is the idea that leaders have natural styles and, consequently, companies need to change the leader's environment to suit his or her style. The theory of leadership substitutes identifies contingencies that either limit the leader's ability to influence subordinates or make that particular leadership style unnecessary. This idea will become more important as organizations remove supervisors and shift toward team-based structures.

❧ Transformational leaders create a strategic vision, communicate that vision through framing and use of metaphors, model the vision by walking the talk and acting consistently, and build commitment to the vision. This leadership style contrasts with transactional leadership, which involves linking job performance to valued rewards and ensuring that employees have the resources needed to get the job done. The contingency and behavioral perspectives adopt the transactional view of leadership.

According to the romance perspective, people inflate the importance of leadership through attribution, stereotyping, and fundamental needs for human control.

Women generally do not differ from men in the degree of people-oriented or task-oriented leadership. However, female leaders more often adopt a participative style. Research also suggests that people evaluate female leaders on the basis of gender stereotypes.

KEY TERMS

DISCUSSION QUESTIONS

1. Southern Industrials Inc. wants to develop a competency-based approach to executive selection. Which leadership perspective mainly applies to this practice? Also, on the basis of leadership research, identify four competencies that Southern Industrials will probably identify in effective executives.

2. Consider your favorite teacher. What people-oriented and task-oriented leadership behaviors does he or she use effectively? In general, do you prefer an instructor who is more people-oriented or more task-oriented? Explain your preference.

3. Your employees are skilled and experienced customer service representatives who perform nonroutine tasks, such as solving unique customer problems or special needs with the company's equipment. Use path–goal theory to identify the most appropriate leadership style(s) you should use in this situation. Be sure to explain your answer fully and discuss why other styles are inappropriate.

4. Discuss the accuracy of the following statement: Contingency theories don't work because they assume leaders can adjust their style to the situation. In reality, people have a preferred leadership style that they can't easily change.

5. Is it possible to be a transformational leader and have poor communication skills? Why or why not?

6. Transformational leadership is currently the most popular perspective of leadership. However, it is far from perfect. Discuss three concerns with transformational leadership.

7. Identify a current political leader (e.g., president, governor, mayor) and his or her recent accomplishments. Now, using the romance of leadership perspective, think of ways that these accomplishments of the leader may be overstated. In other words, explain why they may be due to factors other than the leader.

8. You hear two people debating the merits of women as leaders. One person claims that women make better leaders than do men because women are more sensitive to their employees' needs and involve them in organizational decisions. The other person counters that although these leadership styles may be increasingly important, most women have trouble gaining acceptance as leaders when they face tough situations in which a more autocratic style is required. Discuss the accuracy of the comments made in this discussion.

JEREMIAH BIGATALLIO'S LEADERSHIP CHALLENGE

By Alvin Turner, Brock University

Jeremiah Bigatallio was eager to start his new job at InterContinental Communication, a high-tech company near Boston. Jeremiah, a civil engineer, joined the organization because it was a relatively young, growing, and dynamic organization that claimed in a brochure five years ago that its work environment was modeled on that of Microsoft. Jeremiah was hired as director of engineering services to supervise a staff of 25. The staff includes 10 engineers, seven technicians, and eight lab assistants.

Mr. Bigatallio's predecessor was John Angle, who was fired for just cause. The official reason for his dismissal was not made public, but it is well known that he was having trouble managing his staff as well as interacting with other departments. First, most of the engineers did not get along with one another; some have not spoken to each other for more than two years. Second, the technicians disliked the engineers because they were seen as arrogant prima donnas who were concerned only about themselves. The engineers did not have any respect for or confidence in the technicians. They felt that the technicians were a group of bungling incompetents who should all be sent back to trade school. Third, both of these teams were in almost complete harmony in their contempt for the lab assistants, all of whom they felt were lacking in initiative, vastly overpaid, vastly underqualified, and more concerned with abusing overtime privileges and being promoted than achieving and maintaining minimum productivity standards.

Other line and staff departments' heads were very upset with John Angle. The head of corporate financial control was dissatisfied with him because his department was constantly over budget allocations, particularly because of the excessive amount of overtime worked by his staff. He did not keep good records and did not submit accounting information on time. A recent audit revealed major financial irregularities of more than $300,000 in salaries. And there were also

concerns about potential misappropriation of $250,000 of a government grant program. People in other departments (research and development, manufacturing, quality assurance) were very displeased with John Angle because the internecine warfare ongoing in his department made it difficult to work with anyone in engineering. This lack of communication, and frequent substandard lathes, dies, and design surveys, resulted in backlogged work and unnecessary overtime expenses. And when communication did occur, the engineering unit's performance was generally unreliable.

John Angle believed in self-directing and autonomous work teams. Consequently, he believed in empowering his subordinates to make decisions and to feel responsible for the successes of the department as well as their own successes. John provided little or no direction or support for his subordinates. He did not articulate his vision, leadership style, or expectations to his subordinates. He felt that they were highly trained professionals who should know what is expected of them and should be willing to do the right thing. He also felt that by being self-regulating and solving their own problems as they arose, employees would learn from their own mistakes. He saw this as the best way for employees to grow and develop on the job and for the organization to realize maximum output from workers.

John Angle viewed himself as a progressive liberal thinker whose new-age leadership style would transform and motivate employees to achieve great things. He believed that sharing power would enhance employees' self-worth and energize them. He also believed in maintaining a convivial work atmosphere. Thus, absenteeism and lateness were overlooked. Angle was also fairly lax in enforcing work rules and work productivity standards. As a consequence of the laxity in discipline and absence of enforcement of work standards, employees took advantage of the situation and worked at their leisure; they were frequently late or absent and (mis)managed other aspects of their own work schedule. They also took frequent coffee breaks and tended to work substantially higher amounts of overtime relative to other employees in the organization.

When Jeremiah was hired, he was told that he had the full confidence of the CEO and his vice presidents to clean up the mess in the engineering department. He was given four months to fix all the existing problems in the department.

On his first day on the job, Jeremiah sat down in his office and typed on his laptop: What type of leadership style should I use on this diverse team of individuals? Then he stopped to retrieve from his pocket a note that he found under his door that morning. It said: "Try changing our overtime around here and we will cut you down to size!"

Discussion Questions

1. In what way was John Angle's leadership style ineffective? In what way may the existing span of control be considered too broad or too narrow? What impact does the existing structure have on a manager's leadership style?

2. Use the path–goal leadership model to identify the best leadership style(s) for Jeremiah Bigatallio in this situation at InterContinental Communication.

3. What other type of leadership style could Jeremiah use in leading his staff? Explain why and how you believe the style you have selected will be effective in resolving the conflicts and other problems within the department and between departments.

C A S E   S T U D Y   14.2

GE'S JEFF IMMELT: HIS OWN MAN

BusinessWeek If anyone embodies the cliché of a tough act to follow, it's General Electric Company's former chief executive officer Jack Welch. Welch was widely respected not only by his employees but also by businesspeople around the world. This audience of Welch fans therefore paused to watch as Jeffrey R. Immelt moved to center stage as Welch's replacement at GE. A question on many minds was whether Immelt could match Jack Welch as leader of the giant conglomerate.

This *Business Week* case study describes Jeffrey Immelt and the leadership challenges he faces as GE's new chief executive. The author interviewed GE managers and business analysts to learn about Immelt's leadership style and goals. Read through this *Business Week* case study at www.mhhe.com/mcshane2e and prepare for the discussion questions below.

Discussion Questions

1. What leadership competencies do the author and the people she interviewed see in Jeffrey Immelt?

2. How might Immelt apply path–goal theory to his leadership role at GE? Consider contingencies from this theory that are relevant in this case.

3. How can transformational leadership benefit GE in its early years under Immelt? Does Immelt show potential for such leadership? Explain, on the basis of evidence from the article.

Source: D. Brady, "GE's Jeff Immelt: His Own Man," *Business Week*, September 17, 2001.

LEADERSHIP DIAGNOSTIC ANALYSIS

Purpose This exercise is designed to help you learn about the different path–goal leadership styles and when to apply each style.

Instructions

- *Step 1*—Students individually write down two incidents in which someone has been an effective manager or leader over them. The leader and situation might be from work, a sports team, a student work group, or any other setting where leadership might emerge. For example, students might describe how their supervisor in a summer job pushed them to reach higher performance goals than they would have done otherwise. Each incident should state the actual behaviors that the leader used, not just general statements (e.g., "My boss sat down with me and we agreed on specific targets and deadlines; then he said several times over the next few weeks that I was capable of reaching those goals"). Each incident requires only two or three sentences.
- *Step 2*—After everyone has written her or his two incidents, the instructor will form small groups (typically between four or five

students). Each team will answer the following questions for each incident presented in that team:
  - a. Which path–goal theory leadership style(s)—directive, supportive, participative, or achievement-oriented—did the leader apply in this incident?
  - b. What were the conditions that made this leadership style (or these styles, if more than one was used) appropriate in this situation? The team should list these contingency factors clearly and, where possible, connect them to the contingencies described in path–goal theory. (*Note:* The team might identify path–goal leadership contingencies that are not described in the book. These, too, should be noted and discussed.)
- *Step 3*—After the teams have diagnosed the incidents, each team will describe to the entire class the most interesting incident as well as its diagnosis of that incident. Other teams will critique the diagnosis. Any leadership contingencies not mentioned in the textbook should also be presented and discussed.

SELECTING THE BEST LEADER

By Robert Cunningham, University of Tennessee

Purpose This team exercise is designed to help you understand the competency (trait) and romance perspectives of leadership.

Instructions You are on a task force responsible for selecting a new chief executive officer for your organization. The instructor may provide

more details about the type of organization (e.g., large private-sector firm, manager of a suburban city).

- *Step 1*—The instructor will place students in teams, preferably with between five and eight people in each team. Each team will have an opportunity to meet one of the candidates, identify the candidate's observable characteristics, and evaluate from these characteristics the candidate's leadership qualities (both positive and negative). Each team member should have an opportunity to inspect the candidate. The team will document the characteristics and leadership qualities identified for other teams to view later (e.g., on an overhead transparency or a flip chart).

■ *Step 2*—Each team will report to the class on the characteristics and leadership qualities

as well as the appropriateness of the candidate that it evaluated for the position.
■ *Step 3*—Students will discuss the assessments of each candidate and try to reach agreement on the best candidate. If time does not permit this extended discussion, or if the class cannot reach consensus, the instructor may call for a vote on the best candidate.

Source: Adapted from R. Cunningham, "Meet Dr. Clay and Dr. Glass: A Leadership Exercise," *Journal of Management Education* 21 (May 1997), pp. 262–64.

SELF-ASSESSMENT EXERCISE 14.5

LEADERSHIP DIMENSIONS INSTRUMENT

Purpose This self-assessment exercise is designed to help you understand two important dimensions of leadership and to identify which of these dimensions is more prominent in your supervisor, team leader, coach, or other person to whom you are accountable.

Instructions Read each of the following statements and circle the response that you believe

best describes your supervisor. You may substitute "supervisor" with anyone else to whom you are accountable, such as a team leader, CEO, course instructor, or sports coach. Then use the scoring key in Appendix B to calculate the results for each leadership dimensions. After completing this assessment, be prepared to discuss in class the distinctions between these leadership dimensions.

Leadership dimensions					
My supervisor . . .	Strongly agree ▼	Agree ▼	Neutral ▼	Disagree ▼	Strongly disagree ▼
1. Focuses attention on irregularities, mistakes, exceptions, and deviations from what is expected of me.	1	2	3	4	5
2. Engages in words and deeds that enhance his or her image of competence.	1	2	3	4	5
3. Monitors performance for errors needing correction.	1	2	3	4	5
4. Serves as a role model for me.	1	2	3	4	5
5. Points out what I will receive if I do what is required.	1	2	3	4	5
6. Instills pride in being associated with him or her.	1	2	3	4	5
7. Keeps careful track of mistakes.	1	2	3	4	5
8. Can be trusted to help me overcome any obstacle.	1	2	3	4	5
9. Tells me what to do to be rewarded for my efforts.	1	2	3	4	5
10. Makes me aware of strongly held values, ideals, and aspirations that we have in common.	1	2	3	4	5

—continued

My supervisor . . .	Strongly agree ▼	Agree ▼	Neutral ▼	Disagree ▼	Strongly disagree ▼
11. Is alert for failure to meet standards.	1	2	3	4	5
12. Mobilizes a collective sense of mission.	1	2	3	4	5
13. Works out agreements with me on what I will receive if I do what needs to be done.	1	2	3	4	5
14. Articulates a vision of future opportunities.	1	2	3	4	5
15. Talks about special rewards for good work.	1	2	3	4	5
16. Talks optimistically about the future.	1	2	3	4	5

Source: Items and dimensions are adapted from D. N. Den Hartog, J. J. Van Muijen, and P. L. Koopman, "Transactional versus Transformational Leadership: An Analysis of the MLQ," *Journal of Occupational and Organizational Psychology* 70 (March 1997), pp. 19–34. Den Hartog et al. label transactional leadership as "rational-objective leadership" and transformational leadership as "inspirational leadership." Many of their items may have originated from B. M. Bass and B. J. Avolio, *Manual for the Multifactor Leadership Questionnaire* (Palo Alto, CA: Consulting Psychologists Press, 1989).

After studying the preceding material, be sure to check out our website at
www.mhhe.com/mcshane2e
for more in-depth information and interactivities that correspond to this chapter.

Organizational Processes

4

15

Organizational Culture

AFTER READING THIS CHAPTER, YOU SHOULD BE ABLE TO:

■ Describe the elements of organizational culture.

■ Discuss the importance of organizational subcultures.

■ List four categories of artifacts through which corporate culture is communicated.

■ Identify three functions of organizational culture.

■ Discuss the conditions under which cultural strength improves corporate performance.

■ Discuss the effect of organizational culture on business ethics.

■ Compare and contrast four strategies for merging organizational cultures.

■ Identify five strategies to strengthen an organization's culture.

Carly Fiorina is taking Hewlett-Packard back to the future by reformulating the California-based technology company's legendary culture, known as the H-P Way. "The H-P Way is about innovation; trust and respect and integrity; contribution to community; and performance," says Fiorina, H-P's first CEO hired from outside the company. The problem, she argues, is that employees have distorted these values over the years. "The H-P Way has been misinterpreted and twisted as a gentle bureaucracy of entitlement instead of a performance-based meritocracy."

To reinstate a more performance-based culture, Fiorina launched the "Rules of the Garage," a set of cultural values with symbolic reference to the Palo Alto garage where founders William Hewlett and David Packard started the company in 1939. To reinforce these values, Fiorina introduced a customer-focused bonus system, integrated the company's 83 decentralized business units, and laid off thousands of employees.

Hewlett-Packard CEO Carly Fiorina (shown here with Compaq Computer CEO Michael Capellas) is trying to reformulate the company's famous "H-P Way" culture, even to the point of merging with former rival Compaq Computer. (© Reuters/New Media, Inc./CORBIS)

If the Rules of the Garage don't change H-P's culture, Fiorina is betting that a merger with Houston-based Compaq Computer will do the trick. Fiorina calls the merger "a catalyst that would rejuvenate the H-P Way," forcing H-P employees to adopt Compaq's fast-moving culture. Some industry observers are more concerned that the merger will produce a monumental clash between Compaq's "cowboy mentality" culture and H-P's consensus-driven culture. "It's an awkward match," says Laurie McCabe, vice president of Summit Strategies. "At a party, Compaq is the outgoing guy shaking everyone's hand, while H-P is the introspective, analytical guy." Mark Specker of SoundView Technology agrees, suggesting that combining these two firms will be like "merging the Texas big hair and the California granola."[1] ■

arly Fiorina and her executive team at Hewlett-Packard are facing a force much more powerful than marketplace competitors. They are facing the H-P Way, a deeply entrenched organizational culture. **Organizational culture** is the basic pattern of shared assumptions, values, and beliefs considered the correct way of thinking about and acting on problems and opportunities facing the organization. Organizational culture defines what is important and unimportant in the company. You might think of it as the organization's DNA—invisible to the naked eye, yet a powerful template that shapes what happens in the workplace.[2]

This chapter begins by examining the elements of organizational culture and how culture is deciphered through artifacts. That section is followed by a discussion of the relationship between organizational culture and corporate performance, including the effects of cultural strength, fit, and adaptability. Then we turn to the issue of mergers and corporate culture. The last section of this chapter looks at specific strategies for maintaining a strong organizational culture.

ELEMENTS OF ORGANIZATIONAL CULTURE

As Exhibit 15.1 illustrates, the assumptions, values, and beliefs that represent organizational culture operate beneath the surface of organizational behavior. They are not directly observed, yet their effects are everywhere. Assumptions

EXHIBIT 15.1

Elements of organizational culture

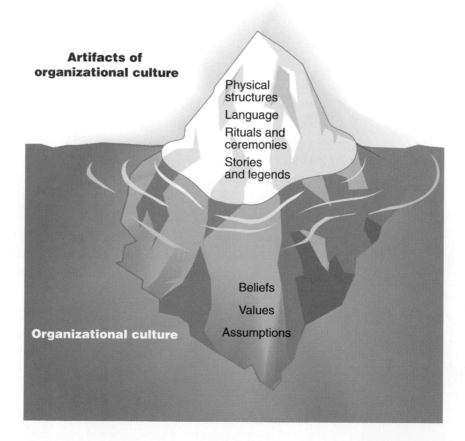

Artifacts of organizational culture

Physical structures
Language
Rituals and ceremonies
Stories and legends

Organizational culture

Beliefs
Values
Assumptions

represent the deepest part of organizational culture because they are unconscious and taken for granted. Assumptions are the shared mental models, the broad worldviews or theories in use that people rely on to guide their perceptions and behaviors (see Chapter 3). At Hewlett-Packard, for example, employees expect a high degree of job security and involvement in corporate decisions. These assumptions are ingrained, taken for granted. In other high-technology companies, employees might assume less security and involvement.

Because people are aware of them, an organization's cultural beliefs and values are somewhat easier to decipher than are assumptions. *Beliefs* represent the individual's perceptions of reality. *Values* are more stable, long-lasting beliefs about what is important. They help define what is right or wrong, or good or bad, in the world (see Chapter 4).[3] For example, employees at Sparks.com—the San Francisco provider of Internet greeting cards—think it's "cool" to spend long hours at the office with a fuzzy distinction between work and play. In contrast, the corporate culture at **SAS Institute**, the Cary, North Carolina–based statistical software firm, values work–life balance and locking up the office by 5 P.M. each day.[4]

We can't determine an organization's cultural values just by asking employees and other people about them. Values are socially desirable, so what people say they value (called *espoused values*) may differ from what they truly value (*enacted values*).[5] Espoused values do not represent an organization's culture. Rather, they establish the public image that corporate leaders want to display. Enacted values, on the other hand, are values in use. They are the values that guide individual decisions and behavior in the workplace.

Content of Organizational Culture

Organizations differ in their cultural content, that is, the relative ordering of beliefs, values, and assumptions. Consider the following companies and their apparent dominant cultures:

■ *SAS Institute*—SAS Institute has one of the most employee-friendly cultures on the planet. Located on a 200-acre campus in Cary, North Carolina, the world's largest privately held software company supports employee well-being with free on-site medical care, unlimited sick days, heavily subsidized day care, ski trips, personal trainers, inexpensive gourmet cafeterias, and tai chi classes. Unlike other software companies, SAS encourages its employees to stick to a 35-hour workweek. "You can't be a programmer 15 and 16 hours a day," says Jim Goodnight, SAS chief executive and co-founder. "By the end of the day you are just producing total garbage." Little wonder that SAS Institute is rated as one of the best companies to work for.[6]

■ *Rand Merchant Bank*—Employees at this South African financial institution were recently handed a booklet entitled *The Complete Book of Rules*. But instead of a long list of dos and don'ts, all the pages inside were blank. The message here is that Rand Merchant Bank has a culture that empowers employees to make their own decisions. "We trust that in any given situation an employee who has freedom to make choices will inherently do the best for the company," explains Rand chairman Paul Harris. This cultural assumption seems to work: Rand Merchant Bank is rated the best company to work for in South Africa and tends to outperform the marketplace in terms of earnings.[7]

■ *Amazon.com*—Frugality is clearly a corporate value at Amazon.com. Beyond the online bookseller's popular website is a drab 1960s four-story headquarters in downtown Seattle. All desks are made from doors (total cost: $130). Monitors are propped up on telephone books to avoid the cost of monitor stands. Extra chairs are considered an extravagance. "By watching your overhead you can spend more on business expansion," explains Amazon.com founder and CEO Jeff Bezos.[8]

Employee-friendly. Empowered. Frugal. How many corporate cultural values are there? No one knows for certain. There are dozens of individual and cross-cultural values, so there are likely as many organizational values. Some writers and consultants have attempted to classify organizational cultures into a few categories with catchy labels, such as "mercenaries" and "communes." Although these typologies might reflect the values of a few organizations, they oversimplify the diversity of cultural values in organizations. Worse, they tend to distort rather than clarify our attempts to diagnose corporate culture.

Organizational Subcultures

When discussing organizational culture, we are actually referring to the *dominant culture*, that is, the themes shared most widely by the organization's members. However, organizations are also composed of *subcultures* located throughout their various divisions, geographic regions, and occupational groups.[9] Some subcultures enhance the dominant culture by espousing parallel assumptions, values, and beliefs; others, called *countercultures*, directly oppose the organization's core values.

Subcultures, particularly countercultures, potentially create conflict and dissension among employees, but they also serve two important functions. First, they maintain the organization's standards of performance and ethical behavior. Employees who hold countercultural values are an important source of surveillance over and critique of the dominant order.[10] They encourage constructive controversy and more creative thinking about how the organization should interact with its environment. Subcultures prevent employees from blindly following one set of values, thereby helping the organization abide by society's ethical values.

The second function of subcultures is that they are the spawning grounds for emerging values that keep the firm aligned with the needs of customers, suppliers, society, and other stakeholders. Companies eventually need to replace their dominant values with ones that are more appropriate for the changing environment. If subcultures are

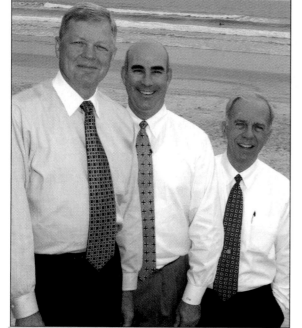

Aggressive is too mild a word to describe the corporate culture of Brown & Brown, Inc. The unofficial mascot of this Daytona Beach, Florida–based insurance company is a cheetah. On the back cover of a recent annual report is the warning, in Latin, "No Egg-Sucking Dogs," a not-so-subtle reminder that poor performers will not be tolerated. This is not an idle threat. At the company's annual sales meeting, managers of poorly performing divisions are led to a podium by employees dressed as medieval executioners, while a funeral dirge plays over loudspeakers. These managers have to explain to an audience of 1,000 employees why they failed to meet their annual goals. "It does sound a bit harsh, but that's the culture," says Brown & Brown's chief executive. "This is not a warm and fuzzy world."[11] Would Brown & Brown's aggressive culture work well in every company? Why or why not? *(Eileen Marie Samelson/Orlando Sentinel)*

suppressed, the organization may take longer to discover and adopt values aligned with the emerging environment.

DECIPHERING ORGANIZATIONAL CULTURE THROUGH ARTIFACTS

artifacts

The observable symbols and signs of an organization's culture.

We can't directly see an organization's cultural assumptions, values, and beliefs. Instead, as Exhibit 15.1 illustrated, organizational culture is deciphered indirectly through **artifacts.** Artifacts are the observable symbols and signs of an organization's culture, such as the way visitors are greeted, the physical layout, and the way employees are rewarded.[12] "You show your corporate culture in everything—the way the building looks, the way people act, the names of the conference rooms," says the CEO of a California-based web portal company.[13] In other words, the symbols of corporate culture are all around us.

Understanding an organization's culture requires painstaking assessment of many artifacts because they are subtle and often ambiguous.[14] The process is very much like an anthropological investigation of a new society. Some scholars extract organizational values from the narratives of everyday corporate life.[15] Others survey employees, observe workplace behavior, and study written documents. We probably need to do all these things to accurately assess an organization's culture. Although this book tries to present accurate examples, we should remain cautious about public statements regarding a company's culture. Most often, these statements are based on no more than a journalist's quick scan or the company's own public relations pronouncements of its espoused values. With this caution in mind, let's consider four broad categories of artifacts: organizational stories and legends, rituals and ceremonies, language, and physical structures and symbols.

Organizational Stories and Legends

A decade ago, Southwest Airlines introduced an ad campaign with the phrase "Just Plane Smart." Unknowingly, the Dallas-based airline had infringed on the "Plane Smart" slogan at Stevens Aviation, an aviation sales and maintenance company in Greensville, South Carolina. Rather than paying buckets of money to lawyers, Stevens chairman Kurt Herwald and Southwest CEO Herb Kelleher decided to settle the dispute with an old-fashioned arm wrestling match at a run-down wrestling stadium in Dallas. A boisterous crowd watched the "Malice in Dallas" event as "Smokin" Herb Kelleher and "Kurtsey" Herwald battled their designates, and then each other. When Kelleher lost the final round to Herwald, he jested (while being carried off on a stretcher) that his defeat was due to a cold and the strain of walking up a flight of stairs. Stevens Aviation later decided to let Southwest Airlines continue to use its ad campaign, and both companies donated funds from the event to charities.[16]

Malice in Dallas is a legendary story that almost every Southwest employee knows by heart. It is a tale that communicates one of the maverick airline's core values—that having fun is part of doing business. Stories and legends about past corporate incidents serve as powerful social prescriptions of the way things should (or should not) be done. They provide human realism to corporate expectations, individual performance standards, and assumptions about the way things should work around the organization.

Four Seasons Hotels and Resorts hires, trains, and rewards employees for (like the doorman shown in the photo) superior customer service. Yet founder Isadore Sharp will tell you that the company's legendary service is also ingrained in the Four Seasons corporate culture. There is certainly evidence of the customer service value in stories and legends. One story recounts an incident in which rock star Rod Stewart called Four Seasons staff while he was a guest to find someone to play the bagpipes in his suite. The employees were able to find a bagpipe player, even though Stewart phoned in the request at *midnight!*[17] In what ways do such stories and legends support organizational culture? *(Courtesy of Four Seasons Hotel)*

Not all stories and legends are positive. Some are repeated to demonstrate what is wrong with the corporate culture. For instance, General Motors (GM) employees who rejected the automaker's dominant culture liked to tell about how dozens of GM people would arrive at the airport to meet a senior executive. An executive's status was symbolized by the number of vehicles leaving the airport with the executive.[18] This story didn't just symbolize respect for authority; it was repeated because it highlighted the decadence and waste that characterized GM's dominant culture.

Organizational stories and legends are most effective at communicating cultural values when they describe real people, are assumed to be true, and are known by employees throughout the organization. Stories are also prescriptive—they advise people what to do or not to do.[19] Research on organizational stories reveals that they tend to answer one or more of the following questions: How does the boss react to mistakes? What events are so important that people get fired? Who, if anyone, can break the rules? How do people rise to the top of this organization? How much help can employees expect from the organization for transfers and other events? How will the organization deal with crises?[20]

Rituals and Ceremonies

Soon after moving from IBM to Digital Equipment Corporation (now part of Hewlett-Packard through its merger with Compaq Computer) several years ago, Peter DeLisi noticed that Digital employees seemed to fight a lot with each other. "Shouting matches were a frequent occurrence, and I came to conclude that Digital people didn't like one another," he recalls. Eventually, DeLisi learned that Digital employees didn't dislike each other; they were engaging in the ritual of "pushing back"—defending ideas until truth ultimately prevailed.[21]

rituals

The programmed routines of daily organizational life that dramatize the organization's culture.

Pushing back at Digital was a ritual that reflected the firm's belief that constructive conflict is useful. **Rituals** are the programmed routines of daily organizational life that dramatize the organization's culture. Along with shouting matches at Digital, rituals include how visitors are greeted, how often senior executives visit subordinates, how people communicate with each other, and how much time employees take for lunch. **Ceremonies** are more formal artifacts than rituals. Ceremonies are planned activities conducted specifically for the benefit of an audience, such as publicly rewarding (or punishing) employees, or celebrating the launch of a new product or a newly won contract.[22]

ceremonies

Planned and usually dramatic displays of organizational culture, conducted specifically for the benefit of an audience.

Organizational Language

The language of the workplace speaks volumes about the company's culture. How employees address co-workers, describe customers, express anger, and greet stakeholders are all verbal symbols of cultural values. Employees at The Container Store compliment each other about "being Gumby," meaning that they are being as flexible as the once-popular green toy—going outside their regular job to help a customer or another employee. (A human-sized Gumby is displayed at the retailer's headquarters.)[23]

Organizational leaders also use phrases, metaphors, and other special vocabularies to symbolize the company's culture.[24] For example, Jack Welch often talked about General Electric as a "grocery store." The former CEO of the giant conglomerate wanted everyone to think of GE as a small business where customer service and the constant search for new opportunities keeps the "shop" in business.[25] Of course, metaphors and catchphrases often reflect the leader's espoused values rather the company's than enacted values (see Chapter 4).

Language also highlights values held by organizational subcultures. This concept was recently apparent to consultants working at Whirlpool. They kept hearing employees talk about the appliance company's "PowerPoint culture." This phrase, which names Microsoft's presentation software, is a critique of Whirlpool's hierarchical culture in which communication is one-way (from executives to employees). PowerPoint presentations tend to be one-way conversations from the presenter to the audience, and Whirlpool employees see themselves as the "audience" with limited opportunity to voice opinions or concerns to senior management (the "presenters").[26]

Oakley, Inc., is at war. At least, that's the impression you get when visiting its recently built headquarters in Foothill Ranch, California. The maker of ultra-hip eyewear and footwear has a front lobby (right) that looks like a bomb shelter. Sleek pipes, watertight doors, and towering metallic walls studded with oversize bolts suggest a place that is routinely subjected to laser fire and floods. Ejection seats from a B-52 bomber furnish the waiting area. A full-size torpedo lies in a rack behind the receptionist's armored desk. "We've always had a fortress mentality," says an Oakley executive. "What we make is gold, and people will do anything to get it, so we protect it."[27] Go to Oakley's website (www.oakley.com). In what ways does the information at this website reflect Oakley's warlike and protective culture? *(Courtesy of Oakley, Inc.)*

Physical Structures and Symbols

British Airways (BA) is changing its corporate culture by changing its headquarters building. The old multistory headquarters near London's Heathrow Airport reinforced hierarchical and bureaucratic values that the airline was trying to cast off. The new headquarters is designed with a central village square and work units spreading out from it. Executives are located with their units, not cloistered on a separate executive floor. In the words of a British Airways executive, "move the office, change the culture."[28]

British Airways is part of the recent wave in which corporate leaders are redesigning the workplace to fit the culture (or create a new one). The size, shape, location, and age of buildings might suggest the organization's emphasis on teamwork, risk aversion, flexibility, or any other set of values. Such structures may be designed deliberately to shape the culture, or they may merely be artifacts of the existing culture.[29]

Even if the building doesn't make much of a statement, a treasure trove of physical artifacts inside may do so. Desks, chairs, office space, and wall hangings (or lack of them) are just a few of the items that might convey cultural meaning. Stroll through IDEO's offices in Palo Alto, California, and you soon realize that the industrial design firm has an innovative, team-oriented, egalitarian culture. All employee cubicles are similar in size and are grouped into neighborhoods facing an asymmetrical table that serves as a central "park" for the team. One employee has hung dozens of strands of beads over the doorway to her workstation. Others suspend patio umbrellas from the ceiling to reduce computer glare from the skylights. To save space, some employees hoist their bicycles overhead on pulleys.[30] Each of these artifacts alone might not say much, but put enough of them together and the company's cultural values become easier to decipher.

ORGANIZATIONAL CULTURE AND PERFORMANCE

Does organizational culture affect corporate performance? Bob Gett thinks so. The chief executive officer of consulting firm Viant, Inc., prefers to be called "chief cultural officer" because he believes a strong corporate culture shapes the organization's success. Several writers on this subject also conclude that a strong corporate culture is good for business.[31] Generally, they argue that culture serves three important functions.

First, corporate culture is a deeply embedded form of social control that influences employee decisions and behavior.[32] Culture is pervasive and operates unconsciously. You might think of it as an automatic pilot, directing employees in ways that are consistent with organizational expectations. Second, corporate culture is the social glue that bonds people together and makes them feel part of the organizational experience.[33] Employees are motivated to internalize the organization's dominant culture because it fulfills their need for social identity. This social glue is increasingly important as a way to attract new staff and retain top performers.

Finally, corporate culture assists the sense-making process.[34] It helps employees understand organizational events. They can get on with the task at hand rather than spend time trying to figure out what is expected of them. Employees can also communicate more efficiently and reach higher levels of cooperation with each other because they share common mental models of reality.

Organizational Culture Strength and Fit

Each of these functions of organizational culture assumes that a strong culture is better than a weak one. A *strong organizational culture* exists when most employees across all subunits hold the dominant values. The values are also institutionalized through well-established artifacts, thereby making it difficult for those values to change. Lastly, strong cultures are long-lasting. In many cases, they can be traced back to the beliefs and values established by the company's founder.[35] In contrast, companies have weak cultures when the dominant values are short-lived and held mainly by a few people at the top of the organization.

In spite of the popular view about the benefits of strong organizational cultures, studies have found only a modestly positive relationship between culture strength and organizational performance.[36] One reason for the weak relationship is that a strong culture increases organizational performance only when the cultural content is appropriate for the organization's environment (see Exhibit 15.2). Global Connections 15.1 describes how Infosys

EXHIBIT 15.2

Organizational culture and performance

Silicon Valley Culture Aligns Infosys with Its Environment

Infosys Technologies has an impressive 42-acre campus. Around the massive green courtyard connecting the six low-rise buildings, you can see employees playing on the miniature golf green, cooling off in the mammoth swimming pool, or munching on a freshly made Dominos pizza from one of the two huge food courts. There is also a huge video wall, a leading-edge training center, and a complete medical center. Not bad, even by Silicon Valley standards.

But Infosys isn't located in Silicon Valley, or even in the United States. India's third-largest information technology firm has its headquarters 15 miles south of Bangalore. To compete and survive in the global marketplace, Infosys has built a campus and adopted a culture that matches its Silicon Valley clients and competitors. This "valley culture" values employees as a scarce resource, so providing a lavish workplace is a worthwhile investment in becoming the employer of choice. Such "culture and caring aspects are really the emotional glue that holds employees together," explains Hema Ravichandar, head of human resources at Infosys.

Infosys also has an egalitarian culture, somewhat unusual in Indian companies. "Everyone has e-mail access," says Infosys CEO Narayana Murthy. "Everyone eats in the same canteen. We all share the same gymnasium. So there is much less hierarchical mind-set than in the traditional company." Infosys became the first Indian company to offer employee stock options, another artifact of this egalitarian culture.

Customer focus through quality is another cultural value that has helped Infosys succeed in the global

Infosys has a strong "valley culture" that is aligned with its external environment. (*James Bagnall and Sanjay Chetty Naidu*/The Ottawa Citizen)

marketplace. "We're symbolic of the coming of age of Indian companies and technology," says Infosys president Nandan Nilekani. "We focus on customer service and deadlines, and that's a valley kind of culture. It's exciting. Incredibly exciting."

Sources: "Islands of Quality," *The Economist*, June 2, 2001, p. 17; J. Bagnall, "The Modern Face of India," *Ottawa Citizen*, March 5, 2001, p. B2; J. Slater, "The Battle to Retain IT Talent," *Far Eastern Economic Review*, February 15, 2001, p. 70; R. Sukumar, "Infosys: Wealth and Values," *Business Today*, January 7, 2001, p. 131; S. Bodow, "Murthy's Law," *Business 2.0*, November 28, 2000; M. McDonald, "Software Companies in India Turn Problem into Tidy Profits," *San Jose Mercury*, January 2, 2000.

Technologies has been successful partly because its culture is aligned with the demands of its environment in the global software marketplace. This "valley culture" values employees as the source of competitive advantage, egalitarian workplace practices, and high levels of quality service. Without these cultural values, Infosys would have difficulty keeping talented software engineers or attracting American clients.

When a firm's strong culture is misaligned with its environment, employees have difficulty anticipating and responding to the needs of customers or other dominant stakeholders. Lego seems to face this problem.[37] The Danish maker of Lego blocks has a fiercely independent culture that has created problems in an era of increasing globalization. Until recently, Lego refused to license products through partnerships with movie studios. When one executive proposed a partnership with Lucasfilms Ltd. to make Star Wars products, other executives were horrified, arguing that this "wasn't the Lego way." One executive threatened, "Over my dead body will you be launching Star Wars in Europe." Lego's chief executive eventually approved the deal and Lego Star Wars became the company's most successful product launch in recent memory. Yet Lego's corporate culture nearly killed this important initiative.

A second reason companies with strong cultures aren't necessarily more effective is that strong cultures lock decision makers into mental models that blind them to opportunities and unique problems. When an organization's culture intensely emphasizes customer service, for example, employees tend to see problems as customer service problems, even though some are really problems about efficiency or technology. Thus, strong cultures might cause decision makers to overlook or incorrectly define subtle misalignments between the organization's activities and the changing environment.[38]

Finally, very strong cultures tend to suppress dissenting subcultural values. In the long term, this prevents organizations from nurturing new cultural values that should become dominant values as the environment changes. In the short term, a strong culture might undermine constructive controversy (see Chapter 13). Procter & Gamble CEO Durk I. Jager thinks a strong organizational culture is a problem at the giant consumer products firm. He complains that recruits are quickly "Procterized"—they eventually sound alike, think alike, and look alike. With common values, the company lacks conflict. "Great ideas generally come from conflict—a dissatisfaction with the status quo," explains Jager. "I'd like to have an organization where there are rebels."[39] Thus, corporate leaders need to recognize that healthy organizations have subcultures with dissenting values that may produce dominant values in the future.

Adaptive Cultures

So far, we have learned that strong cultures are more effective when the cultural values are aligned with the organization's environment. Also, no corporate culture should be so strong that it blinds employees to alternative viewpoints or completely suppresses dissenting subcultures. One last point to add to this discussion is that organizations are more likely to succeed when they have an adaptive culture.[40] An **adaptive culture** exists when employees focus on the changing needs of customers and other stakeholders, and support initiatives to keep pace with these changes.

Organizational culture experts are starting to piece together the elements of adaptive cultures.[41] First and foremost, adaptive cultures have an external focus. Employees hold a common mental model that the organization's success depends on continuous change to support stakeholders. Nortel Networks has shifted from telephones to Internet gear. Nokia has moved from toilet paper and rubber boots to cellular telephones. Both of these firms have maintained an adaptive culture because employees believe that change is both necessary and inevitable to keep pace with a changing external environment.

Second, employees in adaptive cultures pay as much attention to organizational processes as they do to organizational goals. They engage in continuous improvement of internal processes (production, customer service, etc.) to serve external stakeholders. Third, employees in adaptive cultures have a strong sense of ownership. They assume responsibility for the organization's performance. In other words, they believe that "it's our job" rather than "it's not my

adaptive culture
An organizational culture in which employees focus on the changing needs of customers and other stakeholders, and support initiatives to keep pace with these changes.

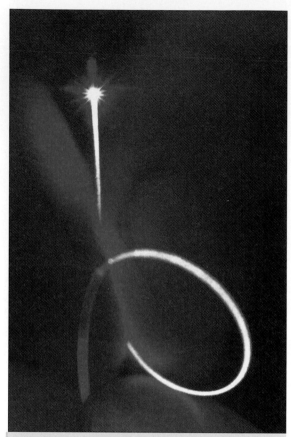

Corning, Inc., has a remarkable knack for reinventing itself. Once known for its Pyrex heat-resistant glass kitchenware, Revere metal cookware, and Corelle laminated glass tableware, Corning is now a leader in fiber-optic technology, pumping out optical technologies at breathtaking speed. The company's destroy-and-create strategy is possible because of its adaptive culture. For example, just weeks after completing a new state-of-the-art fiber manufacturing facility in Concord, North Carolina, Corning's designers were asked to create a next-generation plant that would outperform it. "We've told them to go off and make obsolete that $1 billion we just spent," says Corning's vice president for optical communications.[44] What characteristics would indicate that Corning has an adaptive culture? *(AP/Wide World)*

job." Fourth, adaptive cultures are proactive and quick. Employees seek out opportunities, rather than wait for them to arrive. They act quickly to learn through discovery rather than engage in paralysis by analysis.

Organizational Culture and Business Ethics

Along with other forms of performance, an organization's culture can potentially influence ethical conduct.[42] This idea makes sense because, as we learned in Chapter 4, good behavior is driven by ethical values. An organization can guide the conduct of its employees by embedding ethical values in its dominant culture.

Shiseido provides a good example. For more than 100 years, Shiseido's corporate culture has valued beauty and knowledge. "For us, beauty is art and knowledge is science," explains Akira Gemma, president of Japan's largest cosmetics company. "It is who we are. It is our corporate culture." But after the complaints in the mid-1990s about its sales methods, Shiseido is also trying to make business ethics part of its corporate culture. A new set of corporate values, called "The Shiseido Code," was developed, and several hundred employees have become standard-bearers of this code throughout Shiseido's 250 Japanese offices. When the ethics code was distributed, the company designated two months as "a period of reflection" during which employees were asked to reflect on all their past activities in light of business ethics. Shiseido hopes that these practices, along with training and communication, will embed the ethics code in the company's culture.[43]

Although organizational culture can support ethical values, it can also become the source of ethical problems. As we mentioned earlier, corporate culture is a form of control because it guides employee decisions and behavior. All organizations require some control to ensure that employee actions are aligned with organizational objectives. But as Connections 15.2 describes, a few organizations imprint their cultural values so strongly on employees that they risk becoming corporate cults. They take over employee lives and rob a person's individualism. Thus, an organization's culture should be consistent with society's ethical values, and the culture should not be so strong that it undermines individual freedom.

When Corporate Culture Becomes a Corporate Cult

Andrew Brenner is still troubled by an interview he had a few years ago for a lawyer's job at Microsoft. "All the lawyers seemed to think it was a foregone conclusion Microsoft would take over the world," says Brenner. Ultimately, Brenner decided not to pursue the job. "It's a very strong culture. Too strong for me."

While many writers seem to celebrate organizations with strong cultures, a few are worried that some firms are becoming corporate cults. A recent book on the subject suggests that employees are victims of corporate cults when they work crushingly long hours, have few friends outside the workplace, develop emotional attitudes about their job, and have difficulty distinguishing who they are from what they do.

Microsoft has been accused of being a corporate cult. Some employees practically live at the software giant's campus in Redmond, Washington. "There [are] people working here 24 hours a day," says a Microsoft manager. "It's set up so you never have to go home."

Consultancy McKinsey & Company apparently has an equally strong culture. Says one senior McKinseyite:

"It's like being a Catholic. Once baptized, there is no escape." A reporter from Britain's *Financial Times* newspaper suggests that the firm's training for new recruits looks more like a brainwashing camp. "It's as if they are Moonies," says the journalist. "That's slightly scary."

Razorfish, an Internet professional services organization, also has the characteristics of a corporate cult. "We've been accused of creating a cultlike atmosphere here, but to us there's Razorfish and not-Razorfish," says Len Sellers, managing director of Razorfish's San Francisco office.

Sellers defends the strong culture at Razorfish, but he also describes how it has taken over his life. "I used to be an avid sailor, but haven't been on a boat in a year," he admits. "I used to have girlfriends, but they left out of boredom and frustration. I used to have a cat, but it moved in with a neighbor. It's one thing when a girlfriend leaves, but it's another when a cat goes."

Sources: T. C. Doyle, "New Economy, New Culture," *VarBusiness*, July 10, 2000, p. 26; J. Useem, "Welcome to the New Company Town," *Fortune*, January 10, 2000, pp. 62–70; D. Arnott, *Corporate Cults* (New York: AMACOM, 1999); "The Cult of the Firm," *The Express on Sunday (UK)*, August 15, 1999.

MERGING ORGANIZATIONAL CULTURES

Corporate culture was on the minds of executives at Billiton plc in South Africa and BHP in Australia when they met to discuss a proposed merger into the world's largest mining company. "Obviously one of the questions when you get into a merger is: Is one culture going to dominate or do you create a new one?" says Tom Brown, BHP's human resources director. "Lots of mergers have failed to realize what they purported to [do] because they failed to look at the people or culture side of the business." To ensure that the BHP–Billiton merger wasn't another casualty, the two firms set up a committee to address the cultural issues and plan integration of the two firms. The committee began by taking a "cultural swab" from both companies. What they found was two businesses in cultural transition, so it was possible to form a composite culture that takes the best of both firms.[45]

The BHP–Billiton merger started on the right track from a corporate cultural perspective. Unfortunately, it is also the exception. Between 1997 and 2000, U.S. mergers and acquisitions had an equity value of more than $4.6 trillion—nearly equal to the combined annual gross domestic products of Japan and Germany. Yet more than two-thirds of these combined firms underperformed their industry peers in the following years. The main problem is that corporate leaders are so focused on the financial or marketing logistics of a merger that they fail to conduct due-diligence audits on their respective corporate cultures. One survey recently reported that over half of executives in major U.S. companies identified integrating organizational cultures as the top challenge in a merger.[46]

"It's the people stuff that trips up mergers," says an executive at Astra-Zeneca U.S., one of the world's largest pharmaceutical companies after the merger of Astra AB and Zeneca Group PLC. "You can do the deal because it looks really good on paper, but if you don't engage the minds of the people from each culture, you won't get the productivity you need to be successful."[47]

The corporate world is littered with mergers that failed or had a difficult gestation because of clashing organizational cultures. One such example is 3Com's acquisition of modem manufacturer U.S. Robotics Corporation. Wall Street analysts applauded the deal, yet two years later, 3Com's stock sank to one-third of its pre-merger value and U.S. Robotics was spun off into a private firm. The failed acquisition was partly due to declining demand for modems, and partly due to the two firms' having significantly different cultures. "If Robotics was an army, we were so aggressive we were outrunning supply lines, while 3Com was stuck inside the tent looking at maps while the enemy was destroying villages," quips a U.S. Robotics manager who left after the merger.[48]

bicultural audit
Diagnoses cultural relations between companies prior to a merger and determines the extent to which the cultural clashes will likely occur.

The merger of Detroit-based Chrysler and German automaker Daimler-Benz has become one of the most famous culture clashes in recent history. Chrysler values lean efficiency, empowerment, and fairly egalitarian relations among staff. In contrast, Daimler seems to value respect for authority, bureaucratic precision, and centralized decision making. Chrysler executives quickly became frustrated with the attention Daimler executives gave to trivial matters, such as the shape of a pamphlet sent to employees. Daimler executives were equally perplexed when Robert Eaton, Chrysler's chairman at the time of the merger, showed his emotions with tears in a speech to other executives. Adding to the culture clash, Daimler-Chrysler CEO Jürgen Schrempp (shown in photo) revealed that Daimler always intended the so-called merger of equals to be Daimler's acquisition of Chrysler. Most of Chrysler's top executives and many other talented staff have since left Chrysler.[51] What steps should companies take to minimize culture clashes in mergers and acquisitions? *(Reuters/New Media Inc./CORBIS)*

Bicultural Audit

Organizational leaders can minimize these cultural collisions and fulfill their duty of due diligence by conducting a bicultural audit, similar to what BHP and Billiton did prior to their merger. A **bicultural audit** diagnoses cultural relations between the companies and determines the extent to which cultural clashes will likely occur.[49] "The process [of addressing cultural issues] really starts during due diligence," advises Barry Griswell, CEO of The Principal Financial Group, which acquired Bankers Trust Australia. BT Funds Management CEO Ian Martin agrees. "Cultural considerations have been high on our agenda throughout our integration with The Principal," says Martin. "Management on both sides has been sensitive to, and interested in, the unique cultures of each organization."[50]

The bicultural audit process begins with interviews, questionnaires, focus groups, and observation to identify cultural differences between the merging companies. This process includes carefully examining artifacts of each organization—how the office is laid out, how the company bills customers, how decisions are made, how information is shared, and so on. Next, the bicultural audit data are analyzed to determine which differences between the two firms will result in conflict and which cultural values provide common ground on which to build a cultural foundation in the merged organization. The final stage of the bicultural audit involves identifying strategies and preparing action plans to bridge the two organizations' cultures.

Strategies to Merge Different Organizational Cultures

In some cases, the bicultural audit results in a decision to end merger talks because the two cultures are too different to merge effectively. For instance, GE Capital has rejected potential acquisitions when it became apparent that the other firm's cultural values were incompatible. Nortel Networks also walked away from a joint venture, with Cisco Systems, because it wasn't comfortable with the other firm's cultural values.[52] However, even with substantially different cultures, two companies may form a workable union if they apply the appropriate merger strategy. The four main strategies for merging different corporate cultures are assimilation, deculturation, integration, and separation (see Exhibit 15.3).[53]

Assimilation   Assimilation occurs when employees at the acquired company willingly embrace the cultural values of the acquiring organization. This strategy works best when the acquired company has a weak culture that is dysfunctional, whereas the acquiring company's culture is strong and focused on clearly defined values. Sun Microsystems has acquired many smaller organizations using this strategy. The California high-technology company refuses to digest larger firms because in that situation, it would be much more difficult to apply Sun's aggressive culture.[54] Culture clash is rare with assimilation because the acquired firm's culture is weak and employees are looking for better cultural alternatives.

Deculturation   Assimilation is rare. Employees usually resist organizational change, particularly when they are asked to throw away personal and cultural values. Under these conditions, some acquiring companies apply a *deculturation* strategy by imposing their culture and business practices on the acquired

EXHIBIT 15.3   Strategies for merging different organizational cultures

Merger strategy	Description	Works best when . . .
Assimilation	Acquired company embraces acquiring firm's culture.	Acquired firm has a weak culture.
Deculturation	Acquiring firm imposes its culture on unwilling acquired firm.	Acquired firm's culture doesn't work but employees don't realize it. (But, in fact, this strategy rarely works.)
Integration	Two or more cultures are combined into a new composite culture.	Both cultures can be improved and are relatively weak.
Separation	Merging companies remain distinct entities with minimal exchange of culture or organizational practices.	Firms operate successfully in different businesses requiring different cultures.

Source: Based on ideas in K. W. Smith, "A Brand-New Culture for the Merged Firm," *Mergers and Acquisitions* 35 (June 2000), pp. 45–50; A. R. Malekazedeh and A. Nahavandi, "Making Mergers Work by Managing Cultures," *Journal of Business Strategy,* May–June 1990, pp. 55–57.

organization. The acquiring firm strips away artifacts and reward systems that support the old culture. People who cannot adopt the acquiring company's culture are often terminated.

Deculturation may be necessary when the acquired firm's culture doesn't work but employees aren't convinced of this reality. However, this strategy rarely works because it increases the risk of socioemotional conflict (see Chapter 13). Employees from the acquired firm resist the cultural intrusions from the buying firm, thereby delaying or undermining the merger process.

The problems of deculturation were apparent soon after AT&T's hostile takeover of NCR Corporation. AT&T antagonized NCR employees by changing NCR's name to AT&T Global Information Solutions, installing AT&T executives to run the acquired firm, and generally trying to make NCR's culture become more like AT&T's. The merger strategy failed. AT&T eventually divested NCR (which returned to its original name) after piling up nearly $4 billion in losses at the Dayton, Ohio–based cash register and computer systems company.[55]

Integration   A third strategy is to integrate the corporate cultures of both organizations. This strategy involves combining the two or more cultures into a new composite culture that preserves the best features of the previous cultures. Integration is slow and potentially risky, because there are many forces preserving the existing cultures. However, this strategy should be considered when the companies have relatively weak cultures or when their cultures include several overlapping values. Integration also works best when people realize that their existing cultures are ineffective and are therefore motivated to adopt a new set of dominant values.

Nortel Networks' acquisition of Bay Networks is a case in point. The telecommunications manufacturer bought Bay Networks partly because Nortel wanted a bigger piece of the Internet hardware business. But CEO John Roth also candidly says that he wanted to shake off Nortel's slower, more bureaucratic ways by acquiring some of Bay Networks' culture that was moving at "Web speed."[56]

Separation   A separation strategy occurs when the merging companies agree to remain distinct entities with minimal exchange of culture or organizational practices. This strategy is most appropriate when the two merging companies are in unrelated industries or operate in different countries, because the most appropriate cultural values tend to differ by industry and national culture. Distinct cultures within an organization can also lead to the separation strategy of demerging. For example, Baltimore-based Constellation Energy Group Inc. created a holding company (called BGE Corporation) to separate its slow-moving public utility business from its high-flying merchant energy firm because their cultures are so different.[57]

CHANGING AND STRENGTHENING ORGANIZATIONAL CULTURE

Whether merging two cultures or reshaping the firm's existing values, corporate leaders need to understand how to change and strengthen the organization's dominant culture. Indeed, some organizational scholars conclude that the only way to ensure any lasting change is to realign cultural values with those changes. In other words, changes "stick" when they become "the way we do things around here."[58]

Changing organizational culture requires the change management tool kit that we will learn about in the next chapter (Chapter 16). Corporate leaders need to make employees aware of the urgency for change. Then they need to "unfreeze" the existing culture by removing artifacts that represent that culture and "refreeze" the new culture by introducing artifacts that communicate and reinforce the new values.

Strengthening Organizational Culture

Artifacts communicate and reinforce the new corporate culture, but we also need to consider ways to further strengthen that culture. Five approaches that are commonly cited in the literature are the actions of founders and leaders, introducing culturally consistent rewards, maintaining a stable workforce, managing the cultural network, and selecting and socializing new employees (see Exhibit 15.4).

Actions of Founders and Leaders   Founders establish an organization's culture.[59] You can see this at Southwest Airlines, where founder Herb Kelleher has established a culture that is both fun and efficient. Founders develop the systems and structures that support their personal values. They are also typically the visionaries whose energetic style provides a powerful role model for others to follow.

In spite of the founder's effect, subsequent leaders can break the organization away from the founder's values if they apply the transformational leadership concepts that were described in Chapter 14. Transformational leaders alter and strengthen organizational culture by communicating and enacting their vision of the future.[60] The opening vignette in this chapter described how Carly Fiorina is trying to change Hewlett-Packard's culture because she believes H-P employees hide behind their corporate culture to avoid tough decisions. "The phrase 'The H-P Way' became a way of resisting change and resisting radical ideas," argues Fiorina. "One of the things I've been able to do as an outsider is challenge it."[61]

EXHIBIT 15.4

Strategies for strengthening organizational culture

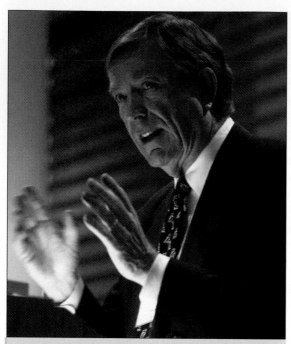

Ray Anderson (shown in photo) admits that he didn't pay much attention to environmentalism when he launched Atlanta-based Interface Inc. in the 1970s. But after reading *The Ecology of Commerce* in 1994, Anderson's newfound environmental values have reshaped the culture of the world's largest floor covering company. "[W]e've got a company full of people who've really bought in to that vision," Anderson says. Today, Interface has solar- powered looms in California, a weaving plant in Maine that uses recycled plastics, and an R&D department that experiments with hemp, sugar cane, and other renewable resources. Most of the company's 8,000 employees on four continents have received environmental training, and many of them have created environmental organizations in their communities. Anderson even replaced his Bentley and Jaguar with a fuel-efficient Toyota that runs on batteries and gas.[65] In what ways do founders and leaders influence their organization's culture? *(Pierre Roussel/The Ottawa Citizen)*

Introducing Culturally Consistent Rewards Reward systems strengthen corporate culture when they are consistent with cultural values.[62] For example, paternalistic cultures would emphasize employee assistance programs, medical insurance, and other benefits that support employee well-being. Home Depot has stock options to support an ownership culture. "We've always wanted this to be part of our culture," explains Home Depot CEO and co-founder Arthur Blank, "that associates feel that they own the stores, that they own the merchandise, that they have total responsibility for the customers in their aisles, and that they create the value."[63]

Maintaining a Stable Workforce An organization's culture is embedded in the minds of its employees. Organizational stories are rarely written down; rituals and ceremonies do not usually exist in procedure manuals; organizational metaphors are not found in corporate directories. Thus, organizations depend on a stable workforce to communicate and reinforce the dominant beliefs and values. The organization's culture can literally disintegrate during periods of high turnover and precipitous downsizing because the corporate memory leaves with those employees.[64]

Conversely, corporate leaders who want to change the corporate culture have accelerated the turnover of senior executives and older employees, those who held the cultural values in place. For instance, the two executives who revived Continental Airlines claim that they introduced a more customer-focused culture partly by replacing most of the 60 executives with people who had more compatible values. Hoechst, the German chemical company, also seems to be applying this tactic through early retirement of its older employees. "The company is trying to lower the average age of the workforce," says a Hoechst spokesperson. "Perhaps the main reason for replacing older workers is that it makes it easier to 'defrost' the corporate culture."[66]

Managing the Cultural Network Organizational culture is learned, so an effective network of cultural transmission is necessary to strengthen the company's underlying assumptions, values, and beliefs. According to Max DePree, former CEO of furniture manufacturer Herman Miller Inc., every organization needs "tribal storytellers" to keep the organization's history and culture alive.[67] The cultural network exists through the organizational grapevine. It is also supported through frequent opportunities for interaction so that employees can share stories and reenact rituals. Senior executives must tap into the cultural network, sharing their own stories and creating new ceremonies and other opportunities to demonstrate shared meaning. Company magazines and other media can also strengthen organizational culture by communicating cultural values and beliefs more efficiently.

Selecting and Socializing Employees   People at Bristol-Myers recently noticed that executives hired from the outside weren't as successful as those promoted from within. Within a year, many quit or were fired. Ben Dowell, who runs Bristol-Myers's Center for Leadership Development, looked closely at the problem and arrived at the following conclusion: "What came through was, those who left were uncomfortable in our culture or violated some core area of our value system." From this discovery, Bristol-Myers assessed its culture—it's team-oriented, consistent with the firm's research and development roots. Now applicants are carefully screened to ensure they have compatible values.[68]

Bristol-Myers and a flock of other organizations strengthen their corporate cultures by hiring people with beliefs, values, and assumptions similar to those cultures. They realize that a good fit of personal and organizational values makes it easier for employees to adopt the corporate culture. A good person–organization fit also improves job satisfaction and organizational loyalty because new hires with values compatible with the corporate culture adjust more quickly to the organization.[69]

Job applicants are also paying more attention to corporate culture during the hiring process. According to one survey, job applicants ask corporate culture questions more than any other topic, aside from pay and benefits.[70] They realize that employees must feel comfortable with the company's values, not just the job duties and hours of work.

Kathy Wheeler learned this important point the hard way. A few years ago, the Hewlett-Packard engineer accepted a career opportunity at Apple Computer. Apple's headquarters is just two miles away from H-P's, but its corporate culture is on another planet. H-P's culture emphasizes collaboration, consensus, and advanced engineering technology, whereas Apple's culture applauds marketers rather than engineers and slick user interfaces rather than advanced technology. Fourteen months later, Wheeler was back at H-P. "I admire Apple to a large extent," says Wheeler. "But I wouldn't work there again because of the cultural issues."[71] The point here is that applicants need to look at corporate culture artifacts when deciding whether to join a particular organization. By diagnosing the company's dominant culture, they are more likely to determine whether its values are compatible with their own.

Along with selecting people with compatible values, companies maintain strong cultures through the effective socialization of new employees. **Organizational socialization** refers to the process by which individuals learn the values, expected behaviors, and social knowledge necessary to assume their roles in the organization.[72] By communicating the company's dominant values, organizations can ensure that new hires are more likely to internalize these values quickly and deeply.

We will learn more about the organizational socialization process in Chapter 18, on employment relations and career dynamics. At this point, you

organizational socialization
The process by which individuals learn the values, expected behaviors, and social knowledge necessary to assume their roles in the organization.

should know that socialization includes the process of learning about the company's culture and adopting its set of values. For example, Carolyn Arnott has lived and breathed the IKEA culture almost all her working life. She started as a cashier and soon got her first lessons about the Scandinavian home furnishing company's values through its mandatory Culture Days. Today, as an IKEA manager, Arnott easily recites the cultural values that make the company unique: thrift, hard work, fair play, and inventiveness.[73]

Throughout this chapter, we have learned that organizational culture is pervasive and powerful. For corporate leaders, it is either a force for change or an insurmountable barrier to it. For employees, it is either the glue that bonds people together or a force that drives them away from the organization. So many artifacts communicate and reinforce the existing culture that it requires monumental effort to replace the current values. Transformational leadership can assist this process, as can the effective management of change, which we explore in the next chapter.

CHAPTER SUMMARY

Organizational culture is the basic pattern of shared assumptions, values, and beliefs that govern behavior within a particular organization. Assumptions are the shared mental models or theories in use that people rely on to guide their perceptions and behaviors. *Beliefs* represent the individual's perceptions of reality. Values are more stable, long-lasting beliefs about what is important. They help us define what is right or wrong, or good or bad, in the world. Cultural content refers to the relative ordering of beliefs, values, and assumptions.

Organizations have subcultures as well as the dominant culture. Some subcultures enhance the dominant culture, whereas others, called countercultures, have values that oppose the organization's core values. Subcultures maintain the organization's standards of performance and ethical behavior. They are also the source of emerging values that replace aging core values.

Artifacts are the observable symbols and signs of an organization's culture. Four broad categories of artifacts are organizational stories and legends, rituals and ceremonies, organizational language, and physical structures and symbols. Understanding an organization's culture requires painstaking assessment of many artifacts, because they are subtle and often ambiguous.

Organizational culture has three main functions. First, it is a deeply embedded form of social control. Second, it is the social glue that bonds people together and makes them feel part of the organizational experience. Third, corporate culture helps employees make sense of the workplace.

Companies with strong cultures generally perform better than those with weak cultures, but only when the cultural content is appropriate for the organization's environment. Also, the culture should not be so strong that it drives out dissenting values, which may form emerging values for the future. Organizations should have adaptive cultures so that employees focus on the need for change and support initiatives and leadership that keep pace with these changes.

Organizational culture relates to business ethics in two ways. First, corporate cultures can support the ethical values of society, thereby reinforcing ethical conduct. Second, some cultures are so strong that they rob a person's individualism and discourage constructive controversy.

Mergers should include a bicultural audit to diagnose the compatibility of the organizational cultures. The four main strategies for merging different corporate cultures are integration, deculturation, assimilation, and separation.

Organizational culture is very difficult to change. However, change may be possible by creating an urgency for change and replacing artifacts that support the old culture with artifacts aligned more with the desired future culture. Organizational culture may be strengthened through the actions of founders and leaders, introducing culturally consistent rewards, maintaining a stable workforce, managing the cultural network, and selecting and socializing employees.

KEY TERMS

adaptive culture, p. 457
artifacts, p. 451
bicultural audit, p. 460

ceremonies, p. 453
organizational culture, p. 448

organizational socialization, p. 465
rituals, p. 453

DISCUSSION QUESTIONS

1. Superb Consultants has submitted a proposal to analyze the cultural values of your organization. The proposal states that Superb has developed a revolutionary new survey to tap the company's true culture. The survey takes just 10 minutes to complete, and the consultants say results can be based on a small sample of employees. Discuss the merits and limitations of this proposal.

2. Some people suggest that the most effective organizations have the strongest cultures. What do we mean by the strength of organizational culture, and what possible problems are there with a strong organizational culture?

3. The chief executive of a midsized food products company wants everyone to support the organization's dominant culture of lean efficiency and hard work. The CEO introduced a new reward system to reinforce this culture and personally interviews all professional and managerial applicants to ensure that they bring similar values to the organization. Some employees who criticized these values have had their careers sidelined, leading to their leaving the company. Two mid-level managers were fired for supporting contrary values, such as work–life balance. On the basis of your knowledge of organizational subcultures,

what potential problems is the CEO of this company creating?

4. Identify four types of artifacts used to communicate organizational culture. Why are artifacts used for this purpose?

5. Acme Corporation is planning to acquire Beta Corporation, which operates in a different industry. Acme's culture is entrepreneurial and fast-paced, whereas Beta employees value slow, deliberate decision making by consensus. Which merger strategy would you recommend to minimize culture shock when Acme acquires Beta? Explain your answer.

6. Under what conditions is assimilation likely to occur when two companies merge? Your answer should clearly describe the assimilation strategy.

7. Explain how transformational leadership strengthens corporate culture.

8. Suppose that you are asked by senior executives of a large city government to identify ways to reinforce a new culture of teamwork and collaboration. The senior executive group clearly supports these values, and it wants everyone in the organization to embrace them. Identify four types of activities that would strengthen these cultural values.

CASE STUDY 15.1

ASSETONE BANK

AssetOne Bank is one of Asia's largest financial institutions, but it had difficulty entering the personal investment business, where several other companies dominate the market. To gain entry to this market, AssetOne decided to acquire TaurusBank, a much smaller financial institution that had aggressively developed investment funds (mutual funds) and online banking in the

region. Taurus was owned by a European conglomerate that wanted to exit the financial sector, so the company was quietly put up for sale. The opportunity to acquire Taurus seemed like a perfect fit to AssetOne's executives, who saw the purchase as an opportunity to finally gain a competitive position in the personal investment market. In particular, the acquisition would give

AssetOne valuable talent in online banking and investment fund businesses.

Negotiations between AssetOne and TaurusBank occurred secretly, except for communication with government regulatory agencies, and took several months as AssetOne's executive team deliberated over the purchase. When AssetOne finally decided in favor of the acquisition, employees of both companies were notified only a few minutes before the merger was announced publicly. During the public statement, AssetOne's CEO boldly announced that TaurusBank would become a "seamless extension of AssetOne." He explained that, like AssetOne, Taurus employees would learn the value of detailed analysis and cautious decision making.

The comments by AssetOne's CEO shocked many employees at Taurus, which was an aggressive and entrepreneurial competitor in online banking and personal investments. Taurus was well known for its edgy marketing, innovative products, and tendency to involve employees to generate creative ideas. The company didn't hesitate to hire people from other industries who would bring different ideas to the investment and online banking business. AssetOne, on the other hand, almost completely promoted its executives from within the ranks. Everyone on the senior executive team had started at AssetOne. The company also emphasized decision making at the top to maintain better control and consistency.

Frustration was apparent within a few months after the merger. Several Taurus executives quit after repeated failure of AssetOne's executive team to decide quickly on critical online banking initiatives. For example, at the time of the acquisition, Taurus was in the process of forming affinity alliances with several companies. Yet, six months later, AssetOne's executive team still had not decided whether to proceed with these partnerships.

The biggest concerns occurred in the investment fund business, where 20 of TaurusBank's 60 fund managers were lured away by competitors within the first year. Some left for better opportunities. Six fund managers left with the Taurus executive in charge of the investment fund business, who joined an investment firm that specialized in investment funds. Several employees left Taurus after AssetOne executives insisted that all new investment funds must be approved by AssetOne's executive group. Previously, Taurus had given the investment fund division enough freedom to launch new products without approval of the entire executive team.

Two years later, AssetOne's CEO admitted that the acquisition of TaurusBank did not provide the opportunities that the company had originally hoped for. AssetOne had more business in investment funds and online banking, but many of the more talented people in these areas had left the firm. Overall, the merged company had not kept pace with other innovative financial institutions in the market.

Discussion Questions

1. On the basis of your understanding of mergers and organizational culture, discuss the problems that occurred in this case.

2. What strategies would you recommend to AssetOne's executives to avoid these corporate culture clashes in future mergers and acquisitions?

C A S E S T U D Y 15.2

AVON'S NEW CALLING

BusinessWeek Avon Products pioneered direct selling when Mrs. P. F. E. Albee became the first "Avon lady" in 1886. Since then, Avon representatives have helped the company grow into a multibillion-dollar beauty products business and enter international markets. Those same direct salespeople are at the heart of Avon's organizational culture. As the company struggles to adapt to the Internet age and the busy lives of its customers (today, rarely is anyone home when the Avon lady comes calling), business changes incorporate respect for the central role of Avon representatives.

This *Business Week* case study describes Avon's business plans and organizational culture. It details the role of Avon's CEO, Andrea Jung, in identifying, managing, and embodying that culture. Read through this *Business Week* case study at www.mhhe.com/mcshane2e and prepare for the discussion questions at right.

Discussion Questions

1. What elements of Avon's organizational culture does the author describe?

2. What evidence can you find that Avon's culture is strong? That it is adaptive? Does it seem to be a good fit with its environment?

3. How can Andrea Jung change or strengthen Avon's culture to make it a better fit with the modern environment?

Source: N. Byrnes, "Avon's New Calling," *Business Week*, September 18, 2000.

TEAM EXERCISE 15.3

ORGANIZATIONAL CULTURE METAPHORS

By David L. Luechauer, Butler University, and Gary M. Shulman, Miami University

Purpose Both parts of this exercise are designed to help you understand, assess, and interpret organizational culture using metaphors.

Part A: Assessing Your School's Culture

Instructions A metaphor is a figure of speech that contains an implied comparison between a word or phrase that is ordinarily used for one thing but can be applied to another. Metaphors also carry a great deal of hidden meaning—they say a lot about what we think and feel about that object. This activity asks you to use several metaphors to define the organizational culture of your university, college, or institute. (Alternatively, the instructor might ask students to assess another organization that most students know about.)

- *Step 1*—The class will be divided into teams of four to six members.
- *Step 2*—Each team will reach consensus on which words or phrases should be inserted in the blanks of the statements presented below. This information should be recorded on a flip chart or overhead acetate for class presentation. The instructor will provide 15 to 20 minutes for teams to determine which words best describe the college's culture.

  If our school were an animal, it would be _____ because _____.

  If our school were a food, it would be _____ because _____.

If our school were a place, it would be _____ because _____.

If our school were a season, it would be _____ because _____.

If our school were a TV show or movie, it would be _____ because _____.

- *Step 3*—The class will listen to each team present the metaphors that it believes symbolize the school's culture. For example, a team that picks winter for a season might mean they are feeling cold or distant about the school and its people.
- *Step 4*—The class will discuss the questions below.

Discussion Questions (Part A)

1. How easy was it for your group to reach consensus regarding these metaphors? What does that imply about the culture of your school?

2. How do you see these metaphors in action? In other words, what are some critical school behaviors or other artifacts that reveal the presence of the school's culture?

3. Think of another organization to which you belong (e.g., work, religious congregation). What are its dominant cultural values, how do you see them in action, and how do they affect the effectiveness of that organization?

Part B: Analyzing and Interpreting Cultural Metaphors

Instructions Previously, you completed a metaphor exercise to describe the organizational culture of your school. That exercise gave you a taste of how to administer such a diagnostic tool and draw inferences from the results generated. This activity builds on that experience and is designed to help refine your ability to analyze such data and make suggestions for improvement. Five work teams (four to seven members of mixed gender in all groups) of an organization located in Cincinnati completed a metaphor exercise similar to the exercise you completed in class (see Part A above). Their responses are shown in the table below. Working in teams, analyze the information in this table and answer the questions below.

Discussion Questions (Part B)

1. In your opinion, what are the dominant cultural values in this organization? Explain your answer.

2. What are the positive aspects of this type of culture?

3. What are the negative aspect of this type of culture?

4. What do you think this organization's main business is? Explain your answer.

5. These groups all reported to one manager. What advice would you give to her about this unit?

Metaphor results of five teams in a Cincinnati organization					
Team	Animal	Food	Place	TV show or movie	Season
1	Rabbit	Big Mac	Casino	*48 Hours* (movie)	Spring
2	Horse	Taco	Racetrack	*Miami Vice*	Spring
3	Elephant	Ribs	Circus	*Roseanne*	Summer
4	Eagle	Big Mac	Las Vegas	CNN	Spring
5	Panther	Chinese	New York	*LA Law*	Racing

Source: Adapted from D. L. Luechauer and G. M. Shulman, "Using a Metaphor Exercise to Explore the Principles of Organizational Culture," *Journal of Management Education* 22 (December 1998), pp. 736–44.

SELF-ASSESSMENT EXERCISE 15.4

CORPORATE CULTURE PREFERENCE SCALE

Purpose This self-assessment exercise is designed to help you identify a corporate culture that fits most closely with your personal values and assumptions.

Instructions Read each pair of statements in the corporate culture preference scale, and circle the statement that describes the organization you would prefer to work in. Then use the scoring key in Appendix B to calculate your results for each subscale. This exercise is completed alone so that students assess themselves honestly without concerns of social comparison. However, class discussion will focus on the importance of matching job applicants to the organization's dominant values.

I would prefer to work in an organization . . .

1a. Where employees work well together in teams.

OR

1b. That produces highly respected products or services.

2a. Where top management maintains a sense of order in the workplace.

OR

2b. Where the organization listens to customers and responds quickly to their needs.

3a. Where employees are treated fairly.

OR

3b. Where employees continually search for ways to work more efficiently.

4a. Where employees adapt quickly to new work requirements.

OR

4b. Where corporate leaders work hard to keep employees happy.

5a. Where senior executives receive special benefits not available to other employees.

OR

5b. Where employees are proud when the organization achieves its performance goals.

6a. Where employees who perform the best get paid the most.

OR

6b. Where senior executives are respected.

7a. Where everyone gets his or her job done like clockwork.

OR

7b. That is on top of innovations in the industry.

8a. Where employees receive assistance to overcome any personal problems.

OR

8b. Where employees abide by company rules.

9a. That is always experimenting with new ideas in the marketplace.

OR

9b. That expects everyone to put in 110 percent for peak performance.

10a. That quickly benefits from market opportunities.

OR

10b. Where employees are always kept informed of what's happening in the organization.

11a. That can respond quickly to competitive threats.

OR

11b. Where most decisions are made by the top executives.

12a. Where management keeps everything under control.

OR

12b. Where employees care for each other.

After studying the preceding material, be sure to check out our website at

www.mhhe.com/mcshane2e

for more in-depth information and interactivities that correspond to this chapter.

16

Organizational Change and Development

AFTER READING THIS CHAPTER, YOU SHOULD BE ABLE TO:

- Identify four forces for change in the business environment.

- Describe the elements of Lewin's force field analysis model.

- Outline six reasons people resist organizational change.

- Discuss six strategies to minimize resistance to change.

- Outline the conditions for effectively diffusing change from a pilot project.

- Define *organization development*.

- Discuss three things consultants need to determine in a client relationship.

- Explain how appreciative inquiry differs from the more traditional approach to OD.

- Discuss four ethical issues in organization development.

When Richard H. "Dick" Brown was hired as CEO of Electronic Data Systems (EDS) Corporation, the board of directors gave him an additional title: change agent. The Plano, Texas–based computer services giant was floundering in the industry it created 40 years ago. IBM's Global Services division had steamrolled over EDS to become the market leader, while nimble start-ups ate away at other parts of EDS's market share.

Brown wasted no time transforming EDS into a more responsive, customer-focused company. Within weeks, he was visiting the company's largest clients, hearing their complaints, and replacing account teams to correct the problems. Brown had a "service excellence dashboard" installed on executive computers to monitor the status of major clients. A special task force took just six weeks to create four new client-centered organizational units to replace EDS's previous structure of 48 inward-looking fiefdoms.

Brown replaced most of the executive team he had inherited. "We had too many leaders who didn't believe we could grow," says Brown. "Those people either had to change their beliefs or leave." Brown introduced several challenging financial goals for his new executive team and introduced monthly conference calls in which 125 top worldwide EDS executives reviewed their financial accomplishments.

But Brown emphasizes that "you can't change a business with numbers. Numbers are the end result. You change a business by changing the behavior of its people." To change the people and culture, Brown holds quarterly "Straight Talk" sessions via satellite to discuss the change process and answer employee questions. He also sends e-mail messages every two weeks to all 128,000 EDS employees, telling them where EDS is going, how it will get there, and what challenges lie ahead.

When Richard H. "Dick" Brown was hired as CEO of Electronic Data Systems (EDS) Corporation, the board of directors gave him an additional title: change agent. *(AP/Wide World)*

EDS employees are now embracing Brown's urgency for continual change. "Change is a constant," says Steve Smith, an EDS client delivery executive in Colorado Springs. "In our business, it's the only way we remain competitive because our technology changes every half hour. Our customers look to us to stay on the forefront."[1]

hange is difficult enough in small firms. At EDS and other large organizations, it requires monumental effort and persistence. Organizational change is also very messy. The change process that Dick Brown launched at EDS looks like a well-executed strategy, but all organizational transformations are buffeted by uncertain consequences, organizational politics, and various forms of employee resistance.

This chapter examines ways to bring about meaningful change in organizations. After considering some of the more significant forces for organizational change, we introduce Lewin's model of change and its component parts: identifying sources of resistance to change, minimizing this resistance, and stabilizing desired behaviors. The latter part of this chapter introduces the field of organization development (OD). In particular, we review the OD process, introduce recent OD trends, and identify issues relating to OD effectiveness.

EXTERNAL FORCES FOR CHANGE

Today's business environment is changing so rapidly that it leaves almost everyone breathless. "We're really aggressive at moving at the notion of speed—not only because it's important for internal purposes, but it's also important to our clients," says Joe Forehand, managing partner and chief executive of global consulting firm Accenture. In other words, Accenture's clients are facing rapid change in the marketplace, and they expect Accenture to keep pace with that change.[2]

To illustrate how fast organizations are changing, consider this: American companies that were on the S&P 500 list in the 1920s stayed on the list an average of 67 years. Today, the average company life cycle on the S&P 500 is about 12 years. In other words, your grandparents could work for the same organization all their lives, whereas you will likely outlive two or three companies.[3] Similarly, the most valued companies today—such as Microsoft, Cisco Systems, Capital One Financial, and EMC—were either junior start-ups or nonexistent 20 years ago.[4] And unless these firms anticipate and adapt to continual change, few of them will be around 20 years from now. As open systems (see Chapter 1), successful organizations monitor their environments and take appropriate steps to maintain a compatible fit with the new external conditions. This adaptability requires continual change. It is an ongoing process because environmental change does not end.[5]

There are many forces for change in the external environment, but the prominent forces are information technology, globalization, competition, and demographics. Not surprisingly, most of these are emerging organizational behavior issues that we discussed in the opening chapter of this book.

Information Technology

The network of computers linked around the world has become a major driver of rapid environmental change.[6] Amazon.com, Yahoo!, and other firms are leveraging the power of the Internet to offer a variety of electronic commerce experiences. Intranets have also made it easy and inexpensive to transfer information throughout the organization.[7] Suppliers are hooked up to computer-based networks (called *extranets*) to accelerate just-in-time management deliveries. Major clients are also hooked up to the organization's product database for direct ordering and deliver.[8]

Nokia is a classic example of how companies survive and remain competitive by adapting to environmental changes. The Finnish conglomerate started in 1865 as a pulp and paper company in a mill town near Helsinki (see photo, taken around 1890). The company bought into the rubber business 30 years later and into cable wiring in the 1920s. Many Finns still associate Nokia with the rubber snow boots they wore as children. In the 1960s, Nokia invested in electronics and was soon making televisions and computer monitors. In the 1980s, Nokia executives sensed an emerging market for mobile telecommunications and took enormous risks by investing in that environmental shift. Today, people around the world know of Nokia for its sleek cellular telephones.[9] What factors do you think helped Nokia executives anticipate opportunities and change the organization to realize those opportunities? *(Courtesy of Nokia and the National Museum of Finland)*

Information technology does more than open up business opportunities. It forces corporate leaders to rethink how their organizations are configured, as well as which competencies and expectations employees must have in these emerging organizational forms.[10] Information technology creates new structures that allow companies to compete globally through network alliances (see Chapter 17). It facilitates telecommuting and opens up new employment relationships with employees. It places emphasis on knowledge management rather than physical presence and manufacturing capacity as a driver of competitive advantage.

Global and Local Competition

Betty Coulter is a typical 21-year-old college grad from Illinois. She wears the lastest jeans and is a faithful fan of the TV shows "Friends" and "Buffy the Vampire Slayer." At least, that's what Betty will say, if asked, when Americans call her about a broken appliance or an incorrect sweater ordered from a store catalog. In reality, Betty is Savitha Balasubramanyam, an employee at a call center in Bangalore, India. "It doesn't matter if I'm really Betty or Savitha," says Balasubramanyam with a well-practiced American accent. "What matters is that at the end of the day I've helped the customer."[11]

Welcome to the world of globalization! Whether they are software giants in Europe or call centers in India, competitors are just as likely to be located in a distant part of the world than within your country. SAP, the German software giant, is the leader in enterprise software. Wipro Technologies, India's leading software company, routinely wins multimillion-dollar contracts from the likes of General Electric, Home Depot, and Nokia. CustomerAsset, where Savitha Balasubramanyam works, provides seamless customer service—complete with American accent!—from India's technology hub.

Global and domestic competition often leads to corporate restructuring. To increase their competitiveness, companies reduce layers of management, sell entire divisions of employees, and reduce payroll through downsizing. Global competition has also fueled an unprecedented number of mergers and acquisitions in recent years. Liquor dynasty Seagram Company acquired Universal Studios and other entertainment companies, and then was acquired by Vivendi, based in France. Germany's Daimler-Benz merged with Chrysler, which then increased its stake in Japan's Mitsubishi Motors. These and other mergers potentially improve a firm's competitive advantage through greater efficiency and global reach, but they also result in significant disruptions and changes in employment relationships and the way people work.

Demography

While firms adjust to global competition, they are also adapting to changes in the workforce. Employees are more educated and, consequently, expect more involvement and interesting work. Generation-X and Generation-Y employees are less intimidated by management directives, and they work to live more than live to work. In Japan and other Asian countries, corporate leaders must adjust to a younger workforce that is more individualistic and less patient with cumbersome hierarchies. Meanwhile, in many parts of the world, companies employ a far more diverse workforce than a few decades ago (see Chapter 1). These changes have put pressure on organizational leaders to alter work practices, develop more compatible structures and rewards, and discover new ways to lead.

LEWIN'S FORCE FIELD ANALYSIS MODEL

force field analysis
Lewin's model of systemwide change that helps change agents diagnose the forces that drive and restrain proposed organizational change.

It is easy to see that these environmental forces push companies to change the way they operate. What is more difficult to see is the complex interplay of these forces against other organizational dynamics. Psychologist Kurt Lewin developed the **force field analysis** model to help us understand how the change process works (see Exhibit 16.1).[12] Although developed over 50 years ago, Lewin's force field analysis model remains the prominent way of viewing this process.

One side of the force field model represents the *driving forces,* which push organizations toward a new state of affairs. We began this chapter by describing some of the driving forces in the external environment: information technology, globalization, competition, and demographics. Along with these external forces are driving forces that originate from within the organization, such as competition across divisions of the company and the leader's need to make his or her mark on the company.

EXHIBIT 16.1

Lewin's force field
analysis model

The other side of Lewin's model represents the *restraining forces,* which maintain the status quo. These restraining forces are commonly called "resistance to change" because they appear as employee behaviors that block the change process. Stability occurs when the driving and restraining forces are roughly in equilibrium, that is, when they are of approximately equal strength in opposite directions.

Lewin's force field model emphasizes that effective change occurs by **unfreezing** the current situation, moving to a desired condition, and then **refreezing** the system so that it remains in this desired state. Unfreezing involves producing a disequilibrium between the driving and restraining forces. As we will describe later, this change may occur by increasing the driving forces, reducing the restraining forces, or having a combination of both. Refreezing occurs when the organization's systems and structures are aligned with the desired behaviors. They must support and reinforce the new role patterns and prevent the organization from slipping back into the old way of doing things. This stabilization does not occur automatically; rather, organizational leaders must continually stabilize the desired behaviors. Over the next few pages, we use Lewin's model to understand why change is blocked and how the process can evolve more smoothly.

unfreezing
The first part of the change process whereby the change agent produces disequilibrium between the driving and restraining forces.

refreezing
The latter part of the change process in which systems and conditions are introduced that reinforce and maintain the desired behaviors.

Restraining Forces

BP Norge, the Norwegian subsidiary of British Petroleum, faced more resistance from employees than from the infamous North Sea weather when it introduced self-directed work teams (SDWTs) on its drilling rigs. Many skeptical employees claimed that previous attempts to create SDWTs didn't work. Others were convinced that they already had SDWTs, so why change anything? Several people complained that SDWTs required more responsibility, so they wanted more status and pay. Still others were worried that they lacked the skills to operate in SDWTs. Some BP Norge supervisors were slow to embrace SDWTs because they didn't want to give away their cherished power.[13]

In his two tumultuous years as CEO, Jacques Nasser (left in photo) heaped a lot of change on employees at Ford Motor Company. He tried to shift the automaker from engineering prowess to cyber savvy, from quality to efficiency, and from an old-boys' club to a performance-focused competitor. In one year, Nasser rammed through a performance review system that took General Electric nearly a decade to implement. The changes were too much for many Ford employees. Some engineers grumbled that quality declined; employees stung by the performance system launched age discrimination lawsuits. "When you induce change, you get a reaction," explains a senior Ford executive. "I have letters from employees congratulating us. I have letters from employees doing the opposite." In the latter group was the Ford family, who replaced Nasser with William Clay Ford (right in photo) as CEO.[14] How can corporate leaders change their organizations quickly without experiencing the level of resistance experienced at Ford? *(AP/Wide World)*

BP Norge isn't the only company where employees block organizational change. In one survey, 43 percent of U.S. executives identified employee resistance as the main reason their organization is not more productive.[15] This resistance takes many forms, including passive noncompliance, complaints, absenteeism, turnover, and collective action (e.g., strikes, walkouts). In extreme cases, such as at Ford, Xerox, and Kodak, the chief change agent eventually leaves or is pushed out.[16]

Some organizational behavior scholars suggest that employee resistance represents symptoms of underlying restraining forces that need to be removed.[17] Employees may be worried about the *consequences* of change, such as how the new conditions will take away their power and status. Some are concerned about the *process* of change itself, such as the effort required to break old habits and learn new skills. The main reasons people create obstacles to change are shown in Exhibit 16.2 and are described below. They are direct

EXHIBIT 16.2

Forces resisting
organizational change

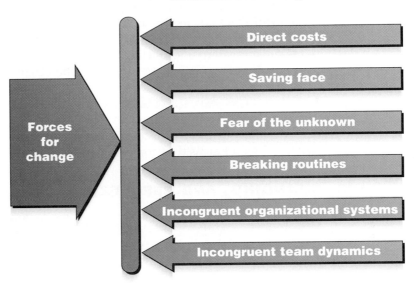

EXHIBIT 16.2

Forces resisting organizational change

costs, saving face, fear of the unknown, breaking routines, incongruent organizational systems, and incongruent team dynamics:[18]

Direct costs—People tend to block actions that result in higher direct costs or lower benefits than the existing situation. For instance, Ford employees who received low performance ratings resisted change because it threatened their job security and career development.

Saving face—Some people resist change as a political strategy to "prove" that the decision is wrong or that the person encouraging change is incompetent. For example, senior executives in a manufacturing firm bought a computer other than the system recommended by the information systems department. Soon after the system was in place, several information systems employees let minor implementation problems escalate to demonstrate that senior management had made a poor decision.

Fear of the unknown—People resist change because they are worried that they cannot adopt the new behaviors. This fear of the unknown increases the *risk* of personal loss. This situation happened at a company where the owner wanted sales staff to telephone rather than personally visit prospective customers. With no experience in telephone sales, the sales staff complained about the changes. Some even avoided the training program that taught them how to make telephone sales. "The salespeople were afraid of failing," explained the owner. "Each of them was very successful in the field, but they had never been exposed to a formalized telephone lead development program."[19]

Breaking routines—Chapter 1 described how organizations need to unlearn, not just learn.[20] Employees need to abandon the behavioral routines that are no longer appropriate. Unfortunately, people are creatures of habit. They like to stay within their comfort zones by continuing routine role patterns that make life predictable.[21] Consequently, many employees resist organizational changes that force them out of their comfort zones and require investing time and energy learning new role patterns.

▸ *Incongruent organizational systems*—Rewards, selection, training, and other control systems ensure that employees maintain desired role patterns. Yet the organizational systems that maintain stability also discourage employees from adopting new ways.[22] The implication, of course, is that organizational systems must be altered to fit the desired change. Unfortunately, control systems can be difficult to change, particularly when they have supported role patterns that worked well in the past.[23]

▸ *Incongruent team dynamics*—Teams develop and enforce conformity to a set of norms that guide behavior (see Chapter 8). However, conformity to existing team norms may discourage employees from accepting organizational change. Team norms that conflict with the desired changes need to be altered.

UNFREEZING, CHANGING, AND REFREEZING

According to Lewin's force field analysis model, effective change occurs by unfreezing the current situation, moving to a desired condition, and then refreezing the system so that it remains in this desired state. Unfreezing occurs when the driving forces are stronger than the restraining forces. This process involves making the driving forces stronger, weakening or removing the restraining forces, or having a combination of both.

Certainly, driving forces must be strong enough to motivate employees to change their current ways. However, change rarely occurs by increasing driving forces alone, because the restraining forces often adjust to counterbalance the driving forces. The harder corporate leaders push for change, the stronger the restraining forces push back. This antagonism threatens the change effort by producing tension and conflict within the organization.

The preferred option is to both increase the driving forces and reduce or remove the restraining forces. Increasing the driving forces creates an urgency for change, whereas reducing the restraining forces minimizes resistance to change. "The only way to have people change is because they choose to," explains Carly Fiorina, chief executive of Hewlett-Packard. "You cannot force change onto people—not lasting change, not real change."[24]

Creating an Urgency for Change

Driving forces represent the booster rockets that push employees out of their comfort zones. They energize people to face the risks that change presents to them. Driving forces must be real, not contrived; otherwise, employees will doubt the change agent's integrity. Some threats are well known to employees. PepsiCo employees never forget about their archrivals at Coca-Cola. EDS staff members are always aware of the competitive pressures from IBM Global Services in the computer services business.

However, many driving forces are unknown to anyone below the top ranks of the organization. Thus, the change process must begin by informing employees about competitors, changing consumer trends, impending government regulations, and other driving forces.[25] For instance, James Donald had to communicate the urgency for change when he took over Pathmark Stores. The New Jersey–based supermarket chain was in financial trouble, but few of the company's 28,000 employees knew about these problems. To get employees ready for change and avoid bankruptcy, Donald prepared a video that told everyone about Pathmark's tremendous financial debt. Some employees quit, fearing that the company wasn't going to make it. But the remaining 99 percent quickly developed a commitment to get the company back to health.[26]

Customer Driven Change   Another powerful driver of change is customer expectations.[27] Dissatisfied customers represent a compelling force for change because of the adverse consequences for the organization's survival and success. Customers also provide a human element that further energizes employees to change current behavior patterns. The opening vignette in this chapter described how Dick Brown met with major clients soon after he arrived as CEO of Electronic Data Systems. The purpose of these visits wasn't just to learn about the problems; it was also to let employees know that the problems were real and required urgent change. Al Galdi, CEO of the New Jersey architectural design firm ARCNET, also relied on customer-driven change by having employees listen to a voice mail message from an angry customer. "I played it to the entire staff. It's not something for me to fix, it's something for all of us to fix," he says.[28]

Joel Kocher, CEO of Micron Electronics, also engaged in customer-driven change in his previous job as an executive with Texas-based Power Computing. At a large employee meeting, Kocher read an angry customer letter. Some employees responded defensively by suggesting the customer installed or used the equipment incorrectly, or that the problem is never as serious as customers say. Then, to everyone's surprise, Kocher brought the customer who wrote the letter into the meeting. "We actually brought the customer to the meeting, to personalize it for every single person in the room," says Kocher. "And it was very, very interesting to see the metamorphosis that occurred within the context of these several hundred people when you actually had a customer talking about how their foul-up had hurt this person and hurt their business."[29]

Reducing the Restraining Forces

Effective change involves more than making employees aware of the driving forces. It also involves reducing or removing the restraining forces. Exhibit 16.3 identifies six ways to overcome employee resistance. Communication, training, employee involvement, and stress management try to reduce the restraining forces and, if feasible, should be attempted first.[30] However, negotiation and coercion are necessary for people who will clearly lose something from the change and when the speed of change is critical.

Communication   Communication is the highest priority and the first strategy required for any organizational change. It reduces the restraining forces by keeping employees informed about what to expect from the change effort. Although time-consuming and costly, communication can potentially reduce fear of the unknown and develop team norms that are more consistent with the change effort.

DuPont recognized the importance of communication when it decided to outsource most of its 3,100 information systems (IS) employees to information systems service providers. The chemical giant informed everyone of this decision six months before the change, and it continually communicated with employees throughout the process using e-mail, videos, and face-to-face meetings. By the time the transition took place, employees knew thoroughly what was happening and how it would affect them personally. The result was that

EXHIBIT 16.3   Methods for dealing with resistance to change

Strategy	Example	When used	Problems
Communication	Customer complaint letters are shown to employees.	When employees don't feel an urgency for change or don't know how the change will affect them.	Time-consuming and potentially costly.
Training	Employees learn how to work in teams as the company adopts a team-based structure.	When employees need to break old routines and adopt new role patterns.	Time-consuming and potentially costly.
Employee involvement	Company forms a task force to recommend new customer service practices.	When the change effort needs more employee commitment, some employees need to save face, and/or employee ideas would improve decisions about the change strategy.	Very time-consuming. May also lead to conflict and poor decisions if employees' interests are incompatible with organizational needs.
Stress management	Employees attend sessions to discuss their worries about the change.	When communication, training, and involvement do not sufficiently ease employee worries.	Time-consuming and potentially expensive. Some methods may not reduce stress for all employees.
Negotiation	Employees agree to replace strict job categories with multiskilling in return for increased job security.	When employees will clearly lose something of value from the change and would not otherwise support the new conditions. Also necessary when the company must change quickly.	May be expensive, particularly if other employees want to negotiate their support. Also tends to produce compliance, but not commitment to the change.
Coercion	Company president tells managers to get on board and accept the change or leave.	When other strategies are ineffective and the company needs to change quickly.	Can lead to more subtle forms of resistance, as well as long-term antagonism with the change agent.

Sources: Adapted from J. P. Kotter and L. A. Schlesinger, "Choosing Strategies for Change," *Harvard Business Review* 57 (1979), pp. 106–14; P. R. Lawrence, "How to Deal with Resistance to Change," *Harvard Business Review* (May–June 1954), pp. 49–57.

97 percent of DuPont's IS staff went along with the change. "The communication was so thorough that, by the time we got the offer letter, it was an absolute nonevent," says an outsourced DuPont employee.[31]

Training Training is an important process in most change initiatives because employees need to learn new knowledge and skills. When a company introduces a new sales database, for instance, representatives need to learn how to adapt their previous behavior patterns to benefit from the new system. Coaching is a variation of training that provides more personalized feedback and direction during the learning process. Global Connections 16.1 describes how an executive at Unilever's Elida Fabergé factory in Seacroft, United Kingdom, brought about significant change by hiring team coaches to train employees. Coaching and other forms of training are time-consuming, but they help employees break routines by learning new role patterns.

Coaching for Change at Unilever's Elida Fabergé Factory in Seacroft

Gary Calveley announced a bold vision soon after he arrived as works director at Unilever's Elida Fabergé factory in Seacroft, United Kingdom. Calveley wanted the facility to apply European quality practices, win the Best Factory award, and become the safest Unilever site in Europe. What's surprising isn't that Calveley set such audacious goals; the surprise is that the plant actually achieved them in three years.

One of the key strategies in Elida Fabergé's success was the introduction of team coaches to guide the change process. Calveley recruited Gene Toner as an independent change agent, who then recruited 10 people with coaching skills from sports, police, teaching, and psychology. Two people were appointed from within the factory.

The coaching process began with "lots of tension and questioning" as employees openly wondered why they needed coaches when experts already worked on the production line. To address these doubts, Calveley worked with a theater company to produce a play portraying current and past work in the factory, and how it could be improved using European quality management practices. After watching the play, coaches guided employees through the process of finding ways to turn this vision of a quality-focused factory into a reality.

The theatrical production helped employees realize that the coaches were there to guide employees toward their goals, just like sports coaches. Another contributing factor to the coaches' role was the variable pay system Calveley negotiated with the union. The new reward system tied pay increases to measurable goals in each employee's personal development plan (PDP). The coaches worked with employees to develop these PDPs

Change consultant Gene Toner (left) and plant manager Gary Calveley (right) introduced coaching to make Unilever's Elida Fabergé factory the best in Europe. *(Dean Smith/The Camera Crew)*

and provided feedback so that they could reach them. This made the coaches valuable allies to both employees and management in the change process.

"[O]nce the targets had been set and people were committed to them, they started coming to the coaches," recalls one coach. "[T]hey came in early, stayed late, or came over during stoppages—it was a bit of a turnaround from being seen as a nuisance factor before." Only 3 employees out of the workforce of 600 didn't get a pay increase in the first year. And by the third year, the entire plant had achieved Calveley's audacious goals.

Source: Adapted from P. Baker, "Change Catalysts," *Works Management* 54 (July 2001), pp. 18–21.

Some training programs, such as action learning projects (see Chapter 2), can also minimize employee resistance caused by saving face, because employees are actively involved in the change process through this type of learning process. In Ford Motor Company's Capstone action learning program, for instance, global teams of six mid-level Ford executives are formed and given six months to tackle a strategic challenge. At the end of six months, team members present their findings and receive feedback from senior Ford executives as well as fellow participants.[32]

Employee Involvement Employee involvement can be an effective way to reduce the restraining forces because it creates a psychological ownership of the decision (see Chapter 9). Rather than viewing themselves as agents of someone else's decision, staff members feel personally responsible for the success of the decision. Employee involvement also minimizes resistance to change by reducing problems of saving face and fear of the unknown. "It is important to have employees take ownership of this," says Colleen Arnold, an executive at IBM Global Services. "It won't work if it's just coming from the top 10 people in the company."[33]

Employee involvement is fairly easy in small organizations, but how do you involve everyone in large firms? One solution is to have representative employees directly involved in the change process. Celestica, Inc., followed this change strategy when it was spun off from IBM a few years ago. Nearly two dozen design teams targeted specific change initiatives by diagnosing Celestica's work processes against the company's critical success factors. Numerous study teams then developed recommendations and implementation strategies in the areas that required change.[34]

Search conferences represent another way to involve a large number of employees and other stakeholders in the change process. Search conferences are large group sessions, usually lasting a few days, in which participants identify the environmental trends and establish strategic solutions for those conditions.[35] Experts on various topics are sometimes brought in to speak during lunch or dinner. Search conferences "put the entire system in the room," meaning that they try to involve as many employees and other stakeholders associated with the organizational system as possible. For instance, Eicher Motors, a large manufacturer of light commercial vehicles in central India, holds an annual three-day search conference that includes a representation of suppliers, buyers, and shareholders, as well as all employees.[36]

Various organizations, such as Microsoft, the U.S. Forest Service, and Peco Energy, have used search conferences to assist the change process.[37] Of course, search conferences and other forms of employee involvement require follow-up action by decision makers. If employees do not see meaningful decisions and actions resulting from these meetings, they begin to question the credibility of the process and are more cynical of similar change strategies in the future.

search conferences

Systemwide group sessions, usually lasting a few days, in which participants identify the environmental trends and establish strategic solutions for those conditions.

Stress Management   For most people, organizational change is a stressful experience.[38] It threatens self-esteem and creates uncertainty about the future. Communication, training, and employee involvement can reduce some of these stressors, but companies also need to introduce stress management practices to help employees cope with the changes. Stress management minimizes resistance by removing some of the direct costs and fear of the unknown associated with the change process. Stress also saps energy, so minimizing stress potentially increases employee motivation to support the change process.

Negotiation   Organizational change is, in large measure, a political activity.[39] People have vested interests and apply their power to ensure that the emerging conditions are consistent with their personal values and needs. Consequently, negotiation may be necessary for employees who will clearly lose out from the change activity. This negotiation offers certain benefits to offset some of the cost of the change.

Coercion   By any account, EDS is one of the most dramatic corporate turnarounds in the computer services industry. As we read in the opening vignette in this chapter, Dick Brown relied on various change management strategies

Executives at Wachovia Corporation knew that its merger with First Union would be stressful for employees, and that stress can make the change process more difficult. To ease the stress, the Winston-Salem–based financial institution set up a toll-free number that employees and other stakeholders could call for updates on the merger process. It also dispatched 400 middle and upper-level managers, called ambassadors, to keep everyone informed. Wachovia offered special sessions to help employees deal with change and stress. Shortly after the merger was announced, the company sent out a memo reminding people about the company's employee assistance counseling service. "I've encouraged people to take care of themselves," says L. M. "Bud" Baker, Wachovia's chairman and chief executive officer (front in photo). "This is a physically and emotionally demanding time."[40] Use Lewin's force field model to explain why stress management strategies improve the change management process. *(AP/Wide World)*

to transform EDS into a more responsive, customer-focused company. Although his change process included communication, training, and employee involvement, it also involved some tough decisions about removing senior executives who didn't fit the new culture.

EDS is not an isolated example. One survey reported that two-thirds of senior management in large U.S. firms were replaced by the time the businesses were revived.[41] Replacing people is the least desirable way to change organizations. However, dismissals and other forms of coercion are sometimes necessary when speed is essential and other tactics are ineffective. For example, it may be necessary to remove several members of an executive team who are unwilling or unable to change their existing mental models of the ideal organization.

Dismissal is also a radical form of organizational "unlearning" (see Chapter 1) because when executives leave, they take knowledge of the organization's past routines, potentially opening up opportunities for new practices to take hold.[42] At the same time, we should keep in mind that coercion is a risky strategy because survivors (employees who are not fired) may have less trust in corporate leaders and engage in more political tactics to protect their own job security. In general, various forms of coercion may change behavior through compliance, but they won't develop commitment to the change effort (see Chapter 12).

Changing to the Desired Future State

Organizational change takes many forms. Dick Brown changed EDS's culture to become more customer-focused, requiring changes in behavior as well as in attitudes and values. Change was more dramatic at Celestica, the IBM spin-off that manufactures high-technology products. Task forces identified specific changes, which resulted in new tasks and roles in the organization. Overall, change results in new behaviors that employees must learn and internalize.

Refreezing the Desired Conditions

After unfreezing and changing behavior patterns, we need to refreeze desired behaviors so that people do not slip back into their old work practices.[43] Refreezing occurs when organizational systems and team dynamics are realigned with the desired changes. The desired patterns of behavior can be nailed down by changing the physical structure and situational conditions. Organizational rewards are also powerful systems that refreeze behaviors.[44] If the change process is supposed to encourage efficiency, then rewards should be realigned to motivate and reinforce efficient behavior. Information systems play a complementary role in the change process, particularly as conduits for feedback.[45]

Feedback mechanisms help employees learn how well they are moving toward the desired objectives, and they provide a permanent architecture to support the new behavior patterns in the long term. Alberto-Culver Company North America transformed into a performance-oriented firm by measuring employees' attitudes toward the top executive team and change agents, called growth development leaders. "I'm a firm believer that you change what you measure," says Carol Lavin Bernick, North American president of the personal care products company.[46]

STRATEGIC VISIONS, CHANGE AGENTS, AND DIFFUSION OF CHANGE

Kurt Lewin's force field analysis model provides a rich understanding of the dynamics of organizational change. But it overlooks three other ingredients in effective change processes: strategic visions, change agents, and diffusion of change.

Strategic Visions

Every successful change requires a clear, well-articulated vision of the desired future state. This vision provides a sense of direction and establishes the critical success factors against which the real changes are evaluated. It also minimizes employee fear of the unknown and provides a better understanding of which behaviors employees must learn for the future state.[47] Although some executives say that strategic visions are too "fluffy," most executives in large U.S. organizations believe a clear vision of the proposed change is the most important feature of successful change initiatives.[48]

You can see the importance of a strategic vision in the change process at EDS. Dick Brown began the turnaround at EDS with a clear vision of a more responsive, customer-focused organization. "[Dick Brown] is the finest communicator I have ever worked with" says Don Uzzi, EDS senior vice president of global marketing, communications, and government affairs. "He has a vision and a mission and employees well know it."[49]

Change Agents

change agent
Anyone who possesses enough knowledge and power to guide and facilitate the change effort.

Organizational change also requires change agents to help form, communicate, and build commitment toward the desired future state. A change agent is anyone who possesses enough knowledge and power to guide and facilitate the change effort. Some organizations rely on external consultants to serve as change agents. However, change agents are typically people within the organization who possess the leadership competencies necessary to bring about meaningful change. Corporate executives certainly need to be change agents. However, as companies rely increasingly on self-directed work teams, most employees will become change agents from time to time.

Effective change agents such as Dick Brown are transformational leaders (see Chapter 14).[50] They form a vision of the desired future state, communicate that vision in ways that are meaningful to others, behave in ways that are consistent with the vision, and build commitment to the vision.

Diffusion of Change

Change agents often test the transformation process with a pilot project, then diffuse what has been learned from this experience to other parts of the organization. Pilot projects are more flexible and less risky than centralized, organizationwide programs.[51] Scholars have identified several conditions that effectively diffuse change from the pilot project to the rest of the organization.[52] Diffusion is more likely to occur when the pilot project is successful within one or two years and receives visibility (e.g., favorable news media coverage). These conditions tend to increase top management support for the change program and persuade other managers to introduce the change effort in their operations. Successful diffusion also depends on labor union support and active involvement in the diffusion process.

organization development (OD)
A planned system-wide effort, managed from the top with the assistance of a change agent, that uses behavioral science knowledge to improve organizational effectiveness.

Another important condition is that the diffusion strategy isn't described too abstractly. If the strategy is too abstract, the instructions may be too vague to allow introduction of the change elsewhere. Neither should the strategy be stated too precisely, because it might not seem relevant to other areas of the organization. Finally, without producing excessive turnover in the pilot group, people who have worked under the new system should be moved to other areas of the organization. These employees transfer their knowledge and commitment of the change effort to work units that have not yet experienced it.

ORGANIZATION DEVELOPMENT

So far, we have discussed the dynamics of change that occur every day in organizations. However, an entire field of study, called **organization development (OD)**, tries to understand how to manage planned change in organizations. OD is a planned systemwide effort, managed from the top with the

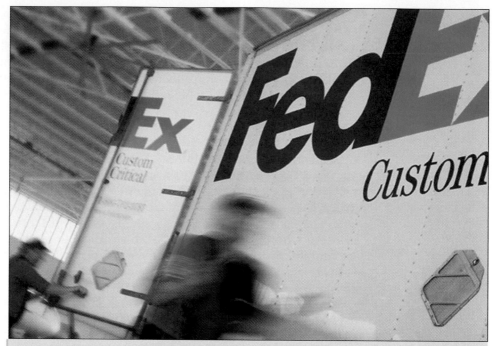

FedEx Custom Critical (formerly Roberts Express) introduced self-directed work teams through a pilot project. Seven employees from operations, customer service, and safety/recruiting at the Akron, Ohio–based expedited delivery service firm agreed to form a pilot team, representing the first cross-functional customer service unit. As problems were ironed out, the company transferred what it learned about forming SDWTs in the pilot group to form other teams. Today, the entire work process is operated by self-directed teams.[53] What conditions would help FedEx Custom Critical diffuse the pilot project to other parts of the organization? *(Courtesy of FedEx Custom Critical)*

assistance of a change agent, that uses behavioral science knowledge to improve organizational effectiveness.[54]

OD relies on many of the organizational behavior concepts described in this book, such as team dynamics, perceptions, job design, and conflict management. OD also takes an open systems perspective, because it recognizes that organizations have many interdependent parts and must adapt to their environments. Thus, OD experts try to ensure that all parts of the organization are compatible with the change effort, and that the change activities help the company fit its environment.[55]

Most OD activities rely on **action research** as the primary blueprint for planned change. As depicted in Exhibit 16.4, action research is a data-based, problem-oriented process that diagnoses the need for change, introduces the OD activity, and then evaluates and stabilizes the desired changes.[56]

Action research is a highly participative process, involving the client throughout the various stages.[57] It typically includes an action research team consisting of people both affected by the organizational change and having the power to facilitate it. This participation, a fundamental philosophy of OD, also increases commitment to the change process and provides valuable

action research
A data-based, problem-orientated process that diagnoses the need for change, introduces the OD intervention, and then evaluates and stabilizes the desired changes.

EXHIBIT 16.4 The action research approach to organization development

information for conducting organizational diagnosis and evaluation. Let's look at the main elements of the action research process.

Establish the Client–Consultant Relationship

The organization development process begins by forming a relationship between the client and the consultant. External consultants might become change agents, but they are usually retained as facilitators to assist an internal change agent (usually a senior executive or team leader). Consultants need to determine three things when forming a client relationship in organization development: the client's readiness for change, the consultant's power base, and the consultant's role in the relationship.

First, consultants need to determine the client's readiness for change, including whether people are motivated to participate in the process, are open to meaningful change, and possess the abilities to complete the process. They watch out for people who enter the process with preconceived ideas before the situation is fully diagnosed, or who intend to use the change effort to their personal advantage (e.g., closing down a department or firing a particular employee).

Second, consultants need to establish their power base in the client relationship.[58] Effective consultants rely on expertise and perhaps referent power to have any influence on the participants (see Chapter 12). However, they *should not* use reward, legitimate, or coercive power, because these bases may weaken trust and neutrality in the client–consultant relationship.

Third, consultants need to agree with their clients on the most appropriate role in the relationship.[59] A consultant's role might range from providing technical expertise on a specific change activity to facilitating the change process. Many OD experts prefer the latter role, commonly known as **process consultation**.[60] Process consultation involves helping the organization solve its own problems by making it aware of organizational processes, the consequences of those processes, and the means by which they can be changed. Rather than providing expertise about the content of the change—such as how to introduce continuous improvement teams—process consultants help participants learn how to solve their own problems by guiding them through the change process.[61]

process consultation

Involves helping the organization solve its own problems by making it aware of organizational processes, the consequences of those processes, and the means by which they can be changed.

Diagnose the Need for Change

Action research is a problem-oriented activity that carefully diagnoses the problem (or opportunity) through systematic analysis of the situation. *Organizational diagnosis* involves gathering and analyzing data about an ongoing system. Organizational diagnosis is important because it establishes the appropriate direction for the change effort.[62] Data collection may occur through interviews, survey questionnaires, direct observation, analysis of documents, or any combination of these.

Along with gathering and analyzing data, the diagnostic process involves agreeing on specific prescriptions for action, including the appropriate change method and the schedule for these actions. This process, known as *joint action planning,* ensures that everyone knows what is expected of him or her and that standards are established to properly evaluate the process after the transition.[63]

Introduce Change

incremental change

An evolutionary strategy whereby the organization fine-tunes the existing organization and takes small steps toward the change effort's objectives.

An important issue in any change process is whether to implement incremental or quantum change.[64] **Incremental change** is an evolutionary strategy whereby the organization fine-tunes the existing organization and takes small steps toward the change effort's objectives. Incremental change is generally less threatening and stressful to employees because they have time to adapt to the new conditions. Moreover, any problems in the process can be corrected while the change process is occurring, rather than afterward. However, incremental change may be inadequate where companies face extreme environmental turbulence. Instead, they may require **quantum change** (also called *episodic change*) in which the organization breaks out of its existing ways and moves toward a totally different configuration of systems and structures.[65] Organizational restructuring and reengineering are common forms of quantum change.

quantum change

A revolutionary approach to change in which the organization breaks out of its existing ways and moves toward a totally different configuration of systems and structures.

Executives at Nestlé, the Swiss food giant, prefer continuous improvement because quantum change potentially creates more problems within organizations.[66] Quantum change can be costly as organizational systems and structures and torn apart and replaced. Employees typically need to learn completely new roles, which are not known until the change process has begun. Quantum change is usually traumatic and rapid, so change agents rely more on coercion and negotiation than on employee involvement to build support for the change effort.

Evaluate and Stabilize Change

OD activities can be very expensive, so it makes sense that we should measure their effectiveness. To evaluate an OD process, we need to recall its objectives, which were developed during the organizational diagnosis and action planning stages. But even when these goals are clearly stated, the effectiveness of an OD activity might not be apparent for several years. It is also difficult to separate the effects of the activity from external factors (e.g., improving economy, introduction of new technology).

If the activity has the desired effect, then the change agent and participants need to stabilize the new conditions. This element refers to the refreezing process that we described earlier. Rewards, information systems, team norms, and other conditions are redesigned so that they support the new values and behaviors. Even with stabilizing systems and structures in place, the desired conditions may erode without the ongoing support of a change champion.

For example, Alcoa's magnesium plant in Addy, Washington, became a model of efficiency under the guidance of its plant manager and human resource manager. Then Alcoa transferred both of them to other turnaround projects and cut back on the number of department heads at the plant. These actions unintentionally had the effect of removing the change champions and undermining the previous four years of change effort. "[Alcoa] stripped away the leadership that could have supported the change efforts afterwards," says one of the original change agents.[67]

TRENDS IN ORGANIZATION DEVELOPMENT

Organization development includes any planned change intended to make a firm more effective. In theory, this means that OD covers almost every area of organizational behavior, as well as many aspects of strategic and human resource management. In practice, OD consultants have favored one perspective and level of process more than others at various periods in OD's history.

When the field of organization development emerged in the 1940s and 1950s, OD practitioners focused almost exclusively on interpersonal and small group dynamics. The field was equated with T-groups, encounter groups, and other forms of sensitivity training. **Sensitivity training** is an unstructured and agendaless session in which a small group of people meet face-to-face, often for a few days, to learn more about themselves and their relations with others.[68] Learning occurs as participants disclose information about themselves and receive feedback from others during the session. Few OD activities were involved with macro-level, organizationwide changes.

Today, the reverse is true.[69] OD processes now are aimed mostly at improvements in service quality, corporate restructuring, and organizational learning. They are typically organizationwide, affecting organizational systems and structures, with less emphasis on individual emotions and values. OD practitioners are paying more attention to productivity, customer service, product or service quality, and related business outcomes.[70] Although surveys suggest that OD consultants still value their humanistic roots, there is also increasing awareness that the field's values have shifted to a more bottom-line focus.

There are numerous OD activities. Some are discussed elsewhere in this book, such as job design (Chapter 6), team building (Chapter 8), dialogue meetings (Chapter 13), and changes in organizational culture (Chapter 15). In this section, we briefly discuss two increasingly popular OD activities: parallel learning structures and appreciative inquiry.

Parallel Learning Structures

Parallel learning structures are highly participative arrangements, composed of people from most levels of the organization who follow the action research model to produce meaningful organizational change. They are social structures developed alongside the formal hierarchy with the purpose of increasing the organization's learning.[71] Ideally, parallel learning structure participants are sufficiently free from the constraints of the larger organization so that they can more effectively solve organizational issues.

sensitivity training

An unstructured and agendaless session in which a small group of people meet face to face, often for a few days, to learn more about themselves and their relations with others.

parallel learning structures

Highly participative groups constructed alongside (i.e., parallel to) the formal organization with the purpose of increasing the organization's learning and producing meaningful organizational change.

Royal Dutch/Shell Changes through Parallel Learning Structures

A few years ago, competitors were threatening Royal Dutch/Shell's market share. The oil company's executives in London and The Hague spent two years reorganizing, downsizing, and educating several layers of management, but this top-down approach had minimal effect. Managers in charge of Shell's operations for a particular country resisted changes that threatened their autonomy, and headquarters managers couldn't break out of the routines that worked for them in the past.

So Steve Miller, head of Shell's worldwide oil products business, decided to apply a parallel learning structure and change the company from the bottom up. He and his executive team held several five-day workshops, each attended by six-country teams of frontline people (e.g., gas station managers, truck drivers, marketing professionals). Participants at these "retailing boot camps" learned about worrisome competitive trends in their regions and were taught powerful marketing tools to identify opportunities. The teams then returned home to study their markets and develop proposals for improvement. For example, a team in South Africa proposed ways to increase liquid gas market share. The Malaysian team developed plans to increase gasoline sales in that country.

Four months later, the teams returned for a second workshop, where each proposal was critiqued by Miller's executive team in "fishbowl" sessions with the other teams watching. Videotapes from these sessions became socialization tools for other employees back in the home country. Each team had 60 days to put its ideas into action. The team returned for a third workshop to analyze what worked and what didn't.

These workshops, along with field tours and several other grassroots activities, had a tremendous effect.

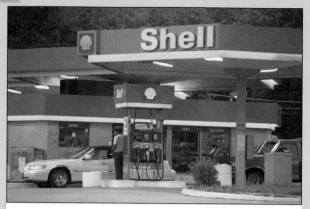

Royal Dutch/Shell relied on a parallel learning structure to change the company from the bottom up. *(John Thoeming)*

Frontline employees developed an infectious enthusiasm and a stronger business approach to challenging the competition. "I can't overstate how infectious the optimism and energy of these committed employees was on the many managers above them," says Miller. The change process also resulted in solid improvements in profitability and market share in most regions where employees had attended the sessions.

Sources: R. Pascale, M. Millemann, and L. Gioja, *Surfing on the Edge of Chaos* (London: Texere, 2000); R. T. Pascale, "Leading from a Different Place," in J. A. Conger, G. M. Spreitzer, and E. E. Lawler III, eds., *The Leader's Change Handbook* (San Francisco: Jossey-Bass, 1999), pp. 301–20; D. J. Knight, "Strategy in Practice: Making It Happen," *Strategy and Leadership* 26 (July–August 1998), pp. 29–33; R. T. Pascale, "Grassroots Leadership—Royal Dutch/Shell," *Fast Company* 14 (April–May 1998), pp. 110–20.

The change process at EDS relied on a parallel learning structure. CEO Dick Brown formed Project Breakaway—a team of seven people from different units, each with different industry expertise—to develop a customer-focused organizational structure that would increase productivity, promote accountability, and drive a collaborative culture across the entire enterprise. The team was given six weeks to resolve their differences and draft the new structure that would break away from the old ways of doing business.[72] Project Breakaway became a microcosm of the larger organization, complete with internal rivalries that had to be resolved before the new structure took shape.

Connections 16.2 describes how Royal Dutch/Shell's retail boot camp teams represent a form of parallel structure because they work outside the normal structure. These teams represent various countries and establish a more entrepreneurial approach to getting things done at Shell. The retail teams are separated from the traditional hierarchy so that it is easier to instill new attitudes, role patterns, and work behaviors.

Appreciative Inquiry

appreciative inquiry
An organization development intervention that directs the group's attention away from its own problems and focuses participants on the group's potential and positive elements.

The action research process described earlier in this chapter is based on the traditional problem-solving model. OD participants focus on problems with the existing organizational system and identify ways to correct those problems. Unfortunately, this deficiency model of the world—in which something is wrong that must be fixed—focuses on the negative dynamics of the group or system rather than its positive opportunities.

Appreciative inquiry tries to break out of the problem-solving mentality by reframing relationships around the positive and the possible.[73] It takes the view that organizations are creative entities in which people are capable of building synergy beyond their individual capabilities. To avoid dwelling on the group's own shortcomings, the process usually directs its inquiry toward successful events and successful organizations. This external focus becomes a form of behavioral modeling, but it also increases open dialogue by redirecting the group's attention away from its own problems. Appreciative inquiry is especially useful when participants are aware of their "problems" or already suffer from enough negativity in their relationships. The positive orientation of appreciative inquiry enables groups to overcome these negative tensions and build a more hopeful perspective of their future by focusing on what is possible.

Exhibit 16.5 outlines the Four-D model of appreciative inquiry, which was developed in Harare, Zimbabwe, by a group working with the U.S. Agency for International Development and the Save the Children Fund.[74] The process begins with *discovery*—identifying the positive elements of the observed events or organization. This stage might involve documenting positive customer experiences elsewhere in the organization. Or it might include interviewing members of another organization to discover its fundamental strengths. As

EXHIBIT 16.5   The appreciative inquiry process

Sources: Based on J. M. Watkins and B. J. Mohr, *Appreciative Inquiry: Change at the Speed of Imagination* (San Francisco: Jossey-Bass, 2001), pp. 25, 42–45; D. Whitney and C. Schau, "Appreciative Inquiry: An Innovative Process for Organization Change," *Employment Relations Today* 25 (Spring 1998), pp. 11–21; F. J. Barrett and D. L. Cooperrider, "Generative Metaphor Intervention: A New Approach for Working with Systems Divided by Conflict and Caught in Defensive Perception," *Journal of Applied Behavioral Science* 26 (1990), p. 229.

participants discuss their findings, they shift into the *dreaming* stage by envisioning what might be possible in an ideal organization. By directing their attention to a theoretically ideal organization or situation, participants feel safer revealing their hopes and aspirations than if they were discussing their own organization or predicament.

As participants make their private thoughts public to the group, the process shifts into the third stage, called *designing*. Designing involves the process of dialogue (see Chapter 8), in which participants listen with selfless receptivity to each other's models and assumptions and eventually form a collective model for thinking within the team.[75] In effect, they create a common image of what should be. As this model takes shape, group members shift the focus back to their own situation. In the final stage of appreciative inquiry, called

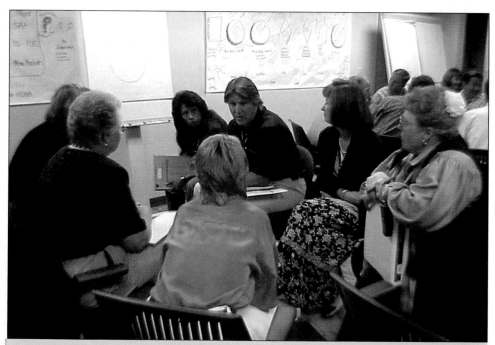

The HunterDouglas Window Fashions Division (WFD) relied on appreciative inquiry to create a collective vision, reinstill a sense of community among employees, and build leadership within the organization. The Broomfield, Colorado–based business unit sent an advisory team to a weeklong training program where they learned about the Four-D process. The WFD advisory team then described appreciative inquiry and its rationale to employees through a series of town meetings. The discovery phase consisted of over 500 interviews with employees, customers, suppliers, and community members. These results were reviewed at an Appreciative Summit, where WFD employees worked through the dream, design, and deliver stages. A second wave of interviews became background data for a subsequent search conference–type of strategic planning summit. WFD executives say that appreciative inquiry improved productivity and cross-departmental collaboration, and created a can-do attitude toward the company's quality management initiative.[76] What problems might occur if HunterDouglas relied on action research rather than appreciative inquiry to facilitate this change process? *(Courtesy of Amanda Trosten-Bloom)*

delivering, participants establish specific objectives and direction for their own organization based on their model of what will be.

Appreciative inquiry is a relatively new approach to organization development, but several organizations have already applied its basic principles. One of these is AVON Mexico, which conducted sessions to develop employment opportunities for women in the top ranks. A team of employees and consultants interviewed people for their stories illustrating best practices in gender equality at AVON Mexico. These stories were presented at two-day sessions, and participants built on these best practices to discover how AVON could extend these experiences. Over the next few years, the company won the Catalyst award for gender equality, its profit increased dramatically (attributed partly to the appreciative inquiry process), and women found their way into more senior positions at AVON Mexico.[77]

EFFECTIVENESS OF ORGANIZATION DEVELOPMENT

Is organization development effective? Considering the incredible range of organization development activities, answering this question is not easy. Nevertheless, a few studies have generally reported that some OD processes have a moderately positive effect on employee productivity and attitudes. According to some reviews, team building and interpersonal dialogue produce the most favorable results when a single activity is applied.[78] One of the most consistent findings is that OD is most effective when it includes two or more change processes.

Cross-Cultural Concerns with OD

One significant concern with OD techniques originating from North America is that they conflict with cultural values in other countries.[79] Some scholars argue that OD practices in North America assume a linear model of change, as shown earlier in the force field analysis, that is punctuated by tension and overt conflict. Indeed, sensitivity training and other OD practices encourage open display of conflict. But these assumptions are incompatible with cultures that view change as a natural, cyclical process with harmony and equilibrium as the objectives.[80] For instance, people in many Asian countries try to minimize conflict in order to respect others and save face.[81] These concerns do not mean that OD is ineffective elsewhere. Rather, it suggests that the field needs to develop a more contingency-oriented perspective with respect to the cultural values of its participants.

Ethical Concerns with OD

The field of organization development also faces ethical concerns with respect to some processes.[82] One ethical concern is that OD activities may threaten the individual's privacy rights. The action research model is built on the idea of collecting information from organizational members, yet this activity requires employees to provide personal information and emotions that they may not want to divulge. The scientific nature of the data collection exercise may mislead employees into believing that their information is confidential when, in reality, executives can sometimes identify opinions of individual employees.[83]

A second ethical concern is that OD activities potentially increase management's power by inducing compliance and conformity in organizational members. This power shift occurs because OD initiatives create uncertainty and reestablish management's position in directing the organization. Moreover, because OD is a systemwide activity, it *requires* employees to participate rather than allowing individuals to get involved voluntarily. Indeed, one of the challenges of OD consultants is to bring on board those who are reluctant to engage in the process.

A third concern is that some OD activities undermine the individual's self-esteem. The unfreezing process requires participants to disconfirm their existing beliefs, sometimes including their own competence at certain tasks or interpersonal relations. Sensitivity training may involve direct exposure to personal critique by co-workers as well as public disclosure of personal limitations and faults.

A fourth ethical dilemma facing OD consultants is their role in the client relationship. Generally, they should occupy marginal positions with the clients they are serving. That is, they must be sufficiently detached from the organization to maintain objectivity and avoid having the client become too dependent on them.[84] However, this can be a difficult objective to satisfy because of the politics of organizational change. OD consultants and clients have their own agendas, and these are not easily resolved without moving beyond the marginal positions that change agents should ideally attain.

The organization development practices described in this section facilitate the change process, and Lewin's force field analysis model provides a valuable template for understanding how the change process works. Still, you can tell from reading this chapter that organizational change is easier said than done. Many corporate leaders have promised more change than they were able to deliver because they underestimated the time and challenges involved with the process. This is certainly true of corporate restructuring, where leaders typically have difficulty redesigning the organization's departments, reporting relationships, and distribution of formal power. The next chapter looks closely at organizational structure and design.

CHAPTER SUMMARY

Organizations face numerous forces for change, because they are open systems that need to adapt to changing environments. Some current environmental dynamics include computer technology, globalization, competition, and demographics.

Lewin's force field analysis model states that all systems have driving and restraining forces. Change occurs through the process of unfreezing, changing, and refreezing. Unfreezing produces disequilibrium between the driving and restraining forces. Refreezing realigns the organization's systems and structures with the desired behaviors.

Almost all organizational change efforts face one or more forms of employee resistance. The main reasons people resist change are direct costs, saving face, fear of the unknown, breaking routines, incongruent organizational systems, and incongruent team dynamics.

Resistance to change may be minimized by keeping employees informed about what to expect from the change effort (communicating); by teaching employees valuable skills for the desired future (training); by involving them in the change process; by helping employees cope with the stress of change; by negotiating trade-offs with those who will clearly lose from the change effort; and by using coercion (sparingly and as a last resort).

A change agent is anyone who possesses enough knowledge and power to guide and facilitate the change effort. Change agents rely on transformational leadership to develop a vision, communicate that vision, and build commitment to the vision of a desirable future state.

Organization development (OD) is a planned systemwide effort, managed from the top with the assistance of a change agent, that uses behavioral science knowledge to improve organizational effectiveness.

When forming a client relationship, OD consultants need to determine the readiness for change, establish their power base in the client relationship, and understand their appropriate role in the change process. An important issue is whether change should be evolutionary (incremental change) or revolutionary (quantum change).

Parallel learning structures are social structures developed alongside the formal hierarchy with the purpose of increasing the organization's learning. They are highly participative arrangements, composed of people from most levels of the organization who follow the action research model to produce meaningful organizational change. Appreciative inquiry focuses participants on the positive and possible. It tries to break out of the problem-solving mentality that dominates OD through the action research model. The four stages of appreciative inquiry are discovery, dreaming, designing, and delivering.

OD activities, particularly those with multiple components, have a moderately positive effect on employee productivity and attitudes. However, there are some cross-cultural concerns with OD processes. Moreover, there are ethical concerns with some OD activities, including increasing management's power over employees, threatening individual privacy rights, undermining individual self-esteem, and making clients dependent on the OD consultant.

KEY TERMS

action research, p. 488
appreciative inquiry, p. 493
change agent, p. 487
force field analysis, p. 476
incremental change, p. 490

organization development (OD), p. 487
parallel learning structures, p. 491
process consultation, p. 489
quantum change, p. 490

refreezing, p. 477
search conferences, p. 484
sensitivity training, p. 491
unfreezing, p. 477

DISCUSSION QUESTIONS

1. Chances are that the school you are attending is currently undergoing some sort of change to adapt more closely to its environment. Discuss the external forces that are driving these changes. What internal drivers for change also exist?
2. Use Lewin's force field analysis to describe the dynamics of organizational change at Unilever's Elida Fabergé factory, described in Global Connections 16.1.
3. Senior management of a large multinational corporation is planning to restructure the organization. Currently, the organization is decentralized around geographical areas so that the executive responsible for each area has considerable autonomy over manufacturing and sales. The new structure will transfer power to the executives responsible for different product groups; the executives responsible for each geographic area will no longer be responsible for manufacturing in their area but will retain control over sales activities. Describe two types of resistance senior management might encounter from this organizational change.
4. Review the organizational change process at EDS (opening vignette in this chapter); then explain how this process reduced resistance to change.
5. Web Circuits, Inc., is a Singapore-based manufacturer of computer circuit boards for high-technology companies. Senior management wants to introduce value-added management practices to reduce production costs and remain competitive. A consultant has recommended that the company start with a pilot project in one department and, when successful, diffuse those practices to other areas of the organization. Discuss the advantages of this recommendation, and identify three conditions (other than the pilot project's success) that would make diffusion of the change effort more successful.
6. You are an organization development consultant who has been asked by the president of Seattle Photonics Inc. to explore the issues that may account for the slow hardware and software development of three teams under the direction of a particular project manager. Before accepting this role, what three things should you consider when forming the client relationship? How would you determine whether the client is well suited to organizational development?
7. Suppose that you are vice president of branch services at the Bank of East Lansing. You notice that several branches have consistently low customer

service ratings even though there are no apparent differences among branches in resources or staff characteristics. Describe an appreciative inquiry process in one of these branches that might help overcome these problems.

8. This chapter suggests that some organization development activities face ethical concerns. Yet several OD consultants actively use these processes

because they believe they benefit the organization and do less damage to employees than it seems on the surface. For example, some OD activities try to open up the employee's hidden area (see Johari Window in Chapter 3) so that there is better mutual understanding with co-workers. Discuss the merits of this argument, and identify where you think OD should limit this process.

CASE STUDY 16.1

TRANSACT INSURANCE CORPORATION

TransAct Insurance Corporation (TIC) provides automobile insurance throughout the Southeastern United States. Last year, a new president was brought in by TIC's board of directors to improve the company's competitiveness and customer service. After spending several months assessing the situation, the new president introduced a strategic plan to improve TIC's competitive position. He also replaced three vice presidents. Jim Leon was hired as vice president of claims, TIC's largest division, with 1,500 employees, 50 claims center managers, and five regional directors.

Jim immediately met with all claims managers and directors, and visited employees at TIC's 50 claims centers. Because he was an outsider, this was a formidable task, but his strong interpersonal skills and uncanny ability to remember names and ideas helped him through the process. Through these visits and discussions, Jim discovered that the claims division had been managed in a relatively authoritarian, top-down manner. He could also see that morale was very low and employee–management relations were guarded. High workloads and isolation (adjusters work in tiny cubicles) were two other common complaints. Several managers acknowledged that the high turnover among claims adjusters was partly due to these conditions.

Following discussions with TIC's president, Jim decided to make morale and supervisory leadership his top priority. He initiated a divisional newsletter with a tear-off feedback form for employees to register their comments. He announced an open-door policy in which any claims division employee could speak to him

directly and confidentially without first going to the immediate supervisor. Jim also fought organizational barriers to initiate a flex-time program so that employees could design work schedules around their needs. This program later became a model for other areas of TIC.

One of Jim's most pronounced symbols of change was the "Claims Management Credo" outlining the philosophy that every claims manager would follow. At his first meeting with the complete claims management team, Jim presented a list of what he thought were important philosophies and actions of effective managers. The management group was asked to select and prioritize items from this list. They were told that the resulting list would be the division's management philosophy and all managers would be held accountable for abiding by its principles. Most claims managers were uneasy about this process, but they also understood that the organization was under competitive pressure and that Jim was using this exercise to demonstrate his leadership.

The claims managers developed a list of 10 items, such as encouraging teamwork, fostering a trusting work environment, setting clear and reasonable goals, and so on. The list was circulated to senior management in the organization for their comment and approval, and sent back to all claims managers for their endorsement. Once this was done, a copy of the final document was sent to every claims division employee. Jim also announced plans to follow up with an annual survey to evaluate each claims manager's performance. This plan concerned the managers, but most of them believed that the credo exercise was a result of Jim's initial enthusiasm and that he would be too busy to introduce a survey after settling into the job.

One year after the credo had been distributed, Jim announced that the first annual survey would be conducted. All claims employees would complete the survey and return it confidentially to the human resources department, where the survey results would be compiled for each claims center manager. The survey asked the extent to which the manager had lived up to each of the 10 items in the credo. Each form also provided space for comments.

Claims center managers were surprised that a survey would be conducted, but they were even more worried about Jim's statement that the results would be shared with employees. What "results" would employees see? Who would distribute these results? What would happen if a manager got poor ratings from his or her subordinates? "We'll work out the details later," said Jim in response to these questions. "Even if the survey results aren't great, the information will give us a good baseline for next year's survey."

The claims division survey had a high response rate. In some centers, every employee completed and returned a form. Each report showed the claim center manager's average score for each of the 10 items as well as how many employees rated the manager at each level of the 5-point scale. The reports also included every comment made by employees at that center.

No one was prepared for the results of the first survey. Most managers received moderate or poor ratings on the 10 items. Very few managers averaged above 3.0 (out of a possible 5.0) on more than a couple of items. These results suggested that, at best, employees were ambivalent about whether their claims center manager had abided by the 10 management philosophy items. The comments were even more devastating than the ratings. Comments ranged from mildly disappointed in to extremely critical of their claims manager. Employees also described their long-standing frustration with TIC, high workloads, and isolated working conditions. Several people bluntly stated that they were skeptical about the changes that Jim had promised. "We've heard the promises before, but now we've lost faith," wrote one claims adjuster.

The survey results were sent to each claims manager, the regional director, and employees at the claims center. Jim instructed managers to discuss the survey data and comments with their regional manager and directly with employees. The claims center managers, who thought employees received only the average scores, went into shock when they realized that the reports included individual comments. Some managers went to their regional director, complaining that revealing the personal comments would ruin their careers. Many directors sympathized, but the results were already available to employees.

When Jim heard about these concerns, he agreed that the results were lower than expected and that the comments should not have been shown to employees. After discussing the situation with his directors, he decided that the discussion meetings between claims managers and their employees should proceed as planned. To delay or withdraw the reports would undermine the credibility and trust that Jim was trying to develop with employees. However, the regional director attended the meeting in each claims center to minimize direct conflict between the claims center manager and employees.

Although many of these meetings went smoothly, a few created harsh feelings between managers and their employees. The sources of some comments were easily identified by their content, creating a few delicate moments in several sessions. A few months after these meetings, two claims center managers quit and three others asked for transfers back to nonmanagement positions in TIC. Meanwhile, Jim wondered how to manage this process more effectively, particularly since employees expected another survey the following year.

Discussion Questions

1. Identify the forces pushing for change and the forces restraining the change effort in this case.

2. Was Jim Leon successful at bringing about change? Why or why not?

3. What should Jim Leon do now?

EMC DISHES OUT A LITTLE MORE TLC

BusinessWeek At a big company, data storage used to involve rooms in which paper files were carefully packed into boxes and organized on shelves. Today, data storage is a computer-driven business for safely maintaining electronic files. A major player in the data storage business is EMC Corporation, which originally won customers solely on the basis of the company's leadership in storage technology. After competitors such as IBM and Hitachi Data Systems caught up in terms of technology, EMC had to rethink the way it treats customers.

This *Business Week* case study describes how EMC is making the move from a technology-driven company to a customer-focused company. It discusses how EMC lost customers to rivals offering better service along with better prices and how it is changing in an attempt to win them back. Read through this *Business Week* case study at www.mhhe.com/mcshane2e and prepare for the discussion questions below.

Discussion Questions

1. What driving forces for change at EMC does the author identify?

2. How are managers at EMC enabling change?

3. What resistance to this change would you expect to see at EMC? What strategies for dealing with the resistance would be appropriate?

Source: F. Keenan, "EMC Dishes Out a Little More TLC," *Business Week*, September 10, 2001.

STRATEGIC CHANGE MANAGEMENT

Purpose This exercise is designed to help you identify strategies to facilitate organizational change in various situations.

Instructions

- *Step 1*—The instructor will place students into teams, and each team will be assigned one of the scenarios presented below.
- *Step 2*—Each team will diagnose its assigned scenario to determine the most appropriate set of change management practices. Where appropriate, these practices should (a) create an urgency to change, (b) minimize resistance to change, and (c) refreeze the situation to support the change initiative. Each scenario is based on real events that occurred in the United States and Canada.
- *Step 3*—Each team will present and defend its change management strategy. Class discussion regarding the appropriateness and feasibility of each strategy will occur after all teams assigned the same scenario have presented their proposals. The instructor will then describe what the organizations actually did in these situations.

Scenario 1: Greener Telco The board of directors at a large telephone company wants its executives to make the organization more environmentally friendly by encouraging employees to reduce waste in the workplace. There are also expectations by government and other stakeholders for the company to take this action and be publicly successful. Consequently, the company president wants to significantly reduce the use of paper, refuse, and other waste throughout the company's many widespread offices. Unfortunately, a survey indicates that employees do not value environmental objectives and do not know how to "reduce, reuse, recycle." As the executive responsible for this change, you have been asked to develop a strategy that might bring about meaningful behavioral change toward these environmental goals. What would you do?

Scenario 2: Go Forward Airline A major airline had experienced a decade of turbulence, including two bouts of bankruptcy protection, 10 executive officers, and morale so low that employees had ripped off company logos from their uniforms out of embarrassment. Service was terrible, and the airplanes rarely arrived or left the terminal on time. Poor performance was costing the airline significant amounts of money in passenger layovers. Managers were paralyzed by anxiety, and many had been with the firm so long that they didn't know how to set strategic goals that worked. One-fifth of all flights were losing money, and the company overall was near financial collapse (just three months from defaulting on payroll obligations). The newly hired CEO and you must get employees to quickly improve operational efficiency and customer service. What actions would you take to bring about these changes?

TEAM EXERCISE 16.4

APPLYING LEWIN'S FORCE FIELD ANALYSIS

Purpose This exercise is designed to help you understand how to diagnose situations using force field analysis, and to identify strategies to facilitate organizational change.

Instructions This exercise involves diagnosing the situation described below, identifying the forces for and against change, and recommending strategies to reduce resistance to change. Although the exercise is described as a team activity, the instructor may choose to have it completed individually. Also, the instructor may choose a situation other than the one presented here.

■ *Step 1*—Students will form teams of four or five people, and everyone will read the following situation. (*Note:* If your school currently has a full trimester or a quarter system, then imagine the situation below as though your school currently has a two-semester system.)

> Your college has two semesters (beginning in September and January) as well as a six-week summer session from early May to mid-June. Instructors typically teach their regular load of courses during the two semesters. The summer session is taught mainly by part-time contract faculty, although some full-time faculty teach for extra pay. After carefully reviewing costs,

student demand, and competition from other institutions, senior administration has decided that your college should switch to a trimester curriculum. In a trimester system, courses are taught in three equal semesters—September to December, January to April, and May to early August. Faculty with research obligations must teach any two semesters in which their courses are offered; teaching-only faculty teach courses in all three semesters. Senior administration has determined that this change will make more efficient use of college resources, particularly because it will allow the institution to admit more students without building additional classrooms or other facilities. Moreover, market surveys indicate that over 50 percent of current students would continue their studies in the revised summer semester (i.e., the second trimester) and the institution would attract more full-fee students from other countries. The faculty association has not yet had time to state its position on this proposed change.

■ *Step 2*—Using Lewin's force field analysis model (see Exhibit 16.6 on next page), identify the forces that seem to support the

EXHIBIT 16.6   Force Field Analysis Model

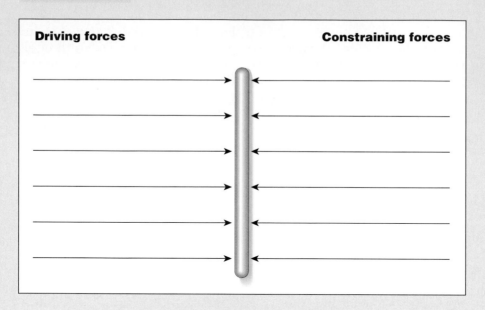

Driving forces   **Constraining forces**

change and the forces that likely oppose the change to a trimester system. Team members should consider all possible sources of support and resistance, not just those stated in the situation on the previous page.

■ *Step 3*—For each source of resistance, identify one or more strategies that would most

effectively manage change. Recall from the textbook that the change management strategies include communication, training, employee involvement, stress management, negotiation, and coercion.

■ *Step 4*—The class will discuss each team's results.

SELF-ASSESSMENT EXERCISE 16.5

TOLERANCE OF CHANGE SCALE

Purpose This self-assessment exercise is designed to help you understand how people differ in their tolerance of change.

Instructions Read each statement in the table on the next page and circle the response that best fits your personal belief. Then use the scoring key in Appendix B of this book to calculate

your results. This self-assessment exercise is completed alone so that students rate themselves honestly without concerns of social comparison. However, class discussion will focus on the meaning of the concept measured by this scale and its implications for managing change in organizational settings.

For each statement, indicate your level of agreement by marking the appropriate response on the right.

	Strongly agree ▼	Moderately agree ▼	Slightly agree ▼	Neutral ▼	Slightly disagree ▼	Moderately disagree ▼	Strongly disagree ▼
1. An expert who doesn't come up with a definite answer probably doesn't know too much.	☐	☐	☐	☐	☐	☐	☐
2. I would like to live in a foreign country for a while.	☐	☐	☐	☐	☐	☐	☐
3. There is really no such thing as a problem that can't be solved.	☐	☐	☐	☐	☐	☐	☐
4. People who fit their lives into a schedule probably miss most of the joy of living.	☐	☐	☐	☐	☐	☐	☐
5. A good job is one where it is always clear what is to be done and how it is to be done.	☐	☐	☐	☐	☐	☐	☐
6. It is more fun to tackle a complicated problem than to solve a simple one.	☐	☐	☐	☐	☐	☐	☐
7. In the long run, it is possible to get more done by tackling small, simple problems rather than large, complicated ones.	☐	☐	☐	☐	☐	☐	☐
8. Often the most interesting and stimulating people are those who don't mind being different and original.	☐	☐	☐	☐	☐	☐	☐
9. What we are used to is always preferable to what is unfamiliar.	☐	☐	☐	☐	☐	☐	☐
10. People who insist on a yes or no answer just don't know how complicated things really are.	☐	☐	☐	☐	☐	☐	☐
11. A person who leads a life in which few surprises or unexpected happenings arise really has a lot to be grateful for.	☐	☐	☐	☐	☐	☐	☐
12. Many of our most important decisions are based on insufficient information.	☐	☐	☐	☐	☐	☐	☐
13. I like parties where I know most of the people more than ones where all or most of the people are complete strangers.	☐	☐	☐	☐	☐	☐	☐
14. Teachers or supervisors who hand out vague assignments give you a chance to show initiative and originality.	☐	☐	☐	☐	☐	☐	☐
15. The sooner everyone acquires similar values and ideals, the better.	☐	☐	☐	☐	☐	☐	☐
16. A good teacher is one who makes you wonder about your way of looking at things.	☐	☐	☐	☐	☐	☐	☐

Source: Adapted from S. Budner, "Intolerance of Ambiguity as a Personality Variable," *Journal of Personality* 30 (1962), pp. 29–50.

 After studying the preceding material, be sure to check out our website at

www.mhhe.com/mcshane2e

for more in-depth information and interactivities that correspond to this chapter.

Organizational Structure and Design

One of Douglas Daft's first actions as Coca-Cola's latest CEO was to cut half of the staff at the soft drink maker's Atlanta headquarters and move the regional chieftains closer to their local markets. Daft spent most of his career working at Coke's far-flung operations, so he knows how centralized decision making has hampered Coke's ability to serve local needs. For example, Coke was several months behind its rivals in launching a new carbonated tea in northeast China: "We had the formula, we had the flavor, we had done all the taste-testing," complains Daft, "but Atlanta kept saying 'are you sure?'"

Coke executives previously made decisions from Atlanta because they thought Coke had global appeal. But Daft argues that Coke isn't "it" in all cultures. "People don't buy drinks globally," Daft explains. "You can't pander to similarities between people: you have to find the differences." Daft believes it will be easier for Coke executives to anticipate and respond to those differences through a more decentralized organizational structure.

Coca-Cola India CEO Alexander Von Behr has taken Daft's strategy further by radically decentralizing decisions down to six regions representing the country's diverse tastes. Marketing and brand building, which were previously decided nationally, are now controlled by the regional heads. Coke India's 36 bottling operations have also been

Coca-Cola decentralized its worldwide operations so that regional executives would be closer to their customers. (© AFP/CORBIS)

organized around these six regions. An area general manager who reports to the regional head has complete profit center responsibility for bottling activities in the region.

"In effect, we have built companies at regional levels and created profit centers with mini-CEOs at area levels," explains Nalin Miglani, Coca-Cola India's vice president of human resources.[1]

Something of a revolution is occurring in how organizations are structured. Driven by global competition and facilitated by information technology, Coca-Cola and many other companies are throwing out the old organizational charts and trying out new designs that they hope will achieve organizational objectives more effectively. **Organizational structure** refers to the division of labor as well as the patterns of coordination, communication, work flow, and formal power that direct organizational activities. An organizational structure reflects the organization's culture and power relationships.[2] Our knowledge of this subject provides the tools to engage in **organizational design**, that is, to create and modify organizational structures.

Organizational structures are frequently used as tools for change. Structures support or inhibit communication and relationships across the organization.[3] They also serve either as sources of resistance to change or supportive mechanisms that refreeze the desired state. They establish new communication patterns and refreeze the change initiatives. For example, Ford Motor Company restructured its many business units so that employees are closer to specific types of customers, such as luxury car buyers (Jaguar, Volvo), services (Hertz, e-commerce), and Ford's mainstream car buyers.[4]

We begin this chapter by considering the two fundamental processes in organizational structure: division of labor and coordination. This discussion is followed by a detailed investigation of the four main elements of organizational structure: span of control, centralization, formalization, and departmentalization. The latter part of this chapter examines the contingencies of organizational design, including organizational size, technology, external environment, and organizational strategy.

organizational structure
The division of labor as well as the patterns of coordination, communication, work flow, and formal power that direct organizational activities.

organizational design
The process of creating and modifying organizational structures.

DIVISION OF LABOR AND COORDINATION

All organizational structures include two fundamental requirements: the division of labor into distinct tasks and the coordination of that labor so that employees are able to accomplish common goals.[5] Organizations are groups of people who work interdependently toward some purpose (see Chapter 1). To accomplish their goals efficiently, these groups typically divide the work into manageable chunks, particularly when there are many different tasks to perform. They also introduce various coordinating mechanisms to ensure that everyone is working effectively toward the same objectives.

Division of Labor

Division of labor refers to the subdivision of work into separate jobs assigned to different people. Subdivided work leads to job specialization, because each job now includes a narrow subset of the tasks necessary to complete the product or service (see Chapter 6). Launching a space shuttle at NASA, for example, requires tens of thousands of specific tasks that are divided among thousands of people. Tasks are also divided vertically, such as having supervisors coordinate work while employees perform the work.

Work is divided into specialized jobs because doing so potentially increases work efficiency.[6] Job incumbents can master their tasks quickly because work cycles are shorter. Less time is wasted changing from one task to another. Training costs are reduced because employees require fewer physical and mental skills to accomplish the assigned work. Finally, job specialization makes it easier to match people with specific aptitudes or skills to the jobs for which they are best suited.

Coordinating Work Activities

As soon as people divide work among themselves, coordinating mechanisms are needed to ensure that everyone works in concert.[7] Every organization—from the two-person corner convenience store to the largest corporate entity—uses one or more of the following coordinating mechanisms: informal communication, formal hierarchy, and standardization (see Exhibit 17.1).

Coordination through Informal Communication   Informal communication is a coordinating mechanism in all organizations.[8] It includes sharing information on mutual tasks as well as forming common mental models so that employees synchronize work activities using the same mental road map.[9] Informal communication permits considerable flexibility because employees transmit a large volume of information through face-to-face communication and other media-rich channels (see Chapter 11). Consequently, informal communication is a vital coordinating mechanism in nonroutine and ambiguous situations.

Coordination through informal communication is easiest in small firms and work units where employees face few communication barriers. Emerging information technologies have further leveraged this coordinating mechanism in large organizations, even where employees are scattered around the globe. Larger organizations can also support informal communication by forming temporary cross-functional teams and moving team members into a common physical area (called *co-locating*). For example, **concurrent engineering** (also called *platform teams*) involves assigning product development to a cross-functional project team consisting of people from marketing, design, manufacturing, customer service, and other areas.[10] These employees are typically

concurrent engineering
Involves assigning product development to a cross-functional project team consisting of people from marketing, design, manufacturing, customer service, and other areas.

EXHIBIT 17.1	Coordinating mechanisms in organizations

Form of coordination	Description	Subtypes
Informal communication	Sharing information on mutual tasks; forming common mental models to synchronize work activities	• Direct communication • Liaison roles • Integrator roles
Formal hierarchy	Assigning legitimate power to individuals, who then use this power to direct work processes and allocate resources	• Direct supervision • Corporate structure
Standardization	Creating routine patterns of behavior or output	• Standardized skills • Standardized processes • Standardized output

Sources: Based on information in D. A. Nadler and M. L. Tushman, *Competing by Design: The Power of Organizational Architecture* (New York: Oxford University Press, 1997), chap. 6; H. Mintzberg, *The Structuring of Organizations* (Englewood Cliffs, NJ: Prentice Hall, 1979), chap. 1; J. Galbraith, *Designing Complex Organizations* (Reading, MA: Addison-Wesley, 1973), pp. 8–19.

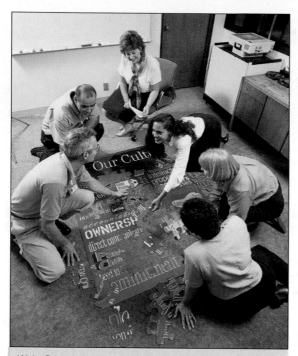

W. L. Gore & Associates Inc. avoids hierarchies and formal supervision. Instead, the maker of Gore-Tex fabric and other high-tech products encourages informal communication to coordinate most work activities among its nearly 6,000 employees in 45 locations. It does this by limiting the size of each facility to about 200 people and ensuring that each unit is self-sufficient. "People sometimes get concerned and worried that there is no structure and no organization, and I don't think that is true at all," says a senior Gore associate. Project leaders serve as integrators by coordinating the work of various individuals and work units.[12] Could the coordinating mechanism used at Gore work at a General Motors assembly plant? *(W. L. Gore & Associates, Inc.)*

co-located to improve cross-functional coordination, whereas more formal and less flexible coordinating mechanisms are used when product development occurs through several departments.

Larger organizations also encourage coordination through informal communication by creating *integrator roles.* These people are responsible for coordinating a work process by encouraging employees in each work unit to share information and informally coordinate work activities. Integrators do not have authority over the people involved in that process, so they must rely on persuasion and commitment.[11] Brand managers at Procter & Gamble coordinate work among marketing, production, and design groups. Project leaders at W. L. Gore & Associates and other companies also serve as integrators by encouraging people from various work units to work together on a project.

Coordination through Formal Hierarchy Informal communication is the most flexible form of coordination, but it can be time-consuming. Consequently, as organizations grow, they develop a second coordinating mechanism in the shape of a formal hierarchy. Hierarchy assigns legitimate power to individuals, who then use this power to direct work processes and allocate resources (see Chapter 12). In other words, work is coordinated through direct supervision.

Any organization with a formal structure coordinates work to some extent through the formal hierarchy. For instance, team leaders at Microsoft coordinate work by ensuring that employees in their group remain on schedule and that their respective tasks are compatible with tasks completed by others in the group. The team leader has direct authority to reassign people to different work activities and to resolve conflicts by dictating solutions. The formal hierarchy also coordinates work among executives through the division of organizational activities. If the organization is divided into geographic areas, the structure gives the heads of those regional groups legitimate power over executives responsible for production, customer service, and other activities in those areas. If the organization is divided into product groups, then the heads of those groups have the right to coordinate work across regions.

The formal hierarchy has traditionally been applauded as the optimal coordinating mechanism for large organizations. Henri Fayol, an early scholar on the subject, argued that organizations are most effective when managers exercise their authority and employees receive orders from only one supervisor. Coordination should occur through the chain of command, that is, up the hierarchy and across to the other work unit.[13] This approach to coordination is practiced at the British conglomerate Rentokil Initial. Rentokil operates like a military organization, with eight levels of management and a strict chain of command. "I don't encourage people to pick up the phone directly to me because that is attempting to bypass their boss," warns Rentokil CEO Sir Clive Thompson.[14]

Coordination through formal hierarchy may have been popular with classic organizational theorists, but it is often a very inefficient coordinating mechanism. Later in this chapter, we will learn that there are limits to how many employees a supervisor can coordinate. Furthermore, the chain of command is rarely as fast or accurate as direct communication between employees. And, as recent scholars have warned, today's educated and individualistic workforce is less tolerant of rigid structures and legitimate power.[15]

Coordination through Standardization Standardization—creating routine patterns of behavior or output—is the third means of coordination. Many organizations try to improve the quality and consistency of a product or service by standardizing work activities through job descriptions and procedures.[16] Standardization coordinates work requiring routine and simple tasks, but is not effective in complex and ambiguous situations. In these situations,

Each member of this medical team at Duke University Medical Center performs specialized jobs requiring special knowledge and skills. To some extent, operating room staff coordinate through informal communication. However, much of the work activity can occur without discussion because team members also coordinate through standardization of skills. Through extensive training, each medical professional has learned precise role behaviors so that his or her task activities are coordinated with the activities of others on the surgical team. What other types of organizations make extensive use of standardization of skills to coordinate work? *(Charles Ledford/Black Star/TimePix)*

companies might coordinate work by standardizing the individual's or team's goals and product or service output (e.g., customer satisfaction, production efficiency). For instance, to coordinate the work of salespeople, companies assign sales targets rather than specific behaviors.

When work activities are too complex to standardize through procedures or goals, companies often coordinate work effort by extensively training employees or hiring people who have learned precise role behaviors from educational programs. This form of coordination is used in hospital operating rooms. Surgeons, nurses, and other operating room professionals coordinate their work more through training than goals or company rules.

Division of labor and coordination of work represent the two fundamental ingredients of all organizations. How work is divided, who makes decisions, which coordinating mechanisms are emphasized, and other issues are related to the four elements of organizational structure.

ELEMENTS OF ORGANIZATIONAL STRUCTURE

Every company is configured in terms of four basic elements of organizational structure. This section introduces three of them: span of control, centralization, and formalization. The fourth element—departmentalization—is presented in the next section.

Span of Control

span of control
The number of people directly reporting to the next level in the hierarchy.

Span of control refers to the number of people reporting directly to the next level in the hierarchy. As we mentioned earlier, Henri Fayol strongly recommended the formal hierarchy as the primary coordinating mechanism. Consequently, he and other theorists of that time prescribed a relatively narrow span of control, typically no more than 20 employees per supervisor and six supervisors per manager. These prescriptions were based on the assumption that managers simply cannot monitor and control closely enough any more subordinates.

Today, we know better. The best-performing manufacturing facilities currently have an average of 31 employees per supervisor—a much wider span of control than past scholars had recommended. Yet these operations plan to stretch this span to an average of 75 employees per supervisor over the next few years.[17]

What's the secret here? Did Fayol and others miscalculate the optimal span of control? The answer is that early scholars thought in terms of Frederick Taylor's scientific management model (see Chapter 6). They believed that employees should do the work, whereas supervisors and other management personnel should monitor employee behavior and make most of the decisions. This division of labor limited the span of control. It is very difficult to directly supervise 75 people. It is much easier to *oversee* 75 subordinates who are grouped into several self-directed work teams. Employees manage themselves, thereby releasing supervisors from the time-consuming tasks of monitoring behavior and making everyone else's decisions.[18]

Vancom Zuid-Limburg, a joint venture that operates a public bus company in The Netherlands, illustrates this point. Vancom has about 40 bus drivers for each manager, whereas other bus companies have 8 drivers per manager. Vancom is able to operate with a much wider span of control because bus drivers are organized into self-directed work teams that manage their own schedules and budgets.[19]

The underlying principle here is that the span of control depends on the presence of other coordinating mechanisms. Self-directed work teams supplement direct supervision with informal communication and specialized knowledge. This also explains why dozens of surgeons and other medical professionals may report to the head surgeon in a major hospital. The head surgeon doesn't engage in much direct supervision because the standardized skills of medical staff coordinate the unit's work. A wider span of control is possible when employees perform similar tasks or have routine jobs. In these situations, the organization relies more on standardization of work processes to coordinate work, thereby reducing the need for hands-on supervision.[20]

Tall and Flat Structures   The Development Bank of South Africa increased employee productivity by restructuring and flattening the organization. In particular, the government-owned financial institution slashed the number of managers from 74 to 27 and cut out one of its four management layers. "[T]he essence of transformation was not to shift the chairs, but to ensure that some of the chairs came out of the room," says a bank executive.[21]

Ducks Unlimited Canada recently flattened its organizational structure by removing layers of management. The Winnipeg-based environmental conservation group wanted to help empower employees, making it easier for the professionals in the field to make decisions quickly without having to go up and down the proverbial hierarchy. "I think by having that flattened structure there is more job enrichment," says Cheryl Barber, Ducks Unlimited Canada's human resources administrator. "People feel that they are in control of what they are doing and that also helps to retain the employees."[22] What conditions should corporate leaders consider when determining the optimal number of layers of management? *(Courtesy of Ducks Unlimited Canada)*

The Development Bank of South Africa joins a long list of companies that are moving toward flatter organizational structures. Royal Mail, which delivers mail throughout Great Britain, went from 16 layers of management to 6 layers. Varian X-Ray Tube Products reduced its five management tiers to three.[23] This trend toward delayering—moving from a tall to a flat structure—is partly in response to the recommendations of management gurus. For example, management guru Tom Peters challenged corporate leaders to cut the number of layers to three within a facility and to five within the entire organization.[24]

The main arguments in favor of delayering are that it potentially cuts overhead costs and puts decision makers closer to frontline staff and information about customer needs. "American corporations have come to realize that they need to have fewer layers of management if they are to communicate daily with their organizations and if they are to become closer to the customer," advises Lawrence A. Bossidy, CEO of AlliedSignal.[25] However, some organizational experts warn that corporate leaders may be cutting out too much hierarchy. They argue that the much maligned middle managers serve a valuable function by controlling work activities and managing corporate growth. Moreover, companies will always need hierarchy because someone has to make quick decisions and represent a source of appeal over conflicts.[26]

One last point before leaving this topic: The size of an organization's hierarchy depends on both the average span of control and the number of people employed by the organization. As shown in Exhibit 17.2, a tall structure has many hierarchical levels, each with a relatively narrow span of control, whereas a flat structure has few levels, each with a wide span of control.[27] Larger organizations that depend on hierarchy for coordination necessarily develop taller structures. For instance, Microsoft is considered a high-involvement organization, yet it has at least seven levels of corporate hierarchy to coordinate its tens of thousands of employees.[28]

Centralization and Decentralization

Centralization and decentralization represent a second element of organizational design. **Centralization** means that formal decision-making authority is held by a small group of people, typically those at the top of the organizational hierarchy. Most organizations begin with centralized structures, as the founder makes most of the decisions and tries to direct the business toward his or her vision. But as organizations grow, they diversify and their environments become more complex. Senior executives aren't able to process all the decisions that significantly influence the business. Consequently, larger organizations tend to *decentralize;* that is, they disperse decision-making authority and power throughout the organization.

The opening vignette in this chapter described how Coca-Cola CEO Douglas Daft decentralized the world's largest soft drink maker because consumers are more diverse than Coke executives had previously believed. Daft and other corporate leaders decentralized to make the organization more entrepreneurial and responsive to the local environments in which it operates. However, executives are just as likely to centralize during times of turbulence and organizational crisis. When the problems are over, these leaders are reluctant to decentralize decision making to lower levels.

Both centralization and decentralization can occur within large organizations. Nestlé has a decentralized structure with respect to marketing, yet some

centralization
The degree to which formal decision authority is held by a small group of people, typically those at the top of the organizational hierarchy.

EXHIBIT 17.2   Span of control and tall flat structures

**Tall structure/
Narrow span of control**

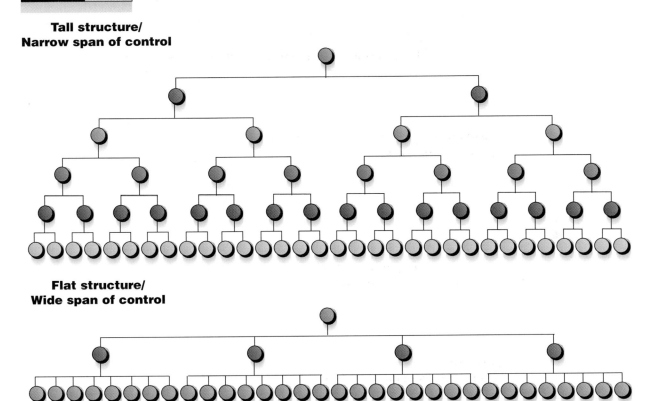

**Flat structure/
Wide span of control**

parts of the giant Swiss food company are centralized. "If you are too decentralized, you can become too complicated—you get too much complexity in your production system," explains Nestlé CEO Peter Brabeck. Nestlé centralizes its production, logistics, and supply chain management to leverage the economies of scale of a large organization.[29]

Formalization

Have you ever wondered why a McDonald's hamburger in Seattle looks and tastes the same as one in Singapore? The fast-food company has engineered out all variation through formalization. **Formalization** is the degree to which organizations standardize behavior through rules, procedures, formal training, and related mechanisms.[30] In other words, formalization represents the establishment of standardization as a coordinating mechanism.

McDonald's has a formalized structure because it prescribes every activity in explicit detail. Each McDonald's franchise must dole out five perfect drops of mustard, a quarter ounce of onions, and two pickles—three if they're small—on each hamburger. Drink cups are filled with ice up to a point just below the arches on their sides. Cooking and bagging fries are explained in 19 steps. Employees who work on the grill must put the hamburger patties in six rows of six patties each. A Big Mac is supposed to be assembled in 25 seconds from the time that it appears on the order screen.[31]

formalization
The degree to which organizations standardize behavior through rules, procedures, formal training, and related mechanisms.

Older companies tend to become more formalized because work activities become routinized, making them easier to document into standardized practices. Larger companies formalize as a coordinating mechanism, because direct supervision and informal communication among employees do not operate as easily. External influences, such as government safety legislation and strict accounting rules, also encourage formalization.

Problems with Formalization   Formalization may increase efficiency, but it can also create problems. Rules and procedures reduce organizational flexibility, so employees follow prescribed behaviors even when the situation clearly calls for a customized response. Some work rules become so convoluted that organizational efficiency would decline if they were actually followed as prescribed. Labor unions sometimes call work-to-rule strikes, in which their members closely follow the formalized rules and procedures established by an organization. This tactic increases union power, because the company's productivity falls significantly when employees follow the rules that are supposed to guide their behavior.

Another concern is that although employees with very strong security needs and a low tolerance for ambiguity like working in highly formalized organizations, others become alienated and feel powerless in these structures. Finally, rules and procedures have been known to take on a life of their own in some organizations. They become the focus of attention rather than the organization's ultimate objectives of producing a product or service and serving its dominant stakeholders.

Mechanistic versus Organic Structures

You may have noticed that organizations seem to cluster around their span of control, centralization, and formalization. Some companies, such as McDonald's, have a **mechanistic structure**.[32] Mechanistic structures are characterized by a narrow span of control and a high degree of formalization and centralization. They have many rules and procedures, limited decision making at lower levels, tall hierarchies of people in specialized roles, and vertical rather than horizontal communication flows. Tasks are rigidly defined and are altered only when sanctioned by higher authorities.

Companies with an **organic structure** have the opposite characteristics. They have a wide span of control, little formalization, and decentralized decision making. Tasks are fluid, adjusting to new situations and organizational needs. The organic structure values knowledge and takes the view that information may be located anywhere in the organization rather than only among senior executives. Thus, communication flows in all directions with little concern for the formal hierarchy. St. Luke's is an example of a company with an extreme organic structure. As described in Global Connections 17.1, the award-winning British advertising agency is completely decentralized and has minimal hierarchy and formalization.

Mechanistic structures operate best in stable environments because they rely on efficiency and routine behaviors. However, as we have emphasized throughout this book, most organizations operate in a world of dramatic change. Information technology, globalization, a changing workforce, and other factors have strengthened the need for more organic structures that are

mechanistic structure
An organizational structure with a narrow span of control and high degrees of formalization and centralization.

organic structure
An organizational structure with a wide span of control, little formalization, and decentralized decision making.

The Extreme Organic Structure of St. Luke's

A few years ago, American advertising company Chiat/Day was acquired by a larger firm, which intended to lay off most of Chiat/Day's 35 London staff. But these employees had other plans. They held a retreat to design their concept of the ideal organization; then they applied that ideal model to their newly formed advertising agency, called St. Luke's.

Named after the patron saint of artists, St. Luke's is a highly organic structure fashioned after a medieval guild. "We wanted to do something radical," explains St. Luke's co-founder David Abraham. "Many ad agencies have a very hierarchical structure and exist only to benefit shareholders that you never meet or owners with little direct involvement, so we created a corporate structure to match our ideals."

St. Luke's doesn't have any bosses or corporate hierarchy—just apprentices and practitioners. David Abraham and Andy Law are the company's main co-founders (Law is also company chairman), but no one reports to either of them. "Neither of us can tell people what to do," explains Law. "In fact, we report to them. We have to tell everybody openly all the time what we're doing." A five-member board elected by employees governs the agency, but almost all the 115 people now

employed at St. Luke's are company owners and have equal say in how the company is run.

Anyone who joins St. Luke's contractually agrees to be flexible in his or her job duties, including moving to different tasks on the basis of feedback from peers. The company's headquarters—a converted toffee factory in London—supports this organic structure because it doesn't have any offices. The only work spaces, other than the front reception area and cafeteria, are client rooms with visual themes to support creative thinking.

"Working without a formal structure presents pressures—ambiguity is stressful," explains Abraham. Still, Britain's most unusual ad agency has become its most successful. St. Luke's has grown 25 percent faster than any competitor and has been recognized as Britain's top advertising agency.

Sources: A. Law, "Creating the Most Frightening Company on Earth: An Interview with Andy Law of St. Luke's," *Harvard Business Review* 78 (September–October 2000), p. 142; A. Law, *Creative Company* (New York: Wiley, 2000); J. P. Flintoff, "Keeping Faith in St. Luke," *Guardian (London),* September 19, 1998, p. 22; F. Jebb, "Don't Call Me Sir," *Management Today,* August 1998, pp. 44–47; H. Jones, "Selling Space," *Design Week,* April 10, 1998, pp. 18–21; A. R. Sorkin, "Gospel According to St. Luke's," *New York Times,* February 12, 1998, pp. D1, D7; S. Caulkin, "The Advertising Gospel According to St. Luke's," *Observer (London),* August 24, 1997, p. 8; M. Carter, "In St. Luke's We Trust," *The Independent (London),* April 21, 1997, p. 6.

flexible and responsive to these changes. Moreover, organic structures are more consistent with knowledge management because they emphasize information sharing rather than hierarchy and status.[33]

FORMS OF DEPARTMENTALIZATION

Span of control, centralization, and formalization are important elements of organizational structure, but most people think about organizational charts when the discussion of organizational structure arises. The organizational chart represents the fourth element in the structuring of organizations, called departmentalization. Departmentalization specifies how employees and their activities are grouped together. It is a fundamental strategy for coordinating organizational activities because it influences organizational behavior in the following ways:[34]

■ Departmentalization establishes a system of common supervision among positions and units within the organization. It establishes formal work teams, as described in Chapter 8. Departmentalization typically determines which positions and units must share resources. Thus, it establishes interdependencies among employees and subunits (see Chapter 13).

- Departmentalization usually creates common measures of performance. Members of the same work team, for example, share common goals and budgets, giving the company standards against which to compare subunit performance.
- Departmentalization encourages coordination through informal communication among people and subunits. With common supervision and resources, members within each configuration typically work near each other so that they can use frequent and informal interaction to get the work done.

There are almost as many organizational charts as there are businesses, but we can identify five pure types of departmentalization: simple, functional, divisional, matrix, and team-based. Few companies fit exactly into any of these categories, but they represent a useful framework for discussing more complex hybrid forms of departmentalization. Also discussed are emerging variations of network structures, including affiliate networks and virtual corporations.

Simple Structure

Most companies begin with a *simple structure*.[35] They employ only a few people and typically offer only one distinct product or service. There is minimal hierarchy—usually just employees reporting to the owners. Employees are grouped into broadly defined roles because there are insufficient economies of scale to assign them to specialized roles. Simple structures are flexible, yet they usually depend on the owner's direct supervision to coordinate work activities. Consequently, this structure is very difficult to operate under complex conditions.

Functional Structure

functional structure
An organizational structure that organizes employees around specific knowledge or other resources.

A **functional structure** organizes employees around specific knowledge or other resources. Employees with marketing expertise are grouped into a marketing unit, those with production skills are located in manufacturing, engineers are found in product development, and so on. Organizations with functional structures are typically centralized to coordinate their activities effectively. Standardization of work processes is the most common form of coordination used in a functional structure. Most organizations use functional structures at some level or at some time in their development.

Advantages and Disadvantages   An important advantage of functional structures is that they foster professional identity and clarify career paths. They permit greater specialization so that the organization has expertise in each area. Direct supervision is easier, because managers have backgrounds in that functional area and employees approach them with common problems and issues. Finally, functional structures create common pools of talent that typically serve everyone in the organization. This creates an economy of scale that would not exist if functional specialists were spread over different parts of the organization.[36]

Functional structures also have limitations. Because people with common interests and backgrounds are grouped together, these designs tend to emphasize subunit goals over superordinate organizational goals. Employees in purchasing, accounting, engineering, and other functional units are less likely to give priority to the company's product or service than to the goals of their specific department. Unless people are transferred from one function to another, they fail to develop a broader understanding of the business. A related concern is that functional structures emphasize differences across work units. For this reason, functional structures tend to have higher dysfunctional conflict and poorer coordination with other work units. Together, these problems require substantial formal controls and coordination when functional structures are used.

Divisional Structure

divisional structure

An organizational structure that groups employees around geographic areas, clients, or outputs.

A **divisional structure** groups employees around geographic areas, clients, or outputs (products/services). Divisional structures are sometimes called *strategic business units* (SBUs), because they are normally more autonomous than functional structures and may operate as subsidiaries rather than departments of the enterprise. Exhibit 17.3 illustrates the three pure forms of divisional structure.[37] *Geographic divisionalized structures* organize employees around distinct areas of the country or globe. Exhibit 17.3 (a) illustrates a geographic divisionalized structure similar to McDonald's global structure. *Product/service structures* organize work around distinct outputs. Exhibit 17.3 (b) illustrates this type of structure at Agilent Technologies. The California-based spin-off from Hewlett-Packard divides its workforce into product divisions, ranging from test and measurement to chemical and life sciences products. *Client structures* represent the third form of divisional structure, in which employees are organized around specific customer groups. Exhibit 17.3 (c) illustrates the client structure that Microsoft has adopted.[38]

Which form of divisionalization should large organizations adopt? At one time, most companies with international operations adopted a geographic divisionalized structure. McDonald's, Coca-Cola, Nestlé, and other food companies are still organized by region because consumer tastes vary across cultures. However, a recent survey of executives indicates that most corporations are now restructuring around clients rather than around geography or products.[39] One reason for the decline in geographic divisionalization is that information technology reduces the need for local representation. Clients can purchase online and communicate with businesses from almost anywhere in the world.

Geographical structures are also waning because freer trade has reduced government intervention in some products, and consumer preferences may be quite similar around the world. For example, Nortel Networks shifted from geographic to client divisions as fiber optics and telecommunications systems developed more global standards with less government intervention. A third reason geographic divisions are less common today is that business customers are becoming more global, and they want one global point of purchase, not one in every country or region. Axa Group is moving toward global profit centers for its services (e.g., reinsurance) because clients increasingly expect the London-based insurer to provide global (not regional) expertise and support.[40]

Advantages and Disadvantages   The divisional form is a building block structure, because it accommodates growth relatively easily. Related products

EXHIBIT 17.3   Three types of divisional structure

(a) Geographic structure

Chief Executive Officer

European operations | Asia Pacific operations | U.S. operations | Latin American operations

(b) Product/service structure

Chief Executive Officer

Test and measurement | Semiconductor products | Chemical/ life sciences | Communications solutions

(c) Client structure

Chief Executive Officer

Business enterprise | Consumers | Knowledge workers | Software developers

Note: Diagram (a) is similar to the geographic divisional structure of McDonald's; diagram (b) shows the product/service division at Aligent Technologies; diagram (c) shows the customer groups at Microsoft Corporation.

or clients can be added to existing divisions with little need for additional learning, whereas increasing diversity may be accommodated by sprouting a new division. Organizations typically reorganize around divisional structures as they expand into distinct products, services, and domains of operation, because coordinating functional units becomes too unwieldy with increasing diversity.[41]

Organizations tend to adopt divisional structures as they grow and become more complex, but this structural configuration is not perfect. The most common complaint is that divisional structures duplicate and underutilize resources. This structure creates silos of knowledge because functional specialists are spread throughout the various business units. Consequently,

A few years ago, Chicago-based advertising company Leo Burnett USA replaced its functional structure with a client-based divisional structure consisting of seven mini-agencies serving different client industries. The idea, said Burnett USA's CEO at the time, was to "get people closer to clients, to get people to sit cross-functionally so things would happen faster." The mini-agency structure did improve collaboration by moving together creative, client service, planning, and production staff. Unfortunately, this structure duplicated resources, and clients complained they weren't getting the best talent across the entire agency. "In the end, our clients didn't see a lot of benefit from the structure, and it wasn't as flexible as we wanted it to be," says a senior Burnett executive. Leo Burnett USA has since drifted back to a functional structure, although temporary teams are formed to serve specific clients.[42] Why would a client-based divisional structure be less effective at Leo Burnett than at Microsoft (which currently has a client structure)? *(www.leoburnett.com)*

matrix structure

A type of departmentalization that overlays a divisionalized structure (typically a project team) with a functional structure.

new knowledge and practices in one part of the organization are not shared elsewhere. Divisional structures also tend to reduce cooperation across groups. Nortel Networks recognized this problem, so it developed a special communication program, called Come Together, to remind employees in each division of their responsibility to work more closely with employees from other divisions.[43]

Matrix Structure

When Wolfgang Kemna became head of SAP America, he soon discovered that the German software giant's U.S. subsidiary was too inward-looking. "What I found was a highly defocused company," says Kemna. Much of the problem was SAP America's organizational structure, which was configured around the company's main product. The trouble with this structure is that SAP has five main software applications—such as customer relationship management and supply chain management. Moreover, SAP's products require unique marketing and application in different industries. So Kemna and his executive team introduced a **matrix structure that organizes employees around both the five main software applications and various industry groups.**[44]

A matrix structure overlays two organizational structures to leverage the benefits of both types of structure. There are two main forms of matrix structure. One form, shown in Exhibit 17.4, overlaps a functional structure with project teams.[45] In this example, employees are assigned to a cross-functional project team, yet they also belong to a permanent functional unit (e.g., engineering, marketing) to which they return when a project is completed.

The second form of matrix structure is found in corporations that want to balance power between two divisional groups. SAP America relies on this type of matrix structure because it overlaps product and client divisions. Many other global corporations adopt a matrix structure that combines geographical with product divisions. The product-based structure allows the company to exploit global economies of scale, whereas the geographic structure keeps knowledge close to the needs of individual countries. Asea Brown Boveri (ABB) is widely known for this global matrix structure. The Swiss/Swedish manufacturer of industrial electrical systems has country managers as well as managers responsible for specific product lines.[46]

Matrix structures create the unusual situation where employees have two bosses. A project team member reports not only to the project leader on a

EXHIBIT 17.4   A simplified matrix structure

Team member ■

daily basis, but also to the functional leader (engineering, marketing, etc.). Some companies give these managers equal power; more often, each has authority over different elements of the employee's or work unit's tasks.[47] Matrix structures that combine two divisionalized forms also have a dual-boss reporting system, but only for some employees. The manager of ABB's transformer plant in the United States would report to both the U.S. country manager and the global manager of ABB's transformer business. Only about 500 plant managers and group leaders at ABB have two bosses as a result of the matrix structure. The other 200,000 ABB employees work in direct authority structures below the matrix structure.

Advantages and Disadvantages   Matrix structures usually optimize the use of resources and expertise, making them ideal for project-based organizations with fluctuating workloads.[48] When properly managed, they improve communication efficiency, project flexibility, and innovation, compared with purely functional designs. Matrix structures focus technical specialists on the goals of serving clients and creating marketable products. Yet by maintaining a link to their functional unit, employees are able to interact and coordinate with others in their technical specialty.

In spite of these advantages, matrix structures require more coordination than functional or pure divisional structures. The existence of two bosses can also dilute accountability. Royal Dutch/Shell has moved away from a matrix design for these reasons.[49] Matrix structures also tend to generate conflict, organizational politics, and stress.[50] In project-based firms, for example, project leaders must have a general management orientation and conflict resolution skills to coordinate people with diverse functional backgrounds. They also need good negotiation and persuasive communication skills to gain support from functional leaders. Employees who feel comfortable in structured bureaucracies tend to have difficulty adjusting to the relatively fluid nature of matrix structures. Stress is a common symptom of poorly managed matrix structures, because employees must cope with two managers with potentially divergent needs and expectations.

Hybrid Structure

Very few organizations adopt a purely functional, divisional, or matrix structure. Instead, they combine some parts of various designs into a hybrid structure. Research suggests that multinational corporations need to develop structures and systems that maintain some balance of power and effectiveness across functional, product, geographic, and client-focused units.[51] In other words, they must ensure that functional executives do not dominate product executives, product executives do not dominate regional executives, and so forth.

Team-Based (Lateral) Structure

Harley-Davidson, Inc., has reinvented the wheel. More specifically, the motorcycle company designed three overlapping circles to represent its new organizational structure: a Create Demand Circle, a Produce Products Circle, and a Support Circle. In the center where the three circles intersect, Harley has a Leadership and Strategy Council. Each circle represents a team (or set of teams) responsible for specific work processes.[52]

team-based organization

A type of departmentalization with a flat span of control and relatively little formalization, consisting of self-directed work teams responsible for various work processes.

Harley-Davidson has embraced the **team-based organizational structure** (introduced in Chapter 8). Some writers call this a *lateral structure* because, with few organizational levels, it is very flat and relies on extensive lateral communication. Others refer to it as a *cluster structure*, because it is composed of a cluster of teams. Harley-Davidson refers to its team-based organization as a *circle structure* because the organization has several circles of activity with free-floating teams operating within each domain.[53] Exhibit 17.5 illustrates two of these views of team-based organizations.

No matter what name is used or how it is drawn, the team-based structure has a few features that distinguish it from other organizational forms. First, it uses self-directed work teams rather than individuals as the basic building blocks of the organization. Second, teams are typically organized around work processes, such as making a specific product or serving a specific client group. For instance, Harley-Davidson has platform teams that design new products and are responsible for the life cycle of their particular line. Each platform team includes a design engineer, manufacturing lead, purchasing lead, and marketing lead.[54]

A third distinguishing feature of team-based organizational structures is that they have a very flat hierarchy, usually with no more than two or three

EXHIBIT 17.5   Two perspectives of a team-based (lateral) structure

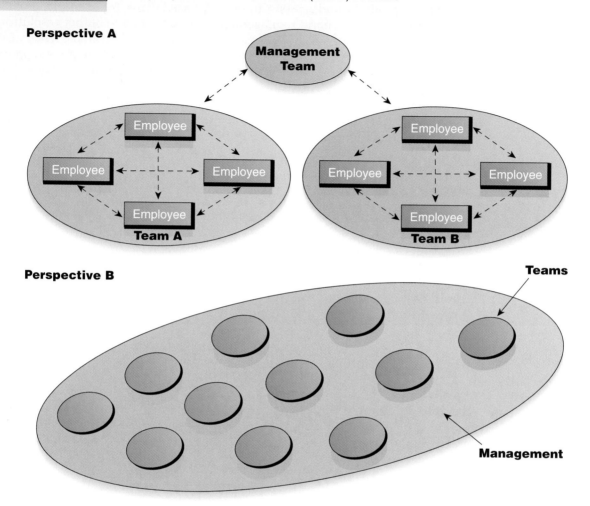

Perspective A

Perspective B

management levels. Harley-Davidson and other organizations delegate most supervisory activities to the team by having members take turns as the coordinator. Finally, this type of structure has very little formalization. Almost all day-to-day decisions are made by team members rather than someone farther up the organizational hierarchy. Teams are given relatively few rules about how to organize their work. Instead, the executive team typically assigns output goals to the team, such as the volume and quality of product or service, or productivity improvement targets for the work process. Teams are then encouraged to use available resources and their own initiative to achieve those objectives.

Team-based structures are usually found within the manufacturing operations of larger divisionalized structures. For example, aircraft components maker Pratt & Whitney has a divisionalized structure, but some of the manufacturing plants within those divisions have team-based organizational structures. Much less common are companies with a team-based structure from top to bottom. Flight Center is a unique example of this totally team-based organization. Global Connections 17.2 describes how this Brisbane, Australia–based travel agency organizes its global operations into teams based on the concepts of families, villages, and tribes.

Advantages and Disadvantages   The team-based organization represents an increasingly popular structure because it is usually responsive and flexible.[55] Teams empower employees and reduce reliance on a managerial hierarchy, thereby reducing costs. A cross-functional team structure improves communication and cooperation across traditional boundaries. With greater autonomy, this structure also allows quicker and more informed decision making.[56] Some hospitals have shifted from functional departments to cross-functional teams for this reason. Teams composed of nurses, radiologists, anesthetists, a pharmacology representative, and, possibly, social workers, a rehabilitation therapist, and other specialists communicate and coordinate more efficiently, therefore reducing delays and errors.[57]

One concern with team-based structures is that they can be costly to maintain because of the need for ongoing interpersonal skills training. Teamwork potentially takes more time to coordinate than formal hierarchy during the early stages of team development (see Chapter 8). Employees may experience more stress as a result of increased ambiguity in their roles. Team leaders also experience more stress because of increased conflict, loss of functional power, and unclear career progression ladders.[58]

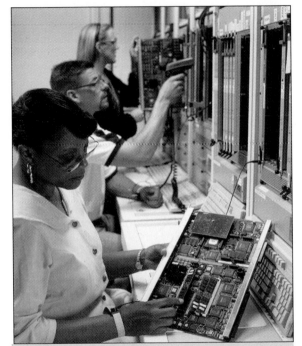

Jabil Circuits relies on a team organizational structure at its manufacturing operations in St. Petersburg, Florida, and Auburn Hills, Michigan. "Our manufacturing environment is team-oriented," says Jabil Circuits' operations manager in Michigan. "Employees are organized into teams of from three to 14 or 15 people." Each production team is responsible for a specific customer group. For example, one team makes circuit boards that go into car dashboards. Team members have a high degree of autonomy to stop production when they see quality problems. They are also cross-trained to perform several tasks so that they can cover for each other.[59] What advantages and potential problems might Jabil Circuits have with its team-based organizational structure? *(Courtesy of Jabil Circuits)*

Network Structures

To the outside world, Cisco Systems is one company. But the world's leading provider of business-to-business computer networks is mostly a constellation of suppliers, contract manufacturers, assemblers, and other partners connected through an intricate web of computer technology. Cisco's network springs into action as soon as a customer places an order (usually through the Internet). Suppliers send the required materials to assemblers, who ship the product directly to the client, usually the same day. Seventy percent of Cisco's product is outsourced this way. In many cases, Cisco employees never touch the product. "Partnerships are key to the new world strategies of the 21st century," says a Cisco senior vice president.

Tribal Organizing at Flight Center

Flight Center is a runaway success story in the travel industry. The Brisbane, Australia–based company has had eight straight years of profitability and at least 20 percent annual growth. In spite of its rapid growth, Flight Center has only three layers of hierarchy and provides consistent service at each of its approximately 600 travel shops in several countries.

What's the secret to Flight Center's success? According to chief executive and co-founder Graham Turner, Flight Center's unique "tribal" organizational structure facilitates easy replication and fuels organic growth. Each shop, as well as each administrative group, represents a "family" of three to seven people. Between 7 and 10 families in an area form a village with a village leader. Three or four villages form a tribal country, rather like a regional office. As a region (tribal country) becomes overpopulated with Flight Center families and villages, it splits into smaller countries. Tribal countries are part of tribes representing the various brands, such as Flight Center, Corporate Traveler, and Student Flights.

Flight Center is highly decentralized. Each tribal country (region) has control of its own recruitment, marketing, and training. Tribal countries also have the freedom to buy services from other Flight Center business units, or to buy holiday packages from outside wholesalers instead. Further decentralization occurs down to each Flight Center shop. The shop's team leader takes 10 percent of the shop's profit and may own up to 20 percent of the shop. The team structure is supported by

Flight Center has a team-based structure that organizes employees around families, villages, and tribes. *(AAP Image/Dave Hunt)*

a reward system in which the shop is its own profit center and employees take a share of those profits on top of their guaranteed base salary.

Sources: E. Johnston, "Elf Boys," *Boss Magazine,* June 8, 2001, p. 26; S. K. Witcher, "Flight Center Founder Prides Company on Being Deliberately Unconventional," *Wall Street Journal,* December 11, 2000, p. C15; J. Palmer, "Flight Center Has an Unusual Team Culture," *Business Day (South Africa),* April 20, 2000, p. 28; M. Massey, "Travel Agency Succeeds by Going Tribal," *Business Review Weekly,* March 22, 1999, p. 69.

---

network structure

An alliance of several organizations for the purpose of creating a product or serving a client.

"Partners collapse time because they allow you to take on more things and bring them together quicker."[60]

Cisco is an example of the **network structure.** A network structure (also known as a *modular structure*) is an alliance of several organizations for the purpose of creating a product or serving a client.[61] As Exhibit 17.6 illustrates, this collaborative structure typically consists of several satellite organizations beehived around a hub or core firm. The core firm coordinates the network process and provides one or two other core competencies, such as marketing or product development. For instance, Cisco mainly designs and markets new products. Nike, another network organization, mainly provides marketing expertise for its sports footwear and apparel.

The core firm might be the main contact with customers, but most of the product or service delivery and support activities are farmed out to satellite organizations which may be located anywhere in the world. Extranets (Web-based

EXHIBIT 17.6

A network structure

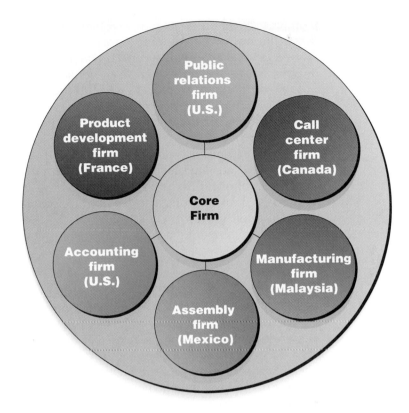

networks with partners) and other technologies ensure that information flows easily and openly between the core firm and its array of satellites. For instance, Nokia, the Finnish company, entered the U.S. video display market with only five employees. All the major tasks—marketing, sales, logistics, and technical support—were contracted out to specialists around the country. This diverse network was then connected through information technology to a common database.[62]

One of the main forces pushing toward a network structure is the recognition that an organization has only a few *core competencies*. A core competency is a knowledge base that resides throughout the organization and provides a strategic advantage. Exxon's core competency is its ability to distribute and market oil products. Most people think of Yahoo! as a search engine, but the Internet company's core competency is really Internet-based marketing. Yahoo! relies on Inktomi, a Web-based search engine to provide the technology.[63]

As companies discover their core competency, they outsource noncritical tasks to other organizations that have a core competency in performing those tasks. Many firms have outsourced information systems for this reason. Many also rely on independent sales agencies to provides sales support in certain territories. Several have their manufacturing done by outside firms, such as Solectron and Celestica. Each of these relations represents part of a network organization structure.[64]

affiliate networks
Network organizations where the satellite companies have a special affiliation with the core firm, such as investment or start-up support.

Affiliate Networks   Some network organizations are called **affiliate networks** because they have a special historical or financial affiliation with the core company. Affiliates may be former departments or divisions of the core firm that have been spun off to form independent businesses. Other affiliates are recent start-ups that receive financial support from the core firm. For example, Nortel Networks has an in-house incubator called the Business Ventures Group where employees develop their ideas to the point of being spun off into a separate company. In either case, affiliate networks have a special relationship with the core firm that distinguishes them from arm's-length network structures.[65]

Microsoft Corporation also provides start-up funding for several affiliate companies, such as Teledesic, a satellite-based telecommunications company. However, many affiliates were launched by former Microsoft employees with generous stock options earned at the software giant. These "Baby Bills" (named after Microsoft CEO Bill Gates) became affiliates by working with—rather than competing against—Microsoft on emerging technology.[66]

Virtual Corporations   The network structures that exist at Cisco Systems, Nortel Networks, Nike, Dell Computer, and other firms generally perform a patterned set of tasks for all clients. When you order a computer from Dell, the network partners follow the same set of transactions as for the next person who orders a computer. The specific computer configuration may change, but the relationships among the partners and the production process are fairly standardized until the partnership is reconfigured every few years.

In contrast, some network structures—known as **virtual corporations** (also called *cellular organizations*)—represent several independent companies that form unique partnership teams to provide customized products or services, usually to specific clients, for a limited time.[67] For example, several British and North American businesses in the marine technology industry have formed the NewSouth Alliance to compete for contracts larger than those each firm could manage alone. "By networking, smaller firms can act like a large firm, reduce costs, spread risk and compete more effectively," explains Clayton Burry, broker for NewSouth Alliance.[68]

Virtual corporations exist temporarily and reshape themselves quickly to fit immediate needs. When an opportunity emerges, a unique combination of partners in the alliance forms a virtual corporation that works on the assignment until it is completed. Virtual corporations are self-organizing, meaning that they rearrange their own communication patterns and roles to fit the situation. The relationship among the partners is mutually determined rather than imposed by a core firm.

> **virtual corporations**
>
> Network structures that represent several independent companies that form unique partnerships teams to provide customized products or services, usually to specific clients, for a limited time.

Advantages and Disadvantages   For several years, scholars have argued that organizational leaders must develop a metaphor of organizations as plasmalike organisms rather than rigid machines.[69] Network structures come close to the organism metaphor because they offer the flexibility to realign their structure with changing environmental requirements. If customers demand a new product or service, the core firm forms new alliances with other firms offering the appropriate resources. For example, by finding partners with available plant facilities, Cisco Systems expanded its business much

Five years ago, DRS Communications Company. took a bold step forward when it faced dramatic cutbacks in U.S. military spending. The Wyndmoor, Pennsylvania, producer of military communications equipment formed an alliance, called Agile Web, Inc., with 20 other small manufacturers in northeastern Pennsylvania. Agile Web forms a virtual corporation with some alliance members to bid on contracts that individual partners could not do alone. For example, DRS recently teamed up with Paramount Industries and Blue Mountain Structures to produce a forklift lever. Paramount provided the plastic handle, Blue Mountain fabricated the metal components, and DRS soldered and tested the switches. Over the past five years, DRS has participated in several dozen commercial contracts through Agile Web's virtual corporation structure.[71] How do these virtual corporations differ from the network structure that Cisco uses to manufacture and distribute its products? *(Gary Buss/ FPG International/Getty Images)*

more rapidly than if it had built its own production facilities. When Cisco's needs change, it isn't saddled with nonessential facilities and resources.

These virtual organizations also offer efficiencies because the core firm becomes globally competitive as it shops worldwide for subcontractors with the best people and the best technology at the best price. Indeed, the pressures of global competition have made network structures more vital, and computer-based information technology has made them possible.[70]

A potential disadvantage of network structures is that they expose the core firm to market forces. Other companies may bid up the price for subcontractors, whereas the short-term cost would be lower if the company hired its own employees to provide this function. Another problem is that although information technology makes worldwide communication much easier, it will never replace the degree of control organizations have when manufacturing, marketing, and other functions are in-house. The core firm can use arm's-length incentives and contract provisions to maintain the subcontractor's quality, but these actions are relatively crude compared with those used to maintain performance of in-house employees.

CONTINGENCIES OF ORGANIZATIONAL DESIGN

Organizational theorists and practitioners are interested not only in the elements of organizational structure but also in the contingencies that determine or influence the optimal design. In this section, we introduce four contingencies of organizational design: size, technology, environment, and strategy.

Organizational Size

Larger organizations have structures considerably different from those of smaller organizations.[72] As the number of employees increases, job specialization increases as a result of a greater division of labor. Larger firms also have more elaborate coordinating mechanisms to manage the greater division of labor. They are more likely to use standardization of work processes and outputs to coordinate work activities. These coordinating mechanisms create an administrative hierarchy and greater formalization. Informal communication has traditionally decreased as a coordinating mechanism as organizations get larger. However, emerging computer technologies and increased emphasis on empowerment have caused informal communication to regain its importance in large firms.[73]

Larger organizations also tend to be more decentralized. As we noted earlier in this chapter, neither founders nor senior managers have sufficient time or expertise to process all the decisions that significantly influence the business as it grows. Therefore, decision-making authority is pushed down to lower levels, where incumbents are able to cope with the narrower range of issues under their control.[74]

Technology

From the description of the open systems model (see Chapter 1), we know that an organization's structure needs to be aligned with its dominant technology. Two important technological contingencies that influence the best type of organizational structure are the variety and analyzability of work activities.[75] *Variety* refers to the number of exceptions to standard procedure that can occur in the team or work unit. *Analyzability* refers to the extent that the transformation of input resources to outputs can be reduced to a series of standardized steps.

Some jobs are routine, meaning that employees perform the same tasks all the time and rely on set rules (standard operating procedures) when exceptions do occur. Almost everything is predictable. These situations, such as automobile assembly lines, have high formalization and centralization as well as standardization of work processes. When employees perform tasks with high variety and low analyzability, they apply their skills to unique situations with little opportunity for repetition. Research project teams operate under these conditions. These situations call for an organic structure, one with low formalization, highly decentralized decision-making authority, and coordination mainly through informal communication among team members.

High variety and high analyzability tasks have many exceptions to routines, but these exceptions can usually be resolved through standard procedures. Maintenance groups and engineering design teams experience these conditions. Work units that fall into this category should use an organic structure, but it is possible to have somewhat greater formalization and centralization because of the analyzability of problems.

Skilled tradespeople tend to work in situations with low variety and low analyzability. Their tasks involve few exceptions, but the problems that arise are difficult to resolve. This situation allows more centralization and formalization than in a purely organic structure, but coordination must include informal communication among the skilled employees so that unique problems can be resolved.

External Environment

The best structure for an organization depends on its external environment. The external environment includes anything outside the organization, including most stakeholders (e.g., clients, suppliers, government), resources (e.g., raw materials, human resources, information, finances), and competitors. Four relatively distinct characteristics of external environments influence the type of organizational structure best suited to a particular situation: dynamism, complexity, diversity, and hostility.[76]

■ *Dynamic versus stable environments*—Dynamic environments have a high rate of change, leading to novel situations and a lack of identifiable patterns. Organic structures are better suited to this type of environment so that the organization can adapt more quickly to changes.[77] Network and team-based structures seem to be most effective in dynamic environments, because they usually have these features. In contrast, stable environments are characterized by regular cycles of activity and steady changes in supply and demand for inputs and outputs. Events are more predictable, enabling the firm to apply rules and procedures. Thus, more mechanistic structures tend to work best under these conditions.

■ *Complex versus simple environments*—Complex environments have many elements, whereas simple environments have few things to monitor. For instance, a multinational corporation has a complex environment because it has many stakeholders. Decentralized structures seem to be better suited to complex environments, because these subunits are close to their local environment and are able to make more informed choices.

■ *Diverse versus integrated environments*—Organizations located in diverse environments have a greater variety of products or services, clients, and regions. In contrast, an integrated environment has only one client, product, and geographic area. The more diversified the environment, the more the firm needs to use a divisionalized form aligned with that diversity. If the firm sells a single product around the world, a geographic divisionalized structure would align best with the firm's geographic diversity.

■ *Hostile versus munificent environments*—Firms located in a hostile environment face resource scarcity and more competition in the marketplace. Hostile environments are typically dynamic ones because they reduce the predictability of access to resources and demand for outputs. Organic structures tend to be best in hostile environments. However, when the environment is extremely hostile—such as a severe shortage of supplies or lower market share—organizations tend to centralize temporarily so that decisions can be made more quickly and executives feel more comfortable being in control.[78] Ironically, centralization may result in lower-quality decisions during organizational crises, because top management has less information, particularly when the environment is complex.

organizational strategy
The way an organization positions itself in its setting in relation to its stakeholders, given the organization's resources, capabilities, and mission.

Organizational Strategy

Although size, technology, and environment influence the optimal organizational structure, these contingencies do not necessarily determine structure. Instead, there is increasing evidence that corporate leaders formulate and implement strategies that shape both the characteristics of these contingencies as well as the organization's resulting structure. **Organizational strategy** refers to the way the organization positions itself in its setting in relation to its stakeholders, given the organization's resources, capabilities, and mission.[79] The idea that an organization interacts with its environment rather than being totally determined by it is known as **strategic choice**.[80] In other words, organizational leaders take steps to define and manipulate their environments, rather than let the organization's fate be determined entirely by external influences.

The notion of strategic choice can be traced back to the work of Alfred Chandler in the early 1960s.[81] Chandler's proposal was that structure follows strategy. He observed that organizational structures follow the growth strategy developed by the organization's decision makers. Moreover, he noted that organizational structures change only after decision makers decide to do so. This recognizes that the link between structure and the contingency factors described earlier is mediated by organizational strategy.

Chandler's thesis that structure follows strategy has become the dominant perspective of business policy and strategic management. An important aspect of this view is that organizations can choose the environments in which they want to operate. Some businesses adopt a *differentiation strategy* by bringing unique products to the market or attracting clients who want customized goods and services. They try to distinguish their outputs from those provided by other firms through marketing, provision of special services, and innovation. Others adopt a cost leadership strategy, in which they maximize productivity and thereby are able to offer popular products or services at a competitive price.[82]

The type of organizational strategy selected leads to the best organizational structure to adopt.[83] Organizations with a cost leadership strategy should adopt a mechanistic, functional structure with high levels of job specialization and standardized work processes. A differentiation strategy, on the other hand, requires more customized relations with clients. A matrix or team-based structure with less centralization and formalization is most appropriate here so that technical specialists are able to coordinate their work activities more closely with the client's needs. Overall, it is now apparent that organizational structure is influenced by size, technology, and environment, but the organization's strategy may reshape these elements and loosen their connection to organizational structure.

CHAPTER SUMMARY

Organizational structure refers to the division of labor as well as the patterns of coordination, communication, work flow, and formal power that direct organizational activities. All organizational structures divide labor into distinct tasks and coordinate that labor to accomplish common goals. The primary means of coordination are informal communication, formal hierarchy, and standardization.

The four basic elements of organizational structure are span of control, centralization, formalization, and departmentalization. At one time, scholars suggested that firms should have a tall hierarchy with a narrow span of control. Today, most organizations have the opposite because they rely on informal communication and standardization, rather than direct supervision, to coordinate work processes.

Centralization means that formal decision-making authority is held by a small group of people, typically senior executives. Many companies decentralize as they become larger and more complex because senior executives lack the necessary time and expertise to process all the decisions that significantly influence the business. Companies also tend to become more formalized over time because work activities become routinized. Formalization increases in larger firms because standardization works more efficiently than informal communications and direct supervision.

A functional structure organizes employees around specific knowledge or other resources. This structure fosters greater specialization and improves direct supervision, but makes it more difficult for people to see the organization's larger picture or to coordinate across departments. A divisional structure groups employees around geographic areas, clients, or outputs. This structure accommodates growth and focuses employee attention on products or customers rather than tasks. However, this structure creates silos of knowledge and duplication of resources.

The matrix structure combines two structures to leverage the benefits of both types of structure. However, this approach requires more coordination than functional or pure divisional structures, may dilute accountability, and increases conflict.

Another form of departmentalization is the team-based structure. This structure is very flat, has low formalization, and organizes self-directed teams around work processes rather than functional specialties.

A network structure is an alliance of several organizations for the purpose of creating a product or serving a client. Virtual corporations are network structures that can quickly reorganize themselves to suit the client's requirements.

The best organizational structure depends on the firm's size, technology, and environment. Generally, larger organizations are decentralized and more formalized, with greater job specialization and elaborate coordinating mechanisms. The work unit's technology—including variety of work and analyzability of problems—influences the decision to adopt either an organic or a mechanistic structure. Also necessary to consider is whether the external environment is dynamic, complex, diverse, or hostile.

Although size, technology, and environment influence the optimal organizational structure, these contingencies do not necessarily determine structure. Rather, organizational leaders formulate and implement strategies to define and manipulate their environments. These strategies, rather than the other contingencies, directly shape the organization's structure.

KEY TERMS

affiliate networks, p. 525
centralization, p. 512
concurrent engineering, p. 507
divisional structure, p. 517
formalization, p. 513
functional structure, p. 516

matrix structure, p. 519
mechanistic structure, p. 514
network structure, p. 524
organic structure, p. 514
organizational design, p. 506
organizational strategy, p. 529

organizational structure, p. 514
span of control, p. 510
strategic choice, p. 530
team-based organizational structure, p. 521
virtual corporations, p. 526

DISCUSSION QUESTIONS

1. Why are organizations moving toward flatter structures?
2. Diversified Technologies, Inc. (DTI) makes four types of products, each type to be sold to different types of clients. For example, one product is sold exclusively to automobile repair shops, whereas another is used mainly in hospitals. Customer expectations and needs are surprisingly similar throughout the world. However, the company has separate marketing, product design, and manufacturing facilities in North America, Europe, Asia, and South America because, until recently, each jurisdiction had unique regulations governing the production and sales of these products. However, several governments have begun the process of deregulating the products that DTI designs and manufactures, and trade agreements have opened several markets to foreign-made products. Which form of departmentalization

might be best for DTI if deregulation and trade agreements occur?
3. Why don't all organizations group people around geographic-based divisions?
4. Several global organizations have tried implementing a matrix structure to balance the power of their functional and divisional groups. However, many of these firms experienced problems and eventually switched to a hybrid form of divisionalized structure. Identify some of the problems that these companies may have experienced with a matrix structure.
5. Flight Center has a team-based structure from top to bottom. Is this typical? Could such a structure exist at IBM or Intel?
6. Some writers believe that a network structure is an effective design for global competition. Is this true, or are there situations where this organizational structure may be inappropriate?

7. Suppose that you have been hired as a consultant to diagnose the environmental characteristics of your college. How would you describe the college's external environment? Is the college's existing structure appropriate for this environment?

8. What is meant by the expression "structure follows strategy"?

THE RISE AND FALL OF PMC AG

Founded in 1930, PMC AG is a German manufacturer of high-priced sports cars. During the early years, PMC was a small consulting engineering firm that specialized in solving difficult automotive design problems for clients. At the end of World War II, however, the son of PMC's founder decided to expand the business beyond consulting engineering. He was determined that PMC would build its own precision automobiles.

In 1948, the first PMC prototypes rolled out of the small manufacturing facility. Each was handmade by highly skilled craftspeople. For several years, the engine and other parts were designed and built by other companies and assembled at the PMC plant. By the 1960s, however, PMC had begun to design and build its own parts.

PMC grew rapidly during the 1960s to mid-1980s. The company designed a completely new car in the early 1960s, launched a lower-priced model in 1970, and added a mid-priced model in 1977. By the mid-1980s, PMC had become very profitable as its name became an icon for wealthy entrepreneurs and jet-setters. In 1986, the year of highest production, PMC sold 54,000 cars. Nearly two-thirds of these were sold in North America.

PMC's Structure

PMC's organizational structure expanded with its success. During the early years, the company consisted of only an engineering department and a production department. By the 1980s, employees were divided into more than 10 functional departments representing different stages of the production process as well as upstream (e.g., design, purchasing) and downstream (e.g., quality control, marketing) activities. Employees worked exclusively in one department. It was almost considered treason for an employee to move voluntarily into another department.

PMC's production staff were organized into a traditional hierarchy. Frontline employees reported to work group leaders, who reported to supervisors, who reported to group supervisors in each area. Group supervisors reported to production managers, who reported to production directors, who reported to PMC's executive vice president of manufacturing. At one point, nearly 20 percent of production staff members were involved in supervisory tasks. In the early 1990s, for example, there were 48 group supervisors, 96 supervisors, and 162 work group leaders supervising about 2,500 frontline production employees.

PMC's Craft Tradition

PMC had a long tradition and culture that supported craft expertise. This set of values appealed to Germany's skilled workforce because it gave employees an opportunity to test and further develop their skills. PMC workers were encouraged to master long work cycles, often as much as 15 minutes per unit. Their ideal was to build as much of the automobile as possible alone. For example, a few masters were able to assemble an entire engine. Their reward was to personally sign their name on the completed component.

The design engineers worked independently of the production department, with the result that production employees had to adjust designs to fit the available parts. Rather than being a nuisance, the production employees viewed this situation as a challenge that would further test their well-developed craft skills. Similarly, manufacturing engineers occasionally redesigned the product to fit manufacturing capabilities.

To improve efficiency, the company introduced a moving track assembly system in 1977. Even then, the emphasis on craft skills was apparent. Employees were encouraged to put all the parts on the car quickly, knowing that highly skilled troubleshooting craftspeople would discover and repair defects after the car came off the line. This approach was much more costly and time-consuming than assembling the vehicle correctly the first time, but it provided yet another challenging set of tasks for skilled craftspeople. And as a result, PMC vehicles were known for their few defects by the time they were sold to customers.

The End of Success?

PMC sports cars filled a small niche in the automobile market for those who wanted a true sports car just tame enough for everyday use. PMCs were known for their superlative performance based on excellent engineering technology, but they were also becoming very expensive. Although Japanese sports cars were not quite in the same league as a PMC, the cost of manufacturing the Japanese vehicles was a small fraction of the cost of manufacturing a vehicle at PMC.

This cost inefficiency hit PMC's sales during the late 1980s and early 1990s. First, the German currency appreciated against the U.S. dollar, which made PMC sports cars even more expensive in the North American market. By 1990, PMC was selling half the number of cars it had sold just four years earlier. Then the North American recession hit, driving PMC sales down further. In 1993, PMC sold just 14,000 vehicles, compared with 54,000 in 1987. And although sales rebounded to 20,000 by 1995, the high price tag put PMCs out of reach of many potential customers. It was clear to PMC's founding family that changes were needed, but they weren't sure where to begin.

Discussion Questions

1. Describe PMC's organizational structure in terms of the four organizational design features (i.e., span of control, centralization, formalization, and departmentalization).

2. Discuss the problems with PMC's current structure.

3. Identify and justify an organizational structure that, in your opinion, would be more appropriate for PMC.

Source: Written by Steven L. McShane based on information from several sources about "PMC." The company name and some details of actual events have been altered to provide a fuller case discussion.

CASE STUDY 17.2

CLICKING AT GRAYBAR

BusinessWeek   Sometimes the solution to performance problems begins with an organization's structure and design. Realigning the structure can help employees focus on the most important objectives. That was the way Graybar Electric Company's management set out to improve sales and profits. Graybar distributes communications and electrical products to big customers such as telephone companies.

When e-commerce stimulated a surge in demand, Graybar struggled to fill orders quickly and efficiently, so the company created a more centralized distribution system.

This *Business Week* case study describes the changes in Graybar's distribution system. Along with details about the new organizational structure, the article discusses the reasons for the change and the impact on Graybar's organizational culture. Read through this *Business Week* case study at www.mhhe.com/mcshane2e and prepare for the discussion questions below.

Discussion Questions

1. What changes to Graybar's organizational structure do the authors describe? Do the changes make Graybar's structure more organic or more mechanistic?

2. How appropriate are these changes in view of Graybar's technology, external environment, and business strategy?

3. In making this change in the organization's design, what other aspects of organizational behavior are Graybar's managers considering (or should they consider)?

Source: F. Keenan and T. J. Mullaney, "Clicking at Graybar," *Business Week*, June 18, 2001.

TEAM EXERCISE 17.3

ORGANIZATIONAL STRUCTURE AND DESIGN: THE CLUB ED EXERCISE

By Cheryl Harvey and Kim Morouney, Wilfrid Laurier University

Purpose This exercise is designed to help you understand the issues to consider when designing organizations at various stages of growth.

Materials Each student team should have enough overhead transparencies or flip chart sheets to display several organizational charts.

Instructions Each team will discuss several scenarios. The first scenario appears below. The instructor will facilitate discussion and advise teams when to begin the next step. This exercise may be continued over two class sessions.

■ *Step 1*—Students are placed in teams (typically of four or five people).
■ *Step 2*—After reading scenario 1, each team will design an organizational chart (departmentalization) that is most appropriate for this situation. Students should be able to describe the type of structure drawn and explain why it is appropriate. The structure should be drawn on an overhead transparency or flip chart for others to see during later class discussion. The instructor will set a fixed time (e.g., 15 minutes) to complete this task.

Scenario 1—Determined never to shovel snow again, you are establishing a new resort business on a small Caribbean island. The resort is under construction and is scheduled to open one year from now. You decide it is time to draw up an organizational chart for this new venture, called Club Ed.

■ *Step 3*—At the end of the time allowed, the instructor will present scenario 2, and each team will be asked to draw another organizational chart to suit that situation. Again, students should be able to describe the type of structure drawn and explain why it is appropriate.
■ *Step 4*—At the end of the time allowed, the instructor will present scenario 3, and each team will be asked to draw another organizational chart to suit that situation.
■ *Step 5*—Depending on the time available, the instructor might present a fourth scenario. The teams will gather to present their designs for each scenario. During each presentation, teams should describe the type of structure drawn and explain why it is appropriate.

Source: Adapted from C. Harvey and K. Morouney, *Journal of Management Education* 22 (June 1998), pp. 425–29. Used with permission of the authors.

IDENTIFYING YOUR PREFERRED ORGANIZATIONAL STRUCTURE

Purpose This self-assessment exercise is designed to help you understand how an organization's structure influences the personal needs and values of people working in that structure.

Instructions Personal values influence how comfortable you are working in different organizational structures. You might prefer an organization with clearly defined rules or one with no rules at all. You might prefer a firm where almost any employee can make important decisions or one where important decisions are screened by senior executives. Read each statement below and indicate the extent to which you would like to work in an organization with that characteristic. When finished, use the scoring key in Appendix B to calculate your results. This self-assessment exercise is completed alone so that students will complete the exercise honestly without concerns of social comparison. However, class discussion will focus on the elements of organizational design and their relationship to personal needs and values.

Organizational structure preference scale					
I would like to work in an organization where . . .	Not at all	A little	Some-what	Very much	Score
1. A person's career ladder has several steps toward higher status and responsibility.	0	1	2	3	_____
2. Employees perform their work with few rules to limit their discretion.	0	1	2	3	_____
3. Responsibility is pushed down to employees who perform the work.	0	1	2	3	_____
4. Supervisors have few employees, so they work closely with each person.	0	1	2	3	_____
5. Senior executives make most decisions to ensure that the company is consistent in its actions.	0	1	2	3	_____
6. Jobs are clearly defined so that there is no confusion over who is responsible for various tasks.	0	1	2	3	_____
7. Employees have their say on issues, but senior executives make most of the decisions.	0	1	2	3	_____
8. Job descriptions are broadly stated or nonexistent.	0	1	2	3	_____
9. Everyone's work is tightly synchronized around top management operating plans.	0	1	2	3	_____
10. Most work is performed in teams without close supervision.	0	1	2	3	_____
11. Work gets done through informal discussion with co-workers rather than through formal rules.	0	1	2	3	_____
12. Supervisors have so many employees that they can't watch anyone very closely.	0	1	2	3	_____
13. Everyone has clearly understood goals, expectations, and job duties.	0	1	2	3	_____

—continued

Organizational structure preference scale—*cont.*					
I would like to work in an organization where . . .	Not at all	A little	Some-what	Very much	Score
14. Senior executives assign overall goals but leave daily decisions to frontline teams.	0	1	2	3	_____
15. Even in a large company, the CEO is only three or four levels above the lowest position.	0	1	2	3	_____

After studying the preceding material, be sure to check out our website at

www.mhhe.com/mcshane2e

for more in-depth information and interactivities that correspond to this chapter.

18

Employment Relationship and Career Dynamics

AFTER READING THIS CHAPTER, YOU SHOULD BE ABLE TO:

- Discuss the different types of psychological contracts.

- Identify three types of trust in organizational settings.

- Discuss the employment trends of employability and contingent work.

- Discuss the two primary functions of organizational socialization.

- Describe the stages of organizational socialization.

- Explain how realistic job previews and socialization agents assist the socialization process.

- Describe the main features of Holland's theory of occupational choice.

- Identify three conditions that would encourage lateral career development.

- Explain why boundaryless careers have become more common.

- List five strategies that assist personal career development.

A few years ago, Dan Schmitt worked as operations manager at the Richmond Coliseum. He then jumped over to Interim Services Inc. selling temporary labor, then moved on to a job as marketing manager at the Richmond Athletic Club. Schmitt also picked up some freelance work, providing various services for special entertainment events. Schmitt's career path might look messy, but the pieces fell into place when he launched RMC Events Inc., a Richmond, Virginia–based entertainment events security firm.

"I sold temporary labor at Interim, so I had the staffing experience, and I had the sports-entertainment-business background from the Coliseum, so I started thinking, 'Why can't I combine them?'" Schmitt explains. As founder and head of RMC Events, Schmitt has also found work that matches his needs and values. "I love what I do now," says Schmitt, whose company employs over 200 contract staff. "I wake up every day and am thrilled to do what I do."

Unlike Dan Schmitt, Rich Preziotti has worked for one employer, Honeywell, since graduating from business school a decade ago. But his career is also quite different from that of the "company man" of yesteryear. Starting as a financial analyst, Preziotti has moved through seven diverse jobs in which he mastered various chemicals, engineered turnarounds, moved overseas and back, sat on a board, negotiated acquisitions, and handled major customers.

Today, as vice president of a $450-million-a-year specialty waxes division, Preziotti has an employment relationship with Honeywell

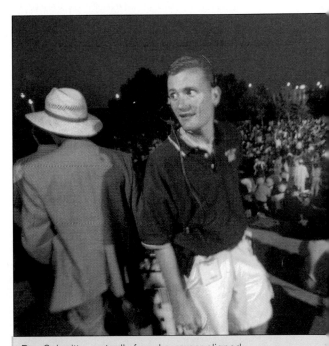

Dan Schmitt eventually found a career aligned with his needs and values as founder and head of Richmond, Virginia–based entertainment security firm RMC Events Inc. *(D. Hoffmeyer/ Richmond Times-Dispatch)*

that is also quite different from the job-for-life guarantee of the past. His long-term employment depends on how well he keeps his competencies up-to-date, not on his loyalty to Honeywell. "The employer–employee contract that used to exist 25 years ago doesn't exist today," Preziotti warns. "It's too competitive a work environment."[1] ■

Dan Schmitt and Rich Preziotti reflect the divergent realities of employment relationships and career dynamics in today's workforce. Schmitt has followed a boundaryless career, picking up valuable skills that he eventually leveraged into his own business. Preziotti's career path looks more traditional, but only because Honeywell has been able to replicate the career challenges of a free agent within the organization. Preziotti's employment relationship is also more characteristic of the "new deal" that replaces the old job-for-life guarantee.[2] To some extent, Schmitt's and Preziotti's career experiences are more similar than they first appear.

This chapter begins by looking at the most fundamental element of the employment relationship: the psychological contract. We consider the types of contracts, the ways contracts change, the importance of trust in employment relationships, and the dynamics of contingent work. Next, this chapter examines the process of employee socialization, including the stages of socialization and specific socialization strategies. We then turn to the topic of career development, including Holland's model of occupational choice, as well as the emerging trends toward lateral and boundaryless career development. This chapter closes with an overview of specific strategies to guide your career development.

THE PSYCHOLOGICAL CONTRACT

Karl Morris once believed that organizations would repay hard work and loyalty with long-term employment. Not any more. The manager at Quokka Sports lost his job when the San Francisco pioneer in Internet-based sports programming filed for bankruptcy. "I had a reputation I would sacrifice . . . anything [for Quokka]," says Morris. "I'd run through the fire for these guys, and they shot me down." Soon after, Morris landed a consulting job at Broadchoice, a Web graphics and media company. "We thought Karl would work 90 days as a contractor at Broadchoice and then be full-time," says Morris's wife. It didn't work out that way. Morris was laid off just four weeks into his job with Broadchoice.[3]

Karl Morris experienced the shock of having his psychological contract violated. This situation isn't unusual. According to one university study, 24 percent of employees are "chronically" angry at work, mostly because they felt their employer violated basic promises and didn't fulfill the psychological contract.[4] The **psychological contract** refers to the individual's beliefs about the terms and conditions of a reciprocal exchange agreement between that person and another party.[5] This contract is inherently perceptual, so one person's understanding of the psychological contract may differ from the other party's understanding. In employment relationships, psychological contracts consist of beliefs about what the employee is entitled to receive and is obliged to offer the employer in return. For example, Karl Morris believed that his hard work and loyalty at Quokka would result in long-term employment. He also assumed that his contract with Broadchoice would eventually turn into an offer of full-time employment.[6]

Everyone has a unique psychological contract, but one British study has found some common elements. Specifically, employers expect employees to work contracted hours, perform quality work, deal honestly with clients, guard the organization's reputation, treat property carefully, dress and behave cor-

psychological contract

The individual's beliefs about the terms and conditions of a reciprocal exchange agreement between that person and another party.

rectly, and engage in some organizational citizenship. The psychological contract for most British employees emphasizes fairness in decisions (e.g., selection, promotion, and layoffs), the application of rules, and allocation of pay and benefits. Employees also expect enough personal time off, consultation on matters affecting them, minimal interference in how they do their job, supportive leadership, reward for long service and good performance, a safe work environment, and as much job security as the organization can reasonably provide.[7]

Types of Psychological Contracts

Psychological contracts vary in many ways. One of the most fundamental differences is the extent to which they are transactional or relational.[8] As Exhibit 18.1 describes, *transactional contracts* are primarily short-term economic exchanges. Responsibilities are well defined around a fairly narrow set of obligations that do not change over the life of the contract. People hired in temporary positions and as consultants tend to have transactional contracts. To some extent, new employees also form transactional contracts until they develop a sense of continuity with the organization.

Relational contracts, on the other hand, are rather like marriages; they are long-term attachments that encompass a broad array of subjective mutual obligations. Employees with a relational psychological contract are more willing to contribute their time and effort without expecting the organization to pay back this debt in the short term. Relational contracts are also dynamic, meaning that the parties tolerate and expect that mutual obligations are not necessarily balanced in the short run. Not surprisingly, organizational citizenship behaviors are more likely to prevail under relational than transactional contracts. Permanent employees are more likely to believe they have a relational contract.

EXHIBIT 18.1 Types of psychological contracts in employment	Contract characteristics	Transactional contracts	Relational contracts
	Focus	Economic	Economic and socioemotional
	Time frame	Closed-ended and short-term	Open-ended and indefinite
	Stability	Static	Dynamic
	Scope	Narrow	Pervasive
	Tangibility	Well-defined	More subjective

Source: Based on information in D. M. Rousseau and J. M. Parks, "The Contracts of Individuals and Organizations," *Research in Organizational Behavior* 15 (1993), pp. 1–43.

Psychological Contracts across Cultures

Psychological contracts are influenced by the social contexts in which the contracting process occurs.[9] Organizations maintain their status as good corporate citizens by recognizing and applying the prevailing social norms. In other words, psychological contracts vary across cultures, and employers must align their employment expectations with those societal norms.

For instance, employees in low power distance cultures (such as the United States) are less likely than employees in high power distance cultures (such as Singapore or Mexico) to accept arbitrary commands from their supervisors. Taking an afternoon siesta is a cultural norm (although quickly disappearing) in Spain, so this norm is embedded in most psychological contracts in that country.[10] Mexicans generally assume that organizations in their society have a strong obligation to provide "life, health, dignity and liberty." Overall, we must be sensitive to cultural differences in the psychological contracting process as well as interpretations and assumptions about the content of those contracts.

Trust and the Psychological Contract

Any relationship—including an employment relationship—depends on a certain degree of trust between the parties.[11] Trust occurs when we have positive expectations about another party's intentions and actions toward us in risky situations (see Chapter 4). A high level of trust occurs when the other party's actions affect you in situations where you are vulnerable, but you believe they will not adversely affect your needs.

There are many trust relationships in organizations.[12] Employees learn to trust their co-workers, team leaders, and subordinates, as well as representatives from suppliers and customers. Organizational behavior scholars also refer to *institutional trust,* which is the employee's trust of the organization's CEO and top management. Along with relationships involving whom to trust, there are three types of trust, each representing a different level and form of relationship.[13]

■ *Calculus-based trust,* the minimal level of trust, refers to an expected consistency of behavior based on deterrence. Each party believes that the other will deliver on its promises because punishments will be administered if they fail. For example, most of us trust our employer enough to expect a paycheck at the end of the work period because we believe the company will face government sanctions if payment isn't received.

■ *Knowledge-based trust* is grounded in the other party's predictability. This predictability develops from meaningful communication and experience with the other party. The better you know senior management's past actions, the more accurately you can predict what they will do in the future. Similarly, the more consistent the leader's behavior—the more he or she "walks the talk"— the more employees are willing to trust that person.[14]

■ *Identification-based trust* is based on mutual understanding and an emotional bond between the parties. Identification occurs when one party thinks like, feels like, and responds like the other party. High-performance teams exhibit this level of trust. To some extent, employees can have a high level of identification-based trust in organizations with strong cultures. By identifying

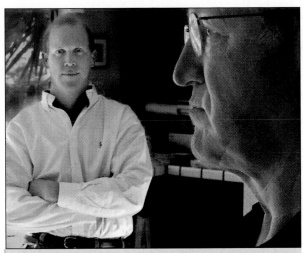

Terry Akre (right) put in 37 years as a technician at AT&T, waking up at 5:30 A.M. each day to be on the job by 7:30. Then he was laid off without any warning. Terry's son Daniel (left), who was 18 at the time, vowed never to let that happen to him. "I said then and there, I'm going to 'employ' my employers," Daniel recalls. So Daniel, a top-performing salesman, has worked for seven employers since graduating from college a dozen years ago. Each job hop resulted in higher pay or more challenging work.[15] How does Daniel Akre's psychological contract differ from his father's? What level of trust do you think he has with his employer compared with the trust his father had in AT&T? *(Kat Wade/*San Francisco Chronicle*)*

with the company's dominant values, employees understand what to expect and what is expected of them.

Calculus-based trust is the weakest of the three because it is easily broken by a violation of expectations and the subsequent application of sanctions against the violating party. It is difficult to develop a strong level of trust based on the threat of punishment if one party fails to deliver its promises. Generally, calculus-based trust alone cannot sustain a relational type of psychological contract.

Knowledge-based trust is more stable than calculus-based trust because it is developed over time. Suppose an employer hires someone from outside the company rather than promoting from within, as it almost always did in the past. A trusting employee "knows" that this is probably an exception because it deviates from the employer's past actions. Identification-based trust is the most robust of all three. Because the individual identifies with the organization (or any other party), he or she is more likely to forgive transgressions. Moreover, the individual is reluctant to acknowledge a violation of this high-level trust because it strikes at the heart of her or his self-image.

Trust is important in the employment relationship because it affects the type of psychological contract. When employees experience psychological contract violations, they lose trust in the employer and are less likely to engage in organizational citizenship behaviors.[16] If violations continue, the loss of trust shifts the employee's psychological contract from open and dynamic to precise and static. In other words, loss of trust moves the psychological contract from relational to transactional.

TRENDS IN EMPLOYMENT RELATIONSHIPS

Trust is critical during changing times, and few things are changing more rapidly than employment relationships. People with relational psychological contracts tolerate some change as a normal part of the employment relationship. The parties believe the original contract is still in place and has minor additions or modifications. How much change can occur to the original contract, yet still maintain this sense of continuity? The answer depends on the flexibility of the employer and employee, which is largely determined by the degree of trust between them.[17]

Some employment relationships are changing so radically that they move beyond the boundaries of relational contracts. These transformations occur when one party—usually the employer—wants to significantly change the employee's expectations regarding rewards, career development, corporate culture, or other important elements of the employment relationship. Over the next few pages, we look at two trends in employment relationships: employability and contingent work.

From Security to Employability

The most dramatic transition in recent years is the shift away from a psychological contract that emphasizes job security in return for loyalty. The old contract established the expectation that if you are loyal to the company, the company will be loyal to you by providing job security and managing your career development.[18] Many employees could expect lifelong career progression through the ranks with ever-increasing salaries. Although this paternalistic contract didn't exist for everyone, it was considered the norm for most knowledge-based workers.

The emerging psychological contract is employability, whereby employees must take responsibility for their own careers by continually developing new competencies for future work opportunities within and beyond the organization (see Chapter 1). In this new deal, jobs are temporary events and organizations are no longer perceived as paternalistic institutions that take care of their employees. Rather, organizations are customers, and employees keep their jobs by continuing to offer valuable skills and knowledge to their clients. From this perspective, individuals must anticipate future organizational needs and develop new competencies accordingly.[19]

Consider Rich Preziotti's employment relationship with Honeywell, described in the opening vignette in this chapter. Preziotti may have an increasingly rare career with one company, but his long-term employment depends on continually developing his competencies. "Employees are developing the view that their only job security in the future must be based on their ability and their competence, and not on keeping a job at some particular company," says Gary L. Howard, Motorola vice president. Career consultant Barbara Moses agrees with that assessment. "Today's career emphasizes self-reliance," she says. Moses suggests that career security (not job security) originates with the individual's self-confidence and proactive effort to keep pace with changing organizational needs.[20]

Permanence of Employability   Some people might argue that the pendulum will swing from employability back to job security as low unemployment gives employees enough power to push for more job guarantees. After all, employability began in the early 1990s when unemployment rates were high and companies could demand more favorable employment relationships. With low unemployment, won't employees demand those job guarantees again?

So far, the evidence suggests that low unemployment might increase job security somewhat, but other factors will tend to preserve the psychological contracts of employability. One important factor is increasing turbulence in the business environment. Global competition, deregulation, and information technologies have made it difficult for employers to provide the job security that was possible in more stable conditions. Organizations need employability to remain flexible and adaptive.

Another factor is changing employee expectations. Some scholars suggest that job security has less value to Generation-X and Generation-Y employees

Japan's New Psychological Contract

Ogura Junpei is looking for a job after graduating from Japan's Keio University. But he isn't interested in a career with one of the traditional job-for-life Japanese companies. Instead, Ogura-san has found more challenging work and better pay at a consulting firm and a foreign investment bank. "I'm not just looking for a job," explains Ogura-san, "but a place where I find it worthwhile to work."

Japan's well-known psychological contract—lifetime employment, steady advancement, and seniority-based pay increases—is starting to fall apart. One reason is that Japan's long recession has forced Honda, Sony, NEC, and other major corporations to introduce performance-based relationships, which weaken job security guarantees. The other reason is that many younger Japanese employees want challenging work and better pay now, not after waiting a decade or more. "I'm suffocating from the rigid seniority system in my office," complains a young electronics engineer with a major Japanese company.

Not every young Japanese employee is abandoning the lifetime employment relationship. "Lifelong employment is suitable to the Japanese character," explains Kentaro Takahashi, a 23-year-old engineering graduate. "From long ago, people donated their whole lives to the company. So we should give our full support to our new firm."

Still, Takahashi's psychological contract is becoming the exception. One recent survey revealed that 80 percent of Japanese employees in their twenties strongly intend to switch jobs within the next 10 years. Further proof was the recent turnout of hundreds of job seekers at one of Japan's first international job fairs where more than 50 foreign firms were recruiting. "The young urban Japan is already voting for change with their careers," says Kenneth Courtis, strategist and chief economist at Deutsche Bank Group in Tokyo.

Sources: J-I. Lee, "Recent Exodus of Core Human Resources Disturbing Trend for Domestic Companies," *Korea Herald,* May 14, 2001; "Trend of Caring for Employees Waning among Japan's Companies," *Japan Weekly Monitor,* May 7, 2001; M. Zielenziger, "The Fading Salary Man," *National Post,* April 5, 2000, p. C15; M. Mutsuko, "Who Needs Life Employment?" *AsiaWeek,* March 17, 2000; B. McKenna, "Restructuring Fever Sweeps Japan," *Globe and Mail,* May 29, 1999.

than to baby boomers. Workforce newcomers have experienced a psychological contract based mainly on employability and are comfortable with minimal employment guarantees.[21] In fact, younger employees say the old psychological contract would be stifling—rather like serving time—because it offers less opportunity to steer one's career through personal achievement. "My friends today, they're on their fourth or fifth company," says a thirty-something Walgreen district manager in Tucson. "People are more willing to change jobs. My generation is the 'me' generation—instant gratification and how fast can I get ahead."[22]

Of course, we can't say that all Gen-X or Gen-Y employees want the new deal psychological contract, but they seem to be more comfortable with the career risks and opportunities offered by employability. Thus, in spite of an economic downturn, over half of American employees are either actively looking for another job or continually scanning the job market for better opportunities.[23] This trend is also apparent in Japan, traditionally a stalwart of company loyalty and lifetime employment. Global Connections 18.1 describes how some recent Japanese university graduates prefer challenging work and performance-based pay over lifelong employment.

Contingent Work

The world's largest employer isn't General Motors or IBM. It's Manpower Inc., a temporary services agency that provides contingent workers in almost any

contingent work
Any job in which the individual does not have an explicit or implicit contract for long-term employment, or one in which the minimum hours of work can vary in a nonsystematic way.

occupation a company would want. Manpower annually provides 2 million temps to over 250,000 employers around the globe.[24] Manpower is riding the trend toward a contingent workforce. **Contingent work** is any job in which the individual does not have an explicit or implicit contract for long-term employment, or one in which the minimum hours of work can vary in a nonsystematic way.[25]

The contingent workforce includes employees with a fixed-term contract or those who work for a client organization through an employment agency. It also includes self-employed individuals who contract their services directly to organizations. Contingent work excludes permanent part-time employees because their employment is stable and long-term. However, it does include on-call part-timers because their work hours can vary considerably from one month to the next.

How many people are in the contingent workforce? No one agrees on the answer. The U.S. Bureau of Labor Statistics estimates that 6 million people—about 5 percent of the labor force—are in "alternative work arrangements."[26] However, this number excludes on-call part-time staff and leased employees (those who work in one organization but are employed by another), and may underestimate the number of temporary and subcontracted workers. Other studies estimate that contingent workers represent up to one-quarter of the U.S. workforce. The correct number is probably somewhere in between. However, we do know that temporary workers are the fastest-growing segment of the nonpermanent workforce. Today, 91 percent of U.S. companies use some form of temporary help. This trend is growing even more quickly in Europe, where labor laws make it difficult to lay off or fire permanent employees.[27]

Types of Contingent Workers   Exhibit 18.2 illustrates the three main types of contingent workers based on their motivation and ability to find permanent

EXHIBIT 18.2

Types of contingent workers

Note: Those who want permanent employment and have high-demand skills are shown in parentheses because they tend to leave the contingent workforce quickly.

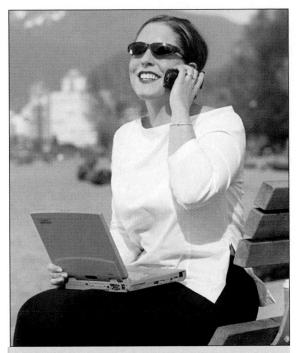

Adina Trowhill Smith describes herself as a "virtual assistant." Her company, North American Exec-Works, provides administrative support to people who are starting their own businesses or need extra help on quick notice. "A lot of people just starting out their own business want someone on call, but they can't afford, or don't need, a full-time administrative assistant, so they come to me," explains Smith, who lives in Vancouver, Canada. Smith fell into the job almost by accident. "I quit my old job and started looking around, but I couldn't find anything I was interested in, so I started thinking about what I could do," she says. That's when Smith discovered a large demand for virtual assistants. "I had no idea I would do so well," Smith admits. She also admits appreciating the flexibility of scheduling and working at home that her new career offers.[30] What factors affect the job satisfaction of free agents such as Adina Trowhill? *(Rob Kruyt/ Vancouver Sun)*

employment. The largest group, representing approximately two-thirds of all contingent workers, are those who have a high motivation but low ability to secure permanent employment.[28] These "temporary temporaries" have been laid off or contracted out and cannot easily find a permanent job. Some have outdated skills; others are young people who lack work experience. These people accept contract work to meet basic economic needs, gain work experience, and find leads to more permanent employment.

A smaller, but growing, cadre of professional contingent workers are known as free agents. Free agents possess valued competencies, so they have the expert power to command desired work in the marketplace. These people are usually confident in their independence and are less interested in permanent employment. They recognize that their career success depends on maintaining up-to-date knowledge and skills rather than seeking a paternalistic employment relationship.[29] Free agents are typically found in technical fields, such as accounting or information systems management. Many of these professionals eventually return to permanent employment to avoid the nuisance of continually marketing themselves.

Lastly, some people in the contingent workforce have neither the motivation nor the ability to obtain permanent employment. These transients lack the skills or experience to command much power over work opportunities, but they are also unwilling or unable to abide by the confined work schedules and organizational control systems of permanent employment. Work opportunities beyond basic needs are not important to them because they reject the idea that long-term employment is a sign of career success.[31]

Reasons for Relying on Contingent Workers
Contingent work has become more common because it provides companies with greater numerical and skill flexibility.[32] It provides numerical flexibility by easily increasing or decreasing the workforce through contingent work contracts rather than by hiring and firing permanent employees. With respect to skill flexibility, organizations respond faster to market demands by temporarily contracting skilled people than by retraining current staff in the new skills. Consultants and other skilled contractors bring valuable knowledge to the organization that is immediately applied and shared with others. This knowledge can also have a catalytic effect on the knowledge creation process because permanent employees learn the foundations for further knowledge acquisition.[33]

A second reason for the increasing reliance on contingent workers is that many organizations offer fewer employer-paid benefits and lower wages to contingent workers than to permanent staff. Some employers also reduce administrative costs by outsourcing and leasing back noncore employees from a large professional company specializing in that field (e.g., information technology services).[34] A third reason for the increase in contingent work is that information technology makes it easier for people in some professions to contract out their services without worrying about commuting or traveling. Some writers speculate that telecommuting will produce a new regime of electronically connected freelancers—called e-lancers—who come together into temporary organizations.[35]

Contingent Workforce Issues   The literature tends to either glamorize or vilify contingent work, but this emerging employment relationship is much more complex than that. Free agents usually cherish their freedom, yet many also appreciate the social connectedness of more permanent employment. They dislike the rigid boundaries of organizational careers, yet they may complain about the lack of career boundaries in contingent work.[36]

It is also difficult to say that contingent workers are more or less satisfied with their work. Satisfaction depends on the individual's personal needs and the type of contingent work. Some studies report that contingent workers are equally satisfied as people in more permanent employment. Other studies point to less satisfaction and feelings of inequity among contingent workers. Some writers argue that both contingent and permanent employees feel inequity when they work side by side because they receive different compensation, benefits, and job security for performing the same work.[37] "The message implicit in contract work is that the company is not doing well enough to elevate you to a job," warns Judy Davis, who was laid off as a contingent worker from a surgical instruments company in Cincinnati. "Layoff looms as a possibility."[38]

Another concern is that contingent workers may have less ability or motivation to perform their jobs. Some writers argue that contingent workers are less motivated because their tenuous employment creates transactional psychological contracts.[39] Others suggest that contingent workers have less training and work experience, which leads to lower-quality products or services and higher accident rates.[40] With less psychological connection to the organization, some contingent workers may also pose a higher security risk. For instance, one university replaced its security department with a contracted security firm, but fired the firm just three months later. The institution discovered that several employees at the contracted firm were stealing from the offices they were supposed to protect.[41]

Against these criticisms are arguments that contingent workers may be more productive than permanent employees under certain conditions. Many professionals are contracted precisely because they have better skills and experience than permanent employees with specific equipment or situations. To increase their probability of future contract or permanent employment, some contingent workers may also be highly motivated to perform the job well. This applies particularly to free agent professionals because the perceived value of their work—their reputational capital—affects future contract opportunities. And although professionals may have low commitment to the contracting organization, they typically have a strong sense of loyalty and obligation to the standards of their profession.

8-30
© 1992 Farcus Cartoons/dist. by Universal Press Syndicate   WAISGLASS/COULTHART

Minimizing Contingent Workforce Problems   One way to minimize the organizational problems with contingent workers is to give them the same respect and treatment as permanent staff.[42] Where possible, they should receive similar pay and prorated benefits. If this isn't possible, then it may be better to staff an entire work activity with either temps or core staff, but not both. This strategy reduces the likelihood that the other type of worker is a comparison other in equity perceptions.

Careful selection of temporary employees is another way to minimize problems, particularly in situations with high turnover and risk of theft. For example, one study of temporary service workers at a theme park reported that those with a high work ethic had higher organizational commitment and were less likely to quit before their contract ended.[43] Lastly, contingent workers can develop a stronger relational contract and make a better contribution to the organization when they learn the values, expected behaviors, and social knowledge necessary to assume their roles in the organization. In other words, they should receive support in their organizational socialization, which is discussed next.

ORGANIZATIONAL SOCIALIZATION

organizational socialization

The process by which individuals learn the values, expected behaviors, and social knowledge necessary to assume their roles in the organization.

Organizational socialization refers to the process by which individuals learn the values, expected behaviors, and social knowledge necessary to assume their roles in the organization.[44] The effectiveness of this socialization process may increase or hinder job performance and job satisfaction, whether the recruits are unskilled and new to the workforce or are highly skilled and have many years of work experience.[45]

Socialization as a Learning Process

Organizational socialization is a process of learning and of change. It is a learning process because newcomers try to make sense of the company's physical workplace, social dynamics, and strategic/cultural environment. Organizational behavior research has identified six content dimensions of organizational socialization.[46] Newcomers need to learn about the organization's performance expectations, power dynamics, corporate culture, company history, and jargon. They also need to form successful and satisfying relationships with other people from whom they can learn the ropes.[47]

Intel includes many of these content elements in its employee socialization process. The world's largest computer chip manufacturer sends new hires a complete package of materials about the company before they begin their first day. On day one, recruits learn about Intel's corporate strategy and get a clear message about performance expectations. A month later, they spend an entire day learning about Intel's corporate culture. At the six-month mark, employees experience a two-hour review of how much they have learned about Intel.[48] The idea is to transmit knowledge in a way that enables new recruits to form a cognitive map of the physical, social, and strategic/cultural dynamics of the organization without information overload.

Socialization as a Change Process

Organizational socialization is also a process of change, because individuals need to adapt to their new work environment.[49] They develop new work roles, adopt new team norms, and practice new behaviors. To varying degrees, newcomers also acquire the values and assumptions of the organization's dominant culture as well as the local subculture. Some people quickly internalize the company's culture; a few others rebel against these attempts to change their mental models and values. Ideally, newcomers adopt a level of creative individualism in which they accept the essential elements of the organization's culture and team norms, yet maintain a healthy individualism that challenges the allegedly dysfunctional elements of organizational life.

Socialization is a continuous process, beginning long before the first day of employment and continuing throughout one's career within the company. However, it is most intense when people move across organizational boundaries, such as when they first join a company, move to a new department or regional branch office, get transferred to (or back from) an international assignment, or get promoted to a higher level in the firm. For each of these transitions, employees need to adjust to an entirely new work context as well as learn role-specific behaviors.[50]

STAGES OF SOCIALIZATION

The organizational socialization process can be divided into three stages: preemployment socialization, encounter, and role management (see Exhibit 18.3).

EXHIBIT 18.3   Stages of organizational socialization

Preemployment socialization (outsider)	Encounter (newcomer)	Role management (insider)	Socialization outcomes
• Learn about the organization and job • Form the psychological contract	• Test expectations against perceived workplace realities	• Strengthen work relationships • Practice new role behaviors • Resolve conflicts between work and nonwork	• Higher motivation • Higher loyalty • Higher satisfaction • Lower stress • Lower turnover

These stages parallel the individual's transition from outsider, to newcomer, and then to insider.[51]

Stage 1: Preemployment Socialization

Think back to the months and weeks before you began working in a new job (or attending a new school). You actively searched for information about the company, formed expectations about working there, and felt some anxiety about fitting into that environment. The preemployment socialization stage encompasses all the learning and adjustment that occurs before the first day of work in a new position.[52]

This socialization adjustment is not an easy process, however. Individuals are outsiders, so they must rely on friends, employment interviews, recruiting literature, and other indirect information to form expectations about what it is like to work in the organization. The employer also forms a set of expectations about the job applicant, such as the unique skills and vitality that he or she will bring to the organization.

Conflicts When Exchanging Information   Job applicants and employers need an open exchange of accurate information during preemployment socialization to ensure that they form the same psychological contract. Unfortunately, as Exhibit 18.4 illustrates, four conflicts make it difficult for both parties to send or receive accurate information.[53]

Conflict A occurs between the employer's need to attract qualified applicants and the applicant's need for complete information to make accurate employment decisions. Many firms use a "flypaper" approach by describing only positive aspects of the job and company and neglecting to mention the undesirable elements in the hope that the best applicants will get "stuck" on the organization. This approach may lead applicants to accept job offers on the basis of incomplete or false expectations.[54]

Conflict B occurs between the applicant's need to look attractive to employers and the organization's need for complete information to make accurate selection decisions. The problem is that applicants sometimes emphasize

EXHIBIT 18.4

Information exchange conflicts during preemployment socialization

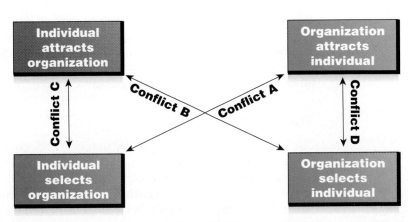

Source: L. W. Porter, E. E. Lawler III, and J. R. Hackman, *Behavior in Organizations* (New York: McGraw-Hill, 1975), p. 134. Reprinted by permission.

favorable employment experiences and leave out less favorable events in their careers. This tactic provides employers with inaccurate data, thereby distorting their expectations of the job candidate and weakening the quality of organizational selection decisions.

Conflict C occurs when applicants refrain from asking important career decision questions to avoid conveying an unfavorable image. For instance, applicants usually don't like to ask about starting salaries and promotion opportunities because they assume that doing so makes them sound greedy or overaggressive. Yet, unless the employer presents this information, applicants might fill in the missing information with false assumptions that produce an inaccurate psychological contract.

Finally, conflict D occurs when employers avoid asking certain questions or using potentially valuable selection devices because doing so might put the organization in a bad light. For instance, some employers refuse to use aptitude or ability tests, because they don't want to give the impression that the organization treats employees like mice running through a maze. Unfortunately, without the additional information, employers may form a less accurate opinion of the job candidate's potential as an employee.

In spite of these conflicts, job applicants do manage to discover some information about the organization. They learn from casual acquaintances with current and former employees. They receive some information from brochures, advertisements, public news about the company, and initial recruitment visits. Job applicants also learn from their visits to the organization. For example, after leaving a senior marketing position at Sun Microsystems, Peter Kestenbaum arranged to interview with a start-up company in New York. When he arrived in his $1,000 suit, he discovered that everyone was wearing sandals and shorts. There was no receptionist, so Kestenbaum had to wander through the place to find the person he was supposed to meet. But the deciding factor was the bathrooms. They were so filthy that Kestenbaum was convinced that the company would not fit his style.[55]

Postdecisional Justification   Both employers and job applicants further distort their perceptions of the psychological contract through the process of postdecisional justification (see Chapter 9). To maintain a positive self-identity, new hires tend subconsciously to increase the importance of favorable elements of the job and justify or completely forget about some negative elements. At the same time, they reduce the quality of job offers that they turned down. Employers often distort their expectations of new hires in the same way. The result is that both parties develop higher expectations of each other than they will actually experience during the encounter stage.

Stage 2: Encounter

reality shock
When newcomers perceive discrepancies between their preemployment expectations and on-the-job reality.

The first day on the job typically marks the beginning of the encounter stage of organizational socialization. This is the stage in which newcomers test their prior expectations with the perceived realities. Many jobs fail the test, resulting in varying degrees of **reality shock.** Reality shock occurs when newcomers perceive discrepancies between their preemployment expectations and on-the-job reality.[56] The larger the gap, the stronger the reality shock.

Consider Duncan McNee, the high school English and gym teacher from Brisbane, Australia, who accepted a teaching post in the United Kingdom.

McNee expected a challenging new adventure teaching in another country. Instead, he was soon shocked by the severity of student behavior problems. "Even in the worst schools where I taught in Australia, the kids still had some respect," says McNee. "But over here there seems to be a complete lack of it. I've had chairs being thrown around, textbooks thrown out of windows and fights."[57]

Duncan McNee experienced reality shock because student behavior problems were much worse than he had imagined. This reality shock doesn't necessarily occur on the first day; it might develop over several weeks as newcomers form a better understanding of their new work environment. Along with the experience of unmet expectations, reality shock occurs when newcomers are overwhelmed by sudden entry into a new work environment. They experience the stress of information overload and have difficulty adjusting quickly to their new role.

Reality shock is common in many organizations.[58] Unmet expectations sometimes occur because the employer is unable to live up to its promises, such as failing to provide challenging projects or resources to get the work done. Reality shock also occurs because new hires develop a distorted psychological contract through the previously described information exchange conflicts and postdecisional justification. Whatever the cause, reality shock impedes the socialization process because the newcomer's energy is directed toward managing the stress rather than learning and accepting organizational knowledge and roles.[59]

Stage 3: Role Management

During the role management stage in the socialization process, employees settle in as they make the transition from newcomers to insiders. They strengthen relationships with co-workers and supervisors, practice new role behaviors, and adopt attitudes and values consistent with their new position and organization.

Role management also involves resolving the conflicts between work and nonwork activities. In particular, employees must redistribute their time and energy between work and family, reschedule recreational activities, and deal with changing perceptions and values in the context of other life roles. They must address any discrepancies between their existing values and those emphasized by the organizational culture. New self-identities are formed that are more compatible with the work environment.

IMPROVING THE SOCIALIZATION PROCESS

Organizational socialization has a profound effect on individual performance, organizational commitment, and turnover, so companies should consider various ways to guide this process. Two important strategies are providing realistic job previews and effectively engaging socialization agents.

Realistic Job Previews

As noted earlier, many companies use a flypaper approach to recruiting. In reality, this strategy of exaggerating positive features and ignoring negative aspects of the job tends to produce a distorted psychological contract that eventually leads to lower trust and higher turnover.[60] A better approach is to give job applicants a **realistic job preview (RJP),** that is, a balance of positive and negative information about the job and work context.[61]

For example, one public transit company shows job applicants a video depicting angry riders, knife attacks, and other abuses that bus drivers must endure on their routes. Applicants then meet with a union representative who explains, among other things, that new drivers are typically assigned night shifts and the poorest routes. Finally, applicants are given the opportunity to drive a bus.

Although RJPs scare away some applicants, they tend to reduce turnover and increase job performance.[62] RJPs help applicants develop more accurate preemployment expectations that, in turn, minimize reality shock. RJPs prepare employees for the more challenging and troublesome aspects of work life. Moreover, applicants engage in self-selection when given realistic

Ford Motor Company pulled out all the stops when it invited 360 top-rated college seniors and MBA candidates to a special "leadership conference." The event was really a recruitment drive where potential job applicants were flown in to Detroit, housed at the Ritz, shuttled back and forth in shiny black Lincoln Continental sedans, and treated to dinners at fancy restaurants. They also test-drove Jaguars and had a meeting with Ford's chief executive officer. Ford executives initially considered holding the event in Florida, but decided that the visitors needed some workplace reality during the January event. "We are not trying to hide the fact we are in Detroit," says a Ford executive. "We are not telling them, 'It's wonderful here all the time and the climate is great.' We tell the truth."[63] Does it sound like Ford Motor Company is providing realistic job previews in its recruiting process? What are the consequences of providing RJPs under these conditions? *(R. Buckson/Detroit News)*

information. There is also some evidence that RJPs increase organizational loyalty. A possible explanation is that companies providing candid information are easier to trust. They also show respect for the psychological contract and concern for employee welfare.[64]

Socialization Agents

Ask new employees what most helped them adjust to their job and chances are they will mention helpful co-workers, bosses, or maybe even friends who work for the company. The fact is, a lot of organizational socialization occurs informally through these socialization agents.[65] Supervisors tend to provide technical information, performance feedback, and information about job duties. They also improve the socialization process by giving newcomers reasonably challenging first assignments, buffering them from excessive demands, and helping them form social ties with co-workers.[66]

Co-workers are also important socialization agents because they are easily accessible, can answer questions when problems arise, and serve as role models for appropriate behavior. New employees tend to receive this information and support when co-workers integrate them into the work team. Co-workers also aid the socialization process by being flexible and tolerant in their interactions with these new hires.

Several organizations rely on a buddy system, whereby newcomers are assigned to co-workers for sources of information and social support. Every nurse who joins Children's Memorial Hospital in Chicago is assigned a mentor to help ease the transition into the new culture. ExtendMedia also has a formal buddy system, but equally valuable is the box of doughnuts put on every newcomer's desk on the first day of work. "The [doughnuts] are there to break the ice so that other people come and talk to [the new hires]. We are introducing people through their stomachs," explains an executive at the interactive media company. Progressive Inc., the Mayfield, Ohio–based insurance firm, relies on current employees to recruit and socialize job applicants. "I think candidates can trust and respect people who already work here," says Jennifer Cohen, Progressive's national employment director. "They know they aren't being sold a bill of goods. They have someone to talk to about the opportunities, and they get a lot of honest information about the company."[67]

Newcomers who quickly form social relations with co-workers tend to have a less traumatic socialization experience and are less likely to quit their jobs within the first year of employment.[68] However, co-workers sometimes engage in hazing—the practice of fooling or intimidating newcomers as a practical joke or initiation ritual. Connections 18.2 describes how employees at a McDonald's restaurant haze new employees by asking them to look for "steam mix." This initiation seems innocent enough and certainly provides entertainment for other staff members, but it can further stress new hires and interfere with their need to form social bonds with co-workers.

Organizational socialization is an ongoing process as employees make adjustments through different jobs and organizations. As we learn in the next section, we must also view careers as dynamic and multiorganizational processes in a rapidly changing environment.

Separating the Steam from the Haze

"We need more steam mix for our hamburger buns," a veteran employee calls out to the new hire at a McDonald's restaurant. "Get another package of mix, please."

For the newly hired McDonald's employee, this is just another task to learn in the confusing world of fast-food restaurants. For seasoned employees, it is a ritual for newcomers that usually brings hilarity to the otherwise serious work-oriented setting.

Some new employees get the joke immediately, but most scurry to the food storage area in search of the elusive package of steam mix. They check among the stacks of hamburger buns and in the freezer around the boxes of french fries for any package that says "steam mix" on it. After 5 or 10 minutes, the discouraged recruits return empty-handed and ask for further directions.

Sometimes, if it isn't too busy, co-workers might say: "It's the big bag clearly marked 'Steam Mix!'—the one with the picture of a kettle on it." Occasionally, the hazing might go one step further. With a straight face, an employee might reply, "Oh, that's right. We're out of steam mix. Here, take this bucket and go next door to the Wendy's restaurant. We often borrow some of their mix."

Eager to please their fellow employees, newcomers jaunt across the parking lot with a McDonald's bucket in hand and politely ask a Wendy's employee for some of their steam mix. A few Wendy's staff members have learned to play along with the game by telling the visitor that Wendy's steam mix is different from McDonald's. More often, the new McDonald's worker is politely reminded that steam comes from boiled water and doesn't require any other ingredients.

Hazing new employees at McDonald's can potentially undermine the socialization process. *(John Thoeming)*

Across the parking lot, co-workers watch the embarrassed (and occasionally angry) newcomer return with the empty McDonald's bucket. Somehow, the hazing ritual never loses its appeal, maybe because it provides a welcome break from the work. No one has quit over the experience, although most newcomers are cautious whenever co-workers ask them to retrieve anything from the storage area.

Source: Based on information provided to Steven L. McShane by a student who survived this hazing ritual and watched many others experience it.

ORGANIZATIONAL CAREERS

If changing jobs is one of life's greatest stresses, then someone forgot to tell Steve Koskie. The 30-year-old has worked for 10 employers over the past dozen years. With each move, he gained experience and new career challenges that the previous employer couldn't offer. Today, Koskie is founder of Ocean-Lake Commerce Inc., which makes Internet transaction verification software for the banking industry. His career challenge now is to keep his own employees. "[Employees] are looking out for themselves and making sure they're in the best position they can be in," says Koskie.[69]

Steve Koskie may be your above-average job-hopper, but his career pattern is becoming more the norm than the exception. A **career** is no longer just a series of moves up a career ladder within one organization. It is a sequence of work-related experiences that people participate in over the span of their working lives.[70] A person's career might include moving across the organiza-

career
A sequence of work-related experiences that people participate in over the span of their working lives.

tion (i.e., moving laterally) or temporarily moving down the hierarchy to acquire new skills. Increasingly, Steve Koskie and other people are extending their careers across organizational boundaries.[71]

Effective career development improves employee satisfaction and self-esteem, minimizes stress, and strengthens the employee's psychological and physical health. Effective career development benefits organizations because employees adapt more quickly to changing organizational needs.[72] These benefits explain why Honeywell (described in this chapter's opening vignette) tries to develop careers within the organization. Vanguard Group also emphasizes career development so that employees become "lifers." "We believe in careers, not jobs," says Jack Brennan, CEO of the nation's second-largest mutual fund company. "There's a difference between being a place to work and a place to build a career."[73] In this section, we explore the prominent career development concepts, starting with Holland's model of occupational choice and following through to the emerging trends in lateral and boundaryless career paths.

Holland's Theory of Occupational Choice

Miriam Goldberger produced sound effects for movies, then ran a prenatal and postpartum women's fitness program, and later edited books for a publisher. She performed each job well but was frustrated with the work environment (dark, cramped sound rooms), lack of job autonomy, or people. That's when Goldberger took stock of what she liked and didn't like. "I can't behave in meetings," Goldberger admits. "I can't use diplomatic doublespeak. I'm movement-oriented; I enjoy physical hard work, and I like to do something different every day."

With that self-assessment, Miriam Goldberger decided to turn her favorite hobby—gardening—into a full-time career. Today, she and her husband (a former advertising executive) landscape gardens, design meadows, and sell low-maintenance wildflowers. The couple gave up stable paychecks and scaled back their lifestyle, but now earn more than ever before.[74]

Miriam Goldberger and many other people have discovered that a career is not just about matching your skills with job requirements. It is a complex alignment of personality, values, and competencies with the requirements of work and conditions of the work environment. Goldberger may have been talented in her other jobs, but her personality and values were more aligned with physical work that produces tangible results.

John Holland, a career development scholar, was an early proponent of the notion that career success depends on the degree of fit between the person and his or her work environment.[75] Specifically, Holland's theory of occupational choice states that the degree of congruence between an individual's personality traits and the work environment has a significant effect on the person's performance, satisfaction, and length of time in that career. Moreover, a person's occupational choice is an expression of his or her personality.[76] Thus, we would expect that medical doctors have similar traits and interests, which differ from the traits and interests of, say, marketing analysts. With similar personality characteristics, people in a particular occupational group will respond in similar ways to problems and situations.

Holland's Six Types Holland's theory contends that there are six types, or themes, that represent characteristics of both the work environment and the

| EXHIBIT 18.5 | Holland's six types of personality and work environment |

Holland type	Personality traits	Work environment characteristics	Sample occupations
Realistic	Practical, shy, materialistic, stable	Work involves using hands, machines, or tools; focus on tangible results	Assembly worker, dry cleaner, mechanical engineer
Investigative	Analytic, introverted, reserved, curious, precise, independent	Work involves discovering, collecting, and analyzing; focus on solving problems	Biologist, dentist, systems analyst
Artistic	Creative, impulsive, idealistic, intuitive, emotional	Work involves creation of new products or ideas, typically in an unstructured setting	Journalist, architect, advertising executive
Social	Sociable, outgoing, conscientious; need for affiliation	Work involves serving or helping others; focus on working in teams	Social worker, nurse, teacher, counselor
Enterprising	Confident, assertive, energetic; need for power	Work involves leading others; focus on achieving goals through others in a results-oriented setting	Salesperson, stockbroker, politician
Conventional	Dependable, disciplined, orderly, practical, efficient	Work involves systematic manipulation of data or information	Accountant, banker, administrator

Sources: Based on information in D. H. Montross, Z. B. Leibowitz, and C. J. Shinkman, *Real People, Real Jobs* (Palo Alto, CA: Davies-Black, 1995); J. H. Greenhaus, *Career Management* (Chicago, IL: Dryden, 1987).

personality traits and interests of people working in those environments. These six categories are realistic, investigative, artistic, social, enterprising, and conventional. Exhibit 18.5 defines these types of people and work environments, and lists sample occupations representing those environments.

Before trying to categorize your occupational preference, you should be aware that few people fall squarely into only one type. Thus, Holland refers to a person's degree of *differentiation,* that is, the extent to which the individual fits into one or several types. A highly differentiated person is aligned with a single category, whereas most people relate to two or more categories.

Since most people have more than one career type, Holland developed a hexagonal model that helps people determine the consistency of their personality in the career model (see Exhibit 18.6). *Consistency* refers to the extent that a person is aligned with similar rather than dissimilar types. Similar types are adjacent to each other in the hexagon, whereas dissimilar types are opposite each other. For instance, individuals with enterprising personalities are more similar to social people than to investigative people. Those who fit mainly into the enterprising category but also relate to the social type are considered consistent, whereas enterprising people who also relate to the investigative type are inconsistent.

Practical Implications of Holland's Theory   Debate is ongoing regarding how well Holland's categories represent personality traits and whether his model should be hexagonal.[77] Holland's personality types represent only two

EXHIBIT 18.6

Holland's
hexagon model

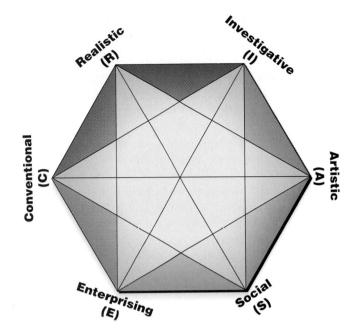

Source: J. L. Holland, *Making Vocational Choices: A Theory of Vocational Personalities and Work Environments*, 2nd ed. (Englewood Cliffs, NJ: Prentice Hall, 1985).

of the Big Five personality dimensions—openness and extroversion (see Chapter 3). This aspect of his theory raises the question of whether Holland's types are incomplete because the three other personality dimensions are not represented. In addition, research has reported that Holland's model should look more like a skewed polygon than a hexagon. In other words, some opposing categories are less opposite than others. Aside from these concerns, research using Holland's concepts has found that job stress is related to a lack of congruence between personality and work environment.[78]

Holland's model of occupational choice has laid the foundation for many career development activities in use today. If you take a vocational interest test, there is a good chance that the results are presented around Holland's six dimensions.[79] The idea that an individual's personality should be congruent with the work environment is now well established in research and practice. Holland's hexagonal model (Exhibit 18.6) helps identify the degree of congruence between an individual's dominant personality type and his or her work environment. Someone who fits mostly in the realistic category would, of course, be most congruent with a realistic environment. The adjacent environments (conventional and investigative) would offer the next best degree of congruence. The lowest congruence occurs for realistic people working in a social environment. Overall, Holland's theory emphasizes the point that effective career development involves finding a good fit between the individual's personality and the work environment. This notion of fit is increasingly important as companies replace the traditional career ladder with more diverse work experiences through lateral career development, which we will discuss next.

Lateral Career Development

lateral career development

The traditional career path up the corporate ladder is not as common as it once was. Instead, many firms now define career success in terms of **lateral career development** rather than how many steps employees have taken up the corporate hierarchy. The idea behind lateral career development is that people can fulfill their personal needs in different jobs across the organization. Employees must think about their careers as a lattice rather than a ladder. They must also redefine career success in terms of the variety of challenging work assignments a person completes across the few organizational levels that still remain. "The emphasis would be on discontinuous activity, a continuous series of challenging projects that excites employees and helps them grow," explains Nalin Miglani, vice president (human resources) of Coca-Cola India.[80]

lateral career development
The view that career success occurs when employees fulfill their personal needs in different jobs across the organization rather than by moving through the organizational hierarchy.

One reason organizations encourage lateral career development is that much of the existing career ladder is still filled with baby boomers who aren't going anywhere.[81] Lateral career development helps employees fulfill their personal needs in different jobs across the organization when promotional opportunities are limited. A second reason for lateral career development is that many organizations have transformed their tall hierarchies into flattened team-based structures. In these structures, employees tend to move to different projects across the organization rather than to higher management levels.

Consider Debbie McNamara's first five years at Lend Lease Corporation, the global real estate development and financial services company. The 26-year-old's first job was working with financial advisors who sell Lend Lease products. A year later, she became project manager to simplify business processes in the fund management division's call center group. When that project was near completion, McNamara was transferred to the United Kingdom, where she helped retailers open their businesses at Lend Lease's Bluewater development. McNamara's career path across the organization is typical at Lend Lease, because the company wants "careening careers" where employees continually acquire new competencies.[82]

A third reason for the increasing emphasis on lateral career development is that it is consistent with the shifting emphasis from job status to competencies. Promotions through the traditional corporate ladder tend to reinforce job status, whereas lateral career development helps people learn new competencies and remain competitive in the labor market. This emphasis on competencies is also aligned with the trend toward employability rather than job security. Employees must anticipate future demand for skills and knowledge, and manage their careers accordingly by seeking out work opportunities that develop those competencies.

Consider IBM in the United States, Glaxo Wellcome in the United Kingdom, Volkswagen in Germany, and Michelin in France. Each of these firms has developed fewer and wider pay grades to reflect the fewer promotional opportunities in the organization (see Chapter 6).[83] Instead, these companies advise employees to broaden their knowledge and experience through lateral career paths. The result is a more flexible workforce with multiple skills.

Encouraging Lateral Career Development   Many people have difficulty adjusting to lateral career development. Baby boomers, in particular, have learned to praise the linear career concept in which career success is defined in terms of how high you go up the corporate hierarchy. Employees are also reluctant to engage in lateral career development because it involves the risk of leaving their longtime jobs and departments. Moreover, they may face interference from supervisors who don't want to see their prized staff move elsewhere.

To encourage lateral career development, companies need to regularly communicate new job openings and help employees with career self-assessments. For example, Starbucks Coffee Company posts all job openings every week. Many firms also have virtual career centers where employees can assess their skills online, determine how those skills fit in the organization, and learn how they can gain the skills needed to meet their career goals. Raychem offers career seminars that encourage employees to think of themselves as self-employed and to explore many career options. The Menlo Park, California, electronics company also has a career development center where employees explore their potential through self-assessments, career workshops, and referrals to career resources. Employees compare their current competencies with current and future market demands.[84]

Boundaryless Careers

Nearly 50 years ago, in his best-selling book *Organization Man,* William H. Whyte painted a satirical picture of American white-collar career success in terms of secure employment with slow, steady promotions through several professional and management layers. These people devoted their entire lives to the same company, slowly working their way up the corporate ladder.[85]

boundaryless career

The idea that careers operate across company and industry boundaries rather than just within a single organizational hierarchy.

Some people still follow this structured model of career development, but most do not. Instead, there is a growing trend toward the **boundaryless career**—the idea that careers operate across company and industry boundaries rather than just within a single organizational hierarchy.[86] It is the view that careers unfold throughout one's life, not necessarily throughout one company. Dan Schmitt, described in the opening vignette in this chapter, developed his competencies in the entertainment events services business by job-hopping rather than waiting for the next great challenge within one organization. In fact, the average employee has 12 to 15 jobs over the course of a career, including between 5 and 7 jobs by age 30.[87]

At the same time, career experts warn that too much job-hopping could undermine the individual's career. The challenge is to find the right balance between career development within and between organizations. "Employers don't want to employ job-hoppers, but if they can see that you're increasing your repertoire of skills each time then it's not so bad," says career coach Paula Stenberg. "But you do have to be careful not to be too ruthless or brash about it."[88]

Reasons Why People Adopt Boundaryless Careers Boundaryless careers are more common today than 10 years ago, but this trend does not imply that employees enjoy changing jobs. On the contrary, by a two-to-one margin, high-tech job-hoppers would rather stay with one employer for 20 years than have five jobs for 4 years each.[89] This behavior suggests that the boundaryless career is more a function of necessity than motivation. The trend toward boundaryless careers accelerated with massive corporate downsizing over the past decade.[90] These layoffs and early retirements forced people to realign their careers with other organizations. From this painful experience, many people developed the attitude that it is better to accept career opportunities as they come along rather than remain loyal to one employer.

A related explanation for the rise in boundaryless careers is that many psychological contracts have shifted from job security to employability. As we mentioned earlier in this chapter, the new deal rewards people who take control of their own career development.[91] But moving away from a loyalty-based contract also weakens the internal labor market. Thus, employees are more likely to seek career development opportunities outside the organization.

What can organizations do about boundaryless careers and the trend toward job-hopping? One obvious solution is to provide enough career opportunities within the organization to make external job-hopping unnecessary. Although this approach may seem impossible in smaller firms, we must remember that career opportunities can be created through new projects and challenges, not just existing positions elsewhere in the company.

In general, corporate leaders need to reexamine the drivers of organizational loyalty that were identified in Chapter 4. Employees are more likely to keep their careers in-house when they have positive and equitable work experiences, a reasonable level of job security, continual understanding of organizational activities, involvement in organizational decisions, and a high level of trust in corporate leaders and co-workers.

Finally, we need to recognize that it is natural and desirable for some employees to leave for better career opportunities elsewhere. Connections 18.3 describes how many employers are adapting to the emerging reality of boundaryless careers by welcoming back "boomerangers" who have left for opportunities elsewhere. In this wired world, where employees quickly gain information about career opportunities through Monster.com and other websites, organizations need to recognize the benefits of rehiring former employees versus losing them forever.

CAREER DEVELOPMENT: RULES FOR THE ROAD AHEAD

Whether you are just starting your career or are already well along the road, the following ideas should help you improve both your prospects and long-term career satisfaction. These points do not cover everything you need to remember about developing your career. Instead, they highlight some of the key strategies that will help you along the road ahead.

Understand Your Needs and Values

Career development begins with understanding your personal needs and values.[92] "If you're in the wrong career, it doesn't matter if the economy is good or bad, you're still unhappy," advises Atlanta career consultant Deborah R. Brown.[93]

How do you know what type of career is most fulfilling for you? To answer this question, you need to complete self-assessments of your vocational interests and recount experiences that you enjoyed. Holland's occupational choice model, presented earlier in this chapter, helps align your personality and interests with the work environment. It may also be useful to get feedback from others regarding activities that they notice you like or dislike. This approach

Boundaryless Careers Boomerang Back

Lured by the dot-com excitement and potential fortunes, Michael Czyz quit his job at DiamondCluster International and joined TheSauce.com, an Internet marketplace for restaurant vendors. But when TheSauce.com ran out of money less than a year later, Czyz was looking for another job. Fortunately, he found a good employment opportunity—back at DiamondCluster International.

DiamondCluster International and many other companies are opening their doors to boomerangers—former employees who want to come back. "It used to be you couldn't really go home again—you betrayed your company . . . [by] leaving for a better opportunity," says John Challenger, CEO of Chicago placement firm Challenger, Gray and Christmas. "Many companies are [now] welcoming people back with open arms, or they are at least willing to talk to them."

One survey reported that 90 percent of employers in Fortune 1000 companies would consider rehiring a former employee who left their firm in good standing. Corporate leaders reason that boomerangers have lower hiring costs than other job applicants because they adjust more easily to their former work environment and their track record is already known. Moreover, former employees bring additional knowledge to the organization from their experience.

Some employers are bending over backward to bring their wayward staff back into the fold. When discount stockbroker Charles Schwab reluctantly laid off 2,100 staff, it offered a $7,500 rehiring bonus to anyone who returned within 18 months. Consulting firms Accenture and PricewaterhouseCoopers have established alumni lists and actively keep track of former employees. "We are very aggressively seeking them out," says

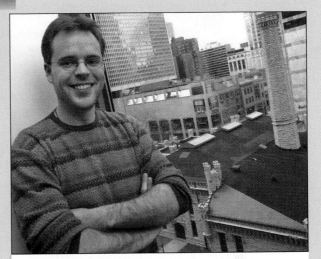

Michael Czyz tried out a boundaryless career that boomeranged him back to his former employer, Diamond-Cluster International. *(Ellyn Domke. Reprinted with special permission from the Chicago Sun-Times, Inc. © 2001)*

a PricewaterhouseCoopers partner. Accenture has rehired at least 200 boomerangers, particularly the entrepreneurial types who left for dot-com start-ups. "It's a rich source of talent for us," says Steve Colbourn, an industry recruiting director for Accenture. "We would certainly welcome them back."

Sources: K. Clark, "You're Laid Off! Kind Of," *U.S. News & World Report,* July 2, 2001; M. Duvall, "You Look Like You Need a Rest," *Interactive Week,* June 21, 2001; D. Newbart, "Dot-Boomerang Time," *Chicago Sun-Times,* March 5, 2001, p. 46; "Welcome Back!" *PR Newswire,* June 13, 2000.

---

applies the Johari Window model described in Chapter 3, whereby you learn more about yourself through information presented by close associates.

Understand Your Competencies

Knowing yourself also involves knowing what you are capable of doing.[94] In Chapter 2, we learned that each of us has a set of aptitudes—natural talents that help us learn specific tasks quickly and perform them well. Although we might visualize our future as an engineering wizard or president of the United States, we need to take our abilities into account. The more careers are aligned with our personal competencies, the more we develop a strong sense of self-efficacy—the can-do attitude that further empowers our career.

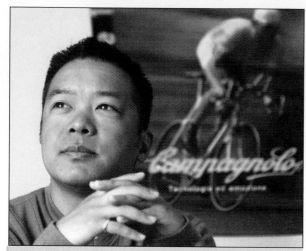

The recent economic downturn put a damper on job prospects for many business graduates, but Andrew Wang is philosophical. "It's not fun, but at least it forces you to figure out what it is you really want to do," says the graduating MBA student at UCLA's Anderson School of Management. So, rather than jumping into a dot-com start-up, Wang is thinking about joining a company more aligned with his personal interests. "I've had this lifelong interest in cycling, so I'm now looking at the recreational industry for product-management positions," he says. "I've learned [they] don't pay as well, but you're doing something that you like."[96] How can you tell when a particular career path fulfills your personal needs? (Robert Harbison, © The Christian Science Monitor)

Self-assessments, performance results, and constructive feedback from friends can help us identify our capabilities. Also, keep in mind that employers look beyond technical skills to generic competencies, such as communication, problem solving, and interpersonal relations. Indeed, some recruiters say they pay more attention to these foundations and assume employees will develop job-specific skills at work.

Set Career Goals

Soon after Mary Morse joined Autodesk as a software engineer, the manager above her immediate supervisor asked Morse to draw up a list of short-term and long-term career goals. Then the manager at the California software firm provided Morse with a list of training courses, both inside and outside the company, that would help her meet those career objectives. The manager also spoke to Morse's immediate supervisor to ensure she would have time to complete those courses.[95]

Mary Morse was lucky. She joined an organization that helps employees identify and achieve their career goals. But we usually can't count on others to guide our career development. We need to set our own goals to realize our potential and ultimately fulfill our needs. Goal setting is a powerful way to motivate and achieve results, and this applies as much to careers as to any other activity. Career goals are benchmarks against which we evaluate our progress and identify strategies to develop our competencies.

Career consultant Barbara Moses emphasizes that career goal setting is a fundamental element in becoming a "career activist." It involves writing your own script rather than waiting for someone to write it for you, being vigilant by identifying and preparing for opportunities, and becoming an independent agent by separating your self-identity from your job title, your organization, or what other people think you should be.[97]

Maintain Networks

As people develop boundaryless careers, their career opportunities depend more on trusting relationships than documented information about their performance. For example, a survey by Drake Beam Morin revealed that 64 percent of the 7,435 people in the placement firm's executive career transition programs found new employment through networking. As one successful job hunter advises: "Be prepared, know your story, and network, network, network."[98]

Several research studies have confirmed that networking is an increasingly important feature of career development. In particular, people with large, nonredundant networks tend to be more successful job seekers and receive greater organizational rewards. One important piece of advice is to network in areas beyond your current sphere of work. Careers change much more than in the past, so you need to establish connections to other fields where you may someday find yourself.[99]

Get a Mentor

So far, our discussion has emphasized self-leadership in career development (see Chapter 6). We need to set our own goals, motivate ourselves for career advancement, and visualize where we want to go. But career development also benefits from the help of others. Mentoring involves learning the ropes of organizational life from a senior person within the company (see Chapter 12.) Mentors give protégés more visible and meaningful work opportunities, but they also provide career guidance. You might think of them as career coaches because they provide ongoing advice and feedback.[100]

Mentoring is so important at McKinsey & Company that several offices of the management consulting firm regularly ask all associates to identify which partners they view as mentors. The first of these surveys was a shock because each partner was identified by fewer than five associates as a mentor. In other words, McKinsey partners provided less mentoring than they had assumed. This survey was a wake-up call for McKinsey's partners, who now spend significantly more time and effort mentoring junior staff at the consulting firm.[101]

CAREERS AND ORGANIZATIONAL BEHAVIOR

Wherever your career leads, you will invariably remain inside or close to those abstract constructs called organizations. As a result, the topics discussed throughout this book will continually relate to your career success and personal fulfillment. You will discover how organizational behavior topics are interrelated. It is difficult to discuss motivation without referring to personality. We can't understand communication without noting power and politics. Leadership embraces change. Change embraces knowledge management. And as you apply organizational behavior throughout your career, remember that organizations are the people in them. They are human entities—full of life, sometimes fragile, always exciting.

CHAPTER SUMMARY

The psychological contract is a set of perceived mutual obligations about the employer's and employee's exchange relationship. Some contracts are transactional, whereas others are more relational. Trust is an important factor in the employment relationship. Three levels of trust are calculus-based, knowledge-based, and identification-based. Knowledge-based and identification-based trust are stronger and more flexible than calculus-based trust.

One trend in employment relationships is the shift from job security to employability. This "new deal" psychological contract says that employees must take

responsibility for their own careers by continually developing new competencies for future work opportunities within and beyond the organization. The other trend is the increase in contingent work—any job in which the individual does not have an explicit or implicit contract for long-term employment or in which the minimum hours of work can vary in a nonsystematic way. Contingent work is growing because companies want more flexibility and lower payroll costs, and many are outsourcing noncore work activities.

Organizational socialization is the process by which individuals learn the values, expected behaviors, and social knowledge necessary to assume their roles in the organization. It is a learning process because newcomers need to acquire information about performance proficiency, people, politics, language, organizational goals and values, and history. Socialization is also a process of change as newcomers develop new work roles, adopt new team norms, and practice new behaviors.

Employees typically pass through three socialization stages. Preemployment socialization occurs before the first day of work and includes conflicts between the organization's and applicant's needs to collect information and attract the other party. Encounter begins on the first day and typically involves adjusting to reality shock. Role management involves resolving work–nonwork conflicts and settling in to the workplace. To manage the socialization process, organizations should introduce realistic job previews (RJPs) and recognize the value of socialization agents in the process. RJPs give job applicants a realistic balance of positive and negative information about the job and work context. Socialization agents provide information and social support during the socialization process.

A career is a sequence of work-related experiences in which people participate over the span of their working lives. Holland's theory of occupational choice states that the degree of congruence between an individual's personality traits and the work environment affects career performance, satisfaction, and longevity. The theory includes six personality types and work environments: realistic, investigative, artistic, social, enterprising, and conventional. Individuals are differentiated if they fit mainly in one of these categories, and they are consistent if they relate to adjacent rather than opposite types.

Companies are encouraging lateral career development rather than the climb up the traditional corporate ladder, because there are fewer steps on the corporate ladder, baby boomers block upward mobility of employees farther down the hierarchy, and lateral career development is consistent with the shifting emphasis from job status to competencies.

Boundaryless careers operate across company and industry boundaries. They are becoming more common as a result of corporate downsizing and the shift from job security to employability. Five strategies that assist personal career development are the following: Understand your needs and values, understand your competencies, set career goals, maintain networks, and get a mentor.

KEY TERMS

boundaryless career, p. 561
career, p. 556
contingent work, p. 546
lateral career development, p. 560
organizational socialization, p. 549
psychological contract, p. 540
realistic job preview (RJP), p. 554
reality shock, p. 552

DISCUSSION QUESTIONS

1. Jack Santoni works on the field production crew at Gusher Drilling Company. When he joined the company five years ago, the supervisor who hired him said Jack could use the company's old pickup truck on weekends. Now the company plans to sell the truck and won't replace it, leaving Jack without a vehicle on the weekends. Discuss the implications of this action on Jack's psychological contract with Gusher Drilling Company.

2. Many organizations are moving toward a psychological contract based on employability. What does this trend mean, and how does a contract based on employability differ from the psychological contract that most employees believed in a few decades ago? Do you think this employability-based contract will continue, or will it revert to a security-based contract in the future?

3. WestFoods, a major food company, has just decided that its core competency is in food processing, so it will outsource most of its support services (human resources, information systems). This decision will result in a large contingent workforce in these functions. What issues should WestFoods consider before moving to a contingent workforce?

4. The textbook states that organizational socialization is a process of learning and of change. What does this mean, and how do organizations facilitate both learning and change for new employees?

5. After three months on the job, you feel that the company has violated the psychological contract. The job is not as exciting as you originally expected, and your current boss is no better than the supervisor in your previous job. The people

who interviewed you are concerned about your feelings, but say that they didn't misrepresent either the job or the fact that some supervisors are not as good as others. Explain how your perceived psychological contract may have been distorted during preemployment socialization.

6. Progressive, Inc., ExtendMedia, and other organizations rely on current employees to socialize new recruits. What are the advantages of relying on this type of socialization agent? What problems can you foresee (or you have personally experienced) with co-worker socialization practices?

7. You have just completed a vocational test which concludes that you have an enterprising personality, along with fairly high levels of the artistic and investigative types in Holland's model. Assuming that this vocational test is accurate, what are its implications for your career?

8. Although companies encourage lateral career development, many baby boom–generation employees still prefer the opportunity to climb the corporate ladder. Do you think that these employees are correct in thinking that "real" career development occurs only when you are promoted? Will Generation-X and Generation-Y employees develop a similar attachment to promotions later in their careers?

CASE STUDY 18.1

QUANTOR CORPORATION'S CONTINGENT WORKFORCE POLICY

Three years ago, Quantor Corporation, a large manufacturer of computer printers and other peripherals, established a task force to determine the most appropriate use of contingent workers throughout the company. The company had started to rely on contract, part-time, and temporary help agency people to fill temporary jobs. At the time, these workers represented less than 1 percent of Quantor's workforce, and the company wanted to review these practices to ensure consistency and effectiveness.

After reviewing current ad hoc practices, the task force concluded that Quantor needed contingent workers when demand for the company's products expanded rapidly or a new product was launched. Quantor needed this workforce flexibility because of uncertain production demand beyond the short term. At the same time, the task force warned that treating contingent workers the same as permanent employees would undermine the benefits of flexibility, create false hopes of permanent employment among contingent workers, and possibly create feelings of inequity between the two groups. Thus, policies were introduced that treated contingent workers differently from permanent employees.

Quantor's task force established two contingent worker categories: on-call and on-contract. On-call people are employed by Quantor as part-time staff. They work a full day, but only up to two-thirds of the hours of a full-time permanent employee. Their managers can alter their work schedules at will to suit production demands. On-contract people are employed full-time by Quantor for a fixed period, usually six months. Their contract may be renewed up to three times for a maximum employment of two years.

On-call and on-contract employees receive no employee benefits other than the government-mandated minimum vacation and holiday pay. Benefits therefore represent approximately 10 percent of their total pay, compared with nearly 40 percent for permanent employees. However, contingent workers earn the midpoint of the pay grade for their job group, which represents 15 percent above the entry rate. This rate is paid even when the contingent worker lacks experience in the job.

Quantor's Contingent Workforce Problems

Three years after the initiation of Quantor's task force recommendations, the contingent workforce policy was in trouble. Current practices succeeded in creating a more flexible workforce, and there was some evidence that using contingent workers increased profitability. However, these practices created unanticipated problems that became apparent as the percentage of contingent workers increased.

One problem was that few people wanted only contract employment. Most were seeking full-time permanent work and were using their contingent position as a stepping-stone to those jobs at Quantor. The result was that many contract workers remained for the entire two-year maximum period and beyond. The company was reluctant to apply the task force's recommendation of not renewing contracts beyond two years because of the perceived arbitrariness of this action as well as loss of knowledge to the organization. Several contract staff members asked the company for an employee-paid benefit package (benefits are mainly employer-paid for permanent employees). However, Quantor rejected this request because it would add further permanence to their employment relationship.

Quantor's managers also began to complain about the company policy that contingent workers could not be offered permanent employment. They appreciated the opportunity to select permanent employees based on observations of their performance in on-contract or on-call positions. Quantor's task force had warned against this practice because it might create inequities and raise false expectations about the likelihood of permanent employment. Managers acknowledged this risk, but the inability to permanently hire good contract staff was frustrating to them.

The third problem was that Quantor's treatment of contingent workers was incompatible with its organizational culture. Quantor had a strong culture based on the philosophy of employee well-being. The company had a generous benefits package, supportive leadership, and a belief system that made employees a top priority in corporate decisions. The company did not treat contingent workers in a way that was consistent with this philosophy. Yet if Quantor treated contingent workers the same as permanent staff members, then flexibility would be lost. For example, managers would continue renewing contract workers even when their employment was not essential and would be reluctant to schedule on-call people at awkward times.

Quantor's team orientation was also incompatible with its use of contingent workers. Permanent staff members frequently gathered to discuss organizational and group decisions. Contingent workers were not invited to these team activities because they might be working at Quantor for only a few more months. This barrier created some awkward moments for managers as contingent workers continued working while permanent employees went to meetings and team sessions.

As these problems intensified, senior management formed another task force to reexamine Quantor's contingent workforce policy. The company needed contingent workers, but it was increasingly apparent that the current practices were not working.

Discussion Questions

1. Identify the problems that Quantor experienced with its contingent workforce practices. Also identify other possible contingent workforce problems that have not been explicitly mentioned in this case.

2. Discuss the problems with contingent workers at Quantor in terms of the psychological contract and organizational commitment.

3. What alternative strategies might allow Quantor to include a contingent workforce with fewer problems?

Source: This case was prepared by Steven L. McShane based on information about an actual experience. The company name and some details have been altered.

CASE STUDY 18.2

ANNE MULCAHY: SHE'S HERE TO FIX THE XEROX

BusinessWeek Anne M. Mulcahy may not know how to repair a copier, but Xerox Corporation's board of directors evidently thinks she knows how to fix the company. After Xerox reported its first quarterly loss in a decade and a half, the board appointed Mulcahy to the post of chief executive. That job marks the peak of a very successful career at Xerox. After earning a degree in English and journalism, Mulcahy joined Xerox as a sales representative, then worked her way up through the company's retail division, and held a job as vice president for human resources. The directors considered Mulcahy a decisive leader and charged her with restoring the company's profitability.

This *Business Week* case study describes Mulcahy's career at Xerox and her objectives as the company's CEO. Those objectives will require changes in Xerox's relationships with its employees. Read through this *Business Week* case study at www.mhhe.com/mcshane2e and prepare for the discussion questions below.

Source: P. L. Moore, "Anne Mulcahy: She's Here to Fix the Xerox," *Business Week*, August 6, 2001.

Discussion Questions

1. How do Anne Mulcahy's objectives to eliminate unprofitable operations and focus more on business solutions change the psychological contract at Xerox?

2. Assuming Xerox succeeds in shifting from a focus on selling "boxes" to selling "solutions," how does this new focus change the work environment characteristics at Xerox and the career types needed? Refer to the categories in Exhibit 18.5, detailing John Holland's theory of occupational choice.

TEAM EXERCISE 18.3

ORGANIZATIONAL SOCIALIZATION DIAGNOSTIC EXERCISE

Purpose This exercise is designed to help students understand the socialization strategies that organizations should use for new employees, and learn about the impediments to forming an accurate psychological contract.

Instructions The instructor will form teams (typically of four or five people). Each team will follow these steps:

- *Step 1*—Each team member will describe one particularly memorable positive or negative experience encountered when entering an organization. (Students with limited organizational experience may describe entry to school.) Entry to the organization would include any interaction with the company up to, including, and a short while after the first day of work. The incident might describe how the individual was greeted during the first day of work, how the company kept him or her informed before the first day of work, how the company did (or didn't) tell the person about negative aspects of the work or job context, and so forth. The team will consider all these experiences, but will pick the most interesting one for description in class.

- *Step 2*—On the basis of these experiences, the team will develop a list of strategies that companies should use to improve the organizational entry process. Some experiences will reflect effective management of this process. Other experiences will indicate what companies have done ineffectively, so the team must identify strategies to avoid those problems.

- *Step 3*—In class, one person from each team will describe his or her organizational entry experience. (This person is chosen in Step 1.) The team will explain what the company did well or poorly with respect to that incident. After each team has presented one anecdote, the class will discuss other ideas from the team discussion.

TEAM EXERCISE 18.4

TRUTH IN ADVERTISING

Purpose This team exercise is designed to help you diagnose the degree to which recruitment advertisements and brochures provide realistic previews of the job and/or organization.

Materials The instructor will bring to class either recruiting brochures or newspaper advertisements.

Instructions The instructor will place students into teams and give them copies of recruiting brochures and/or advertisements. The instructor might assign one lengthy brochure; alternatively, several newspaper advertisements may be assigned. All teams should receive the same materials so that everyone is familiar with the items and results can be compared. Teams will evaluate the recruiting material(s) and answer the questions at right for each item:

1. What information in the text of this brochure/advertisement identifies conditions or activities in this organization or job that some applicants may not like?
2. If there are photographs or images of people at work, do they show only positive conditions, or do any show conditions or events that some applicants may not like?
3. After reading this item, would you say that it provides a realistic preview of the job and/or organization?

SELF-ASSESSMENT EXERCISE 18.5

MATCHING HOLLAND'S CAREER TYPES

Purpose This self-assessment exercise is designed to help you understand Holland's career types.

Instructions Holland's theory identifies six types of work environments. A brief description of each type appears below. Although few jobs fit purely into a single category, all have a dominant work environment type. In the table below, for each occupation, circle the letter representing the Holland type that you believe *best* fits that occupation's work environment.

Descriptions of Holland's six work environments

R Realistic—Work involves using hands, machines, or tools; focus on tangible results

I Investigative—Work involves discovering, collecting, and analyzing; focus on solving problems

A Artistic—Work involves creation of new products or ideas, typically in an unstructured setting

S Social—Work involves serving or helping others; focus on working in teams

E Enterprising—Work involves leading others; focus on achieving goals through others in a results-oriented setting

C Conventional—Work involves systematic manipulation of data or information

Occupation	Holland category						Occupation	Holland category					
Actuary	R	I	A	S	E	C	Mathematics teacher	R	I	A	S	E	C
Archeologist	R	I	A	S	E	C	Medical illustrator	R	I	A	S	E	C
Buyer	R	I	A	S	E	C	Minister/priest/rabbi	R	I	A	S	E	C
Computer operator	R	I	A	S	E	C	Pediatrician	R	I	A	S	E	C
Corporate executive	R	I	A	S	E	C	Pharmacist	R	I	A	S	E	C
Corporate trainer	R	I	A	S	E	C	Pilot	R	I	A	S	E	C
Dietitian	R	I	A	S	E	C	Production manager	R	I	A	S	E	C
Economist	R	I	A	S	E	C	Professional athlete	R	I	A	S	E	C
Elementary school teacher	R	I	A	S	E	C	Public relations director	R	I	A	S	E	C
Fashion model	R	I	A	S	E	C	Recreation leader	R	I	A	S	E	C
Firefighter	R	I	A	S	E	C	School administrator	R	I	A	S	E	C
Foreign exchange trader	R	I	A	S	E	C	Sculptor	R	I	A	S	E	C
Jeweler	R	I	A	S	E	C	Tax auditor	R	I	A	S	E	C
Life insurance agent	R	I	A	S	E	C	Veterinarian	R	I	A	S	E	C
Lobbyist	R	I	A	S	E	C	Wine maker	R	I	A	S	E	C

Interpreting Your Score When everyone is finished, the instructor will provide the correct answers. Add up the number of occupations that you matched correctly to determine your score. Then use your score to find out how well you understand Holland's career types.

Number Correct	Interpretation
26–30	Excellent understanding of Holland's career types
21–25	Good understanding of Holland's career types
16–20	Fair understanding of Holland's career types
11–15	Need to look more closely at Holland's descriptions
<11	Career counseling might not be your calling!

After studying the preceding material, be sure to check out our website at
www.mhhe.com/mcshane2e
for more in-depth information and interactivities that correspond to this chapter.

CASE 1   Arctic Mining Consultants

Tom Parker enjoyed working outdoors. At various times in the past, he worked as a ranch hand, high steel rigger, headstone installer, prospector, and geological field technician. Now 43, Parker is a geological field technician and field coordinator with Arctic Mining Consultants. He has specialized knowledge and experience in all nontechnical aspects of mineral exploration, including claim staking, line cutting and grid installation, soil sampling, prospecting, and trenching. He is responsible for hiring, training, and supervising field assistants for all of Arctic Mining Consultants' programs. Field assistants are paid a fairly low daily wage (no matter how long they work, which may be up to 12 hours or more) and are provided meals and accommodations. Many of the programs are operated by a project manager who reports to Parker.

Parker sometimes acts as a project manager, as he did on a job that involved staking 15 claims near Eagle Lake, Alaska. He selected John Talbot, Greg Boyce, and Brian Millar, all of whom had previously worked with Parker, as the field assistants. To stake a claim, the project team

marks a line with flagging tape and blazes along the perimeter of the claim, cutting a claim post every 500 yards (called a length). The 15 claims would require almost 60 miles of line. Parker had budgeted seven days (plus mobilization and demobilization) to complete the job. This schedule meant that each of the four stakers (Parker, Talbot, Boyce, and Millar) would have to complete a little over seven lengths each day. The following is a chronology of the project.

Day 1

The Arctic Mining Consultants crew assembled in the morning and drove to Eagle Lake, from where they were flown by helicopter to the claim site. On arrival, they set up tents at the edge of the area to be staked and agreed on a schedule for cooking duties. After supper, they pulled out the maps and discussed the job—how long it would take, the order in which the areas were to be staked, possible helicopter landing spots, and areas that might be more difficult to stake.

Parker pointed out that with only a week to complete the job, everyone would have to average seven and a half lengths per day. "I know that is a lot," he said, "but you've all staked claims before and I'm confident that each of you is capable of it. And it's only for a week. If we get the job done in time, there's a $300 bonus for each man." Two hours later, Parker and his crew members had developed what seemed to be a workable plan.

Day 2

Millar completed six lengths; Boyce, six lengths; Talbot, eight; and Parker, eight. Parker was not pleased with Millar's or Boyce's production. However, he didn't make an issue of it, thinking that they would develop their rhythm quickly.

Day 3

Millar completed five and a half lengths; Boyce, four; and Talbot, seven. Parker, who was nearly twice as old as the other three, completed eight lengths. He also had enough time remaining to walk over and check the quality of stakes that Millar and Boyce had completed, then walk back to his own area for helicopter pickup back to the tent site.

That night Parker exploded with anger. "I thought I told you that I wanted seven and a half lengths a day!" he shouted at Boyce and Millar. Boyce said that he was slowed down by unusually thick underbrush in his assigned area. Millar said that he had done his best and would try to pick up the pace. Parker did not mention that he had inspected their work. He explained that, as far as he was concerned, the field assistants were supposed to finish their assigned area for the day, no matter what.

Talbot, who was sharing a tent with Parker, talked to him later. "I think that you're being a bit hard on them, you know. I know that it has been more by luck than anything else that I've been able to do my quota. Yesterday I had only five lengths done after the first seven hours, and there was only an hour before I was supposed to be picked up. Then I hit a patch of really open bush and was able to do three lengths in 70 minutes. Why don't I take Millar's area tomorrow and he can have mine? Maybe that will help."

"Conditions are the same in all the areas," replied Parker, rejecting Talbot's suggestion. "Millar just has to try harder."

Day 4

Millar did seven lengths, and Boyce completed six and a half. When they reported their production that evening, Parker grunted uncommunicatively. Parker and Talbot did eight lengths each.

Day 5

Millar completed six lengths; Boyce, six; Talbot, seven and a half; and Parker, eight. Once again Parker blew up, but he concentrated his diatribe on Millar. "Why don't you do what you say you are going to do? You know that you have to do seven and a half lengths a day. We went over that when we first got here, so why don't you do it? If you aren't willing to do the job, then you never should have taken it in the first place!"

Millar replied by saying that he was doing his best, that he hadn't even stopped for lunch, and that he didn't know how he could possibly do any better. Parker launched into him again: "You have to work harder! If you put enough effort into it, you will get the area done!"

Later Millar commented to Boyce, "I hate getting dumped on all the time! I'd quit if it didn't mean that I'd have to walk 50 miles to the highway. And besides, I need the bonus money. Why doesn't he pick on you? You don't get any more done than I do; in fact, you usually do less. Maybe if you did a bit more he wouldn't be so bothered about me."

"I work only as hard as I have to," Boyce replied.

Day 6

Millar raced through breakfast, was the first one to be dropped off by the helicopter, and arranged to be the last one picked up. That evening the production figures were Millar, eight and a quarter lengths; Boyce, seven; and Talbot and Parker, eight each. Parker remained silent when the field assistants reported their performance for the day.

Day 7

Millar was again the first out and last in. That night, he collapsed in an exhausted heap at the table, too tired to eat. After a few moments, he announced in an abject tone, "Six lengths. I worked like a dog all day and I got only a lousy six lengths!" Boyce completed five lengths; Talbot, seven; and Parker, seven and a quarter.

Parker was furious. "That means we have to do a total of 34 lengths tomorrow if we are to finish this job on time!" With his eyes directed at Millar, he added: "Why is it that you never finish the job? Don't you realize that you are part of a team, and that you are letting the rest of the team down? I've been checking your lines, and you're doing too much blazing and wasting too much time making picture-perfect claim posts! If you worked smarter, you'd get a lot more done!"

Day 8

Parker cooked breakfast in the dark. The helicopter drop-offs began as soon as morning light appeared on the horizon. Parker instructed each assistant to complete eight lengths and, if they finished early, to help the others. Parker said

that he would finish the other 10 lengths. Helicopter pickups were arranged for one hour before dark.

By noon, after working as hard as he could, Millar had completed only three lengths. "Why bother," he thought to himself, "I'll never be able to do another five lengths before the helicopter comes, and I'll catch the same amount of abuse from Parker for doing six lengths as for seven and a half." So he sat down and had lunch and a rest. "Boyce won't finish his eight lengths either, so even if I did finish mine, I still wouldn't get the bonus. At least I'll get one more day's pay this way."

That night, Parker was livid when Millar reported that he had completed five and a half lengths. Parker had done ten and a quarter lengths, and Talbot had completed eight. Boyce proudly announced that he finished seven and a half lengths, but sheepishly added that Talbot had helped him with some of it. All that remained were the two and a half lengths that Millar had not completed.

The job was finished the next morning, and the crew was demobilized. Millar has never worked for Arctic Mining Consultants again, despite being offered work several times by Parker. Boyce sometimes does staking for Arctic, and Talbot works full-time with the company.

CASE 2   A Window on Life

For Gilbert LaCrosse, there is nothing quite as beautiful as a handcrafted wood-framed window. LaCrosse's passion for windows goes back to his youth in Eau Claire, Wisconsin, where he learned how to make residential windows from an elderly carpenter. He learned about the characteristics of good wood, the best tools to use, and how to choose the best glass from local suppliers. LaCrosse apprenticed with the carpenter in his small workshop and, when the carpenter

retired, was given the opportunity to operate the business himself.

LaCrosse hired his own apprentice as he built up business in the local area. His small operation soon expanded as the quality of windows built by LaCrosse Industries Ltd. became better known. Within eight years, the company employed nearly 25 people, and the business had moved to larger facilities to accommodate the increased demand throughout Wisconsin. In these early years, LaCrosse spent most of his time in the production shop, teaching new apprentices the unique skills that he had mastered and applauding the journeymen for their accomplishments. He would constantly repeat the point that LaCrosse products had to be of the highest quality because they gave families a "window on life."

After 15 years, LaCrosse Industries employed over 200 people. A profit-sharing program was introduced to give employees a financial reward for their contribution to the organization's success. As a result of the company's expansion, headquarters had to be moved to another area of the city, but the founder never lost touch with the workforce. Although new apprentices were now taught entirely by the master carpenters and other craftspeople, LaCrosse would still chat with plant and office employees several times each week.

When a second work shift was added, LaCrosse would show up during the evening break with coffee and boxes of donuts and discuss how the business was doing and how it became so successful through quality workmanship. Production employees enjoyed the times when he would gather them together to announce new contracts with developers from Chicago and New York. After each announcement, LaCrosse would thank everyone for making the business a success. They knew that LaCrosse quality had become a standard of excellence in window manufacturing across the eastern part of the country.

It seemed that almost every time he visited, LaCrosse would repeat the now well-known phrase that LaCrosse products had to be of the highest quality because they provided a window on life to so many families. Employees never grew tired of hearing this phrase from the company founder. However, it gained extra meaning when LaCrosse began posting photos of families looking through LaCrosse windows. At first, LaCrosse would personally visit developers and homeowners with a camera in hand. Later, as the "window on life" photos became known by developers and customers, people would send in photos of their own families looking through elegant front windows made by LaCrosse Industries. The company's marketing staff began using this idea, as well as LaCrosse's famous phrase, in their advertising. After one such marketing campaign, hundreds of photos were sent in by satisfied customers. Production and office employees took time after work to write personal letters of thanks to those who had submitted photos.

As the company's age reached the quarter-century mark, LaCrosse, now in his mid-fifties, realized that the organization's success and survival depended on expansion to other parts of the United States. After consulting with employees, LaCrosse made the difficult decision to sell a majority share to Build-All Products, Inc., a conglomerate with international marketing expertise in building products. As part of the agreement, Build-All brought in a vice president to oversee production operations while LaCrosse spent more time meeting with developers. LaCrosse would return to the plant and office at every opportunity, but often this would be only once a month.

Rather than visiting the production plant, Jan Vlodoski, the new production vice president, would rarely leave his office in the company's downtown headquarters. Instead, production orders were sent to supervisors by memorandum. Although product quality had been a priority throughout the company's history, less attention had been paid to inventory controls. Vlodoski introduced strict inventory guidelines and outlined procedures on using supplies for each shift. Goals were established for supervisors to meet specific inventory targets. Whereas employees previously tossed out several pieces of warped wood, they would now have to justify this action, usually in writing.

Vlodoski also announced new procedures for purchasing production supplies. LaCrosse Industries had highly trained purchasing staff who worked closely with senior craftspeople when selecting suppliers, but Vlodoski wanted to bring in Build-All's procedures. The new purchasing methods removed production leaders from the decision process and, in some cases, resulted in trade-offs that LaCrosse's employees would not have made earlier. A few employees quit during this time, saying that they did not feel comfortable about producing a window that would not stand the test of time. However, there were few jobs for carpenters at the time, so most staff members remained with the company.

After one year, inventory expenses decreased by approximately 10 percent, but the number of defective windows returned by developers and wholesalers had increased markedly. Plant employees knew that the number of defective windows would increase as they used somewhat lower-quality materials to reduce inventory costs. However, they heard almost no news about the seriousness of the problem until Vlodoski sent a memo to all production staff saying that quality must be maintained. During the latter part of the first year under Vlodoski, a few employees had the opportunity to personally ask LaCrosse about the changes and express their concerns. LaCrosse apologized, saying that as a result of his travels to new regions, he had not heard about the problems, and that he would look into the matter.

Exactly 18 months after Build-All had become majority shareholder of LaCrosse Industries, LaCrosse called together five of the original staff in the plant. The company founder looked pale and shaken as he said that Build-All's actions were inconsistent with his vision of the company, and, for the first time in his career, he did not know what to do. Build-All was not pleased with the arrangement either. Although LaCrosse windows still enjoyed a healthy market share and were competitive for the value, the company did not quite provide the minimum 18 percent return on equity that the conglomerate expected. LaCrosse asked his long-time companions for advice.

CASE 3   Maelstrom Communications

Sales manager Roger Todd was fuming. Thanks to, as he put it, "those nearsighted addleheads in service," he had nearly lost one of his top accounts. When told of Todd's complaint, senior serviceperson Ned Rosen retorted, "That figures. Anytime Mr. Todd senses even the remotest possibility of a sale, he immediately promises the customer the world on a golden platter. We can't possibly provide the service they request under the time constraints they give us and do an acceptable job."

Feelings of this sort were common in the departments both Roger and Ned worked for in Maelstrom Communications. Sales and service, the two dominant functions in the company, never saw eye to eye on anything, it seemed. The problems dated well back in the history of the company, even before Roger and Ned were hired some years ago.

Maelstrom Communications is a franchised distributorship belonging to a nationwide network of communications companies that sell products such as intercom, paging, sound, and interconnect telephone systems. Maelstrom competes directly with companies in the telephone hardware market. Equipment installation and maintenance service are an integral part of the total package Maelstrom offers.

Modern telephone system hardware is highly sophisticated, and few, if any, system users have the technological know-how to do their own equipment servicing. An excellent service record is crucial to the success of any company in the field. After the direct sale of a Maelstrom system, the sales force maintains contacts with customers. There is nothing the salespeople dislike so much as hearing that a customer hasn't received the type of service promised at the time of sale. On the other hand, service technicians complain of being hounded by the salespeople whenever a preferred customer needs a wire spliced. As Ned Rosen put it, "I can't remember the last time a service request came through that *wasn't* an emergency from a preferred customer."

Maelstrom's owner and president, Al Whitfield, has a strong sales background and views sales as the bread-and-butter department of the company. He is in on all major decisions and has final say on any matter brought to his attention. He spends most of his time working with sales and marketing personnel, and rarely concerns himself with the day-to-day activities of the service department unless a major problem of some sort crops up.

Next in line in Maelstrom's corporate hierarchy is the vice president in charge of production, Lawrence Henderson. Henderson is responsible for the acquisition and distribution of all job-related equipment and materials and for the scheduling of all service department activities. His sympathies lie primarily with the service department.

Each week Whitfield, Henderson, and all members of the sales force hold a meeting in Maelstrom's conference room. The sales personnel present their needs to Henderson so that equipment can be ordered and jobs scheduled. Service requests reported to salespeople from customers are also relayed to Henderson at this point. Once orders for service have been placed with production, sales personnel receive no feedback on the disposition of them (unless a customer complains to them directly) other than at these weekly meetings. It is common for a salesperson to think all is well with his or her accounts when, in fact, they are receiving delayed service or none at all. When an irate customer phones the sales representative to complain, it sets in motion the machinery that leads to disputes such as the one between Roger Todd and Ned Rosen.

It has become an increasingly common occurrence at Maelstrom for sales personnel to go to Henderson to complain when their requests are not met by the service department. Henderson has exhibited an increasing tendency to side with the service department and to tell the salespeople that existing service department priorities must be adhered to and that any sales requests will have to wait for rescheduling. At this point, a salesperson's only recourse is to go to Whitfield, who invariably agrees with the salesperson and instructs Henderson to take appropriate action. All of this is time-consuming and only serves to produce friction between the president and the vice president in charge of production.

Source: Written by Daniel Robey, Georgia State University, in collaboration with Todd Anthony. Used with permission.

CASE 4   Perfect Pizzeria

Perfect Pizzeria in Southville, deep in southern Illinois, is the chain's second-largest franchise. The headquarters is located in Phoenix, Arizona. Although the business is prospering, it has employee and managerial problems.

Each operation has one manager, an assistant manager, and from two to five night managers. The managers of each pizzeria work under an area supervisor. There are no systematic criteria for being a manager or becoming a manager trainee. The franchise has no formalized training period for the manager. No college education is required. The managers for whom the case observer worked during a four-year period were relatively young (ages 24 to 27), and only one had completed college. They came from the ranks of night managers, assistant managers, or both. The night managers were chosen for their ability to perform the duties of the regular employees. The assistant managers worked a two-hour shift during the luncheon period five days a week to gain knowledge about bookkeeping and management. Those becoming managers remained at that level unless they expressed interest in investing in the business.

The employees were mostly college students, with a few high school students performing the less challenging jobs. Because Perfect Pizzeria was located in an area with few job opportunities, it had a relatively easy task of filling its employee quotas. All the employees, with the exception of the manager, were employed part-time. Consequently, they earned only the minimum wage.

The Perfect Pizzeria system is devised so that food and beverage costs and profits are set up according to a percentage. If the percentage of food unsold or damaged in any way is very low, the manager gets a bonus. If the percentage is high, the manager does not receive a bonus; rather, he or she receives only his or her normal salary.

There are many ways in which the percentage can fluctuate. Because the manager cannot be in the store 24 hours a day, some employees make up for their paychecks by helping themselves to the food. When a friend comes in to order a pizza, extra ingredients are put on the friend's pizza. Occasional nibbles by 18 to 20 employees throughout the day at the meal table also raise the percentage figure. An occasional bucket of sauce may be spilled or a pizza accidentally burned. Sometimes the wrong size of pizza may be made.

In the event of an employee mistake or a burned pizza by the oven person, the expense is supposed to come from the individual. Because of peer pressure, the night manager seldom writes up a bill for the erring employee. Instead, the establishment takes the loss and the error goes unnoticed until the end of the month when the inventory is taken. That's when the manager finds out that the percentage is high and that there will be no bonus.

In the present instance, the manager took retaliatory measures. Previously, each employee was entitled to a free pizza, salad, and all the soft drinks he or she could drink for every 6 hours of work. The manager raised this figure from 6 to 12 hours of work. However, the employees had received these 6-hour benefits for a long time. Therefore, they simply took advantage of the situation whenever the manager or the assistant was not in the building. Although the night managers theoretically had complete control of the operation in the evenings, they did not command the respect that the manager or assistant manager did. That was because night managers received the same pay as the regular employees, could not reprimand other employees, and were basically the same age or sometimes even younger than the other employees.

Thus, apathy grew within the pizzeria. There seemed to be a further separation between the manager and his workers, who started out to be a closely knit group. The manager made no attempt to alleviate the problem, because he felt it would iron itself out. Either the employees who were dissatisfied would quit or they would be content to put up with the new regulations. As it turned out, there was a rash of employee dismissals. The manager had no problem in filling the vacancies with new workers, but the loss of key personnel was costly to the business.

With the large turnover, the manager found he had to spend more time in the building, supervising and sometimes taking the place of inexperienced workers. This was in direct violation of the franchise regulation, which stated that a manager would act as a supervisor and at no time take part in the actual food preparation. Employees were not placed under strict supervision with the manager working alongside them. The operation no longer worked smoothly because of differences between the remaining experienced workers and the manager concerning the way in which a particular function should be performed.

Within a two-month period, the manager was again free to go back to his office and leave his subordinates in charge of the entire operation. During this two-month period, in spite of the differences between experienced workers and the manager, the unsold/damaged food percentage had returned to the previous low level and the manager received a bonus each month. The manager felt that his problems had been resolved and that conditions would remain the same, since the new personnel had been properly trained.

It didn't take long for the new employees to become influenced by the other employees. Immediately after the manager had returned to his supervisory role, the unsold/damaged food percentage began to rise. This time the manager took a bolder step. He cut out any benefits that the employees had—no free pizzas, salads, or drinks. With the job market at an even lower ebb than usual, most employees were forced to stay. The appointment of a new area supervisor made it impossible for the manager to "work behind the counter," because the supervisor was centrally located in Southville.

The manager tried still another approach to alleviate the rising unsold/damaged food percentage problem and maintain his bonus. He placed a notice on the bulletin board, stating that if the percentage remained at a high level, a lie detector test would be given to all employees. All those found guilty of taking or purposefully wasting food or drinks would be immediately terminated. This did not have the desired effect on the employees, because they knew if they were all subjected to the test, all would be found guilty and the manager would have to dismiss all of them. This would leave him in a worse situation than ever.

Even before the following month's percentage was calculated, the manager knew it would be high. He had evidently received information from one of the night managers about the employees' feelings toward the notice. What he did not expect was that the percentage would reach an all-time high. That is the state of affairs at the present time.

Source: J. E. Dittrich and R. A. Zawacki, *People and Organizations* (Plano, TX: Business Publications, 1981), pp. 126–28. Used by permission of Irwin/McGraw-Hill.

CASE 5   TriVac Industries Inc.

TriVac Industries Inc., an Akron, Ohio based manufacturer of centralized vacuum systems, was facing severe cash flow problems due to increasing demand for its products and rapid expansion of production facilities. Steve Heinrich, TriVac's founder and majority shareholder, flew to Germany to meet with management of Rohrtech Gmb to discuss the German company's willingness to become majority shareholder of TriVac Industries in exchange for an infusion of much-needed cash. A deal was struck whereby Rohrtech would become majority shareholder while Heinrich would remain as TriVac's president. One of Rohrtech's senior executives would become the chairperson of TriVac's board of directors and Rohrtech would appoint two other board members.

This relationship worked well until Rohrtech was acquired by a European conglomerate two years later. Rohrtech's new owner wanted more precise financial information and controls placed on its holdings, including TriVac Industries, but Heinrich resented this imposition and refused to provide the necessary information. Relations between Rohrtech and TriVac Industries quickly soured to the point where Heinrich refused to let Rohrtech representatives into the TriVac Industries plant. He also instituted legal proceedings to regain control of the company.

According to the original agreement between TriVac and Rohrtech, any party who possessed over two-thirds of a company's shares could force the others to sell their shares to the majority shareholder. Heinrich owned 29 percent of TriVac's shares, whereas Rohrtech owned 56 percent. The remaining 15 percent of TriVac Industries shares were held by Tex Weston, TriVac's vice president of sales and marketing. Weston was one of TriVac's original investors and a long-time executive at TriVac Industries, but he had remained quiet throughout most of the battle between Rohrtech and Heinrich. However, Weston finally agreed to sell his shares to Rohrtech, thereby forcing Heinrich to give up his shares. When Heinrich's bid for control failed, Rohrtech purchased all remaining shares and TriVac's board of directors (now dominated by Rohrtech) fired Heinrich as president. The board immediately appointed Weston as TriVac Industries' new president.

Searching for a New COO

Several months before Heinrich was fired as president, the chairman of TriVac's board of directors privately received instructions from Rohrtech to hire an executive search firm in New York to identify possible outside candidates for the new position of chief operating officer

(COO) at TriVac Industries. The successful candidate would be hired after the conflict with Heinrich had ended (presumably with Heinrich's departure). The COO would report to the president (the person eventually replacing Heinrich) and would be responsible for day-to-day management of the company. Rohrtech's management correctly believed that most of TriVac's current managers were loyal to Heinrich, and, by hiring an outsider, the German firm would gain more inside control over its American subsidiary (TriVac).

The executive search firm identified several qualified executives interested in the COO position, and three candidates were interviewed by TriVac's chairman and another Rohrtech representative. One of these candidates, Kurt Devine, was vice president of sales at an industrial packaging firm in Albany, New York, and, at 52 years of age, was looking for one more career challenge before retirement. The Rohrtech representatives explained the current situation and said that they were offering stable employment after the problem with Heinrich was resolved so that the COO could help settle TriVac's problems. When Devine expressed his concern about rivalry with internal candidates, the senior Rohrtech manager stated: "We have a bookkeeper, but he is not our choice. The sales manager is capable, but he is located in California and doesn't want to move to Ohio."

One week after Heinrich was fired and Weston was appointed president, TriVac's chairman invited Devine to a meeting at a posh hotel attended by the chairman, another Rohrtech manager on TriVac's board of directors, and Weston. The chairman explained the recent events at TriVac Industries and formally invited Devine to accept the position of chief operating officer. After discussing salary and details about job duties, Devine asked the others whether he had their support as well as the support of TriVac's employees. The two Rohrtech representatives said yes while Weston remained silent. When the chairman left the room to get a bottle of wine to toast the new COO, Devine asked Weston how long he had known about the decision to hire him. Weston replied: "Just last week when I became president. I was surprised . . . I don't think I would have hired you."

Confrontation with Tom O'Grady

Devine began work at TriVac Industries in early October and, within a few weeks, noticed that the president and two other TriVac Industries managers were not giving him the support he needed to accomplish his work. For example, Weston would call the salespeople almost daily yet spoke to Devine only when Devine approached him first. The vice president of sales acted cautiously toward Devine, whereas Tom O'Grady, the vice president of finance and administration, seemed to resent his presence the most. O'Grady had been promoted from the position of controller in October and now held the highest rank at TriVac Industries below Devine. After Heinrich's departure, TriVac's board of directors had placed O'Grady in charge of day-to-day operations until Devine took over.

Devine depended on O'Grady for general operations information because he had more knowledge than anyone else about many aspects of the business. However, O'Grady provided incomplete information on many occasions and would completely refuse to educate the COO on some matters. O'Grady was also quick to criticize many of Devine's decisions and made indirect statements to Devine about his appropriateness as a COO. He also mentioned how he and other TriVac managers didn't want the German company (Rohrtech) to interfere with their company.

Devine would later learn about other things O'Grady had said and done to undermine his position. For example, O'Grady actively spoke to office staff and other managers about the problems with Devine and encouraged them to tell the president about their concerns. Devine overheard O'Grady telling another manager that Devine's memoranda were a "complete joke" and that "Devine didn't know what he was talking about most of the time." On one occasion, O'Grady let Devine present incorrect information to resellers (companies that sold TriVac products to customers) even though O'Grady knew that it was incorrect "just to prove what an idiot Rohrtech had hired."

Just six weeks after joining TriVac Industries, Devine confronted O'Grady with his concerns. O'Grady was quite candid with the COO, saying everyone felt that Devine was a "plant" by Rohrtech and was trying to turn TriVac Industries into a branch office of the German company. He said that some employees would quit if Devine did not leave because they wanted TriVac Industries to maintain its independence from Rohrtech. In a later meeting with Devine and Weston, O'Grady repeated these points and added that Devine's management style was not appropriate for TriVac Industries. Devine responded that he had not received any support from TriVac Industries since the day he had arrived even though Rohrtech had sent explicit directions to Weston and other TriVac Industries managers that he was to have complete support in managing the company's daily operations. Weston told the two men that they should work together and that, of course, Devine was the more senior person.

Decision by TriVac's Board of Directors

As a member of TriVac's board of directors, Weston included Devine's performance on the January meeting's agenda and invited O'Grady to provide comments at that meeting. On the basis of this this testimony, the board decided to remove Devine from the COO job and give him a special project instead. O'Grady was immediately named acting COO. The chairman and other Rohrtech representatives on TriVac's board were disappointed that events did not unfold as they had hoped, but they agreed to remove Devine rather than face the mass exodus of TriVac managers that Weston and O'Grady had warned about.

In late April, Devine attended a morning meeting of TriVac's board of directors to present his interim report on the special project. The board agreed to give Devine until mid-June to complete the project. However, the board recalled Devine into the boardroom in the afternoon and Weston bluntly asked Devine why he didn't turn in his resignation. Devine replied: "I can't think of a single reason why I should. I will not resign. I joined your company six months ago as a challenge. I have not been allowed to do my job. My decision to come here was based on support from Rohrtech and upon a great product." The next day, Weston came to Devine's office with a letter of termination signed by the chairman of TriVac's board of directors.

Theory Building and Scientific Research Methods

People need to make sense of their world, so they form theories about the way the world operates. A **theory** is a general set of propositions that describes interrelationships among several concepts. We form theories for the purpose of predicting and explaining the world around us.[1] What does a good theory look like? First, it should be stated as clearly and simply as possible so that the concepts can be measured and no ambiguity exists regarding the theory's propositions. Second, the elements of the theory must be logically consistent with each other, because we cannot test anything that doesn't make sense. Finally, a good theory provides value to society; it helps people understand their world better than they could without the theory.[2]

The Process of Theory Building

Theory building is a continuous process that typically includes the inductive and deductive stages shown in Exhibit A.1.[3] The inductive stage draws on personal experience to form a preliminary theory, whereas the deductive stage uses the scientific method to test the theory.

The inductive stage of theory building involves observing the world around us, identifying a pattern of relationships, and then forming a theory from these personal observations. For example, you might casually notice that new employees want their supervisor to give direction, whereas this leadership style irritates long-service employees. From these observations, you form a theory about the effectiveness of directive leadership. (See Chapter 14 for a discussion of this leadership style.)

Positivism versus Interpretivism Research requires an interpretation of reality, and researchers tend to perceive reality in one of two ways. A common view, called **positivism,** is that reality exists independent of people. It is "out there" to be discovered and tested. Positivism is the foundation for most quantitative research (statistical analysis). It assumes that we can measure variables and that those variables have fixed relationships with other variables. For example, the positivist perspective says that we could study whether a supportive style of leadership reduces stress. If we find evidence of this connection, then someone else studying leadership and stress would "discover" the same relationship.

Interpretivism takes a different view of reality. It suggests that reality comes from shared

582

EXHIBIT A.1

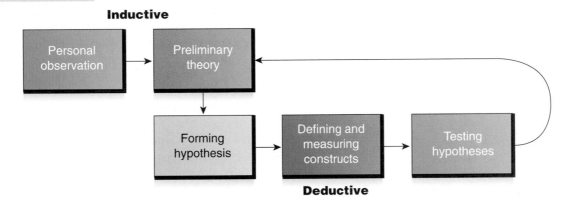

meaning among people in that environment. For example, supportive leadership is a personal interpretation of reality, not something that can be measured across time and people. Interpretivists rely mainly on qualitative data, such as observation and nondirective interviews. They particularly listen to the language people use to understand the common meaning that people have toward various events or phenomena. For example, they might argue that you need to experience and observe supportive leadership to study it effectively. Moreover, you can't really predict relationships because the specific situation shapes reality.[4]

Most OB scholars identify themselves somewhere in between the extreme views of positivism and interpretivism. Many believe that inductive research should begin with an interpretivist angle. We should enter a new topic with an open mind and search for shared meaning of people in that situation. In other words, researchers should let the participants define reality rather than let the researcher's preconceived notions shape that reality. This process involves gathering qualitative information and letting this information shape the theory.[5] After the theory emerges, researchers shift to a positivist perspective by quantitatively testing relationships in that theory.

Theory Testing: The Deductive Process   Once a theory has been formed, we shift into the deductive stage of theory building. This process includes forming hypotheses, defining and measuring constructs, and testing hypotheses (see Exhibit A.1). **Hypotheses** make empirically testable declarations that certain variables and their corresponding measures are related in a specific way proposed by the theory. For instance, to find support for the directive leadership theory described earlier, we need to form and then test a specific hypothesis from that theory. One such hypothesis might be: "New employees are more satisfied with supervisors who exhibit a directive rather than a nondirective leadership style." Hypotheses are indispensable tools of scientific research, because they provide the vital link between the theory and empirical verification.

Defining and measuring constructs   Hypotheses are testable only if we can define and then form measurable indicators of the concepts stated in those hypotheses. Consider the hypothesis in the previous paragraph about new employees and directive leadership. To test this hypothesis, we first need to define the concepts, such as "new employees," "directive leadership," and "supervisor." These concepts are known as **constructs,** because they are abstract ideas constructed by the researcher that can be linked to observable information. Organizational behavior scholars developed the construct called *directive leadership* to help them understand the different effects that leaders have over followers. We can't directly see, taste, or smell directive leadership; instead, we rely on indirect indicators that it exists, such as observing someone giving directions, maintaining clear performance standards, and ensuring that procedures and practices are followed.

As you can see, defining constructs well is very important, because these definitions become the foundation for finding or developing acceptable measures of those constructs. We can't measure directive leadership if we have only a vague idea about what this concept means. The better the definition is, the better our chances are of applying a measure that adequately represents that construct. However, even with a good definition, constructs can be difficult to measure, because the empirical representation must capture several elements in the definition. A measure of directive leadership must be able to identify not only people who give directions but also those who maintain performance standards and ensure that procedures are followed.

Testing hypotheses   The third step in the deductive process is to collect data for the empirical measures of the variables. Following our directive leadership example, we might conduct a formal survey in which new employees indicate the behavior of their supervisors and their attitudes toward their supervisor. Alternatively, we might design an experiment in which people work with someone who applies either a directive or nondirective leadership style. When the data have been collected, we can use various procedures to test our hypotheses statistically.

A major concern in theory building is that some researchers might inadvertently find support for their theory simply because they use the same information used to form the theory during the inductive stage. Consequently, the deductive stage must collect new data that are completely independent of the data used during the inductive stage. For instance, you might decide to test your theory of directive leadership by studying employees in another organization. Moreover, the inductive process may have relied mainly on personal observation, whereas the deductive process might use survey questionnaires. By studying different samples and using different measurement tools, we minimize the risk of conducting circular research.

Using the Scientific Method   Earlier, we said that the deductive stage of theory building follows the scientific method. The **scientific method** is a systematic, controlled, empirical, and critical investigation of hypothetical propositions about the presumed relationships among natural phenomena.[6] There are several elements to this definition, so let's look at each one. First, scientific research is systematic and controlled, because researchers want to rule out all but one explanation for a set of interrelated events. To rule out alternative explanations, we need to control them in some way, such as by keeping them constant or removing them entirely from the environment.

Second, we say that scientific research is empirical because researchers need to use objective reality—or as close as they can get to it—to test a theory. Researchers measure observable elements of the environment, such as what a person says or does, rather than rely on their own subjective opinion to draw conclusions. Moreover, scientific research analyzes these data using acceptable principles of mathematics and logic.

Finally, scientific research involves critical investigation. This aspect means that the study's hypotheses, data, methods, and results are openly described so that other experts in the field can properly evaluate this research. It also means that scholars are encouraged to critique and build on previous research. The scientific method encourages the refinement and, eventually, the replacement of a particular theory with one that better suits our understanding of the world.

Selected Issues in Organizational Behavior Research

There are many issues to consider in theory building, particularly when we use the deductive process to test hypotheses. Some of the more important issues are sampling, causation, and ethical practices in organizational research.

Sampling in Organizational Research   When finding out why things happen in organizations, we typically gather information from a few sources and then draw conclusions about the larger population. If we survey several employees and determine that older employees are more loyal to their company, then we would like to generalize this statement to all older employees in our population, not just those whom we surveyed. Scientific inquiry generally requires researchers to engage in **representative sampling**—that is, sampling a population in such a way that we can extrapolate the results of that sample to the larger population.

One factor that influences representativeness is whether the sample is selected in an unbiased way from the larger population. Let's suppose that you want to study organizational commitment among employees in your organization. A casual procedure might result in sampling too few employees from the head office and too many located elsewhere in the country. If head office employees actually have higher loyalty than employees located elsewhere, then the biased sampling would cause the results to underestimate the true level of loyalty among employees in the company. If you repeat the process again next year but somehow overweight employees from the head office, the results might wrongly suggest that employees have increased their organizational commitment over the past year. In reality, the only change may be the direction of sampling bias.

How do we minimize sampling bias? The answer is to randomly select the sample. A randomly drawn sample gives each member of the population an equal probability of being chosen, so there is less likelihood that a subgroup within that population dominates the study's results.

The same principle applies to random assignment of subjects to groups in experimental designs. If we want to test the effects of a team development training program, we need to randomly place some employees in the training group and randomly place others in a group that does not receive training. Without this random selection, each group might have different types of employees, so we wouldn't know whether the training explains the differences between the two groups. Moreover, if employees respond differently to the training program, we couldn't be sure that the training program results are representative of the larger population. Of course, random sampling does not necessarily produce a perfectly representative sample, but we do know that this is the best approach to ensure unbiased selection.

The other factor that influences representativeness is sample size. Whenever we select a portion of the population, there will be some error in our estimate of the population values. The larger the sample, the less error will occur in our estimate. Let's suppose that you want to find out how employees in a 500-person firm feel about smoking in the workplace. If you ask 400 of those employees, the information would provide a very good estimate of how the entire workforce in that organization feels. If you survey only 100 employees, the estimate might deviate more from the true population. If you ask only 10 people, the estimate could be quite different from what all 500 employees feel.

Notice that sample size goes hand in hand with random selection. You must have a sufficiently large sample size for the principle of randomization to work effectively. In our example of attitudes toward smoking, we would do a poor job of random selection if our sample consisted of only 10 employees from the 500-person organization. These 10 people probably wouldn't capture the diversity of employees throughout the organization. In fact, the more diverse the population, the larger the sample size should be, to provide adequate representation through random selection.

Causation in Organizational Research   Theories present notions about relationships among constructs. Often, these propositions suggest a causal relationship, namely, that one variable has an effect on another variable. When discussing causation, we refer to variables as being independent or dependent. Independent variables are the presumed causes of dependent variables, which are the presumed effects. In our earlier example of directive leadership, the main independent variable (although there might be others) would be the supervisor's directive or nondirective leadership style, because we presume that it causes the dependent variable (satisfaction with supervision).

In laboratory experiments (described later), the independent variable is always manipulated by the experimenter. In our research on directive leadership, we might have subjects (new employees) work with supervisors who exhibit directive or nondirective leadership behaviors.

If subjects are more satisfied under the directive leaders, then we would be able to infer an association between the independent and dependent variables.

Researchers must satisfy three conditions to provide sufficient evidence of causality between two variables.[7] The first condition of causality is that the variables are empirically associated with each other. An association exists whenever one measure of a variable changes systematically with a measure of another variable. This condition of causality is the easiest to satisfy, because there are several well-known statistical measures of association. A research study might find, for instance, that heterogeneous groups (in which members come from diverse backgrounds) produce more creative solutions to problems. This association would be observed when the measure of creativity (such as number of creative solutions produced within a fixed time) is higher for teams that have a high score on the measure of group heterogeneity. They are statistically associated or correlated with each other.

The second condition of causality is that the independent variable precedes the dependent variable in time. Sometimes, this condition is satisfied through simple logic. In our group heterogeneity example, it doesn't make sense to say that the number of creative solutions caused the group's heterogeneity, because the group's heterogeneity existed before it produced the creative solutions. In other situations, however, the temporal relationship among variables is less clear. One example is the ongoing debate about job satisfaction and organizational commitment. Do companies develop more loyal employees by increasing their job satisfaction, or do changes in organizational loyalty cause changes in job satisfaction? Simple logic does not answer these questions; instead, researchers must use sophisticated longitudinal studies to build up evidence of a temporal relationship between these two variables.

The third requirement for evidence of a causal relationship is that the statistical association between two variables cannot be explained by a third variable. There are many associations that we quickly dismiss as being causally related. For example, there is a statistical association between the number of storks in an area

and the birthrate in that area. We know that storks don't bring babies, so something else must cause the association between these two variables. The real explanation is that both storks and birthrates have a higher incidence in rural areas.

In other studies, the third variable effect is less apparent. Many years ago, before polio vaccines were available, a study in the United States reported a surprisingly strong association between consumption of a certain soft drink and the incidence of polio. Was polio caused by drinking this soft drink, or did people with polio have a unusual craving for this beverage? Neither. Both polio and consumption of the soft drink were caused by a third variable: climate. There was a higher incidence of polio in the summer months and in warmer climates, and people drink more liquids in these climates.[8] As you can see from this example, researchers have a difficult time supporting causal inferences, because third variable effects are sometimes difficult to detect.

Ethics in Organizational Research   Organizational behavior researchers need to abide by the ethical standards of the society in which the research is conducted. One of the most important ethical considerations is the individual subject's freedom to participate in the study. For example, it is inappropriate to force employees to fill out a questionnaire or attend an experimental intervention for research purposes only. Moreover, researchers have an obligation to tell potential subjects about any potential risks inherent in the study so that participants can make an informed choice about whether or not to be involved.

Finally, researchers must be careful to protect the privacy of those who participate in the study. Researchers should let people know when they are being studied as well as guaranteeing that their individual information will remain confidential (unless publication of identities is otherwise granted). Researchers maintain anonymity through careful security of data. The research results usually aggregate data in numbers large enough that they do not reveal the opinions or characteristics of any specific individual. For example, we would report the average absenteeism of employees in a department rather than state the absence rates of each person. When data are shared with other researchers, it is usually necessary to specially code each case so that individual identities are not known.

Research Design Strategies

So far, we have described how to build a theory, including the specific elements of empirically testing that theory within the standards of scientific inquiry. But what are the different ways to design a research study so that we get the data necessary to achieve our research objectives? There are many strategies, but they fall mainly under three headings: laboratory experiments, field surveys, and observational research.

Laboratory Experiments   A **laboratory experiment** is any research study in which independent variables and variables outside the researcher's main focus of inquiry can be controlled to some extent. Laboratory experiments are usually located outside the everyday work environment, such as a classroom, simulation lab, or any other artificial setting in which the researcher can manipulate the environment. Organizational behavior researchers sometimes conduct experiments in the workplace (called *field experiments*) in which the independent variable is manipulated. However, the researcher has less control over the effects of extraneous factors in field experiments than in laboratory situations.

Advantages of laboratory experiments   There are many advantages of laboratory experiments. By definition, this research method offers a high degree of control over extraneous variables that would otherwise confound the relationships being studied. Suppose we want to test the effects of directive leadership on the satisfaction of new employees. One concern might be that employees are influenced by how much leadership is provided, not just the type of leadership style. An experimental design would allow us to control how often the supervisor exhibited this style so that this extraneous variable does not confound the results.

A second advantage of lab studies is that the independent and dependent variables can be developed more precisely than in field settings.

For example, the researcher can ensure that supervisors in a lab study apply specific directive or nondirective behaviors, whereas real-life supervisors would use a more complex mixture of leadership behaviors. By using more precise measures, we are more certain that we are measuring the intended construct. Thus, if new employees are more satisfied with supervisors in the directive leadership condition, we are more confident that the independent variable was directive leadership rather than some other leadership style.

A third benefit of laboratory experiments is that the independent variable can be distributed more evenly among participants. In our directive leadership study, we can ensure that approximately half of the subjects have a directive supervisor, whereas the other half have a nondirective supervisor. In natural settings, we might have trouble finding people who have worked with a nondirective leader and, consequently, we couldn't determine the effects of this condition.

Disadvantages of laboratory experiments   With these powerful advantages, you might wonder why laboratory experiments are the least appreciated form of organizational behavior research.[9] One obvious limitation of this research method is that it lacks realism and, consequently, the results might be different in the real world. One argument is that laboratory experiment subjects are less involved than their counterparts in an actual work situation. This argument is sometimes true, although many lab studies have highly motivated participants. Another criticism is that the extraneous variables controlled in the lab setting might produce a different effect of the independent variable on the dependent variables. This might also be true, but remember that the experimental design controls variables in accordance with the theory and its hypotheses. Consequently, this concern is really a critique of the theory, not the lab study.

Finally, there is the well-known problem that participants are aware they are being studied and this awareness causes them to act differently than they normally would. Some participants try to figure out how the researcher wants them to behave and then deliberately try to act that way. Other participants try to upset the experiment by doing just the opposite of what they believe the researcher expects. Still others might act unnaturally simply because they know they are being observed. Fortunately, experimenters are well aware of these potential problems and are usually (although not always) successful at disguising the study's true intent.

Field Surveys   **Field surveys** collect and analyze information in a natural environment—an office, factory, or other existing location. The researcher takes a snapshot of reality and tries to determine whether elements of that situation (including the attitudes and behaviors of people in that situation) are associated with each other as hypothesized. Everyone does some sort of field research. You might think that people from some states are better drivers than others, so you "test" your theory by looking at the way people with out-of-state license plates drive. Although your methods of data collection might not satisfy scientific standards, this is a form of field research because it takes information from a naturally occurring situation.

Advantages and disadvantages of field surveys One advantage of field surveys is that the variables often have a more powerful effect than they would in a laboratory experiment. Consider the effect of peer pressure on the behavior of members within the team. In a natural environment, team members would form very strong cohesive bonds over time, whereas a researcher would have difficulty replicating this level of cohesiveness and corresponding peer pressure in a lab setting.

Another advantage of field surveys is that the researcher can study many variables simultaneously, thereby permitting a fuller test of more complex theories. Ironically, this is also a disadvantage of field surveys, because it is difficult for the researcher to contain his or her scientific inquiry. There is a tendency to shift from deductive hypothesis testing to more inductive exploratory browsing through the data. If these two activities become mixed, the researcher can lose sight of the strict covenants of scientific inquiry.

The main weakness of field surveys is that it is very difficult to satisfy the conditions for causal conclusions. One reason is that the data are usually collected at one point in time, so the researcher must rely on logic to decide whether the independent variable really preceded the dependent variable. Contrast this situation with the lab study, in which the researcher can usually be confident that the independent variable was applied before the dependent variable occurred. Increasingly, organizational behavior studies use longitudinal research to provide a better indicator of temporal relations among variables, but this is still not as precise as the lab setting. Another reason causal analysis is difficult in field surveys is that extraneous variables are not controlled as they are in lab studies. Without this control, there is a higher chance that a third variable might explain the relationship between the hypothesized independent and dependent variables.

Observational Research   In their study of brainstorming and creativity, Robert Sutton and Andrew Hargadon observed 24 brainstorming sessions at IDEO, a product design firm in Palo Alto, California. They also attended a dozen "Monday morning meetings," conducted 60 semistructured interviews with IDEO executives and designers, held hundreds of informal discussions with these people, and read through several dozen magazine articles about the company.[10]

Sutton and Hargadon's use of observational research and other qualitative methods was quite appropriate for their research objectives, which were to reexamine the effectiveness of brainstorming beyond the number of ideas generated. Observational research generates a wealth of descriptive accounts about the drama of human existence in organizations. It is a useful vehicle for learning about the complex dynamics of people and their activities, such as brainstorming. (The results of Sutton and Hargadon's study are discussed in Chapter 10.)

Participant observation takes the observation method one step further by having the observer take part in the organization's activities. This experience gives the researcher a fuller understanding of the activities compared with just watching others participate in those activities.

Disadvantages of observational research   In spite of its intuitive appeal, observational research has a number of weaknesses. The main problem is that the observer is subject to the perceptual screening and organizing biases that we discuss in Chapter 6 of this textbook. There is a tendency to overlook the routine aspects of organizational life, even though they may prove to be the most important data for research purposes. Instead, observers tend to focus on unusual information, such as activities that deviate from what the observer expects. Because observational research usually records only what the observer notices, valuable information is often lost.

Another concern with the observation method is that the researcher's presence and involvement may influence the people whom he or she is studying. This factor can be a problem in short-term observations, but in the long term people tend to return to their usual behavior patterns. With ongoing observations, such as Sutton and Hargadon's study of brainstorming sessions at IDEO, employees eventually forget that they are being studied.

Finally, observation is usually a qualitative process, so it is more difficult to empirically test hypotheses with the data. Instead, observational research provides rich information for the inductive stages of theory building. It helps us form ideas about the way things work in organizations. We begin to see relationships that lay the foundation for new perspectives and theory. We must not confuse this inductive process of theory building with the deductive process of theory testing.

Scoring Keys for Self-Assessment Exercises

CHAPTER 2
Scoring Key for Assessing Your General Self-Efficacy
To calculate your score on the general self-efficacy scale, use the table below to assign the appropriate number to each statement. For example, if you indicated "Disagree" for statement 1, assign a 2 to that statement. Then add the numbers for all statements. Higher scores indicate that you have a higher level of self-efficacy; that is, you have a stronger can-do attitude toward new tasks and other challenges in life.

For statement items 1, 3, 8, 9, 13, 15	For statement items 2, 4, 5, 6, 7, 10, 11, 12, 14, 16, 17
Strongly agree = 5	Strongly agree = 1
Agree = 4	Agree = 2
Neutral = 3	Neutral = 3
Disagree = 2	Disagree = 4
Strongly disagree = 1	Strongly disagree = 5

CHAPTER 4
Scoring Key for Individualism–Collectivism Scale

Individualism: Add your circled numbers for the odd-numbered items (i.e., items 1, 3, 5, 7, 9, 11, 13, and 15). The maximum score is 40. Higher scores indicate more individualism.

Collectivism: Add your circled numbers for the even-numbered items (i.e., items 2, 4, 6, 8, 10, 12, 14, and 16). The maximum score is 40. Higher scores indicate more collectivism.

CHAPTER 5
Scoring Key for Growth Need Strength Scale
Step 1: The growth need strength scale yields a number from 1 ("Strongly prefer A") to 5 ("Strongly prefer B"). Write your circled numbers for the items indicated below, and add them to determine subtotal A.

$$\underline{\quad} + \underline{\quad} + \underline{\quad} + \underline{\quad} + \underline{\quad} + \underline{\quad} = \underline{\qquad}$$
$$\text{(1)} \quad \text{(5)} \quad \text{(7)} \quad \text{(10)} \quad \text{(11)} \quad \text{(12)} \quad \text{Subtotal A}$$

Step 2: The remaining items in the growth need strength scale need to be reverse-scored. To calculate a reverse score, subtract the direct score from 6. For example, if you circled 4 in one of these items, the reverse score would be 2 (i.e., $6 - 4 = 2$). If you circled 1, the reverse score would be 5 (i.e., $6 - 1 = 5$). Calculate the *reverse score* for the items indicated below and write them in the spaces provided. Then calculate subtotal B by adding these reverse scores.

$$\underline{\quad} + \underline{\quad} + \underline{\quad} + \underline{\quad} + \underline{\quad} + \underline{\quad} = \underline{\qquad}$$
$$\text{(2)} \quad \text{(3)} \quad \text{(4)} \quad \text{(6)} \quad \text{(8)} \quad \text{(9)} \quad \text{Subtotal B}$$

Step 3: Calculate the total scores by summing subtotal A and subtotal B. A total score below 30 indicates relatively low growth need strength, whereas a score above 42 indicates a relatively high growth need strength. Growth need strength indicates the strength of your growth needs, including self-esteem, personal achievement, and self-actualization.

$$\underline{\hspace{2cm}} + \underline{\hspace{2cm}} = \underline{\hspace{2cm}}$$
Subtotal A   Subtotal B   Total

CHAPTER 5

Scoring Key for Equity Sensitivity   To score this equity scale, called the Equity Preference Questionnaire (EPQ), complete the three steps below.

Step 1: Write your circled numbers for the items indicated below, and add them to determine subtotal A.

$$\underline{\hspace{0.5cm}} + \underline{\hspace{0.5cm}} + \underline{\hspace{0.5cm}} + \underline{\hspace{0.5cm}} + \underline{\hspace{0.5cm}} + \underline{\hspace{0.5cm}} + \underline{\hspace{0.5cm}} + \underline{\hspace{0.5cm}} = \underline{\hspace{1cm}}$$
(1) (2) (3) (4) (5) (6) (7) (10) Subtotal A

Step 2: The remaining items in the Equity Preference Questionnaire need to be reverse-scored. To calculate a reverse score, subtract the direct score from 6. For example, if you circled 4 in one of these items, the reverse score would be 2 (i.e., $6 - 4 = 2$). If you circled 1, the reverse score would be 5 (i.e., $6 - 1 = 5$). Calculate the *reverse score* for the items indicated below and write them in the spaces provided. Then calculate subtotal B by adding these reverse scores.

$$\underline{\hspace{0.5cm}} + \underline{\hspace{0.5cm}} + \underline{\hspace{0.5cm}} + \underline{\hspace{0.5cm}} + \underline{\hspace{0.5cm}} + \underline{\hspace{0.5cm}} + \underline{\hspace{0.5cm}} + \underline{\hspace{0.5cm}} = \underline{\hspace{1cm}}$$
(8) (9) (11) (12) (13) (14) (15) (16) Subtotal B

Step 3: Calculate the total score by summing subtotal A and subtotal B.

$$\underline{\hspace{2cm}} + \underline{\hspace{2cm}} = \underline{\hspace{2cm}}$$
Subtotal A   Subtotal B   Total

The Equity Preference Questionnaire measures the extent to which you are a "benevolent," an "equity sensitive," or an "entitled." Use the table below to determine your category as indicated by your total score.

EPQ score	Equity preference category
16–37	Entitleds—want to receive proportionately more than others (i.e., like to be overrewarded)
38–58	Equity Sensitives—want an outcome/input ratio equal to the ratio of the comparison other
59–80	Benevolents—are tolerant of situations where they are underrewarded

CHAPTER 6
Scoring Key for Money Attitude Scale   This instrument presents three dimensions with a smaller set of items than the original five-dimension, 62-item money attitude scale. However, this scale will provide some estimate of your money attitude on these three dimensions.

To calculate your score on each dimension, write the number that you circled in the scale to the corresponding item number in the scoring key below. For example, write the number you circled in the scale's first statement ("I sometimes purchase things . . .") on the line above "Item 1." Then add up the numbers for that dimension. The money attitude total score is calculated by adding up all scores for all dimensions.

Money attitude dimension	Calculation				Your score
Money as power/prestige	___ Item 1	+ ___ Item 4	+ ___ Item 7	+ ___ Item 10	= ___
Retention time	___ Item 2	+ ___ Item 5	+ ___ Item 8	+ ___ Item 11	= ___
Money anxiety	___ Item 3	+ ___ Item 6	+ ___ Item 9	+ ___ Item 12	= ___
Money Attitude Total	Add up all dimension scores =				___

The three money attitude scale dimensions measured here, as well as the total score, are defined as follows:

Money as power/prestige: People with higher scores (between 13 and 20 points) on this dimension tend to use money to influence and impress others.

Retention time: People with higher scores (between 13 and 20 points) on this dimension tend to be careful financial planners.

Money anxiety: People with higher scores (between 13 and 20 points) on this dimension tend to view money as a source of anxiety.

Money attitude total: This is a general estimate of how much respect and attention you give to money.

CHAPTER 6
Scoring Key for Self-Leadership Questionnaire   To calculate your score on the self-leadership questionnaire, write the number that you circled in the scale to the corresponding item number in the scoring key on the next page. For example, write the number you circled in the scale's third statement ("I like to work toward specific goals . . .") on the line above "Item 3." Then add the numbers for each dimension. Calculate the self-leadership total score by adding up all scores for all dimensions.

Self-leadership dimension	Calculation	Your score
Personal goal setting	—— + —— + —— = Item 3 Item 9 Item 15	——
Mental practice	—— + —— + —— = Item 6 Item 12 Item 18	——
Designing natural rewards	—— + —— + —— = Item 5 Item 11 Item 17	——
Self-monitoring	—— + —— + —— = Item 1 Item 7 Item 13	——
Self-reinforcement	—— + —— + —— = Item 4 Item 10 Item 16	——
Cueing strategies	—— + —— + —— = Item 2 Item 8 Item 14	——
Self-Leadership Total	Add up all dimension scores =	——

The six self-leadership dimensions measured here, as well as the total score, are defined as follows:

Personal goal setting: People with higher scores (10 or more points) have a strong tendency to set their own performance-oriented goals.

Mental practice: Mental practice is similar to constructive thought patterns. People with higher scores (10 or more points) have a strong tendency to rehearse future events and practice behaviors in their mind.

Designing natural rewards: People with higher scores (10 or more points) have a strong tendency to organize their work and seek out work activities that maximize their need fulfillment.

Self-monitoring: People with higher scores (10 or more points) have a strong tendency to keep track of how well they are performing a task.

Self-reinforcement: People with higher scores (10 or more points) have a strong tendency to reward themselves after successfully completing a task.

Cueing Strategies: People with higher scores (10 or more points) have a strong tendency to create symbols or indicators that remind them of their task or keep them focused on the task. Although not explicitly described in Chapter 6, cueing strategies are similar to "antecedents" in the A-B-C model of organizational behavior modification described in Chapter 2. The only difference is that these antecedents are self-developed or self-controlled rather than introduced and controlled by others.

Self-leadership (total): Self-leadership is the process of influencing oneself to establish the self-direction and self-motivation needed to perform a task. People with higher scores (60 or more points) have a high incidence of self-leadership.

CHAPTER 7

Scoring Key for Time Stress Scale To estimate how time-stressed you are, add the number of items for which you circled "Yes." You are considered time-stressed if you answered "Yes" to seven or more of these items. Low time-stress is indicated by fewer than four "yes" answers.

CHAPTER 8

Scoring Key for Team Roles Preferences Scale Write your circled score for each statement on the appropriate line below (statement numbers are in parentheses), and add the numbers for each role category. These roles are described in Chapter 8.

Encourager	—— + —— + —— = —— (6) (9) (11)
Gatekeeper	—— + —— + —— = —— (4) (10) (13)
Harmonizer	—— + —— + —— = —— (3) (8) (12)
Initiator	—— + —— + —— = —— (1) (5) (14)
Summarizer	—— + —— + —— = —— (2) (7) (15)

The five team roles dimensions measured here are defined as follows:

Encourager: People who score higher (10 points or above) in this dimension have a strong tendency to praise and support the ideas of other team members, thereby showing warmth and solidarity to the group.

Gatekeeper: People who score higher (10 points or above) in this dimension have a strong tendency to encourage all team members to participate in discussions.

Harmonizer: People who score higher (10 points or above) in this dimension have a strong tendency to mediate intragroup conflicts and reduce tension.

Initiator: People who score higher (10 points or above) in this dimension have a strong tendency to identify goals for meetings, including ways to work on goals.

Summarizer: People who score higher (10 points or above) in this dimension have a strong tendency to keep track of what was said in meetings (i.e., act as the team's memory).

CHAPTER 9

Scoring Key for Decision Making Style Inventory Write your circled score for each statement on the appropriate line (statement numbers are in parentheses), and add the numbers for each decision style.

Rational
decision style   ___ + ___ + ___ + ___ = ___
                  (1)   (2)   (6)   (8)

Intuitive
decision style   ___ + ___ + ___ + ___ = ___
                  (3)   (4)   (5)   (7)

CHAPTER 10
Scoring Key for Assessing Your Creative Disposition

Assign +1 to the following words if you marked them: capable, clever, confident, egotistical, humorous, individualistic, informal, insightful, intelligent, inventive, original, reflective, resourceful, self-confident, sexy, snobbish, unconventional, wide interests.

Assign −1 to the following words if you marked them: affected, cautious, commonplace, conservative, conventional, dissatisfied, honest, mannerly, narrow interests, sincere, submissive, suspicious.

Add the numbers to determine the total score, which will range from −12 to +18. Generally, people who score above +5 on this scale have more creative personalities than typical college students or people working in most professional occupations.

CHAPTER 11
Scoring Key for Active Listening Skills Inventory

Step 1: Using the table below, assign the appropriate number to each statement. For example, if you indicated "Very much" for statement 1, assign a 3 to that statement.

For statement items 3, 4, 6, 7, 10, 13	For statement items 1, 2, 5, 8, 9, 11, 12, 14, 15
Not at all = 3	Not at all = 0
A little = 2	A little = 1
Somewhat = 1	Somewhat = 2
Very much = 0	Very much = 3

Step 2: Write the score for each statement on the appropriate line below (statement numbers are in parentheses), and add the scores for each dimension.

Then calculate the overall score by summing the scores for all dimensions.

Avoiding
interruption (AI)   ___ + ___ + ___ = ___
                     (3)   (7)   (15)   (AI)

Maintaining
interest (MI)   ___ + ___ + ___ = ___
                 (6)   (9)   (14)   (MI)

Postponing
evaluation (PE)   ___ + ___ + ___ = ___
                   (1)   (5)   (13)   (PE)

Organizing
information (OI)   ___ + ___ + ___ = ___
                   (2)   (10)   (12)   (OI)

Showing
interest (SI)   ___ + ___ + ___ = ___
                 (4)   (8)   (11)   (SI)

Total score   ___ + ___ + ___ + ___ + ___ = ___
               (AI) (MI) (PE) (OI) (SI) Total

The five active listening dimensions and the overall active listening scale measured here are defined as follows:

Avoiding interruption: People who score higher (10 points or above) in this dimension have a strong tendency to let the speaker finish his or her statements before responding.

Maintaining interest: People who score higher (10 points or above) in this dimension have a strong tendency to remain focused and concentrate on what the speaker is saying even when the conversation is boring or the information is well known.

Postponing evaluation: People who score higher (10 points or above) in this dimension have a strong tendency to keep an open mind and avoid evaluating what the speaker is saying until the speaker has finished.

Organizing information: People who score higher (10 points or above) in this dimension have a strong tendency to actively organize the speaker's ideas into meaningful categories.

Showing interest: People who score higher (10 points or above) in this dimension have a strong tendency to use nonverbal gestures or brief verbal acknowledgments to demonstrate that they are paying attention to the speaker.

Active listening (total): People who score higher (50 points or above) in this dimension have a strong tendency to actively sense the sender's signals, evaluate them accurately, and respond appropriately.

Note: This scale does not explicitly measure two other dimensions of active listening, namely, empathizing and providing feedback. Empathizing is difficult to measure, and providing feedback involves behaviors similar to those for showing interest.

CHAPTER 12
Scoring Key for Perceptions of Politics Scale (POPS)

Step 1: To calculate your score on the Perceptions of Politics Scale, use the table below to assign the appropriate number to each statement.

People who score 7 or above on the "General political behavior" dimension believe that their school has a politicized culture. People who score 25 or higher on the "Go along to get ahead" dimension believe that employees at this school get ahead by avoiding disagreements.

For statement items 1, 4, 5, 6, 7, 8, 9	For statement items 2, 3
Strongly agree = 5	Strongly agree = 1
Agree = 4	Agree = 2
Neutral = 3	Neutral = 3
Disagree = 2	Disagree = 4
Strongly disagree = 1	Strongly disagree = 5

Step 2: Write the score for each statement on the appropriate line below (statement numbers are in parentheses), and add the scores to determine subtotals A and B. Then calculate the total score by summing subtotals A and B.

General political behavior __ (1) + __ (5) = _____ Subtotal A

Go along to get ahead __ (2) + __ (3) + __ (4) + __ (6) + __ (7) + __ (8) + __ (9) = _____ Subtotal B

Total score: _____ Subtotal A + _____ Subtotal B = _____ Total

CHAPTER 13
Scoring Key for Conflict Management Style Orientation Scale

Write your circled score for each statement on the appropriate line (statement numbers are in parentheses), and add the numbers for each style category. Higher scores indicate that you are stronger in that conflict management style.

Competing __ (1) + __ (9) + __ (12) = __

Accommodating __ (2) + __ (7) + __ (11) = __

Compromising __ (3) + __ (6) + __ (15) = __

Avoiding __ (4) + __ (8) + __ (14) = __

Collaborating __ (5) + __ (10) + __ (13) = __

CHAPTER 14
Scoring Key for Leadership Dimensions Instrument

Transactional leadership: Add your circled numbers for the odd-numbered items (i.e., items 1, 3, 5, 7, 9, 11, 13, and 15). The maximum score is 40. High scores indicate that your supervisor has a strong inclination toward transactional leadership.

Transformational leadership: Add your circled numbers scores for the even-numbered items (i.e., items 2, 4, 6, 8, 10, 12, 14, and 16). The maximum score is 40. High scores indicate that your supervisor has a strong inclination toward transformational leadership.

CHAPTER 15
Scoring Key for Corporate Culture Preference Scale

All item numbers are listed in parentheses in the equations below. For each item, in the space provided, write a 1 if you circled that item and a 0 if you did not. Then add the numbers for each subscale. The maximum score for each subscale is 6, and the minimum is 0. The higher the score, the more that you would likely feel comfortable in that type of culture.

Control culture __ (2a) + __ (5a) + __ (6b) + __ (8b) + __ (11b) + __ (12a) = __

Performance culture __ (1b) + __ (3b) + __ (5b) + __ (6a) + __ (7a) + __ (9b) = __

Relationship culture __ (1a) + __ (3a) + __ (4b) + __ (8a) + __ (10b) + __ (12b) = __

Responsive culture __ (2b) + __ (4a) + __ (7b) + __ (9a) + __ (10a) + __ (11a) = __

These subscales, which be found in many organizations, represent only four of the many possible organizational culture values. Keep in mind that none of these subscales is inherently good or bad. Each is effective in different situations.

Control culture: This culture values the role of senior executives to lead the organization. Its goal is to keep everyone aligned and under control.

Performance culture: This culture values individual and organizational performance and strives for effectiveness and efficiency.

Relationship culture: This culture values nurturing and well-being. It considers open communication, fairness, teamwork, and sharing vital parts of organizational life.

Responsive culture: This culture values its ability to keep in tune with the external environment, including being competitive and realizing opportunities.

CHAPTER 16
Scoring Key for Tolerance of Change Scale

This measurement instrument is formally known as the Tolerance of Ambiguity Scale. Although it was developed 40 years ago, the instrument is still used today in research. People with a high tolerance of ambiguity are comfortable with uncertainty, sudden change, and new situations. These are characteristics of the hyperfast changes occurring in many organizations today.

To calculate your tolerance of change score, use the table below to assign the appropriate number to each statement. For example, if you indicated "Strongly agree" for statement 2, assign a 7 to that statement. Then add the numbers for all statements. Higher scores indicate that you have a higher tolerance of ambiguity.

For statement items 2, 4, 6, 8, 10, 12, 14, 16	For statement items 1, 3, 5, 7, 9, 11, 13, 15
Strongly agree = 7	Strongly agree = 1
Moderately agree = 6	Moderately agree = 2
Slightly agree = 5	Slightly agree = 3
Neutral = 4	Neutral = 4
Slightly disagree = 3	Slightly disagree = 5
Moderately disagree = 2	Moderately disagree = 6
Strongly disagree = 1	Strongly disagree = 7

CHAPTER 17
Scoring Key for Organizational Structure Preference Scale

Step 1: Using the table below, assign the appropriate number to each statement. For example, if you indicated "Very much" for statement 1, assign a 3 to that statement.

For statement items 2, 3, 8, 10, 11, 12, 14, 15	For statement items 1, 4, 5, 6, 7, 9, 13
Not at all = 3	Not at all = 0
A little = 2	A little = 1
Somewhat = 1	Somewhat = 2
Very much = 0	Very much = 3

Step 2: Write the score for each statement on the appropriate line below (statement numbers are in parentheses), and add the scores for each scale. Then calculate the overall score by summing the scores for all scales.

Tall hierarchy (H)   __ + __ + __ + __ + __ = __
(1)   (4)   (10)   (12)   (15)   (H)

Formalization (F)   __ + __ + __ + __ + __ = __
(2)   (6)   (8)   (11)   (13)   (F)

Centralization (C)   __ + __ + __ + __ + __ = __
(3)   (5)   (7)   (9)   (14)   (C)

Total score   __ + __ + __ = ____
(H)   (F)   (C)   Total

A higher total score indicates a preference for mechanistic organizations, whereas a lower score indicates a preference for more organic organizations.

The number following each definition indicates the chapter in which the term receives the fullest description.

A

ability The natural aptitudes and learned capabilities required to successfully complete a task. (2)

action learning A variety of experiential learning activities in which employees are involved in a real, complex, and stressful problem, usually in teams, with immediate relevance to the company. (2)

action research A data-based, problem-oriented process that diagnoses the need for change, introduces the organization development (OD) intervention, and then evaluates and stabilizes the desired changes. (16)

adaptive culture An organizational culture in which employees focus on the changing needs of customers and other stakeholders, and support initiatives to keep pace with those changes. (15)

affiliate networks Network organizations in which the satellite companies have a special affiliation with the core firm, such as investment or start-up support. (17)

alternative dispute resolution (ADR) A third-party dispute resolution process that includes mediation, typically followed by arbitration. (13)

appreciative inquiry An organization development intervention that directs the group's attention away from its own problems and focuses participants on the group's potential and positive elements. (16)

artifacts The observable symbols and signs of an organization's culture. (15)

attitudes The cluster of beliefs, assessed feelings, and behavioral intentions toward an object. (4)

attribution process The perceptual process of deciding whether an observed behavior or event is caused largely by internal or by external factors. (3)

autonomy The degree to which a job gives employees the freedom, independence, and discretion to schedule their work and determine the procedures used in completing it. (6)

B

behavior modification A theory that explains learning in terms of the antecedents and consequences of behavior. (2)

bicultural audit A process used to diagnose cultural relations between the companies in a potential merger and determine the extent to which cultural clashes are likely to occur. (15)

Big Five personality dimensions The five abstract dimensions representing most personality traits: conscientiousness, emotional stability, openness to experience, agreeableness, and extroversion. (3)

boundaryless career A career that operates across company and industry boundaries rather than just within a single organizational hierarchy. (18)

brainstorming A team decision-making process in which team members, in a freewheeling, face-to-face meeting, generate as many ideas as possible, piggyback on the ideas of others, and avoid evaluating anyone's ideas during the idea-generation stage. (10)

C

career A sequence of work-related experiences that people participate in over the span of their working lives. (18)

centrality The degree and nature of interdependence between the power holder and others. (12)

centralization The degree to which formal decision authority is held by a small group of people, typically those at the top of the organizational hierarchy. (17)

ceremonies Planned and usually dramatic displays of organizational culture, conducted specifically for the benefit of an audience. (15)

change agent Anyone who possesses enough knowledge and power to guide and facilitate the organizational change effort. (16)

coalition An informal group that attempts to influence people outside the group by pooling the resources and power of its members. (8)

codetermination A form of employee involvement required by some governments that typically operates at the work site as works councils and at the corporate level as supervisory boards. (9)

coercive power The ability to apply punishment. (12)

cognitive dissonance The conflict that occurs when people perceive an inconsistency between their beliefs and feelings and their behavior. (4)

communication The process by which information is transmitted and understood between two or more people. (11)

communication competence A person's ability to identify appropriate communication patterns in a given situation and to achieve goals by applying that knowledge. (11)

communities of practice Informal groups bound by shared expertise and a passion for a particular activity or interest. (1, 8)

competencies The abilities, values, personality traits, and other characteristics of people that lead to superior performance. (2)

concurrent engineering The cross-functional integration and concurrent development of a product or service and its associated processes, usually guided by a cross-functional project team consisting of people from marketing, design, manufacturing, customer service, and other areas. (17)

conflict The process in which one party perceives that its interests are being opposed or negatively affected by another party. (13)

conflict management Interventions that alter the level and form of conflict in ways that maximize its benefits and minimize its dysfunctional consequences. (13)

conscientiousness A Big Five personality dimension that characterizes people who are careful, dependable, and self-disciplined. (3)

constructive controversy Any situation in which people debate their differing opinions about an issue in a way that keeps the conflict focused on the task rather than the people. (10)

constructs Abstract ideas constructed by researchers that can be linked to observable information. (Appendix A)

content theories of motivation Theories that explain the dynamics of employee needs, such as why people have different needs at different times. (5)

contingency approach The idea that a particular action may have different consequences in different situations. (1)

contingent work Any job in which the individual does not have an explicit or implicit contract for long-term employment, or one in which the minimum hours of work can vary in a nonsystematic way. (1, 18)

continuous reinforcement A behavior modification schedule that reinforces every occurrence of a desired behavior. (2)

counterpower The capacity of a person, team, or organization to keep a more powerful person or group in the exchange relationship. (12)

creativity The capacity to develop an original product, service, or idea that makes a socially recognized contribution. (10)

D

decision making A conscious process of making choices among one or more alternatives with the intention of moving toward some desired state of affairs. (9)

Delphi technique A structured team decision-making process of systematically pooling the collective knowledge of experts on a particular subject to make decisions, predict the future, or identify opposing views. (10)

dialogue A process of conversation among team members in which they learn about each other's mental models and assumptions, and eventually form a common model for thinking within the team. (8, 13)

divergent thinking The creative ability to reframe a problem in a unique way and generate different approaches to the issue. (10)

divisional structure An organizational structure that groups employees around geographic areas, clients, or outputs. (17)

E

effort-to-outcome (E→P) expectancy The individual's perceived probability that his or her effort will result in a particular level of performance. (5)

electronic brainstorming A team decision-making process whereby participants individually generate ideas by using special computer software that posts each participant's ideas or opinions anonymously, thereby minimizing the team dynamics problems inherent in traditional brainstorming sessions. (10)

emotional contagion The automatic and subconscious tendency to mimic and synchronize one's own nonverbal behaviors with those of other people. (11)

emotional dissonance The conflict between required and true emotions. (4)

emotional intelligence (EQ) The ability to monitor one's own and others' feelings and emotions, to discriminate among them, and to use this information to guide one's thinking and actions. (4)

emotional labor The effort, planning, and control needed to express organizationally desired emotions during interpersonal transactions. (4)

emotions The feelings experienced toward an object, person, or event that create a state of readiness. (4)

empathy A person's ability to understand and be sensitive to the feelings, thoughts, and situations of others. (3)

employability An employment relationship in which employees are expected to continually develop their skills to remain employed. (1)

employee assistance programs (EAPs) Counseling services that help employees overcome personal or organizational stressors and adopt more effective coping mechanisms. (7)

employee involvement The degree to which employees share information, knowledge, rewards, and power throughout the organization. (9)

employee stock ownership plans (ESOPs) Reward systems that encourage employees to buy shares of the company. (6)

empowerment A feeling of control and self-efficacy that emerges when people are given power in a previously powerless situation. (6)

equity sensitivity One's outcome–input preferences and reaction to various outcome–input ratios. (5)

equity theory A process motivation theory that explains how people develop perceptions of fairness in the distribution and exchange of resources. (5)

ERG theory Alderfer's content motivation theory of three instinctive needs arranged in a hierarchy, in which people progress to the next higher need when a lower one is fulfilled, and regress to a lower need if unable to fulfill a higher one. (5)

escalation of commitment The tendency to repeat an apparently bad decision or allocate more resources to a failing course of action. (9)

ethical sensitivity A personal characteristic that enables people to recognize the presence and determine the relative importance of an ethical issue. (4)

ethics The study of moral principles or values that determine whether actions are right or wrong and outcomes are good or bad. (1)

evaluation apprehension An individual's reluctance to mention ideas that seem silly because the individual believes (often correctly) that other team members are silently evaluating him or her. (10)

existence needs A person's physiological and physically related safety needs, such as the needs for food, shelter, and safe working conditions. (5)

expectancy theory The process motivation theory based on the idea that work effort is directed toward behaviors that people believe will lead to desired outcomes. (5)

expert power   Power that originates from within the person and is the individual's or work unit's capacity to influence others by possessing knowledge or skills that others want. (12)

extinction   The contingency of reinforcement in which the target behavior decreases because no consequence follows it. (2)

extroversion   A Big Five personality dimension that characterizes people who are outgoing, talkative, sociable, and assertive. (3)

F

feedback   Any information that people receive about the consequences of their behavior. (2)

Fiedler's contingency model   A contingency theory of leadership developed by Fred Fiedler, which states that leader effectiveness depends on whether the person's natural leadership style is appropriately matched to the situation. (14)

field surveys   A research design strategy that involves collecting and analyzing information in a natural environment, an office, a factory, or other existing location. (Appendix A)

fixed interval schedule   A behavior modification schedule that reinforces a behavior after a fixed time. (2)

fixed ratio schedule   A behavior modification schedule that reinforces a behavior after a fixed number of times. (2)

flaming   The act of sending an emotionally charged electronic mail message to others. (11)

force field analysis   Lewin's model of systemwide change that helps change agents diagnose the forces that drive and restrain proposed organizational change. (16)

formalization   The degree to which organizations standardize behavior through rules, procedures, formal training, and related mechanisms. (17)

frustration-regression process   In ERG theory, a process whereby a person who is unable to satisfy a higher need becomes frustrated and regresses to the next lower need level. (5)

functional structure   An organizational structure that organizes employees around specific knowledge or other resources. (17)

fundamental attribution error   The tendency to attribute the behavior of other people more to internal than to external factors. (3)

G

gainsharing plan   A system that rewards team members with a bonus for reducing costs and increasing labor efficiency in their work process. (6)

general adaptation syndrome   A model of the stress experience, consisting of three stages: alarm reaction, resistance, and exhaustion. (7)

globalization   The trend in organizations toward extending activities to other parts of the world, actively participating in other markets, and competing against organizations located in other countries. (1)

goal setting   The process of motivating employees and clarifying their role perceptions by establishing performance objectives. (5)

goals   The immediate or ultimate objectives that employees are trying to accomplish from their work effort. (5)

grafting   The process of acquiring knowledge by hiring individuals or buying entire companies. (1)

grapevine   An unstructured and informal communication network founded on social relationships rather than organizational charts or job descriptions. (11)

group polarization   The tendency of teams to make more extreme decisions than individuals working alone. (10)

groups   People with a unifying relationship. (8)

groupthink   The tendency of highly cohesive groups to value consensus at the price of decision quality. (10)

growth needs   A person's needs for self-esteem through personal achievement as well as for self-actualization. (5)

H

halo error   A perceptual error whereby one's general impression of a person, usually based on one prominent characteristic, colors the perception of other characteristics of that person. (3)

heterogeneous teams   Teams that include members with diverse personal characteristics and backgrounds. (8)

homogeneous teams   Teams that include members with common technical expertise, demographics (age, gender), ethnicity, experiences, or values. (8)

hypotheses   Statements making empirically testable declarations that certain variables and their corresponding measures are related in a specific way proposed by theory. (Appendix A)

I

impression management   The practice of actively shaping one's public image. (12)

incremental change   An evolutionary strategy whereby the organization fine-tunes the existing organization and takes small steps toward the change effort's objectives. (16)

individualism versus collectivism   The degree to which people value their individual versus their group goals. (4)

informal groups   Two or more people who interact primarily to meet their personal (rather than organizational) needs. (8)

information overload   A condition in which the volume of information received exceeds the person's capacity to process it. (11)

inoculation effect   A persuasive communication strategy of warning listeners that others will try to influence them in the future and that they should be wary about the opponents' arguments. (12)

intellectual capital   The sum of an organization's human capital, structural capital, and relationship capital. (1)

interpretivism   The view held in many qualitative studies that reality comes from shared meaning among people in that environment. (Appendix A)

introversion   A Big Five personality dimension that characterizes people who are quiet, shy, and cautious. (3)

intuition   The ability to know when a problem or opportunity exists and select the best course of action without conscious reasoning. (9)

J

jargon   The technical language and acronyms as well as recognized words with specialized meanings in specific organizations or groups. (11)

job burnout The emotional exhaustion, depersonalization, and reduced personal accomplishment resulting from prolonged exposure to stress. (7)

job characteristics model A job design model that relates the motivational properties of jobs to specific personal and organizational consequences of those properties. (6)

job design The process of assigning tasks to a job, including the interdependency of those tasks with other jobs. (6)

job enlargement The process of increasing the number of tasks employees perform within their job. (6)

job enrichment The process of giving employees more responsibility for scheduling, coordinating, and planning their own work. (6)

job evaluation The process of systematically evaluating the worth of jobs within an organization by measuring their required skill, effort, responsibility, and working conditions. Job evaluation results create a hierarchy of job worth. (6)

job feedback Direct sensory information from the job itself, which allows employees to tell how well they are doing. (6)

job rotation The practice of moving employees from one job to another. (6)

job satisfaction A person's attitude regarding his or her job and work content. (2)

job specialization The result of division of labor in which each job includes a subset of the tasks required to complete the product or service. (6, 17)

Johari Window The model of personal and interpersonal understanding that encourages disclosure and feedback to increase the open area and reduce the blind, hidden, and unknown areas of oneself. (3)

K

knowledge management Any structured activity that improves an organization's capacity to acquire, share, and use knowledge in ways that improve its survival and success. (1)

L

laboratory experiment Any research study in which independent variables and variables outside the researcher's main focus of inquiry can be controlled to some extent. (Appendix A)

lateral career development Career success that occurs when employees fulfill their personal needs in different jobs across the organization rather than by moving through the organizational hierarchy. (18)

law of effect A principle stating that the likelihood that an operant behavior will be repeated depends on its consequences. (2)

law of telecosm A principle stating that as the web of computer networks expands, distances will shrink and eventually become irrelevant. (8, 11)

leadership The process of influencing people and providing an environment for them to achieve team or organizational objectives. (14)

Leadership Grid® A model of leadership that assesses an individual's leadership effectiveness in terms of his or her concern for people and production. (14)

leadership substitutes Contingencies that either limit the leader's ability to influence subordinates or make that particular leadership style unnecessary. (14)

learning A relatively permanent change in behavior that occurs as a result of a person's interaction with the environment. (2)

learning orientation The extent that an organization or individual supports knowledge management, particularly opportunities to acquire knowledge through experience and experimentation. (2)

legitimate power The capacity to influence others through formal authority. (12)

locus of control A personality trait referring to the extent to which people believe that events are within their control. (3)

M

Machiavellian values The belief that deceit is a natural and acceptable way to influence others. (12)

management by objectives (MBO) A participative goal-setting process in which organizational objectives are cascaded down to work units and individual employees. (5)

management by walking around (MBWA) A communication practice in which executives get out of their offices and learn from others in the organization through face-to-face dialogue. (11)

matrix structure A type of departmentalization that overlays a divisionalized structure (typically a project team) with a functional structure. (17)

mechanistic structure An organizational structure with a narrow span of control and high degrees of formalization and centralization. (17)

media richness The data-carrying capacity of a communication medium, including the volume and variety of information it can transmit. (11)

mental imagery The process of mentally practicing a task and visualizing its successful completion. (6)

mental models The broad worldviews or theories in use that people rely on to guide their perceptions and behaviors. (3, 9)

mentoring The process of learning the ropes of organizational life from a senior person within the company. (12)

moral intensity The degree to which an issue demands the application of ethical principles. (4)

motivation The forces within a person that affect his or her direction, intensity, and persistence of voluntary behavior. (2, 5)

motivator–hygiene theory Herzberg's theory stating that employees are motivated primarily by growth and esteem needs, not by lower-level needs. (5)

Myers-Briggs Type Indicator (MBTI) A personality test that measures each of the traits in Jung's personality theory. (3)

N

need for achievement (nAch) A learned need in which people want to accomplish reasonably challenging goals through their own efforts, like to be successful in competitive situations, and desire unambiguous feedback regarding their success. (5)

need for affiliation (nAff) A learned need in which people seek approval from others, conform to their wishes and expectations, and avoid conflict and confrontation. (5)

need for power (nPow) A learned need in which people want to control their environment, including people and material resources, to benefit either themselves (personalized power) or others (socialized power). (5)

needs Deficiencies that energize or trigger behaviors to satisfy those needs. (5)

needs hierarchy theory Maslow's content motivation theory of five instinctive needs arranged in a hierarchy, whereby people are motivated to fulfill a higher need as a lower one becomes gratified. (5)

negative affectivity (NA) The tendency to experience negative emotions. (4)

negative reinforcement The contingency of reinforcement in which the removal or avoidance of a consequence increases or maintains the frequency or future probability of a behavior. (2)

negotiation An attempt by two or more conflicting parties to resolve their divergent goals by redefining the terms of their interdependence. (13)

network structure An alliance of several organizations for the purpose of creating a product or serving a client. (1, 17)

networking Cultivating social relationships with others to accomplish one's goals. (12)

nominal group technique A structured team decision-making process whereby team members independently write down ideas, describe and clarify them to the group, and then independently rank or vote on them. (10)

nonprogrammed decision The process applied to unique, complex, or ill-defined situations whereby decision makers follow the full decision-making process, including a careful search for and/or development of unique solutions. (9)

norms The informal rules and expectations that groups establish to regulate the behavior of their members. (8)

O

open book management An employee involvement approach that involves sharing financial information with employees and encouraging them

to recommend ideas that improve those financial results. (9)

open systems Organizations that take their sustenance from the environment and, in turn, affect that environment through their output. (1)

organic structure An organizational structure with a wide span of control, little formalization, and decentralized decision making. (17)

organization development (OD) A planned systemwide effort, managed from the top with the assistance of a change agent, that uses behavioral science knowledge to improve organizational effectiveness. (16)

organizational behavior (OB) The study of what people think, feel, and do in and around organizations. (1)

organizational citizenship Organizational membership characterized by behaviors that extend beyond the employee's normal job duties. (2)

organizational commitment The employee's emotional attachment to, identification with, and involvement in a particular organization. (4)

organizational culture The basic pattern of shared assumptions, values, and beliefs governing the way employees within an organization think about and act on problems and opportunities. (1, 15)

organizational design The process of creating and modifying organizational structures. (17)

organizational memory The storage and preservation of intellectual capital. (1)

organizational politics The attempts to influence others using discretionary behaviors to promote personal objectives. (12)

organizational socialization The process by which individuals learn the values, expected behaviors, and social knowledge necessary to assume their roles in the organization. (15, 18)

organizational strategy The way an organization positions itself in its setting in relation to its stakeholders, given the organization's resources, capabilities, and mission. (17)

organizational structure The division of labor and the patterns of coordination, communication, work flow, and formal power that direct organizational activities. (17)

organizations Groups of people who work interdependently toward some purpose. (1)

P

parallel learning structures Highly participative groups constructed alongside (i.e., parallel to) the formal organization with the purpose of increasing the organization's learning and producing meaningful organizational change. (16)

path–goal leadership theory A contingency theory of leadership based on expectancy theory of motivation that relates several leadership styles to specific employee and situational contingencies. (14)

perception The process of selecting, organizing, and interpreting information to make sense of the world around us. (3)

perceptual defense A psychological process in which emotions screen out large blocks of information that threaten one's beliefs and values. (3)

perceptual grouping The perceptual organization process of placing people and objects into recognizable and manageable patterns or categories. (3)

performance-to-outcome (P→O) expectancy The perceived probability that a specific behavior or performance level will lead to specific outcomes. (5)

personality The relatively stable pattern of behaviors and consistent internal states that explain a person's behavioral tendencies. (3)

persuasive communication The process of having listeners accept rather than just understand a sender's message. (12)

positive affectivity (PA) The tendency to experience positive emotional states. (4)

positive reinforcement The contingency of reinforcement in which the introduction of a consequence increases or maintains the frequency or future probability of a behavior. (2)

positivism A view held in quantitative research in which reality exists independent of the perceptions and interpretations of people. (Appendix A)

postdecisional justification The tendency to justify choices by unconsciously inflating the quality of the selected option and deflating the quality of the discarded options. (9)

power The capacity of a person, team, or organization to influence others. (12)

power distance The extent to which people accept unequal distribution of power in a society. (4)

prejudice The unfounded negative emotions toward people belonging to a particular stereotyped group. (3)

primacy effect A perceptual error in which one quickly forms an opinion of people based on the first information received about them. (3)

procedural fairness Perceptions of fairness regarding the dispute resolution process, whether or not the outcome is favorable to the person. (13)

process consultation A method of helping the organization solve its own problems by making it aware of organizational processes, the consequences of those processes, and the means by which they can be changed. (16)

process losses Resources (including time and energy) expended toward team development and maintenance rather than the task. (8)

process theories of motivation Theories that describe the processes through which needs are translated into behavior. (5)

production blocking A time constraint in team decision making due to the procedural requirement that only one person may speak at a time. (10)

profit-sharing plan A reward system that pays bonuses to employees based on the previous year's level of corporate profits. (6)

programmed decision The process whereby decision makers follow standard operating procedures to select the preferred solution without the need to identify or evaluate alternative choices. (9)

projection bias A perceptual error in which an individual believes that other people have the same beliefs and behaviors that he or she has. (3)

psychological contract The individual's beliefs about the terms and conditions of a reciprocal exchange agreement between that person and another party. (18)

punishment The contingency of reinforcement in which a consequence decreases the frequency or future probability of a behavior. (2)

Q

quality circles Small teams of employees who meet for a few hours each week to identify quality and productivity problems, propose solutions to management, and monitor the implementation and consequences of those solutions in their work area. (8)

quantum change A revolutionary approach to change in which the organization breaks out of its existing ways and moves toward a totally different configuration of systems and structures. (16)

R

realistic job preview (RJP) A recruiting strategy that involves giving job applicants a balance of positive and negative information about the job and the work context. (18)

reality shock The reaction of newcomers to perceived discrepancies between their preemployment expectations and on-the-job reality. (18)

recency effect A perceptual error in which the most recent information dominates one's perception of others. (3)

referent power The capacity to influence others based on the identification and respect they have for the power holder. (12)

refreezing The latter part of the change process in which systems and conditions are introduced that reinforce and maintain the desired behaviors. (16)

relatedness needs A person's needs to interact with other people, receive public recognition, and feel secure around other people. (5)

representative sampling The process of sampling a population in such a way that one can extrapolate the results of that sample to the larger population. (Appendix A)

reward power The capacity to influence others by controlling the allocation of rewards valued by others them and removing negative sanctions. (12)

rituals The programmed routines of daily organizational life that dramatize the organization's culture. (15)

role The set of behaviors that people are expected to perform because they hold certain positions in a team and organization. (8)

role ambiguity Uncertainty about job duties, performance expectations, level of authority, and other job conditions. (7)

role conflict A situation in which an individual faces competing demands. (7)

role perceptions A person's beliefs about the behaviors that are appropriate or necessary in a particular situation, including the specific tasks that make up the job, their relative importance, and the preferred behaviors to accomplish those tasks. (2)

S

satisfaction-progression process A process whereby people become increasingly motivated to fulfill a higher need as a lower need is gratified. (5)

satisficing Selecting a solution that is satisfactory, or "good enough," rather than optimal, or "the best." (9)

scenario planning A systematic process of thinking about alternative futures and determining what the organization should do to anticipate and react to those environments. (9)

scientific management The process of systematically partitioning work into its smallest elements and standardizing tasks to achieve maximum efficiency. (6)

scientific method A systematic, controlled, empirical, and critical investigation of hypothetical propositions about the presumed relationships among natural phenomena. (Appendix A)

search conference A systemwide group session, usually lasting a few days, in which participants identify the environmental trends and establish strategic solutions for those conditions. (16)

selective attention The process of filtering information received by the senses. (3)

self-directed work teams (SDWTs) Cross-functional work groups that are organized around work processes, that complete an entire piece of work requiring several interdependent tasks, and that have substantial autonomy over the execution of those tasks. (8, 9)

self-efficacy A person's belief that he or she has the ability, motivation, and resources to complete a task successfully. (2)

self-fulfilling prophecy The perceptual process in which one's expectations about another person cause that person to act in a way that is consistent with those expectations. (3)

self-leadership The process of influencing oneself to establish the self-direction and self-motivation needed to perform a task. (6)

self-monitoring A personality trait referring to an individual's level of sensitivity and ability to adapt to situational cues. (3)

self-serving bias A perceptual error whereby people tend to attribute our their favorable outcomes to internal factors and our their failures to external factors. (3)

self-talk Talking to oneself about one's own thoughts or actions for the purpose of increasing self-efficacy and navigating through decisions in a future event. (6)

sensitivity training An unstructured and agendaless session in which a small group of people need meet face-to-face, often for a few days, to learn more about themselves and their relations with others. (16)

servant leadership The belief that leaders serve followers by understanding their needs and facilitating their work performance. (14)

sexual harassment Unwelcome conduct of a sexual nature that detrimentally affects the work environment or leads to adverse job-related consequences for its victims. (7)

situational leadership model A leadership model developed by Hersey and Blanchard suggesting that effective leaders vary their style according to the readiness of followers. (14)

skill variety The extent to which employees must use different skills and talents to perform tasks within their job. (6)

skill-based pay Pay structures in which employees earn higher pay rates according to the number of skill modules they have mastered. (6)

skunkworks Temporary teams formed spontaneously to develop products or solve complex problems. (8)

social identity theory A model that explains self-perception and social perception in terms of the person's unique characteristics (personal identity) and membership in various social groups (social identity.) (3)

social learning theory A theory stating that much learning occurs by observing others and then modeling the behaviors that lead to favorable outcomes and avoiding the behaviors that lead to punishing consequences. (2)

social loafing A phenomenon in which people exert less effort (and usually perform at a lower level) when working in groups than when working alone. (8)

social responsibility A person's or an organization's moral obligation toward others who are affected by that person's or organization's actions. (2)

sociotechnical systems (STS) theory A theory stating that effective work sites have joint optimization of their social and technological systems, and that teams should have sufficient autonomy to control key variances in the work process. (9)

span of control The number of people directly reporting to the next level in the organizational hierarchy. (17)

splatter vision The process of perceiving everything in as a whole rather than focusing on specific elements of the perceptual field. (3)

stakeholders Shareholders, customers, suppliers, governments, and any other groups with a vested interest in the organization. (1)

stereotyping The process of assigning traits to people based on their membership in a social category. (3)

stock options The right given to employees to purchase company stock at a future date at a predetermined price. (6)

strategic choice The idea that an organization interacts with its environment rather than being totally determined by it. (17)

stress An individual's adaptive response to a situation that is perceived as challenging or threatening to the person's well-being. (7)

stressors The causes of stress, including any environmental conditions that place a physical or emotional demand on the person. (7)

substitutability The extent to which people dependent on a resource have alternatives. (12)

superordinate goal A common objectives held by conflicting parties that is more important than their conflicting departmental or individual goals. (13)

synergy A phenomenon in which people generate more and better solutions by working together and sharing ideas than if they worked alone. (9)

T

tacit knowledge Knowledge embedded in actions and ways of thinking, and transmitted only through observation and experience. (2)

task identity The degree to which a job requires completion of a whole or an identifiable piece of work. (6)

task interdependence The degree to which a task requires employees to share common inputs or outcomes, or to interact in the process of executing their work. (8)

task performance An individual's level of performance with regard to goal-directed activities that are under that individual's control. (2)

task significance The degree to which the job has a substantial impact on the organization and/or larger society. (6)

team-based organization A type of departmentalization with a flat span of control and relatively little formalization, consisting of self-directed work teams responsible for various work processes. (8)

team building Any formal activity intended to improve the development and functioning of a work team. (8)

team cohesiveness The degree of attraction people feel toward the team and their motivation to remain members of that team. (8)

team effectiveness The extent to which a team achieves its objectives, fulfills the needs and objectives of its members, and sustains itself over time. (8)

teams Groups of two or more people who interact and influence each other, are mutually accountable for achieving common objectives, and perceive themselves as a social entity within an organization. (8)

telecommuting Working from home, usually with a computer connection to the office; also called *teleworking*. (1)

theory A general set of propositions that describes interrelationships among several concepts. (Appendix A)

third-party conflict resolution Any attempt by a relatively neutral person to help the parties resolve their differences. (13)

360-degree feedback Performance feedback received from a full circle of people around an employee. (2)

transactional leadership Leadership that helps organizations achieve their current objectives more efficiently, such as linking job performance to valued rewards and ensuring that employees have the resources needed to get the job done. (14)

transformational leadership A leadership perspective that explains how leaders change teams or organizations by creating, communicating, and modeling a vision for the organization or work unit, and inspiring employees to strive for that vision. (14)

trust Positive expectations about another party's intentions and actions in risky situations. (4)

type A behavior pattern A behavior pattern associated with people having premature coronary heart disease; type A's tend to be impatient, lose their temper, talk rapidly, and interrupt others. (7)

type B behavior pattern A behavior pattern associated with people having a low risk of coronary heart disease; type B's tend to work steadily, take a relaxed approach to life, and be even-tempered. (7)

U

uncertainty avoidance The degree to which people tolerate ambiguity or feel threatened by ambiguity and uncertainty. (4)

unfreezing The first part of the change process whereby the change agent produces disequilibrium between the driving and restraining forces. (16)

utilitarianism A moral principle stating that decision makers should seek the greatest good for the greatest number of people when choosing among alternatives. (4)

V

valence The anticipated satisfaction or dissatisfaction that an individual feels toward an outcome. (5)

values Stable, long-lasting beliefs about what is important in a variety of situations. (1)

variable interval schedule A behavior modification schedule that reinforces behavior after it has occurred for a varying length of time around some average. (2)

variable ratio schedule A behavior modification schedule that reinforces behavior after it has occurred a varying number of times around some average. (2)

virtual corporations Network structures that represent several independent companies that form unique partnership teams to provide customized products or services, usually to specific clients, for a limited time. (17)

virtual teams Cross-functional groups that operate across space, time, and organizational boundaries with members who communicate mainly through electronic technologies. (1, 8)

W

win–lose orientation The belief that conflicting parties are drawing from a fixed pie, so the more one party receives, the less the other party will receive. (13)

win–win orientation The belief that conflicting perception that parties will find a mutually beneficial solution to their disagreement. (13)

workplace bullying Offensive, intimidating, or humiliating behavior that degrades, ridicules, or insults another person at work. (7)

NOTES

CHAPTER ONE

1. B. Broadway, "Good for the Soul—and for the Bottom Line," *Washington Post*, August 19, 2001, p. A1; L. Kline, "The Secret of Their Success," *D Magazine–Dallas/Fort Worth* 28 (July 2001), p. 32; "Container Store to Open in Walnut Creek," *East Bay (CA) Business Times*, May 4, 2001, p. 5; J. Laabs, "Thinking Outside the Box at The Container Store," *Workforce* 80 (March 2001), pp. 34–38; M. Mazzetti, "Managing, Texas-Style," *Texas Monthly*, December 2000, p. 64; M. Forseter, "Associates Keep Score at The Container Store," *Chain Store Age* 76 (May 2000), p. 18; K. M. Kroll, "Container Store a Hit with Customers, Employees," *Shopping Centers Today*, May 2000; Daniel Roth, "My Job at The Container Store," *Fortune*, January 10, 2000, pp. 74–78.

2. M. Warner, "Organizational Behavior Revisited," *Human Relations* 47 (October 1994), pp. 1151–66. The various historical sources are described in T. Takala, "Plato on Leadership," *Journal of Business Ethics* 17 (May 1998), pp. 785–98; R. Kanigel, *The One Best Way: Frederick Winslow Taylor and the Enigma of Efficiency* (New York: Viking, 1997); M. Weber, *The Theory of Social and Economic Organization*, A. M. Henderson and T. Parsons, trans., (New York: Oxford University Press, 1947); N. Machiavelli, *The Prince and the Discourses* (New York: Modern Library, 1940); F. J. Roethlisberger and W. J. Dickson, *Management and the Worker* (Cambridge, MA: Harvard University Press, 1939); A. Smith, *The Wealth of Nations* (London: Dent, 1910).

3. R. Harley, "The Man in the Hot Seat for the Games," *Australian Financial Review*, September 16, 2000, p. 14; T. Harris, "The Men Whose Reputations Rise and Fall with the Olympics," *Australian Financial Review*, September 16, 2000, p. 22; E. Wilson, "Big Blue in the Balance," *Sydney Morning Herald*, September 12, 2000, p. 38; T. Condon, "Exit the Circus, Enter the Games," *Business Review Weekly*, September 1, 2000, p. 66; S. A. Teicher, "It's Not Just Games at 'Olympics U.,'" *Christian Science Monitor*, June 20, 2000, p. 15.

4. L. E. Greiner, "A Recent History of Organizational Behavior," in S. Kerr, ed., *Organizational Behavior* (Columbus, OH: Grid, 1979), pp. 3–14.

5. B. Schlender, "The Three Faces of Steve," *Fortune*, November 9, 1998.

6. R. N. Stern and S. R. Barley, "Organizations as Social Systems: Organization Theory's Neglected Mandate," *Administrative Science Quarterly* 41 (1996), pp. 146–62; D. Katz and R. L. Kahn, *The Social Psychology of Organizations* (New York: Wiley, 1966), chap. 2.

7. J. Pfeffer, *New Directions for Organization Theory* (New York: Oxford University Press, 1997), pp. 7–9.

8. A. Etzioni, *Modern Organizations* (Englewood Cliffs, NJ: Prentice Hall, 1964), p. 1.

9. P. R. Lawrence, "Historical Development of Organizational Behavior," in L. W. Lorsch, ed., *Handbook of Organizational Behavior* (Englewood Cliffs, NJ: Prentice Hall, 1987), pp. 1–9; D. S. Pugh, "Modern Organizational Theory: A Psychological and Sociological Study," *Psychological Bulletin* 66 (1966), pp. 235–51. For a contrary view, see A. P. Brief and J. M. Dukerich, "Theory in Organizational Behavior: Can It Be Useful?" *Research in Organizational Behavior* 13 (1991), pp. 327–52.

10. M. S. Myers, *Every Employee a Manager* (New York: McGraw-Hill, 1970). The phrase "adult supervision" as a derogatory term for managers is mentioned in T. A. Stewart, "Just Think: No Permission Needed," *Fortune*, January 8, 2001, p. 190.

11. A. Edgecliffe-Johnson, "Two Brains May Be Better Than One Big Cheese," *Financial Times (London)*, September 3, 2001, p. 9; P. Brabeck, "The Business Case against Revolution: An Interview with Nestlés Peter Brabeck," *Harvard Business Review* 79 (February 2001), p. 112; P. Stevenson, "Cheers End Dairy Merger Pain," *New Zealand Herald*, December 23, 2000.

12. H. Schachter, "The 21st Century CEO," *Profit* 18 (April 1999), pp. 25–35; M. A. Hitt, B. W. Keats, and S. M. DeMarie, "Navigating in the New Competitive Landscape: Building Strategic Flexibility and Competitive Advantage in the 21st Century," *Academy of Management Executive* 12 (November 1998), pp. 22–42.

13. J. Garten, *The Mind of the CEO* (New York: Perseus, 2001), chap. 3.

14. E. Van Bronhorst, "On Eve of Turning 30, Starbucks Exports Seattle 'Coffee Culture' to the Globe," *Associated Press Newswire*, September 9, 2001.

15. A. Teo, "Creating a Global Real Estate Player," *Business Times (Singapore)*, October 18, 2000.

16. T. H. Wagar, "Consequences of Work Force Reduction: Some Employer and Union Evidence," *Journal of Labor Research* 22 (Fall 2001), pp. 851–62; T. D. Allen et al., "Survivor Reactions to Organizational Downsizing: Does Time Ease the Pain?" *Journal of Occupational and Organizational Psychology* 74 (June 2001), pp. 145–64; M. L. Marks and P. H. Mirvis, "Making Mergers and Acquisitions Work: Strategic and Psychological Preparation," *Academy of Management Executive* 15 (May 2001), pp. 80–94; J. Vahtera, M. Kivimaki, and J. Pentti, "Effect of Organizational Downsizing on Health of Employees," *Lancet* 350 (1997), pp. 1124–28.

17. C. Kleiman, "Work Issues the Same the Whole World Over," *Seattle Times*, September 2, 2001.

18. K. L. Newman and S. D. Nollen, "Culture and Congruence: The Fit

between Management Practices and National Culture," *Journal of International Business Studies* 27 (1996), pp. 753–78. Early warnings came from A. R. Negandhi and B. D. Estafen, "A Research Model to Determine the Applicability of American Management Knowhow in Different Cultures and/or Environment," *Academy of Management Journal* 8 (1965), pp. 309–18.

19. P. R. Sparrow, "Reappraising Psychological Contracting: Lessons for the Field of Human-Resource Development from Cross-Cultural and Occupational Psychology Research," *International Studies of Management and Organization* 28 (March 1998), pp. 30–63; R. Schuler and N. Rogovsky, "Understanding Compensation Practice Variations across Firms: The Impact of National Culture," *Journal of International Business Studies* 29 (1998), pp. 159–77.

20. F. Swoboda, "Trust in Employers Is Eroding, Survey Finds," *Washington Post*, August 31, 2001, p. E2.

21. "Managing a Multicultural Workforce," *Black Enterprise*, July 2001, p. 121; M. F. Riche, "America's Diversity and Growth: Signposts for the 21st Century," *Population Bulletin*, June 2000, pp. 3–43; C. Bowman, "BLS Projections to 2006: A Summary," *Monthly Labor Review*, November 1997, pp. 3–5.

22. N. Glazer, "American Diversity and the 2000 Census," *The Public Interest*, Summer 2001, pp. 3–18.

23. J. Milicia, "Companies Change to Fit Muslim Employees' Needs," *Detroit News*, May 16, 2001.

24. D. Mangan, "Remember When . . . a Women Doctor Was a Rarity?" *Medical Economics* 75 (May 11, 1998), pp. 225–26; P. M. Flynn, J. D. Leeth, and E. S. Levy, "The Accounting Profession in Transition," *CPA Journal* 67 (May 1997), pp. 42–45.

25. Most writers define Generation X as people born immediately after the baby boom generation ended (1964) through around 1977. See B. Losyk, "Generation X: What They Think and What They Plan to Do," *The Futurist* 31 (March–April 1997), pp. 29–44.

26. N. Mui, "Here Come the Kids," *New York Times*, February 4, 2001, p. 1; R. Zemke and B. Filipczak, *Genera-*

tions at Work: Managing the Clash of Veterans, Boomers, Xers, and Nexters in Your Workplace (New York: AMACOM, 2000); B. R. Kupperschmidt, "Multigeneration Employees: Strategies for Effective Management," *Health Care Manager*, September 2000, pp. 65–76; S. Hays, "Generation X and the Art of the Reward," *Workforce* 78 (November 1999), pp. 44–48; Losyk, "Generation X: What They Think and What They Plan to Do."

27. D. C. Lau and J. K. Murnighan, "Demographic Diversity and Faultlines: The Compositional Dynamics of Organizational Groups," *Academy of Management Review* 23 (April 1998), pp. 325–40; G. Robinson and K. Dechant, "Building a Business Case for Diversity," *Academy of Management Executive* 11 (August 1997), pp. 21–31; J. R. W. Joplin and C. S. Daus, "Challenges of Leading a Diverse Workforce," *Academy of Management Executive* 11 (August 1997), pp. 32–47.

28. "Mixing Nationalities in the Workplace," *Guardian (London)*, November 11, 1999, p. 23.

29. D. L. Nelson and R. J. Burke, "Women Executives: Health, Stress, and Success," *Academy of Management Executive* 14, May 2000, pp. 107–21; "What Blacks Think of Corporate America," *Fortune*, July 6, 1998, pp. 140–43.

30. D. Woodruff, "Crossing Culture Divide Early Clears Merger Paths," *Asian Wall Street Journal*, May 28, 2001, p. 9; S. J. A. Talvi, "Stars of All Stripes," *Christian Science Monitor*, November 13, 2000, p. 11; Hays, "Generation X and the Art of the Reward."

31. J. Dionne-Proulx, J.-C. Bernatchez, and R. Boulard, "Attitudes and Satisfaction Levels Associated with Precarious Employment," *International Journal of Employment Studies* 6 (1998), pp. 91–114; P. Cappelli et al., *Change at Work* (New York: Oxford University Press, 1997). Employability is also extending into parts of Asia. For example, see R. Ong, "Skills and Lifelong Employability," *Business Times (Singapore)*, March 20, 2001.

32. A. E. Polivka, "Contingent and Alternative Work Arrangements, Defined," *Monthly Labor Review* 119 (October 1996), pp. 3–10; S. Nollen

and H. Axel, *Managing Contingent Workers* (New York: AMACOM, 1996), pp. 4–9.

33. M. Saville, "The Future is e-Me," *Sydney Morning Herald*, February 26, 2000.

34. D. H. Pink, "Land of the Free," *Fast Company* 46 (May 2001), pp. 125–33; D. H. Pink, "Free Agent Nation," *Fast Company* 12 (December–January 1998), pp. 131–47; S. B. Gould, K. J. Weiner, and B. R. Levin, *Free Agents: People and Organizations Creating a New Working Community*, (San Francisco: Jossey-Bass, 1997).

35. K. Voigt, "Virtual Work: Some Telecommuters Take Remote Work to the Extreme," *Wall Street Journal Europe*, February 1, 2001, p. 1.

36. D. Stafford, "Workplace Policies about Snow- and Ice-Related Absences Vary Widely," *Kansas City Star*, December 21, 2000.

37. N. B. Kurland and D. E. Bailey, "Telework: The Advantages and Challenges of Working Here, There, Anywhere, and Anytime," *Organizational Dynamics* 28 (Autumn 1999), pp. 53–68; A. Dunkin, "Saying Adios to the Office," *Business Week*, October 12, 1998; J. A. Challenger, "There Is No Future for the Workplace," *Futurist* 32 (October 1998), pp. 16–20; A. Mahlon, "The Alternative Workplace: Changing Where and How People Work," *Harvard Business Review* 76 (May–June 1998), pp. 121–30.

38. J. Lipnack and J. Stamps, *Virtual Teams: People Working across Boundaries with Technology*, (New York: Wiley, 2001); D. J. Armstrong and P. Cole, "Managing Distances and Differences in Geographically Distributed Work Groups," in S. E. Jackson and M. N. Ruderman, eds., *Diversity in Work Teams: Research Paradigms for a Changing Workplace* (Washington, DC: American Psychological Association, 1995), pp. 187–215.

39. R. D. Foster, "Internet Takes Ancient Craft Global," *Christian Science Monitor*, September 7, 2001, p. 7.

40. J. A. Byrne, "The Corporation of the Future," *Business Week*, August 31, 1998, pp. 102–4.

41. A. Sagie and D. Elizur, "Work Values: A Theoretical Overview and a Model of Their Effects," *Journal of*

Organizational Behavior 17 (1996), pp. 503–14; W. H. Schmidt and B. Z. Posner, *Managerial Values in Perspective* (New York: American Management Association, 1983).

42. Cited in T. Schubert, "Stop Bad Vibes Rising," *New Zealand Management* 47 (September 2000), pp. 32–35.

43. For early writing on values in the context of organizations, see E. H. Schein, *Organizational Culture and Leadership* (San Francisco: Jossey-Bass, 1985); G. Hofstede, *Culture's Consequences: International Differences in Work-Related Values* (Beverly Hills, CA: Sage, 1980); A. M. Pettigrew, "On Studying Organizational Cultures," *Administrative Science Quarterly* 24 (1979), pp. 570–81; G. W. England, "Personal Value Systems of American Managers," *Academy of Management Journal* 10 (1967), pp. 53–68; W. D. Guth and R. Tagiuri, "Personal Values and Corporate Strategy," *Harvard Business Review* 43 (1965), pp. 123–32.

44. B. R. Agle and C. B. Caldwell, "Understanding Research on Values in Business," *Business and Society* 38 (September 1999), pp. 326–87; B. M. Meglino and E. C. Ravlin, "Individual Values in Organizations: Concepts, Controversies, and Research," *Journal of Management* 24 (May 1998), pp. 351–89.

45. C. Pearson and L. Entrekin, "Structural Properties, Work Practices, and Control in Asian Businesses: Some Evidence from Singapore and Malaysia," *Human Relations* 51 (October 1998), pp. 1285–1306.

46. S. R. Chatterjee and C. A. L. Pearson, "Indian Managers in Transition: Orientations, Work Goals, Values and Ethics," *Management International Review*, January 2000, pp. 81–95.

47. M. N. Zald, "More Fragmentation? Unfinished Business in Linking the Social Sciences and the Humanities," *Administrative Science Quarterly* 41 (1996), pp. 251–61.

48. J. Barbian, "The Charit Able Worker," *Training*, July 2001, p. 50.

49. T. S. Kuhn, *The Structure of Scientific Revolutions* (Chicago: University of Chicago Press, 1970).

50. For an excellent critique of the "one best way" approach by past scholars, see P. F. Drucker, "Management's New Paradigms," *Forbes*, October 5, 1998, pp. 152–77.

51. H. L. Tosi and J. W. Slocum, Jr., "Contingency Theory: Some Suggested Directions," *Journal of Management* 10 (1984), pp. 9–26.

52. D. M. Rousseau and R. J. House, "Meso Organizational Behavior: Avoiding Three Fundamental Biases," in C. J. Cooper and D. M. Rousseau, eds., *Trends in Organizational Behavior*, vol. 1 (Chichester, UK: Wiley, 1994), pp. 13–30.

53. H. Trinca, "Her Way," *Australian Financial Review (Boss Supplement)*, October 9, 2000.

54. R. T. Pascale, M. Millemann, and L. Gioja, *Surfing the Edge of Chaos* (New York: Crown, 2000); P. Senge et al., *The Dance of Change* (New York: Currency Doubleday, 1999), pp. 137–48; A. De Geus, *The Living Company* (Boston: Harvard Business School Press, 1997); A. Waring, *Practical Systems Thinking*, (Boston : International Thomson Business Press, 1997); P. M. Senge, *The Fifth Discipline: The Art and Practice of the Learning Organization* (New York: Doubleday, 1990), chap. 4; F. E. Kast and J. E. Rosenweig, "General Systems Theory: Applications for Organization and Management," *Academy of Management Journal* 00 (1972), pp. 447–65.

55. S. G. Scott and V. R. Lane, "A Stakeholder Approach to Organizational Identity," *Academy of Management Review* 25 (January 2000), pp. 43–62; A. A. Atkinson, J. H. Waterhouse, and R. B. Wells, "A Stakeholder Approach to Strategic Performance Measurement," *Sloan Management Review* 38 (Spring 1997), pp. 25–37; G. T. Savage, T. W. Nix, C. J. Whitehead, and J. D. Blair, "Strategies for Assessing and Managing Organizational Stakeholders," *Academy of Management Executive* 5 (May 1991), pp. 61–75; R. E. Freeman, *Strategic Management: A Stakeholder Approach* (Marshfield, MA: Pitman, 1984).

56. H. Mintzberg, *The Rise and Fall of Strategic Planning* (New York: Free Press, 1994).

57. M. L. Tushman, M. B. Nadler, and D. A. Nadler, *Competing by Design: The Power of Organizational Architecture* (New York: Oxford University Press, 1997).

58. E. P. Lima, "Pioneering in People," *Air Transport World*, April 1995, pp. 51–54; "British Airways Encourages Employees to Be Conceited," *Travel Weekly*, October 8, 1992, pp. 41, 42; K. Macher, "Creating Commitment," *Training and Development Journal* (April 1991), pp. 45–52; J. Aspery, "British Companies Meet the Challenge of Change," *IABC Communication World* 7 (December 1990), pp. 39–41.

59. G. F. B. Probst, "Practical Knowledge Management: A Model That Works," *Prism* (Second Quarter 1998), pp. 17–23; G. Miles, R. E. Miles, V. Perrone, and L. Edvinsson, "Some Conceptual and Research Barriers to the Utilization of Knowledge," *California Management Review* 40 (Spring 1998), pp. 281–88; E. C. Nevis, A. J. DiBella, and J. M. Gould, "Understanding Organizations as Learning Systems," *Sloan Management Review* 36 (Winter 1995), pp. 73–85; G. Huber, "Organizational Learning: The Contributing Processes and Literature," *Organizational Science* 2 (1991), pp. 88–115.

60. F. Belaire, "IC: The Ultimate Renewable Resource," *Silicon Valley North* 2 (December 1998), p. 16; T. A. Stewart, *Intellectual Capital: The New Wealth of Organizations* (New York: Doubleday, 1997); H. Saint-Onge, "Tacit Knowledge: The Key to the Strategic Alignment of Intellectual Capital," *Strategy and Leadership* 24 (March/April 1996), pp. 10–14; G. Petrash, "Dow's Journey to a Knowledge Value Management Culture," *European Management Journal* 14 (August 1996), pp. 365–73.

61. Relationship capital was initially called customer capital in the knowledge management literature. However, the concept is evolving to include relationships among external stakeholders. For example, see D. Halloran, "Putting Knowledge Management Initiatives into Action at Motorola," Presentation by Motorola Vice President and Director of Human Resources Dan Halloran at the Future of Business in the New Knowledge Economy Conference, March 22–23, 2000, Pan Pacific Hotel, Singapore.

62. P. N. Bukh, H. T. Larsen, and J. Mouritsen, "Constructing Intellectual Capital Statements," *Scandinavian*

Journal of Management 17 (March 2001), pp. 87–108.

63. There is no complete agreement on the meaning of organizational learning, and the relationship between organizational learning and knowledge management is still somewhat ambiguous. For writing on organizational learning, see Huber, "Organizational Learning"; Senge, *The Fifth Discipline*, pp. 3–5.

64. Huber, "Organizational Learning."

65. A. L. Brown, "In Economic Slowdown, Wal-Mart Counts on Its Cultural Roots," *Detroit News*, June 9, 2001; L. Wah, "Behind the Buzz," *Management Review* 88 (April 1999), pp. 16–19; C. W. Wick and L. S. Leon, "From Ideas to Actions: Creating a Learning Organization," *Human Resource Management* 34 (Summer 1995), pp. 299–311; D. Ulrich, T. Jick, and M. Von Glinow, "High Impact Learning: Building and Diffusing Learning Capability," *Organizational Dynamics* 22 (Autumn 1993), pp. 52–66. Experimentation is similar to synthetic learning described in D. Miller, "A Preliminary Typology of Organizational Learning: Synthesizing the Literature," *Journal of Management* 22 (1996), pp. 485–505.

66. C. O'Dell and C. J. Grayson, "If Only We Knew What We Know: Identification and Transfer of Internal Best Practices," *California Management Review* 40 (Spring 1998), pp. 154–74; R. Ruggles, "The State of the Notion: Knowledge Management in Practice," *California Management Review* 40 (Spring 1998), pp. 80–89; G. S. Richards and S. C. Goh, "Implementing Organizational Learning: Toward a Systematic Approach," *The Journal of Public Sector Management* (Autumn 1995), pp. 25–31.

67. E. C. Wenger and W. M. Snyder, "Communities of Practice: The Organizational Frontier," *Harvard Business Review* 78 (January–February 2000), pp. 139–45; O'Dell and Grayson, "If Only We Knew What We Know."

68. M. Hopkins, "Zen and the Art of the Self-Managing Company," *Inc.*, November 2000, p. 55.

69. G. Barker, "High Priest of the PC," *The Age*, April 4, 2001; N. Way, "Talent War," *Business Review Weekly*, August 18, 2000, p. 64.

70. J. McKay, "The Smell of Success," *Pittsburgh (PA) Post-Gazette*, October 28, 1999.

71. Stewart, *Intellectual Capital*, chap. 7.

72. B. P. Sunoo, "The Sydney Challenge," *Workforce*, September 2000, pp. 70–76.

73. D. Lei, J. W. Slocum, and R. A. Pitts, "Designing Organizations for Competitive Advantage: The Power of Unlearning and Learning," *Organizational Dynamics* 27 (Winter 1999), pp. 24–38; M. E. McGill and J. W. Slocum, Jr., "Unlearn the Organization," *Organizational Dynamics* 22 (2) (1993), pp. 67–79.

CHAPTER TWO

1. S. Silver, "Behind Many Successful Business Leaders Is an Executive Coach," *AP Worldstream*, June 5, 2001; D. C. Feldman, "Career Coaching: What HR Professionals and Managers Need to Know," *Human Resource Planning* 24 (June 2001), p. 26; K. Kicklighter, "Put Me In, Coach," *Atlanta Journal and Constitution*, January 12, 2001, p. E1; D. E. Lewis, "Companies Are Hiring Coaches to Teach Executives How to Sharpen Management Skills and Communicate Effectively Leading the Corporate League," *Boston Globe*, November 26, 2000, p. G1; J. Laabs, "Need Peak HR Performance? Consider a Coach," *Workforce* 79 (October 2000), pp. 132–35.

2. C. C. Pinder, *Work Motivation in Organizational Behavior* (Upper Saddle River, NJ: Prentice Hall, 1998); E. E. Lawler III, *Motivation in Work Organizations* (Monterey, CA: Brooks/Cole, 1973), pp. 2–5.

3. J. Kochanski, "Competency-Based Management," *Training and Development*, October 1997, pp. 40–44; Hay Group et al., *Raising the Bar: Using Competencies to Enhance Employee Performance* (Scottsdale, AZ: American Compensation Association, 1996); L. M. Spencer and S. M. Spencer, *Competence at Work: Models for Superior Performance* (New York: Wiley, 1993).

4. T. Hellström, "Knowledge and Competence Management at Ericsson: Decentralization and Organizational Fit," *Journal of Knowledge Management* 4 (2000).

5. J. R. Edwards, "Person-Job Fit: A Conceptual Integration, Literature Review, and Methodological Critique," *International Review of Industrial and Organizational Psychology* 6 (1991), pp. 283–357; J. E. Hunter and R. F. Hunter, "Validity and Utility of Alternative Predictors of Job Performance," *Psychological Bulletin* 96 (1984), pp. 72–98.

6. S. Pearlstein, "Canadian Stores Take On U.S. Rivals," *Plain Dealer (Cleveland)*, January 24, 1999, p. H1. For research on customer service and training, see J. W. Johnson, "Linking Employee Perceptions of Service Climate to Customer Satisfaction," *Personnel Psychology* 49 (1996), pp. 831–51; A. Sharma and D. Sarel, "The Impact of Customer Satisfaction Based Incentive Systems on Salespeople's Customer Service Response: An Empirical Study," *Journal of Personal Selling and Sales Management* 15 (Summer 1995), pp. 17–29; R. A. Guzzo, R. D. Jette, and R. A. Katzell, "The Effects of Psychologically Based Intervention Programs on Worker Productivity: A Meta-Analysis," *Personnel Psychology* 38 (1985), pp. 275–91.

7. B. Riggs and M. E. Thyfault, "The Modern Call Center—Customer Relationships and Loyalty Take Center Stage," *Information Week*, October 4, 1999.

8. L. Welch, "Watch Out for That Ice!" *Capital Times (Madison, WI)*, February 27, 2001, p. A1.

9. S. P. Brown and R. A. Peterson, "The Effect of Effort on Sales Performance and Job Satisfaction," *Journal of Marketing* 58 (April 1994), pp. 70–80.

10. Gary Johns discusses situational factors in terms of constraints both on behavior and on the complexities of organizational research. G. Johns, "Commentary: In Praise of Context," *Journal of Organizational Behavior* 22 (2001), pp. 31–42; Also see S. B. Bacharach and P. Bamberger, "Beyond Situational Constraints: Job Resources Inadequacy and Individual Performance at Work," *Human Resource Management Review* 5 (1995), pp. 79–102; K. F. Kane, ed., "Special Issue: Situational Constraints and Work Performance," *Human Resource Management Review* 3 (Summer 1993), pp. 83–175.

11. J. H. Sheridan, "Lockheed Martin Corp.," *Industry Week* 247 (October 19, 1998), pp. 54–56.

12. D. Yankelovich, "Got to Give to Get," *Mother Jones* 22 (July 1997), pp. 60–63.

13. B. Clements, "Skilled-Labor Shortage Compels Tacoma, Wash.–Area Photo Lab to Close for Good," *News Tribune* (*Tacoma, WA*), October 21, 2000.

14. "War for Talent II: Seven Ways to Win," *Fast Company* 42 (January 2001).

15. S. M. Jacoby, "Most Workers Find a Sense of Security in Corporate Life," *Los Angeles Times*, September 7, 1998, p. B5.

16. S. Patrick, "D–FW Hospitals in 'Quicksand' over Worsening Nurse Shortage," *Dallas Business Journal*, May 25, 2001; N. M. Moore, "Outside Agencies Offer Nursing Relief, but at What Cost?" *Cleveland Sun*, May 3, 2001; S. A. Webster, "Area Short of Nurses; Care Suffers," *Detroit News*, January 11, 2001.

17. T. Romita, "The Talent Search," *Business 2.0*, June 12, 2001; K. Dobbs, "Knowing How to Keep Your Best and Brightest," *Workforce* 80 (April 2001), pp. 56–60.

18. S. K. Witcher, "Asian Companies Grasp at Ways to Keep Staff," *Asian Wall Street Journal*, August 22, 2000, p. 8. Also see R. W. Griffeth and P. W. Hom, "The Employee Turnover Process," *Research in Personnel and Human Resource Management* 13 (1995), pp. 245–93.

19. P. Eaton-Robb, "For Employees, Solutions That Work," *Providence (RI) Journal*, January 10, 2001, p. E1; D. Stafford, "Workplace Policies about Snow- and Ice-Related Absences Vary Widely," *Kansas City Star*, December 21, 2000. For details about the causes of absenteeism, see S. R. Rhodes and R. M. Steers, *Managing Employee Absenteeism* (Reading, MA: Addison-Wesley, 1990).

20. D. A. Harrison and J. J. Martocchio, "Time for Absenteeism: A 20-Year Review of Origins, Offshoots, and Outcomes," *Journal of Management* 24 (Spring 1998), pp. 305–50; R. D. Hackett and P. Bycio, "An Evaluation of Employee Absenteeism as a Coping Mechanism among Hospital Nurses," *Journal of Occupational and Organizational Psychology* 69 (December 1996) pp. 327–38; R. G. Ehrenberg, R. A. Ehrenberg, D. I. Rees, and E. L. Ehrenberg, "School District Leave Policies, Teacher Absenteeism, and Student Achievement," *Journal of Human Resources* 26 (Winter 1991), pp. 72–105.

21. J. P. Campbell, R. A. McCloy, S. H. Oppler, and C. E. Sager, "A Theory of Performance," in N. Schmitt, W. C. Borman, and Associates, eds., *Personnel Selection in Organizations* (San Francisco: Jossey-Bass, 1993), pp. 35–70.

22. S. T. Hunt, "Generic Work Behavior: An Investigation into the Dimensions of Entry-Level, Hourly Job Performance," *Personnel Psychology* 49 (1996), pp. 51–83.

23. A. Czarnecki, "Customer Service Training: More Than an 'Event,'" *Learning for the Workplace* (*Canadian HR Reporter*, Supplement), May 20, 1996, pp. L4–L7.

24. C. I. Barnard, *The Functions of the Executive* (Cambridge, MA: Harvard University Press, 1938), pp. 83–84; D. Katz and R. L. Kahn, *The Social Psychology of Organizations* (New York: Wiley, 1966), pp. 337–40.

25. P. M. Podsakoff, M. Ahearne, and S. B. MacKenzie, "Organizational Citizenship Behavior and the Quantity and Quality of Work Group Performance," *Journal of Applied Psychology* 82 (1997), pp. 262–70; D. W. Organ, "The Motivational Basis of Organizational Citizenship Behavior," *Research in Organizational Behavior* 12 (1990), pp. 43–72. The discussion of altruism is also based on R. N. Kanungo and J. A. Conger, "Promoting Altruism as a Corporate Goal," *Academy of Management Executive* 7, no. 3 (1993), pp. 37–48.

26. G. Fauntleroy, "Top Education Employee Runs Office with Celestial Precision," *Santa Fe New Mexican*, July 22, 2001, p. E5.

27. P. Cappelli and N. Rogovsky, "Employee Involvement and Organizational Citizenship: Implications for Labor Law Reform and 'Lean Production,'" *Industrial and Labor Relations Review* 51 (July 1998), pp. 633–53; R. H. Moorman, G. L. Blakely, and B. P. Niehoff, "Does Perceived Organizational Support Mediate the Relationship between Procedural Justice and Organizational Citizenship Behavior?" *Academy of Management Journal* 41 (1998), pp. 351–57; Organ, "The Motivational Basis of Organizational Citizenship Behavior," pp. 60–63.

28. Kanungo and Conger, "Promoting Altruism as a Corporate Goal," p. 42.

29. K. Hanson, "Perks Help Keep Four Seasons Staff Pampering Guests," *National Post*, January 13, 2001, p. D8.

30. T. A. Stewart, "Gray Flannel Suit? Moi?" *Fortune*, March 16, 1998, pp. 76–82.

31. D. M. Harris and R. L. DeSimone, *Human Resource Development* (Fort Worth, TX: Harcourt Brace, 1994), p. 54; B. Bass and J. Vaughn, *Training in Industry: The Management of Learning* (Belmont, CA: Wadsworth, 1966), p. 8; W. McGehee and P. W. Thayer, *Training in Business and Industry* (New York: Wiley, 1961), pp. 131–34.

32. G. F. B. Probst, "Practical Knowledge Management: A Model That Works," *Prism* (Second Quarter 1998), pp. 17–23; G. Miles, R. E. Miles, V. Perrone, and L. Edvinsson, "Some Conceptual and Research Barriers to the Utilization of Knowledge," *California Management Review* 40 (Spring 1998), pp. 281–88; E. C. Nevis, A. J. DiBella, and J. M. Gould, "Understanding Organizations as Learning Systems," *Sloan Management Review* 36 (Winter 1995), pp. 73–85; D. Ulrich, T. Jick, and M. Von Glinow, "High Impact Learning: Building and Diffusing Learning Capability," *Organizational Dynamics* 22 (Autumn 1993), pp. 52–66; G. Huber, "Organizational Learning: The Contributing Processes and Literature," *Organizational Science* 2 (1991), pp. 88–115.

33. W. L. P. Wong and D. F. Radcliffe, "The Tacit Nature of Design Knowledge," *Technology Analysis and Strategic Management*, December 2000, pp. 493–512; R. Madhavan and R. Grover, "From Embedded Knowledge to Embodied Knowledge: New Product Development as Knowledge Management," *Journal of Marketing* 62 (October 1998), pp. 1–12; D. Leonard and S. Sensiper, "The Role of Tacit Knowledge in Group Innovation," *California Management Review* 40 (Spring 1998), pp. 112–32;

I. Nonaka and H. Takeuchi, *The Knowledge-Creating Company* (New York: Oxford University Press, 1995); R. K. Wagner and R. J. Sternberg, "Practical Intelligence in Real-World Pursuits: The Role of Tacit Knowledge," *Journal of Personality and Social Psychology* 49 (1985), pp. 436–58.

34. A. Lam, "Tacit Knowledge, Organizational Learning and Societal Institutions: An Integrated Framework," *Organization Studies,* May 2000.

35. M. J. Kerr, "Tacit Knowledge as a Predictor of Managerial Success: A Field Study," *Canadian Journal of Behavioral Science* 27 (1995), pp. 36–51.

36. W. F. Dowling, "Conversation with B. F. Skinner," *Organizational Dynamics,* Winter 1973, pp. 31–40.

37. R. G. Miltenberger, *Behavior Modification: Principles and Procedures* (Pacific Grove, CA: Brooks/Cole, 1997); J. Komaki, T. Coombs, and S. Schepman, "Motivational Implications of Reinforcement Theory," in R. M. Steers, L. W. Porter, and G. A. Bigley, eds., *Motivation and Leadership at Work* (New York: McGraw-Hill, 1996), pp. 34–52; H. P. Sims and P. Lorenzi, *The New Leadership Paradigm: Social Learning and Cognition in Organizations* (Newbury Park, CA: Sage, 1992), part II.

38. B. F. Skinner, *The Behavior of Organisms* (New York: Appleton-Century-Crofts, 1938).

39. F. Luthans and R. Kreitner, *Organizational Behavior Modification and Beyond* (Glenview, IL: Scott, Foresman, 1985); pp. 85–88; T. K. Connellan, *How to Improve Human Performance* (New York: Harper & Row, 1978), pp. 48–57.

40. Miltenberger, *Behavior Modification,* chaps. 4–6.

41. T. C. Mawhinney and R. R. Mawhinney, "Operant Terms and Concepts Applied to Industry," in R. M. O'Brien, A. M. Dickinson, and M. P. Rosow, eds., *Industrial Behavior Modification: A Management Handbook* (New York: Pergamon Press, 1982), p. 117; R. Kreitner, "Controversy in OBM: History, Misconceptions, and Ethics," in L. W. Frederiksen, ed., *Handbook of Organizational Behavior Management* (New York: Wiley, 1982), pp. 76–79.

42. Luthans and Kreitner, *Organizational Behavior Modification and Beyond,* pp. 53–54.

43. K. D. Butterfield, L. K. Trevino, and G. A. Ball, "Punishment from the Manager's Perspective: A Grounded Investigation and Inductive Model," *Academy of Management Journal* 39 (1996), pp. 1479–1512; L. K. Trevino, "The Social Effects of Punishment in Organizations: A Justice Perspective," *Academy of Management Review* 17 (1992), pp. 647–76.

44. B. S. Klaas and H. N. Wheeler, "Managerial Decision Making about Employee Discipline: A Policy-Capturing Approach," *Personnel Psychology* 43 (1990), pp. 117–34.

45. Butterfield et al., "Punishment from the Manager's Perspective"; Luthans and Kreitner, *Organizational Behavior Modification and Beyond,* pp. 139–44; J. M. Beyer and H. M. Trice, "A Field Study of the Use and Perceived Effects of Discipline in Controlling Work Performance," *Academy of Management Journal* 27 (1984), pp. 743–64.

46. G. P. Latham and V. L. Huber, "Schedules of Reinforcement: Lessons from the Past and Issues for the Future," *Journal of Organizational Behavior Management* 13 (1992), pp. 125–49.

47. A. Zipkin, "Kinder, Gentler Workplace Replaces Era of Tough Boss," *New York Times,* June 26, 2000.

48. F. Luthans and A. D. Stajkovic, "Reinforce for Performance: The Need to Go Beyond Pay and Even Rewards," *Academy of Management Executive* 13 (May 1999), pp. 49–57; A. D. Stajkovic and F. Luthans, "A Meta-Analysis of the Effects of Organizational Behavior Modification on Task Performance, 1975–95," *Academy of Management Journal* 40 (1997), pp. 1122–49.

49. P. Eaton-Robb, "For Employees, Solutions That Work," *Providence Journal,* January 10, 2001, p. E1; D. Behar, "Firm Launches Lottery to Beat 'Sickies' Plague," *Daily Mail (UK),* January 8, 2001, p. 27; G. Masek, "Dana Corp.," *Industry Week,* October 19, 1998, p. 48.

50. G. A. Merwin, J. A. Thomason, and E. E. Sanford, "A Methodological and Content Review of Organizational Behavior Management in the Private Sector: 1978–1986," *Journal of Organizational Behavior Management* 10 (1989), pp. 39–57.

51. P. Drucker, *Management: Tasks, Responsibilities, Practices* (New York: Harper & Row, 1974).

52. R. Curren, "Lottery Helps Solve Absenteeism," *Winnipeg Free Press,* November 6, 1999. Further information about NOVA Chemicals was provided by Ms. Roxann Good, NOVA Chemicals Ltd., July 2000. All amounts are in U.S. dollars.

53. Latham and Huber, "Schedules of Reinforcement," pp. 132–33.

54. T. C. Mawhinney, "Philosophical and Ethical Aspects of Organizational Behavior Management: Some Evaluative Feedback," *Journal of Organizational Behavior Management* 6 (Spring 1984), pp. 5–31; F. L. Fry, "Operant Conditioning in Organizational Settings: Of Mice or Men?" *Personnel* 51 (July–August 1974), pp. 17–24.

55. A. N. Kluger and A. DeNisi, "The Effects of Feedback Interventions on Performance: A Historical Review, A Meta-Analysis, and a Preliminary Feedback Intervention Theory," *Psychological Bulletin* 119 (March 1996), pp. 254–84; A. A. Shikdar and B. Das, "A Field Study of Worker Productivity Improvements," *Applied Ergonomics* 26 (1995), pp. 21–27; L. M. Sama and R. E. Kopelman, "In Search of a Ceiling Effect on Work Motivation: Can Kaizen Keep Performance 'Risin'?" *Journal of Social Behavior and Personality* 9 (1994), pp. 231–37.

56. R. Waldersee and F. Luthans, "The Impact of Positive and Corrective Feedback on Customer Service Performance," *Journal of Organizational Behavior* 15 (1994), pp. 83–95; P. K. Duncan and L. R. Bruwelheide, "Feedback: Use and Possible Behavioral Functions," *Journal of Organizational Behavior Management* 7 (Fall 1985), pp. 91–114; J. Annett, *Feedback and Human Behavior* (Baltimore: Penguin, 1969).

57. M. C. Andrews and K. M. Kacmar, "Confirmation and Extension of the Sources of Feedback Scale in Service-Based Organizations," *Journal of Business Communication* 38 (April 2001), pp. 206–26.

58. For discussion of multisource feedback, see W. W. Tornow and M. London, *Maximizing the Value of 360-degree Feedback: A Process for Successful Individual and Organizational Development* (San

Francisco: Jossey-Bass, 1998); D. A. Waldman and L. E. Atwater, *The Power of 360 Feedback: How to Leverage Performance Evaluations for Top Productivity* (Houston: Gulf, 1998); M. Edwards and A. Ewan, *360 Feedback: The Powerful New Model for Employee Assessment and Performance Improvement* (New York: AMACOM, 1996).

59. P. G. Dominick, R. R. Reilly, and J. W. McGourty, "The Effects of Peer Feedback on Team Member Behavior," *Group and Organization Management* 22 (December 1997), pp. 508–20. Employee concerns with 360-degree feedback are reported in B. Usher and J. Morley, "Overcoming the Obstacles to a Successful 360-Degree Feedback Program," *Canadian HR Reporter*, February 8, 1999, p. 17.

60. The problems with 360-degree feedback are discussed in M. A. Peiperl, "Getting 360 Degree Feedback Right," *Harvard Business Review* 79 (January 2001), pp. 142–47; A. S. DeNisi and A. N. Kluger, "Feedback Effectiveness: Can 360-Degree Appraisals Be Improved?" *Academy of Management Executive* 14 (February 2000), pp. 129–39; J. Ghorpade, "Managing Five Paradoxes of 360-Degree Feedback," *Academy of Management Executive* 14 (February 2000), pp. 140–50.

61. D. M. Herold, R. C. Linden, and M. L. Leatherwood, "Using Multiple Attributes to Assess Sources of Performance Feedback," *Academy of Management Journal* 30 (December 1987), pp. 826–35.

62. M. London, "Giving Feedback: Source-Centered Antecedents and Consequences of Constructive and Destructive Feedback," *Human Resource Management Review* 5 (1995), pp. 159–88; D. Antonioni, "The Effects of Feedback Accountability on 360-Degree Appraisal Ratings," *Personnel Psychology* 47 (1994), pp. 375–90; S. J. Ashford and G. B. Northcraft, "Conveying More (or Less) Than We Realize: The Role of Impression Management in Feedback Seeking," *Organizational Behavior and Human Decision Processes* 53 (1992), pp. 310–34; E. W. Morrison and R. J. Bies, "Impression Management in the Feedback-Seeking Process: A Literature Review and Research Agenda," *Academy of Management Review* 16 (1991), pp. 522–41.

63. J. R. Williams, C. E. Miller, L. A. Steelman, and P. E. Levy, "Increasing Feedback Seeking in Public Contexts: It Takes Two (or More) to Tango," *Journal of Applied Psychology* 84 (December 1999), pp. 969–76; G. B. Northcraft and S. J. Ashford, "The Preservation of Self in Everyday Life: The Effects of Performance Expectations and Feedback Context on Feedback Inquiry," *Organizational Behavior and Human Decision Processes* 47 (1990), pp. 42–64.

64. R. D. Pritchard, P. L. Roth, S. D. Jones, and P. G. Roth, "Implementing Feedback Systems to Enhance Productivity: A Practical Guide," *National Productivity Review* 10 (Winter 1990–1991), pp. 57–67.

65. P. M. Posakoff and J. Fahr, "Effects of Feedback Sign and Credibility on Goal Setting and Task Performance," *Organizational Behavior and Human Decision Processes* 44 (1989), pp. 45–67.

66. R. D. Guzzo and B. A. Gannett, "The Nature of Facilitators and Inhibitors of Effective Task Performance," in F. D. Schoorman and B. Schneider, eds., *Facilitating Work Effectiveness* (Lexington, MA.: Lexington Books, 1988), p. 23; R. C. Linden and T. R. Mitchell, "Reactions to Feedback: The Role of Attributions," *Academy of Management Journal* 28 (June 1985), pp. 291–308.

67. S. Robinson and E. Weldon, "Feedback Seeking in Groups: A Theoretical Perspective," *British Journal of Social Psychology* 32 (1993), pp. 71–86; S. J. Ashford and L. L. Cummings, "Feedback as an Individual Resource: Personal Strategies of Creating Information," *Organizational Behavior and Human Performance* 32 (1983), pp. 370–98; S. J. Ashford, "Feedback Seeking in Individual Adaptation: A Resource Perspective," *Academy of Management Journal* 29 (1986), pp. 465–87.

68. J. M. Mishra and S. M. Crampton, "Employee Monitoring: Privacy in the Workplace?" *SAM Advanced Management Journal* 63 (June 1998), pp. 4–14.

69. A. Miller, "Being Sued? Roll Video," *Broward Daily Business Review*, August 15, 2001, p. A9; T. Joyner, "Work Hard, Step Straight: Big Boss Is Watching," *Chattanooga (TN) Times*, July 29, 2001, p. G1; G. T. Pakulski, "The Boss Is Watching," *Toledo (OH)*

Blade, May 27, 2001; "CT Employees Sue Airline over Hidden Camera," *Amarillo (TX) Globe*, May 20, 2001.

70. K. D. Grimsley, "35% of Firms Found to Monitor Workers Electronically," *Washington Post*, May 24, 1997, p. F1. For discussion of the ethical issues of monitoring, see N. B. Fairweather, "Surveillance in Employment: The Case of Teleworking," *Journal of Business Ethics* 22 (October 1999), pp. 39–49; B. E. Bohling, "Workplace Video Surveillance," *Monthly Labor Review* 120 (July 1997), p. 41.

71. J. M. Stanton and E. M. Weiss, "Electronic Monitoring in Their Own Words: An Exploratory Study of Employees' Experiences with New Types of Surveillance," *Computers in Human Behavior* 16 (July 2000), pp. 423–40; D. Lyon, *The Electronic Eye: The Rise of the Surveillance Society* (Minneapolis: University of Minnesota Press, 1994); B. P. Niehoff and R. H. Moorman, "Justice as a Mediator of the Relationship between Methods of Monitoring and Organizational Citizenship Behavior," *Academy of Management Journal* 36 (1993), pp. 527–56; J. Chalykoff and T. A. Kochan, "Computer-Aided Monitoring: Its Influence on Employee Job Satisfaction and Turnover," *Personnel Psychology* 42 (1989), pp. 807–34.

72. A. Bandura, *Social Foundations of Thought and Action: A Social Cognitive Theory* (Englewood Cliffs, NJ: Prentice Hall, 1986).

73. A. Pescuric and W. C. Byham, "The New Look of Behavior Modeling," *Training and Development* 50 (July 1996), pp. 24–30; H. P. Sims, Jr., and C. C. Manz, "Modeling Influences on Employee Behavior," *Personnel Journal*, January 1982, pp. 58–65.

74. A. D. Stajkovic and F. Luthans, "Social Cognitive Theory and Self-Efficacy: Going Beyond Traditional Motivational and Behavioral Approaches," *Organizational Dynamics* 26 (Spring 1998), pp. 62–74; A. Bandura, *Self-Efficacy: The Exercise of Control* (New York: Freeman, 1996); M. E. Gist and T. R. Mitchell, "Self-Efficacy: A Theoretical Analysis of Its Determinants and Malleability," *Academy of Management Review* 17 (1992), pp. 183–211; R. F. Mager, "No Self-Efficacy, No Performance," *Training* 29 (April 1992), pp. 32–36.

75. L. K. Trevino, "The Social Effects of Punishment in Organizations: A Justice Perspective," *Academy of Management Review* 17 (1992), pp. 647–76; M. E. Schnake, "Vicarious Punishment in a Work Setting," *Journal of Applied Psychology* 71 (1986), pp. 343–45.

76. M. Foucault, *Discipline and Punish: The Birth of the Prison* (Harmondsworth, UK: Penguin, 1977).

77. L. K. Trevino, "The Social Effects of Punishment in Organizations: A Justice Perspective," *Academy of Management Review* 17 (1992), pp. 647–76; M. E. Schnake, "Vicarious Punishment in a Work Setting," *Journal of Applied Psychology* 71 (1986), pp. 343–45.

78. A. W. Logue, *Self-Control: Waiting until Tomorrow for What You Want Today.* (Englewood Cliffs, NJ: Prentice Hall, 1995); A. Bandura, "Self-Reinforcement: Theoretical and Methodological Considerations," *Behaviorism* 4 (1976), pp. 135–55.

79. C. A. Frayne, "Improving Employee Performance through Self-Management Training," *Business Quarterly* 54 (Summer 1989), pp. 46–50.

80. D. Woodruff, "Putting Talent to the Test," *Wall Street Journal Europe*, November 14, 2000, p. 25. The simulation events described here were experienced by the author of this article, but we reasonably assume that Mandy Chooi, who also completed the simulation, went through similar events in her simulation.

81. S. Gherardi, D. Nicolini, and F. Odella, "Toward a Social Understanding of How People Learn in Organizations," *Management Learning* 29 (September 1998), pp. 273–97; Ulrich, Jick, and Von Glinow, "High Impact Learning."

82. D. A. Kolb, *Experiential Learning* (Englewood Cliffs, NJ: Prentice Hall, 1984).

83. The learning orientation concept is the focus of current attention in marketing. See M. A. Farrell, "Developing a Market-Oriented Learning Organization," *Australian Journal of Management* 25 (September 2000); W. E. Baker and J. M. Sinkula, "The Synergistic Effect of Market Orientation and Learning Orientation," *Journal of the Academy of Marketing Science* 27 (1999), pp. 411–27.

84. A. Lee, "Mock City Rises in Mich.," *Detroit News*, May 4, 2001, p. 1.

85. J. Jusko, "Always Lessons to Learn," *Industry Week*, February 15, 1999, p. 23; A. C. Edmondson, "Learning from Mistakes Is Easier Said Than Done: Group and Organizational Influences on the Detection and Correction of Human Error," *Journal of Applied Behavioral Science* 32 (1996), pp. 5–28.

86. R. W. Revans, *The Origin and Growth of Action Learning* (London: Chartwell Bratt, 1982), pp. 626–27.

87. V. J. Marsick, "The Many Faces of Action Learning," *Management Learning* 30 (June 1999), pp. 159–76.

88. R. M. Fulmer, P. Gibbs, and J. B. Keys, "The Second Generation Learning Organizations: New Tools for Sustaining Competitive Advantage," *Organizational Dynamics* 27 (Autumn 1998), pp. 6–20; A. L. Stern "Where the Action Is," *Across the Board* 34 (September 1997), pp. 43–47; R. W. Revans, "What Is Action Learning?" *Journal of Management Development* 15 (1982), pp. 64–75.

89. R. M. Fulmer, P. A. Gibbs and M. Goldsmith, "Developing Leaders: How Winning Companies Keep On Winning," *Sloan Management Review*, October 2000, pp. 49–59; J. A. Conger and K. Xin, "Executive Education in the 21st Century," *Journal of Management Education* (February 2000), pp. 73ff.

90. T. T. Baldwin, C. Danielson, and W. Wiggenhorn, "The Evolution of Learning Strategies in Organizations: From Employee Development to Business Redefinition," *Academy of Management Executive* 11 (November 1997), pp. 47–58.

CHAPTER THREE

1. N. Bendavid, "Report Criticizes Work in Lee Case," *Chicago Tribune*, August 14, 2001, p. N1; E. Lichtblau, "Report Assails Botched Probe of Lee Spy Case," *Los Angeles Times*, August 14, 2001, p. A1; F. Davila, "Prejudice Stings 'Model Minority,'" *Baltimore Sun*, July 29, 2001, p. C5; S. Hepinstall, "Chinese-Americans Face Stereotyping—Survey," *Reuters English News Service*, April 25, 2001; O. Barker, "The Asianization of America," *USA Today*, March 22, 2001, p. A1; J. Glanz, "Amid Race Profiling Claims, Asian-Americans Avoid Labs," *New York Times*, July 16, 2000, p. 1. Dr. Wen Ho Lee was detained for nine months and eventually pleaded guilty to one count of downloading classified information on his computer. The other 58 counts of mishandling classified information were dropped.

2. Plato, *The Republic*, trans. D. Lee (Harmondsworth, UK: Penguin, 1955), part VII, sec. 7.

3. S. F. Cronshaw and R. G. Lord, "Effects of Categorization, Attribution, and Encoding Processes on Leadership Perceptions," *Journal of Applied Psychology* 72 (1987), pp. 97–106.

4. R. H. Fazio, D. R. Roskos-Ewoldsen, and M. C. Powell, "Attitudes, Perception, and Attention," in P. M. Niedenthal and S. Kitayama, eds., *The Heart's Eye: Emotional Influences in Perception and Attention* (San Diego, CA: Academic Press, 1994), pp. 197–216.

5. D. Goleman, *Vital Lies, Simple Truths: The Psychology of Deception* (New York: Touchstone, 1985); M. Haire and W. F. Grunes, "Perceptual Defenses: Processes Protecting an Organized Perception of Another Personality," *Human Relations* 3 (1950), pp. 403–12.

6. C. N. Macrae, G. V. Bodenhausen, A. M. Schloerscheidt, and A. B. Milne, "Tales of the Unexpected: Executive Function and Person Perception," *Journal of Personality and Social Psychology* 76 (1999), pp. 200–13; J. M. Beyer et al., "The Selective Perception of Managers Revisited," *Academy of Management Journal* 40 (June 1997), pp. 716–37; C. N. Macrae and G. V. Bodenhausen, "The Dissection of Selection in Person Perception: Inhibitory Processes in Social Stereotyping," *Journal of Personality and Social Psychology* 69 (1995), pp. 397–407; J. P. Walsh, "Selectivity and Selective Perception: An Investigation of Managers' Belief Structures and Information Processing," *Academy of Management Journal* 31 (1988), pp. 873–96; D. C. Dearborn and H. A. Simon, "Selective Perception: A Note on the Departmental Identification of Executives," *Sociometry* 21 (1958), pp. 140–44.

7. J. Rupert, "We Haven't Forgotten about Her," *Ottawa Citizen*, December 6, 1999; W. Burkan, "Developing Your Wide-Angle Vision; Skills for Anticipating the Future," *Futurist* 32 (March

1998), pp. 35–38. For splatter vision applied to professional bird watchers, see E. Nickens, "Window on the Wild," *Backpacker* 25 (April 1997), pp. 28–32.

8. D. Gurteen, "Knowledge, Creativity and Innovation," *Journal of Knowledge Management* 2 (September 1998), p. 5; C. Argyris and D. A. Schön, *Organizational Learning II* (Reading, MA: Addison-Wesley, 1996); P. M. Senge, *The Fifth Discipline: The Art and Practice of the Learning Organization* (New York: Doubleday Currency, 1990), chap. 10; P. N. Johnson-Laird, *Mental Models* (Cambridge, UK: Cambridge University Press, 1984). Mental models are widely discussed in the philosophy of logic. For example, see J. L. Aronson, "Mental Models and Deduction," *American Behavioral Scientist* 40 (May 1997), pp. 782–97.

9. Burkan, "Developing Your Wide-Angle Vision."

10. "What Are Mental Models?" *Sloan Management Review* 38 (Spring 1997), p. 13; P. Nystrom and W. Starbuck, "To Avoid Organizational Crises, Unlearn," *Organizational Dynamics* 12 (Winter 1984), pp. 53–65.

11. T. Abate, "Meet Bill Gates, Stand-up Comic," *San Francisco Examiner*, March 13, 1996, p. D1; P. J. H. Schoemaker, "Scenario Planning: A Tool for Strategic Thinking," *Sloan Management Review* 36 (Winter 1995), pp. 25–40.

12. P. Roberts, "Sony Changes the Game," *Fast Company* 10 (1997), p. 116.

13. M. A. Hogg and D. J. Terry, "Social Identity and Self-Categorization Processes in Organizational Contexts," *Academy of Management Review* 25 (January 2000), pp. 121–40; B. E. Ashforth and F. Mael, "Social Identity Theory and the Organization," *Academy of Management Review* 14 (1989), pp. 20–39; H. Tajfel, *Social Identity and Intergroup Relations* (Cambridge, UK: Cambridge University Press, 1982).

14. The interaction between personal and social identity is quite complex, as researchers are now discovering. See J. A. Howard, "Social Psychology of Identities," *Annual Review of Sociology* 26 (2000), pp. 367–93.

15. J. E. Dutton, J. M. Dukerich, and C. V. Harquail, "Organizational Images and Member Identification," *Administrative Science Quarterly* 39 (June 1994), pp. 239–63. For recent research on the selection of identity groups, see B. Simon and C. Hastedt, "Self-Aspects as Social Categories: The Role of Personal Importance and Valence," *European Journal of Social Psychology* 29 (1999), pp. 479–87.

16. J. W. Jackson and E. R. Smith, "Conceptualizing Social Identity: A New Framework and Evidence for the Impact of Different Dimensions," *Personality and Social Psychology Bulletin* 25 (January 1999), pp. 120–35.

17. G. Brenneman, "Right Away and All at Once: How We Saved Continental," *Harvard Business Review* 76 (September–October 1998), pp. 162–79; T. Kennedy, "Confidence Returns with Continental's Strong Comeback," *Minneapolis Star Tribune*, February 1, 1998, p. 1A.

18. C. N. Macrae and G. V. Bodenhausen, "Social Cognition: Thinking Categorically about Others," *Annual Review of Psychology* 51 (2000), pp. 93–120; W. G. Stephan and C. W. Stephan, *Intergroup Relations* (Boulder, CO: Westview, 1996), chap. 1; L. Falkenberg, "Improving the Accuracy of Stereotypes within the Workplace," *Journal of Management* 16 (1990), pp. 107–18; D. L. Hamilton, S. J. Sherman, and C. M. Ruvolo, "Stereotype-Based Expectancies: Effects on Information Processing and Social Behavior," *Journal of Social Issues* 46 (1990), pp. 35–60.

19. F. T. McAndrew et al., "A Multicultural Study of Stereotyping in English-Speaking Countries," *Journal of Social Psychology* 740 (August 2000), pp. 487–502; S. Madon et al., "The Accuracy and Power of Sex, Social Class, and Ethnic Stereotypes: A Naturalistic Study in Person Perception," *Personality and Social Psychology Bulletin* 24 (December 1998), pp. 1304–18; Y. Lee, L. J. Jussim, and C. R. McCauley, eds., *Stereotype Accuracy: Toward Appreciating Group Differences* (Washington, DC: American Psychological Association, 1996). For an early discussion of stereotypes, see W. Lippmann, *Public Opinion* (New York: Macmillan, 1922).

20. D. L. Stone and A. Colella, "A Model of Factors Affecting the Treatment of Disabled Individuals in Organizations," *Academy of Management Review* 21 (1996), pp. 352–401.

21. C. Stangor and D. McMillan, "Memory for Expectancy-Congruent and Expectancy-Incongruent Information: A Review of the Social and Social Development Literatures," *Psychological Bulletin* 111 (1992), pp. 42–61; C. Stangor, L. Lynch, C. Duan, and B. Glass, "Categorization of Individuals on the Basis of Multiple Social Features," *Journal of Personality and Social Psychology* 62 (1992), pp. 207–18.

22. P. J. Oaks, S. A. Haslam, and J. C. Turner, *Stereotyping and Social Reality* (Cambridge, MA: Blackwell, 1994).

23. J. W. Sherman, A. Y. Lee, G. R. Bessenoff, and L. A. Frost, "Stereotype Efficiency Reconsidered: Encoding Flexibility under Cognitive Load," *Journal of Personality and Social Psychology* 75 (1998), pp. 589–606; C. N. Macrae, A. B. Milne, and G. V. Bodenhausen, "Stereotypes as Energy-Saving Devices: A Peek Inside the Cognitive Toolbox," *Journal of Personality and Social Psychology* 66 (1994), pp. 37–47; S. T. Fiske, "Social Cognition and Social Perception," *Annual Review of Psychology* 44 (1993), pp. 155–94.

24. Z. Kunda and P. Thagard, "Forming Impressions from Stereotypes, Traits, and Behaviors: A Parallel-Constraint Satisfaction Theory," *Psychological Review* 103 (1996), pp. 284–308.

25. S. O. Gaines and E. S. Reed, "Prejudice: From Allport to DuBois," *American Psychologist* 50 (February 1995), pp. 96–103; L. Jussim and T. E. Nelson, "Prejudice, Stereotypes, and Labeling Effects: Sources of Bias in Person Perception," *Journal of Personality and Social Psychology* 68 (February 1995), pp. 228–46.

26. P. Porco, "Intolerance Claims Mount," *Anchorage Daily News*, July 19, 2001, p. A1; K. Sinclair, "New Laws Unlikely to Stamp Out Racial Prejudice," *South China Morning Post*, April 25, 2001, p. 17; M. C. Quinn, "Southern's Big Day," *Atlanta Journal–Constitution*, April 1, 2001, p. G1; L. Hunt, "Racism in Hong Kong Seen Tarnishing Territory's Reputation," *Agence France Presse*, January 29, 2001.

27. A. P. Brief et al., "Beyond Good Intentions: The Next Steps toward Racial Equality in the American Workplace," *Academy of Management Executive* 11 (November 1997), pp. 59–72; M. J.

Monteith, "Self-Regulation of Prejudiced Responses: Implications for Progress in Prejudice-Reduction Efforts," *Journal of Personality and Social Psychology* 65 (1993), pp. 469–85.

28. P. M. Buzzanell, "Reframing the Glass Ceiling as a Socially Constructed Process: Implications for Understanding and Change," *Communication Monographs* 62 (December 1995), pp. 327–54; M. E. Heilman, "Sex Stereotypes and Their Effects in the Workplace: What We Know and What We Don't Know," *Journal of Social Behavior and Personality* 10 (1995), pp. 3–26.

29. Age bias is also making headlines in the United States. See M. Ortiz, "Age-Bias Claims Jolt Ford Culture Change," *Detroit News*, April 29, 2001; L. B. Song, "Technology Workers Say Age Bias Becoming More Noticeable," *Chicago Tribune*, April 13, 2001; R. Pogrebin, "At 40, They're Finished, Television Writers Say," *New York Times*, January 30, 2001, p. 9.

30. S. T. Fiske and P. Glick, "Ambivalence and Stereotypes Cause Sexual Harassment: A Theory with Implications for Organizational Change," *Journal of Social Issues* 51 (1995), pp. 97–115; K. Deaux, "How Basic Can You Be? The Evolution of Research on Gender Stereotypes," *Journal of Social Issues* 51 (1995), pp. 11–20.

31. E. Rosell and K. Miller, "Firefighting Women and Sexual Harassment," *Public Personnel Management* 24 (Fall 1995), pp. 339–50.

32. H. H. Kelley, *Attribution in Social Interaction* (Morristown, NJ: General Learning Press, 1971).

33. H. H. Kelley, "The Processes of Causal Attribution," *American Psychologist* 28 (1973), pp. 107–28; J. M. Feldman, "Beyond Attribution Theory: Cognitive Processes in Performance Appraisal," *Journal of Applied Psychology* 66 (1981), pp. 127–48.

34. J. D. Ford, "The Effects of Causal Attributions on Decision Makers' Responses to Performance Downturns," *Academy of Management Review* 10 (1985), pp. 770–86; M. J. Martinko and W. L. Gardner, "The Leader/Member Attribution Process," *Academy of Management Review* 12 (1987), pp. 235–49.

35. J. Martocchio and J. Dulebohn, "Performance Feedback Effects in

Training: The Role of Perceived Controllability," *Personnel Psychology* 47 (1994), pp. 357–73; J. M. Crant and T. S. Bateman, "Assignment of Credit and Blame for Performance Outcomes," *Academy of Management Journal* 36 (1993), pp. 7–27; D. R. Norris and R. E. Niebuhr, "Attributional Influences on the Job Performance–Job Satisfaction Relationship," *Academy of Management Journal* 27 (1984), pp. 424–31.

36. H. J. Bernardin and P. Villanova, "Performance Appraisal," in E. A. Locke, ed., *Generalising from Laboratory to Field Settings* (Lexington, MA: Lexington Books, 1986), pp. 43–62; S. G. Green and T. R. Mitchell, "Attributional Processes of Leader-Member Interactions," *Organizational Behavior and Human Performance* 23 (1979), pp. 429–58.

37. P. J. Taylor and J. L. Pierce, "Effects of Introducing a Performance Management System on Employees' Subsequent Attitudes and Effort," *Public Personnel Management* 28 (Fall 1999), pp. 423–52.

38. J. R. Bettman and B. A. Weitz, "Attributions in the Board Room: Causal Reasoning in Corporate Annual Reports," *Administrative Science Quarterly* 28 (1983), pp. 165–83.

39. P. Rosenthal and D. Guest, "Gender Difference in Managers' Causal Explanations for Their Work Performance: A Study in Two Organizations," *Journal of Occupational and Organizational Psychology* 69 (1996), pp. 145–51.

40. B. McElhinny, "Printing Plant Makes Its Mark," *Charleston (WV) Daily Mail*, May 6, 1997, p. D1.

41. J. M. Darley and K. C. Oleson, "Introduction to Research on Interpersonal Expectations," in P. D. Blanck, ed., *Interpersonal Expectations: Theory, Research, and Applications* (Cambridge, UK: Cambridge University Press, 1993), pp. 45–63; D. Eden, *Pygmalion in Management* (Lexington, MA: Lexington, 1990); L. Jussim, "Self-Fulfilling Prophecies: A Theoretical and Integrative Review," *Psychological Review* 93 (1986), pp. 429–45.

42. D. Eden and A. B. Shani, "Pygmalion Goes to Boot Camp: Expectancy, Leadership, and Trainee Performance," *Journal of Applied Psychology* 67 (1982), pp. 194–99.

43. Similar models are presented in R. H. G. Field and D. A. Van Seters, "Management by Expectations (MBE): The Power of Positive Prophecy," *Journal of General Management* 14 (Winter 1988), pp. 19–33; D. Eden, "Self-Fulfilling Prophecy as a Management Tool: Harnessing Pygmalion," *Academy of Management Review* 9 (1984), pp. 64–73.

44. M. J. Harris and R. Rosenthal, "Mediation of Interpersonal Expectancy Effects: 31 Meta-Analyses," *Psychological Bulletin* 97 (1985), pp. 363–86.

45. D. Eden, "Interpersonal Expectations in Organizations," in , ed., *Interpersonal Expectations: Theory, Research, and Applications* (Cambridge, UK: Cambridge University Press, 1993), pp. 154–78.

46. A. Bandura, *Self-Efficacy: The Exercise of Control* (New York: Freeman, 1996); M. E. Gist and T. R. Mitchell, "Self Efficacy: A Theoretical Analysis of Its Determinants and Malleability," *Academy of Management Review* 17 (1992), pp. 183–211.

47. J-F. Manzoni, "The Set-Up-to-Fail Syndrome," *Harvard Business Review* 76 (March–April 1998), pp. 101–13; J. S. Livingston, "Retrospective Commentary," *Harvard Business Review* 66 (September–October 1988), p. 125.

48. The earlier advice on positive expectations is found in S. Oz and D. Eden, "Restraining the Golem: Boosting Performance by Changing the Interpretation of Low Scores," *Journal of Applied Psychology* 79 (1994), pp. 744–54; D. Eden, "OD and Self-Fulfilling Prophecy: Boosting Productivity by Raising Expectations," *Journal of Applied Behavioral Science* 22 (1986), pp. 1–13.

49. S. S. White and E. A. Locke, "Problems with the Pygmalion Effect and Some Proposed Solutions," *Leadership Quarterly* 11 (Autumn 2000), pp. 389–415. This source also cites recent studies on the failure of traditional Pygmalion training. For an early application of self-efficacy in self-fulfilling prophecy, see K. S. Crawford, E. D. Thomas, and J. J. Fink, "Pygmalion at Sea: Improving the Work Effectiveness of Low Performers," *Journal of Applied Behavioral Science* 16 (1980), pp. 482–505.

50. T. Hill, P. Lewicki, M. Czyzewska, and A. Boss, "Self-Perpetuating

Development of Encoding Biases in Person Perception," *Journal of Personality and Social Psychology* 57 (1989), pp. 373–87; C. L. Kleinke, *First Impressions: The Psychology of Encountering Others* (Englewood Cliffs, NJ: Prentice Hall, 1975).

51. R. Wright, "Great X-pectations," *Canadian Banker* 106 (January–February 1999), pp. 11–15.

52. D. D. Steiner and J. S. Rain, "Immediate and Delayed Primacy and Recency Effects in Performance Evaluation," *Journal of Applied Psychology* 74 (1989), pp. 136–42; R. L. Heneman and K. N. Wexley, "The Effects of Time Delay in Rating and Amount of Information Observed in Performance Rating Accuracy," *Academy of Management Journal* 26 (1983), pp. 677–86.

53. W. H. Cooper, "Ubiquitous Halo," *Psychological Bulletin* 90 (1981), pp. 218–44; K. R. Murphy, R. A. Jako, and R. L. Anhalt, "Nature and Consequences of Halo Error: A Critical Analysis," *Journal of Applied Psychology* 78 (1993), pp. 218–25.

54. S. Kozlowski, M. Kirsch, and G. Chao, "Job Knowledge, Ratee Familiarity, Conceptual Similarity, and Halo Error: An Exploration," *Journal of Applied Psychology* 71 (1986), pp. 45–49; H. C. Min, "Country Image: Halo or Summary Construct?" *Journal of Marketing Research* 26 (1989), pp. 222–29.

55. W. K. Balzer and L. M. Sulsky, "Halo and Performance Appraisal Research: A Critical Examination," *Journal of Applied Psychology* 77 (1992), pp. 975–85; H. J. Bernardin and R. W. Beatty, *Performance Appraisal: Assessing Human Behavior at Work* (Boston: Kent, 1984).

56. R. L Gross and S. E. Brodt, "How Assumptions of Consensus Undermine Decision Making," *Sloan Management Review* 42 (January 2001), pp. 86–94; G. G. Sherwood, "Self-Serving Biases in Person Perception: A Re-examination of Projection as a Mechanism of Defense," *Psychological Bulletin* 90 (1981), pp. 445–59.

57. "Women Flourish in Schwab's Climate," *San Francisco Business Times*, April 27, 2001, p. S10.

58. "Diversity Initiatives Help Keep a Competitive Edge," *PR Newswire*, June 4, 2001; R. M. Wentling and N. Palma-

Rivas, "Current Status of Diversity Initiatives in Selected Multinational Corporations," *Human Resource Development Quarterly* 11 (Spring 2000), pp. 35–60; J. A. Gilbert, B. A. Stead, and J. M. Ivancevich, "Diversity Management: A New Organizational Paradigm," *Journal of Business Ethics* 21 (August 1999), pp. 61–76; G. Robinson and K. Dechant, "Building a Business Case for Diversity," *Academy of Management Executive* 11 (August 1997), pp. 21–31.

59. J. Neff, "Johnson Layers Diversity," *Advertising Age*, February 19, 2001, pp. S1–S2.

60. R. Hudson, "Employers Find a More Diverse Work Force Brings a Variety of Religious Beliefs," *St. Louis Post-Dispatch*, August 6, 2001, p. 10.

61. D. E. Owens, "Walt Disney Resort: Winner—Cutting Edge Award," *Orlando Sentinel*, August 5, 2001, p. 35; L. Eckelbecker, "Raytheon Celebrates Diversity," *Telegram and Gazette* (Worcester, MA), June 8, 2001, p. E1.

62. H. Hemphill and R. Haines, *Discrimination, Harassment, and the Failure of Diversity Training: What to Do Now* (Westport, CT: Quorum Books, 1997); J. R. W. Joplin and C. S. Daus, "Challenges of Leading a Diverse Workforce," *Academy of Management Executive* 11 (August 1997), pp. 32–47.

63. B. Parks, "Club Swinging a Sticky Situation in NHL," *Star-Ledger (Newark, NJ)*, March 28, 2000, p. 61; L. Hornby, "Racism Meeting Hits Home with Leafs Players," *Toronto Sun*, September 27, 1999, p. 81; K. C. Johnson, "When Words Collide," *Chicago Tribune*, May 2, 1999, p. 7.

64. B. Whitaker, "United Parcel's School for Hard Hearts, Sort Of," *New York Times*, July 26, 2000; M. J. Reid, "Profit Motivates Corporate Diversity," *San Francisco Examiner*, March 15, 1998, p. W42.

65. W. G. Stephen and K. A. Finlay, "The Role of Empathy in Improving Intergroup Relations," *Journal of Social Issues* 55 (Winter 1999), pp. 729–43; D. B. Fedor and K. M. Rowland, "Investigating Supervisor Attributions of Subordinate Performance," *Journal of Management* 15 (1989), pp. 405–16; G. Egan, *The Skilled Helper: A Model for Systematic Helping and*

Interpersonal Relating (Belmont, CA: Brooks/Cole, 1975).

66. D. Goleman, "What Makes a Leader?" *Harvard Business Review* 76 (November–December 1998), pp. 92–102.

67. C. Tsai, "Molly Maid President Calls It an Honor to Serve," *Associated Press Newswire*, October 6, 1999.

68. L. Beamer, "Learning Intercultural Communication Competence," *Journal of Business Communication* 29 (1992), pp. 285–303; D. Landis and R. W. Brislin, eds., *Handbook of Intercultural Training* (New York: Pergamon, 1983).

69. T. W. Costello and S. S. Zalkind, *Psychology in Administration: A Research Orientation* (Englewood Cliffs, NJ: Prentice Hall, 1963), pp. 45–46.

70. J. Luft, *Group Processes* (Palo Alto, CA: Mayfield, 1984). For a variation of this model, see J. Hall, "Communication Revisited," *California Management Review* 15 (Spring 1973), pp. 56–67.

71. L. C. Miller and D. A. Kenny, "Reciprocity of Self-Disclosure at the Individual and Dyadic Levels: A Social Relations Analysis," *Journal of Personality and Social Psychology* 50 (1986), pp. 713–19.

72. L. Himelstein, "The General Says 'Charge!'" *Business Week*, February 19, 2001, p. 34.

73. R. T. Hogan, "Personality and Personality Measurement," in M. D. Dunnette and L. M. Hough, eds., *Handbook of Industrial and Organizational Psychology*, 2nd ed., vol. 2 (Palo Alto, CA: Consulting Psychologists Press, 1991), pp. 873–919. Also see W. Mischel, *Introduction to Personality* (New York: Holt, Rinehart & Winston, 1986).

74. H. M. Weiss and S. Adler, "Personality and Organizational Behavior," *Research in Organizational Behavior* 6 (1984), pp. 1–50.

75. W. Revelle, "Personality Processes," *Annual Review of Psychology* 46 (1995), pp. 295–328.

76. R. M. Guion and R. F. Gottier, "Validity of Personality Measures in Personnel Selection," *Personnel Psychology* 18 (1965), pp. 135–64. Also see N. Schmitt, R. Z. Gooding, R. D. Noe, and M. Kirsch, "Meta-Analyses of Validity Studies Published between 1964 and 1982 and the Investigation of

Study Characteristics," *Personnel Psychology* 37 (1984), pp. 407–22.

77. P. G. Irving, "On the Use of Personality Measures in Personnel Selection," *Canadian Psychology* 34 (April 1993), pp. 208–14.

78. K. M. DeNeve and H. Cooper, "The Happy Personality: A Meta-Analysis of 137 Personality Traits and Subjective Well-Being," *Psychological Bulletin* 124 (September 1998), pp. 197–229; M. K. Mount and M. R. Barrick, "The Big Five Personality Dimensions: Implications for Research and Practice in Human Resources Management," *Research in Personnel and Human Resources Management* 13 (1995), pp. 153–200; B. M. Bass, *Stogdill's Handbook of Leadership: A Survey of Theory and Research*, 3rd ed. (New York: Free Press, 1990); J. L. Holland, *Making Vocation Choices: A Theory of Careers* (Englewood Cliffs, NJ: Prentice Hall, 1973).

79. C. Daniels, "Does This Man Need a Shrink?" *Fortune*, February 5, 2001, p. 205.

80. This historical review and the trait descriptions in this section are discussed in R. J. Schneider and L. M. Hough, "Personality and Industrial/Organizational Psychology," *International Review of Industrial and Organizational Psychology* 10 (1995), pp. 75–129; Mount and Barrick, "The Big Five Personality Dimensions"; J. M. Digman, "Personality Structure: Emergence of the Five-Factor Model," *Annual Review of Psychology* 41 (1990), pp. 417–40.

81. G. M. Hurtz and J. J. Donovan, "Personality and Job Performance: The Big Five Revisited," *Journal of Applied Psychology* 85 (December 2000), pp. 869–79; M. K. Mount, M. R. Barrick, and J. P. Strauss, "Validity of Observer Ratings of the Big Five Personality Factors," *Journal of Applied Psychology* 79 (1994), pp. 272–80; R. P. Tett, D. N. Jackson, and M. Rothstein, "Personality Measures as Predictors of Job Performance: A Meta-Analytic Review," *Personnel Psychology* 44 (1991), pp. 703–42.

82. J. M. Howell and C. A. Higgins, "Champions of Change: Identifying, Understanding, and Supporting Champions of Technological Innovations," *Organizational Dynamics* 19 (Summer 1990), pp. 40–55.

83. M. Dalton and M. Wilson, "The Relationship of the Five-Factor Model of Personality to Job Performance for a Group of Middle Eastern Expatriate Managers," *Journal of Cross-Cultural Psychology* 31 (March 2000), pp. 250–58; K. P. Carson and G. L. Stewart, "Job Analysis and the Sociotechnical Approach to Quality: A Critical Examination," *Journal of Quality Management* 1 (1996), pp. 49–64; Mount and Barrick, "The Big Five Personality Dimensions," pp. 177–78.

84. I. B. Myers, *The Myers-Briggs Type Indicator* (Palo Alto, CA: Consulting Psychologists Press, 1987); C. G. Jung, *Psychological Types*, trans. H. G. Baynes, rev. R. F. C. Hull (Princeton, NJ: Princeton University Press, 1971) (Original work published 1921).

85. L. R. Offermann and R. K. Spiros, "The Science and Practice of Team Development: Improving the Link," *Academy of Management Journal* 44 (April 2001), pp. 376–92.

86. G. Potts, "Oklahoma City Employers Use Personality Tests to Improve Placement," *Daily Oklahoman*, February 26, 2001.

87. D. W. Salter and N. J. Evans, "Test-Retest of the Myers-Briggs Type Indicator: An Examination of Dominant Functioning," *Educational and Psychological Measurement* 57 (August 1997), pp. 590–97; W. L. Gardner and M. J. Martinko, "Using the Myers-Briggs Type Indicator to Study Managers: A Literature Review and Research Agenda," *Journal of Management* 22 (1996), pp. 45–83; R. Zemke, "Second Thoughts about the MBTI," *Training*, April 1992, pp. 42–47; M. H. McCaulley, "The Myers-Briggs Type Indicator: A Measure for Individuals and Groups," *Measurement and Evaluation in Counseling and Development* 22 (1990), pp. 181–95.

88. C. Caggiano, "Psycho Path," *Inc.* 20 (July 1998), pp. 76–85.

89. Gardner and Martinko, "Using the Myers-Briggs Type Indicator to Study Managers."

90. S. S. K. Lam and J. Schaubroeck, "The Role of Locus of Control in Reactions to Being Promoted and to Being Passed Over: A Quasi Experiment," *Academy of Management Journal* 43 (February 2000), pp. 66–78; J. M. How-

ell and B. J. Avolio, "Transformational Leadership, Transactional Leadership, Locus of Control, and Support for Innovation: Key Predictors of Consolidated-Business-Unit Performance," *Journal of Applied Psychology* 78 (1993), pp. 891–902; D. Miller and J-M. Toulouse, "Chief Executive Personality and Corporate Strategy and Structure in Small Firms," *Management Science* 32 (1986), pp. 1389–1409; P. E. Spector, "Behavior in Organizations as a Function of Employee's Locus of Control," *Psychological Bulletin* 91 (1982), pp. 482–97.

91. M. Snyder, *Public Appearances/Private Realities: The Psychology of Self-Monitoring* (New York: Freeman, 1987).

92. M. A. Warech, J. W. Smither, R. R. Reilly, R. E. Millsap, and S. P. Reilly, "Self-Monitoring and 360-Degree Ratings," *Leadership Quarterly* 9 (Winter 1998), pp. 449–73; M. Kilduff and D. V. Day, "Do Chameleons Get Ahead? The Effects of Self-Monitoring on Managerial Careers," *Academy of Management Journal* 37 (1994), pp. 1047–60; R. J. Ellis and S. E. Cronshaw, Self-Monitoring and Leader Emergence: A Test of Moderator Effects," *Small Group Research* 23 (1992), pp. 113–29; S. J. Zaccaro, R. J. Foti, and D. A. Kenny, "Self-Monitoring and Trait-Based Variance in Leadership: An Investigation of Leader Flexibility across Multiple Group Situations," *Journal of Applied Psychology* 76 (1991), pp. 308–15.

93. H. A. Simon, *Administrative Behavior* (New York: Free Press, 1957), p. xv.

CHAPTER FOUR

1. J. Doebele, "Kiwi Category Killer," *Forbes*, August 20, 2001; S. Fea, "Tindall Pushes Zero Waste," *Southland Times (Chistchurch, NZ)*, May 11, 2001, p. 3; A. Miriyana, "A Southern Man," *Sunday Star-Times (Auckland, NZ)*, March 4, 2001, p. A3; "Warehouse Grasps the Bigger Picture," *New Zealand Herald*, January 4, 2001; M. Alexander, "Warehouse Boss Just Loves Seeing Red," *Sunday Star-Times (Auckland, NZ)*, December 31, 2000; J. E. Hilsenrath, "Value Creators: In the Company of Asia's Superheroes," *Asian Wall Street Journal*, December 8, 2000, p. P3; S. Hendery, "Warehouse Plans to Give Us All a Foot in the Store," *New Zealand Herald*, November 25, 2000; S. Hendery, "Expansion Hits

Warehouse Sales," *New Zealand Herald*, November 8, 2000.

2. A. Sagie and D. Elizur, "Work Values: A Theoretical Overview and a Model of Their Effects," *Journal of Organizational Behavior* 17 (1996), pp. 503–14; S. H. Schwartz, "Are There Universal Aspects in the Structure and Contents of Human Values?" *Journal of Social Issues* 50 (1994), pp. 19–45; W. H. Schmidt and B. Z. Posner, *Managerial Values in Perspective* (New York: American Management Association, 1983); M. Rokeach, *The Nature of Human Values* (New York: Free Press, 1973); F. Kluckhorn and F. L. Strodtbeck, *Variations in Value Orientations* (Evanston, IL: Row, Peterson, 1961).

3. C. Kleiman, "Self-Assessment Essential Aspect of Balanced Life," *Chicago Tribune*, May 1, 2001.

4. M. Rokeach, *Understanding Human Values* (New York: Free Press, 1979).

5. B. M. Meglino and E. C. Ravlin, "Individual Values in Organizations: Concepts, Controversies, and Research," *Journal of Management* 24 (May 1998), pp. 351–89.

6. Meglino and Ravlin, "Individual Values in Organizations"; C. Argyris and D. A. Schön, *Organizational Learning: A Theory of Action Perspective* (Reading, MA: Addison-Wesley, 1978).

7. B. R. Agle and C. B. Caldwell, "Understanding Research on Values in Business," *Business and Society* 38 (September 1999), pp. 326–87; P. McDonald and J. Gandz, "Getting Value from Values," *Organizational Dynamics*, Winter 1992, pp. 64–77.

8. S. R. Chatterjee and C. A. L. Pearson, "Indian Managers in Transition: Orientations, Work Goals, Values and Ethics," *Management International Review* 40 (January 2000), pp. 81–95.

9. The role of values as a control system is discussed in T. M. Begley, "Articulating Corporate Values through Human Resource Policies," *Business Horizons*, July 2000; J. C. McCune, "Exporting Corporate Culture," *Management Review* 88 (December 1999), pp. 52–56; M. S. Fenwick, H. L. DeCieri, and D. E. Welch, "Cultural and Bureaucratic Control in MNEs: The Role of Expatriate Performance Management," *Management International Review* 39 (1999), Special Issue no. 3.

10. P. Pruzan, "The Question of Organizational Consciousness: Can Organizations Have Values, Virtues and Visions?" *Journal of Business Ethics* 29 (February 2001), pp. 271–84.

11. Chatterjee and Pearson, "Indian Managers in Transition"; K. F. Alam, "Business Ethics in New Zealand Organizations: Views from the Middle and Lower Level Managers," *Journal of Business Ethics* 22 (November 1999), pp. 145–53.

12. C. Salter, "This Is One Fast Factory," *Fast Company* 49 (August 2001), pp. 32–33; M. Howard, "All About Attitude," *Richmond (VA) Times-Dispatch*, May 7, 2001, p. D16.

13. B. Pheasant, "Business Searches for a Soul," *Australian Financial Review*, April 21, 2001, p. 28; H. Trinca, "The McKinsey Rapport," *Boss Magazine*, March 9, 2001, p. 34.

14. C. Fox, "Firms Go Warm and Fuzzy to Lure Staff," *Australian Financial Review*, May 15, 2001, p. 58.

15. A. Gove, "Culture Club," *Red Herring*, November 1998.

16. K. L. Newman and S. D. Nolan, "Culture and Congruence: The Fit between Management Practices and National Culture," *Journal of International Business Studies* 27 (1996), pp. 753–79; G. Hofstede, "Cultural Constraints in Management Theories," *Academy of Management Executive* 7 (1993), pp. 81–94; G. Hofstede, *Culture's Consequences: International Differences in Work-Related Values* (Beverly Hills, CA: Sage, 1980).

17. F. S. Niles, "Individualism-Collectivism Revisited," *Cross-Cultural Research* 32 (November 1998), pp. 315–41; C. P. Earley and C. B. Gibson, "Taking Stock in Our Progress on Individualism-Collectivism: 100 Years of Solidarity and Community," *Journal of Management* 24 (May 1998), pp. 265–304; J. A. Wagner III, "Studies of Individualism-Collectivism: Effects of Cooperation in Groups," *Academy of Management Journal* 38 (1995), pp. 152–72; H. C. Triandis, *Individualism and Collectivism* (Boulder, CO: Westview, 1995). Some research suggests that individualism and collectivism are two separate values, not polar opposites of one value. At the risk of being too traditional, we have kept these as

one value until research leads to more definitive conclusions. See D. A. Ralston, V. T. Nguyen, and N. K. Napier, "A Comparative Study of the Work Values of North and South Vietnamese Managers," *Journal of International Business Studies* 30 (October 1999), pp. 655–72.

18. M. Erez and P. Christopher Earley, *Culture, Self-Identity, and Work* (New York: Oxford University Press, 1993), pp. 126–27.

19. G. Hofstede, *Cultures and Organizations: Software of the Mind* (New York: McGraw-Hill, 1991), p. 124. Hofstede used the terms *masculinity* and *femininity* for achievement and nurturing orientation, respectively. We have adopted the latter terminology to minimize the sexist perspective of these concepts. The achievement and nurturing orientation labels are also used in G. R. Jones, J. M. George, and C. W. L. Hill, *Contemporary Management* (Burr Ridge, IL: Irwin/McGraw-Hill, 1998), pp. 112–13.

20. For counterarguments to these criticisms, see G. Hofstede, "Attitudes, Values and Organizational Culture: Disentangling the Concepts," *Organization Studies* 19 (June 1998), pp. 477–92.

21. C. W. Stephan, W. G. Stephan, I. Saito, and S. M. Barnett, "Emotional Expression in Japan and the United States: The Nonmonolithic Nature of Individualism and Collectivism," *Journal of Cross-Cultural Psychology* 29 (November 1998), pp. 728–48; D. Matsumoto, T. Kudoh, and S. Takeuchi, "Changing Patterns of Individualism and Collectivism in the United States and Japan," *Culture and Psychology* 2 (1996), pp. 77–107. For a discussion of Americanization, see C. McGregor, "It's the United States of Australia, and Let Us All Rejoice," *The Age*, April 11, 2001.

22. S. S. Sarwono and R. W. Armstrong, "Microcultural Differences and Perceived Ethical Problems: An International Business Perspective," *Journal of Business Ethics* 30 (March 2001), pp. 41–56; C. J. Robertson, "The Global Dispersion of Chinese Values: A Three-Country Study of Confucian Dynamism," *Management International Review* 40 (Third Quarter 2000), pp. 253–68; J. S. Osland, A. Bird, J. Delano, and M. Jacob, "Beyond Sophisticated

Stereotyping: Cultural Sensemaking in Context," *Academy of Management Executive* 14 (February 2000), pp. 65–79.

23. C. Hess and K. Hey, " 'Good' Doesn't Always Mean 'Right,' " *Across the Board* 38 (July–August 2001), pp. 61–64.

24. For a discussion of the relationship between work values and ethics, see J. J. Dose, "Work Values: An Integrative Framework and Illustrative Application to Organizational Socialization," *Journal of Occupational and Organizational Psychology* 70 (September 1997), pp. 219–40.

25. C. Savoye, "Workers Say Honesty Is Best Company Policy," *Christian Science Monitor*, June 15, 2000.

26. L. Koss-Feder, "The Good Works Perk," *Time*, January 22, 2001, p. B1.

27. W. H. Shaw and V. Barry, *Moral Issues in Business*, 5th ed. (Belmont, CA: Wadsworth, 1992), chaps. 1–3; M. G. Velasquez, *Business Ethics*, 2nd ed. (Englewood Cliffs, NJ: Prentice Hall, 1988), chap. 2.

28. R. Berenbeim, "The Search for Global Ethics," *Vital Speeches of the Day* 65 (January 1999), pp. 177–78.

29. B. H. Frey, "The Impact of Moral Intensity on Decision Making in a Business Context," *Journal of Business Ethics* 26 (August 2000), pp. 181–95; J. M. Dukerich, M. J. Waller, E. George, and G. P. Huber, "Moral Intensity and Managerial Problem Solving," *Journal of Business Ethics* 24 (March 2000), pp. 29–38; T. J. Jones, "Ethical Decision Making by Individuals in Organizations: An Issue Contingent Model," *Academy of Management Review* 16 (1991), pp. 366–95.

30. J. R. Sparks and S. D. Hunt, "Marketing Researcher Ethical Sensitivity: Conceptualization, Measurement, and Exploratory Investigation," *Journal of Marketing* 62 (April 1998), pp. 92–109.

31. B. Stoneman and K. K. Holliday, "Pressure Cooker," *Banking Strategies*, January–February 2001, p. 13; Alam, "Business Ethics in New Zealand Organizations"; K. Blotnicky, "Is Business in Moral Decay?" *Halifax (Nova Scotia) Chronicle-Herald*, June 11, 2000; D. McDougall and B. Orsini, "Fraudbusting Ethics," *CMA Management* 73 (June 1999), pp. 18–21; J. Evensen, "Ethical Behavior in Business and Life Is Its Own Reward," *Desert News (Salt Lake City, UT)*, October 19, 1997. For a discussion of the situational effects on ethical conduct, see C. J. Thompson, "A Contextualist Proposal for the Conceptualization and Study of Marketing Ethics," *Journal of Public Policy and Marketing* 14 (1995), pp. 177–91.

32. P. Haapaniemi and W. R. Hill, "Not Just for the Big Guys!" *Chief Executive*, September 1998, pp. 62–73.

33. M. Milliet-Einbinder, "Writing Off Tax Deductibility," *OECD Observer*, April 2000, pp. 38–40; F. Rotherham, "NZ Moves to Curb Corruption by Ending Tax Deductible Bribes," *Independent Business Weekly*, June 30, 1999, p. 27.

34. T. H. Stevenson and C. D. Bodkin, "A Cross-National Comparison of University Students' Perceptions Regarding the Ethics and Acceptability of Sales Practices," *Journal of Business Ethics* 17 (January 1998), pp. 45–55; T. Jackson and M. C. Artola, "Ethical Beliefs and Management Behavior: A Cross-Cultural Comparison," *Journal of Business Ethics* 16 (August 1997), pp. 1163–73; M.-K. Nyaw and I. Ignace, "A Comparative Analysis of Ethical Beliefs: A Four Country Study," *Journal of Business Ethics* 13 (1994), pp. 543–55; W. R. Swinyard, H. Rinne, and A. K. Kau, "The Morality of Software Piracy: A Cross-Cultural Analysis," *Journal of Business Ethics* 9 (1990), pp. 655–64.

35. P. F. Buller, J. J. Kohls, and K. S. Anderson, "A Model for Addressing Cross-Cultural Ethical Conflicts," *Business and Society* 36 (June 1997), pp. 169–93.

36. F. T. McCarthy, "Doing Well by Doing Good," *The Economist*, April 22, 2000; Institute of Business Ethics, *Report on Business Ethics Codes 1998* (from www.ibe.org.uk). J. Alexander, "On the Right Side," *Worldbusiness* 3 (January–February 1997), pp. 38–41.

37. M. S. Schwartz, "The Nature of the Relationship between Corporate Codes of Ethics and Behavior," *Journal of Business Ethics* 32 (August 2001), pp. 247–62; M. A. Clark and S. L. Leonard, "Can Corporate Codes of Ethics Influence Behavior?" *Journal of Business Ethics* 17 (April 1998), pp. 619–30.

38. K. Hirani, "B'lore Firms Keen on Ethics Code for Employees," *Times of India*, April 28, 2001.

39. For a discussion of additional ethical practices, see McCarthy, "Doing Well by Doing Good"; E. Van Zyl and K. Lazenby, "Ethical Behavior in the South African Organizational Context: Essential and Workable," *Journal of Business Ethics* 21 (August 1999), pp. 15–22.

40. N. M. Ashkanasy, C. E. Haertel, and W. J. Zerbe, eds., *Emotions in the Workplace: Research, Theory, and Practice* (Westport, CT: Quorum, 2000); B. E. Ashforth and R. H. Humphrey, "Emotion in the Workplace: A Reappraisal," *Human Relations* 48 (1995), pp. 97–125.

41. This definition is based on material in H. M. Weiss and R. Cropanzano, "Affective Events Theory: A Theoretical Discussion of the Structure, Causes, and Consequences of Affective Experiences at Work," *Research in Organizational Behavior* 18 (1996), pp. 1–74; S. Kitayama and P. M. Niedenthal, "Introduction," in P. M. Niedenthal and S. Kitayama, eds., *The Heart's Eye: Emotional Influences in Perception and Attention* (San Diego, CA: Academic Press, 1994), pp. 6–7.

42. R. B. Zajonc, "Emotions," in D. T. Gilbert, S. T. Fiske, and L. Gardner, eds., *Handbook of Social Psychology* (New York: Oxford University Press, 1998), pp. 591–634; K. Oatley and J. M. Jenkins, "Human Emotions: Function and Dysfunction," *Annual Review of Psychology* 43 (1992), pp. 55–85.

43. For a fuller discussion of specific emotions, see R. Pekrun and M. Frese, "Emotions in Work and Achievement," *International Review of Industrial and Organizational Psychology* 7 (1992), pp. 153–200.

44. J. M. George and A. P. Brief, "Motivational Agendas in the Workplace: The Effects of Feelings on Focus of Attention and Work Motivation," *Research in Organizational Behavior* 18 (1996), pp. 75–109; J. M. George, "Mood and Absence," *Journal of Applied Psychology* 74 (1989), pp. 317–24.

45. J. M. George and G. R. Jones, "Experiencing Work: Values, Attitudes, and Moods," *Human Relations* 50 (April 1997), pp. 393–416; J. M. Olson and M. P. Zama, "Attitudes and Attitude Change," *Annual Review of Psychology* 44 (1993), pp. 117–54; M. Fishbein and I. Ajzen, *Belief, Attitude, Intention,*

and Behavior (Reading, MA: Addison-Wesley, 1975).

46. M. D. Zalesny and J. K. Ford, "Extending the Social Information Processing Perspective: New Links to Attitudes, Behaviors, and Perceptions," *Organizational Behavior and Human Decision Processes* 52 (1992), pp. 205–46; G. Salancik and J. Pfeffer, "A Social Information Processing Approach to Job Attitudes and Task Design," *Administrative Science Quarterly* 23 (1978), pp. 224–53.

47. Weiss and Cropanzano, "Affective Events Theory."

48. For a full discussion of several theories on this topic, see K. T. Strongman, *The Psychology of Emotion: Theories of Emotion in Perspective*, 4th ed. (Chichester, UK: Wiley, 1996), chap. 6.

49. D. M. Irvine and M. G. Evans, "Job Satisfaction and Turnover among Nurses: Integrating Research Findings across Studies," *Nursing Research* 44 (1995), pp. 246–53.

50. Weiss and Cropanzano, "Affective Events Theory," pp. 52–57.

51. L. Festinger, *A Theory of Cognitive Dissonance* (Evanston, IL: Row, Peterson, 1957); G. R. Salancik, "Commitment and the Control of Organizational Behavior and Belief," in B. M. Staw and G. R. Salancik, eds., *New Directions in Organizational Behavior* (Chicago: St. Clair, 1977), pp. 1–54.

52. T. A. Judge, E. A. Locke, and C. C. Durham, "The Dispositional Causes of Job Satisfaction: A Core Evaluations Approach," *Research in Organizational Behavior* 19 (1997), pp. 151–88; A. P. Brief, A. H. Butcher, and L. Roberson, "Cookies, Disposition, and Job Attitudes: The Effects of Positive Mood-Inducing Events and Negative Affectivity on Job Satisfaction in a Field Experiment," *Organizational Behavior and Human Decision Processes* 62 (1995), pp. 55–62.

53. J. Schaubroeck, D. C. Ganster, and B. Kemmerer, "Does Trait Affect Promote Job Attitude Stability?" *Journal of Organizational Behavior* 17 (1996), pp. 191–96; R. D. Arvey, B. P. McCall, T. L. Bouchard, and P. Taubman, "Genetic Differences on Job Satisfaction and Work Values," *Personality and Individual Differences* 17 (1994), pp. 21–33; B. M. Staw and J. Ross, "Stabil-ity in the Midst of Change: A Dispositional Approach to Job Attitudes," *Journal of Applied Psychology* 70 (1985), pp. 469–80.

54. D. Matheson, "A Vancouver Cafe Where Rudeness Is Welcomed," *CTV Television*, "Canada AM," January 11, 2000; R. Corelli, "Dishing Out Rudeness," *Maclean's*, January 11, 1999, p. 44.

55. J. A. Morris and D. C. Feldman, "The Dimensions, Antecedents, and Consequences of Emotional Labor," *Academy of Management Review* 21 (1996), pp. 986–1010; B. E. Ashforth and R. H. Humphrey, "Emotional Labor in Service Roles: The Influence of Identity," *Academy of Management Review* 18 (1993), pp. 88–115.

56. J. A. Morris and D. C. Feldman, "Managing Emotions in the Workplace," *Journal of Managerial Issues* 9 (Fall 1997), pp. 257–74.

57. J. S. Sass, "Emotional Labor as Cultural Performance: The Communication of Caregiving in a Nonprofit Nursing Home," *Western Journal of Communication* 64 (Summer 2000), pp. 330–58; R. I. Sutton, "Maintaining Norms about Expressed Emotions: The Case of Bill Collectors," *Administrative Science Quarterly* 36 (1991), pp. 245–68.

58. J. Strasburg, "The Making of a Grand Hotel," *San Francisco Chronicle*, March 25, 2001, p. B1.

59. E. Forman, "'Diversity Concerns Grow as Companies Head Overseas,' Consultant Says," *Fort Lauderdale (FL) Sun-Sentinel*, June 26, 1995.

60. J. Schaubroeck and J. R. Jones, "Antecedents of Workplace Emotional Labor Dimensions and Moderators of Their Effects on Physical Symptoms," *Journal of Organizational Behavior* 21 (2000), 163–83; R. Buck, "The Spontaneous Communication of Interpersonal Expectations," in P. D. Blanck, ed., *Interpersonal Expectations: Theory, Research, and Applications* (Cambridge, UK: Cambridge University Press, 1993), pp. 227–41. The quotation from George Burns comes from the Buck source. However, this line has also been attributed to Groucho Marx.

61. K. Pugliesi, "The Consequences of Emotional Labor: Effects on Work Stress, Job Satisfaction, and Well-Being," *Motivation and Emotion* 23 (June 1999), pp. 125–54; A. S. Wharton, "The Psychosocial Consequences of Emotional Labor," *Annals of the American Academy of Political and Social Science* 561 (January 1999), pp. 158–76; J. A. Morris and D. C. Feldman, "Managing Emotions in the Workplace," *Journal of Managerial Issues* 9 (Fall 1997), pp. 257–74; P. K. Adelmann "Emotional Labor as a Potential Source of Job Stress," in S. Sauter and L. R. Murphy, eds., *Organizational Risk Factors for Job Stress* (Washington, DC: American Psychological Association, 1995), chap. 24.

62. M. Savidge, "Retailers Focus on Quality Workers," *The Morning Call (Allentown, PA)*, December 10, 2000, p. D1. The "hire for attitude, train for skills" phrase is also widely recognized as the policy of Southwest Airlines. See M. Brelis, "Herb's Way," *Boston Globe*, November 5, 2000, p. F1.

63. T. Schwartz, "'How Do You Feel?'" *Fast Company*, June 2000, p. 296; J. Stuller, "Unconventional Smarts," *Across the Board* 35 (January 1998), pp. 22–23.

64. D. Goleman, "What Makes a Leader?" *Harvard Business Review* 76 (November–December 1998), pp. 92–102. The definition of *emotional intelligence* appears in J. D. Mayer and P. Salovey, "The Intelligence of Emotional Intelligence," *Intelligence* 17 (1993), pp. 433–42. The levels of emotional intelligence are discussed in J. D. Mayer and P. Salovey, "What Is Emotional Intelligence," in P. Salovey and D. Sluyter, eds., *Emotional Development and Emotional Intelligence: Educational Implications* (New York: Basic Books, 1997), pp. 3–34.

65. A brief history of emotional intelligence is presented in S. Newsome, A. L. Day, and V. M. Catano, "Assessing the Predictive Validity of Emotional Intelligence," *Personality and Individual Differences* 29 (December 2000), pp. 1005–16.

66. R. J. Grossman, "Emotions at Work," *Health Forum Journal* 43 (September–October 2000), pp. 18–22; D. Swift, "Do Doctors Have an Emotional Handicap?" *Medical Post*, March 9, 1999, p. 30.

67. J. V. Ciarrochi, A. Y. C. Chan, and P. Caputi, "A Critical Evaluation of the

Emotional Intelligence Construct," *Personality and Individual Differences* 28 (2000) 539–61; S. Fox and P. E. Spector, "Relations of Emotional Intelligence, Practical Intelligence, General Intelligence, and Trait Affectivity with Interview Outcomes: It's Not All Just G," *Journal of Organizational Behavior* 21 (2000), pp. 203–20; R. Bar-On, J. M. Brown, B. D. Kirkcaldy, and E. P. Thomé, "Emotional Expression and Implications for Occupational Stress: An Application of the Emotional Quotient Inventory," *Personality and Individual Differences* 28 (2000) 1107–18.

68. D. Dawda and S. D. Hart, "Assessing Emotional Intelligence: Reliability and Validity of the Bar-On Emotional Quotient Inventory (EQ-i) in University Students," *Personality and Individual Differences* 28 (2000), pp. 797–812.

69. J. Brown, "School Board, Employment Centers Test Emotional Intelligence," *Technology in Government* 8 (April 2001), p. 9; Grossman, "Emotions at Work."

70. "Emotional Intelligence (EQ) Gets Better with Age," EQi News Release, March 3, 1997.

71. Weiss and Cropanzano, "Affective Events Theory." The *job satisfaction* definition is still being debated. This definition captures the most popular view that job satisfaction is an evaluation and represents both beliefs and feelings. For details, see A. P. Brief, *Attitudes In and Around Organizations* (Thousand Oaks, CA: Sage, 1998), chaps. 2 and 4.

72. E. A. Locke, "The Nature and Causes of Job Satisfaction," in M. Dunnette, ed., *Handbook of Industrial and Organizational Psychology* (Chicago: Rand McNally, 1976), pp. 1297–1350.

73. D. W. Moore, "Most American Workers Satisfied with Their Job," *Gallup News Service*, August 31, 2001. Also see T. Lemke, "Poll Data Show Americans' Long-Term Positive Attitude toward Jobs," *Washington Times*, August 28, 2001, p. B8.

74. S. MacDonald, "Do You Really Enjoy Your Work?" *Times of London*, January 15, 1998.

75. See G. Law, "If You're Happy and You Know It, Tick the Box," *Management-Auckland* 45 (March 1998), pp. 34–37. The problems with measuring work attitudes across cultures are also discussed in K. Bae and C. Chung, "Cultural Values and Work Attitudes of Korean Industrial Workers in Comparison with Those of the United States and Japan," *Work and Occupations* 24 (February 1997), pp. 80–96.

76. A. J. Rucci, S. P. Kirn, and R. T. Quinn, "The Employee-Customer-Profit Chain at Sears," *Harvard Business Review* 76 (January–February 1998), pp. 83–97; W. Bole, "Workers Getting Say in CEOs' Pay," *Orlando (FL) Sentinel*, September 14, 1997, p. H1; M. Kerr, "Developing a Corporate Culture for the Maximum Balance between the Utilization of Human Resources and Employee Fulfillment in Canada," *Canada–United States Law Journal* 22 (1996), pp. 169–76.

77. R. D. Hackett and P. Bycio, "An Evaluation of Employee Absenteeism as a Coping Mechanism among Hospital Nurses," *Journal of Occupational and Organizational Psychology* 69 (December 1996), pp. 327–38; J. Barling, "The Prediction, Psychological Experience, and Consequences of Workplace Violence," in G. R. VandenBos and E. Q. Bulatao, eds., *Violence on the Job* (Washington, DC: American Psychological Association, 1996), pp. 29–49. S. D. Bluen, "The Psychology of Strikes," *International Review of Industrial and Organizational Psychology* 9 (1994), pp. 113–45; P. Y. Chen and P. E. Spector, "Relationships of Work Stressors with Aggression, Withdrawal, Theft and Substance Use: An Exploratory Study," *Journal of Occupational and Organizational Psychology* 65 (1992), pp. 177–84.

78. B. M. Staw and S. G. Barsade, "Affect and Managerial Performance: A Test of the Sadder-but-Wiser vs. Happier-and-Smarter Hypotheses," *Administrative Science Quarterly* 38 (1993), pp. 304–31; M. T. Iaffaldano and P. M. Muchinsky, "Job Satisfaction and Job Performance: A Meta-Analysis," *Psychological Bulletin* 97 (1985), pp. 251–73; D. P. Schwab and L. L. Cummings, "Theories of Performance and Satisfaction: A Review," *Industrial Relations* 9 (1970), pp. 408–30.

79. E. E. Lawler III and L. W. Porter, "The Effect of Performance on Job Satisfaction," *Industrial Relations* 7 (1967), pp. 20–28.

80. J. I. Heskett, W. E. Sasser, and L. A. Schlesinger, *The Service Profit Chain*, (New York: Free Press, 1997). For recent support of this model, see D. J. Koys, "The Effects of Employee Satisfaction, Organizational Citizenship Behavior, and Turnover on Organizational Effectiveness: A Unit-Level, Longitudinal Study," *Personnel Psychology* 54 (April 2001), pp. 101–14.

81. "Happy, Passionate Employees Key to Good Business, Top Executives Say," *Ascribe News*, April 16, 2001; S. Chandler, "Sears' System of Rewards Has Ups and Downs," *Chicago Tribune*, February 15, 1998, p. C1; Rucci, Kirn, and Quinn, "The Employee-Customer-Profit Chain at Sears."

82. T. Kirchofer, "Firm Takes Boat of Confidence," *Boston Herald*, March 20, 2001, p. 27.

83. K. Gwinner, D. Gremier, and M. Bitner, "Relational Benefits in Services Industries: The Customer's Perspective," *Journal of the Academy of Marketing Science* 26 (1998), pp. 101–14.

84. R. T. Mowday, L. W. Porter, and R. M. Steers, *Employee Organization Linkages: The Psychology of Commitment, Absenteeism, and Turnover* (New York: Academic Press, 1982).

85. C. W. Mueller and E. J. Lawler, "Commitment to Nested Organizational Units: Some Basic Principles and Preliminary Findings," *Social Psychology Quarterly* (December 1999), pp. 325–46; T. E. Becker, R. S. Billings, D. M. Eveleth, and N. L. Gilbert, "Foci and Bases of Employee Commitment: Implications for Job Performance," *Academy of Management Journal* 39 (1996), pp. 464–82.

86. J. P. Meyer, "Organizational Commitment," *International Review of Industrial and Organizational Psychology* 12 (1997), pp. 175–228. Along with affective and continuance commitment, Meyer identifies normative commitment, which refers to employee feelings of obligation to remain with the organization. This commitment has been excluded so that students focus on the two most common perspectives of commitment.

87. R. D. Hackett, P. Bycio, and P. A. Hausdorf, "Further Assessments of Meyer and Allen's (1991) Three-Component Model of Organizational

Commitment," *Journal of Applied Psychology* 79 (1994), pp. 15–23.

88. K. Phillips, "The Loyalty Trap," *Boss Magazine*, May 8, 2000, pp. 33–37; Watson Wyatt, "Survey Says Employee Commitment Declining," News Release, March 14, 2000; C. W. Mueller and E. J. Lawler, "Commitment to Nested Organizational Units: Some Basic Principles and Preliminary Findings," *Social Psychology Quarterly* 62 (December 1999), pp. 325–46; "Employees' Morale Plummets," *Management Services* 41 (February 1997), p. 6. In contrast, the Gallup Organization has reported consistently high loyalty ratings for the past decade. See Moore, "Most American Workers Satisfied with Their Job."

89. F. F. Reichheld, "Lead for Loyalty," *Harvard Business Review* 79 (July–August 2001), p. 76; D. S. Bolon, "Organizational Citizenship Behavior among Hospital Employees: A Multidimensional Analysis Involving Job Satisfaction and Organizational Commitment," *Hospital and Health Services Administration* 42 (Summer 1997), pp. 221–41; Meyer, "Organizational Commitment," pp. 203–15; F. F. Reichheld, *The Loyalty Effect* (Boston: Harvard Business School Press, 1996), chap. 4.

90. Phillips, "The Loyalty Trap."

91. J. P. Meyer and N. J. Allen, *Commitment in the Workplace: Theory, Research, and Application* (Thousand Oaks, CA: Sage, 1997), chap. 4.

92. E. W. Morrison and S. L. Robinson, "When Employees Feel Betrayed: A Model of How Psychological Contract Violation Develops," *Academy of Management Review* 22 (1997), pp. 226–56.

93. C. Hendry and R. Jenkins, "Psychological Contracts and New Deals," *Human Resource Management Journal* 7 (1997), pp. 38–44; D. M. Noer, *Healing the Wounds* (San Francisco: Jossey-Bass, 1993); S. Ashford, C. Lee, and P. Bobko, "Content, Causes, and Consequences of Job Insecurity: A Theory-Based Measure and Substantive Test," *Academy of Management Journal* 32 (1989), pp. 803–29.

94. R. J. Lewicki and B. B. Bunker, "Developing and Maintaining Trust in Work Relationships," in R. M. Kramer and T. R. Tyler, eds., *Trust in Organizations: Frontiers of Theory and Research*, (Thousand Oaks, CA: Sage, 1996), pp. 114–39; S. L. Robinson, "Trust and Breach of the Psychological Contract," *Administrative Science Quarterly* 41 (1996), pp. 574–99; J. M. Kouzes and B. Z. Posner, *The Leadership Challenge* (San Francisco: Jossey-Bass, 1987), pp. 146–52.

95. P. Mackey, "Old Ireland Tries New Hooks," *Computerworld*. April 23, 2001, p. 46.

96. A. A. Luchak and I. R. Gellatly, "Employer-Sponsored Pensions and Employee Commitment," *Proceedings of the Annual ASAC Conference, Human Resource Management Division* 17 (9) (1996), pp. 64–71; H. L. Angle and M. B. Lawson, Organizational Commitment and Employees' Performance Ratings: Both Type of Commitment and Type of Performance Count," *Psychological Reports* 75 (1994), pp. 1539–51; L. M. Shore and S. J. Wayne, "Commitment and Employee Behavior: Comparison of Affective Commitment and Continuance Commitment with Perceived Organizational Support," *Journal of Applied Psychology* 78 (1993), pp. 774–80; J. P. Meyer, S. V. Paunonen, I. R. Gellatly, R. D. Goffin, and D. N. Jackson, "Organizational Commitment and Job Performance: It's the Nature of the Commitment That Counts," *Journal of Applied Psychology* 74 (1989), pp. 152–56.

CHAPTER FIVE

1. M. Leuchter, "Capital One: Fanaticism That Works," *US Banker* 111 (August 2001), pp. 24–29; N. Pandya, "Cool Companies: No 60: Capital One," *The Guardian (London)*, July 14, 2001, p. 5; P. Knight, "Capital One Shows How to Keep Its Staff," *Computer Weekly*, June 7, 2001; M. Zelsman, "Most Likely to Succeed," *InfoWorld*, May 7, 2001, p. 45.

2. C. C. Pinder, *Work Motivation in Organizational Behavior* (Upper Saddle River, NJ: Prentice Hall, 1998); E. E. Lawler III, *Motivation in Work Organizations* (Monterey, CA: Brooks/Cole, 1973), pp. 2–5.

3. "Towers Perrin Study Finds, Despite Layoffs and Slow Economy, a New, More Complex Power Game Is Emerging between Employers and Employees," *Business Wire*, August 30, 2001.

4. T. D. Allen et al., "Survivor Reactions to Organizational Downsizing: Does Time Ease the Pain?" *Journal of Occupational and Organizational Psychology* 74 (June 2001), pp. 145–64; R. Burke, "Downsizing and Restructuring in Organizations: Research Findings and Lessons Learned—Introduction," *Canadian Journal of Administrative Sciences* 15 (December 1998), pp. 297–99.

5. R. Zemke and B. Filipczak, *Generations at Work: Managing the Clash of Veterans, Boomers, Xers, and Nexters in Your Workplace* (New York: AMACOM, 2000); B. Losyk, "Generation X: What They Think and What They Plan to Do," *The Futurist* 31 (March–April 1997), pp. 29–44; B. Tulgan, *Managing Generation X: How to Bring Out the Best in Young Talent* (Oxford, UK: Capstone, 1996).

6. S. H. Schwartz, "Are There Universal Aspects in the Structure and Contents of Human Values?" *Journal of Social Issues* 50 (1994), pp. 19–45; W. H. Schmidt and B. Z. Posner, *Managerial Values in Perspective* (New York: American Management Association, 1983); M. Rokeach, *The Nature of Human Values* (New York: Free Press, 1973); F. Kluckhorn and F. L. Strodtbeck, *Variations in Value Orientations* (Evanston, IL: Row, Peterson, 1961).

7. Pinder, *Work Motivation in Organizational Behavior*, chap. 3.

8. A. H. Maslow, "A Theory of Human Motivation," *Psychological Review* 50 (1943), pp. 370–96; A. H. Maslow, *Motivation and Personality* (New York: Harper & Row, 1954).

9. J. Sidener, "Easter Eggs Turning Up in Software for DVDs," *Arizona Republic*, April 10, 2001, p. F4; L. Kahney, "Taking the Fun Out of Win2000," *Wired News*, February 16, 2000; "Cracking Open the Eggs," *The Economist*, December 18, 1999; D. Claymon, "Apple Tradition Dies As Named Credits End," *Arizona Republic*, December 6, 1999, p. E5; L. Gornstein, "Software Harbors Treasures," *Arizona Republic*, March 9, 1998, p. E1; T. Standage "Easter Eggs beyond a Joke," *Daily Telegraph (London)*, February 19, 1998, p. 4. Some information was also collected from the website http://www.eeggs.com.

10. M. A. Wahba and L. G. Bridwell, "Maslow Reconsidered: A Review of

Research on the Need Hierarchy Theory," *Organizational Behavior and Human Performance* 15 (1976), pp. 212–40.

11. C. P. Alderfer, *Existence, Relatedness, and Growth* (New York: Free Press, 1972).

12. J. P. Wanous and A. A. Zwany, "A Cross-Sectional Test of Need Hierarchy Theory," *Organizational Behavior and Human Performance* 18 (1977), pp. 78–97.

13. H. M. Weiss and R. Cropanzano, "Affective Events Theory: A Theoretical Discussion of the Structure, Causes, and Consequences of Affective Experiences at Work," *Research in Organizational Behavior* 18 (1996), pp. 1–74.

14. F. Herzberg, B. Mausner, and B. B. Snyderman, *The Motivation to Work* (New York: Wiley, 1959).

15. The motivational value of money is effectively argued in T. Kinni, "Why We Work," *Training* 35 (August 1998), pp. 34–39. For critiques of Herzberg's theory, see A. K. Korman, *Industrial and Organizational Psychology* (Englewood Cliffs, NJ: Prentice Hall, 1971), p. 149; N. King, "Clarification and Evaluation of the Two Factor Theory of Job Satisfaction," *Psychological Bulletin* 74 (1970), pp. 18–31.

16. R. Beck, "Pop Go Those Pricey Perks," *Toronto Star*, August 7, 2001, p. E7; S. Caudron, "Be Cool!" *Workforce* 77 (April 1998), pp. 50–61.

17. J. Jacobs, "Helping 'Small Guys' Compete with Big Firms," *Business Times (Malaysia)*, April 6, 2001.

18. R. M. Steers and L. W. Porter, *Motivation and Work Behavior*, 5th ed. (New York: McGraw-Hill, 1991), p. 413.

19. D. C. McClelland, *The Achieving Society* (New York: Van Nostrand Reinhold, 1961); M. Patchen, *Participation, Achievement, and Involvement on the Job* (Englewood Cliffs, NJ: Prentice Hall, 1970).

20. For example, see J. Langan-Fox and S. Roth, "Achievement Motivation and Female Entrepreneurs," *Journal of Occupational and Organizational Psychology* 68 (1995), pp. 209–18; H. A. Wainer and I. M. Rubin, "Motivation of Research and Development Entrepreneurs: Determinants of Company Success, Part I," *Journal of Applied Psychology* 53 (June 1969), pp. 178–84.

21. D. C. McClelland, "Retrospective Commentary," *Harvard Business Review* 73 (January–February 1995), pp. 138–39; D. McClelland and R. Boyatzis, "Leadership Motive Pattern and Long-Term Success in Management," *Journal of Applied Psychology* 67 (1982), pp. 737–43.

22. G. Scotton, "Pamela Grof's InterVisual on the Fast Lane to Success," *Calgary Herald*, January 10, 2000.

23. McClelland, *The Achieving Society*; R. deCharms and G. H. Moeller, "Values Expressed in American Children's Readers: 1800–1950," *Journal of Abnormal and Social Psychology* 64 (1962), pp. 136–42.

24. R. J. House and R. N. Aditya, "The Social Scientific Study of Leadership: Quo Vadis?" *Journal of Management* 23 (1997), pp. 409–73; D. C. McClelland and D. H. Burnham, "Power Is the Great Motivator," *Harvard Business Review* 73 (January–February 1995), pp. 126–39 (Reprinted from *Harvard Business Review*, 1976).

25. D. Vredenburgh and Y. Brender, "The Hierarchical Abuse of Power in Work Organizations," *Journal of Business Ethics* 17 (September 1998), pp. 1337–47; McClelland and Burnham, "Power Is the Great Motivator."

26. D. G. Winter, "A Motivational Model of Leadership: Predicting Long-Term Management Success from TAT Measures of Power Motivation and Responsibility," *Leadership Quarterly* 2 (1991), pp. 67–80.

27. House and Aditya, "The Social Scientific Study of Leadership."

28. D. C. McClelland and D. G. Winter, *Motivating Economic Achievement* (New York: Free Press, 1969); D. Miron and D. McClelland, "The Impact of Achievement Motivation Training on Small Business," *California Management Review* 21 (1979), pp. 13–28.

29. A. Kohn, *Punished by Rewards* (New York: Houghton Mifflin, 1993).

30. D. S. Elenkov, "Can American Management Concepts Work in Russia? A Cross-Cultural Comparative Study," *California Management Review* 40 (Summer 1998), pp. 133–56; N. J. Adler, *International Dimensions of Organizational Behavior*, 3rd ed. (Cincinnati, OH: South-Western, 1997), chap. 6; G. Hofstede, "Motivation, Leadership, and Organization: Do American Theories Apply Abroad?" *Organizational Dynamics*, Summer 1980, pp. 42–63.

31. A. Sagie, D. Elizur, and H. Yamauchi, "The Structure and Strength of Achievement Motivation: A Cross-Cultural Comparison," *Journal of Organizational Behavior* 17 (September 1996), pp. 431–44; D. Elizur, I. Borg, R. Hunt, and I. M. Beck, "The Structure of Work Values: A Cross Cultural Comparison," *Journal of Organizational Behavior* 12 (1991), pp. 21–38.

32. Expectancy theory of motivation in work settings originated in V. H. Vroom, *Work and Motivation* (New York: Wiley, 1964). The version of expectancy theory presented here was developed by Edward Lawler. Lawler's model provides a clearer presentation of the model's three components. P→O expectancy is similar to instrumentality in Vroom's original expectancy theory model. The difference is that instrumentality is a correlation whereas P→O expectancy is a probability. See D. A. Nadler and E. E. Lawler, "Motivation: A Diagnostic Approach," in J. R. Hackman, E. E. Lawler III, and L. W. Porter, eds., *Perspectives on Behavior in Organizations*, 2nd ed. (New York: McGraw-Hill, 1983), pp. 67–78; J. P. Campbell, M. D. Dunnette, E. E. Lawler, and K. E. Weick, *Managerial Behavior, Performance, and Effectiveness* (New York: McGraw-Hill, 1970), pp. 343–48; E. E. Lawler, *Motivation in Work Organizations* (Monterey, CA: Brooks/Cole, 1973), chap. 3.

33. Nadler and Lawler, "Motivation."

34. K. A. Karl, A. M. O'Leary-Kelly, and J. J. Martoccio, "The Impact of Feedback and Self-Efficacy on Performance in Training," *Journal of Organizational Behavior* 14 (1993), pp. 379–94; T. Janz, "Manipulating Subjective Expectancy through Feedback: A Laboratory Study of the Expectancy-Performance Relationship," *Journal of Applied Psychology* 67 (1982), pp. 480–85.

35. D. Jones, "Firms Spend Billions to Fire Up Workers—with Little Luck," *USA Today*, May 10, 2001, p. A1.

36. J. B. Fox, K. D. Scott, and J. M. Donohoe, "An Investigation into Pay Valence and Performance in a Pay-for-

Performance Field Setting," *Journal of Organizational Behavior* 14 (1993), pp. 687–93.

37. J.-I. Lee, "Recent Exodus of Core Human Resources Disturbing Trend for Domestic Companies," *Korea Herald*, May 14, 2001; Y. Ghahremani, "In the Company of Millionaires," *Asia Week*, March 17, 2000; B. McKenna, "Restructuring Fever Sweeps Japan," *Globe and Mail*, May 29, 1999; M. Tanikawa, "The Corporate Samurai Are Getting Less Loyal," *Business Week*, March 16, 1998; R. M. Hodgetts, "Discussing Incentive Compensation with Donald Hastings of Lincoln Electric," *Compensation and Benefits Review* 29 (September 1997), pp. 60–66.

38. W. Van Eerde and H. Thierry, "Vroom's Expectancy Models and Work-Related Criteria: A Meta-Analysis," *Journal of Applied Psychology* 81 (1996), pp. 575–86; T. R. Mitchell, "Expectancy Models of Job Satisfaction, Occupational Preference and Effort: A Theoretical, Methodological, and Empirical Appraisal," *Psychological Bulletin* 81 (1974), pp. 1053–77.

39. Elenkov, "Can American Management Concepts Work in Russia?"; N. A. Boyacigiller and N. J. Adler, "The Parochial Dinosaur: Organizational Science in a Global Context," *Academy of Management Review* 16 (1991), pp. 262–90; N. J. Adler, *International Dimensions of Organizational Behavior*, 3rd ed. (Cincinnati, OH: South-Western, 1997), chap. 6.

40. D. H. B. Welsh, F. Luthans, and S. M. Sommer, "Managing Russian Factory Workers: The Impact of U.S.–Based Behavioral and Participative Techniques," *Academy of Management Journal* 36 (1993), pp. 58–79; T. Matsui and I. Terai, "A Cross-Cultural Study of the Validity of the Expectancy Theory of Motivation," *Journal of Applied Psychology* 60 (1979), pp. 263–65.

41. M. L. Ambrose and C. T. Kulik, "Old Friends, New Faces: Motivation Research in the 1990s," *Journal of Management* 25 (May 1999), pp. 231–92; K. C. Snead and A. M. Harrell, "An Application of Expectancy Theory to Explain a Manager's Intention to Use a Decision Support System," *Decision Sciences* 25 (1994), pp. 499–513.

42. J. S. Adams, "Toward an Understanding of Inequity," *Journal of Abnormal and Social Psychology* 67 (1963), pp. 422–36; R. T. Mowday, "Equity Theory Predictions of Behavior in Organizations," in R. M. Steers and L. W. Porter, eds., *Motivation and Work Behavior*, 5th ed. (New York: McGraw-Hill, 1991), pp. 111–31. The incident involving Tracy Jones is described in M. W. Walsh, "Workers Challenge Employer Policies on Pay Confidentiality," *New York Times*, July 28, 2000.

43. G. Blau, "Testing the Effect of Level and Importance of Pay Referents on Pay Level Satisfaction," *Human Relations* 47 (1994), pp. 1251–68; C. T. Kulik and M. L. Ambrose, "Personal and Situational Determinants of Referent Choice," *Academy of Management Review* 17 (1992), pp. 212–37; J. Pfeffer, "Incentives in Organizations: The Importance of Social Relations," in O. E. Williamson, ed., *Organization Theory: From Chester Barnard to the Present and Beyond* (New York: Oxford University Press, 1990), pp. 72–97.

44. P. P. Shah, "Who Are Employees' Social Referents? Using a Network Perspective to Determine Referent Others," *Academy of Management Journal* 41 (June 1998), pp. 249–68; K. S. Law and C. S. Wong, "Relative Importance of Referents on Pay Satisfaction: A Review and Test of a New Policy-Capturing Approach," *Journal of Occupational and Organizational Psychology* 71 (March 1998), pp. 47–60.

45. T. P. Summers and A. S. DeNisi, "In Search of Adams' Other: Reexamination of Referents Used in the Evaluation of Pay," *Human Relations* 43 (1990), pp. 497–511.

46. J. S. Adams, "Inequity in Social Exchange," in L. Berkowitz, ed., *Advances in Experimental Psychology* (New York: Academic Press, 1965), pp. 157–89.

47. J. Barling, C. Fullagar, and E. K. Kelloway, *The Union and Its Members: A Psychological Approach* (New York: Oxford University Press, 1992).

48. L. Greenberg and J. Barling, "Employee Theft," in C. L. Cooper and D. M. Rousseau, eds., *Trends in Organizational Behavior* 3 (1996), pp. 49–64.

49. J. Greenberg, "Cognitive Reevaluation of Outcomes in Response to Underpayment Inequity," *Academy of Management Journal* 32 (1989), pp. 174–84; E. Hatfield and S. Sprecher, "Equity Theory and Behavior in Organizations," *Research in the Sociology of Organizations* 3 (1984), pp. 94–124.

50. Cited in *Canadian Business*, February 1997, p. 39.

51. J. Rawls, *A Theory of Justice* (Cambridge, MA: Harvard University Press, 1971). For a recent discussion of justice and ethics, see M. Schminke, M. L. Ambrose, and T. W. Noel, "The Effect of Ethical Frameworks on Perceptions of Organizational Justice," *Academy of Management Journal* 40 (October 1997), pp. 1190–1207.

52. K. Crawford, "Bonus Puts Apple Boss Way above High Flyers," *Sydney Morning Herald*, January 21, 2000, p. 3; J. Fortt, "Apple Gives CEO Steve Jobs a Jet," *San Jose (CA) Mercury*, January 20, 2000.

53. M. Gordon, "CEOs Still Getting Big Pay," *AP Online*, August 28, 2001.

54. T. W. Gerdel, "Paying for the Privilege," *Cleveland (OH) Plain Dealer*, February 15, 1998, p. H1.

55. M. N. Bing and S. M. Burroughs, "The Predictive and Interactive Effects of Equity Sensitivity in Teamwork-Oriented Organizations," *Journal of Organizational Behavior* 22 (2001), pp. 271–90; K. S. Sauleya and A. G. Bedeian, "Equity Sensitivity: Construction of a Measure and Examination of Its Psychometric Properties," *Journal of Management* 26 (September 2000), pp. 885–910; P. E. Mudrack, E. S. Mason, and K. M. Stepanski, "Equity Sensitivity and Business Ethics," *Journal of Occupational and Organizational Psychology* 72 (December 1999), pp. 539–60; R. P. Vecchio, "An Individual-Differences Interpretation of the Conflicting Predictions Generated by Equity Theory and Expectancy Theory," *Journal of Applied Psychology* 66 (1981), pp. 470–81.

56. The meaning of these three groups has evolved over the years. These definitions are based on W. C. King, Jr., and E. W. Miles, "The Measurement of Equity Sensitivity," *Journal of Occupational and Organizational Psychology* 67 (1994), pp. 133–42.

57. L. Y. Fok, S. J. Hartman, M. F. Villere, and R. C. Freibert III, "A Study of the Impact of Cross Cultural Differences on Perceptions of Equity and Organizational Citizenship Behavior," *International Journal of Management* 13 (1996), pp. 3–14.

58. R. Folger and R. A. Baron, "Violence and Hostility at Work: A Model of Reactions to Perceived Injustice," in G. R. VandenBos and E. Q. Bulatao, eds., *Violence on the Job: Identifying Risks and Developing Solutions* (Washington, DC: American Psychological Association, 1996); J. Greenberg, "Stealing in the Name of Justice: Informational and Interpersonal Moderators of Theft Reactions to Underpayment Inequity," *Organizational Behavior and Human Decision Processes* 54 (1993), pp. 81–103; R. D. Bretz, Jr., and S. L. Thomas, "Perceived Equity, Motivation, and Final-Offer Arbitration in Major League Baseball," *Journal of Applied Psychology* 77 (1993), pp. 280–87. For a summary of recent equity theory studies, see M. L. Ambrose and C. T. Kulik, "Old Friends, New Faces: Motivation Research in the 1990s," *Journal of Management* 25 (May 1999), pp. 231–92.

59. Walker Information, *The 1999 U.S. National Employee Relationship Benchmark Report* (Indianapolis, IN: Walker Information, 2000). Similar levels of inequity are reported in Australia, as reported in *The Australian* survey, "Overworked and Underpaid," Morgan and Banks News Release, January 2001.

60. R. P. Vecchio and J. R. Terborg, "Salary Increment Allocation and Individual Differences," *Journal of Organizational Behavior* 8 (1987), pp. 37–43.

61. D. Beardsley, "This Company Doesn't Brake for (Sacred) Cows," *Fast Company* 16 (August 1998), p. 66.

62. For recent research on the effectiveness of goal setting, see L. A. Wilk and W. K. Redmon, "The Effects of Feedback and Goal Setting on the Productivity and Satisfaction of University Admissions Staff," *Journal of Organizational Behavior Management* 18 (1998), pp. 45–68; K. H. Doerr and T. R. Mitchell, "Impact of Material Flow Policies and Goals on Job Outcomes," *Journal of Applied Psychology* 81 (1996), pp. 142–52; A. A. Shikdar and B. Das, "A Field Study of Worker Productivity Improvements," *Applied Ergonomics* 26 (February 1995), pp. 21–27; M. D. Cooper and R. A. Phillips, "Reducing Accidents Using Goal Setting and Feedback: A Field Study," *Journal of Occupational and Organizational Psychology* 67 (1994), pp. 219–40.

63. T. H. Poister and G. Streib, "MBO in Municipal Government: Variations on a Traditional Management Tool," *Public Administration Review* 55 (1995), pp. 48–56.

64. E. A. Locke and G. P. Latham, *A Theory of Goal Setting and Task Performance* (Englewood Cliffs, NJ: Prentice Hall, 1990); A. J. Mento, R. P. Steel, and R. J. Karren, "A Meta-Analytic Study of the Effects of Goal Setting on Task Performance: 1966–1984," *Organizational Behavior and Human Decision Processes* 39 (1987), pp. 52–83; M. E. Tubbs, "Goal-Setting: A Meta-Analytic Examination of the Empirical Evidence," *Journal of Applied Psychology* 71 (1986), pp. 474–83.

65. I. R. Gellatly and J. P. Meyer, "The Effects of Goal Difficulty on Physiological Arousal, Cognition, and Task Performance," *Journal of Applied Psychology* 77 (1992), pp. 694–704; A. Mento, E. A. Locke, and H. Klein, "Relationship of Goal Level to Valence and Instrumentality," *Journal of Applied Psychology* 77 (1992), pp. 395–405.

66. R. Kaiser, "Human Touch Selling Online," *Chicago Tribune*, September 10, 2001, p. CN1; F. Knowles "CDW Chief Gung-Ho," *Chicago Sun-Times*, April 23, 2001, p. 51.

67. J. T. Chambers, "The Future of Business," *Executive Excellence* 17 (February 2000), pp. 3–4; K. R. Thompson, W. A. Hochwarter, and N. J. Mathys, "Stretch Targets: What Makes Them Effective?" *Academy of Management Executive* 11 (August 1997), pp. 48–60; S. Sherman, "Stretch Goals: The Dark Side of Asking for Miracles," *Fortune* 132 (November 13, 1995), pp. 231–32.

68. H. J. Klein, "Further Evidence of the Relationship between Goal Setting and Expectancy Theory," *Organizational Behavior and Human Decision Processes* 49 (1991), pp. 230–57.

69. M. E. Tubbs, "Commitment as a Moderator of the Goal-Performance Relation: A Case for Clearer Construct Definition," *Journal of Applied Psychology* 78 (1993), pp. 86–97.

70. G. P. Latham, D. C. Winters, and E. A. Locke, "Cognitive and Motivational Effects of Participation: A Mediator Study," *Journal of Organizational Behavior* 15 (1994), pp. 49–63.

71. J. Chowdhury, "The Motivational Impact of Sales Quotas on Effort," *Journal of Marketing Research* 30 (1993), pp. 28–41; Locke and Latham, *A Theory of Goal Setting and Task Performance*, chaps. 6 and 7; E. A. Locke, G. P. Latham, and M. Erez, "The Determinants of Goal Commitment," *Academy of Management Review* 13 (1988), pp. 23–39.

72. P. M. Wright, "Goal Setting and Monetary Incentives: Motivational Tools That Can Work Too Well," *Compensation and Benefits Review* 26 (May–June, 1994), pp. 41–49.

73. F. M. Moussa, " Determinants and Process of the Choice of Goal Difficulty," *Group and Organization Management* 21 (1996), pp. 414–38.

CHAPTER SIX

1. J. Mayne, "Bonuses Abound," *Seattle Post-Intelligencer*, December 5, 2000, p. C5; J. Mayne, "IKEA Workers in Renton Looking Like $1 Million," *Seattle Post-Intelligencer*, December 2, 2000, p. C5; K. Richter, "IKEA's Successful One-Day Bonus May Have Been a One-Time Deal," *Wall Street Journal Europe*, October 19, 1999, p. 4; N. R. Brooks, "IKEA Bonus Day Exceeds Expectations," *Los Angeles Times*, October 12, 1999, p. 3; "IKEA Puts $118m into Workers' Pay," *Edmonton (Alberta) Sun*, October 12, 1999, p. 51.

2. M. C. Bloom and G. T. Milkovich, "Issues in Managerial Compensation Research," in C. L. Cooper and D. M. Rousseau, eds., *Trends in Organizational Behavior*, vol. 3 (Chicester, UK: Wiley, 1996), pp. 23–47.

3. T. Kinni, "Why We Work," *Training* 35 (August 1998), pp. 34–39; A. Furnham and M. Argyle, *The Psychology of Money* (London: Routledge, 1998); T. L-P. Tang, "The Meaning of Money Revisited," *Journal of Organizational Behavior* 13 (March 1992), pp. 197–202.

4. Cited in T. R. Mitchell and A. E. Mickel, "The Meaning of Money: An Individual-Difference Perspective," *Academy of Management Review* (July 1999), pp. 568–78.

5. A. Furnham, B. D. Kirkcaldy, and R. Lynn, "National Attitudes to Competitiveness, Money, and Work among Young People: First, Second, and Third

World Differences," *Human Relations* 47 (January 1994), pp. 119–32; R. Lynn, *The Secret of the Miracle Economy* (London: SAE, 1991), cited in A. Furnham and R. Okamura, "Your Money or Your Life: Behavioral and Emotional Predictors of Money Pathology," *Human Relations* 52 (September 1999), pp. 1157–77.

6. M. Leder, "Better Perks Resonate in Boom Times," *New York Times*, November 21, 1999, p. 24; J. Juergens, "Corporate Spotlight: ARCNET," *Incentive* 173 (September 1999), pp. 68–69.

7. Furnham and Okamura, "Your Money or Your Life." For discussion of the money ethic, see T. L-P. Tang, J. K. Kim, and D. S-H. Tang, "Does Attitude toward Money Moderate the Relationship between Intrinsic Job Satisfaction and Voluntary Turnover?" *Human Relations* 53 (February 2000), pp. 213–45; T. L-P. Tang and J. K. Kim, "The Meaning of Money among Mental Health Workers: The Endorsement of Money Ethic as Related to Organizational Citizenship Behavior, Job Satisfaction, and Commitment," *Public Personnel Management* 28 (Spring 1999), pp. 15–26.

8. A. K. Kau, S. J. Tan and J. Wirtz, *Seven Faces of Singaporeans: Their Values, Aspirations, and Lifestyles* (Singapore: Prentice Hall, 1998); Furnham, Kirkcaldy, and Lynn, "National Attitudes to Competitiveness, Money, and Work among Young People." However, one recent study reported that "belief in the wonders of money" was higher among a sample of Canadian university students than students in Singapore, Hong Kong, or Hawaii. See S. H. Ang, "The Power of Money: A Cross-Cultural Analysis of Business-Related Beliefs," *Journal of World Business* 35 (March 2000), pp. 43–60.

9. C. Fox, "Never Fear, Aussies Are Here," *Australian Financial Review*, June 29, 2000, p. 38.

10. O. Mellan, "Men, Women and Money," *Psychology Today* 32 (February 1999), pp. 46–50.

11. Lynn, *The Secret of the Miracle Economy*, cited in Furnham and Okamura, "Your Money or Your Life."

12. M. Steen, "Study Looks at What Good Employees Want from a Company," *San Jose (CA) Mercury*, December 19, 2000; J. O'Rourke, "Show Boys the Money and Tell Girls You Care," *Sydney Morning Herald*, December 10, 2000.

13. Steen, "Study Looks at What Good Employees Want from a Company"; Mellan, "Men, Women and Money"; V. K. G. Lim and T. S. H. Teo, "Sex, Money and Financial Hardship: An Empirical Study of Attitudes towards Money among Undergraduates in Singapore," *Journal of Economic Psychology* 18 (1997), pp. 369–86; A. Furnham, "Attitudinal Correlates and Demographic Predictors of Monetary Beliefs and Behaviors," *Journal of Organizational Behavior* 17 (1996), 375–88.

14. Y. Park, "A Comparative Analysis of Work Incentives in U.S. and Japanese Firms," *Multinational Business Review* 4 (Fall 1996), pp. 59–70. Longevity pay in some Nevada counties is described in F. Greary, "Salary Incentives: County May Replace Longevity Pay," *Las Vegas Review-Journal*, August 14, 2001, p. B1.

15. J. M. Newman and F. J. Krzystofiak, "Value-Chain Compensation," *Compensation and Benefits Review* 30 (May 1998), pp. 60–66.

16. Q. Chan and C. Wan, "Equal Pay under the Microscope," *South China Morning Post*, May 31, 2001, p. 4.

17. "A Fair Day's Pay," *Economist*, May 8, 1999, p. 12; F. F. Reichheld, *The Loyalty Effect* (Boston, MA: Harvard Business School Press, 1996), p. 137. On the problems with job evaluation, see M. Quaid, *Job Evaluation: The Myth of Equitable Assessment* (Toronto: University of Toronto Press, 1993); S. L. McShane, "Two Tests of Direct Gender Bias in Job Evaluation Ratings," *Journal of Occupational Psychology* 63 (1990), pp. 129–40.

18. J. Kochanski, "Competency-Based Management," *Training and Development*, October 1997, pp. 40–44; Hay Group et al., *Raising the Bar: Using Competencies to Enhance Employee Performance* (Scottsdale, AZ: American Compensation Association, 1996).

19. E. Lawler, *Rewarding Excellence* (San Francisco: Jossey-Bass, 2000); R. Shareef, "A Midterm Case Study Assessment of Skill-Based Pay in the Virginia Department of Transportation," *Review of Public Personnel Administration* 18 (Winter 1998), pp. 5–22; D. Hofrichter, "Broadbanding: A 'Second Generation' Approach," *Compensation and Benefits Review* 25 (September–October 1993), pp. 53–58.

20. B. Murray and B. Gerhart, "Skill-Based Pay and Skill Seeking," *Human Resource Management Review* 10 (Autumn 2000), pp. 271–87; J. R. Thompson and C. W. LeHew, "Skill-Based Pay as an Organizational Innovation," *Review of Public Personnel Administration* 20 (Winter 2000), pp. 20–40; D-O. Kim and K. Mericle, "From Job-Based Pay to Skill-Based Pay in Unionized Establishments: A Three-Plant Comparative Analysis," *Relations Industrielles* 54 (Summer 1999), pp. 549–80; E. E. Lawler III, "From Job-Based to Competency-Based Organizations," *Journal of Organizational Behavior* 15 (1994), pp. 3–15.

21. C. T. Crumpley, "Skill-Based Pay Replaces Traditional Ranking," *Kansas City Star*, June 30, 1997, p. B6.

22. E. E. Lawler III, G. E. Ledford, Jr., and L. Chang, "Who Uses Skill-Based Pay, and Why," *Compensation and Benefits Review* 25 (March–April 1993), pp. 22–26.

23. E. E. Lawler III, "Competencies: A Poor Foundation for the New Pay," *Compensation and Benefits Review*, November–December 1996, pp. 20, 22–26.

24. E. B. Peach and D. A. Wren, "Pay for Performance from Antiquity to the 1950s," *Journal of Organizational Behavior Management*, 1992, pp. 5–26. Bank One's incentive is described in S. Brenowitz, "Bank One Launches Effort to Lure Customers with Bounties, Contests," *Columbus (OH) Dispatch*, June 7, 2001, p. E1.

25. S. Jones, "The Wages of Compression," *News and Observer (Raleigh, NC)*, December 14, 1999, p. D1.

26. F. Russo, "Aggression Loses Some of Its Punch," *Time*, July 30, 2001.

27. J. S. DeMatteo, L. T. Eby, and E. Sundstrom, "Team-Based Rewards: Current Empirical Evidence and Directions for Future Research," in B. M. Staw and L. L. Cummings, eds., *Research in Organizational Behavior* 20 (1998), pp. 141–83; P. Pascarella, "Compensating Teams," *Across the Board* 34 (February 1997), pp. 16–23; D. G. Shaw and C. E. Schneier, "Team Measurement and Rewards: How Some Companies Are Getting It Right," *Human Resource Planning* (1995), pp. 34–49.

28. L. R. Gomez-Mejia, T. M. Welbourne, and R. M. Wiseman, "The Role of Risk Sharing and Risk Taking under Gainsharing," *Academy of Management Review* 25 (July 2000), pp. 492–507.

29. J. Creswell, "America's Elite Factories," *Fortune*, September 3, 2001.

30. A. Miller, "St. Joseph's to Reward Surgeons for Savings," *Atlanta Journal-Constitution*, January 20, 2001, p. F1.

31. D. P. O'Bannon and C. L. Pearce, "An Exploratory Examination of Gainsharing in Service Organizations: Implications for Organizational Citizenship Behavior and Pay Satisfaction," *Journal of Managerial Issues* 11 (Fall 1999), pp. 363–78; C. Cooper and B. Dyck, "Improving the Effectiveness of Gainsharing: The Role of Fairness and Participation," *Administrative Science Quarterly* 37 (1992), pp. 471–90.

32. M. Jarman, "Stock Plans for Workers," *Arizona Republic*, June 14, 1998; D. Bencivenga, "Employee-Owners Help Bolster the Bottom Line," *HRMagazine* 42 (February 1997), pp. 78–83.

33. J. M. Newman and M. Waite, "Do Broad-Based Stock Options Create Value?" *Compensation and Benefits Review* 30 (July 1998), pp. 78–86.

34. H. Hamid, "Tien Wah's Flexi-Wage a Success," *Business Times (Malaysia)*, December 7, 2000.

35. S. J. Marks, "Incentives that Really Reward and Motivate," *Workforce* 80 (June 2001), pp. 108–14; "A Fair Day's Pay," *Economist*, May 8, 1999, p. 12; Bencivenga, "Employee-Owners Help Bolster the Bottom Line"; J. Chelius and R. S. Smith, "Profit Sharing and Employment Stability," *Industrial and Labor Relations Review* 43 (1990), pp. 256s–273s.

36. A. Leckey, "Some Are Left Sizing Up Their Options," *Chicago Tribune*, May 9, 2001.

37. A. Kohn, "Challenging Behaviorist Dogma: Myths about Money and Motivation," *Compensation and Benefits Review* 30 (March 1998), pp. 27–33; A. Kohn, *Punished by Rewards* (Boston: Houghton Mifflin, 1993); W. C. Hamner, "How to Ruin Motivation with Pay," *Compensation Review* 7, no. 3 (1975), pp. 17–27.

38. M. O'Donnell and J. O'Brian, "Performance-Based Pay in the Australian Public Service," *Review of Public Personnel Administration* 20 (Spring 2000), pp. 20–34.

39. B. Nelson, *1001 Ways to Reward Employees* (New York: Workman, 1994), p. 148.

40. "Global Survey Finds Common Trends in Ways Top Companies Reward High Performers," *Business Wire*, May 22, 2000; J. Pfeffer, *The Human Equation* (Boston: Harvard Business School Press, 1998). For an early summary of research supporting the motivational value of performance-based rewards, see E. E. Lawler III, *Pay and Organizational Effectiveness: A Psychological View* (New York: McGraw-Hill, 1971).

41. S. Kerr, "Organization Rewards: Practical, Cost-Neutral Alternatives That You May Know, but Don't Practice," *Organizational Dynamics* 28 (Summer 1999), pp. 61–70.

42. "New Survey Finds Variable Pay Has Yet to Deliver on Its Promise," *Pay for Performance Report*, March 2000, p. 1. The politics of pay is discussed in D. Collins, *Gainsharing and Power? Lessons from Six Scanlon Plans* (Ithaca, NY: Cornell University Press, 1998); K. M. Bartol and D. C. Martin, "When Politics Pays: Factors Influencing Managerial Compensation Decisions," *Personnel Psychology* 43 (1990), pp. 599–614.

43. Kerr, "Organization Rewards."

44. "New Survey Finds Variable Pay Has Yet to Deliver on Its Promise."

45. S. Chandler, "Sears' System of Rewards Has Ups and Downs," *Chicago Tribune*, February 15, 1998, p. C1.

46. DeMatteo et al., "Team-Based Rewards."

47. R. Wageman, "Interdependence and Group Effectiveness," *Administrative Science Quarterly* 40 (1995), pp. 145–80.

48. "Dream Teams," *Human Resources Professional*, November 1994, pp. 17–19.

49. S. Kerr, "On the Folly of Rewarding A, While Hoping for B," *Academy of Management Journal* 18 (1975), pp. 769–83.

50. D. R. Spitzer, "Power Rewards: Rewards That Really Motivate," *Management Review*, May 1996, pp. 45–50.

51. P. M. Perry, "Holding Your Top Talent," *Research Technology Management* 44 (May 2001), pp. 26–30; "Strong Leaders Make Great Workplaces," *(Minneapolis–St. Paul) CityBusiness*, August 28, 2000.

52. This definition is more consistent with popular use of the word *job* and with the definition in *Random House Webster's College Dictionary*. However, some scholars have used this definition for *position* and have defined *job* as a group of similar positions. See K. Pearlman, "Job Families: A Review and Discussion of Their Implications for Personnel Selection," *Psychological Bulletin* 87 (January 1980), pp. 1–28.

53. M. Bensaou and M. Earl, "The Right Mind-Set for Managing Information Technology," *Harvard Business Review*, September–October 1998, pp. 118–28; B. B. Arnetz, "Technological Stress: Psychophysiological Aspects of Working with Modern Information Technology," *Scandinavian Journal of Work and Environmental Health* 23, suppl. 3 (1997), pp. 97–103; J. W. Medcof, "The Effect of Extent of Use and Job of the User upon Task Characteristics," *Human Relations* 42 (1989), pp. 23–41, R. J. Long, *New Office Information Technology: Human and Managerial Implications* (London: Crom Helm, 1987).

54. G. L. Dalton, "The Collective Stretch: Workforce Flexibility," *Management Review* 87 (December 1998), pp. 54–59; C. Hendry and R. Jenkins, "Psychological Contracts and New Deals," *Human Resource Management Journal* 7 (1997), pp. 38–44.

55. D. Whitford, "A Human Place to Work," *Fortune*, January 8, 2001, pp. 108–19.

56. A. Smith, *The Wealth of Nations* (London: Dent, 1910). Earlier examples are described in "Scientific Management: Lessons from Ancient History through the Industrial Revolution" (www.accel-team.com).

57. M. A. Campion, "Ability Requirement Implications of Job Design: An Interdisciplinary Perspective," *Personnel Psychology* 42 (1989), pp. 1–24; H. Fayol, *General and Industrial Management*, trans. C. Storrs (London: Pitman, 1949); E. E. Lawler III, *Motivation in Work Organizations* (Monterey, CA: Brooks/Cole, 1973), chap. 7.

58. For a review of Taylor's work and life, see R. Kanigel, *The One Best Way: Frederick Winslow Taylor and the Enigma of Efficiency* (New York:

Viking, 1997). See also C. R. Littler, "Taylorism, Fordism, and Job Design," in D. Knights, H. Willmott, and D. Collinson, eds., *Job Design: Critical Perspectives on the Labor Process* (Aldershot, UK: Gower, 1985), pp. 10–29; F. W. Taylor, *The Principles of Scientific Management* (New York: Harper & Row, 1911).

59. E. E. Lawler III, *High-Involvement Management* (San Francisco: Jossey-Bass, 1986), chap. 6; C. R. Walker and R. H. Guest, *The Man on the Assembly Line* (Cambridge, MA: Harvard University Press, 1952).

60. W. F. Dowling, "Job Redesign on the Assembly Line: Farewell to Blue-Collar Blues?" *Organizational Dynamics*, Autumn 1973, pp. 51–67; Lawler, *Motivation in Work Organizations*, p. 150.

61. M. Keller, *Rude Awakening* (New York: Harper Perennial, 1989), p. 128.

62. C. S. Wong and M. A. Campion, "Development and Test of a Task Level Model of Motivational Job Design," *Journal of Applied Psychology* 76 (1991), pp. 825–37; R. W. Griffin, "Toward an Integrated Theory of Task Design," *Research in Organizational Behavior* 9 (1987), pp. 79–120.

63. F. Herzberg, B. Mausner, and B. B. Snyderman, *The Motivation to Work* (New York: Wiley, 1959).

64. J. R. Hackman and G. Oldham, *Work Redesign* (Reading, MA: Addison-Wesley, 1980).

65. Whitford, "A Human Place to Work."

66. M. C. Andrews and K. M. Kacmar, "Confirmation and Extension of the Sources of Feedback Scale in Service-Based Organizations," *Journal of Business Communication* 38 (April 2001), pp. 206–26.

67. G. Johns, J. L. Xie, and Y. Fang, "Mediating and Moderating Effects in Job Design," *Journal of Management* 18 (1992), pp. 657–76.

68. P. E. Spector, "Higher-Order Need Strength as a Moderator of the Job Scope–Employee Outcome Relationship: A Meta Analysis," *Journal of Occupational Psychology* 58 (1985), pp. 119–27.

69. S. Shepard, "Safety Program at Carrier Plant in Collierville Paying Dividends," *Memphis Business Journal*, May 25, 2001, p. 38.

70. J. L. White, "Police Practice: The Work Itself as a Motivator," *FBI Law Enforcement Bulletin*, February 2001, pp. 7–9.

71. N. G. Dodd and D. C. Ganster, "The Interactive Effects of Variety, Autonomy, and Feedback on Attitudes and Performance," *Journal of Organizational Behavior* 17 (1996), pp. 329–47; M. A. Campion and C. L. McClelland, "Follow-up and Extension of the Interdisciplinary Costs and Benefits of Enlarged Jobs," *Journal of Applied Psychology* 78 (1993), pp. 339–51.

72. This point is emphasized in C. Pinder, *Work Motivation* (Glenview, IL: Scott Foresman, 1984), p. 244; and F. Herzberg, "One More Time: How Do You Motivate Employees?" *Harvard Business Review* 46 (January–February 1968), pp. 53–62. For a full discussion of job enrichment, also see R. W. Griffin, *Task Design: An Integrative Approach* (Glenview, IL: Scott Foresman, 1982); J. R. Hackman, G. Oldham, R. Janson, and K. Purdy, "A New Strategy for Job Enrichment," *California Management Review* 17 (4) (1975), pp. 57–71.

73. S. Ross, "Workers Turn Off Autopilot and Take Charge on Assembly Lines of the 21st Century," *Globe and Mail*, September 3, 2001, p. B12; M. Truby, "Change Becomes Mantra of Ford's New Leaders," *Detroit News*, August 20, 2000.

74. M. Grotticelli, "CNN Moves to Small-Format ENG," *Broadcasting and Cable*, May 14, 2001, p. 46.

75. For a full discussion of empowerment, including its many definitions, see W. A. Randolph, "Re-Thinking Empowerment: Why Is It So Hard to Achieve?" *Organizational Dynamics* 29 (November 2000), pp. 94–107; R. Forrester, "Empowerment: Rejuvenating a Potent Idea," *Academy of Management Executive* 14 (August 2000), pp. 67–80; C. S. Koberg, R. W. Boss, J. C. Senjem, and E. A. Goodman, "Antecedents and Outcomes of Empowerment," *Group and Organization Management* 24 (1999), pp. 71–91; R. C. G. M. Spreitzer, "Psychological Empowerment in the Workplace: Dimensions, Measurement, and Validation," *Academy of Management Journal* 38 (1995), pp. 1442–65; J. A. Conger and R. N. Kanungo, "The Empowerment Process: Integrating

Theory and Practice," *Academy of Management Review* 13 (1988), pp. 471–82.

76. J-C. Chebat and P. Kollias, "The Impact of Empowerment on Customer Contact Employees' Role in Service Organizations," *Journal of Service Research* 3 (August 2000), pp. 66–81.

77. Hackman and Oldham, *Work Redesign*, pp. 137–38.

78. S. L. Paulson, "Training for Change," *American Gas* 79 (December 1997–January 1998), pp. 26–29.

79. R. Saavedra and S. K. Kwun, "Affective States in Job Characteristics Theory," *Journal of Organizational Behavior* 21 (2000), pp. 131–46; P. Osterman, "How Common Is Workplace Transformation and Who Adopts It?" *Industrial and Labor Relations Review* 47 (1994), pp. 173–88; D. E. Bowen and E. E. Lawler III, "The Empowerment of Service Workers: What, Why, How, and When," *Sloan Management Review* Spring 1992, pp. 31–39; P. E. Spector and S. M. Jex, "Relations of Job Characteristics from Multiple Data Sources with Employee Affect, Absence, Turnover Intentions, and Health," *Journal of Applied Psychology* 76 (1991), pp. 46–53; Y. Fried and G. R. Ferris, "The Validity of the Job Characteristics Model: A Review and Meta-analysis," *Personnel Psychology* 40 (1987), pp. 287–322.

80. C-S. Wong, C. Hui, and K. S. Law, "A Longitudinal Study of the Job Perception–Job Satisfaction Relationship: A Test of the Three Alternative Specifications," *Journal of Occupational and Organizational Psychology* 71 (June 1998), pp. 127–46.

81. Forrester, "Empowerment"; D. I. Levine, *Reinventing the Workplace* (Washington, DC: Brookings, 1995), pp. 63–66, 86. However, a more complex curvilinear relationship between employee empowerment and supervisor reactions is reported in M. Fenton-O'Creevy, "Employee Involvement and the Middle Manager: Saboteur or Scapegoat?" *Human Resource Management Journal* 11 (2001), pp. 24–40.

82. R. Hodson, "Dignity in the Workplace under Participative Management: Alienation and Freedom Revisited," *American Sociological Review* 61 (1996), pp. 719–38; J. Rinehart, "Improving the Quality of Working Life through Job Redesign: Work Humanization or Work

Rationalization?" *Canadian Review of Sociology and Anthropology* 23 (1986), pp. 507–30.

83. Campion, "Ability Requirement Implications of Job Design," p. 20; R. B. Dunham, "Relationships of Perceived Job Design Characteristics to Job Ability Requirements and Job Value," *Journal of Applied Psychology* 62 (1977), pp. 760–63.

84. R. Martin and T. D. Wall, "Attentional Demand and Cost Responsibility as Stressors in Shopfloor Jobs," *Academy of Management Journal* 32 (1989), pp. 69–86; D. P. Schwab and L. L. Cummings, "Impact of Task Scope on Employee Productivity: An Evaluation Using Expectancy Theory," *Academy of Management Review* 1 (1976), pp. 23–35.

85. M. Heroux, "CEOs Try Better Ways to Hire, Motivate Employees," *Akron (OH) Beacon Journal,* November 21, 1999.

86. T. Romita, "The Talent Search," *Business 2.0,* June 12, 2001.

87. C. P. Neck and C. C. Manz, "Thought Self-Leadership: The Impact of Mental Strategies Training on Employee Cognition, Behavior, and Affect," *Journal of Organizational Behavior* 17 (1996), pp. 445–67.

88. C. C. Manz and H. P. Sims, Jr., *Superleadership: Leading Others to Lead Themselves* (Englewood Cliffs, NJ: Prentice Hall, 1989); C. C. Manz, "Self-Leadership: Toward an Expanded Theory of Self-Influence Processes in Organizations," *Academy of Management Review* 11 (1986), pp. 585–600.

89. H. P. Sims, Jr., and C. C. Manz, *Company of Heroes: Unleashing the Power of Self-Leadership* (New York: Wiley, 1996); A. M. Saks, R. R. Haccoun, and D. Laxer, "Transfer Training: A Comparison of Self-Management and Relapse Prevention Interventions," *ASAC 1996 Conference Proceedings, Human Resources Division* 17 (9) (1996), pp. 81–91; M. E. Gist, A. G. Bavetta, and C. K. Stevens, "Transfer Training Method: Its Influence on Skill Generalization, Skill Repetition, and Performance Level," *Personnel Psychology* 43 (1990), pp. 501–23.

90. R. M. Duncan and J. A. Cheyne, "Incidence and Functions of Self-Reported Private Speech in Young Adults: A Self-Verbalization Questionnaire," *Canadian Journal of Behavioral Science* 31 (April 1999), pp. 133–36. For an organizational behavior discussion of constructive thought patterns, see C. P. Neck and C. C. Manz, "Thought Self-Leadership: The Influence of Self-Talk and Mental Imagery on Performance," *Journal of Organizational Behavior* 13 (1992), pp. 681–99.

91. G. E. Prussia, J. S. Anderson, and C. C. Manz, "Self-Leadership and Performance Outcomes: The Mediating Influence of Self-Efficacy," *Journal of Organizational Behavior,* September 1998, pp. 523–38; Neck and Manz, "Thought Self-Leadership: The Impact of Mental Strategies Training on Employee Cognition, Behavior, and Affect."

92. Early scholars seem to distinguish mental practice from mental imagery, whereas recent literature combines mental practice with visualizing positive task outcomes within the meaning of mental imagery. For recent discussion of this concept, see C. P. Neck, G. L. Stewart, and C. C. Manz, "Thought Self-Leadership as a Framework for Enhancing the Performance of Performance Appraisers," *Journal of Applied Behavioral Science* 31 (September 1995), pp. 278–302; W. P. Anthony, R. H. Bennett III, E. N. Maddox, and W. J. Wheatley, "Picturing the Future: Using Mental Imagery to Enrich Strategic Environmental Assessment," *Academy of Management Executive* 7 (2) (1993), pp. 43–56.

93. C. Salter, "This Is Brain Surgery," *Fast Company* 13 (February–March 1998), pp. 147–50.

94. J. E. Driscoll, C. Cooper, and A. Moran, "Does Mental Practice Enhance Performance?" *Journal of Applied Psychology* 79 (1994), pp. 481–92.

95. A. Wrzesniewski and J. E. Dutton, "Crafting a Job: Revisioning Employees as Active Crafters of Their Work," *Academy of Management Review* 26 (April 2001), pp. 179–201; Manz, "Self-Leadership."

96. M. I. Bopp, S. J. Glynn, and R. A. Henning, "Self-Management of Performance Feedback during Computer-Based Work by Individuals and Two-Person Work Teams," Paper presented at the APA-NIOSH conference, March 1999.

97. A. W. Logue, *Self-Control: Waiting until Tomorrow for What You Want Today* (Englewood Cliffs, NJ: Prentice Hall, 1995).

98. J. Bauman, "The Gold Medal Mind," *Psychology Today* 33 (May 2000), pp. 62–69; K. E. Thiese and S. Huddleston, "The Use of Psychological Skills by Female Collegiate Swimmers," *Journal of Sport Behavior,* December 1999, pp. 602–10; D. Landin and E. P. Hebert, "The Influence of Self-Talk on the Performance of Skilled Female Tennis Players," *Journal of Applied Sport Psychology* 11 (September 1999), pp. 263–82; C. Defrancesco and K. L. Burke, "Performance Enhancement Strategies Used in a Professional Tennis Tournament," *International Journal of Sport Psychology* 28 (1997), pp. 185–95; S. Ming and G. L. Martin, "Single-Subject Evaluation of a Self-Talk Package for Improving Figure Skating Performance," *Sport Psychologist* 10 (1996), pp. 227–38.

99. A. M. Saks and B. E. Ashforth, "Proactive Socialization and Behavioral Self-Management." *Journal of Vocational Behavior* 48 (1996), pp. 301–23; Neck and Manz, "Thought Self-Leadership: The Impact of Mental Strategies Training on Employee Cognition, Behavior, and Affect."

100. A. L. Kazan, "Exploring the Concept of Self-Leadership: Factors Impacting Self-Leadership of Ohio Americorps Members," *Dissertation Abstracts International* 60 (June 2000); S. Ross, "Corporate Measurements Shift from Punishment to Rewards," *Reuters* February 28, 2000; M. Castaneda, T. A. Kolenko, and R. J. Aldag, "Self-Management Perceptions and Practices: A Structural Equations Analysis," *Journal of Organizational Behavior* 20 (1999), pp. 101–20; G. L. Stewart, K. P. Carson, and R. L. Cardy, "The Joint Effects of Conscientiousness and Self-Leadership Training on Employee Self-Directed Behavior in a Service Setting," *Personnel Psychology* 49 (1996), pp. 143–64.

CHAPTER SEVEN

1. G. Hassell, "Energy Trading Fast, Furious and Lucrative," *Houston Chronicle,* May 20, 2001, p. 25; J. Warren, "Secrecy Cloaks State's Buyers on Their Prowl for Power," *Los Angeles Times,* February 23, 2001, p. A1.

2. "CareerBuilder Survey Finds Growing Worker Disenchantment, Long Hours and Stress," *PR Newswire*, August 30, 2001; D. Stafford, "Nearly One-Third of Workers Often Feel Overworked, Study Says," *Philadelphia Inquirer*, May 21, 2001; E. Galinsky, S. S. Kim, J. T. Bond, *Feeling Overworked: When Work Becomes Too Much* (New York: Families and Work Institute, 2001); American Institute of Stress (www.stress.org).

3. S. Lem, "Snowed Under by Stress," *London Free Press*, February 3, 2000, p. C4; "Good Bosses Are Hard to Find," Morgan & Banks news release, August 2000; S. Efron, "Jobs Take a Deadly Toll on Japanese," *Los Angeles Times*, April 12, 2000, p. A1; N. Chowdhury and S. Menon, "Beating Burnout," *India Today*, June 9, 1997, p. 86; Cross-National Collaborative Group, "The Changing Rate of Major Depression: Cross-National Comparisons," *JAMA: The Journal of the American Medical Association* 268 (December 2, 1992), pp. 3098–3105.

4. R. S. DeFrank and J. M. Ivancevich, "Stress on the Job: An Executive Update," *Academy of Management Executive* 12 (August 1998), pp. 55–66; J. C. Quick and J. D. Quick, *Organizational Stress and Prevention Management* (New York: McGraw-Hill, 1984).

5. J. C. Quick, J. D. Quick, D. L. Nelson, and J. J. Hurrell, Jr., *Preventive Stress Management in Organizations* (Washington, DC: American Psychological Association, 1997).

6. S. Sauter and L. R. Murphy (eds.), *Organizational Risk Factors for Job Stress* (Washington, DC: American Psychological Association, 1995).

7. H. Selye, *Stress without Distress* (Philadelphia: Lippincott, 1974).

8. S. E. Taylor, R. L. Repetti, and T. Seeman, "Health Psychology: What Is an Unhealthy Environment and How Does It Get under the Skin?" *Annual Review of Psychology*, 48 (1997), pp. 411–47.

9. K. Danna and R. W. Griffin, "Health and Well-being in the Workplace: A Review and Synthesis of the Literature," *Journal of Management*, Spring 1999, pp. 357–84; Quick and Quick, *Organizational Stress and Prevention Management*, p. 3.

10. S. Cassidy, "Record Payouts for Assaults and Accidents in Class," *The Independent (London)*, May 12, 2001, p. 13; R. Hancock, "Teachers Top Stress Bill," *Sunday Mail (Adelaide)*, March 25, 2001, p. 19; "Teacher Payouts," *Sunday Telegraph (Sydney)*, March 4, 2001, p. 27; N. Webber, "Teachers Terrorized," *Herald Sun (Melbourne)*, February 26, 2001, p. 11; N. Webber, "Stressed Teachers Win $34m Compo," *Herald Sun (Melbourne)*, February 22, 2001; S. O'Connell, "Too Tense to Teach," *Times of London*, December 7, 2000, p. 22; L. Lightfoot, "Teacher Receives Record £254,000 Payout for Stress," *The Telegraph (London)*, December 5, 2000; J. Judd, "Teacher Awarded £250,000 over Stress Illnesses," *The Independent (London)*, December 5, 2000, p. 5.

11. G. Evans and D. Johnson, "Stress and Open-Office Noise," *Journal of Applied Psychology* 85 (2000), pp. 779–83; S. Melamed and S. Bruhis, "The Effects of Chronic Industrial Noise Exposure on Urinary Cortisol, Fatigue, and Irritability: A Controlled Field Experiment," *Journal of Occupational and Environmental Medicine* 38 (1996), pp. 252–56.

12. M. Siegall and L. L. Cummings, "Stress and Organizational Role Conflict," *Genetic, Social, and General Psychology Monographs* 12 (1995), pp. 65–95; E. K. Kelloway and J. Barling, "Job Characteristics, Role Stress and Mental Health," *Journal of Occupational Psychology* 64 (1991), pp. 291–304; R. L. Kahn, D. M. Wolfe, R. P. Quinn, J. D. Snoek, and R. A. Rosenthal, *Organizational Stress: Studies in Role Conflict and Ambiguity* (New York: Wiley, 1964).

13. B. Stoneman and K. K. Holliday, "Pressure Cooker," *Banking Strategies*, January–February, 2001, p. 13.

14. G. R. Cluskey and A. Vaux, "Vocational Misfit: Source of Occupational Stress among Accountants," *Journal of Applied Business Research* 13 (Summer 1997), pp. 43–54; J. R. Edwards, "An Examination of Competing Versions of the Person–Environment Fit Approach to Stress," *Academy of Management Journal* 39 (1996), pp. 292–339; B. E. Ashforth and R. H. Humphrey, "Emotional Labor in Service Roles: The Influence of Identity," *Acad-*

emy of Management Review 18 (1993), pp. 88–115.

15. A. M. Saks and B. E. Ashforth, "Proactive Socialization and Behavioral Self-Management," *Journal of Vocational Behavior* 48 (1996), pp. 301–23; D. L. Nelson and C. Sutton, "Chronic Work Stress and Coping: A Longitudinal Study and Suggested New Directions," *Academy of Management Journal* 33 (1990), pp. 859–69.

16. J. Vahtera, M. Kivimaki, J. Pentti, and T. Theorell, "Effect of Change in the Psychosocial Work Environment on Sickness Absence: A Seven-Year Follow-up of Initially Healthy Employees," *Journal of Epidemiology & Community Health* 54 (July 2000), pp. 482–83; L. D Sargent and D. J. Terry, "The Effects of Work Control and Job Demands on Employee Adjustment and Work Performance," *Journal of Occupational and Organizational Psychology* 71 (September 1998), pp. 219–36; M. G. Marmot, H. Bosma, H. Hemingway, E. Brunner, and S. Stansfeld, "Contribution of Job Control and Other Risk Factors to Social Variations in Coronary Heart Disease Incidence," *Lancet* 350 (July 26, 1997), pp. 235–39; P. M. Elsass and J. F. Veiga, "Job Control and Job Strain: A Test of Three Models," *Journal of Occupational Health Psychology* 2 (July 1997), pp. 195–211; B. B. Arnetz, "Technological Stress: Psychophysiological Aspects of Working with Modern Information Technology," *Scandinavian Journal of Work and Environment Health* 23 (1997, suppl. 3), pp. 97–103; R. Karasek and T. Theorell, *Healthy Work: Stress, Productivity, and the Reconstruction of Working Life* (New York: Basic Books, 1990).

17. B. Lubinger, "Even on Vacation, There's No Getting Away," *Plain Dealer (Cleveland)*, June 10, 2001, p. L1.

18. J. MacFarland, "Many Are Called, But What Are the Choices: Working in New Brunswick's 1-800 Call Centres," *New Maritimes* 14 (July/August 1996), pp. 10–19.

19. D. F. Elloy and A. Randolph, "The Effect of Superleader Behavior on Autonomous Work Groups in a Government Operated Railway Service," *Public Personnel Management* 26 (June 1997), pp. 257+.

20. J. T. Madore, C. Mason-Draffen, and R. Feigenbaum, "When Work Turns Ugly," *Newsday*, April 5, 1998, p. A4.

21. V. Schultz, "Reconceptualizing Sexual Harassment," *Yale Law Journal* 107 (April 1998), pp. 1683–1805. Several U.S. court cases have discussed these two causes for action, including *Lehman v. Toys 'R' Us Inc.* (1993) 132 N.J. 587; 626 A. (2nd) 445; *Meritor Savings Bank v. Vinson*, 477 U.S. 57 (1986) (U.S.S.C.).

22. L. J. Munson, C. Hulin, and F. Drasgow, "Longitudinal Analysis of Dispositional Influences and Sexual Harassment: Effects on Job and Psychological Outcomes," *Personnel Psychology* (Spring 2000), pp. 21–46; C. S. Piotrkowski, "Gender Harassment, Job Satisfaction, and Distress among Employed White and Minority Women," *Journal of Occupational Health Psychology* 3 (January 1998), pp. 33–43; L. F. Fitzgerald, F. Drasgow, C. L. Hulin, M. J. Gelfand, and V. Magley, "The Antecedents and Consequences of Sexual Harassment in Organizations: A Test of an Integrated Model," *Journal of Applied Psychology* 82 (1997), pp. 578–89; J. Barling, I. Dekker, C. A. Loughlin, E. K. Kelloway, C. Fullagar, and D. Johnson, "Prediction and Replication of the Organizational and Personal Consequences of Workplace Sexual Harassment," *Journal of Managerial Psychology* 11 (5) (1996), pp. 4–25.

23. H. W. French, "Fighting Sex Harassment, and Stigma, in Japan," *New York Times*, July 15, 2001, p. 1.

24. J. H. Neuman and R. A. Baron, "Workplace Violence and Workplace Aggression: Evidence Concerning Specific Forms, Potential Causes, and Preferred Targets," *Journal of Management* 24 (May 1998), pp. 391–419.

25. D. Reiss-Koncar, "The War against Nurses," *Salon.com*, July 27, 2001.

26. G. Lardner, Jr., "Violence at Work Is Largely Unreported," *Washington Post*, July 27, 1998, p. A2; "ILO Survey Reveals Extent of Violence at Work," *Agence France-Presse*, July 19, 1998.

27. J. Barling, "The Prediction, Experience, and Consequences of Workplace Violence," In G. R. VandenBos and E. Q. Bulatao, eds., *Violence on the Job: Identifying Risks and Developing Solutions* (Washington, DC: American Psychological Association, 1996), pp. 29–49.

28. C. A. Duffy and A. E. McGoldrick, "Stress and the Bus Driver in the UK Transport Industry," *Stress and Work* 4 (1990), pp. 17–27.

29. C. M. Pearson, L. M. Andersson, and C. L. Porath, "Assessing and Attacking Workplace Incivility," *Organizational Dynamics* 29 (November 2000), pp. 123–37. We would like to thank Dr. Michael Sheehan at Griffith University, Queensland, Australia, for assisting the research on this topic.

30. The University of Michigan study of workplace bullying is cited in M. Fletcher Stoeltje, "Jerks at Work," *San Antonio (TX) Express-News*, August 31, 2001, p. F1. M. Kivimaki, M. Elovainio, and J. Vahtera, "Workplace Bullying and Sickness Absence in Hospital Staff," *Occupational and Environmental Medicine* 57 (October 2000), pp. 656–60.

31. Kivimaki et al., "Workplace Bullying and Sickness Absence in Hospital Staff"; P. McCarthy and M. Barker, "Workplace Bullying Risk Audit," *Journal of Occupational Health and Safety, Australia and New Zealand* 16 (2000), pp. 409–18; M. O'Moore, E. Seigne, L. McGuire, and M. Smith, "Victims of Bullying at Work in Ireland," *Journal of Occupational Health and Safety* 14 (1998), pp. 569–74; G. Namie, "Hostile Workplace Survey" (http://www.bullybusters.org/home/twd/bb/res/surv2000.html).

32. S. Einarsen, "Harassment and Bullying at Work: A Review of the Scandinavian Approach," *Aggression and Violent Behavior* 5 (2000), pp. 379–401.

33. Pearson et al., "Assessing and Attacking Workplace Incivility."

34. M. Schorr, "Left in Limbo," *ABC News*, October 26, 2000; M. Kivimaki, J. Vahtera, J. Pentti, and J. E. Ferrie, "Factors Underlying the Effect of Organizational Downsizing on Health of Employees: Longitudinal Cohort Study," *BMJ: British Medical Journal* 320 (April 8, 2000), pp. 971–75.

35. G. A. Adams, L. A. King, and D. W. King, "Relationships of Job and Family Involvement, Family Social Support, and Work–Family Conflict with Job and Life Satisfaction," *Journal of Applied Psychology* 81 (August 1996), pp. 411–20; S. Lewis and C. L. Cooper, "Balancing the Work/Home Interface: A European Perspective," *Human Resource Management Review* 5 (1995), pp. 289–305; K. J. Williams and G. M. Alliger, "Role Stressors, Mood Spillover, and Perceptions of Work–Family Conflict in Employed Parents," *Academy of Management Journal* 37 (1994), pp. 837–68.

36. L. Washburn, "Sleepless in America," *Bergen (NJ) Record*, March 28, 2001, p. A1.

37. D. S. Carlson, "Work–Family Conflict in the Organization: Do Life Role Values Make a Difference?" *Journal of Management*, September 2000; M. Jamal and V. V. Baba, "Shiftwork and Department Type Related to Job Stress, Work Attitudes and Behavioral Intentions: A Study of Nurses," *Journal of Organizational Behavior* 13 (1992), pp. 449–64; C. Higgins, L. Duxbury, and R. Irving, "Determinants and Consequences of Work–Family Conflict," *Organizational Behavior and Human Decision Processes* 51 (February 1992), pp. 51–75.

38. D. L. Nelson and R. J. Burke, "Women Executives: Health, Stress, and Success," *Academy of Management Executive* 14 (May 2000), pp. 107–21; C. S. Rogers, "The Flexible Workplace: What Have We Learned?" *Human Resource Management* 31 (Fall 1992), pp. 183–99; L. E. Duxbury and C. A. Higgins, "Gender Differences in Work–Family Conflict," *Journal of Applied Psychology* 76 (1991), pp. 60–74; A. Hochschild, *The Second Shift* (New York: Avon, 1989).

39. M. P. Leiter and M. J. Durup, "Work, Home, and In-Between: A Longitudinal Study of Spillover," *Journal of Applied Behavioral Science* 32 (1996), pp. 29–47; W. Stewart and J. Barling, "Fathers' Work Experiences' Effect on Children's Behaviors via Job-Related Affect and Parenting Behaviors," *Journal of Organizational Behavior* 17 (1996), pp. 221–32; C. A. Beatty, "The Stress of Managerial and Professional Women: Is the Price Too High?" *Journal of Organizational Behavior* 17 (1996), pp. 233–51. See also: D. L. Morrison and R. Clements, "The Effect of

One Partner's Job Characteristics on the Other Partner's Distress: A Serendipitous, but Naturalistic, Experiment," *Journal of Occupational and Organizational Psychology* 70 (December 1997), pp. 307–24; Higgins, Duxbury, and Irving, "Determinants and Consequences of Work–Family Conflict."

40. A. S. Wharton and R. J. Erickson, "Managing Emotions on the Job and at Home: Understanding the Consequences of Multiple Emotional Roles," *Academy of Management Review* 18 (1993), pp. 457–86; S. E. Jackson and C. Maslach, "After-Effects of Job-Related Stress: Families as Victims," *Journal of Occupational Behavior* 3 (1982), pp. 66–77.

41. "Office Workers More Stressed Than Nurses," *The Independent (London)*, August 7, 2000, p. 8; B. Keil, "The 10 Most Stressful Jobs in NYC," *New York Post*, April 6, 1999, p. 50; International Labor Office (ILO), *World Labor Report* (Geneva: ILO, 1993), chap. 5; Karasek and Theorell, *Healthy Work*.

42. Quick et al., *Preventive Stress Management in Organizations*, chap. 3.

43. J. A. Roberts, R. S. Lapidus, and L. B. Chonko, "Salespeople and Stress: The Moderating Role of Locus of Control on Work Stressors and Felt Stress," *Journal of Marketing Theory and Practice* 5 (Summer 1997), pp. 93–108; J. Schaubroeck and D. E. Merritt, "Divergent Effects of Job Control on Coping with Work Stressors: The Key Role of Self-Efficacy," *Academy of Management Journal* 40 (June 1997), pp. 738+; A. O'Leary and S. Brown, "Self-Efficacy and the Physiological Stress Response," in J. E. Maddux, ed., *Self-Efficacy, Adaptation, and Adjustment: Theory, Research, and Application* (New York: Plenum, 1995).

44. S. C. Segerstrom, S. E. Taylor, M. E. Kemeny, and J. L. Fahey, "Optimism Is Associated with Mood, Coping, and Immune Change in Response to Stress," *Journal of Personality and Social Psychology* 74 (June 1998), pp. 1646–55.

45. K. R. Parkes, "Personality and Coping as Moderators of Work Stress Processes: Models, Methods and Measures," *Work and Stress* 8 (April 1994), pp. 110–29; S. J. Havlovic and J. P.

Keenen, "Coping with Work Stress: The Influence of Individual Differences," in P. L. Perrewé, ed., "Handbook on Job Stress" [Special Issue], *Journal of Social Behavior and Personality* 6 (1991), pp. 199–212.

46. B. C. Long and S. E. Kahn, eds., *Women, Work, and Coping: A Multidisciplinary Approach to Workplace Stress* (Montreal: McGill-Queen's University Press, 1993); E. R. Greenglass, R. J. Burke, and M. Ondrack, "A Gender-Role Perspective of Coping and Burnout," *Applied Psychology: An International Review* 39 (1990), pp. 5–27; T. D. Jick and L. F. Mitz, "Sex Differences in Work Stress," *Academy of Management Review* 10 (1985), pp. 408–20.

47. B. Bergman, R. Sheppard, and J. DeMont, "Pressure Point," *Maclean's*, February 7, 2000, p. 48.

48. M. Friedman and R. Rosenman, *Type A Behavior and Your Heart* (New York: Knopf, 1974). For a more recent discussion, see P. E. Spector and B. J. O'Connell, "The Contribution of Personality Traits, Negative Affectivity, Locus of Control" and Type A to the Subsequent Reports of Job Stressors and Job Strains," *Journal of Occupational and Organizational Psychology* 67 (1994), pp. 1–11; Parkes, "Personality and Coping as Moderators of Work Stress Processes."

49. M. Jamal, "Type A Behavior and Job Performance: Some Suggestive Findings," *Journal of Human Stress* 11 (Summer 1985), pp. 60–68; C. Lee, P. C. Earley, and L. A. Hanson, "Are Type A's Better Performers?" *Journal of Organizational Behavior* 9 (1988), pp. 263–69.

50. S. Cohen, D. A. Tyrrell, and A. P. Smith, "Psychological Stress and Susceptibility to the Common Cold," *New England Journal of Medicine* 325 (August 29, 1991), pp. 654–56.

51. S. A. Everson et al., "Stress-Induced Blood Pressure Reactivity and Incident Stroke in Middle-Aged Men," *Stroke* 32 (June 2001), pp. 1263–70; R. J. Benschop et al., "Cardiovascular and Immune Responses to Acute Psychological Stress in Young and Old Women: A Meta-Analysis," *Psychosomatic Medicine* 60 (May–June 1998), pp. 290–96; H. Bosma, R. Peter, J. Siegrist, and M. Marmot, "Two Alter-

native Job Stress Models and the Risk of Coronary Heart Disease," *American Journal of Public Health* 88 (January 1998), pp. 68–74.

52. A. Dabrow, "Improving the Odds against Hypertension," *Nursing* 31 (August 2001), p. 36; *National Vital Statistics Reports*, vol. 48, no. 11, July 24, 2000, pp. 26–36. Many of these statistics are also available at the website of the National Center for Health Statistics (www.cdc.gov/nchs/).

53. D. K. Sugg, "Study Shows Link between Minor Stress, Early Signs of Coronary Artery Disease," *Baltimore Sun*, December 16, 1997, p. A3.

54. R. C. Kessler, "The Effects of Stressful Life Events on Depression," *Annual Review of Psychology* 48 (1997), pp. 191–214; H. M. Weiss and R. Cropanzano, "Affective Events Theory: A Theoretical Discussion of the Structure, Causes, and Consequences of Affective Experiences at Work," *Research in Organizational Behavior* 18 (1996), pp. 1–74.

55. R. T. Lee and B. E. Ashforth, "A Meta-Analytic Examination of the Correlates of the Three Dimensions of Job Burnout," *Journal of Applied Psychology*, 81 (1996) pp. 123–33; R. J. Burke, "Toward a Phase Model of Burnout: Some Conceptual and Methodological Concerns," *Group and Organization Studies* 14 (1989), pp. 23–32; and C. Maslach, *Burnout: The Cost of Caring* (Englewood Cliffs, NJ: Prentice Hall, 1982).

56. C. L. Cordes and T. W. Dougherty, "A Review and Integration of Research on Job Burnout," *Academy of Management Review* 18 (1993), pp. 621–56.

57. R. T. Lee and B. E. Ashforth, "A Further Examination of Managerial Burnout: Toward an Integrated Model," *Journal of Organizational Behavior* 14 (1993), pp. 3–20.

58. M. Jamal, "Job Stress and Job Performance Controversy: An Empirical Assessment," *Organizational Behavior and Human Performance* 33 (1984), pp. 1–21; G. Keinan, "Decision Making under Stress: Scanning of Alternatives under Controllable and Uncontrollable Threats," *Journal of Personality and Social Psychology* 52 (1987), pp. 638–44; S. J. Motowidlo, J. S. Packard, and M. R. Manning, "Occupational Stress:

Its Causes and Consequences for Job Performance," *Journal of Applied Psychology* 71 (1986), pp. 618–29.

59. R. D. Hackett and P. Bycio, "An Evaluation of Employee Absenteeism as a Coping Mechanism among Hospital Nurses," *Journal of Occupational and Organizational Psychology* 69 (December 1996) pp. 327–38; V. V. Baba and M. J. Harris, "Stress and Absence: A Cross-Cultural Perspective," *Research in Personnel and Human Resources Management*, suppl. 1 (1989), pp. 317–37.

60. DeFrank and Ivancevich, "Stress on the Job"; Neuman and Baron, "Workplace Violence and Workplace Aggression."

61. L. Greenberg and J. Barling, "Predicting Employee Aggression against Coworkers, Subordinates and Supervisors: The Roles of Person Behaviors and Perceived Workplace Factors," *Journal of Organizational Behavior* 20 (1999), pp. 897–913; M. A. Diamond, "Administrative Assault: A Contemporary Psychoanalytic View of Violence and Aggression in the Workplace," *American Review of Public Administration* 27 (September 1997), pp. 228–47.

62. Neuman and Baron, "Workplace Violence and Workplace Aggression"; L. Berkowitz, *Aggression: Its Causes, Consequences, and Control* (New York: McGraw-Hill, 1993).

63. "Stressed Out: How the Big Shots Get Some Stability," *Wall Street Journal Europe*, January 18, 2001, p. 21.

64. Siegall and Cummings, "Stress and Organizational Role Conflict"; Havlovic and Keenen, "Coping with Work Stress."

65. T. Newton, J. Handy, and S. Fineman, *Managing Stress: Emotion and Power at Work* (Newbury Park, CA: Sage, 1995).

66. N. Elkes, "Hospital Tackles Health of Stressed-Out Staff," *Birmingham (UK) Evening Mail*, August 24, 2001, p. 73.

67. N. Terra, "The Prevention of Job Stress by Redesigning Jobs and Implementing Self-Regulating Teams," in L. R. Murphy, ed., *Job Stress Interventions* (Washington, DC: American Psychological Association, 1995); T. D. Wall and K. Davids, "Shopfloor Work Organization and Advanced Manufac-

turing Technology," *International Review of Industrial and Organizational Psychology* 7 (1992), pp. 363–98; Karasek and Theorell, *Healthy Work*.

68. T. Layman, "Minimizing Travel's Toll Helps Retain Consultants," *Atlanta Business Chronicle*, September 17, 2001.

69. B. S. Watson, "Share and Share Alike," *Management Review*, October 1995, pp. 50–52.

70. E. J. Hill, B. C. Miller, S. P. Weiner, and J. Colihan, "Influences of the Virtual Office on Aspects of Work and Work/Life Balance," *Personnel Psychology* 51 (Autumn 1998), 667–83; A. Mahlon, "The Alternative Workplace: Changing Where and How People Work," *Harvard Business Review* (May–June 1998), pp. 121–30.

71. D. Coates, "Ford Exec Turns Work Day to Fit Children's Life," *Detroit News*, June 17, 2001.

72. Over 100 countries have paid maternity leave. Among the industrialized countries, only the United States, Australia, and New Zealand do not provide this support. See T. Allard and L. Glendinning, "For Now, Aussie Mums Are Still a World Apart," *Sydney Morning Herald*, August 16, 2001; J. Satterfield, "U.S. Lags Behind Other Nations on Family Leave," *Knoxville (TN) News-Sentinel*, May 7, 2001, p. A1. For discussion of the FMLA, see S. Kim, "Toward Understanding Family Leave Policy in Public Organizations: Family Leave Use and Conceptual Framework for the Family Leave Implementation Process," *Public Productivity and Management Review* 22 (September 1998), pp. 71–87.

73. "Work/Life Balance a Key to Productivity," *Employee Benefit Plan Review* 53 (September 1998), pp. 30–31.

74. S. Hale, "Execs Embrace Wide-Open Spaces," *Los Angeles Times*, May 13, 2001; P. DeMont, "Too Much Stress, Too Little Time," *Ottawa Citizen*, November 12, 1999.

75. E. Cowing, "Get Richer by Keeping Your Staff Happy," *Sunday Times (London)*, November 28, 1999, p. 20.

76. R. Levering and M. Moskowitz, "The 100 Best Companies to Work For," *Fortune*, January 8, 2001, p. 148.

77. M. Stobbe, "Charlotte, N.C., Workers Find Ways to Beat Stress, 'Pump

Up Their Own Morale,'" *Charlotte (NC) Observer*, September 21, 2001.

78. A. M. Saks and B. E. Ashforth, "Proactive Socialization and Behavioral Self-Management," *Journal of Vocational Behavior* 48 (1996), pp. 301–23; M. Waung, "The Effects of Self-Regulatory Coping Orientation on Newcomer Adjustment and Job Survival," *Personnel Psychology* 48 (1995), pp. 633–50; J. E. Maddux, ed. *Self-Efficacy, Adaptation, and Adjustment: Theory, Research, and Application* (New York: Plenum, 1995).

79. A. J. Daley and G. Parfitt, "Good Health—Is It Worth It? Mood States, Physical Well-Being, Job Satisfaction and Absenteeism in Members and Non-Members of British Corporate Health and Fitness Clubs," *Journal of Occupational and Organizational Psychology* 69 (1996), pp. 121–34; L. E. Falkenberg, "Employee Fitness Programs: Their Impact on the Employee and the Organization," *Academy of Management Review* 12 (1987), pp. 511–22; R. J. Shephard, M. Cox, and P. Corey, "Fitness Program Participation: Its Effect on Workers' Performance," *Journal of Occupational Medicine* 23 (1981), pp. 359–63.

80. For a more detailed discussion of stress and wellness in organizations, see K. Danna and R. W. Griffin, "Health and Well-Being in the Workplace: A Review and Synthesis of the Literature," *Journal of Management* 25 (May 1999), pp. 357–84

81. A. S. Sethi, "Meditation for Coping with Organizational Stress," in A. S. Sethi and R. S. Schuler, eds., *Handbook of Organizational Stress Coping Strategies* (Cambridge, MA: Ballinger, 1984), pp. 145–65; M. T. Matteson and J. M. Ivancevich, *Managing Job Stress and Health* (New York: Free Press, 1982), pp. 160–66.

82. J. J. L. van der Klink, R. W. B. Blonk, A. H. Schene, and F. J. H. van Dijk, "The Benefits of Interventions for Work-Related Stress," *American Journal of Public Health* 91 (February 2001), pp. 270–76; T. Rotarius, A. Liberman, and J. S. Liberman, "Employee Assistance Programs: A Prevention and Treatment Prescription for Problems in Health Care Organizations," *Health Care Manager* 19 (September 2000), pp. 24–31.

83. P. D. Bliese and T. W. Britt, "Social Support, Group Consensus, and Stressor–Strain Relationships: Social Context Matters," *Journal of Organizational Behavior* 22 (2001), pp. 425–36; B. N. Uchino, J. T. Cacioppo, and J. K. Kiecolt-Glaser, "The Relationship Between Social Support and Physiological Processes: A Review with Emphasis on Underlying Mechanisms and Implications for Health," *Psychological Bulletin* 119 (May 1996), pp. 488–531; M. R. Manning, C. N. Jackson, and M. R. Fusilier, "Occupational Stress, Social Support, and the Costs of Health Care," *Academy of Management Journal* 39 (June 1996), pp. 738–50.

84. J. S. House, *Work Stress and Social Support* (Reading, MA: Addison-Wesley, 1981); S. Cohen and T. A. Wills, "Stress, Social Support, and the Buffering Hypothesis," *Psychological Bulletin* 98 (1985), pp. 310–57.

85. S. Schachter, *The Psychology of Affiliation* (Stanford, CA: Stanford University Press, 1959).

86. L. Tickner, "Miners Take Health Road," *West Australian*, March 17, 2001, pp. 1, 4.

CHAPTER EIGHT

1. S. Carney, "DaimlerChrysler Launches Product Teams," *Detroit News*, July 13, 2001, p. 1; J. Dixon, "Lean, Mean Is Theme for Chrysler," *Detroit Free Press*, July 12, 2001; E. Garsten, "Chrysler Has New Product Process," *AP Online*, July 12, 2001.

2. R. Kulwiec, "Self-Managed Work Teams—Reality or Fad?" *Material Handling Management—Strategies for Top Management Supplement*, April 2001, pp. 15–22; J. Sung, "Designed for Interaction," *Fortune*, January 8, 2001; S. Kirsner, "Every Day, It's a New Place," *Fast Company*, April–May 1998, pp. 130–34.

3. M. Orton, "Enamoured with Creativity," *Ottawa Citizen* [High Tech Supplement], May 30, 1999.

4. S. G. Cohen and D. E. Bailey, "What Makes Teams Work: Group Effectiveness Research from the Shop Floor to the Executive Suite," *Journal of Management* 23 (May 1997), pp. 239–90; M. A. West, "Preface: Introducing Work Group Psychology," in M. A. West, ed., *Handbook of Work Group Psychology* (Chichester, UK: Wiley, 1996), p. xxvi; S. A. Mohrman, S. G. Cohen, and A. M. Mohrman, Jr., *Designing Team-Based Organizations: New Forms for Knowledge Work* (San Francisco: Jossey-Bass, 1995), pp. 39–40; J. R. Katzenbach and K. D. Smith, "The Discipline of Teams," *Harvard Business Review* 71 (March–April 1993), pp. 111–20; M. E. Shaw, *Group Dynamics*, 3rd ed. (New York: McGraw-Hill, 1981), p. 8.

5. L. R. Offermann and R. K. Spiros, "The Science and Practice of Team Development: Improving the Link," *Academy of Management Journal* 44 (April 2001), pp. 376–92. David Nadler similarly distinguishes *crowds* from *groups* and *teams*. See D. A. Nadler, "From Ritual to Real Work: The Board as a Team," *Directors and Boards* 22 (Summer 1998), pp. 28–31.

6. The preference for using the term *team* rather than *group* is also discussed in Cohen and Bailey, "What Makes Teams Work"; R. A. Guzzo and M. W. Dickson, "Teams in Organizations: Recent Research on Performance and Effectiveness," *Annual Review of Psychology* 47 (1996), pp. 307–38.

7. A. R. Jassawalla and G. H. C. Sashittal, "The Role of Senior Management and Team Leaders in Building Collaborative New Product Teams," *Engineering Management Journal* 13 (June 2001), pp. 33–39.

8. G. E. Huszczo, *Tools for Team Excellence* (Palo Alto, CA: Davies-Black, 1996), pp. 9–15; R. Likert, *New Patterns of Management* (New York: McGraw-Hill, 1961), pp. 106–8.

9. D. E. Yeatts and C. Hyten, *High-Performing Self-Managed Work Teams: A Comparison of Theory and Practice* (Thousand Oaks, CA: Sage, 1998); Mohrman, Cohen, and Mohrman, Jr., *Designing Team-Based Organizations*, p. 6; J. H. Shonk, *Team-Based Organizations: Developing a Successful Team Environment* (Homewood, IL: Business Irwin One, 1992).

10. N. S. Bruning and P. R. Liverpool, "Membership in Quality Circles and Participation in Decision Making," *Journal of Applied Behavioral Science* 29 (March 1993), pp. 76–95.

11. Mohrman, Cohen, and Mohrman, Jr., *Designing Team-Based Organizations*, chap. 2; R. S. Wellins, W. C. Byham, and G. R. Dixon, *Inside Teams* (San Francisco: Jossey-Bass, 1994), pp. 9–10.

12. R. Pascale, M. Millemann, and L. Gioja, *Surfing on the Edge of Chaos* (London: Texere, 2000), pp. 181–95, 223–26; R. Pascale, "Change How You Define Leadership, and You Change How You Run a Company," *Fast Company*, April–May 1998, pp. 110–20.

13. T. Peters, *Thriving on Chaos* (New York: Knopf, 1987), pp. 211–18; T. Kidder, *Soul of a New Machine* (Boston: Little, Brown, 1981); T. Peters and N. Austin, *A Passion for Excellence* (New York: Random House, 1985), chaps. 9 and 10.

14. S. Zesiger, "Dial 'M' For Mystique," *Fortune*, January 12, 1998, p. 175; R. Hertzberg, "No Longer a Skunkworks," *Internet World*, November 3, 1997; R. Lim, "Innovation, Innovation, Innovation," *Business Times (Singapore)*, October 27, 1997, p. 18.

15. J. Kurlantzick, "New Balance Stays a Step Ahead," *U.S. News & World Report*, July 2, 2001, p. 34; A. Bernstein, "Low-Skilled Jobs: Do They Have to Move?" *Business Week*, February 26, 2001, p. 92; G. Gatlin, "Firm Boasts of New Balance of Power," *Boston Herald*, January 24, 2001, p. 27.

16. S. Alexander, "Virtual Teams Going Global," *InfoWorld*, November 13, 2000, pp. 55–56.

17. J. Lipnack and J. Stamps, *Virtual Teams: People Working across Boundaries with Technology* (New York: Wiley, 2001); D. J. Armstrong and P. Cole, "Managing Distances and Differences in Geographically Distributed Work Groups," in S. E. Jackson and M. N. Ruderman, eds., *Diversity in Work Teams: Research Paradigms for a Changing Workplace* (Washington, DC: American Psychological Association, 1995), pp. 187–215.

18. D. Robey, H. M. Khoo, and C. Powers, "Situated Learning in Cross-Functional Virtual Teams," *Technical Communication*, February 2000, pp. 51–66.

19. G. Gilder, *Telecosm: How Infinite Bandwidth Will Revolutionize Our*

World (New York: Free Press, 2001); J. S. Brown, "Seeing Differently: A Role for Pioneering Research," *Research Technology Management* 41 (May–June 1998), pp. 24–33.

20. A. M. Townsend, S. M. DeMarie, and A. R. Hendrickson, "Virtual Teams: Technology and the Workplace of the Future," *Academy of Management Executive* 12 (August 1998), pp. 17–29.

21. J. Pollard, "Anyway, Anyhow, Anywhere," *Observer (London),* September 3, 2000, p. 16.

22. J. A. Wagner III, C. R. Leana, E. A. Locke, and D. M. Schweiger, "Cognitive and Motivational Frameworks in U.S. Research on Participation: A Meta-Analysis of Primary Effects," *Journal of Organizational Behavior* 18 (1997), pp. 49–65.

23. W. B. Stevenson, J. L. Pearce, and L. W. Porter, "The Concept of 'Coalition' in Organization Theory and Research," *Academy of Management Review* 10 (1985), pp. 256–68; Shaw, *Group Dynamics,* pp. 105–10.

24. E. C. Wenger and W. M. Snyder, "Communities of Practice: The Organizational Frontier," *Harvard Business Review* 78 (January–February 2000), pp. 139–45; J. W. Botkin, *Smart Business: How Knowledge Communities Can Revolutionize Your Company* (New York: Free Press, 1999).

25. M. Finlay, "Panning for Gold," *ComputerUser,* July 1, 2001.

26. M. A. Hogg and D. J. Terry, "Social Identity and Self-Categorization Processes in Organizational Contexts," *Academy of Management Review* 25 (January 2000), pp. 121–40; B. E. Ashforth and F. Mael, "Social Identity Theory and the Organization," *Academy of Management Review* 14 (1989), pp. 20–39.

27. A. S. Tannenbaum, *Social Psychology of the Work Organization* (Belmont, CA: Wadsworth, 1966), p. 62; S. Schacter, *The Psychology of Affiliation* (Stanford, CA: Stanford University Press, 1959), pp. 12–19.

28. R. Forrester and A. B. Drexler, "A Model for Team-based Organization Performance," *Academy of Management Executive* 13 (August 1999), pp. 36–49; M. A. West, C. S. Borrill, and K. L. Unsworth, "Team Effectiveness in Organizations," *International Review of Industrial and Organizational Psychology* 13 (1998), pp. 1–48; R. A. Guzzo and M. W. Dickson, "Teams in Organizations: Recent Research on Performance and Effectiveness," *Annual Review of Psychology* 47 (1996), pp. 307–38.

29. West et al., "Team Effectiveness in Organizations"; Mohrman, Cohen, and Mohrman, Jr., *Designing Team-Based Organizations,* pp. 58–65; J. E. McGrath, "Time, Interaction, and Performance (TIP): A Theory of Groups," *Small Group Research* 22 (1991), pp. 147–74; G. P. Shea and R. A. Guzzo, "Group Effectiveness: What Really Matters?" *Sloan Management Review* 27 (1987), pp. 33–46.

30. D. K. Denton, "How a Team Can Grow," *Quality Progress,* June 1999, p. 53.

31. S. Sarin and V. Mahajan, "The Effect of Reward Structures on the Performance of Cross-Functional Product Development Teams," *Journal of Marketing* 65 (April 2001), pp. 35–53; J. S. DeMatteo, L. T. Eby, and E. Sundstrom, "Team-Based Rewards: Current Empirical Evidence and Directions for Future Research," *Research in Organizational Behavior* 20 (1998), pp. 141–83; R. L. Heneman and C. von Hippel, "Balancing Group and Individual Rewards: Rewarding Individual Contributions to the Team," *Compensation and Benefits Review* 27 (July–August 1995), pp. 63–68.

32. P. Bordia, "Face-to-Face versus Computer-Mediated Communication: A Synthesis of the Experimental Literature," *Journal of Business Communication* 34 (January 1997), pp. 99–120; A. D. Shulman, "Putting Group Information Technology in its Place: Communication and Good Work Group Performance," in S. R. Clegg, C. Hardy, and W. R. Nord, eds., *Handbook of Organization Studies* (London: Sage, 1996), pp. 357–74; J. E. McGrath and A. B. Hollingshead, *Groups Interacting with Technology* (Thousand Oaks, CA: Sage, 1994).

33. S. Alexander, "Virtual Teams Going Global," *InfoWorld,* November 13, 2000, pp. 55–56. For further discussion of communication in virtual teams, see W. G. Cascio, "Managing a Virtual Workplace," *Academy of Management Executive,* August 2000, pp. 81–90.

34. J. Hansen, "Wide Open Spaces," *AsiaWeek,* May 25, 2001.

35. R. Wageman, "Case Study: Critical Success Factors for Creating Superb Self-Managing Teams at Xerox," *Compensation and Benefits Review* 29 (September–October 1997), pp. 31–41; D. Dimancescu and K. Dwenger, "Smoothing the Product Development Path," *Management Review* 85 (January 1996), pp. 36–41.

36. E. F. McDonough III, "Investigation of Factors Contributing to the Success of Cross-Functional Teams," *Journal of Product Innovation Management* 17 (May 2000), pp. 221–35; A. Edmondson, "Psychological Safety and Learning Behavior in Work Teams," *Administrative Science Quarterly* 44 (1999), pp. 350–83; D. G. Ancona and D. E. Caldwell, "Demography and Design: Predictors of New Product Team Performance," *Organization Science* 3 (August 1992), pp. 331–41.

37. M. A. Campion, E. M. Papper, and G. J. Medsker, "Relations between Work Team Characteristics and Effectiveness: A Replication and Extension," *Personnel Psychology* 49 (1996), pp. 429–52; S. Worchel and S. L. Shackelford, "Groups Under Stress: The Influence of Group Structure and Environment on Process and Performance," *Personality and Social Psychology Bulletin* 17 (1991), pp. 640–47; E. Sundstrom, K. P. De Meuse, and D. Futrell, "Work Teams: Applications and Effectiveness," *American Psychologist* 45 (1990), pp. 120–33.

38. G. van der Vegt, B. Emans, and E. van de Vliert, "Motivating Effects of Task and Outcome Interdependence in Work Teams," *Group and Organization Management* 23 (June 1998), pp. 124–43; R. C. Liden, S. J. Wayne, and L. K. Bradway, "Task Interdependence as a Moderator of the Relation between Group Control and Performance," *Human Relations* 50 (1997), pp. 169–81; R. Wageman, "Interdependence and Group Effectiveness," *Administrative Science Quarterly* 40 (1995), pp. 145–80; M. A. Campion, G. J. Medsker, and A. C. Higgs, "Relations between Work Group Characteristics and Effectiveness: Implications for Designing Effective Work Groups," *Personnel Psychology* 46 (1993), pp. 823–50; M. N. Kiggundu, "Task Interdependence and the Theory

of Job Design," *Academy of Management Review* 6 (1981), pp. 499–508.

39. A. Muoio, "Growing Smart," *Fast Company* 16 (August 1998); A. R. Sorkin, "Gospel According to St. Luke's," *New York Times*, February 12, 1998, p. D1.

40. G. R. Hickman and A. Creighton-Zollar, "Diverse Self-Directed Work Teams: Developing Strategic Initiatives for 21st-Century Organizations," *Public Personnel Management* 27 (Spring 1998), pp. 187–200; J. R. Katzenbach and D. K. Smith, *The Wisdom of Teams: Creating the High-Performance Organization* (Boston: Harvard University Press, 1993), pp. 45–47; G. Stasser, "Pooling of Unshared Information during Group Discussion," in S. Worchel, W. Wood, and J. A. Simpson, eds., *Group Process and Productivity* (Newbury Park, CA: Sage, 1992), pp. 48–67.

41. T. Willmert, "Smart Workplace Design Should Bring People, and Their Ideas, Together," *Minneapolis Star Tribune*, January 28, 2001, p. D11.

42. D. Huynh, "Central Market Caters to Hungry Shoppers on the Run," *Houston Chronicle*, June 1, 2001, p. 2; "Creative Hiring Replaces Yesterday's Staid Interview," *Houston Business Journal*, March 9, 2001, p. 35.

43. L. T. Eby and G. H. Dobbins, "Collectivist Orientation in Teams: An Individual and Group-Level Analysis," *Journal of Organizational Behavior* 18 (1997), pp. 275–95; P. C. Earley, "East Meets West Meets Mideast: Further Explorations of Collectivistic and Individualistic Work Groups," *Academy of Management Journal* 36 (1993), pp. 319–48.

44. Mohrman, Cohen, and Mohrman, Jr., *Designing Team-Based Organizations*, pp. 248–54; M. J. Stevens and M. A. Campion, "The Knowledge, Skill and Ability Requirements for Teamwork: Implications for Human Resources Management," *Journal of Management* 20 (1994), pp. 503–30; A. P. Hare, *Handbook of Small Group Research*, 2nd ed. (New York: Free Press, 1976), pp. 12–15.

45. B. Buzaglo and S. Wheelan, "Facilitating Work Team Effectiveness: Case Studies from Central America," *Small Group Research* 30 (1999), pp. 108–29; B. Schultz, "Improving Group Communication Performance: An Overview of Diagnosis and Intervention," in L. Frey, D. Gouran, and M. Poole, eds., *Handbook of Group Communication Theory and Research* (Thousand Oaks, CA: Sage, 1999), pp. 371–94.

46. "New Anchor Hocking Plant Incorporates 'Socio-Tech' Work Environment Philosophy," *Business Wire*, October 19, 1995. For a comprehensive discussion of selecting people for team-based work, see R. J. Klimoski and L. B. Zukin, "Selection and Staffing for Team Effectiveness," in E. Sundstrom and Associates, eds., *Supporting Work Team Effectiveness* (San Francisco: Jossey-Bass, 1998), pp. 63–91.

47. D. C. Hambrick, S. C. Davison, S. A. Snell, and C. C. Snow, "When Groups Consist of Multiple Nationalities: Towards a New Understanding of the Implications," *Organization Studies* 19 (1998), pp. 181–205; F. J. Milliken and L. L. Martins, "Searching for Common Threads: Understanding the Multiple Effects of Diversity in Organizational Groups," *Academy of Management Review* 21 (1996), pp. 402–33; J. K. Murnighan and D. Conlon, "The Dynamics of Intense Work Groups: A Study of British String Quartets," *Administrative Science Quarterly* 36 (1991), pp. 165–86.

48. P. C. Earley and E. Mosakowski, "Creating Hybrid Team Cultures: An Empirical Test of Transnational Team Functioning," *Academy of Management Journal* 43 (February 2000), pp. 26–49; D. C. Lau and J. K. Murnighan, "Demographic Diversity and Faultlines: The Compositional Dynamics of Organizational Groups," *Academy of Management Review* 23 (April 1998), pp. 325–40.

49. L. H. Pelled, K. M. Eisenhardt, and K. R. Xin, "Exploring the Black Box: An Analysis of Work Group Diversity, Conflict, and Performance," *Administrative Science Quarterly* 44 (March 1999), pp. 1–28; K. Y. Williams and C. A. O'Reilly III, "Demography and Diversity in Organizations: A Review of 40 Years of Research," *Research in Organizational Behavior* 20 (1998), pp. 70–140; B. Daily, A. Wheatley, S. R. Ash, and R. L. Steiner, "The Effects of a Group Decision Support System on Culturally Diverse and Culturally Homogeneous Group Decision Making," *Information and Management* 30 (1996), pp. 281–89; W. E. Watson, K. Kumar, and L. K. Michaelson, "Cultural Diversity's Impact on Interaction Process and Performance: Comparing Homogeneous and Diverse Task Groups," *Academy of Management Journal* 36 (1993), pp. 590–602.

50. L. Tucci, "Owens Drake Consulting Fosters Systematic Change," *St. Louis Business Journal*, May 25, 1998.

51. B. W. Tuckman and M. A. C. Jensen, "Stages of Small-Group Development Revisited," *Group and Organization Studies* 2 (1977), pp. 419–42. For a humorous and somewhat cynical discussion of team dynamics through these stages, see H. Robbins and M. Finley, *Why Teams Don't Work* (Princeton, NJ: Peterson's/Pacesetters, 1995), chap. 21.

52. J. E. Mathieu and G. F. Goodwin, "The Influence of Shared Mental Models on Team Process and Performance," *Journal of Applied Psychology* 85 (April 2000), pp. 273–84; J. A. Cannon-Bowers, S. I. Tannenbaum, E. Salas, and C. E. Volpe, "Defining Competencies and Establishing Team Training Requirements," in Guzzo, Salas, and Associates, eds., *Team Effectiveness and Decision Making in Organizations* (San Francisco: Jossey-Bass, 1995), pp. 333–80.

53. A. Edmondson, "Psychological Safety and Learning Behavior in Work Teams," *Administrative Science Quarterly* 44 (1999), pp. 350–83.

54. D. L. Miller, "Synergy in Group Development: A Perspective on Group Performance," *Proceedings of the Annual ASAC Conference, Organizational Behavior Division* 17, pt. 5 (1996), pp. 119–28; S. Worchel, D. Coutant-Sassic, and M. Grossman, "A Developmental Approach to Group Dynamics: A Model and Illustrative Research," in Worchel et al., eds., *Group Process and Productivity*, pp. 181–202; C. J. G. Gersick, "Time and Transition in Work Teams: Toward a New Model of Group Development," *Academy of Management Journal* 31 (1988), pp. 9–41.

55. D. C. Feldman, "The Development and Enforcement of Group Norms," *Academy of Management Review* 9 (1984), pp. 47–53; L. W. Porter, E. E.

Lawler III, and J. R. Hackman, *Behavior in Organizations* (New York: McGraw-Hill, 1975), pp. 391–94.

56. I. R. Gellatly, "Individual and Group Determinants of Employee Absenteeism: Test of a Causal Model," *Journal of Organizational Behavior* 16 (1995), pp. 469–85; G. Johns, "Absenteeism Estimates by Employees and Managers: Divergent Perspectives and Self-Serving Perceptions," *Journal of Applied Psychology* 79 (1994), pp. 229–39.

57. "Employees Terrorized by Peer Pressure in the Workplace," Morgan & Banks news release, September 2000. See also B. Latané, "The Psychology of Social Impact," *American Psychologist* 36 (1981), pp. 343–56; C. A. Kiesler and S. B. Kiesler, *Conformity* (Reading, MA: Addison-Wesley, 1970).

58. Porter, Lawler, and Hackman, *Behavior in Organizations*, pp. 399–401.

59. Feldman, "The Development and Enforcement of Group Norms," pp. 50–52.

60. Katzenbach and Smith, *The Wisdom of Teams*, pp. 121–23.

61. K. L. Bettenhausen and J. K. Murnighan, "The Development of an Intragroup Norm and the Effects of Interpersonal and Structural Challenges," *Administrative Science Quarterly* 36 (1991), pp. 20–35.

62. R. S. Spich and K. Keleman, "Explicit Norm Structuring Process: A Strategy for Increasing Task-Group Effectiveness," *Group and Organization Studies* 10 (March 1985), pp. 37–59.

63. L. Y. Chan and B. E. Lynn, "Operating in Turbulent Times: How Ontario's Hospitals Are Meeting the Current Funding Crisis," *Health Care Management Review* 23 (June 1998), p. 7.

64. D. I. Levine, "Piece Rates, Output Restriction, and Conformism," *Journal of Economic Psychology* 13 (1992), pp. 473–89.

65. L. Coch and J. R. P. French, Jr., "Overcoming Resistance to Change," *Human Relations* 1 (1948), pp. 512–32.

66. D. Katz and R. L. Kahn, *The Social Psychology of Organizations* (New York: Wiley, 1966), chap. 7; J. W. Thibault and H. H. Kelley, *The Social Psychology of Groups* (New York: Wiley, 1959), chap. 8.

67. D. Vinokur-Kaplan, "Treatment Teams That Work (and Those That Don't): An Application of Hackman's Group Effectiveness Model to Interdisciplinary Teams in Psychiatric Hospitals," *Journal of Applied Behavioral Science* 31 (1995), pp. 303–27; Shaw, *Group Dynamics*, pp. 213–26; D. S. Goodman, E. Ravin, and M. Schminke, "Understanding Groups in Organizations," *Research in Organizational Behavior* 9 (1987), pp. 144–46.

68. S. Lembke and M. G. Wilson, "Putting the 'Team' into Teamwork: Alternative Theoretical Contributions for Contemporary Management Practice," *Human Relations* 51 (July 1998), pp. 927–44; B. E. Ashforth and R. H. Humphrey, "Emotion in the Workplace: A Reappraisal," *Human Relations* 48 (1995), pp. 97–125; P. R. Bernthal and C. A. Insko, "Cohesiveness without Groupthink: The Interactive Effects of Social and Task Cohesiveness," *Group and Organization Management* 18 (1993), pp. 66–87.

69. A. Lott and B. Lott, "Group Cohesiveness as Interpersonal Attraction: A Review of Relationships with Antecedent and Consequent Variables," *Psychological Bulletin* 64 (1965), pp. 259–309.

70. S. E. Jackson, "Team Composition in Organizational Settings: Issues in Managing an Increasingly Diverse Work Force," in Worchel et al., eds., *Group Process and Productivity*, pp. 138–73; J. Virk, P. Aggarwal, and R. N. Bhan, "Similarity versus Complementarity in Clique Formation," *Journal of Social Psychology* 120 (1983), pp. 27–34.

71. M. B. Pinto, J. K. Pinto, and J. E. Prescott, "Antecedents and Consequences of Project Team Cross-Functional Cooperation," *Management Science* 39 (1993), pp. 1281–96; W. Piper, M. Marrache, R. Lacroix, A. Richardson, and B. Jones, "Cohesion as a Basic Bond in Groups," *Human Relations* 36 (1983), pp. 93–108.

72. M. Frase-Blunt, "The Cubicles Have Ears. Maybe They Need Earplugs," *Washington Post*, March 6, 2001, p. HE7.

73. F. G. Mangrum, M. S. Fairley, and D. L. Wieder, "Informal Problem Solving in the Technology-Mediated Work Place," *Journal of Business Communication* 38 (July 2001), pp. 315–36;

Robey et al., "Situated Learning in Cross-Functional Virtual Teams"; E. J. Hill, B. C. Miller, S. P. Weiner, and J. Colihan, "Influences of the Virtual Office on Aspects of Work and Work/Life Balance," *Personnel Psychology* 51 (Autumn 1998), pp. 667–83; S. B. Gould, K. J. Weiner, and B. R. Levin, *Free Agents: People and Organizations Creating a New Working Community* (San Francisco: Jossey-Bass, 1997), pp. 158–60.

74. J. Zbar, "Home Base," *Network World Fusion,* March 12, 2001.

75. J. E. Hautaluoma and R. S. Enge, "Early Socialization into a Work Group: Severity of Initiations Revisited," *Journal of Social Behavior and Personality* 6 (1991) pp. 725–48; E. Aronson and J. Mills, "The Effects of Severity of Initiation on Liking for a Group," *Journal of Abnormal and Social Psychology* 59 (1959), pp. 177–81.

76. B. Mullen and C. Copper, "The Relation between Group Cohesiveness and Performance: An Integration," *Psychological Bulletin* 115 (1994), pp. 210–27; Shaw, *Group Dynamics*, p. 215.

77. M. Rempel and R. J. Fisher, "Perceived Threat, Cohesion, and Group Problem Solving in Intergroup Conflict," *International Journal of Conflict Management* 8 (1997), pp. 216–34.

78. J. M. McPherson and P. A. Popielarz, "Social Networks and Organizational Dynamics," *American Sociological Review* 57 (1992), pp. 153–70; Piper et al., "Cohesion as a Basic Bond in Groups," pp. 93–108.

79. C. A. O'Reilly III, D. F. Caldwell, and W. P. Barnett, "Work Group Demography, Social Integration, and Turnover," *Administrative Science Quarterly* 34 (1989), pp. 21–37.

80. R. D. Banker, J. M. Field, R. G. Schroeder, and K. K. Sinha, "Impact of Work Teams on Manufacturing Performance: A Longitudinal Study," *Academy of Management Journal* 39 (1996), pp. 867–90; Vinokur-Kaplan, "Treatment Teams That Work (and Those That Don't)"; Mullen and Copper, "The Relation between Group Cohesiveness and Performance"; C. R. Evans and K. L. Dion, "Group Cohesion and Performance: A Meta-Analysis," *Small Group Research,* 22 (1991), pp. 175–86.

81. C. Langfred, "Is Group Cohesiveness a Double-Edged Sword? An Investigation of the Effects of Cohesiveness on Performance," *Small Group Research* 29 (1998), pp. 124–43.

82. Robbins and Finley, *Why Teams Don't Work*, chap. 20; "The Trouble with Teams," *Economist*, January 14, 1995, p. 61; A. Sinclair, "The Tyranny of Team Ideology," *Organization Studies* 13 (1992), pp. 611–26. For discussion of the benefits of teams, see J. Pfeffer, "Seven Practices of Successful Organizations," *California Management Review* 40 (1998), pp. 96–124.

83. P. Panchak, "The Future Manufacturing," *Industry Week* 247 (September 21, 1998), pp. 96–105; B. Dumaine, "The Trouble with Teams," *Fortune*, September 5, 1994, pp. 86–92.

84. J. Pappone, "Sometimes Life's Truly a Beach . . . ," *Ottawa Citizen*, February 3, 2000.

85. I. D. Steiner, *Group Process and Productivity*, (New York: Academic Press, 1972).

86. D. Dunphy and B. Bryant, "Teams: Panaceas or Prescriptions for Improved Performance?" *Human Relations* 49 (1996), pp. 677–99. For discussion of Brooke's Law, see M. A. Cusumano, "How Microsoft Makes Large Teams Work Like Small Teams," *Sloan Management Review* 39 (Fall 1997), pp. 9–20.

87. R. Cross, "Looking before You Leap: Assessing the Jump to Teams in Knowledge-Based Work," *Business Horizons*, September 2000.

88. M. Erez and A. Somech, "Is Group Productivity Loss the Rule or the Exception? Effects of Culture and Group-Based Motivation," *Academy of Management Journal* 39 (1996), pp. 1513–37; S. J. Karau and K. D. Williams, "Social Loafing: A Meta-Analytic Review and Theoretical Integration," *Journal of Personality and Social Psychology* 65 (1993), pp. 681–706; J. M. George, "Extrinsic and Intrinsic Origins of Perceived Social Loafing in Organizations," *Academy of Management Journal* 35 (1992), pp. 191–202; R. Albanese and D. D. Van Fleet, "Rational Behavior in Groups: The Free- Riding Tendency," *Academy of Management Review* 10 (1985), pp. 244–55.

89. Erez and Somech, "Is Group Productivity Loss the Rule or the Exception?"; P. C. Earley, "Social Loafing and Collectivism: A Comparison of the U.S. and the People's Republic of China," *Administrative Science Quarterly* 34 (1989), pp. 565–81.

90. T. A. Judge and T. D. Chandler, "Individual-Level Determinants of Employee Shirking," *Relations Industrielles* 51 (1996), pp. 468–86; J. M. George, "Asymmetrical Effects of Rewards and Punishments: The Case of Social Loafing," *Journal of Occupational and Organizational Psychology* 68 (1995), pp. 327–38; R. E. Kidwell and N. Bennett, "Employee Propensity to Withhold Effort: A Conceptual Model to Intersect Three Avenues of Research," *Academy of Management Review* 19 (1993), pp. 429–56; J. A. Shepperd, "Productivity Loss in Performance Groups: A Motivation Analysis," *Psychological Bulletin* 113 (1993), pp. 67–81.

91. W. G. Dyer, *Team Building: Issues and Alternatives*, 2nd ed. (Reading, MA: Addison-Wesley, 1987); S. J. Liebowitz and K. P. De Meuse, "The Application of Team Building," *Human Relations* 35 (1982), pp. 1–18.

92. Sundstrom et al., "Work Teams," p. 128; M. Beer, *Organizational Change and Development: A Systems View* (Santa Monica, CA: Goodyear, 1980), pp. 143–46.

93. Beer, *Organizational Change and Development*, p. 145.

94. G. Coetzer, *A Study of the Impact of Different Team Building Techniques on Work Team Effectiveness*, Unpublished MBA research project, Simon Fraser University, Burnaby, British Columbia, 1993.

95. T. G. Cummings and C. G. Worley, *Organization Development and Change*, 6th ed. (Cincinnati: South-Western, 1997), pp. 218–19; P. F. Buller and C. H. Bell, Jr., "Effects of Team Building and Goal Setting on Productivity: A Field Experiment," *Academy of Management Journal* 29 (1986), pp. 305–28.

96. C. J. Solomon, "Simulation Training Builds Teams through Experience," *Personnel Journal* 72 (June 1993), pp. 100–1.

97. D. Goh, "Firms Strike Out for Adventure Learning," *Sunday Times (Singapore)*, April 8, 2001, pp. 7, 29.

98. M. J. Brown, "Let's Talk About It, Really Talk About It," *Journal for Quality and Participation* 19, no. 6 (1996), pp. 26–33; E. H. Schein, "On Dialogue, Culture, and Organizational Learning," *Organizational Dynamics*, Autumn 1993, pp. 40–51; P. M. Senge, *The Fifth Discipline* (New York: Doubleday Currency, 1990), pp. 238–49.

99. B. Oaff, "Team Games Take Turn for the Verse," *Mail on Sunday (UK)*, January 28, 2001, p. 56; K. Cross, "Adventure Capital," *Business 2.0*, July 11, 2000; C. Prystay, "Executive Rearmament: Tempering Asia's Executive Mettle," *Asian Business*, October 1996.

100. R. W. Woodman and J. J. Sherwood, "The Role of Team Development in Organizational Effectiveness: A Critical Review," *Psychological Bulletin* 88 (1980), pp. 166–86; Sundstrom et al., "Work Teams," p. 128.

101. Robbins and Finley, *Why Teams Don't Work*, chap. 17.

102. P. McGraw, "Back from the Mountain: Outdoor Management Development Programs and How to Ensure the Transfer of Skills to the Workplace," *Asia Pacific Journal of Human Resources* 31 (Spring 1993), pp. 52–61; G. E. Huszczo, "Training for Team Building," *Training and Development Journal* 44 (February 1990), pp. 37–43.

CHAPTER NINE

1. R. Beck, "Jet Blue Takes Wing on Low Rates, Hip Jets," *Baton Rouge (LA) Advocate*, August 7, 2001; S. B. Donnelly, "Is JetBlue the Next Great Airline—Or Just a Little Too Good to Be True?" *Time*, July 30, 2001, p. 24; R. Mowbray, "Blue Skies Ahead," *Times-Picayune (New Orleans)*, July 27, 2001, p. 1.

2. F. A. Shull, Jr., A. L. Delbecq, and L. L. Cummings, *Organizational Decision Making* (New York: McGraw-Hill, 1970), p. 31. See also J. G. March, "Understanding How Decisions Happen in Organizations," in Z. Shapira, ed., *Organizational Decision Making* (New York: Cambridge University Press, 1997), pp. 9–32.

3. B. M. Bass, *Organizational Decision Making* (Homewood, IL: Irwin, 1983), chap. 3; W. F. Pounds, "The Process of Problem Finding," *Industrial Management Review* 11 (Fall 1969), pp. 1–19; C. Kepner and B. Tregoe, *The Rational*

Manager (New York: McGraw-Hill, 1965).

4. This model is adapted from several sources: H. Mintzberg, D. Raisinghani, and A. Théorét, "The Structure of 'Unstructured' Decision Processes," *Administrative Science Quarterly* 21 (1976), pp. 246–75; H. A. Simon, *The New Science of Management Decision* (New York: Harper & Row, 1960); C. Kepner and B. Tregoe, *The Rational Manager* (New York: McGraw-Hill, 1965); W. C. Wedley and R. H. G. Field, "A Predecision Support System," *Academy of Management Review* 9 (1984), pp. 696–703.

5. J. W. Dean, Jr., and M. P. Sharfman, "Does Decision Process Matter? A Study of Strategic Decision-Making Effectiveness," *Academy of Management Journal* 39 (1996), pp. 368–96.

6. P. F. Drucker, *The Practice of Management* (New York: Harper & Brothers, 1954), pp. 353–57.

7. Wedley and Field, "A Predecision Support System," p. 696; Drucker, *The Practice of Management*, p. 357; L. R. Beach and T. R. Mitchell, "A Contingency Model for the Selection of Decision Strategies," *Academy of Management Review* 3 (1978), pp. 439–49.

8. I. L. Janis, *Crucial Decisions* (New York: Free Press, 1989), pp. 35–37; Simon, *The New Science of Management Decision*, pp. 5–6.

9. I. Nonaka and H. Takeuchi, *The Knowledge-Creating Company* (New York: Oxford University Press, 1995), p. 69.

10. Mintzberg, Raisinghani, and Théorét, "The Structure of 'Unstructured' Decision Processes," pp. 255–56.

11. B. Fischhoff and S. Johnson, "The Possibility of Distributed Decision Making," in Shapira, ed., *Organizational Decision Making*, pp. 216–37.

12. J. E. Dutton, "Strategic Agenda Building in Organizations," in Shapira, ed., *Organizational Decision Making*, pp. 81–107; M. Lyles and H. Thomas, "Strategic Problem Formulation: Biases and Assumptions Embedded in Alternative Decision-Making Models," *Journal of Management Studies* 25 (1988), pp. 131–45; I. I. Mitroff, "On Systematic Problem Solving and the Error of the Third Kind," *Behavioral Science* 9 (1974), pp. 383–93.

13. D. Gurteen, "Knowledge, Creativity and Innovation," *Journal of Knowledge Management* 2 (September 1998), pp. 5–13; P. M. Senge, *The Fifth Discipline: The Art and Practice of the Learning Organization* (New York: Doubleday Currency, 1990), chap. 10.

14. D. Domer, *The Logic of Failure* (Reading, MA: Addison-Wesley, 1996); M. Basadur, "Managing the Creative Process in Organizations," in M. A. Runco, ed., *Problem Finding, Problem Solving, and Creativity* (Norwood, NJ: Ablex, 1994), pp. 237–68.

15. P. C. Nutt, "Preventing Decision Debacles," *Technological Forecasting and Social Change* 38 (1990), pp. 159–74.

16. J. A. Byrne, *Chainsaw* (New York: HarperCollins, 1999).

17. P. C. Nutt, *Making Tough Decisions* (San Francisco: Jossey-Bass, 1989).

18. J. Conlisk, "Why Bounded Rationality?" *Journal of Economic Literature* 34 (1996), pp. 669–700; B. L. Lipman, "Information Processing and Bounded Rationality: A Survey," *Canadian Journal of Economics* 28 (1995), pp. 42–67.

19. L. T. Pinfield, "A Field Evaluation of Perspectives on Organizational Decision Making," *Administrative Science Quarterly* 31 (1986), pp. 365–88. The recent survey, conducted by Kepner-Tregoe, is described in D. Sandahl and C. Hewes, "Decision Making at Digital Speed," *Pharmaceutical Executive* 21 (August 2001), p. 62.

20. H. A. Simon, *Administrative Behavior*, 2nd ed. (New York: Free Press, 1957), pp. xxv, 80–84; and J. G. March and H. A. Simon, *Organizations* (New York: Wiley, 1958), pp. 140–41.

21. P. O. Soelberg, "Unprogrammed Decision Making," *Industrial Management Review* 8 (1967), pp. 19–29; H. A. Simon, "A Behavioral Model of Rational Choice," *Quarterly Journal of Economics* 69 (1955), pp. 99–118.

22. J. E. Russo, V. H. Medvec, and M. G. Meloy, "The Distortion of Information during Decisions," *Organizational Behavior and Human Decision Processes*, 66 (1996), pp. 102–10.

23. H. A. Simon, *Models of Man: Social and Rational* (New York: Wiley, 1957), p. 253.

24. Y. Ganzach, A. H. Kluger, and N. Klayman, "Making Decisions from an Interview: Expert Measurement and Mechanical Combination," *Personnel Psychology* 53 (Spring 2000), pp. 1–20.

25. J. Gregoire, "Leading the Charge for Change," *CIO*, June 1, 2001.

26. A. Rangaswamy and G. L. Lilien, "Software Tools for New Product Development," *Journal of Marketing Research* 34 (1997), pp. 177–84.

27. G. H. Anthes, "Learning How to Share," *Computerworld* 32 (February 23, 1998), pp. 75–77.

28. P. Goodwin and G. Wright, "Enhancing Strategy Evaluation in Scenario Planning: A Role for Decision Analysis," *Journal of Management Studies* 38 (January 2001), pp. 1–16; R. Rosen, P. Digh, M. Singer, and C. Phillips, *Global Literacies* (New York: Simon & Schuster, 2000), pp. 269–70; C. Pratt, "Planning Noranda's Future," *Research Technology Management* 42 (January–February 1999), pp. 15–18; P. J. H. Schoemaker, "Disciplined Imagination: From Scenarios to Strategic Options," *International Studies of Management and Organization* 27 (Summer 1997), pp. 43–70; K. Van Der Heijden, *Scenarios: The Art of Strategic Conversation* (New York: Wiley, 1996).

29. This incident is described in B. Breen, "What's Your Intuition?" *Fast Company* 38 (September 2000), p. 290.

30. L. A. Burke and M. K. Miller, "Taking the Mystery out of Intuitive Decision Making," *Academy of Management Executive* 13 (November 1999), pp. 91–99.

31. O. Behling and N. L. Eckel, "Making Sense out of Intuition," *Academy of Management Executive* 5 (February 1991), pp. 46–54; Nutt, *Making Tough Decisions*, p. 54; H. A. Simon, "Making Management Decisions: The Role of Intuition and Emotion," *Academy of Management Executive* (February 1987), pp. 57–64; W. H. Agor, "The Logic of Intuition," *Organizational Dynamics* (Winter 1986), pp. 5–18.

32. N. Khatri, "The Role of Intuition in Strategic Decision Making," *Human Relations* 53 (January 2000), pp. 57–86; Burke and Miller, "Taking the Mystery out of Intuitive Decision Making."

33. E. N. Brockmann and W. P. Anthony, "The Influence of Tacit

Knowledge and Collective Mind on Strategic Planning," *Journal of Managerial Issues* 10 (Summer 1998), pp. 204–22; D. Leonard and S. Sensiper, "The Role of Tacit Knowledge in Group Innovation," *California Management Review* 40 (Spring 1998), pp. 112–32. For a discussion of the problems with intuition in business start-ups, see L. Broderick and M. Sponer, "The Death of Gut Instinct," *Inc.* 23 (January 2001), pp. 38–42.

34. A. M. Hayashi, "When to Trust Your Gut," *Harvard Business Review* 79 (February 2001), pp. 59–65; E. Gubbins and B. Quinton, "Serial Entrepreneurs: They're Grrreat!" *Upstart*, January 30, 2001.

35. R. N. Taylor, *Behavioral Decision Making* (Glenview, IL: Scott Foresman, 1984), pp. 163–66.

36. D. R. Bobocel and J. P. Meyer, "Escalating Commitment to a Failing Course of Action: Separating the Role of Choice and Justification," *Journal of Applied Psychology* 79 (1994), pp. 360–63; G. Whyte, "Escalating Commitment in Individual and Group Decision Making: A Prospect Theory Approach," *Organizational Behavior and Human Decision Processes* 54 (1993), pp. 430–55; G. Whyte, "Escalating Commitment to a Course of Action: A Reinterpretation," *Academy of Management Review* 11 (1986), pp. 311–21.

37. M. Keil and R. Montealegre, "Cutting Your Losses: Extricating Your Organization When a Big Project Goes Awry," *Sloan Management Review* 41, Spring 2000, pp. 55–68; M. Fackler, "Tokyo's Newest Subway Line a Saga of Hubris, Humiliation," *Associated Press Newswires*, July 20, 1999; P. Ayton and H. Arkes, "Call It Quits," *New Scientist*, June 20, 1998.

38. F. D. Schoorman and P. J. Holahan, "Psychological Antecedents of Escalation Behavior: Effects of Choice, Responsibility, and Decision Consequences," *Journal of Applied Psychology* 81 (1996), pp. 786–93.

39. S. W. Geiger, C. J. Robertson, and J. G. Irwin, "The Impact of Cultural Values on Escalation of Commitment," *International Journal of Organizational Analysis* 6 (April 1998), pp. 165–76; D. K. Tse, K. Lee, I. Vertinsky, and D. A. Wehrung, "Does Culture Matter? A Cross-Cultural Study of Executives' Choice, Decisiveness, and Risk Adjustment in International Marketing," *Journal of Marketing* 52 (1988), pp. 81–95.

40. M. Keil and D. Robey, "Turning around Troubled Software Projects: An Exploratory Study of the Deescalation of Commitment to Failing Courses of Action," *Journal of Management Information Systems* 15 (Spring 1999), pp. 63–87.

41. B. M. Staw, K. W. Koput, and S. G. Barsade, "Escalation at the Credit Window: A Longitudinal Study of Bank Executives' Recognition and Write-Off of Problem Loans," *Journal of Applied Psychology* 82 (1997), pp. 130–42.

42. W. Boulding, R. Morgan, and R. Staelin, "Pulling the Plug to Stop the New Product Drain," *Journal of Marketing Research* 34 (1997), pp. 164–76; I. Simonson and B. M. Staw, "Deescalation Strategies: A Comparison of Techniques for Reducing Commitment to Losing Courses of Action," *Journal of Applied Psychology* 77 (1992), pp. 419–26.

43. D. Ghosh, "De-Escalation Strategies: Some Experimental Evidence," *Behavioral Research in Accounting* 9 (1997), pp. 88–112.

44. W. A. Randolph, "Re-Thinking Empowerment: Why Is It So Hard to Achieve?" *Organizational Dynamics* 29 (November 2000), pp. 94–107; G. C. McMahon and E. E. Lawler III, "Effects of Union Status on Employee Involvement: Diffusion and Effectiveness," *Research in Organizational Change and Development* 8 (1995), pp. 47–76; V. H. Vroom and A. G. Jago, *The New Leadership: Managing Participation in Organizations* (Englewood Cliffs, NJ: Prentice Hall, 1988), p. 15.

45. B. Broadway, "Good for the Soul—and for the Bottom Line," *Washington Post*, August 19, 2001, p. A1; M. Forseter, "Associates Keep Score at The Container Store," *Chain Store Age* 76 (May 2000), p. 18.

46. R. O. Esler and D. A. Nipp, "Worker Designed Culture Change," *Nursing Economics* 19 (July 2001), pp. 161ff. C. Hymowitz, "How to Keep Innovation Alive," *The Wall Street Journal*, May 23, 2001, p. N1; C. Brenner, "Pride in Ownership Is Byword for Bank's Employees," *News-Sun (Waukegan, IL)*, February 11, 1997, p. A3.

47. A. M. Berg, "Participatory Strategies in Quality Improvement Programs," *Public Productivity & Management Review* 21 (September 1997), pp. 30–43; D. I. Levine, *Reinventing the Workplace* (Washington, DC: Brookings, 1995), chap. 3; E. A. Locke and D. M. Schweiger, "Participation in Decision-Making: One More Look," *Research in Organizational Behavior* 1 (1979), pp. 265–339.

48. V. A. Sun, "Great Plains Software Phils. Inc.: Workplace of the 21st Century," *BusinessWorld (Philippines)*, May 15, 2000, p. 30.

49. J. T. Addison, "Nonunion Representation in Germany," *Journal of Labor Research* 20 (Winter 1999), pp. 73–92; G. Strauss, "Collective Bargaining, Unions, and Participation," in F. Heller, E. Pusic, G. Strauss, and B. Wilpert, eds., *Organizational Participation: Myth and Reality* (New York: Oxford University Press, 1998), pp. 97–143; Levine, *Reinventing the Workplace*, pp. 47–48.

50. L. Zuckerman, "Management: Employee–Ownership Experiment Unravels at United," *New York Times*, March 14, 2001; J. Singer and S. Duvall, "High-Performance Partnering by Self-Managed Teams in Manufacturing," *Engineering Management Journal* 12 (December 2000), pp. 9–15.

51. R. C. Liden and S. Arad, "A Power Perspective of Empowerment and Work Groups: Implications for Human Resources Management Research," *Research in Personnel and Human Resources Management* 14 (1996), pp. 205–51; R. C. Ford and M. D. Fottler, "Empowerment: A Matter of Degree," *Academy of Management Executive* 9 (August 1995), pp. 21–31; R. W. Coye and J. A. Belohlav, "An Exploratory Analysis of Employee Participation," *Group and Organization Management* 20 (1995), pp. 4–17; Vroom and Jago, *The New Leadership*.

52. P. E. Rossler and C. P. Koelling, "The Effect of Gainsharing on Business Performance at a Papermill," *National Productivity Review* 12 (Summer 1993), pp. 365–82; C. R. Gowen, III, "Gainsharing Programs: an Overview of History and Research," *Journal of*

Organizational Behavior Management 11 (2) (1990), pp. 77–99; F. G. Lesieur, ed., *The Scanlon Plan: A Frontier in Labor–Management Cooperation.* (Cambridge, MA: MIT Press, 1958).

53. Open book management at The Container Store, American Brass, and Voyant Technologies is described in C. Hymowitz, "How to Keep Innovation Alive," *The Wall Street Journal*, May 23, 2001, p. N1; M. Forseter, "Associates Keep Score at The Container Store," *Chain Store Age* 76 (May 2000), p. 18; W. Royal, "A Factory's Crash Course in Economics Pays Off," *New York Times*, April 25, 2001, p. 9.

54. J. Case, "Opening the Books," *Harvard Business Review* 75 (March–April 1997), pp. 118–27; T. R. V. Davis, "Open-Book Management: Its Promise and Pitfalls," *Organizational Dynamics*, Winter 1997, pp. 7–20; J. Case, *Open Book Management: The Coming Business Revolution* (New York: Harper Business, 1995).

55. D. E. Yeatts and C. Hyten, *High-Performing Self-Managed Work Teams: A Comparison of Theory and Practice* (Thousand Oaks, CA: Sage, 1998); S. A. Mohrman, S. G. Cohen, and A. M. Mohrman, Jr., *Designing Team-Based Organizations: New Forms for Knowledge Work* (San Francisco: Jossey-Bass, 1995); E. E. Lawler III, *High-Involvement Management* (San Francisco: Jossey-Bass, 1986), chaps. 11 and 12; L. C. Plunkett and R. Fournier, *Participative Management: Implementing Empowerment* (New York: Wiley, 1991).

56. Singer and Duvall, "High-Performance Partnering by Self-Managed Teams in Manufacturing"; D. Fields, "Harley Teams Shoot for Better Bike," *Akron (OH) Beacon Journal*, June 15, 1998; M. Savage, "Harley Irons Out an Innovative Way of Working," *Milwaukee Journal Sentinel*, May 25, 1998, p. 12; L. Ziegler, "Labor's Role at New Harley Plant," National Public Radio, "All Things Considered," February 25, 1998, 8:00 P.M., EST; C. Eberting, "The Harley Mystique Comes to Kansas City," *Kansas City Star*, January 6, 1998, p. A1.

57. E. E. Lawler III, *Organizing for High Performance* (San Francisco: Jossey-Bass, 2001).

58. The SDT attributes discussed here are discussed in Yeatts and Hyten, *High-Performing Self-Managed Work Teams*; B. L. Kirkman and D. L. Shapiro, "The Impact of Cultural Values on Employee Resistance to Teams: Toward a Model of Globalized Self-Managing Work Team Effectiveness," *Academy of Management Review* 22 (July 1997), pp. 730–57; Mohrman et al., *Designing Team-Based Organizations*.

59. L. Rittenhouse, "Dennis W. Bakke—Empowering a Workforce with Principles," *Electricity Journal*, January 1998, pp. 48–59.

60. P. S. Goodman, R. Devadas, and T. L. G. Hughson, "Groups and Productivity: Analyzing the Effectiveness of Self-Managing Teams," in J. P. Campbell, R. J. Campbell, and Associates, eds., *Productivity in Organizations*, (San Francisco: Jossey-Bass, 1988), pp. 295–327.

61. D. Tjosvold, *Teamwork for Customers* (San Francisco: Jossey-Bass, 1993); D. E. Bowen and E. E. Lawler III, "The Empowerment of Service Workers: What, Why, How, and When," *Sloan Management Review*, Spring 1992, pp. 31–39.

62. E. L. Trist, G. W. Higgin, H. Murray, and A. B. Pollock, *Organizational Choice* (London: Tavistock, 1963). The origin of SDTs from sociotechnical systems research is also noted in R. Beckham, "Self-Directed Work Teams: The Wave of the Future?" *Hospital Materiel Management Quarterly* 20 (August 1998), pp. 48–60.

63. The main components of sociotechnical systems are discussed in M. Moldaschl and W. G. Weber, "The 'Three Waves' of Industrial Group Work: Historical Reflections on Current Research on Group Work," *Human Relations* 51 (March 1998), pp. 347–88; W. Niepce and E. Molleman, "Work Design Issues in Lean Production from a Sociotechnical Systems Perspective: Neo-Taylorism or the Next Step in Sociotechnical Design?" *Human Relations* 51 (March 1998), pp. 259–87.

64. E. Ulich and W. G. Weber, "Dimensions, Criteria, and Evaluation of Work Group Autonomy," in M. A. West, ed., *Handbook of Work Group Psychology* (Chichester, UK: Wiley, 1996), pp. 247–82.

65. C. C. Manz and G. L. Stewart, "Attaining Flexible Stability by Integrating Total Quality Management and Socio-Technical Systems Theory," *Organization Science* 8 (1997), pp. 59–70; K. P. Carson and G. L. Stewart, "Job Analysis and the Sociotechnical Approach to Quality: A Critical Examination," *Journal of Quality Management* 1 (1996), pp. 49–65.

66. D. Zell, *Changing by Design: Organizational Innovation at Hewlett-Packard* (Ithaca, NY: ILR Press, 1997); "New Anchor Hocking Plant Incorporates 'Socio-Tech' Work Environment Philosophy," *Business Wire*, October 19, 1995; R. Reese, "Redesigning for Dial Tone: A Socio-Technical Systems Case Study," *Organizational Dynamics* 24 (Autumn 1995), pp. 80+.

67. K. Kane, "L.L. Bean Delivers the Goods," *Fast Company* 10 (August 1997), p. 104.

68. P. S. Adler and R. E. Cole, "Designed for Learning: A Tale of Two Auto Plants," *Sloan Management Review* 34 (Spring 1993), pp. 85–94; O. Hammarström and R. Lansbury, "The Art of Building a Car: The Swedish Experience Re-examined," *New Technology, Work and Employment* 2 (Autumn 1991), pp. 85–90; J. P. Womack, D. T. Jones, and D. Roos, *The Machine That Changed the World* (New York: Macmillan, 1990). For more favorable evaluations of Volvo's plants, see I. Magaziner and M. Patinkin, *The Silent War* (New York: Random House, 1988); P. G. Gyllenhammar, *People at Work* (Reading, MA: Addison-Wesley, 1977).

69. M. Evans, T. Hamilton, L. Surtees, and S. Tuck, "The Road to a Billion," *Globe and Mail*, January 6, 2000; R. Dyck and N. Halpern, "Team-Based Organizations Redesign at Celestica," *Journal for Quality and Participation* 22 (September–October 1999), pp. 36–40.

70. R. Likert, *New Patterns of Management* (New York: McGraw-Hill, 1961); D. McGregor, *The Human Side of Enterprise* (New York: McGraw-Hill, 1960); C. Argyris, *Personality and Organization* (New York: Harper & Row, 1957).

71. J. A. Wagner III, C. R. Leana, E. A. Locke, and D. M. Schweiger, "Cognitive and Motivational Frameworks in U.S. Research on Participation: A Meta-Analysis of Primary Effects," *Journal of Organizational Behavior* 18 (1997), pp. 49–65; G. P. Latham, D. C. Winters, and E. A. Locke, "Cognitive

and Motivational Effects of Participation: A Mediator Study," *Journal of Organizational Behavior* 15 (1994), pp. 49–63; J. L. Cotton, *Employee Involvement: Methods for Improving Performance and Work Attitudes* (Newbury Park, CA: Sage, 1993), chap. 8; S. J. Havlovic, "Quality of Work Life and Human Resource Outcomes," *Industrial Relations*, 1991, pp. 469–79; K. I. Miller and P. R. Monje, "Participation, Satisfaction, and Productivity: A Meta-Analytic Review," *Academy of Management Journal* 29 (1986), pp. 727–53.

72. K. Y. Williams and C. A. O'Reilly III, "Demography and Diversity in Organizations: A Review of 40 Years of Research," *Research in Organizational Behavior* 20 (1998).

73. J. P. Walsh and S-F. Tseng, "The Effects of Job Characteristics on Active Effort at Work," *Work and Occupations* 25 (February 1998), pp. 74–96; K. T. Dirks, L. L. Cummings, and J. L. Pierce, "Psychological Ownership in Organizations: Conditions under Which Individuals Promote and Resist Change," *Research in Organizational Change and Development* 9 (1996), pp. 1–23.

74. C. L. Cooper, B. Dyck, and N. Frohlich, "Improving the Effectiveness of Gainsharing: The Role of Fairness and Participation," *Administrative Science Quarterly* 37 (1992), pp. 471–90.

75. J. P. Guthrie, "High-Involvement Work Practices, Turnover, and Productivity: Evidence from New Zealand," *Academy of Management Journal* 44 (February 2001), pp. 180–90. See also R. Hodson, *Working with Dignity* (Cambridge, UK: Cambridge University Press, 2000); D. J. Glew, A. M. O'Leary-Kelly, R. W. Griffin, and D. D. Van Fleet, "Participation in Organizations: A Preview of the Issues and Proposed Framework for Future Analysis," *Journal of Management* 21 (1995), pp. 395–421. The limits of employee involvement for improving employee satisfaction are discussed in J. A. Wagner III, C. R. Leana, E. A. Locke, and D. Schweiger, "Cognitive and Motivational Frameworks in U.S. Research on Participation: A Meta-Analysis of Primary Effects," *Journal of Organizational Behavior*, 1997, pp. 49–65.

76. Vroom and Jago, *The New Leadership*, pp. 151–52.

77. Vroom and Jago, *The New Leadership*.

78. C. Robert and T. M. Probst, "Empowerment and Continuous Improvement in the United States, Mexico, Poland, and India," *Journal of Applied Psychology* 85 (October 2000), pp. 643–58; B. L. Kirkman and D. L. Shapiro, "The Impact of Cultural Values on Employee Resistance to Teams: Toward a Model of Globalized Self-Managing Work Team Effectiveness," *Academy of Management Review* 22 (July 1997), pp. 730–57; C. Pavett and T. Morris, "Management Styles within a Multinational Corporation: A Five Country Comparative Study," *Human Relations* 48 (1995) pp. 1171–91; M. Erez and P. C. Earley, *Culture, Self-Identity, and Work* (New York: Oxford University Press, 1993), pp. 104–12.

79. X. Chen and W. Barshes, "To Team or Not to Team?" *China Business Review* 27 (March–April 2000), pp. 30–34; C. E. Nicholls, H. W. Lane, and M. B. Brechu, "Taking Self-Managed Teams to Mexico," *Academy of Management Executive* 13 (August 1999), pp. 15–25.

80. "The Changing Workplace," *Business Line (The Hindu)*, February 24, 2001.

81. H. Hamid, "Tien Wah's Flexi-Wage a Success," *Business Times (Malaysia)*, December 7, 2000.

82. This quotation is found at www.quoteland.com

83. J. D. Orsburn and L. Moran, *The New Self-Directed Work Teams: Mastering the Challenge* (New York: McGraw-Hill, 2000), chap. 11; C. C. Manz, D. E. Keating, and A. Donnellon, "Preparing for an Organizational Change to Employee Self-Management: The Managerial Transition," *Organizational Dynamics* 19 (Autumn 1990), pp. 15–26.

84. D. Gerwin, "Team Empowerment in New Product Development," *Business Horizons*, July 1999, p. 29.

85. G. T. Fairhurst, S. Green, and J. Courtright, "Inertial Forces and the Implementation of a Socio-Technical Systems Approach: A Communication Study," *Organization Science* 6 (1995), pp. 168–85; Manz et al., "Preparing for an Organizational Change to Employee Self-Management," pp. 23–25.

86. J. Jusko, "Always Lessons to Learn," *Industry Week*, February 15, 1999,

pp. 23–30. Another manager made a similar comment in R. Cross, "Looking before You Leap: Assessing the Jump to Teams in Knowledge-Based Work," *Business Horizons*, September 2000.

87. M. Fenton-O'Creevy, "Employee Involvement and the Middle Manager: Saboteur or Scapegoat?" *Human Resource Management Journal* 11 (2001), pp. 24–40.

88. R. Yonatan and H. Lam, "Union Responses to Quality Improvement Initiatives: Factors Shaping Support and Resistance," *Journal of Labor Research* 20 (Winter 1999), pp. 111–31; Levine, *Reinventing the Workplace*, pp. 66–69; I. Goll and N. B. Johnson, "The Influence of Environmental Pressures, Diversification Strategy, and Union/Nonunion Setting on Employee Participation," *Employee Responsibilities and Rights Journal* 10 (1997), pp. 141–54; R. Hodson, "Dignity in the Workplace under Participative Management: Alienation and Freedom Revisited," *American Sociological Review* 61 (1996), pp. 719–38.

89. E. C. Rosenthal, "Sociotechnical Systems and Unions: Nicety or Necessity," *Human Relations* 50 (May 1997), pp. 585–604; R. E. Allen and K. L. Van Norman, "Employee Involvement Programs: The Noninvolvement of Unions Revisited," *Journal of Labor Research* 17 (Summer 1996), pp. 479–95; B. Gilbert, "The Impact of Union Involvement on the Design and Introduction of Quality of Working Life," *Human Relations* 42 (1989), pp. 1057–78; T. A. Kochan, H. C. Katz, and R. B. McKersie, *The Transformation of American Industrial Relations* (New York: Basic Books, 1986), pp. 238–45.

CHAPTER TEN

1. T. Kelley, *The Art of Innovation* (New York: Doubleday Currency, 2001); B. Roberts, "Innovation Quotient," *Electronic Business*, December 2000, p. 96; A. Hargadon and R. I. Sutton, "Building an Innovation Factory," *Harvard Business Review* 78 (May–June 2000), pp. 157–66; R. Garner, "Innovation for Fun and Profit," *Upside Magazine*, March 2000; P. Sinton, "Teamwork the Name of the Game for IDEO," *San Francisco Chronicle*, February 23, 2000; E. Brown, "A Day at Innovation U.," *Fortune*, April 12, 1999,

pp. 163–65; R. I. Sutton and A. Hargadon, "Brainstorming Groups in Context: Effectiveness in a Product Design Firm," *Administrative Science Quarterly* 41 (December 1996), pp. 685–718.

2. D. Gurteen, "Knowledge, Creativity and Innovation," *Journal of Knowledge Management* 2 (September 1998), pp. 5–13.

3. A. Cummings and G. R. Oldham, "Enhancing Creativity: Managing Work Contexts for the High Potential Employee," *California Management Review* 40 (Fall 1997), pp. 22–38; T. M. Amabile, *The Social Psychology of Creativity* (New York: Springer-Verlag, 1983), pp. 32–35.

4. P. Swisher, "Soaring Creativity," *Successful Meetings* 50 (August 2001), p. 83; A. Tizon, "Spirit at Work," *Seattle Times*, September 13, 2000.

5. R. Grover, T. Lowry, and L. Armstrong, "Henry Yuen: TV Guy," *Business Week*, March 12, 2001; A. MacKensie, "Innovate or Be Damned," *Asian Business*, January 1995, pp. 30–34.

6. B. Kabanoff and J. R. Rossiter, "Recent Developments in Applied Creativity," *International Review of Industrial and Organizational Psychology* 9 (1994), pp. 283–324.

7. J. R. Hayes, "Cognitive Processes in Creativity," in J. A. Glover, R. R. Ronning, and C. R. Reynolds, eds., *Handbook of Creativity* (New York: Plenum, 1989), pp. 135–45.

8. R. S. Nickerson, "Enhancing Creativity," in R. J. Sternberg, ed., *Handbook of Creativity* (New York: Cambridge University Press, 1999), pp. 392–430; A. Hiam, "9 Obstacles to Creativity—and How You Can Remove Them," *Futurist* 32 (October 1998), pp. 30–34.

9. R. T. Brown, "Creativity: What Are We to Measure?" in Glover, Ronning, and Reynolds, eds., *Handbook of Creativity*, pp. 3–32.

10. Hargadon and Sutton, "Building an Innovation Factory."

11. For a thorough discussion of insight, see R. J. Sternberg and J. E. Davidson, eds., *The Nature of Insight* (Cambridge, MA: MIT Press, 1995).

12. V. Parv, "The Idea Toolbox: Techniques for Being a More Creative Writer," *Writer's Digest* 78 (July 1998), p. 18; J. Ayan, *Aha! 10 Ways to Free Your Creative Spirit and Find Your Great Ideas* (New York: Crown Trade, 1997), pp. 50–56.

13. A. Chandrasekaran, "Bye, Bye Serendipity," *Business Standard*, March 28, 2000, p. 1; K. Cottrill, "Reinventing Innovation," *Journal of Business Strategy*, March–April 1998, pp. 47–51.

14. C. Martindale, "Biological Bases of Creativity," in Sternberg, ed., *Handbook of Creativity*, pp. 137–52. For a critical view of "right-brained thinking," see T. Hines, "Left Brain/Right Brain Mythology and Implications for Management and Training," *Academy of Management Review* 12 (1987), pp. 600–6.

15. R. J. Sternberg and L. A. O'Hara, "Creativity and Intelligence," in Sternberg, ed., *Handbook of Creativity*, pp. 251–72.

16. R. J. Sternberg, L. A. O'Hara, and T. I. Lubart, "Creativity as Investment," *California Management Review* 40 (Fall 1997), pp. 8–21.

17. R. W. Weisberg, "Creativity and Knowledge: A Challenge to Theories," in Sternberg, ed., *Handbook of Creativity*, pp. 226–50.

18. R. J. Sternberg, *Thinking Styles* (New York: Cambridge University Press, 1997).

19. M. Michalko, "Thinking Like a Genius: Eight Strategies Used by the Supercreative, from Aristotle and Leonardo to Einstein and Edison," *The Futurist* 32 (May 1998), pp. 21–25; J. S. Dacey, "Peak Periods of Creative Growth across the Lifespan," *Journal of Creative Behavior* 23 (1989), pp. 224–47; F. Barron and D. M. Harrington, "Creativity, Intelligence, and Personality," *Annual Review of Psychology* 32 (1981), pp. 439–76.

20. P. Roberts, "Sony Changes the Game," *Fast Company* 10 (1997), p. 116.

21. G. J. Feist, "The Influence of Personality on Artistic and Scientific Creativity," in Sternberg, ed., *Handbook of Creativity*, pp. 273–96; M. A. West, *Developing Creativity in Organizations* (Leicester, UK: BPS Books, 1997), pp. 10–19.

22. D. C. McClelland, *The Achieving Society* (New York: Van Nostrand Reinhold, 1961); M. Patchen, *Participation, Achievement, and Involvement on the Job* (Englewood Cliffs, NJ: Prentice Hall, 1970).

23. B. Breen, "Rapid Motion," *Fast Company* 49 (August 2001), p. 49; L. Pratt, "Persistence in Motion," *Profit Magazine* 20 (May 2001), pp. 18–22.

24. D. K. Simonton, "Creativity: Cognitive, Personal, Developmental, and Social Aspects," *American Psychologist* 55 (January 2000), pp. 151–58; Cummings and Oldham, "Enhancing Creativity."

25. S. Long, "They Slaughter Sacred Cows," *Straits Times (Singapore)*, February 28, 1999, p. 3.

26. S. Bharadwaj and A. Menon, "Making Innovation Happen in Organizations: Individual Creativity Mechanisms, Organizational Creativity Mechanisms or Both?" *Journal of Product Innovation Management* 17 (November 2000), pp. 424–34; M. D. Mumford, "Managing Creative People: Strategies and Tactics for Innovation," *Human Resource Management Review* 10 (Autumn 2000), pp. 313–51; T. M. Amabile, R. Conti, H. Coon, J. Lazenby, and M. Herron, "Assessing the Work Environment for Creativity," *Academy of Management Journal* 39 (1996), pp. 1154–84; G. R. Oldham and A. Cummings, "Employee Creativity: Personal and Contextual Factors at Work," *Academy of Management Journal* 39 (1996), pp. 607–34.

27. C. Sams, "The Difference Is Graphic," *Sun Herald (Sydney, Australia)*, November 19, 2000, p. 7; G. Maddox, "Oz Fx in Effect, the Best," *Sydney Morning Herald*, April 1, 2000, p. 39; S. Pipe, "Animal Logic Drives Budding Artists," *The Australian*, November 16, 1999, p. C9; H. Jacobs, "Up from Down Under," *Shoot* 40 (October 1999), pp. 19–22; I. Cuthbertson, "Wizards of Oz," *Weekend Australian*, June 26, 1999, p. 48.

28. D. Maitra, "Livio D. Desimone: We Do Not See Failures As Failure," *Business Today (India)*, June 22, 1998, p. 66.

29. T. M. Amabile, "Changes in the Work Environment for Creativity during Downsizing," *Academy of Management Journal* 42 (December 1999), pp. 630–40.

30. P. Luke, "Business World's a Stage," *Vancouver Province*, September 2, 2001.

31. Cummings and Oldham, "Enhancing Creativity."

32. C. E. Shalley, L. L. Gilson, and T. C. Blum, "Matching Creativity Requirements and the Work Environment: Effects on Satisfaction and Intentions to Leave," *Academy of Management Journal*, April 2000, pp. 215–23; R. Tierney, S. M. Farmer, and G. B. Graen, "An Examination of Leadership and Employee Creativity: The Relevance of Traits and Relationships," *Personnel Psychology* 52 (Autumn 1999), pp. 591–620; Cummings and Oldham, "Enhancing Creativity."

33. Michalko, "Thinking Like a Genius."

34. T. M. Amabile, "Motivating Creativity in Organizations: On Doing What You Love and Loving What You Do," *California Management Review* 40 (Fall 1997), pp. 39–58.

35. M. Csikszentmihalyi, *Creativity—Flow and the Psychology of Discovery and Invention* (New York: HarperCollins, 1996).

36. T. M. Amabile, "A Model of Creativity and Innovation in Organizations," *Research in Organizational Behavior* 10 (1988), pp. 123–67. The survey about time pressure in advertising and marketing is summarized in "No Time for Creativity," *London Free Press*, August 7, 2001, p. D3.

37. S. M. Rostan, "Problem Finding, Problem Solving, and Cognitive Controls: An Empirical Investigation of Critically Acclaimed Productivity," *Creativity Research Journal* 7 (1994), pp. 97–110. See also S. Z. Dudek and R. Côté, "Problem Finding Revisited," in M. A. Runco, ed., *Problem Finding, Problem Solving, and Creativity* (Norwood, NJ: Ablex, 1994), pp. 130–50.

38. Sternberg et al., "Creativity as Investment."

39. J. Kao, *Jamming* (New York: HarperCollins Business, 1996).

40. Hiam, "Obstacles to Creativity—and How You Can Remove Them."

41. West, *Developing Creativity in Organizations*, pp. 33–35.

42. Cathy Olofson, "Monster Board Has Fun," *Fast Company* 16 (August 1998), p. 50.

43. P. Brown, "Across the Table into the Bedroom," *Times of London*, March 1, 2001, p. D4.

44. K. W. Jesse, "A Creative Approach to Doing Business," *Dayton (OH) Daily News,* June 19, 1998, p. C1.

45. W. J. J. Gordon, *Synectics: The Development of Creative Capacity* (New York: Harper & Row, 1961).

46. J. Neff, "At Eureka Ranch, Execs Doff Wing Tips, Fire Up Ideas," *Advertising Age* 69 (March 9, 1998), pp. 28–29.

47. A. G. Robinson and S. Stern, *Corporate Creativity, How Innovation and Improvement Actually Happen* (San Francisco: Berrett-Koehler, 1997).

48. Kelley, *The Art of Innovation*, pp. 158–62; Hargadon and Sutton, "Building an Innovation Factory."

49. D. Beardsley, "This Company Doesn't Brake for (Sacred) Cows," *Fast Company* 16 (August 1998).

50. V. H. Vroom and A. G. Jago, *The New Leadership* (Englewood Cliffs, NJ: Prentice Hall, 1988), pp. 28–29.

51. R. B. Gallupe, W. H. Cooper, M. L. Grisé, and L. M. Bastianutti, "Blocking Electronic Brainstorms," *Journal of Applied Psychology* 79 (1994), pp. 77–86; M. Diehl and W. Stroebe, "Productivity Loss in Idea-Generating Groups: Tracking Down the Blocking Effects," *Journal of Personality and Social Psychology* 61 (1991), pp. 392–403.

52. Kelley, *The Art of Innovation*, p. 70; Hargadon and Sutton, "Building an Innovation Factory."

53. P. W. Mulvey, J. F. Veiga, and P. M. Elsass, "When Teammates Raise a White Flag," *Academy of Management Executive* 10 (February 1996), pp. 40–49.

54. S. Plous, T*he Psychology of Judgment and Decision Making* (Philadelphia: Temple University Press, 1993), pp. 200–2.

55. B. Mullen, T. Anthony, E. Salas, and J. E. Driskell, "Group Cohesiveness and Quality of Decision Making: An Integration of Tests of the Groupthink Hypothesis," *Small Group Research 25* (1994), pp. 189–204; I. L. Janis, *Crucial Decisions* (New York: Free Press, 1989), pp. 56–63; I. L. Janis, Groupthink: *Psychological Studies of Policy Decisions and Fiascoes*, 2nd ed. (Boston: Houghton Mifflin, 1982).

56. M. E. Turner and A. R. Pratkanis, "Threat, Cohesion, and Group Effectiveness: Testing a Social Identity Maintenance Perspective on Group-think," *Journal of Personality and Social Psychology* 63 (1992), pp. 781–96.

57. M. Rempel and R. J. Fisher, "Perceived Threat, Cohesion, and Group Problem Solving in Intergroup Conflict," *International Journal of Conflict Management* 8 (1997), pp. 216–34.

58. G. Moorhead, R. Ference, and C. P. Neck, "Group Decision Fiascoes Continue: Space Shuttle *Challenger* and a Revised Groupthink Framework," *Human Relations* 44 (1991), pp. 539–50; Janis, *Crucial Decisions*, pp. 76–77.

59. C. McGarty, J. C. Turner, M. A. Hogg, B. David, and M. S. Wetherell, "Group Polarization as Conformity to the Prototypical Group Member," *British Journal of Social Psychology* 31 (1992), pp. 1–20; D. Isenberg, "Group Polarization: A Critical Review and Meta-analysis," *Journal of Personality and Social Psychology* 50 (1986), pp. 1141–51; D. G. Myers and H. Lamm, "The Group Polarization Phenomenon," *Psychological Bulletin* 83 (1976), pp. 602–27.

60. D. Friedman, "Monty Hall's Three Doors: Construction and Deconstruction of a Choice Anomaly," *American Economic Review* 88 (September 1998), pp. 933–46; D. Kahneman and A. Tversky, "Prospect Theory: An Analysis of Decision under Risk," *Econometrica* 47 (1979), pp. 263–91.

61. Janis, *Crucial Decisions*, pp. 244–49.

62. F. A. Schull, A. L. Delbecq, and L. L. Cummings, *Organizational Decision Making* (New York: McGraw-Hill, 1970), pp. 144–49.

63. A. C. Amason, "Distinguishing the Effects of Functional and Dysfunctional Conflict on Strategic Decision Making: Resolving a Paradox for Top Management Teams," *Academy of Management Journal* 39 (1996), pp. 123–48; G. Katzenstein, "The Debate on Structured Debate: Toward a Unified Theory," *Organizational Behavior and Human Decision Processes* 66 (1996), pp. 316–32; D. Tjosvold, *Team Organization: An Enduring Competitive Edge* (Chichester, UK: Wiley, 1991).

64. K. M. Eisenhardt, J. L. Kahwajy, and L. J. Bourgeois III, "Conflict and Strategic Choice: How Top Management Teams Disagree," *California Management Review* 39 (Winter 1997), pp. 42–62.

65. J. S. Valacich and C. Schwenk, "Structuring Conflict in Individual, Face-to-Face, and Computer-Mediated Group Decision Making: Carping versus Objective Devil's Advocacy," *Decision Sciences* 26 (1995), pp. 369–93; D. M. Schweiger, W. R. Sandberg, and P. L. Rechner, "Experiential Effects of Dialectical Inquiry, Devil's Advocacy, and Consensus Approaches to Strategic Decision Making," *Academy of Management Journal* 32 (1989), pp. 745–72.

66. P. J. H. Schoemaker, "Disciplined Imagination: From Scenarios to Strategic Options," *International Studies of Management and Organization* 27 (Summer 1997), pp. 43–70.

67. A. F. Osborn, *Applied Imagination* (New York: Scribner, 1957).

68. A. Chandrasekaran, "Bye, Bye Serendipity," *Business Standard,* March 28, 2000, p. 1.

69. B. Oaff, "Great Idea, Even if It Can Get You Fired," *Mail on Sunday* (UK), May 6, 2001, p. 43.

70. B. Mullen, C. Johnson, and E. Salas, "Productivity Loss in Brainstorming Groups: A Meta-Analytic Integration," *Basic and Applied Psychology* 12 (1991), pp. 2–23.

71. R. I. Sutton and A. Hargadon, "Brainstorming Groups in Context: Effectiveness in a Product Design Firm," *Administrative Science Quarterly* 41 (1996), pp. 685–718; P. B. Paulus and M. T. Dzindolet, "Social Influence Processes in Group Brainstorming," *Journal of Personality and Social Psychology* 64 (1993), pp. 575–86; B. Mullen, C. Johnson, and E. Salas, "Productivity Loss in Brainstorming Groups: A Meta-Analytic Integration," *Basic and Applied Psychology* 12 (1991), pp. 2–23.

72. Gallupe et al., "Blocking Electronic Brainstorms."

73. P. Bordia, "Face-to-Face versus Computer-Mediated Communication: A Synthesis of the Experimental Literature," *Journal of Business Communication* 34 (1997), pp. 99–120; J. S. Valacich, A. R. Dennis, and T. Connolly, "Idea Generation in Computer-Based Groups: A New Ending to an Old Story," *Organizational Behavior and Human Decision Processes* 57 (1994), pp. 448–67; Gallupe et al., "Blocking Electronic Brainstorms."

74. A. R. Dennis and J. S. Valacich, "Electronic Brainstorming: Illusions and Patterns of Productivity," *Information Systems Research* 10 (1999), pp. 375–77; R. B. Gallupe, A. R. Dennis, W. H. Cooper, J. S. Valacich, L. M. Bastianutti, and J. F. Nunamaker, Jr., "Electronic Brainstorming and Group Size," *Academy of Management Journal* 35 (June 1992), pp. 350–69; R. B. Gallupe, L. M. Bastianutti, and W. H. Cooper, "Unblocking Brainstorms," *Journal of Applied Psychology* 76 (1991), pp. 137–42.

75. A. Pinsoneault, H. Barki, R. B. Gallupe, and N. Hoppen. "Electronic Brainstorming: The Illusion of Productivity," *Information Systems Research* 10 (1999), pp. 110–33; B. Kabanoff and J. R. Rossiter, "Recent Developments in Applied Creativity," *International Review of Industrial and Organizational Psychology* 9 (1994), pp. 283–324.

76. H. A. Linstone and M. Turoff, eds., *The Delphi Method: Techniques and Applications* (Reading, MA: Addison-Wesley, 1975).

77. C. Critcher and B. Gladstone, "Utilizing the Delphi Technique in Policy Discussion: A Case Study of a Privatized Utility in Britain," *Public Administration* 76 (Autumn 1998), pp. 431–49; S. R. Rubin et al., "Research Directions Related to Rehabilitation Practice: A Delphi Study," *Journal of Rehabilitation* 64 (Winter 1998), p. 19.

78. A. L. Delbecq, A. H. Van de Ven, and D. H. Gustafson, *Group Techniques for Program Planning: A Guide to Nominal Group and Delphi Processes* (Middleton, WI: Green Briar Press, 1986).

79. A. B. Hollingshead, "The Rank-Order Effect in Group Decision Making," *Organizational Behavior and Human Decision Processes* 68 (1996), pp. 181–93.

80. S. Frankel, "NGT + MDS: An Adaptation of the Nominal Group Technique for Ill-Structured Problems," *Journal of Applied Behavioral Science* 23 (1987), pp. 543–51; D. M. Hegedus and R. Rasmussen, "Task Effectiveness and Interaction Process of a Modified Nominal Group Technique in Solving an Evaluation Problem," *Journal of Management* 12 (1986), pp. 545–60.

CHAPTER ELEVEN

1. P. Tam, "The Bulldog Unchained," *Ottawa Citizen,* July 24, 2000; K. Goff, "Workers Ponder Their Futures," *Ottawa Citizen,* February 24, 2000; K. Standen, "Just What the Doctor Ordered," *Ottawa Citizen,* November 3, 1999; E. Mulqueen, "The Director's Chair—Pearse Flynn, Vice-President, Newbridge," *Irish Times,* August 27, 1999, p. 64; J. Bagnall, "Shaking Newbridge to the Core," *Ottawa Citizen,* March 17, 1999. Pearse Flynn is now CEO of Damovo, a spin-off from Ericsson that sells and services call center telecommunications systems. See J. Boxell, "Man Who Sold $7bn Newbridge in Fresh Challenge," *Financial Times (London),* September 10, 2001.

2. N. Sriussadaporn-Charoenngam and F. M. Jablin, "An Exploratory Study of Communication Competence in Thai Organizations," *Journal of Business Communication* 36 (October 1999), pp. 382–418; F. M. Jablin et al., "Communication Competence in Organizations: Conceptualization and Comparison across Multiple Levels of Analysis," in L. Thayer and G. Barnett, eds., *Organization Communication: Emerging Perspectives,* vol. 4 (Norwood, NJ: Ablex, 1994), pp. 114–40.

3. S. L. Pan and H. Scarbrough, "Knowledge Management in Practice: An Exploratory Case Study," *Technology Analysis and Strategic Management* 11 (September 1999), pp. 359–74; S. Greengard, "Will Your Culture Support KM?" *Workforce* 77 (October 1998), pp. 93–94; M. N. Martinez, "The Collective Power of Employee Knowledge," *HRMagazine* 43 (February 1998), pp. 88–94; R. K. Buckman, "Knowledge Sharing at Buckman Labs," *Journal of Business Strategy,* January–February 1998, pp. 11–15.

4. H. Mintzberg, *The Nature of Managerial Work* (New York: Harper & Row, 1973); E. T. Klemmer and F. W. Snyder, "Measurement of Time Spent Communicating," *Journal of Communication* 22 (June 1972), pp. 142–58.

5. R. T. Barker and M. R. Camarata, "The Role of Communication in Creating and Maintaining a Learning Organization: Preconditions, Indicators, and Disciplines," *Journal of Business Communication* 35 (October 1998), pp. 443–67.

6. R. Grenier and G. Metes, "Wake Up and Smell the Syzygy," *Business Communications Review* 28 (August 1998), pp. 57–60; "We Are the World," *CIO* 9 (August 1996), p. 24.

7. G. Calabrese, "Communication and Co-operation in Product Development: A Case Study of a European Car Producer," *R&D Management* 27 (July 1997), pp. 239–52; C. Downs, P. Clampitt, and A. L. Pfeiffer, "Communication and Organizational Outcomes," in G. Goldhaber and G. Barnett, eds., *Handbook of Organizational Communication* (Norwood, NJ: Ablex, 1988), pp. 171–211.

8. V. L. Shalin, and G. V. Prabhu, "A Cognitive Perspective on Manual Assembly," *Ergonomics* 39 (1996), pp. 108–27; I. Nonaka and H. Takeuchi, The *Knowledge-Creating Company* (New York: Oxford University Press, 1995).

9. L. K. Lewis and D. R. Seibold, "Communication during Intraorganizational Innovation Adoption: Predicting User's Behavioral Coping Responses to Innovations in Organizations," *Communication Monographs* 63 (2) (1996), pp. 131–57; R. J. Burke and D. S. Wilcox, "Effects of Different Patterns and Degrees of Openness in Superior—Subordinate Communication on Subordinate Satisfaction," *Academy of Management Journal* 12 (1969), pp. 319–26.

10. C. E. Shannon and W. Weaver, *The Mathematical Theory of Communication* (Urbana: University of Illinois Press, 1949). For a more recent discussion, see K. J. Krone, F. M. Jablin, and L. L. Putnam, "Communication Theory and Organizational Communication: Multiple Perspectives," in F. M. Jablin, L. L. Putnam, K. H. Roberts, and L. W. Porter, eds., *Handbook of Organizational Communication: An Interdisciplinary Perspective* (Newbury Park, CA: Sage, 1987), pp. 18–40.

11. S. Axley, "Managerial and Organizational Communication in Terms of the Conduit Metaphor," *Academy of Management Review* 9 (1984), pp. 428–37.

12. D. Jones, "Corning Chief Says Keep Open Mind, Challenge Strategy," *USA Today*, June 1, 2001, p. B5; The George Bernard Shaw quotation is cited at the website www.synco.com/communct.html.

13. M. Meissner, "The Language of Work," in R. Dubin, ed., *Handbook of Work, Organization, and Society* (Chicago: Rand McNally, 1976), pp. 205–79.

14. M. J. Glauser, "Upward Information Flow in Organizations: Review and Conceptual Analysis," *Human Relations* 37 (1984), pp. 613–43.

15. L. Larwood, "Don't Struggle to Scope Those Metaphors Yet," *Group and Organization Management* 17 (1992), pp. 249–54; L. R. Pondy, P. J. Frost, G. Morgan, and T. C. Dandridge, eds., *Organizational Symbolism* (Greenwich, CT: JAI Press, 1983).

16. L. Sahagun, "Cold War Foes Find Harmony in Satellite Launch Partnership," *Los Angeles Times*, July 25, 2001, p. B1.

17. B. Robins, "Why 'Sell' Is Now a Four-Letter Word," *The Age (Melbourne)*, June 16, 2001.

18. A. Markham, "Designing Discourse: A Critical Analysis of Strategic Ambiguity and Workplace Control," *Management Communication Quarterly* 9 (1996), pp. 389–421; Larwood, "Don't Struggle to Scope Those Metaphors Yet"; R. Mead, *Cross-Cultural Management Communication* (Chichester, UK: Wiley, 1990), pp. 130–37; E. M. Eisenberg, "Ambiguity as a Strategy in Organizational Communication," *Communication Monographs* 51 (1984), pp. 227–42; R. Daft and J. Wiginton, "Language and Organization," *Academy of Management Review* 4 (1979), pp. 179–91.

19. M. J. Hatch, "Exploring the Empty Spaces of Organizing: How Improvisational Jazz Helps Redescribe Organizational Structure," *Organization Studies* 20 (1999), pp. 75–100; G. Morgan, *Images of Organization*, 2nd ed. (Thousand Oaks, CA: Sage, 1997); L. L. Putnam, N. Phillips, and P. Chapman, "Metaphors of Communication and Organization," in S. R. Clegg, C. Hardy, and W. R. Nord, eds., *Handbook of Organization Studies* (London: Sage, 1996), pp. 373–408.

20. B. Beaupre, "You've Got Too Much Mail," *Chicago Sun-Times*, August 7, 2000.

21. J. T. Koski, "Reflections on Information Glut and Other Issues in Knowledge Productivity," *Futures* 33 (August 2001), pp. 483–95; C. Norton

and A. Nathan, "Computer-Mad Generation Has a Memory Crash," *Sunday Times (London)*, February 4, 2001; S. Bury, "Does E-mail Make You More Productive?" *Silicon Valley North*, September 1999.

22. From "The Best of Ideas," CBC Radio, 1967. (Cited at the website www.mcluhan4managers.com).

23. K. Alesandrini, *Survive Information Overload* (Homewood, IL: Business One–Irwin, 1993); A. G. Schick, L. A. Gordon, and S. Haka, "Information Overload: A Temporal Approach," *Accounting, Organizations and Society* 15 (1990), pp. 199–220.

24. Schick et al., "Information Overload," pp. 209–14; C. Stohl and W. C. Redding, "Messages and Message Exchange Processes," in Jablin et al., eds., *Handbook of Organizational Communication*, pp. 451–502.

25. J. H. E. Andriessen, "Mediated Communication and New Organizational Forms," *International Review of Industrial and Organizational Psychology* 6 (1991), pp. 17–70; L. Porter and K. Roberts, "Communication in Organizations," in M. Dunnette, ed., *Handbook of Industrial and Organizational Psychology* (Chicago: Rand McNally, 1976), pp. 1553–89.

26. F. Moore, "Storage Faces Newest Challenge—Coping with Success," *Computer Technology Review* 21 (September 2001), p. 1; S. D. Kennedy, "Finding a Cure for Information Anxiety," *Information Today*, May 1, 2001, p. 40; M. R. Overly, "E-Policy," *Messaging Magazine*, January–February 1999. For a discussion of the merits of e-mail, see J. Hunter and M. Allen, "Adaptation to Electronic Mail," *Journal of Applied Communication Research*, August 1992, pp. 254–74; M. Culnan and M. L. Markus, "Information Technologies," in Jablin et al., eds., *Handbook of Organizational Communication*, pp. 420–43.

27. C. S. Saunders, D. Robey, and K. A. Vaverek, "The Persistence of Status Differentials in Computer Conferencing," *Human Communications Research* 20 (1994), pp. 443–72; D. A. Adams, P. A. Todd, and R. R. Nelson, "A Comparative Evaluation of the Impact of Electronic and Voice Mail on Organizational Communication,"

Information and Management 24 (1993), pp. 9–21.

28. "Eisner: E-mail Is Biggest Threat," *Associated Press*, May 12, 2000; A. D. Shulman, "Putting Group Information Technology in Its Place: Communication and Good Work Group Performance," in Clegg et al., eds., *Handbook of Organization Studies*, pp. 373–408.

29. S. Schafer, "Misunderstandings @ the Office," *Washington Post*, October 31, 2000, p. E1; M. Gibbs, "Don't Say It with Smileys," *Network World*, August 9, 1999, p. 62.

30. A. Gumbel, "How E-mail Puts Us in a Flaming Bad Temper," *The Independent (London)*, January 3, 1999, p. 14; J. Kaye, "The Devil You Know," *Computer Weekly*, March 19, 1998, p. 46; S. Kennedy, "The Burning Issue of Electronic Hate Mail," *Computer Weekly*, June 5, 1997, p. 22

31. A. C. Poe, "Don't Touch That 'Send' Button!" *HRMagazine* 46 (July 2001), pp. 74–80. Problems with e-mail are discussed in M. M. Extejt, "Teaching Students to Correspond Effectively Electronically: Tips for Using Electronic Mail Properly," *Business Communication Quarterly* 61 (June 1998), pp. 57–67; V. Frazee, "Is E-mail Doing More Harm Than Good?" *Personnel Journal* 75 (May 1996), p. 23.

32. J. L. Locke, "Q: Is E-Mail Degrading Public and Private Discourse? Yes: Electronic Mail Is Making Us Rude, Lonely, Insensitive and Dishonest," *Insight on the News*, October 19, 1998, p. 24.

33. S. Stellin, "The Intranet Is Changing Many Firms from Within," *New York Times*, January 30, 2001.

34. Stellin, "The Intranet Is Changing Many Firms from Within"; A. Mahlon, "The Alternative Workplace: Changing Where and How People Work," *Harvard Business Review*, May–June 1998, pp. 121–30; C. Meyer and S. Davis, *Blur: The Speed of Change in the Connected Economy* (Reading, MA: Addison-Wesley, 1998); P. Bordia, "Face-to-Face versus Computer-Mediated Communication: A Synthesis of the Experimental Literature," *Journal of Business Communication* 34 (January 1997), pp. 99–120.

35. M. McCance, "IM: Rapid, Risky," *Richmond (VA) Times-Dispatch*, July 19, 2001, p. A1; C. Hempel, "Instant-Message Gratification Is What People Want," *Ventura County (CA) Star*, April 9, 2001.

36. D. Robb, "Ready or Not . . . Instant Messaging Has Arrived as a Financial Planning Tool," *Journal of Financial Planning*, July 2001, pp. 12–14.

37. W. Boei, "The Most Wired Person in Nunavut," *Ottawa Citizen*, November 13, 1999; S. De Santis, "Across Tundra and Cultures, Entrepreneur Wires Arctic," *The Wall Street Journal*, October 19, 1998, p. B1; T. Saito, "Internet Helps Keep Scattered Inuit in Touch," *Daily Yomiuri (Tokyo)*, June 7, 1997.

38. J. S. Brown, "Seeing Differently: A Role for Pioneering Research," *Research Technology Management* 41 (May–June 1998), pp. 24–33; See G. Gilder, *Telecosm: How Infinite Bandwidth will Revolutionize Our World* (New York: Free Press, 2001).

39. "New Age Heralds End of Information Overload," *Financial News*, December 8, 1998.

40. T. E. Harris, *Applied Organizational Communication: Perspectives, Principles, and Pragmatics* (Hillsdale, NJ: Erlbaum, 1993), chap. 5; R. E. Rice and D. E. Shook, "Relationships of Job Categories and Organizational Levels to Use of Communication Channels, Including Electronic Mail: A Meta-Analysis and Extension," *Journal of Management Studies* 27 (1990), pp. 195–229; S. B. Sitkin, K. M. Sutcliffe, and J. R. Barrios-Choplin, "A Dual-Capacity Model of Communication Media Choice in Organizations," *Human Communication Research* 18 (June 1992), pp. 568–98.

41. B. Parkinson, *Ideas and Realities of Emotion* (London: Routledge, 1995), pp. 182–83; E. Hatfield, J. T. Cacioppo, and R. L. Rapson, *Emotional Contagion* (Cambridge, UK: Cambridge University Press, 1993).

42. D. Goodsire, "Seconds from Disaster, the Captain Aborts," *The Age (Melbourne)*, April 25, 2001.

43. R. L. Daft, R. H. Lengel, and L. K. Tevino, "Message Equivocality, Media Selection, and Manager Performance: Implications for Information Systems," *MIS Quarterly* 11 (1987), pp. 355–66.

44. I. Lamont, "Do Your Far-Flung Users Want to Communicate as if They Share an Office?" *Network World*, November 13, 2000.

45. R. Lengel and R. Daft, "The Selection of Communication Media as an Executive Skill," *Academy of Management Executive* 2 (1988), pp. 225–32; G. Huber and R. Daft, "The Information Environments of Organizations," in Jablin et al., eds., *Handbook of Organizational Communication*, pp. 130–64; R. Daft and R. Lengel, "Information Richness: A New Approach to Managerial Behavior and Organization Design," *Research in Organizational Behavior* 6 (1984), pp. 191–233.

46. R. E. Rice, "Task Analyzability, Use of New Media, and Effectiveness: A Multi-Site Exploration of Media Richness," *Organization Science* 3 (1992), pp. 475–500; J. Fulk, C. W. Steinfield, J. Schmitz, and J. G. Power, "A Social Information Processing Model of Media Use in Organizations," *Communication Research* 14 (1987), pp. 529–52.

47. R. Madhavan and R. Grover, "From Embedded Knowledge to Embodied Knowledge: New Product Development As Knowledge Management," *Journal of Marketing* 62 (October 1998), pp. 1–12; D. Stork and A. Sapienza, "Task and Human Messages over the Project Life Cycle: Matching Media to Messages," *Project Management Journal* 22 (December 1992), pp. 44–49.

48. J. R. Carlson and R. W. Zmud, "Channel Expansion Theory and the Experiential Nature of Media Richness Perceptions," *Academy of Management Journal* 42 (April 1999), pp. 153–70.

49. M. McLuhan, *Understanding Media: The Extensions of Man* (New York: McGraw-Hill, 1964).

50. Sitkin et al., "A Dual-Capacity Model of Communication Media Choice in Organizations"; J. Schmitz and J. Fulk, "Organizational Colleagues, Media Richness, and Electronic Mail: A Test of the Social Influence Model of Technology Use," *Communication Research* 18 (1991), pp. 487–523.

51. M. Misra and P. Misra, "Hughes Software: Fun and Flexibility," *Business Today*, January 7, 2001, p. 182.

52. B. Sosnin, "Digital Newsletters 'E-volutionize' Employee Communications," *HRMagazine* 46 (May 2001), pp. 99–107; G. Grates, "Is the Employee Publication Extinct?" *Communication*

World 17 (December 1999–January 2000), pp. 27–30.

53. R. Hotch, "Put the 'Quality' in Equality," *Success* 48 (April 2001), pp. 28ff.; N. Hulsman, "Farewell, Corner Office," *BC Business*, June 1999, pp. 48ff.; L. Stuart, "Why Space Is the New Frontier," *The Guardian (London)*, October 31, 1998, p. 24.

54. G. Evans and D. Johnson, "Stress and Open-Office Noise," *Journal of Applied Psychology* 85 (2000), pp. 779–83.

55. F. Russo, "My Kingdom for a Door," *Time*, October 23, 2000, p. B1. The TBWA Chiat/Day office design and its problems are described in Hulsman, "Farewell, Corner Office"; "Why Chiat/Day Is Putting Down Its Binoculars," *Creative Review*, April 1998, p. 67; C. Knight, "Gone Virtual," *Canadian HR Reporter*, December 16, 1996, pp. 24, 26.

56. J. Sung, "Designed for Interaction," *Fortune*, January 8, 2001; S. Kirsner, "Every Day, It's a New Place," *Fast Company*, April–May, 1998, pp. 130–34; J. S. Russell, "A Company Headquarters Planned for Flexibility," *New York Times*, September 7, 1997, p. 7.

57. B. Schneider, S. D. Ashworth, A. C. Higgs, and L. Carr, "Design, Validity, and Use of Strategically Focused Employee Attitude Surveys," *Personnel Psychology* 49 (1996), pp. 695–705; T. Geddie, "Surveys Are a Waste of Time . . . Until You Use Them," *Communication World*, April 1996, pp. 24–26; D. M. Saunders and J. D. Leck, "Formal Upward Communication Procedures: Organizational and Employee Perspectives," *Canadian Journal of Administrative Sciences* 10 (1993), pp. 255–68.

58. L. Girion, "Employee Inner Views," *Los Angeles Times*, September 10, 2000, p. G1.

59. The original term is "management by *wandering* around," but "wandering" has been replaced with "walking" over the years. T. Peters and R. Waterman, *In Search of Excellence* (New York: Harper & Row, 1982), p. 122; W. Ouchi, *Theory Z* (New York: Avon, 1981), pp. 176–77.

60. J. Hansen, "Wide Open Spaces," *AsiaWeek*, May 25, 2001; S. Bongiorni, "LSU Students Get Business Tips," *Louisiana State Times/Morning Advocate*, November 11, 2000, p. C1; M. Goldberg,

"Cisco's Most Important Meal of the Day," *Fast Company* 13 (February 1998), p. 56.

61. M. Duffy, "Jobs Cloud Lifts for Staff at Mitsubishi," *The Advertiser (Adelaide, Australia)*, April 3, 2001, p. 12; M. Duffy, "Contract a Lifeline for Mitsubishi," *Herald Sun (Melbourne)*, April 3, 2001; M. Duffy, "Welcome to the Future," *The Advertiser (Adelaide, Australia)*, November 29, 2000, p. 1; M. Duffy, "Japan Backs Mitsubishi," *The Advertiser (Adelaide, Australia)*, November 28, 2000, pp. 1, 6; M. Duffy, "Let Us Get On with It," *The Advertiser (Adelaide, Australia)*, November 18, 2000, p. 1.

62. "Survey Finds Good and Bad Points on Worker Attitudes," *Eastern Pennsylvania Business Journal*, May 5, 1997, p. 13.

63. G. Kreps, *Organizational Communication* (White Plains, NY: Longman, 1986), pp. 202–6; W. L. Davis and J. R. O'Connor, "Serial Transmission of Information: A Study of the Grapevine," *Journal of Applied Communication Research* 5 (1977), pp. 61–72; K. Davis, "Management Communication and the Grapevine," *Harvard Business Review* 31 (September–October 1953), pp. 43–49.

64. D. Krackhardt and J. R. Hanson, "Informal Networks: The Company Behind the Chart," *Harvard Business Review* 71 (July–August 1993), pp. 104–11; H. Mintzberg, *The Structuring of Organizations* (Englewood Cliffs, NJ: Prentice Hall, 1979), pp. 46–53.

65. M. Noon and R. Delbridge, "News from Behind My Hand: Gossip in Organizations," *Organization Studies* 14 (1993), pp. 23–36; R. L. Rosnow, "Inside Rumor: A Personal Journey," *American Psychologist* 46 (May 1991), pp. 484–96; C. J. Walker and C. A. Beckerle, "The Effect of State Anxiety on Rumor Transmission," *Journal of Social Behavior and Personality* 2 (August 1987), pp. 353–60.

66. J. N. Lynem, "Sex, Lies and Message Boards," *San Francisco Chronicle*, July 1, 2001, p. W1; D. E. Lewis, "Firms Try to Cope with Rumors, Gossip on Online Message Boards," *Boston Globe*, May 17, 2001; M. Schrage, "If You Can't Say Anything Nice, Say It Anonymously," *Fortune*, December 6, 1999, p. 352; S. Caudron, "Employeechat.com:

Bashing HR on the Web," *Workforce* 78 (December 1999), pp. 36–42.

67. Lewis, "Firms Try to Cope with Rumors, Gossip on Online Message Boards." The banning of office gossip in Cascavel, Brazil, is described in "Odd Spot," *The Age (Melbourne)*, July 20, 2001, p. 1.

68. G. Dutton, "One Workforce, Many Languages," *Management Review* 87 (December 1998), pp. 42–47.

69. D. Woodruff, "Crossing Culture Divide Early Clears Merger Paths," *Asian Wall Street Journal*, May 28, 2001, p. 9.

70. Mead, *Cross-Cultural Management Communication*, pp. 161–62; J. V. Thill and C. L. Bovée, *Excellence in Business Communication*, 2nd ed. (New York: McGraw-Hill, 1993), chap. 17.

71. F. Cunningham, "A Touch of the Tartan Treatment for Mazda," *The Scotsman*, October 14, 1997, p. 27.

72. R. M. March, *Reading the Japanese Mind* (Tokyo: Kodansha International, 1996), chap. 1; H. Yamada, *American and Japanese Business Discourse: A Comparison of Interaction Styles* (Norwood, NJ: Ablex, 1992), p. 34.

73. One writer explains that Aboriginal people tend to avoid conflict, so differences are discussed over an open campfire, which absorbs some of the potential conflict and allows people to avoid direct eye contact. See H. Blagg, "A Just Measure of Shame?" *British Journal of Criminology* 37 (Autumn 1997), pp. 481–501. For other differences in cross-cultural communication, see R. Axtell, *Gestures: The Do's and Taboos of Body Language around the World* (New York: Wiley, 1991); P. Harris and R. Moran, *Managing Cultural Differences* (Houston: Gulf, 1987); P. Ekman, W. V. Friesen, and J. Bear, "The International Language of Gestures," *Psychology Today*, May 1984, pp. 64–69.

74. H. Yamada, *Different Games, Different Rules* (New York: Oxford University Press, 1997), pp. 76–79; Yamada, *American and Japanese Business Discourse*, chap. 2; D. Tannen, *Talking from 9 to 5* (New York: Avon, 1994), pp. 96–97; D. C. Barnlund, *Communication Styles of Japanese and Americans: Images and Realities* (Belmont, CA: Wadsworth, 1988).

75. D. Goleman, What Makes a Leader?" *Harvard Business Review* 76 (November–December 1998), pp. 92–102.

76. S. Herring, "Gender Differences in Computer-Mediated Communication: Bringing Familiar Baggage to the New Frontier," Paper presented at the American Library Association Annual Conference, Miami, June 27, 1994.

77. M. Crawford, *Talking Difference: On Gender and Language* (Thousand Oaks, CA: Sage, 1995), pp. 41–44; Tannen, *Talking from 9 to 5;* D. Tannen, *You Just Don't Understand: Men and Women in Conversation* (New York: Ballantine, 1990); S. Helgesen, *The Female Advantage: Women's Ways of Leadership* (New York: Doubleday, 1990).

78. A. Mulac et al., "'Uh-Huh. What's That All About?' Differing Interpretations of Conversational Backchannels and Questions as Sources of Miscommunication across Gender Boundaries," *Communication Research* 25 (December 1998), pp. 641–68; G. H. Graham, J. Unruh, and P. Jennings, "The Impact of Nonverbal Communication in Organizations: A Survey of Perceptions," *Journal of Business Communication* 28 (1991), pp. 45–61; J. Hall, "Gender Effects in Decoding Nonverbal Cues," *Psychological Bulletin* 68 (1978), pp. 845–57.

79. This stereotypic notion is prevalent throughout J. Gray, *Men Are from Mars, Women Are from Venus* (New York: HarperCollins, 1992). For a critique of this view, see Crawford, *Talking Difference,* chap. 4; D. J. Canary and T. M. Emmers-Sommer, *Sex and Gender Differences in Personal Relationships* (New York: Guilford 1997), chap. 1.

80. P. Tripp-Knowles, "A Review of the Literature on Barriers Encountered by Women in Science Academia," *Resources for Feminist Research* 24 (Spring–Summer 1995) pp. 28–34.

81. R. J. Grossman, "Emotions at Work," *Health Forum Journal* 43 (September–October 2000), pp. 18–22.

82. Cited in K. Davis and J. W. Newstrom, *Human Behavior at Work: Organizational Behavior,* 7th ed. (New York: McGraw-Hill, 1985), p. 438.

83. The three components of listening discussed here are based on several recent studies in the field of marketing, including K. de Ruyter and M. G. M. Wetzels, "The Impact of Perceived Listening Behavior in Voice-to-Voice Service Encounters," *Journal of Service Research* 2 (February 2000), pp. 276–84; S. B. Castleberry, C. D. Shepherd, and R. Ridnour, "Effective Interpersonal Listening in the Personal Selling Environment: Conceptualization, Measurement, and Nomological Validity," *Journal of Marketing Theory and Practice* 7 (Winter 1999), pp. 30–38; L. B. Comer and T. Drollinger, "Active Empathetic Listening and Selling Success: A Conceptual Framework," *Journal of Personal Selling and Sales Management* 19 (Winter 1999), pp. 15–29.

84. S. Silverstein, "On the Job, but Do They Listen?" *Los Angeles Times,* July 19, 1998.

CHAPTER TWELVE

1. T. Wanless, "Business and Golfing—Par for the Course," *Vancouver Province,* June 10, 2001; S. J. Wells, "Smoothing the Way," *HRMagazine* 46 (June 2001), pp. 52–58; C. Kleiman, "Women's Networks Play Essential Role in Career Advancement," *The Record (Bergen County, NJ),* October 15, 2000, p. 5; D. L Nelson and R. J. Burke, "Women Executives: Health, Stress, and Success," *Academy of Management Executive* 14 (May 2000), pp. 107–21.

2. C. Hardy and S. Leiba-O'Sullivan, "The Power behind Empowerment: Implications for Research and Practice," *Human Relations* 51 (April 1998), pp. 451–83; R. Farson, *Management of the Absurd* (New York: Simon & Schuster, 1996), chap. 13; R. M. Cyert and J. G. March, *A Behavioral Theory of the Firm* (Englewood Cliffs, NJ: Prentice Hall, 1963).

3. For a discussion of the definition of *power,* see J. Pfeffer, *New Directions in Organizational Theory* (New York: Oxford University Press, 1997), chap. 6; J. Pfeffer, *Managing with Power* (Boston: Harvard Business University Press, 1992), pp. 17, 30; H. Mintzberg, *Power In and Around Organizations* (Englewood Cliffs, NJ: Prentice Hall, 1983), chap. 1.

4. A. M. Pettigrew, *The Politics of Organizational Decision-Making* (London: Tavistock, 1973); R. M. Emerson, "Power-Dependence Relations," *American Sociological Review* 27 (1962), pp. 31–41; R. A. Dahl, "The Concept of Power," *Behavioral Science* 2 (1957), pp. 201–18.

5. D. J. Brass and M. E. Burkhardt, "Potential Power and Power Use: An Investigation of Structure and Behaviour," *Academy of Management Journal* 36 (1993), pp. 441–70; K. M. Bartol and D. C. Martin, "When Politics Pays: Factors Influencing Managerial Compensation Decisions," *Personnel Psychology* 43 (1990), pp. 599–614.

6. P. P. Carson and K. D. Carson, "Social Power Bases: A Meta-Analytic Examination of Interrelationships and Outcomes," *Journal of Applied Social Psychology* 23 (1993), pp. 1150–69; P. Podsakoff and C. Schreisheim, "Field Studies of French and Raven's Bases of Power: Critique, Analysis, and Suggestions for Future Research," *Psychological Bulletin* 97 (1985), pp. 387–411; J. R. P. French and B. Raven, "The Bases of Social Power," in D. Cartwright, ed., *Studies in Social Power* (Ann Arbor: University of Michigan Press, 1959), pp. 150–67.

7. For example, see S. Finkelstein, "Power in Top Management Teams: Dimensions. Measurement, and Validation," *Academy of Management Journal* 35 (1992), pp. 505–38.

8. G. Yukl and C. M. Falbe, "Importance of Different Power Sources in Downward and Lateral Relations," *Journal of Applied Psychology* 76 (1991), pp. 416–23.

9. G. A. Yukl, *Leadership in Organizations,* 3rd ed. (Englewood Cliffs, NJ: Prentice Hall, 1994), p. 13; B. H. Raven, "The Bases of Power: Origins and Recent Developments," *Journal of Social Issues* 49 (1993), pp. 227–51.

10. C. Hardy and S. R. Clegg, "Some Dare Call It Power," in S. R. Clegg, C. Hardy, and W. R. Nord, eds., *Handbook of Organization Studies* (London: Sage, 1996), pp. 622–41; C. Barnard, *The Function of the Executive* (Cambridge, MA: Harvard University Press, 1938).

11. I. Nonaka and H. Takeuchi, *The Knowledge-Creating Company* (New York: Oxford University Press, 1995), pp. 138–39.

12. J. A. Conger, *Winning 'Em Over: A New Model for Managing in the Age of Persuasion* (New York: Simon & Schuster, 1998), Appendix A.

13. "Employees Terrorized by Peer Pressure in the Workplace," Morgan & Banks news release, September 2000. For a discussion of peer pressure at work, see R. Hodson, "Group Relations at Work: Solidarity, Conflict, and Relations with Management," *Work and Occupations* 24 (November 1997), pp. 426–52.

14. G. Sewell, "The Discipline of Teams: The Control of Team-Based Industrial Work through Electronic and Peer Surveillance," *Administrative Science Quarterly* 43 (June 1998), pp. 397–428.

15. "Empowerment Torture to Some," *Tampa (FL) Tribune*, October 5, 1997, p. 6.

16. P. Panchak, "The Future of Manufacturing," *Industry Week* 247 (September 21, 1998), pp. 96–105.

17. J. D. Kudisch and M. L. Poteet, "Expert Power, Referent Power, and Charisma: Toward the Resolution of a Theoretical Debate," *Journal of Business and Psychology* 10 (Winter 1995), pp. 177–95.

18. Information was identified as a form of influence, but not power, in the original French and Raven writing. Information was added as a sixth source of power in subsequent writings by Raven, but this textbook takes the view that information power is derived from the original five sources. See B. H. Raven, "Kurt Lewin Address: Influence, Power, Religion, and the Mechanisms of Social Control," *Journal of Social Issues* 55, Spring 1999, pp. 161–86; Yukl and Falbe, "Importance of Different Power Sources in Downward and Lateral Relations."

19. "Corporate Culture Instilled Online," *The Economist*, November 11, 2000.

20. Pitney Bowes, "Study Finds Growth of Communication Options Is Fundamentally Changing Work," Pitney Bowes news release, April 8, 1997 (www.pitneybowes.com).

21. D. J. Brass, "Being in the Right Place: A Structural Analysis of Individual Influence in an Organization," *Administrative Science Quarterly* 29 (1984), pp. 518–39; N. M. Tichy, M. L. Tuchman, and C. Frombrun, "Social Network Analysis in Organizations," *Academy of Management Review* 4 (1979), pp. 507–19; H. Guetzkow and

H. Simon, "The Impact of Certain Communication Nets upon Organization and Performance in Task-Oriented Groups," *Management Science* 1 (1955), pp. 233–50.

22. C. S. Saunders, "The Strategic Contingency Theory of Power: Multiple Perspectives," *Journal of Management Studies* 27 (1990), pp. 1–21; D. J. Hickson, C. R. Hinings, C. A. Lee, R. E. Schneck, and J. M. Pennings, "A Strategic Contingencies Theory of Intraorganizational Power," *Administrative Science Quarterly* 16 (1971), pp. 216–27; J. D. Thompson, *Organizations in Action* (New York: McGraw-Hill, 1967).

23. C. R. Hinings, D. J. Hickson, J. M. Pennings, and R. E. Schneck, "Structural Conditions of Intraorganizational Power," *Administrative Science Quarterly* 19 (1974), pp. 22–44.

24. Hickson et al., "A Strategic Contingencies Theory of Intraorganizational Power"; Hinings et al., "Structural Conditions of Intraorganizational Power"; and R. M. Kanter, "Power Failure in Management Circuits," *Harvard Business Review*, July–August 1979, pp. 65–75.

25. M. Crozier, *The Bureaucratic Phenomenon* (London: Tavistock, 1964).

26. M. F. Masters, *Unions at the Crossroads: Strategic Membership, Financial, and Political Perspectives* (Westport, CT: Quorum Books, 1997).

27. Brass and Burkhardt, "Potential Power and Power Use"; Hickson et al., "A Strategic Contingencies Theory of Intraorganizational Power," pp. 219–21; J. D. Hackman, "Power and Centrality in the Allocation of Resources in Colleges and Universities," *Administrative Science Quarterly* 30 (1985), pp. 61–77.

28. D. Beveridge, "Job Actions Hit World's Airlines during Year's Busiest Flying Season," *Canadian Press*, July 10, 2001; M. O'Dell, "Airlines Grounded by the Rise of Pilot Power," *Financial Times (UK)*, July 3, 2001.

29. L. Holden, "European Managers: HRM and an Evolving Role," *European Business Review* 12 (2000); Kanter, "Power Failure in Management Circuits," p. 68; B. E. Ashforth, "The Experience of Powerlessness in Organizations," *Organizational Behaviour*

and Human Decision Processes 43 (1989), pp. 207–42.

30. M. L. A. Hayward and W. Boeker, "Power and Conflicts of Interest in Professional Firms: Evidence from Investment Banking," *Administrative Science Quarterly* 43 (March 1998), pp. 1–22.

31. R. Madell, "Ground Floor," *Pharmaceutical Executive (Women in Pharma Supplement)*, June 2000, pp. 24–31.

32. L. A. Perlow, "The Time Famine: Toward a Sociology of Work Time," *Administrative Science Quarterly* 44 (March 1999), pp. 5–31.

33. Perlow, "The Time Famine."

34. Raven, "The Bases of Power," pp. 237–39.

35. B. R. Ragins, "Diversified Mentoring Relationships in Organizations: A Power Perspective," *Academy of Management Review* 22 (1997), pp. 482–521; G. R. Ferris, D. D. Frink, D. P. S. Bhawuk, J. Zhou, and D. C. Gilmore, "Reactions of Diverse Groups to Politics in the Workplace," *Journal of Management* 22 (1996), pp. 23–44.

36. C. M. Falbe and G. Yukl, "Consequences for Managers of Using Single Influence Tactics and Combinations of Tactics," *Academy of Management Journal* 35 (1992), pp. 638–52.

37. D. Kipnis, *The Powerholders* (Chicago: University of Chicago Press, 1976); G. R. Salancik and J. Pfeffer, "The Bases and Use of Power in Organizational Decision Making: The Case of a University," *Administrative Science Quarterly* 19 (1974), pp. 453–73.

38. K. Voigt, "When Work Is a Beach," *Asian Wall Street Journal*, January 26, 2001, p. W1; J. K. Stewart, "Out-of-Sight Telecommuters Might Be Out of Mind," *Chicago Tribune*, April 5, 1998, p. 7; S. Fea, "Boss Moves Office to Lakeside," *Southland Times (Christchurch, NZ)*, February 26, 1998, p. 1.

39. G. E. G. Catlin, *Systematic Politics* (Toronto: University of Toronto Press, 1962), p. 71.

40. G. Kalogerakis, "Fired Manager Fined over Office Pass," *National Post*, May 9, 2000, p. A5.

41. B. James, "EU Drafts Measure to Outlaw Sexual Harassment," *International Herald Tribune*, June 8, 2000; C. S. Piotrkowski, "Gender Harassment, Job Satisfaction, and Distress among Em-

ployed White and Minority Women," *Journal of Occupational Health Psychology* 3 (January 1998), pp. 33–43.

42. D. E. Terpstra, "The Effects of Diversity on Sexual Harassment: Some Recommendations on Research," *Employee Responsibilities and Rights Journal* 9 (1996), pp. 303–13; J. A. Bargh and P. Raymond, "The Naive Misuse of Power: Nonconscious Sources of Sexual Harassment," *Journal of Social Issues* 51 (1995), pp. 85–96; R. A. Thacker and G. R. Ferris, "Understanding Sexual Harassment in the Workplace: The Influence of Power and Politics with the Dyadic Interaction of Harasser and Target," *Human Resource Management Review* 1 (1991), pp. 23–37.

43. For a discussion of the ethical implications of sexual harassment, see T. I. White, "Sexual Harassment: Trust and the Ethic of Care," *Business and Society Review* (January 1998), pp. 9–20; J. Keyton and S. C. Rhodes, "Sexual Harassment: A Matter of Individual Ethics, Legal Definitions, or Organizational Policy?" *Journal of Business Ethics* 16 (February 1997), pp. 129–46.

44. T. L. Tang and S. L. McCollum, "Sexual Harassment in the Workplace," *Public Personnel Management* 25 (1996), pp. 53–58; Bargh and Raymond, "The Naive Misuse of Power."

45. C. M. Schaefer and T. R. Tudor, "Managing Workplace Romances," *SAM Advanced Management Journal* 66, July 2001, pp. 4–10; S. Ulfelder, "Cupid Hits Cubeland," *Boston Globe*, February 11, 2001, p. H1; R. Dhooma, "Taking Care of Business and Pleasure," *Toronto Sun*, September 20, 1999, p. 38; E. Edmonds, "Love and Work," *Ottawa Sun*, February 14, 1999, p. S10. See also G. N. Powell and S. Foley, "Something to Talk About: Romantic Relationships in Organizational Settings," *Journal of Management* 24 (1998), pp. 421–28.

46. "Work Life," *Arizona Daily Star*, February 18, 2001, p. D1. For a discussion of perceived justice and office romance, see S. Foley and G. N. Powell, "Not All Is Fair in Love and Work: Coworkers' Preferences for and Responses to Managerial Interventions Regarding Workplace Romances," *Journal of Organizational Behavior* 20 (1999), pp. 1043–56.

47. Ulfelder, "Cupid Hits Cubeland."

48. M. Solomon, "The Secret's Out: How to Handle the Truth of Workplace Romance," *Workforce* 7 (July 1998), pp. 42–50. See also C. A. Pierce and H. Aguinis, "A Framework for Investigating the Link between Workplace Romance and Sexual Harassment," *Group and Organization Management* 26 (June 2001), pp. 206–29; N. Nejat-Bina, "Employers as Vigilant Chaperones Armed with Dating Waivers: The Intersection of Unwelcomeness and Employer Liability in Hostile Work Environment Sexual Harassment Law," *Berkeley Journal of Employment and Labor Law*, December 22, 1999, pp. 325ff.

49. T. Petzinger, Jr., *The New Pioneers: The Men and Women Who Are Transforming the Workplace and Marketplace* (New York: Simon & Schuster, 1999), chap. 1.

50. K. M. Kacmar and R. A. Baron, "Organizational Politics: The State of the Field, Links to Related Processes, and an Agenda for Future Research," *Research in Personnel and Human Resources Management* 17 (1999), pp. 1–39; K. M. Kacmar and G. R. Ferris, "Politics at Work: Sharpening the Focus of Political Behaviour in Organizations," *Business Horizons* 36 (July–August 1993), pp. 70–74; A. Drory and T. Romm, "The Definition of Organizational Politics: A Review," *Human Relations* 43 (1990), pp. 1133–54.

51. K. Ohlson, "Leadership in an Age of Mistrust," *Industry Week* 247 (February 2, 1998), pp. 37–46.

52. D. J. Burrough, "Office Politics Mirror Popular TV Program," *Arizona Republic*, February 4, 2001, p. EC1. See also T. H. Davenport, R. G. Eccles, and L. Prusak, "Information Politics," *Sloan Management Review*, Fall 1992, pp. 53–65; Pfeffer, *Managing with Power*, chap. 17.

53. D. Sandahl and C. Hewes, "Decision Making at Digital Speed," *Pharmaceutical Executive* 21 (August 2001), p. 62; "Notes about Where We Work and How We Make Ends Meet," *Arizona Daily Star*, February 18, 2001, p. D1.

54. J. C. Howes, A. A. Grandey, and P. Toth, "The Relationship of Organizational Politics and Support to Work Behaviours, Attitudes, and Stress," *Journal of Organizational Behaviour* 18

(March 1997), pp. 159–80; G. R. Ferris and D. D. Frink, "Reactions of Diverse Groups to Politics in the Workplace," *Journal of Management* 22 (Spring 1996), pp. 23–44; P. Kumar and R. Ghadially, "Organizational Politics and Its Effects on Members of Organizations," *Human Relations* 42 (1989), pp. 305–14.

55. M. Velasquez, D. J. Moberg, and G. F. Cavanaugh, "Organizational Statesmanship and Dirty Politics: Ethical Guidelines for the Organizational Politician," *Organizational Dynamics* 11 (1983), pp. 65–79.

56. R. W. Allen, D. L. Madison, L. W. Porter, P. A. Renwick, and B. T. Mayes, "Organizational Politics: Tactics and Characteristics of Its Actors," *California Management Review* 22 (Fall 1979), pp. 77–83; V. Murray and J. Gandz, "Games Executives Play: Politics at Work," *Business Horizons*, December 1980, pp. 11–23.

57. B. E. Ashforth and R. T. Lee, "Defensive Behaviour in Organizations: A Preliminary Model," *Human Relations* 43 (1990), pp. 621–48.

58. For examples and discussion of these information turf wars, see A. Simmons, *Territorial Games: Understanding and Ending Turf Wars* (New York: AMACOM, 1998).

59. "Be Part of the Team if You Want to Catch the Eye," *Birmingham Post (UK)*, August 31, 2000, p. 14.

60. Y. Gabriel, "An Introduction to the Social Psychology of Insults in Organizations," *Human Relations* 51 (November 1998), pp. 1329–54.

61. M. Warshaw, "The Good Guy's Guide to Office Politics," *Fast Company* 14 (April–May 1998), pp. 157–78.

62. E. A. Mannix, "Organizations as Resource Dilemmas: The Effects of Power Balance on Coalition Formation in Small Groups," *Organizational Behaviour and Human Decision Processes* 55 (1993), pp. 1–22; A. T. Cobb, "Toward the Study of Organizational Coalitions: Participant Concerns and Activities in a Simulated Organizational Setting," *Human Relations* 44 (1991), pp. 1057–79; W. B. Stevenson, J. L. Pearce, and L. W. Porter, "The Concept of 'Coalition' in Organization Theory and Research," *Academy of Management Review* 10 (1985), pp. 256–68.

63. Falbe and Yukl, "Consequences for Managers of Using Single Influence Tactics and Combinations of Tactics."

64. D. Krackhardt and J. R. Hanson, "Informal Networks: The Company behind the Chart," *Harvard Business Review* 71 (July–August 1993), pp. 104–11; R. E. Kaplan, "Trade Routes: The Manager's Network of Relationships," *Organizational Dynamics*, Spring 1984, pp. 37–52.

65. M. Linehan, "Barriers to Women's Participation in International Management," *European Business Review* 13 (2001); R. J. Burke and C. A. McKeen, "Women in Management," *International Review of Industrial and Organizational Psychology* 7 (1992), pp. 245–83; B. R. Ragins and E. Sundstrom, "Gender and Power in Organizations: A Longitudinal Perspective," *Psychological Bulletin* 105 (1989), pp. 51–88.

66. D. M. McCracken, "Winning the Talent War for Women: Sometimes It Takes a Revolution," *Harvard Business Review* 78 (November–December 2000), pp. 159–67.

67. A. R. Cohen and D. L. Bradford, "Influence without Authority: The Use of Alliances, Reciprocity, and Exchange to Accomplish Work," *Organizational Dynamics* 17 (3) (1989), pp. 5–17.

68. A. Rao and S. M. Schmidt, "Upward Impression Management: Goals, Influence Strategies, and Consequences," *Human Relations* 48 (1995), pp. 147–67; R. A. Giacalone and P. Rosenfeld, eds., *Applied Impression Management* (Newbury Park, CA: Sage, 1991); J. T. Tedeschi, ed., *Impression Management Theory and Social Psychological Research* (New York: Academic, 1981).

69. W. L. Gardner III, "Lessons in Organizational Dramaturgy: The Art of Impression Management," *Organizational Dynamics*, Summer 1992, pp. 33–46; R. C. Liden and T. R. Mitchell, "Ingratiatory Behaviours in Organizational Settings," *Academy of Management Review* 13 (1988), pp. 572–87.

70. A. Vuong, "Job Applicants Often Don't Tell Whole Truth," *Denver Post*, May 30, 2001, p. C1. For a discussion of research on false résumés, see S. L. McShane, "Applicant Misrepresentation in Résumés and Interviews," *Labor Law Journal* 45 (January 1994), pp. 15–24.

71. S. Romero and M. Richtel, "Second Chance," *New York Times*, March 5, 2001, p. C1; L. Faught, J. Collins, and R. Srisavasdi, "Senior Center Head Fired in Costa Mesa," *Orange County (CA) Register*, May 18, 2000, p. A1.

72. C. Hardy, *Strategies for Retrenchment and Turnaround: The Politics of Survival* (Berlin: de Gruyter, 1990), chap. 14; J. Gandz and V. V. Murray, "The Experience of Workplace Politics," *Academy of Management Journal* 23 (1980), pp. 237–51.

73. P. Dillon, "Failure Is an Option," *Fast Company* 22 (February–March 1999), pp. 154–71.

74. G. R. Ferris, G. S. Russ, and P. M. Fandt, "Politics in Organizations," in R. A. Giacalone and P. Rosenfeld, eds., *Impression Management in the Organization* (Hillsdale, NJ: Erlbaum, 1989), pp. 143–70; H. Mintzberg, "The Organization as Political Arena," *Journal of Management Studies* 22 (1985), pp. 133–54.

75. R. J. House, "Power and Personality in Complex Organizations," *Research in Organizational Behaviour* 10 (1988), pp. 305–57; L. W. Porter, R. W. Allen, and H. L. Angle, "The Politics of Upward Influence in Organizations," *Research in Organizational Behaviour* 3 (1981), pp. 120–22.

76. K. S. Sauleya and A. G. Bedeian "Equity Sensitivity: Construction of a Measure and Examination of Its Psychometric Properties," *Journal of Management* 26 (September 2000), pp. 885–910; S. M. Farmer, J. M. Maslyn, D. B. Fedor, and J. S. Goodman, "Putting Upward Influence Strategies in Context," *Journal of Organizational Behaviour* 18 (1997), pp. 17–42; P. E. Mudrack, "An Investigation into the Acceptability of Workplace Behaviours of a Dubious Ethical Nature," *Journal of Business Ethics* 12 (1993), pp. 517–24; R. Christie and F. Geis, *Studies in Machiavellianism* (New York: Academic Press, 1970).

77. D. Tannen, *Talking from 9 to 5* (New York: Avon, 1995), pp. 137–41, 151–52.

78. N. Martin, "Men 'Gossip More than Women to Boost Their Egos,'" *Daily Telegraph (UK)*, June 15, 2001, p. P13; Tannen, *Talking from 9 to 5*, chap. 2; M. Crawford, *Talking Difference: On Gen-* der and Language (Thousand Oaks, CA: Sage, 1995), pp. 41–44; D. Tannen, *You Just Don't Understand: Men and Women in Conversation* (New York: Ballantine, 1990); S. Helgesen, *The Female Advantage: Women's Ways of Leadership* (New York: Doubleday, 1990).

79. S. Mann, "Politics and Power in Organizations: Why Women Lose Out," *Leadership and Organization Development Journal* 16 (1995), pp. 9–15; L. Larwood and M. M. Wood, "Training Women for Management: Changing Priorities," *Journal of Management Development* 14 (1995), pp. 54–65. A recent popular-press book serves as a guide for women to learn organizational politics; see H. Rubin, *The Princessa: Machiavelli for Women* (New York: Doubleday Currency, 1996).

80. G. R. Ferris et al., "Perceptions of Organizational Politics: Prediction, Stress-Related Implications, and Outcomes," *Human Relations* 49 (1996), pp. 233–63.

81. A. P. Brief, *Attitudes In and Around Organizations* (Thousand Oaks, CA: Sage, 1998), pp. 69–84; K. K. Reardon, *Persuasion in Practice* (Newbury Park, CA: Sage, 1991); P. Zimbardo and E. B. Ebbeson, *Influencing Attitudes and Changing Behavior* (Reading, MA: Addison-Wesley, 1969).

82. J. J. Jiang, G. Klein, and R. G. Vedder, "Persuasive Expert Systems: The Influence of Confidence and Discrepancy," *Computers in Human Behavior* 16 (March 2000), pp. 99–109; J. Cooper and R. T. Coyle, "Attitudes and Attitude Change," *Annual Review of Psychology* 35 (1984), pp. 395–426; N. MacLachlan, "What People Really Think about Fast Talkers," *Psychology Today* 113 (November 1979), pp. 112–17.

83. J. A. Conger, *Winning 'Em Over*.

84. D. B. Freeland, "Turning Communication into Influence," *HRMagazine* 38 (September 1993), pp. 93–96; M. Snyder and M. Rothbart, "Communicator Attractiveness and Opinion Change," *Canadian Journal of Behavioural Science* 3 (1971), pp. 377–87.

85. E. Aronson, *The Social Animal* (San Francisco: Freeman, 1976), pp. 67–68; R. A. Jones and J. W. Brehm, "Persuasiveness of One- and Two-Sided Communications as a Function of Awareness That There Are Two Sides,"

Journal of Experimental Social Psychology 6 (1970), pp. 47–56.

86. D. G. Linz and S. Penrod, "Increasing Attorney Persuasiveness in the Courtroom," Law and Psychology Review 8 (1984), pp. 1–47; R. B. Zajonc, "Attitudinal Effects of Mere Exposure," *Journal of Personality and Social Psychology Monograph* 9 (1968), pp. 1–27; R. Petty and J. Cacioppo, *Attitudes and Persuasion: Classic and Contemporary Approaches* (Dubuque, IA: Brown, 1981).

87. Conger, *Winning 'Em Over.*

88. Zimbardo and Ebbeson, *Influencing Attitudes and Changing Behavior.*

89. M. Zellner, "Self-Esteem, Reception, and Influenceability," *Journal of Personality and Social Psychology* 15 (1970), pp. 87–93.

CHAPTER THIRTEEN

1. M. King and S. Stripling, "Blend of Generations," *Seattle Times*, March 12, 2001; T. S. Taylor, "An Age-Old Conflict," *Chicago Tribune*, January 7, 2001, p. C1; T. Aeppel, "Power Generation: Young and Old See Technology Sparking Friction on Shop Floor," *The Wall Street Journal*, April 7, 2000, p. A1; V. Uhland, "Generations at Crossroads," *Denver Rocky Mountain News*, February 6, 2000, p. J1.

2. J. A. Wall and R. R. Callister, "Conflict and Its Management," *Journal of Management* 21 (1995), pp. 515–58; D. Tjosvold, *Working Together to Get Things Done* (Lexington, MA: Lexington, 1986), pp. 114–15.

3. The conflict process is described in K. W. Thomas, "Conflict and Negotiation Processes in Organizations," in M. D. Dunnette and L. M. Hough, eds., *Handbook of Industrial and Organizational Psychology*, 2nd ed., vol. 3 (Palo Alto, CA: Consulting Psychologists Press, 1992), pp. 651–718; L. Pondy, "Organizational Conflict: Concepts and Models," *Administrative Science Quarterly* 2 (1967), pp. 296–320.

4. A. C. Ward, "Another Look at How Toyota Integrates Product Development," *Harvard Business Review*, July–August 1998, pp. 36–49.

5. L. H. Pelled, K. R. Xin, and A. M. Weiss, "No Es Como Mi: Relational Demography and Conflict in a Mexican Production Facility," *Journal of*

Occupational and Organizational Psychology 74 (March 2001), pp. 63–84; L. H. Pelled, K. M. Eisenhardt, and K. R. Xin, "Exploring the Black Box: An Analysis of Work Group Diversity, Conflict, and Performance," *Administrative Science Quarterly* 44 (March 1999), pp. 1–28; A. C. Amason, "Distinguishing the Effects of Functional and Dysfunctional Conflict on Strategic Decision Making: Resolving a Paradox for Top Management Teams," *Academy of Management Journal* 39 (1996), pp. 123–48; K. A. Jehn, "A Multimethod Examination of the Benefits and Detriments of Intragroup Conflict," *Administrative Science Quarterly* 40 (1995), pp. 256–82.

6. J. M. Brett, D. L. Shapiro, and A. L. Lytle, "Breaking the Bonds of Reciprocity in Negotiations," *Academy of Management Journal* 41 (August 1998), pp. 410–24; G. E. Martin and T. J. Bergman, "The Dynamics of Behavioral Response to Conflict in the Workplace," *Journal of Occupational and Organizational Psychology* 69 (December 1996), pp. 377–87; G. Wolf, "Conflict Episodes," in M. H. Bazerman and R. J. Lewicki , eds., *Negotiating in Organizations* (Beverly Hills, CA: Sage, 1983), pp. 135–40; L. R. Pondy, "Organizational Conflict: Concepts and Models," *Administrative Science Quarterly* 12 (1967), pp. 296–320.

7. H. Witteman, "Analyzing Interpersonal Conflict: Nature of Awareness, Type of Initiating Event, Situational Perceptions, and Management Styles," *Western Journal of Communications* 56 (1992), pp. 248–80; F. J. Barrett and D. L. Cooperrider, "Generative Metaphor Intervention: A New Approach for Working with Systems Divided by Conflict and Caught in Defensive Perception," *Journal of Applied Behavioral Science* 26 (1990), pp. 219–39.

8. Wall and Callister, "Conflict and Its Management," pp. 526–33.

9. T. Wallace, "Fear and Loathing," *Australian Financial Review (Boss Magazine)*, April 12, 2001, p. 42.

10. R. R. Blake and J. S. Mouton, *Solving Costly Organizational Conflicts* (San Francisco: Jossey-Bass, 1984).

11. F. Rose, "The Eisner School of Business," *Fortune*, July 6, 1998, pp. 29–30. For a more favorable interpretation of conflict at Disney, see

S. Wetlaufer, "Common Sense and Conflict: An Interview with Disney's Michael Eisner," *Harvard Business Review* 78 (January–February 2000), pp. 114–24.

12. M. Rempel and R. J. Fisher, "Perceived Threat, Cohesion, and Group Problem Solving in Intergroup Conflict," *International Journal of Conflict Management* 8 (1997), pp. 216–34.

13. Amason, "Distinguishing the Effects of Functional and Dysfunctional Conflict on Strategic Decision Making"; L. L. Putnam, "Productive Conflict: Negotiation as Implicit Coordination," *International Journal of Conflict Management* 5 (1994), pp. 285–99; D. Tjosvold, *The Conflict-Positive Organization* (Reading, MA: Addison-Wesley, 1991); R. A. Baron, "Positive Effects of Conflict: A Cognitive Perspective," *Employee Responsibilities and Rights Journal* 4 (1991), pp. 25–36.

14. K. M. Eisenhardt, J. L. Kahwajy, and L. J. Bourgeois III, "Conflict and Strategic Choice: How Top Management Teams Disagree," *California Management Review* 39 (Winter 1997), pp. 42–62; J. K. Bouwen and R. Fry, "Organizational Innovation and Learning: Four Patterns of Dialog between the Dominant Logic and the New Logic," *International Studies of Management and Organizations* 21 (1991), pp. 37–51.

15. R. Rosen, P. Digh, M. Singer, and C. Phillips, *Global Literacies* (New York: Simon & Schuster, 2000), pp. 285–89; "Face Value: Tractebel the Intractable," *The Economist*, February 27, 1999, p. 66.

16. S. Armour, "Moderate Amounts of Conflict Contribute to Healthy Workplace," *Des Moines (IA) Register*, May 20, 1997, p. 8.

17. R. E. Walton and J. M. Dutton, "The Management of Conflict: A Model and Review," *Administrative Science Quarterly* 14 (1969), pp. 73–84.

18. D. Evans, "Team Players," *Canadian Business*, August 1991, pp. 28–31.

19. D. M. Brock, D. Barry, and D. C. Thomas, "'Your Forward Is Our Reverse, Your Right, Our Wrong': Rethinking Multinational Planning Processes in Light of National Culture," *International Business Review* 9 (December 2000), pp. 687–701.

20. For a fuller discussion of conflict across the generations, see R. Zemke and B. Filipczak, *Generations at Work: Managing the Clash of Veterans, Boomers, Xers, and Nexters in Your Workplace* (New York: AMACOM, 1999).

21. R. C. Liden, S. J. Wayne, and L. K. Bradway, "Task Interdependence as a Moderator of the Relation between Group Control and Performance," *Human Relations* 50 (1997), pp. 169–81; R. Wageman, "Interdependence and Group Effectiveness," *Administrative Science Quarterly* 40 (1995), pp. 145–80; M. A. Campion, G. J. Medsker, and A. C. Higgs, "Relations between Work Group Characteristics and Effectiveness: Implications for Designing Effective Work Groups," *Personnel Psychology* 46 (1993), pp. 823–50; M. N. Kiggundu, "Task Interdependence and the Theory of Job Design," *Academy of Management Review* 6 (1981), pp. 499–508.

22. K. Jelin, "A Multimethod Examination of the Benefits and Detriments of Intragroup Conflict," *Administrative Science Quarterly* 40 (1995), pp. 245–82; P. C. Earley and G. B. Northcraft, "Goal Setting, Resource Interdependence, and Conflict Management," in M. A. Rahim, ed., *Managing Conflict: An Interdisciplinary Approach* (New York: Praeger, 1989), pp. 161–70.

23. J. D. Thompson, *Organizations in Action* (New York: McGraw-Hill, 1967), pp. 54–56.

24. K. H. Doerr, T. R. Mitchell, and T. D. Klastorin, "Impact of Material Flow Policies and Goals on Job Outcomes," *Journal of Applied Psychology* 81 (1996), pp. 142–52.

25. W. W. Notz, F. A. Starke, and J. Atwell, "The Manager as Arbitrator: Conflicts over Scarce Resources," in Bazerman and Lewicki, eds., *Negotiating in Organizations*, pp. 143–64.

26. P. Roberts, "Sony Changes the Game," *Fast Company* 10 (1997), p. 116.

27. A. Risberg, "Employee Experiences of Acquisition Processes," *Journal of World Business* 36 (March 2001), pp. 58–84.

28. Brett et al., "Breaking the Bonds of Reciprocity in Negotiations"; R. A. Baron, "Reducing Organizational Conflict: An Incompatible Response Approach," *Journal of Applied Psychology* 69 (1984), pp. 272–79.

29. K. D. Grimsley, "Slings and Arrows on the Job," *Washington Post*, July 12, 1998, p. H1; "Flame Throwers," *Director* 50 (July 1997), p. 36.

30. T. A. Abma, "Stakeholder Conflict: A Case Study," *Evaluation and Program Planning* 23 (May 2000), pp. 199–210; J. W. Jackson and E. R. Smith, "Conceptualizing Social Identity: A New Framework and Evidence for the Impact of Different Dimensions," *Personality and Social Psychology Bulletin* 25 (January 1999), pp. 120–35.

31. D. C. Dryer and L. M. Horowitz, "When Do Opposites Attract? Interpersonal Complementarity versus Similarity," *Journal of Personality and Social Psychology* 72 (1997), pp. 592–603.

32. S. Vaughn, "Common Ground for Differences," *Los Angeles Times*, July 15, 2001, p. W1.

33. K. W. Thomas, "Conflict and Conflict Management," in M. D. Dunnette, ed., *Handbook of Industrial and Organizational Psychology* (Chicago: Rand McNally, 1976), pp. 889–935; R. R. Blake and J. S. Mouton, *The Managerial Grid* (Houston: Gulf, 1964); M. A. Rahim, "A Measure of Styles of Handling Interpersonal Conflict," *Academy of Management Journal* 26 (1983), pp. 368–76. A more complex variation of eight conflict styles is discussed in E. Van de Vliert and O. Janssen, "Description, Explanation, and Prescription of Intragroup Conflict Behaviors," in M. E. Turner, ed., *Groups at Work: Theory and Research* (Mahwah, NJ: Lawrence Erlbaum, 2001), pp. 267–97.

34. R. J. Lewicki and J. A. Litterer, Negotiation (Homewood, IL: Irwin, 1985), pp. 102–6; K. W. Thomas, "Toward Multi-Dimensional Values in Teaching: The Example of Conflict Behaviors," *Academy of Management Review* 2 (1977), pp. 484–90.

35. Jehn, "A Multimethod Examination of the Benefits and Detriments of Intragroup Conflict," p. 276.

36. M. Lyster et al., "The Changing Guard," *Orange County (CA) Business Journal*, May 7, 2001, p. 31.

37. L. Xiaohua and R. Germain, "Sustaining Satisfactory Joint Venture Relationships: The Role of Conflict Resolution Strategy," *Journal of International Business Studies* 29 (March 1998), pp. 179–96.

38. Tjosvold, *Working Together to Get Things Done*, chap. 2; D. W. Johnson, G. Maruyama, R. T. Johnson, D. Nelson, and S. Skon, "Effects of Cooperative, Competitive, and Individualistic Goal Structures on Achievement: A Meta-Analysis," *Psychological Bulletin* 89 (1981), pp. 47–62; R. J. Burke, "Methods of Resolving Superior–Subordinate Conflict: The Constructive Use of Subordinate Differences and Disagreements," *Organizational Behavior and Human Performance* 5 (1970), pp. 393–441.

39. K. Leung and D. Tjosvold, eds., *Conflict Management in the Asia Pacific* (Singapore: Wiley, 1998); M. A. Rahim and A. A. Blum, eds., *Global Perspectives on Organizational Conflict* (Westport, CT: Praeger, 1995); M. Rabie, *Conflict Resolution and Ethnicity* (Westport, CT: Praeger, 1994).

40. C. C. Chen, X. P. Chen, and J. R. Meindl, "How Can Cooperation Be Fostered? The Cultural Effects of Individualism–Collectivism," *Academy of Management Review* 23 (1998), pp. 285–304; S. M. Elsayed-Ekhouly and R. Buda, "Organizational Conflict: A Comparative Analysis of Conflict Styles across Cultures," *International Journal of Conflict Management* 7 (1996), pp. 71–81; D. K. Tse, J. Francis, and J. Walls, "Cultural Differences in Conducting Intra- and Inter-Cultural Negotiations: A Sino-Canadian Comparison," *Journal of International Business Studies* 25 (1994), pp. 537–55; S. Ting-Toomey et al., "Culture, Face Management, and Conflict Styles of Handling Interpersonal Conflict: A Study in Five Cultures," *International Journal of Conflict Management* 2 (1991), pp. 275–96.

41. L. Karakowsky, "Toward an Understanding of Women and Men at the Bargaining Table: Factors Affecting Negotiator Style and Influence in Multi-Party Negotiations," *Proceedings of the Annual ASAC Conference, Women in Management Division*, 1996, pp. 21–30; W. C. King, Jr., and T. D. Hinson, "The Influence of Sex and Equity Sensitivity on Relationship Preferences, Assessment of Opponent, and Outcomes in a Negotiation Experiment," *Journal of Management* 20 (1994), pp. 605–24; R. Lewicki, J. Litterer, D. Saunders, and J. Minton, eds., *Negotiation: Readings,*

Exercises, and Cases (Homewood, IL: Irwin, 1993).

42. E. Van de Vliert, "Escalative Intervention in Small Group Conflicts," *Journal of Applied Behavioral Science* 21 (Winter 1985), pp. 19–36.

43. M. B. Pinto, J. K. Pinto, and J. E. Prescott, "Antecedents and Consequences of Project Team Cross-Functional Cooperation," *Management Science* 39 (1993), pp. 1281–97; M. Sherif, "Superordinate Goals in the Reduction of Intergroup Conflict," *American Journal of Sociology* 68 (1958), pp. 349–58.

44. L. Mulitz, "Flying Off over Office Politics," *InfoWorld*, November 6, 2000.

45. X. M. Song, J. Xile, B. Dyer, "Antecedents and Consequences of Marketing Managers' Conflict-Handling Behaviors," *Journal of Marketing* 64, January 2000, pp. 50–66; K. M. Eisenhardt, J. L. Kahwajy, and L. J. Bourgeois III, "How Management Teams Can Have a Good Fight," *Harvard Business Review*, July–August 1997, pp. 77–85.

46. Song et al., "Antecedents and Consequences of Marketing Managers' Conflict-Handling Behaviors."

47. "Teamwork Polishes This Diamond," *Philippine Daily Inquirer*, October 4, 2000, p. 10.

48. "American Factories Halt Their Assembly Lines," *Globe and Mail (Toronto)*, January 7, 1995, p. D4.

49. This strategy and other conflict management practices in joint military operations are fully discussed in E. Elron, B. Shamir, and E. Ben-Ari, "Why Don't They Fight Each Other? Cultural Diversity and Operational Unity in Multinational Forces," *Armed Forces and Society* 26 (October 1999), pp. 73–97.

50. R. J. Fisher, E. Maltz, and B. J. Jaworski, "Enhancing Communication between Marketing and Engineering: The Moderating Role of Relative Functional Identification," *Journal of Marketing* 61 (1997), pp. 54–70. For a discussion of minimizing conflict through understanding as "other point multiplicity," see T. A. Abma, "Stakeholder Conflict: A Case Study," *Evaluation and Program Planning* 23 (May 2000), pp. 199–210.

51. A. Zurcher, "Techies and Non-Techies Don't Always Interface Well," *Washington Post*, September 3, 2000, p. L5.

52. D. Woodruff, "Crossing Culture Divide Early Clears Merger Paths," *Asian Wall Street Journal*, May 28, 2001, p. 9.

53. L. Ellinor and G. Gerard, *Dialogue: Rediscovering the Transforming Power of Conversation* (New York: Wiley, 1998); W. N. Isaacs, "Taking Flight: Dialog, Collective Thinking, and Organizational Learning," *Organizational Dynamics*, Autumn 1993, pp. 24–39; E. H. Schein, "On Dialog, Culture, and Organizational Learning," *Organizational Dynamics*, Autumn 1993, pp. 40–51; P. M. Senge, *The Fifth Discipline* (New York: Doubleday Currency, 1990), pp. 238–49.

54. P. R. Lawrence and J. W. Lorsch, *Organization and Environment* (Homewood, IL: Irwin, 1969).

55. E. Horwitt, "Knowledge, Knowledge, Who's Got the Knowledge?" *Computerworld*, April 8, 1996, pp. 80, 81, 84.

56. D. G. Pruitt and P. J. Carnevale, *Negotiation in Social Conflict* (Buckingham, UK: Open University Press, 1993), p. 2; J. A. Wall, Jr., *Negotiation: Theory and Practice* (Glenview, IL: Scott Foresman, 1985), p. 4.

57. L. Edson, "The Negotiation Industry," *Across the Board*, April 2000, pp. 14–20.

58. For a critical view of collaboration in negotiation, see J. M. Brett, "Managing Organizational Conflict," *Professional Psychology: Research and Practice* 15 (1984), pp. 664–78.

59. R. E. Fells, "Overcoming the Dilemmas in Walton and McKersie's Mixed Bargaining Strategy," *Industrial Relations* (Laval) 53 (March 1998), pp. 300–25; R. E. Fells, "Developing Trust in Negotiation," *Employee Relations* 15 (1993), pp. 33–45.

60. L. Thompson, *The Mind and Heart of the Negotiator* (Upper Saddle River, NJ: Prentice Hall, 1998), chap. 2; R. Stagner and H. Rosen, *Psychology of Union—Management Relations* (Belmont, CA: Wadsworth, 1965), pp. 95–96, 108–10; R. E. Walton and R. B. McKersie, *A Behavioral Theory of Labor Negotiations: An Analysis of a Social In-*

teraction System (New York: McGraw-Hill, 1965), pp. 41–46.

61. J. Mayfield, M. Mayfield, D. Martin, and P. Herbig, "How Location Impacts International Business Negotiations," *Review of Business* 19 (December 1998), pp. 21–24; J. W. Salacuse and J. Z. Rubin, "Your Place or Mine? Site Location and Negotiation," *Negotiation Journal* 6 (January 1990), pp. 5–10; Lewicki and Litterer, *Negotiation*, pp. 144–46.

62. Lewicki and Litterer, *Negotiation*, pp. 146–51; B. Kniveton, *The Psychology of Bargaining* (Aldershot, UK: Avebury, 1989), pp. 76–79.

63. Pruitt and Carnevale, *Negotiation in Social Conflict*, pp. 59–61; Lewicki and Litterer, *Negotiation*, pp. 151–54.

64. B. M. Downie, "When Negotiations Fail: Causes of Breakdown and Tactics for Breaking the Stalemate," *Negotiation Journal*, April 1991, pp. 175–86.

65. Pruitt and Carnevale, *Negotiation in Social Conflict*, pp. 56–58; Lewicki and Litterer, *Negotiation*, pp. 215–22.

66. V. V. Murray, T. D. Jick, and P. Bradshaw, "To Bargain or Not to Bargain? The Case of Hospital Budget Cuts," in Brazerman and Lewicki, eds., *Negotiating in Organizations*, pp. 272–95.

67. S. Doctoroff, "Reengineering Negotiations," *Sloan Management Review* 39 (March 1998), pp. 63–71; R. L. Lewicki, A. Hiam, and K. Olander, *Think before You Speak: The Complete Guide to Strategic Negotiation* (New York: Wiley, 1996); G. B. Northcraft and M. A. Neale, "Joint Effects of Assigned Goals and Training on Negotiator Performance," *Human Performance* 7 (1994), pp. 257–72.

68. M. A. Neale and M. H. Bazerman, *Cognition and Rationality in Negotiation* (New York: Free Press, 1991), pp. 29–31; L. L. Thompson, "Information Exchange in Negotiation," *Journal of Experimental Social Psychology* 27 (1991), pp. 161–79.

69. Y. Paik and R. L. Tung, "Negotiating with East Asians: How to Attain 'Win-Win' Outcomes," *Management International Review* 39 (1999), pp. 103–22; L. Thompson, E. Peterson, and S. E. Brodt, "Team Negotiation: An Examination of Integrative and Distributive Bargaining," *Journal of Personality and Social Psychology* 70 (1996), pp. 66–78.

70. L. L. Putnam and M. E. Roloff, eds., *Communication and Negotiation* (Newbury Park, CA: Sage, 1992).

71. L. Hall, ed., *Negotiation: Strategies for Mutual Gain* (Newbury Park, CA: Sage, 1993); D. Ertel, "How to Design a Conflict Management Procedure That Fits Your Dispute," *Sloan Management Review* 32 (Summer 1991), pp. 29–42.

72. Lewicki and Litterer, *Negotiation*, pp. 89–93.

73. J. J. Zhao, "The Chinese Approach to International Business Negotiation," *Journal of Business Communication*, July 2000, pp. 209–37; Paik and Tung, "Negotiating with East Asians"; N. J. Adler, *International Dimensions of Organizational Behavior*, 2nd ed., (Belmont, CA: Wadsworth, 1991), pp. 180–81.

74. Kniveton, *The Psychology of Bargaining*, pp. 100–1; J. Z. Rubin and B. R. Brown, *The Social Psychology of Bargaining and Negotiation* (New York: Academic, 1976), chap. 9; Brett, "Managing Organizational Conflict," pp. 670–71.

75. B. H. Sheppard, R. J. Lewicki, and J. W. Monton, *Organizational Justice: The Search for Fairness in the Workplace* (New York: Lexington, 1992).

76. L. B. Bingham, "Mediating Employment Disputes: Perceptions of Redress at the United States Postal Service," *Review of Public Personnel Administration* 17 (Spring 1997), pp. 20–30; R. Folger and J. Greenberg, "Procedural Justice: An Interpretive Analysis of Personnel Systems," *Research in Personnel and Human Resources Management* 3 (1985), pp. 141–83.

77. A. R. Elangovan, "The Manager as the Third Party: Deciding How to Intervene in Employee Disputes," in R. Lewicki, J. Litterer, and D. Saunders, eds., *Negotiation: Readings, Exercises, and Cases*, 3rd ed., (New York: McGraw-Hill, 1999), pp. 458–69; L. L. Putnam, "Beyond Third Party Role: Disputes and Managerial Intervention," *Employee Responsibilities and Rights Journal* 7 (1994), pp. 23–36; Sheppard et al., *Organizational Justice*.

78. M. A. Neale and M. H. Bazerman, *Cognition and Rationality in Negotiation* (New York: Free Press, 1991), pp. 140–42.

79. B. H. Sheppard, "Managers as Inquisitors: Lessons from the Law," in M. Bazerman and R. J. Lewicki, eds., *Bargaining inside Organizations* (Beverly Hills, CA: Sage, 1983), pp. 193–213.

80. R. Cropanzano, H. Aguinis, M. Schminke, and D. L. Denham, "Disputant Reactions to Managerial Conflict Resolution Tactics," *Group and Organization Management* 24 (June 1999), pp. 124–53; R. Karambayya and J. M. Brett, "Managers Handling Disputes: Third Party Roles and Perceptions of Fairness," *Academy of Management Journal* 32 (1989), pp. 687–704.

81. A. R. Elangovan, "Managerial Intervention in Organizational Disputes: Testing a Prescriptive Model of Strategy Selection," *International Journal of Conflict Management* 4 (1998), pp. 301–35.

82. J. P. Meyer, J. M. Gemmell, and P. G. Irving, "Evaluating the Management of Interpersonal Conflict in Organizations: A Factor-Analytic Study of Outcome Criteria," *Canadian Journal of Administrative Sciences* 14 (1997), pp. 1–13.

83. C. Hirschman, "Order in the Hearing!" *HRMagazine* 46 (July 2001), p. 58; S. L. Hayford, "Alternative Dispute Resolution," *Business Horizons* 43 (January–February 2000), pp. 2–4.

84. D. Hechler, "No Longer a Novelty: ADR Winning Corporate Acceptance," *Fulton County (GA) Daily Report*, June 29, 2001.

85. M. Barrier, "A Working Alternative for Settling Disputes," *Nation's Business* 86 (July, 1998) pp. 43–46.

CHAPTER FOURTEEN

1. L. Veit, "Ethical Matters," *Credit Union Management* 24 (June 2001), pp. 18–20; P. Gallagher, "How Can You Be a Great Leader—Drive the Vision," *Success* 48 (April 2001), pp. 28ff.; S-J. Yim, "Behind the Mystique at the Top," *Portland Oregonian*, April 29, 2001, p. L11; C. Fox, "CEOs Slipping into Old Habits," *Australian Financial Review*, February 6, 2001, p. 38; "New Economy, Old Values," *Corporate Report Wisconsin* 16 (October 2000), pp. 12ff.; "Leadership A to Z" (Interview), *Training and Development*, March 2000, p. 58; P. Clark and E. Mychasuk, "The New Leadership," *Boss Magazine*, September 11, 2000, p. 32.

2. R. A. Barker, "How Can We Train Leaders if We Do Not Know What Leadership Is?" *Human Relations* 50 (1997), pp. 343–62; P. C. Drucker, "Foreward," in F. Hesselbein et al., *The Leader of the Future* (San Francisco, CA: Jossey-Bass, 1997).

3. D. Miller, M. F. R. Ket de Vries, and J. M. Toulouse, "Top Executive Locus of Control and Its Relationship to Strategy-Making, Structure, and Environment," *Academy of Management Journal* 25 (1982), pp. 237–53; P. Selznick, *Leadership in Administration* (Evanston, IL: Row, Peterson, 1957), p. 37.

4. M. Groves, "Cream Rises to the Top, but from a Small Crop," *Los Angeles Times*, June 8, 1998. A recent study also reported that only 3 percent of executives in large firms agreed that their companies develop leadership talent quickly and effectively. See H. Handfield-Jones, "How Executives Grow," *McKinsey Quarterly*, January 2000, pp. 116–23.

5. C. L. Cole, "Eight Values Bring Unity to a Worldwide Company," *Workforce* 80 (March 2001), pp. 44–45.

6. C. A. Beatty, "Implementing Advanced Manufacturing Technologies: Rules of the Road," *Sloan Management Review*, Summer 1992, pp. 49–60; J. M. Howell and C. A. Higgins, "Champions of Technological Innovation," *Administrative Science Quarterly* 35 (1990), pp. 317–41.

7. Many of these perspectives are summarized in R. N. Kanungo, "Leadership in Organizations: Looking Ahead to the 21st Century," *Canadian Psychology* 39 (Spring 1998), pp. 71–82.

8. L. Ortiz, "Karenann Terrell Was a GM Loyalist, until DCX Called," *Automotive News*, May 21, 2001, p. 18T-B; S. Carney and D. Howes, "Exodus Reshapes Chrysler," *Detroit News*, March 18, 2001, p. 1; L. Vaas, "Putting Pedal to the Metal," *EWeek*, September 11, 2000, p. 67; C. J. Murray, "Auto Engineer Helps Steer Carmaker to Internet Era," *Electronic Engineering Times*, May 22, 2000, pp. 34–37.

9. J. Kochanski, "Competency-Based Management," *Training and Development*, October 1997, pp. 40–44; Hay Group et al., *Raising the Bar: Using Competencies to Enhance Employee Performance* (Scottsdale, AZ: American Compensation Association, 1996); L. M. Spencer and S. M. Spencer, *Competence*

at Work: Models for Superior Performance (New York: Wiley, 1993).

10. T. Takala, "Plato on Leadership," *Journal of Business Ethics* 17 (May 1998), pp. 785–98.

11. R. M. Stogdill, *Handbook of Leadership* (New York: Free Press, 1974), chap. 5.

12. Most elements of this list were derived from S. A. Kirkpatrick and E. A. Locke, "Leadership: Do Traits Matter?" *Academy of Management Executive* 5 (May 1991), pp. 48–60. Several of these ideas are also discussed in H. B. Gregersen, A. J. Morrison, and J. S. Black, "Developing Leaders for the Global Frontier," *Sloan Management Review* 40 (Fall 1998), pp. 21–32; R. J. House and R. N. Aditya, "The Social Scientific Study of Leadership: Quo Vadis?" *Journal of Management* 23 (1997), pp. 409–73; R. J. House and M. L. Baetz, "Leadership: Some Empirical Generalizations and New Research Directions," *Research in Organizational Behavior* 1 (1979), pp. 341–423.

13. House and Aditya, "The Social Scientific Study of Leadership."

14. C. Savoye, "Workers Say Honesty Is Best Company Policy," *Christian Science Monitor*, June 15, 2000; "Canadian CEOs Give Themselves Top Marks for Leadership!" *Canada NewsWire*, September 9, 1999; J. M. Kouzes and B. Z. Posner, *Credibility: How Leaders Gain and Lose It, Why People Demand It* (San Francisco: Jossey-Bass, 1993).

15. J. George, "Emotions and Leadership: The Role of Emotional Intelligence," *Human Relations* 53 (August 2000), pp. 1027–55; D. Goleman, What Makes a Leader?" *Harvard Business Review* 76 (November–December 1998), pp. 92–102; J. D. Mayer and P. Salovey, "The Intelligence of Emotional Intelligence," *Intelligence* 17 (1993), pp. 433–42.

16. J. A. Kolb, "The Relationship between Self-Monitoring and Leadership in Student Project Groups," *Journal of Business Communication* 35 (April 1998), pp. 264–82; S. J. Zaccaro, R. J. Foti, and D. A. Kenny, "Self-Monitoring and Trait-Based Variance in Leadership: An Investigation of Leader Flexibility across Multiple Group Situations," *Journal of Applied Psychology* 76 (1991), pp. 308–15; S. E. Cronshaw and R. J.

Ellis, "A Process Investigation of Self-Monitoring and Leader Emergence," *Small Group Research* 22 (1991), pp. 403–20; S. J. Zaccaro, R. J. Foti, and D. A. Kenny, "Self-Monitoring and Trait-Based Variance in Leadership: An Investigation of Leader Flexibility across Multiple Group Situations," *Journal of Applied Psychology* 76 (1991); pp. 308–15; G. H. Dobbins, W. S. Long, E. J. Dedrick, and T. C. Clemons, "The Role of Self-Monitoring and Gender on Leader Emergence: A Labouratory and Field Study," *Journal of Management* 16 (1990), pp. 609–18.

17. "S Korea H&CB's Kim Jung-tae Named New Kookmin Bank CEO," *Dow Jones International News*, July 25, 2001; L. Nakarmi, "Here Come the Mavericks," *Asiaweek*, April 9, 1999; "Korea's Kim Jung Tae," *Business Week*, June 29, 1998.

18. R. G. Lord and K. J. Maher, *Leadership and Information Processing: Linking Perceptions and Performance* (Cambridge, MA: Unwin Hyman, 1991).

19. W. C. Byham, "Grooming Next-Millennium Leaders," *HRMagazine* 44 (February 1999), pp. 46–50; R. Zemke and S. Zemke, "Putting Competencies to Work," *Training* 36 (January 1999), pp. 70–76.

20. G. A. Yukl, *Leadership in Organizations*, 3rd ed. (Englewood Cliffs, NJ: Prentice Hall, 1994), pp. 53–75; R. Likert, *New Patterns of Management* (New York: McGraw-Hill, 1961).

21. M. D. Abrashoff, "Retention through Redemption," *Harvard Business Review* 79 (February 2001), pp. 136–41.

22. A. K. Korman, "Consideration, Initiating Structure, and Organizational Criteria—A Review," *Personnel Psychology* 19 (1966), pp 349–62; E. A. Fleishman, "Twenty Years of Consideration and Structure," in E. A. Fleishman and J. C. Hunt, eds., *Current Developments in the Study of Leadership* (Carbondale, IL: Southern Illinois University Press, 1973), pp. 1–40.

23. V. V. Baba, "Serendipity in Leadership: Initiating Structure and Consideration in the Classroom," *Human Relations* 42 (1989), pp. 509–25.

24. P. Weissenberg and M. H. Kavanagh, "The Independence of Initiating Structure and Consideration: A Review

of the Evidence," *Personnel Psychology* 25 (1972), pp. 119–30; Stogdill, *Handbook of Leadership*, chap. 11; R. L. Kahn, "The Prediction of Productivity," *Journal of Social Issues* 12 (2) (1956), pp. 41–49.

25. R. R. Blake and A. A. McCanse, Leadership Dilemmas—Grid Solutions (Houston: Gulf, 1991); R. R. Blake and J. S. Mouton, "Management by Grid Principles or Situationalism: Which?" *Group and Organization Studies* 7 (1982), pp. 207–10.

26. L. L. Larson, J. G. Hunt, and R. N. Osborn, "The Great Hi–Hi Leader Behavior Myth: A Lesson from Occam's Razor," *Academy of Management Journal* 19 (1976), pp. 628–41; S. Kerr, C. A. Schriesheim, C. J. Murphy, and R. M. Stogdill, "Towards a Contingency Theory of Leadership Based upon the Consideration and Initiating Structure Literature," *Organizational Behavior and Human Performance* 12 (1974), pp. 62–82; A. K. Korman, "Consideration, Initiating Structure, and Organizational Criteria—A Review," *Personnel Psychology* 19 (1966), pp. 349–62.

27. R. Tannenbaum and W. H. Schmidt, "How to Choose a Leadership Pattern," *Harvard Business Review*, May–June 1973, pp. 162–80.

28. For a recent discussion of the contingency perspective of leadership and emotional intelligence, see D. Goleman, "Leadership That Gets Results," *Harvard Business Review* 78 (March–April 2000), pp. 78–90.

29. M. G. Evans, "The Effects of Supervisory Behavior on the Path–Goal Relationship," *Organizational Behavior and Human Performance* 5 (1970), pp. 277–98; M. G. Evans, "Extensions of a Path–Goal Theory of Motivation," *Journal of Applied Psychology* 59 (1974), pp. 172–78; R. J. House, "A Path–Goal Theory of Leader Effectiveness," *Administrative Science Quarterly* 16 (1971), pp. 321–38.

30. R. J. House and T. R. Mitchell, "Path–Goal Theory of Leadership," *Journal of Contemporary Business*, Autumn 1974, pp. 81–97.

31. M. Fulmer, "Learning across a Living Company: The Shell Companies' Experiences," *Organizational Dynamics* 27 (Autumn 1998), pp. 61–69; R. Wageman, "Case Study: Critical Success

Factors for Creating Superb Self-Managing Teams at Xerox," *Compensation and Benefits Review* 29 (September–October 1997), pp. 31–41.

32. M. E. McGill and J. W. Slocum, Jr., "A Little Leadership, Please?" *Organizational Dynamics* 39 (Winter 1998), pp. 39–49; R. J. Doyle, "The Case of a Servant Leader: John F. Donnelly, Sr." in R. P. Vecchio, ed., *Leadership: Understanding the Dynamics of Power and Influence in Organizations* (Notre Dame, IN: University of Notre Dame Press, 1997), pp. 439–57.

33. R. J. House, "Path–Goal Theory of Leadership: Lessons, Legacy, and a Reformulated Theory," *Leadership Quarterly* 7 (1996), pp. 323–52.

34. J. C. Wofford and L. Z. Liska, "Path–Goal Theories of Leadership: A Meta-Analysis," *Journal of Management* 19 (1993), pp. 857–76; J. Indvik, "Path–Goal Theory of Leadership: A Meta-Analysis," *Academy of Management Proceedings*, 1986, pp. 189–92.

35. R. T. Keller, "A Test of the Path–Goal Theory of Leadership with Need for Clarity as a Moderator in Research and Development Organizations," *Journal of Applied Psychology* 74 (1989), pp. 208–12.

36. J. M. Jermier, "The Path–Goal Theory of Leadership: A Subtextural Analysis," *Leadership Quarterly* 7 (1996), pp. 311–16.

37. House, "Path–Goal Theory of Leadership."

38. Wofford and Liska, "Path–Goal Theories of Leadership"; Yukl, *Leadership in Organizations*, pp. 102–4; Indvik, "Path–Goal Theory of Leadership."

39. C. A. Schriesheim and L. L. Neider, "Path–Goal Leadership Theory: The Long and Winding Road," *Leadership Quarterly* 7 (1996), pp. 317–21. One of the more prominent studies that found evidence against path–goal theory is H. K. Downey, J. E. Sheridan, and J. W. Slocum, "Analysis of Relationships among Leader Behavior, Subordinate Job Performance and Satisfaction: A Path–Goal Approach," *Academy of Management Journal* 18 (1975), pp. 253–62.

40. P. Hersey and K. H. Blanchard, *Management of Organizational Behavior: Utilizing Human Resources*, 5th ed. (Englewood Cliffs, NJ: Prentice Hall, 1988).

41. C. L. Graeff, "Evolution of Situational Leadership Theory: A Critical Review," *Leadership Quarterly* 8 (1997), pp. 153–70; W. Blank, J. R. Weitzel, and S. G. Green, "A Test of the Situational Leadership Theory," *Personnel Psychology* 43 (1990), pp. 579–97; R. P. Vecchio, "Situational Leadership Theory: An Examination of a Prescriptive Theory," *Journal of Applied Psychology* 72 (1987), pp. 444–51.

42. F. E. Fiedler, *A Theory of Leadership Effectiveness* (New York: McGraw-Hill, 1967); F. E. Fiedler and M. M. Chemers, *Leadership and Effective Management* (Glenview, IL: Scott Foresman, 1974).

43. F .E. Fiedler, "Engineer the Job to Fit the Manager," *Harvard Business Review* 43 (5) (1965), pp. 115–22.

44. For a summary of criticisms, see Yukl, *Leadership in Organizations*, pp. 197–98.

45. N. Nicholson, *Executive Instinct* (New York: Crown, 2000).

46. P. M. Podsakoff and S. B. MacKenzie, "Kerr and Jermier's Substitutes for Leadership Model: Background, Empirical Assessment, and Suggestions for Future Research," *Leadership Quarterly* 8 (1997), pp. 117–32; P. M. Podsakoff, B. P. Niehoff, S. B. MacKenzie, and M. L. Williams, "Do Substitutes Really Substitute for Leadership? An Empirical Examination of Kerr and Jermier's Situational Leadership Model," *Organizational Behavior and Human Decision Processes* 54 (1993), pp. 1–44.

47. This observation has also been made by C. A. Schriesheim, "Substitutes-for-Leadership Theory: Development and Basic Concepts," *Leadership Quarterly* 8 (1997), pp. 103–8.

48. D. Anfuso, "Core Values Shape W. L. Gore's Innovative Culture," *Workforce* 78 (March 1999), pp. 48–53; A. Dominguez, "Employees Flourish at No-Boss Firm," *Deseret News (Salt Lake City, UT)*, July 4, 1998; M. Kaplan, "You Have No Boss," *Fast Company* 11 (November 1997), p. 226.

49. D. F. Elloy and A. Randolph, "The Effect of Superleader Behavior on Autonomous Work Groups in a Government Operated Railway Service," *Public Personnel Management* 26 (Summer 1997), pp. 257–72.

50. C. Manz and H. Sims, *Superleadership; Getting to the Top by Motivating Others* (San Francisco, CA: Berkley, 1990).

51. C. P. Neck and C. C. Manz, "Thought Self-Leadership: The Impact of Mental Strategies Training on Employee Cognition, Behavior, and Affect," *Journal of Organizational Behavior* 17 (1996), pp. 445–67.

52. D. Tarrant, "Boss Aha!" *Australian Financial Review*, December 29, 2000, p. 24.

53. R. Eglin, "Leadership Success: The Key Ingredient," *Sunday Times (London)*, July 22, 2001; A. R. Gold, M. Hirano, and Y. Yokoyama, "An Outsider Takes On Japan: An Interview with Nissan's Carlos Ghosn," *McKinsey Quarterly*, January 2001, p. 95; P. Sellers, "The 50 Most Powerful Women in American Business," *Fortune*, October 12, 1998, pp. 76–98; R. Slater, *Jack Welch and the GE Way: Management Insights and Leadership Secrets of the Legendary CEO* (New York: McGraw-Hill, 1998); K. Freiberg and J. Freiberg, *Nuts! Southwest Airlines' Crazy Recipe for Business and Personal Success* (New York: Bantam Doubleday Dell, 1998).

54. J. M. Howell and B. J. Avolio, "Transformational Leadership, Transactional Leadership, Locus of Control, and Support for Innovation: Key Predictors of Consolidated-Business-Unit Performance," *Journal of Applied Psychology* 78 (1993), pp. 891–902; J. A. Conger and R. N. Kanungo, "Perceived Behavioral Attributes of Charismatic Leadership," *Canadian Journal of Behavioral Science* 24 (1992), pp. 86–102; J. Seltzer and B. M. Bass, "Transformational Leadership: Beyond Initiation and Consideration," *Journal of Management* 16 (1990), pp. 693–703.

55. B. J. Avolio and B. M. Bass, "Transformational Leadership, Charisma, and Beyond," in J. G. Hunt, H. P. Dachler, B. R. Baliga, and C. A. Schriesheim, eds., *Emerging Leadership Vistas* (Lexington, MA: Lexington, 1988), pp. 29–49.

56. J. Kotter, *A Force for Change* (Cambridge, MA: Harvard Business School Press, 1990); W. Bennis and B. Nanus, *Leaders: The Strategies for Taking Charge* (New York: Harper & Row, 1985), p. 21; A. Zaleznik, "Managers and Leaders: Are They Different?" *Harvard Business Review* 55 (5) (1977), pp. 67–78.

57. C. P. Egri and S. Herman, "Leadership in the North American Environmental Sector: Values, Leadership Styles, and Contexts of Environmental Leaders and Their Organizations," *Academy of Management Journal* 43 (August 2000), pp. 571–604.

58. For discussion on the tendency to slide from transformational to transactional leadership, see W. Bennis, *An Invented Life: Reflections on Leadership and Change* (Reading, MA: Addison-Wesley, 1993).

59. L. Rittenhouse, "Dennis W. Bakke— Empowering a Workforce with Principles," *Electricity Journal,* January 1998, pp. 48–59.

60. J. A. Conger and R. N. Kanungo, "Toward a Behavioral Theory of Charismatic Leadership in Organizational Settings," *Academy of Management Review* 12 (1987), pp. 637 47; R. J. House, "A 1976 Theory of Charismatic Leadership," in J. G. Hunt and L. L. Larson, eds., *Leadership: The Cutting Edge* (Carbondale, IL: Southern Illinois University Press, 1977), pp. 189–207.

61. Y. A. Nur, "Charisma and Managerial Leadership: The Gift That Never Was," *Business Horizons* 41 (July 1998), pp. 19–26; J. E. Barbuto, Jr., "Taking the Charisma out of Transformational Leadership," *Journal of Social Behavior and Personality* 12 (September 1997), pp. 689–97.

62. L. Sooklal, "The Leader as a Broker of Dreams," *Organizational Studies,* 1989, pp. 833–55.

63. I. M. Levin, "Vision Revisited," *Journal of Applied Behavioral Science* 36 (March 2000), pp. 91–107; J. M. Stewart, "Future State Visioning—A Powerful Leadership Process," *Long Range Planning* 26 (December 1993), pp. 89–98; Bennis and Nanus, *Leaders,* pp. 27–33, 89.

64. T. J. Peters, "Symbols, Patterns, and Settings: An Optimistic Case for Getting Things Done," *Organizational Dynamics* 7 (Autumn 1978), pp. 2–23.

65. I. R. Baum, E. A. Locke, and S. A. Kirkpatrick, "A Longitudinal Study of the Relation of Vision and Vision Communication to Venture Growth in Entrepreneurial Firms," *Journal of Applied Psychology* 83 (1998), pp. 43–54; S. A. Kirkpatrick and E. A. Locke, "Direct and Indirect Effects of Three Core Charismatic Leadership Components on Performance and Attitudes," *Journal of Applied Psychology* 81 (1996), pp. 36–51.

66. G. T. Fairhurst and R. A. Sarr, *The Art of Framing: Managing the Language of Leadership* (San Francisco: Jossey-Bass, 1996); J. A. Conger, "Inspiring Others: The Language of Leadership," *Academy of Management Executive* 5 (February 1991), pp. 31–45.

67. R. S. Johnson, "Home Depot Renovates," *Fortune,* November 23, 1998, pp. 200–6.

68. Fairhurst and Sarr, *The Art of Framing,* chap. 5; J. Pfeffer, "Management as Symbolic Action: The Creation and Maintenance of Organizational Paradigms," *Research in Organizational Behavior* 3 (1981), pp. 1–52.

69. L. Black, "Hamburger Diplomacy," *Report on Business Magazine* 5 (August 1988), pp. 30–36; S. Franklin, *The Heroes: A Saga of Canadian Inspiration* (Toronto: McClelland and Stewart, 1967), p. 53.

70. McGill and Slocum, Jr., "A Little Leadership, Please?"; N. H. Snyder and M. Graves, "Leadership and Vision," *Business Horizons* 37 (January 1994), pp. 1–7; D. E. Berlew, "Leadership and Organizational Excitement," in D. A. Kolb, I. M. Rubin, and J. M. McIntyre, eds., *Organizational Psychology: A Book of Readings* (Englewood Cliffs, NJ: Prentice Hall, 1974).

71. M. F. R. Kets de Vries "Charisma in Action: The Transformational Abilities of Virgin's Richard Branson and ABB's Percy Barnevik," *Organizational Dynamics* 26 (Winter 1998), pp. 6–21; M. F. R. Kets de Vries, "Creative Leadership: Jazzing Up Business," *Chief Executive,* March 1997, pp. 64–66; F. Basile, "Hotshots in Business Impart Their Wisdom," *Indianapolis Business Journal,* July 21, 1997, p. A40.

72. E. M. Whitener, S. E. Brodt, M. A. Korsgaard, and J. M. Werner, "Managers as Initiators of Trust: An Exchange Relationship Framework for Understanding Managerial Trustworthy Behavior," *Academy of Management Review* 23 (July 1998), pp. 513–30; Bennis and Nanus, *Leaders,* pp. 43–55; Kouzes and Posner, *Credibility.*

73. J. J. Sosik, S. S. Kahai, and B. J. Avolio, "Transformational Leadership and Dimensions of Creativity: Motivating Idea Generation in Computer-Mediated Groups," *Creativity Research Journal* 11 (1998), pp. 111–21; P. Bycio, R. D. Hackett, and J. S. Allen, "Further Assessments of Bass's (1985) Conceptualization of Transactional and Transformational Leadership," *Journal of Applied Psychology* 80 (1995), pp. 468–78; W. L. Koh, R. M. Steers, and J. R. Terborg, "The Effects of Transformational Leadership on Teacher Attitudes and Student Performance in Singapore," *Journal of Organizational Behavior* 16 (1995), pp. 319–33; Howell and Avolio, "Transformational Leadership, Transactional Leadership, Locus of Control, and Support for Innovation."

74. J. Barling, T. Weber, and E. K. Kelloway, "Effects of Transformational Leadership Training on Attitudinal and Financial Outcomes: A Field Experiment," *Journal of Applied Psychology* 81 (1996), pp. 827–32.

75. A. Bryman, "Leadership in Organizations," in S. R. Clegg, C. Hardy, and W. R. Nord, eds., *Handbook of Organization Studies* (Thousand Oaks, CA: Sage, 1996), pp. 276–92.

76. Egri and Herman, "Leadership in the North American Environmental Sector"; B. S. Pawar and K. K. Eastman, "The Nature and Implications of Contextual Influences on Transformational Leadership: A Conceptual Examination," *Academy of Management Review* 22 (1997), pp. 80–109.

77. K. Boehnke, A. C. DiStefano, J. J. DiStefano, and N. Bontis, "Leadership for Extraordinary Performance," *Business Quarterly* 61 (Summer 1997), pp. 56–63.

78. For a review of this research, see House and Aditya, "The Social Scientific Study Of Leadership."

79. R. J. Hall and R. G. Lord, "Multilevel Information Processing Explanations of Followers' Leadership Perceptions," *Leadership Quarterly* 6 (1995), pp. 265–87; R. Ayman, "Leadership Perception: The Role of Gender and Culture," in M. M. Chemers and R. Ayman, eds., *Leadership Theory and Research: Perspectives and Directions* (San Diego: Academic, 1993), pp. 137–66; J. R. Meindl, "On Leadership: An Alternative to the Conventional Wisdom," *Research in Organizational Behavior* 12 (1990), pp. 159–203.

80. G. R. Salancik and J. R. Meindl, "Corporate Attributions as Strategic Illusions of Management Control," *Administrative Science Quarterly* 29 (1984), pp. 238–54; J. M. Tolliver, "Leadership and Attribution of Cause: A Modification and Extension of Current Theory," *Proceedings of the Annual ASAC Conference, Organizational Behavior Division* 4, pt. 5 (1983), pp. 182–91.

81. L. M. Ah Chong and D. C. Thomas, "Leadership Perceptions in Cross-Cultural Context: Pakeha and Pacific Islanders in New Zealand," *Leadership Quarterly* 8 (1997), pp. 275–93; J. L. Nye and D. R. Forsyth, "The Effects of Prototype-Based Biases on Leadership Appraisals: A Test of Leadership Categorization Theory," *Small Group Research* 22 (1991), pp. 360–79; S. F. Cronshaw and R. G. Lord, "Effects of Categorization, Attribution, and Encoding Processes on Leadership Perceptions," *Journal of Applied Psychology* 72 (1987), pp. 97–106.

82. Meindl, "On Leadership," p. 163.

83. J. Pfeffer, "The Ambiguity of Leadership," *Academy of Management Review* 2 (1977), pp. 102–12; Yukl, *Leadership in Organizations*, pp. 265–67.

84. Cronshaw and Lord, "Effects of Categorization, Attribution, and Encoding Processes on Leadership Perceptions," pp. 104–5.

85. D. Barboza, "Teacher, Cheerleader and C.E.O," *New York Times*, May 28, 2000.

86. The study was conducted by the Conference Board of Canada and was reported in L. Elliott, "Women Switch Jobs to Climb the Power Ladder," *Toronto Star*, June 15, 2000, p. NE1.

87. N. Wood, "Venus Rules," *Incentive* 172 (February 1998), pp. 22–27; S. H. Appelbaum and B. T. Shapiro, "Why Can't Men Lead Like Women?" *Leadership and Organization Development Journal* 14 (1993), pp. 28–34; J. B. Rosener, "Ways Women Lead," *Harvard Business Review* 68 (November–December 1990), pp. 119–25.

88. K. Goff, "The Muscle behind Martha," *Ottawa Citizen*, October 21, 1999.

89. G. N. Powell, "One More Time: Do Female and Male Managers Differ?" *Academy of Management Executive* 4 (August 1990), pp. 68–75; G. H. Dobbins and S. J. Platts, "Sex Differences in Leadership: How Real Are They?" *Academy of Management Review* 11 (1986), pp. 118–27. In contrast to these studies, one review cites an unpublished study reporting that women demonstrate more people-oriented leadership and are rated higher than men on their leadership. See M-T. Claes, "Women, Men and Management Styles," *International Labour Review* 138 (1999), pp. 431–46.

90. A. H. Eagly and B. T. Johnson, "Gender and Leadership Style: A Meta-Analysis," *Psychological Bulletin* 108 (1990), pp. 233–56.

91. J. Eckberg, "When It's Time to Get Tough—It's Tough," *Cincinnati Enquirer*, August 28, 2000, p. B18; A. H. Eagly, S. J. Karau, and M. G. Makhijani, "Gender and the Effectiveness of Leaders: A Meta-Analysis," *Psychological Bulletin* 117 (1995), pp. 125–45; M. E. Heilman and C. J. Block, "Sex Stereotypes: Do They Influence Perceptions of Managers?" *Journal of Social Behavior and Personality* 10 (1995), pp. 237–52; R. L. Kent and S. E. Moss, "Effects of Sex and Gender Role on Leader Emergence," *Academy of Management Journal* 37 (1994), pp. 1335–46; A. H. Eagly, M. G. Makhijani, and B. G. Klonsky, "Gender and the Evaluation of Leaders: A Meta-Analysis," *Psychological Bulletin* 111 (1992), pp. 3–22.

92. M. Sappenfield, "Women, It Seems, Are Better Bosses," *Christian Science Monitor*, January 16, 2001. R. Sharpe, "As Leaders, Women Rule," *Business Week*, November 20, 2000, C. D'Nan Bass, "Women May Outdo Men As Sales Managers, Study Says," *Chicago Tribune*, January 26, 2000.

CHAPTER FIFTEEN

1. B. Pimentel, "The HP–Compaq Deal: Losing Their Way?" *San Francisco Chronicle*, September 6, 2001; J. Swartz, "How Will Compaq, H-P Fit Together?" *USA Today*, September 6, 2001, p. 3B; D. Olive, "Fiorina: A Woman in a Hurry," *National Post*, September 5, 2001; M. Veverka, "Carly's Challenge," *Barron's*, August 13, 2001, pp. 21–27; "H-P's Employee-Friendly Culture in Flux," *Sacramento (CA) Business Journal*, August 3, 2001, p. 3; J. Foley, "Hewlett-Packard Reaches a Cultural Crossroads," *InformationWeek*, July 23, 2001, p. 40.

2. T. O. Davenport, "The Integration Challenge: Managing Corporate Mergers," *Management Review* 87 (January 1998), pp. 25–28; E. H. Schein, "What Is Culture?" in P. J. Frost, L. F. Moore, M. R. Louis, C. C. Lundberg, and J. Martin, eds., *Reframing Organizational Culture* (Beverly Hills, CA: Sage, 1991), pp. 243–53; A. Williams, P. Dobson, and M. Walters, *Changing Culture: New Organizational Approaches* (London: Institute of Personnel Management, 1989).

3. A. Sagie and D. Elizur, "Work Values: A Theoretical Overview and a Model of Their Effects," *Journal of Organizational Behavior* 17 (1996), pp. 503–14; W. H. Schmidt and B. Z. Posner, *Managerial Values in Perspective* (New York: American Management Association, 1983).

4. M. Fan, "Cary, N.C., Software Firm Posts Steady Growth without IPO," *San Jose (CA) Mercury News*, July 29, 2001; K. S. Hymowitz, "Ecstatic Capitalism's Brave New Work Ethic," *City Journal* 11 (Winter 2001), pp. 33–43.

5. B. M. Meglino and E. C. Ravlin, "Individual Values in Organizations: Concepts, Controversies, and Research," *Journal of Management* 24 (May 1998), pp. 351–89; C. Argyris and D. A. Schön, *Organizational Learning: A Theory of Action Perspective* (Reading, MA: Addison-Wesley, 1978).

6. Fan, "Cary, N.C., Software Firm Posts Steady Growth without IPO"; E. P. Dalesio, "A Quiet Software Company Considers Raising Its Profile," *Philadelphia Inquirer*, May 6, 2001.

7. "Job Satisfaction Means More Than Pay," *Business Day (South Africa)*, December 6, 2000, p. 14; S. Planting, "Mirror, Mirror . . . Here Are the Fairest of Them All," *Financial Mail (South Africa)*, November 24, 2000, p. 48.

8. K. Doler, "Interview: Jeff Bezos, Founder and CEO of Amazon.com Inc.," *Upside* 10 (September 1998), pp. 76–80.

9. S. Sackmann, "Culture and Subcultures: An Analysis of Organizational Knowledge," *Administrative Science Quarterly* 37 (1992), pp. 140–61; J. Martin and C. Siehl, "Organizational Culture and Counterculture: An Un-

easy Symbiosis," *Organizational Dynamics*, Autumn 1983, pp. 52–64; J. S. Ott, *The Organizational Culture Perspective* (Pacific Grove, CA: Brooks/Cole, 1989), pp. 45–47; T. E. Deal and A. A. Kennedy, *Corporate Cultures* (Reading, MA: Addison-Wesley, 1982), pp. 138–39.

10. A. Sinclair, "Approaches to Organizational Culture and Ethics," *Journal of Business Ethics* 12 (1993), pp. 63–73.

11. M. Cooke, "Humiliation as Motivator?" *Meetings and Conventions* 36 (July 2001), p. 26; G. Groeller, "Eat or Be Eaten Ethic Boosts Bottom Line," *Orlando (FL) Sentinel*, April 30, 2001, p. 16.

12. M. O. Jones, *Studying Organizational Symbolism: What, How, Why?* (Thousand Oaks, CA: Sage, 1996); Ott, *The Organizational Culture Perspective*, chap. 2; J. S. Pederson and J. S. Sorensen, *Organizational Cultures in Theory and Practice* (Aldershot, UK: Gower, 1989), pp. 27–29.

13. "Making Work Fun," *Minneapolis Star Tribune*, August 18, 1998, p. E9

14. E. H. Schein, *The Corporate Culture Survival Guide* (San Francisco: Jossey-Bass, 1999), chap. 4; A. Furnham and B. Gunter, "Corporate Culture: Definition, Diagnosis, and Change," *International Review of Industrial and Organizational Psychology* 8 (1993), pp. 233–61; E. H. Schein, "Organizational Culture," *American Psychologist*, February 1990, pp. 109–19; Ott, *The Organizational Culture Perspective*, chap. 2; W. J. Duncan, "Organizational Culture: 'Getting a Fix' on an Elusive Concept," *Academy of Management Executive* 3 (1989), pp. 229–36.

15. J. C. Meyer, "Tell Me a Story: Eliciting Organizational Values from Narratives," *Communication Quarterly* 43 (1995), pp. 210–24.

16. K. Frieberg and J. Frieberg, *Nuts! Southwest Airlines' Crazy Recipe for Business and Personal Success* (New York: Bantam Doubleday Dell, 1998).

17. This story is cited in K. Foss, "Isadore Sharp," *Foodservice and Hospitality*, December 1989, pp. 20–30; J. DeMont, "Sharp's Luxury Empire," *Maclean's*, June 5, 1989, pp. 30–33. See also S. Kemp and L. Dwyer, "An Examination of Organizational Culture—The Regent Hotel, Sydney," *International*

Journal of Hospitality Management 20 (March 2001), pp. 77–93.

18. J. Z. DeLorean, *On a Clear Day You Can See General Motors* (Grosse Pointe, MI: Wright Enterprises, 1979).

19. R. Zemke, "Storytelling: Back to a Basic," *Training* 27 (March 1990), pp. 44–50; A. L. Wilkins, "Organizational Stories as Symbols Which Control the Organization," in L. R. Pondy, P. J. Frost, G. Morgan, and T. C. Dandridge, eds., *Organizational Symbolism* (Greenwich, CT: JAI Press, 1984), pp. 81–92; J. Martin and M. E. Powers, "Truth or Corporate Propaganda: The Value of a Good War Story," in Pondy et al., eds., *Organizational Symbolism*, pp. 93–107.

20. J. Martin et al., "The Uniqueness Paradox in Organizational Stories," *Administrative Science Quarterly* 28 (1983), pp. 438–53.

21. P. S. DeLisi, "A Modern-Day Tragedy: The Digital Equipment Story," *Journal of Management Inquiry* 7 (June 1998), pp. 118–30. Digital's famous shouting matches are also described in E. Schein, "How to Set the Stage for a Change in Organizational Culture," in P. Senge et al., *The Dance of Change* (New York: Doubleday Currency, 1999), pp. 334–44.

22. J. M. Beyer and H. M. Trice, "How an Organization's Rites Reveal Its Culture," *Organizational Dynamics* 15 (4) (1987), pp. 5–24; L. Smirchich, "Organizations as Shared Meanings," in Pondy et al., eds., *Organizational Symbolism*, pp. 55–65.

23. D. Roth, "My Job at The Container Store," *Fortune*, January 10, 2000, pp. 74–78.

24. L. A. Krefting and P. J. Frost, "Untangling Webs, Surfing Waves, and Wildcatting," in P. J. Frost, L. F. Moore, M. R. Louis, C. C. Lundberg, and J. Martin, eds., *Organizational Culture* (Beverly Hills, CA: Sage, 1985), pp. 155–68.

25. J. A. Byrne, "How Jack Welch Runs GE," *Business Week*, June 8, 1998.

26. R. E. Quinn and N. T. Snyder, "Advance Change Theory: Culture Change at Whirlpool Corporation," in J. A. Conger, G. M. Spreitzer, and E. E. Lawler III, eds., *The Leader's Change Handbook* (San Francisco: Jossey-Bass, 1999), pp. 162–93.

27. Adapted from P. Roberts, "The Empire Strikes Back," *Fast Company* 22 (February–March 1999), pp. 122–31.

28. J. Myerson, "Britain's Most Creative Offices," *Management Today*, April 1999, pp. 62–67.

29. J. M. Kouzes and B. Z. Posner, *The Leadership Challenge* (San Francisco: Jossey-Bass, 1995), pp. 230–31.

30. G. Levitch, "Rethinking the Office," *Report on Business Magazine*, September 2001; T. Kelley, *The Art of Innovation* (New York: Doubleday Currency, 2001), chap. 7.

31. C. Siehl and J. Martin, "Organizational Culture: A Key to Financial Performance?" in B. Schneider, ed., *Organizational Climate and Culture* (San Francisco: Jossey-Bass, 1990), pp. 241–81; J. B. Barney, "Organizational Culture: Can It Be a Source of Sustained Competitive Advantage?" *Academy of Management Review* 11 (1986), pp. 656–65; V. Sathe, *Culture and Related Corporate Realities* (Homewood, IL: Irwin, 1985), chap. 2; Deal and Kennedy, *Corporate Cultures*, chap. 1. Information about Viant, Inc., comes from L. Daniel, "Within the Viant Experiment," *WebTechniques*, April 2000 (www.webtechniques.com).

32. C. A. O'Reilly and J. A. Chatman, "Culture as Social Control: Corporations, Cults, and Commitment," *Research in Organizational Behavior* 18 (1996), pp. 157–200. For a discussion of organizational culture as social control at The Regent, Sydney, see S. Kemp and L. Dwyer, "An Examination of Organizational Culture—The Regent Hotel, Sydney," *International Journal of Hospitality Management* 20 (March 2001), pp. 77–93.

33. B. Ashforth and F. Mael, "Social Identity Theory and the Organization," *Academy of Management Review* 14 (1989), pp. 20–39.

34. S. G. Harris, "Organizational Culture and Individual Sensemaking: A Schema-Based Perspective," *Organization Science* 5 (1994), pp. 309–21; M. R. Louis, "Surprise and Sensemaking: What Newcomers Experience in Entering Unfamiliar Organizational Settings," *Administrative Science Quarterly* 25 (1980), pp. 226–51.

35. G. S. Saffold III, "Culture Traits, Strength, and Organizational Perfor-

mance: Moving Beyond 'Strong' Culture," *Academy of Management Review* 13 (1988), pp. 546–58; Williams et al., *Changing Culture*, pp. 24–27.

36. J. P. Kotter and J. L. Heskett, *Corporate Culture and Performance* (New York: Free Press, 1992); G. G. Gordon and N. DiTomasco, "Predicting Corporate Performance from Organizational Culture," *Journal of Management Studies* 29 (1992), pp. 783–98; D. R. Denison, *Corporate Culture and Organizational Effectiveness* (New York: Wiley, 1990).

37. C. Fishman, "Why Can't Lego Click?" *Fast Company* 50 (September 2001), p. 144.

38. E. H. Schein, "On Dialogue, Culture, and Organizational Learning," *Organization Dynamics*, Autumn 1993, pp. 40–51.

39. T. Parker-Pope, "New CEO Preaches Rebellion for P&G's 'Cult,'" *The Wall Street Journal*, December 11, 1998.

40. J. Kotter, "Cultures and Coalitions," *Executive Excellence* 15 (March 1998), pp. 14–15; Kotter and Heskett, *Corporate Culture and Performance*.

41. The features of adaptive cultures are described in W. F. Joyce, *Mega-Change: How Today's Leading Companies Have Transformed Their Workforces* (New York: Free Press, 1999), pp. 44–47.

42. S. Peck and J. Larson, "Making Change: Some Major Corporations Are Making Sustainability Their Business," *Alternatives* 27 (Spring 2001), pp. 17–20; S. J. Carroll and M. J. Gannon, *Ethical Dimensions of International Management* (Thousand Oaks, CA: Sage, 1997), chap. 5; A. Sinclair, "Approaches to Organizational Culture and Ethics," *Journal of Business Ethics* 12 (1993), pp. 63–73.

43. J. Mizuo, "Business Ethics and Corporate Governance in Japanese Corporations," *Business and Society Review*, March 1999, p. 65; "Shiseido," *Forbes (Supplement)*, January 11, 1999, p. S6.

44. W. J. Holstein, "Dump the Cookware," *Business 2.0*, May 2001; S. N. Mehta, "Can Corning Find Its Optic Nerve?" *Fortune*, March 19, 2001, pp. 148–50.

45. C. Fox, "Mergers and Desires II," *Business Review Weekly*, May 11, 2001.

46. D. B. Marron, "Is This Marriage Made in Heaven?" *Chief Executive*, May 2001, pp. 50–52; P. Troiano, "Post-Merger Challenges," *Management Review* 88 (January 1999), p. 6. For a discussion of corporate culture issues in mergers, see M. L. Marks, "Mixed Signals," *Across the Board*, May 2000, pp. 21–26; M. L. Marks, "Adding Cultural Fit to Your Diligence Checklist," *Mergers and Acquisitions*, December 1999; E. H. Schein, *The Corporate Culture Survival Guide* (San Francisco: Jossey-Bass, 1999), chap. 8; A. F. Buono and J. L. Bowditch, *The Human Side of Mergers and Acquisitions* (San Francisco: Jossey-Bass, 1989), chap. 6.

47. E. Krell, "Merging Corporate Cultures," *Training* 38 (May 2001), pp. 68–78; J. K. Stewart, "Imperfect Partners," *Chicago Tribune*, March 18, 2001, p. 1.

48. J. K. Stewart, "3COM–Robotics Merger a Lesson in Frustration," *Chicago Tribune*, March 21, 2001, p. N1.

49. Marks, "Adding Cultural Fit to Your Diligence Checklist"; S. Greengard, "Due Diligence: The Devil in the Details," *Workforce*, October 1999, p. 68; Schein, *The Corporate Culture Survival Guide*. A corporate culture audit is also recommended for joint ventures. For details, see K. J. Fedor and W. B. Werther, Jr., "The Fourth Dimension: Creating Culturally Responsive International Alliances," *Organizational Dynamics* 25 (Autumn 1996), pp. 39–53.

50. D. Kramer-Kawakami, "Merging Cultures: The Challenges of Convergence," *LIMRA's MarketFacts* 19 (September–October 2000), pp. 24.

51. T. Evanoff, "Crash of a Titan," *Indianapolis Star*, April 15, 2001, p.E1; J. Mann, J. Flock, and R. Charles, "The Crashing of Chrysler," *CNN International*, January 30, 2001; H. Greimel, "Merger Woes at DaimlerChrysler," *Associated Press*, December 24, 2000; J. Hyde, "Chrysler's New Boss Faces Same Merger Problems as Old Boss," *Associated Press*, November 16, 2000; J. Ball and S. Miller, "DaimlerChrysler Isn't Living Up to Its Promise," *Wall Street Journal Europe*, July 26, 2000; B. Vlasic and B. A. Stertz, "Taken for a Ride," *Business Week*, June 5, 2000, pp. 80–92.

52. D. Buckner, "Nortel versus Cisco," *Venture*, CBC TV, January 4, 2000; R. N. Ashkenas, L. J. DeMonaco, and S. C. Francis, "Making the Deal Real: How GE Capital Integrates Acquisitions," *Harvard Business Review* 76 (January–February 1998), pp. 165–76.

53. K. W. Smith, "A Brand-New Culture for the Merged Firm," *Mergers and Acquisitions* 35 (June 2000), pp. 45–50; A. R. Malekazedeh and A. Nahavandi, "Making Mergers Work by Managing Cultures," *Journal of Business Strategy*, May–June 1990, pp. 55–57.

54. A. Levy, "Mergers Spread Despite Failures," *Plain Dealer (Cleveland, OH)*, August 9, 1998, p. H1.

55. S. F. Walker and J. W. Marr, *Stakeholder Power* (New York: Perseus, 2001); S. Silverstein and D. Vrana, "After Back-Slapping Wanes, Mega-Mergers Often Fail," *Los Angeles Times*, April 19, 1998, p. 1.

56. "Nortel Uses Acquisition to Transform Role," *Wall Street Journal Europe*, July 26, 2000, p. 13.

57. "Split Personality," *Baltimore Business Journal*, July 20, 2001, p. 1.

58. J. P. Kotter, "Leading Change: The Eight Steps of Transformation," in Conger et al., eds., *The Leader's Change Handbook*, pp. 87–99.

59. E. H. Schein, "The Role of the Founder in Creating Organizational Culture," *Organizational Dynamics* 12 (1) (Summer 1983), pp. 13–28.

60. E. H. Schein, *Organizational Culture and Leadership* (San Francisco, CA: Jossey-Bass, 1985), chap. 10; T. J. Peters, "Symbols, Patterns, and Settings: An Optimistic Case for Getting Things Done," *Organizational Dynamics* 7 (2) (Autumn 1978), pp. 2–23.

61. A. Effinger, "With Charm, Poise and Attitude Fiorina Rousting Hewlett-Packard," *Seattle-Post Intelligencer*, January 3, 2000, p. E1.

62. J. Kerr and J. W. Slocum, Jr., "Managing Corporate Culture Through Reward Systems," *Academy of Management Executive* 1 (May 1987), pp. 99–107; Williams et al., *Changing Culture*, pp. 120–24; K. R. Thompson and F. Luthans, "Organizational Culture: A Behavioral Perspective," in Schneider, ed., *Organizational Climate and Culture*, pp. 319–44.

63. "Get Rich? Work at Home Depot," *Baltimore Sun*, July 27, 1998.

64. W. G. Ouchi and A. M. Jaeger, "Type Z Organization: Stability in the Midst of Mobility," *Academy of Management Review* 3 (1978), pp. 305–14; K. Mc-

Neil and J. D. Thompson, "The Regeneration of Social Organizations," *American Sociological Review* 36 (1971), pp. 624–37.

65. B. Broadway, "Good for the Soul—and for the Bottom Line," *Washington Post*, August 19, 2001, p. A1; N. Hoogeveen, "Reinventing Industry," *Business Record*, April 10, 2001, p. 22; M. Haskell, "It's Incredibly Important That Businesses Wake Up Now and Get It Straight," *Maine Times*, October 12, 2000, p. 3.

66. "A Full Life," *The Economist*, September 4, 1999.

67. M. De Pree, *Leadership Is an Art* (East Lansing: Michigan State University Press, 1987).

68. C. Daniels, "Does This Man Need a Shrink?" *Fortune*, February 5, 2001, pp. 205–8.

69. A. E. M. Van Vianen, "Person–Organization Fit: The Match between Newcomers' and Recruiters' Preferences for Organizational Cultures," *Personnel Psychology* 53 (Spring 2000), pp. 113–49; C. A. O'Reilly III, J. Chatman, and D. F. Caldwell, "People and Organizational Culture: A Profile Comparison Approach to Assessing Person-Organization Fit," *Academy of Management Journal* 34 (1991), pp. 487–516.

70. "Corporate Culture Rivals Company Benefits in Importance to Job Applicants," Robert Half International news release, May 1, 1996.

71. M. Siegal, "The Perils of Culture Conflict," *Fortune*, November 9, 1998, pp. 257–62.

72. J. Van Maanen, "Breaking In: Socialization to Work," in R. Dubin, ed., *Handbook of Work, Organization, and Society* (Chicago: Rand McNally, 1976), p. 67.

73. P. Tam, "Frugal Founder Rewards Employees," *Ottawa Citizen*, November 21, 1999.

CHAPTER SIXTEEN

1. B. Breen, "How EDS Got Its Groove Back," *Fast Company* 51 (October 2001), pp. 106–17; L. B. Ward, "EDS Chief Confident in Role as Change Agent," *Dallas Morning News*, August 14, 2001, p. 1D; C. Hymowitz, "Executive Action Drafting a Winning Team," *Asian Wall Street Journal*, March 30, 2001, p. W3; W. Zellner, "Meet the 'Completely Different EDS,'" *Business Week*, December 18, 2000, p. 204; D. Callaghan, "Everything Old Is New Again. Really," *MC Technology Marketing Intelligence* 20 (April 2000), pp. 70–76; J. Bean, "EDS Trying to Shed Buttoned-down Image," *Montreal Gazette*, March 20, 2000, p. IB8.

2. J. P. Donlon, "Built for Speed," *Chief Executive*, October 2000, pp. 58–68.

3. R. Mitchell, "Feeding the Flames," *Business 2.0*, May 1, 2001.

4. These four companies appear on recent *Business Week* "Best Performers" lists. See J. Weber, "The Best Performers," *Business Week*, April 7, 2001, p. 10; A. Barrett, "The 50 Best Performers," *Business Week*, March 27, 2000, p. 124.

5. R. T. Pascale, M. Millemann, and L. Gioja, *Surfing on the Edge of Chaos* (London: Texere, 2000).

6. D. Tapscott, A. Lowy, and D. Ticoll, eds., *Blueprint to the Digital Economy: Creating Wealth in the Era of E-business* (New York: McGraw-Hill, 1998); C. Meyer and S. Davis, *Blur: The Speed of Change in the Connected Economy* (Reading, MA: Addison-Wesley, 1998). For an excellent discussion of how computer networks are changing the world of business, see also K. Kelly, *New Rules for the New Economy* (New York: Viking, 1998).

7. D. Tapscott and A. Laston, *Paradigm Shift* (New York: McGraw-Hill, 1993); W. H. Davidow and M. S. Malone, *The Virtual Corporation* (New York: Harper-Business, 1992).

8. Tapscott et al., *Blueprint to the Digital Economy.*

9. N. Bannister, "Nokia: From Start to Finnish," *The Age (Melbourne)*, October 26, 1999; K. Lyytinen and S. Goodman, "Finland: The Unknown Soldier on the IT Front," *Communications of the ACM* 42 (March 1999), pp. 13–17; S. Baker, "Can CEO Ollila Keep the Cellular Superstar Flying High?" *Business Week*, August 10, 1998, pp. 54–61; J. Dromberg, "Nokia's Line to the Top Slot," *Independent (London)*, August 9, 1998, p. 5.

10. T. Keller, "Reinventing the Firm," *National Post Business Magazine*, June 1, 2000, p. 68.

11. B. Duff-Brown, "Service Centers Booming in India," *Chicago Tribune*, July 9, 2001, p. 6; M. Landler, "Hi, I'm in Bangalore (but I Can't Say So)," *New York Times*, March 21, 2001, p. A1.

12. K. Lewin, *Field Theory in Social Science* (New York: Harper & Row, 1951).

13. M. Moravec, O. J. Johannessen, and T. A. Hjelmas, "The Well-Managed SMT," *Management Review* 87 (June 1998), pp. 56–58; M. Moravec, O. J. Johannessen, and T. A. Hjelmas, "Thumbs Up for Self-Managed Teams," *Management Review*, July 17, 1997, p. 42.

14. M. Riley, "High-Revving Nasser Undone by a Blind Spot," *Sydney Morning Herald*, November 3, 2001; J. McCracken, "Nasser Out; Ford In," *Detroit Free Press*, October 30, 2001; M. Truby, "Can Ford Chief Ride Out Storm?" *Detroit News*, June 24, 2001; M. Truby, "Ford Revolution Spawns Turmoil," *Detroit News*, April 29, 2001.

15. C. O. Longenecker, D. J. Dwyer, and T. C. Stansfield, "Barriers and Gateways to Workforce Productivity," *Industrial Management* 40 (March–April 1998), pp. 21–28. Several sources discuss resistance to change, including D. A. Nadler, Champions of Change (San Francisco: Jossey-Bass, 1998), chap. 5; P. Strebel, "Why Do Employees Resist Change?" *Harvard Business Review*, May–June 1996, pp. 86–92; R. Maurer, *Beyond the Wall of Resistance: Unconventional Strategies to Build Support for Change* (Austin, TX: Bard Books, 1996); C. Hardy, *Strategies for Retrenchment and Turnaround: The Politics of Survival* (Berlin: de Gruyter, 1990), chap. 13.

16. F. Vogelstein and P. Sloan, "Corporate Dowagers Go for a Makeover," *U.S. News & World Report*, November 6, 2000.

17. E. B. Dent and S. G. Goldberg, "Challenging 'Resistance to Change,'" *Journal of Applied Behavioral Science* 35 (March 1999), pp. 25–41.

18. D. A. Nadler, "The Effective Management of Organizational Change," in J. W. Lorsch, ed., *Handbook of Organizational Behavior* (Englewood Cliffs, NJ: Prentice Hall, 1987), pp. 358–69; D. Katz and R. L. Kahn, *The Social Psychology of Organizations*, 2nd ed. (New York: Wiley, 1978).

19. "Making Change Work for You—Not against You," *Agency Sales Magazine* 28 (June 1998), pp. 24–27.

20. M. E. McGill and J. W. Slocum, Jr., "Unlearn the Organization," *Organizational Dynamics* 22 (2) (1993), pp. 67–79.

21. R. Katz, "Time and Work: Toward an Integrative Perspective," *Research in Organizational Behavior* 2 (1980), pp. 81–127.

22. D. Nicolini and M. B. Meznar, "The Social Construction of Organizational Learning: Conceptual and Practical Issues in the Field," *Human Relations* 48 (1995), pp. 727–46.

23. D. Miller, "What Happens after Success: The Perils of Excellence," *Journal of Management Studies* 31 (1994), pp. 325–58.

24. H. Trinca, "Her Way," *Boss Magazine*, October 9, 2000.

25. T. G. Cummings, "The Role and Limits of Change Leadership," in J. A. Conger, G. M. Spreitzer, and E. E. Lawler III, eds., *The Leader's Change Handbook* (San Francisco: Jossey-Bass, 1999), pp. 301–20.

26. J. P. Donlon et al., "In Search of the New Change Leader," *Chief Executive*, November 1997, pp. 64–75.

27. L. D. Goodstein and H. R. Butz, "Customer Value: The Linchpin of Organizational Change," *Organizational Dynamics* 27 (June 1998), pp. 21–35.

28. J. Juergens, "Corporate Spotlight: ARCNET," *Incentive* 173 (September 1999), pp. 68–69.

29. A. Gore, "Joel Kocher: Power COO Says It's Time to Evolve," *MacUser*, April 1997.

30. J. P. Kotter and L. A. Schlesinger, "Choosing Strategies for Change," *Harvard Business Review*, March–April 1979, pp. 106–14.

31. J. Moad, "Dupont's People Deal," *PC Week* 14 (September 29, 1997), pp. 751.

32. K. H. Hammonds, "Grassroots Leadership–Ford Motor Company," *Fast Company*, April 2000, p. 138; S. Wetlaufer, "Driving Change: An Interview with Ford Motor Company's Jacques Nasser," *Harvard Business Review* 77 (March–April 1999), pp. 76–88.

33. D. Tarrant, "Boss Aha!" *Australian Financial Review*, December 29, 2000, p. 24. For a discussion of employee involvement in change management, see J. P. Walsh and S-F. Tseng, "The Ef-fects of Job Characteristics on Active Effort at Work," *Work and Occupations* 25 (February 1998), pp. 74–96; K. T. Dirks, L. L. Cummings, and J. L. Pierce, "Psychological Ownership in Organizations: Conditions under Which Individuals Promote and Resist Change," *Research in Organizational Change and Development* 9 (1996), pp. 1–23.

34. M. Evans, T. Hamilton, L. Surtees, and S. Tuck, "The Road to a Billion," *Globe and Mail*, January 6, 2000; R. Dyck and N. Halpern, "Team-Based Organizations Redesign at Celestica," *Journal for Quality & Participation* 22 (September–October 1999), pp. 36–40; "Celestica Nurtures Strong Corporate Culture Within," *Northern Colorado Business Report*, July 16, 1999, p. B5; K. Damsell, "Celestica Escapes from Its Cage," *National Post*, September 1, 1998, p. 9.

35. B. B. Bunker and B. T. Alban, *Large Group Interventions: Engaging the Whole System for Rapid Change* (San Francisco: Jossey-Bass, 1996); M. Emery and R. E. Purser, *The Search Conference: A Powerful Method for Planning Organizational Change and Community Action* (San Francisco: Jossey-Bass, 1996). For a description of Trist and Emery's first search conference, see M. R. Weisbord, "Inventing the Search Conference: Bristol Siddeley Aircraft Engines, 1960," in M. R. Weisbord, ed., *Discovering Common Ground* (San Francisco: Berret-Koehler, 1992), pp. 19–33.

36. R. Dubey, "The CEO Who Walked Away," *Business Today (India)*, May 22, 1998, p. 98.

37. R. E. Purser and S. Cabana, *The Self-Managing Organization* (New York: Free Press, 1998), chap. 7; "Making Organizational Changes Effective and Sustainable," *Educating for Employment*, August 7, 1998; R. Larson, "Forester Defends 'Feel-Good' Meeting," *Washington Times*, November 28, 1997, p. A9; W. Kaschub, "PECO Energy Redesigns HR," *HR Focus* 74 (March 1997), p. 3; A. Crombie, "Empowering People with Diabetes," in Weisbord, ed., *Discovering Common Ground*, pp. 249–64.

38. P. H. Mirvis and M. L. Marks, *Managing the Merger* (Englewood Cliffs, NJ: Prentice Hall, 1992).

39. R. Greenwood and C. R. Hinings, "Understanding Radical Organizational Change: Bringing Together the Old and the New Institutionalism," *Academy of Management Review* 21 (1996), pp. 1022–54.

40. T. Joyner, "Merger Toil Replaced Fun in Sun," *Atlanta Journal and Constitution*, August 5, 2001, p. A1.

41. J. Lublin, "Curing Sick Companies Better Done Fast," *Globe and Mail (Toronto)*, July 25, 1995, p. B18.

42. Nicolini and Meznar, "The Social Construction of Organizational Learning."

43. The importance of systems and structure in reinforcing change is discussed in W. F. Joyce, *MegaChange: How Today's Leading Companies Have Transformed Their Workforces* (New York: Free Press, 1999), chaps. 4 and 5.

44. E. E. Lawler III, "Pay Can Be a Change Agent," *Compensation and Benefits Management* 16 (Summer 2000), pp. 23–26.

45. R. H. Miles, "Leading Corporate Transformation: Are You Up to the Task?" in Conger et al., eds., *The Leader's Change Handbook*, pp. 221–67; Goodstein and Butz, "Customer Value," pp. 21–34.

46. C. L. Bernick, "When Your Culture Needs a Makeover," *Harvard Business Review* 79 (June 2001), pp. 53–61.

47. D. A. Nadler, "Implementing Organizational Changes," in D. A. Nadler, M. L. Tushman, and N. G. Hatvany, eds., *Managing Organizations: Readings and Cases* (Boston: Little, Brown, 1982), pp. 440–59.

48. B. McDermott and G. Sexton, "Sowing the Seeds of Corporate Innovation," *Journal for Quality and Participation* 21 (November–December 1998), pp. 18–23.

49. Callaghan, "Everything Old Is New Again. Really."

50. J. P. Kotter, "Leading Change: The Eight Steps to Transformation," in Conger et al., eds., *The Leader's Change Handbook*, pp. 221–67; J. P. Kotter, "Leading Change: Why Transformation Efforts Fail," *Harvard Business Review*, March–April 1995, pp. 59–67.

51. M. Beer, R. A. Eisenstat, and B. Spector, *The Critical Path to Corpo-*

rate Renewal (Boston, MA: Harvard Business School Press, 1990).

52. R. E. Walton, *Innovating to Compete: Lessons for Diffusing and Managing Change in the Workplace* (San Francisco: Jossey-Bass, 1987); Beer et al., *The Critical Path to Corporate Renewal*, chap. 5; R. E. Walton, "Successful Strategies for Diffusing Work Innovations," *Journal of Contemporary Business*, Spring 1977, pp. 1–22.

53. J. Childs, "Five Years and Counting: The Path to Self-Directed Work Teams," *Hospital Materiel Management Quarterly* 18 (May 1997), pp. 34–43.

54. R. Beckhard, *Organization Development: Strategies and Models* (Reading, MA: Addison-Wesley, 1969), chap. 2. See also T. G. Cummings and E. F. Huse, *Organization Development and Change*, 4th ed. (St. Paul, MN: West, 1989), pp. 1–3. There is some debate about the distinction between OD and change management. For example, see N. A. M. Worren, K. Ruddle, and K. Moore, "From Organizational Development to Change Management: The Emergence of a New Profession," *Journal of Applied Behavioral Science* 35 (September 1999), pp. 273–86.

55. W. W. Burke, *Organization Development: A Normative View* (Reading, MA: Addison-Wesley, 1987), pp. 12–14.

56. L. Dickens and K. Watkins, "Action Research: Rethinking Lewin," *Management Learning* 30 (June 1999), pp. 127–40; J. B. Cunningham, *Action Research and Organization Development* (Westport, CT: Praeger, 1993). For a discussion of early applications of action research, see R. Sommer, "Action Research: From Mental Hospital Reform in Saskatchewan to Community Building in California," *Canadian Psychology* 40 (February 1999), pp. 47–55.

57. A. B. Shani and G. R. Bushe, "Visionary Action Research: A Consultation Process Perspective," *Consultation: An International Journal* 6 (1) (1987), pp. 3–19.

58. M. L. Brown, "Five Symbolic Roles of the Organizational Development Consultant: Integrating Power, Change, and Symbolism," *Proceedings of the Annual ASAC Conference, Organizational Behavior Division* 14, pt. 5 (1993), pp. 71–81; D. A. Buchanan and D. Boddy, *The Expertise of the Change Agent: Public Performance and Backstage Activity* (New York: Prentice Hall, 1992); L. E. Greiner and V. E. Schein, *Power and Organization Development: Mobilizing Power to Implement Change* (Reading, MA: Addison-Wesley, 1988).

59. D. F. Harvey and D. R. Brown, *An Experiential Approach to Organization Development*, 5th ed. (Upper Saddle River, NJ: Prentice Hall, 1996), chap. 4.

60. M. Beer and E. Walton, "Developing the Competitive Organization: Interventions and Strategies," *American Psychologist* 45 (February 1990), pp. 154–61.

61. E. H. Schein, *Process Consultation: Its Role in Organization Development* (Reading, MA: Addison-Wesley, 1969).

62. For a case study of poor diagnosis, see M. Popper, "The Glorious Failure," *Journal of Applied Behavioral Science* 33 (March 1997), pp. 27–45.

63. M. Beer, *Organization Change and Development: A Systems View* (Santa Monica, CA: Goodyear, 1980), pp. 101–1.

64. K. E. Weick and R. E. Quinn, "Organizational Change and Development," *Annual Review of Psychology* 1999, pp. 361–86; D. A. Nadler, "Organizational Frame Bending: Types of Change in the Complex Organization," in R. H. Kilmann, T. J. Covin, and Associates, eds., *Corporate Transformation: Revitalizing Organizations for a Competitive World* (San Francisco: Jossey-Bass, 1988), pp. 66–83.

65. C. R. Hinings and R. Greenwood, *The Dynamics of Strategic Change* (Oxford, UK: Basil Blackwell, 1988), chap. 6; D. Miller and P. H. Friesen, "Structural Change and Performance: Quantum versus Piecemeal-Incremental Approaches," *Academy of Management Journal* 25 (1982), pp. 867–92.

66. P. Brabeck, "The Business Case against Revolution: An Interview with Nestlés Peter Brabeck," *Harvard Business Review* 79 (February 2001), pp. 112–18.

67. S. R. Olberding, "Turnaround Drama Instills Leadership," *Journal for Quality and Participation* 21 (January–February 1998), pp. 52–55.

68. Cummings and Huse, *Organization Development and Change*, pp. 158–61.

69. A. H. Church and W. W. Burke, "Practitioner Attitudes about the Field of Organization Development," *Research in Organizational Change and Development* 8 (1995), pp. 1–46.

70. A. H. Church, W. W. Burke, and D. F. Van Eynde, "Values, Motives, and Interventions of Organization Development Practitioners," *Group and Organization Management* 19 (1994), pp. 5–50.

71. E. M. Van Aken, D. J. Monetta, and D. S. Sink, "Affinity Groups: The Missing Link in Employee Involvement," *Organization Dynamics* 22 (Spring 1994), pp. 38–54; G. R. Bushe and A. B. Shani, *Parallel Learning Structures* (Reading, MA: Addison-Wesley, 1991).

72. Breen, "How EDS Got Its Groove Back."

73. J. M. Watkins and B. J. Mohr, *Appreciative Inquiry: Change at the Speed of Imagination* (San Francisco: Jossey-Bass, 2001); G. Johnson and W. Leavitt, "Building on Success: Transforming Organizations through an Appreciative Inquiry," *Public Personnel Management* 30 (March 2001), pp. 129–36; D. Whitney and D. L. Cooperrider, "The Appreciative Inquiry Summit: Overview and Applications," *Employment Relations Today* 25 (Summer 1998), pp. 17–28.

74. The history of this and other aspects of appreciative inquiry are outlined in Watkins and Mohr, *Appreciative Inquiry*, pp. 15–21. For other descriptions of the appreciative inquiry model, see D. Whitney and C. Schau, "Appreciative Inquiry: An Innovative Process for Organization Change," *Employment Relations Today* 25 (Spring 1998), pp. 11–21; F. J. Barrett and D. L. Cooperrider, "Generative Metaphor Intervention: A New Approach for Working with Systems Divided by Conflict and Caught in Defensive Perception," *Journal of Applied Behavioral Science* 26 (1990), pp. 219–39.

75. G. R. Bushe and G. Coetzer, "Appreciative Inquiry as a Team-Development Intervention: A Controlled Experiment," *Journal of Applied Behavioral Science* 31 (1995), pp. 13–30; L. Levine, "Listening with Spirit and the Art of Team Dialogue," *Journal of Organizational Change Management* 7 (1994), pp. 61–73.

76. A. Trosten-Bloom, "Case Study: HunterDouglas Window Fashions Division," in Watkins and Mohr, *Appreciative Inquiry*, pp. 176–80. For more details about the HunterDouglas appreciative inquiry intervention, see

D. Whitely and A. Trosten-Bloom; *Positive Change @ Work: The Appreciative Inquiry Approach to Whole System Change* (Euclid, OH: Lakeshore Communications, 2002).

77. M. Schiller, "Case Study: AVON Mexico," in Watkins and Mohr, *Appreciative Inquiry*, pp. 123–26.

78. G. A. Neuman, J. E. Edwards, and N. S. Raju, "Organizational Development Interventions: A Meta-Analysis of Their Effects on Satisfaction and Other Attitudes," *Personnel Psychology* 42 (1989), pp. 461–89; R. A. Guzzo, R. D. Jette, and R. A. Katzell, "The Effects of Psychologically Based Intervention Programs on Worker Productivity: A Meta-Analysis," *Personnel Psychology* 38 (1985), pp. 275–91.

79. C-M. Lau, "A Culture-Based Perspective of Organization Development Implementation," *Research in Organizational Change and Development* 9 (1996), pp. 49–79.

80. R. J. Marshak, "Lewin Meets Confucius: A Review of the OD Model of Change," *Journal of Applied Behavioral Science* 29 (1993), pp. 395–415; T. C. Head and P. F. Sorenson, "Cultural Values and Organizational Development: A Seven-Country Study," *Leadership and Organization Development Journal* 14 (1993), pp. 3–7; J. M. Putti, "Organization Development Scene in Asia: The Case of Singapore," *Group and Organization Studies* 14 (1989), pp. 262–70; A. M. Jaeger, "Organization Development and National Culture: Where's the Fit?" *Academy of Management Review* 11 (1986), pp. 178–90.

81. For an excellent discussion of conflict management and Asian values, see several articles in K. Leung and D. Tjosvold, eds., *Conflict Management in the Asia Pacific: Assumptions and Approaches in Diverse Cultures* (Singapore: Wiley, 1998).

82. C. M. D. Deaner, "A Model of Organization Development Ethics," *Public Administration Quarterly* 17 (1994), pp. 435–46; and M. McKendall, "The Tyranny of Change: Organizational Development Revisited," *Journal of Business Ethics* 12 (February 1993), pp. 93–104.

83. G. A. Walter, "Organization Development and Individual Rights," *Journal of Applied Behavioral Science* 20 (1984), pp. 423–39.

84. Burke, *Organization Development*, pp. 149–51; Beer, *Organization Change and Development*, pp. 223–24.

CHAPTER SEVENTEEN

1. P. R. Chowdhury, "The Unbottling of Coke," *Business Today*, January 2001; P. O'Kane, "Coca Cola's Canny Man," *The Herald (Glasgow)*, June 18, 2000, p. 3; "Debunking Coke," *The Economist*, February 12, 2000; "World Has Changed at Coca-Cola as 6,000 Lose Jobs," *National Post*, January 27, 2000, p. C10.

2. S. Ranson, R. Hinings, and R. Greenwood, "The Structuring of Organizational Structure," *Administrative Science Quarterly* 25 (1980), pp. 1–14.

3. J-E. Johanson, "Intraorganizational Influence," *Management Communication Quarterly* 13 (February 2000), pp. 393–435.

4. "Ford Motor Company Announces Consumer-Focused Organization for the 21st Century," *Auto Channel* (online), October 18, 1999.

5. H. Mintzberg, *The Structuring of Organizations* (Englewood Cliffs, NJ: Prentice Hall, 1979), pp. 2–3.

6. H. Fayol, *General and Industrial Management*, trans. C. Storrs (London: Pitman, 1949); E. E. Lawler III, *Motivation in Work Organizations* (Monterey, CA: Brooks/Cole, 1973), chap. 7; M. A. Campion, "Ability Requirement Implications of Job Design: An Interdisciplinary Perspective," *Personnel Psychology* 42 (1989), pp. 1–24.

7. A. N. Maira, "Connecting across Boundaries: The Fluid-Network Organization," *Prism*, First Quarter 1998, pp. 23–26; D. A. Nadler and M. L. Tushman, *Competing by Design: The Power of Organizational Architecture* (New York: Oxford University Press, 1997), chap. 6; Mintzberg, *The Structuring of Organizations*, pp. 2–8.

8. C. Downs, P. Clampitt, and A. L. Pfeiffer, "Communication and Organizational Outcomes," in G. Goldhaber and G. Barnett, eds., *Handbook of Organizational Communication* (Norwood, NJ: Ablex, 1988), pp. 171–211; H. C. Jain, "Supervisory Communication and Performance in Urban Hospitals," *Journal of Communication* 23 (1973), pp. 103–17.

9. V. L. Shalin, and G. V. Prabhu, "A Cognitive Perspective on Manual Assembly," *Ergonomics* 39 (1996), pp. 108–27; I. Nonaka and H. Takeuchi, *The Knowledge-Creating Company* (New York: Oxford University Press, 1995).

10. A. L. Patti, J. P. Gilbert, and S. Hartman, "Physical Co-location and the Success of New Product Development Projects," *Engineering Management Journal* 9 (September 1997), pp. 31–37; M. L. Swink, J. C. Sandvig, and V. A. Mabert, "Customizing Concurrent Engineering Processes: Five Case Studies," *Journal of Product Innovation Management* 13 (1996), pp. 229–44; W. I. Zangwill, *Lightning Strategies for Innovation: How the World's Best Firms Create New Products* (New York: Lexington, 1993).

11. For a recent discussion of the role of brand manager at Procter & Gamble, see C. Peale, "Branded for Success," *Cincinnati (OH) Enquirer*, May 20, 2001, p. A1.

12. D. Anfuso, "Core Values Shape W. L. Gore & Associates' Innovative Culture," *Workforce* 78 (March 1999), pp. 48–53; M. Kaplan. "You Have No Boss," *Fast Company* 11 (November 1997), p. 226; D. M. Price, "Gore-Tex Gets Hip," *Minneapolis (MN) Star Tribune*, May 5, 1997, p. D1.

13. Fayol's work is summarized in J. B. Miner, *Theories of Organizational Structure and Process* (Chicago: Dryden, 1982), pp. 358–66.

14. F. Jebb, "Rentokil Initial: A Place for Everyone and Everyone in Their Place," *Management Today*, August 1998, p. 46.

15. J. A. Conger, *Winning 'Em Over: A New Model for Managing in the Age of Persuasion* (New York: Simon & Shuster, 1998), Appendix A.

16. Y-M. Hsieh and A. Tien-Hsieh, "Enhancement of Service Quality with Job Standardization," *Service Industries Journal* 21 (July 2001), pp. 147–66.

17. J. H. Sheridan, "Lessons from the Best," *Industry Week*, February 20, 1995, pp. 13–22.

18. J. P. Starr, "Reintroducing Alcoa to Economic Reality," in W. E. Halal, ed., *The Infinite Resource* (San Francisco: Jossey-Bass, 1998), pp. 57–67.

19. J. Pfeffer, "Seven Practices of Successful Organizations," *California Management Review* 40 (1998), pp. 96–124.

20. D. D. Van Fleet and A. G. Bedeian, "A History of the Span of Management," *Academy of Management Review* 2 (1977), pp. 356–72; Mintzberg, *The Structuring of Organizations*, chap. 8; D. Robey, *Designing Organizations*, 3rd ed. (Homewood, IL: Irwin, 1991), pp. 255–59.

21. B. Simon, "Bank Leads by Example in Transformation," *Business Day (South Africa)*, July 30, 1998, p. 17.

22. "Taking Care of the People," *Canadian Healthcare Manager* 6 (April–May 1999), pp. 5–9.

23. S. Ellis, "A New Role for the Post Office: An Investigation into Issues behind Strategic Change at Royal Mail," *Total Quality Management* 9 (May 1998), pp. 223–34; R. H. Kluge, "An Incentive Compensation Plan with an Eye on Quality," *Quality Progress* 29 (December 1996), pp. 65–68.

24. T. Peters, *Thriving on Chaos* (New York: Knopf, 1987), p. 359.

25. L. A. Bossidy, "Reality-Based Leadership," *Executive Speeches* 13 (August–September 1998), pp. 10–15.

26. Q. N. Huy, "In Praise of Middle Managers," *Harvard Business Review* 79 (September 2001), pp. 72–79; L. Donaldson and F. G. Hilmer, "Management Redeemed: The Case against Fads That Harm Management," *Organizational Dynamics* 26 (Spring 1998), pp. 6–20.

27. Mintzberg, *The Structuring of Organizations*, p. 136.

28. The number of layers at Microsoft is inferred from an example in F. Jebb, "Don't Call Me Sir," *Management Today*, August 1998, pp. 44–47.

29. P. Brabeck, "The Business Case against Revolution: An Interview with Nestlés Peter Brabeck," *Harvard Business Review* 79 (February 2001), p. 112.

30. Mintzberg, *The Structuring of Organizations*, chap. 5.

31. B. Victor and A. C. Boynton, *Invented Here* (Boston: Harvard Business School Press, 1998), chap. 2; M. Hamstra, "McD Speeds Up Drive-Thru with Beefed Up Operations," *Nation's Restaurant News*, April 6, 1998, p. 3; G. Morgan, *Creative Organization Theory: A Resourcebook* (Newbury, Park, CA: Sage, 1989), pp. 271–73; K. Deveny, "Bag Those Fries, Squirt That Ketchup, Fry That Fish," *Business Week*, October 13, 1986, p. 86.

32. T. Burns and G. Stalker, *The Management of Innovation* (London: Tavistock, 1961).

33. A. Lam, "Tacit Knowledge, Organizational Learning and Societal Institutions: An Integrated Framework," *Organization Studies* 21 (May 2000), pp. 487–513.

34. Mintzberg, *The Structuring of Organizations*, p. 106.

35. Mintzberg, *The Structuring of Organizations*, chap. 17.

36. Robey, *Designing Organizations*, pp. 186–89.

37. M. Hamstra, "McD's to Decentralize US Management Team," *Nation's Restaurant News*, June 2, 1997, p. 1

38. "Microsoft Splits into Five Groups in Reorganization," *Reuters*, March 29, 1999; "Microsoft Plans Realignment to Focus on Customers," *Reuters*, February 8, 1999.

39. T. H. Davenport, J. G. Harris, and A. K. Kohli, "How Do They Know Their Customers So Well?" *Sloan Management Review* 42 (Winter 2001), pp. 63–73.

40. "Axa Executive Says Global Insurers Must Pool Local Expertise," *Best's Insurance News*, May 1, 2001. The evolution of organizational structures in global organizations is further discussed in J. R. Galbraith, "Structuring Global Organizations," in S. A. Mohrman, J. R. Galbraith, E. E. Lawler III, and Associates, eds., *Tomorrow's Organization* (San Francisco: Jossey-Bass, 1998), pp. 103–29.

41. Robey, *Designing Organizations*, pp. 191–97; A. G. Bedeian and R. F. Zammuto, *Organizations: Theory and Design* (Hinsdale, IL: Dryden, 1991), pp. 162–68.

42. K. Maddox, "Reinventing the Ad Agency," *B to B*, April 30, 2001, p. 1; C. Marshall, "The Kings of Madison Avenue," *Campaign*, April 27, 2001, p. 12; A. Baar, "Burnett USA Reorganizes, Names New Leaders," *Adweek*, October 25, 1999, p. 5; H. Shura, "Reorganization Positions Haupt to Lead Leo Group," *Advertising Age*, September 20, 1999, p. 25.

43. "Tearing Down Silos to Build a Corporate-wide Communication Plan," *PR News*, July 10, 2000.

44. R. Waters, "SAP America Faces Up to Challenge of Change," *Financial Times*, June 13, 2001.

45. R. C. Ford and W. A. Randolph, "Cross-Functional Structures: A Review and Integration of Matrix Organization and Project Management," *Journal of Management* 18 (1992), pp. 267–94.

46. J. Belanger, C. Berggren, T. Bjorkman, and C. Kohler, eds., *Being Local Worldwide: ABB and the Challenge of Global Management* (Ithaca, NY: Cornell University Press, 1999); M. F. R. Kets de Vries "Charisma in Action: The Transformational Abilities of Virgin's Richard Branson and ABB's Percy Barnevik," *Organizational Dynamics* 26 (Winter 1998), pp. 6–21; D. A. Nadler and M. L. Tushman, *Competing by Design* (New York: Oxford University Press, 1997), chap. 6.

47. H. F. Kolodny, "Managing in a Matrix," *Business Horizons*, March–April 1981, pp. 17–24; S. M. Davis and P. R. Lawrence, *Matrix* (Reading, MA: Addison-Wesley, 1977).

48. K. Knight, "Matrix Organization: A Review," *Journal of Management Studies*, May 1976, pp. 111–30.

49. C. Herkströter, "Royal Dutch/Shell: Rewriting the Contracts," in G. W. Dauphinais and C. Price, eds., *Straight from the CEO* (New York: Simon & Schuster, 1998), pp. 86–93.

50. G. Calabrese, "Communication and Co-operation in Product Development: A Case Study of a European Car Producer," *R&D Management* 27 (July 1997), pp. 239–52; J. L. Brown and N. M. Agnew, "The Balance of Power in a Matrix Structure," *Business Horizons*, November–December 1982, pp. 51–54.

51. C. A. Bartlett and S. Ghoshal, "Managing across Borders: New Organizational Responses," *Sloan Management Review*, Fall 1987, pp. 43–53.

52. G. Imperato, "Harley Shifts Gears," *Fast Company* 9 (1997). Harley-Davidson's team-based structure in the Kansas plant is described slightly differently in J. Singer and S. Duvall, "High-Performance Partnering by Self-Managed Teams in Manufacturing," *Engineering Management Journal* 12 (December 2000), pp. 9–15.

53. J. R. Galbraith, *Competing with Flexible Lateral Organizations* (Boston, MA: Addison-Wesley, 1994); J. B. Rieley, "The Circular Organization: How Leadership Can Optimize Organizational Effectiveness," *National Productivity Review* 13 (Winter 1993–1994), pp. 11–19; J. A. Byrne, "The Horizontal Corporation," *Business Week*, December 20, 1993, pp. 76–81; R. Tomasko, *Rethinking the Corporation* (New York: AMACOM, 1993); D. Q. Mills (with G. B. Friesen), *Rebirth of the Corporation* (New York: Wiley, 1991), pp. 29–30.

54. M. A. Brunelli, "How Harley-Davidson Uses Cross-Functional Teams," *Purchasing*, November 4, 1999, p. 148.

55. R. Bettis and M. Hitt, "The New Competitive Landscape," *Strategic Management Journal* 16 (1995), pp. 7–19; J. R. Galbraith, E. E. Lawler III, and Associates, *Organizing for the Future: The New Logic for Managing Complex Organizations* (San Francisco: Jossey-Bass, 1993).

56. P. C. Ensign, "Interdependence, Coordination, and Structure in Complex Organizations: Implications for Organization Design," *Mid-Atlantic Journal of Business* 34 (March 1998), pp. 5–22

57. L. Y. Chan and B. E. Lynn, "Operating in Turbulent Times: How Ontario's Hospitals Are Meeting the Current Funding Crisis," *Health Care Management Review* 23 (June 1998), pp. 7–18; M. M. Fanning, "A Circular Organization Chart Promotes a Hospital-Wide Focus on Teams," *Hospital and Health Services Administration* 42 (June 1997), pp. 243–54.

58. R. Cross, "Looking before You Leap: Assessing the Jump to Teams in Knowledge-Based Work," *Business Horizons*, September, 2000; W. F. Joyce, V. E. McGee, and J. W. Slocum, Jr., "Designing Lateral Organizations: An Analysis of the Benefits, Costs, and Enablers of Nonhierarchical Organizational Forms," *Decision Sciences* 28 (Winter 1997), pp. 1–25.

59. J. King, "Employers Quickly Hire Circuit Board Assemblers," *Detroit News*, October 15, 2000, p. 1; J-A. Johnston, "The Faces of Productivity," *Tampa (FL) Tribune*, September 4, 2000, p. 7.

60. R. Hacki and J. Lighton, "The Future of the Networked Company," *Business Review Weekly*, August 30, 2001, p. 58; A. M. Porter, "The Virtual Corporation: Where Is It?" *Purchasing*, March 23, 2000, pp. 40–48; J. A. Byrne, "The Corporation of the Future," *Business Week*, August 31, 1998, pp. 102–4.

61. J. R. Galbraith, "Designing the Networked Organization," in Mohrman et al., eds., *Tomorrow's Organization*, p. 102; C. Baldwin and K. Clark, "Managing in an Age of Modularity," *Harvard Business Review* 75 (September–October 1997), pp. 84–93; R. E. Miles and C. C. Snow, "The New Network Firm: A Spherical Structure Built on a Human Investment Philosophy," *Organizational Dynamics* 23 (4) (1995), pp. 5–18; W. Powell, "Neither Market nor Hierarchy: Network Forms of Organization," *Research in Organizational Behavior* 12 (1990), pp. 295–336.

62. T. W. Malone and R. J. Laubacher, "The Dawn of the E-lance Economy," *Harvard Business Review* 76 (September–October 1998), pp. 144–52.

63. T. Arsenault, "Return of the Rich Man," *Halifax-Chronicle Herald*, November 5, 1999; J. Hagel III and M. Singer, "Unbundling the Corporation," *Harvard Business Review* 77 (March–April 1999), pp. 133–41. For a discussion of core competencies, see G. Hamel and C. K. Prahalad, *Competing for the Future* (Boston: Harvard Business School Press, 1994), chap. 10.

64. D. Egbert, "Label Says 'Nortel,' but Somebody Else Probably Made It," *News and Observer (Raleigh, NC)*, June 15, 2000, p. D1.

65. R. Lieber, "Startups: The 'Inside' Stories," *Fast Company* 32 (March 2000), p. 284.

66. J. Matthews, " 'Baby Bills' Follow Leader to Success," *Baltimore Sun*, August 14, 1998; J. F. Moore, "The Rise of a New Corporate Form," *Washington Quarterly* 21 (Winter 1998), pp. 167–81.

67. L. Fried, *Managing Information Technology in Turbulent Times* (New York: Wiley, 1995); W. H. Davidow and M. S. Malone, *The Virtual Corporation* (New York: HarperBusiness, 1992).

68. P. Doyle, "Getting Their Act Together," *St. John's (Newfoundland) Telegram*, October 29, 1999.

69. G. Morgan, *Imagin-I-Zation: New Mindsets for Seeing, Organizing and Managing* (Thousand Oaks, CA: Sage, 1997); G. Morgan, *Images of Organization*, 2nd ed. (Newbury Park: Sage, 1996).

70. C. Meyer and S. Davis, *Blur: The Speed of Change in the Connected Economy* (Reading, MA: Addison-Wesley, 1998); P. M. J. Christie and R. Levary, "Virtual Corporations: Recipe for Success," *Industrial Management* 40 (July 1998), pp. 7–11; H. Chesbrough and D. J. Teece, "When Is Virtual Virtuous? Organizing for Innovation," *Harvard Business Review*, January–February 1996, pp. 65–73.

71. A. Gilbert, "Virtual Company Wins New Business," *InformationWeek*, April 2, 2001, p. 79.

72. Mintzberg, *The Structuring of Organizations*, chap. 13; D. S. Pugh and C. R. Hinings, eds., *Organizational Structure: Extensions and Replications* (Farnborough, UK: Lexington, 1976).

73. T. A. Stewart, *Intellectual Capital: The New Wealth of Organizations* (New York: Doubleday Currency, 1997), chap. 10.

74. Robey, *Designing Organizations*, p. 102.

75. C. Perrow, "A Framework for the Comparative Analysis of Organizations," *American Sociological Review* 32 (1967), pp. 194–208.

76. Mintzberg, *The Structuring of Organizations*, chap. 15.

77. Burns and Stalker, *The Management of Innovation*; P. R. Lawrence and J. W. Lorsch, *Organization and Environment* (Homewood, IL: Irwin, 1967); D. Miller and P. H. Friesen, *Organizations: A Quantum View* (Englewood Cliffs, NJ: Prentice Hall, 1984), pp. 197–98.

78. Mintzberg, *The Structuring of Organizations*, p. 282.

79. R. H. Kilmann, *Beyond the Quick Fix* (San Francisco: Jossey-Bass, 1984), p. 38.

80. J. Child, "Organizational Structure, Environment, and Performance: The Role of Strategic Choice," *Sociology* 6 (1972), pp. 2–22.

81. A. D. Chandler, *Strategy and Structure* (Cambridge, MA: MIT Press, 1962).

83. M. E. Porter, *Competitive Strategy* (New York: Free Press, 1980).

84. D. Miller, "Configurations of Strategy and Structure," *Strategic Management Journal* 7 (1986), pp. 233–50.

CHAPTER EIGHTEEN

1. M. Ruggieri, "Security Courtesy of Dan Schmitt and Company," *Richmond (VA) Times-Dispatch*, July 29, 2001; A. K. Smith, "Charting Your Own Course," *U.S. News & World Report*, November 6, 2000.

2. P. Cappelli, *The New Deal at Work* (Boston: Harvard Business School Press, 1999).

3. P. Stinton, "Double Disaster," *San Francisco Chronicle*, May 25, 2001, p. B1.

4. P. Kruger, "Betrayed by Work," *Fast Company*, November 1999, p. 182.

5. E. W. Morrison and S. L. Robinson, "When Employees Feel Betrayed: A Model of How Psychological Contract Violation Develops," *Academy of Management Review* 22 (1997), pp. 226–56.

6. S. L. Robinson, M. S. Kraatz, and D. M. Rousseau, "Changing Obligations and the Psychological Contract: A Longitudinal Study," *Academy of Management Journal* 37 (1994), pp. 137–52; D. M. Rousseau and J. M. Parks, "The Contracts of Individuals and Organizations," *Research in Organizational Behavior* 15 (1993), pp. 1–43.

7. P. Herriot, W. E. G. Manning, and J. M. Kidd, "The Content of the Psychological Contract," *British Journal of Management* 8 (1997), pp. 151–62.

8. J. McLean Parks and D. L. Kidder, "'Till Death Us Do Part . . . ' Changing Work Relationships in the 1990s," in C. L. Cooper and D. M. Rousseau, eds., *Trends in Organizational Behavior*, vol. 1 (Chichester, UK: Wiley, 1994), pp. 112–36.

9. H. J. Van Buren III, "The Bindingness of Social and Psychological Contracts: Toward a Theory of Social Responsibility in Downsizing," *Journal of Business Ethics* 25 (June 2000), pp. 205–19; P. R. Sparrow, "Reappraising Psychological Contracting: Lessons for the Field of Human-Resource Development from Cross-Cultural and Occupational Psychology Research," *International Studies of Management and Organization* 28 (March 1998), pp. 30–63.

10. L. Stevens, "Believers in the Midday Doze Are Stripping Away Stigma of Siestas," *Fort Worth (TX) Star-Telegram*, March 24, 2001; R. Hogan, "A Daytime Nap Could Make You More Productive," *Los Angeles Times*, January 15, 2001; S. M. Handelsblatt, "Stressed Out and Stranded in Barcelona?" *Wall Street Journal Europe*, August 4, 2000, p. 32; R. Boudreaux, "Spaniards Are Missing Their Naps," *Los Angeles Times*, March 28, 2000.

11. S. L. Robinson, "Trust and Breach of the Psychological Contract," *Administrative Science Quarterly* 41 (1996), pp. 574–99. For a discussion of the antecedents of trust, see E. M Whitener, S. E. Brodt, M. A. Korsgaard, and J. M. Werner, "Managers As Initiators of Trust: An Exchange Relationship Framework for Understanding Managerial Trustworthy Behavior," *Academy of Management Review* 23 (July 1998), pp. 513–30.

12. R. D. Costigan, S. S. Ilter, and J. J. Berman, "A Multi-Dimensional Study of Trust in Organizations," *Journal of Managerial Issues* 10 (Fall 1998), pp. 303–17.

13. D. M. Rousseau, S. B. Sitkin, R. S. Burt, and C. Camerer, "Not So Different After All: A Cross-Discipline View of Trust," *Academy of Management Review* 23 (July 1998), pp. 393–404; R. J. Lewicki and B. B. Bunker, "Developing and Maintaining Trust in Work Relationships," in R. M. Kramer and T. R. Tyler, eds., *Trust in Organizations: Frontiers of Theory and Research* (Thousand Oaks, CA: Sage, 1996), pp. 114–39.

14. Whitener et al., "Managers As Initiators of Trust"; W. Bennis and B. Nanus, *Leaders: The Strategies for Taking Charge* (New York: Harper & Row, 1986), pp. 43–55; J. M. Kouzes and B. Z. Posner, *Credibility: How Leaders Gain and Lose It, Why People Demand It* (San Francisco: Jossey-Bass, 1993). Knowledge-based trust is sometimes called history-based trust in the psychological literature. See R. M. Kramer, "Trust and Distrust in Organizations: Emerging Perspectives, Enduring Questions," *Annual Review of Psychology* 50 (1999), pp. 569–98.

15. I. DeBare, "Keeping a Packed Bag at Work," *San Francisco Chronicle*, April 30, 1999.

16. S. L. Robinson and E. W. Morrison, "Psychological Contracts and OCB: The Effect of Unfulfilled Obligations on Civic Virtue Behavior," *Journal of Organizational Behavior* 16 (1995), pp. 289–98.

17. D. M. Rousseau, "Changing the Deal While Keeping the People," *Academy of Management Executive* 10 (February 1996), pp. 50–61.

18. C. Hendry and R. Jenkins, "Psychological Contracts and New Deals," *Human Resource Management Journal* 7 (1997), pp. 38–44; P. Herriot and C. Pemberton, *New Deals: The Revolution in Managerial Careers* (New York: Wiley, 1995), chap. 3; W. H. Whyte, *The Organization Man* (New York: Simon & Schuster, 1956), p. 129.

19. J. C. Meister, "The Quest for Lifetime Employability," *Journal of Business Strategy* 19 (May–June 1998), pp. 25–28; T. A. Stewart, "Gray Flannel Suit? Moi?" *Fortune*, March 16, 1998, pp. 76–82; A. Rajan, "Employability in the Finance Sector: Rhetoric vs. Reality," *Human Resource Management Journal* 7 (1997), pp. 67–78.

20. L. Uchitelle, "As Job Cuts Spread, Tears Replace Anger," *New York Times*, August 5, 2001; B. Moses, *The Good News about Careers: How You'll Be Working in the Next Decade* (Toronto: Stoddart, 1999).

21. P. Herriot and C. Pemberton, "Facilitating New Deals," *Human Resource Management Journal* 7 (1997), pp. 45–56; P. R. Sparrow, "Transitions in the Psychological Contract: Some Evidence from the Banking Sector," *Human Resource Management Journal* 6 (1996), pp. 75–92.

22. M. E. Podmolik, "Talkin' 'Bout My Generation," *Crain's Chicago Business*, June 4, 2001, p. E18.

23. "Towers Perrin Study Finds, Despite Layoffs and Slow Economy, a New, More Complex Power Game Is Emerging between Employers and Employees," *Business Wire*, August 30, 2001.

24. Facts about Manpower, Inc., are from its website (www.manpower.com). This observation is also noted in T. W. Malone and R. J. Laubacher, "The Dawn of the E-lance Economy," *Harvard Business Review* 76 (September–October 1998), pp. 144–52.

25. M. Mallon and J. Duberley, "Managers and Professionals in the Contingent Workforce," *Human Resource Management Journal*, January 2000, p. 33; A. E. Polivka, "Contingent and Alternative Work Arrangements, Defined," *Monthly Labor Review* 119 (Oc-

tober 1996), pp. 3–10. For further discussion of the meaning of *contingent work*, see S. Nollen and H. Axel, *Managing Contingent Workers* (New York: AMACOM, 1996), pp. 4–9.

26. S. Hipple, "Contingent Work: Results from the Second Survey," *Monthly Labor Review* 121 (November 1998), pp. 22–35.

27. For a discussion of contingent work, including estimates of the American workforce percentage in this category, see K. Barker and K. Christensen, eds., *Contingent Work: American Employment in Transition* (Ithaca, NY: ILR Press, 1998). Contingent work in Europe is discussed in G. Edmondson et al., "A Tidal Wave of Temps," *Business Week (International)*, November 24, 1997; Sparrow, "Reappraising Psychological Contracting."

28. C. von Hippel, S. L. Mangum, D. B. Greenberger, R. L. Heneman, and J. D. Skoglind, "Temporary Employment: Can Organizations and Employees Both Win?" *Academy of Management Executive* 11 (February 1997), pp. 93–104; A. E. Polivka "Into Contingent and Alternative Employment: By Choice?" *Monthly Labor Review* 119 (October 1996), pp. 55–74. A recent U.S. government study revealed that the percentage of contingent workers who want permanent employment is dropping. However, most of these people still prefer permanent employment. See "Gains in Job Security," *Monthly Labor Review* 121 (March 1998), pp. 74–75.

29. F. Buffini, "The Free Agent Nation," *Boss Magazine*, June 8, 2001, p. 38; D. H. Pink, "Land of the Free," *Fast Company*, May 2001, pp. 125–33; S. B. Gould, K. J. Weiner, and B. R. Levin, *Free Agents: People and Organizations Creating a New Working Community* (San Francisco: Jossey-Bass, 1997); von Hippel et al., "Temporary Employment," pp. 94–96; W. J. Byron, "Coming to Terms with the New Corporate Contract," *Business Horizons* 38 (January 1995), pp. 8–15.

30. P. Luke, "From Secretary to Cyber Queen," *Vancouver Province*, May 14, 2000; A. Daniels, "Virtual Assistant," *Vancouver Sun*, March 27, 2000, p. C10.

31. S. J. Hartman, A. C. Yrle, and A. R. Yrle, "Turnover in the Hotel Industry: Is There a Hobo Phenomenon at

Work?" *International Journal of Management* 13 (1996), pp. 340–48; T. A. Judge and S. Watanabe, "Is the Past Prologue? A Test of Ghiselli's Hobo Syndrome," *Journal of Management* 21 (1995), pp. 211–29.

32. J. Walsh and S. Deery, "Understanding the Peripheral Workforce: Evidence from the Service Sector," *Human Resource Management Journal* 9 (1999), pp. 50–63; von Hippel et al., "Temporary Employment," pp. 93–104.

33. S. F. Matusik and C. W. L. Hill, "The Utilization of Contingent Work, Knowledge Creation, and Competitive Advantage," *Academy of Management Review* 23 (October 1998), pp. 680–97.

34. J. Larson, "Temps Are Here to Stay," *American Demographics* 18 (February 1996), pp. 26–30.

35. Malone and Laubacher, "The Dawn of the E-lance Economy."

36. For a recent survey on the complex array of problems and benefits of contingent work, see Mallon and Duberley, "Managers and Professionals in the Contingent Workforce."

37. J. Dionne-Proulx, J-C. Bernatchez, and R. Boulard, "Attitudes and Satisfaction Levels Associated with Precarious Employment," *International Journal of Employment Studies* 6, no. 2 (1998), pp. 91–114. The contingencies of contingent work attitudes are reviewed in M. Armstrong-Stassen, "Alternative Work Arrangements: Meeting the Challenges," *Canadian Psychology* 39 (1998), pp. 108–23. Potential organizational behavior problems with contingent work are discussed in J. Pfeffer, *New Directions in Organizational Theory* (New York: Oxford University Press, 1997), pp. 18–20.

38. L. Uchitelle, "As Job Cuts Spread, Tears Replace Anger," *New York Times*, August 5, 2001.

39. K. M. Beard and J. R. Edwards, "Employees at Risk: Contingent Work and the Psychological Experience of Contingent Workers," in C. L. Cooper and D. M. Rousseau, eds., *Trends in Organizational Behavior*, vol. 2 (Chichester, UK: Wiley, 1995), pp. 109–26.

40. Y-S. Park and R. J. Butler, "The Safety Costs of Contingent Work: Evidence from Minnesota," *Journal of Labor Research* 22 (Fall 2001), pp. 831–49; D. M. Rousseau and C. Libuser, "Contingent Workers in High Risk Environ-

ments," *California Management Review* 39 (Winter 1997), pp. 103–23.

41. "Four Arrested as Campus 'Theft Ring' Is Exposed," *Simon Fraser News (Burnaby, BC)*, September 5, 1996.

42. Armstrong-Stassen, "Alternative Work Arrangements"; D. C. Feldman and H. I. Doerpinghaus, "Managing Temporary Workers: A Permanent HRM Challenge," *Organizational Dynamics* 23 (Fall 1994), pp. 49–63.

43. A. M. Saks, P. E. Mudrack, and B. E. Ashforth, "The Relationship between the Work Ethic, Job Attitudes, Intentions to Quit, and Turnover for Temporary Service Workers," *Canadian Journal of Administrative Sciences* 13 (1996), pp. 226–36.

44. J. Van Maanen, "Breaking In: Socialization to Work," in R. Dublin, ed., *Handbook of Work, Organization, and Society* (Chicago: Rand McNally, 1976), p. 67.

45. C. L. Adkins, "Previous Work Experience and Organizational Socialization: A Longitudinal Examination," *Academy of Management Journal* 38 (1995), pp. 839–62; T. N. Bauer and S. G. Green, "The Effect of Newcomer Involvement in Work Related Activities: A Longitudinal Study of Socialization," *Journal of Applied Psychology* 79 (1994), pp. 211–23.

46. E. F. Holton III, "New Employee Development: A Review and Reconceptualization," *Human Resource Development Quarterly* 7 (Fall 1996), pp. 233–52; G. T. Chao, A. O'Leary-Kelly, S. Wolf, H. J. Klein, and P. D. Gardner, "Organizational Socialization: Its Content and Consequences," *Journal of Applied Psychology* 79 (1994), pp. 450–63.

47. J. T. Mignerey, R. B. Rubin, and W. I. Gorden, "Organizational Entry: An Investigation of Newcomer Communication Behavior and Uncertainty," *Communication Research* 22 (1995), pp. 54–85.

48. K. Mieszkowski, "Get with the Program!" *Fast Company* 13 (February–March 1998), pp. 28–30.

49. B. E. Ashforth and A. M. Saks, "Socialization Tactics: Longitudinal Effects on Newcomer Adjustment," *Academy of Management Journal* 39 (1996), pp. 149–78; C. D. Fisher, "Organizational Socialization: An Integrative View," *Research in Personnel and Human Re-

sources Management 4 (1986), pp. 101–45; N. Nicholson, "A Theory of Work Role Transitions," *Administrative Science Quarterly* 29 (1984), pp. 172–91.

50. C. C. Pinder and K. G. Schroeder, "Time to Proficiency Following Job Transfers," *Academy of Management Journal* 30 (1987), pp. 336–53; N. J. Adler, *International Dimensions of Organizational Behavior*, 2nd ed. (Belmont, CA: Wadsworth, 1991), chap. 8.

51. Van Maanen, "Breaking In," pp. 67–130; L. W. Porter, E. E. Lawler III, and J. R. Hackman, *Behavior in Organizations* (New York: McGraw-Hill, 1975), pp. 163–67; D. C. Feldman, "The Multiple Socialization of Organization Members," *Academy of Management Review* 6 (1981), pp. 309–18.

52. M. K. Gibson and M. J. Papa, "The Mud, the Blood, and the Beer Guys: Organizational Osmosis in Blue-Collar Work Groups," *Journal of Applied Communication Research*, February 2000, p. 68; Ashforth and Saks, "Socialization Tactics"; T. N. Bauer and S. G. Green, "Effect of Newcomer Involvement in Work-Related Activities: A Longitudinal Study of Socialization," *Journal of Applied Psychology* 79 (1994), pp. 211–23.

53. Porter et al., *Behavior in Organizations*, chap. 5.

54. D. M. Cable, L. Aiman-Smith, P. W. Mulvey, and J. R. Edwards, "The Sources and Accuracy of Job Applicants' Beliefs about Organizational Culture," *Academy of Management Journal* 43 (December 2000), pp. 1076–85.

55. J. Stites, "Going from the Corporate World to Silicon Alley Can Prove Tough," *New York Times*, August 31, 1998, p. 3.

56. M. R. Louis, "Surprise and Sensemaking: What Newcomers Experience in Entering Unfamiliar Organizational Settings," *Administrative Science Quarterly* 25 (1980), pp. 226–51.

57. E. Fitzmaurice, "A Hard Lesson," *Sun Herald (Sydney)*, March 11, 2001, p. 50.

58. C. A. Young and C. C. Lundberg, "Creating a Good First Day on the Job," *Cornell Hotel and Restaurant Administration Quarterly* 37 (December 1996), pp. 26–33; S. L. Robinson and D. M. Rousseau, "Violating the Psychological Contract: Not the Exception but the Norm," *Journal of Organizational Behavior* 15 (1994), pp. 245–59.

59. D. L. Nelson, "Organizational Socialization: A Stress Perspective," *Journal of Occupational Behavior* 8 (1987), pp. 311–24.

60. Morrison and Robinson, "When Employees Feel Betrayed," p. 251.

61. J. A. Breaugh, *Recruitment: Science and Practice* (Boston: PWS-Kent, 1992), chap. 7; J. P. Wanous, *Organizational Entry*, 2nd ed. (Reading, MA: Addison-Wesley, 1992), chap. 3; A. M. Saks and S. F. Cronshaw, "A Process Investigation of Realistic Job Previews: Mediating Variables and Channels of Communication," *Journal of Organizational Behavior* 11 (1990), pp. 221–36.

62. M. Truby, "Ford Romances Top Prospects," *Detroit News*, January 7, 2001.

63. J. M. Phillips, "Effects of Realistic Job Previews on Multiple Organizational Outcomes: A Meta-Analysis," *Academy of Management Journal* 41 (December 1998), pp. 673–90.

64. J. P. Wanous and A. Colella, "Organizational Entry Research: Current Status and Future Directions," *Research in Personnel and Human Resources Management* 7 (1989), pp. 59–120.

65. C. Ostroff and S. W. J. Koslowski, "Organizational Socialization as a Learning Process: The Role of Information Acquisition," *Personnel Psychology* 45 (1992), pp. 849–74; N. J. Allen and J. P. Meyer, "Organizational Socialization Tactics: A Longitudinal Analysis of Links to Newcomers' Commitment and Role Orientation," *Academy of Management Journal* 33 (1990), pp. 847–58; F. M. Jablin, "Organizational Entry, Assimilation, and Exit," in F. M. Jablin, L. L. Putnam, K. H. Roberts, and L. W. Porter, eds., *Handbook of Organizational Communication* (Beverly Hills, CA: Sage, 1987), pp. 679–740.

66. E. W. Morrison, "Newcomer Information Seeking: Exploring Types, Modes, Sources, and Outcomes," *Academy of Management Journal* 36 (1993), pp. 557–89; Fisher, "Organizational Socialization," pp. 135–36; Porter et al., *Behavior in Organizations*, pp. 184–86.

67. C. Goforth, "Still Recruiting Staff," *Akron (OH) Beacon Journal*, July 15, 2001; A. L. Stern, "Bridging the Workforce Shortage," *Trustee*, July 2001, p. 8; D. Francis, "Work Is a Warm Puppy," *National Post*, May 27, 2000, p. W20.

68. S. L. McShane, "Effect of Socialization Agents on the Organizational Adjustment of New Employees," Paper presented at the Annual Conference of the Western Academy of Management, Big Sky, Montana, March 1988.

69. "Employee Loyalty a Fading Virtue," *Canadian Press*, April 9, 2000.

70. M. B. Arthur, D. T. Hall, and B. S. Lawrence, "Generating New Directions in Career Theory: The Case for a Transdisciplinary Approach," in M. B. Arthur, D. T. Hall, and B. S. Lawrence, eds., *Handbook of Career Theory* (Cambridge, UK: Cambridge University Press, 1989), pp. 7–25.

71. M. B. Arthur, "The Boundaryless Career: A New Perspective for Organizational Inquiry," *Journal of Organizational Behavior* 15 (1994), pp. 295–306.

72. D. T. Hall, *Careers in Organizations* (Glenview, IL: Scott Foresman, 1976), pp. 93–97.

73. M. Hinkelman, "Loyalty Pays for Vanguard," *Philadelphia Daily News*, September 4, 2001.

74. T. Snyder, "Take This Job and Love It," *Chatelaine*, October 1999, p. 97.

75. J. Holland, *Making Vocational Choices: A Theory of Careers* (Englewood Cliffs, NJ: Prentice Hall, 1973).

76. G. D. Gottfredson and J. L. Holland, "A Longitudinal Test of the Influence of Congruence: Job Satisfaction, Competency Utilization, and Counterproductive Behavior," *Journal of Counseling Psychology* 37 (1990), pp. 389–98.

77. J. Arnold, "The Psychology of Careers in Organizations," *International Review of Industrial and Organizational Psychology* 12 (1997), pp. 1–37.

78. For example, see G. R. Cluskey and A. Vaux, "Vocational Misfit: Source of Occupational Stress among Accountants," *Journal of Applied Business Research* 13 (Summer 1997), pp. 43–54.

79. R. A. Young and C. P. Chen, "Annual Review: Practice and Research in Career Counseling and Development—1998," *Career Development Quarterly*, December 1999, p. 98.

80. P. R. Chowdhury, "The New Worker," *Business Today*, January 2001,

p. 68. For early discussion of lateral career development, see D. T. Hall and J. Richter, "Career Gridlock: Baby Boomers Hit the Wall," *Academy of Management Executive* 4 (August 1990), pp. 7–22.

81. B. Kaye and C. Farren, "Up Is Not the Only Way," *Training and Development* 50 (February 1996), pp. 48–53.

82. P. LaBarre, "The Company without Limits," *Fast Company* 27 (September 1999), p. 160.

83. P. Baker, "A Sideways Move Could Bring You out of Your Shell," *The Observer (UK)*, March 22, 1998, p. 8; "De-Layered Pay Systems Encourage Employees to Move Sideways," *Universal News Services*, January 24, 1997.

84. J. C. Meister, "The Quest for Lifetime Employability," *Journal of Business Strategy* 19 (May–June 1998), pp. 25–28.

85. Whyte, *Organization Man*.

86. M. B. Arthur and D. M. Rousseau, *The Boundaryless Career: A New Employment Principle for a New Organizational Era* (New York: Oxford University Press, 1996); Arthur, "The Boundaryless Career."

86. A. K. Smith, "Charting Your Own Course," *U.S. News & World Report*, November 6, 2000.

88. P. Oliver, "Shifting to Find a Job That Fits," *New Zealand Herald*, January 21, 2001. The backlash of job-hopping in Silicon Valley is discussed in J. Palmer, "Marry Me a Little," *Barron's*, July 24, 2000, p. 24.

89. Stewart, "Gray Flannel Suit? Moi?"

90. New York Times Staff, *The Downsizing of America* (New York: Times Books, 1996); R. J. Defillippi and M. B. Arthur,

"The Boundaryless Career: A Competency-Based Perspective," *Journal of Organizational Behavior* 15 (1994), pp. 307–24.

91. B. O'Reilly, "The New Deal: What Companies and Employees Owe One Another," *Fortune*, June 13, 1994, pp. 44–52.

92. J. P. Sampson, Jr., J. G. Lenz, R. C. Reardon, and G. W. Peterson, "A Cognitive Information Processing Approach to Employment Problem Solving and Decision Making," *Career Development Quarterly* 48 (September 1999), pp. 3–18.

93. "A Career with 'Karma,'" *ABC News*, May 3, 2001 (www.abcnews.com).

94. S. Terry, "Job Outlook for Grads: Off Peak, but Not Bleak," *Christian Science Monitor*, May 21, 2001.

95. B. Moses, "Give People Belief in the Future," *Workforce*, June 2000, pp. 134–41.

96. A. Zipkin, "Tough Bosses Don't Cut It in Today's Workplace," *San Jose (CA) Mercury*, May 31, 2000.

97. B. Moses, "Career Activists Take Command," *Globe and Mail (Toronto)*, March 20, 2000, p. B6.

98. F. T. McCarthy "Career Evolution," *The Economist*, January 29, 2000. The survey is reported in Drake Beam Morin, "1999 DBM Career Transition Study," November 2000 (www.dbm.com).

99. S. E. Sullivan, "The Changing Nature of Careers: A Review and Research Agenda," *Journal of Management*, May 1999, pp. 457–84; Moses, *The Good News about Careers*.

100. N. Beech and A. Brockbank, "Power/Knowledge and Psychosocial Dynamics in Mentoring," *Management*

Learning 30 (March 1999), pp. 7–24; S-C. Van Collie, "Moving Up through Mentoring," *Workforce* 77 (March 1998), pp. 36–40.

101. H. Handfield-Jones, "How Executives Grow," *McKinsey Quarterly*, January 2000, p. 117.

APPENDIX A

1. F. N. Kerlinger, *Foundations of Behavioral Research* (New York: Holt, Rinehart & Winston, 1964), p. 11.

2. J. B. Miner, *Theories of Organizational Behavior* (Hinsdale, IL: Dryden, 1980), pp. 7–9.

3. Miner, *Theories of Organizational Behavior*, pp. 6–7.

4. J. Mason, *Qualitative Researching* (London: Sage, 1996).

5. A. Strauss and J. Corbin, eds., *Grounded Theory in Practice* (London: Sage, 1997); B. G. Glaser and A. Strauss, *The Discovery of Grounded Theory: Strategies for Qualitative Research* (Chicago, IL: Aldine, 1967).

6. Kerlinger, *Foundations of Behavioral Research*, p. 13.

7. P. Lazarsfeld, *Survey Design and Analysis* (New York: Free Press, 1955).

8. This example is cited in D. W. Organ and T. S. Bateman, *Organizational Behavior*, 4th ed. (Homewood, IL: Irwin, 1991), p. 42.

9. Organ and Bateman, *Organizational Behavior*, p. 45.

10. R. I. Sutton and A. Hargadon, "Brainstorming Groups in Context: Effectiveness in a Product Design Firm," *Administrative Science Quarterly* 41 (1996), pp. 685–718.

COMPANY INDEX